PROPERTY LAW AND POLICY:
A COMPARATIVE INSTITUTIONAL PERSPECTIVE

by

JOHN P. DWYER
John H. Boalt Professor of Law,
University of California at Berkeley

PETER S. MENELL
Professor of Law,
University of California at Berkeley

WESTBURY, NEW YORK

THE FOUNDATION PRESS, INC.

1998

For June,

J.P.D.

For my parents, Carole and Allan, and my sister, Jill, and
for Claire and the most wonderful little guys in the world, Dylan and Noah,

P.S.M.

*

PREFACE

Professors and students increasingly lament that the first-year property course has devolved into a disparate set of doctrinal areas loosely tied together by their relationship to land. The traditional property course lacks the theoretical and structural coherence of the other first-year courses, and consequently it has lost the central importance that it once commanded in the curriculum.

Given the fundamental importance of resources—land, natural resources, intellectual creativity—to the structure of legal, social, market, and political institutions in our society, property law, properly conceived, is integral to the understanding and resolution of many fundamental issues. **Property Law and Policy** reestablishes the primacy of property law in the curriculum by developing a coherent framework to survey and analyze the many elements that constitute the field of property. Rather than defining the course by reference to a particular resource, *i.e.*, land, **Property Law and Policy** conceptualizes the course through the comparative analysis of the major institutions—legal, social, market, and political—governing resources. In this way, the course prepares students to address not only issues regarding land, but also the many other resources, including natural resources and intellectual property, that are increasingly important in our society. The book's emphasis on governance and comparative institutional analysis provides intellectual coherence to the subject.

Comparative institutional analysis integrates legal, philosophical, economic, sociological, political, anthropological, and historical perspectives to form a coherent framework to understand law and policy. Drawing upon the insights and analytical tools of these various fields, **Property Law and Policy** provides students a firm grounding in the principal institutions that society uses to allocate resources, as well as a thorough survey of property law. Our approach recognizes the interplay of common law, statutory, and constitutional regimes, the growing significance of non-land forms of property (especially intellectual property), the emergence of environmental values, and the central importance of public policy analysis to the resolution of complex social problems. This modern approach breathes new life into the basic property course.

Property Law and Policy also provides students with the analytical skills that they will need for the upper level curriculum. The heavy emphasis of traditional property texts on common law is both anachronistic and poorly suited to preparing students for the challenges of the second and third years of law school and for the demands of modern law practice. The principal courses in the upper level curriculum are centered around statutory regimes, administrative process, and the comparative analysis of a range of legal, market, and political institutions. This is particularly true of the courses that build upon the basic property course—real estate transactions, land use, trusts and estates, landlord-tenant law, family law/marital property, local government law, environmental law, public lands, water law, intellectual property, and constitutional law. (It is also true of other courses, including administrative law, corporate and partnership law, and legislation, for which this text provides important background and introduction.) Moreover, most states today have codified basic property law in ways that reflect the detailed statutory and regulatory regimes studied in the upper level curriculum rather than the traditional common law fields of the 19th century. By integrating common law and statutory materials, **Property Law and Policy** provides a balanced treatment of today's legal landscape.

Organization

Property Law and Policy is structured around the key institutions that society uses to allocate resources. The first chapter develops the basic framework for the course. Rather than defining property simply as rights in land or other resources, the book presents property as reflecting a triadic relation among institutions, resources, and culture.

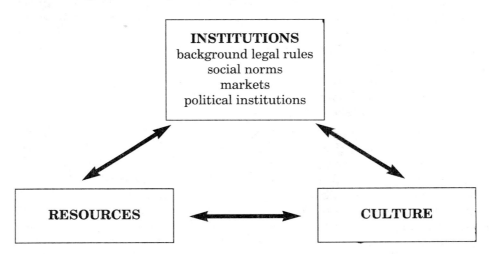

Chapter I introduces the basic themes of the book by first surveying the major philosophical perspectives on property. It then builds upon a rich historical account of early New England society to highlight the manner in which property is socially constructed. Native Americans and colonists lived upon and used the same resources, yet their notions of property—the set of rights and institutions governing access to material resources—were quite varied. The rules and institutions that the different societies developed to govern resources flowed from the nature of the resources (*i.e.*, undeveloped land, water, forests, and wildlife) and the distinct cultures (history, social and economic arrangements, religious beliefs, population density, and knowledge of ecology, agriculture, and technology). The historical account provides a rich backdrop against which to define four distinct categories of institutions: background legal rules, social norms, markets, and political institutions.

Subsequent chapters are structured around these four fundamental institutions. Chapter II surveys the principal background legal rules and institutions that have developed in the United States, including rules governing the acquisition and transfer of property, defining ownership interests (*i.e.*, present and future interests, concurrent interests, and marital property), and delineating property rights and obligations. Chapter III explores the manner in which informal social norms and conventions augment, influence, and even supplant background legal rules in the allocation and governance of resources. We use a range of rich case studies—including Professor Robert Ellickson's pathbreaking study of the role of social norms in resolving property disputes in Shasta County, Professor Elinor Ostrom's seminal work on the governance of common property resources, the evolution of the fair use doctrine of copyright law as applied to photocopying, and the ways in which law firms structure work incentives, profit sharing, and property interests within the firm—to highlight the role of social norms in governing resources. Chapter IV surveys how parties can make formal, private arrangements—under both contract and property law—to vary the background legal rules. The chapter focuses upon landlord-tenant law, nonpossessory interests, and the increasingly important field of common interest communities (condominiums, cooperatives, and gated communities), areas in which legislatures and the courts have regulated the range of available contractual instruments. Chapter V looks at the way political institutions govern resources, focusing upon land use planning and zoning.

We are grateful to many people for contributions, direct and indirect, to the completion of this book. As the many excerpts and references to Robert Ellickson's work throughout the text reflect, we are deeply indebted to Bob for his many significant contributions to property scholarship during the past two and a half decades. Bob has reshaped the landscape of property law and his work inspired much of the reconceptualization of the property field reflected in this text. We have also benefitted from the scholarly contributions of many others in the field, many of whose work is included in this book. A number of colleagues have provided input, constructive criticism, and encouragement, including Vicki Been, Bob Cooter, Bob Ellickson, Dan Ernst, Bill Eskridge, Bob Kagan, Herma Hill Kay, David Kirp, Mark Lemley, Rob Merges, Andrea Peterson, Peggy Radin, Eric Rakowski, Dan Rodriguez, Carol Rose, Larry Rosenthal, Joe Sax, Harry Scheiber, Dick

Stewart, Claire Sylvia, and Jeremy Waldron. We also wish to thank Osa Armi, Jonathan Dowell, Nadia Wetzler, and Chris Scanlan for research assistance and Michele Co and Larry Trask for administrative and secretarial assistance. Finally, we wish to express our deep gratitude to Dick Fenton and Foundation's Board for encouraging us to pursue this project and for the efficiency and professionalism with which Foundation Press brought this work to fruition.

JOHN P. DWYER
PETER S. MENELL

Berkeley, California
June 1997

FORMATTING NOTE

Text that the authors have omitted is indicated by asterisks (* * *). Standard ellipses (. . .) indicates text omitted in the original material. The authors have omitted footnotes without indication; footnotes are numbered consecutively within each chapter and hence do not correspond with footnote numbers in the original material (except by coincidence).

*

COPYRIGHT PERMISSIONS

Acheson, James M., The Lobster Gangs of Maine (1988). Excerpts © 1988 by University Press of New England.

Agnello & Donnelley, Property Rights and Efficiency in the Oyster Industry, 18 J. Law & Econ. 521, 522-23 (1975).

Arnott, Richard J., Time for Revisionism on Rent Control? 9 J. Econ. Perspectives 99, 100-02 (1995).

Been, Vicki, "Exit" As a Constraint on Land Use Exactions: Rethinking the Unconstitutional Conditions Doctrine, 91 Colum. L. Rev. 473, 486-92, 504, 509-10 (1991). Reprinted by permission.

Berger, Curtis J., Beyond Homelessness: An Entitlement to Housing, 45 U. Miami L.Rev. 315, 316-26, 334-35 (1991).

Berger, Lawrence, Unification of the Law of Servitudes, 55 S. Cal. L. Rev. 1339-43 (1982), reprinted with the permission of the Southern California Law Review.

Brill, Steven, Bye, Bye, Finley, Kumble: The firm everone loves to hate is falling apart. Steven Brill is Chairman and CEO of American Lawyer Media. This article is reprinted with permission from the September 1987 issue of *The American Lawyer*. © 1987 *American Lawyer Media, L.P.*

Calabresi & Melamed, Property Rules, Liability Rules and Inalienability: One View of the Cathedral, 85 Harvard Law Review 1089, 1090, 1092-98, 1105-08, 1110 (1972). Copyright © 1972 by The Harvard Law Review Association.

Cronon, William, Changes in the Land: Indians, Colonists, and the Ecology of New England (1983). Copyright © 1983 by William Cronon. Reprinted by permission of Hill and Wang, a division of Farrar, Straus & Giroux, Inc.

Demsetz, Harold, Toward a Theory of Property Rights, 57 Am. Econ. Rev., Papers & Proceedings 347, 350-57 (1967).

Dunham, Allison, Statutory Reformation of Land Obligations, 55 S. Cal. L. Rev. 1345-52 (1982), reprinted with the permission of the Southern California Law Review.

Ellickson, Robert C., The Untenable Case for an Unconditional Right to Shelter, 15 Harv. J.L. & Pub. Pol'y, 20-28, 32-34 (1992).

SUMMARY OF CONTENTS

*

TABLE OF CONTENTS

189–198

199–215

216–233

257–272

274–281

*

TABLE OF CASES

Principal cases are in bold type. Non-principal cases are in roman type. References are to Pages.

*

PROPERTY LAW AND POLICY:
A COMPARATIVE INSTITUTIONAL PERSPECTIVE

*

CHAPTER I

INTRODUCTION

Property is notoriously difficult to define. Although notions of property and ownership are deeply ingrained in our social thought and our legal system, a precise definition is elusive.

It is common enough to recognize that although property has to do with tangibles and certain intangibles—"things"—property is not the thing itself. Rather, property is often described as a "bundle of rights" concerning things. Some of the more notable sticks in the bundle include the right to exclude others from occupying or using the "thing," the right to use, and the right to transfer.

One problem in arriving at a general definition of property is that no stick in the bundle seems to be essential. Consider the right to use. A car owner normally has a right to use a car, but safety laws impose limitations on that use (*e.g.,* speed limits), or even prohibit use altogether in some circumstances (*e.g.,* if the owner is drunk or under age). From the opposite angle, having the authority or right to use or control the use of something does not necessarily establish property rights. A police officer who uses a police cruiser to patrol the city does not own the car. Pedestrians have rights to prevent drivers from using their cars negligently, but we would never say that pedestrians own the cars. Moreover, different jurisdictions put different sticks in the property bundle, and even within a single jurisdiction, the precise content of the bundle may depend on the particular resource. A landowner's right to destroy vegetation on his land may depend on whether the plant is a common dandelion or the endangered Sacramento prickly-poppy. The indeterminacy threatens to render the term "property" meaningless. [1]

Professor Jeremy Waldron has suggested that property be viewed as a "system of rules governing access to and control of material resources."[2] In a world of scarce resources, property rules help (Hobbes would say property rules are necessary) to determine how material resources are allocated.

---

1. *See* Grey, The Disintegration of Property, XXII Nomos 69, 81 (1980) (arguing that the bundle-of-rights metaphor has eliminated "property" as "an important category in legal and political theory").

2. Waldron, What Is Private Property?, 5 Oxford J. Leg. Stud. 313, 318 (1985). Property certainly involves tangibles, such as land, cars, and books, and intangibles, such as stock, copyrights, trademarks, and patents. Some authors have argued that property should include governmental largesse, such as welfare entitlements, jobs, subsidies, and licenses. *See* Reich, The New Property, 73 Yale L.J. 733 (1964). Should it also include one's reputation?

Waldron argues that not all rules governing resources should be considered property rules. Safety rules, for example, which delimit appropriate uses of a car regardless of the user's entitlement to use it, normally are not considered property rules. Property rights, in this example, concern the entitlement to use the car.[3] In other cases, clear categorization is not so easy or even possible. As you will see later, a lease has characteristics of both contract and property.

Having defined the general concept of property, Waldron then shows that different permutations of the bundle of rights are just different conceptions of property.[4] While the right to exclude and the right to transfer are not essential to the general concept of property—one can easily imagine communal or statist property systems in which these rights do not exist with respect to significant resources—they are pretty basic in market-based economies.

The balance of this chapter explores the jurisprudential underpinnings of property, particularly private property. Part A surveys the principal philosophical justifications of private property. Part B is a case study of the development of Indian and colonial European property regimes in New England. The case study attempts to test the proposition that a society's conception of property adapts to promote the beneficial use of resources, from that society's perspective. Finally, Part C compares different property regimes that have developed to allocate particular resources—whales, oyster beds, and lobster territories.

A.   PHILOSOPHICAL PERSPECTIVES

In market economies, such as ours, four competing justifications are commonly offered for private property. These justifications are Locke's natural rights theory that one owns property in resources when he has mixed his labor with Nature; Hegel's theory that private property rights over some resources are necessary to ensure proper development as a person; Rawls' theory of distributive justice; and utilitarianism.

1.   NATURAL RIGHTS

In this excerpt, Locke develops a natural law theory to explain and justify the origins of private property. As you read the excerpt, think carefully about the limits of Locke's theory.

3. 5 Oxford J.L.Stud. at 320–21. At one point, the American Law Institute defined property as including any "rights, privileges, powers and immunities." The definition was so broad that it was meaningless.

4. *Id.* at 334–40. Waldron also points out that in contrast to the legal philosopher, the technical lawyer generally is less concerned with "property" and "ownership," which are too indeterminate for most practical problems, than with specific legal entitlements or obligations that may attach to particular resources.

John Locke, Second Treatise of Government

Chapter 5 (3rd ed. 1698).

Though the earth and all inferior creatures be common to all men, yet every man has a "property" in his own "person." This nobody has any right to but himself. The "labour" of his body and the "work" of his hands, we may say, are properly his. Whatsoever, then, he removes out of the state that Nature hath provided and left it in, he hath mixed his labor with it, and joined to it something that is his own, and thereby makes it his property. It being by him removed from the common state Nature placed it in, it hath by this labour something annexed to it that excludes the common right of other men. For this "labour" being the unquestionable property of the labourer, no man but he can have a right to what that is once joined to, at least where there is enough, and as good left in common for others.

He that is nourished by the acorns he picked up under an oak, or the apples he gathered from the trees in the wood, has certainly appropriated them to himself. * * * That labour put a distinction between them and common. * * * And will any one say he had no right to those acorns or apples he thus appropriated because he had not the consent of all mankind to make them his? Was it a robbery thus to assume to himself what belonged to all in common? If such a consent as that was necessary, man had starved, notwithstanding the plenty God had given him. We see in commons, which remain so by compact, that it is the taking any part of what is common, and removing it out of the state Nature leaves it in, which begins the property, without which the common is of no use. And the taking of this or that part does not depend on the express consent of all the commoners. * * *

It will, perhaps, be objected to this, that if gathering the acorns or other fruits, of the earth, etc., makes a right to them, then any one may engross as much as he will. To which I answer, Not so. The same law of Nature that does by this means give us property, does also bound that property too. * * * As much as any one can make use of to any advantage of life before it spoils, so much he may by his labor fix his property in. Whatever is beyond this is more than his share, and belongs to others. * * *

As much land as a man tills, plants, improves, cultivates, and can use the product of, so much is his property. He by his labor does, as it were, enclose it from the common. * * *

Nor was this appropriation of any parcel of land, by improving it, any prejudice to any other man, since there was still enough and as good left, and more than the yet unprovided could use. So that, in effect, there was never the less left for others because of his enclosure for himself. For he that leaves as much as another can make use of does as good as take nothing at all.

1.   Locke asserts at the beginning of his argument that every person has property in his or her own body. Is his assertion accurate? Is a person free to inject heroin? Is a person free to sell his organs—an extra kidney or some bone marrow—during his lifetime?

Is property the best legal concept to decide such issues? Suppose a medical researcher collected some cells from a patient in the normal course of medical treatment. Without the patient's agreement or even knowledge, the researcher used the cells to develop a cell line that became commercially and medically valuable. Should the patient have the right to sue for conversion (theft of his property) for damages or injunctive relief? *See Moore v. Regents of University of California*, 51 Cal.3d 120, 271 Cal.Rptr. 146, 793 P.2d 479 (1990).

Suppose a married couple, anticipating future problems about fertility, had some of the husband's sperm frozen and stored for later use. Thereafter, the husband died. Is the wife entitled to the frozen sperm on the ground that it is property and therefore passes to her in her husband's will? *See Hecht v. Superior Court*, 16 Cal.App.4th 836, 850, 20 Cal.Rptr.2d 275, 283 (1993). Would your answer change if the legal dispute were a divorce and the soon-to-be-former wife claimed that she was entitled to half of the frozen sperm under the state laws requiring equal division of marital property upon divorce?

Suppose the couple had not frozen sperm but embryos. Should the spouses base their claims to possession on the theory that the embryos are property? *See York v. Jones*, 717 F.Supp. 421 (E.D.Va.1989) (suit by married couple against hospital for possession of frozen embryos); *Davis v. Davis*, 842 S.W.2d 588, 597 (Tenn.1992) (spouses' claims for possession of frozen embryos in divorce). *See generally* Ramaden, Frozen Semen As Property in *Hecht v. Superior Court*: One Step Forward, Two Steps Backward, 62 UMKC L. Rev. 377 (1994) (arguing that courts should rely more heavily on property rights to decide issues involving "reproductive materials").

2.   What limits does Locke's theory impose on an individual's ability to appropriate previously unclaimed resources? Is even the most trivial amount of labor enough to acquire the resource? Does it matter if the labor is inefficient or unproductive? *See* R. Nozick, Anarchy and Utopia 175 (1974). Would minor or unproductive amounts of labor not suffice to create property because Locke's theory really rests on a notion of "desert," that is, reward for useful labor? *See* L. Becker, Property Rights: Philosophic Foundations 49 (1977).

3.   How would Locke's theory apply where different people want to make different uses of the same resource—*e.g.*, a farm versus a factory, or a fishery versus a canal?

4.   How would Locke's theory apply to the ownership of things other than land and its fruits? Would a person who used a fishery thereby own the fishery, or just the fish he caught? Would it apply to ideas?

5. Locke's theory is built upon value creation and productive use of resources. To what extent does it recognize passive or non-developmental uses of land, such as recreation and habitat protection?

6. Locke asserts that property arises when a person mixes his labor with a material resource; as a result of the mixing, the person "removes" the resource from its "common state" and becomes "bound" with it. Could labor reasonably be viewed as serving a different or perhaps additional function—a "clear statement" that reduces wasteful conflict over competing claims? Consider the common law doctrine of "first possession," which gives property rights to the first person to possess unowned material resources. Regarding this doctrine and its relationship to Locke's labor theory of property, Carol Rose argues:

> The doctrine of first possession * * * reflects the attitude that human beings are outsiders to nature. It gives the earth and its creatures over to those who mark them so clearly as to transform them, so that no one else will mistake them for unsubdued nature.
>
> We may admire nature and enjoy wilderness, but those sentiments find little resonance in the doctrine of first possession. Its texts are those of cultivation, manufacture, and development. * * * The common law gives preference to those who convince the world that they have caught the fish and hold it fast. This may be a reward to useful labor, but it is more precisely the articulation of a specific vocabulary within a structure of symbols approved and understood by a commercial people. It is this commonly understood and shared set of symbols that gives significance and form to what might seem the quintessentially individualistic act: the claim that one has, by possession, separated oneself property from the great commons of unowned things.

Rose, Possession as the Origin of Property, 52 U. Chi. L. Rev. 73, 87–88 (1985).

---

2. PERSONHOOD

Professor Margaret Radin's article explores the relationship between property and personhood, a relationship that has commonly been both ignored and taken for granted in legal thought. The premise underlying the personhood perspective is that to achieve proper self-development—to be *a person*—an individual needs some control over resources in the external environment. The necessary assurances of control take the form of property rights. Although explicit elaboration of this perspective is wanting in modern writing on property, the personhood perspective is often implicit in the connections that courts and commentators find between property and privacy or between property and liberty. In addition to its power to explain certain aspects of existing schemes of property entitlement, the personhood perspective can also serve as an explicit source of values for making moral distinctions in property disputes, and hence for either justifying or criticizing current law.

Margaret Jane Radin, Property and Personhood

34 Stanford Law Review 957, 958–60, 972–73, 976–78, 1003–06 (1982).

* * *

In what follows I shall discuss the personhood perspective as Hegel developed it in *Philosophy of Right*, trace some of its later permutations and entanglements with other perspectives on property, and try to develop a contemporary view useful in the context of the American legal system.
* * *

I.   Property for Personhood: An Intuitive View

Most people possess certain objects they feel are almost part of themselves. These objects are closely bound up with personhood because they are part of the way we constitute ourselves as continuing personal entities in the world. They may be as different as people are different, but some common examples might be a wedding ring, a portrait, an heirloom, or a house.

One may gauge the strength or significance of someone's relationship with an object by the kind of pain that would be occasioned by its loss. On this view, an object is closely related to one's personhood if its loss causes pain that cannot be relieved by the object's replacement. If so, that particular object is bound up with the holder. For instance, if a wedding ring is stolen from a jeweler, insurance proceeds can reimburse the jeweler, but if a wedding ring is stolen from a loving wearer, the price of a replacement will not restore the status quo—perhaps no amount of money can do so.

The opposite of holding an object that has become a part of oneself is holding an object that is perfectly replaceable with other goods of equal market value. One holds such an object for purely instrumental reasons. The archetype of such a good is, of course, money, which is almost always held only to buy other things. A dollar is worth no more than what one chooses to buy with it, and one dollar bill is as good as another. Other examples are the wedding ring in the hands of the jeweler, the automobile in the hands of the dealer, the land in the hands of the developer, or the apartment in the hands of the commercial landlord. I shall call these theoretical opposites—property that is bound up with a person and property that is held purely instrumentally—personal property and fungible property respectively.

* * *

III.   Hegel, Property, and Personhood

A.   *Hegel's Philosophy of Right*

* * *

Because the person in Hegel's conception is merely an abstract unit of free will or autonomy, it has no concrete existence until that will acts on the external world. * * *

Hegel concludes that the person becomes a real self only by engaging in a property relationship with something external. Such a relationship is the goal of the person. In perhaps the best-known passage from this book, Hegel says:

> The person has for its substantive end the right of placing its will in any and every thing, which thing is thereby mine; [and] because that thing has no such end in itself, its destiny and soul take on my will. [This constitutes] mankind's absolute right of appropriation over all things.

Hence, "property is the first embodiment of freedom and so is in itself a substantive end." * * *

Hegel seems to make property "private" on the same level as the unit of autonomy that is embodying its will by holding it. He argues that property is private to individuals when discussing it in the context of the autonomous individual will and that it is essentially common within a family, when discussing it in the context of the autonomous family unit. He does not make the leap to state property, however, even though his theory of the state might suggest it. For Hegel, the properly developed state (in contrast to civil society) is an organic moral entity * * * and individuals within the state are subsumed into its community morality. * * *

B. *Hegel and Property for Personhood*

[A] theory of personal property can build upon some of Hegel's insights. First, the notion that the will is embodied in things suggests that the entity we know as a person cannot come to exist without both differentiating itself from the physical environment and yet maintaining relationships with portions of that environment. The idea of embodied will, cut loose from Hegel's grand scheme of absolute mind, reminds us that people and things have ongoing relationships which have their own ebb and flow, and that these relationships can be very close to a person's center and sanity. If these relationships justify ownership, or at least contribute to its justification, Hegel's notion that ownership requires continuous embodiment of the will is appealing.

Second, Hegel's incompletely developed notion that property is held by the unit to which one attributes autonomy has powerful implications for the concept of group development and group rights. Hegel thought that freedom (rational self-determination) was only possible in the context of a group (the properly organized and fully developed state). Without accepting this role for the state, one may still conclude that in a given social context certain groups are likely to be constitutive of their members in the sense that the members find self-determination only within the groups. This might have political consequences for claims of the group on certain resources of the external world (*i.e.,* property).

Third, there may be an echo of Hegel's notion of an objective community morality in the intuition that certain kinds of property relationships can be presumed to bear close bonds to personhood. If property in one's body is not too close to personhood to be considered property at all, then it is the clearest case of property for personhood. The property/privacy nexus of the home is also a relatively clear case in our particular history and culture.

* * *

V.   Two Kinds of Property: A Selective Survey

[T]he personhood theory helps us understand the nature of the right dictating that discrete units [*i.e.,* an undivided, individual asset] ought to be protected.

An argument that discrete units are more important than total assets takes the following form. A person cannot be fully a person without a sense of continuity of self over time. To maintain that sense of continuity over time and to exercise one's liberty or autonomy, one must have an ongoing relationship with the external environment, consisting of both "things" and other people. One perceives the ongoing relationship to the environment as a set of individual relationships, corresponding to the way our perception separates the world into distinct "things." Some things must remain stationary if anything is to move; some points of reference must be constant or thought and action is not possible. In order to lead a normal life, there must be some continuity in relating to "things." One's expectations crystallize around certain "things," the loss of which causes more disruption and disorientation than does a simple decrease in aggregate wealth. For example, if someone returns home to find her sofa has disappeared, that is more disorienting than to discover that her house has decreased in market value by 5%. If, by magic, her white sofa were instantly replaced by a blue one of equal market value, it would cause no loss in net worth but would still cause some disruption in her life.

This argument assumes that all discrete units one owns and perceives as part of her continuing environment are to some degree personal. If the white sofa were totally fungible, then magically replacing it with a blue one would cause no disruption. In fact, neither would replacing it with money.

* * *

[G]ranting relief for object-loss permits line-drawing. Courts can perceive whether or not an object has been taken, but cannot in the same way discern whether "too much" wealth has been taken. But the argument above suggests that another element in the explanation is courts' understanding of the necessity of object relations in ordinary life. Object-loss is more important than wealth-loss because object-loss is specially related to personhood in a way that wealth-loss is not. The cases economists find mysterious are mysterious just because economists generally treat property as fungible, and those cases treat it as personal.

But the theory of personal property suggests that not all object-loss is equally important. Some objects may approach the fungible end of the continuum so that the justification for protecting them as specially related to persons disappears. They might just as well be treated by whatever general moral rules govern wealth-loss at the hands of the government. If the moral rules governing wealth-loss correspond to Michelman's utilitarian suggestion—government may take whatever wealth is necessary to generate higher welfare in which the individual can confidently expect to share—then the government could take some fungible items without compensation. In general, the moral inquiry for whether fungible property could be taken would be the same as the moral inquiry for whether it is fair to impose a tax on this particular person.

On the other hand, a few objects may be so close to the personal end of the continuum that no compensation could be "just." That is, hypothetically, if some object were so bound up with me that I would cease to be "myself" if it were taken, then a government that must respect persons ought not to take it. If my kidney may be called my property, it is not property subject to condemnation for the general public welfare. Hence, in the context of a legal system, one might expect to find the characteristic use of standards of review and burdens of proof designed to shift risk of error away from protected interests in personal property. For instance, if there were reason to suspect that some object were close to the personal end of the continuum, there might be a prima facie case against taking it. That prima facie case might be rebutted if the government could show that the object is not personal, or perhaps that the object is not "too" personal compared with the importance to the government of acquiring that particular object for social purposes.

This suggests that if the personhood perspective is expressed in law, one might expect to find an implied limitation on the eminent domain power. That is, one might expect to find that a special class of property like a family home is protected against the government by a "property rule" and not just a "liability rule." Or one might expect to find that a special class of property is protected against taking unless the government shows a "compelling state interest" and that taking it is the "least intrusive alternative."

This general limitation has not developed. Perhaps the personhood perspective is not strong enough to outweigh other concerns, especially the government's need to appear even-handed and the lower administrative costs associated with simpler rules. * * * On the other hand, perhaps the personhood perspective is so deeply embedded that, without focusing on the problem, we expect that the condemning authority will take fungible property where possible. * * * Still, the fact that the personhood perspective has not surfaced to give some explicit protection to family homes from government taking, such as stricter scrutiny, seems to be anomalous.

―――――――――――

1. Is personhood theory sufficiently objective to provide a workable basis for legislatures, government agencies, or courts to make predictable

and equitable decisions regarding property rights? Does the theory anticipate a bright line between "fungible" and "personal" objects? What are the criteria to be used to draw that line?

2.   What types of property disputes seem most appropriate for applying personhood theory? Consider the following examples:

(a) whether to allow a city to use its power of eminent domain to condemn part of a closely knit neighborhood to build a new sports complex that will provide enhanced job opportunities and revitalize a depressed inner city (see *Poletown Neighborhood Council v. City of Detroit*, 410 Mich. 616, 304 N.W.2d 455 (1981));

(b) whether to relax rent control laws so as to encourage investment, thereby spurring the gentrification of decaying housing stock;

(c) whether to enact amendments to the copyright law to allow creators of black and white films (or their estates) to block colorization of their work for an unlimited term.

How does personhood theory help to make the appropriate social choices?

3.   Does personhood theory provide a comprehensive theory of property rights? Does it explain how to define rights in resources that are at "the fungible end of the continuum"?   For further elaboration and refinements of Radin's work, see M. Radin, Reinterpreting Property (1993).

---

3.   DISTRIBUTIVE JUSTICE

In A Theory of Justice (1971)—probably the most influential work of political philosophy written in the past century—John Rawls offers an "ideal contractarian" theory of distributive shares. To determine the just allocation of the benefits and burdens of social life, he asks what distributive principles would suitably disinterested persons choose. To ask what *selfish* people would want, or what social contract would *actually* result from a convocation of all members of society, Rawls argues, would ensure that the naturally smart or strong, or people who shared a particular race, nationality, religion, or ideology, dominated the rest, if any agreement could be reached at all. Rawls rejects this construction of the "original position" for choosing social rules—which more libertarian philosophers, such as David Gauthier, come closer to favoring—because he finds this consequence intuitively unacceptable. He assumes instead that the resources and opportunities a person should have available should not depend primarily on how fortunate he or she was in the natural lottery of talents and parents, or in what group that person happens to be born.

Rawls therefore tries to determine principles that rational people behind a "veil of ignorance" would choose. Rawls contends that the veil must be quite opaque. It must, for example, exclude from the minds of those choosing principles of justice all knowledge of their own abilities, desires, parentage, and social stratum.

Rawls concludes that people behind the veil of ignorance would adopt what he calls the "difference principle." They would agree, he says, that the fundamental institutions of society should be arranged so that the distribution of "primary goods"—not only wealth, income, and opportunities for work or leisure, but also what Rawls terms the "bases of self-respect"—is to the maximal advantage of a representative member of the least advantaged social class. Defining the least advantaged class and the proper set of primary goods is difficult and contentious. Rawls has attempted to do so with care over the last twenty years; the results appear in his new book, Political Liberalism (1993). Rawls refines his theory of distributive justice in the following passage:

> * * * [M]easures are required to assure that the basic needs of all citizens can be met so that they can take part in political and social life.

> About this last point, the idea is not that of satisfying needs as opposed to mere desires and wants; nor is it that of redistribution in favor of greater equality. The constitutional essential here is rather that below a certain level of material and social well-being, and of training and education, people simply cannot take part in society as citizens, much less equal citizens.

Id. at 166.

James Q. Wilson, The Moral Sense
73–76 (1993).

* * * As I understand him everybody in Rawls's universe is averse to risk; each wants to make certain that, if he winds up on the bottom of the heap, the bottom is as attractive as possible.

But many people are in fact not averse to risk, they are risk takers; to them, a just society would be one in which inequalities in wealth were acceptable provided that the people at the top of the heap got there as a result of effort and skill. And even people who are not risk takers may endorse this position because they think it fair that rewards should be proportional to effort, even if some people lose out entirely. (These same people might also expect their church or government to take care of those who lost out.) They have this view of fairness because they recognize that people differ in talent, energy, temperament, and interests; that conflicts among such people are inevitable; and that matching, as best one can, rewards to contributions is the best way of handling that conflict.

To test this view, let us imagine a society in which property is distributed more or less equally. * * * Indeed, we can more than imagine such a society, we can study it.

The San are African bushmen who live in small groups, or bands, that until quite recently foraged widely through inhospitable parts of Namibia,

Botswana, and Angola, hunting animals and picking edibles. Only a few simple possessions were required by their livelihood or permitted by their mobility. With few fixed places of abode, their sense of land tenure was more directed to the broad territory that they canvassed than to a specific residence that they occupied. Under these circumstances it is not surprising that most differences among people were not thought sufficiently great to warrant large differences in treatment. Food brought back to the camp was distributed equally among all, with the successful hunter having no greater claim than anyone else. Arrowheads that had killed animals did not remain as trophies of the hunter but were exchanged among other members of the band, women as well as men. Contrary to what some Western observers have suggested, San life was not idyllic, nor were they quite the "harmless people" sometimes depicted: not only were the San very poor, their children (although raised in the most tender fashion) were cruel to animals, husbands (although sharing in child care) occasionally beat their wives, and adults (though they were hospitable to strangers and unfamiliar with war) committed homicides at a rate that exceeds that found in many American cities.

But if not idyllic, San society was indisputably egalitarian. The weak division of labor, the need for cooperation, and the difficulty of accumulating or transporting possessions fostered the view that everyone's contribution (or in terms of equity theory, input) was roughly the same as everybody else's, and so everyone's benefits (or output) should be about the same. Culture reinforced necessity: the San engaged in ritual joking designed to deflate any claims to status or prowess. Though the San are the best-known hunter-gatherer societies, there are others and once were many others and, insofar as we can tell, most tended toward an egalitarian structure.

When these peoples became settled, however, things changed. They may have acquired a sedentary life voluntarily (as when it became possible to raise crops and keep cattle), involuntarily (as when an outside power compelled them to live on reservations), or opportunistically (as when the chance arose to work for cash wages for other people). Whatever the process, the people now live in fixed abodes from whence they herd the cattle, raise crops, or earn cash incomes. Living in one place requires less cooperation and permits a greater division of labor than being on the move. Cash, unlike fresh meat, can be stored and hidden. Proximity to industrial societies means that cash and crops can be exchanged for manufactured goods, not the least of which is alcohol. They can even become actors in movies such as *The Gods Must Be Crazy*. One San woman who had a part in that film used her wages to buy things that she would not share with her kin, thereby provoking a fight.

Jean–Jacques Rousseau might have had the settled San [in] mind when he wrote, with heavy sarcasm, this famous line to explain the origin of human inequality: "The first man who, having enclosed a piece of ground, bethought himself of saying, *This is mine*, and found people simple enough to believe him, was the real founder of civil society." The entire *Discourse on the Origin of Inequality* [1758] can be read as a commentary on what we know about the transition from hunter-gatherer to sedentary societies. Building huts meant acquiring property, "the source of a thousand quarrels and conflicts." Settled into those huts, the men "went abroad in search of their common subsistence" while the women "became more sedentary and accustomed themselves to mind the hut and their children." Tools become valuable and their possession possible, and so men became beholden to them and alert to the differences in status implied by differences in their ownership.

The many contemporary followers of Rousseau read these words as an argument against inequality, but if anything, they are an argument against civilization, by which I mean settled living and the division of labor. Rousseau clearly preferred premodern man to modern man and opposed political society, which, arising out of the need to protect property, "bound new fetters on the poor and gave new powers to the rich; irretrievably destroyed natural liberty, fixed externally the law of property and inequality, converted clever usurpation into unalterable right, and, for the advantage of a few ambitious individuals, subjected all mankind to perpetual labour, slavery, and wretchedness."

But this unhappy state of affairs did not arise because men were naturally equal; rather, it arose because the conditions of settled life forced men to recognize, act upon, and reinforce their natural inequalities, inequalities that hunter-gatherers could afford—indeed, were obliged—to overlook. In settled societies, Rousseau wrote, "equality might have been sustained, had the talents of individuals been equal." But they are not: Once the division of labor took effect, "the strongest did the most work; the most skillful turned his labour to best account; the most ingenious devised methods of diminishing his labour." While all might work equally, the one would gain much while the other "could hardly support himself." Though laws may legitimate and even magnify these differences, "all the inequality which now prevails owes it strength and growth to the development of our faculties and the advance of the human mind."

Equality is a special and, as it turns out, rare and precarious case of equity. Settled living, and in particular the accumulation of private property, makes equality of outcomes impossible because inequality of contributions become manifest. The task of settled societies is to devise ways of assuring that outcomes are proportional to worth, reasonably defined.

---

1. Do you agree with Rawls that people behind the veil of ignorance would agree that the fundamental institutions of society should be arranged so that the distribution of "primary goods"—including property—is to the maximal advantage of a representative member of the least advan-

taged social class? Would you agree to this principle if you were behind a veil of ignorance?

2.   What do Rawls' principles of distributive justice imply for the rights in real property? Do they necessarily imply a mechanism to redistribute wealth equally? Could his principles tolerate substantial differences in wealth?

3.   Under Rawls' principles, what obligations does society have to provide shelter? Should such an obligation extend to all who desire shelter? To what extent should the effect of a "right to shelter" on work incentives be considered in developing a homelessness policy? *See* Ellickson, The Untenable Case for an Unconditional Right to Shelter, 15 Harv. J.L. & Pub. Pol'y 17 (1992) (arguing that unconditional welfare rights would substantially reduce individuals' incentive to work and would, by reducing the total economic productivity of society, hurt poor people); Berger, Beyond Homelessness: An Entitlement to Housing, 45 U. Miami L. Rev. 315 (1990) (arguing for a statutory right to housing); Michelman, Welfare Rights in a Constitutional Democracy, 1979 Wash. U.L.Q. 659 (arguing for unconditional welfare rights).

---

4.   Utilitarianism

The utilitarian framework, on which neoclassical economic theory is based, views the goal of society to allocate resources so as to maximize the aggregate welfare or satisfaction ("utility" in the jargon of economists) of its citizens. In contrast to distributive justice frameworks, utilitarianism focuses upon average utility rather than its distribution. Utilitarianism is a consequentialist perspective, evaluating social policies solely by reference to their impact on citizens' welfare as opposed to independent moral imperatives or precepts.

A fundamental principle of economics is that free market competition will ensure an efficient allocation of resources in the absence of market failures, such as monopoly or high transaction or information costs. Through an auctioning mechanism, markets allocate resources to their most valued use, as measured by willingness to pay. The market thus provides a strong incentive for the creation of valuable goods. *See generally* P. Samuelson & W. Nordhaus, Economics 678 (12th ed. 1985).

According to utilitarianism, legal institutions should be principally concerned with establishing and enforcing property rights and fostering the voluntary exchange of goods and services through contract. The first excerpt below highlights this dimension. Legal rules and institutions, however, must also play a role in addressing market failures—those circumstances in which social costs and benefits are not adequately reflected in market exchange. The second excerpt provides a classic introduction to this set of problems.

Richard A. Posner, Economic Analysis of Law

10–13 (1973).*

I.   THE ECONOMIC THEORY OF PROPERTY RIGHTS

Imagine a society in which all property rights have been abolished. A farmer plants corn, fertilizes it, and erects scarecrows, but when the corn is ripe his neighbor reaps and sells it. The farmer has no legal remedy against his neighbor's conduct since he owns neither the land that he sowed nor the crop. After a few such incidents the cultivation of land will be abandoned and the society will shift to methods of subsistence (such as hunting) that involve less preparatory investment.

This example suggests that the legal protection of property rights has an important economic function: to create incentives to use resources efficiently. Although the value of the crop in our example, as measured by consumer willingness to pay, may have greatly exceeded the cost in labor, materials, and forgone alternative uses of the land, without property rights there is no incentive to incur these costs because there is no reasonably assured reward for incurring them. The proper incentives are created by the parceling out among the members of society of mutually exclusive rights to the use of particular resources. If every piece of land is owned by someone, in the sense that there is always an individual who can exclude all others from access to any given area, then individuals will endeavor by cultivation or other improvements to maximize the value of land.

The creation of exclusive rights is a necessary rather than sufficient condition for the efficient use of resources. The rights must be transferable. Suppose the farmer in our example owns the land that he sows but is a bad farmer; his land would be more productive in someone else's hands. The maximization of value requires a mechanism by which the farmer can be induced to transfer rights in the property to someone who can work it more productively. A transferable property right is such a mechanism.

An example will illustrate. Farmer A owns a piece of land that he anticipates will yield him $100 a year, in excess of labor and other costs, indefinitely. The value of the right to a stream of future earnings can be expressed as a present sum. Just as the price of a share of common stock expresses the present value of the anticipated earnings to which the shareholder will be entitled, so the present value of a parcel of land that yields an annual net income of $100 can be calculated and is the minimum price that A will accept in exchange for his property right. Farmer B believes that he can use A's land more productively than A. Stated another way, B thinks he could net more than $100 a year from working A's land. The present value of B's higher expected earnings stream will, of course, exceed the present value calculated by A. Assume the present value calculated by A is $1000 and B $1500. Then sale of the property right by A to B will yield benefits to both parties if the price is anywhere between

$1000 and $1500. At a price of $1250, for example, A receives $250 more than the land is worth to him and B pays $250 less than the land is worth to *him*. Thus, there are strong incentives for the parties voluntarily to exchange A's land for B's money, and if B is as he believes a better farmer than A, the transfer will result in an increase in the productivity of the land. Through a succession of such transfers, resources are shifted to their highest valued, most productive uses and efficiency in the use of economic resources is maximized.

The foregoing discussion suggests three criteria of an efficient system of property rights. The first is *universality*. Ideally, all resources should be owned, or ownable, by someone, except resources so plentiful that everybody can consume as much of them as he wants without reducing consumption by anyone else (sunlight is a good, but not perfect, example—why?). No issue of efficient use arises in such a case.

The second criterion—but one that requires, as we shall see, careful qualification—is *exclusivity*. We have assumed so far that either the farmer can exclude no one or he can exclude everyone, but of course there are intermediate stages: the farmer may be entitled to exclude private individuals from reaping his crop, but not the government in time of war. It might appear that the more exclusive the property right, the greater the incentive to invest the right amount of resources in the development of the property. Suppose our farmer estimates that he can raise a hog with a market value of $100 at a cost of only $50 in labor and materials. Suppose further that there is no alternative combination of resources and land use that would yield a greater excess of value over cost: in the next best use his net income from the land would be only $20. He will raise the hog. But now suppose his property right is less than exclusive in two respects. First, he has no right to prevent an adjacent railroad from accidentally emitting engine sparks that may set fire to the hog's pen, killing it prematurely. Second, he has no right to prevent the local government from rezoning his land from agricultural to residential use and compelling him to sell the hog at disadvantageous terms before it is grown. In light of these contingencies he must reevaluate the yield of his land: he must discount the $100 to reflect the probability that the yield may be much less, perhaps zero. Suppose, after discounting, the expected revenue from raising the hog (market value times the probability that it will reach the market) is only $60. He will not raise the hog. He will shift to the next best use of the land, which we said was less valuable.[5]

The analysis, however, is incomplete. While the farmer will be induced, as a consequence of no longer enjoying an exclusive property right, to shift to an alternative land use that *seems* less efficient, overall efficiency may be increased. The removal of the hog my result in an increase in the value of surrounding residential land greater than the reduction in the value of the farmer's parcel. The cost of preventing the emission of engine sparks may

---

5. The profit from raising the hog is now $10, since his costs are $50. The next best use, we said, yields a profit of $20.

be larger than the reduction in the value of the farmer's land when he switches from hog raising to, say, growing radishes. To this, the very alert reader may be tempted to reply that if the increase in value to others from a different use of the farmer's land exceeds the decrease to him, they can buy his right: the railroad can purchase an easement to emit sparks; the surrounding homeowners can purchase a covenant from the farmer not to raise hogs. Often, however, the costs of effecting a transfer of rights—transaction costs—are prohibitive; but more on this shortly.

The third criterion of an efficient system of property rights is *transferability*. If a property right cannot be transferred, there is no way of shifting a resource from a less productive to a more productive use through voluntary exchange. The cost of transfer may be high to begin with; a legal prohibition against transferring may, depending on the penalties for violation, make the costs utterly prohibitive. We shall see that when the costs of transferring property rights are high, the attempt to achieve our second criterion, exclusivity, may actually reduce the efficiency of the property rights system. * * *

Garrett Hardin, The Tragedy of the Commons

162 Science 1243, 1244–45 (1968).*

    * * *

The tragedy of the commons develops in this way. Picture a pasture open to all. It is to be expected that each herdsman will try to keep as many cattle as possible on the commons. Such an arrangement may work reasonably satisfactorily for centuries because tribal wars, poaching, and disease keep the numbers of both man and beast well below the carrying capacity of the land. Finally, however, comes the day of reckoning, that is, the day when the long-desired goal of social stability becomes a reality. At this point, the inherent logic of the commons remorselessly generates tragedy.

As a rational being, each herdsman seeks to maximize his gain. Explicitly or implicitly, more or less consciously, he asks, "What is the utility *to me* of adding one more animal to my herd?" This utility has one negative and one positive component.

(1) The positive component is a function of the increment of one animal. Since the herdsman receives all the proceeds from the sale of the additional animal, the positive utility is nearly $+1$.

(2) The negative component is a function of the additional overgrazing created by one more animal. Since, however, the effects of overgrazing are

* Reprinted with permission from Garrett Hardin, "The Tragedy of the Commons," 162 Science 1243, 1244–45 (1986) © 1986 American Association for the Advancement of Science.

shared by all the herdsmen, the negative utility for any particular decision-making herdsman is only a fraction of –1.

Adding together the component partial utilities, the rational herdsman concludes that the only sensible course for him to pursue is to add another animal to his herd. And another; and another.... But this is the conclusion reached by each and every rational herdsman sharing a commons. Therein is the tragedy. Each man is locked into a system that compels him to increase his herd without limit—in a world that is limited. Ruin is the destination toward which all men rush, each pursuing his own best interest in a society that believes in the freedom of the commons. Freedom in a commons brings ruin to all.

Some would say that this is a platitude. Would that it were! In a sense, it was learned thousands of years ago, but natural selection favors the forces of psychological denial. The individual benefits as an individual from his ability to deny the truth even though society as a whole, of which he is a part, suffers. Education can counteract the natural tendency to do the wrong thing, but the inexorable succession of generations requires that the basis for this knowledge be constantly refreshed.

A simple incident that occurred a few years ago in Leominster, Massachusetts, shows how perishable the knowledge is. During the Christmas shopping season the parking meters downtown were covered with plastic bags that bore tags reading: "Do not open until after Christmas. Free parking courtesy of the mayor and the city council." In other words, facing the prospect of an increased demand for already scarce space, the city fathers reinstated the system of the commons. (Cynically, we suspect that they gained more votes than they lost by this retrogressive act.)

In an approximate way, the logic of the commons has been understood for a long time, perhaps since the discovery of agriculture or the invention of private property in real estate. But it is understood mostly only in special cases which are not sufficiently generalized. Even at this late date, cattlemen leasing national land on the western ranges demonstrate no more than an ambivalent understanding, in constantly pressuring federal authorities to increase the head count to the point where overgrazing produces erosion and weed-dominance. Likewise, the oceans of the world continue to suffer from the survival of the philosophy of the commons. Maritime nations still respond automatically to the shibboleth of the "freedom of the seas." Professing to believe in the "inexhaustible resources of the oceans," they bring species after species of fish and whales closer to extinction.

The National Parks present another instance of the working out of the tragedy of the commons. At present, they are open to all, without limit. The parks themselves are limited in extent—there is only one Yosemite Valley—whereas population seems to grow without limit. The values that visitors seek in the parks are steadily eroded. Plainly, we must soon cease to treat the parks as commons or they will be of no value to anyone.

What shall we do? We have several options. We might sell them off as private property. We might keep them as public property, but allocate the right to enter them. The allocation might be on the basis of wealth, by the use of an auction system. It might be on the basis of merit, as defined by some agreed upon standards. It might be by lottery. Or it might be on a first-come, first-served basis, administered to long queues. These, I think, are all the reasonable possibilities. They are all objectionable. But we must choose—or acquiesce in the destruction of the commons that we call our National Parks.

Pollution

In a reverse way, the tragedy of the commons reappears in problems of pollution. Here it is not a question of taking something out of the commons, but of putting something in—sewage, or chemical, radioactive, and heat wastes into water; noxious and dangerous fumes into the air; and distracting and unpleasant advertising signs into the line of sight. The calculations of utility are much the same as before. The rational man finds that his share of the cost of the wastes he discharges into the commons is less than the cost of purifying his wastes before releasing them. Since this is true for everyone, we are locked into a system of "fouling our own nest," so long as we behave only as independent, rational, free-enterprisers.

The tragedy of the commons as a food basket is averted by private property, or something formally like it. But the air and waters surrounding us cannot readily be fenced, and so the tragedy of the commons as a cesspool must be prevented by different means, by coercive laws or taxing devices that make it cheaper for the polluter to treat his pollutants than to discharge them untreated. We have not progressed as far with the solution of this problem as we have with the first. Indeed, our particular concept of private property, which deters us from exhausting the positive resources of the earth, favors pollution. The owner of a factory on the bank of a stream—whose property extends to the middle of the stream—often has difficulty seeing why it is not his natural right to muddy the waters flowing past his door. The law, always behind the times, requires elaborate stitching and fitting to adapt it to this newly perceived aspect of the commons.
* * *

---

1.   A utilitarian perspective applies readily to the allocation of tangible resources such as land and physical objects. The boundaries surrounding these resources can be clearly defined and property rights assigned and enforced. But as Hardin suggests, many resources cannot be so easily demarcated—air, water, ideas. What does utilitarian theory or economic analysis tell us about how to allocate these resources?

2. Does the City of Berkeley understand the "Tragedy of the Commons" any better than the Mayor of Leominster?

City of Berkeley

```
┌─────────────────────────────────────┐
│ ┌─────────────────────────────────┐ │
│ │                                 │ │
│ │      FREE PARKING EVERY         │ │
│ │    SATURDAY IN DECEMBER         │ │
│ │    ─────────────────────        │ │
│ │       2 HOUR LIMIT              │ │
│ │        ENFORCED!                │ │
│ │                                 │ │
│ └─────────────────────────────────┘ │
└─────────────────────────────────────┘
```

Downtown Berkeley Association

3. Does utilitarianism always imply a preference for private property? Professor Ellickson argues that in some circumstances there are efficiency advantages to group ownership. He points out that setting boundaries and settling boundary disputes can be expensive, and under the right circumstances it may be more efficient to engage in cooperative behavior. Group ownership may also be useful as a means to capture economies of scale (such as with grazing lands) or to spread risks, especially when risks are high (*e.g.*, external security) and individuals do not have alternative means of ensuring against those risks. Robert Ellickson, Property in Land, 102 Yale L.J. 1315, 1332–44 (1993). In what specific instances would utilitarianism favor group ownership?

4. What values would be served by public ownership or open access to resources that would not be served by private property? *See* Joseph Sax, Mountains Without Handrails: Reflections on the National Parks (1980) (arguing that the undeveloped national parks are important in part because of their capacity for providing "reflective or contemplative recreation").

5. Does the utilitarian framework provide an adequate basis to structure property institutions and rights? In what circumstances does utilitarianism particularly succeed? In what circumstances does it particularly fail?

B.   INSTITUTIONS TO MANAGE AND ALLOCATE RESOURCES: A CASE STUDY OF NATIVE AMERICAN AND COLONIST PROPERTY INSTITUTIONS

As you read through the following historical account of early New England, assess the validity of the following proposition: *A society's conception of property and its associated institutions adapt to promote the beneficial use of the society's resources (from the perspective of the particular society).* If you find this proposition wanting, what alternative(s) best characterizes the nature of property institutions?

William Cronon, Changes in the Land: Indians, Colonists, and the Ecology of New England

37–49, 53–75, 128–31 (1983).

Chapter 3

SEASONS OF WANT AND PLENTY

A central fact of temperate ecosystems like those of New England is their periodicity: they are tied to overlapping cycles of light and dark, high and low tides, waxing and waning moons, and especially the long and short days which mean hot and cold seasons. Each plant and animal species makes its adjustments to these various cycles, so that the flowing of sap in trees, the migration of birds, the spawning of fish, the rutting of deer, and the fruiting of plants all have their special times of the year. A plant that stores most of its food energy in its roots during the winter will transfer much of that energy first to its leaves and then to its seeds as the warmer months progress. Such patterns of energy concentration are crucial to any creature which seeks to eat that plant. Because animals, including people, feed on plants and other animals, the ways they obtain their food are largely determined by the cycles in which other species lead their lives. Just as a fox's summer diet of fruit and insects shifts to rodents and birds during the winter, so too did the New England Indians seek to obtain their food wherever it was seasonally most concentrated in the New England ecosystem. Doing so required an intimate understanding of the habits and ecology of other species, and it was this knowledge that the English discovered they lacked.

Indian communities had learned to exploit the seasonal diversity of their environment by practicing mobility: their communities characteristically refused to stay put. The principal social and economic grouping for precolonial New England Indians was the village, a small settlement with perhaps a few hundred inhabitants organized into extended kin networks. Villages, rather than the larger and better-known units called tribes or confederacies, were the centers around which Indian interactions with the environment revolved. But villages were not fixed geographical entities:

their size and location changed on a seasonal basis, communities breaking up and reassembling as social and ecological needs required. Wherever villagers expected to find the greatest natural food supplies, there they went. When fish were spawning, many Indian families might gather at a single waterfall to create a dense temporary settlement in which feasting and celebration were the order of the day; when it was time to hunt in the fall, the same families might be found scattered over many square miles of land. All aspects of Indian life hinged on this mobility. Houses, consisting of wooden frames covered by grass mats or bark, were designed to be taken apart and moved in a few hours. For some groups, the shape of houses changed from season to season to accommodate different densities of population: small wigwams housing one or two families in the summer became in the winter extended longhouses holding many families. When food had to be stored while a village moved elsewhere, it was left in carefully constructed underground pit-barns, where it could be retrieved when needed. Tools and other property were either light and easily carried or just as readily abandoned and remade when needed in a new location. As Thomas Morton observed, "They love not to bee cumbered with many utensilles."

The seasonal cycles within which a village moved depended on the habitats available to it: Indians who had access to the seashore, for instance, could lead rather different lives than their inland counterparts. Important as habitat differences were, however, the crucial distinction between Indian communities was whether or not they had adopted agriculture. In general, Indians south of the Kennebec River in Maine raised crops as part of their annual subsistence cycles; more northern Indians, on the other hand, as Verrazzano noted in 1524 showed "no sign of cultivation." Verrazzano quite reasonably attributed the absence of agriculture in the north to soil which would produce neither fruit nor grain "on account of its sterility": climatic conditions in fact made grain raising an increasingly risky business the farther north an Indian people lived. Because the ability to grow crops had drastic implications for the way a village conducted the rest of its food-gathering activities, it is best to begin our description of Indian subsistence strategies in the north, where Indians were entirely dependent on the natural abundance of the ecosystem. Only in the north did Indians live entirely as hunter-gatherers, people who bore at least superficial resemblance to the creatures of English fantasy who captured nature's bounties with "small labor but great pleasure."

In the north, spring commenced "when the leaves begin to sprout, when the wild geese appear, when the fawns of moose attain to a certain size in the bellies of their mothers, and when the seals bear their young." Most especially, the northern spring began when the ice broke up; then inland populations moved to coastal sites where they repaired fishing gear—nets, tackle, weirs, birchbark canoes—in anticipation of the spawning runs. For Maine Indians who had access to the coast, probably well over half the yearly food supply came from the rivers and seashore. In late March, the smelt arrived in streams and rivers in such quantities that one could not put a "hand into the water, without encountering them." They were followed in April by the alewives, sturgeon, and salmon, so that spawning runs furnished a major share of the food supply from March through May. By early May, nonspawning fish were also providing food. Offshore were cod which had to be caught with hook and line. Closer to land were tidewater and ground fish, such as brook trout, smelt, striped bass, and flounder, all of which could be caught with weirs and nets, and the larger sturgeon and salmon, which were usually harpooned. In the tidal zone were the scallops, clams, mussels, and crabs which women and children gathered as a steady base for the village diet. As described by the Jesuit Pierre Biard, this phase of the northern Indians' subsistence cycle was especially flush: "From the month of May up to the middle of September, they are free from all anxiety about their food; for the cod are upon the coast, and all kinds of fish and shellfish."

The arrival of the alewives also heralded the coming of the migratory birds, including the large ducks which Biard called bustards, whose eggs were over twice as large as ordinary European hens' eggs. Not only could women and children gather birds' eggs while men fished; they could capture the birds themselves with snares or clubs. Bird migrations made their biggest contribution to Indian food supplies in April, May, September, and October, when Canada geese, brants, mourning doves, and miscellaneous ducks passed through; other birds, albeit in fewer numbers, could be caught during the summer as well. By July and August, strawberries, raspberries, and blueberries were ripening, providing food not only for Indians but for flocks of passenger pigeons and other birds which nested in the area. In addition to birds, various coastal mammals—whales, porpoises, walruses, and seals—were hunted and eaten. Nuts, berries, and other wild plants were gathered as they became available. In all ways, the summer was a time of plenty.

Things changed in September. Toward the middle of the month, Indian populations moved inland to the smaller creeks, where eels could be caught as they returned from their spawning in the sea. From October through March, villages broke into small family bands that subsisted on beaver, caribou, moose, deer, and bear. Men were responsible for killing these animals, while women maintained the campsite and did all hauling and processing of the slaughtered meat. If snows were heavy and animals could be easily tracked, hunting provided an adequate food supply; if the snow failed to stay on the ground, on the other hand, it was easy to starve. Northern Indians accepted as a matter of course that the months of February and March, when the animals they hunted were lean and relatively scarce, would be times of little food.

European visitors had trouble comprehending this Indian willingness to go hungry in the late winter months. They were struck by the northern Indians' apparent refusal to store more than a small amount of the summer's plenty for winter use. As the Jesuit Chrétien Le Clercq remarked:

> They are convinced that fifteen to twenty lumps of meat, or of fish
> dried or cured in the smoke, are more than enough to support

them for the space of five to six months. Since, however, they are a
people of good appetite, they consume their provisions very much
sooner than they expect. This exposes them often to the danger of
dying from hunger, through lack of the provision which they could
easily possess in abundance if they would only take the trouble to
gather it.

Here again was the paradox of want in a land of plenty. To a European
sensibility, it made no sense to go hungry if one knew in advance that there
would be little food in winter. Colonists who starved did so because they
learned too late how ill informed they had been about the New World's
perpetual abundance. Although the myth died hard, those who survived it
were reasonably quick to revise their expectations. When Europeans inquired why nonagricultural Indians did not do the same, the Indians
replied, "It is all the same to us, we shall stand it well enough; we spend
seven and eight days, even ten sometimes, without eating anything, yet we
do not die." What they said was true: Indians died from starvation much
less frequently than did early colonists, so there was a certain irony in
European criticisms of Indians on this score. Whatever the contradictions
of their own position, however, the colonists could not understand Indian
attitudes toward winter food shortages. Consciously choosing hunger, rather than working harder in the leisurely times of summer, seemed a fool's
decision.

One effect of that choice, however, was to hold northern Indians to low
population densities. The ecological principle known as Liebig's Law states
that biological populations are limited not by the total annual resources
available to them but by the minimum amount that can be found at the
scarcest time of the year. Different species meet this restriction in different
ways, and the mechanism—conscious or unconscious—whereby northern
Indians restrained their fertility is not clear. However they accomplished
this feat, its effects were self-evident: the low Indian populations of the
precolonial northern forests had relatively little impact on the ecosystems
they inhabited. The very abundance which so impressed the Europeans was
testimony to this fact. By keeping population densities low, the food
scarcities of winter guaranteed the abundance of spring, and contributed to
the overall stability of human relationships to the ecosystem. In this,
northern New England Indians were typical of hunting and gathering
peoples around the world.

The farming Indians of southern New England, among whom the
earliest English colonists made their settlements, also engaged in hunting
and gathering, but their ability to raise crops put them in a fundamentally
different relationship with their environment. The very decision to engage
in agriculture requires the creation of at least enough seed surplus to
assure that planting can be done the following year, and opens the
possibility of growing and storing enough food to carry a population
through the winter with much less dependence on the vagaries of the hunt.
Grain made up perhaps one-half to two-thirds of the southern New England diet, thereby reducing southern reliance on other foodstuffs; in com-

parison, northern Indians who raised no grain at all had to obtain two to three times more food energy from hunting and fishing. More importantly, nothing in the northern diet could be stored through the scarce times of winter as effectively as grain, making starvation a much less serious threat in the south than in the north.

The ability of agriculture to smooth out the seasonal scarcities of wild foodstuffs had major consequences for the sizes of Indian populations in New England. The nonagricultural Indians of Maine sustained population densities, on average, of perhaps 41 persons per hundred square miles. The crop-raising Indians of southern New England, on the other hand, probably maintained 287 persons on an identical amount of land, a sevenfold difference. When these two broad groups were combined, the total Indian population of New England probably numbered somewhere between 70,000 and 100,000 people in 1600. (Lest this seem unimpressive, one should remember that the *English* population of New England was smaller than this even at the beginning of the eighteenth century, having reached only 93,000 people by 1700.) The crucial role of agriculture in maintaining so large an Indian population in precolonial New England is clear: although agricultural and nonagricultural peoples inhabited roughly equal areas of southern and northern New England respectively, those who raised crops contributed over 80 percent of the total population.

Although southern Indians engaged in many of the same annual hunting and fishing activities as northern ones, their concentration on the raising of crops can be seen even in the names they gave their months. Northern Indians named their lunar months in terms of seasonal changes in animal populations, referring to the egg laying of birds, the running of salmon, the molting of geese, the hibernation of bears, and so on. By contrast, southern Indians chose the names of their months with an entirely different emphasis. The fur trader John Pynchon recorded that the Agawam Indian village near Springfield, Massachusetts, began its year with the month of Squannikesos, which included part of April and part of May, and whose name meant "when they set Indian corn." This was followed by various months whose names indicated the weeding of corn, the hilling of corn, the ripening of corn, the coming of the frost, the middle of winter, the thawing of ice, and the catching of fish. The southern cycle of months was thus remarkable in having only a single reference to the animals which so dominated the northern calendar, an indication of how much agriculture had transformed Indian lives there.

As the Agawam calendar shows, southern Indians began their annual subsistence cycles by moving to their summer fields and preparing the ground by working it with clamshell hoes. According to the Dutch traveler Isaack de Rasieres, the Indians "make heaps like molehills, each about two and a half feet from the others, which they sow or plant in April with maize, in each heap five or six grains." Because the earth was not stirred deeply by this method, much of the soil was left intact and erosion was thereby held to a minimum. As the young plants grew, soil was raised around them to create low mounds which strengthened their roots against the attacks of birds. Maize was not an easy crop to raise: as de Rasieres noted, it was "a grain to which much labor must be given, with weeding and earthing-up, or it does not thrive." Perhaps partly for this reason, Indian farmers, unlike European ones, used their cornfields to raise more than just corn. When Champlain observed Indian fields near the mouth of the Saco River, he noted that

> with the corn they put in each hill three or four Brazilian beans [kidney beans], which are of different colors. When they grow up, they interlace with the corn, which reaches to the height of from five to six feet; and they keep the ground very free from weeds. We saw there many squashes, and pumpkins, and tobacco, which they likewise cultivate.

It was not an agriculture that looked very orderly to a European eye accustomed to monocultural fields. Cornstalks served as beanpoles, squashes sent their tendrils everywhere, and the entire surface of the field became a dense tangle of food plants. But, orderly or not, such gardens had the effect, as John Winthrop, Jr., said, of "loading the Ground with as much as it will beare," creating very high yields per acre, discouraging weed growth and preserving soil moisture. Moreover, although Indians may or may not have realized it, the resulting harvest of beans and corn provided the amino acids necessary for a balanced diet of vegetable protein.

* * * * *

Crops were planted between March and late June, the event often being timed by the leafing of certain trees or the arrival of the alewives. While women worked the fields, men erected weirs on the rivers and fished the spring spawning runs. By March, most beans and corn remaining from the previous harvest were probably needed as seed for planting, so that fish and migratory birds became the chief sources of food from late winter through midsummer.

* * * * *

Once crops were planted and weeded, they needed less attention for two or three months, until the ripening corn had to be guarded against marauding birds before being harvested. (De Rasieres explained how some birds, probably passenger pigeons, were known as "maize thieves" because "they flatten the corn in any place where they alight, just as if cattle had lain there.") During these months, villages tended to disperse and families moved their individual wigwams to other planting and gathering sites. Women, who owned the wigwams and most household goods, moved their camps from field to field as necessary, and then to points along the coast where they gathered seafood and the cattails used in making mats for wigwams. Camps occasionally had to be moved in the summer simply to escape the fleas which tended to breed around human habitations. Wigwams were also moved if a death occurred in one, or if a settlement was threatened by war.

Men fanned out from these bases for extended fishing and hunting trips. They might disappear into the woods for ten days at a time to build a dugout canoe that would allow them to fish deep water with harpoon or hook and line. Southern New England boats were made from decay-resistant chestnut and were heavy enough to require several hands to launch; in the north, paper birch, which did not grow in southeastern New England, was used to create the much lighter and more familiar birchbark canoes. Whether birch or chestnut, these tippy boats might be taken a mile or more offshore at night to hunt sturgeon by torchlight, or be run down the rapids of rivers in search of salmon or eels. Used for these purposes, canoes could be very dangerous indeed. Roger Williams spoke from personal experience when he said, "It is wonderfull to see how they will venture in those Canoes, and how (being oft overset as I have myself been with them) they will swim a mile, yea two or more safe to Land." Such danger was typical of male work. Whereas the relatively steady labor of agriculture and gathering allowed women to provide the largest share of a village's food without moving far from home, the hunting and fishing of animal protein had much different requirements. These activities took men far from the main camp for many days at a time, and exposed them to much greater risk of injury or death. Hunting and fishing both had irregular work rhythms which sometimes required many intense hours of labor under hard conditions, and sometimes long hours of idleness. Times in camp were often periods of relative leisure and recuperation for men.

As summer drew to a close, female food production reached a climax and male hunting activities began to contribute a greater share of the village's food. Autumn saw the harvesting of corn in addition to the gathering of acorns, chestnuts, groundnuts, and other wild plants. It was a time of extensive festivals when many hundreds of people gathered in dense settlements and consumed much of this surplus food. Gambling, dancing, and eating were combined with rituals—similar to the potlatch ceremonies of the Pacific Northwest—in which wealthy individuals gave away much of what they owned to establish reciprocal relations of obligation with potential followers or allies. The harvest saw greater surplus than any other time of year, and so was often the preferred season for going to war, when food stores both at home and in enemy territory would be at their peak. But once the harvest celebrations were over, Indian households struck their wigwams, stored the bulk of their corn and beans, and moved to campsites to conduct the fall hunt.

From October to December, when animals like bear and deer were at their fattest, southern villages, much like their counterparts in the north, broke into small bands to assure maximum coverage of the hunting territory. Again the sexual division of labor came into play. Men hunted steadily, using a variety of techniques. Game might be stalked with bow and arrow by a lone hunter or by groups of two or three hundred men working together. It might be snared with traps specially designed to capture a single species; William Bradford, for instance, accidentally walked into a trap strong enough to hold a full-grown deer. Or game might be run between specially planted hedges more than a mile in length until it was finally driven onto the weapons of waiting hunters. Nothing required a greater knowledge of animal behavior than the winter hunt. While men remained in the field, women hauled dead game back to camp. There they butchered and processed it, preparing the hides for clothing, cooking the meat, and smoking some of it for use later in the winter.

By late December, when the snows finally came, the village had probably reassembled in heavily wooded valleys well protected from the weather, where fuel for campfires was easy to obtain. For the rest of the winter, men continued to hunt and fish the surrounding area on snowshoes, while women remained in camp making garments and living on meat and stored grain. Especially for men away from camp, winter was a time of occasional hunger between kills; most carried only a small store of parched corn flour called *nocake* as traveling fare. Like their hunting kindred to the north, they accepted such hunger as inevitable and bore it with stoicism. As Samuel Lee reported, the Indians were "very patient in fasting, & will gird in their bellies till they meet with food; but then none more gluttons or drunk on occasion. Theyle eat 10 times in 24 houres, when they have a beare or a deere."

The hunt provided a crucial source of protein and vitamins during the winter. A single season's catch for a southern New England village of about 400 inhabitants might bring in over 8,500 pounds of edible deer meat and over 7,000 pounds of bear, the two animals which together contributed more than three-fourths of an inland village's winter meat supply. (Coastal Indians who relied more heavily on seafood killed smaller amounts of large game.) Whether or not this meat was essential to a community's survival—given the availability of stored beans and grain—the skins of these and other furbearing animals would furnish the village's clothing for the following year. Simple measurements of caloric content thus tend to undervalue the importance of the fall and winter hunt to an agricultural village's subsistence cycle. Hundreds of square miles had to be stalked to obtain skins for the skirts, leggings, shirts, moccasins, and other articles of clothing Indians would need in the months ahead.

The relationship of the southern New England Indians to their environment was thus, if anything, even more complicated than that of the northern Indians. To the seasons of hunting and fishing shared by both groups were added the agricultural cycles which increased the available food surplus and so enabled denser populations to sustain themselves. In both areas, the mobility of village sites and the shift between various subsistence bases reduced potential strains on any particular segment of the ecosystem, keeping the overall human burden low. But in clearing land for planting and thus concentrating the food base, southern Indians were taking a most important step in reshaping and manipulating the ecosystem.

Clearing fields was relatively easy. By setting fire to wood piled around the base of standing trees, Indian women destroyed the bark and so killed the trees; the women could then plant corn amid the leafless skeletons that were left. During the next several years, many of the trees would topple and could be entirely removed by burning. As one Indian remembered, "An industrious woman, when great many dry logs are fallen, could burn off as many logs in one day as a smart man can chop in two or three days time with an axe." However efficient they were at such clearing, Indian women were frugal with their own labor, and sought to avoid even this much work for as long as they could. That meant returning to the same field site for as long as possible, usually eight to ten years. In time, the soil gradually lost its fertility and eventually necessitated movement to a new field. (Soil exhaustion was to some extent delayed by the action of the nitrogen-fixing beans which Indian women planted with the corn; whether they were aware of it or not, this was one of the side benefits of planting multicrop fields.)

The annual reoccupation of fixed village and planting sites meant that the area around field and camp experienced heavy human use: intensive food gathering, the accumulation of garbage, and, most importantly, the consumption of firewood. One of the main reasons Indians moved to winter camps was that their summer sites had been stripped of the fuel essential for winter fires. Indians believed in big fires—one colonist said that "their Fire is instead of our bed cloaths"—and burned wood heavily all night long, both summer and winter. Such practices could not long be maintained on a single site. * * * * *

The relationships of the New England Indians to their environment, whether in the north or the south, revolved around the wheel of the seasons: throughout New England, Indians held their demands on the ecosystem to a minimum by moving their settlements from habitat to habitat. As one of the earliest European visitors noted, "They move ... from one place to another according to the richness of the site and the season." By using other species when they were most plentiful, Indians made sure that no single species became overused. It was a way of life to match the patchwork of the landscape. On the coast were fish and shellfish, and in the salt marshes were migratory birds. In the forests and lowland thickets were deer and beaver; in cleared upland fields were corn and beans; and everywhere were the wild plants whose uses were too numerous to catalog. For New England Indians, ecological diversity, whether natural or artificial, meant abundance, stability, and a regular supply of the things that kept them alive.

The ecological relationships which the English sought to reproduce in New England were no less cyclical than those of the Indians; they were only simpler and more concentrated. The English too had their seasons of want and plenty, and rapidly adjusted their false expectations of perpetual natural wealth to match New World realities. But whereas Indian villages moved from habitat to habitat to find maximum abundance through minimal work, and so reduce their impact on the land, the English believed in and required permanent settlements. Once a village was established, its improvements—cleared fields, pastures, buildings, fences, and so on—were regarded as more or less fixed features of the landscape. English fixity sought to replace Indian mobility; here was the central conflict in the ways Indians and colonists interacted with their environments. The struggle was over two ways of living and using the seasons of the year, and it expressed itself in how two peoples conceived of property, wealth, and boundaries on the landscape.

Chapter 4

BOUNDING THE LAND

To take advantage of their land's diversity, Indian villages had to be mobile. This was not difficult as long as a family owned nothing that could not be either stored or transported on a man's or—more probably—a woman's back. Clothing, baskets, fishing equipment, a few tools, mats for wigwams, some corn, beans, and smoked meat: these constituted most of the possessions that individual Indian families maintained during their seasonal migrations. Even in southern New England, where agriculture created larger accumulations of food than existed among the hunter-gatherer peoples of the north, much of the harvest was stored in underground pits to await later visits and was not transported in large quantities. The need for diversity and mobility led New England Indians to avoid acquiring much surplus property, confident as they were that their mobility and skill would supply any need that arose.

This, then, was a solution to the riddle Thomas Morton had posed his European readers. If English visitors to New England thought it a paradox that Indians seemed to live like paupers in a landscape of great natural wealth, then the problem lay with English eyesight rather than with any real Indian poverty. To those who compared Massachusetts Indians to English beggars, Morton replied, "If our beggers of England should, with so much ease as they, furnish themselves with foode at all seasons, there would not be so many starved in the streets." Indians only *seemed* impoverished, since they were in fact "supplied with all manner of needefull things, for the maintenance of life and lifelyhood." Indeed, said Morton, the leisurely abundance of Indian life suggested that there might be something wrong with *European* notions of wealth: perhaps the English did not know true riches when they saw them. In a passage undoubtedly intended to infuriate his Puritan persecutors, Morton counterposed to the riddle of Indian poverty a riddle of Indian wealth: "Now since it is but foode and rayment that men that live needeth (though not all alike,) why should not the Natives of New England be sayd to live richly, having no want of either?"

Why not indeed? It was not a question that sat well with the New England Puritans, who had banished Morton for just such irreverence (not to mention his rival trade with the Indians). Criticism of Indian ways of life was a near-constant element in early colonial writing, and in that criticism we may discover much about how colonists believed land should be used. "The *Indians*," wrote Francis Higginson, "are not able to make use of the one fourth part of the Land, neither have they any setled places, as Townes to dwell in, nor any ground as they challenge for their owne possession, but change their habitation from place to place." A people who moved so much and worked so little did not deserve to lay claim to the land they inhabited. Their supposed failure to "improve" that land was a token not of their chosen way of life but of their laziness. "Much might they benefit themselves," fumed William Wood, "if they were not strong fettered in the chains of idleness; so as that they had rather starve than work, following no employments saving such as are sweetened with more pleasures and profit than pains or care." Few Indians, of course, had actually starved in precolonial times, so Wood's criticism boiled down to an odd tirade against Indians who chose to subsist by labor they found more pleasurable than hateful. (Ironically, this was exactly the kind of life that at least some colonists fantasized for themselves in their visions of the natural bounty of the New World.) Only the crop-planting (and therefore supposedly over-worked) women were exempted from such attacks. As we have seen, the full scorn of English criticism was reserved for Indian males, whose lives were perhaps too close to certain English pastoral and aristocratic fantasies for Calvinists to tolerate. At a time when the royalist Izaak Walton would soon proclaim the virtues of angling and hunting as pastimes, the Puritan objections to these "leisure" activities carried political as well as moral overtones.

More importantly, English colonists could use Indian hunting and gathering as a justification for expropriating Indian land. To European eyes, Indians appeared to squander the resources that were available to them. Indian poverty was the result of Indian waste: underused land, underused natural abundance, underused human labor. In his tract defending "the Lawfulness of Removing Out of England into the Parts of America," the Pilgrim apologist Robert Cushman argued that the Indians were "not industrious, neither have art, science, skill or faculty to use either the land or the commodities of it; but all spoils, rots, and is marred for want of manuring, gathering, ordering, etc." Because the Indians were so few, and "do but run over the grass, as do also the foxes and wild beasts," Cushman declared their land to be "spacious and void," free for English taking.

Colonial theorists like John Winthrop posited two ways of owning land, one natural and one civil. Natural right to the soil had existed "when men held the earth in common every man sowing and feeding where he pleased." This natural ownership had been superseded when individuals began to raise crops, keep cattle, and improve the land by enclosing it; from such actions, Winthrop said, came a superior, civil right of ownership. That these notions of land tenure were ideological and inherently Eurocentric was obvious from the way Winthrop used them: "As for the Natives in New England," he wrote, "they inclose noe Land, neither have any setled habytation, nor any tame Cattle to improve the Land by, and soe have noe other but a Naturall Right to those Countries." By this argument, only the fields planted by Indian women could be claimed as property, with the happy result, as Winthrop said, that "the rest of the country lay open to any that could and would improve it." The land was a *vacuum Domicilium* waiting to be inhabited by a more productive people. "In a vacant soyle," wrote the minister John Cotton, "hee that taketh possession of it, and bestoweth culture and husbandry upon it, his Right it is."

This was, of course, little more than an ideology of conquest conveniently available to justify the occupation of another people's lands. Colonists occasionally admitted as much when they needed to defend their right to lands originally purchased from Indians: in order for Indians legitimately to sell their lands, they had first to own them. Roger Williams, in trying to protect Salem's claim to territory obtained from Indians rather than from the English Crown, argued that the King had committed an "injustice, in giving the Countrey to his *English* Subjects, which belonged to the Native *Indians.*" Even if the Indians used their land differently than did the English, Williams said, they nevertheless possessed it by right of first occupancy and by right of the ecological changes they had wrought in it. Whether or not the Indians conducted agriculture, they "hunted all the Countrey over, and for the expedition of their hunting voyages, they burnt up all the underwoods in the Countrey, once or twice a yeare." Burning the woods, according to Williams, was an improvement that gave the Indians as much right to the soil as the King of England could claim to the royal forests. If the English could invade Indian hunting grounds and claim right of ownership over them because they were unimproved, then the Indians could do likewise in the royal game parks.

It was a fair argument. Williams's opponents could only reply that English game parks were not just hunted but also used for cutting timber and raising cattle; besides, they said, the English King (along with lesser nobles holding such lands) performed other services for the Common-wealth, services which justified his large unpeopled holdings. If these assertions seemed a little lame, designed mainly to refute the technical details of Williams's argument, that was because the core of the dispute lay elsewhere. Few Europeans were willing to recognize that the ways Indians inhabited New England ecosystems were as legitimate as the ways Europeans *intended* to inhabit them. Colonists thus rationalized their conquest of New England: by refusing to extend the rights of property to the Indians, they both trivialized the ecology of Indian life and paved the way for destroying it. "We did not conceive," said Williams's opponents with fine irony, "that it is a just Title to so vast a Continent, to make no other improvement of millions of Acres in it, but onely to burn it up for pastime."

Whether denying or defending Indian rights of land tenure, most English colonists displayed a remarkable indifference to what the Indians themselves thought about the matter. As a result, we have very little direct evidence in colonial records of the New England Indians' conceptions of property. To try to reconstruct these, we must use not only the few early fragments available to us but a variety of evidence drawn from the larger ethnographic literature. Here we must be careful about what we mean by "property," lest we fall into the traps English colonists have set for us. Although ordinary language seems to suggest that property is generally a simple relationship between an individual person and a thing, it is actually a far more complicated social institution which varies widely between cultures. Saying that A owns B is in fact meaningless until the society in which A lives agrees to allow A a certain bundle of rights over B and to impose sanctions against the violation of those rights by anyone else. The classic definition is that of Huntington Cairns: "the property relation is triadic: 'A owns B against C,' where C represents all other individuals." Unless the people I live with recognize that I own something and so give me certain unique claims over it, I do not possess it in any meaningful sense. Moreover, different groups will permit me different bundles of rights over the same object. To define property is thus to represent boundaries between people; equally, it is to articulate at least one set of conscious ecological boundaries between people and things.

This suggests that there are really two issues involved in the problem of Indian property rights. One is individual *ownership*, the way the inhabitants of a particular village conceived of property vis-à-vis each other; and the other is collective *sovereignty*, how everyone in a village conceived of their territory (and political community) vis-à-vis other villages. An individual's or a family's rights to property were defined by the community which recognized those rights, whereas the community's territorial claims were made in opposition to those of other sovereign groups. Distinctions here can inevitably become somewhat artificial. Because kin networks might also have territorial claims—both *within* and *across* villages—even the village is sometimes an arbitrary unit in which to analyze property rights: ownership and sovereignty among Indian peoples could shade into each other in a way Europeans had trouble understanding. For this reason, the nature of Indian political communities is crucial to any discussion of property rights.

A village's right to the territory which it used during the various seasons of the year had to be at least tacitly accepted by other villages or, if not, defended against them. Territorial rights of this kind, which were expressions of the entire group's collective right, tended to be vested in the person of the sachem, the leader in whom the village's political identity at least symbolically inhered. Early English visitors who encountered village sachems tended to exaggerate their authority by comparing them to European kings: Roger Williams and John Josselyn both baldly asserted of New England Indians that "their Government is Monarchicall." Comparison might more aptly have been made to the relations between lords and retainers in the early Middle Ages of Europe. In reality, sachems derived their power in many ways: by personal assertiveness; by marrying (if male) several wives to proliferate wealth and kin obligations; by the reciprocal exchange of gifts with followers; and, especially in southern New England, by inheriting it from close kin. Although early documents are silent on this score, kin relations undoubtedly cemented networks both of economic exchange and of political obligation, and it was on these rather than more formal state institutions that sachems based their authority. As William Wood remarked, "The kings have not many laws to command by nor have they any annual revenues."

Polity had less the abstract character of a monarchy, a country or even a tribe, than of a relatively fluid set of personal relationships. Although those relationships bore some resemblance to the dynastic politics of early modern Europe—a resemblance several historians have recently emphasized—they were crucially different in not being articulated within a state system. Kinship and personality rather than any alternative institutional structure organized power in Indian communities. Both within and between villages, elaborate kin networks endowed individuals with greater or lesser degrees of power. A sachem—who could be either male or female—asserted authority only in consultation with other powerful individuals in the village. Moreover, the sachem of one village might regularly pay tribute to the sachem of another, thus acknowledging a loose hierarchy between villages and sachems. Such hierarchies might be practically unimportant until some major conflict or external threat arose, whereupon the communities assembled into a larger confederacy until the problem was solved. The result, like Indian subsistence patterns, entailed a good deal more flexibility and movement than Europeans were accustomed to in their political institutions. As the missionary Daniel Gookin indicated, it was a very shifting politics:

> Their sachems have not their men in such subjection, but that very frequently their men will leave them upon distaste or harsh dealing, and go and live among other sachems that can protect them: so that their princes endeavour to carry it obligingly and lovingly unto their people, lest they should desert them, and thereby their strength, power, and tribute would be diminished.

Insofar as a village "owned" the land it inhabited, its property was expressed in the sovereignty of the sachem. "Every sachem," wrote Edward Winslow, "knoweth how far the bounds and limits of his own Country extendeth." For all of their differences, a sachem "owned" territory in a manner somewhat analogous to the way a European monarch "owned" an entire European nation: less as personal real estate than as the symbolic possession of a whole people. A sachem's land was coterminous with the area within which a village's economic subsistence and political sanctions were most immediately expressed. In this sovereign sense, villages were fairly precise about drawing boundaries among their respective territories. When Roger Williams wrote that "the *Natives* are very exact and punctuall in the bounds of their Lands, belonging to this or that Prince or People," he was refuting those who sought to deny that legitimate Indian property rights existed. But the rights of which he spoke were not ones of individual ownership; rather, they were sovereign rights that defined a village's political and ecological territory.

The distinction becomes important in the context of how such territorial rights could be alienated. Williams said that he had "knowne them make bargaine and sale amongst themselves for a small piece, or quantity of Ground," suggesting that Indians were little different from Europeans in their sense of how land could be bought or sold. When two sachems made an agreement to transfer land, however, they did so on behalf of their two political or kinship communities, as a way of determining the customary rights each village would be allowed in a given area. An instructive example of this is the way Roger Williams had to correct John Winthrop's confusion over two islands which Winthrop thought Williams had bought from the Narragansett sachem Miantonomo. Williams had indeed gotten permission to use the islands for grazing hogs—a land transaction of sorts had taken place—but it was emphatically not a purchase. "Be pleased to understand,"

cautioned Williams, "your great mistake: neither of them were sold properly, for a thousand fathom [of wampum] would not have bought either, by
strangers. The truth is, not a penny was demanded for either, and what
was paid was only gratuity, though I choose, for better assurance and form,
to call it sale." What had been transacted, as Williams clearly understood,
was more a diplomatic exchange than an economic one. Miantonomo, like
other New England sachems, had no intention of conducting a market in
real estate.

That this was so can best be seen by examining how a village's
inhabitants conceived of property *within* its territory. Beginning with
personal goods, ownership rights were clear: people owned what they made
with their own hands. Given the division labor, the two sexes probably
tended to possess the goods that were most closely associated with their
respective tasks: women owned baskets, mats, kettles, hoes, and so on,
while men owned bows, arrows, hatchets, fishing nets, canoes, and other
hunting tools. But even in the case of personal goods, there was little sense
either of accumulation or of exclusive use. Goods were owned because they
were useful, and if they ceased to be so, or were needed by someone else,
they could easily be given away. "Although every proprietor knowes his
own," said Thomas Morton "yet all things, (so long as they will last), are
used in common amongst them." Not surprisingly, theft was uncommon in
such a world.

This relaxed attitude toward personal possessions was typical throughout New England. Chrétien Le Clercq described it among the Micmac of
Nova Scotia by saying that they were "so generous and liberal towards one
another that they seem not to have any attachment to the little they
possess, for they deprive themselves thereof very willingly and in very good
spirit the very moment when they know that their friends have need of it."
Europeans often interpreted such actions by emphasizing the supposed
generosity of the noble savage, but the Indians' relative indifference to
property accumulation is better understood as a corollary of the rest of
their political and economic life. Personal goods could be easily replaced,
and their accumulation made little sense for the ecological reasons of
mobility we have already examined; in addition, gift giving was a crucial
lubricant in sustaining power relationships within the community. As
Pierre Biard noted, guests thanked their hosts by giving gifts that were
expressions of relative social status, and did so "with the expectation that
the host will reciprocate, when the guest comes to depart, if the guest is a
Sagamore, otherwise not." Willingness to give property away with alacrity
was by no means a sign that property did not exist; rather, it was a crucial
means for establishing and reproducing one's position in society.

When it came to land, however, there was less reason for gift giving or
exchange. Southern New England Indian families enjoyed exclusive use of
their planting fields and of the land on which their wigwams stood, and so
might be said to have "owned" them. But neither of these were permanent
possessions. Wigwams were moved every few months, and planting fields
were abandoned after a number of years. Once abandoned, a field returned

to brush until it was recleared by someone else, and no effort was made to set permanent boundaries around it that would hold it indefinitely for a single person. What families possessed in their fields was the use of them, the crops that were produced by a woman's labor upon them. When lands were traded or sold in the way Williams described, what were exchanged were usufruct rights, acknowledgments by one group that another might use an area for planting or hunting or gathering. Such rights were limited to the period of use, and they did not include many of the privileges Europeans commonly associated with ownership: a user could not (and saw no need to) prevent other village members from trespassing or gathering nonagricultural food on such lands, and had no conception of deriving rent from them. Planting fields were "possessed" by an Indian family only to the extent that it would return to them the following year. In this, they were not radically different in kind from other village lands; it was *European* rather than Indian definitions of land tenure that led the English to recognize agricultural land as the only legitimate Indian property. The Massachusetts Court made its ownership theories quite clear when it declared that "what landes any of the Indians, within this jurisdiction, have by possession or improvement, by subdueing of same, they have just right thereunto, accordinge to that Gen: 1: 28, chap: 9: 1, Psa: 115, 16."

The implication was that Indians did *not* own any other kind of land: clam banks, fishing ponds, berry-picking areas, hunting lands, the great bulk of a village's territory. (Since the nonagricultural Indians of the north had *only* these kinds of land, English theories assigned them no property rights at all.) Confusion was easy on this point, not only because of English ideologies, but because the Indians themselves had very flexible definitions of land tenure for such areas. Here again, the concept of usufruct right was crucial, since different groups of people could have different claims on the same tract of land depending on how they used it. Any village member, for instance, had the right to collect edible wild plants, cut birchbark or chestnut for canoes, or gather sedges for mats, wherever these things could be found. No special private right inhered in them. Since village lands were usually organized along a single watershed, the same was true of rivers and the coast: fish and shellfish could generally be taken anywhere, although the nets, harpoons, weirs, and tackle used to catch them—and hence sometimes the right to use the sites where these things were installed—might be owned by an individual or a kin group. Indeed, in the case of extraordinarily plentiful fishing sites—especially major inland waterfalls during spawning runs—several villages might gather at a single spot to share the wealth. All of them acknowledged a mutual right to use the site for that specific purpose, even though it might otherwise lie within a single village's territory. Property rights, in other words, shifted with ecological use.

Hunting grounds are the most interesting case of this shifting nonagricultural land tenure. The ecological habits of different animals were so various that their hunting required a wide range of techniques, and rights to land use had to differ accordingly. The migratory birds in the ponds and salt marshes, for example, were so abundant that they could be treated much like fish: whoever killed them owned them, and hunters could range over any tract of land to do so, much like the birds themselves. (In this, Indian practices bore some resemblance to European customs governing the right of hunters, when in pursuit of game, to cross boundaries which were otherwise legally protected.) Likewise, flocks of turkeys and the deer herds were so abundant in the fall that they were most efficiently hunted by collective drives involving anywhere from twenty to three hundred men. In such cases, the entire village territory was the logical hunting region, to which all those involved in the hunt had an equal right.

The same was not true, on the other hand, of hunting that involved the setting of snares or traps. The animals prey to such techniques were either less numerous, as in the case of winter deer or moose, or sedentary creatures, like the beaver, which lived in fixed locales. These were best hunted by spreading the village population over as broad a territory as possible, and so usufruct rights had to be designed to hold the overlap of trapped areas to a reasonable minimum. Roger Williams described how, after the harvest, ten or twenty men would go with their wives and children to hunting camps which were presumably organized by kin lineage groups. There, he said, "each man takes his bounds of two, three, or foure miles, where hee sets thirty, forty, or fiftie Traps, and baits his Traps with that food the Deere loves, and once in two dayes he walks his round to view his Traps."

At least for the duration of the winter hunt, the kin group inhabiting a camp probably had a clear if informal usufruct right to the animals caught in its immediate area. Certainly a man (or, in the north, his wife) owned the animals captured in the traps he set, though he might have obligations to share which created *de facto* limits to his claims on them. The collective activities of a camp thus tended to establish a set of rights which at least temporarily divided the village territory into hunting areas. The problem is to know how such rights were allocated, how permanent and exclusive they were, and—most crucially—how much their interaction with the European fur trade altered them. The full discussion of this issue, which anthropologists have debated for decades, must wait for the next chapter. For now, we can conclude that, however exclusive hunting territories originally were and however much the fur trade changed them, they represented a different kind of land use—and so probably a different set of usufruct rights—than planting fields, gathering areas, or fishing sites.

What the Indians owned—or, more precisely, what their villages gave them claim to—was not the land but the things that were on the land during the various seasons of the year. It was a conception of property shared by many of the hunter-gatherers and agricultural peoples of the world, but radically different from that of the invading Europeans. In nothing is this more clear than in the names they attached to their landscape, the great bulk of which related not to possession but to use. In south New England, some of these names were agricultural. Pokanoket, in Plymouth County, Massachusetts, was "at or near the cleared lands." Anitaash Pond, near New London, Connecticut meant, literally, "rotten corn," referring to a swampy location where corn could be buried until it blackened to create a favorite Indian delicacy. Mittineag, in Hampden County, Massachusetts meant "abandoned fields," probably a place where the soil had lost its fertility and a village had moved its summer encampment elsewhere. * * *

Boundaries between the Indians and these intruding "strangers" differed in fundamental ways from the ones between Indian villages, largely because the two interpreted those boundaries using very different cultural concepts. The difference is best seen in early deeds between the two groups. On July 15, 1636, the fur trader William Pynchon purchased from the Agawam village in central Massachusetts a tract of land extending four or five miles along the Connecticut River in the vicinity of present-day Springfield, leaving one of the earliest Indian deeds in American history to record the transaction. Several things are striking about the document. No fewer than thirteen Indians signed it, two of whom, Commucke and Matanchon, were evidently sachems able to act "for and in the name of al the other Indians" in the village. In defining their claims to the land being sold, they said that they acted "in the name of Cuttonus the right owner of Agaam and Quana, and in the Name of his mother Kewenusk the Tamasham or wife of Wenawis, and Niarum the wife of Coa," suggesting that both men and women had rights to the land being transferred. On the Indian side, then, an entire kin group had to concur in an action which thus probably had more to do with sovereignty than ownership.

Moreover, village members evidently conceived of that action in strictly limited terms. Though they gave permission to Pynchon and his associates "for ever to trucke and sel al that ground," they made a number of revealing reservations: in addition to the eighteen coats, eighteen hatchets, eighteen hoes, and eighteen knives they received as payment, they extracted the concession that

> they shal have and enjoy all that cottinackeesh [planted ground], or ground that is now planted; And have liberty to take Fish and Deer, ground nuts, walnuts akornes and sasachiminesh or a kind of pease.

Understood in terms of the usufruct rights discussed above, it is clear that the Indians conceived of this sale as applying only to very specific uses of the land. They gave up none of their most important hunting and gathering privileges, they retained right to their cornfields, and evidently intended to keep living on the land much as they had done before. The rights they gave Pynchon were apparently to occupy the land jointly with them, to establish a village like their own where cornfields could be planted, to conduct trade there, and perhaps to act as a superior sachem who could negotiate with other villages about the land so long as he continued to recognize the reserved rights of the Agawam village. The Agawam villagers gave up none of their sovereignty over themselves, and relinquished few of their activities on the land. What they conferred on Pynchon was a right ownership identical to their own: not to possess the land as a tradeable commodity, but to use it as an ecological cornucopia. Save for cornfields, no Indian usufruct rights were inherently exclusive, and transactions such as this one had more to do with sharing possession than alienating it.

On the English side, the right "for ever to trucke and sel al that ground" of course carried rather different connotations. In the first place, the transaction was conducted not by a sovereign kin group but by a trading partnership operating under the much larger sovereignty of the Massachusetts Bay Company and the English Crown. None of the three partners who acquired rights to the land—William Pynchon, Henry Smith, or Jehu Burr—was actually present at the transaction, which was conducted for them by several men in their employ. Insofar as we can make a valid distinction, what the Indians perceived as a political negotiation between two sovereign groups the English perceived as an economic transaction wholly within an English jurisdiction. As we have seen, Massachusetts recognized that Indians might have limited natural rights to land, and so provided that such rights could be alienated *under the sanctions of Massachusetts law*. No question of an Indian village's own sanctions could arise, for the simple reason that Indian sovereignty was not recognized. The Massachusetts Bay Company was careful very early to instruct its agents on this point, telling them "to make composition with such of the salvages as did pretend any tytle or lay clayme to any of the land." Indian rights were not real, but pretended, because the land had already been granted the company by the English Crown.

Land purchases like Pynchon's were thus interpreted under English law, and so were understood as a fuller transfer of rights than Indian communities probably ever intended. Certainly Pynchon's deed is unusual in even mentioning rights reserved to the Indians. Later deeds describe exchanges in which English purchasers appeared to obtain complete and final ownership rights, however the Indian sellers may have understood those exchanges. In 1637, for instance, John Winthrop received lands in Ipswich, Massachusetts, from the Indian Maskonomett, who declared that "I doe fully resigne up all my right of the whole towne of Ipswich as farre as the bounds thereof shall goe all the woods meadowes, pastures and broken up grounds unto the said John Winthrop in the name of the rest of the English there planted." Deeds in eastern Massachusetts—when they existed at all—typically took this form, extinguishing all Indian rights and transferring them either to an English purchaser or, as in this case, to an English group with some corporate identity. As the English understood these transactions, what was sold was not a bundle of usufruct rights, applying to a range of different "territories," but the land itself, an abstract area whose bounds in theory remained fixed no matter what the use to which it was put. Once the land was bounded in this new way, a host of ecological changes followed almost inevitably.

European property systems were much like Indian ones in expressing the ecological purposes to which a people intended to put their land; it is crucial that they not be oversimplified if their contribution to ecological history is to be understood. The popular idea that Europeans had private property, while the Indians did not, distorts European notions of property as much as it does Indian ones. The colonists' property systems, like those of the Indians, involved important distinctions between sovereignty and ownership, between possession by communities and possession by individuals. They too dealt in bundles of culturally defined rights that determined what could and could not be done with land and personal property. Even the fixity they assigned to property boundaries, the quality which most distinguished them from Indian land systems, was at first fuzzier and less final than one might expect. They varied considerably depending on the region of England from which a group of colonists came, so that every New England town, like every Indian village, had idiosyncratic property customs of its own. All of these elements combined to form what is usually called "the New England land system." The phrase is misleading, since the "system" resided primarily at the town level and was in fact many systems, but there were nevertheless common features which together are central to the subject of this book. Their development was as much a product as a cause of ecological change in colonial New England.

Colonial claims to ownership of land in New England had two potential sources: purchases from Indians or grants from the English Crown. The latter tended quickly to absorb the former. The Crown derived its own claim to the region from several sources: Cabot's "discovery" of New England in 1497–98; the failure of Indians adequately to subdue the soil as Genesis 1.28 required; and from the King's status—initially a decidedly speculative one—as the first Christian monarch to establish colonies there. Whether or not a colony sought to purchase land from the Indians— something which Plymouth, Connecticut, and Rhode Island, in the absence of royal charters, felt compelled as a matter of expediency or ethics to do— all New England colonies ultimately derived their political rights of sovereignty from the Crown.

The distinction between sovereignty and ownership is crucial here. When a colony purchased land from Indians, it did so under its own system of sovereignty: whenever ownership rights were deeded and purchased, they were immediately incorporated into English rather than Indian law. Indian land sales, operating as they did at the interface of two different sovereignties, one of which had trouble recognizing that the other existed, thus had a potentially paradoxical quality. Because Indians, at least in the beginning, thought they were selling one thing and the English thought they were buying another, it was possible for an Indian village to convey what it regarded as identical and nonexclusive usufruct rights to several different English purchasers. Alternatively, several different Indian groups might sell to English ones rights to the same tract of land. Uniqueness of title as the English understood it became impossible under such circumstances, so colonies very early tried to regulate the purchase of Indian lands. Within four years of the founding of Massachusetts Bay, the General Court had ordered that "noe person whatsoever shall buy any land of any Indean without leave from the Court." The other colonies soon followed suit. The effect was not only to restrict the right of English individuals to engage in Indian land transactions but—more importantly, given the problem of sovereignty—to limit the rights of Indians to do so as well.

Illegal individual sales nevertheless persisted, and titles in some areas became so confused that the Connecticut Court in 1717 made a formal declaration:

> That all lands in this government are holden of the King of Great Britain as the lord of the fee: and that no title to any lands in this Colony can accrue by any purchase made of Indians on pretence of their being native proprietors thereof.

Even by the late seventeenth century, Indian lands were regarded as being entirely within English colonial jurisdiction; indeed, the logic of the situation seemed to indicate that, for Indians to own land at all, it had first to be granted them by the English Crown.

If all colonial lands derived from the Crown, how did this affect the way they were owned and used? As with an Indian sachem, albeit on a larger and more absolute scale, the King did not merely possess land in his own right but also represented in his person the collective sovereignty which defined the system of property rights that operated on that land. In the case of the Massachusetts Bay Company's charter, the King conferred the lands of the grant "as of our manor of Eastgreenewich, in the County of Kent, in free and common Socage, and not in Capite, nor by knightes service." Land tenure as of the manor of East Greenwich put a colony under Kentish legal custom and was the most generous of feudal grants, involving the fewest obligations in relation to the Crown. It was ideally suited to mercantile trading companies, since it allowed easy alienation of the land and did not impose the burden of feudal quitrents on its holders. Both of these features made Kentish tenure attractive to would-be settlers and promoted the early development of a commercial market in land. As opposed to tenure in capite or by knight's service, which carried various civil and military obligations for their holders, free and common socage—in some senses, the least feudal of medieval tenures—conceived of land simply as property carrying an economic rent, a rent which was often negligible. In Massachusetts, the Crown's only claim was to receive one-fifth of all the gold and silver found there. Given New England geology the burden did not prove onerous.

The royal charter drew a set of boundaries on the New England landscape. Unlike those of the Indians, these were not "boundary or ending places" between the territories of two peoples. Rather, they were defined by lines of latitude—40 and 48 degrees north—that in theory stretched from "sea to sea." Between those lines, the Massachusetts Bay Company was given the right

> TO HAVE and to houlde, possesse, and enjoy all and singuler the aforesaid continent, landes, territories, islands, hereditaments, and precincts, seas, waters, fishings, with all and all manner their commodities, royalties, liberties, prehemynences, and profitts that should from thenceforth arise from thence, with all and singuler their appurtenances, and every parte and parcell thereof, unto the saide Councell and their successors and assignes for ever.

It was an enormous grant, no doubt in part because the King's personal claim to the territory was so tenuous. For our purposes, its significance lies in the sweeping extent and abstraction of its rights and boundaries, its lack of concern for the claims of existing inhabitants, its emphasis on the land's profits and commodities, and its intention that the land being granted could and would remain so bounded "forever." In all of these ways, it implied conceptions of land tenure drastically different from those of the Indians.

Because the King's grant was so permissive, and gave so little indication as to how land should be allocated within the new colony, the company and its settlers found themselves faced with having to devise their own method for distributing lands. Initially, the company thought to make grants to each shareholder and settler individually, as had been done in Virginia, but this idea was rapidly—though not completely—replaced with grants to groups of settlers acting together as towns. The founding proprietors of each town were collectively granted an average of about six square miles of land, and from then on were more or less free to dispose of that land as they saw fit. In terms of sovereignty, the chief difference between Indian and English villages lay in the formal hierarchy by which the latter derived and maintained their sovereign rights. But in terms of ownership— the way property and usufruct rights were distributed *within* a village—the two differed principally in the ways they intended ecologically to use the land. When the Agawam villagers reserved hunting and gathering rights in their deed to William Pynchon, they revealed how they themselves thought that particular tract of land best used. Likewise, John Winthrop's deed to Ipswich—clearly an English rather than an Indian document—in speaking of "woods meadowes, pastures and broken up grounds," betrayed the habits of thought of an English agriculturalist who was accustomed to raising crops, building fences, and keeping cattle. Conceptions of land tenure mimicked systems of ecological use.

The proprietors of a new town initially held all land in common. Their first act was to determine what different types of land were present in their territory, types which were understood to be necessary to English farming in terms of the categories mentioned in Winthrop's deed: forested lands for timber and firewood, grassy areas for grazing, salt marshes for cutting hay, potential planting fields, and so on. Like their Indian counterparts, English villages made their first division of land to locate where houses and cornfields should be; unlike the Indians, that division was conducted formally and was intended to be a permanent one, the land passing forever into private hands. Land was allocated to inhabitants using the same biblical philosophy that had justified taking it from the Indians in the first place: individuals should only possess as much land as they were able to subdue and make productive. The anonymous "Essay on the Ordering of Towns" declared that each inhabitant be given "his due proportion, more or lesse according unto his present or apparent future occasion of Imployment." A person with many servants and cattle could "improve" more land than one who had few, and so was granted more land, although the quantities varied from town to town. In this way, the social hierarchy of the

English class system was reproduced, albeit in modified form, in the New World. Grants of house lots and planting grounds were followed by grants of pastures, hay meadows, and woodlots, all allocated on the same basis of one's ability to use them.

In these and later grants as well, the passage of land from town commons to individual property was intended to create permanent private rights to it. These rights were never absolute, since both town and colony retained sovereignty and could impose a variety of restrictions on how land might be used. Burning might be prohibited on it during certain seasons of the year. A grant might be contingent on the land being used for a specific purpose—such as the building of a mill—and there was initially a require- ment in Massachusetts that all land be improved within three years or its owner would forfeit rights to it. Regulations might forbid land from being sold without the town's permission. But compared with Indian villages, grants made by New England towns contemplated much more extensive privileges for each individual landholder, with greater protection from trespass and more exclusive rights of use. The "Essay on the Ordering of Towns" saw such private ownership as the best way to promote fullest use of the land: "he that knoweth the benefit of incloseing," it said, "will omit noe dilligence to brenge him selfe into an inclusive condicion, well under- standing that one acre inclosed, is much more beneficiall than 5 falling to his share in Common."

Different towns acted differently at first in relation to their common lands, their behavior usually depending on the land practices of the regions of England from which their inhabitants came. Some settlers, like those of Rowley or Sudbury, came from areas with open-field systems, where strong manorial control had been exercised over lands held in common by peasant farmers. They initially re-created such systems in New England, making relatively few small divisions of common holdings, regulating closely who could graze and gather wood on unenclosed land, and not engaging exten- sively in the buying or selling of real estate. Settlers in towns like Ipswich or Scituate, on the other hand, came from English regions where closed- field systems gave peasant proprietors more experience with owning their lands in severalty. They proved from the start to be much interested in transferring lands from common to private property as rapidly as possible, so that their land divisions were more frequent and involved more land at an earlier date. In these towns, a market in real estate developed very early, both to allow the consolidation of scattered holdings and to facilitate limited speculative profits in land dealings.

In the long run, it was this latter conception of land—as private commodity rather than public commons—that came to typify New England towns. Initial divisions of town lands, with their functional classifications of woodlot and meadow and cornfield, bore a superficial resemblance to Indian usufruct rights, since they seemed to define land in terms of how it was to be used. Once transferred into private hands, however, most such lands became abstract parcels whose legal definition bore no inherent relation to their use: a person owned everything on them, not just specific activities which could be conducted within their boundaries. Whereas the earliest deeds tended to describe land in terms of its topography and use—for instance, as the mowing field between a certain two creeks—later deeds described land in terms of lots held by adjacent owners, and marked territories using the surveyor's abstractions of points of the compass and metes and bounds. Recording systems, astonishingly sloppy in the beginning because there was little English precedent for them, became increasingly formalized so that boundaries could be more precisely defined. Even Indian deeds showed this transformation. The land Pynchon purchased from the Agawam village was vaguely defined in terms of cornfields, meadows, and the Connecticut River; an eighteenth-century deed from the same county, on the other hand, transferred rights to two entire townships which it defined precisely but abstractly as "the full Contents of Six miles in Weadth and Seven miles in length," starting from a specified point.

The uses to which land could be put vanished from such descriptions, and later land divisions increasingly ignored actual topography. What was on the land became largely irrelevant to its legal identity, even though its contents—and the rights to them—might still have great bearing on the price it would bring if sold. Describing land as a fixed parcel with purely arbitrary boundaries made buying and selling it increasingly easy, as did the recording systems—an American innovation—which kept track of such transactions. Indeed, legal descriptions, however abstracted, had little effect on everyday life *until* land was sold. People did not cease to be intimately a part of the land's ecology simply by reason of the language with which their deeds were written. But when it came time to transfer property rights, those deeds allowed the alienation of land as a commodity, an action with important ecological consequences. To the abstraction of legal boundaries was added the abstraction of price, a measurement of property's value assessed on a unitary scale. More than anything else, it was the treatment of land and property as commodities traded at market that distinguished English conceptions of ownership from Indian ones.

Chapter 7

A WORLD OF FIELDS AND FENCES

What made Indian and European subsistence cycles seem so different from one another had less to do with their use of plants than their use of animals. Domesticated grazing mammals—and the tool which they made possible, the plow—were arguably the single most distinguishing characteristic of European agricultural practices. The Indians' relationships to the deer, moose, and beaver they hunted were far different from those of the Europeans to the pigs, cows, sheep, and horses they owned. Where Indians had contented themselves with burning the woods and concentrating their hunting in the fall and winter months, the English sought a much more total and year-round control over their animals' lives. The effects of that control ramified through most aspects of New England's rural economy, and by the end of the colonial period were responsible for a host of changes in the New England landscape: the seemingly endless miles of fences, the silenced voices of vanished wolves, the system of country roads, and the new fields filled with clover, grass, and buttercups.

Livestock were initially so rare in Plymouth and Massachusetts Bay that both William Bradford and John Winthrop noted in their journals the arrival of each new shipment of animals. Plymouth was over three years old before it obtained the "three heifers and a bull" which Bradford described as "the first beginning of any cattle of that kind in the land." Massachusetts Bay had a larger number of livestock almost from the start, but there were by no means enough to satisfy colonial demand for more animals. One colonist explained to an English patron that cattle were "wonderful dear here," and another argued that the most profitable investment a merchant could make in New England would be "to venture a sum of moneys to be turned into cattle." As a result, ship after ship arrived laden with upward of fifty animals in a load. By 1634, William Wood was able to define the wealth of the Massachusetts Bay Colony simply by referring to its livestock. "Can they be very poor," he asked, "where for four thousand souls there are fifteen hundred head of cattle, besides four thousand goats and swine innumerable? "

The importance of these various animals to the English colonists can hardly be exaggerated. Hogs had the great virtues of reproducing them-selves in large numbers and—like goats—of being willing to eat virtually anything. Moreover, in contrast to most other English animals, they were generally able to hold their own against wolves and bears, so that they could be turned out into the woods for months at a time to fend for themselves almost as wild animals. They required almost no attention until the fall slaughter, when—much as deer had been hunted by Indians—they could be recaptured, butchered, and used for winter meat supplies. Cattle needed somewhat more attention, but they too were allowed to graze freely during the warmer months of the year. In addition to the meat which they furnished, their hides were a principal source of leather, and milch cows provided dairy products—milk, cheese, and butter—that were unknown to the Indians. Perhaps most importantly, oxen were a source of animal power for plowing, clearing, and other farmwork. The use of such animals ultimately enabled English farmers to till much larger acreages than Indians had done, and so produce greater marketable surpluses. When oxen were attached to wheeled vehicles, those surpluses could be taken to market and sold. Horses were another, speedier source of power, but they were at first not as numerous as oxen because they were used less for farmwork than for personal transportation and military purposes. Finally, sheep, which required special attention because of their heavy wear on pastures and their vulnerability to predators, were the crucial supplier of the wool which furnished (with flax) most colonial clothing. Each of these animals in its own way represented a significant departure from Indian subsistence practices.

What most distinguished a hog or a cow from the deer hunted by Indians was the fact that the colonists' animal was owned. Even when it grazed in a common herd or wandered loose in woodlands or open pastures, a fixed property right inhered in it. The notch in its ear or the brand on its flanks signified to the colonists that no one other than its owner had the right to kill or convey rights to it. Since Indian property systems granted rights of personal ownership to an animal only at the moment it was killed, there was naturally some initial conflict between the two legal systems concerning the new beasts brought by the English. In 1631, for instance, colonists complained to the sachem Chickatabot that one of his villagers had shot an English pig. After a month of investigation, a colonial court ordered that a fine of one beaver skin be paid for the animal. Although the fine was paid by Chickatabot rather than the actual offender—suggesting the confusion between diplomatic relations and legal claims which necessarily accompanied any dispute between Indian and English communities—the effect of his action was to acknowledge the English right to own animal flesh. Connecticut went so far as to declare that Indian villages adjacent to English ones would be held liable for "such trespasses as shalbe committed by any Indian"—whether a member of the village or not—"either by spoilinge or killinge of Cattle or Swine either with Trappes, dogges or arrowes." Despite such statutes, colonists continued for many years to complain that Indians were stealing their stock. As late as 1672, the Massachusetts Court was noting that Indians "doe frequently sell porke to the English, and there is ground to suspect that some of the Indians doe steale and sell the English mens swine." Nevertheless, most Indians appear to have recognized fairly quickly the colonists' legal right to own animals.

Ironically, legal disputes over livestock arose as frequently when Indians *acknowledged* English property rights as when they denied them. One inevitable consequence of an English agricultural system that mixed the raising of crops with the keeping of animals was the necessity of separating the two—or else the animals would eat the crops. The obvious means for accomplishing this task was the fence, which to colonists represented perhaps the most visible symbol of an "improved" landscape: when John Winthrop had denied that Indians possessed anything more than a "natural" right to property in New England, he had done so by arguing that "they inclose noe Land" and had no "tame Cattle to improve the Land by." Fences and livestock were thus pivotal elements in the English rationale for taking Indian lands. But this rationale could cut both ways. If the absence of "improvements"—fences—meant to the colonists that Indians could claim to own only their cornfields, it also meant that those same cornfields lay open to the ravages of English grazing animals. Indians were quick to point out that, since colonists claimed ownership of the animals, colonists should be responsible for any and all damages caused by them.

Much as they might have preferred not to, the English had to admit the justice of this argument, which after all followed unavoidably from English conceptions of animal property. Colonial courts repeatedly sought some mechanism for resolving the perennial conflict between English grazing animals and Indian planting fields. In 1634, for instance, the Massachusetts Court sent an investigator "to examine what hurt the swyne of Charlton hath done amongst the Indean barnes of corne," and declared that "accordingly the inhabitants of Charlton promiseth to give them satisfaction.'' Courts regularly ordered payment of compensation to Indians whose crops had been damaged by stock, but this was necessarily a temporary solution, administered after the fact, and one which did nothing to prevent further incidents. Colonists for this reason sometimes found themselves building fences on behalf of Indian villages: in 1653, the town of New Haven promised to contribute sixty days of labor toward the construction of fences around fields planted by neighboring Indians.

Robert C. Ellickson, Property in Land
102 Yale Law Journal 1315, 1338–39 (1993).

The land story of the colony at Plymouth, Massachusetts parallels the history of Jamestown, except that events unfolded more briskly. To finance their voyage, the Pilgrims formed a joint-stock company with London investors. At the investors' insistence, the settlers agreed to pool output, lands, capital, and profits during the first seven years abroad. From this ''common stock,'' residents of the colony were to receive food and other necessities, and, at the end of the seven-year period, the land and other assets were to be ''equally divided betwixt'' the investors and settlers. The colonists initially complied with the spirit of this contract. Although they planted household gardens almost from the start, they collectivized initial field and livestock operations. The settlers had some agricultural successes, but they were unable to grow corn in their common field. Within six months of reaching Plymouth, almost one-half of the population had perished form disease.

In 1624 the Plymouth colonists deviated from the investors' plan and assigned each family from one to ten acres, depending on the number of family members. This greatly increased productivity.

> [Parcelization] had very good success; for it made all hands very industrious, so as much more corne was planted than other waise . . . The women now wente willingly into the field, and tooke their litle-ones with them to set corne, which before would aledge weakne and inabilitie; whom to have compelled would have bene though tiranie and oppression.

In 1627 Plymouth's inhabitants, at last able to liquidate the joint-stock company, followed up by parcelling out a freehold of twenty acres per member to each family. Even Plymouth's common meadows had been privatized by the early 1630's.

Other towns in colonial Massachusetts also tended to parcelize their lands as time passed. Settlers usually started by replicating the forms of land tenure they had known in their home villages in England. In some instances, these plots were laid out as strips in open field, following the familiar medieval practice. After a generation or two of land sales, consolidated family farmsteads typically began to supplant the scattered-plot systems. Nevertheless, New Englanders hardly exhibited an unrelenting drive to privatize land. Many towns set aside common greens, pastures, and woodlots. For the first generation or two, towns restricted use of these lands to the original settlers and their descendants; later, access was granted to all town householders.

---

1.   What is the significance of the distinction that Cronon makes between private property and sovereignty?

2.   Did the New England Indians have private property? Did they have private property in land? How would you characterize the Indians' conception of property with regard to land, food, tools, dwellings, and other personal items, *i.e.,* the system of rules governing access to material resources? What were the differences in property systems between the northern and southern New England Indians? What characteristics of Indian culture and society allowed them to thrive using this form of property?

Did the Colonists have common property in land? How did the colonists' view of property evolve over time?

3.   In what respects did the European conception of proper land use differ from the Native American conception? How do these differences relate to their conceptions of property in land?

4.   In Western societies, property rights have traditionally been divided into six categories: (1) the right to possess; (2) the right to exclude; (3) the right to dispose/transfer; (4) the right to use; (5) the right to enjoy fruits or profits; and (6) the right to alter/destroy. Pound, The Law of Property and Recent Jurisitic Thought, 25 A.B.A.J. 993, 997 (1939). The rights are sometimes referred to as "sticks" within the bundle that constitutes ownership. *See generally,* Waldron, What Is Private Property, 5 Oxford J. Leg. Studies 313 (1985); Cohen, Dialogue on Private Property, 9 Rutgers L. Rev. 357 (1954).

Using this division of rights, how would you classify the property interest recognized by the various Native American communities in early New England? How would you classify the interests recognized by the Colonists?

5.   Do the competing systems of rights and institutions that Cronon discusses support the hypothesis set forth at the outset of this unit: *A society's conception of property and its associated institutions adapt to promote the beneficial use of the society's resources (from the perspective of the particular society)?* If you find this proposition wanting, what alternative(s) best characterizes the nature of property institutions?

Harold Demsetz, Toward a Theory of Property Rights

57 American Economic Review Papers and Proceedings 347, 350–57 (1967).

* * *

The Emergence of Property Rights

* * *

[P]roperty rights develop to internalize externalities when the gains of internalization become larger than the cost of internalization. Increased internalization, in the main, results from changes in economic values, changes which stem from the development of new technology and the opening of new markets, changes to which old property rights are poorly attuned. A proper interpretation of this assertion requires that account be taken of a community's preferences for private ownership. Some communities will have less well-developed private ownership systems and more highly developed state ownership systems. But, given a community's tastes in this regard, the emergence of new private or state-owned property rights will be in response to changes in technology and relative prices.

I do not mean to assert or to deny that the adjustments in property rights which take place need be the result of a conscious endeavor to cope with new externality problems. These adjustments have arisen in Western societies largely as a result of gradual changes in social mores and in common law precedents. At each step of this adjustment process, it is unlikely that externalities per se were consciously related to the issue being resolved. These legal and moral experiments may be hit-and-miss procedures to some extent, but in a society that weights the achievement of efficiency heavily, their viability in the long run will depend on how well they modify behavior to accommodate to the externalities associated with important changes in technology or market values.

A rigorous test of this assertion will require extensive and detailed empirical work. A broad range of examples can be cited that are consistent with it: the development of air rights, renters' rights, rules for liability in automobile accidents, etc. In this part of the discussion, I shall present one group of such examples in some detail. They deal with the development of private property rights in land among American Indians. These examples are broad ranging and come fairly close to what can be called convincing evidence in the field of anthropology.

The question of private ownership of land among aboriginals has held a fascination for anthropologists. It has been one of the intellectual battle-grounds in the attempt to assess the "true nature" of man unconstrained by the "artificialities" of civilization. In the process of carrying on this debate, information has been uncovered that bears directly on the thesis with which we are now concerned. What appears to be accepted as a classic treatment and a high point of this debate is Eleanor Leacock's memoir on

The Montagnes: "Hunting Territory" and the Fur Trade.[6] Leacock's research followed that of Frank G. Speck[7] who had discovered that the Indians of the Labrador Peninsula had a long-established tradition of property in land. This finding was at odds with what was known about the Indians of the American Southwest and it prompted Leacock's study of the Montagnes who inhabited large regions around Quebec.

Leacock clearly established the fact that a close relationship existed, both historically and geographically, between the development of private rights in land and the development of the commercial fur trade. The factual basis of this correlation has gone unchallenged. However, to my knowledge, no theory relating privacy of land to the fur trade has yet been articulated. The factual material uncovered by Speck and Leacock fits the thesis of this paper well, and in doing so, it reveals clearly the role played by property right adjustments in taking account of what economists have often cited as an example of an externality—the overhunting of game.

Because of the lack of control over hunting by others, it is in no person's interest to invest in increasing or maintaining the stock of game. Overly intensive hunting takes place. Thus a successful hunt is viewed as imposing external costs on subsequent hunters—costs that are not taken into account fully in the determination of the extent of hunting and of animal husbandry.

Before the fur trade became established, hunting was carried on primarily for purposes of food and the relatively few furs that were required for the hunter's family. The externality was clearly present. Hunting could be practiced freely and was carried on without assessing its impact on other hunters. But these external effects were of such small significance that it did not pay for anyone to take them into account. There did not exist anything resembling private ownership in land. And in the *Jesuit Relations*, particularly Le Jeune's record of the winter he spent with the Montagnes in 1633–34 and in the brief account given by Father Druilletes in 1647–48, Leacock finds no evidence of private land holdings. Both accounts indicate a socioeconomic organization in which private rights to land are not well developed.

We may safely surmise that the advent of the fur trade had two immediate consequences. First, the value of furs to the Indians was increased considerably. Second, and as a result, the scale of hunting activity rose sharply. Both consequences must have increased considerably the importance of the externalities associated with free hunting. The property right system began to change, and it changed specifically in the direction required to take account of the economic effects made important by the fur trade. The geographical or distributional evidence collected by Leacock indicates an unmistakable correlation between early centers of fur trade

6. Eleanor Leacock, American Anthropologist (American Anthropological Ass'n), Vol. 56, No. 5, Part 2, Memoir No. 78.

7. *Cf.* Frank G. Speck, The Basis of American Indian Ownership of Land, Old Penn Weekly Rev. (Univ. of Pennsylvania), Jan. 16, 1915, pp. 491–495.

and the oldest and most complete development of the private hunting territory.* * *

The principle that associates property right changes with the emergence of new and reevaluation of old harmful and beneficial effects suggests in this instance that the fur trade made it economic to encourage the husbanding of fur-bearing animals. Husbanding requires the ability to prevent poaching and this, in turn, suggests that socioeconomic changes in property in hunting land will take place. The chain of reasoning is consistent with the evidence cited above. Is it inconsistent with the absence of similar rights in property among the southwestern Indians?

Two factors suggest that the thesis is consistent with the absence of similar rights among the Indians of the southwestern plains. The first of these is that there were no plains animals of commercial importance comparable to the fur-bearing animals of the forest, at least not until cattle arrived with Europeans. The second factor is that animals of the plains are primarily grazing species whose habit is to wander over wide tracts of land. The value of establishing boundaries to private hunting territories is thus reduced by the relatively high cost of preventing the animals from moving to adjacent parcels. Hence both the value and cost of establishing private hunting lands in the Southwest are such that we would expect little development along these lines. The externality was just not worth taking into account.

The lands of the Labrador Peninsula shelter forest animals whose habits are considerably different from those of the plains. Forest animals confine their territories to relatively small areas, so that the cost of internalizing the effects of husbanding these animals is considerably reduced. This reduced cost, together with the higher commercial value of fur-bearing forest animals, made it productive to establish private hunting lands. Frank G. Speck finds that family proprietorship among the Indians of the Peninsula included retaliation against trespass. Animal resources were husbanded. Sometimes conservation practices were carried on extensively. Family hunting territories were divided into quarters. Each year the family hunted in a different quarter in rotation, leaving a tract in the center as a sort of bank, not to be hunted over unless forced to do so by a shortage in the regular tract. * * *

The Coalescence and Ownership of Property Rights

I have argued that property rights arise when it becomes economic for those affected by externalities to internalize benefits and costs. But I have not yet examined the forces which will govern the particular form of right ownership. Several idealized forms of ownership must be distinguished at the outset. These are communal ownership, private ownership, and state ownership.

By communal ownership, I shall mean a right which can be exercised by all members of the community. Frequently the rights to till and to hunt the land have been communally owned. The right to walk on a city sidewalk is communally owned. Communal ownership means that the community denies to the state or to individual citizens the right to interfere with any person's exercise of communally-owned rights. Private ownership implies that the community recognizes the right of the owner to exclude others from exercising the owner's private rights. State ownership implies that the state may exclude anyone from the use of a right as long as the state follows accepted political procedures for determining who may not use state-owned property. * * *

It will be best to begin by considering a particularly useful example that focuses our attention on the problem of land ownership. Suppose that land is communally owned. Every person has the right to hunt, till, or mine the land. This form of ownership fails to concentrate the cost associated with any person's exercise of his communal right on that person. If a person seeks to maximize the value of his communal rights, he will tend to overhunt and overwork the land because some of the costs of his doing so are borne by others. The stock of game and the richness of the soil will be diminished too quickly. It is conceivable that those who own these rights, *i.e.*, every member of the community, can agree to curtail the rate at which they work the lands if negotiating and policing costs are zero. * * *

Negotiating costs will be large because it is difficult for many persons to reach a mutually satisfactory agreement, especially when each hold-out has the right to work the land as fast as he pleases. But, even if an agreement among all can be reached, we must yet take account of the costs of policing the agreement . * * *

The land ownership example confronts us immediately with a great disadvantage of communal property. The effects of a person's activities on his neighbors * * * will not be taken into account fully. Communal property results in great externalities. The full costs of the activities of an owner of a communal property right are not borne directly by him, nor can they be called to his attention easily by the willingness of others to pay him an appropriate sum. Communal property rules out a "pay-to-use-the-property" system and high negotiation and policing costs make ineffective a "pay-him-not-to-use-the-property" system.

The state, the courts, or the leaders of the community could attempt to internalize the external costs resulting from communal property by allowing private parcels owned by small groups of persons with similar interests. The logical groups in terms of similar interests are, of course, the family and the individual. * * *

[P]rivate ownership of land will internalize many of the external costs associated with communal ownership, for now an owner, by virtue of his power to exclude others, can generally count on realizing the rewards associated with husbanding the [resources] and increasing the [value] of his land. This concentration of benefits and costs on owners creates incentives to utilize resources more efficiently.

But we have yet to contend with externalities. Under the communal property system the maximization of the value of communal property rights will take place without regard to many costs, because the owner of a communal right cannot exclude others from enjoying the fruits of his efforts and because negotiation costs are too high for all to agree jointly on optimal behavior. The development of private rights permits the owner to economize on the use of those resources from which he has the right to exclude others. Much internalization is accomplished in this way. But the owner of private rights to one parcel does not himself own the rights to the parcel of another private sector. Since he cannot exclude others from their private rights to land, he has no direct incentive (in the absence of negotiations) to economize in the use of his land in a way that takes into account the effects he produces on the land rights of others. If he constructs a dam on this land, he has no direct incentive to take into account the lower water levels produced on his neighbor's land.

This is exactly the same kind of externality that we encountered with communal property rights, but it is present to a lesser degree. Whereas no one had an incentive to store water on any land under the communal system, private owners now can take into account directly those benefits and costs to their land that accompany water storage. But the effect on the land of others will not be taken into account directly.

The partial concentration of benefits and costs that accompany private ownership is only part of the advantage [a private property] system offers. * * * The cost of negotiating over the remaining externalities will be reduced greatly. Communal property rights allow anyone to use the land. Under this system it becomes necessary to reach an agreement on land use. But the externalities that accompany private ownership of property do not affect all owners, and, generally speaking, it will be necessary for only a few to reach an agreement that takes these effects into account. * * *

The reduction in negotiation cost that accompanies the private right to exclude others allows most externalities to be internalized at rather low cost. Those that are not are associated with activities that generate external effects impinging upon many people. The soot from smoke affects many homeowners, none of whom might be willing to pay enough to the factory to get its owner to reduce smoke output. All homeowners together might be willing to pay enough, but the cost of their getting together may be enough to discourage effective market bargaining. The negotiating problem is compounded even more if the smoke comes not from a single smoke stack but from an industrial district. In such cases, it may be too costly to internalize effects through the marketplace.

---

1. What is the essence of Demsetz's theory of the evolution of property rights? Why, in Demsetz's view, do private property rights reduce externalities while communal or collective rights regimes encourage or exacerbate externalities? What assumptions does he make about social relations and community governance?

2. In choosing between communal and private property systems, what is the relevance of: (1) transaction costs of decision making; (2) incentives

for and costs of monitoring boundaries; (3) rewards for productive labor and punishment for inefficient use of resources; (4) scarcity of land; (5) levels of technology; and (6) literacy?

3. Is the choice between private and communal property systems simply about efficiency? Does private property serve functions other than wealth maximization? Consider the following overlapping arguments:

> "In a society that favors individualism, private property helps to ensure economic independence, protect privacy from interference by the government and other persons, and ensure that individuals can control their own environment. Communitarianism, by contrast, promotes community, solidarity against external threats, and frequently (although not always) egalitarianism, at some expense to individualism." Robert Ellickson, Property in Land, 102 Yale L.J. 1315, 1352–57 (1993).

> "One of [the functions of private property] is to draw a boundary between public and private power. * * * Outside, [the property owner] must justify any interference. * * * Thus, property performs the function of maintaining independence, dignity and pluralism in society by creating zones within which the majority has to yield to the owner." Reich, The New Property, 73 Yale L.J. 733, 771 (1964). *See also* M. Friedman, Capitalism and Freedom 7–21 (1962) (private property is a necessary precondition to political freedom).

> Private property "prevents monopolization of the means of intellectual and political production by the state * * * It means that individuals have places other than the state to turn to for their employment and their subsistence if they become suspect in the eyes of the authorities. * * *" It improves the "general morale of a society" because it "helps foster people's sense that their well-being depends on their own efforts and that they should take responsibility for the risks they run and the losses and successes they incur." Private property "fosters an attractive conception of social cooperation—one in which individuals work with others and exchange goods and services back and forth because they want to and conceive some advantage in doing so not because they are forced to whether they see the sense in it or not." Waldron, Property, Justification, and Need, 6 Can. J. L. & Juris. 185, 189 (1993).

> Private "property function[s] to foster the independence and civic participation of a morally committed citizenry." Rose, *Mahon* Reconstructed: Why the Takings Issue Is Still a Muddle, 57 S. Cal. L. Rev. 561, 590 (1984).

Do you find these arguments persuasive?

4. Do communal property systems necessarily lead to tragedy? What are some counter-examples? Consider the following passage:

> Insofar as recreation educates and socializes us, it acts as a "social glue" for everyone, not just those immediately engaged; and of course, the more people involved in any socializing activity, the better. Like commerce, then, recreation has social and political overtones. The

contemplation of nature elevates our minds above the workaday world, and thus helps us to cope with that very world; recreational play trains us in the democratic give-and-take that makes our regime function. If these arguments are true, we should not worry that people engage in too much recreation, but too little. This again argues that recreation should be open to all at minimal costs, or at costs to be borne by the general public, since all of us benefit from the greater sociability of our fellow citizens. If we accept these arguments, we might believe that unique recreational sites ought not be private property; their greatest value lies in civilizing and socializing all members of the public, and this value should not be "held up" by private owners. * * *

Perhaps the chief lesson from the nineteenth century doctrines of "inherently public property," then, is that while we may change our minds about which activities are socializing, we always accept that the public requires access to some physical locations for some of these activities. Our law consistently allocates that access to the public, because public access to those locations is as important as the general privatization of property in other spheres of our law. In the absence of the socializing activities that take place on "inherently public property," the public is a shapeless mob, whose members neither trade nor converse nor play, but only fight, in a setting where life is, in Hobbes' all too famous phrase, solitary, poor, nasty, brutish, and short.

Rose, The Comedy of the Commons: Custom, Commerce, and Inherently Public Property, 53 U. Chi. L. Rev. 711, 779–81 (1986).

5.   Does Cronon's historical study tend to support or refute Demsetz's theory of property rights formation? Or do Cronon and Demsetz focus upon different variables to explain the evolution of property institutions?

6.   Recently discovered archaeological evidence indicates that Iroquois Indians living near Niagara Falls in the early 17th century bred and raised deer in pens in order to trade deer skins with European colonists in exchange for whelk shells from the Chesapeake Bay. The relatively high proportion of male deer bones found at the site suggests that the Iroquois were resourceful in their management of stocks. This evidence corroborates historical references to the Iroquois as "those who tend deer." Rensberger, Iroquois as Deer Managers, Wash. Post, May 16, 1988, at A.3. How do these findings relate to Cronon's? Demsetz's? What theory of property institutions encompasses these findings? Consider, in this regard, Robert Ellickson's argument:

[A] close-knit group tends to create, through custom and law, a cost-minimizing land regime that adaptively responds to changes in risk, technology, demand, and other economic conditions. In so doing, the group opportunistically mixes private, group, and open-access lands. According to the private property thesis, a close-knit group invariably entitles its individual members, households, or narrow family lines to obtain exclusive rights to sites suitable for dwellings, agriculture, and other intensive uses. The key utilitarian advantage of private land tenure, in comparison to collective ownership, is that it is far simpler to monitor boundary crossings than to appraise the behavior of individuals who are privileged to be where they are. * * *

As a group becomes literate and its lands become more scarce, its standard bundle of private land rights tends to evolve from the time-limited and inalienable usufruct to something like the perpetual and alienable fee simple. * * *

But a private-property regime is not always best. To exploit scale economies, and perhaps to spread risks, a group may gravitate toward governing some territories, such as a pasture in a medieval village or a recreation area in a homeowners' association, as limited-access commonses. * * *

Ellickson, Property in Land, 102 Yale L.J. 1315, 1397–98 (1993).

C.   COMPARING PROPERTY REGIMES IN DIFFERENT RESOURCES

1.   A CASE STUDY OF PROPERTY RIGHTS IN THE WHALING INDUSTRY

The 18th–19th century whaling industry provides a particularly interesting case study of the development of property rights in a valuable, elusive, and dangerous resource.[8] From 1750 to 1870, whale oil and bone were valuable commodities. A single whale might be worth from $2000–$3000, roughly 3–5 times the mean annual income for a family in the late nineteenth century.

American whaling communities were close-knit, largely because they were concentrated in a few ports in southern New England. The relative remoteness of the ports and intermarriage reinforced the common goals and values that developed in the whaling industry.

Over time, the whaling industry developed rules to resolve disputes over the ownership of whales that had been chased, harpooned, or killed by more than one ship. In numerous reported cases, American courts deferred to these industry-developed property rules. In the following excerpt from Moby–Dick, Melville describes some of these rules and uses them to raise larger questions about the meaning of property.

8. The description of the whaling community is drawn from Ellickson, A Hypothesis of Wealth–Maximizing Norms: Evidence from the Whaling Industry 5 J. L. Econ. & Org. 83 (1989).

Herman Melville, Moby–Dick

(1851).

Chapter 89.

FAST–FISH AND LOOSE–FISH

The allusion to the waifs[9] and waif-poles in the last chapter but one, necessitates some account of the laws and regulations of the whale fishery, of which the waif may be deemed the grand symbol and badge.

It frequently happens that when several ships are cruising in company, a whale may be struck by one vessel, then escape, and be finally killed and captured by another vessel; and herein are indirectly comprised many minor contingencies, all partaking of this one grand feature. For example,—after a weary and perilous chase and capture of a whale, the body may get loose from the ship by reason of a violent storm: and drifting far away to leeward, be retaken by a second whaler, who in a calm, snugly tows it alongside, without risk of life or line. Thus the most vexatious and violent disputes would often arise between the fishermen, were there not some written or unwritten, universal, undisputed law applicable to all cases.

Perhaps the only formal whaling code authorized by legislative enactment, was that of Holland. It was decreed by the States–General in A.D. 1695. But though no other nation has ever had any written whaling law, yet the American fishermen have been their own legislators and lawyers in this matter. They have provided a system which for terse comprehensiveness surpasses Justinian's Pandeets and the By-laws of the Chinese Society for the Suppression of Meddling with other People's Business. Yes: these laws might be engraved on a Queen Anne's farthing, or the barb of a harpoon, and worn round the neck, so small are they.

I.   A Fast–Fish belongs to the party fast to it.

II.   A Loose–Fish is fair game for anybody who can soonest catch it.

But what plays the mischief with this masterly code is the admirable brevity of it, which necessitates a vast volume of commentaries to expound it.

First: What is a Fast–Fish? Alive or dead a fish is technically fast, when it is connected with an occupied ship or boat, by any medium at all controllable by the occupant or occupants,—a mast, an oar, a nine-inch cable, a telegraph wire, or a strand of cobweb, it is all the same. Likewise a fish is technically fast when it bears a waif, or any other recognized symbol of possession; so long as the party waifing it plainly evince their ability at any time to take it alongside, as well as their intention so to do.

These are scientific commentaries; but the commentaries of the whalemen themselves sometimes consist in hard words and harder knocks—the

---

9. [A "waif" is a small pole with a flag. Whalers would stick the waif in a dead whale to signify their claim and intention to return later to harvest the whale.]

Coke-upon-Littleton[10] of the fist. True, among the more upright and honorable whalemen allowances are always made for peculiar cases, where it would be an outrageous moral injustice for one party to claim possession of a whale previously chased or killed by another party. But others are by no means so scrupulous.

Some fifty years ago there was a curious case of whale-trover litigated in England wherein the plaintiffs set forth that after a hard chase of a whale in the northern seas, they (the plaintiffs) had succeeded in harpooning the fish; but at last, through peril of their lives, were obliged to forsake, not only their lines, but their boat itself,—Furthermore: ultimately the defendants (the crew of another ship) came up with the whale; struck, killed, seized, and finally appropriated it before the very eyes of the plaintiffs;—Yet again:—and when those defendants were remonstrated with, their captain snapped his fingers in the plaintiffs' teeth, and assured them that by way of doxology to the deed he had done, he would now retain their line, harpoons, and boat, all of which had remained attached to the whale at the time of the seizure. Wherefore, the plaintiffs now sued for the recovery of the value of their whale, line, harpoons, and boat.

* * *

These pleadings, and the counter pleadings, being duly heard, the very learned judge in set terms decided, to wit:—That as for the boat, he awarded it to the plaintiffs, because they had merely abandoned it to save their lives; but that with regard to the controverted whale, harpoons, and line, they belonged to the defendants; the whale, because it was a Loose–Fish at the time of the final capture; and the harpoons and line because when the fish made off with them, it (the fish) acquired a property in those articles; and hence anybody who afterwards took the fish had a right to them. Now, the defendants afterwards took the fish; ergo, the aforesaid articles were theirs.

A common man looking at this decision of the very learned Judge, might possibly object to it. But ploughed up to the primary rock of the matter, the two great principles laid down in the twin whaling laws previously quoted, and applied and elucidated by Lord Ellenborough in the above cited case; these two laws touching Fast–Fish and Loose–Fish, I say, will, on reflection, be found the fundamentals of all human jurisprudence; for notwithstanding its complicated tracery of sculpture, the Temple of the Law, like the Temple of the Philistines, has but two props to stand on.

Is it not a saying in every one's mouth, Possession is half of the law: that is, regardless of how the thing came into possession? But often possession is the whole of the law. What are the sinews and souls of Russian serfs and Republican slaves but Fast–Fish, whereof possession is the whole of the law? What to the rapacious landlord is the widow's last mite but a Fast–Fish? What is yonder undetected villain's marble mansion with a door-plate for a waif; what is that but a Fast-Fish? What is the

---

10. [This refers to Sir Edward Coke's authoritative early seventeenth-century commentary upon a fifteenth-century work on real property by Sir Thomas Littleton.]

ruinous discount which Mordecai, the broker, gets from poor Woebegone, the bankrupt, on a loan to keep Woebegone's family from starvation; what is that ruinous discount but a Fast–Fish? What is the Archbishop of Savesoul's income of £100,000 seized from the scant bread and cheese of hundreds of thousands of broken-backed laborers (all sure of heaven without any of Savesouls help) what is that globular 100,000 but a Fast–Fish? What are the Duke of Dunder's hereditary towns and hamlets but Fast–Fish? What to that redoubted harpooner, John Bull, is poor Ireland, but a Fast–Fish? What to that apostolic lancer, Brother Jonathan, is Texas but a Fast–Fish? And concerning all these, is not Possession the whole of the law? But if the doctrine of Fast–Fish be pretty generally applicable, the kindred doctrine of Loose–Fish is still more widely so. That is internationally and universally applicable.

What was America in 1492 but a Loose–Fish, in which Columbus struck the Spanish standard by way of waifing it for his royal master and mistress? What was Poland to the Czar? What Greece to the Turk? What India to England? What at last will Mexico be to the United States? All Loose-Fish.

What are the Rights of Man and the Liberties of the World but Loose–Fish? What all men's minds and opinions but Loose–Fish? What is the principle of religious belief in them but a Loose-Fish? What to the ostentatious smuggling verbalists are the thoughts of thinkers but Loose–Fish? And what are you, reader, but a Loose–Fish and a Fast–Fish, too?

Problem: Choosing Rules to Determine the Ownership of Whales

Two of the most important whales were "right whales" and "sperm whales." Right whales, which were hunted off the coast of Greenland, are slow swimmers that do not put up much of a fight when harpooned. They usually do not swim in schools. In many cases, dead right whales sink before they can be butchered, thus forcing boatsmen to cut their lines. Several days later, the bloated carcasses float to the surface. By that time, of course, the whale ship may be gone.

Sperm whales, which were the whales in Moby–Dick, are faster, dive deeper, and fight harder than right whales. They swim in schools. When hunting sperm whales, boatsmen often used "drogues"—floats at the end of harpoon lines—to tire the whales and mark them. When hunting with drogues, boatsmen did not attach the harpoon to the harpooning boat. Even when boatsmen hunted with harpoons attached to the boat, lines often broke or the boatsmen had to cut their lines to avoid serious damage to the boat.

First identify the objectives of the whaling industry. Second, in light of these objectives, choose among the following rules[11] the ones that best allocate property interests for each type of whale:

11. Robert Ellickson developed these rules as part of his paper, A Hypothesis of Wealth–Maximizing Norms: Evidence from the Whaling Industry, 5 J. L. Econ. & Org. 83 (1989).

1. *Share the wealth*: equal division of the whale among the ships that had lowered at least one boat to pursue the whale, regardless of their contributions to the capture.

2. *Reward useful labor*: equal division of the whale among ships that made substantial contributions to its capture.

3. *Line holds the whale*: a ship has an exclusive right to possession of the whale so long as the whale (whether dead or alive) is connected by a line to one of the ship's whaling boats.

4. *Possession of carcass*: the first ship to have unmistakable control over the whale after its death has exclusive right to possession.

5. *Lowered boat holds the whale*: the first ship to lower a boat to pursue the whale has an exclusive right to possession, so long as it maintains a fresh pursuit of the whale.

6. *Reasonable prospect*: the first ship to achieve a "reasonable prospect" of capturing the whale has an exclusive right to possession, so long as it maintains a fresh pursuit of the whale.

7. *Harpoon holds the whale*: the first ship to affix a harpoon to the whale, whether or not the harpoon is attached by line to a whaling boat, has an exclusive right to possession, so long as it maintains a fresh pursuit of the whale.

8. *Brand holds the whale*: the first ship to place its identifying brand on the tail of the whale, whether dead or alive, has an exclusive right to possession, so long as it maintains a fresh pursuit of the whale.

9. *Mortal wounding*: the ship whose crew mortally wounds the whale has an exclusive right to possession, so long as it maintains a fresh pursuit of the whale.

---

2.   A Case Study of Property Rights in the Oyster Industry

Richard J. Agnello & Lawrence P. Donnelley, Property Rights and Efficiency in the Oyster Industry

18 Journal of Law and Economics 521, 522–23, 524–25, 532–33 (1975).

The American Easter oyster represents the resource base of both the Gulf and Atlantic coast oyster industries. Following a brief larva stage (spat), the oyster connects permanently to a firm subaqueous material such as rock or shell deposits (cultch). Its habitat is the intermediate salinity waters of the seacoast's intertidal zone and of inland rivers and bays. Water current, temperature and biological productivity, in addition to salinity, are determinants of the resource productivity of a given parcel of subaqueous land.

Two property right structures characterizing the oyster industry in each of the Atlantic and Gulf states can be identified, a private right structure based mainly on leaseholds and a common right system. The courts have long recognized rights to subaqueous land for the people of each state for their common use. State legislatures have confirmed and modified these rights. Although the federal government claims jurisdiction over a three mile coastal zone, Congress has ceded jurisdiction over land and resource use rights within this zone back to the states. The states have exercised their jurisdiction over the oyster resource in similar ways. In general, natural oyster beds have been set aside as a common fishery for state residents whereas other submerged land parcels are available for private leasing.

The distinction made by each state between natural oyster beds and other land permits the development of an empirical measure of a state's property right variable used in subsequent sections of this paper. Oysters found on subaqueous land classified as a "natural oyster bed" are in general an open access (common property) fishery for state residents. Other areas may be leased and used exclusively by the lessee for the cultivation of oysters. Regardless of how a state arrives at the determination of which lands are natural oyster beds and which are available for leasing, each state makes a clear demarcation of its common from leasable land. However, great variation among the states exists in the proportion of area and quality of land set aside for public or common use versus private use depending on how broadly administrators define the term "natural oyster bed." An examination of the proportion of oyster catch by weight on private grounds to total catch by state reveals ratios ranging from a maximum of 1 to almost zero during the 1950's and 1960's.* * *

In a world where transactions costs are significant and resources are scarce common property right systems result in less efficient resource allocation than private right systems. This occurs because communal rights do not ensure that the costs of an individual harvester's actions in exploiting the resource are borne fully by him. In attempting to maximize the value of his common right, the individual can be expected to over-exploit the resource leading to depletion of the stock, and in the extreme case to extinction of even replenishable resources. Private property internalizes the costs of the harvester's actions. In a similar way, a private right enables the producer to capture a greater proportion of the benefit of his activity in comparison to a communal right.

The type of externality manifested by communal rights to oysters depends on the stage at which the production process is being examined. In general, an oysterman can separate production into two stages: establishment of suitable conditions for oysters to mature, and second, the act of harvesting oysters for the market.

The most important requirement under the control of an individual oysterman for ensuring maturation of oysters is that a cultch be established. Other things equal, an individual could transform barren subaqueous land into productive grounds by depositing rock or shells on to it. He could then plant seed oysters on the material to hasten maturity. It should be obvious, however, that this kind of activity is minimal unless the planter is given the exclusive right of harvesting oysters from that land parcel. Under a communal right system, such a guarantee is nonexistent.

Three problems arise at the harvesting stage. First, the harvesting process typically removes cultch. Unless replaced, cultch removal implies disinvestment. On communal property once again, incentive to replenish this material is minimal. In practice, most states stipulate that some proportion of shells be redeposited on communal oyster grounds. In many states, however, processors rather than harvesters bear this cost. Frequently, states also subsidize the communal system by undertaking cultch rehabilitation programs. Second, overcrowding of vessels on particularly rich water areas leads to congestion. Finally, immature oysters are caught indiscriminately with the mature. Consequently, the growth behavior of the stock is affected. Most states set a minimum size restriction and require that culling of undersized oysters be done immediately upon being caught. Culling restrictions are also accompanied by stipulations that any cultch that was removed by the act of harvesting also be replaced immediately.
* * *

The empirical findings suggest that private property rights do in general make a significant difference in a state's average labor productivity in oyster harvesting. Common property rights are associated with low labor productivity resulting from disinvestment, congestion, over exploitation and government restrictions. Regulation in common property rights states aims at conserving the oyster resource by mandating labor intensive technologies. If labor opportunity costs are roughly equal across states, it is likely that labor intensive methods in common property states are inefficient, and that social benefit could be increased by encouraging private leasing of oyster beds as an alternative to the common property structure utilized by many states.

The regression results provide an indication of the magnitude of the welfare loss due to common property rights. * * * [A] 10 per cent increase in private property rights across states could be expected to increase average physical product by 338 pounds per man and average income by $179. Furthermore if all coastal states had relied entirely on private property in oyster harvesting in 1969, * * * an increase in average oystermen's incomes of around $1300 or almost fifty per cent of 1969 average income [would be predicted by the analysis]. Since costs of enforcing private rights do not seem to be a serious problem for sessile species in intertidal coastal waters, one can conclude that considerations other than economic efficiency are used by states relying on common property for the oyster industry.

3. A Case Study of Property Rights in the Lobster Industry

James M. Acheson, The Lobster Gangs of Maine
48–49, 73–76, 142–144 (1988).

While lobstermen themselves often subscribe to the stereotype of the independent man-at-sea, they are in fact part of a complicated social network. The industry has rules that all men are expected to obey, its own standards of conduct, and its own mythology. To succeed in lobstering a man not only must have certain technical skills and work hard, but also must be able to operate in a particular social milieu.

Beyond the kinship group, the most important people in a lobster fisherman's life are the men who fish from the same harbor. Such social groupings, while they are recognized by everyone in the lobster-fishing industry, have no universally accepted name. People refer to the "Monhegan boys," or the "Friendship fishermen," or the "Port Clyde gang." Sometimes men refer to those in their own harbor as "the men I fish with." I have called these groups "harbor gangs," although this term is only rarely used by the fishermen themselves.

Membership in a harbor gang strongly influences many aspects of a lobster fisherman's career. Most importantly, it controls entry into the industry. To go lobster fishing, a man must first become a member of a harbor gang. Once he has gained admission, he can go fishing only in the territory "owned" communally by members of that gang. Fishermen who place their traps in the territory of another gang can expect swift retribution, normally the purposeful destruction of their gear. Although these territories and the gangs that own them are completely unrecognized by the state, they are a longstanding reality. Fishermen identify with a particular harbor gang and are identified as members of it. Members of harbor gangs obtain a great deal of valuable information from one another on fishing locations and innovations. They also assist one another in times of emergency at sea. If a motor breaks down or someone runs out of gas, other members of the gang are called for a tow. This is one of the reasons that people in a harbor gang keep their radios on the same channel. * * *

Lobster fishermen in the same harbor gang ordinarily have long-term, multistrand ties with one another. Almost all live in the town where the harbor is located. Many are members of long-established families and share kinship ties as well. The men of the same generation have grown up together, and members of their families have known one another and intermarried for generations. * * *

Defense of Boundaries

Violation of territorial boundaries meets with no fixed response. An older person from an established family with a long history of fishing might infringe on the territorial rights of others almost indefinitely. Those being infringed upon are especially reluctant to accuse a gang leader or the member of a large family, either of whom could have a large number of allies. An unpopular person, a young fisherman, or a newcomer encounters trouble more quickly. Sooner or later, however, someone decides to take action against the interloper. Sometimes a small group of fishermen decide to act in concert, but boundary defense is often effected by one person acting alone.

The violator is usually warned, sometimes by verbal threats and abuse, but usually by surreptitious molestation of lobstering gear. Two half-hitches of rope may be tied around the spindle of the buoy, or legal-sized lobsters may be taken out and the doors of the traps left open. Fishermen have been known to leave threatening notes in bottles inside the offending traps, and one colorful islander carves a representation of female genitalia in the styrofoam buoys. Most interlopers move their gear when warned in these ways. If the violations persist, the traps are destroyed. Fishermen have destroyed traps by "carving them up a little" with a chain saw or by smashing them with sledge hammers. When such traps are pulled, the owner has little doubt as to what has happened. Usually, however, the offending traps are cut off: they are pulled, the buoy toggles and warp line are cut, and the trap is pushed into deep water, where there is little chance of finding it. There is no practical way to protect traps in the water. Removing the traps not only removes the symbol of another person's intrusion but also limits the intruder's capacity to reduce the defender's own catch. Destruction of traps does not usually lead to direct confrontation since the owner can only guess who destroyed them or even whether they were destroyed on purpose.

In a few instances, gangs defend their boundaries as a group. It is well known that anyone invading the traditional territories of such islands as Metinic, Monhegan, and Green Island can expect coordinated resistance from men fishing those islands. Once in a while, groups goaded beyond endurance launch a full scale "cut war" in which hundreds of traps are destroyed, boats sunk, and even docks and fish houses burnt. These so-called lobster wars lead to long-standing bitterness, violence, and court action.

It is a rare day in a harbor when someone does not suspect that his traps have been tampered with. Many incidents occur as a result of feuds and competition within a particular area. Much of this small-scale molestation stems from the fact that maintaining territorial lines means constantly utilizing one's own territory and perhaps a little more—a process known as "pushing the lines." Even in slow months, a few traps are left in certain peripheral areas to maintain local territorial claims. However, fishermen touch another's gear only with great reluctance, knowing that their own gear is vulnerable to retaliation. The whole industry is aware that the individuals whose traps have been cut off may well take vengeance, but frequently against the wrong person. The result, they know, can be a comic and costly chain of events in which the innocent and the guilty retaliate blindly against one another. The norms are therefore widely obeyed, and although the entire coast is patrolled by only a few wardens, there is little trouble. Fishermen are very careful to punish intruders in ways that will not provoke a massive, violent response. According to one fisherman, "The trick to driving a man [out of the area] is to cut off just one or two traps at a time." This harassment makes it unprofitable to fish an area but does not challenge a man to open warfare, since he can only guess who cut his traps.

A conspiracy of silence surrounds all trap-cutting incidents and efforts to enforce boundaries. Those who resort to cutting traps rarely advertise their "skill with the knife," to reduce both the possibility of retaliation and the chance of losing their lobster licenses for destroying the traps of other men. Destruction of another's gear is always considered immoral, regardless of the circumstances, because it interferes with the victim's ability to feed his family. Victims may growl and threaten but they rarely report the incident to any law enforcement agency. The culprit's identity may be unknown, and chances of successful prosecution are small. Fishermen feel strongly that the law should be kept at bay and that people should handle their own problems. Any fisherman who goes to the police to complain about trap cuttings not only looks ineffectual and ridiculous but is somewhat of a threat. When a man's traps are missing, taking the law into his own hands is not only more effective but also maintains his standing among fellow fishermen. * * *

Fishermen say that a man is allowed to fish within the entire territory owned by the harbor gang to which he belongs. This statement is not strictly accurate. A man is expected to keep his distance from other fishermen and not "dump" his traps on top of another's, where they can become entangled. Fishermen with traps in a saturated location have usufructuary rights; others cannot enter until someone leaves. The older, more skilled fishermen are likely to have their traps prepositioned in the best locations. When lobsters do appear, those who have "camped out" in good spots have monopolized all or most of the available space. Younger fishermen—particularly those who have joined the gang recently—are well advised to stay out of the way of men with status in the hierarchy of skill and prestige. Men of lower status can lose a great deal by coming into conflict with highliners.

Sometimes groups of men use a particular spot or set of spots for such a long time that they begin to feel proprietary rights over these locations. Within harbor gangs in the study area, however, such men have only usufructuary rights no permanent ownership. Should the men who regularly fish in a location move their traps elsewhere, others from the harbor gang can move their traps into it. * * *

Common-Property Resources

According to the theory of common-property resources, resources such as fish, air, water, and publicly owned parks and forests are overexploited and abused in ways that privately owned resources are not. Owners of private property protect their resources, while those exploiting publicly owned or open-access resources are locked into a system that makes unlimited exploitation rational. Why should one cattleman, logger, or polluter conserve the resources, since he cannot capture the benefits for himself? Under these circumstances, it is only logical for such a person to expand the amount of capital he uses and strive to use as much of the resources as possible and as fast as possible. The result is what Garrett Hardin has called the "tragedy of the commons." In the case of fisheries, the "tragedy" is said to result in overexploitation of fish stocks, decline of the breeding stock, "overcapitalization," and "economic inefficiency." Two different kinds of solutions have been suggested for such common-property problems. Many of the economists who have developed this body of theory see salvation in establishing private property rights of one kind or another. Hardin, a biologist, is more pessimistic. He believes such problems can be solved only by draconian government controls.

Although the theory of common-property resources has played a key role in shaping current conceptions of resource management, little empirical work has been done to verify this theory. * * * One axiom of the theory is that property rights help to conserve resources, promote economic efficiency, and result in higher incomes. This case study confirms this axiom. In the perimeter-defended areas, where access is more limited and property rights are more vigorously enforced, the stock of lobsters is larger, catches of fishermen are larger, and the breeding stock is larger. However, the theory assumes that there are really only two kinds of ownership: private ownership and having no control over access at all. As * * * a number of other authors have recently pointed out, there are really three different kinds of property: private property, communal or jointly owned property, and "open access." Maine lobstering territories are an instance of joint or communal property. Such institutions, which can be generated by local communities operating on their own, can be effective in conserving the resources. This case study reinforces [the] point * * * that the problem is not "common property" but "open access," or no controls at all on usage. It also helps to modify Hardin's theory by pointing out that governmental action and private property are not the only solutions to resource problems. An alternative solution is a communal property arrangement.

Maine lobster territories are not unique in this respect. A large number of local communities have generated a wide variety of institutions to control exploitation of the resources on which their livelihood depends. Though tragedies of the commons (more accurately, tragedies of "open access") do exist in both the third world and the developed world, they are not inevitable in the absence of private property.

Maine lobstering territories have not been an unqualified success in conserving the resource. They have limited the numbers of fishermen entering the fishery, but except in those few places where informal or formal trap limits are imposed (e.g., Swans Island), they have not helped to limit the number of traps and the escalation of fishing effort.

---

1.   How do you reconcile the relative success of the private property regime in the oyster industry with the apparent success of a communal property regime for lobsters? If private property in the oyster industry succeeds because it provides incentives to make the beds more productive, what are the characteristics of the lobster industry that allow it to survive and perhaps even thrive? Are there characteristics of lobstering that make a private property regime less tenable than in the oyster industry?

2.   Does a regime of communal or joint property, as opposed to open access, always solve the tragedy of the commons? Drawing on the lessons of the lobster industry, what factors favor the success of communal property regimes? What factors threaten to undermine the lobster industry?

3.   What are the implications of this theory of property institutions for other contexts? Consider the organization of law firms, farming cooperatives, compensation/ownership arrangements in different types of businesses, grazing rules for federal lands, and fishing in international waters.

CHAPTER II

BACKGROUND LEGAL RULES AND INSTITUTIONS

The foundation of every property system is the set of background legal rules and institutions that define the rights and remedies regarding resources. These background rules both reflect and shape social, market, and political institutions.

Many of the property rules in our society reflect their historic origins in medieval England. Although most of these rules—through the common law or the enactment of statutes—have evolved to keep pace with changes in social, market, and political institutions, their archaic labels and less-than-intuitive definitions bedevil students. Nonetheless, these background rules are simply part of the new vocabulary and grammar that every lawyer must master to be technically proficient in the law.

As we will see in Chapters III–V, most background rules may be altered by social norms, private agreements (*e.g.*, through market transactions), or political decisions (*e.g.*, zoning). The background legal rules, however, establish the default rules that courts will apply in the absence of private or public modification and therefore form the foundation upon which modern governance regimes are built.

We begin Chapter II with a survey of the ways in which property rights are acquired. The rules for acquiring property vary dramatically in different contexts and with regard to different resources, such as land, water, or ideas. Nonetheless, in each case the rules flow from and reflect many of the theoretical principles that we explored in Chapter I—the nature of the resources and the social, economic, and political setting. Part B of this Chapter surveys the key forms of property ownership and their historical origins, including present and future interests, concurrent interests, and marital property. Part C covers the rights and limitations of property ownership. This Part applies economic principles to analyze the common law rights against nuisance and trespass, examines the constitutional right against governmental takings, and considers important limitations on the rights of property owners. Part D surveys the distinctive rules and institutions governing the transfer of real property interests.

A. Acquisition of Property

1. Acquisition of Land

a. DISCOVERY OR CONQUEST

A logical starting point for our study of the law governing the acquisition of property is the set of doctrines governing rights in land in early America. Real property was and continues to be among the most important property interests in our society. In addition, the allocation of real property significantly determines community formation and other essential elements of human society.

Johnson and Graham's Lessee v. M'Intosh involved a suit to establish legal title to a parcel of land. The plaintiff's claim derived from a grant from the Illinois and Piankeshaw Tribes to a European–American settler. The defendant's claim derived from a subsequent grant (called a patent) from the United States to another European–American. Thus, the validity of the plaintiff's and the defendant's claims depended on the validity of the initial grants, which in turn depended on the legal authority of the Tribes and the United States to make those grants. The Court framed the legal issue as whether title was vested in the Tribes or the United States.

The decision is a minor aftershock in the far more momentous collision between Indian and European cultures between the fifteenth and nineteenth centuries. Nevertheless, it raises (even if it does not satisfactorily answer) some important questions about the cultural contingency of every conception of property and about the origin and justification of property rights.

Johnson and Graham's Lessee v. M'Intosh

Supreme Court of the United States, 1823.
21 U.S. (8 Wheat.) 543, 5 L.Ed. 681.

ERROR to the District Court of Illinois. This was an action of ejectment for lands in the State and District of Illinois, claimed by the plaintiffs under a purchase and conveyance from the Piankeshaw Indians, and by the defendant, under a grant from the United States. It came up on a case stated, upon which there was a judgment below for the defendant. * * *

■ MR. CHIEF JUSTICE MARSHALL delivered the opinion of the Court.

The plaintiffs in this cause claim the land, in their declaration mentioned, under two grants, purporting to be made, the first in 1773, and the last in 1775, by the chiefs of certain Indian tribes, constituting the Illinois and the Piankeshaw nations; and the question is, whether this title can be recognised in the Courts of the United States?

The facts, as stated in the case agreed, show the authority of the chiefs who executed this conveyance, so far as it could be given by their own people; and likewise show, that the particular tribes for whom these chiefs acted were in rightful possession of the land they sold. The inquiry, therefore, is, in a great measure, confined to the power of Indians to give, and of private individuals to receive, a title which can be sustained in the Courts of this country.

As the right of society, to prescribe those rules by which property may be acquired and preserved is not, and cannot be drawn into question; as the title to lands, especially, is and must be admitted to depend entirely on the law of the nation in which they lie; it will be necessary, in pursuing this inquiry, to examine, not singly those principles of abstract justice, which the Creator of all things has impressed on the mind of his creature man, and which are admitted to regulate, in a great degree, the rights of civilized nations, whose perfect independence is acknowledged; but those principles also which our own government has adopted in the particular case, and given us as the rule for our decision.

On the discovery of this immense continent, the great nations of Europe were eager to appropriate to themselves so much of it as they could respectively acquire. Its vast extent offered an ample field to the ambition and enterprise of all; and the character and religion of its inhabitants afforded an apology for considering them as a people over whom the superior genius of Europe might claim an ascendancy. The potentates of the old world found no difficulty in convincing themselves that they made ample compensation to the inhabitants of the new, by bestowing on them civilization and Christianity, in exchange for unlimited independence. But, as they were all in pursuit of nearly the same object, it was necessary, in order to avoid conflicting settlements, and consequent war with each other, to establish a principle, which all should acknowledge as the law by which the right of acquisition, which they all asserted, should be regulated as between themselves. This principle was, that discovery gave title to the government by whose subjects, or by whose authority, it was made, against all other European governments, which title might be consummated by possession.

The exclusion of all other Europeans, necessarily gave to the nation making the discovery the sole right of acquiring the soil from the natives, and establishing settlements upon it. It was a right with which no Europeans could interfere. It was a right which all asserted for themselves, and to the assertion of which, by others, all assented.

Those relations which were to exist between the discoverer and the natives, were to be regulated by themselves. The rights thus acquired being exclusive, no other power could interpose between them.

In the establishment of these relations, the rights of the original inhabitants were, in no instance, entirely disregarded; but were necessarily, to a considerable extent, impaired. They were admitted to be the rightful occupants of the soil, with a legal as well as just claim to retain possession of it, and to use it according to their own discretion; but their rights to complete sovereignty, as independent nations, were necessarily diminished, and their power to dispose of the soil at their own will, to whomsoever they pleased, was denied by the original fundamental principle, that discovery gave exclusive title to those who made it.

While the different nations of Europe respected the right of the natives, as occupants, they asserted the ultimate dominion to be in themselves; and claimed and exercised, as a consequence of this ultimate dominion, a power to grant the soil, while yet in possession of the natives. These grants have been understood by all, to convey a title to the grantees, subject only to the Indian right of occupancy.

The history of America, from its discovery to the present day, proves, we think, the universal recognition of these principles.

Spain did not rest her title solely on the grant of the Pope. Her discussions respecting boundary, with France, with Great Britain, and with the United States, all show that she placed in on the rights given by discovery. Portugal sustained her claim to the Brazils by the same title.

France, also, founded her title to the vast territories she claimed in America on discovery. However conciliatory her conduct to the natives may have been, she still asserted her right of dominion over a great extent of country not actually settled by Frenchmen, and her exclusive right to acquire and dispose of the soil which remained in the occupation of Indians. * * *

No one of the powers of Europe gave its full assent to this principle, more unequivocally than England. The documents upon this subject are ample and complete. So early as the year 1496, her monarch granted a commission to the Cabots, to discover countries then unknown to *Christian people*, and to take possession of them in the name of the king of England. Two years afterwards, Cabot proceeded on this voyage, and discovered the continent of North America, along which he sailed as far south as Virginia. To this discovery the English trace their title.

In this first effort made by the English government to acquire territory on this continent, we perceive a complete recognition of the principle which has been mentioned. The right of discovery given by this commission, is confined to countries "then unknown to all Christian people;" and of these countries Cabot was empowered to take possession in the name of the king of England. Thus asserting a right to take possession, notwithstanding the occupancy of the natives, who were heathens, and, at the same time, admitting the prior title of any Christian people who may have made a previous discovery.

The same principle continued to be recognised. * * *

Thus has our whole country been granted by the crown while in the occupation of the Indians. These grants purport to convey the soil as well as the right of dominion to the grantees. In those governments which were denominated royal, where the right to the soil was not vested in individuals, but remained in the crown, or was vested in the colonial government, the king claimed and exercised the right of granting lands, and of dismembering the government at his will. The grants made out of the two original colonies, after the resumption of their charters by the crown, are examples of this. The governments of New–England, New–York, New–Jersey, Pennsylvania, Maryland, and a part of Carolina, were thus created. In all of them, the soil, at the time the grants were made, was occupied by the Indians. Yet almost every title within those governments is dependent on these grants. In some instances, the soil was conveyed by the crown unaccompanied by the powers of government, as in the case of the northern neck of Virginia. It has never been objected to this, or to any other similar grant, that the title as well as possession was in the Indians when it was made, and that it passed nothing on that account. * * *

By the treaty which concluded the war of our revolution, Great Britain relinquished all claim, not only to the government, but to the "propriety and territorial rights of the United States," whose boundaries were fixed in the second article. By this treaty, the powers of government, and the right to soil, which had previously been in Great Britain, passed definitively to these States. We had before taken possession of them, by declaring independence; but neither the declaration of independence, nor the treaty confirming it, could give us more than that which we before possessed, or to which Great Britain was before entitled. It has never been doubted, that either the United States, or the several States, had a clear title to all the lands within the boundary lines described in the treaty, subject only to the Indian right of occupancy, and that the exclusive power to extinguish that right, was vested in that government which might constitutionally exercise it.

Virginia, particularly, within whose chartered limits the land in controversy lay, passed an act, in the year 1779, declaring her "exclusive right of pre-emption from the Indians, of all the lands within the limits of her own chartered territory, and that no person or persons whatsoever, have, or ever had, a right to purchase any lands within the same, from any Indian nation, except only persons duly authorized to make such purchase; formerly for the use and benefit of the colony, and lately for the Commonwealth." The act then proceeds to annul all deeds made by Indians to individuals, for the private use of the purchasers.

Without ascribing to this act the power of annulling vested rights, or admitting it to countervail the testimony furnished by the marginal note opposite to the title of the law, forbidding purchases from the Indians, in the revisals of the Virginia statutes, stating that law to be repealed, it may safely be considered as an unequivocal affirmance, on the part of Virginia, of the broad principle which had always been maintained, that the exclusive right to purchase from the Indians resided in the government.

In pursuance of the same idea, Virginia proceeded, at the same session, to open her land office, for the sale of that country which now constitutes Kentucky, a country, every acre of which was then claimed and possessed by Indians, who maintained their title with as much persevering courage as was ever manifested by any people.

The States, having within their chartered limits different portions of territory covered by Indians, ceded that territory, generally, to the United States, on conditions expressed in their deeds of cession, which demonstrate the opinion, that they ceded the soil as well as jurisdiction, and that in doing so, they granted a productive fund to the government of the Union. The lands in controversy lay within the chartered limits of Virginia, and were ceded with the whole country northwest of the river Ohio. This grant contained reservations and stipulations, which could only be made by the owners of the soil; and concluded with a stipulation, that "all the lands in the ceded territory, not reserved, should be considered as a common fund, for the use and benefit of such of the United States as have become, or shall become, members of the confederation," & c. "according to their usual respective proportions in the general charge and expenditure, and shall be faithfully and *bona fide* disposed of for that purpose, and for no other use or purpose whatsoever."

The ceded territory was occupied by numerous and warlike tribes of Indians; but the exclusive right of the United States to extinguish their title, and to grant the soil, has never, we believe, been doubted. * * *

The United States, then, have unequivocally acceded to that great and broad rule by which its civilized inhabitants now hold this country. They hold, and assert in themselves, the title by which it was acquired. They maintain, as all others have maintained, that discovery gave an exclusive right to extinguish the Indian title of occupancy, either by purchase or by conquest; and gave also a right to such a degree of sovereignty, as the circumstances of the people would allow them to exercise.

The power now possessed by the government of the United States to grant lands, resided, while we were colonies, in the crown, or its grantees. The validity of the titles given by either has never been questioned in our Courts. It has been exercised uniformly over territory in possession of the Indians. The existence of this power must negative the existence of any right which may conflict with, and control it. An absolute title to lands cannot exist, at the same time, in different persons, or in different governments. An absolute, must be an exclusive title, or at least a title which excludes all others not compatible with it. All our institutions recognise the absolute title of the crown, subject only to the Indian right of occupancy, and recognise the absolute title of the crown to extinguish that right. This is incompatible with an absolute and complete title in the Indians.

We will not enter into the controversy, whether agriculturists, merchants, and manufacturers, have a right, on abstract principles, to expel hunters from the territory they possess, or to contract their limits. Conquest gives a title which the Courts of the conqueror cannot deny, whatever the private and speculative opinions of individuals may be, respecting the original justice of the claim which has been successfully asserted. The British government, which was then our government, and whose rights have passed to the United States, asserted title to all the lands occupied by Indians, within the chartered limits of the British colonies. It asserted also a limited sovereignty over them, and the exclusive right of extinguishing the title which occupancy gave to them. These claims have been maintained and established as far west as the river Mississippi, by the sword. The title to a vast portion of the lands we now hold, originates in them. It is not for the Courts of this country to question the validity of this title, or to sustain one which is incompatible with it.

Although we do not mean to engage in the defence of those principles which Europeans have applied to Indian title, they may, we think, find some excuse, if not justification, in the character and habits of the people whose rights have been wrested from them.

The title by conquest is acquired and maintained by force. The conqueror prescribes its limits. Humanity, however, acting on public opinion, has established, as a general rule, that the conquered shall not be wantonly oppressed, and that their condition shall remain as eligible as is compatible with the objects of the conquest. Most usually, they are incorporated with the victorious nation, and become subjects or citizens of the government with which they are connected. The new and old members of the society mingle with each other; the distinction between them is gradually lost, and they make one people. Where this incorporation is practicable, humanity demands, and a wise policy requires, that the rights of the conquered to property should remain unimpaired; that the new subjects should be governed as equitably as the old, and that confidence in their security should gradually banish the painful sense of being separated from their ancient connexions, and united by force to strangers.

When the conquest is complete, and the conquered inhabitants can be blended with the conquerors, or safely governed as a distinct people, public opinion, which not even the conqueror can disregard, imposes these restraints upon him; and he cannot neglect them without injury to his fame, and hazard to his power.

But the tribes of Indians inhabiting this country were fierce savages, whose occupation was war, and whose subsistence was drawn chiefly from the forest. To leave them in possession of their country, was to leave the country a wilderness; to govern them as a distinct people, was impossible, because they were as brave and as high spirited as they were fierce, and were ready to repel by arms every attempt on their independence.

What was the inevitable consequence of this state of things? The Europeans were under the necessity either of abandoning the country, and relinquishing their pompous claims to it, or of enforcing those claims by the sword, and by the adoption of principles adapted to the condition of a people with whom it was impossible to mix, and who could not be governed as a distinct society, or of remaining in their neighbourhood, and exposing themselves and their families to the perpetual hazard of being massacred.

Frequent and bloody wars, in which the whites were not always the aggressors, unavoidably ensued. European policy, numbers, and skill, prevailed. As the white population advanced, that of the Indians necessarily receded. The country in the immediate neighbourhood of agriculturists became unfit for them. The game fled into thicker and more unbroken forests, and the Indians followed. The soil, to which the crown originally claimed title, being no longer occupied by its ancient inhabitants, was parcelled out according to the will of the sovereign power, and taken possession of by persons who claimed immediately from the crown, or mediately, through its grantees or deputies.

That law which regulates, and ought to regulate in general, the relations between the conqueror and conquered, was incapable of application to a people under such circumstances. The resort to some new and different rule, better adapted to the actual state of things, was unavoidable. Every rule which can be suggested will be found to be attended with great difficulty.

However extravagant the pretension of converting the discovery of an inhabited country into conquest may appear; if the principle has been asserted in the first instance, and afterwards sustained; if a country has been acquired and held under it; if the property of the great mass of the community originates in it, it becomes the law of the land, and cannot be questioned. So, too, with respect to the concomitant principle, that the Indian inhabitants are to be considered merely as occupants, to be protected, indeed, while in peace, in the possession of their lands, but to be deemed incapable of transferring the absolute title to others. However this restriction may be opposed to natural right, and to the usages of civilized nations, yet, if it be indispensable to that system under which the country has been settled, and be adapted to the actual condition of the two people, it may, perhaps, be supported by reason, and certainly cannot be rejected by Courts of justice. * * *.

It has never been contended, that the Indian title amounted to nothing. Their right of possession has never been questioned. The claim of government extends to the complete ultimate title, charged with this right of possession, and to the exclusive power of acquiring that right. * * *

After bestowing on this subject a degree of attention which was more required by the magnitude of the interest in litigation, and the able and elaborate arguments of the bar, than by its intrinsic difficulty, the Court is decidedly of opinion, that the plaintiffs do not exhibit a title which can be sustained in the Courts of the United States; and that there is no error in the judgment which was rendered against them in the District Court of Illinois.

Judgment affirmed, with costs.

---

1. *Relativity of Title.* In a typical action to quiet title, a court determines which of the parties before it has superior title to the land in question. Why does the court limit its focus solely to the parties before it? Does this adequately protect the interests of others who may have claims on the land? Shouldn't a court seek to establish correct title with regard to all potential claimants, and not merely those who happen to be involved in the particular dispute?

2. *Chain of Title.* What claims do the parties in *Johnson* make to establish the superiority of their title? What is the chain of title under which each party bases his claim?

3. What is the philosophical basis of Marshall's analysis of ownership? Why were Native Americans incapable, according to Marshall's reasoning, of passing valid title to other people? Does this reasoning justify the severe limits the Court places upon aboriginal rights to property?

4. Recall Melville's discussion of property rights in whales. Does Marshall's opinion adopt the "Fast Fish–Loose Fish" rule? Were the Indians, in Marshall's view, not making adequately productive use of the land (by European standards) to establish the full complement of property rights? If Justice Marshall had read and accepted Cronon's account of early New England, would Marshall's reasoning have compelled a different result in the case?

5. *Bundle of Sticks.* Property rights have often been analogized to sticks in a bundle. There are six traditional sticks—the right to possess, the right to exclude, the right to transfer, the right to use, the right to enjoy fruits, and the right to alter. The metaphor reinforces the notion that property rights can be held as a bundle or divided up among different people and over time. What "sticks" within the bundle of property rights does Marshall recognize in Native Americans?

6. What is the principle of "discovery" that Marshall is at such pains to establish? Is it simply a principle to allocate property rights among various European nations? How does it relate to the competing claims of the United States and the Tribes for title to land?

Is the real basis for the decision that conquest necessarily diminishes (nearly to the point of elimination) the property rights of conquered peoples, and the courts are in no position to decide in favor of pre-conquest claims? Why does the Court not make this point explicitly?

b. ADVERSE POSSESSION

Perhaps the most startling means of acquiring property is adverse possession. If all of the technical requirements of the doctrine are met, a trespasser may obtain title to someone else's land through deliberate or inadvertent occupancy. The doctrine of adverse possession can be found in English statutes as early as 1275. *See* Statute of Westminster I, Edward I, Ch. 39 (1275).

In its modern form, adverse possession works both as a statute of limitations that bars the true owner from bringing a suit for possession against the occupier, and as a means to establish the adverse possessor's legal title to the land. The successful adverse possessor is thus not only immune from a suit for ejection, he or she may use or transfer the land as would any owner.[1]

---

1. As soon as the adverse possessor has met the criteria, he holds title to the land.

The adverse possessor is under no obligation to file suit to establish title (known as a quiet

At common law, an occupier could establish title by adverse possession by showing that his possession has been: (1) actual; (2) hostile and with a claim of right; (3) open and notorious; (4) exclusive; and (5) continuous for the statutory period. Powell on Real Property, ¶¶ 1012–1013 (1986); Thompson on Real Property, chpt. 38, § 2543 (1979). Many state legislatures and courts have modified these criteria somewhat,[2] but the basic requirements are similar in every state.

1. **Actual Possession**. The adverse possessor must show that he actually possessed the land. The purpose of this requirement is to award the occupier title only if he has been making actual, productive use of the land. *See Wijas v. Clorfene*, 126 Ill.App.2d 315, 262 N.E.2d 83 (1970) (using a fish pond, garden, and sidewalk and making repairs to a fence are adequate to show actual possession of a lot adjacent to the adverse possessor's land); *Nutting v. Herman Timber Co.*, 214 Cal.App.2d 650, 657–58, 29 Cal.Rptr. 754, 758–59 (1963) (posting "No Trespassing" signs is insufficient to establish actual possession). Generally, the type and scope of a claimant's use must be consistent with the particular characteristics of the land. In *City of South Greenfield v. Cagle*, 591 S.W.2d 156 (Mo.App. 1979), the claimant had the grass mowed, planted decorative trees, and travelled across the property to go to her garden. The court found that these activities were "normal incidences of possession to a residential front yard" and so constituted actual possession. *Id.* at 160. *See also Doty v. Chalk*, 632 P.2d 644, 645 (Colo.App.1981) (using the land for farming or grazing or keeping it fallow in a government soil bank program was "commensurate with [the] particular attributes" of the land and this satisfied actual possession).

One exception to the requirement of actual possession is the doctrine of "constructive possession." Under this doctrine, an adverse possessor who holds "color of title"[3] gains title to all land described in the deed, not just the land he actually possesses. *See Devlin v. Powell*, 67 Cal.App. 165, 172, 227 P. 231, 233 (1924); *Campbell v. Gregory*, 200 Ga. 684, 38 S.E.2d 295 (1946). Several states have codified this exception. *See, e.g.*, Ark. Code Ann. § 37–102; Fla. Stat. ch. 95.16.

title action). *See Marriage v. Keener*, 26 Cal. App.4th 186, 31 Cal.Rptr.2d 511 (1994) (rejecting the true owners' defense of laches because the adverse possessor had waited several years after the statutory period before asserting title through adverse possession).

2. *See, e.g.*, Wash.Rev.Code § 7.28.080 (giving title to a person who in good faith paid assessed taxes on vacant and unoccupied land for seven successive years); Ark. Code Ann. § 18–11–106(a) (requiring payment of taxes as an element of adverse possession); Fla. Stat. ch. 95.16 (deeming property possessed when it is "cultivated or improved"; "protected by a substantial enclosure"; or

used for supply of fuel, fencing, or ordinary use).

3. "Color of title" refers to a claim based on a document (such as a deed or court judgment) that turns out to be defective. A claim may not be based on color of title if the claimant has actual knowledge that the document is invalid. *Yuba River Sand Co. v. City of Marysville*, 78 Cal.App.2d 421, 430, 117 P.2d 642, 647 (1947). *See also Bergesen v. Clauss*, 15 Ill.2d 337, 342, 155 N.E.2d 20, 23 (1958) ("A forged deed, when taken in good faith, may constitute color of title if, at the time of the purchase of the deed, the grantee believed it to be genuine.").

2. **Hostile with a Claim of Right**. As discussed in the case that follows, "hostile possession" normally does not require proof of animosity between the claimant and the true owner. Rather, possession is hostile if the occupier claims the land as his own, in derogation of the true owner's claim. According to one case, possession is hostile if it is "unaccompanied by any recognition, express or inferable from the circumstances, of the right in the latter." *Estate of Williams*, 73 Cal.App.3d 141, 147, 140 Cal.Rptr. 593, 596 (1977). Put differently, the adverse possessor must possess the land without express or implied permission of the true owner.

Good faith. A few states require the occupier to have acted in "good faith" in asserting a claim to the land. *See* Ga. Code Ann. §§ 44–5–161, 44–5–162 (actual or positive fraud will bar a claim for adverse possession). Most states, however, require only that the adverse possessor claim ownership, whether or not that claim is mistaken or intentionally false.

Nonetheless, many of these states give favorable treatment to claims based on "color of title." For example, some states have a reduced limitations period for such claims. *See, e.g.*, Colo. Rev. Stat. §§ 38–41–108, 38–41–109 (reducing the period from 18 to 7 years); Ga. Code Ann. §§ 44–5–164 (reducing the period from 20 to 7 years). In addition, as mentioned above, a claimant with color of title may invoke the doctrine of "constructive possession" to claim a larger portion of land.

Presumed or implied permissive use. Courts will presume permission in a range of circumstances. For example, if possession began with the true owner's permission, it is presumed to continue permissively until the occupier openly claims, or takes an action clearly indicating that he claims, title to the property. If the possessor remains in possession after a judicial decree awarding the property to another person, "the possessor's occupation is deemed subordinate to the true owner until express notice is given to the owner of the possessor's adverse claim." *Buic v. Buic*, 5 Cal.App.4th 1600, 1605, 7 Cal.Rptr.2d 738, 741 (1992). *See also Sweeten v. Park*, 154 Tex. 266, 276 S.W.2d 794 (1955) (a person who accepted a court decree divesting him of title but remained in possession cannot claim adverse possession since he did not repudiate the owner's rights). Similarly, if a grantor remains in possession after transferring the interest, or if a tenant remains in possession after termination of the lease, the possession is presumed to be permissive. *Reid v. Reid*, 219 Or. 500, 348 P.2d 29 (1959) (continued possession by the grantor is presumed to be with the grantee's permission, absent evidence of grantor's contrary intent); Cal. Code Civ. Proc. § 326 (tenant's holding over presumed permissive for 5 years).

In other circumstances, a court will imply permission from the relationship of the parties. *See Berg v. Fairman*, 107 Idaho 441, 443, 690 P.2d 896, 898 (1984) ("when one occupies the land of a blood relative, such occupation is presumptively with the permission of the true owner"); *Herzog v. Boykin*, 148 Ariz. 131, 133, 713 P.2d 332, 334 (App.1985) ("where such implied permissive use of the land continued through 'the neighborly indulgence of its owner,' it could not ripen into a prescriptive use without 'a distinct and positive assertion of a right hostile to the owner [being] brought home to him by words or acts' ").

3. **Open and Notorious**. This criterion requires the adverse possessor to use the land openly, without any attempt to hide or disguise his use. "Open and notorious" use (along with actual use) gives the true owner an opportunity (if he is properly monitoring the land) to detect adverse possessors. *Commonwealth Dep't of Parks v. Stephens*, 407 S.W.2d 711, 713 (Ky.1966) (the adverse possessor's use must be "so conspicuous that it is generally known and talked of by the public or the people in the neighborhood"); *Adams v. Slattery*, 156 Tex. 433, 443, 295 S.W.2d 859, 865 (1956) (adverse possessor's payment of property taxes for 17 years is sufficient to meet this criterion); *Bramlett v. Harris & Eliza Kempner Fund*, 462 S.W.2d 104, 105 (Tex.Civ.App.1970) (weekend camping and construction of a lean-to wind break and duck blind does not meet open and notorious criterion). Most states, however, do not require the adverse possessor to give the true owner actual notice of his use. *Lobro v. Watson*, 42 Cal.App.3d 180, 116 Cal.Rptr. 533 (1974) (adverse possession claim is not defeated even though the true owner was not aware she owned the land, and thus had no actual notice that the land was being possessed adversely to her interests).

Ambiguous actions may not be deemed "open and notorious." In *Custis Fishing and Hunting Club, Inc. v. Johnson*, 214 Va. 388, 393–94, 200 S.E.2d 542, 546–47 (1973), the hunting club owned land adjoining a pond. The club hired a caretaker to tend to the pond, stocked it with fish, posted "no fishing" signs, and raised and lowered the water level repeatedly. The court held that these actions were not sufficient to meet this requirement and establish title by adverse possession in the pond since the actions could be viewed as consistent with the other party's riparian interests in the pond.

4. **Exclusive Possession**. The adverse possessor's use must be exclusive of the true owner throughout the statutory period. If the true owner exercises his ownership rights to the land, the adverse possessor's use has not been exclusive. *See, e.g.*, *Miller v. Doheny*, 50 Cal.App. 413, 195 P. 745 (1920) (overhanging eaves built by true owner during claimant's actual possession and use of the land is a sufficient basis for court to find claimant's use is not exclusive); *Dzuris v. Kucharik*, 164 Colo. 278, 434 P.2d 414 (1967) (because water from the true owner's nearby reservoir periodically inundated the land claimed by the adverse possessor, the adverse possessor could not show exclusive possession).

The question arises what the true owner can do (before expiration of the statutory period) to prevent adverse possession. In general, a letter demanding that the adverse possessor quit the premises is insufficient. Rather, the true owner should file and successfully prosecute a suit to quiet title or to eject the claimant. Filing the suit alone is insufficient; the owner must successfully prosecute the case. *Dong Chun Len v. Luke Kow Lee*, 7 Cal.App.2d 194, 196, 45 P.2d 827, 828 (1935). If the suit eventually is decided against the adverse possessor, the interruption is deemed to "relate back" to the date on which the suit was filed.

5. **Continuous for the Statutory Period**. Possession must be continuous for the statutory period.

Continuous. The claimant's use of the land must be continuous, but it does not have to be constant. Rather, the claimant must use the land as would an "ordinary occupant." *Compare Park v. Powers*, 2 Cal.2d 590, 595, 42 P.2d 75, 77 (1935) (where land was "adapted and customarily used" for grazing, use of the land for that purpose during the grazing season is sufficient to establish continuous use) *with Madson v. Cohn*, 122 Cal.App. 704, 705–07, 10 P.2d 531, 532 (1932) (finding continuous possession lacking even though the claimant cleared the vacant lot of weeds on one occasion and planted and watered several rose bushes and trees on other occasions). *See also Nickman v. Kirschner*, 202 Neb. 78, 84, 273 N.W.2d 675, 679 (1979) ("where drainage of surface waters into an artificial drain occurs only on those occasions when such waters exist in sufficient quantity to so flow, such use would be continuous for that purpose"); *White v. Boydstun*, 91 Idaho 615, 621–22, 428 P.2d 747, 753–54 (1967) (summertime use of property normally used only for summer residences is sufficient to meet continuous use requirement). Temporary absences, in the course of otherwise regular use, will not bar a claim for adverse possession. In *Helton v. Cook*, 27 N.C.App. 565, 568, 219 S.E.2d 505, 507 (1975), the adverse possessor, who had made her home on the true owner's land, twice went to jail, once for four months and then for nine months. The court nonetheless held that her occupancy of the land was "continuous."

Tacking. The criterion of continuous possession need not be made by a single claimant. Successive occupiers may "tack" their periods of possession together so long as there has been some "privity" between them (*e.g.*, transfer by will, grant, or inheritance). *See, e.g., Noel v. Jumonville Pipe & Machinery Co.*, 245 La. 324, 338–39, 158 So.2d 179, 184–85 (1963) (children, as heirs, may tack their father's prior adverse possession); *Cutliff v. Densmore*, 354 Mich. 586, 592–93, 93 N.W.2d 307, 311 (1958) (an occupier who wishes to tack the prior adverse possession of his grantor must show "an express reference to * * * the disputed property in the grantor's deed"). Several states have codified this requirement. *See* Ga. Code Ann. § 44–5–172 (an "inchoate prescriptive title may be transferred by a person in possession to his successor so that successive possessions may be tacked to make out the prescription"); Ariz. Rev. Stat. § 12–521(B) (adverse possession "need not be continued in the same person, but when held by different persons successively there must be privity of estate between them"). The notion that adverse possessors must convey their interests is a bit peculiar since before the limitations period expires they have no interest in the property.

Statutory Period. At common law, the statutory period was 20 years, and in most eastern states the statutory period is 15–30 years. *See, e.g.*, Conn. Gen. Stat. § 52–575 (15 years); Del. Code Ann., tit. 10, §§ 7901–7902 (20 years); Ohio Rev. Code Ann. § 2305.04 (21 years). In many western states, by contrast, the period is 10 years or less. *See, e.g.*, Alaska Stat.

§ 09.45.052 (7 years); Cal. Code of Civ. Pro. § 318 (5 years); Idaho Code Ann. § 5–203 (5 years); Or. Rev. Stat. § 12.050 (10 years).

States with shorter limitations periods, however, typically also require the occupier to have paid the property taxes assessed and levied during the statutory period. *See, e.g.*, Cal. Code Civ. Pro. § 325; Idaho Code Ann. § 5–210; Or. Rev. Stat. § 105.615. The tax requirement frequently limits the availability of adverse possession to cases where the claimant took possession under color of title, for it is usually only in that circumstance that the claimant would receive a tax bill for the disputed land.[4] Absent color of title, adverse possession is restricted to those cases in which the tax assessor based the assessment not "on the record boundary but valued the land and improvements visibly possessed by the parties." *Gilardi v. Hallam*, 30 Cal.3d 317, 327, 178 Cal.Rptr. 624, 629, 636 P.2d 588, 593 (1981).

Tolling. As far back as the fifteenth century, English adverse possession statutes provided that the statute of limitations is tolled if the true owner is incapacitated when the claimant first takes possession. All states continue to recognize the importance of legal disabilities such as insanity, imprisonment, and legal infancy. *See, e.g.*, Cal. Code Civ. Proc. §§ 328, 328.5 (maximum tolling period of 20 years in cases of legal infancy and insanity, but only two years for imprisonment). In a few states, the statute is also tolled for a short period of time if the true owner dies before expiration of the statutory period. *See, e.g.*, Ind. Code § 34–1–2–7 (extending the period for 18 months); Va. Code Ann. § 8.01–229(B)(1) (1 year extension). Some states provide a longer extension if the owner was under a disability at the time of his death. *See, e.g.*, Del. Code Ann. tit. 10, § 7904 (10 years); Nev. Rev. Stat. Ann. § 11.180 (2 years).

At common law, disabilities that arose after the occupier took possession did not, and today in most states do not, toll the period. For example, in *Eubanks v. Zimmerman*, 255 Ark. 53, 498 S.W.2d 655 (1973), the claimant began possession during the true owner's minority. By the time the true owner reached majority, he was in the army, which normally tolls the statute of limitations under federal law (thus superseding any state law barring tacking of disabilities under state common law). Before he was discharged from the army, the true owner had become mentally incompetent. The court held that the owner could not use the latter disability to toll the statute since that disability did not exist when the claimant first began possession. *Id.* at 55, 498 S.W. 2d at 656–57. *See also Dickson v. Caruso*, 31 Misc.2d 1050, 1056 224 N.Y.S.2d 33, 39 (1961) (infancy of successor in interest will not toll statute); *Johnson v. Biegelmeier*, 409 N.W.2d 379, 381 (S.D.1987) (mental incompetency will toll statute only if present when

---

4. One author has argued that the original purpose of the property tax requirement, which exists mostly in western states, was to defeat the otherwise valid claims of squatters on range lands. *See* Comment, The Payment of Taxes Requirement in Adverse Possession Statutes, 37 Cal. L. Rev. 477 (1949). *See also* Comment, Payment of Taxes as a Condition of Title by Adverse Possession: A Nineteenth Century Anachronism, 9 Santa Clara Law. 244 (1969) (arguing that the tax requirement was adopted to provide an additional means of giving large landowners notice of adverse possession by squatters).

adverse possession began or when true owner acquired property); *Westphal v. Arnoux*, 51 Cal.App. 532, 535, 197 P. 395, 396 (1921) (dictum stating that transfer of property by inheritance to a minor during period of adverse possession would not suspend period). In addition, the statute of limitations is not tolled by successive disabilities. Once the disability is lifted, the remaining period of possession needed to acquire title is reduced in some states. Iowa Code Ann. § 614.8 (1 year from termination of disability); Mo. Ann. Stat. § 516.030 (3 years from termination of disability); Ohio Rev. Code Ann. § 2305.04 (10 years).

---

1.   *Justifications for Adverse Possession.* What are the justifications for the doctrine of adverse possession? Does it reward those who make land productive? If so, does the doctrine denigrate owners who prefer to "use" the land by letting it lie dormant? *See* Sprankling, An Environmental Critique of Adverse Possession, 79 Cornell L. Rev. 816 (1994) (arguing that adverse possession promotes an "ideology of exploitative utilitarianism," particularly against wild lands, and that such lands should be exempt from adverse possession). Does the requirement in many western states that adverse possessors pay taxes on the land adequately address Sprankling's concern?

Is adverse possession a utilitarian doctrine designed to encourage landowners to police their land and to eliminate old claims (for which evidence has faded) and thus reduce litigation? Does adverse possession help to minimize boundary errors by encouraging would-be adverse possessors to survey the land before making substantial investments? *See* Miceli & Sirmans, An Economic Theory of Adverse Possession, 15 Int'l Rev. L. & Econ. 161 (1995). Or would these purposes be entirely served by a statute of limitations?

Is adverse possession a means to protect personhood interests? Consider in this regard the words of Oliver Wendell Holmes:

> A thing which you have enjoyed and used as your own for a long time, whether property or an opinion, takes root in your being and cannot be torn away without your resenting the act and trying to defend yourself, however you came by it. The law can ask no better justification than the deepest instincts of man. It is only by way of reply to the suggestion that you are disappointing the former owner, that you refer to his neglect having allowed the gradual dissociation between himself and what he claims, and the gradual association of it with another. If he knows that another is doing acts which on their face show that he is on the way toward establishing such an association, I should argue that in justice to that other he was bound at his peril to find out whether the other was acting under his permission, to see that he was warned, and, if necessary, stopped.

Holmes, The Path of the Law, 10 Harv. L. Rev. 457, 477 (1897). *See also* Radin, Time, Possession, and Alienation, 64 Wash. U. L.Q. 739, 748–49 (1986) ("the possessor's interest, initially fungible, becomes more and more personal as time passes. At the same time, the titleholder's interest fades from personal to fungible and finally to nothingness"). Is this argument a persuasive justification for adverse possession? Is it consistent with a doctrine that permits successive occupiers to "tack" their time? Is it consistent with a doctrine that permits occupiers acting in bad faith? Would a "personhood theory" help to justify adverse possession by corporations?

For other articles discussing the function and importance of adverse possession, see Epstein, Past and Future: The Temporal Dimension in the Law of Property, 64 Wash. U. L.Q. 667, 669–93 (1986); Ellickson, Adverse Possession and Perpetuities Law: Two Dents in the Libertarian Model of Property Rights, 64 Wash. U. L.Q. 723, 725–34 (1986); Merrill, Property Rules, Liability Rules, and Adverse Possession, 79 Nw. U.L. Rev. 1122 (1986).

2. *Government-Owned Land.* At common law, there was no adverse possession against government-owned lands. Today, most states still bar adverse possession of state-owned lands and lands held by public service corporations for public use. *See, e.g.,* Cal. Civ. Code § 1007; Mich. Stat. Ann. § 27A.5821; N.H. Rev. Stat. Ann. § 539:6. What are the justifications for a broad exemption of government-owned lands from adverse possession?

If you were to allow *some* adverse possession against government-owned lands, what limitations or restrictions would you impose?

The states that allow adverse possession of state lands often make adverse possession of such lands more difficult than adverse possession of privately owned lands. Some states, for example, lengthen the period of possession required to establish title. S.D. Codified Laws § 15–3–4 (doubling the period to 40 years); Mont. Code Ann. § 70–19–302 (doubling the period to 10 years). Other states distinguish lands held in public trust (*i.e.,* lands the state cannot grant to private individuals) or held for use by the public generally from lands held in a private or proprietary character. *See, e.g., Brown v. Trustees of Schools,* 224 Ill. 184, 79 N.E. 579 (1906) (holding that since the state land was the subject of a commercial joint venture between the state and private parties, it was subject to adverse possession). Other courts apply the same criteria that are used with privately held lands, but apply the criteria so conservatively that adverse possession is blocked in most cases. *See, e.g., Hinckley v. New York,* 234 N.Y. 309, 137 N.E. 599 (1922). *See generally* Comment, Encouraging the Responsible Use of Land by Municipalities: The Erosion of *Nullum Tempus Occurrit Regi* and the Use of Adverse Possession Against Municipal Land Owners, 99 Dick. L. Rev. 197 (1994) (comparing adverse possession against municipal lands in several jurisdictions).

3. *Doctrine of Dedication.* In some circumstances, the state may claim title to a private roadway through the doctrine of dedication. Dedication can occur in one of two ways. First, the owner may offer explicitly to

dedicate the road and the government may accept. Developers commonly dedicate roadways upon completion of commercial development projects (indeed, such dedications usually are a condition of obtaining necessary permits). The owner's offer also may be inferred from the owner's acquiescence in the public use of the property. Second, a court may find a dedication if the public has used the road openly and continuously for the statutory prescriptive period. *Hays v. Vanek*, 217 Cal.App.3d 271, 281, 266 Cal.Rptr. 856, 860 (1989). What are the justifications for a doctrine that facilitates *public* acquisition of private property, while generally preventing private adverse possession of government-owned lands?

4.   *Doctrine of Agreed Boundaries.* In addition to adverse possession, many states have a doctrine of "agreed boundaries." *See generally* Browder, The Practical Location of Boundaries, 56 Mich. L. Rev. 487 (1958). In contrast to adverse possession, which is based on the absence of permission, the agreed boundaries doctrine relies on implied agreement and estoppel. It applies only to contiguous parcels of land where the owners are uncertain about the correct boundary line and have agreed to an incorrect boundary line. *See, e.g., Grappo v. Mauch,* 110 Nev. 1396, 1399, 887 P.2d 740, 742 (1994) (requiring only a dispute between the landowners); *Duff v. Seubert,* 110 Idaho 865, 867, 719 P.2d 1125, 1127 (1985) (requiring uncertainty or dispute between parties). *But see Faulkner v. Lloyd*, 253 S.W.2d 972, 974 (Ky.1952) (doctrine applies only when the boundary line is "not susceptible of certain determination"); *Bryant v. Blevins,* 9 Cal.4th 47, 36 Cal.Rptr.2d 86, 884 P.2d 1034 (1994) (doctrine applies only when there is "no reliable legal description"). An owner will be estopped from later asserting the correct boundary if both owners adhered to the agreed boundary line for a specified statutory period or if one owner detrimentally relied on the agreed boundary. *See Ernie v. Trinity Lutheran Church*, 51 Cal.2d 702, 707, 336 P.2d 525, 528 (1959). Longstanding acquiescence in a particular boundary line is evidence that owners (or their predecessors) used the line to settle an uncertainty about the actual boundary. *Vella v. Ratto*, 17 Cal.App.3d 737, 741, 95 Cal.Rptr. 72, 75 (1971).

Under what circumstances would a person assert the agreed boundaries doctrine rather than adverse possession?

Because the agreed boundaries doctrine involves an agreement, it essentially involves a voluntary transfer of title. Why do courts not require compliance with the statute of frauds?

Mannillo v. Gorski

Supreme Court of New Jersey, 1969.
54 N.J. 378, 255 A.2d 258.

■ HANEMAN, J.

Plaintiffs filed a complaint in the Chancery Division seeking a mandatory and prohibitory injunction against an alleged trespass upon their lands. Defendant counterclaimed for a declaratory judgment which would adjudicate that she had gained title to the disputed premises by adverse possession under N.J.S. 2A:14–6, N.J.S.A., which provides:

> Every person having any right or title of entry into real estate shall make such entry within 20 years next after the accrual of such right or title of entry, or be barred therefrom thereafter.

After plenary trial, judgment was entered for plaintiffs. *Mannillo v. Gorski*, 100 N.J.Super. 140, 241 A.2d 276 (Ch.Div.1968). Defendant appealed to the Appellate Division. Before argument there, this Court granted defendant's motion for certification.

 proc

The facts are as follows: In 1946, defendant and her husband entered into possession of premises in Keansburg known as Lot No. 1007 in Block 42, under an agreement to purchase. Upon compliance with the terms of said agreement, the seller conveyed said lands to them on April 16, 1952. Defendant's husband thereafter died. The property consisted of a rectangular lot with a frontage of 25 feet and a depth of 100 feet. Plaintiffs are the owners of the adjacent Lot 1008 in Block 42 of like dimensions, to which they acquired title in 1953.

In the summer of 1946 Chester Gorski, one of the defendant's sons, made certain additions and changes to the defendant's house. He extended two rooms at the rear of the structure, enclosed a screened porch on the front, and put a concrete platform with steps on the west side thereof for use in connection with a side door. These steps were built to replace existing wooden steps. In addition, a concrete walk was installed from the steps to the end of the house. In 1953, defendant raised the house. In order to compensate for the resulting added height from the ground, she modified the design of the steps by extending them toward both the front and the rear of the property. She did not change their width.

Defendant admits that the steps and concrete walk encroach upon plaintiffs' lands to the extent of 15 inches. She contends, however, that she has title to said land by adverse possession. N.J.S.A. 2A:14–6, quoted above. Plaintiffs assert contrawise that defendant did not obtain title by adverse possession as her possession was not of the requisite hostile nature. They argue that to establish title by adverse possession, the entry into and continuance of possession must be accompanied by an intention to invade the rights of another in the lands, i.e., a knowing wrongful taking. They assert that, as defendant's encroachment was not accompanied by an intention to invade plaintiffs' rights in the land, but rather by the mistaken belief that she owned the land, and that therefore an essential requisite to establish title by adverse possession, i.e., an intentional tortious taking, is lacking.

The trial court concluded that defendant had clearly and convincingly proved that her possession of the 15–inch encroachment had existed for more than 20 years before the institution of this suit and that such possession was "exclusive, continuous, uninterrupted, visible, notorious and against the right and interest of the true owner." There is ample evidence to sustain this finding except as to its visible and notorious nature, of which more hereafter. However, the judge felt impelled by existing New Jersey case law, holding as argued by plaintiffs above, to deny defendant's claim and entered judgment for plaintiffs. 100 N.J.Super, at 150, 241 A.2d 276. The first issue before this Court is, therefore, whether an entry and continuance of possession under the mistaken belief that the possessor has title to the lands involved, exhibits the requisite hostile possession to sustain the obtaining of title by adverse possession.

The first detailed statement and acceptance by our then highest court, of the principle that possession as an element of title by adverse possession cannot be bottomed on mistake, is found in *Folkman v. Myers*, 93 N.J.Eq. 208, 115 A. 615 (E. & A. 1921), which embraced and followed that thesis as expressed in *Myers v. Polkman*, 89 N.J.L. 390, 99 A. 97 (Sup.Ct.1916). It is not at all clear that this was the common law of this State prior to the latter case. An earlier opinion, *Davock v. Nealon*, 58 N.J.L. 21, 32 A. 675 (Sup.Ct.1895), held for an adverse possessor who had entered under the mistaken belief that he had title without any discussion of his hostile intent. However, the court in *Myers v. Folkman, supra*, at p. 393, 99 A. at p. 98, distinguished *Davock* from the case then under consideration by referring to the fact that "Charles R. Myers *disclaims* any intent to claim what did not belong to him, and apparently never asserted a right to land outside the bounds of his title * * *." (Emphasis supplied.) The factual distinction between the two cases, according to *Myers*, is that in the later case there was not only an entry by mistake but also an articulated disclaimer of an intent by the entrant to claim title to lands beyond his actual boundary. *Polkman*, although apparently relying on *Myers*, eliminated the requirement of that decision that there be expressed an affirmative disclaimer, and expanded the doctrine to exclude from the category of hostile possessors those whose entry and continued possession was under a mistaken belief that the lands taken were embraced within the description of the possessor's deed. In so doing, the former Court of Errors and Appeals aligned this State with that branch of a dichotomy which traces its genesis to *Preble v. Maine Cent. R. Co.*, 85 Me. 260, 27 A. 149, 21 L.R.A. 829 (Sup.Jud.Ct.Me.1893) and has become known as the Maine doctrine. In *Preble*, the court said at 27 A. at p. 150:

> There is every presumption that the occupancy is in subordination to the true title, and, if the possession is claimed to be adverse, the act of the wrongdoer must be strictly construed, and the character of the possession clearly shown. *Roberts v. Richards*, 84 Me. 1, 24 Atl.Rep. 425, and authorities cited. "The intention of the possessor to claim adversely," says Mellen, C.J., in *Ross v. Gould, supra* (5 Me. 204), "is an essential ingredient in disseisin." And in *Worcester v. Lord, supra* (56 Me. at 266) the court says: "To make a disseisin in fact, there must be an intention on the part of the party assuming possession to assert title in himself." Indeed, the authorities all agree that this intention of the occupant to claim the ownership of land not embraced in his title is a necessary element of adverse possession; and in case of occupancy

by mistake beyond a line capable of being ascertained this intention to claim title to the extent of the occupancy must appear to be absolute, and not conditional; otherwise the possession will not be deemed adverse to the true owner. It must be an intention to claim title to all land within a certain boundary on the face of the earth, whether it shall eventually be found to be the correct one or not. If, for instance, one in ignorance of his actual boundaries takes and holds possession by mistake up to a certain fence beyond his limits, upon the claim and in the belief that it is the true line, with the intention to claim title, and thus, if necessary, to acquire "title by possession" up to that fence, such possession, having the requisite duration and continuity, will ripen into title. *Hitchings v. Morrison*, 72 Me. 331, is a pertinent illustration of this principle. *See also, Abbott v. Abbott*, 51 Me. 575; *Ricker v. Hibbard*, 73 Me. 105.

If, on the other hand, a party through ignorance, inadvertence, or mistake occupies up to a given fence beyond his actual boundary, because he believes it to be the true line, but has no intention to claim title to that extent if it should be ascertained that the fence was on his neighbor's land, an indispensable element of adverse possession is wanting. In such a case the intent to claim title exists only upon the condition that the fence is on the true line. The intention is not absolute, but provisional, and the possession is not adverse. This thesis, it is evident, rewards the possessor who entered with a premeditated and predesigned "hostility"—the intentional wrongdoer and disfavors an honest, mistaken entrant.

The other branch of the dichotomy relies upon *French v. Pearce*, 8 Conn. 439 (Sup.Ct.Conn.1831). The court said in *Pearce* on the question of the subjective hostility of a possessor, at pp. 442, 445–446:

Into the recesses of his (the adverse claimant's) mind, his motives or purposes, his guilt or innocence, no enquiry is made. * * *

* * * The very nature of the act (entry and possession) is an assertion of his own title, and the denial of the title of all others. It matters not that the possessor was mistaken, and had he been better informed, would not have entered on the land. 8 Conn. at 442, 445–446.

The Maine doctrine has been the subject of much criticism in requiring a knowing wrongful taking. The criticism of the Maine and the justification of the Connecticut branch of the dichotomy is well stated in 6 Powell, Real Property (1969) ¶ 1015, pp. 725–28:

Do the facts of his possession, and of his conduct as if he were the owner, make immaterial his mistake, or does such a mistake prevent the existence of the prerequisite claim of right? The leading case holding the mistake to be of no importance was *French v. Pearce*, decided in Connecticut in 1831. * * * This viewpoint has gained increasingly widespread acceptance. The more subjectively oriented view regards the "mistake" as necessarily preventing the existence of the required claim of right. The leading case on this position is *Preble v. Maine Central R.R.,* decided in 1893. This position is still followed in a few states. It has been strongly criticized as unsound historically, inexpedient practically, and as resulting in better treatment for a ruthless wrongdoer than for the honest landowner. * * * On the whole the law is simplified, in the direction of real justice, by a following of the Connecticut leadership on this point.

* * *

We are in accord with the criticism of the Maine doctrine and favor the Connecticut doctrine for the above quoted reasons. As far as can be seen, overruling the former rule will not result in undermining any of the values which *stare decisis* is intended to foster. The theory of reliance, a cornerstone of *stare decisis*, is not here apt, as the problem is which of two mistaken parties is entitled to land. Realistically, the true owner does not rely upon entry of the possessor by mistake as a reason for not seeking to recover possession. Whether or not the entry is caused by mistake or intent, the same result eventuates—the true owner is ousted from possession. In either event his neglect to seek recovery of possession, within the requisite time, is in all probability the result of a lack of knowledge that he is being deprived of possession of lands to which he has title.

Accordingly, we discard the requirement that the entry and continued possession must be accompanied by a knowing intentional hostility and hold that any entry and possession for the required time which is exclusive, continuous, uninterrupted, visible and notorious, even though under mistaken claim of title, is sufficient to support a claim of title by adverse possession.

However, this conclusion is not dispositive of the matter *sub judice*. Of equal importance under the present factual complex, is the question of whether defendant's acts meet the necessary standard of "open and notorious" possession. It must not be forgotten that the foundation of so-called "title by adverse possession" is the failure of the true owner to commence an action for the recovery of the land involved, within the period designated by the statute of limitations. The justifications for the doctrine are aptly stated in 4 Tiffany, Real Property (3d ed. 1939) § 1134, p. 406 as follows:

> The desirability of fixing, by law, a definite period within which claims to land must be asserted has been generally recognized, among the practical considerations in favor of such a policy being the prevention of the making of illegal claims after the evidence necessary to defeat them has been lost, and the interest which the community as a whole has in the security, of title. The moral justification of the policy lies in the consideration that one who has reason to know that land belonging to him is in the possession of another, and neglects, for a considerable period of time, to assert his right thereto, may properly be penalized by his

preclusion from thereafter asserting such right. It is, apparently, by reason of the demerit of the true owner, rather than any supposed merit in the person who has acquired wrongful possession of the land, that this possession, if continued for the statutory period, operates to debar the former owner of all right to recover the land.

See also 5 Thompson, Real Property (1957 Replacement), 497.

In order to afford the true owner the opportunity to learn of the adverse claim and to protect his rights by legal action within the time specified by the statute, the adverse possession must be visible and notorious. In 4 Tiffany, *supra* (Supp.1969, at 291), the character of possession for that purpose, is stated to be as follows:

> * * * it must be public and based on physical facts, including known and visible lines and boundaries. Acts of dominion over the land must be so open and notorious as to put an ordinarily prudent person on notice that the land is in actual possession of another. Hence, title may never be acquired by mere possession, however long continued, which is surreptitious or secret or which is not such as will give unmistakable notice of the nature of the occupant's claim.

See also 5 Thompson, *supra*, § 2546; 6 Powell, Real Property, 1013 (1969).

Generally, where possession of the land is clear and unequivocal and to such an extent as to be immediately visible, the owner may be presumed to have knowledge of the adverse occupancy. In *Foulke v. Bond*, 41 N.J.L. 527, 545 (E. & A. 1879), the court said:

> Notoriety of the adverse claim under which possession is held, is a necessary constituent of title by adverse possession, and therefore the occupation or possession must be of that nature that the real owner is *presumed to have known* that there was a possession adverse to his title, under which it was intended to make title against him. (Emphasis supplied.)

However, when the encroachment of an adjoining owner is of a small area and the fact of an intrusion is not clearly and self-evidently apparent to the naked eye but requires an on-site survey for certain disclosure as in urban sections where the division line is only infrequently delineated by any monuments, natural or artificial, such a presumption is fallacious and unjustified. *See* concurring opinion of Judge (now Justice) Francis in *Predham v. Holfester*, 32 N.J.Super. 419, 428–429, 108 A.2d 458 (App.Div. 1954). The precise location of the dividing line is then ordinarily unknown to either adjacent owner and there is nothing on the land itself to show by visual observation that a hedge, fence, wall or other structure encroaches on the neighboring land to a minor extent. Therefore, to permit a presumption of notice to arise in the case of minor border encroachments not exceeding several feet would fly in the face of reality and require the true owner to be on constant alert for possible small encroachments. The only method of certain determination would be by obtaining a survey each time the adjacent owner undertook any improvement at or near the boundary, and this would place an undue and inequitable burden upon the true owner. Accordingly we hereby hold that no presumption of knowledge arises from a minor encroachment along a common boundary. In such a case, only where the true owner has actual knowledge thereof may it be said that the possession is open and notorious.

It is conceivable that the application of the foregoing rule may in some cases result in undue hardship to the adverse possessor who under an innocent and mistaken belief of title has undertaken an extensive improvement which to some extent encroaches on an adjoining property. In that event the situation falls within the category of those cases of which *Riggle v. Skill*, 9 N.J.Super. 372, 74 A.2d 424 (Ch.Div.1950), *affirmed* 7 N.J. 268, 81 A.2d 364 (1951) is typical and equity may furnish relief. Then, if the innocent trespasser of a small portion of land adjoining a boundary line cannot without great expense remove or eliminate the encroachment, or such removal or elimination is impractical or could be accomplished only with great hardship, the true owner may be forced to convey the land so occupied upon payment of the fair value thereof without regard to whether the true owner had notice of the encroachment at its inception. Of course, such a result should eventuate only under appropriate circumstances and where no serious damage would be done to the remaining land as, for instance, by rendering the balance of the parcel unusable or no longer capable of being built upon by reason of zoning or other restrictions.

We remand the case for trial of the issues (1) whether the true owner had actual knowledge of the encroachment, (2) if not, whether plaintiffs should be obliged to convey the disputed tract to defendant, and (3) if the answer to the latter question is in the affirmative, what consideration should be paid for the conveyance. The remand, of course, contemplates further discovery and a new pretrial.

Remanded for trial in accordance with the foregoing.

———————

1. *Hostility Requirement.* Do you agree with the court's rejection of the Maine doctrine? In what sense is "adversity" an element of the adverse possession doctrine? Does hostility as defined in the Maine doctrine serve any valuable purpose in resolving property disputes? Does such a requirement undermine important social values?

2. *Good Faith.* After a review of all adverse possession cases decided in this country since 1966, Professor Richard Helmholz concluded that in practice courts find a way to deny a claimant's title when he has acted in "bad faith" in occupying the land, and thus hold for the claimant only when his possession is mistaken, that is, in "good faith." Helmholz, Adverse Possession and Subjective Intent, 61 Wash. U. L.Q. 331 (1983). *But see* Cunningham, Adverse Possession and Subjective Intent: A Reply to Professor Helmholz, 64 Wash. U.L.Q. 1 (1986) (vigorously disagreeing with

Helmholz's analysis and conclusions). Should the adverse possession doctrine be renamed the "mistaken possession" doctrine?

3. *Open and Notorious Requirement.* Does the *Manillo* court's strict interpretation of the "open and notorious" requirement in the context of an encroachment foster the purposes of the adverse possession doctrine? What incentives does it create for landowners to know their property boundaries? Improve their land?

4. *Good Faith Improver.* In view of the court's interpretation of the open and notorious possession requirement, the defendants are at risk of losing their investments. How have New Jersey courts mitigated the harshness of the "all-or-nothing" adverse possession rules? Is this supplemental doctrine, a form of good faith improver exception, fair? In what ways does this remedy differ from the doctrine of adverse possession? Several states have enacted legislation addressing the "good faith" improver problem. *See, e.g.,* Cal. Civ. Code § 1013.5, Cal. Code Civ. Proc. §§ 741(b), 871.1–871.5; Kan. Stat. Ann. § 60–1004 (requiring compensation); *Board of County Commissioners of Wyandotte County v. Adkins*, 12 Kan.App.2d 522, 749 P.2d 1056 (1988) (requiring compensation for cost, not value, of improvements); *Somerville v. Jacobs*, 153 W.Va. 613, 626–29, 170 S.E. 2d 805, 812–14 (1969) (equity requires that a landowner who keeps improvements to compensate good faith improver for the value of the improvements). *See generally* Dickinson, Mistaken Improvers of Real Estate, 64 N.C.L. Rev. 37 (1985). We will examine such legislation in our discussion of the rights of property owners, *infra* pp. 292–96.

5. *Indemnity.* Should courts permit landowners who have been dispossessed of title to seek indemnity against the adverse possessor for the value of the land taken? *See* Merrill, Property Rules, Liability Rules, and Adverse Possession 79 Nw. U.L. Rev. 1122 (1986). Would such a rule unreasonably increase the costs of litigation by encouraging new claims (*i.e.,* for indemnity) and by requiring the court to determine market value at the time of dispossession? Should there be a separate statute of limitations for such indemnity claims? If so, do you think there would be many such claims?

6. *Rights of Other Interest Holders.* The adverse possessor holds title to the land if she meets all the applicable criteria. Does she also take title subject to other existing claims to the property, such as easements, liens, and mortgages? *See New England Home for Deaf Mutes v. Leader Filling Stations Corp.*, 276 Mass. 153, 177 N.E. 97 (1931) (easement). What if the easement, lien, or mortgage is not imposed until after the adverse possessor first takes possession?

Problem

In 1901, Smith acquired a deed describing the western half of lot 7, Block 51 in the town of Benicia, California. The block was undeveloped at that point in time. By mistake, Smith took possession and built a home on the eastern half of lot 8. In 1928, Rose acquired title to the eastern half of lot 7. By mistake, she built her home later that year on the western half of lot 7, leaving the eastern half of lot 7 unimproved. In 1940, Rose transferred her interest to Jones.

At a tax sale in September 1940, Smith acquired title to the eastern half of lot 8. He had the land surveyed and discovered that the tax deed actually described the land on which he had been living for almost 50 years. Smith then realized that Jones was occupying the western half of lot 7, for which Smith held the deed. Jones brought an action to quiet title to the property he occupied. The tax records show that both parties (and their predecessors) received property tax bills at their proper addresses, that they paid the property taxes assessed, and that the amount of the tax bills for both parties (and their predecessors) have been assessed on the basis of improved lots (dating back to 1901 for Smith and 1928 for Jones).

Adverse possession claims in California are governed by the following statutory provisions:

California Code of Civil Procedure

318. **Seisin within five years, when necessary for real property.**

No action for the recovery of real property, or for the recovery of the possession thereof, can be maintained, unless it appear that the plaintiff, his ancestor, predecessor, or grantor, was seised or possessed of the property in question, within five years before the commencement of the action.

320. **Entry on real estate.**

No entry upon real estate is deemed sufficient or valid as a claim, unless an action be commenced thereupon within one year after making such entry, and within five years from the time when the right to make it descended or accrued.

322. **Occupation under written instrument or judgment, when deemed adverse.**

When it appears that the occupant, or those under whom he claims, entered into the possession of the property under claim of title, exclusive of other right, founding such claim upon a written instrument, as being a conveyance of the property in question, or upon the decree or judgment of a competent Court, and that there has been a continued occupation and possession of the property included in such instrument, decree, or judgment, of some part of the property, under such claim, for five years, the property so included is deemed to have been held adversely, except that when it consists of a tract divided into lots, the possession of one lot is not deemed a possession of any other lot of the same tract.

323. **What constitutes adverse possession under written instrument or judgment.**

For the purpose of constituting an adverse possession by any person claiming a title, founded upon a written instrument, or a judgment or decree, land is deemed to have been possessed and occupied in the following cases:

1. Where it has been usually cultivated or improved;

2. Where it has been protected by a substantial inclosure;

3. Where, although not inclosed, it has been used for the supply of fuel, or of fencing-timber for the purposes of husbandry, or for pasturage, or for the ordinary use of the occupant;

4. Where a known farm or single lot has been partly improved, the portion of such farm or lot that may have been left not cleared, or not inclosed according to the usual course and custom of the adjoining country, shall be deemed to have been occupied for the same length of time as the part improved and cultivated.

324. **Premises actually occupied under claim of title deemed to be held adversely.**

Where it appears that there has been an actual continued occupation of land, under a claim of title, exclusive of any other right, but not founded upon a written instrument, judgment, or decree, the land so actually occupied, and no other, is deemed to have been held adversely.

325. **Claim of title not founded upon written instrument, etc.; occupancy of land.**

For the purpose of constituting an adverse possession by a person claiming title, not founded upon a written instrument, judgment, or decree, land is deemed to have been possessed and occupied in the following cases only:

First—Where it has been protected by a substantial inclosure.

Second—Where it has been usually cultivated or improved.

Provided, however, that in no case shall adverse possession be considered established under the provisions of any section or sections of this Code, unless it shall be shown that the land has been occupied and claimed for the period of five years continuously, and the party or persons, their predecessors and grantors, have paid all the taxes, State, county, or municipal, which have been levied and assessed upon such land.

How would a court resolve this dispute? Should the court base its decision on §§ 322–323 or §§ 324–325? What is the most difficult criterion for Jones to satisfy? *See Sorensen v. Costa,* 32 Cal.2d 453, 196 P.2d 900 (1948).

---

2.   ACQUISITION OF OTHER RESOURCES

a.   WILD ANIMALS

Pierson v. Post

Supreme Court of New York, 1805.
3 Cai. R. 175.

This was an action of trespass on the case commenced in a justice's court, by the present defendant against the now plaintiff.

The declaration stated that *Post*, being in possession of certain dogs and hounds under his command, did, upon a certain wild and uninhabited, unpossessed and waste land, called the beach, whilst there hunting, chasing and pursuing the same with his dogs and hounds, and when in view thereof, *Pierson*, well knowing the fox was so hunted and pursued, did in the sight of *Post*, to prevent his catching the same, kill and carry it off. A verdict having been rendered for the plaintiff below, the defendant there sued out a *certiorari*, and now assigned for error, that the declaration and the matters therein contained were not sufficient in law to maintain an action.

Sanford, for the now plaintiff. It is firmly settled that animals, *ferae naturae*, belong not to anyone. If, then, *Post* had not acquired any property in the fox, when it was killed by *Pierson*, he had no right in it which could be the subject of injury. As, however, a property may be gained in such an animal, it will be necessary to advert to the facts set forth, to see whether they are such as could give a legal interest in the creature, that was the cause of the suit below. Finding, hunting, and pursuit, are all that the plaint enumerates. To create a title [to an] animal *ferae naturae*, occupancy is indispensable. It is the only mode recognised by our system. 2 *Black. Com.* 403. The reason of the thing shows it to be so. For whatever is not appropriated by positive institutions, can be exclusively possessed by natural law alone. Occupancy is the sole method this code acknowledges. Authorities are not wanting to this effect. *Just.* liv. 2. tit. 1. s. 12. "*Ferae igitur bestiae, simul atque ab aliquo captae fuerint jure gentium statim illius esse incipiunt.*" There must be a taking; and even that is not in all cases sufficient, for in the same section he observes, "*Quicquid autem corum ceperis, eo usque tuum esse intelligitur, donec tua custodia coercetur; cum vero tuam evaserit custodiam, et in libertatem naturalem sese receperit, tuam esse desinit, et rursus occumpantis fit.*" It is also that this natural liberty my be regained even if in sight of the pursuer, "*ita sit, ut difficilis sit ejus persecutio.*" In section 13. it is laid down, that even wounding will not give a right of property in an animal that is unreclaimed. For, notwithstanding the wound, "*multa accidere soleant ut eam non capia;*" and "*non alter tuam esse, quam si eam ceperis.*" *Fleta*, b. 3. p. 175. and *Bracton*, b.2.c.1. p.86 are in unison with the *Roman* lawgiver. It is manifest, then from the record, that there was no title in *Post*, and the action, therefore, not maintainable.

Colden, contra. I admit with *Fleta*, that pursuit alone does not give a right of property in animals *ferae naturae*, and I admit also that occupancy is to give a title to them. But then, what kind of occupancy? and here I shall contend it is not such as is derived from manucaption alone. In *Puffendorf's Law of Nature and of Nations*, b.4. c.6. s. 2. n. 2. *Ibid.* s. 7. n. 2. demonstrated that manucaption is only one of many means to declare the intention of exclusively appropriating that, which was before in a state of nature. Any continued act which does this, is equivalent to occupancy. Pursuit, therefore, by a person who starts a wild animal, gives an exclusive right whilst it is followed. It is all the possession the nature of the subject admits; it declares the intention of acquiring dominion, and is as much to be respected as manucaption itself. The contrary idea, requiring actual taking, proceeds, as Mr. *Barbeyrac* observes, in *Puffendorf*, b. 4. c.6. s. 10. on a "false notion of possession."

Sanford, in reply. The only authority relied on is that of an annotator. On the question now before the court, we have taken our principles from the civil code, and nothing has been urged to impeach those quoted from the authors referred to.

■ TOMPKINS, J. delivered the opinion of the court. This cause comes before us on a return to a *certiorari* directed to one of the justices of *Queens* County.

The question submitted by the counsel in this cause for our determination is, whether *Lodivick Post*, by the pursuit with his hounds in the manner alleged in his declaration, acquired such a right to, or property in, the fox, as will sustain an action against *Pierson* for killing and taking him away?

The cause was argued with much ability by the counsel on both sides, and presents for our decision a novel and nice question. It is admitted that a fox is an animal *ferae naturae*, and that property in such animals is acquired by occupancy only. These admissions narrow the discussion to the simple question of what acts amount to occupancy, applied to acquiring right to wild animals?

If we have recourse to the ancient writers upon general principles of law, the judgment below is obviously erroneous. *Justinian's Institutes*, liv. 2. tit. 1. s. 13 and *Fleta*, lib. 3. c. 2. p. 175. adopt the principle, that pursuit alone vests no property or right in the huntsman; and that even pursuit, accompanied with wounding, is equally ineffectual for that purpose, unless the animal be actually taken. The same principle is recognised by *Bracton*, lib. 2. c. 1. p. 8.

Puffendorf, lib. 4. c. 6. s. 2. and 10. defines occupancy of beasts *ferae naturae*, to be the actual corporal possession of them, and *Bynkershoek* is cited as coinciding in this definition. It is indeed with hesitation that *Puffendorf* affirms that a wild beast mortally wounded, or greatly maimed, cannot be fairly intercepted by another, whilst the pursuit of the person inflicting the wound continues. The foregoing authorities are decisive to show that mere pursuit gave *Post* no legal right to the fox, but that he became the property of *Pierson*, who intercepted and killed him.

It therefore only remains to inquire whether there are any contrary principles, or authorities, to be found in other books, which ought to induce a different decision. Most of the cases which have occurred in *England*, relating to property in wild animals, have either been discussed and decided upon the principles of their positive statute regulations, or have arisen between the huntsman and the owner of the land upon which beasts *ferae naturae* have been apprehended; the former claiming them by title of occupancy, and the latter *ratione soli*. Little satisfactory aid can, therefore, be derived from the *English* reporters.

Barbeyrac, in hist notes on *Puffendorf*, does not accede to the definition of occupancy by the latter, but, on the contrary, affirms, that actual bodily seizure is not, in all cases, necessary to constitute possession of wild animals. He does not, however, *describe* the acts which, according to his ideas, will amount to an appropriation of such animals to private use, so as to exclude the claims of all other persons, by title of occupancy, to the same animals; and he is far from averring that pursuit alone is sufficient for that purpose. To a certain extent, and as far as *Barbeyrac* appears to me to go, his objections to *Puffendorf's* definition of occupancy are reasonable and correct. That is to say, that actual bodily seizure is not indispensable to acquire right to, or possession of, wild beasts; but that, on the contrary, the mortal wounding of such beasts, by one not abandoning his pursuit, may, with the utmost propriety, be deemed possession of him; since, thereby, the pursuer manifests an unequivocal intention of appropriating the animal to his individual use, has deprived him of his natural liberty, and brought him within his certain control. So also, encompassing and securing such animals with nets and toils, or otherwise intercepting them in such a manner as to deprive them of their natural liberty, and render escape impossible, may justly be deemed to give possession of them to those persons who, by their industry and labour, have used such means of apprehending them. *Barbeyrac* seems to have adopted, and had in view in his notes, the more accurate opinion of *Grotius*, with respect to occupancy. That celebrated author, lib. 2. c. 8. s. 3. p. 309. speaking of occupancy, proceeds thus: "*Requiritur autem corporalis quoedam possessio ad dominium adipiscendum; atque ideo, vulnerasse non sufficit.*" But in the following section he explains and qualifies this definition of occupancy: "*Sed possessio illa potest non solis manibus, sed instrumentis, ut decipulis, retibus, laqueis dum duo adsint: primum ut ipsa instrumenta sint in nostra potestate, deinde ut fera, ita inclusa sit, ut exire inde nequeat.*" This qualification embraces the full extent of *Barbeyrac's* objection to *Puffendorf's* definition, and allows as great a latitude to acquiring property by occupancy, as can reasonably be inferred from the words or ideas expressed by *Barbeyrac* in his notes. The case now under consideration is one of mere pursuit, and presents no circumstances or acts which can bring it within the definition of occupancy by *Puffendorf*, or *Grotius*, or the ideas of *Barbeyrac* upon that subject.

The case cited from 11 *Mod*. 74–130. I think clearly distinguishable from the present; inasmuch as there the action was for maliciously hindering and disturbing the plaintiff in the exercise and enjoyment of a private franchise; and in the report of the same case, 3 *Salk*. 9. *Holt*, Ch. J. states, that the ducks were in the plaintiff's decoy pond, and *so in his possession*, from which it is obvious the court laid much stress in their opinion upon the plaintiff's possession of the ducks, *ratione soli*.

We are the more readily inclined to confine possession or occupancy of beasts *ferae naturae*, within the limits prescribed by the learned authors above cited, for the sake of certainty, and preserving peace and order in society. If the first seeing, starting, or pursuing such animals, without having so wounded, circumvented or ensnared them, so as to deprive them of their natural liberty, and subject them to the control of their pursuer, should afford the basis of actions against others for intercepting and killing them, it would prove a fertile source of quarrels and litigation.

However uncourteous or unkind the conduct of *Pierson* towards *Post*, in this instance, may have been, yet his act was productive of no injury or damage for which a legal remedy can be applied. We are of opinion the judgment below was erroneous, and ought to be reversed.

■ LIVINGSTON, J. My opinion differs from that of the court. Of six exceptions, taken to the proceedings below, all are abandoned except the third, which reduces the controversy to a single question.

Whether a person who, with his own hounds, starts and hunts a fox on waste and uninhabited ground, and is on the point of seizing his prey, acquires such an interest in the animal, as to have a right of action against another, who in view of the huntsman and his dogs in full pursuit, and with knowledge of the chase, shall kill and carry him away?

This is a knotty point, and should have been submitted to the arbitration of sportsmen, without poring over *Justinian, Fleta, Bracton, Puffendorf, Locke, Barbeyrac,* or *Blackstone*, all of whom have been cited; they would have had no difficulty in coming to a prompt and correct conclusion. In a court thus constituted, the skin and carcass of poor *reynard* would have been properly disposed of, and a precedent set, interfering with no usage or custom which the experience of ages has sanctioned, and which must be so well known to every votary of *Diana*. But the parties have referred the question to our judgment, and we must dispose of it as well as we can, from the partial lights we possess, leaving to a higher tribunal, the correction of any mistake which we may be so unfortunate as to make. By the pleadings it is admitted that a fox is a "wild and noxious beast." Both parties have regarded him, as the law of nations does a pirate, *"hostem humani generis,"* and although *"de mortuis nil nisi bonum,"* be a maxim of our profession, the memory of the deceased has not been spared. His depredations on farmers and on barn yards, have not been forgotten; and to put him to death wherever found, is allowed to be meritorious, and of public benefit. Hence it follows, that our decision should have in view the greatest possible encouragement to the destruction of an animal so cunning and ruthless in his career. But who would keep a pack of hounds; or what gentleman, at the sound of the horn, and at peep of day, would mount his steed, and for hours together, "*sub jove frigido*," or a vertical sun, pursue the windings of this wily quadruped, if, just as night came on, and his stratagems and strength were nearly exhausted, a saucy intruder, who had not shared in the honours or labours of the chase, were permitted to come in at the death, and bear away in triumph the object of pursuit? Whatever *Justinian* may have thought of the matter, it must be recollected that his code was compiled many hundred years ago, and it would be very hard indeed, at the distance of so many centuries, not to have a right to establish a rule for ourselves. In his day, we read of no order of men who made it a business, in the language of the declaration in this cause, "with hounds and dogs to find, start, pursue, hunt, and chase," these animals, and that, too, without any other motive than the preservation of *Roman* poultry; if this diversion had been then in fashion, the lawyers who composed his institutes, would have taken care not to pass it by, without suitable encouragement. If anything, therefore, in the digests or pandects shall appear to militate against the defendant in error, who, on this occasion, was the foxhunter, we have only to say *tempora mutantur*; and if men themselves change with the times, why should not laws also undergo an alteration?

It may be expected, however, by the learned counsel, that more particular notice be taken of their authorities. I have examined them all, and feel great difficulty in determining, whether to acquire dominion over a thing, before in common, it be sufficient that we barely see it, or know where it is, or wish for it, or make a declaration of our will respecting it; or whether, in the case of wild beasts, setting a trap, or lying in wait, or starting, or pursuing, be enough; or if an actual wounding, or killing, or bodily tact and occupation be necessary. Writers on general law, who have favoured us with their speculations on these points, differ on them all; but, great as is the diversity of sentiment among them, some conclusion must be adopted on the question immediately before us. After mature deliberation, I embrace that of *Barbeyrac*, as the most rational, and least liable to objection. If at liberty, we might imitate the courtesy of a certain emperor, who, to avoid giving offence to the advocates of any of these different doctrines, adopted a middle course, and by ingenious distinctions, rendered it difficult to say (as often happens after a fierce and angry contest) to whom the palm of victory belonged. He ordained, that if a beast be followed with *large dogs and hounds*, he shall belong to the hunter, not to the chance occupant; and in like manner, if he be killed or wounded with a lance or sword; but if chased with *beagles only*, then he passed to the captor, not to the first pursuer. If slain with a dart, a sling, or a bow, he fell to the hunter, if still in chase, and not to him whom might afterwards find and seize him.

Now, as we are without any municipal regulations of our own, and the pursuit here, for aught that appears on the case, being with dogs and hounds of *imperial stature*, we are at liberty to adopt one of the provisions just cited, which comports also with the learned conclusion of *Barbeyrac*, that property in animals *ferae naturae* may be acquired without bodily touch or manucaption, provided the pursuer be within reach, or have a *reasonable* prospect (which certainly existed here) of taking, what he has *thus* discovered an intention of converting to his own use.

When we reflect also that the interest of our husbandmen, the most useful of men in any community, will be advanced by the destruction of a beast so pernicious and incorrigible, we cannot greatly err, in saying, that a pursuit like the present, through waste and unoccupied lands, and which must inevitably and speedily have terminate in corporal possession, or bodily *seisin*, confers such a right to the object of it, as to make any one a wrongdoer, who shall interfere and shoulder the spoil. The *justice's* judgment ought, therefore, in my opinion to be affirmed.

Judgment of reversal.

---

1. *Majority Rule*. What did the majority decide? What was the majority's reasoning? What assumptions underlie the court's analysis? What is the philosophical basis for this rule?

2. *Dissent Rule*. What did the dissent argue? What was the dissent's reasoning? What assumptions underlie its analysis? What is the philosophical basis for the dissent's proposed rule?

3. *Decision Process*. Justice Livingston suggests that this case would have been better decided by "sportsmen." In what way would such people be more likely to arrive at a better result? Are there disadvantages to having sportsmen decide these types of cases? By what criteria should society select the proper institutions to decide such disputes? Are administrability and efficiency relevant considerations? What other considerations are important?

Contrast the handling of this dispute with the norms that developed in the whaling and lobster industries. What type of disputes are best suited to "arbitration" of the type Livingston proposes? Which are least suited? When are non-judicial decision processes particularly prone to abuse?

---

b. OIL AND NATURAL GAS

The formation of oil reservoirs began hundreds of millions of years ago in ancient seas and rivers. These bodies of water dumped marine organisms, sand, and silt into basins where they mixed and settled to form sedimentary deposits. The Gulf of Mexico, where the Mississippi River dumps millions of tons of sediment daily, is a current example of an active sedimentary basin. As more sediment is buried, increasing pressure and temperature compact the sediment into "source rock" and convert the organic material embedded in the source rock into oil and natural gas.

Source rock is porous so it permits movement of oil, natural gas, and water. The great pressure within the source rock causes the oil and natural gas, which are less dense than water, to rise through the pores in the rock. Oil reservoirs form in traps where impermeable rock prevents the oil and gas from rising further.

The middle panel of Diagram 2.1 illustrates an anticlinal trap, the most common type of oil trap. Anticlinal traps occur where impermeable rock is folded upward, forming an inverted bowl shape. Natural gas and oil accumulate at the crest of the fold where the impermeable rock prevents further migration. Oil reservoirs also commonly occur at faults in the earth's crust ("fault traps"—panel a) and where wedge-shaped layers of sandstone, which once may have been beaches, are sandwiched between layers of impermeable rock ("stratigraphic traps"—panel c).

Diagram 2.1

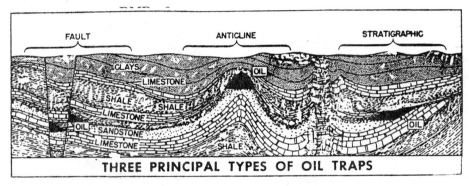

THREE PRINCIPAL TYPES OF OIL TRAPS

Reprinted courtesy of the American Petroleum Institute.

Oil and gas are extracted by drilling through the rock layer that traps the resource. The natural upward pressure of the oil and natural gas usually drives the resource out. The high pressure of some reservoirs cannot be contained, thus causing "gushers." The natural pressure of a reservoir releases between a few percent and as much as 70 percent of the resource from the ground. Inefficient extraction efforts, such as poor placement of drilling platforms and excessive drilling, can reduce the amount of recoverable resources by dissipating the reservoir's natural pressure at an excessive rate. On average, approximately 30 percent of the oil in place is recoverable through natural pressure. In the early years of the petroleum industry, extraction would end when the natural pressure declined to a low level. In the past 50 years, as oil has become more valuable and technology has developed, geologists and engineers have developed numerous enhanced recovery methods, such as gas and water injection, steam injection, and *in situ* combustion, to release some of the remaining petroleum left after the reservoir's natural pressure has dissipated.

In view of the difficulty of identifying, mapping, and extracting subsurface oil and gas resources the rules governing ownership of oil and natural gas are more complex than traditional real property law. In *Westmoreland*

and Cambria Natural Gas Co. v. De Witt, 130 Pa. 235, 18 A. 724, 725 (1889), the Pennsylvania Supreme Court described the law as follows:

> Water and oil, and still more strongly [natural] gas, may be classed by themselves, if the analogy be not too fanciful, as minerals *ferae naturae*. In common with animals, and unlike other minerals [such as hard minerals like coal or iron], they have the power and the tendency to escape without the volition of the owner. Their "fugitive and wondering existence within the limits of a particular tract was uncertain" * * * They belong to the owner of the land, and are part of it, so long as they are on or in it, and are subject to his control; but when they escape, and go into other land, or come under another's control, the title of the former owner is gone. Possession of the land, therefore, is not necessarily possession of the gas [or oil]. If an adjoining, or even a distant, owner drills his own land, and taps your gas [or oil], so that it comes into his well and under his control, it is no longer yours, but his * * * [T]he one who controls the gas [or oil]—has it in his grasp, so to speak—is the one who has possession in the legal as well as the ordinary sense of the word.

This doctrine has come to be known as the "rule of capture."

---

1. What are the philosophical bases for the rule of capture?

2. Is the rule of capture a good way to allocate oil and gas resources? Why or why not? What problems can you foresee from such a rule? How could they be addressed? Consider the following problems:

Common Pool. Suppose that a pool of oil lay beneath two, separately owned tracts of land. The owner of Tract 1 drills straight down and begins to pump oil from the pool. The owner of Tract 2 claims that the owner of Tract 1 is taking more than his fair share of the oil. Under *Westmoreland* should the owner of the second tract be able to collect damages or obtain an injunction? What would you propose as an alternative rule? Are there any difficulties with a rule that prohibits "excessive" drilling? *See Union Gas & Oil Co. v. Fyffe*, 219 Ky. 640, 294 S.W. 176 (1927) (barring excessive drilling).

Slant Drilling. Suppose that a pool of oil lay directly beneath Tract 1. The owner of Tract 2, an adjacent tract, drills downward at a slant toward the pool and begins to extract the oil. When he learns what is going on, the owner of Tract 1 sues for damages and injunctive relief. Should the owner of Tract 1 have a legal remedy? Despite the rule of capture, is there any reason to treat this example differently than the previous problem? Does a capture rule make any sense here?

---

c. WATER

The value of land is often intertwined with access to and control of water. Water is necessary for drinking and sanitation, and for growing crops and raising livestock. It provides a key mode of transportation and power generation, and it is essential for the operation of most industries. As a result, the nature of water resources and the rules that have evolved (and continue to evolve) to govern its allocation have played central roles in determining the economic structure, population density, and land-use patterns of many communities.

The law governing the control of water resources always has reflected elements of both private and public property systems. Water law has traditionally limited water use to that which is "reasonable" or "beneficial," although the meaning of these general concepts in particular settings is often variable, evolving, controversial, and subject to the limitations of the institutions applying the standards. The great importance of water has generated its share of political, legal, and economic battles in the development of our nation. Mark Twain crisply captured the contentiousness surrounding water disputes in the early West: "Whiskey is for drinkin' and water is for fightin'."

Water law remains a vital area today because of the increasing demands on water resources, changes in technology and industrial organization, and evolving social values. Whereas water traditionally has been seen as a resource to be harnessed for agriculture, commerce, power generation, and transportation, a growing awareness of the role of water resources in the sustainability of critical ecosystems has more recently channeled water law in new directions. Particularly in the past decade, water law and policy have shifted from an exclusive focus on direct human uses toward the inclusion of watershed and habitat protection in the balance.

The field of water law is far too expansive to survey comprehensively in this course.[5] Our purpose here is to examine through some illustrative cases the manner in which early water law evolved in this country. Although water has a singular definition in scientific terms—two parts hydrogen and one part oxygen—its nature in the social, economic, political and legal realms is far more variable and complex. As you read these cases, carefully consider the essential nature of the water resource at issue and examine the extent to which legal rules and institutions governing that resource have responded to the needs of the particular community.

---

5. For a survey of water law, see J. Sax, R. Abrams, & B. Thompson, Legal Control of Water Resources (2d ed. 1991); Scott & Coustalin, The Evolution of Water Rights, 35 Nat. Res. J. 821 (1995).

Evans v. Merriweather

Supreme Court of Illinois, 1842.
4 Ill. 492.

■ LOCKWOOD, JUSTICE, delivered the opinion of the Court: This was an action on the *case*, brought in the Greene Circuit Court, by Merriweather against Evans, for obstructing and diverting a water course. The plaintiff obtained a verdict, and judgment was rendered thereon. On the trial the defendant excepted to the instructions asked for and given, at the instance of the plaintiff. The defendant also excepted, because instructions, that were asked by him, were refused. After the cause was brought into this Court, the parties agreed upon the following statement of facts, as having been proved on the trial, to wit:

It is agreed between the parties to this suit, that the following is the statement of facts proved at the trial in this case, and that the same shall be considered as part of the record by the Court, in the adjudication of this cause. . . . Smith & Baker, in 1834, bought of T. Carlin six acres of land, through which a branch ran and erected a steam mill thereon. They depended upon a well and the branch for water in running their engine. . . . About one or two years afterwards, John Evans bought of T. Carlin six acres of land, on the same branch, above and immediately adjoining the lot owned by Smith & Baker, and erected thereon a steam mill, depending upon a well and the branch for water in running his engine.

Smith & Baker, after the erection of Evans' mill, in 1836 or 1837, sold the mill and appurtenances to Merriweather, for about $8,000. Evans' mill was supposed to be worth $12,000. Ordinarily there was an abundance of water for both mills; but in the fall of 1837, there being a drought, the branch failed, so far that it did not afford water sufficient to run the upper mill continually. Evans directed his hands not to stop, or divert the water, in the branch; but one of them employed about the mill did make a dam across the branch, just below Evans' mill, and thereby diverted all the water in the branch into Evans' well. Evans was at home, half a mile from the mill, and was frequently about his mill, and evidence was introduced conducing to prove that he might have known that the water of the branch was diverted into his well. After the diversion of the water into Evans' well, as aforesaid, the branch went dry below, and Merriweather's mill could not and did not run, in consequence of it, more than one day in a week, and was then supplied with water from his well. Merriweather then brought this suit, in three or four weeks after the putting of the dam across the branch for the diversion of the water, and obtained a verdict for $150. This suit, it is admitted, is the first between the parties litigating the right as to the use of the water. It is further agreed, that the branch afforded usually sufficient water for the supply of both mills, without materially affecting the size of the current, though the branch was not depended upon exclusively for that purpose. Furthermore, that at the time of the grievances complained of by the plaintiff below, the defendant had water hauled in part for the supply of his boilers. That the dam was made below the defendant's well, across the branch, which diverted as well the water hauled and poured out into the branch above the well, as the water of the branch, into the defendant's well.

Upon this state of facts, the question is presented, as to what extent riparian proprietors, upon a stream not navigable, can use the water of such stream? The branch mentioned in the agreed statement of facts, is a small natural stream of water, not furnishing, at all seasons of the year, a supply of water sufficient for both mills. There are no facts in the case showing that the water is wanted for any other than milling purposes, and for those purposes to be converted into steam, and thus entirely consumed. In an early case decided in England, it is laid down that "A water course begins '*ex jure naturae*,' and having taken a certain course naturally, cannot be diverted." The language of all the authorities is, that water flows in its natural course, and should be permitted thus to flow, so that all through whose land it naturally flows, may enjoy the privilege of using it. The property in the water, therefore, by virtue of the riparian ownership, is in its nature usufructuary, and consists, in general, not so much of the fluid itself, as of the advantage of its impetus. A riparian proprietor, therefore, though he has an undoubted right to use the water for hydraulic or manufacturing purposes, must so use it as to do no injury to any other riparian proprietor. Some decisions, in laying down the rights of riparian proprietors of water courses, have gone so far as to restrict their right in the use of water flowing over their land, so that there shall be no diminution in the quantity of the water, and no obstruction to its course. The decisions last referred to cannot, however, be considered as furnishing the true doctrine on this subject. Mr. Justice Story, in delivering the opinion of the Court, in the case of *Tyler v. Wilkinson*, says,

I do not mean to be understood as holding the doctrine that there can be no diminution whatever, and no obstruction of impediment whatever, by a riparian proprietor in the use of water as it flows; for that would be to deny any valuable use of it. There may be, and there must be, of that which is common to all, a reasonable use. The true test of the principle and extent of the use is, whether it is to the injury of the other proprietors or not. There may be diminution in quantity, or a retardation or acceleration of the natural current, indispensable for the general and valuable use of the water, perfectly consistent with the use of the common right. The diminution, retardation, or acceleration, not positively and sensibly injurious, by diminishing the value of the common right, is an implied element in the right of using the stream at all. The law here, as in many other cases, acts with a reasonable reference to public convenience and general good, and is not betrayed into a narrow strictness, subversive of common use, nor into an extravagant looseness, which would destroy private rights.

The same learned judge further says, "That of a thing common by nature, there may be an appropriation by general consent or grant. Mere priority of appropriation of running water, without such consent or grant, confers no exclusive right" * * *

Each riparian proprietor is bound to make such a use of running water, as to do as little injury to those below him, as is consistent with a valuable benefit to himself. The use must be a reasonable one. Now the question fairly arises, is that a reasonable use of running water by the upper proprietor, by which the fluid itself is entirely consumed? To answer this question satisfactorily, it is proper to consider the wants of man in regard to the element of water. These wants are either natural or artificial. Natural are such as are absolutely necessary * * * to his existence. Artificial, such only, as by supplying them, his comfort and prosperity are increased. To quench thirst, and for household purposes, water is absolutely indispensable. In civilized life, water for cattle is also necessary. These wants must be supplied, or both man and beast will perish.

The supply of man's artificial wants is not essential to his existence; it is not indispensable; he could live if water was not employed in irrigating lands, or in propelling his machinery. In countries differently situated from ours, with a hot and arid climate, water doubtless is absolutely indispensable to the cultivation of the soil, and in them, water for irrigation would be natural want. Here it might increase the products of the soil, but it is by no means essential, and cannot therefore be considered a natural want of man. So of manufacturers, they promote the prosperity and comfort of mankind, but cannot be considered absolutely necessary to his existence; nor need the machinery which he employs be set in motion by steam.

From these premises would result this conclusion; that an individual owning a spring on his land, from which water flows in a current through his neighbor's land, would have the right to use the whole of it, if necessary to satisfy his natural wants. He may consume all the water for his domestic purposes, including water for his stock. If he desires to use it for irrigation or manufactures, and there be a lower proprietor to whom its use is essential to supply his natural wants, or for his stock, he must use the water so as to leave enough for such lower proprietor. Where the stream is small, and does not supply water more than sufficient to answer the natural wants of the different proprietors living on it, none of the proprietors can use the water for either irrigation or manufactures. So far then as natural wants are concerned, there is no difficulty in furnishing a rule by which riparian proprietors may use flowing water to supply such natural wants. Each proprietor in his turn may, if necessary, consume all the water for these purposes. But where the water is not wanted to supply natural wants, and there is not sufficient for each proprietor living on the stream, to carry on his manufacturing purposes, how shall the water be divided? We have seen that without a contract or grant, neither has a right to use all the water; all have a right to participate in its benefits. Where all have a right to participate in a common benefit, and none can have an exclusive enjoyment, no rule, from the very nature of the case, can be laid down, as to how much each may use without infringing upon the rights of others. In such cases, the question must be left to the judgment of the jury, whether the party complained of has used, under all the circumstances, more than his just proportion.

It appears from the facts agreed on, that Evans obstructed the water by a dam, and diverted the whole into his well. This diversion, according to all the cases, both English and American, was clearly illegal. For this diversion, an action will lie. It, however, was contended that Evans forbid the construction of the dam, by which the water was diverted into his well. If a servant do an act against the consent of the master, the latter is not liable. In this case, however, a jury might fairly infer from the fact, that as Evans lived near the mill, and was frequently at it, he must have been conversant of the manner in which his mill was supplied with water, and that he either countermanded the instructions, or acquiesced in the construction of the dam, after it was erected. Having availed himself of the illegal act of his servant, the law presumes he authorized it. Having arrived at the conclusion that an action will lie in behalf of Merriweather against Evans, for obstructing and diverting the water course mentioned in the plaintiff's declaration, I have not deemed it necessary to examine the instructions given by the Court, to see if they accord with the principles above laid down. Having decided that the plaintiff below has a right to recover on the facts, whether the instructions were right or wrong, would not vary that result. It is possible that if the true principles which govern this action had been correctly given to the jury, the damages might have been either less or more than the jury have given; but in this case, as the damages are small, the Court ought not, where justice has upon the whole been done, to send the case back, to see if a jury, upon another trial, would not give less.

For these reasons, I am of opinion that the judgment ought to be affirmed with costs.

———

1. *Doctrine of Riparian Rights.* What are the rights of landowners adjoining non-navigable streams in mid–19th century Illinois? What institutions administer this doctrine? Is the doctrine practicable? What are the limitations of this doctrine? What are the factual assumptions underlying the doctrine?

2. What are the philosophical bases for the rule described by the court? Does it comport with the nature of the resources, the developing economic structure, and the social culture of the place and times?

———

Coffin v. The Left Hand Ditch Co.

Supreme Court of Colorado, 1882.
6 Colo. 443.

■ HELM, J.

Appellee, who was plaintiff below, claimed to be the owner of certain water by virtue of an appropriation thereof from the south fork of the St.

Vrain creek. It appears that such water, after its diversion, is carried by means of a ditch to the James creek, and thence along the bed of the same to Left Hand creek, where it is again diverted by lateral ditches and used to irrigate lands adjacent to the last named stream. Appellants are the owners of lands lying on the margin and in the neighborhood of the St. Vrain below the mouth of said south fork thereof, and naturally irrigated therefrom.

In 1879 there was not a sufficient quantity of water in the St. Vrain to supply the ditch of appellee and also irrigate the said lands of appellant. A portion of appellee's dam was torn out, and its diversion of water thereby seriously interfered with by appellants. The action is brought for damages arising from the trespass, and for injunctive relief to prevent repetitions thereof in the future.

* * *

It is contended by counsel for appellants that the common law principles of riparian proprietorship prevailed in Colorado until 1876, and that the doctrine of priority of right to water by priority of appropriation thereof was first recognized and adopted in the constitution. But we think the latter doctrine has existed from the date of the earliest appropriations of water within the boundaries of the state. The climate is dry, and the soil, when moistened only by the usual rainfall, is arid and unproductive; except in a few favored sections, artificial irrigation for agriculture is an absolute necessity. Water in the various streams thus acquires a value unknown in moister climates. Instead of being a mere incident to the soil, it rises, when appropriated, to the dignity of a distinct usufructuary estate, or right of property. It has always been the policy of the national, as well as the territorial and state governments, to encourage the diversion and use of water in this country for agriculture; and vast expenditures of time and money have been made in reclaiming and fertilizing by irrigation portions of our unproductive territory. Houses have been built, and permanent improvements made; the soil has been cultivated, and thousands of acres have been rendered immensely valuable, with the understanding that appropriations of water would be protected. Deny the doctrine of priority or superiority of right by priority of appropriation, and a great part of the value of all this property is at once destroyed.

The right to water in this country, by priority of appropriation thereof, we think it is, and has always been, the duty of the national and state governments to protect. The right itself, and the obligation to protect it, existed prior to legislation on the subject of irrigation. It is entitled to protection as well after patent to a third party of the land over which the natural stream flows, as when such land is a part of the public domain; and it is immaterial whether or not it be mentioned in the patent and expressly excluded from the grant.

The act of congress protecting in patents such right in water appropriated, when recognized by local customs and laws, "was rather a voluntary recognition of a pre-existing right of possession, constituting a valid claim to its continued use, than the establishment of a new one." *Broder v. Natoma W. & M. Co.* 11 Otto, 274.

We conclude, then, that the common law doctrine giving the riparian owner a right to the flow of water in its natural channel upon and over his lands, even though he makes no beneficial use thereof, is inapplicable to Colorado. Imperative necessity, unknown to the countries which gave it birth, compels the recognition of another doctrine in conflict therewith. And we hold that, in the absence of express statutes to the contrary, the first appropriator of water from a natural stream for a beneficial purpose has, with the qualifications contained in the constitution, a prior right thereto, to the extent of such appropriation. *See Schilling v. Rominger*, 4 Col. 103.

The territorial legislature in 1864 expressly recognizes the doctrine. It says: "Nor shall the water of any stream be diverted from its original channel to the detriment of any miner, millmen or others along the line of said stream, *who may have a priority of right*, and there shall be at all times left sufficient water in said stream for the use of miners and agriculturists along said stream." Session Laws of 1864, p. 68, § 32.

The priority of right mentioned in this section is acquired by priority of appropriation, and the provision declares that appropriations of water shall be subordinate to the use thereof by prior appropriators. This provision remained in force until the adoption of the constitution; it was repealed in 1868, but the repealing act re-enacted it *verbatim*.

But the rights of appellee were acquired, in the first instance, under the acts of 1861 and 1862, and counsel for appellants urge, with no little skill and plausibility, that these statutes are in conflict with our conclusion that priority of right is acquired by priority of appropriation. The only provision, however, which can be construed as referring to this subject is § 4 on page 68, Session Laws of 1861. This section provides for the appointment of commissioners, in times of scarcity, to apportion the stream "in a just and equitable proportion," to the best interests of all parties, *"with a due regard to the legal rights of all."* What is meant by the concluding phrases of the foregoing statute? What are the legal rights for which the commissioners are enjoined to have a "due regard?" Why this additional limitation upon the powers of such commissioners?

It seems to us a reasonable inference that these phrases had reference to the rights acquired by priority of appropriation. This view is sustained by the universal respect shown at the time said statute was adopted, and subsequently by each person, for the prior appropriations of others, and the corresponding customs existing among settlers with reference thereto. This construction does not, in our judgment, detract from the force or effect of the statute. It was the duty of the commissioners under it to guard against extravagance and waste, and to so divide and distribute the water as most economically to supply all of the earlier appropriators thereof according to their respective appropriations and necessities, to the extent of the amount remaining in the stream.

It appears from the record that the patent under which appellant George W. Coffin holds title was issued prior to the act of congress of 1866, hereinbefore mentioned. That it contained no reservation or exception of vested water rights, and conveyed to Coffin through his grantor the absolute title in fee simple to his land, together with all incidents and appurtenances thereunto belonging; and it is claimed that therefore the doctrine of priority of right by appropriation cannot, at least, apply to him. We have already declared that water appropriated and diverted for a beneficial purpose is, in this country, not necessarily an appurtenance to the soil through which the stream supplying the same naturally flows. If appropriated by one prior to the patenting of such soil by another, it is a vested right entitled to protection, though not mentioned in the patent. But we are relieved from any extended consideration of this subject by the decision in *Broder v. Notoma W. & M. Co., supra.*

It is urged, however, that even if the doctrine of priority or superiority of right by priority of appropriation be conceded, appellee in this case is not benefited thereby. Appellants claim that they have a better right to the water because their lands lie along the margin and in the neighborhood of the St. Vrain. They assert that, as against them, appellee's diversion of said water to irrigate lands adjacent to Left Hand creek, though prior in time, is unlawful.

In the absence of legislation to the contrary, we think that the right to water acquired by priority of appropriation thereof is not in any way dependent upon the locus of its application to the beneficial use designed. And the disastrous consequences of our adoption of the rule contended for, forbid our giving such a construction to the statutes as will concede the same, if they will properly bear a more reasonable and equitable one.

The doctrine of priority of right by priority of appropriation for agriculture is evoked, as we have seen, by the imperative necessity for artificial irrigation of the soil. And it would be an ungenerous and inequitable rule that would deprive one of its benefit simply because he has, by large expenditure of time and money, carried the water from one stream over an intervening watershed and cultivated land in the valley of another. It might be utterly impossible, owing to the topography of the country, to get water upon his farm from the adjacent stream; or if possible, it might be impracticable on account of the distance from the point where the diversion must take place and the attendant expense; or the quantity of water in such stream might be entirely insufficient to supply his wants. It sometimes happens that the most fertile soil is found along the margin or in the neighborhood of the small rivulet, and sandy and barren land beside the larger stream. To apply the rule contended for would prevent the useful and profitable cultivation of the productive soil, and sanction the waste of water upon the more sterile lands. It would have enabled a party to locate upon a stream in 1875, and destroy the value of thousands of acres, and the improvements thereon, in adjoining valleys, possessed and cultivated for the preceding decade. Under the principle contended for, a party owning land ten miles from the stream, but in the valley thereof, might deprive a prior appropriator of the water diverted therefrom whose lands are within a thousand yards, but just beyond an intervening divide.

We cannot believe that any legislative body within the territory or state of Colorado ever *intended* these consequences to flow from a statute enacted. Yet two sections are relied upon by counsel as practically producing them. These sections are as follows:

> All persons who claim, own or hold a possessory right or title to any land or parcel of land within the boundary of Colorado territory, * * * when those claims are on the bank, margin or neighborhood of any stream of water, creek or river, shall be entitled to the use of the water of said stream, creek or river for the purposes of irrigation, and making said claims available to the full extent of the soil, for agricultural purposes. Session Laws 1861, p. 67, § 1.

> Nor shall the water of any stream be diverted from its original channel to the detriment of any miner, millmen or others along the line of said stream, and there shall be at all times left sufficient water in said stream for the use of miners and farmers along said stream. Latter part of § 13, p. 48, Session Laws 1862.

The two statutory provisions above quoted must, for the purpose of this discussion, be construed together. The phrase "along said stream," in the latter, is equally comprehensive, as to the extent of territory, with the expression "on the bank, margin or neighborhood," used in the former, and both include all lands in the immediate valley of the stream. The latter provision sanctions the diversion of water from one stream to irrigate lands adjacent to another, provided such diversion is not to the "detriment" of parties along the line of the stream from which the water is taken. If there is any conflict between the statutes in this respect, the latter, of course, must prevail. We think that the "use" and "detriment" spoken of are a use existing at the time of the diversion, and a detriment immediately resulting therefrom. We do not believe that the legislature intended to prohibit the diversion of water to the "detriment" of parties who might at some future period conclude to settle upon the stream; nor do we think that they were legislating with a view to preserving in such stream sufficient water for the "use" of settlers who might never come, and consequently never have use therefor.

But "detriment" at the time of diversion could only exist where the water diverted had been previously appropriated or used; if there had been no previous appropriation or use thereof, there could be no present injury or *"detriment."*

Our conclusion above as to the intent of the legislature is supported by the fact that the succeeding assembly, in 1864, hastened to insert into the latter statute, without other change or amendment, the clause, *"who have a priority of right."* in connection with the idea of *"detriment"* to adjacent owners. This amendment of the statute was simply the acknowledgment by the legislature of a doctrine already existing, under which rights had accrued that were entitled to protection. In the language of Mr. Justice Miller, above quoted, upon a different branch of the same subject, it "was rather a voluntary recognition of a pre-existing right constituting a valid claim, than the creation of a new one."

* * *

But this is an action of trespass; the defendants below were, according to the verdict of the jury, and according to the view herein expressed, wrong-doers * * *

---

1. *Doctrine of Prior Appropriation.* What are the rights of landowners adjoining non-navigable streams in mid-late 19th century Colorado? What institutions delineate and administer this doctrine? Is it workable? What are the factual assumptions underlying the doctrine?

2. What are the philosophical bases for the rule described by the court? Does it comport with the nature of the resources, the developing economic structure of the West, and the social culture of the place and times?

3. *Mode of Analysis.* What legal authority provides the basis for the Colorado court's decision? How does the court approach its adjudicatory function in this case? What distinguishes the court's function in this case from the court's role in *Evans v. Merriweather* and *Pierson v. Post*?

4. *The Evolution of Law.* Justice Benjamin Cardozo described the evolution of water law in the following metaphorical terms:

> Sooner or later, if the demands of social utility are sufficiently urgent, if the operation of an existing rule is sufficiently productive of hardship or inconvenience, utility will tend to triumph. * * * We have a conspicuous illustration in the law of waters in our western states. "Two systems of water law are in force within the United States—the riparian and the appropriation systems." The system first named prevails in thirty-one of the forty-eight states. Its fundamental principle is "that each riparian proprietor has an equal right to make a reasonable use of the waters of the stream, subject to the equal right of the other riparian proprietors likewise to make a reasonable use." Some of the arid states of the west found this system unsuited to their needs. Division of the water "into small quantities among the various water users and on the general principle of equality of right" would be a division "so minute as not to be of advantage to anybody." "It is better in such a region that some have enough and others go without, than that the division should be so minute as to be of no real economic value." The appropriation system built upon the recognition of this truth. Its fundamental principle is "that the water user who first puts to beneficial use—irrigation, mining, manufacturing, power, household, or other economic use—the water of a stream,

acquires thereby the first right to the water, to the extent reasonably necessary to his use, and that he who is the second to put the water of the stream to beneficial use, acquires the second right, a third to put it to use acquires the third right, a right subordinate to the other two, and so on throughout the entire series of uses.'' Here we have the conscious departure from a known rule, and the deliberate adoption of a new one, in obedience to the promptings of a social need so obvious and so insistent as to overrun the ancient channel and cut a new one for itself.

B. Cardozo, The Growth of the Law 117–20 (1924).

5. *Modern Water Law in the West.* Resource and social conditions in the West have changed markedly since the 19th century. Over the past 100 years, an extraordinarily complex system of federal, state, and local controls and subsidies have evolved to allocate increasingly scarce supplies of water. As the pressure on scarce water resources has continued to increase, and as the environmental damage has become more evident, federal and state policies have slowly changed to permit greater emphasis on water conservation and protection of watersheds. *See generally* Mark Reisner, Cadillac Desert: The American West and Its Disappearing Water (1986).

Some state statutes now restrict appropriations to protect fish and wildlife, *see, e.g.*, Cal. Water Code §§ 1253–1257, and state courts increasingly rely on the public trust doctrine to limit appropriations when public values, such as environmental protection, are threatened. *See National Audubon Society v. Superior Court*, 33 Cal.3d 419, 189 Cal.Rptr. 346, 658 P.2d 709 (1983) (the public trust doctrine requires reconsideration of appropriations rights in the Mono Basin). *See generally*, Sax, The Public Trust Doctrine in National Resources Law: Effective Judicial Intervention, 68 Mich. L. Rev. 471 (1970); Johnson, Public Trust Protections for Stream Flows and Lake Levels, 14 U.C. Davis L. Rev. 233 (1980); Selvin, The Public Trust Doctrine in American Law and Economic Policy, 1789–1920, 1980 Wis. L. Rev. 1403. Federal law—especially reserved rights doctrine—helps to ensure that water is not entirely appropriated for developmental purposes, although the courts do not always find reserved water rights. *See, e.g., Cappaert v. United States*, 426 U.S. 128 (1976) (finding reserved federal right in unappropriated water at Devil's Hole national monument); *United States v. New Mexico*, 438 U.S. 696 (1978) (federal reserved right for Gila National Forest does not include water for recreation, aesthetics, wildlife or cattle grazing). What problems do you foresee with these doctrines and the institutions that administer them? What other legal regimes or institutions would you propose?

The most recent and substantial changes have more to do with changing the means for transferring water interests than with the underlying system of appropriation. To a significant extent, the private property model has been fostered, with emphasis on promoting the trading of water. In essence, those with a use right have obtained a right to transfer such interest. *See* Thompson, Institutional Perspectives on Water Policy and Markets, 81 Cal. L. Rev. 671 (1993); Gray, Driver & Wahl, Economic

Incentives for Environmental Protection: Transfers of Federal Reclamation Water: A Case Study of California's San Joaquin Valley, 21 Envt'l L. 911 (1991). Why has policy reform taken this turn? How might such a system serve the priorities of the current generation? How well will the strengthening of private property rights serve future generations?

---

d. INTELLECTUAL RESOURCES

i. *Ideas*

Downey v. General Foods Corp.

Court of Appeals of New York, 1972.
31 N.Y.2d 56, 334 N.Y.S.2d 874, 286 N.E.2d 257, 175 U.S.P.Q. 374.

■ FULD, CHIEF JUDGE.

The plaintiff, an airline pilot, brought this action against the defendant General Foods Corporation to recover damages [of $2,800,000] for the alleged misappropriation of an idea. It is his claim that he suggested that the defendant's own gelatin product, "Jell–O," be named "Wiggley" or a variation of that word, including "Mr. Wiggle," and that the product be directed towards the children's market; that, although the defendant disclaimed interest in the suggestion, it later offered its product for sale under the name "Mr. Wiggle." The defendant urges—by way of affirmative defense—that the plaintiff's "alleged 'product concept and name' was independently created and developed" by it. The plaintiff moved for partial summary judgment "on the question of liability" on 5 of its 14 causes of action and the defendant cross-moved for summary judgment dismissing the complaint. The court at Special Term denied both motions, and the Appellate Division affirmed, 37 A.D.2d 250, 323 N.Y.S.2d 578, granting leave to appeal to this court on a certified question.

The plaintiff relies chiefly on correspondence between himself and the defendant, or, more precisely, on letters over the signature of a Miss Dunham, vice-president in charge of one of its departments. On February 15, 1965, the plaintiff wrote to the defendant, stating that he had an "excellent idea to increase the sale of your product JELL–O * * * making it available for children." Several days later, the defendant sent the plaintiff an "Idea Submittal Form" (ISF) which included a form letter and a space for explaining the idea.[6] In that form, the plaintiff suggested, in essence, that the product "be packaged & distributed to children under the name 'WIG–L–E' (meaning wiggly or wiggley) or 'WIGGLE–E' or 'WIG-

---

6. The form letter—signed and returned by the plaintiff—recited that "I submit this suggestion with the understanding, which is conclusively evidenced by my use and transmittal to you of this form, that this suggestion is not submitted to you in confidence, that no confidential relationship has been or will be established between us and that the use, if any, to be made of this suggestion by you and the compensation to be paid therefor, if any, if you use it, are matters resting solely in your discretion."

GLE–EEE' or 'WIGLEY.' " He explained that, although his children did not "get especially excited about the Name JELL–O, or wish to eat it" when referred to by that name, "the kids really took to it fast" when his wife "called it 'wiggle-y,' " noting that they then "associate[d] the name to the 'wiggleing' dessert." Although this is the only recorded proof of his idea, the plaintiff maintains that he sent Miss Dunham two handwritten letters in which he set forth other variations of "Wiggiley," including "Mr. Wiggley, Wiggle, Wiggle-e."[7]

A letter, dated March 8, 1965, over the signature of Miss Dunham, acknowledged the submission of the ISF and informed the plaintiff that it had no interest in promoting his suggestion. However, in July, the defendant introduced into the market a Jell–O product which it called "Mr. Wiggle." The plaintiff instituted the present action some months later. In addition to general denials, the answer contains several affirmative defenses, one of which, as indicated above, recites that the defendant independently created the product's concept and name before the plaintiff's submission to it.

In support of its position, the defendant pointed to depositions taken by the plaintiff from its employees and from employees of Young & Rubicam, the firm which did its advertising. From these it appears that the defendant first began work on a children's gelatin product in May, 1965— three months after the plaintiff had submitted his suggestion—in response to a threat by Pillsbury Company to enter the children's market with a product named "Jiggly." Those employees of the defendant in charge of the project enlisted the aid of Young & Rubicam which, solely on its own initiative, "came up with the name 'Mr. Wiggle.' " In point of fact, Miss Dunham swore in her deposition that she had had no knowledge whatever of the plaintiff's idea until late in 1966, shortly before commencement of his suit; that ideas submitted by the general public were kept in a file by an assistant of hers "under lock and key"; and that no one from any other of the defendant's departments ever asked to research those files. The assistant, who had alone handled the correspondence with the plaintiff over Miss Dunham's signature—reproduced by means of a signature duplicating machine—deposed that she had no contact whatsoever with Young & Rubicam and had never discussed the name "Wiggle" or "Mr. Wiggle" with any one from that firm.

In addition to the depositions of its employees and the employees of its advertising agency, the defendant submitted documentary proof of its prior use of some form of the word "wiggle" in connection with its endeavor to sell Jell–O to children. Thus, it submitted (1) a copy of a report which Young & Rubicam furnished it in June of 1959 proposing "an advertising program directed at children as a means of securing additional sales volume"; (2) a copy of a single dimensional reproduction of a television commercial, prepared in 1959 and used thereafter by the defendant in

---

7. Neither of these letters was found in the defendant's files, nor did the plaintiff have the originals or copies.

national and local television broadcasts, which contained the phrase, "ALL THAT WIGGLES IS NOT JELL–O"; and (3) a copy of a newspaper advertisement that appeared in 1960, depicting an Indian "squaw" puppet and her "papoose" preparing Jell–O—the "top favorite in every American tepee"—and suggesting to mothers that they "[m]ake a wigglewam of Jell–O for your tribe tonight!"

The critical issue in this case turns on whether the idea suggested by the plaintiff was original or novel. An idea may be a property right. But, when one submits an idea to another, no promise to pay for its use may be implied, and no asserted agreement enforced, if the elements of novelty and originality are absent, since the property right in an idea is based upon these two elements. (*See Soule v. Bon Ami Co.*, 201 App.Div. 794, 796, 195 N.Y.S. 574, 575, *aff'd* 235 N.Y. 609, 139 N.E. 754; *Bram v. Dannon Milk Prods.*, 33 A.D.2d 1010, 307 N.Y.S.2d 571.) * * * The *Bram* case is illustrative; in reversing Special Term and granting summary judgment dismissing the complaint, the Appellate Division made it clear that, despite the asserted existence of an agreement, the plaintiff could not recover for his idea if it was not original and had been used before (33 A.D.2d, at p. 1010, 307 N.Y.S.2d 571):

> The idea submitted by the plaintiff to the defendants, the concept of depicting an infant in a highchair eating and enjoying yogurt, was lacking in novelty and had been utilized by the defendants * * * prior to its submission. Lack of novelty in an idea is fatal to any cause of action for its unlawful use. In the circumstances a question of fact as to whether there existed an oral agreement between the parties would not preclude summary judgment.

In the case before us, the record indisputably establishes, first, that the idea submitted—use of a word ("wiggley" or "wiggle") descriptive of the most obvious characteristic of Jell–O, with the prefix "Mr." added—was lacking in novelty and originality and, second, that the defendant had envisaged the idea, indeed had utilized it, years before the plaintiff submitted it. As already noted, it had made use of the word "wiggles" in a 1959 television commercial and the word "wigglewam" in a 1960 newspaper advertisement. It was but natural, then, for the defendant to employ some variation of it to combat Pillsbury's entry into the children's market with its "Jiggly." Having relied on its own previous experience, the defendant was free to make use of "Mr. Wiggle" without being obligated to compensate the plaintiff. * * *

The order appealed from should be reversed . * * *

---

1. Should society bestow property interests upon people who develop good ideas? Why or why not? What requirements should they have to meet to obtain such property interests? What rights should attach to these property interests?

2.   What must a creator establish under the *Downey* opinion to obtain property interests in an idea? What goals do these requirements serve?

Problem

The Washington humorist and columnist Art Buchwald submitted an eight-page summary of a film idea entitled "It's a Crude, Crude World" to executives at Paramount. The summary described in some detail the storyline, which involved a rich, educated, arrogant, extravagant, despotic African prince who comes to America for a state visit. After a grand tour of the United States, the potentate arrives at the White House. A gaffe in remarks made by the President infuriates the African leader. A State Department officer assigned to him rebuffs his sexual advances. While in the United States, the potentate is deposed, deserted by his entourage, and left destitute. He ends up in the Washington ghetto, is stripped of his clothes, and befriended by a woman in the neighborhood. The potentate experiences a number of incidents and he obtains employment as a waiter. To avoid deportation, he marries the woman who befriended him, becomes the emperor of the ghetto, and lives happily ever after.

Paramount subsequently entered into a contract with Buchwald whereby Paramount bought the rights to Buchwald's story and concept, with the aim of making a movie, starring Eddie Murphy, to be called "King for a Day." Another person would write the actual script, but "King for a Day" was to be based on "It's a Crude, Crude World." Because of various production difficulties, Paramount abandoned the project in March 1985. In May 1986, Buchwald gave an option on his film idea to the Warner Brothers Studio.

In the summer of 1987, Paramount began development of a similar script by Eddie Murphy. In this movie—which became the successful film "Coming to America"—Murphy portrayed a pampered prince of a mythical African Kingdom who wakes up on his 21st birthday to find that the day for his prearranged marriage has arrived. Upon discovering his bride-to-be to be subservient, and being unhappy about that fact, he convinces his father to permit him to go to America for the ostensible purpose of having one last fling. In fact, the prince intends to go to America to find an independent woman to marry. The prince and his friend go to Queens, New York, where their property is stolen. They begin living in a slum area. The prince meets his true love, Lisa, whose father operates a fast-food restaurant. The prince and his friend begin to work for Lisa's father. The prince and Lisa fall in love, but when the King and Queen come to New York and it is disclosed who the prince is, Lisa initially rejects the prince's marriage invitation. The film ends with Lisa appearing in the African Kingdom, marrying the prince, and apparently living happily ever after.

Because of Paramount's "Coming to America," Warner Brothers decided not to pursue Buchwald's story. Buchwald then sued Paramount for stealing his idea. What should the court decide?

Idea theft cases are extremely common. It seems as though every hit film spawns a half dozen claims in this vein. *See* Joy Horowitz, *Hollywood Law: Whose Idea Is It, Anyway?*, N.Y. Times, March 15, 1992, § 2, at 1. If you were an independent script writer, how would you protect your ideas while trying to market them? Under what circumstances would the career damage from obtaining a reputation for litigiousness be worth it? For a description of an institutional response to the theft of idea problem, *see infra* pp. 504–06 (chapter 3); Cynthia Craft, *Hollywood's Storehouse of Scripts, Ideas, Movies*, L.A. Times, March 18, 1992, at F3 (describing the "script registry" system of the Writers Guild of America (Western Division) which allows script writers to register a copy of submitted materials for proof that a certain idea was submitted in a certain form on a certain date).

---

ii. Inventions

U.S. Constitution, Article 1

The Congress shall have Power * * *

(8) To Promote the Progress of Science and useful Arts, by securing for limited Times to Authors and Inventors the exclusive Right to their respective Writings and Discoveries * * *

Pursuant to the constitutional authorization, Congress has adopted statutes giving inventors a limited monopoly in their inventions—processes, machines, and compositions of matter. The purpose of the monopoly is to encourage new inventions; inventors generally profit from their work by selling or licensing their patent rights. Society benefits directly through the spur to innovation and disclosure of the patented invention. After the term of the patent expires (20 years after filing), the innovation becomes part of the public domain, freely available to all. 35 U.S.C. § 154. What philosophical perspective does the patent law most clearly reflect?

To obtain a utility patent, an inventor must submit an application to the Patent and Trademark Office (PTO) meeting four requirements: patentable subject matter, novelty, non-obviousness, and usefulness. The inventor must also disclose the innovation to the public in a way that would enable others to make and use the invention. While the threshold for usefulness is low, the novelty and non-obviousness standards are exacting, and the PTO conducts an independent review of the application to ensure that it meets these requirements. If the PTO grants the patent, the inventor obtains exclusive rights to make, use, and sell the innovation for a term of up to 20 years. The patent grant is near-absolute, barring even those who independently develop the invention from practicing its art.

Hughes Aircraft Co. v. United States

United States Court of Appeals, Federal Circuit, 1983.
717 F.2d 1351.

■ MARKEY, CHIEF JUDGE.

Hughes Aircraft Company (Hughes) appeals that part of a judgment of the United States Claims Court finding non-infringement of U.S. patent No. 3,758,051 (the Williams patent) by the government's "store and execute" (S/E) spacecraft. * * *

Background

Throughout the late 1950's and early 1960's, the Department of Defense and the National Aeronautics and Space Administration (NASA) engaged in an intense effort to build a synchronous communications satellite with an orbital period equalling the rotational period of the earth. The goal was a satellite moving in a west-to-east orbit with a radius of 22,750 nautical miles and having a linear velocity of 10,090 feet per second, so that it could "hover" above a fixed point on earth.

Despite huge expenditures, the government never solved the technical problem of attitude control. That problem is described as the need to orient the satellite in space, without exceeding weight limitations, while insuring that (1) its directional antennas were always pointed toward the earth, and (2) that it would obtain a reliable, adequate fuel supply from the sun.

Working for Hughes, Williams solved the problem. He created a practical system for attitude control of a spin-stabilized satellite. In the Williams system, signals sent by a ground crew control the satellite by causing a jet on the satellite to pulse at a selected satellite position in successive spin cycles, thereby "precessing" the satellite in a selected direction. Williams taught how a jet valve on the satellite's periphery could discharge gas in brief, successive pulses on command. He taught that an on-board V-beam sun sensor (vertical slit and canted slit) could collect raw data from the sun and transmit it to earth, enabling a ground crew to determine the satellite's existing and desired orientations.

When, using conventional radio signals, the ground crew pulses the attitude jet, torque is applied to the satellite and its spin axis is "precessed" parallel to the earth's axis, causing the beam of the satellite's antenna to point to the earth continuously during the 24–hour period of each orbit, and insuring that the satellite's solar cells receive maximum light from the sun.

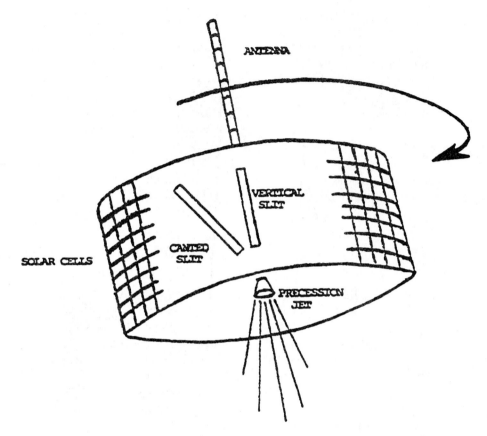

On April 2, 1960, Williams successfully operated a laboratory model, known as the "dynamic wheel," in demonstration of his invention.

Hughes disclosed the invention to NASA, seeking its participation in building a satellite with the unique attitude control system. In its "Sole Source Justification," NASA stated:

> Hughes has submitted the only proposal to NASA indicating that a 24–hour lightweight synchronous satellite having a two-way voice communication capability is practicable. This design is achieved through the use of a unique attitude and orbital velocity vernier system which allows an optimized communication system to meet the requirements for two-way voice communication within the weight limitations.
>
> Utilization of the development team and design approaches established at Hughes will result in a savings in time and money to the Government. It is therefore recommended that a sole source

procurement of a spacecraft for Project SYNCOM be awarded to Hughes Aircraft Corporation.

In August, 1961, Hughes and NASA entered a contract for engineering and construction of the SYNCOM satellite. On July 26, 1963, SYNCOM II, the world's first synchronous communications satellite, was launched and placed in orbit. On July 31, 1963, the attitude control system was successfully employed and radio transmission continued 24 hours per day.

On April 18, 1960, Williams had filed the parent application of that which resulted in the Williams patent. The examiner allowed some claims, but rejected others based on prior art and an inadequate disclosure of ground control apparatus. * * *

By amendment filed April 29, 1966, Williams canceled the rejected broad claims and inserted three independent claims that became claims 1–3 of the patent in suit. Representative claim 1 reads:

1. Apparatus comprising:

    a. a body adapted to spin about an axis;

    b. fluid supply means associated with said body;

    c. a valve connected to said fluid supply means;

    d. fluid expulsion means disposed on said body and coupled with said valve and oriented to expel said fluid substantially along a line parallel to said axis and separated therefrom;

    e. means disposed on said body for providing an indication to a location external to said body of the instantaneous spin angle position of said body about said axis and the orientation of said axis with reference to a fixed external coordinate system;

    f. and means disposed on said body for receiving from said location control signals synchronized with said indication;

    g. said valve being coupled to said last-named means and responsive to said control signals for applying fluid to said fluid expulsion means in synchronism therewith for precessing said body to orient said axis in a predetermined desired relationship with said fixed external coordinate system.

In accompanying remarks, Williams said "[t]hese claims were re-written . . . so that the claims more clearly distinguish over the newly-cited reference, McLean" and "[a]s to McLean, he does not teach or suggest the elements and relationships set out in [paragraphs (e), (f), and (g)]." Placing emphasis on paragraph (e), Williams said: "McLean's infrared telescope does not indicate the instantaneous spin angle position of his body *with reference to a fixed external coordinate system, and it does not indicate the orientation of the axis with reference to a fixed external coordinate system.* [Emphasis in original.]" On May 4, 1966, the examiner allowed the claims. * * *

On September 11, 1973, the Williams patent issued, with Hughes as assignee. On November 13, 1973, Hughes filed this action in the Court of

Claims under 28 U.S.C. § 1498, seeking reasonable and entire compensation for the unauthorized manufacture or use by the United States of the claimed invention in the government's SKYNET II, NATO II, DSCS II, IMP (H and J), SOLRAD (9 and 10), and PIONEER (10 and 11) spacecraft. The government disputed validity and denied infringement.

. . .

Issues

* * *

Whether Williams' claims are infringed by any of the accused "store and execute" spacecraft.

Opinion

* * *

II. Infringement

(A) Literal Infringement

In the "real-time" satellite disclosed by Williams, sun pulses (signals from the V-beam sun sensor) are transmitted to earth, enabling the ground crew to simulate the rotation of the satellite and to calculate the satellite's spin rate, sun angle, and ISA [instantaneous spin angle] position, *i.e.*, the measure of where the satellite is in its spin cycle at any instant of time. The sun pulses are known in "real time" and are used as reference points by the ground crew in transmitting firing signals to the jet, causing it to fire immediately and to produce precession.

In the accused S/E spacecraft, sun pulses are transmitted, but to a computer on board the spacecraft rather than to the ground. The computer calculates spin rate and transmits it to the ground. The computer also transmits sufficient information from which a ground crew can calculate the sun angle. With most S/E spacecraft, the ground crew does not know the spacecraft's ISA position. The ground crew does not need to know ISA position because the computer does and the ground crew knows the computer knows. * * *

The sun pulses present on S/E spacecraft provide reference points for firing the jet to effect precession just as they do in the Williams invention, but after, not upon, receipt from earth of spaced firing signals: (1) an "information" signal telling the on-board computer when in each revolution the jet should be fired and how many firings (one per revolution) should be made; and (2) an "execute" signal telling the computer when to begin firing.

The trial judge correctly found, and it is here undisputed, that there are only two distinctions in the structure of the claimed Williams satellite from that of the S/E spacecraft: (1) the SKYNET II, NATO II, and DSCS II spacecraft do not include Williams' means for providing to the ground crew an indication of ISA position, having substituted computer-retention of that information; and (2) in all S/E systems, Williams' means for receiving synchronized control signals for immediate execution are substituted for by an on-board computer for receiving control signals and storing them for later execution. Because the claims speak of means for "providing an indication" of ISA position "to a location external" to the satellite, and to means for receiving from the external location firing signals "synchronized with said indication," there can be no literal infringement. At trial, Hughes conceded the absence of literal infringement and predicated its case for infringement on the doctrine of equivalents.

(B) Doctrine of Equivalents * * *

The doctrine of equivalents comes into play only when actual literal infringement is not present. Under the doctrine of equivalents, an accused product that does not literally infringe a structural claim may yet be found an infringement "if it performs substantially the same function in substantially the same way to obtain the same result" as the claimed product or process. *Graver Tank & Mfg. Co. v. Linde Air Products Co.*, 339 U.S. 605, 608 (1950) (quoting from *Sanitary Refrigerator Co. v. Winters*, 280 U.S. 30, 42). The doctrine is judicially devised to do equity. "Courts have also recognized that to permit imitation of a patented invention which does not copy every literal detail would be to convert the protection of the patent grant into a hollow and useless thing," *id.* 339 U.S. at 607 * * *

Hughes, having the burden of proving infringement by a preponderance of the evidence, characterizes as "inconsequential" the differences in operation of the claimed invention and the accused S/E spacecraft. It asserts that the Williams satellite and S/E spacecraft are "obvious and exact equivalents." Hughes argues that: (1) though sun pulses are not sent to the ground by the SKYNET II, NATO II, or DSCS II spacecraft, they are retained in the on-board computer and used in the spacecraft for the same purpose as in Williams' "real-time" satellite, *i.e.*, as reference points to fire the precession jet; (2) respecting immediate and delayed firing, the Williams satellite and all S/E spacecraft require "synchronization of jet firing with spin position"; and (3) "[i]f there were doubt as to whether the S/E spacecraft are obvious and exact equivalents of Williams, the S/E spacecraft nevertheless fall within the broad range of equivalents to which the pioneer Williams patent is entitled."

Addressing the last argument first, we agree with the trial judge that Williams' invention is not of such "pioneer" status as to entitle the invention to the very broad range of equivalents to which pioneer inventions are normally entitled. McLean, not Williams, was the first to disclose the basic operational concept in which a pulsed jet is used to precess the spin axis of a spin-stabilized body. That does not mean, as discussed below, that the Williams invention is entitled to no range of equivalents. Nor is the Williams invention entitled only to that very narrow range of equivalents applicable to improvement patents in a crowded art.

* * *

Application of the Doctrine of Equivalents

The issue, as above indicated, is whether the accused S/E spacecraft infringe the claims under the doctrine of equivalents. That question turns on whether the S/E spacecraft employ substantially the same means which "perform substantially the same function" as that performed by the claimed invention, and do so "in substantially the same way" the claimed invention does, and "obtain the same result" as that obtained by the claimed invention.

In his opinion, exhaustive in respect of other issues, the trial judge treated the subject of equivalency in a single conclusory paragraph:

> There is no obvious or exact equivalent of plaintiff's means for providing an indication of the ISA to an external location in either of the SKYNET II, NATO II or DSCS II systems. Nor is there an obvious or exact equivalent of the means for pulsing the precession jet within a fixed time period after the receipt of a control signal in any of the accused store and execute systems.

The trial judge declined to supply reasoning in support of that conclusion and did not apply the "substantially the same function, in substantially the same way, to obtain the same result" guidance set forth in *Graver*, *supra*. He also declined, as have the parties here, the opportunity to define "obvious or exact equivalent." That phrase is not defined, moreover, in the case on which he relied, *Eastern Rotorcraft Corp. v. United States*, 154 USPQ 43, 46 (Trial Div., Ct.Cl. 1967), *aff'd* 158 USPQ 294 (Ct.Cl. 1968), or in the case cited therein, *Southern Textile Machinery Co. v. United Hosiery Mills Corp.*, 33 F.2d 862, 866 (6th Cir.1929). Neither the trial judge nor the government, for example, has explained why employment of the now-well-known store and execute capabilities of a computer was not an employment of substantially the same means or an "obvious" equivalent, or why the performance thereby of the functions of the Williams' claimed elements did not render the S/E spacecraft "exact" equivalents.

However the phrase "obvious and exact equivalents" may be defined, it was effectively and improperly applied here as a substitute for literal infringement, the absence of which was conceded. The failure to apply the doctrine of equivalents to the claimed invention as a whole, and the accompanying demand for "obvious and exact" equivalents of two elements the presence of which would have effectively produced literal infringement, was error.

In *Eastern Rotorcraft*, the Court of Claims afforded the patentee a limited application of the doctrine of equivalents, concluding that the range of equivalents of the claimed invention there encompassed the accused device. We hold that the trial judge erred as a matter of law in not so interpreting the scope of Williams' claims 1, 2, and 3 in their entirety, and in applying an appropriate range of equivalents to the entirety of the accused S/E spacecraft.

There are striking overall similarities between Williams' claimed satellite and the S/E spacecraft: (1) each is spin-stabilized; (2) each contains a jet on the periphery, connected by a valve to a tank containing fluid for expulsion substantially parallel to the spin axis; (3) each employs sun sensors to sense ISA position; (4) each requires knowledge of orientation relative to a fixed external coordinate system; (5) each contains radio equipment for communicating with the ground; (6) each transmits spin rate and sun angle information to a ground crew; and (7) in each, jet firing is synchronized with ISA position to effect controlled precession and thus to achieve a desired orientation. Only elements (1) and (2) are found in McLean. Clearly, the S/E spacecraft are much closer to Williams' satellite than they are to McLean's space vehicle. It is clear also that, in constructing its S/E spacecraft, the government followed the teachings of Williams much more than it did those of McLean. In following Williams' teachings, the government merely employed a modern day computer to do indirectly what Williams taught it to do directly.

The dispute as presented centers on what appears in paragraphs (e), (f), and (g), of representative claim 1:

> e. means disposed on said body for providing an indication to a location external to said body of the instantaneous spin angle position of said body about said axis and the orientation of said axis with reference to a fixed external coordinate system;

> f. and means disposed on said body for receiving from said location control signals synchronized with said indication;

> g. said valve being coupled to said last-named means and responsive to said control signals for applying fluid to said fluid expulsion means in synchronism therewith for precessing said body to orient said axis in a predetermined desired relationship with said fixed external coordinate system.

Paragraph (E) "Providing an Indication"

Based on the testimony of its expert, Arthur E. Bryson, Jr., Hughes argues that the S/E spacecraft, with the ISA position indication retained on-board, are equivalents of Williams' claimed satellite, with the ISA position indication sent to ground, performance of the function involving the ISA position being substantially the same in each. We agree. Once an on-board computer became available, as Bryson said, "any intelligent engineer designing this [S/E] system would say 'Look, I don't need to send the value of that ISA position to the ground, it's right there in the spacecraft. I'll just key my firing signal to that on board the spacecraft.'"

The S/E spacecraft are identical with the Williams satellite, except for the employment of sophisticated, post-Williams equipment (computers) to achieve attitude control in the basic manner taught by Williams. Advanced computers and digital communications techniques developed since Williams permit doing on-board a part of what Williams taught as done on the ground. As one of our predecessor courts, the Court of Claims, has thrice made clear, that partial variation in technique, an embellishment made possible by post-Williams technology, does not allow the accused spacecraft to escape the "web of infringement." *Bendix Corp. v. United States*, 600 F.2d 1364, 1382, 204 USPQ 617, 631 (Ct.Cl.1979); *see Decca Ltd. v. United States*, 544 F.2d 1070, 1080–81, 191 USPQ 439, 447–48 (Ct.Cl.1976); *Eastern Rotorcraft Corp. v. United States*, 397 F.2d at 981, 154 USPQ at 45.

That an appropriate range of equivalents of the claims extends beyond devices that send the ISA position indication to ground is consistent with Williams' patent specification:

> As an example of one means of controlling the starting time and duration of pulses to the jet control valves ... in such a way as to result in thrust during the correct portion of each spin revolution, cam-controlled contacts or switches may be used.

In the operation of the S/E spacecraft, the information that is transmitted to the ground crew, to enable them to determine and provide thrust during "the correct portion of each spin revolution," is the modern-day equivalent of sending the ISA position indication to the ground for that same purpose in Williams. Put another way, retention of the ISA position in an on-board computer, while transmitting sufficient information to enable the ground crew to use that computer-retained information to control the satellite, is the modern-day equivalent of providing an indication of ISA to ground as taught by Williams.

The government asserts only that its S/E spacecraft do not send an indication of the ISA position to the ground. That argument is clearly effective against an allegation of literal infringement, for if the S/E spacecraft did send an ISA position to the ground, literal infringement of that element of the claims would be clear. Williams controls his satellite, and the government controls its S/E spacecraft, from the ground. That Williams does so in "real time" and the government does so in a delayed reaction made possible by the advent of computers does not establish that the S/E spacecraft do not perform the same function in substantially the same way to obtain the same result.

Paragraphs (F) & (G) "Direct" vs. "Indirect" Firing

The distinction emphasized by the government between "direct" firing and its own "indirect" firing, phrased also as a distinction between "external" and "internal" synchronization of command signals with ISA position, and as a distinction between firing in "fixed" time and in "computer-set" time, rests on the government's use of modern memory circuits on-board S/E spacecraft to store commands for later use. As above indicated, mere substitution of an embellishment made possible by post-Williams technology does not avoid infringement. *See Bendix Corp., Decca Ltd.*, and *Eastern Rotorcraft, supra*. Applying the guidance of those cases, along with that in *Graver, supra*, the range of equivalents of the present claims reaches the S/E spacecraft, wherein sun pulses, though retained on-board, are derived and used in the same way as in Williams to perform the same function, jet firing, which, though "indirect," is synchronized with ISA position precisely as taught by Williams.

The S/E spacecraft and the Williams claimed satellite each have on-board means for transmitting to ground the sun angle and spin rate. In each, the ground crew determines: (1) present orientation; (2) desired orientation; and (3) where in the spin cycle and how many times the jet must be pulsed to change (1) to (2). Each system, furthermore, provides for receipt of command signals to cause firing of the precession jet. The S/E spacecraft uses sun pulses retained on-board as reference points to fire the jet. Williams uses sun pulses sent to ground as reference points to fire the jet. The difference between operation by retention and operation by sending is achieved by relocating the function, making no change in the function performed, or in the basic manner of operation, or in the result obtained.

Conclusion on Equivalents

The S/E spacecraft and the claimed Williams satellite reflect the precise circumstance envisaged in *Graver, supra,* for they perform the same function (receipt of and response to command signals from an external location to accomplish precession), in substantially the same way (jet firings synchronized, albeit later and internally, with ISA position) to obtain substantially the same result (controlled precession of spin axis in a predetermined direction to orient a hovering satellite). * * *

Accordingly, we hold that Hughes has proven that the government's S/E spacecraft infringe Williams' claims 1, 2, and 3 under the doctrine of equivalents. * * *

■ DAVIS, CIRCUIT JUDGE, concurring in part and dissenting in part.

* * *

My difference with the majority is that I would hold the doctrine of equivalents inapplicable to the S/E spacecraft involved here because, to find equivalence as the majority does, that doctrine has to be stretched far too broadly for the Williams patent.

The status and history of the patent is very important. I agree with the majority that Williams is not a pioneer patent; accordingly, it is not entitled to the broad range of equivalents allowable for pioneer inventions. In addition, the prosecution history shows that, after the citation of McLean, the Williams inventors cancelled several of their original, broad claims and substituted new claims (now claims 1–3) containing new limiting elements directly relevant to the charge of infringement by the S/E satellites: (1) means for providing an indication of ISA to an external location; and (2) means for applying fluid to fluid expulsion means within a fixed time period after the receipt of a control signal from the external location. The accused S/E spacecraft do not contain those elements which were expressly included to overcome prior art.[8] As the majority says, these new claims show that Williams did not submit claims broadly covering all ground controllable

---

8. SKYNET II, NATO II and DSCS II do not have either means; none of the accused S/E spacecraft (including the three just mentioned plus IMP (H and J)) has the second means.

spacecraft. An infringing article must embody the two elements I have mentioned, either literally or through an appropriate equivalent. * * *

The Supreme Court upheld the doctrine of equivalents in a recent patent case. *Warner-Jenkinson Co. v. Hilton Davis Chemical Co.,* ___ U.S. ___, 117 S.Ct. 1040, 137 L.Ed.2d 146 (1996). Although the Court narrowed the scope of the doctrine by requiring that it be applied to each element of an invention, not simply to the invention as a whole, it affirmed lower-court rulings finding no requirement of intent in the doctrine.

---

1. What factors determine the scope of property rights in patented inventions? Does this approach make sense?

2. The issue in this case can be framed in a number of ways:

- As in *Pierson v. Post* or the whaling norms in *Moby Dick*, the case may be seen as determining the point at which a person obtains property rights to the object of a hunt. How well does this analogy fit? How does the framing and application of a rule in *Hughes* affect the incentives to "capture" new ideas?

- Alternatively, the issue in this case can be seen as defining the scope of property rights to *use* ideas. Under a "prospect theory," a patentee would be granted a substantial scope to "mine" his or her claim. *See* Kitch, The Nature and Function of the Patent System, 20 J.L. & Econ. 265 (1977). According to Kitch, such an approach spurs creativity by (1) providing an inventor "breathing room" to invest in development without fear that another firm will preempt her or steal her work and (2) allowing the inventor to coordinate her activities with those of potential imitators to reduce inefficient duplication of inventive effort. Thus, the prospect model favors broadly awarding property rights to a single developer. Other scholars suggest that strong competition for second and third generation inventions are a better way of spurring technology. They would more tightly circumscribe the scope of patents. *See* Merges & Nelson, On the Complex Economics of Patent Scope, 90 Colum. L. Rev. 839 (1990). Which of these models seems most appropriate for satellite technology? In general?

Which of these ways of framing the issue in *Hughes* is most helpful? Can these frameworks be reconciled?

3. Should the courts use a clear rule regarding patent scope or a more flexible rule specific to the particular area of technology and industry structure? In answering this question, recall the dissent in *Pierson v. Post* and the discussion of decisionmaking institutions in *Moby Dick* and the

lobster industry. What do these examples add to your consideration of this question?

———————

In addition to common law idea protection and patent law, the intellectual property field comprises trade secret law, copyright law, trademark law, unfair competition law, and a variety of more specialized areas. *See generally* R. Merges, P. Menell, M. Lemley, & T. Jorde, Intellectual Property in the New Technological Age (1997).

Trade Secret. Trade secret laws are state law doctrines that protect against the misappropriation of certain confidential information. As such, they are more akin to traditional tort and contract law than to patent or copyright law. While protection for trade secrets has long been a part of the common law, most states today protect trade secrets by statute. The basic purpose behind protecting trade secrets is to prevent "theft" of information by unfair or commercially unreasonable means. In essence, trade secret law is a form of *private* intellectual property law under which creators establish contractual limitations or build legal "fences" that afford protection from misappropriation.

The definition of subject matter eligible for protection is quite broad—business or technical information of any sort. To benefit from trade secret protection, the information must be a secret. However, only relative and not absolute secrecy is required. In addition, the owner of a trade secret must take reasonable steps to maintain its secrecy. Trade secrets have no definite term of protection, but may be protected only as long as they are secret. Once a trade secret is disclosed, protection is lost.

There is no state agency in charge of "issuing" (or even registering) trade secrets. Rather, any information that meets the above criteria can be protected. Courts will find misappropriation of trade secrets in two circumstances: where the defendant obtained the secrets by theft or other improper means, or where the defendant used or disclosed the secrets in violation of a confidential relationship. Trade secret laws do not protect against independent discovery or invention, nor do they prevent competitors from "reverse engineering" a legally obtained product to determine the secrets contained inside. Violations of trade secret law entitle the owner to damages and in some cases injunctions against use or further disclosure.

Copyright. Although the copyright and patent laws flow from the same constitutional basis and share the same general approach—statutorily created monopolies to foster progress—they feature different elements and rights, reflecting the very different fields of creativity that they seek to encourage. In general, copyrights are easier to secure and last substantially longer than patents, although copyrights are narrower and less absolute. *See generally* Copyright Act of 1976, 17 U.S.C. §§ 1–702.

Copyright law covers the broad range of literary and artistic expression—including books, poetry, song, dance, dramatic works, movies, sculpture, and painting. 17 U.S.C. § 102(a). Copyright also covers the expressive element of computer programs. Ideas themselves are not copyrightable, *id.* § 102(b), but the author's particular expression of an idea is protectible. A work must exhibit a modicum of originality and be fixed in a "tangible medium of expression" to receive protection. *Id.* § 102(a). Copyright protection attaches as soon as a work is fixed. There is no examination by a governmental authority, although the Copyright Office registers copyrightable works. Such registration is no longer required for a copyright to be valid, but U.S. authors must register their works before filing an infringement suit. *Id.* §§ 408–412. A copyright lasts for the life of the author plus 50 years, or a total of 75 years in the case of entity authors. *Id.* § 302.

The breadth and ease of acquisition of copyright protection are balanced by the more limited rights copyright law confers. Ownership of a valid copyright protects a copyright holder from unauthorized copying, public performance, and display, and it entitles the holder to make derivative works and control sale and distribution of the work. *Id.* § 106. These rights, however, are limited in a number ways. For example, others may make "fair use" of the material protected, which is determined by a balancing test. *Id.* § 107; *see infra*, Chapter III. The Copyright Act also establishes compulsory licensing for musical compositions and cable television. *Id.* §§ 111, 115.

Copyright law protects only against copying, hence independent creation of a copyrighted work does not violate the Act. This means that copyright law must have some mechanism to determine when a work has been copied illegally. While in rare cases direct proof of copying may be available, usually it is not. In its place, courts infer copying from proof that the defendant had *access* to the plaintiff's work combined with evidence that the two works are *substantially similar*.

Trademark/Trade Dress. Trademarks are also protected by federal statute, although the source of constitutional authority is different from the Patent and Copyright Acts. Federal power to regulate trademarks and unfair competition stems from the Commerce Clause, which authorizes Congress to regulate interstate commerce. Unlike patent and copyright protection, trademark law grew not out of a desire to stimulate particular types of economic activity, but to protect consumers in a world of mass merchandising from unscrupulous sellers attempting to fly under the banner of a well-known logo or identifying symbol. Only in recent years has trademark law begun to embrace the incentive, personhood, and natural rights rationales.

The Lanham Act, 15 U.S.C. §§ 1051–1127, protects words, symbols and other attributes which serve to identify the nature and source of goods or services. Examples of marks protectible under the Lanham Act include corporate and product names, symbols, logos, slogans, pictures and designs, product configurations, colors, and even smells. Not all such marks are protectible, however. To receive trademark protection, an identifying mark need not be new or previously unused, but it must represent to consumers the source of the good or service identified. It cannot be merely a description of the good itself, or a generic term for the class of goods or services offered. Further, the identifying mark may not be a functional element of the product itself, but must serve a purely identifying purpose. Finally, trademark protection is directly tied to the use of the mark to identify goods in commerce. Trademarks do not expire on any particular date, but continue in force until they are "abandoned" by their owner or become unprotectable (*e.g.*, by becoming generic).

The PTO examines trademark applications and issues trademark registrations that confer significant benefits upon the registrants, including: *prima facie* evidence of validity; constructive notice to others of the claim of ownership; federal subject matter jurisdiction; incontestability after five years, which confers exclusive right to use the mark; authorization to seek treble damages and attorney fees; and the right to bar importation of goods bearing the infringing mark. Federal trademark registration, however, is not necessary to obtain trademark protection. A trademark owner who believes that another is using the same or a similar mark to identify competing goods can bring suit for trademark infringement. Unlike patent and copyright law, the outcome does not turn on the similarity between the marks or on whether the defendant copied the mark from the trademark owner. Rather, infringement turns on whether consumers are likely to be confused as to the origin of the goods or services. If so, the trademark owner is entitled to an injunction against the confusing use, damages for past infringement, and in some cases the seizure and destruction of infringing goods.

Problems

1. A botanist exploring a remote region of a small tropical country stumbled across a field full of beautiful flowers, the likes of which he had never seen. He plucked one of the flowers and, when he returned to his encampment that night, he showed it to a fellow scientist, who is an expert in the biochemistry of plants. After smelling and tasting the flower, the biochemist said that it smelled faintly like Substance P, a medicine widely used to treat a variety of serious diseases. She remarked that Substance P is easy to detect; it turns a bright yellow when exposed to intense heat. The botanist put the flower over the campfire that night, and sure enough it turned bright yellow.

Upon his return home, the botanist worked for months to isolate the active ingredient in the flower, a chemical that is a close structural analog to Substance P. In various lab experiments he discovered that the chemical shows an amazing degree of activity in fighting many of the same diseases that Substance P is used to treat.

    A. What rights should the botanist have in the new chemical? Should his rights prevent anyone else from going back to the tropical country, finding the flower, and isolating the active chemical he discovered?

B.   What if a highly skilled chemist could have isolated the active ingredient in less than a day, at essentially no cost, instead of the months it took the botanist? Should this affect the existence or scope of the botanist's rights in the substance?

C.   Assume indigenous people in the tropical country have been using this same flower to treat various diseases for centuries. Should they have the right to receive a portion of the botanist's profits from the sale of the new chemical? Should he be able to charge these indigenous people a royalty for using their traditional medicines based on the chemical isolate?

D.   Assume that some members of the public who come to rely on the new chemical as a treatment for their diseases become addicted to it; after using it for a short period of time, they cannot go back to preexisting treatments without serious risk of severe medical complications, even death. Should this affect the botanist's ability to remove the chemical from the market if he wishes, or to charge whatever price he wants for it?

2.   Steven Simitar contracted the HIV virus in 1982. After almost a decade of minimal reaction, Simitar's doctor sent him to see a leading AIDS researcher, Dr. Illinois Jones. Dr. Jones took some blood and tissue samples from Steve for research purposes. Simitar signed a consent form authorizing Dr. Jones to use these samples solely for research. Dr. Jones discovered that Simitar possessed a cell line that resisted the HIV virus. Dr. Jones cloned the cell line and has developed a therapy that may help to treat AIDS patients. In addition, Dr. Jones is hopeful that he can develop an AIDS vaccine using products of Simitar's cell line. Should Dr. Jones and/or Steve Simitar have property rights in the AIDS treatment or vaccine based on the Simitar cell line? If so, should they have the right to exercise unfettered monopoly control over the markets for the treatment and vaccine? *See Moore v. Regents of University of California*, 51 Cal.3d 120, 271 Cal.Rptr. 146, 793 P.2d 479 (1990).

3.   The Internet has become an important and valuable means by which many people search for information. Many companies, government agencies, universities, and other organizations have created web pages to serve this purpose. A major controversy has arisen over the manner in which "domain names," *i.e.*, the addresses for web sites and electronic mail (e-mail) directories, are allocated. The National Science Foundation, which administers the Internet, contracted with Network Solutions, Inc. (NSI) to register domain names. NSI has followed a first-come, first-served approach to registering domain names. It charges $100 to register a name and $50 per year to maintain the name. Under this system, site names contain a suffix which designates the type of entity registering the name: ".com" for companies, ".gov" for government agencies, ".org" for organizations, and ".edu" for educational institutions. The popularity of the Internet has fueled a rush to register names, and many companies have been disappointed to find that their preferred domain names (often their trade names) have already been registered by others. Consider the following disputes:

- Hasbro Inc., maker of the popular children's game "Candyland," was horrified to learn that "Candyland.com" had been registered by a company that markets adult movies and sex toys and solicits members for "Club Love."

- Stanley H. Kaplan Education Center, a leading standardized test-preparation company, sought to register "Kaplan.com," only to learn that it had already been registered by one its chief competitors, Princeton Review. Princeton Review used the site to provide testimonials of disgruntled Kaplan customers, along with linkage to Princeton Review's main web site.

- Many company names have common terms, such as Sun Oil, Sun Photo, and Sun Microsystems. Because they are in different product markets, they can all maintain trademarks featuring the term "Sun." There necessarily is, however, a one-to-one relationship between a term and an internet address. Therefore, there can only be one "Sun.com," which Sun Microsystems successfully registered first.

- Domain name "prospectors" have registered hundreds of corporate and other names, including "mcdonalds.com," and have offered the names for sale on the open market. "Wallstreet.org" has been listed for $375,000; "Gratefuldead.org" for $175,000; and "Videodating.com" for $30,000.

- One individual has registered more than 200 domain names, including "deltaairlines.com," "saturdaynightlive.com," "nationalparks.com," "tourdefrance.com," "neiman-marcus.com," and "elmerfudd.com." He has sought to sell these names to interested parties.

Is this first-come, first-served approach an efficient or fair way to allocate domain names? How should these property rights to cyberspace be allocated? To what extent does or should existing trademark law resolve disputes involving domain names?

4. Manna Gray, a famous fashion model for ShiShi Cosmetics, is hired by the game show, Maze of Luck, to point gracefully at the various prizes the contestants may win. The show and Manna become household names. Knock–Off Software develops a computer simulation of the game which features a video image of a model who bears striking resemblance to Manna. Manna sues, alleging that Knock–Off is unjustly profiting from her image. What rights should Manna have? What if a t-shirt entrepreneur were to sell shirts with Manna's likeness? What if the shirt had a derogatory caption below Manna's picture? *See White v. Samsung Electronics*, 989 F.2d 1512 (9th Cir.1993); *Midler v. Ford Motor Co.*, 849 F.2d 460 (9th Cir.1988).

B. FORMS OF PROPERTY OWNERSHIP

Property rights in a given resource can be divided up in numerous ways. For example, two people may share the resource in an undivided manner (*e.g.*, as marital property), or one person may have only a limited right to use a resource (*e.g.*, a right of way) that is owned principally by another. In addition, property rights can be divided temporally, such as when one person has rights to possess and use the resource until some stated event, at which point the rights are forfeited automatically to someone else.

The skein of potential property rights requires a detailed system for classifying property ownership. The system that has evolved (and continues to evolve) in the United States reflects its roots in feudal land relationships of medieval England as well as dramatic cultural changes over the past century (*e.g.*, recognition of married women's property rights). The resulting system is neither tidy nor free from anachronism, but it does form a body of law that all lawyers must understand. These materials summarize the key historical developments that have shaped the forms of property ownership as a background for understanding the present day rules and institutions. We make heavy use of problems to develop your abilities to classify property interests within this arcane system and to apply the various rules governing property ownership competently.

1. ESTATES IN LAND

a. HISTORICAL BACKGROUND

American property law has deep roots in the English common law. Indeed, many of the property concepts and terms used in the United States today are derived directly from English practices and laws that began to take shape in the eleventh century.[1]

The Rise of the Estate in Fee Simple

The most important event in the legal history of English feudalism was the Norman Conquest of England in 1066. The singular importance of the Conquest is partly attributable to the fact that England was never subsequently conquered by another invader. The English legal culture remained secure from sudden or discontinuous changes; the only changes were those associated with the generally gradual changes in English society.

Property Rights and Obligations in Feudal England. After his victory at Hastings, William faced two problems: (1) how to control the politically decentralized country that was not rich in any particular re-

---

1. If you are interested in pursuing the relevant feudal history underlying estates in land, *see* T. Plucknett, A Concise History of the Common Law (5th ed. 1956); R. Palmer, The Whilton Dispute, 1264–1380: A Social–Legal Study of Dispute Settlement in Medieval England (1984); Thorne, English Feudalism and Estates in Land, 10 Cambridge L.J. 193 (1959); Riesenfeld, Individual and Family Rights in Land During the Formative Period

of the Common Law, in Essays in Jurisprudence in Honor of Roscoe Pound 439 (1962); Seipp, The Concept of Property in the Early Common Law, 12 Law & Hist. Rev. 29 (1994).

For a study of the growth of literacy and the use of documents in legal transactions shortly following the Norman Conquest of England, *see* M.T. Clanchy, From Memory to Written Record: England 1066–1307 (1979).

source, other than the land itself; and (2) how to maintain sufficient military strength to repel invaders. William's solution, following similar practices prevalent on the Continent, was to redistribute the conquered lands to the Norman barons and English landowners who had supported William against Harold. To control these new landowners (who were potential enemies), William retained certain ownership rights in the land. While the grantees were in many respects landowners (as we use that expression today), technically they held the land as tenants of William. In return for the land, these grantees owed William loyalty and military obligations, called the "knight services." Traitorous actions or failure to fulfill these services could result in forfeiture of the land to the king. In less serious cases, the king would seize the tenant's personal property to force compliance, a legal action called "distraint of chattels."

In accordance with Norman feudal customs, William required each grantee to provide a fixed number of knights for the king's army. To secure the required number of knights, the barons generally "subinfeudated" portions of their lands to individual knights on condition that they spend a fixed amount of time each year in the king's or baron's military service. The knights in turn repeated this process to find people to work the land. The knights often demanded a fixed amount of labor, agricultural produce, or money. These non-military tenures were known as socage.[2]

Another important form of tenure was "villeinage tenure." This tenure arose in "demesne lands," those lands that the lord did not subinfeudate. The laborers who worked and lived on these lands were called villeins.

The holders of tenure by knight service and socage were considered to have "free tenure," and the holders of these interests were called "freehold tenants." Villeinage tenure was considered "unfree" because the services required were not fixed, but depended on the will of the lord, and thus were not worthy of a free person. A principal legal difference between the two was that the freehold tenant's rights were protected by the king's courts, whereas the tenant in villeinage had protection only from the lord's manorial courts.

The freehold estates were the forerunners of our present system of land ownership. The villeinage tenure, or non-freehold estates, evolved into our modern landlord-tenant relationship.

Within a few generations, heavily armored knights became obsolete in warfare, largely because of the invention of the longbow (as the French learned at Agincourt). Moreover, the English kings, especially John, found it more convenient to maintain military strength through mercenaries. As a result, the military obligations were replaced by an annual payment of money, known as "scutage." By the fourteenth century, the amount of scutage became fixed by custom and statute; inflation gradually devalued it so that it became more of a nuisance than a serious economic burden.

---

2. In addition to tenure by knight service and socage, there were tenures of ser- jeanty (for nonagricultural personal services) and frankalmoin (for religious services).

Inheritability of Land. Immediately after the Conquest, English lands probably were not inheritable. *See* Thorne, English Feudalism and Estates in Land, 10 Cambridge L.J. 193, 193 (1959). Thus, the baron would receive from the king the right to use the land for his life, after which the land would escheat to the king. The same arrangement applied between barons and knights, and knights and farmers. This arrangement, however, undermined the economic security of families by leaving them dependent upon the continued life of a single person. As a result, by the thirteenth century, tenants were bargaining with their lords for a promise that when the tenant died, the tenant's heir would succeed to the tenant's land. The lords exacted a price for this promise, called "relief." In time, relief was required whenever the land passed by descent, from tenant to heir. The relief thus became a form of inheritance tax.

The lord's promise to accept the tenant's heir as a substitute for the tenant initially extended only to the eldest surviving son, a system known as primogeniture.[3] (In a few areas, all land went to the youngest son, a practice known a ultimogeniture.) Gradually, the promise to accept heirs as substitutes extended to female lineal heirs and collateral heirs. If the tenant had no heirs, or if the tenant had committed a felony, the land escheated to the lord. If the tenant committed treason, the land was forfeited to the Crown. The "incidents" (*i.e.*, benefits of lordship) of forfeiture and escheat were not abolished until the nineteenth and twentieth centuries.

The legal means to express the lord's promise to accept the tenant's lineal and collateral heirs as new tenants was to add the words "and his heirs" to a grant at the time of a transfer. Thus, at common law a grant "to Jones" only guaranteed that Jones could use the land during his lifetime. When he died the land escheated to the lord. This form of ownership became known as a "life estate." By contrast, a grant "to Jones and his heirs" guaranteed that so long as there were heirs who would perform the services, the tenancy continued. This estate became know as the "fee simple"; it corresponds most closely to our current notion of ownership. The life estate and the fee simple were two of the three types of freehold estates, the other being the "fee tail," described below.[4]

---

3. Although originally restricted to the military tenures, primogeniture eventually spread to the socage tenures.

4. Because reliable land records were unknown, land was transferred with considerable ceremony, both to help the participants remember the event and to give notice to other interested parties, such as the lord above the grantor. The ceremony involved making a ritual "livery" of "seisin," or delivery of possession.

Although the ritual varied from locale to locale, it went something like this: the grantor and the grantee, together with witnesses, would go to the land in question, and the grantor would hand the grantee a lump of dirt (in some areas, a branch or a knife) while stating the terms of the grant, including the words "and his heirs" if that was part of the agreement. The grantee—the proud new owner of some interest in land—usually had to do something to demonstrate this ownership, *e.g.*, work the land for some period of time. No written documents were required, although a charter might be given as evidence of the conveyance. The ritual was called "feoffment with livery of seisin." From the word feoffment we get the modern word "fee," which today designates an interest in

Feudal Incidents. As the feudal system developed, mesne lords began to derive other benefits—"incidents"—in addition to the services, or scutage, required under the terms of the tenancy, and the incidents of relief, escheat, and forfeiture already described. *See* T. Plucknett, A Concise History of the Common Law 531–45 (5th ed. 1956).

Two incidents applied only to military tenures. "Wardship" arose when the tenant's heir was a minor. The incident gave the feudal lord guardianship of the deceased tenant's minor heir until that heir became an adult. This incident entitled the lord to treat the heir's lands as his own (and thus collect the profits of the land) until the heir reached the age of majority.

The other potentially profitable incident was marriage, which gave the lord the right to approve the marriage partner of the tenant's child. Although this incident eventually extended to include male children, it primarily applied to female children. Because the husband had full control of the wife's lands, suitors often were willing to pay considerable sums to become the new spouse. The wife-to-be could refuse the marriage arrangement, but only upon payment of the established price.

These incidents of wardship and marriage, as well as the annual scutage payment, were abolished in 1660 (Tenures Abolition Act), when the military tenures were converted to socage. Thus, until the middle of the seventeenth century, the lord could expect regular profits from scutage, and irregular windfalls from the incidents of relief, escheat, wardship, and marriage.

Transference of Land. There were two principal ways to transfer land—subinfeudation and substitution. Substitution was similar to the way we transfer land today. The tenant transferred the entire interest to another person in exchange for a sum of money. Substitution, however, was not very attractive to prospective tenants because the substituted tenant would owe the same services and incidents the original tenant once owed. The mesne lords also were uncomfortable with substitution when the required services were economically substantial; they feared that the new tenant would be dishonest or less able to provide the services. As a result, lords often refused to consent to substitution unless the tenant gave the lord a substantial payment, or fine, on every transfer.

Subinfeudation, which is the creation of an interest in land in a subtenant, allowed the tenant to transfer virtually all of his interest in the land without transferring the incidents of wardship, relief, marriage, and escheat. The tenant would do this by creating an interest in land that contained only nominal services and no incidents running to himself. Although the lord was entitled to the original scutage payment while the

land of potentially infinite duration (*i.e.*, an inheritable interest).

Feoffment with livery of seisin was not the only method of transferring estates. Because the ritual was so cumbersome, the common law lawyers developed two types of feigned lawsuits to convey property, the "fine" and the "common recovery." More on these methods later.

tenant was alive, it stopped when the tenant died. More importantly to the lord, his opportunity to profit from the incidents was seriously impaired by subinfeudation. For example, when the old tenant died, the heir would not be willing to pay the customary relief for the tenant's interest (called a "seignory"), for the tenant (and thus his heir) received practically nothing from the subtenant. If the tenant's heir refused to accept the property, that interest escheated to the lord. But the lord received only what the old tenant had: a promise for nominal services and no incidents.

This situation did not last long. In 1290 a statute, *Quia Emptores*, expressly forbade subinfeudation of land held in fee simple, although it expressly permitted free substitution (*i.e.*, without consent of the lord; a separate statute, however, forbade free alienation by the Crown's tenants). This statute marked the beginning of the end of feudal property arrangements. Because of the availability of free substitution, the relationship between tenants and lords eventually became wholly economic, and the personal bond that was the hallmark of feudalism dissipated. Moreover, with the prohibition of new subinfeudation, the pyramid of land ownership that had characterized feudal England began to collapse as land escheated every time a tenant had no heirs or committed a felony.

By the end of the thirteenth century, then, feudal law had created the "fee simple," a freehold estate that was both inheritable and freely alienable. And following the 1540 Statute of Wills, land held by such grants was devisable.

The Rise and Fall of the Estate in Fee Tail

Well before the 1290 *Quia Emptores* statute, it was generally understood that a grant such as "to Jones and his heirs" created an interest in land that was both inheritable and transferable (although not freely transferable). Many grantors, however, believed that this sort of grant did not give them sufficient control over who held the interest in question. Grantors wanted a legal device to ensure that only the grantee's lineal heirs got the land when the grantee died, and that if there were no lineal heirs the land reverted to the grantor or his heirs.

A limited form of this type of grant already existed. When fathers endowed their daughters with grant of land as part of a marriage agreement, the grant was conditioned on the birth of children. Absent a live birth, the land reverted to the grantor on the couple's death. Grantors eventually extended this condition to conventional grants in fee simple. Grants were now made "to Jones and the heirs of his body," signifying the grantor's intent that only lineal heirs of the grantee were to get the property. If there were no lineal heirs, the land reverted to the original grantor.

However, the King's courts were attentive to the tenants' demands to be able to alienate the land without restriction. They readily misconstrued the language in these grants to allow the grantee to make an *inter vivos* transfer of his interest in the land on condition that a child was first born live to the grantee. That is, the courts misconstrued the expression "heirs of his body" as words of limitation when clearly words of purchase were intended.[5] If no child was born to the grantee, or if the grantee subsequently failed to transfer the land before he died, the grantor's intent was given effect. This sort of estate became known as a fee simple conditional. It was a fee conditioned on the birth of a child.

Large landowners were unhappy with this judicial sleight of hand and sought statutory relief. In 1285, a statute known as *De Donis Conditionalibus* authorized creation of a new estate in land that restored the grantors' original intent to the language and thus took away the grantees' power to transfer estates in fee simple absolute after the birth of a child. This new estate was called a "fee tail," a term that probably derived from the Norman French word "tailler," which means "to cut." A grant in fee tail literally cut the fee simple absolute into a series of "life estates," with the possibility that some day the original grantor—or his heirs (or devisees after 1540)—would retake possession of the land. The grantee could sell only his life estate; upon his death the land came back into the chain of inheritance. The grantor's residual interest in the land was called a "reversion."

This statute remained effective for almost 200 years. It generated two sources of opposition in that period. The first source was the class of grantees, who wanted the right to alienate land freely. The second source was the Crown. By ensuring that land remained in the family, the fee tail estate also ensured the continued power of the landed families. For example, even when an interest in fee tail was forfeited to the king for a felony or treason, he got only the life estate of the wrongdoer. Because of this continued concentration of wealth, these landed families proved to be a great source of political opposition to the crown. Thus, it hardly came as a surprise when in *Taltarum's Case* (1472) the king's judges approved of a means to avoid the effects of a fee tail estate, the common recovery. *See* Spinosa, The Legal Reasoning Behind the Common, Collusive Recovery: *Taltarum's Case* (1472), 36 Am. J. Leg. Hist. 70 (1992).

The common recovery was a sham suit to allow the grantee to "disentail" the grant. It was made possible by two unrelated changes in legal doctrine. First, courts allowed tenants to substitute lands of equal value for the entailed estate. That is, the fee tail tenant could swap entailed land with another owner, and the newly acquired parcel would become the entailed estate. Second, courts allowed tenants to substitute a money judgment of sufficient value for the entailed estate. Essentially, the money judgment was passed along to the grantee's lineal heirs as if it were an estate in land. Thus, if the line of heirs ran out, the original grantor would get only the judgment. The judgment was potentially uncollectible if, for example, the debtor had no money or could not be found.

---

5. "Words of limitation" is language in the grant denoting the duration of the estate, *i.e.*, the estate becomes freely alienable if there is live issue. "Words of purchase" de- note who gets the estate, *i.e.*, the grantors meant that the lineal descendants were the only persons who could acquire the estate.

Now you can see how the common recovery works. It begins with a collusive suit. A third party "C" sues the grantee of the fee tail, falsely claiming that the grantee's lands belong to C. The grantee responds by claiming, just as falsely, that he had acquired the land from someone else, call him "X," who had warranted title to the land. That is, X gave a warranty to the grantee—a promise that could make X liable in damages—that the land belonged to X when he sold it to the grantee. X would appear at trial and admit giving and breaching the warranty. The court would then award C title to the land, and award the grantee a money judgment against X for breach of warranty. This judgment replaced the entailed land. C would later reconvey the land in fee simple to the grantee, who was now free to dispose of the land as he pleased.

The grantor had little recourse so long as the courts were willing to participate in this charade. For example, the grantor could not move immediately against X and garnish his wages or seize his property to satisfy the judgment. Because the money judgment substituted for the land, and thus passed from heir to heir, the grantor had no right to collect on the judgment until there were no heirs. At that point, X might be dead or unfindable. Moreover, X often was judgment proof to begin with; in practice he was paid a small fee by the grantee and C to perform his role in the sham suit. As you might have guessed from this description, the common recovery was a great source of artificially created litigation, and thus was quite lucrative for lawyers.

Another collusive method to disentail an estate was the "fine," which became available in the sixteenth century. "A," who held the land in fee tail, would covenant to transfer the land to "B," his co-conspirator, in fee simple absolute. Upon A's failure to make the transfer, B would sue for possession. After A admitted the breach of the covenant, the parties would reach a "final accord," approved by the court, which recognized title in fee simple absolute in B. Shortly thereafter, B, who now held title in fee simple absolute, would regrant the land to A in fee simple absolute.

These two methods of disentailing were not abolished in England until the 1833 Fines and Recoveries Act. Today in England a fee tail owner can disentail his estate by deed. Fee tail estates have been abolished or were never permitted in virtually all states in the United States. In the majority of states, fee tail estates are converted automatically to fee simple estates. *See, e.g.,* West's Ann. Cal. Civ. Code §§ 763–764; West's Colo. Rev. Stat. Ann. §§ 38–30–106; 20 Pa. Cons. Stat. § 2516. A few states permit fee tail estates, but they also permit the holders to transfer the interest in fee simple. *See, e.g.,* Mass. Gen. Laws Ann. ch. 193, § 45. In a few other states, grant of a fee tail estate creates a life estate in the grantee and a remainder in fee simple in the grantee's children. R.I. Gen. Laws § 33–6–10 (applied only to devises); West's Fla. Stat. Ann. ch. 689.14. Fee tail estates thus are of almost no consequence in American property law.

b.   PRESENT INTERESTS AND ESTATES IN LAND IN MODERN LAW[6]

Interests in land can be divided along several axes. First, a property right may be either a "present" or a "future" interest, depending on whether the holder is entitled to immediate or future use of the resource. As we will see, there are numerous types of future interests (*i.e.*, reversion, possibility of reverter, power of termination, remainder, and executory interest).[7] Second, property rights in land are classified either as an "estate" or a nonpossessory interest. The nonpossessory interests involve rights to use or restrict the use of land (*i.e.*, easement, real covenant, and equitable servitude).[8] Third, estates may be further divided into freehold and nonfreehold estates. The freehold estates, with which we deal in this chapter, are the fee simple and the life estate. The nonfreehold estates are the leasehold estates.[9]

Fee Simple

An estate in *fee simple* is the type of interest that most people associate with ownership. Its principal characteristic is that it is inheritable. If continued ownership of the fee is not subject to any conditions, the interest is a *fee simple absolute*. If a fee simple is subject to a condition that could terminate the present interest, it is a *fee simple defeasible*.

Although at common law the grant had to include the words "and his heirs" to create a fee simple, such words are unnecessary today. Courts assume, absent explicit language creating a life estate, that a grant of property "to Jones" is in fee simple. Adding the words "and his heirs" does *not* give the heirs a future interest in the property.

Distribution After Death

Modern property systems allow property owners to leave their estate to heirs through testamentary disposition, *i.e.*, a will. This power came late in England because of the feudal system, but is now firmly established. At the death of a property owner, the estate goes into probate, a judicial process for establishing the validity of a will. Where a valid will exists, the court distributes the estate according to the testator's instructions. Where a property owner dies without leaving a will (or if the only testamentary instruments are invalid), the estate is distributed according to the state's intestacy statute. Under the Uniform Probate Code, the surviving spouse receives the entire estate if there are no surviving issue or parents of the decedent, but in no circumstances less than one half of the estate, with the remainder divided among the surviving issue if any, then surviving parents

---

6. Excellent sources for estates in land are C. Moynihan, Introduction to the Law of Real Property (2d ed. 1988), and T. Bergin & P. Haskell, Preface to Estates in Land and Future Interests (2d ed. 1984).

7. Future interests are discussed in the next section.

8. Nonpossessory interests are discussed in Chapter IV.

9. Nonfreehold estates are discussed in Chapter IV.

if any, then the surviving issue of the parents if any, and so forth. If there is no surviving spouse, the estate is distributed entirely to surviving issue if any, then to surviving parents if any, then to issue of the parents if any, and so forth. If no kin survive the decedent, then the estate passes to the state. (Uniform Probate Code §§ 2–101 to 103, 2–105 (1990). Analogous rules exist in community property states.

Life Estates

A *life estate* normally is created by a grant "to Jones for life," or "to Jones for life, remainder to Smith."[10] In each example, the life estate exists for the life of the grantee, Jones. In the first example, the grantor has a future interest called a *reversion*, which becomes a present interest upon Jones' death. In the second example, Smith has a future interest called a *remainder*, which also becomes a present interest on Jones' death.

Less commonly, a *life estate pur autre vie*[11] can be created for the life of another person, for example "to Jones for the life of Smith." In this example, Jones' interest would last only so long as Smith was alive. You can readily see a potential problem: If Jones died, but Smith was still alive, it is unclear who would get the life estate for the period between Jones' death and Smith's death. Jones' heirs? The grantor?

At common law, the first person to occupy the land—the so-called "common" or "general" occupant—held a present interest until the estate terminated (*i.e.*, Smith died). However, if the original grant had been to "Jones *and his heirs* for the life of Smith," Jones' heirs would take the land until Smith's death as "special" occupants. In most states today, even without the "and his heirs" language, Jones' heirs or beneficiaries under the will would take the property until Smith's death. *See, e.g., The Union National Bank of Pasadena v. Hunter*, 93 Cal.App.2d 669, 675, 209 P.2d 621, 624 (1949) (dicta); *Harrison v. Marden*, 298 Mass. 148, 150, 10 N.E.2d 109, 110–11 (1937) (heirs of the life tenant take the property unless the will expresses contrary intent); *Oak Park Trust & Savings Bank v. Baumann*, 108 Ill.App.3d 322, 327, 64 Ill.Dec. 35, 38–39, 438 N.E.2d 1354, 1357–58 (1982) (same).

10. The first life estates probably were the common law marital estates, dower and curtesy. *Dower* is the interest a wife retains in land upon her husband's death—at common law an interest for life in one-third of the lands that her husband possessed as freehold estates during the marriage. The dower interest could not be defeated by *inter vivos* transfer during his life or by will. If he sold the land, at his death one third of those lands would revert to the wife, for her life. *Curtesy* gave the husband an interest for life in all, not just one-third, of the lands that his wife possessed as freehold estates during the marriage. Again, his interest could not be defeated by *inter vivos* transfer or will.

Most states have abolished dower and curtesy. *See, e.g.*, Ala. Stat. § 43–8–57; West's Ann. Cal. Prob. Code § 6412; Del. Code tit. 12, § 511; West's Ann. Ind. Code 29–1–2–11; Wyo. Stat. § 2–4–101. States that have retained dower and curtesy treat the husband's and wife's interest identically; they usually restrict that interest to lands owned by the deceased spouse at his or her death. *See, e.g.*, Ark. Code Ann. § 28–11–305 (one-third of land owned at death); Mass. Gen. Laws Ann. ch. 189, § 1 (one-third of lands owned at death).

11. *"Pur autre vie"* is the French Norman expression for "for another life."

Life estates are often created in connection with trusts to provide economic security for the grantees.[12] For example, the grantor (known as the "settlor" in trust law), may create a trust giving the beneficiary use of (or income or interest from) the property during his life, with a remainder to the beneficiary's children. Such a grant might read, "To T, to be held in trust for B for his life." The trustee, T, holds legal title in the fee; the trustee's job is to make appropriate investment and management decisions. The beneficiary, B, holds an equitable life interest, and can use or receive the income from (but not transfer) the property.

Waste. Conflict can arise between the life tenant and the remainderman (or reversioner if there is no remainder) over the use of the property. The life tenant, for example, may want to use or exploit the property in ways that interfere with the future interest of the remainderman or the reversioner.[13] Under the doctrine of "waste," the future interest holder may seek damages, or injunctive relief when the life tenant commits waste. *See, e.g.*, West's Ann. Cal. Code Civ. Proc. § 732 (treble damages); Mich. Comp. Laws Ann. § 600.2919(2) (double damages); Ky. Rev. Stat. § 381.350 (treble damages).

The problem is deciding what activities constitute waste. The owner of a life estate should have some rights to use the land, but at the same time, he should be under some obligation to preserve the land for the remainderman or reversioner.

At common law, waste is either "affirmative" or "permissive." *Permissive waste* occurs when the life tenant fails to take reasonable steps to preserve or protect the property, such as making necessary repairs or paying certain financial obligations. In general, the life tenant must pay the property taxes and the costs of necessary repairs, and is solely responsible for improvements made at her behest. Governmental assessments for permanent improvements (*e.g.*, sidewalks) are apportioned between the present and future interest holders (the key factor is the life expectancy of the life tenant). *See, e.g.*, West's Ann. Cal. Civ. Code § 840 (taxes, repairs, and other annual charges and a "just proportion of extraordinary assessments"); Idaho Code § 55–311 (same); S.D. Codified Laws 43–8–2 (same).

If the property was granted with an encumbrance (such as a mortgage), the financial obligations are split. The life tenant must pay the interest, which is viewed as an "annual charge," and the remainderman must pay the principal. *See, e.g.*, *Stroh v. O'Hearn*, 176 Mich. 164, 179, 142 N.W. 865, 870 (1913); *Boggs v. Boggs*, 63 Cal.App.2d 576, 580, 147 P.2d 116, 118 (1944). As the *Boggs* case makes clear, if the present interest holder fails to fulfill his financial obligation and the future interest holder

---

12. A trust is a legal device by which one person holds property for the benefit of another, often a minor.

13. Judge (formerly Professor) Richard Posner has characterized the problem in economic terms: "A life tenant will have an incentive to maximize not the value of the property, that is, the present value of the entire stream of future earnings obtainable from it, but only the present value of the earnings stream obtainable during his expected lifetime." R. Posner, Economic Analysis of Law 73 (4th ed. 1992).

makes the necessary payments (usually in order to avoid foreclosure), then the future interest holder may obtain a lien on the property and foreclose on that interest. *Id.* at 584–85.

Affirmative Waste (also called "active" or "voluntary" waste) includes the intentional or negligent exploitation of resources, destruction of existing buildings, or other activities that cause permanent injury to or devaluation of the land.[14] A difficult problem arises when a life tenant (or tenant for a substantial number of years) makes extensive alterations to structures on the property that enhance the market value of the property yet change the essential character of the property, a circumstance sometimes referred to by the oxymoron "ameliorative waste." In *Melms v. Pabst Brewing Co.*, 104 Wis. 7, 79 N.W. 738 (1899), the present interest holder (a brewery that held a life estate *pur autre vie*) tore down a once-elegant mansion and graded the land to better suit its use of the land in what had become an industrial neighborhood. The future interest holder sued for waste. The court held that the life tenant may make substantial alterations to or even destroy a structure "when . . . there has occurred a complete and permanent change of surrounding conditions, which has deprived the property of its value and usefulness," and the tenant is not required under the grant to "restore the property to the same condition in which he received it." *Id.* at 15–16, 79 N.W. at 741.

Brokaw v. Fairchild

Supreme Court, Special Term, New York County, 1929.
135 Misc. 70, 237 N.Y.S. 6.

■ Hammer, J.

This is an action * * * in which plaintiff asks that it be declared and adjudged that the plaintiff, upon giving such security as the court may direct, has the right and is authorized to remove the present structures and improvements on or affecting the real property No. 1 East Seventy–Ninth street, or any part thereof, except the party wall, and to erect new structures and improvements thereon in accordance with certain proposed plans and specifications. * * *

In the year 1886 the late Isaac V. Brokaw bought for $199,000 a plot of ground in the borough of Manhattan, City of New York, opposite Central Park, having a frontage of 102 feet 2 inches on the easterly side of Fifth avenue and a depth of 150 feet on the northerly side of Seventy–Ninth street. Opposite there is an entrance to the park and Seventy–Ninth street is a wide crosstown street running through the park. Upon the corner portion, a plot of ground 51 feet 2 inches on Fifth avenue and a depth of 110 feet on Seventy–Ninth street, Mr. Brokaw erected in the year 1887, for

---

14. Although present interest holders were at one time responsible to future interest holders for the actions of trespassing strangers, modern cases limit the present interest holder's liability to those acts for which the present interest holder is at fault.

his own occupancy, a residence known as No. 1 East Seventy–Ninth street, at a cost of over $300,000. That residence and corner plot is the subject-matter of this action. The residence, a three-story, mansard and basement granite front building, occupies the entire width of the lot. The mansard roof is of tile. On the first floor are two large drawing rooms on the Fifth avenue side, and there are also a large hallway running through from south to north, a reception room, dining room, and pantry. The dining room is paneled with carved wood. The hallway is in Italian marble and mosaic. There are murals and ceiling panels. There is a small elevator to the upper portion of the house. On the second floor are a large library, a large bedroom with bath on the Fifth avenue side, and there are also four other bedrooms and baths. The third floor has bedrooms and baths. The fourth floor has servants' quarters, bath, and storage rooms. The building has steam heat installed by the plaintiff, electric light and current, hardwood floors, and all usual conveniences. It is an exceedingly fine house, in construction and general condition as fine as anything in New York. It is contended by plaintiff that the decorations are heavy, not of a type now required by similar residences, and did not appeal to the people to whom it was endeavored to rent the building. See S. M. pp. 79, 130, 131, 132, and 133. (S. M. p. 33): It is "a masonry house of the old-fashioned type with very thick walls and heavy reveals in the windows, very high ceilings, monumental staircase and large rooms." (S. M. p. 53): "Such as has not been built for probably twenty-five years." (S. M. p. 54): "Utterly impractical to remodel for occupancy by more than one family." It "was offered to a great many people for rental at $25,000 with the statement that a lower figure might be considered and no offer of rental was obtained (S. M. p. 27). Mr. Brokaw (the plaintiff) directed that the asking rental be $30,000 to start and finally reduced to $20,000. There is no demand for rental of private houses. There is a sporadic demand for purchase and sale on Fifth avenue for use as private homes. Once in a while somebody will want a private house." The taxes are $16,881, upkeep for repairs $750, and watchman $300. The taxes for 1913 were $8,950.77 (S. M. p. 92).

Since 1913, the year of the death of Isaac V. Brokaw and the commencement of the life estate of plaintiff, there has been a change of circumstances and conditions in connection with Fifth avenue properties. Apartments were erected with great rapidity and the building of private residences has practically ceased. Forty-four apartments and only 2 private residences have been erected on Fifth avenue from Fifty–Ninth street to 110th street. There are to-day but 8 of these 51 blocks devoted exclusively to private residences. Plaintiff's expert testified: "It is not possible to get an adequate return on the value of that land by any type of improvement other than an apartment house. The structure proposed in the plans of plaintiff is proper and suitable for the site and show 172 rooms which would rent for $1,000 per room. There is an excellent demand for such apartments. * * * There is no corner in the City of New York as fine for an apartment house as that particular corner."

The plaintiff testified also that his expenses in operating the residence which is unproductive would be at least $70,542 greater than if he resided in an apartment. He claims such difference constitutes a loss and contends that the erected apartment house would change this loss into an income or profit of $30,000. Plaintiff claims that under the facts and changed conditions shown the demolition of the building and erection of the proposed apartment is for the best interests of himself as life tenant, the inheritance, and the remaindermen. The defendants deny these contentions and assert certain affirmative defenses: (1) That the proposed demolition of the residence is waste, which against the objection of the adult defendant remaindermen plaintiff cannot be permitted to accomplish. * * *

Coming, therefore, to plaintiff's claimed right to demolish the present residence and to erect in its place the proposed apartment, I am of the opinion that such demolition would result in such an injury to the inheritance as under the authorities would constitute waste. The life estate given to plaintiff under the terms of the will and codicil is not merely in the corner plot of ground with improvements thereon, but, without question, in the residence of the testator. Four times in the devising clause the testator used the words "my residence." This emphasis makes misunderstanding impossible. The identical building which was erected and occupied by the testator in his lifetime and the plot of ground upon which it was built constitute that residence. By no stretch of the imagination could "my residence" be in existence at the end of the life tenancy were the present building demolished and any other structure, even the proposed 13–story apartment, erected on the site.

It has been generally recognized that any act of the life tenant which does permanent injury to the inheritance is waste. The law intends that the life tenant shall enjoy his estate in such a reasonable manner that the land shall pass to the reversioner or remainderman as nearly as practicable unimpaired in its nature, character, and improvements. The general rule in this country is that the life tenant may do whatever is required for the general use and enjoyment of his estate as he received it. The use of the estate he received is contemplated, and not the exercise of an act of dominion or ownership. What the life tenant may do in the future in the way of improving or adding value to the estate is not the test of what constitutes waste. The act of the tenant in changing the estate, and whether or not such act is lawful or unlawful, *i.e.*, whether the estate is so changed as to be an injury to the inheritance, is the sole question involved. The tenant has no right to exercise an act of ownership. In the instant case the inheritance was the residence of the testator—"my residence"—consisting of the present building on a plot of ground 51 feet 2 inches on Fifth avenue by 110 feet on Seventy–Ninth street. "My residence," such is what the plaintiff under the testator's will has the use of for life. He is entitled to use the building and plot reasonably for his own convenience or profit. To demolish that building and erect upon the land another building, even one such as the contemplated 13–story apartment house, would be the exercise of an act of ownership and dominion. It would change the inheritance or thing, the use of which was given to the plaintiff as tenant for life, so that the inheritance or thing could not be delivered to the remaindermen or reversioners at the end of the life estate. The receipt by them at the end of the life estate of a 13–story $900,000 apartment house might be more beneficial to them. Financially, the objecting adults may be unwise in not consenting to the proposed change. They may be selfish and unmindful that in the normal course of time and events they probably will not receive the fee. With motives and purposes the court is not concerned. *In Matter of Brokaw's Will*, 219 App. Div. 337, 219 N.Y.S. 734; *Id.*, 245 N. Y. 614, 157 N. E. 880, their right to object to a proposed building loan and mortgage for the erection of the proposed apartment was established by decision. They have the same right of objection in this action. To tear down and demolish the present building, which cost at least $300,000 to erect and would cost at least as much to replace, under the facts in this case, is clearly and beyond question an act of waste. In *Winship v. Pitts*, 3 Paige, Ch. 259, Chancellor Walworth, although holding that an injunction was properly refused to restrict the erection of a building upon premises where the lease did not specifically limit the use thereof, nevertheless (at page 262 of 3 Paige Ch.) said: "I have no hesitation in saying, that by the law of this state, as now understood, it is not waste for the tenant to erect a new edifice upon the demised premises; provided it can be done without destroying or materially injuring the buildings or other improvements already existing thereon. I admit he has no right to pull down valuable buildings, or to make improvements or alterations which will materially and permanently change the nature of the property, so as to render it impossible for him to restore the same premises, substantially, at the expiration of the term."

In *Agate v. Lowenbein*, 57 N. Y. 604, 607, the court said: "Had there been no license given to the defendants to do the acts of which the plaintiff complains, the injuries done to the property would have been, apparently, acts of waste, for which the plaintiff could, by the rules of the common law, have brought an action on the case in the nature of waste. (2 R. S., 384; Taylor on Landlord and Tenant, § 348, and cases.) The right which the tenant has is to make use of the property. The power of making an alteration does not arise out of a mere right of user; it is, therefore, incompatible with his interest for a tenant to make any alteration, unless he is justified by the express permission of his landlord. (Taylor, § 348.) Holroyd, J., in *Farrant v. Thompson* (5 B. & Ald. 826) defines the extent of a lessee's rights. By a lease, the use, not dominion of the property demised, is conferred. If a tenant exercises an act of ownership, he is no longer protected by his tenancy."

And at page 614 of 57 N. Y., the court said: "It is, in general, no justification for an act of waste that a party will, at some future time, put the premises in the same condition as they were when the lease was made. The question is, whether the tenant, at the time the wrongful act was done, caused an injury which then affected the plaintiff as to his reversion. * * * The tenant has no right to exercise an act of ownership."

In *Kidd v. Dennison*, 6 Barb. 9, 13, the court said: "So if the tenant materially changes the nature and character of the buildings, it is waste, although the value of the property should be enhanced by the alteration. * * * The tenant has no authority to assume the right of judging what may be an improvement to the inheritance. He must confine himself to the conditions of his lease." [the court then cited numerous cases].

The cases given by plaintiff are either cases where a prohibitory injunction against future waste has been sought and the parties have been refused the injunction and relegated to an action for damages for waste, or where, in condemnation proceedings or actions in equity, it appears that the equities between the parties are such that the technical waste committed has been ameliorated. [Plaintiff relies on] *Melms v. Pabst Brewing Co.,* 104 Wis. 7, 79 N. W. 738, 46 L. R. A. 478. * * * [It is] readily distinguishable from the case at bar. In *Melms v. Pabst Brewing Co., supra,* there was a large expensive brick dwelling house build by one Melms in the year 1864. He also owned the adjoining real estate and a brewery upon part of the premises. He died in 1869. The brewery and dwelling were sold and conveyed to Pabst Brewing Company. The Pabst Company used the brewery part of the premises. About the year 1890 the neighborhood about the dwelling house had so changed in character that it was situated on an isolated lot standing from 20 to 30 feet above the level of the street, the balance of the property having been graded down to fit it for business purposes. It was surrounded by business property, factories, and railroad tracks with no other dwellings in the neighborhood. Pabst Brewing Company, in good faith regarding itself as the owner, tore down the building and graded down the ground for business purposes. Thereafter it was held, in the action of *Melms v. Pabst Brewing Co.,* 93 Wis. 140, 66 N. W. 244, that the brewing company had only acquired a life estate in the homestead, although in another action between the same parties (93 Wis. 153, 66 N. W. 518, 57 Am. St. Rep. 899) it was held that as to the other property the brewing company had acquired full title in fee. The action for waste in which the decision of 104 Wis. was delivered was brought and decided after the decisions in the other actions. We find it there said at page 9 (79 N. W. 738): "The action was tried before the court without a jury, and the court found, in addition to the facts above stated, that the removal of the building and the grading down of the earth was done by the defendant in 1891 and 1892, believing itself to be the owner in fee simple of the property, and that by the said acts the estate of the plaintiffs in the property was substantially increased, and that the plaintiffs have been in no way injured thereby."   Again, it was stated at page 13 of 104 Wis., 79 N.W. at 740, 46 L. R. A. at 478:

> There are no contract relations in the present case. The defendants are the grantees of a life estate, and their rights may continue for a number of years. The evidence shows that the property became valueless for the purpose of residence property as the result of the growth and development of a great city. Business and manufacturing interests advanced and surrounded the once elegant mansion, until it stood isolated and alone, standing upon just enough ground to support it, and surrounded by factories and railroad tracks, absolutely undesirable as a residence, and incapable of any use as business property. Here was a complete change of conditions, not produced by the tenant, but resulting from causes

which none could control. Can it be reasonably or logically said that this entire change of condition is to be completely ignored, and the ironclad rule applied that the tenant can make no change in the uses of the property because he will destroy its identity? Must the tenant stand by, and preserve the useless dwelling house, so that he may at some future time turn it over to the reversioner, equally useless?

The facts in the above case are clearly not analogous to the facts here. Especially is this recognized from the fact that the plaintiff's dwelling house is far from being "isolated and alone, standing upon just enough ground to support it, surrounded by factories and railroad tracks, absolutely undesirable as a residence." It is located on the northeast corner of Fifth avenue and Seventy–Ninth street. Across the avenue to the west is Central Park. To the south across Seventy–Ninth street the block Seventy–Eighth to Seventy–Ninth streets is restricted to private dwellings. The residence itself is surrounded by the three other palatial Brokaw dwellings, forming a magnificent residential layout of the four plots. It may, of course, be that the situation will change in the future. The decision here is concerned only with the present.

* * *

The facts, it is seen, in [*Melms* are not] analogous to the case at bar. The law and procedure therein also contain no analogy. *Melms v. Pabst Brewing Co.* was a law action for waste claimed to have been committed prior to the action. Upon the existing facts proved at the trial it was found as fact and in equity that the claimed waste was ameliorated and the plaintiff not damaged. * * *

From the foregoing I am of the opinion, and it will accordingly be adjudged and declared, that upon the present facts, circumstances, and conditions as they exist and are shown in this case, regardless of the proposed security and the expressed purpose of erecting the proposed 13–story apartment, or any other structure, the plaintiff has no right and is not authorized to remove the present structures on or affecting the real estate in question.

———————

1.   How does the doctrine of waste limit the life tenant's rights to use her land? What guidance does *Brokaw v. Fairchild* give in applying the doctrine? Does it conflict with *Melms*?

2.   Should there be any restrictions on activities that transform the land to a more valuable use, sometimes called "ameliorative waste?" Is the grantor's intent or purpose a relevant factor? How relevant should it be that land uses in the neighborhood have changed substantially since the time of the grant?

3. How can a grantor ensure that the structures and land not be significantly altered during a life tenant's occupancy?

———————

Partition. Conflict also arises when one party—either the life tenant or the future interest holder—wants to sell the entire fee simple and split the proceeds. Historically, courts would not intervene to force a sale and apportion the proceeds. Today, however, most states permit the life tenant to petition the court to sell the property and divide the proceeds of the sale between the parties. *See, e.g.,* Alaska Stat. 09.45.260 (allowing the life tenant to petition for sale and division of proceeds); West's Ann. Cal. Code Civ. Proc. § 872.210(a)(2) (allowing the life tenant to seek partition); Official Code Ga. Ann. § 44–6–172 (life tenant may compel partition); Mass. Gen.Laws Ann. ch. 241, § 1 (life tenant may seek partition). *But see Monroe v. Monroe*, 226 Ark. 805, 294 S.W.2d 338 (1956) (interpreting Ark. Code Ann. § 18–60–401 to permit the remainderman, but not the life tenant, to seek partition). In most states, the judge has some discretion to grant or deny the petition. *See, e.g.,* West's Ann. Cal. Code Civ. Proc. § 872.710 (the court must find that partition "is in the best interests of all the parties * * * having in mind the intent of the creator of the successive estates and the interests and needs of the successive owners").

———————

Problems

1. Suppose that the grantor conveyed to "A" a life estate and also conveyed to "B" the right to possession upon A's death (a future interest known as a "remainder"). If, after the grantor's conveyance, an adverse possessor has occupied the land for the requisite period, and A is still alive after that period, what interest if any does the adverse possessor have? What would be the justification for giving the adverse possessor only a life estate for A's life? What would be the justification for giving the adverse possessor a fee simple absolute? *See Thompson v. Pacific Elec. R.R. Co.*, 203 Cal. 578, 265 P. 220 (1928).

2. Suppose instead that the property was not divided into present and future interests when adverse possession first began (in other words, the true owner held the land in "fee simple absolute"). Thereafter, the owner transferred his estate so as to create a life estate in A and a remainder in B. If the period ran while A was still alive, what interest, if anything, should the claimant have? What right of action, if any, should B have against the potential adverse possessor before the period ran?

———————

Defeasible Estates

Any interest in property may be created subject to express conditions. Upon violation of such a condition, the property is forfeited to either the grantor or a third-party grantee. Such interests are called "defeasible" interests.[15]

An important defeasible interest is the *fee simple subject to a condition subsequent*.[16] This interest is created when, for example, R grants property "to E, provided that the property is not used as a commercial establishment, and if it is used as a commercial establishment, then the grantor has the right to reenter and take possession of the property." Notice that E still receives a fee simple–"to E"–but the grant also contains an express condition, violation of which will lead to forfeiture to the grantor, R. The grantee's rights in a fee simple subject to a condition subsequent are almost identical to the rights he would have in a fee simple absolute. The only restriction on the grantee in the former case is that the grantee may not violate the stated condition.

R's future interest, which is discussed in more detail in the section on future interests, is called a *power of termination* or a *right of entry*. Note that the grant expressly creates the power of termination.[17] R's interest becomes a present interest in fee simple (and E's interest comes to an end) only when R takes some appropriate action (*e.g.*, filing a suit for ejection or physically retaking the land) exercising her power of termination. At common law there was no time limit by which the grantor must exercise her power, although the exercise was subject to equitable defenses, such as laches, waiver, and estoppel. Some legislatures have provided that the grantor must exercise the power of termination within a fixed number of years of the breach of the condition. *See, e.g.*, West's Ann. Cal. Civ. Code § 885.050 (5 years, unless the parties agree to an extension); Md. Code, Real Prop., § 6–103 (7–year statute of limitations); Va. Code Ann. § 8.01–255.1 (10–year statute of limitations).

A closely related defeasible fee is the *fee simple determinable*. This interest is created when, for example, R grants property "to E so long as the property is not used as a commercial establishment."[18] Again, E has a fee simple–"to E"–but the grant also contains an express restriction on the use of the property. The corresponding future interest in the grantor is called a *possibility of reverter*. Note that the grant does not expressly create the possibility of reverter; it is implied in the grant.

---

15.   The typical life estate is *not* a defeasible fee. A life estate "expires naturally" upon the holder's death; a defeasible interest, by contrast, is divested or cut short by some event other than the owner's death. While there may be no obvious logical distinction, it is an important legal distinction.

16.   Although this discussion focuses on defeasible fees, *any* interest can be created as a defeasible interest.

17.   Many states require the grant to include language expressly creating a power of termination. A minority of states do not require such language if the grant is clearly conditional. *E.g.*, *Fitzgerald v. Modoc County*, 164 Cal. 493, 495, 129 P. 794, 795 (1913); *Suffolk Business Center, Inc. v. Applied Digital Data Systems*, 78 N.Y.2d 383, 388, 576 N.Y.S.2d 65, 67, 581 N.E.2d 1320, 1322 (1991) ("an express reentry provision is not essential").

18.   Some states have abolished the determinable fee, converting it to a fee simple subject to a condition subsequent. *See* West's Ann. Cal. Civ. Code § 885.020; Ky. Rev. Stat. Ann. § 381.218.

The difference between the two types of defeasible fees is slight. With a fee simple determinable, the interest ends automatically (and reverts to the grantor) upon the happening of the specified event. With a fee simple subject to a condition subsequent, the interest reverts to the grantor only if the grantor takes some action terminating the grantee's interest (*i.e.*, exercises his power of termination or right of entry).

Most courts hold that the grantor's intent is controlling as to whether a grant is a fee simple determinable or a fee simple subject to a condition subsequent. In practice, intent may be difficult to discern, particularly when disputes arise years after the grantor has died. In such cases, courts will rely on relatively minor distinctions in wording. Words expressing a condition—such as, "on condition that," "provided that," and "but if"— frequently are read as creating a fee simple subject to a condition subsequent. Words expressing duration—such as, "so long as," "during," "while," and "until"—are read as creating a fee simple determinable. When ambiguity remains, the courts will construe the grant as a fee simple subject to a condition subsequent; with this construction, the grantee's expectations are less likely to be disrupted by a later claim.

A third type of defeasible fee is the *fee simple subject to an executory limitation*. This interest is created when R grants the property "to E, but if E should use alcohol on the property, then to X." E's interest is virtually identical to the corresponding interest in a fee simple determinable. In this example, the grantor, R, has no future interest; X's future interest is called an *executory interest*. The executory interest is similar to the possibility of reverter. There is no need to "exercise" the power; upon a violation of the condition, X's interest automatically becomes a present interest even if E is still in possession.

Rules of Construction. Courts are uncomfortable with defeasible fees because the land is forfeited if the grantee violates the condition; the court has no discretion. Forfeiture not only can disrupt long-settled expectations, it also does not always seem to fulfill the grantor's intent.

For example, if a grant made in 1900 provided that "It is the understanding of the parties to this conveyance that the land is conveyed solely for the purpose of being used for the construction and maintenance of a public school," the grantor clearly wanted the school board to build and maintain a school on the property. But it is difficult to be confident how long the grantor wanted the school board to maintain a school (*e.g.*, did he want a school until the 21st century?), or whether the grantor really intended forfeiture if the school board concluded 100 years later that a school was no longer needed at that location. Moreover, changed circumstances and the lapse of time can render the grantor's intent obsolete or impractical.

As a result, courts and legislatures have adopted rules of construction to restrict defeasance. *See* West's Ann. Cal. Civ. Code § 1442 ("A condition involving forfeiture must be strictly interpreted against the party for whose benefit it is created."); Mont. Code Ann. 28–1–408; *Rowell v. Gulf, M. & O.R. Co.*, 248 Ala. 463, 465, 28 So.2d 209, 211 (1946) (conditions "will be construed strictly and will be most strongly construed against the grantor'').

First, a court will inquire whether the language is "precatory." Precatory language denotes only a request or a desire, such as, "the grantor wants" or "the grantor wishes." Precatory language is legally unenforceable. For example, in *In re Will of Saulpaugh*, 15 Misc.2d 856, 858, 180 N.Y.S.2d 623, 625 (1958), the court held that a testamentary provision that the property was "to be used as a Veteran's Home" was "precatory (a recommendation) in nature and does not restrict the prior words of absolute devise."

Second, if the language in the grant is not precatory, the court will ask whether it clearly is a condition, *i.e.*, a defeasible interest. If not, the court will construe the language as a covenant. *See, e.g., Rosecrans v. Pacific Elec. Ry. Co.*, 21 Cal.2d 602, 605, 134 P.2d 245, 246 (1943) (a deed restriction will be construed as a covenant unless there is "clear and unmistakable" evidence that the parties intended to create a condition subsequent); *In re Conference of Congregational and Christian Churches*, 352 Pa. 470, 474, 43 A.2d 1, 3 (1945) (because the law "prefers the free and untrammeled use of property" ambiguous restrictions are construed as a covenant rather than a condition); *Kinney v. State*, 238 Kan. 375, 380, 710 P.2d 1290, 1295 (1985). The distinction is critical. A covenant is a legally enforceable promise to do or to refrain from doing something with some land.[19] The remedy for breach of the covenant is damages or, if damages are inadequate, an injunction to obey the terms of the promise. In many cases, damages are nominal and the equitable defenses of laches, waiver, unclean hands, estoppel, and changed conditions prevent a court from issuing an injunction. Violation of a condition, by contrast, results in forfeiture and there are no equitable defenses.

Whereas construction of the document as a defeasible interest leaves the court virtually no flexibility if the condition is violated (the interest must be forfeited), construction as a covenant allows the court much more room to shape appropriate relief through equitable principles.

Finally, in those states that have the fee simple determinable in addition to the fee simple subject to a condition subsequent, courts have a constructional preference for the latter since forfeiture is not automatic. *See, e.g., Oldfield v. Stoeco Homes*, 26 N.J. 246, 257, 139 A.2d 291, 297 (1958); *Storke v. Penn Mutual Life Ins. Co.*, 390 Ill. 619, 623, 61 N.E.2d 552, 555–56 (1945); *State v. Berklund*, 217 Mont. 218, 223, 704 P.2d 59, 61 (1985).

---

19. Normally, a covenant is denoted by the expressions "the parties agree," "the grantee covenants," or "the grantee promises." But, as explained in the text, a court will also construe ambiguous language as a covenant rather than a condition.

1. What is meant by a "present interest" in property? Does anyone have a "future interest" in a fee simple absolute? Suppose the owner of property owned in fee simple signed a will devising the property to her nephew. Would the nephew have a future interest?

2. Are there any present rights involved in a future interest? Can you identify some ways in which the owner of a future interest might be able to protect her interest now?

3. How should a court apportion costs (*e.g.*, repairs, mortgage payments, property taxes, assessments, and improvements) between the present interest holder and the future interest holder?

Fitzgerald v. Modoc County

Supreme Court of California, 1913.
164 Cal. 493, 129 P. 794.

■ HENSHAW, J.

In its form, this is a simple action to quiet title, brought against the county of Modoc and T. F. Dunaway; the complaint alleging title in plaintiff to nine acres of land in the county of Modoc, and asserting that the defendants set up some claim of right or title thereto. The county of Modoc disclaimed. Defendant Dunaway answered, alleging title in himself. The findings declare plaintiff to be the owner of the land; that Dunaway's claim is without right; and judgment followed accordingly. Defendant Dunaway appeals.

By the evidence, it appears that the action is in fact one to enforce a forfeiture upon breach by the grantee, the county of Modoc, of an asserted condition subsequent, contained in a deed to the land made by plaintiff to the county of Modoc. * * *

Plaintiff made a deed to the county of Modoc, which conveyed, by appropriate description, the land here in controversy, and contained immediately following the description the following clause: "To be used as and for a county high school ground and premises, for the county of Modoc, state of California." Evidence is lacking as to whether or not the land was ever used for the indicated purpose; but the breach of the asserted condition subsequent rests upon the fact that admittedly the county of Modoc did convey this land to the defendant Dunaway.

It is fundamental that conditions subsequent, tending to restrict and defeat an estate, are not favored. They can be created only by apt and appropriate language, which *ex proprio vigore* establishes that only a conditional estate was conveyed; and, when such a condition is shown to have been created, the rule of construction is that of strictness against the grantor and in favor of the holder of the estate. Generally speaking, the apt and appropriate words, evidencing that the grant is on condition subsequent, are found in a provision for forfeiture and right of re-entry.

"Reciting in a deed that it is in consideration of a certain sum, and that the grantee is to do certain things, is not an estate upon condition, not being in terms upon condition, nor containing a clause of re-entry or forfeiture." 2 Washburn, Real Property, 4, 8; *Cullen v. Sprigg*, 83 Cal. 56, 23 Pac. 222. Of course, where the language employed declares a condition and imports a forfeiture, a clause of re-entry is not necessary. *Papst v. Hamilton*, 133 Cal. 631, 66 Pac. 10; *Behlow v. Southern Pacific R. R. Co.*, 130 Cal. 16, 62 Pac. 295; *Hawley v. Kafitz*, 148 Cal. 393, 3 L. R. A. (N. S.) 741, 113 Am. St. Rep. 282; *Cleary v. Folger*, 84 Cal. 316, 24 Pac. 280, 18 Am. St. Rep. 187; *Quatman v. McCray*, 128 Cal. 285, 60 Pac. 855. Under no decision of this or any other court, within our knowledge, has language such as is here used ever been construed to create a condition subsequent. At the least, it is but a declaration of the purpose for which the grantor expected the land would be used. At the most, it is but a covenant. The cases from this court, which respondent contends support his argument that this language created a condition subsequent, are far from sustaining him. In *Parsons v. Smilie*, 97 Cal. 647, 32 Pac. 702, the language of the deed was: "This deed is given and accepted on the following conditions, which are to be binding on the party of the second part, his heirs and assigns forever, to wit, * * * and a failure to comply with the same will render this conveyance null and void, and said premises shall revert to said first party." Here was a clear and complete condition subsequent. In *Papst v. Hamilton, supra*, the conveyance was "upon the conditions, however, that the premises shall be used solely," etc., "and for no other purpose whatever." The indicated purpose was for the maintenance of a college or academy. There had been a failure and abandonment of the premises, and the grantor had re-entered and taken possession of them. It was clear that the estate was created upon condition. There had been an actual re-entry, and the decision of this court was simply to the effect that, under these circumstances, plaintiff is "in a position to maintain his action for the cancellation of the deed and the quieting of his title." In *Liebrand v. Otto*, 56 Cal. 242, an action to have declared and enforced a forfeiture, the declaration of this court is that the plaintiff had granted certain lands to the Santa Cruz Railroad Company upon certain expressed conditions to be performed by the latter. The railroad company had failed to perform, and plaintiff had re-entered. It was held that his re-entry and continued possession excused his delay in resorting to equity to remove the cloud from his title. In *Quatman v. McCray, supra*, the deed declared as follows: "And this conveyance is made upon the following express condition, namely," etc. The defense was merely that there had been no breach of the condition. We have thus briefly considered the California cases upon which respondent relies. Upon the other hand, such cases as *Ecroyd v. Coggeshall*, 21 R. I. 1, 41 Atl. 260, 79 Am. St. Rep. 741; *Packard v. Ames*, 16 Gray (Mass.) 327; *Kilpatrick v. Mayor of Baltimore*, 81 Md. 179, 27 L.R.A. 643, 48 Am.St.Rep. 509; *Faith v. Bowles*, 86 Md. 13, 37 Atl. 711, 63 Am. St. Rep. 489; *Rawson v. School Dist.*, 7 Allen (125, 83 Am. Dec. 670; *Page v. Palmer*, 48 N. H. 385; *Cunningham v. Parker*, 146 N.Y. 29, 40 N.E. 635, 48 Am.St.Rep. 765; *Sumner v. Darnell*, 128 Ind. 38, 27 N.E. 162, 13 L.R.A. 173; *Clement v.*

Burtis, *121 N.Y. 708, 24 N.E. 1013;* Thornton v. Trammell, *39 Ga. 202;* Rainey v. Chambers, *56 Tex. 17; and* Owsley v. Owsley, *78 Ky. 257—are all cases to which many more might be added, which construe language, much more pertinent than that employed in the case at bar, as being insufficient to create a condition subsequent. Here the grantor did no more than to indicate his purpose in making the deed, and the use to which he expected the land to be put. But such language is entirely inadequate to create a condition.* Mauzy v. Mauzy, *79 Va. 537.*

We are not forgetful of the principle which holds in mind the circumstances under which such a deed is made, and the fact whether or not an adequate consideration has been paid therefor by the grantor. *Ecroyd v. Coggeshall, supra; Faith v. Bowles, supra.* These facts and circumstances, of course, cannot tend to enlarge or restrict the estate actually granted. They are of value only as an aid in arriving at the actual intent of the parties. But, whatever that actual intent may have been, it must have found adequate expression in the deed itself before it can be given either legal or equitable efficacy.

The judgment appealed from is therefore reversed, and the cause remanded.

----

1.   Do you agree with the decision in *Fitzgerald v. Modoc County?* Is there much doubt that the grantor would not have given the county the land if he knew the county would sell the property to someone else? Why else would he have included the language about a school in the deed? What is the policy basis for the construction the court gives the deed in this case?

2.   Could the language in *Fitzgerald v. Modoc County* be construed as creating a covenant? If so, what would be the remedy? What are the plaintiff's damages in this case? Would there be any defenses to a claim for injunctive relief?

Problems

1.   Appellants were successors in interest to reversionary interests in two deeds. Under one deed, the original landowner conveyed 4.28 acres of land to the railroad for $1 and "in further consideration of the conditions, provisions and covenants hereinafter contained." Later the grant stated: "Provided that [the railroad] shall complete [the line] and shall also continuously thereafter work and operate the same." Under the second deed, the landowner conveyed the land under the "express conditions" ". . . [t]hat in the event of the abandonment of [the line] the land herein conveyed to [the railroad] shall revert to [the landowners]." Does either of these grants create a fee simple subject to a condition subsequent? *See Sanders v. East Bay Municipal Utility Dist.,* 16 Cal.App.4th 125, 130–33, 20 Cal.Rptr.2d 1, 3–5 (1993).

2.   In 1908 Elizabeth Kraft granted the City of Red Bluff property to be used as a public library.

> To have and to hold the said premises in trust for the uses and purposes of a public library. No portion of said property shall be used for any other purpose. If the property herein shall at any time be abandoned by the said Town of Red Bluff, or if the said property shall cease to be used for library purposes, by said Town, or shall be put to any use other than the uses and purposes, here specifically referred to, then the grant and conveyance herein made shall cease and terminate, and the title to the said property and all the improvements thereon shall at once revert to the party of the first part or to her heir or assigns.

The city so used the property until 1986, at which time the city concluded that it needed a larger, more modern building for its library. The city removed the books from the Kraft property to another building, which it deemed more suitable for a library. The city leased the Kraft property to the Tehama County Literacy Council, a nonprofit corporation that teaches reading skills to illiterate adults.

In 1987, Herbert Kraft Walton, Elizabeth Kraft's sole heir, sued Red Bluff to recover the property. The city defended on the ground that conditions had changed so much that a court should exercise its equitable powers to hold that the city is not bound by the condition and to deny Walton's claim.

What type of interest does Walton own? Who should prevail in the suit *Walton v. City of Red Bluff? See Walton v. City of Red Bluff*, 2 Cal.App.4th 117, 134, 3 Cal.Rptr.2d 275, 286 (1991).

––––––––––––

Classifying Present Interests. An essential skill of lawyering is the ability to apply complex classification schemes accurately. It arises not just in understanding the common law, but throughout the practice of law, especially in interpreting complex regulatory and tax statutes and implementing regulations. The estates in land system provides a good opportunity to begin to develop this skill. Mastering the classification of present interests also is essential to classify future interests, which are the basis for the law of wills and trusts. As we will see in the next section, future interests flow from present interests along designated lines. Therefore, when you successfully classify present interests, you will be far along the path of classifying future interests. And if you can do that, you have an important leg up on applying the Rule Against Perpetuities, one of the more notorious challenges of the first year of law school (and the key to fully appreciating the plot in the film *Body Heat*).

The following chart represents the main elements of present interests—how the interests are created (*i.e.*, the key language) and their principal attributes. Use this chart to answer the questions that follow.

	FSA Fee Simple Absolute	Defeasible Fee Interests			Life Estate	Landlord/ Tenant	Fee Tail
PRESENT INTERESTS							
		FSD Fee Simple Determinable	FSSCS Fee Simple Subject to Condition Subsequent	FSSEL Fee Simple Subject to to an Executory Limitation		Concurrent	
creation:	to B and his heirs (old) to B (modern)	• so long as • while • until • during [note: abolished in some states, becomes FSSCS]	1. **Conditional** • provided • however, if • but if • on condition that 2. **Express Reservation** by grantor of right of entry or power of termination	same as FSD & FSSCS, except shifts from grantee or springs from grantor to third party	ordinary pur autre vie	• term of years • periodic • at will • joint • in common • by entirety • community property	to B and the heirs of his body [note: treated as FSA in most states]
attributes •forfeiture	none	automatic	not automatic	automatic	automatic	varies	upon failure of issue
• transfer	freely	freely	freely	freely	freely (but can't pass by will or intestacy)	varies (transfers of leaseholds and marital property more likely subject to restriction)	only a life interest

---

Problems: Present Interests

Answer the questions and classify the interests created by each of the following grants:

1.   O conveys Blackacre "to A and his heirs." A has one child, C. Blackacre is oil-producing land, and A is using it in a fashion that maximizes his short-term profit to the detriment of future owners of the land. Can C, who is A's heir apparent, enjoin A?

2.   O conveys Blackacre "to A for life, remainder to B." A sells his interest in Blackacre to X. X dies intestate while A is still alive. Who has the immediate right to occupy Blackacre? [handwritten: X heir's hare until A dies then B gets]

3.   O conveys "to A for life or until she goes to law school." What are O's and A's interests immediately after the conveyance?

4.   O conveys Blackacre "to A so long as Blackacre is used only for school purposes." What are A's and O's interests immediately after the conveyance?

5.   O conveys Blackacre "to A on the express condition that Blackacre shall be used only for school purposes, and if it ceases to be used for those purposes then O shall have the right to enter and terminate A's interest." What are A's and O's interests immediately after the conveyance?

6.   O conveys Blackacre "to A so long as A uses the land for school purposes, then to C." What are O's, A's and C's interests immediately after the conveyance?

7. O conveys Blackacre "to A, and it is O's expressed desire that the land be used only for school purposes." What are O's and A's interests immediately after the conveyance?

8. O conveys Blackacre "to A, it being understood and agreed between them that the land will only be used for school purposes." What are O's and A's interests immediately after the conveyance?

9. O conveys Blackacre "to A, subject to the condition that the land will automatically be forfeited to O in the event it is used for other than school purposes, and O shall have the right to enter and terminate A's interest." What are O's and A's interests immediately after the conveyance?

---

c. FUTURE INTERESTS IN LAND

A future interest entitles the holder to possession of the land at some time in the future. Although the holder does not have the right to present possession, he does have a present right to protect the property (waste) and to petition the court to force a sale of the entire estate (partition). Future interests can be created in the grantor or in a grantee, including unidentified grantees. We will take up these interests separately.

Future Interests in Grantors

There are three kinds of future interests in grantors: the *reversion*, the *power of termination*, also called the right of entry (or "right of reentry"), and the *possibility of reverter*.

A *reversion* is the residual future interest left in a grantor (or testator or successor) where she has conveyed less than the entire present interest. The reversion becomes a present interest on the termination of the interest granted or devised. For example, if R (who owns a present interest in a fee simple absolute estate) transfers a life estate to E ("to E for life"), R retains a reversion, which will become a present interest in fee simple when E dies. We say that R has "a reversion in a fee simple absolute." Note that the grantor's future interest exists by operation of law; there is no need to provide explicitly for the grantor's reversion in the grant or will. As with most other future interests, reversions are alienable, devisable, and descendible. *See, e.g.,* West's Ann. Cal. Civ. Code § 699; Official Code Ga. Ann. § 44–5–40; N.Y.—McKinney's Est. Powers & Trusts Law § 6–5.1.

The *power of termination* allows a grantor to terminate an interest to enforce a condition subsequent in a grant. For example, if R grants his present interest in a fee simple absolute "to E on condition that the property is not used as a commercial establishment, and if the property is used as a commercial establishment R has the right to reenter and take the property," R's future interest is called a power of termination. It is possible that the interest will never mature into a present interest. In most states, the grant must contain an express power of termination. In most states, the power of termination is descendible and devisable, but for historical reasons that have no relevance today, it is not alienable. *Restatement of Property* § 160, cmt. a. Because the grantee's interest is not automatically forfeited, but only when the grantor exercises his power of termination, the statute of limitations to bring a suit for ejection or to quiet title does not begin to run until the grantor exercises his right.

The *possibility of reverter* arises in the grantor when she grants a determinable interest. *See, e.g.,* N.Y.—McKinney's Est. Powers & Trusts Law § 6–4.5; *Emrick v. Bethlehem Township*, 506 Pa. 372, 378, 485 A.2d 736, 739 (1984). For example, if R grants "to E so long as the property is never used as a commercial establishment," R has a possibility of reverter even though the grant does not explicitly create the interest. The possibility of reverter is alienable, descendible, and devisable in most states.[20] Because the grantee's interest is forfeited automatically upon violation of the condition, the statute of limitations for the grantor to exercise his rights begins to run immediately upon violation of the condition.

Future Interests in Grantees[21]

There are two types of future interests that can be created in individuals other than the grantor—remainders and executory interests. Common law courts carefully distinguished remainders and executory interests based on the nature of the preceding estate; to a substantial degree, the importance of the distinction has diminished or even disappeared.[22] *See, e.g.,* West's Ann. Cal. Civ. Code § 769 (defining all future interests in third parties as remainders); Mont. Code Ann. § 70–15–211 (same); S.D. Codified Laws 43–9–4 (same). Nonetheless, the common law terminology and classifications remain widely used.

A *remainder* is the interest in a third party that immediately follows the "natural" expiration of the preceding interest.[23] For example, if a grant of a present interest in a fee simple absolute reads "to Jones for life and then to Smith," Smith's interest, which follows the expiration of a life estate, is called a remainder. The key is that Jones' interest ends naturally (*i.e.,* by her death) and is not cut short by some other event (*i.e.,* violation

---

20. *But see* Neb. Rev. Stat. § 76–299 (neither the possibility of reverter nor the power of termination is alienable or devisable).

Some states have abolished the possibility of reverter, converting it to a power of termination. *See, e.g.,* West's Ann. Cal. Civ. Code § 885.020; Ky. Rev. Stat. 381.218.

21. Excellent sources for future interests are C. Moynihan, Introduction to the Law of Real Property (2d ed. 1988); T. Bergin & P. Haskell, Preface to Estates in Land and Future Interests (2d ed. 1984).

22. Executory interests and *contingent* remainders today are quite similar. Rules that applied only to contingent remainders (Rule of Destructibility of Contingent Remainders and Rule in Shelley's Case) have been abolished almost everywhere. The Rule Against Perpetuities applies to both interests. Both interests are alienable, devisable, and descendible.

23. The Restatement says that a remainder is "any future interest limited in favor of a transferee in such a manner that it can become a present interest upon the expiration of all prior interests simultaneously created, and cannot divest an interest except an interest left in the transferor." *Restatement of Property* § 156(1).

of a condition). For most purposes, a remainder is the future interest in a third party that immediately follows the end of a life estate.

If, by contrast, the grant had read "to Jones so long as no one uses alcohol on the property, and then to Smith," there is no natural expiration of Jones' interest; it could go on forever (that is, his successors could own the land, subject to the condition). The use of alcohol, however, would "cut short" Jones' interest or "divest" her of her interest. In this second example, Smith has an *executory interest*. Similarly, if the grant was "to Smith, when he reaches 21," there is no precedent estate that expires naturally. Rather, the grant may cut short the grantor's interest if some specified event occurs in the future (Smith turning 21). Smith thus has an executory interest in this example as well.

i. Remainders

Remainders are classified as either *contingent* or *vested*. The distinction between contingent and vested remainders has little to do with the certainty that the interest holder will come into possession of the property some day; some vested remainders are unlikely to come into the remainderman's actual possession, and some contingent remainders are highly likely to become possessory.

Contingent Remainder. A remainder is *contingent* if either (1) the identity of the remainderman is unknown (*e.g.*, unborn children); or (2) the remainder is subject to a "condition precedent." A condition precedent is an express condition in the grant that must occur before the potential interest can take possession of the property. If the remainder is not contingent, it is vested. *See, e.g.*, Ala. Code § 35–4–211 ("A vested remainder is one limited to a certain person at a certain time or upon the happening of a necessary event. A contingent remainder is one limited to an uncertain person or upon an event which may or may not happen."); Ga. Code Ann. § 44–6–61 (same).

Consider the following examples. In classifying the interests, begin with the present interest and then move to the future interests. In each case, assume the grantor has a present interest in a fee simple absolute.

Example 1: "to Jones for life, then to Jones' children alive at his death." Jones has no children at the time of the grant.

Jones has a life estate. The children have remainders in a fee simple absolute; their interests immediately follow the end of the preceding life estate. They have contingent remainders both because their identities are not currently known (they are not yet born), and because there is a condition precedent (that they survive the life tenant).

Example 2: "to Jones for life, then to Smith if Smith survives Jones, otherwise to Brown."

Jones has a life estate. Smith has a remainder because his interest immediately follows the end of a life estate. It is a contingent remainder because of the condition precedent that he survive Jones. Similarly, Brown has a contingent remainder, contingent on Smith not surviving Jones.

Some things that may look like conditions precedent, in fact are not conditions precedent, and thus do not create contingent remainders. Consider the following examples.

Example 3: "to Jones for life, then to Smith."

The identity of the remainderman, Smith, is ascertained, and there is no condition precedent.[24] Thus, Smith has a vested remainder.

Example 4: "to Jones for life, and if Jones dies then to Smith."

This language does not create a contingent remainder in Smith. Adding unnecessary words ("and if Jones dies") does not convert a vested remainder to a contingent remainder, even though the grant ostensibly includes a condition precedent. Thus, as in the preceding example, Smith has a vested remainder.

Example 5: "to Jones for life, and then to Smith if Smith survives Jones."

This grant, unlike the grants in Examples 3 and 4, creates a contingent remainder in Smith because this grant has added an express condition that Smith survive Jones.

Vested Remainder. If a remainder meets neither of the criteria to be a contingent remainder, it must be a vested remainder. Vested remainders are subdivided into three categories: *indefeasibly vested remainders*; *vested remainders subject to open*; and *vested remainders subject to complete divestment*.

A vested remainder is an *indefeasibly vested remainder* if there is no condition subsequent specified in the grant that might result in the interest going to someone else. *E.g.*, "to Jones for life, then to Smith." At the expiration of the preceding estate (*i.e.*, Jones' life estate), Smith, or his successors, will come into possession of the property.

The *vested remainder subject to open* (also called a vested remainder subject to partial divestment or partial defeasement) involves grants to a class that can potentially expand in number, such as the class of the grantor's children. To characterize the interests in a class gift, you must look not only at the words of the grant, but also at the surrounding facts.

Example 6: "to Albert for life, then to Albert's siblings." Albert has one sibling, Belinda, at the time of the grant, and his parents are still alive.

Belinda's interest is a remainder because it will become possessory immediately after the end of Albert's life estate. It is a vested remainder

---

24. The conclusion that there is no condition precedent in this example assumes that survival is not an implied condition precedent in the grant. Most courts will not imply a condition of survival. *See Estate of Stanford*, 49 Cal.2d 120, 315 P.2d 681 (1957); *Lytle v. Guilliams*, 241 Iowa 523, 41 N.W.2d 668 (1950); *In re Cora P. Falconer Estate*, 109 N.H. 460, 254 A.2d 827 (1969). In other words, if Smith predeceased Jones, Smith's heirs or devisees would acquire the remainder and take possession upon Jones' death.

(the remainderman's identity is known, and there is no condition precedent), but it is subject to "open" because the class of siblings might get larger if their parents have more children before Albert dies.[25] The unborn siblings have executory interests; their interests do not follow the life estate, but cut short Belinda's interest. *See* L. Simes & A. Smith, The Law of Future Interests § 114.

With class gifts, one must determine who is a member of the class (even though a person is a member of the class, she will not necessarily receive a portion of the property if there is also a condition precedent to be satisfied). At some point, the class "closes," and no new members are admitted, under one of two circumstances—the class closes naturally, or by operation of the rule of convenience. A class closes naturally when no new class members can be created. In Example 6, the class would close naturally if Albert's parents died.

According to the "rule of convenience," the class closes when the gift can be distributed (*i.e.*, the previous estate has terminated) and at least one class member is eligible to take possession of his or her share of the property (*i.e.*, a class member exists and has satisfied any conditions precedent). For example, suppose a testator left some property "to A's children" and at T's death, A had only two children, C_1 and C_2. If after T's death C_3 was born, C_3 could not share in the property (assuming the will does not evince a different intent; the rule of convenience is a rule of construction, not a rule of law). Because C_1 and C_2 could take possession at T's death, the class would close and C_3, who was born later, would never be a member of the class and never take possession of the property through the grant.

There are two important caveats to the rule of convenience. First, assuming that the class has not already closed, a person becomes a member of the class upon being conceived, on condition that he is later born alive. Thus even if the class closes during the period of gestation, the later-born person would be a member of the class. Second, if at the time for distribution (*i.e.*, termination of the preceding estate) there are no class members, the rule of convenience does not apply; the class stays open until it closes naturally. It does not close when the first class member becomes eligible to take possession.

A *vested remainder subject to complete divestment* arises when the grant contains a "condition subsequent" (*i.e.*, subsequent to vesting) that could divest the remainderman of the entire interest.

Example 7: "to Jones for life and then to Smith, but if Smith uses alcohol then to Brown."

Smith's interest is a remainder (it immediately follows the expiration of the life estate) and it is considered a vested remainder because his identity is known and the clause creating the remainder—"and then to

---

25. Note that if the parents were dead, Belinda would have an indefeasibly vested remainder.

Smith"—contains no conditions precedent. But note, there is a condition subsequent *in the next clause* that may divest Smith of his interest. If Smith uses alcohol (which could occur before he even comes into possession of the property), he would lose his vested interest. Brown has an executory interest, for his interest becomes possessory only by cutting short or divesting Smith's interest.

The following three examples illustrate the subtle distinction between conditions precedent and conditions subsequent. The distinction depends on the position of the condition in the sentence, either as part of the grant or in the next clause rather than when the condition actually occurs.[26]

Example 8: "to Jones for life, then if Smith survives Jones to Smith, otherwise to Brown."

Example 9: "to Jones for life, then to Smith if Smith survives Jones, and otherwise to Brown."

Example 10: "to Jones for life and then to Smith, but if Smith does not survive Jones then to Brown."

In the first and second cases Smith has a contingent remainder—in the clause creating the remainder there is a condition—whereas in the third case Smith has a vested remainder subject to complete divestment—there is no condition in the clause creating the remainder.[27]

If the condition is part of the granting clause creating the remainder (or comes in a previous clause), as in Examples 8 and 9, the condition is a condition precedent, creating a contingent remainder. But if the remainder is first created without a condition, and the condition is contained in a subsequent clause, as in Example 10, the condition is a condition subsequent, creating a vested remainder subject to complete divestment. Note as well that in Examples 8 and 9, Brown has a contingent remainder, whereas in Example 10, because some event may divest Smith of his interest, Brown has an executory interest.

Brief mention should be made of the remainderman's rights to protect his interest. In addition to actions against the present interest holder for waste and apportionment of expenses, the remainderman has a right against third parties who may permanently damage the property. *See, e.g.,* Alaska Stat. § 34.50.010; Cal. Civ. Code § 826; Idaho Code § 55–306; Okla. Stat. tit. 60, §§ 60, 63. The remainderman, however, cannot maintain an

---

26. Also keep in mind that courts prefer to construe remainders as vested rather than contingent. *See, e.g., In re Estate of Stanford*, 49 Cal.2d 120, 124, 315 P.2d 681, 683 (1957); *In re Question Submitted by the United States Court of Appeals for the Tenth Circuit*, 191 Colo. 406, 409, 553 P.2d 382, 385 (1976); *Howard v. Batchelder*, 143 Conn. 328, 334, 122 A.2d 307, 310 (1956). This preference apparently arose as a counterweight to harsh common law doctrines that held contingent remainders destructible and inalien- able. By construing the remainders as vested, the common law rules nullifying contingent remainders were avoided to some extent. *See In re Estate of Haney*, 174 Cal.App.2d 1, 11, 344 P.2d 16, 22 (1959).

27. Even courts sometimes get this wrong. *See Rhoda v. County of Alameda*, 134 Cal.App. 726, 732, 26 P.2d 691, 694 (1933) (stating in dicta that the last example would create a contingent remainder).

action for possession (*e.g.*, to eject trespassers) since he has no present possessory rights. At the same time, the statute of limitations for ejection does not begin to run against the remainderman until the preceding life estate ends. *See Cotney v. Eason*, 269 Ala. 354, 357, 113 So.2d 512, 515 (1959); *Thompson v. Pacific Electric Ry. Co.*, 203 Cal. 578, 265 P. 220 (1928); *Miller v. Stoppel*, 172 Kan. 391, 241 P.2d 488 (1952); *McDonald v. Burke*, 288 S.W.2d 363, 365–66 (Ky.1955).

ii.   *Executory Interests*

Historical Background. Fourteenth century England had a legal device similar to the modern trust, known as the "use." One person would be the feofee to use (he held legal title), whereas the beneficiary would have the actual use of the land (he held equitable title). Although common law courts refused to enforce grants creating uses (because they were not recognized legal estates), the courts of chancery (the forerunner of the court of equity),[28] developed broad equitable principles to enforce the use, as well as other private agreements not enforceable in the common law courts.[29]

Uses served several functions. One was to avoid the cumbersome ritual "feoffment with livery of seisin." The grantor would simply execute a deed in favor of the grantee. Before 1536, this transaction was a nullity in the common law courts because seisin had not passed to the grantee (common law courts did not recognize the validity of deeds at that time). But the chancery courts, concluding that equitable principles required the grantor to observe the terms of the grant, found that the deed created a use in the grantee, leaving legal title in the grantor. The grantor was said to be seised in the land for the use of the grantee; today we would say the grantor held the land in constructive trust for the grantee.

Another function of the use was to allow the grantor to create an express trust. The feofee to use, who held legal title, was bound to follow the instructions of the grantor, which were often designed to ensure the economic well being of family members (who held equitable title) in his

28. Professor Helmholz has noted that uses were popular well before the chancery courts asserted jurisdiction in the second quarter of the fifteenth century. He concludes from a study of the available records that the ecclesiastical courts enforced uses roughly one hundred years before the chancery courts began to enforce them. *See* Helmholz, The Early Enforcement of Uses, 79 Colum. L. Rev. 1503 (1979).

29. An interesting question arises when the feofee to use, holder of legal title, has transferred his interest, in violation of the agreement with the grantor, to a third party grantee. What remedy, if any, does the beneficial owner have?

To answer this question, the chancery court developed a set of rules, which still apply today in conveyancing. If the grantee had notice of the use, or if the grantee had no notice but did not pay value for the transfer (*e.g.*, he received it by inheritance or gift), the grantee was bound by the use. If, on the other hand, the grantee was a bona fide purchaser for value (*i.e.*, he purchased the property without actual or constructive notice of the use), he took title free of the use. Under these circumstances, the only remedy was a court order for the original feofee to recover the title and refund the grantee's money. Of course, the original feofee might be dead or unable to repurchase the property, thereby leaving the injured party without a remedy.

absence. The use also permitted the grantor to gain testamentary power over property interests;[30] he could grant the interest "to F, for the use of G (grantor)," and then separately write a will disposing of his equitable title, which the chancery court would enforce.

The use also was helpful in creating interests that were unavailable at common law. The most important, to our study of executory interests, were the springing and shifting uses. A *springing use* was one that "sprang" from the grantor at some future date and thus divested the grantor of his interest: "To Smith for the use of the grantor, and then to the use of Jones when Jones has a child." This use would have substantially the same effect as "To Jones when he has a child." The problem with the latter grant is that common law did not allow a grantor to create an estate where seisin passed from the grantor sometime in the future. Rather, the law required a present estate to be created simultaneously to "carry seisin" to the future interest holder. Consequently, people turned to uses, which would be enforced in the chancery courts.

The *shifting use* was designed to overcome the early common law prohibition on future interests that cut short or divested freehold estates. The common law courts would not enforce Smith's interest in the grant "to Jones so long as he does not use alcohol, then to Smith." The doctrinal justification was that livery of seisin was a deliberate transfer, not one that might happen upon some event. Chancery courts, however, enforced the corresponding use: "To Brown for the use of Jones so long as Jones does not use alcohol, then to the use of Smith."

Perhaps the most important reason for the use was as a device to avoid the feudal incidents. The scheme worked this way: the grantor would enfeoff several persons as "joint tenants" for the grantor's use for his life, and then to the use of his heirs in fee tail. In brief, each joint tenant owns the land concurrently with his fellow joint tenants. Each joint tenant also has a right of survivorship. When one joint tenant dies, the surviving joint tenants continue to own the land; they simply absorb the dead joint tenant's interest. The crucial legal point is that seisin was not considered to pass by descent (*i.e.*, inheritance) to the surviving joint tenants; they already were seised of the land. Consequently, because the feudal incidents were invoked only when seisin passed by descent, the original grantor never had to worry about their applicability. The use, which was not a common law estate, would pass by descent without any feudal incidents.

The popularity of the use to avoid the feudal incidents resulted in a drop in revenues to the crown. Henry VIII responded in 1536 with the Statute of Uses, which was designed to convert ("execute") uses to common law estates subject to the feudal incidents. Thus, if a grant had read "to Jones for the use of Smith," Smith now held a fee simple.

The Statute of Uses had three important legal consequences. The first was to authorize indirectly grants in land by deed. Before the statute, a deed "to A and his heirs," would be interpreted by the chancery court as

---

30. Common law estates could not be disposed of by will until 1540.

leaving legal title in the grantor, for the use of A. After the statute, however, A's use became a legal estate—the fee simple absolute. Thus, the ritual of feoffment with livery of seisin was no longer legally required.

This new method of transferring land—in contrast to the old, highly public ritual of feoffment with livery of seisin—permitted secret transfers and thereby created new opportunities for fraud. The legislature attempted to solve this problem by passing the Statute of Enrollments, which required recordation of grants of present freehold estates. The statute was ineffective, however, because it did not apply to leases and future interests. By using the device of "lease and release," landowners could avoid making a public record of their conveyances.[31] In 1677, Parliament enacted the Statute of Frauds, which required a written deed for every transfer of land. Because of the fierce resistance at that time to a public recording system (which would, among other things, subject the parties to a transfer tax), the statute was not a title registration law, but a law governing the evidence that can be used to prove the validity of a transfer.[32]

The second consequence of the Statute of Uses was to eliminate the use as a device to transmit real property through a will. The resulting dissatisfaction compelled the Crown to restore the power to devise property through the Statute of Wills in 1540.

The third consequence was that the springing and shifting uses became acceptable future interests in law, known as the springing and shifting executory interests (*i.e.*, "executed" uses). For example, a grantor might want to create a springing executory interest in a potential in-law as part of a marriage agreement: "to B after the marriage of B and C." Alternatively, a grantor might limit the use of granted property, but shift the property to someone else if the condition were violated: "to Jones so long as he does not use alcohol, then to Smith." The grant to Jones is called a fee simple subject to an executory limitation, and Smith has an executory interest. No matter what words of limitation are used (*e.g.*, either "so long as" or "on condition that") the interest *automatically* goes to Smith upon the occurrence of the stated event.

The abolition of uses made it easier to create a series of executory interests that tie up the land within a family for generations: "To Jones, but if Jones should have children, then to the first one to reach 21, but if that child should have children, then to the first one to reach 21 . . ." The courts responded by adopting the Rule Against Perpetuities, which we will get to shortly.

---

31. To avoid the Statute of Enrollments, A, the holder of a fee simple interest, would grant B a one-year lease of the property and retain the reversion. Since an interest in a term of years was not a freehold estate, there was no obligation to record this transfer. After B took possession, A would release his reversion to B. Because B now held the present and future interests, under the doctrine of merger B now had a fee simple absolute.

32. *See* Hamburger, The Conveyancing Purposes of the Statute of Frauds, 27 Am. J. Legal Hist. 354 (1983).

Executory interests under modern law. Although an executory interest is formally defined as a future interest in a third party that cuts short the preceding estate, it is more easily identified negatively. If a future interest in a third party is not a remainder, it must be an executory interest. As with uses, executory interests may be either shifting or springing.

ESTATES IN LAND

PRESENT INTERESTS		Defeasible Fee Interests			Life Estate	Landlord/Tenant	Fee Tail
	FSA	FSD	FSSCS	FSSEL	Life Estate	Concurrent	Fee Tail
creation:	to B and his heirs (old) to B (modern)	• so long as • while • until • during [note: abolished in CA; becomes FSSCS]	1. Conditional • provided • however, if • but if • on condition that 2. Express Reservation by grantor of right of entry or power of termination	same as FSD & FSSCS, except shifts from grantee or springs from grantor to third party	ordinary pur autre vie	• term of years • periodic • at will • joint • in common • by entirety • community property	to B and the heirs of his body [note: treated as FSA in most states]
attributes: • forfeiture	none	automatic	not automatic	automatic	automatic	varies	upon failure of issue
• transfer	freely	freely	freely	freely	freely (but can't pass by will or intestacy)	varies (transfers of leaseholds and marital property more likely subject to restriction)	only a life interest
FUTURE INTERESTS	none	Possibility of Reverter	Right of Entry/ Power of Termination	Executory Interest 1. Shifting 2. Springing	Remainder: 1. Indefeasibly Vested 2. Contingent 3. Vested subject to complete defeasance 4. Vested subject to partial defeasance		Reversion to Grantor
attributes: • forfeiture	N/A	automatic	grantor must act	automatic	automatic		automatic
• transfer	N/A	freely	not inter vivos	freely	freely		freely
• waste	N/A	rules of waste may apply			rules of waste apply		

Classifying Future Interests. The preceding chart shows which future interests follow specific present interests and the key elements of present and future interests. The following summary describes a straight-forward and systematic way to distinguish among the various types of remainders. Use these aids to answer the questions that follow.

Remainders

Definition: A remainder is a future interest created in someone other than the transferor that, according to the terms of its creation, will become a present estate (if ever) immediately upon, and no sooner than, the natural expiration of all prior particular estates (*i.e.*, estates of limited duration—a life estate, a term of years, or a fee tail) created simultaneously with it.

Thus, there are three principal elements:

1. the interest is created in someone *other than the transferor*;

2. the interest must be *capable of becoming possessory immediately upon the natural termination of the prior estate*; and

3. the interest must *follow a life estate, term of years, or fee tail*.

Types of Remainders

1. **Indefeasibly Vested Remainder**—To find that a person has an *indefeasibly vested remainder*, the following four conditions must be satisfied:

   i. The interest is held by a *born and ascertainable person*;

   ii. The interest is *certain to become possessory immediately* upon the termination of the preceding estate (*i.e.*, not subject to a condition precedent);

   iii. The interest is *indefeasible* (*i.e.*, there is no condition subsequent that will divest the remainder); and

   iv. The interest is *indivisible* (it cannot be diminished in size).

2. **Contingent Remainder**—If conditions (i) or (ii) fail, the remainder is *contingent*.

   Note: Condition (ii) can fail in one of two ways. If it fails because the party does not take unless some condition precedent has been met, then the party has a *contingent remainder*. (*E.g.*, "to A for life, then to A's first child," and A has not yet had any children.) If there is simply a gap in possession, but the party is sure to or may take sometime after the previous estate ends, the party has an *executory interest* (and not a remainder) (*E.g.*, "O to A for life, then five years later to B" gives B a springing executory interest out of O's reversion; "O to A until B reaches 21, then to B" is a shifting executory interest, divesting A before the natural end of some estate.)

3. **Vested Remainder Subject to Complete Defeasance**—Conditions (i) and (ii) are satisfied, but condition (iii) fails. *E.g.*, "To A for life, then to B, but if B does not maintain the property as a farm, then to C."

4. **Vested Remainder Subject to Partial Defeasance** (a/k/a partial divestment, or subject to open)—Conditions (i) and (ii) satisfied, but condition (iv) fails. *E.g.*, "To A for life, then to A's children." A has one child.

Problems: Future Interests

Answer the questions and classify the interests created by each of the following grants:

1. O conveys "to A for life, then to B and his heirs." What interests are created at the time of the conveyance?

2. O conveys "to A for life." In a subsequent conveyance, O conveys his interest "to B." What are the interests after the second conveyance?

3. O conveys "to A and her heirs for so long as A lives in New York, then to B and his heirs." What interests are created at the time of the conveyance?

4. O conveys "to A for life, then to B if B attends A's funeral." What interests are created at of the time of the conveyance?

5. O conveys "to A for life, then to B, but if A goes to law school, then to C" What are the interests created at the time of the conveyance?

6. O conveys "to A, but if B goes to law school, then to B for life, and then to C." What are the interests created at the time of the conveyance? Suppose that B goes to law school; what are the interests?

7. O conveys "to A for life, then to B for life, but if at any time B should cease practicing law, then the grantor may terminate the estate." What are the interests created at the time of the conveyance?

8. O conveys "to A for life, then to B if B becomes a member of the Bar, so long as B remains a member of the Bar." What are the interests created at the time of the conveyance?

9. *Class Gifts.* Classify the interests of the parties, including the grantor:

a. "to A's children who reach age 20." A has one child, C_1, age 10. What are the grantor's and A's child's interests? Suppose that when C_1 reaches 20, he already has another sibling, C_2, and that three years later, he has another sibling, C_3. At that point, what are the interests of A's children?

b. "to the grantor's children who reach age 20." The grantor has one child C_1, age 30, and another child C_2, age 12. What interests do C_1 and C_2 have? Suppose another child is born. What is that child's interest?

    c. "to the grantor's children who reach age 20." At the time of the conveyance, the grantor has no children. The grantor subsequently has three children, each of whom reach age 20. Thereafter the grantor dies. What are the interests of the children?

    10. *Remainders.* What types of remainders are created in each of the following conveyances?

    a. "to A for life, remainder to B."

    b. "to A for life, remainder to B for life, remainder to C."

    c. "to A for life, remainder to B, so long as the land shall be put to residential use only."

    d. "to A for life, remainder to the children of A." At the time that the conveyance is made, A has one child, B.

    e. "to A for life, remainder to the children of B." At the time of the conveyance, B is alive and has one child B_1. B subsequently has a second child, B_2, prior to A's death. After A's death, B has a third child, B_3. Classify the interests before and after A's death.

    f. "to A for life, remainder to the heirs of B." B has two children, B_1 and B_2, at the time of the conveyance.

    g. "to A for life, remainder to the heirs of B." B's will leaves his entire estate to his friend, C.

    h. "to A for life, remainder to B if B survives A."

    i. "to A for life, then to B for life if B survives A, but if B fails to survive A, then to C and his heirs upon A's or B's death, whichever comes later."

    j. "to A for life, then if B attains age 21 to B and his heirs."

    k. "to A for life, then to B for life, but if B goes to law school, then the grantor has the right to terminate the estate." After identifying the remainders in this example, specify the grantor's interest.

    l. "to A for life, then if B graduates from law school, to B so long as B remains a lawyer."

    11. O devises Blackacre "to A for life, remainder over, share and share alike, to my grandsons X and Y, but if either of them is dead at that time, then all to the other."

    a. Assume that X is dead when O dies. What interest does Y have?

    b. Assume that X is dead when A dies. What interest does Y have?

    12. O conveys "to A for life, remainder to B, but if B dies without children that survive him, then to C." What interests are created?

    13. O conveys "to A for life, then to B one year after A's death." What interests are created?

    14. O conveys "to A for life so long as A does not go to law school."

15.   O conveys "to A for life, then to A's children, but if none of A's children reach 20, then to C." A has one child, age 10.

---

d. DOCTRINES LIMITING THE GRANTOR'S POWER TO IMPOSE CONDITIONS ON GRANTS

At common law, a number of important rules were based on the distinction between contingent and vested remainders. Each of these rules evinced hostility to the contingent remainder, but not the vested remainder. Common law judges developed these rules because they resisted arrangements in which nobody was available to perform the required feudal services, which avoided relief and the incidents, or which tied up land in perpetuity.

At first, the common law judges held invalid all contingent remainders at their creation (on the formal ground that the remainderman had no present capacity to take seisin at the expiration of the previous estate), and thus allowed only vested remainders as valid estates. Gradually, however, the courts refined the restrictions on contingent remainders into four basic rules—the Rule Against Perpetuities, the Rule of the Destructibility of Contingent Remainders, the Rule in Shelley's Case, and the Doctrine of Worthier Title. The other major restriction on the grantor's power to impose conditions on grants is the Rule Against Restraints on Alienation, discussed later in this section.

The Rule Against Perpetuities.[33] As the fee tail became less useful as a device to restrict the alienability of land (because of legal devices to disentail the interest), landowners used springing and shifting uses and executory devises to control the use and ownership of land for long periods of time, often several generations. The chancery courts, which initially had jurisdiction over these interests, viewed these "perpetuities" with disfavor and often held them invalid to prevent the "dead hand of the past" from controlling the use of land by future generations. There was, however, no clear definition of what constituted an unenforceable perpetuity; for many years the chancery courts dealt with the perpetuities issue on an *ad hoc* basis.

Development of the Common Law Rule.   The first important case providing a rule of decision was the *Duke of Norfolk's Case*, 22 Eng. Rep. 931 (1682).[34] That case involved a use created by the Earl of Arundel on behalf of his widow and his second and third sons, Henry and Charles. The earl created the use because his eldest son, Thomas, through primogeniture

---

33. For excellent articles discussing and applying the Rule Against Perpetuities, *see* Leach, Perpetuities in a Nutshell, 51 Harv. L. Rev. 638 (1938); Leach, Perpetuities: The Nutshell Revisited, 78 Harv. L. Rev. 973 (1965); Dukeminier, A Modern Guide to Perpetuities, 74 Cal. L. Rev. 1867 (1986); Fletch-er, Perpetuities: Basic Clarity, Muddled Reform, 63 Wash. L. Rev. 791 (1988).

34. For a thorough account of this case, see Barry, The Duke of Norfolk's Case, 23 Va. L. Rev. 538 (1937).

would become the earl and enjoy the estates associated with the earldom, and the old earl wanted to provide for the economic security of his wife and his younger sons.[35]

The use involved the lands associated with the Barony of Grostock, which did not come with the earldom. The use named the old earl as the beneficiary during his lifetime (*i.e.*, a life estate); then to his widow during her life; then, during the life of Thomas and his male issue, if any, to Henry and his male issue. But if Thomas should die without male issue while Henry was still alive, then to Charles and his male issue. The Earl created this trust with successive vested (widow) and contingent (Henry, Charles) remainders because he believed that Thomas, who was mentally incompetent, would never have children and that Henry would succeed to the earldom and acquire all the lands that went with that title. By giving Henry the Barony of Grostock while Thomas was alive, he ensured the financial security of the future earl. The trust also ensured that the Earl's third son, Charles, would be provided for (again with the Barony lands) in the likely event that Henry became the earl.

As planned, everyone died in order, leaving Henry with the earldom. Henry, however, did not want to give up the Barony of Grostock, and he went to court to have Charles' interest declared invalid as a perpetuity. Lord Chancellor Nottingham heard the case, and against the arguments of the advisory judges, held Charles' interest valid as not being a perpetuity. The Chancellor reasoned that a limitation on a fee tail (that is, a contingency—Thomas' death—ending Henry's fee tail and creating a present interest in Charles) did not create a perpetuity so long as the contingency would necessarily occur within a life "in being." In other words, a future interest will be invalid as being too remote, if it *might* not vest during the lives of persons who were alive ("in being") when the contingent interest was first created in the original grant (the fact that a particular grant actually vested within a life in being would be legally irrelevant). On the other hand, if the contingent interest necessarily will vest within that period, the contingent interest is valid. Cases decided over the next 100 years added a period of gestation and an additional period of 21 years so that the grantor or testator could provide economic security for the persons he knew, as well as the next generation during its minority. *See, e.g.*, *Thellusson v. Woodford*, 11 Ves. 112 (1805). As stated by Gray, in the classic formulation, *"No interest is good unless it must vest, if at all, not later than twenty-one years after some life in being at the creation of the interest."* Leach, Perpetuities in a Nutshell, 51 Harv.L.Rev. 638, 639 (1938).

While many state legislatures have added reforms—most importantly, the Uniform Statutory Rule Against Perpetuities—the common law Rule

---

35. After the old earl died and Thomas became the new earl, the King (at Henry's behest) designated Thomas the Duke of Norfolk. The Duke of Norfolk was the premier peer of England; whoever held that position was a powerful political figure in England. When Thomas later died, Henry became the Duke of Norfolk, from which we get the name of this case.

remains the basis of most statutes. In most states, the court must first analyze the grant or devise under the common law Rule, and only if the interest is invalid under the common law Rule, then apply the statutory reforms.

The common law Rule, at least as applied in this country, has some serious shortcomings in meeting its principal objective. For example, in many jurisdictions the common law Rule applies only to contingent remainders, vested remainders subject to open, and executory interests, and not to future interests in the grantor—reversions, powers of termination, or possibilities of reverter. *See, e.g., Collins v. Church of God of Prophecy*, 304 Ark. 37, 41, 800 S.W.2d 418, 419–20 (1990) (the Rule does not apply to possibility of reverter); *Strong v. Shatto*, 45 Cal.App. 29, 35–36, 187 P. 159, 162 (1919) (the Rule does not apply to powers of termination); *Brown v. Independent Baptist Church of Woburn*, 325 Mass. 645, 647–48, 91 N.E.2d 922 (1950) (the Rule does not apply to reversionary interests); *Hornets Nest Girl Scout Council, Inc. v. Cannon Found.*, 79 N.C.App. 187, 191, 339 S.E.2d 26, 29 (1986) (all reversionary interests are vested for purposes of the Rule).[36]

The reason for the selective application of the Rule may be largely historical. The reversionary interests in the grantor existed long before the Rule was created in the seventeenth century, and there may have been no felt need to disturb the validity of these interests. In addition, the Rule was specifically created to deal with problems generated by contingent remainders and executory interests. Nonetheless, omitting reversionary interests from the Rule leaves the dead hand of the past considerable power to control property. In England, where this entire mess began, and in an increasing number of states, the Rule applies to future interests held by the grantor.

Application of the Common Law Rule Against Perpetuities. The common law Rule can be a little tricky to apply properly (and it is essential to read the Rule). The basic strategy is to look at the facts *at the time the*

36. Some states, however, have adopted statutes that subject these interests to a statute of limitations or require persons holding these interests to record their interests periodically (*e.g.,* every 30 years) or have them declared unenforceable. *See, e.g.,* West's Ann. Cal. Civ. Code § 885.030 (record every 30 years); Conn. Gen. Stat. Ann. § 45a–505 (30–statute of limitations for power of termination); N.C. Gen. Stat. § 41–32 (60–year statute of limitations for power of termination); West's Fla. Stat. Ann. § 689.18 (con-verting conditions into covenants after 21 years).

Other statutes declare conditions obsolete if they no longer serve their original purposes. *See, e.g.,* West's Ann. Cal. Civ. Code § 885.040 (void if condition serves "no actual and substantial benefit" or it would be "inequitable" to enforce); Minn. Stat. Ann. § 500.20 (condition void if it serves "no actual and substantial benefit"); Mich. Cod. Laws Ann. § 26.46 (condition void if it is "merely

contingent interest was created in the grant or will.[37] If under some combination of circumstances, no matter how improbable, the contingent interest will not vest until beyond the period—21 years after any life in being (a "life in being" is someone who was alive on the effective date of the grant or will)—the contingent interest is void. Thus, the common law Rule is a rule of proof; for a contingent interest to be valid, you must be able to prove that it is certain either to vest within the period or never to vest at all.[38]

We will illustrate application of the Rule through two examples. Following this discussion are numerous problems to help you develop your skills in applying the Rule.

Example 11: G, who has a present interest in fee simple absolute, grants his interest "to the first child of B to attain the age of 25 years." B is alive with one child, C, who is 24. Is the grant valid under the common law Rule?

First identify the future interest. C (and any unborn children) has a springing executory interest that will not become vested (_i.e._, possessory) until that child reaches age 25. The future interest is not a remainder because it does not immediately follow the natural termination of a life estate. Thus, C's interest is subject to the Rule Against Perpetuities.

Take B as the "measuring life" (_i.e._, one of the persons in existence when the property was conveyed). Do we know for certain—can we prove at the time the property was conveyed—either that the interest will vest within 21 years of B's life or that it will never vest? The answer must be no. Of course, the interest _might_ vest in time. C might live another year, and thus the interest will have vested within 21 years of B's life. But probable timely vesting is not good enough. Under the facts _when the property was first conveyed_ C might die before he reaches 25, and B might have another child, D, and B might die immediately thereafter. D might reach 25 (_i.e._, the gift might vest), but he will not reach 25 within 21 years of B's death. The important point is that we can't be sure, at the time the grant is made, that the interest will either vest within 21 years of a life in being or never vest; it might vest "remotely" beyond the period.

nominal, and evince[s] no intention of actual and substantial benefit").

37. An interest is created in a grant when the grantor delivers the deed to the grantee. An interest is created in a will when the testator dies, _not_ when the testator signs the will.

38. Keep in mind that the Rule applies only to "contingent" interests: contingent remainders, executory interests, and vested remainders subject to open. A contingent remainder vests when it becomes a vested remainder or possessory; an executory interest vests when it becomes possessory; and a vested remainder subject to open becomes a vested remainder when every member of the class has a vested remainder or has a possessory interest.

Under the Uniform Statutory Rule Against Perpetuities, the Rule also generally applies only to donative transfers of property. _See, e.g._, West's Ann. Cal. Prob. Code § 21225(a); _Shaver v. Clanton_, 26 Cal. App.4th 568, 31 Cal.Rptr.2d 595 (1994) (the Act excludes commercial transactions, including perpetual options to renew a 5-year lease).

Taking C as the measuring life yields the same conclusion with a similar analysis. Because there is no measuring life that satisfies the Rule, the gift violates the Rule. Note that if *any* one of the possible measuring lives had satisfied the Rule, then the grant would have been valid. In this case, because the interest might vest remotely with every measuring life, the executory interest in B is invalid, and the grantor retains a fee simple absolute.   Thus, even if C reaches 25, he gets nothing.

Class gifts, which typically arise in wills and trusts, present a special set of problems under the Rule Against Perpetuities. The first problem is to decide which persons are members of the class that will share in the property. In legal terms, we need to decide when the class closes. The rule of convenience, discussed *supra* page 162, provides guidance in many circumstances. Once the membership of the class is determined, the Rule Against Perpetuities is applied to each member of the class. If *any* member's contingent interest might vest remotely, the gift to the entire class is void.

Example 12: G grants a present interest in a fee simple absolute "to A for life, then to A's children for life, and upon the death of the last survivor, to A's surviving grandchildren." At the time of the grant, A is alive and has 2 children, C_1 and C_2. Is the grant to the grandchildren valid under the Rule?

First, identify the interests: A has a present interest in a life estate. A's children have a remainder in a life estate (the interest immediately follows the natural termination of a life estate). C_1 and C_2 have vested remainders since we know their identities and there is no condition precedent to vesting. However, since there may be additional siblings (A is still alive) their remainders are subject to open. The unborn children have executory interests. The grandchildren have a contingent remainder in a fee simple absolute (both because they are unborn and because there is a condition precedent of survival). Thus, the interests in the children and the grandchildren are subject to the Rule Against Perpetuities.

The vested remainder subject to open in A's children will vest indefeasibly at A's death (indeed, the interest will become possessory); at that time, there can be no more children and we will know all of their identities. This time of vesting is well within the period of the Rule, if we take A as the measuring life.   Thus, the children's interest is valid.

The contingent remainder of the grandchildren is invalid under the Rule. After the grant is made, A *might* have another child, call him C_3; it is also possible that A, C_1 and C_2 will suddenly die at this time. C_3, who of course is not a life in being, might have children. Because the class of surviving grandchildren cannot be determined until the last of A's children has died, the grandchildren's interests remain contingent until that point. Since C_3 might not die until more than 21 years after all lives in being—A, C_1 and C_2—have died, the interest in C_3's children might vest remotely and thus the gift to the entire class is void. Because the remainder in the grandchildren is void, it is struck from the grant, leaving a reversion in the grantor (the grandchildren might end up with the property through inheritance—or they might not if they are not the heirs at law or the grantor left the reversion in his will to other people, but they will not get the property through the terms of the grant).

Modern Statutory Reforms. Because of the complexity of the Rule, and the corresponding opportunities to draft grants and wills with invalid gifts,[39] many statutes include provisions designed to salvage part of the grant.

California Probate Code[40]

21200. **Short title.**

This chapter shall be known and may be cited as the Uniform Statutory Rule Against Perpetuities.

21201. **Common law rule superseded.**

This chapter supersedes the common law rule against perpetuities.

21202.

(a) Except as provided in subdivision (b), this part applies to nonvested property interests and unexercised powers of appointment regardless of whether they were created before, on, or after January 1, 1992.

(b) This part does not apply to any property interest or power of appointment the validity of which has been determined in a judicial proceeding or by a settlement among interested persons.

21205. **Nonvested property interests; validity; conditions.**

A nonvested property interest is invalid unless one of the following conditions is satisfied:

(a) When the interest is created, it is certain to vest or terminate no later than 21 years after the death of an individual then alive.

39. In *Lucas v. Hamm*, 56 Cal.2d 583, 592–93, 15 Cal.Rptr. 821, 825–827, 364 P.2d 685 (1961), the California Supreme Court held that an attorney could not be held liable for malpractice for drafting a will with a provision violating the Rule.

Of the California law on perpetuities * * * it has been said that few, if any areas of the law have been fraught with more confusion or concealed more traps for the unwary draftsman; that members of the bar * * * make errors in these matters; that the code provisions adopted in 1872 created a situation worse than if the matter had been left to the common law, and that the legislation adopted in 1951, despite the best of intentions, added further complexities. * * * In view of the state of the law relating to perpetuities * * * it would not be proper to hold that defendant failed to use such skill, prudence, and diligence as lawyers of ordinary skill and capacity commonly exercise.

Id. at 592, 15 Cal.Rptr. at 825. Before you decide that you can forego understanding the Rule Against Perpetuities, beware that at least one court has expressed doubt that the holding in *Lucas* remains valid. *See Wright v. Williams*, 47 Cal.App.3d 802, 809 n. 2, 121 Cal. Rptr. 194, 199 n. 2 (1975).

40. This statute is based on the Uniform Statutory Rule Against Perpetuities (1990), which has been adopted in more than 20 states.

(b) The interest either vests or terminates within 90 years after its creation.

21208.   **Posthumous births.**

In determining whether a nonvested property interest * * * is valid under this [Rule], the possibility that a child will be born to an individual after the individual's death is disregarded.

21209.   **Construction of "later of" language in perpetuity saving clause; application of section.**

(a) If, in measuring a period from the creation of a trust or other property arrangement, language in a governing instrument (1) seeks to disallow the vesting or termination of any interest or trust beyond, (2) seeks to postpone the vesting or termination of any interest or trust until, or (3) seeks to operate in effect in any similar fashion upon, the later of (A) the expiration of a period of time not exceeding 21 years after the death of the survivor of specified lives in being at the creation of the trust or other property arrangement or (B) the expiration of a period of time that exceeds or might exceed 21 years after the death of the survivor of lives in being at the creation of the trust or other property arrangement, that language is inoperative to the extent it produces a period that exceeds 21 years after the death of the survivor of the specified lives.

(b) * * * this section applies only to governing instruments * * * executed on or after January 1, 1992.

21210.   **Nonvested property interests or powers of appointment.**

* * * the time of creation of a nonvested property interest * * * is determined by other applicable statutes or, if none, under general principles of property law.

21220.   **Petition; conditions.**

On petition of an interested person, a court shall reform a disposition in the manner that most closely approximates the transferor's manifested plan of distribution and is within the 90 years allowed by [§§ 21205–21209], if any of the following conditions is satisfied:

(a) A nonvested property interest * * * becomes invalid under the statutory rule against perpetuities * * *

(b) A class gift is not but might become invalid under the statutory rule against perpetuities * * *, and the time has arrived when the share of any class member is to take effect in possession or enjoyment.

(c) A nonvested property interest that is not validated by [21205(a)] can vest but not within 90 years after its creation.

21225.   **Application of specified article.**

[This Rule] does not apply to any of the following:

(a) A nonvested property interest * * * arising out of a nondonative transfer, except a nonvested property interest * * * arising out of (1) a premarital or postmarital agreement, (2) a separation or divorce settlement, (3) a spouse's election, (4) or a similar arrangement arising out of a prospective, existing, or previous marital relationship between the parties, (5) a contract to make or not to revoke a will or trust, * * * (7) a transfer in satisfaction of a duty of support, or (8) a reciprocal transfer.

(b) A fiduciary's power relating to the administration or management of assets, including the power of a fiduciary to sell, lease, or mortgage property, and the power of a fiduciary to determine principal and income.

(c) A power to appoint a fiduciary.

* * *

(e) A nonvested property interest held by a charity, government, or governmental agency or subdivision, if the nonvested property interest is preceded by an interest held by another charity, government, or governmental agency or subdivision. * * *

21230. **Validating lives.**

The lives of individuals selected to govern the time of vesting pursuant to [§§ 21205–21209] may not be so numerous or so situated that evidence of their deaths is likely to be unreasonably difficult to obtain.

21231. **Spouse as life in being.**

In determining the validity of a nonvested property interest pursuant to [§§ 21205–21209], an individual described as the spouse of an individual alive at the commencement of the perpetuities period shall be deemed to be an individual alive when the interest is created, whether or not the individual so described was then alive.

One type of provision permits reformation of the grant or will under certain conditions.[41] *See, e.g.,* West's Ann. Cal. Prob. Code § 2122. This provision does not abolish the common law Rule Against Perpetuities. Rather, it is a broad remedy for gifts that violate the Rule, so long as the creator's general intent can be ascertained. Using this doctrine, a court might have reformed the remainder in Example 12 to read "upon the death of the last survivor to C_1's and C_2's children." It is not perfect—it does not fully carry out the grantor's intent—but it may do so more than invalidating the entire grant to the grandchildren.

41. The doctrine was originally developed for charitable gifts and in some states is known as the *cy pres* doctrine. "Cy pres" are the first two Norman French words in the expression meaning "as near as possible."

Numerous states have adopted a statute permitting equitable reform of interests that violate the Rule. While some statutes, such as the Uniform Rule, give judges broad authority to reform all gifts, West's Ann. Cal. Prob. Code § 21220, others limit that authority to trusts and a few allow judges to change only age contingencies (*e.g.,* "to my first child who reaches 25") to 21 where the contingency would otherwise invalidate the interest. *See, e.g.,* 765 Ill. Comp. Stat. 305/4(c)(2).

Another important reform is the "wait-and-see" doctrine.[42] *See, e.g.,* § 21205(b). For example, a Pennsylvania statute provides that "upon the expiration of the period allowed by the common law rule against perpetuities as measured by actual rather than possible events, any interest not then vested ... shall be void." 20 Pa. Cons. Stat. § 6104(b). Under this provision, a court would first test the future interest under the common law rule; if the interest fails, the court would wait until the expiration of the preceding estate, if necessary, to see if the contingent future interests actually vest within the period. A grant would violate the Rule only if it actually failed to vest in time. In Example 12, if A had no more children, then the grandchildren's interest would vest in time; we would know the identities of the surviving grandchildren as soon as C_1 and C_2 died. Thus, under the right set of facts, the grant would be valid under a wait-and-see doctrine.

One problem with the wait-and-see doctrine is that the grantees may have to wait for a substantial period of time to ascertain the validity of their interests. Another problem (at least in states with a Rule like that in Pennsylvania) is that the validity of an interest depends on the longevity of persons having nothing to do with the grant (a life in being could be anyone on the planet alive on the effective date of the grant). States have tried to deal with this problem by restricting the class of measuring lives to those persons having something to do with the grant, the so-called "causally related" lives. *See, e.g.,* Ky. Rev. Stat. Ann. § 381.216. This expression is often not defined by statute, however, leaving the courts to decide who is causally related. Other statutes list the possible measuring lives. The Uniform Rule takes a different approach, setting a fixed time—90 years—for vesting.

———

1. *Wait-and-See Doctrine.* What are the advantages, if any, of the alternative statutory 90–year period for the vesting of interests provided in Cal. Prob. Code § 21205(b)? How would a lawyer use this provision—in litigation or in drafting?

2. To be valid under the Rule, a future interest must either vest or terminate within the period. West's Ann. Cal. Prob. Code § 21205(a). Consider the following devise: "provided my grandmother survives me and lives on to receive distribution of my estate hereby devised to her, I devise all my property to her." Because of the condition precedent (survival), the gift is not vested. Moreover, it is possible that Granny's interest will never vest; Granny, after all, may die before the estate is distributed. Is Granny's gift nevertheless valid under the Rule? *See Estate of McCollum,* 43 Cal. App.2d 313, 110 P.2d 721 (1941).

42. This doctrine has been adopted in approximately 2 dozen states, including those adopting the Uniform Rule. *See, e.g.,* Alaska Stat. § 34.27.050; Kan. Stat. Ann. § 59–3401.

3. *Options.* Options and contracts for future leases often present perplexing problems under the Rule. The traditional rule is that an option to purchase property or a contract to begin a lease at some indeterminate time in the future is subject to the Rule. *See Alamo School Dist. v. Jones,* 182 Cal.App.2d 180, 191, 6 Cal.Rptr. 272, 279 (1960) ("contingent option [to purchase land] that may be exercised at a time beyond the period of the rule is void as in violation of the rule"); *Haggerty v. City of Oakland,* 161 Cal.App.2d 407, 326 P.2d 957 (1958) (holding that a lease, which would not begin until after a city constructed a building, was void because it might vest remotely). Some courts expressed unease with the mechanical application of the rule. In *Wong v. Di Grazia,* 60 Cal.2d 525, 35 Cal.Rptr. 241, 386 P.2d 817 (1963), the state supreme court held that an "on completion" lease (a lease providing that it would begin "on completion" of the construction of the building) was not void because in all likelihood the lease would begin well before the end of the 21–year period. The *Wong* court took the position—contrary to 200 years of doctrine—that the Rule must bend to business realities. "A lease to commence upon completion of the leased building is a common business arrangement. * * * Surely the courts do not seek to invalidate bona fide transactions by the imported application of esoteric legalisms. Our task is not to block the business pathway but to clear it, defining it by guideposts that are reasonably to be expected." *Id.* at 534, 35 Cal.Rptr. at 247, 386 P.2d at 823.

The issue is moot today under the Uniform Rule. Why? *See* West's Ann. Cal. Prob. Code § 21225(a).

4. All of this may begin to seem like a lot of unnecessary complication. Is there any simpler way to accommodate the policy of free alienability of land with the desire to provide for the economic security of a spouse or children, or to maximize the owner's freedom in disposing of land?

Summary of the Common Law Rule Against Perpetuities

No *future interest in a transferee* (contingent remainder, vested remainder subject to open, or executory limitation) is good unless it *must vest,* if it ever does vest, no later than 21 years after some *life in being* at the creation of the interest.

To resolve a Rule Against Perpetuities (RAP) problem, you must answer each of the following questions:

1. Are you dealing with a *future interest in a transferee*?

    The RAP does not apply to future interests held by a grantor or her successors. Therefore, reversions, possibilities of reverter, and rights of entry are not invalidated by the RAP. If you find that these types of interests are present (and no others), then your work is done—such interests are valid with respect to the RAP.

It should be noted that a number of states now statutorily limit the validity of possibilities of reverter and rights of entry to set periods of time (*e.g.*, 30 years after creation). Since we are concerned with only the RAP, however, you needn't worry about such statutes for present purposes.

2. Are there any interests created that are not *vested* at the time of creation?

   The RAP applies only to interests that are not vested. Therefore, it does not apply to vested remainders. Since reversions, possibilities of reverter, and rights of entry are also not subject to the RAP (see above), the RAP *potentially voids* only the following interests:

   1. contingent remainders
   2. executory interests
   3. vested remainder subject to partial defeasance (this is because of other class members who either are unborn or have not satisfied a condition precedent)

   Therefore, if you don't have any of these interests, the RAP does not apply.

3. What is the first point at which the future interest *must vest*?

   A future interest *vests* when: (1) the person or persons who will be entitled to possession under the future interest are ascertained; and (2) there is no condition that must be met before the interest can become possessory (other than the *natural* termination of the preceding estate).

   N.B.: If the future interest is potentially held by more than one person (*e.g.*, as in a vested remainder subject to partial defeasance), the question is what is the first point at which *every* person's future interest *must vest*.

4. Is the point at which the future interest (contingent remainder or executory interest) must vest *more than 21 years* after the end of some *life in being* at the creation of the interest?

   more than 21 years—including possible gestation period.

   life in being at the creation of the interest—any living person mentioned expressly or impliedly (*e.g.*, if conveyance mentions specific living grandchildren of A, A's living children are implied lives in being), subject to the condition that the measuring lives not be too numerous and/or difficult to locate.

   In answering this question, you need to know whether the jurisdiction applies a *what-might-happen* approach (common law rule) or a *wait-and-see* approach (statutory reform in many jurisdictions).

What-might-happen: view possibilities (*e.g.*, births, deaths) as of the creation of the interest.

Wait-and-see: take account of facts that have occurred after the creation of the interest.

5. Is the future interest in question held by a second charity?

There is a special exception for charities. A grant of a future interest to a charity is void if it is contingent upon an event that might not occur during the perpetuity period *unless* such grant follows a grant to a charity.

6. What happens if the future interest is void?

The offending interest is void at the outset, and is stricken from the grant or will. The good parts of the instrument remain standing unless the invalid gift is essential to the grantor's scheme.

Problems: Rule Against Perpetuities

In the following conveyances, identify the present and future interests. Which interests are subject to the Rule Against Perpetuities? Which of those interests are void under the Rule? If an interest is void, what are the resulting interests after application of the Rule?

1. O conveys Blackacre "to A, but only for so long as Blackacre is used for school purposes, then to B."

2. O conveys Blackacre "to A, but only for so long as Blackacre is used for school purposes." O subsequently conveys his interest in Blackacre "to B."

3. O devises Blackacre "to A, but should liquor be sold on the premises within 21 years of the death of any child of A's born before my death, then to B."

4. O gives Blackacre "to A, but should liquor be sold on the premises within 21 years of the death of any child of A's born before my death, then to B."

5. O devises Blackacre "to all my grandchildren born within the next 40 years." The grantor has no grandchildren.

6. O devises Blackacre "to A, but should liquor be sold on the premises within 21 years of the death of Al Gore, then to B."

7. O devises Blackacre "to A, but should liquor be sold on the premises within 21 years of the death of all of Queen Elizabeth's descendants alive on the effective date of this will, then to B." *See In re Villar*, 1 Ch. 243 (1929); West's Ann. Cal. Prob. Code § 21230.

8. O conveys Blackacre "to A's children who reach age 30." At the time of the conveyance, A is dead, and has two children, ages 5 and 18.

9. O conveys Blackacre "to A's children who reach age 23." At the time of the conveyance, A is still alive, and has three children, ages 1, 10, and 24.

10. O devises Blackacre "to my wife, W, for life, then to her children for their lives, and upon the death of the last child, to my wife's grandchildren." At the time of the testator's death, he and his wife are 80 years old, and they have daughter, D, and a son, S. When the testator dies, there are no grandchildren. *See Jee v. Audley*, 29 Eng. Rep. 1186 (Ch. 1787); *cf.* E.A. Maas, *78–Year–Old Granny Is Expecting Twins*, Weekly World Star, Feb. 10, 1987, at 1.

The preceding problem has come to be known as the case of the fertile octogenarian. Notwithstanding its biological improbability and its contradiction of the intention of the grantor, it is the rule in most states. The other famous example is the case of the unborn widow. Consider a grant from G "to my son for life, then to his widow for life, and then to his children who are then living." At the time of this grant, the son, who is 50, is married and has two children, C_1 and C_2. Why does the gift to the children violate the common law Rule? *See* West's Ann. Cal. Prob. Code § 21231 for a statutory solution.

11. O devises Blackacre "to the Law School at the University of California, Berkeley, but if the premises are not used for legal education, then to Stanford Law School."

12. O devises Blackacre "to A for so long as the premises are not used to sell liquor, then to the Law School at the University of California, Berkeley."

13. O conveys Blackacre "to A for life, then to his widow for life, and then 30 years after termination of the last life estate, to B for life." Would the result change if the remainder to B was in fee simple absolute?

The Rule of the Destructibility of Contingent Remainders held that if a contingent remainder did not vest by the expiration of the preceding estate, the contingent remainder was destroyed by operation of law. Consider the grant "to Jones for life, remainder to the first of Jones' children to reach 21." If at the time of the gift, Jones' children are all under 21, or he has no children, the identity of the child who will get possession is unknown, and thus has a contingent remainder. If, when Jones dies, none of his children has yet reached 21, none of the children has satisfied the age condition, and no one is available to perform the feudal services. Under the Rule, the contingent remainder in the minor children would be destroyed, and the interest would revert to the grantor.

The Rule has been repealed in most jurisdictions. In such states, the interest in the above example would revert to the grantor upon Jones' death; if any child later reached 21, the interest would go to that child (after the reversion to the grantor, we would say that the contingent remainder in the children has become an executory interest).

The Rule in Shelley's Case (1581) was a response to a successful method of avoiding the feudal incidents. The incidents applied only when the land passed by descent (*i.e.*, inheritance). To avoid the incidents, the lawyers drafted grants that transferred the land to the grantee's heirs by purchase: "to Jones for life, then to Jones' heirs." Because the heirs were getting the land not by descent (*i.e.*, they were not inheriting the land), but by purchase (*i.e.*, through a grant or will), the incidents did not apply. The transaction must have seemed almost fraudulent at the time.

The Rule in Shelley's Case dealt with the problem by holding that the remainder in the grantee's heirs was actually a remainder in the grantee. Because in the example above Jones had a life estate and the remainder, a separate doctrine, called the doctrine of merger, converted his interest into a fee simple. The heirs got nothing by purchase; rather, they would take only by inheritance if the property was not otherwise disposed of by will or through a grant during the grantor's lifetime. Today, because the Rule in Shelley's Case has been abolished in most jurisdictions, *see* Marvel, Annotation, Modern Status of the Rule in Shelley's Case, 99 A.L.R.2d 1161, 1165–66 (1965), a grant "to Jones for life, and then to Jones' heirs" would create a contingent remainder in Jones' heirs (contingent because we do not know their identities until Jones is dead).

The Doctrine of Worthier Title applies to *inter vivos* grants (and originally to devises as well, when the incidents mattered) that create any future interest, not just a remainder, in the grantor's heirs. You can see that such a grant was another device to avoid the feudal incidents: "to Jones for life, and then to the grantor's heirs," gives the land to the grantor's heirs by purchase, not by descent. The Doctrine held that if the heirs' interest in the conveyance were identical to what they would have taken by descent, the conveyance to the heirs was void, and the grantor was deemed to have a reversion.

Today the Doctrine, which still exists in about half of the states, is justified as making land more alienable. It often is viewed as a rule of construction, so that if the conveyor's intent is clear, or if the conveyor uses more specific words, such as "children" rather than "heirs," a court is more likely to uphold the grant. *See, e.g., Warren–Boynton State Bank v. Wallbaum* 123 Ill.2d 429, 442, 123 Ill.Dec. 936, 942, 528 N.E.2d 640, 646 (1988) (unless grantor's intention is shown by preponderance of evidence, courts will rely on technical meaning of "heirs").

The Rule Against Restraints on Alienation. The Rule Against Perpetuities is a means to prevent, or limit, "indirect" restraints on alienation. Not surprisingly, given the struggle for free alienability of land, the common law has developed a separate doctrine preventing "direct" restraints on alienation. That is, conditions or covenants in grants that restrain the grantee's right to alienate his interest are void under certain conditions.

Many state statutes simply and unhelpfully provide that conditions restraining alienation are void if "repugnant to the interest created." *See, e.g.*, West's Ann. Cal. Civ. Code § 711; Mont. Code Ann. 70–1–405; N.D. Cent. Code 47–02–26. Courts, in turn, have held that "unreasonable" restraints are void. *See, e.g., Wellenkamp v. Bank of America*, 21 Cal.3d

943, 148 Cal.Rptr. 379, 582 P.2d 970 (1978); *Malouff v. Midland Federal Sav. & Loan Ass'n*, 181 Colo. 294, 299, 509 P.2d 1240, 1243 (1973); *Baker v. Loves Park Sav. & Loan Ass'n*, 61 Ill.2d 119, 123, 333 N.E.2d 1, 3 (1975).

The reasonableness of a purported restraint on alienation depends on the type of restraint (disabling, forfeiture, or promissory), the type of interest being restrained (fee, life estate, or leasehold), and the degree of restraint (absolute or partial as to time, persons, or use).

There are three types of restraints. The *disabling restraint* is a prohibition on alienation. For example: "to A, but A may not alienate the land, and any attempt to alienate the land is void." The *forfeiture restraint* defines an attempted alienation as a condition that either permits the grantor to exercise a power of termination or automatically divests the grantee in favor of a third party or the grantor. For example: "to A, so long as A does not attempt to sell the land." The *promissory restraint* defines the attempted alienation as a breach of a covenant, making the covenantor liable for the breach. For example, "to A, and A covenants not to transfer the land."

In most states all three types of restraints on the alienation of fees are prohibited, even if the restraint is limited in time. *See Wharton v. Mollinet*, 103 Cal.App.2d 710, 713, 229 P.2d 861, 863 (1951) (holding invalid a disabling restraint for 20 years); *Bonnell v. McLaughlin*, 173 Cal. 213, 159 P. 590 (1916) (holding invalid a forfeiture restraint during grantee's lifetime); *Brace v. Black*, 51 N.J.Super. 572, 580–84, 144 A.2d 385, 389–91 (1958) (holding invalid a promissory restraint that required the owner to get the approval of 8 named parties before he or his heirs sold the property).[43]

By contrast, forfeiture and promissory restraints on life estates are generally valid, whereas disabling restraints are void. *See* Powell on Real Property ¶ 844. Traditionally, all restraints on lesser interests (*i.e.*, leaseholds) have been upheld, although an increasing number of jurisdictions limit the landlord's power to refuse substitute tenants. *See, e.g.*, Alaska Stat. § 34.03.060 (specifying exclusive list of "reasonable grounds" to refuse consent); West's Ann. Cal. Civ. Code §§ 1995.010–1195.340 (imposing restrictions on the landlord's ability to restrict transfers of commercial leases); Del. Code Ann. tit 25, § 5512(b) (declaring that a landlord "shall not unreasonably" withhold consent); *Fernandez v. Vazquez*, 397 So.2d 1171, 1174 (Fla.Dist.Ct.App.1981) (landlord may not "unreasonably" withhold consent to sublease).

Partial restraints regarding potential grantees often are held invalid, especially when the number of potential grantees is small. *See, e.g.*, *Taormina Theosophical Community, Inc. v. Silver*, 140 Cal.App.3d 964, 190

---

43. One important exception to this general rule is the "spendthrift trust," which is designed to protect certain beneficiaries (*e.g.*, children, people with serious mental disabilities) from their own indiscretions by prohibiting sale or other disposition of the equitable interest. In most states, such restrictions are not void as unlawful restraints on alienation. *See, e.g.*, Ala. Code § 19–3–1(b)(1); West's Ann. Cal. Prob. Code § 15300; La. Rev. Stat. 9:1923.

Cal.Rptr. 38 (1983) (holding invalid a deed condition limiting ownership in a housing development to Theosophists older than age 50). Of course, provisions that purport to prohibit alienation to or use by a protected category of persons are void. *See, e.g.*, West's Ann. Cal. Civ. Code § 53(a) (declaring void written provisions that "forbid or restrict the [use, occupation,] conveyance, encumbrance, leasing, or mortgaging of * * * real property to any person of a specified sex, race, color, religion, ancestry, national origin or blindness or other physical disability"); Mass. Gen. Ann. Laws ch. 184, § 23B. Here, the issue has less to do with the free alienability of land than other social policies barring certain types of discrimination.

Partial restraints are more likely to be upheld if they are related to the use of the land rather than to whom it may be sold. *See, e.g., Gale v. York Center Community Cooperative*, 21 Ill.2d 86, 92, 171 N.E.2d 30, 33 (1960) (upholding partial restraint on the ability of coop members to transfer their ownership). In some cases, however, the distinctions between legitimate restrictions on use and illegitimate restrictions on the identity of the owner may not be clear.

———————

Riste v. Eastern Washington Bible Camp, Inc.

Court of Appeals of Washington, 1980.
25 Wash.App. 299, 605 P.2d 1294.

■ Roe, Judge.

Eastern Washington Bible Camp, Inc., owns land on Silver Lake in Spokane County. Part of the land was subdivided and lots sold only to people who agreed to subscribe to the tenets of the Assembly of God Church. In 1968, George Riste's parents contracted with Eastern Washington Bible Camp to purchase two lots. In 1974, when the contract was paid in full, at the request of plaintiff's surviving parent, defendant issued the deed to plaintiff Riste. Both the sales contract and the deed contained restrictions on occupancy and resale. Riste later attempted to sell the property contrary to the restrictions. Defendant Bible Camp refused to remove the restrictions and Riste sued for a declaration that the restrictions were invalid and for reformation of the deed.

The trial court granted summary judgment for Riste, holding that as a matter of law the restrictions were void, and ordered the deed reformed.

These restrictions state in part:

6.   No residents or occupants of these premises shall conduct themselves in such a manner as to be in conflict with the general practices and principles of the General and District Council of the Assemblies of God. No building activities or work shall be permitted on these premises on any Sunday of the entire year.

. . .

8. The property described herein shall not be resold to any person without written approval by the Seller or its agent.

Eastern Washington Bible Camp claims that a restriction limiting the sale of land to members of a church is reasonable and may be enforced by the courts.

Restriction No. 8 contains a direct restraint on alienation of land. The rule in Washington is that a clause in a deed prohibiting the grantee from conveying land to another without the approval of the grantor, when the grantor transferred a fee simple estate to the grantee, is void as repugnant to the nature of an estate in fee. As stated in *Richardson v. Danson*, 44 Wash.2d 760, 767, 270 P.2d 802, 807 (1954):

> The great weight of authority is that where the fee simple title to real estate passes under a deed or will, any restraint attempted to be imposed by the instrument upon the grantee or devisee is to be treated as void, and the grantee or devisee takes the property free of the void condition.

An exception allows reasonable restraints that are justified by legitimate interests, such as "due on sale" clauses in real estate mortgages. *Bellingham First Fed. Sav. & Loan Ass'n v. Garrison*, 87 Wash.2d 437, 553 P.2d 1090 (1976).

Defendant Bible Camp asserts as error the failure of the trial court to apply the doctrine of equitable estoppel. It argues that Riste acquired the property with knowledge of the restrictions on his and others' lots, and that the other purchasers in the subdivision bought their lots in reliance thereon.

The fact that Riste acquired the property with knowledge that there were restrictions and that the restrictions were common in the subdivision is irrelevant. This is a disabling restraint upon which there is a presumption of invalidity. It is upon public policy grounds that the restriction is invalidated. *Richardson v. Danson, supra.* The doctrine of equitable estoppel has no application in such a case.

Restriction No. 6 in the deed is also invalid. RCW 49.60.224, Law Against Discrimination, states:

> (1) Every provision in a written instrument relating to real property *which purports* to forbid or *restrict the conveyance,* encumbrance, occupancy, or lease thereof *to individuals of a* specified race, *creed,* color, national origin, or with any sensory, mental, or physical handicap, ... which directly or indirectly limits the use or occupancy of real property on the basis of race, creed, color, national origin, or the presence of any sensory, mental, or physical handicap is void.
>
> (2) It is an unfair practice to ... honor or attempt to honor such a provision in the chain of title.

Defendant Bible Camp places great emphasis on the fact that the deed restrictions were in the 1968 contract of sale between it and Riste's parents and therefore RCW 49.60.224, enacted in 1969, does not apply. There are two answers to this. First, under the rationale of *Shelley v. Kraemer*, 334 U.S. 1, 19–21, 68 S.Ct. 836, 92 L.Ed. 1161, 3 A.L.R.2d 441 (1948), which involved racial restrictions on land ownership, this court will deny access to those seeking enforcement of restrictive covenants which are void by statute. Second, the deed which Riste sought to have reformed was issued by Eastern Washington Bible Camp in 1974, 5 years after the passage of RCW 49.60.224. Clearly the statute applies.

Creed, as used in the statute and in its common dictionary meaning, refers to a system of religious beliefs. *See Augustine v. Anti–Defamation League of B'Nai B'Rith*, 75 Wis.2d 207, 249 N.W.2d 547, 551 (1977). Restriction No. 6 in the deed concerns creed and is void under RCW 49.60.224. * * *

Although we understand the desire of Eastern Washington Bible Camp to have an enclave at a quiet lake where there is no drinking or gambling, Sunday working, etc., and where people can enjoy themselves in their vacations in the warm environment of their church, the outright grant of the fee in this deed is fatal to their hopes. That is the extent of our holding. Even if these covenants were enforced, eventually, transfers by inheritance, dissolution actions, or foreclosures of judgments, etc., would tend to destroy the integrity of the plan.

Nothing in this opinion is to be construed as limiting the right of religious organizations to operate and maintain their own bible camps or church property, access to which is limited to those of the same persuasion.

Summary judgment is affirmed.

———————

1. O writes a will stating "I devise my house to X on condition that X live in the house and on condition that X not sell the house during his lifetime." What interest does X have? O's heirs? Can X sell the house?

2. What were the conditions in the deed in the *Riste* case? What, if any, is the difference between these two conditions?

3. The majority finds that condition 8, requiring prior approval, fits literally within the definition of a restraint on alienation. Why is that? Can you make a persuasive argument that condition 6 is also an illegal restraint on alienation?

4. Should there be any significance in the fact that the appellant was a non-profit corporation? Does the restriction serves some useful purpose?

5. In the *Riste* opinion, the court states that "reasonable" restraints on alienation might not be prohibited. What factors would a court consider in deciding whether a restraint was reasonable? Suppose that the restriction prohibited sales to people who gambled or drank alcohol. Would it be upheld as a reasonable restraint?

6.   A city subsidized the construction of condominiums. In return for the subsidy, the city required the project owners to sell a percentage of the units at below-market rates to low-income residents. In addition, the city required a deed restriction (for the low-income units) that restricted subsequent sales to only other low-income residents. Because of their limited income and other credit problems, however, very few low-income residents qualify for mortgages. In these circumstances, is the deed restriction an illegal restraint on alienation? *See City of Oceanside v. McKenna*, 215 Cal.App.3d 1420, 264 Cal.Rptr. 275 (1989).

---

2.   CONCURRENT INTERESTS

There are two forms of non-marital concurrent interests in property—joint tenancy and tenancy in common.[44] The *joint tenancy* existed as early as the thirteenth century. Under this form of ownership, the joint tenants shared an equal, undivided interest in the property with a right of survivorship. By the fourteenth century, legal doctrine required that a joint tenancy be created and maintained with the "four unities" (discussed below). If one or more of the unities was missing, the co-tenants held as *tenants in common*, a form of joint ownership, but without the right of survivorship.

a.   TENANCY IN COMMON

Tenants-in-common have an undivided interest in the land which gives each co-tenant the right to possess and use the entire property, subject to the rights of the other co-tenants.

Creation. A tenancy in common may be created either expressly in a grant or will (*e.g.,* "to A and B"), or by operation of law. For example, a tenancy in common is created by operation of law if several people inherit a particular piece of property. Similarly, if a grant to two or more persons does not create a valid joint tenancy, or if it is ambiguous as to the type of concurrent interest intended, the court will construe the interest as a tenancy in common. *See, e.g.,* Ark. Stat. Ann. § 18–12–603 (presumption in favor of tenancy in common over joint tenancy); Idaho Code § 55–104 (same); Utah Code Ann. § 57–1–5 (same).[45]

Termination. The death of a co-tenant does not terminate a tenancy-in-common. Rather, the decedent's interest passes to his heirs or devisees, who become tenants in common with the surviving co-tenants. For example, if A and B had a tenancy in common, A's interest would pass on his death to his heirs or to the devisees named in his will, and B would retain

---

44.   *Coparency*, one of the earliest forms of joint ownership, was an undivided interest held by female heirs when there were no male heirs. Coparency has long since been abolished. Two other forms of co-ownership are tenancy by the entirety and community property, both of which are forms of marital property, discussed later in this chapter.

45.   Most states, however, do not have a presumption in favor of tenancy in common for co-executors and co-trustees. *See, e.g.,* Ark. Code Ann. § 18–12–603.

her fractional share of ownership. Thus, B would be a tenant in common with A's successor. Similarly, a sale or gift of a co-tenant's interest to a third party simply makes the grantee a tenant in common.

Thus, the only means of terminating a tenancy in common are by transferring all of the interests to a single person or by "partitioning" the property, as discussed below.

b. JOINT TENANCY

The most significant feature of a joint tenancy is the right of survivorship. If two joint tenants, A and B, own a parcel of land and A dies, B becomes the owner of the entire parcel. B does not inherit the land but rather takes it under the terms of the grant as the only remaining survivor.

Purposes. Joint tenancies served three purposes at common law.[46] First, the mesne lord often preferred a joint tenancy. The right of survivorship in the other joint tenants eliminated the risk that upon the death of a co-tenant heirs of uncertain responsibility would take the land by inheritance.

Second, joint tenancies were useful in avoiding shortcomings in the common law system of estates. For example, as discussed earlier, joint tenancies were used in connection with the use, the forerunner of the modern trust, as a means to avoid the feudal incidents. Several persons would be enfeoffed as joint tenants in the property for the use of a named beneficiary (the intended grantee). When one of the joint tenants died, the legal interest did not pass either by inheritance (which would have triggered the incidents) or to the dead co-tenant's heirs or creditors; the property simply accrued to the remaining feofees. At the same time, the beneficial use could pass by inheritance or will, both of which were enforceable in the chancery courts and not subject to the feudal incidents.

In addition, until 1540, when the Statute of Wills was enacted to permit land to be passed in wills, joint tenancies could be effectively used to devise land. The would-be testator would enfeoff several joint tenants for the testator's use with instructions for final disposition of the use in his will. The reason to use several joint tenants was to reduce the probability that a feoffee would use the property for his own purposes.[47]

The third use for joint tenancies was to protect illegitimate children. Wives and legitimate children were protected by dower, intestate succession, and marriage agreements. Unmarried women and their children, by contrast, received no protection under the common law; unmarried women could not inherit from their mates, and illegitimate children could not inherit from their parents or siblings. The interests belonging to illegitimate children could pass only to their lineal heirs; if an illegitimate child

---

46. For a concise discussion of the historical development of joint tenancies, *see* Spitzer, Joint Tenancy with Right of Survivorship: A Legacy from Thirteenth Century England, 16 Tex. Tech. L. Rev. 629 (1985).

47. In contrast to today, at common law a joint tenancy could be terminated only by agreement of all of the joint tenants.

had no lineal heirs, the interest escheated to the grantor. Finally, the common law rules effectively forbade a childless illegitimate child from alienating the interest. Thus, a grant to the unmarried mother did not protect her children. A grant to an illegitimate child left everyone in a precarious position; the child's grant to his siblings or mother was unenforceable, and, of course, they could not take by intestate succession. If an illegitimate child died childless, the land reverted to the grantor, or the grantor's heirs, who may have lost whatever compassion or sense of duty they once felt toward the illegitimate wing of the family.

The creation of a joint tenancy in the mother and her children alleviated this problem to some extent because the survivor simply absorbed the dead joint tenant's interest. Whether the mother or the children died first, the survivors retained the property.

Of course, the common law reasons for joint tenancies no longer obtain. There are no feudal obligations to be avoided;[48] uses have been eliminated, and trusts are readily available; and land can be transferred by will to anyone the testator chooses. Nevertheless, joint tenancies remain popular today. One author conducted an extensive empirical study of real estate transactions over several decades in Iowa and found that since the nineteenth century, the percentage of land transfers creating joint tenancies increased from virtually zero to nearly 50%. In almost all cases, the joint tenants were married; in virtually no cases were they unrelated. *See* Hines, Real Property Joint Tenancies: Law, Fact, and Fancy, 51 Iowa L. Rev. 582 (1966). He concluded that the popularity can be attributed to the right of survivorship, which provides two advantages. First, it is popularly believed to create a "poor man's will." The property accrues to the surviving joint tenant without the time and expense associated with probate. Second, this form of ownership defeats the claims of unsecured and secured creditors of the deceased co-tenant. When the debtor co-tenant dies, creditors can no longer satisfy their claims against the property.[49]

Creation. By the fourteenth century, a joint tenancy was valid only if it was formed with, and continued to have, the four "unities": (1) *unity of interest* required the interests granted (*i.e.*, type, amount, and duration of estate) to be identical for each owner; (2) *unity of title* required the interests to be created in the same grant, not in successive grants; (3) *unity of time* required the interests to vest at the same moment; and (4) *unity of possession* required the owners to have equal rights of access to and use of all portions of the land.

In many jurisdictions, the four unities remain prerequisites for creating a joint tenancy.[50] Thus, a grant from "A" "to A and B as joint tenants"

48. In addition, modern tax laws ensure that inheritance taxes are imposed on property that accrues through the death of a joint tenant.

49. For a discussion of the risks that creditors face with property held in joint tenancy, *see* Treadwell & Shulkin, Joint Tenancy—Creditor–Debtor Relations, 37 Wash. L. Rev. 58 (1962).

50. *But see* Minn. Stat. Ann. § 500.19 (abolishing unities requirement); Wis. Stat. Ann. 700.19 (abolishing requirements of unity of time and title).

would not create a joint tenancy because the unities of title and time are missing, *i.e.*, A's interest derived from an earlier grant. Common law lawyers avoided this obstacle by having A convey the property to a third party "straw man," who then reconveyed the property to A and B as joint tenants.[51] Some states have discarded this rigid application of the rules. *See* West's Ann. Cal. Civ. Code § 683(a); *Estate of Galletto*, 75 Cal.App.2d 580, 171 P.2d 152 (1946) (wife acquired, by deed, an undivided one-half interest in some property; by another deed, wife and husband acquired the remaining half as joint tenants).

As mentioned earlier, many jurisdictions have created rules of construction disfavoring joint tenancies and favoring tenancies in common; indeed, a few states have abolished joint tenancies altogether.[52] Thus, most courts will construe a grant as a tenancy in common unless the grant explicitly identifies the interest as a "joint tenancy," or the grantees as "joint tenants." In many states, for example, a grant to "A and B jointly" will not create a joint tenancy. *See, e.g.*, West's Ann. Cal. Civ. Code § 686; N.Y.—McKinney's Est. Powers & Trusts Law § 6–2.2. A few states also require an express right of survivorship in the grantees. *See, e.g.*, Ala. Code § 35–4–7.[53]

Severance.[54] A joint tenancy can be severed—and thus transformed into a tenancy in common—by the agreement of all of the joint tenants, *see, e.g.*, *Carson v. Ellis*, 186 Kan. 112, 348 P.2d 807 (1960), or following the simultaneous death of the co-tenants. *See* Uniform Simultaneous Death Act, *e.g.*, Tenn. Code Ann. § 31–3–104. In most states, divorce severs a joint tenancy. (Of course, marital property is divided in most cases by a property settlement, not the rules pertaining to severance.) *See, e.g.*, *Snyder v. Snyder*, 298 Minn. 43, 50, 212 N.W.2d 869, 874 (1973).

More surprisingly to the uninitiated, a joint tenancy can be severed by the unilateral act of one co-tenant. For example, if "A," who is a joint tenant with "B" and "C," conveys her interest to "D," D holds as a tenant in common with B and C, although B and C remain joint tenants as to each other. It makes no difference that A acted without B's and C's consent or even without their knowledge. A joint tenancy may also be severed by an involuntary conveyance, *i.e.*, if a creditor of a co-tenant executes a lien against the debtor's interest to satisfy a debt, the purchaser becomes a

51. The expression "straw man" probably derives from the expression "straw shoes." Individuals who, for a price, were willing to testify for any cause would notify attorneys of their availability by placing straw in their shoes. Obviously, anyone who was willing to commit perjury was also willing to act as a conduit to assist in the lawful transfer of property.

52. Alaska Stat. § 34.15.130 (abolished); Or. Rev. Stat. § 93.180 (abolished); 765 Ill. Comp. Stat. Ann. 1005/2 (retained only for trusts and executors); Ky. Rev. Stat. §§ 381.120, 381.130 (same).

53. An exception to this general presumption is when the grantees are married, or when they are co-trustees or co-executors. *See, e.g.*, N.Y.—McKinney's Est. Powers & Trusts Law § 6–2.2(e).

54. For a general discussion on the severance of joint tenancies, see Swenson & Degnan, Severance of Joint Tenancies, 38 Minn. L. Rev. 466 (1954).

tenant in common with the remaining co-tenants.[55] In some states, a joint tenant can sever the joint tenancy by naming himself as the transferee. West's Ann. Cal. Civ. Code § 683.2(a)(2); Minn. Stat. Ann. § 500.19(4); N.Y.—McKinney's Real Prop. Law § 240–c(1)(b).

Some states protect unsuspecting joint tenants from unilateral severances. *See* Cal. Civ. § Code 683.2(b) (defeats a unilateral severance that is contrary to a written agreement among the joint tenants unless the transferee is a "purchaser * * * for value in good faith and without knowledge of the written agreement"); West's Ann. Cal. Civ. Code § 683.2(c) (a transfer of an interest in a recorded joint tenancy will not defeat the survivorship rights of the remaining joint tenants unless that transfer is also recorded). *See also* N.Y.—McKinney's Real Prop. Law § 240–c(2) (requiring transfer be recorded); Minn. Stat. Ann. § 500.19(5) (same). Requiring recordation of the unilateral severance helps ensure that if the non-severing co-tenant dies first, the severing tenant will not be able to destroy evidence of the severance and assert a right of survivorship to the entire estate.

A special problem arises if one co-tenant takes out a mortgage on his share of the property. Whether this mortgage constitutes a severance depends on whether the transaction takes place in a "lien theory" state (majority rule) or a "title theory" state (minority rule). *See, e.g., D.A.D., Inc. v. Moring*, 218 So.2d 451, 452 (Fla.App.1969) (no severance in a lien theory state); *Eder v. Rothamel*, 202 Md. 189, 192, 95 A.2d 860, 862 (1953) (severance in a title theory state).

People v. Nogarr

Court of Appeal of California, 1958.
164 Cal.App.2d 591, 330 P.2d 858.

■ NOURSE, JUSTICE pro tem.

This appeal presents but one question: Is a mortgage upon real property executed by one of two joint tenants enforceable after the death of that joint tenant?

The facts are not in dispute. The appellant, Elaine R. Wilson, hereinafter called "Elaine," and Calvert S. Wilson, hereinafter called "Calvert," were husband and wife. On April 10, 1950, they acquired the real property in question as joint tenants and the record title remained in them as joint

55. Simply obtaining a lien without completing the sale, however, does not sever the joint tenancy. *See, e.g., Grothe v. Cortlandt Corp.*, 11 Cal.App.4th 1313, 1324, 15 Cal.Rptr.2d 38, 45 (1992) (even though the sheriff had levied the property, "the joint tenancy is not severed until after the grace period is over and the sale completed"); *Knibb v. Security Ins. Co.*, 121 R.I. 406, 411–12, 399 A.2d 1214, 1217 (1979) (if joint tenant dies before foreclosure sale, interest passes to surviving joint tenant); *Northern State Bank v. Toal*, 69 Wis.2d 50, 56, 230 N.W.2d 153, 156 (1975) (no severance absent foreclosure).

tenants until the death of Calvert. In July 1954 Elaine and Calvert separated. On October 11, 1954, Calvert executed his promissory note to his parents, the respondents, Frank H. and Alice B. Wilson, hereinafter called "respondents." This note was in the sum of $6,440. At the same time he executed and delivered to respondents a mortgage upon the real property in question. Elaine did not have knowledge of or give her consent to the execution of this mortgage. On June 23, 1955, Calvert died. On May 8, 1956, the People of the State of California commenced an action to condemn the subject real property. By its complaint the condemner alleged that Elaine R. Wilson was the owner of the subject real property and that respondents were mortgagees thereof. By her answer Elaine alleged that she was the owner of the property, that respondents had no right, title or interest therein. Respondents by their answer alleged that they were the owners and holders of the mortgage executed by Calvert and prayed that the mortgage be satisfied from the proceeds of the condemnation award. By agreement the fair market value of the property was fixed at $13,800 and that amount together with interest was paid into court by the condemner. Thereafter trial was had as to the rights and interests of Elaine and the respondents. No formal findings were made by the court but by a memorandum ruling the court found that there was owing to respondents the sum of $6,440 upon the promissory note executed by Calvert and secured by the aforesaid mortgage and ordered that sum plus interest disbursed to respondents out of 50 per cent of the funds remaining in the hands of the trustee (the county clerk) after the payment of certain liens which were concededly a charge upon the joint estate. Judgment was entered accordingly. As a practical matter this resulted in distribution of 50 per cent of said balance to respondents as the amount found due them was in excess of one-half of the balance remaining after the payment of other liens.

It is appellant's contention that execution of the mortgage by Calvert did not operate to terminate the joint tenancy and sever his interest from that of Elaine but that the mortgage was a charge or lien upon his interest as a joint tenant only and that therefore upon his death his interest having ceased to exist the lien of the mortgage terminated and that Elaine was entitled to the distribution of the entire award exclusive of the sums distributed to other lienholders.

We have reached the conclusion that appellant's contention must be sustained. In order that a joint tenancy may exist four unities are required; unity of interest, unity of title, unity of time and unity of possession. *Hammond v. McArthur*, 30 Cal.2d 512, 514, 183 P.2d 1 and authorities there cited. So long as these unities exist the right of survivorship is an incident of the tenancy and upon the death of one joint tenant the survivor becomes the sole owner in fee by right of survivorship and no interest in the property passes to the heirs, devisees or personal representatives of the joint tenant first to die. *King v. King*, 107 Cal.App.2d 257, 236 P.2d 912; *In re Estate of Zaring*, 93 Cal.App.2d 577, 579–580, 209 P.2d 642.

It is undisputed in the present case that a joint tenancy in fee simple existed between Elaine and Calvert at the time of the execution of the mortgage, that at that time there existed all of the four unities, that consequently Elaine upon the death of Calvert became the sole owner of the property in question and under the doctrine of equitable conversion to the entire award in condemnation, unless the execution by Calvert of the mortgage destroyed one of the unities and thus severed the joint tenancy and destroyed the right of survivorship.

Under the law of this state a mortgage is but a hypothecation of the property mortgaged. It creates but a charge or lien upon the property hypothecated without the necessity of a change of possession and without any right of possession in the mortgagee and does not operate to pass the legal title to the mortgagee. Civ.Code, § 2920; *McMillan v. Richards*, 9 Cal. 365, 406, 411; *Dutton v. Warschauer*, 21 Cal. 609, 621; 33 Cal.Jur.2d 423–424.

Inasmuch as the mortgage was but a lien or charge upon Calvert's interest and as it did not operate to transfer the legal title or any title to the mortgagees or entitle the mortgagees to possession it did not destroy any of the unities and therefore the estate in joint tenancy was not severed and Elaine and Calvert did not become tenants in common. It necessarily follows that as the mortgage lien attached only to such interest as Calvert had in the real property when his interest ceased to exist the lien of the mortgage expired with it. *Application of Gau*, 230 Minn. 235, 41 N.W.2d 444; *Power v. Grace*, 1 D.L.R. 801; *Zeigler v. Bonnell*, 52 Cal.App.2d 217, 219–221, 126 P.2d 118, cited with approval in *Hammond v. McArthur*, *supra*, 30 Cal.2d 512, 183 P.2d 1.

In *Zeigler v. Bonnell, supra*, it was directly held that a judgment lien upon the interest of a joint tenant terminated on the death of the judgment debtor joint tenant. In so holding the court said (52 Cal.App.2d at page 219, 126 P.2d at page 119): "The right of survivorship is the chief characteristic that distinguishes a joint tenancy from other interests in property. The surviving joint tenant does not secure that right from the deceased joint tenant, but from the devise or conveyance by which the joint tenancy was first created. (Citation.) While both joint tenants are alive each has a specialized form of a life estate, with what amounts to a contingent remainder in the fee, the contingency being dependent upon which joint tenant survives. The judgment lien of respondent could attach only to the interest of his debtor, William B. Nash. That interest terminated upon Nash's death. After his death there was no interest to levy upon. Although the title of the execution purchaser dates back to the date of his lien, that doctrine only applies when the rights of innocent third parties have not intervened. Here the rights of the surviving joint tenant intervened between the date of the lien and the date of the sale. On the latter date the deceased joint tenant had no interest in the property, and his judgment creditor has no greater rights. * * * This rule is sound in theory and fair in its operation. When a creditor has a judgment lien against the interest of one joint tenant he can immediately execute and sell the interest of his judgment debtor, and thus sever the joint tenancy, or he can keep his lien alive and wait until the joint tenancy is terminated by the death of one of the joint tenants. If the judgment debtor survives, the judgment lien immediately attaches to the entire property. If the judgment debtor is the first to die, the lien is lost. If the creditor sits back to await this contingency, as respondent did in this case, he assumes the risk of losing his lien."

We are unable to distinguish between the effect of a judgment lien and of a lien of a mortgage executed by one joint tenant only. The only distinction between the two liens is that the mortgage lien is a lien upon specific property while the judgment lien is a general lien upon all real property of the judgment debtor. *McMillan v. Richards, supra*, 9 Cal. 365, 409.

In *Hammond v. McArthur, supra*, in discussing the operation of a mortgage as a severance of joint tenancy, the Supreme Court, in what is undoubtedly dictum, as a mortgage was not there involved, said (30 Cal.2d at page 515, 183 P.2d at page 3): "In jurisdictions where a mortgage ordinarily operates to transfer the legal title, a mortgage by a joint tenant causes a severance of the joint tenancy. (Citation.) Also, in some states where a mortgage is regarded as mere security, a mortgage by a joint tenant brings the tenancy to an end. (Citation.) However, that conclusion is not in accord with the common-law authorities to the effect that the creation by a joint tenant of a mere charge upon the land is a nullity as against the right of survivorship of the other joint tenant. (Citation.)"

Respondents have directed our attention to decisions of other jurisdictions which they assert support their contention that a joint tenant has a right to mortgage his interest and that this operates to sever the joint tenancy. Examination of each of the cases relied upon by respondents discloses that all except one of them were rendered in jurisdictions where a mortgage operated not merely as a lien or charge upon the mortgagor's interest but as a transfer or conveyance of his interest, the conveyance being subject to defeasance upon the payment of the mortgage debt. It is evident that in those jurisdictions where a mortgage operates to convey title to the mortgagee the unity of title is destroyed and in those jurisdictions where it operates not only to transfer title but the right of possession to the mortgagee both the unity of title and of possession are destroyed and that in either case there is a severance of the joint tenancy. * * *

There is nothing inequitable in holding that the lien of respondents' mortgage did not survive the death of the mortgagor. Their note was payable upon demand and they could have enforced the lien and mortgage by foreclosure and sale prior to the death of the mortgagor and thus have severed the joint tenancy. If they chose not to do so but to await the contingency of which joint tenant died first they did so at their own risk. Under that event the lien that they had expired. If the event had been otherwise and the mortgagor had been the survivor the security of their lien would have been doubled.

The judgment is reversed.

1. Are creditors disadvantaged by the existence of joint tenancies? Do you consider these disadvantages to be serious? How can creditors avoid these disadvantages?

2. What is the legal basis for the decision in *People v. Nogarr*? What is the policy basis for concluding that giving a mortgage does not sever the joint tenancy? Note that the court asserts that the decision is "fair" because the note was payable on demand. Would the case have been decided differently if the note were not payable on demand?

3. Do you think that Conn. Gen. Stat. Ann. § 47–14e—which provides that a "mortgage * * * executed by less than all of the joint tenants is a severance only to the extent that, upon the death of any joint tenant joining in the mortgage * * *, the mortgage * * * will continue to encumber the interest accruing for the surviving joint tenants * * *"—is fair?

4. Given the ease with which joint tenancies are severed, how could you create a right of survivorship that was not revocable? *See Hass v. Hass*, 248 Wis. 212, 221, 21 N.W.2d 398, 402 (1946); *Holbrook v. Holbrook*, 240 Or. 567, 570, 403 P.2d 12, 13 (1965).

Problem

As a member of the staff of a state legislative committee, you have been asked to draft a statute to deal with the situation where one joint tenant kills another. The situation frequently arises when one spouse kills another; sometimes the killer commits suicide. The deceased joint tenant frequently leaves minor heirs, who may or may not be the children of the killer.

The legislators are in complete consensus that, with the right degree of culpability, the killer should not take the entire joint tenancy under the right of survivorship. Beyond that, however, the legislators are unsure how to proceed. To draft the statute, you must first answer the following questions:

a. What degree of culpability (*e.g.*, accident, negligent homicide, felonious killing, murder) must be established for the exception to the normal rules of joint tenancy to apply?

b. Should the exception apply only upon the killer's criminal conviction?

c. If not, what should be the burden of proof of the deceased joint tenant's heirs?

d. If the deceased joint tenant's heirs prevail, how much of the property do they get—the deceased joint tenant's fractional share or the entire property?

See, e.g., West's Ann. Cal. Prob. Code §§ 251, 254 (felonious killings, preponderance of the evidence). *See generally* Purver, Annotation, Felonious Killing of One Cotenant or Tenant by the Entireties by the Other as Affecting the Latter's Right in the Property, 42 A.L.R.3d 1116 (1972).

The most complicated severance questions arise when one joint tenant has conveyed a life estate or leasehold without the consent of the other co-tenants. (If all of the joint tenants consented to the lease, there would be no severance). In England and in a few states such a conveyance would sever the joint tenancy. The joint tenant/lessor would become a tenant in common with the remaining co-tenants, who would remain joint tenants with respect to each other. *See, e.g., Alexander v. Boyer*, 253 Md. 511, 521, 253 A.2d 359, 365 (1969) (lease fully severs joint tenancy).

Most courts in this country reject the English rule. In some states, the joint tenancy is not severed at all, but the lease or life estate is considered to be *determinable* by the death of the joint tenant/lessor. If the joint tenant/lessor dies, the lease or life estate is terminated, and the dead joint tenant's interest accrues to the surviving joint tenants. *Tenhet v. Boswell*, 18 Cal.3d 150, 152, 133 Cal.Rptr. 10, 12, 554 P.2d 330, 332 (1976) (lease expires on the death of the joint tenant/lessor). If a non-leasing joint tenant died, that joint tenant's interest would accrue to the survivors. And if the grant or lease ended before the death of the lessor/joint tenant, the original joint tenants would continue as before. This approach has the advantage of simplicity, but bears no relation to the doctrinal requirements of the four unities.

Other courts have held that a lease or a life estate "partially severs" the underlying estate.[56] That is, the lessee is a tenant in common with the remaining co-tenants during the lease or life estate, but all of the original co-tenants are joint tenants in the reversion. When the lease or life estate terminates, the joint tenants in the reversion again become joint tenants in the fee. If, however, *any* co-tenant died before termination of the lease, his interest in the reversion would accrue to the surviving joint tenants. Therefore, if the dead joint tenant was also the lessor, the surviving joint tenants would acquire not only his interest in the reversion, but also his rights under the lease.

In the remaining states, the joint tenants' interest is "conditionally" severed. That is, the joint tenant/lessor now holds only a reversion and becomes a tenant in common with the remaining co-tenants (who remain joint tenants with each other in the fee). If the life estate or lease ends before any of the original co-tenants die, the joint tenancy is revived. If *any* co-tenant dies before the end of the lease, the tenancy in common between the lessor/co-tenant and the remaining co-tenants becomes permanent. If the joint tenant/lessor died, his heir would become the new joint tenant/les-

---

56. For a careful discussion of severance following conveyance of a life estate or a leasehold, *see* Comment, Joint Tenancy in California Revisited: A Doctrine of Partial Severance, 61 Cal. L. Rev. 231, 241–47 (1973).

sor. If a different co-tenant died, his interest would accrue to the remaining joint tenants.

c.   RIGHTS AND OBLIGATIONS OF CO–TENANTS[57]

Partition. A partition is a judicial procedure to end a tenancy in common or a joint tenancy when the co-tenants no longer agree on the management or disposition of the property. It is a matter of right, enforceable by a court. For example, in *Dorazio v. Davis*, 283 Ark. 65, 67, 671 S.W.2d 173, 175 (1984), the court declared that the right to partition could not be defeated by showing that partition "would be inconvenient, injurious, or even ruinous" to the other co-tenants. *See also De Roulet v. Mitchel*, 70 Cal.App.2d 120, 160 P.2d 574 (1945) (right to partition not subject to judicial discretion). However, co-tenants may agree to waive the right to partition. West's Ann. Cal. Code Civ. Proc. § 872.710(b); *Prude v. Lewis*, 78 N.M. 256, 263, 430 P.2d 753, 760 (1967) (right to partition may be waived by express or implied agreement).

Partition may be "in kind" (physical division),[58] "by sale" (property is sold and the proceeds divided in proportion to the co-tenants' fractional interests), or in some states "by appraisal" (permitting one co-tenant to buy out the others at the appraisal price). In principle, the law favors partition in kind,[59] but in practice courts often partition concurrently held property by sale. In a partition proceeding the court can order "compensatory adjustment" among the parties to take into account inequities in expenses incurred or benefits derived from the property. *See, e.g., Jordan v. Ellis*, 278 Ala. 116, 120, 176 So.2d 244, 247 (1965) (allowing an adjustment for rental to third party and sale of timber from the property); *In re Marriage of Leversee*, 156 Cal.App.3d 891, 203 Cal.Rptr. 481 (1984) (ordering compensation along with partition by sale to reflect unequal contributions to down payment on house).

Possession. Under the unity of possession, which is basic to each joint tenancy and tenancy in common, each co-tenant has a right to possess and use the entire property. *State v. Hoskins*, 357 Mo. 377, 379, 208 S.W.2d

---

57. For a good summary of co-tenants' rights and liabilities, see Note, Right of Cotenant to Contribution from Other Cotenants for Unauthorized Repairs and Improvements Made to the Common Property, 32 Notre Dame Law. 493 (1957).

58. Partition in kind does not necessarily mean that the property is divided identically. In some cases, courts have awarded equal co-tenants different amounts of land because some parts of the land were more valuable than other parts. *Richmond v. Dofflemyer*, 105 Cal.App.3d 745, 759–62, 164 Cal. Rptr. 727, 735–37 (1980); *Maddox v. Percy*, 351 So.2d 1249 (La.App.1977) (upholding a partition giving one co-tenant 625 acres and the other co-tenant 317 acres). The goal is to ensure that the co-tenants get an amount of land whose value is proportional to the fractional share of their interests.

59. Ala. Code § 35–6–57 (a sale is permitted, in place of a physical division, if "a just and equal division of the land cannot be made" or if a sale would "better promote the interests of all the cotenants"); Official Code Ga. Ann. § 44–6–166.1 (sale permitted when a division is not "fair and equitable"); Kan. Stat. Ann. § 60–1003(c)(2), (4) (permitting sale if division would produce "manifest injury" or would be "impracticable"). *But see* Iowa Rules Civ. Proc. § 278 (creating a presumption in favor of partition by sale and division of proceeds).

221, 222 (1948) (each co-tenant "holds an undivided fraction in every particle of the whole in common with his co-tenants"). It follows that, absent an agreement to the contrary, each co-tenant has the right to sell, lease, or mortgage his interest. *Haster v. Blair*, 41 Cal.App.2d 896, 898, 107 P.2d 933, 934 (1940) (mortgage); *Fuller v. Dennistoun*, 164 Minn. 160, 165, 204 N.W. 958, 959 (1925) (mortgage); *Lee Chuck v. Quan Wo Chong & Co.*, 91 Cal. 593, 598–99, 28 P. 45, 46 (1891) (lease); *Arbesman v. Winer*, 298 Md. 282, 294, 468 A.2d 633, 639 (1983) (lease).

Moreover, since each co-tenant has a right to possession of the entire property, co-tenants who are not in possession (but who have not been "ousted") may not demand an accounting or receive compensation in a partition proceeding for the reasonable rental value of the property. That is, they cannot force a co-tenant in possession to pay rent during the period of his or her occupation. *DesRoches v. McCrary*, 315 Mich. 611, 615, 24 N.W.2d 511, 513 (1946). They also cannot receive compensation for the "profits derived from the property by means of the occupant's own labors." *See, e.g.*, *Arnold v. De Booy*, 161 Minn. 255, 260, 201 N.W. 437, 439 (1924) (where co-tenant did not exclude other co-tenants, he was not liable to them for the profit he earned from farming). In *Black v. Black*, 91 Cal.App.2d 328, 332–34, 204 P.2d 950, 952–54 (1949), the court justified this rule on the ground that since the farmer/co-tenant took the risks of failure, he is entitled to the profits from his efforts.[60]

The rules are different if there has been an ouster. Generally, an ouster occurs when a co-tenant bars another co-tenant from using the property.[61] Some state courts have held that purporting to convey full title to the property also amounts to an ouster. *Whittington v. Cameron*, 385 Ill. 99, 101, 52 N.E.2d 134, 136 (1943) (purported transfer works as an ouster since it sets up a claim for adverse possession by the grantee); *Witherspoon v. Brummett*, 50 N.M. 303, 307, 176 P.2d 187, 190 (1946) (same). A few courts have even held that an ouster exists if the co-tenant not in possession asks for rent and the co-tenant in possession refuses. *See, e.g.*, *Eldridge v. Wolfe*, 129 Misc. 617, 221 N.Y.S. 508 (1927). In *Estate of Hughes*, 5 Cal.App.4th 1607, 1614–16, 7 Cal.Rptr.2d 742, 747–48 (1992), the court held that a co-tenant ousted his co-tenants when he filed a petition to establish his sole ownership of the property under the community property laws.

An ousted co-tenant may seek an injunction as well as damages (measured by the rental value of his exclusion from the property plus

---

60. A specific agreement among the co-tenants would override these common law rules. Thus, if the co-tenants had agreed previously that the co-tenant in exclusive possession should pay for his use of the property, that agreement would be enforceable.

61. Many statutes provide no useful definition. *See, e.g.*, W. Va. Code § 55–4–15 (prohibiting an "actual ouster or some other

act amounting to a total denial of the plaintiff's right as a co-tenant"); R.S. Mo. S. § 524.090 (must show that "defendant actually ousted him, or did some act amounting to a total denial of his right as a cotenant"); N.M. Stat. Ann. § 42–4–8 (must prove "an actual ouster or act equivalent thereto"). *But cf.* West's Ann. Cal. Civ. Code § 843(b) (establishing a procedure to establish whether an ouster occurred).

consequential damages) in a civil suit or as part of an action for partition. *See Harlan v. Harlan*, 74 Cal.App.2d 555, 562, 168 P.2d 985, 989 (1946) (damages are rental value); *Stylianopoulos v. Stylianopoulos*, 17 Mass.App. Ct. 64, 66–69, 455 N.E.2d 477, 479–81 (1983) (because a divorce constituted an ouster of the husband, the wife had to pay fair rental value on the property they owned in common); *MCI Mining Corp. v. Stacy*, 785 S.W.2d 491, 495 (Ky.App.1989) (measure of damages is rental value for use and occupation).

Under the right circumstances, an ouster can ripen into a claim for adverse possession. It normally is difficult for one co-tenant to establish title to the entire property by adverse possession; because each co-tenant is entitled to use the entire property, exclusive occupancy is presumed to be permissive. In *Hare v. Chisman*, 230 Ind. 333, 342, 101 N.E.2d 268, 271 (1951), a husband remained in sole possession of the house after his wife died. The court found no adverse possession against her heirs (his co-tenants) since it "was not an unnatural act of them to permit their father to occupy this property, collect the income, pay the expense, and enjoy the surplus." *See also Johnson v. James*, 237 Ark. 900, 903, 377 S.W.2d 44, 46 (1964) (presumption is even stronger when co-tenants are related).

However, if the co-tenant in possession shows (in addition to the usual elements for adverse possession) that the other co-tenants had been ousted and had actual or constructive notice of their exclusion, the co-tenant in possession will gain title by adverse possession. *See, e.g.*, Official Code Ga. Ann. § 44–6–123 (a co-tenant can obtain title by adverse possession if the co-tenant "effects an actual ouster, retains exclusive possession after demand, or gives his cotenant express notice of adverse possession"); *Johnson v. James*, 237 Ark. 900, 903, 377 S.W.2d 44, 46–47 (1964) (co-tenant established adverse possession since he had sole possession for 36 years, paid the taxes, collected rents, received insurance payments, and possessed a will purportedly granting him title, and co-tenants knew about the will but made no claim); *West v. Evans*, 29 Cal.2d 414, 418, 175 P.2d 219, 221 (1946) (co-tenant out of possession must have either actual or constructive notice of hostile possession; recordation of a deed is not sufficient notice).

Contribution. A co-tenant may demand contribution from the other co-tenants for certain expenditures—payments of taxes, the mortgage, insurance, and necessary repairs, *i.e.*, "expenditures necessarily made for the protection of the common property." *Beshear v. Ahrens*, 289 Ark. 57, 60, 709 S.W.2d 60, 62 (1986) (contribution for mortgage payments and property taxes); *Shenson v. Shenson*, 124 Cal.App.2d 747, 754–55, 269 P.2d 170, 174 (1954) (taxes, mortgage, and necessary repairs). In some states, a co-tenant can seek contribution for these items only in a final accounting during a partition proceeding. If a co-tenant in sole possession seeks contribution for appropriate expenditures, the claim will be offset by the value of his occupancy. *Hunter v. Schultz*, 240 Cal.App.2d 24, 32, 49 Cal.Rptr. 315, 320 (1966).

A co-tenant may not demand compensation for managing the property. *Combs v. Ritter*, 100 Cal.App.2d 315, 317–19, 223 P.2d 505, 506–508 (1950).

In addition, a co-tenant cannot demand contribution from the other co-tenants for the costs of improving the property.[62] *See Perez v. Hernandez*, 658 S.W.2d 697, 701 (Tex.App. 1983) (co-tenant may not seek contribution for expenses incurred in development of land as a citrus grove). In *Knight v. Mitchell*, 97 Ill.App.2d 178, 181, 240 N.E.2d 16, 18 (1968), a co-tenant who developed and operated oil wells on the property sought contribution for expenses in operating the wells. The court held that although the co-tenant could not receive contribution for his expenses, he could set off *necessary* expenses in an action for accounting (*i.e.*, a suit to force the co-tenant to share profits). Thus, he could set-off operating expenses for wells that produced oil, but not for wells that ran dry.

Fiduciary obligations. Co-tenants have a fiduciary relationship[63] with each other if they receive their interests in the same will or grant, or at the same time by inheritance. *See, e.g., Poka v. Holi*, 44 Haw. 464, 481, 357 P.2d 100, 110 (1960) (co-tenants have a fiduciary obligation to give other co-tenants adequate notice of adverse claims to the property); *Wilson v. S.L. Rey, Inc.*, 17 Cal.App.4th 234, 243, 21 Cal.Rptr.2d 552, 556 (1993) (holding that co-tenants who acquire their interests at different times in different instruments have no fiduciary relationship). This relationship restricts the freedom of co-tenants in acquiring *common property*.[64] Thus, a co-tenant acquiring superior title to the property must give the other co-tenants a reasonable opportunity to acquire their proportional share. Similarly, for example, many but not all courts hold that a co-tenant who acquires title to the common property at an execution, mortgage foreclosure, or tax sale holds title for the benefit of the other co-tenants. That is, they are entitled to a reasonable period of time—possibly beyond the statutory redemption period—to pay their share of the purchase price. *Calkins v. Steinbach*, 66 Cal. 117, 4 P. 1103 (1884); *Stevenson v. Boyd*, 153 Cal. 630, 96 P. 284 (1908) (finding the assertion of a claim as a co-tenant after a delay of 4 years to be barred by laches).

Accounting. (1) *Rents*. The co-tenant out of possession may demand an accounting (or compensation at partition) for his share of net rents collected from third parties who have leased the property. *McWhorter v. McWhorter*, 99 Cal.App. 293, 278 P. 454 (1929).[65] More precisely, non-leasing co-tenants may demand their share of the net rents received if the

---

62. Most states, however, have provisions that award the improving co-tenant the *value* of the improvement at a final partition. *See, e.g.*, West's Ann. Cal. Code Civ. Proc. § 873.220.

63. A fiduciary relationship between two people imposes a higher standard of good faith and reasonable care than would exist between two strangers.

64. The fiduciary obligations extend only to common interests. Nothing prohibits

a co-tenant from purchasing another co-tenant's undivided interest at an execution sale. *Anderson v. T.G. Owen & Son, Inc.*, 231 Miss. 633, 639–40, 97 So.2d 369, 371–72 (1957); *McNutt v. Nuevo Land Co.*, 167 Cal. 459, 466–67, 140 P. 6, 9–10 (1914).

65. This rule dates back to an English statute enacted in the early eighteenth century, known as the Statute of Anne. The statute overrode the common law rule that a co-tenant was not liable to fellow co-tenants for rents received.

lease purports to bind all the co-tenants[66] and if the non-leasing co-tenants have acquiesced in the lease. Of course, one co-tenant cannot lawfully sign a lease that binds the other co-tenants without their consent. *Swartzbaugh v. Sampson*, 11 Cal.App.2d 451, 457–61, 54 P.2d 73, 77–79 (1936). Thus, the non-leasing co-tenants are put to a choice. If they acquiesce in the lease they can share in the rents received. If they refuse to acquiesce in the lease, they can exercise their present right of possession as a co-tenant.

(2) *Depletion*. The most complicated rules arise where one co-tenant is engaged in a productive activity that, by its very nature, injures or devalues the land. The most common examples are cutting timber, drilling for oil or natural gas, and mining minerals.

The most obvious claim a co-tenant out of possession might make for these activities is for waste.[67] At common law, a claim for waste could be made only by future interest holders, not by co-tenants. Many modern decisions and statutes permit co-tenants to bring claims for waste, but they are rarely successful. For example, in *Davis v. Byrd*, 238 Mo.App. 581, 587–88, 185 S.W.2d 866, 869 (1945), the court held that mining by one co-tenant does not constitute waste so long as the other co-tenants are not excluded and the mining co-tenant does not willfully or negligently injure the land. *See also McCord v. Oakland Quicksilver Mining Co.*, 64 Cal. 134, 143, 27 P. 863, 866 (1883) (in a proper case, one co-tenant might be liable to another for waste if the land is exploited destructively or inefficiently; but where the mine existed before the property was acquired in tenancy in common, it is not waste for one co-tenant to work the mine). Other cases find that there is no waste if the resources removed do not exceed the co-tenant's fractional share or if the co-tenant consented or acquiesced in the removal. *See, e.g., Hihn v. Peck*, 18 Cal. 640, 643 (1861) (it is not waste for one co-tenant to remove valuable timber "to an extent corresponding to [his] share of the estate"); *Hoolihan v. Hoolihan*, 193 N.Y. 197, 200–02, 85 N.E. 1103, 1104–05 (1908) (holding that a tenant in common who removed trees without the co-tenant's consent could be liable for waste); *Vicars v. First Virginia Bank–Mountain Empire*, 250 Va. 103, 108–09, 458 S.E.2d 293, 296 (1995) (removing minerals from co-owned land is not waste when the co-tenant consented to the mining).

Even when a court finds non-permissive exploitation of the property to be waste, it normally will not award treble damages (the usual remedy for waste), but instead will hold the tenant in possession accountable for net profits from the operation. Casner, American Law of Property, § 6.15;

---

66. It appears that if the lease only covers the leasing co-tenant's share of the property, the non-leasing co-tenants are not entitled to any rents. *Lee Chuck v. Quan Wo Chong & Co.*, 91 Cal. 593, 598–99, 28 P. 45, 46 (1891). *Cf. Swartzbaugh v. Sampson*, 11 Cal.App.2d 451, 461–62, 54 P.2d 73, 79 (1936) (holding that a non-leasing co-tenant in this circumstance is not entitled to cancel the lease). The lessee, in effect, becomes a co-tenant for the duration of the lease. If, however, the lessee bars the non-leasing co-tenants from using the property, the co-tenants are entitled to an injunction or damages in the amount of rental value.

67. Co-tenants have been allowed to bring an action for waste against each other since the enactment of the Statute of Westminster II, 13 Edward I, chpt. 22 (1285).

McCord v. Oakland Quicksilver Mining Co., 64 Cal. 134, 143, 27 P. 863, 866 (1883); *Payne v. Callahan*, 37 Cal.App.2d 503, 519–20, 99 P.2d 1050, 1057–58 (1940). *But see Eggleston v. Crump*, 150 Va. 414, 420, 143 S.E. 688, 689 (1928) (double damages).

Although a co-tenant might have no claim for waste, she may be able to recover part of the *net profits* in an action for an accounting.

White v. Smyth

Supreme Court of Texas, 1948.
147 Tex. 272, 214 S.W.2d 967.

■ Smedley, Justice.

We follow the Court of Civil Appeals, 214 S.W.2d 953, in adopting the statement of the nature and result of the suit as made by White *et al.*, appellants in that court. It is:

> * * * Appellees [Smyth *et al.*] alleged that they and the appellants owned the fee simple estate (including all rock asphalt) in and to a certain 200 acre tract of land in Uvalde County; that the same parties owned all the rock asphalt estate in and under approximately 30,000 acres of land which is mostly in Uvalde County but is partly in Zavala County; that appellants R. L. White and White's Uvalde Mines had removed a large quantity of rock asphalt from the property owned in common and had failed to account to appellees for their portion of such rock asphalt. Appellees prayed that the 200 acre tract, including the rock asphalt estate therein, and the rock asphalt estate in the 30,000 acres, be found to be incapable of partition in kind and that the same be ordered sold and the proceeds divided among the owners thereof; and that the appellants R. L. White and White's Uvalde Mines be required to account to appellees for the rock asphalt removed from the common property and that appellees have judgment against said appellants for any sums that such accounting showed to be due appellees.

It is undisputed that appellants own an undivided one-ninth interest in the 200 acre tract and in the rock asphalt estate in the tract of approximately 30,000 acres.

The case was tried before a jury; and in answer to special issues the jury found that the rock asphalt estate in the land in question cannot be partitioned in kind; that the reasonable value in the ground of the 397,338.11 tons of rock asphalt mined by appellants during the period of time involved in this controversy, that is from October 29, 1942, to September 30, 1945, was $99,-334.53; that the net profit realized by appellants from the conduct of their rock asphalt business during this period of time was $250,180.56; that appellants' mining operations during the same period were not of such nature as to exclude the other owners of rock asphalt (appellees) from mining; and that appellants had not during the period in question "mined more than one-ninth in value in the ground of the rock asphalt minable from all of the rock asphalt involved in this suit."

The trial court entered a decree reciting that the tract of 200 acres, including the rock asphalt estate therein, and the rock asphalt estate in the tract of approximately 30,000 acres, cannot be partitioned in kind. The decree ordered the common property sold and the proceeds distributed among the owners thereof, and awarded appellees a judgment against appellants R. L. White and White's Uvalde Mines in the sum of $222,382.72 (this being eight-ninths of the net profit realized by appellants from their asphalt business) with interest thereon at six per cent per annum until paid.

The Court of Civil Appeals, in a thorough opinion, affirmed the judgment of the trial court. In this opinion petitioners will be referred to as petitioner or White, since petitioner R. L. White is the active partner and principal owner of White's Uvalde Mines.

The 30,000 acres of land, including the 200 acre tract, known as the Smyth ranch, was the community property of J. G. Smyth and his second wife, Mrs. Espie Belle Smyth. On the death of J. G. Smyth, his one-half interest passed in undivided interests to his nine children, two of whom, Mrs. T. M. West and Mrs. R. L. White, wife of petitioner White, were J. G. Smyth's daughters by his first wife. On September 14, 1923, Mrs. Espie Belle Smyth and the devisees of her deceased husband, except Mrs. R. L. White, executed a lease of the ranch to petitioner White for mining, producing and marketing rock asphalt from the land, the lease providing for the payment to lessors of twenty-five, twenty, and fifteen cents per ton for the rock asphalt sold or taken. The term of the lease is ninety-nine years, but the lessee is given the right to terminate the lease by the execution of a written release and the payment of $1,000.00, with the further sum of $13,222.22 which shall be compensation for 56,000 tons of rock asphalt not then paid for, and the lessee is permitted thereafter to remove from the land all machinery, tools, houses and improvements belonging to him and the rock asphalt for which payment has been made, including the 56,000 tons. The interest of Mrs. Espie Belle Smyth in the lands thereafter passed under her will to respondents, so that respondents became the owners in undivided interests of the entire title except the one-eighteenth interest owned by Mrs. White and the one-eighteenth interest owned by Mrs. West.

Petitioner White entered upon the premises a short time after the execution of the lease and operated under the lease continuously until October 30, 1941. In the year 1932 the owners of the ranch, including Mrs. R. L. White, the wife of petitioner White, both by deeds and by decree in a suit for partition, effected a partition of the land by which specific tracts were set apart to those who had owned the same in undivided interests, except that the 200 acre tract in Survey 122, upon which a mine was being operated by White, and the rock asphalt in all of the lands were excluded from the partition and continued to be owned in undivided interests. The partition decree and some of the pleadings recited that the 200 acre tract and the rock asphalt in the other land were then under rock asphalt mining leases, and further that they were not capable of or subject to equitable partition.

On October 30, 1941, White exercised the right to terminate the lease by executing a release and filing it for record, and by depositing to the credit of the lessors, respondents, $14,222.22. He notified respondents of his action and advised them that when he had mined the rock for which he had prepaid he would then vacate the property.

On October 8, 1942, White acquired by conveyances the undivided one-eighteenth interest of Mrs. T. M. West and the undivided one-eighteenth interest of Mrs. White in the 200 acre tract and in the rock asphalt in all of the lands in the ranch; and on November 13, 1942, he notified respondents by letter that he had finished removing his prepaid rock and further that, having acquired the one-ninth interest from his wife and Mrs. West, he would "now want to take out such part of my share of the rock as is practical before I move my machinery". The letter further stated that he recognized "the right of all other interested parties to do likewise" and that he would keep an accurate account of all that he removed. The position thus taken by White and his continued mining and removal of the rock asphalt after he had terminated the lease and after he had taken all of the prepaid rock asphalt caused the institution of this suit.

The application for writ of error presents under several points three principal contentions: First, that petitioner White owes no duty to account to respondents, because he has not taken more than his fair share of the rock asphalt in place, has not excluded respondents from the premises and in mining has made merely normal use of the property, it having already been devoted to the mining of rock asphalt at the time petitioner acquired his undivided interest therein; second, that if he owes a duty to account, he is liable only for eight-ninths of the value in the ground of the rock asphalt he has mined and not for profits which he has realized; and third, that the jury's findings that the rock asphalt in certain surveys in the ranch and in all of the property outside of certain surveys cannot be equitably partitioned in kind are without evidence to support them. We consider first the points pertaining to partition, since the question whether the property is or is not capable of partition in kind has an important bearing upon the other questions.

[After reviewing the record, the court upheld the jury's finding that the property could not be partitioned in kind. The quantity and quality of the rock asphalt varied significantly over the land, and it would be prohibitively expensive to survey the property accurately].

The amount of the trial court's judgment in favor of respondents against petitioner represents eight-ninths of the net profits realized by petitioner from mining, processing and selling 397,381.11 tons of rock asphalt taken from the land during the period from October 29, 1942, to September 30, 1945. This amount of net profits was found by the jury after deducting from the gross proceeds all expenses incurred by petitioner, together with a reasonable compensation for his personal services and the reasonable value of the use of his plant and other property in the operation of the mine. The judgment follows the weight of authority and the general rule thus stated in American Jurisprudence: "Since any co-owner of a mine or mineral property is at liberty to work it, some courts have intimated that a co-owner who does not choose to avail himself of this right should have no claim upon the production of one who has elected to do so. But this view seems to be contrary to the weight of authority, and the prevailing rule appears to be that the producer must account to his cotenant for all profits made to the extent of his interest in the property." [citing cases]

It seems that there are no decisions in this state as to the duty of a co-owner who takes solid minerals from the property to account to his cotenant. It is held, however, as in most of the other states, that one who takes oil without the consent of his cotenants must account to them for their share of the proceeds of the oil less the necessary and reasonable cost of producing and marketing it. [citing cases]

Petitioner contends that the rule above stated does not apply to this case, and that he need not account to his cotenants, because he has mined no more than his fair share of the rock asphalt in place and has not excluded them from the premises. He relies primarily upon *Kirby Lumber Co. v. Temple Lumber Co.*, 125 Tex. 284, 83 S.W.2d 638, and the text of Lindley (Lindley on Mines, 3rd ed., Vol. 3, §§ 789–789a, pp. 1933–1941) for what he insists is the applicable rule.

In the *Kirby Lumber Company* case the Temple Company owned an undivided two-thirds interest and the Kirby Company owned an undivided one-third interest in a 640 acre tract of land on which there was valuable standing timber. The Temple Company, believing that it owned the entire title to a specific 427 acres of the land, cut all of the timber standing on that tract, amounting to ten million feet, and manufactured it into lumber. There remained uncut on the 640 acres 2,783,325 feet of timber. The court's opinion states that the 640 acres was generally of uniform value as to timber and otherwise. The Kirby Company sued the Temple Company to recover the manufactured value of one-third of the timber that had been cut. The trial court found that the total amount of timber standing on the land before the cutting was 12,783,325 feet, of which the Kirby Company's one-third amounted to 4,261,108 feet, and that the amount left standing was 2,783,325 feet, which was treated as belonging to the Kirby Company, and that thus the Temple Company had cut 1,477,783 feet more than its share. Its judgment awarded to the Kirby Company $43,372.93, being the manufactured value of the 1,477,783 feet. * * * The Supreme Court * * * rendered judgment in favor of the Kirby Company against the Temple Company for the stumpage value, $5.00 per thousand feet, of the 1,477,783 feet of excess timber cut by the Temple Company. Most of the Court's opinion is devoted to a discussion of the question whether the Kirby

Company should be charged with notice that timber had been cut by its predecessor in title and of the question as to the amount of the recovery, that is whether stumpage value or manufactured value. Little is said in the approval of that part of the trial court's judgment which charged the Temple Company with only the amount of the timber cut in excess of its share. The authorities there cited relate to timber and to the question whether stumpage value or manufactured value may be recovered.

The important distinction between the *Kirby Lumber Company* case and the instant case, * * * is that in that case * * * "the 640 acres was generally of uniform value as to timber and otherwise," the timber was fairly subject to partition in kind, whereas in the instant case the rock asphalt is not. The Temple Company's action in cutting the timber up to its share and the Court's approval of that action by the judgment rendered worked in effect a partition of the timber. Here there has not been, and there could not be consistently with the finding that the rock asphalt is not capable of partition in kind, an approval by the court of White's action in taking for himself and disposing of a part of the rock asphalt. The ownership of all of the cotenants extends to all of the rock asphalt, and White was not authorized to make partition of it. We approve the conclusion [of the court below]:

> [Because the mineral estate cannot be partitioned in kind] the title to the severed minerals remains in all the cotenants in their proportionate interests. The minerals not being partitionable in kind, the substantive right of cotenants desiring division or partition is the right to have the estate or minerals sold and the proceeds thereof divided. It follows, therefore, that the title of the non-operating cotenant in and to the extracted minerals does not terminate until said minerals are disposed of by sale, or until they are brought to a place or point where there exists an established market value for such minerals. His rights thereupon attach to the proceeds.

The facts of this case attest the obvious soundness of the rule that a cotenant cannot select and take for himself part of the property jointly owned and thus make partition. While he was lessee under the lease that covered the entire ranch, White selected the site for and developed the present pit, making extensive improvements, including the construction of roads, excavations and grading for private tracks, other excavations and grading, all at great cost and of very substantial value. The location of the plant site was favorable and valuable. The rock asphalt in the pit was both rich rock and lean rock, both of which were necessary to meet market demands and specifications. The east wall of the pit, which was rock asphalt, attained a height of about eighty feet. It was rich in asphalt at the top and lean at the bottom. From this wall much of the rock asphalt for which accounting is sought in this suit was mined and mixed by the simple process of blasting the rock from the face of the wall, so blasting it as to mix the rich rock with the lean rock. When White completed the mining of his prepaid rock the piled overburden was about two hundred feet east of the east wall of the pit, and he was able to mine the rock asphalt from the wall without moving more than the natural overburden, but at the time of the trial he had mined so far east that the toe of the piled overburden was reached and the overburden would have to be removed in order to mine farther east.

When White exercised the right to terminate the lease and completed the taking of his prepaid rock he had no further right or interest in the rock asphalt in the lands, the mine or the mine site, except that he was given by the lease the right to remove his machinery, tools, houses and implements. The rock asphalt estate in all of the lands belonged to all of the cotenants, as did also the added advantages and values to the entire mineral estate created and existing by reason of the developed pit and mine site; but White, taking advantage for himself of the added values, after acquiring the one-ninth interest of his wife and his wife's sister, mined from the pit about four hundred thousand tons of the rich, valuable and readily accessible rock asphalt.

It is true, as contended by petitioner, that in some of the cases cited above which require the producing tenant to account to his cotenants for their share of the profits, it does not affirmatively appear that the mining cotenant has not taken more than his share. In those cases the point made by petitioner seems not to have been made, and the rule is stated and applied that the producer must account, with no reference to the question whether he has taken more or has taken less than his share. In several of the cases, however, the point was made and rejected. In *Campbell v. Homer Ore Co.*, 309 Mich. 693, 16 N.W.2d 125, 127, the defendant claimed that as long as the plaintiff's share of the ore was not removed but was still left, it was not liable to the plaintiff. The court, in rejecting the contention, referred to the fact that the iron ore in its natural situation was not capable of precise determination as to either quality or amount, and said further: "The tenant in common who takes possession is not vested with any superior right to choose what ore is to him most convenient to mine, select what is more profitable and remove and sell without accounting." In overruling the defendants' contention in *Barnum v. Landon*, 25 Conn. 137, 150, that the plaintiffs could not call upon them to account without proving that they had taken more than their share, the court said: "The error of the defendants lies in this; they contend they own absolutely whatever they get out of the ore pit if it is not too much, whereas they own only one-twenty-fourth part of what they get out, and must account at reasonable times, for the other twenty-three parts, to the plaintiffs." It was held in *Cosgriff v. Dewey*, 21 App.Div. 129, 47 N.Y.S. 255, *affirmed* 164 N.Y. 1, 58 N.E. 1, 79 Am.St.Rep. 620, that the tenant who quarried and removed rock from the premises was liable to account to his cotenant for his damages and the profits of the transaction, and that he could not avail himself of the fact that the rock was practically inexhaustible, or that his acts had added value to the property as a whole.

[The court rejects an argument, made in a treatise, that a co-tenant has no duty to account for minerals removed].

Kirby Lumber Co. v. Temple Lumber Co., 125 Tex. 284, 83 S.W.2d 638, is cited by petitioner to sustain his assignment of error that if he owes respondents the duty to account, he must account only for the value in the ground of the rock asphalt mined by him. That case is not an authority for this point. The plaintiff did not ask for an accounting for profits. There were no allegations as to profits and no issue as to profits was submitted. There is nothing to show that any profits were made. The question before the court was whether the defendant should be required to pay for the stumpage value of the timber cut or for its value after having been manufactured into lumber and without deduction for expenditures. The court held that the former, that is stumpage value, was the measure of recovery because the defendant had acted in good faith, believing that it owned all of the timber that it had cut. A fundamental difference between the facts of the *Kirby* case and the instant case, which has been noted herein, has an important bearing here. It is that in the *Kirby* case the standing timber was of uniform value and could readily be partitioned in kind, whereas in this case the rock asphalt cannot be fairly and equitably partitioned in kind.

Three cases are cited by petitioner in which the cotenant who had taken minerals was charged with their value in place: *Appeal of Fulmer*, 128 Pa. 24, 18 A. 493, 15 Am.St.Rep. 662; *McGowan v. Bailey*, 179 Pa. 470, 36 A. 325; and *Clowser v. Joplin*, W.D.Mo., Fed.Cas. No. 2,908a, 4 Dill. 469 note. While the opinions in the two Pennsylvania cases contain reasoning to justify the use of that measure, they also indicate that it was deemed just and equitable under the peculiar facts, and that it might not be applicable to all cases. In the Federal case a memorandum opinion adopts the measure of liability stated in the two Pennsylvania cases as appropriate under the Missouri statute. The three cases depart from the majority rule, supported by the authorities cited and discussed herein, which majority rule is stated in American Jurisprudence as follows:

> When it is claimed that a cotenant in possession of a mine or a mineral property has become liable to his cotenants for profits accruing from his productive operations, the usual mode of settling the account is to charge him with all his receipts and credit him with all his expenses, thereby ascertaining the net profits available for distribution. In other words, the usual basis of an accounting by a cotenant who works the common mine or develops the common oil and gas property is the value of the product, less the necessary expenses of production. 14 Am.Jur., p. 106, § 38.

The text of American Jurisprudence contains also a statement that the weight of authority and the prevailing rule are that when a co-owner of mineral property works the property and disposes of the minerals produced, he must account to his cotenant for all profits made to the extent of his interest in the property. 14 Am.Jur., p. 104, § 36.

* * *

It is argued by petitioner that his receipts have been from sales of a manufactured product, and that respondents should not be permitted, by sharing in the profits, to obtain the benefits of his personal skill and industry and of the flux oil and water used and the machinery, apparatus and equipment belonging to petitioner. We believe that the preparation of the rock asphalt for market, as described by petitioner's testimony and by that of other witnesses, is a processing rather than a manufacturing. The rock asphalt is rock asphalt in the ground, that is, limestone rock impregnated with asphalt. To make it ready for the market and for use in the building of roads it is mixed and crushed, and oil is mixed with it to give the small particles of rock a film of oil, and water is put in the mixture so that it will not become solid in transit. It is rock asphalt when it is sold and when it is used on the roads. The producing tenant is required to account to his cotenants for net profits realized from mining, smelting, crushing, processing or marketing solid minerals taken from the land. *Silver King Coalition Mines Co. v. Silver King Consol. Mining Co.*, 8 Cir., 204 F. 166, Ann.Cas.1918B, 571; *Newman v. Newman*, 27 Grat., Va., 714; *Cosgriff v. Dewey*, 21 App.Div. 129, 47 N.Y.S. 255, *affirmed* 164 N.Y. 1, 58 N.E.1, 79 Am.St.Rep. 620.

[The court concludes that the jury properly credited White for his expenses, including "large sums for flux oil, as well as charges for payrolls, salaries, depreciation, repairs, insurance, commissions, etc. In addition to these expenses, the jury, following the trial court's instructions, allowed substantial credits as reasonable compensation for White's personal services and as the reasonable value of the use of the plant and other property belonging to him."]

The rock asphalt was owned in undivided interests by all of the cotenants. Their ownership extended to all of the rock asphalt and to all of the advantages and peculiar conditions and stages of development of the property at the time when petitioner terminated the lease. This ownership extended to the developed pit with its great wall of easily accessible rock asphalt and to the valuable mining site. It extended to the use value of the rock asphalt and to its profit possibilities. To limit the accounting to the value in place of the rock asphalt mined by petitioner, would be to permit him to use for his own profit the property owned in common and the advantages and opportunities for profit inherent in that ownership and to deprive respondents of a substantial part of its value and benefits. In our opinion, the trial court's judgment, requiring petitioner to account to his co-owners according to their interests for the profits realized from the common property after crediting him with all expenses and with the compensation above mentioned, assures to all of the co-owners the benefits and values of their ownership, is correct in principle and, as has been said, is supported by the decided weight of authority.

The judgments of the district court and the Court of Civil Appeals are affirmed.

■ Simpson, Justice, (dissenting)

It is respectfully submitted that the measure of recovery allowed the respondents by the majority ruling is wrong, and is contrary to the applicable precedents under the established facts. It results in what is earnestly urged to be an unjust exaction of the petitioner White, who should have been required to account for $99,334.53, the value in place of the rock asphalt taken, and not $222,382.72, its net manufactured value.

Petitioner White had spent practically a lifetime in the rock asphalt business. He worked the asphalt deposits on the Smyth ranch from 1923 until 1941 under a contract with the landowners, which he then terminated, as he had the right to do. He had acquired one-ninth interest in the 200–acre tract he was working, as well as one-ninth of the rock asphalt under some 30,000 acres of the Smyth ranch, and continued working the deposits after the contract with his cotenants ended. He notified them what he was doing. He had a complete legal and moral right to be on the land and to mine the rock.

This rock, after mining, has to be manufactured into paving material before it is of any practicable use. It is blasted from its beds in large pieces, which are broken up by further blasting. It is then scooped onto trucks by steam shovels and hauled to and further pulverized by a crushing machine. It is then taken to a storage bin where the rock with high asphaltic content is placed at one end, that with a low content at the other. This bin is equipped with vibrating feeders which drop the rock in proper portions on a conveyor belt which takes it to other grinders for further processing. After the final crushing, the rock, by means of a screen, is separated into three bins according to the size of the particles into which it has been crushed. Then the rock, sizes kept separate, is weighed, dropped into a mixer known as a "pug mill" and oil is introduced into the product under pressures running from 75 to 100 pounds. Powerful paddles churn the material so the oil is thoroughly fused into it. (During the period he is held to account, petitioner mixed oil valued at $120,616.13 with the $99,334.53 worth of crude rock asphalt he removed from the land.) Suitable quantities of water are added and milled into the product. The resulting mixture is a manufactured paving material which petitioner has been selling under the registered trade name of "Valdemix."

The plant and equipment investment of the petitioner exceeded $500,-000.

The asphalt business is highly competitive. So competitive in fact that petitioner's Uvalde Mines and Uvalde Asphalt Company are the only survivors among all who have tried. One adequately capitalized concern, for instance, abandoned the business after losing at least $1,000,000.

In addition to the manufacturing of crude rock asphalt into a finished paving product, petitioner employed his skill and experience in selling it. He would agree in advance with contractors bidding on road work that if the contractor should be the successful bidder he would deliver "Valdemix" in given quantities and at certain prices and times. His lifetime of experience in the business enabled him to succeed where others had failed. He knew how to mine, how to manufacture, and how to sell.

What the complaining cotenants are entitled to get is the value of that which was taken, that is, crude rock asphalt. Any higher figure would no longer be compensatory but punitive. And this is the measure of recovery fixed by the authorities. The cases cited by the majority do not decide differently. Those cases either directly or impliedly hold that a joint owner of a mining lode may recover of his cotenant who works the lode the value of the ore taken at the mouth of the pit less the reasonable cost of getting it there. And that is the same thing, under the authorities which will be later noticed, as the value of the ore in place, the basis of accounting to which White should justly be held. * * *

The rule in Texas as elsewhere in oil and gas cases is that a cotenant producing oil must account to his co-owners for the value of the crude oil produced less the reasonable cost of producing and marketing. [citing a case and a treatise]. None would say that if a joint owner produced crude oil and then refined it, his cotenants would be entitled to an accounting on the basis of the value of the refined products. Yet that is the very result the majority has reached here. The raw rock asphalt when first mined is no doubt as little suited for paving as crude oil when first produced is suitable for automobile fuel. Just as it takes refining to prepare crude oil for motor fuel, so does it take manufacturing and processing, including the addition and blending of other products more valuable than the crude rock asphalt itself, coupled with an experienced skill and knowledge of the business, to ready the raw rock asphalt for paving. The nonmining cotenant is entitled only to the net value of the crude oil in the one case, and certainly to no more than the net value of the crude rock asphalt in the other.

[The dissenting opinion then discussed treatises and cases from other jurisdictions]. So, the virtually uncontradicted rule of decision as well as the better reasoning requires an accounting here on the basis of the value of the crude rock asphalt in place or, what is the same thing, its value before being processed at White's mill less the reasonable cost of getting it there.

In Texas this is the rule of accounting as to innocent trespassers in conversion cases. Shall White, who was certainly no trespasser, be held under a more onerous duty to account than a trespasser who is guilty, though innocently, of conversion? * * *

The duty of a cotenant to account on the basis of the value of the mineral in place is the clear and necessary effect of the holding in *Kirby Lumber Co. v. Temple Lumber Co.*, 125 Tex. 284, 83 S.W.2d 638. There, after a full consideration of the authorities, it was concluded that a cotenant must account for timber innocently cut in excess of his share upon the basis of its value in place, called in that case "stumpage value." * * * The cause was not remanded for a determination of what profits the cotenant had made. This for the obvious reason that the *net manufactured value* of the timber was not the measure of recovery. The majority here states that in the *Kirby-Temple* case the timber was "of uniform value and could readily be partitioned in kind." That situation resulted in the court's crediting Temple Lumber Company with the two-thirds of the timber which it owned, but requiring it to account to its co-owner on the basis of the *value in place* of the timber it cut over its own two-thirds. Here the majority holds that since the asphalt in place was not partible in kind, White must account even if he did take less than his one-ninth portion. This is right. But the opinion then proceeds to apply an improper measure of accounting. * * *

The result in the *Kirby-Temple* case is fair and just. It awards full compensation to co-owners whose property is taken, but refuses to allow a punitive recovery. In the case at bar just such a recovery is adjudged against petitioner, who has violated no law, has (the jury so found) taken even less than his fair share of the minerals, and has openly and in the exercise of a clear legal and moral right worked asphalt pits on his own land.

The respondents ought not to be allowed to share in the capital investment, the experience, enterprise and personal business acumen of the petitioner. To allow this sharing puts a grim penalty upon freedom of enterprise and the risk of one's own capital in a highly hazardous and competitive business. The respondents can be made whole by awarding them the value of their share in place of the crude rock asphalt which was mined. This is fair and just. It allows full compensation for what was taken. Respondents are entitled to this, but certainly not to more.

———

1. To what extent can a tenant in possession be allowed a right of contribution for necessary expenses to preserve the property or for improvements? Could the tenant in possession receive any credit for improvements at partition? Why is there an offset for an occupying co-tenant's use of the property?

2. Can the tenant in possession seek contribution for necessary expenses if he ousted his co-tenants?

On the other hand, can the co-tenants out of possession recover the rental value of the ousting co-tenant's exclusive possession? If so, can the tenant in possession offset the rental value by the necessary expenses of maintaining the property?

3. The doctrine of waste originally gave remaindermen and reversioners rights against life tenants. Although later extended to co-tenants, courts have been reluctant to find that one co-tenant's exploitation of property constitutes waste. Why? Should courts be especially wary of finding waste with extraction of fugacious resources, such as oil or natural gas?

4. The court in *White v. Smyth* rejects White's claim that he has no duty to account. Why? Suppose that the quantity, quality, and distribution of the asphalt were readily ascertained. What would have been White's duty to account?

5. The court held that White had to account for the net profits for his extraction of asphalt rock. How did the majority measure net profits? What was the basis for the court's holding? What was the dissent's position?

Did White do something underhanded in this case, when he terminated the lease and acquired a one-ninth interest in the asphalt? Is this what causes the majority to require White to account not only for the value of the asphalt but the value of the processed asphalt?

6. Would a better measure be the net value of the extracted asphalt (gross value less the costs of extraction) before further processing?

Problem

In 1990, Albert and Bertha, who were romantically involved (but not married), decided to purchase a tract of land together for the purposes of living together and living off the land. They found a nice bungalow on a five acre tract of land which contained a lovely grape vineyard in Napa Valley, California. They purchased the property together and took title as joint tenants. They financed the property by each contributing $50,000 in cash and taking out a 30–year mortgage for $200,000. Loan payments were $15,000 per year, most of which was interest in the early years. They paid $3000 per year for property taxes and $1000 for home insurance. During 1991 and 1992, their romance and their grapes blossomed. They enjoyed toiling in the fields and were able make a good living from the vineyard. They built an addition to the bungalow and made plans to construct a swimming pool the following year. The winter of 1993 was very cold, and the frost damaged the grapes as well as the vines. The financial uncertainties contributed to already growing relational discord (Albert liked chardonnay, Bertha preferred pinot noir) and they had a bitter argument in April 1993. That June, Albert pushed ahead with the plan to build a swimming pool. Bertha decided to end the relationship and she moved out in July, after the hole had been dug but before the cement, tile, and equipment had been installed.

Albert asked Bertha to pay her share of the costs of maintaining the property and completing the swimming pool, but she refused. Because of the poor harvest, Albert had to scramble to raise money quickly to cover the mounting debts. The first thing that he did was to cut down 5 massive redwood trees on the property and sell them for a net profit of $40,000. He discovered that the clay that was excavated in building the swimming pool was valuable and he sold it for $5000. Next, Albert took out an advertisement in a local paper looking for a lessee. Corrine answered the advertisement and moved in in October 1993, paying Albert $500 per month. Albert continued to work the vineyard and with much effort restored it to its former level of productivity. Corrine became interested in the vineyard work as well as in Albert and the two of them began a relationship in January 1994, at which point Corrine stopped paying rent. Their success tending the vines gave them sufficient resources to improve the bungalow, nearly doubling it in size. In January 1998, while Albert and Corrine were on vacation in the south of France, lightning struck the house and burned it to the ground. The insurance contract paid $500,000, which was the estimated value of reconstructing the house. The land, including the vineyard, was recently appraised at $350,000.

Bertha learns of the payout in April 1998 and demands half. Albert refuses. The parties seek counsel.

1. What further information do you need to know to resolve this dispute?

2. What claims would you advise Bertha to bring?

3. What answers should Albert provide? What counterclaims would you advise him to bring?

4. How would a judge likely resolve these disputes?

---

3. MARITAL PROPERTY

This section examines the most prevalent and extensive form of concurrent ownership: marital property. This field of law is extraordinarily detailed[68] and therefore we can only survey its main contours and a few particularly important areas that illuminate the evolving nature of property in our society. Marital property is governed by two different systems in this country—common law marital property derived from the English common law and community property derived from the continental European (primarily Spanish) civil law tradition. Because these systems are conceptually different and have different historical origins, we explore them separately, examining how each system allocates property rights and responsibilities during the marriage, at the death of a spouse, and at the dissolution of a marriage. We then look broadly at three salient issues in the marital property field—whether professional training acquired during a marriage is property subject to division at dissolution, the extent to which prospective spouses may alter the default property rules through pre-marital agreements, and whether society recognizes a property relationship between unmarried cohabitants.

a. COMMON LAW MARITAL PROPERTY[69]

i. *Rights During the Marriage*

A majority of jurisdictions in this country use a system of marital property derived directly from the English common law. Before the mid-nineteenth century, the common law in England and the United States did not permit a married woman to own personal property other than her

---

68. For a more thorough treatment of this area, *see* J. Areen, Family Law, Chpts. 5–6 (3d ed. 1992); I. Ellman, P. Kurtz & K. Bartlett, Family Law, Chpt. 3 (2d ed. 1991); L. Harris, L. Titelbaum & C. Weisbrod, Family Law, Chpt. 5 (1996); M. Glendon, The Transformation of Family Law (1989).

69. For articles on the common law marital property interests, *see* Haskins, The Development of Common Law Dower, 62 Harv. L. Rev. 42 (1948); Haskins, Curtesy at Common Law: Historical Development, 29 B.U.L. Rev. 228 (1949). *See also* The Treatise on the Laws and Customs of the Realm of England Commonly Called Glanvill (G.D.G.

clothing. Her personal property, whether acquired before or during marriage, belonged to her husband. Although a married woman could continue to hold legal title to real property, her husband had an absolute right to use, profit from, and convey the real property held in his wife's name.[70]

Married couples could hold (and in many states today still hold) property in a form of joint ownership, known as tenancy by the entirety.[71] Tenancy by the entirety is a close relative of joint tenancy in that cotenants have a right of survivorship. In contrast to the cotenants' rights in a joint tenancy, the right of survivorship in a tenancy by the entirety cannot be destroyed by the unilateral action of one spouse. Rather, the right is extinguished only as a result of the joint action of the parties or the dissolution of the marriage, which converts the tenancy by the entirety to a tenancy in common. Also, contrary to the law's bias against joint tenancies, many states have a constructional preference favoring a tenancy by the entirety over a tenancy in common.

Married couples hold property in a tenancy by the entirety to provide some economic security for the surviving spouse. Because the right of survivorship may not be conveyed without the surviving spouse's consent, anyone buying land from the husband (including a purchaser at a sheriff's auction seeking to satisfy the husband's debts) would take a risk that the wife would outlive her husband and become entitled to the property.

The Married Women's Property Acts of the nineteenth century eliminated the legal restrictions on a wife's rights to own and manage separate personal and real property, and thus they eventually gave married women the same rights to hold and convey separate property that men and single women had.[72] Their enactment also forced courts and legislatures to reconsider the common law rules regarding joint ownership of marital property.

Hall ed. 1965) (discussing dower in the twelfth century). For a good critique of common law marital property, *see* Johnston, Sex and Property: The Common Law Tradition, the Law School Curriculum, and Developments Toward Equality, 47 N.Y.U. L. Rev. 1033 (1972).

70. Although the common law courts offered wives little protection, the chancery courts at this time permitted wives some opportunity to avoid the legal disabilities by enforcing trusts made on their behalf by their fathers or brothers. In addition, chancery courts enforced prenuptial agreements that gave wives sole control of real and personal property. Only married women were treated as if they were incapable of handling their own affairs. Unmarried women had the same rights as men to own property.

71. Spouses could also agree to hold their property in a joint tenancy or in a tenancy in common.

72. The Married Women's Property Act in any given state was not a single comprehensive statute, but a series of statutes that eliminated the common law disabilities on ownership, use, and disposition of personal and real property. For a discussion of the reaction to the Married Women's Property Acts, *see* Chused, Late Nineteenth Century Married Women's Property Law: Reception of the Early Married Women's Property Acts by Courts and Legislatures, 29 Am. J. Legal Hist. 3 (1985).

Some statutes were more limited in that they exempted the wife's property from the claims of her husband's creditors, but left the husband with actual management and control of her property. Eventually, all states granted married women the right to control their separate property.

In about half of the common law marital property states, the legislatures abolished tenancy by the entirety (and converted existing tenancies by the entirety to tenancies in common) when they enacted the Married Women's Property Acts. As a result, a creditor of one spouse could reach jointly held property and become a tenant in common of the interest with the non-debtor spouse.

In the remaining common law marital property states, courts reformulated the common law rules to accommodate the Married Women's Property Acts. Most of these courts held that each spouse had an equal right to possess and use land held in tenancy by the entirety and that all conveyances of property held in tenancy by the entirety had to be made jointly. This reform has disadvantaged creditors. Since all conveyances (including involuntary ones) must be made jointly, the creditors of the debtor spouse can not reach the debtor's interest in the property while both spouses are alive. The non-debtor spouse would simply refuse to consent to the conveyance of the debtor-spouse's interest. At least one court has even held that the husband and wife can jointly convey property held in tenancy by the entirety to a third party (in that case, their children), free of the creditor's claim. *See Sawada v. Endo*, 57 Haw. 608, 561 P.2d 1291 (1977). As a consequence, creditors now insist that major debts be in the names of both spouses. Unsecured creditors of a single spouse, however, cannot protect themselves in this way.

In a few other states, the courts have held that each spouse can convey his or her interest in the property, and that that interest (including the right of survivorship) can be levied by creditors. *See, e.g., King v. Greene*, 30 N.J. 395, 153 A.2d 49 (1959). These holdings, in effect, convert the tenancy by the entirety to a tenancy in common for the joint lives of the spouses, with alternative contingent remainders. If the creditor levies the debtor-spouse's property, he becomes a tenant in common for life with the non-debtor spouse. If the non-debtor spouse outlives the debtor spouse, the non-debtor spouse succeeds to the entire estate and the creditor's life estate ends. Inversely, if the debtor spouse survives, the creditor succeeds to the entire estate. Since a tenant in common can sue for partition (of the life estate), this rule potentially imposes considerable hardship on the non-debtor spouse. This possibility is mitigated in some states by statutes and decisions forbidding partition (and often levying) when the property is a principal residence.

ii. Distribution of Property Following the Death of One Spouse

The common law recognized two other property interests in surviving spouses.[73] *Curtesy* was the husband's right to a life estate in all of the lands his wife owned during the marriage. The only condition precedent to his acquiring this interest was that his wife give birth to live issue during the

---

73. These interests apply only to property held solely in the name of the deceased spouse. If the property was held in a tenancy by the entirety or a joint tenancy, or if title was entirely in the surviving spouse's name, the surviving spouse would be the sole owner

marriage. *Dower* was the widow's right to a life estate in one-third of the lands in which her husband was seised during the marriage. Although the husband controlled virtually every other aspect of his wife's property, he could not convey or devise his wife's dower rights without her consent. Thus, absent a release from the wife, any purchaser or creditor took his interest from the husband subject to the wife's dower right.[74]

Dower and *curtesy* continue to exist in only a few states, and in those states the rights are treated identically. The surviving spouse is entitled to a one-third life estate in the other spouse's inheritable estates owned during the marriage. In the majority of states today, the legislatures have replaced dower and curtesy with an "elective forced share."[75] Under this approach, the surviving spouse is entitled to decline his or her interest under the will and take a statutorily defined fraction (usually one-third or one-half, depending on whether there are children) of all property that the decedent owned at his or her death.

iii.   Distribution of Property Following Dissolution

During most marriages, formal legal issues of property ownership and control rarely if ever arise (issues of control arise at the personal, non-legal

of the property upon the other spouse's death. In addition, the deceased spouse's will may provide that the surviving spouse take some or all of the devisable property.

74. Dower derived initially from an Old French word meaning "to endow," which in turn derived from the Roman law term "dos." At Roman law, dos had two meanings. The first meaning, called "dower" in English common law, referred to the real property the husband gave to his wife at the beginning of the marriage. If he failed to endow his wife at that time, one third of his real property (one-half in socage tenures) owned on the day they were married was deemed to be her dower. In the twelfth century, land acquired during the marriage did not become part of the dower; later the law provided that dower rights covered all lands in which the husband was seised at any time during the marriage.

Dower did not give the wife any rights during the marriage. Rather, it gave her a life estate in the dower lands following her husband's death. If the lands had been conveyed (*e.g.*, to an heir or purchaser), the widow (known as the tenant in dower, or the dowager) could seek a writ ordering them (or equivalent lands if the conveyee no longer had complete title) delivered to her.

The second meaning of dos was "maritagium," or "marriage portion." The dos, or dowry, was the property given to a husband by the wife's father as part of the marriage agreement. Quite often the dowry was given as a fee simple conditional ("to husband and wife and the heirs of their bodies"); if the couple had live issue during the marriage, the husband was entitled to keep the property if he survived his wife. Otherwise, the property would revert to the grantor upon the death of the wife. The husband's survivorship right was only for a life estate. Following his death, the property either descended to the surviving issue, if any, or reverted to the grantor.

The husband's survivorship right was called a "tenancy by the curtesy." By the thirteenth century, curtesy was transformed to give the husband a life estate interest in all of his deceased wife's lands that she owned (including those she inherited) at any time during the marriage.

75. Most of the states that have retained dower and curtesy permit the surviving spouse to decline the common law entitlements and elect to take the statutorily defined share (one-third to one-half) of the real property owned by the decedent at his or her death. In practice, surviving spouses do not assert their dower or curtesy rights unless most of the real estate must be sold to satisfy debts, or the decedent spouse conveyed a large amount of land during the marriage without a release of dower or curtesy rights.

level, of course, but spouses in an intact marriage rarely sue each other). Even at death, many spouses leave most or all of their estate to the surviving spouse. Property issues often take on paramount importance, however, at the dissolution of a marriage. At that point in time, spouses experience strong emotions relating to the failure of their marriage and the many uncertainties—emotional, social, and financial—about the future. Often, spouses lack clear understandings about premarital agreements or about the background legal rules regarding property division following divorce. The division of property, as well as child custody, child support, and spousal support, can become deeply contentious.

The common law provided that property was distributed according to title upon dissolution of the marriage; the spouse with title kept the property. If property was held in joint tenancy or in a tenancy in common, it remained as such unless one party exercised his or her right to severance or partition (as a practical matter, the property settlement resulted in partition in most cases). Property held in tenancy by the entirety was converted into a tenancy in common.[76]

Since 1970, legislatures and courts have largely abandoned the common law scheme and substituted a doctrine of "equitable distribution." *See* Freed & Foster, Divorce in the Fifty States: An Overview As of August 1, 1980, 6 Fam. L. Rep. (BNA) 4043, 4051 (1980). In effect, this doctrine requires courts to consider a variety of factors, such as the duration of the marriage, the age, health, education, skills, occupation, and future earning potential of the spouses, custody of the children, and other needs. Often state laws create a presumption that property should be equally divided, subject to an adjustment based on the factors listed above.

Painter v. Painter

Supreme Court of New Jersey, 1974.
65 N.J. 196, 320 A.2d 484.

■ Mountain, J.

The parties to this suit were divorced by judgment entered March 14, 1972 upon the ground, urged in defendant's counterclaim, that they had lived separate and apart for at least 18 or more consecutive months and that there was no reasonable prospect of reconciliation. N.J.S.A. 2A:34–2(d).[77]

Thereafter, in accordance with the authority contained in N.J.S.A. 2A:34–23—as amended by the 1971 enactment—the trial court made an equitable distribution of the marital property. 118 N.J.Super. 332, 287 A.2d

---

76. In practice many courts adjusted the final distribution of assets if one spouse was able to prove that the dissolution was predominantly the other spouse's fault (*e.g.*, adultery, abuse).

77. This is the so-called 'no fault' ground for divorce, introduced for the first time into our law by L.1971, c. 212, which became effective September 13, 1971.

467 (Ch.Div.1972). We granted certification, 62 N.J. 192, 299 A.2d 726 (1972), as we did simultaneously in several companion cases, in order to consider the questions these cases raise and that are generally presented by this important legislation.

Stephen and Joan Painter were married October 17, 1953, and lived together as husband and wife until January 23, 1967. Three children were born of the marriage and at the time of the institution of this suit, in October, 1970, they were 15, 12 and 7 years of age. They have always been, and remain, in the custody of the mother.

At the trial it was determined that the total assets of plaintiff, Stephen Painter, had a value of $230,309 and those of defendant, Joan Painter, a value of $99,709. However, in determining the value of property subject to equitable distribution pursuant to N.J.S.A. 2A:34–23, the court excluded assets which were acquired by gift or inheritance during marriage as well as property owned prior to marriage. Pursuant to this formula, the court determined the plaintiff's and defendant's assets available for distribution, as being $82,571 and $58,199, respectively. In addition, plaintiff's income in 1971 was found to have been $32,218.

The court then entered an order directing plaintiff to pay (a) alimony and support in the sum of $12,000 per year, allocated $500 per month as alimony and $166.66 per month as support for each of the three children; (b) all reasonable medical and dental care for the three children and all medical care for the defendant; (c) "twenty per cent (20%) of the difference between plaintiff's and defendant's *available* assets—$4,874." (emphasis added).

The issues presented to the Court on this appeal concern both the constitutionality and the interpretation of L.1971, c. 212. * * *

Pursuant to L.1967, c. 57 (as amended by L.1968, c. 170 and L.1969, c. 25) the Legislature created a Divorce Law Study Commission " ... to study and review the statutes and court decisions concerning divorce and nullity of marriage and related matters ..." L.1967, c. 57, 144–145. In the preamble to this enactment it was noted that not since 1907 had there been any general revision of the statutes of the State relating to divorce, nullity of marriage or other phases of the law of domestic relations. Consequently, it went on to point out, except for the Blackwell Act, (L.1923, c. 187), which added extreme cruelty as a ground for divorce, there had been no significant legislation during this period pertaining to this general subject matter, although during the same interval concepts of marriage and divorce had been drastically altered. Legislative investigation and study were deemed essential as a necessary prerequisite to the drafting of a law that would adequately respond to the felt needs of our present day society in this area. On May 11, 1970 the Final Report of the Commission was submitted to the Governor and the Legislature. In very large part, but not entirely, the resulting statute, L.1971, c. 212, was based upon the proposed Divorce Reform Bill which accompanied and was made part of this Report.

The most significant changes in our matrimonial law that have result-ed from the adoption of this act are the following:

1.   In addition to the pre-existing statutory causes for divorce, *i.e.*, (1) adultery, (2) desertion and (3) extreme cruelty, the act includes as addition-al grounds: (4) separation for at least 18 months where there is no reasonable prospect of reconciliation; (5) voluntarily induced addiction to a narcotic drug, or habitual drunkenness, for a period of 12 months; (6) institutionalization because of mental illness for a period of 24 months; (7) imprisonment of the defendant for 18 months, and (8) deviant sexual conduct voluntarily performed by the defendant without the consent of the plaintiff. N.J.S.A. 2A:34–2. * * *

11.   Incident to the grant of divorce "... the court may make ... [an] award or awards to the parties in addition to alimony and maintenance, to effectuate an equitable distribution of the property, both real and personal, which was legally and beneficially acquired by them or either of them during the marriage." *Id.*

An effort has been made, as is apparent from the Commission Report, to move away from the concept of fault on the part of one spouse as having been solely responsible for the marital breakdown, toward a recognition that in all probability each party has in some way and to some extent been to blame. One objective of the Commission was to make it possible to terminate dead marriages regardless of where the responsibility for the failure lay. Final Report, Divorce Law Study Commission 6. The Legisla-ture accepted this recommendation and provided, as we have noted above, that separation for at least 18 months where there is no reasonable prospect of reconciliation shall be a ground for divorce. At the same time the Legislature concurred in the Commission's recommendation that fault grounds for divorce be retained, although somewhat liberalizing the requi-sites for their availability.

We turn then to the constitutional contentions which have been advanced. * * *

The second basis of constitutional challenge is that the section of the act providing for equitable distribution is impermissibly vague and uncer-tain. The argument here is two-pronged. It is first urged that the term "equitable" is insufficiently precise as a guide to a matrimonial judge in effecting distribution of marital property; secondly, it is contended that there is lacking any sufficient legislative statement as to what property shall be eligible for apportionment between the spouses.

The doctrine that a statute may be declared invalid because of indefi-niteness is well settled, but the rationale upon which it rests has not been very clearly formulated. It has been suggested that there are two important statutory functions which may be significantly affected by indefiniteness. "One of these functions is to guide the adjudication of rights and duties; the other is to guide the individual in planning his own future conduct." Note, "Due Process Requirements of Definiteness in Statutes," 62 Harv. L.Rev. 77 (1948). In other words due process requires that the adjudication of a litigant's rights and duties be governed by rules sufficiently clear and objective to guard against an arbitrary result, and that such rules be sufficiently precise to enable a lawyer to advise a client intelligently as to the probable results of a proposed course of conduct.

Judged by these criteria the words, "equitable distribution" set forth a standard which is not unduly vague. This phrase simply directs and requires that the matrimonial judge apportion the marital assets in such manner as will be just to the parties concerned, under all of the circumstances of the particular case. That a judge shall do equity is a notion understood by lawyer and litigant alike. It was the realization that certain matters must be disposed of "equitably" that led to the creation and rapid rise in influence of the Court of Chancery in the fifteenth and sixteenth centuries. Maitland, Equity (Chaytor & Whittaker ed. 1920) 3–10. The great body of equity jurisprudence that has since developed is a response to the continuing insistence that this need be met.

Nor is it unusual for statutes to employ, without more, words such as "equitable," "fair and equitable," "equitable and just" or phrases of like general import as establishing criteria to govern judicial determination or as describing a prerequisite to judicial approval. * * *

Today in the laws of many other states, in words very similar to those found in our statute, provision is made for the fair and equitable distribution of marital assets in the event of divorce. For example, *see* Alaska Code Ann., sec. 09.55.210(6) ("in the manner as may be just, and without regard as to which of the parties is the owner of the property"); Colo.Rev.Stat. Ann., sec. 46–1–5(2) ("in such proportions as may be fair and equitable"); 13 Del.Code Ann., sec. 1531 ("such share as the court deems reasonable"); Hawaii Rev.Stat., sec. 580–47 ("as shall appear just and equitable"); Iowa Code, sec. 598.21 ("as shall be justified"); Mich.Stat.Ann., sec. 25.99 M.C.L.A. § 552.19 ("as it shall deem just and reasonable"); Minn.Stat. Ann., sec. 518.58 ("as shall appear just and equitable"); N.H.Rev.Stat.Ann., sec. 458:19 ("as may be deemed just"); N.D.Rev.Code, sec. 14–05–24 ("as may seem just and proper"); Ore.Rev.Stat., sec. 107.105(e) ("as may be just and proper in all the circumstances"); Utah Code Ann., sec. 30–3–5 ("as may be [just and] equitable"); Vt.Stat.Ann., Title 15, sec. 751 ("as shall appear just and equitable"). Counsel have cited no case, nor have we found any, in which legislation of this sort has been successfully attacked as affording insufficient guidelines to the judge charged with the responsibility of allocating marital assets upon the dissolution of a marriage. As Justice Peters observed in *Addison v. Addison*, 62 Cal.2d 558, 43 Cal.Rptr. 97, 399 P.2d 897 (1965),

> . . . many common-law jurisdictions have provided for the division of the separate property of the respective spouses in a manner which is "just and reasonable" and none of these statutes have been overturned on a constitutional basis.

We hold that the statute before us is free from any constitutional insufficiency upon this score.

It seems appropriate at this point to suggest some of the criteria which may properly be taken into account by a matrimonial judge in determining in a given case how the distribution may most fairly be made. In his opinion in the trial court Judge Consodine, after examining authorities in other jurisdictions, compiled a list of such factors, which we here quote with approval.

Guideline criteria over the broad spectrum of litigation in this area include: (1) respective age, background and earning ability of the parties; (2) duration of the marriage; (3) the standard of living of the parties during the marriage; (4) what money or property each brought into the marriage; (5) the present income of the parties; (6) the property acquired during the marriage by either or both parties; (7) the source of acquisition; (8) the current value and income producing capacity of the property; (9) the debts and liabilities of the parties to the marriage; (10) the present mental and physical health of the parties; (11) the probability of continuing present employment at present earnings or better in the future; (12) effect of distribution of assets on the ability to pay alimony and support, and (13) gifts from one spouse to the other during marriage. (118 N.J.Super. at 335, 287 A.2d at 469)

Section 307 of the Uniform Marriage and Divorce Act, which has quite recently been approved by the House of Delegates of the American Bar Association contains the following list of criteria:

(1) contribution of each spouse to acquisition of the marital property, including contribution of a spouse as homemaker;

(2) value of the property set apart to each spouse;

(3) duration of the marriage; and

(4) economic circumstances of each spouse when the division of property is to become effective, including the desirability of awarding the family home or the right to live therein for reasonable periods to the spouse having custody of any children.

These factors are obviously intended to be illustrative and not exhaustive. The trial judge must in each case regard all of the particular circumstances of the individuals before the court, and having weighed and evaluated them reach a determination as to how best to fulfill the mandate of the statute. As is made clear in *Chalmers v. Chalmers*, 65 N.J. 186, 320 A.2d 478 (1974), decided this day, fault of a marital nature is not an appropriate criterion for consideration in effecting an equitable distribution of marital assets. The judicial task may upon occasion be a difficult one but it will hardly be novel. Seeking just and equitable results is and has always been inherent in the judicial function; it has been a chief concern of the courts for many centuries.

Many if not most property arrangements incident to divorce will probably be agreed upon between the parties, thus obviating the need for judicial intervention. Where, however, the court is called upon to exercise its powers, either in reviewing a proposed settlement when asked to give its approval, or in effecting the allocation itself, it will not be improper for a judge to give appropriate heed to legitimate tax considerations, nor to view sympathetically a resort to the trust device, with its great flexibility, where the most equitable disposition of property interests can thereby be best attained.

It is finally contended that the enactment must fall because there is a fatal lack of a specificity as to what property shall be eligible for equitable distribution. It will be recalled that the statute authorizes "[an] award or awards to the parties, in addition to alimony and maintenance, to effectuate an equitable distribution of the property, both real and personal, which was legally and beneficially acquired by them or either of them during the marriage." N.J.S.A. 2A:34–23. The general purpose of the legislation is clear. The courts are now empowered to allocate marital assets between the spouses, regardless of ownership. This was not the case before the enactment of the statute. In *Calame v. Calame*, 25 N.J.Eq. 548 (E. & A. 1874) Chief Justice Beasley, writing for a unanimous court, held that the statute permitting the payment of alimony and maintenance to a wife, incident to the grant of a divorce, could not be read to permit the assignment to her of a portion of the husband's real estate in fee or of a sum of money in gross. It was held that the statute comprehended only the grant of power "to give the wife an allowance of money in periodical installments." 25 N.J.Eq. at 549. There was, however, no suggestion in the opinion that the Legislature might not, if it saw fit, authorize the allocation of a husband's property by way of provision for a wife who had successfully sought a divorce. The Legislature simply had not chosen to do so. This rule, limiting the court's power to dispose of marital assets, continued unchanged until the passage of the present statute. *Parmly v. Parmly*, 125 N.J.Eq. 545, 5 A.2d 789 (E. & A. 1939). While the grant of power in the present enactment is expressed in rather comprehensive and general terms, this will not, in itself, in any way derogate from its constitutional validity if judicial interpretation, rendered on a case by case basis if need be, can supply specific guidelines to govern particular situations. This, we conclude, can readily be done.

Clearly any property owned by a husband or wife at the time of marriage will remain the separate property of such spouse and in the event of divorce will not qualify as an asset eligible for distribution. As to this the statute is explicit. We also hold that if such property, owned at the time of the marriage, later increases in value, such increment enjoys a like immunity.[78] Furthermore the income or other usufruct derived from such property, as well as any asset for which the original property may be exchanged or into which it, or the proceeds of its sale, may be traceable shall similarly be considered the separate property of the particular spouse. The burden of establishing such immunity as to any particular asset will rest upon the spouse who asserts it. In reaching these latter conclusions we admittedly

---

78. The immunity of incremental value to which we refer is not necessarily intended to include elements of value contributed by the other spouse, nor those for which husband and wife are jointly responsible.

pass beyond the words of the statute. These determinations are, we conceive, those most consonant with presumed legislative intent.

A further question is presented when we consider assets that have come into the ownership of a spouse, or of both spouses jointly, during coverture. To the extent that such property is attributable to the expenditure of effort by either spouse, it clearly qualifies for distribution. Here we have principally in mind the earnings of husband or wife; such assets are certainly comprehended by the statute. But what of property secured by gift, bequest, devise, descent, or in some other way? The trial court found that such property was not available for distribution. We reach a contrary conclusion essentially for the reasons given below.

In the first place we read the statute on its face to express an intent to include such property as eligible for distribution. In the second place, we believe that the exclusion of such assets would result in importing into our law of property, to a significant extent at least, doctrines of community property law. We discern no intent on the part of the Legislature to do this, and we do not think that such a result, with all that it might portend, should be allowed to come about indirectly or without due deliberation.

The court is authorized to distribute equitably " ... the property, both real and personal, which was legally and beneficially *acquired* by them [the spouses] or either of them during the marriage." (Emphasis added). It will be seen that "acquired" is the key word. The trial court accepted a definition to be found in Webster's Third New International Dictionary (1965) that the word "acquired" means "attained by the individual by his own efforts." We think the Legislature used the word in a more comprehensive sense to include not only property title to which is the direct or indirect result of an expenditure of effort on the part of a spouse, but also, assets title to which is received by gift or inheritance, or indeed in any other way. Had the former, more restricted meaning been intended, we believe that some confining language would have been employed to manifest this purpose. It is certainly a commonplace to say that property has been acquired by gift or that an asset has been acquired by inheritance. In fact the thought is probably most often expressed in this fashion. We think the word should be given this more inclusive meaning in the statute, absent any indication to the contrary.

We are further moved to place this construction upon the statutory language because of a result which would apparently ensue were we to exclude from eligibility for distribution all property a spouse receives, by bequest or gift, during marriage. Were we to adopt such an interpretation the resulting rule would be that property received by gift or inheritance during marriage, as well as that owned before marriage, would be ineligible for distribution, while presumably all other property would be eligible. Compare this with the rule followed in community property states to determine whether an asset is separate or community property. The statutes of the eight community property states provide that all property acquired by a husband or a wife during their marriage is community property, except for what either spouse acquires by gift, descent, or devise.

All property thus acquired, plus that owned before the marriage, is separate property. (4A Powell on Real Property, sec. 626, p. 717) It is true that the rules, otherwise identical, would be used to determine different things. Our rule would decide eligibility for allocation of property between spouses upon the occasion of a divorce[79] the other to determine whether a particular asset is separate or community property. But the probable influence and effect of the latter upon the subsequent development of the former seems plain.

We do not wish to be taken as suggesting that there is anything wrong with adopting a rule of community property law.

Much may be said for the community property theory that the accumulations of property during marriage are as much the product of the activities of the wife as those of the titular breadwinner. [Douglas, J., dissenting in *Fernandez v. Wiener*, 326 U.S. 340, 365, 66 S.Ct. 178, 190, 90 L.Ed. 116, 136 (1945).]

The statute we are considering, providing as it does for a fair allocation of marital assets upon divorce, is to some extent at least a recognition of this point of view. But it nevertheless remains true that community property law is very different from our law of property. Its genius is not that of the common law. Its adoption should not occur unwittingly, but only after study and deliberation. The statutory provision permitting equitable distribution, as has been pointed out, was added to the bill during its passage through the Legislature. No legislative history with respect to this provision exists. We have no reason to suppose that the lawmakers intended to adopt a rule the development and evolution of which would very likely come to be governed by rules of community property law, or that they were aware they might be doing so. Thus we think it preferable to accept the statute literally as written, giving to the word "acquired" the more comprehensive meaning as set forth above.

We therefore hold the legislative intent to be that *all* property, regardless of its source, in which a spouse acquires an interest during the marriage shall be eligible for distribution in the event of divorce. * * *

The only portions of the judgment below that are before us on this appeal relate to the disposition of property. The cause is remanded for the reconsideration of this issue in the light of what has been said above in this opinion. Because of the interrelationship of property distribution and the award of alimony and maintenance, the provision of the judgment touching upon the latter will also be considered reopened for such review, if any, as the trial court may deem appropriate.

---

79. It is important to bear in mind that nothing in our statute effects any change with respect to the ownership of property as between husband and wife prior to the entry of a judgment of allocation. Prior to that event neither spouse, by virtue of this statute, acquires any interest in the property of the other.

1. As interpreted by the *Painter* court, how does New Jersey property law allocate resources of married couples? What is included within the set of resources subject to division? Are the factors used in making an "equitable" distribution appropriate? Would it be better to merely use an equal division rule? Under what circumstances is unequal division appropriate? Was the division of property in the *Painter* case—awarding 20% of the difference between the parties' available assets to the wife—fair?

2. *Gifts During Marriage.* The *Painter* court rejected the "community property" view that gifts received during marriage are the separate property of the recipient. How should such gifts be characterized? Would you distinguish between gifts from a spouse and gifts from others? Should the intent of the donor affect the determination of whether a gift is within the class of divisible property?

New Jersey amended its marital property laws in 1980 as follows:

> However, all such property, real and personal or otherwise, legally or beneficially acquired during the marriage by either party by way of gift, devise or bequest shall not be subject to equitable distribution, except that interspousal gifts shall be subject to equitable distribution.

1980 N.J. Laws ch. 181 § 1. Is this approach more sensible?

3. The appropriateness of marital property law should depend upon how marriage is viewed as a social institution. Marriage is, however, a complex and evolving institution about which there exists a broad range of views reflecting the many cultures and histories of our society. Should marriage be viewed as a full partnership with both parties sharing equally in the product of the marriage? Or should marriage be seen as a limited partnership in which the participants retain separate spheres and substantial economic autonomy? Alternatively, should marriage be seen as a highly idiosyncratic institution, varying from couple to couple, such that the law should leave issues such as control of property and division at dissolution to the expressed intentions of the parties? How would such intentions be expressed? What should the law do if the intentions are not expressed? To what extent should other values and policy concerns—such sex-related inequality, the needs of minor children—come into play? *See generally* M. Fineman, The Illusion of Equality: The Rhetoric and Reality of Divorce Reform (1991); Blumberg, Fineman's The Illusion of Equality: A Review Essay 2 UCLA Women's L.J. 309 (1992); M. Glendon, The Transformation of Family Law (1989); L. Weitzman, The Divorce Revolution (1985); Scott, Rational Decisionmaking About Marriage and Divorce, 76 Va. L. Rev. 9 (1990); Carbone and Brinig, Rethinking Marriage: Feminist Ideology, Economic Change, and Divorce Reform, 65 Tulane L. Rev. 953 (1991); V. Fuchs, Women's Quest for Economic Equality (1988); M. Glendon, The New Family and the New Property (1981); G. Becker, A Treatise on the Family (1981); Prager, Sharing Principles and the Future of Marital Property Law, 25 UCLA L. Rev. 1 (1977).

b.   COMMUNITY PROPERTY

Although the Married Women's Acts and the doctrine of equitable distribution have blurred many of the practical differences between community property and common law marital property, these property systems are based on fundamentally different premises.[80] Common law marital property was based on the "unity" of husband and wife (which meant subservience of the wife to the husband) and placed virtually all control of property during the marriage in the husband. The common law also emphasized separate title to property (which, as a practical matter, frequently meant in the husband's name) and distributed property after death or dissolution accordingly, unless the parties went out of their way to create joint ownership in a tenancy by the entirety.

Community property begins with the presumption that property acquired during the marriage is joint (or "community") property, unless the parties go out of their way to create separate property. However, property brought into the marriage as separate property remains separate property, and gifts, devises, and inheritances to one spouse during the marriage also are classified as separate property. Each spouse has unrestricted authority to manage, use, and dispose of his or her separate property, and the spouses have equal authority to manage, use, and dispose of the community property.

Whereas common law martial property derives from the English marital property system and its feudal origins, community property traces its roots to the civil law jurisdictions of Europe. The civil law influenced the development of marital property through the Spanish settlement of the Southwest and Western states and through the French settlement of the Territory of Orleans (which later became Louisiana). California, Louisiana, Texas, New Mexico, Arizona, Nevada, Idaho, Washington, and Puerto Rico have community property systems. In addition, Wisconsin adopted a version of the Uniform Marital Property Act, which is a modified community property system. *See generally* McClanahan, Community Property Law in the United States (2d ed. 1982).

i.   Rights During Marriage

Community property systems presume that property acquired during the marriage is joint (or "community") property, unless the parties agree in writing to create separate property. As a consequence of this presumption, property acquired as a result of the labors or one or both spouses (*e.g.*, income) is community property. However, property brought into the marriage as separate property remains separate property, and gifts, devises,

---

80.   For a good comparison of the evolution of the common law and civil law marital property systems, *see* Younger, Marital Regimes: A Story of Compromise, and Demoralization, Together with Criticism and Suggestions for Reform, 67 Cornell L. Rev. 45 (1981). For an historical explanation of the differences between common law and civil law marital property systems, *see* Donahue, What Causes Fundamental Legal Ideas? Marital Property in England and France in the Thirteenth Century, 78 Mich. L. Rev. 59 (1979).

and inheritances to one spouse during the marriage are classified as separate property. Ariz. Rev. Stat. § 25–213; West's Ann. Cal. Fam. Code § 770. In addition, property acquired with separate property is deemed separate property (and property acquired with community property is deemed community property). *See, e.g., Boyd v. Oser*, 23 Cal.2d 613, 623, 145 P.2d 312, 317 (1944) (a change in the form of the property "affects neither the character of the property nor the respective rights of the spouses therein"); *In re Marriage of Grinius*, 166 Cal.App.3d 1179, 1186–89, 212 Cal.Rptr. 803, 807–10 (1985) (property acquired with a loan secured by separate property, or where the lender intended the loan would be repaid from separate assets, is separate property). In some states, all income or profits from separate property is deemed community property, *see, e.g.,* Idaho Code § 32–906(1), but in other states it is community property only to the extent it is the product of one or both spouses' labors. Ariz. Rev. Stat. § 25–213 ("the increase, rents, issues and profits" from separate property is also separate property); West's Ann. Cal. Fam. Code § 770 (same).

A number of problems arise when classifying property as separate or community property.

a. *Commingling of Funds*. Spouses often put their separate and community funds into a single bank account. Later, upon divorce or death, a dispute will arise over classification of the funds. The presumption that assets held during marriage are community assets normally settles most disputes, especially if the spouses kept inadequate records and a significant amount of time has passed. However, if the claimant kept accurate records, he or she may be able to *trace* the assets to a separate source, thereby overcoming the presumption. The claimant's case may be strengthened by the "family expense presumption," under which family expenses are presumed to have come from the community assets in the commingled account; if family expenses exceeded deposits of community funds, then the balance must be separate property. *See v. See*, 64 Cal.2d 778, 51 Cal.Rptr. 888, 415 P.2d 776 (1966).

b. *Property Purchased with Mixed Funds*. As mentioned above, if property was acquired in exchange for separate property (*e.g,* with separate funds), the acquired property is classified as separate property. If, however, property is purchased with both separate and community property–most commonly when the property was acquired subject to a mortgage before marriage, but some mortgage payments were made with community funds—the spouses (or, rather, the soon to be ex-spouses) must allocate ownership between separate and community property.

Some states have an "inception of title rule," under which title is fixed at the inception of the credit transaction. *McCurdy v. McCurdy*, 372 S.W.2d 381, 383–84 (Tex.Civ.App.1963) (proceeds of life insurance policy go to husband's estate as indicated in his will, and are not community property, where the husband first acquired the policy before his marriage, and even though the community made premium payments after the marriage). Under a "time of vesting" rule, title is determined by the status of the parties when the last payment is made; thus, if the mortgage is paid off with community funds during the marriage, the asset is considered community property. *Cosey v. Cosey*, 364 So.2d 186 (La.App.1978), *rev'd on the facts*, 376 So.2d 486 (La.1979). Under the *"pro rata* share" rule, the community has a share proportional to its share of the principal payments. *In re Dougherty's Estate*, 27 Wash.2d 11, 22, 176 P.2d 335, 341 (1947) (although the house was acquired in the names of both spouses after the marriage, because the downpayment and some of the mortgage payments were from the wife's separate funds, the house is partly separate property); *In re Marriage of Moore*, 28 Cal.3d 366, 371–73, 168 Cal.Rptr. 662, 664–65, 618 P.2d 208, 210–11 (1980) (although the house was acquired with a mortgage prior to marriage, the community acquired an interest in the house because some of the principal payments were made with community funds; in calculating the community's fractional share, only principal payments, and not taxes, insurance, or interest, are considered). Where the property is classified as solely community or separate property, there is a right of reimbursement. *Hanrahan v. Sims*, 20 Ariz.App. 313, 512 P.2d 617 (1973).

c. *Property Purchased in Another Jurisdiction.* A common problem arises when spouses now residing in a community property state acquired property during their marriage but in another jurisdiction. Several states treat such property as "quasi-community" property if it would have been community property had the spouses acquired it in the community property state. Courts treat quasi-community property like community property for many purposes at death or dissolution. *See, e.g.,* West's Ann. Cal. Fam. Code § 760; West's Ann. Cal. Prob. Code §§ 101, 6401(b) (including both real and personal property); Idaho Code § 15–2–201 (personal property only); Vernon's Tex. Code Ann. Fam. Code § 3.63(b) (real and personal property). During the course of the marriage, however, the rights to control and manage quasi-community property follow title (*e.g.,* one spouse's separate property). *See, e.g.,* West's Ann. Cal. Fam. Code §§ 1100–1103 (referring only to management and control of community property).

d. *Pre-marital Agreements.* Most states permit spouses to allocate property rights (but usually not spousal support or child support) pursuant to pre-marital agreements. *See, e.g.,* Ariz. Rev. Stat. §§ 25–201 to 25–205 (adopting the Uniform Premarital Agreement Act); West's Ann. Cal. Fam. Code §§ 1500–1620 (same). We address this issue in section d, *infra.*

e. *Transmutation.* In most community property states, spouses may freely transmute property from one category to another (*e.g.,* separate property of one spouse to community property, separate property of one spouse to separate property of the other). Some states require such transmutations to be in writing, except with regard to personal items, such as clothing and jewelry. *See, e.g.,* West's Ann. Cal. Fam. Code §§ 850–853.

f. *Management.* Each spouse has unrestricted authority to manage, use, and dispose of his or her separate property, Ariz. Rev. Stat. § 25–214(A); West's Ann. Cal. Fam. Code § 752, and the spouses generally have equal authority to manage, use, and dispose of the community property.

See, e.g., Ariz. Rev. Stat. § 25–214(B); West's Ann. Cal. Fam. Code §§ 751, 1100, 1102; Nev. Rev. Stat. Ann. § 123.225. *See generally* Oldham, Management of the Community Estate During an Intact Marriage, 56 Law & Contemp. Prob. 99 (Spring 1993). Some states make exceptions for businesses run by only one spouse. West's Ann. Cal. Fam. Code § 1100(d). In general, both spouses must join in the transfer of community property. *See, e.g.,* Ariz. Rev. Stat. § 25–214(C) (joinder of both spouses required for acquisition, disposition, or encumbrance of community real property, including leases longer than a year); West's Ann. Cal. Fam. Code §§ 1100(b)-(c), 1102(a) (community real property, but not community personal property; consent required for transfer of certain community personal property); Nev. Rev. Stat. Ann. § 123.230 (both spouses must join in sale of real and personal community property). To limit the possibility that one spouse will take advantage of another, each spouse has a duty of good faith and fair dealing in managing community property. *See, e.g.,* West's Ann. Cal. Fam. Code §§ 721, 1101; Nev. Rev. Stat. Ann. § 123.070.

g. *Creditors' Rights.* Community property also relates to the negative side of a couple's balance sheet: their liabilities to creditors. Creditors of a single spouse (whether the debt was incurred before or during the marriage) may reach that spouse's separate assets, West's Ann. Cal. Fam. Code § 913(a), and in general may not reach the other spouse's separate assets, Ariz. Rev. Stat. § 25–215(A); West's Ann. Cal. Fam. Code § 916(b)(1). There is a limited exception for debts incurred to provide the necessaries of life, West's Ann. Cal. Fam. Code § 914; West's Rev. Code Wash. Ann. 26.16.205. Most states also provide that creditors of a single spouse may reach community assets. West's Ann. Cal. Fam. Code § 910(a); *see also id.* § 911 (the non-debtors earnings are not liable for the debtor-spouse's pre-marital debts so long as the earnings are kept uncommingled in a deposit account to which the debtor spouse has no right of withdrawal).

Creditors of both spouses (*e.g.,* for debts incurred during the marriage) may reach community assets, as well as each spouse's separate assets. West's Ann. Cal. Fam. Code § 913(a); Ariz. Rev. Stat. § 25–215(D) (requiring the creditor first to seek satisfaction from community assets).

ii.   *Distribution of Property Following the Death of One Spouse*

When one spouse dies, the surviving spouse keeps his or her separate property and half of the community property. The decedent is free to dispose of his or her separate property and his or her half of the community property in a will. If the decedent's will purports to dispose of more than his or her share of the community property, the surviving spouse can elect between the will and the statutory share (*i.e.,* one-half) of the community property.

Absent a will, the statutory rules of inheritance dictate the disposition of the decedent's property. In California, Idaho, Nevada, New Mexico, and Washington, all of the community property goes to the surviving spouse and the separate property is divided among the spouse and children. The other community property states distribute the decedent's share of the community property among the surviving spouse and the decedent's children.

iii. *Distribution of Property Following Dissolution*

When the marriage ends in divorce, each party normally takes his or her separate property, and is assigned his or her separate debts. With a few exceptions (such as deliberate misappropriation of community funds), the community property and community debts are divided equally in California, New Mexico, and Louisiana, and through "equitable division" (which affords judges greater discretion) in the other community property states.

Divorcing spouses frequently disagree about the classification of property as separate or community assets. Particularly difficult problems arise where the value of separate property has appreciated during the marriage due in part to labor of one or both spouses, and the jurisdiction holds that the rents, issues and profits from separate property are also separate property. In such cases, the appreciation is a combination of separate and community property. How much of the appreciated value is due to the fact that the business was inherently valuable, regardless of the spouses' efforts during the marriage (and thus is separate property), and how much is due to one or both spouses' efforts (and thus is community property)?

Beam v. Bank of America

Supreme Court of California, 1971.
6 Cal.3d 12, 98 Cal.Rptr. 137, 490 P.2d 257.

■ TOBRINER, JUSTICE.

Mrs. Mary Beam, defendant in this divorce action, appeals from an interlocutory judgment awarding a divorce to both husband and wife on grounds of extreme cruelty. The trial court determined that the only community property existing at the time of trial was a promissory note for $38,000, and, upon the husband's stipulation, awarded this note to the wife; the court found all other property to be the separate property of the party possessing it. The court additionally awarded Mrs. Beam $1,500 per month as alimony and granted custody of the Beam's two minor children to both parents, instructing the husband to pay $250 per month for the support of each child so long as the child remained within the wife's care.

On this appeal, Mrs. Beam attacks the judgment primarily on the grounds that the trial court (1) failed adequately to compensate the community for income attributable to the husband's skill, efforts and labors expended in the handling of his sizable separate estate during the marriage, and (2) erred in suggesting that community living expenses, paid from the income of the husband's separate estate, should be charged against community income in determining the balance of community funds. In addition, the wife challenges the court's categorization of several specific assets as separate property of her husband. For the reasons discussed below, we have concluded that substantial precedent and evidence support the various conclusions under attack; thus we conclude that the judgment must be affirmed.

1. The Facts.

Mr. and Mrs. Beam were married on January 31, 1939; the instant divorce was granted in 1968, after 29 years of marriage. Prior to and during the early years of the marriage, Mr. Beam inherited a total of $1,629,129 in cash and securities, and, except for brief and insignificant intervals in the early 1940's, he was not employed at all during the marriage but instead devoted his time to handling his separate estate and engaging in private ventures with his own capital. Mr. Beam spent the major part of his time studying the stock market and actively trading in stocks and bonds; he also undertook several real estate ventures, including the construction of two hotel resorts, Cabana Holiday I at Piercy, California, and Cabana Holiday II at Prunedale, California. Apparently, Mr. Beam was not particularly successful in these efforts, however, for, according to Mrs. Beam's own calculations, over the lengthy marriage her husband's total estate enjoyed only a very modest increase to $1,850,507.33.

Evidence introduced at trial clearly demonstrated that the only moneys received and spent by the parties during their marriage were derived from the husband's separate estate; throughout the 29 years of marriage Mrs. Beam's sole occupation was that of housewife and mother (the Beams have four children). According to the testimony of both parties, the ordinary living expenses of the family throughout the marriage amounted to $2,000 per month and, in addition, after 1960, the family incurred extraordinary expenses (for travel, weddings, gifts) of $22,000 per year. Since the family's income derived solely from Mr. Beam's separate estate, all of these household and extraordinary expenses were naturally paid from that source.

During the greater part of the marriage (1946 to 1963) the Beams resided in a home on Spencer Lane in Atherton, California. In 1963 the family sold the Spencer Lane house and acquired a smaller residence in Atherton, on Selby Lane. This home was sold in 1966 for a cash down payment, which was apparently divided between the parties, and for a promissory note in the sum of $38,000, payable in monthly installments of $262.56. The trial court concluded that this note was community property but, upon Mr. Beam's stipulation, awarded the entire proceeds of the note to the wife.

On this appeal, Mrs. Beam of course does not question the disposition of the promissory note, but does attack the trial court's conclusion that this asset was the only community property existing at the time of the divorce. Initially, and most importantly, the wife contends that the trial court erred in failing to find any community property resulting from the industry, efforts and skill expended by her husband over the 29 years of marriage. We address this issue first.

2. The trial court did not err in concluding that there was no net community property accumulated during the marriage from the earnings of Mr. Beam's separate property.

Section 5108 of the Civil Code provides generally that the profits accruing from a husband's separate property are also separate property.[81] Nevertheless, long ago our courts recognized that, since income arising from the husband's skill, efforts and industry is community property, the community should receive a fair share of the profits which derive from the husband's devotion of more than minimal time and effort to the handling of his separate property. (*Pereira v. Pereira* (1909) 156 Cal. 1, 7, 103 P. 488; see *Millington v. Millington* (1968) 259 Cal.App.2d 896, 907–908, 67 Cal. Rptr. 128 and cases cited therein.) Furthermore, while this principle first took root in cases involving a husband's efforts expended in connection with a separately owned farm or business (*e.g., Pereira v. Pereira* (1909) 156 Cal. 1, 103 P. 488; *Huber v. Huber* (1946) 27 Cal.2d 784, 792, 167 P.2d 708; *Van Camp v. Van Camp* (1921) 53 Cal.App. 17, 29, 199 P. 885; *Stice v. Stice* (1947) 81 Cal.App.2d 792, 796, 185 P.2d 402) our courts now uniformly hold that "[a]n apportionment of profits is required not only when the husband conducts a commercial enterprise but also when he invests separate funds in real estate or securities. (Citations.)" (*Estate of Neilson* (1962) 57 Cal.2d 733, 740, 22 Cal.Rptr. 1, 5, 371 P.2d 745, 749; see *Margolis v. Margolis* (1952) 115 Cal.App.2d 131, 135, 251 P.2d 396). Without question, Mr. Beam's efforts in managing his separate property throughout the marriage were more than minimal, and thus the trial court was compelled to determine what proportion of the total profits should properly be apportioned as community income.

Over the years our courts have evolved two quite distinct, alternative approaches to allocating earnings between separate and community income in such cases. One method of apportionment, first applied in *Pereira v. Pereira* (1909) 156 Cal. 1, 7, 103 P. 488 and commonly referred to as the *Pereira* approach, "is to allocate a fair return on the [husband's separate property] investment [as separate income] and to allocate any excess to the community property as arising from the husband's efforts." (*Estate of Neilson* (1962) 57 Cal.2d 733, 740, 22 Cal.Rptr. 1, 4, 371 P.2d 745, 748.) The alternative apportionment approach, which traces its derivation to *Van Camp v. Van Camp* (1921) 53 Cal.App. 17, 27–28, 199 P. 885, is "to determine the reasonable value of the husband's services * * *, allocate that amount as community property, and treat the balance as separate property attributable to the normal earnings of the [separate estate]." (*Tassi v. Tassi* (1958) 160 Cal.App.2d 680, 690, 325 P.2d 872, 878.)

In making such apportionment between separate and community property our courts have developed no precise criterion or fixed standard, but have endeavored to adopt a yardstick which is most appropriate and equitable in a particular situation * * *

---

81. Section 5108 (formerly § 163) provides in relevant part: "All property owned by the husband before marriage, and that acquired afterwards by gift, bequest, devise, or descent, with the rents, issues, and profits thereof, is his separate property."

depending on whether the character of the capital investment in the separate property or the personal activity, ability, and capacity of the spouse is the chief contributing factor in the realization of income and profits (citations). * * *

In applying this principle of apportionment the court is not bound either to adopt a predetermined percentage as a fair return on business capital which is separate property [the *Pereira* approach] nor need it limit the community interest only to [a] salary fixed as the reward for a spouse's service [the *Van Camp* method] but may select [whichever] formula will achieve substantial justice between the parties.

The trial court in the instant case was well aware of these apportionment formulas and concluded from all the circumstances that the *Pereira* approach should be utilized. As stated above, under the *Pereira* test, community income is defined as the amount by which the actual income of the separate estate exceeds the return which the initial capital investment could have been expected to earn absent the spouse's personal management. In applying the *Pereira* formula the trial court adopted the legal interest rate of 7 percent simple interest as the "reasonable rate of return" on Mr. Beam's separate property; although the wife now attacks this 7 percent simple interest figure as unrealistically high, at trial she introduced no evidence in support of any other more "realistic" rate of return and, as we stated explicitly in *Weinberg v. Weinberg* (1967) 67 Cal.2d 557, 565, 63 Cal.Rptr. 13, 17, 432 P.2d 709, 713, in the absence of such evidence "the trial court correctly adopted the rate of legal interest." (*See also Pereira v. Pereira* (1909) 156 Cal. 1, 11–12, 103 P. 488, *Haldeman v. Haldeman* (1962) 202 Cal.App.2d 498, 505, fn. 1, 21 Cal.Rptr. 75.)

Testimony at trial indicated that, based upon this 7 percent simple interest growth factor, Mr. Beam's separate property would have been worth approximately 4.2 million dollars at the time of trial if no expenditures had been made during the marriage. Since Mrs. Beam's own calculations indicate that the present estate, plus all expenditures during marriage, would not amount to even 4 million dollars,[82] it appears that, under *Pereira*, the entire increase in the estate's value over the 29–year period would be attributable to the normal growth factor of the property itself, and, thus, using this formula, all income would be designated as separate property. In other words, under the *Pereira* analysis, none of the increased valuation of the husband's separate property during the marriage would be attributable to Mr. Beam's efforts, time or skill and, as a result, no community income would have been received and, consequently, no community property could presently be in existence.

The wife concedes that the use of the *Pereira* formula does sustain the trial court's conclusion that the present remainder of the husband's estate

82. According to defendant's figures, the value of Mr. Beam's estate at the time of trial was $1,850,507.33, ordinary living expenses over the marriage totalled $672,000, extraordinary expenses during this period equalled $176,000, and $610,126.93 was expended on "gifts." These calculations produce a gross total of $3,308,634.26.

is entirely his separate property, but she contends that, under the circumstances, the *Pereira* test cannot be said to "achieve substantial justice between the parties" (*Logan v. Forster* (1952) 114 Cal.App.2d 587, 600, 250 P.2d 730, 738) and thus that the trial court erred in not utilizing the *Van Camp* approach. Although the trial judge did not explicitly articulate his reasons for employing the *Pereira* rather than the *Van Camp* analysis, we cannot under the facts before us condemn as unreasonable the judge's implicit decision that the modest increment of Mr. Beam's estate was more probably attributable to the "character of the capital investment" than to the "personal activity, ability, and capacity of the spouse." (*Cf. Estate of Ney* (1963) 212 Cal.App.2d 891, 898, 28 Cal.Rptr. 442.) In any event, however, we need not decide whether the court erred in applying the *Pereira* test because we conclude, as did the trial court, that even under the *Van Camp* approach, the evidence sufficiently demonstrates that all the remaining assets in the estate constitute separate property.

Under the *Van Camp* test community income is determined by designating a reasonable value to the services performed by the husband in connection with his separate property. At trial Mrs. Beam introduced evidence that a professional investment manager, performing similar functions as those undertaken by Mr. Beam during the marriage, would have charged an annual fee of 1 percent of the corpus of the funds he was managing; Mrs. Beam contends that such a fee would amount to $17,000 per year (1 percent of the 1.7 million dollar corpus) and that, computed over the full term of their marriage, this annual "salary" would amount to $357,000 of community income. Mrs. Beam asserts that under the *Van Camp* approach she is now entitled to one-half of this $357,000.

Mrs. Beam's contention, however, overlooks the fundamental distinction between the total community *income* of the marriage, *i.e.*, the figure derived from the *Van Camp* formula, and the community *estate* existing at the dissolution of the marriage. The resulting community estate is not equivalent to total community income so long as there are any community *expenditures* to be charged against the community income. A long line of California decisions has established that "it is presumed that the expenses of the family are paid from community rather than separate funds (citations) [and] thus, in the absence of any evidence showing a different practice the community earnings are chargeable with these expenses. (Citations.)" * * * This "family expense presumption" has been universally invoked by prior California decisions applying either the *Pereira* or *Van Camp* formula. * * * Under these precedents, once a court ascertains the amount of community income, through either the *Pereira* or the *Van Camp* approach, it deducts the community's living expenses from community income to determine the balance of the community property.

If the "family expense" presumption is applied in the present case, clearly no part of the remaining estate can be considered to be community property. Both parties testified at trial that the family's *normal* living expenses were $2,000 per month, or $24,000 per year, and if those expenditures are charged against the annual community income, $17,000 under the

Van Camp accounting approach, quite obviously there was never any positive balance of community property which could have been built up throughout the marriage.[83]

> When a husband devotes his services to and invests his separate property in an economic enterprise, the part of the profits or increment in value attributable to the husband's services must be apportioned to the community. If the amount apportioned to the community is less than the amount expended for family purposes and if the presumption that family expenses are paid from community funds applies, all assets traceable to the investment are deemed to be the husband's separate property. (*Estate of Neilson* (1962) 57 Cal.2d 733, 742, 22 Cal.Rptr. 1, 6, 371 P.2d 745, 750.)
>
> * * *

The discussion in *See* in no way constitutes a rejection of the rule that, in the absence of other evidence, living expenses are presumed to have been paid out of community property rather than separate property, as Mrs. Beam suggests. Instead *See* merely concludes that if a spouse *does* "elect" to expend his separate property on community expenses, such expenditure "is a gift to the community" (*id.*) for which the spouse is not entitled to reimbursement. The cited portion of the *See* opinion thus does not involve the question of determining which assets, community or separate, have been paid out for living expenses—the subject of the family expense presumption—but instead deals with the distinct issue of the effect of a husband's voluntary decision to expend his separate property, rather than community property, on the community's living expenses.

In the instant case, of course, Mr. Beam made no conscious choice to spend his separate property, rather than the "imputed" community property on the family's living expenses. Only by means of a formula now applied by the court do we divide Mr. Beam's income into theoretical "community"

---

83. The trial court determined that no net community property could be established under the *Van Camp* formula by deducting total community expenses *over the course of the entire marriage* from total community income, *i.e.*, by using a 'total recapitulation' approach. Although Mrs. Beam has not challenged this total recapitulation approach on appeal, some suggestion has arisen that the trial court's resort to this accounting method is contrary to this court's decision in *See v. See* (1966) 64 Cal.2d 778, 51 Cal.Rptr. 888, 415 P.2d 776. Given the facts of the instant case, however, we need not decide whether the *See* decision, barring a husband's resort to a total recapitulation accounting in a case in which he has *voluntarily commingled separate and community income in a single account*, would also pre-

clude total recapitulation under the instant circumstances, involving no conscious commingling. In the present case, so long as the family expense presumption is applicable, there could be no positive balance in the community estate even if the accounting procedures prescribed by *See* were utilized. The uncontradicted evidence of both parties establishes that even if the balance of the community estate were determined on a yearly, or indeed monthly, basis, rather than over the entire marriage, there was never a positive balance in the estate since community living expenses regularly exceeded the community earnings as computed under *Van Camp.* Thus, on this record, the application of *See*'s accounting procedure would not alter the trial court's conclusion.

and "separate" portions; Beam could hardly draw upon a fictionalized separate source to pay family expenses. Thus our decision in *See* is simply not in point. * * *

Mrs. Beam further contends, however, that even if the "family expense" presumption remains intact, the presumption was rebutted in the instant case because Mr. Beam testified at trial that family expenses were paid from his separate property. If Mr. Beam's actions demonstrated that he had made a conscious choice to use separate property, as opposed to available community property, to pay living expenses, such use of his separate property would of course constitute a gift to the community for which he would be entitled to no reimbursement. (*See v. See* (1966) 64 Cal.2d 778, 785, 51 Cal.Rptr. 888, 415 P.2d 776.) The record clearly shows, however, that Mr. Beam's testimony rested totally on his assumption that all of his funds were his separate property; we cannot realistically characterize the husband's testimony as indicating that he consciously chose to pay for community expenses out of income which we now deem purely separate income, rather than from the income which, theoretically under the *Van Camp* formula, may now be designated community income.

If Mrs. Beam is to receive the benefit of the "community income" imputed by virtue of the *Pereira* or *Van Camp* tests, that income in the absence of evidence that Mr. Beam consciously declined to use available community funds, must be charged with the expenses that have been incurred by the community over the marriage; the income cannot fairly be isolated from the correlative expenses. (*Cf.* 1 deFuniak, Principles of Community Property (1943) § 159, p. 445.) Therefore we cannot conclude on this record that the trial court erred in finding that the "living expense" presumption had not been rebutted.

In sum, even if the trial court had utilized the *Van Camp* approach in determining community income, as the wife suggests, the court would still have properly concluded that there was no resulting community property from the earnings of her husband's separate property. We therefore conclude that the wife's initial contention is without merit. * * *

The judgment is affirmed.

---

1.   What are the two principal methods for apportioning appreciated value between separate or community property? Should these methods, in theory, produce the same apportionment? Do they produce the same apportionment in practice?

2.   What guidance or criteria does *Beam* give trial courts in choosing between the *Van Camp* and *Pereira* methods? What factors should a court use?

3.   Suppose the wife had an established business when she married. Five years later, when the couple divorced, the value of the business had tripled. As her attorney, which method should you favor? Isn't your best

argument that your client was an incompetent businessperson and the business increased in value despite her efforts?

4. What is the policy basis for the rule that the income or appreciated value of separate property is also separate property? What is the basis for distinguishing it from income from a spouse's labor, which is deemed to be community property? What are the advantages of a rule holding that *all* appreciation of *any* property of either spouse is community property?

c. PROFESSIONAL TRAINING AS MARITAL PROPERTY

Some scholars have argued that the equal division of marital property works systematically to the disadvantage of women because they traditionally have foregone career opportunities during marriage to raise a family and support their husband's career development. Dr. Lenore Weitzman has written that if a woman has

> few skills, outdated experience, no seniority, and no time for retraining, and if she continued to have the major burden of caring for young children after divorce, it is easy to understand why the divorced woman is likely to be much worse off than her former husband.

L. Weitzman, The Divorce Revolution xii (1985). Although Weitzman's book argues that no-fault divorce has substantially contributed to the impoverishment of divorced women relative to divorced men,[84] her less controversial point is that equal division of assets often will not leave the divorced spouses equally well off. *See also* Stark, Burning Down the House: Toward a Theory of More Equitable Distribution, 40 Rutgers L. Rev. 1173 (1988). Equal division of assets may not matter much when the real wealth is from future cash flow. Weitzman advocates the expansion of the definition of marital property to include "career assets," such as non-vested pensions, goodwill of a business or profession, professional education and license, and future earning capacity. *See* Weitzman, The Economics of Divorce, 28 UCLA L. Rev. 1181, 1210–21 (1981).

Other feminist scholars reach different conclusions by emphasizing the potential for family law to loosen the traditional financial dependence of women upon men. Dean Herma Hill Kay argues that

> since ... Anglo–American family law has traditionally reflected the social division of function by sex within marriage, it will be necessary to withdraw existing legal supports for that arrangement as a cultural norm. No sweeping legal reforms of marriage and divorce will be required, however, to achieve this end. It will be enough ... to continue the present trend begun in the nineteenth century toward the emancipation of married women, and implemented more recently by gender-neutral family laws, as well

---

84. A lively discussion of Weitzman's book, much of it disputing her conclusion that no-fault divorce is to blame for the impoverishment of divorced women, can be found in Review Symposium on Weitzman's Divorce Revolution, 1986 Am. B. Found. Res. J. 759.

as the current emphasis on sharing principles in marital property law.

Kay, Equality and Difference: A Perspective on No–Fault Divorce and its Aftermath, 56 U. Cin. L. Rev. 1, 86 (1987). Dean Kay argues that the law should discourage traditional gender roles in the family. While endorsing compensatory alimony awards for women who followed the traditional housewife model well past their prime career development phase of life, Kay opposes awards based on an assumption of financial dependency for women who make "economically disabling" choices in the future. She also advocates joint child custody of minor children to encourage fathers to take responsibility for the emotional and financial needs of their children. Such an approach would enhance women's ability to achieve economic independence and reduce the large disparity between men's and women's post-divorce standard of living. *See generally* Carbone & Brinig, Rethinking Marriage: Feminist Ideology, Economic Change, and Divorce Reform, 65 Tul. L. Rev. 953 (1991).

The actual treatment of "career assets" at the dissolution of marriage varies substantially across states and remains a matter of great controversy. The materials that follow illustrate three different approaches to the treatment of professional training acquired during a marriage.

In re the Marriage of Graham

Supreme Court of Colorado, 1978.
194 Colo. 429, 574 P.2d 75.

■ Lee, Justice.

This case presents the novel question of whether in a marriage dissolution proceeding a master's degree in business administration (M.B.A.) constitutes marital property which is subject to division by the court. In its opinion in *Graham v. Graham*, 38 Colo.App. 130, 555 P.2d 527, the Colorado Court of Appeals held that it was not. We affirm the judgment.

The Uniform Dissolution of Marriage Act requires that a court shall divide marital property, without regard to marital misconduct, in such proportions as the court deems just after considering all relevant factors. The Act defines marital property as follows:

"For purposes of this article only, 'marital property' means all property acquired by either spouse subsequent to the marriage except:

"(a) Property acquired by gift, bequest, devise, or descent;

"(b) Property acquired in exchange for property acquired prior to the marriage or in exchange for property acquired by gift, bequest, devise, or descent;

"(c) Property acquired by a spouse after a decree of legal separation; and

"(d) Property excluded by valid agreement of the parties."

Section 14–10–113(2), C.R.S.1973.

The parties to this proceeding were married on August 5, 1968, in Denver, Colorado. Throughout the six-year marriage, Anne P. Graham, wife and petitioner here, was employed full-time as an airline stewardess. She is still so employed. Her husband, Dennis J. Graham, respondent, worked part-time for most of the marriage, although his main pursuit was his education. He attended school for approximately three and one-half years of the marriage, acquiring both a bachelor of science degree in engineering physics and a master's degree in business administration at the University of Colorado. Following graduation, he obtained a job as an executive assistant with a large corporation at a starting salary of $14,000 per year.

The trial court determined that during the marriage petitioner contributed seventy percent of the financial support, which was used both for family expenses and for her husband's education. No marital assets were accumulated during the marriage. In addition, the Grahams together managed an apartment house and petitioner did the majority of housework and cooked most of the meals for the couple. No children were born during the marriage.

The parties jointly filed a petition for dissolution, on February 4, 1974, in the Boulder County District Court. Petitioner did not make a claim for maintenance or for attorney fees. After a hearing on October 24, 1974, the trial court found, as a matter of law, that an education obtained by one spouse during a marriage is jointly-owned property to which the other spouse has a property right. The future earnings value of the M.B.A. to respondent was evaluated at $82,836 and petitioner was awarded $33,134 of this amount, payable in monthly installments of $100.

The court of appeals reversed, holding that an education is not itself "property" subject to division under the Act, although it was one factor to be considered in determining maintenance or in arriving at an equitable property division.

I.

The purpose of the division of marital property is to allocate to each spouse what equitably belongs to him or her. *See* H. Clark, Domestic Relations § 14.8. The division is committed to the sound discretion of the trial court and there is no rigid mathematical formula that the court must adhere to *Carlson v. Carlson*, 178 Colo. 283, 497 P.2d 1006; *Greer v. Greer*, 32 Colo.App. 196, 510 P.2d 905. An appellate court will alter a division of property only if the trial court abuses its discretion. This court, however, is empowered at all times to interpret Colorado statutes.

The legislature intended the term "property" to be broadly inclusive, as indicated by its use of the qualifying adjective "all" in section 14–10–

113(2). Previous Colorado cases have given "property" a comprehensive meaning, as typified by the following definition: "In short it embraces anything and everything which may belong to a man and in the ownership of which he has a right to be protected by law." *Las Animas County High School District v. Raye*, 144 Colo. 367, 356 P.2d 237.

Nonetheless, there are necessary limits upon what may be considered "property," and we do not find any indication in the Act that the concept as used by the legislature is other than that usually understood to be embodied within the term. One helpful definition is "everything that has an exchangeable value or which goes to make up wealth or estate." Black's Law Dictionary 1382 (rev. 4th ed. 1968). In *Ellis v. Ellis*, Colo., 552 P.2d 506, this court held that military retirement pay was not property for the reason that it did not have any of the elements of cash surrender value, loan value, redemption value, lump sum value, or value realizable after death. The court of appeals has considered other factors as well in deciding whether something falls within the concept, particularly whether it can be assigned, sold, transferred, conveyed, or pledged, or whether it terminates on the death of the owner. *In re Marriage of Ellis*, 36 Colo.App. 234, 538 P.2d 1347, *aff'd, Ellis v. Ellis, supra*.

An educational degree, such as an M.B.A., is simply not encompassed even by the broad views of the concept of "property." It does not have an exchange value or any objective transferable value on an open market. It is personal to the holder. It terminates on death of the holder and is not inheritable. It cannot be assigned, sold, transferred, conveyed, or pledged. An advanced degree is a cumulative product of many years of previous education, combined with diligence and hard work. It may not be acquired by the mere expenditure of money. It is simply an intellectual achievement that may potentially assist in the future acquisition of property. In our view, it has none of the attributes of property in the usual sense of that term.

II.

Our interpretation is in accord with cases in other jurisdictions. We have been unable to find any decision, even in community property states, which appears to have held that an education of one spouse is marital property to be divided on dissolution. This contention was dismissed in *Todd v. Todd*, 272 Cal.App.2d 786, 78 Cal.Rptr. 131 (Ct.App.), where it was held that a law degree is not a community property asset capable of division, partly because it "cannot have monetary value placed upon it." Similarly, it has been recently held that a person's earning capacity, even where enhanced by a law degree financed by the other spouse, "should not be recognized as a separate, particular item of property." *Stern v. Stern*, 66 N.J. 340, 331 A.2d 257.

Other cases cited have dealt only with related issues. For example, in awarding alimony, as opposed to dividing property, one court has found that an education is one factor to be considered. *Daniels v. Daniels*, 20 Ohio Op.2d 458, 185 N.E.2d 773 (Ct.App.). In another case, the wife supported the husband while he went to medical school. *Nail v. Nail*, 486 S.W.2d 761 (Tex.). The question was whether the accrued good will of his medical practice was marital property, and the court held it was not, inasmuch as good will was based on the husband's personal skill, reputation, and experience. *Contra, Mueller v. Mueller*, 144 Cal.App.2d 245, 301 P.2d 90; *see* Annot., 52 A.L.R.3d 1344.

III.

The trial court relied on *Greer v. Greer*, 32 Colo.App. 196, 510 P.2d 905, for its determination that an education is "property." In that case, a six-year marriage was dissolved in which the wife worked as a teacher while the husband obtained a medical degree. The parties had accumulated marital property. The trial court awarded the wife alimony of $150 per month for four years. The court of appeals found this to be proper, whether considered as an adjustment of property rights based upon the wife's financial contribution to the marriage, or as an award of alimony in gross. The court there stated that "* * * [i]t must be considered as a substitute for, or in lieu of, the wife's rights in the husband's property * * * ." We note that the court did not determine that the medical education itself was divisible property. The case is distinguishable from the instant case in that here there was no accumulation of marital property and the petitioner did not seek maintenance (alimony).

IV.

A spouse who provides financial support while the other spouse acquires an education is not without a remedy. Where there is marital property to be divided, such contribution to the education of the other spouse may be taken into consideration by the court. *Greer v. Greer, supra*. *See also Carlson v. Carlson*, 178 Colo. 283, 497 P.2d 1006. Here, we again note that no marital property had been accumulated by the parties. Further, if maintenance is sought and a need is demonstrated, the trial court may make an award based on all relevant factors. Section 14-10-114(2). Certainly, among the relevant factors to be considered is the contribution of the spouse seeking maintenance to the education of the other spouse from whom the maintenance is sought. Again, we note that in this case petitioner sought no maintenance from respondent.

The judgment is affirmed.

■ CARRIGAN, JUSTICE, dissenting:

I respectfully dissent.

As a matter of economic reality the most valuable asset acquired by either party during this six-year marriage was the husband's increased earning capacity. There is no dispute that this asset resulted from his having obtained Bachelor of Science and Master of Business Administration degrees while married. These degrees, in turn, resulted in large part from the wife's employment which contributed about 70% of the couple's total income. Her earnings not only provided her husband's support but also were "invested" in his education in the sense that she assumed the role of breadwinner so that he would have the time and funds necessary to obtain his education.

The case presents the not-unfamiliar pattern of the wife who, willing to sacrifice for a more secure family financial future, works to educate her husband, only to be awarded a divorce decree shortly after he is awarded his degree. The issue here is whether traditional, narrow concepts of what constitutes "property" render the courts impotent to provide a remedy for an obvious injustice.

In cases such as this, equity demands that courts seek extraordinary remedies to prevent extraordinary injustice. If the parties had remained married long enough after the husband had completed his post-graduate education so that they could have accumulated substantial property, there would have been no problem. In that situation abundant precedent authorized the trial court, in determining how much of the marital property to allocate to the wife, to take into account her contributions to her husband's earning capacity. *Greer v. Greer*, 32 Colo.App. 196, 510 P.2d 905 (1973) (wife supported husband through medical school); *In re Marriage of Vanet*, 544 S.W.2d 236 (Mo.App.1976) (wife was breadwinner while husband was in law school).

A husband's future income earning potential, sometimes as indicated by the goodwill value of a professional practice, may be considered in deciding property division or alimony matters, and the wife's award may be increased on the ground that the husband probably will have substantial future earnings. *Todd v. Todd*, 272 Cal.App.2d 786, 78 Cal.Rptr. 131 (1969) (goodwill of husband's law practice); *Golden v. Golden*, 270 Cal.App.2d 401, 75 Cal.Rptr. 735 (1969) (goodwill of husband's medical practice); *Mueller v. Mueller*, 144 Cal.App.2d 245, 301 P.2d 90 (1956) (goodwill of husband's dental lab); *In re Marriage of Goger*, 27 Or.App. 729, 557 P.2d 46 (1976) (potential earnings of husband's dental practice); *In re Marriage of Lukens*, 16 Wash.App. 481, 558 P.2d 279 (1976) (goodwill of husband's medical practice indicated future earning capacity).

Similarly, the wife's contributions to enhancing the husband's financial status or earning capacity have been considered in awarding alimony and maintenance. *Kraus v. Kraus*, 159 Colo. 331, 411 P.2d 240 (1966); *Shapiro v. Shapiro*, 115 Colo. 505, 176 P.2d 363 (1946). The majority opinion emphasizes that in this case no maintenance was requested. However, the Colorado statute would seem to preclude an award of maintenance here, for it restricts the court's power to award maintenance to cases where the spouse seeking it is unable to support himself or herself. Section 14–10–114, C.R.S.1973.

While the majority opinion focuses on whether the husband's master's degree is marital "property" subject to division, it is not the degree itself which constitutes the asset in question. Rather it is the increase in the husband's earning power concomitant to that degree which is the asset conferred on him by his wife's efforts. That increased earning capacity was the asset appraised in the economist's expert opinion testimony as having a discounted present value of $82,000.

Unquestionably the law, in other contexts, recognizes future earning capacity as an asset whose wrongful deprivation is compensable. Thus one who tortiously destroys or impairs another's future earning capacity must pay as damages the amount the injured party has lost in anticipated future earnings. *Nemer v. Anderson*, 151 Colo. 411, 378 P.2d 841 (1963); Abram, Personal Injury Damages in Colorado, 35 Colo.L.Rev. 332, 338 (1963).

Where a husband is killed, his widow is entitled to recover for loss of his future support damages based in part on the present value of his anticipated future earnings, which may be computed by taking into account probable future increases in his earning capacity. *See United States v. Sommers*, 351 F.2d 354 (10th Cir.1965); *Good v. Chance*, Colo.App., 565 P.2d 217 (1977). *See also* Colo.J.I. (Civil) 10:3.

The day before the divorce the wife had a legally recognized interest in her husband's earning capacity. Perhaps the wife might have a remedy in a separate action based on implied debt, quasi-contract, unjust enrichment, or some similar theory. *See, e.g., Dass v. Epplen*, 162 Colo. 60, 424 P.2d 779 (1967). Nevertheless, the law favors settling all aspects of a dispute in a single action where that is possible. Therefore I would affirm the trial court's award.

O'Brien v. O'Brien

Court of Appeals of New York, 1985.
66 N.Y.2d 576, 498 N.Y.S.2d 743, 489 N.E.2d 712.

■ SIMONS, JUDGE.

In this divorce action, the parties' only asset of any consequence is the husband's newly acquired license to practice medicine. The principal issue presented is whether that license, acquired during their marriage, is marital property subject to equitable distribution under Domestic Relations Law § 236(B)(5). * * *

I

Plaintiff and defendant married on April 3, 1971. At the time both were employed as teachers at the same private school. Defendant had a bachelor's degree and a temporary teaching certificate but required 18 months of postgraduate classes at an approximate cost of $3,000, excluding living expenses, to obtain permanent certification in New York. She claimed, and the trial court found, that she had relinquished the opportunity to obtain permanent certification while plaintiff pursued his education. At the time of the marriage, plaintiff had completed only three and one-half years of college but shortly afterward he returned to school at night to earn his bachelor's degree and to complete sufficient premedical courses to enter medical school. In September 1973 the parties moved to Guadalajara, Mexico, where plaintiff became a full-time medical student. While he pursued his studies defendant held several teaching and tutorial positions and contributed her earnings to their joint expenses. The parties returned to New York in December 1976 so that plaintiff could complete the last two semesters of medical school and internship training here. After they returned, defendant resumed her former teaching position and she remained in it at the time this action was commenced. Plaintiff was licensed to practice medicine in October 1980. He commenced this action for divorce two months later. At the time of trial, he was a resident in general surgery.

During the marriage both parties contributed to paying the living and educational expenses and they received additional help from both of their families. They disagreed on the amounts of their respective contributions but it is undisputed that in addition to performing household work and managing the family finances defendant was gainfully employed throughout the marriage, that she contributed all of her earnings to their living and educational expenses and that her financial contributions exceeded those of plaintiff. The trial court found that she had contributed 76% of the parties' income exclusive of a $10,000 student loan obtained by defendant. Finding that plaintiff's medical degree and license are marital property, the court received evidence of its value and ordered a distributive award to defendant.

Defendant presented expert testimony that the present value of plaintiff's medical license was $472,000. Her expert testified that he arrived at this figure by comparing the average income of a college graduate and that of a general surgeon between 1985, when plaintiff's residency would end, and 2012, when he would reach age 65. After considering Federal income taxes, an inflation rate of 10% and a real interest rate of 3% he capitalized the difference in average earnings and reduced the amount to present value. He also gave his opinion that the present value of defendant's contribution to plaintiff's medical education was $103,390. Plaintiff offered no expert testimony on the subject.

The court, after considering the life-style that plaintiff would enjoy from the enhanced earning potential his medical license would bring and defendant's contributions and efforts toward attainment of it, made a distributive award to her of $188,800, representing 40% of the value of the license, and ordered it paid in 11 annual installments of various amounts beginning November 1, 1982 and ending November 1, 1992. The court also directed plaintiff to maintain a life insurance policy on his life for defendant's benefit for the unpaid balance of the award and it ordered plaintiff to pay defendant's counsel fees of $7,000 and her expert witness fee of $1,000. It did not award defendant maintenance. * * *

II

The Equitable Distribution Law contemplates only two classes of property: marital property and separate property (Domestic Relations Law § 236[B][1][c], [d]). The former, which is subject to equitable distribution, is defined broadly as "all property acquired by either or both spouses during the marriage and before the execution of a separation agreement or the commencement of a matrimonial action, *regardless of the form in which title is held"* (Domestic Relations Law § 236[B][1][c] [emphasis added]; *see* § 236[B][5][b], [c]). Plaintiff does not contend that his license is excluded from distribution because it is separate property; rather, he claims that it is not property at all but represents a personal attainment in acquiring knowledge. He rests his argument on decisions in similar cases from other jurisdictions and on his view that a license does not satisfy common-law concepts of property. Neither contention is controlling because decisions in other States rely principally on their own statutes, and the legislative history underlying them, and because the New York Legislature deliberately went beyond traditional property concepts when it formulated the Equitable Distribution Law (*see generally*, 2 Foster–Freed–Brandes, Law and the Family—New York ch. 33, at 917 *et seq.* [1985 Cum.Supp.]). Instead, our statute recognizes that spouses have an equitable claim to things of value arising out of the marital relationship and classifies them as subject to distribution by focusing on the marital status of the parties at the time of acquisition. Those things acquired during marriage and subject to distribution have been classified as "marital property" although, as one commentator has observed, they hardly fall within the traditional property concepts because there is no common-law property interest remotely resembling marital property. "It is a statutory creature, is of no meaning whatsoever during the normal course of a marriage and arises full-grown, like Athena, upon the signing of a separation agreement or the commencement of a matrimonial action. [Thus] [i]t is hardly surprising, and not at all relevant, that traditional common law property concepts do not fit in parsing the meaning of 'marital property' " (Florescue, "Market Value", Professional Licenses and Marital Property: A Dilemma in Search of a Horn, 1982 N.Y.St.Bar Assn.Fam.L.Rev. 13 [Dec.]). Having classified the "property" subject to distribution, the Legislature did not attempt to go further and define it but left it to the courts to determine what interests come within the terms of section 236[B][1][c].

We made such a determination in *Majauskas v. Majauskas*, 61 N.Y.2d 481, 474 N.Y.S.2d 699, 463 N.E.2d 15, holding there that vested but unmatured pension rights are marital property subject to equitable distribution. Because pension benefits are not specifically identified as marital property in the statute, we looked to the express reference to pension rights contained in section 236[B][5][d][4], which deals with equitable distribution of marital property, to other provisions of the equitable distribution statute and to the legislative intent behind its enactment to determine whether pension rights are marital property or separate property. A similar analysis is appropriate here and leads to the conclusion that marital property encompasses a license to practice medicine to the extent that the license is acquired during marriage.

Section 236 provides that in making an equitable distribution of marital property, "the court shall consider: * * * (6) any equitable claim to, interest in, or direct or indirect contribution made to the acquisition of such marital property by the party not having title, including joint efforts or expenditures and contributions and services as a spouse, parent, wage earner and homemaker, and *to the career or career potential* of the other

249

party [and] * * * (9) the impossibility or difficulty of evaluating any component asset or any interest in a business, corporation or *profession*" (Domestic Relations Law § 236[B][5][d][6], [9] [emphasis added]). Where equitable distribution of marital property is appropriate but "the distribution of an interest in a business, corporation or *profession* would be contrary to law" the court shall make a distributive award in lieu of an actual distribution of the property (Domestic Relations Law § 236[B][5][e] [emphasis added]). The words mean exactly what they say: that an interest in a profession or professional career potential is marital property which may be represented by direct or indirect contributions of the non-title-holding spouse, including financial contributions and nonfinancial contributions made by caring for the home and family.

The history which preceded enactment of the statute confirms this interpretation. Reform of section 236 was advocated because experience had proven that application of the traditional common-law title theory of property had caused inequities upon dissolution of a marriage. The Legislature replaced the existing system with equitable distribution of marital property, an entirely new theory which considered all the circumstances of the case and of the respective parties to the marriage (Assembly Memorandum, 1980 N.Y.Legis.Ann., at 129–130). Equitable distribution was based on the premise that a marriage is, among other things, an economic partnership to which both parties contribute as spouse, parent, wage earner or homemaker (*id.*, at 130; *see,* Governor's Memorandum of Approval, 1980 McKinney's Session Laws of N.Y., at 1863). Consistent with this purpose, and implicit in the statutory scheme as a whole, is the view that upon dissolution of the marriage there should be a winding up of the parties' economic affairs and a severance of their economic ties by an equitable distribution of the marital assets. Thus, the concept of alimony, which often served as a means of lifetime support and dependence for one spouse upon the other long after the marriage was over, was replaced with the concept of maintenance which seeks to allow "the recipient spouse an opportunity to achieve [economic] independence" (Assembly Memorandum, 1980 N.Y.Legis.Ann., at 130).

The determination that a professional license is marital property is also consistent with the conceptual base upon which the statute rests. As this case demonstrates, few undertakings during a marriage better qualify as the type of joint effort that the statute's economic partnership theory is intended to address than contributions toward one spouse's acquisition of a professional license. Working spouses are often required to contribute substantial income as wage earners, sacrifice their own educational or career goals and opportunities for child rearing, perform the bulk of household duties and responsibilities and forego the acquisition of marital assets that could have been accumulated if the professional spouse had been employed rather than occupied with the study and training necessary to acquire a professional license. In this case, nearly all of the parties' nine-year marriage was devoted to the acquisition of plaintiff's medical license and defendant played a major role in that project. She worked continuously during the marriage and contributed all of her earnings to their joint effort, she sacrificed her own educational and career opportunities, and she traveled with plaintiff to Mexico for three and one-half years while he attended medical school there. The Legislature has decided, by its explicit reference in the statute to the contributions of one spouse to the other's profession or career (*see*, Domestic Relations Law § 236[B][5][d][6], [9]; [e]), that these contributions represent investments in the economic partnership of the marriage and that the product of the parties' joint efforts, the professional license, should be considered marital property.

The majority at the Appellate Division held that the cited statutory provisions do not refer to the license held by a professional who has yet to establish a practice but only to a going professional practice. There is no reason in law or logic to restrict the plain language of the statute to existing practices, however, for it is of little consequence in making an award of marital property, except for the purpose of evaluation, whether the professional spouse has already established a practice or whether he or she has yet to do so. An established practice merely represents the exercise of the privileges conferred upon the professional spouse by the license and the income flowing from that practice represents the receipt of the enhanced earning capacity that licensure allows. That being so, it would be unfair not to consider the license a marital asset.

Plaintiff's principal argument, adopted by the majority below, is that a professional license is not marital property because it does not fit within the traditional view of property as something which has an exchange value on the open market and is capable of sale, assignment or transfer. The position does not withstand analysis for at least two reasons. First, as we have observed, it ignores the fact that whether a professional license constitutes marital property is to be judged by the language of the statute which created this new species of property previously unknown at common law or under prior statutes. Thus, whether the license fits within traditional property concepts is of no consequence. Second, it is an overstatement to assert that a professional license could not be considered property even outside the context of section 236[B]. A professional license is a valuable property right, reflected in the money, effort and lost opportunity for employment expended in its acquisition, and also in the enhanced earning capacity it affords its holder, which may not be revoked without due process of law. That a professional license has no market value is irrelevant. Obviously, a license may not be alienated as may other property and for that reason the working spouse's interest in it is limited. The Legislature has recognized that limitation, however, and has provided for an award in lieu of its actual distribution (*see*, Domestic Relations Law § 236[B][5][e]).

Plaintiff also contends that alternative remedies should be employed, such as an award of rehabilitative maintenance or reimbursement for direct financial contributions. The statute does not expressly authorize retrospective maintenance or rehabilitative awards and we have no occasion to decide in this case whether the authority to do so may ever be implied from its provisions. It is sufficient to observe that normally a working spouse should not be restricted to that relief because to do so frustrates the purposes underlying the Equitable Distribution Law. Limiting a working spouse to a maintenance award, either general or rehabilitative, not only is contrary to the economic partnership concept underlying the statute but also retains the uncertain and inequitable economic ties of dependence that the Legislature sought to extinguish by equitable distribution. Maintenance is subject to termination upon the recipient's remarriage and a working spouse may never receive adequate consideration for his or her contribution and may even be penalized for the decision to remarry if that is the only method of compensating the contribution. As one court said so well, "[t]he function of equitable distribution is to recognize that when a marriage ends, each of the spouses, based on the totality of the contributions made to it, has a stake in and right to a share of the marital assets accumulated while it endured, not because that share is needed, but because those assets represent the capital product of what was essentially a partnership entity" (*Wood v. Wood,* 119 Misc.2d 1076, 1079, 465 N.Y.S. 2d 475). The Legislature stated its intention to eliminate such inequities by providing that a supporting spouse's "direct or indirect contribution" be recognized, considered and rewarded (Domestic Relations Law § 236[B][5][d][6]).

Turning to the question of valuation, it has been suggested that even if a professional license is considered marital property, the working spouse is entitled only to reimbursement of his or her direct financial contributions (*see*, Note, Equitable Distribution of Degrees and Licenses: Two Theories Toward Compensating Spousal Contributions, 49 Brooklyn L.Rev. 301, 317–322). By parity of reasoning, a spouse's down payment on real estate or contribution to the purchase of securities would be limited to the money contributed, without any remuneration for any incremental value in the asset because of price appreciation. Such a result is completely at odds with the statute's requirement that the court give full consideration to both direct and indirect contributions "made to the acquisition of such marital property by the party not having title, including joint *efforts* or expenditures and *contributions and services as a spouse, parent,* wage earner *and homemaker*" (Domestic Relations Law § 236[B][5][d][6] [emphasis added]). If the license is marital property, then the working spouse is entitled to an equitable portion of it, not a return of funds advanced. Its value is the enhanced earning capacity it affords the holder and although fixing the present value of that enhanced earning capacity may present problems, the problems are not insurmountable. Certainly they are no more difficult than computing tort damages for wrongful death or diminished earning capacity resulting from injury and they differ only in degree from the problems presented when valuing a professional practice for purposes of a distributive award, something the courts have not hesitated to do. The trial court retains the flexibility and discretion to structure the distributive award equitably, taking into consideration factors such as the working spouse's need for immediate payment, the licensed spouse's current ability to pay and the income tax consequences of prolonging the period of payment (*see*, Internal Revenue Code [26 U.S.C.A.] § 71[a][1]; [c][2]; Treas.Reg. [26 CFR]

§ 1.71–1[d][4]) and, once it has received evidence of the present value of the license and the working spouse's contributions toward its acquisition and considered the remaining factors mandated by the statute (*see*, Domestic Relations Law § 236[B][5][d][1]-[10]), it may then make an appropriate distribution of the marital property including a distributive award for the professional license if such an award is warranted. When other marital assets are of sufficient value to provide for the supporting spouse's equitable portion of the marital property, including his or her contributions to the acquisition of the professional license, however, the court retains the discretion to distribute these other marital assets or to make a distributive award in lieu of an actual distribution of the value of the professional spouse's license. * * *

■ Meyer, Judge (concurring).

I concur in Judge Simons' opinion but write separately to point up for consideration by the Legislature the potential for unfairness involved in distributive awards based upon a license of a professional still in training.

An equity court normally has power to " 'change its decrees where there has been a change of circumstances' " (*People v. Scanlon,* 11 N.Y.2d 459, 462, 230 N.Y.S.2d 708, 184 N.E.2d 302, *on second appeal* 13 N.Y.2d 982, 244 N.Y.S.2d 781, 194 N.E.2d 689). The implication of Domestic Relations Law § 236[B][9][b], which deals with modification of an order or decree as to maintenance or child support, is, however, that a distributive award pursuant to section 236[B][5][e], once made, is not subject to change. Yet a professional in training who is not finally committed to a career choice when the distributive award is made may be locked into a particular kind of practice simply because the monetary obligations imposed by the distributive award made on the basis of the trial judge's conclusion (prophecy may be a better word) as to what the career choice will be leaves him or her no alternative.

The present case points up the problem. A medical license is but a step toward the practice ultimately engaged in by its holder, which follows after internship, residency and, for particular specialties, board certification. Here it is undisputed that plaintiff was in a residency for general surgery at the time of the trial, but had the previous year done a residency in internal medicine. Defendant's expert based his opinion on the difference between the average income of a general surgeon and that of a college graduate of plaintiff's age and life expectancy, which the trial judge utilized, impliedly finding that plaintiff would engage in a surgical practice despite plaintiff's testimony that he was dissatisfied with the general surgery program he was in and was attempting to return to the internal medicine training he had been in the previous year. The trial judge had the right, of course, to discredit that testimony, but the point is that equitable distribution was not intended to permit a judge to make a career decision for a licensed spouse still in training. Yet the degree of speculation involved in the award made is emphasized by the testimony of the expert on which it was based. Asked whether his assumptions and calculations were in any way speculative, he replied: "Yes. They're speculative to the extent of, will Dr. O'Brien practice medicine? Will Dr. O'Brien earn more or less than the average surgeon earns? Will Dr. O'Brien live to age sixty-five? Will Dr. O'Brien have a heart attack or will he be injured in an automobile accident? Will he be disabled? I mean, there is a degree of speculation. That speculative aspect is no more to be taken into account, cannot be taken into account, and it's a question, again, Mr. Emanuelli, not for the expert but for the courts to decide. It's not my function nor could it be."

The equitable distribution provisions of the Domestic Relations Law were intended to provide flexibility so that equity could be done. But if the assumption as to career choice on which a distributive award payable over a number of years is based turns out not to be the fact (as, for example, should a general surgery trainee accidentally lose the use of his hand), it should be possible for the court to revise the distributive award to conform to the fact. And there will be no unfairness in so doing if either spouse can seek reconsideration, for the licensed spouse is more likely to seek reconsideration based on real, rather than imagined, cause if he or she knows that the nonlicensed spouse can seek not only reinstatement of the original award, but counsel fees in addition, should the purported circumstance on which a change is made turn out to have been feigned or to be illusory.

California Family Code

2641(a).   Community contributions to education or training.

"Community contributions to education or training" as used in this section means payments made with community property or quasi-community property for education or training or for the repayment of a loan incurred for education or training, whether the payments were made while the parties were resident in this state or resident outside this state.

(b) Subject to the limitations provided in this section, upon dissolution of marriage or legal separation of the parties:

(1) The community shall be reimbursed for community contributions to education or training of a party that substantially enhances the earning capacity of the party. The amount reimbursed shall be with interest at the legal rate, accruing from the end of the calendar year in which the contributions were made.

(2) A loan incurred during marriage for the education or training of a party shall not be included among the liabilities of the community for the purpose of division pursuant to this division but shall be assigned for payment by the party.

(c) The reimbursement and assignment required by this section shall be reduced or modified to the extent circumstances render such a disposition unjust, including, but not limited to, any of the following:

(1) The community has substantially benefited from the education, training, or loan incurred for the education or training of the party. There is a rebuttable presumption, affecting the burden of proof, that the community has not substantially benefited from community contributions to the education or training made less than 10 years before the commencement of the proceeding, and that the community has substantially benefited from community contributions to the education or training made more than 10 years before the commencement of the proceeding.

(2) The education or training received by the party is offset by the education or training received by the other party for which community contributions have been made.

(3) The education or training enables the party receiving the education or training to engage in gainful employment that substantially reduces the need of the party for support that would otherwise be required.

(d) Reimbursement for community contributions and assignment of loans pursuant to this section is the exclusive remedy of the community or a party for the education or training and any resulting enhancement of the earning capacity of a party. However, nothing in this subdivision limits consideration of the effect of the education, training, or enhancement, or the amount reimbursed pursuant to this section, on the circumstances of the parties for the purpose of an order for support pursuant to Section 4320.

(e) This section is subject to an express written agreement of the parties to the contrary.

4320. **Determination of amount due for support; considerations.**

In ordering spousal support under this part, the court shall consider all of the following circumstances:

(a) The extent to which the earning capacity of each party is sufficient to maintain the standard of living established during the marriage, taking into account all of the following:

(1) The marketable skills of the supported party; the job market for those skills; the time and expenses required for the supported party to acquire the appropriate education or training to develop those skills; and the possible need for retraining or education to acquire other, more marketable skills or employment.

(2) The extent to which the supported party's present or future earning capacity is impaired by periods of unemployment that were incurred during the marriage to permit the supported party to devote time to domestic duties.

(b) The extent to which the supported party contributed to the attainment of an education, training, a career position, or a license by the supporting party.

(c) The ability to pay of the supporting party, taking into account the supporting party's earning capacity, earned and unearned income, assets, and standard of living.

(d) The needs of each party based on the standard of living established during the marriage.

(e) The obligations and assets, including the separate property, of each party.

(f) The duration of the marriage.

(g) The ability of the supported party to engage in gainful employment without interfering with the interests of dependent children in the custody of the party.

(h) The age and health of the parties.

(i) The immediate and specific tax consequences to each party.

(j) The balance of the hardships to each party.

(k) The goal that the supported party shall be self-supporting within a reasonable period of time. A "reasonable period of time" for purposes of this section generally shall be one-half the length of the marriage. However, nothing in this section is intended to limit the court's discretion to order support for a greater or lesser length of time, based on any of the other factors listed in this section and the circumstances of the parties.

(*l*) Any other factors the court determines are just and equitable.

---

1. What are the justifications for each of these three approaches to the division of "career assets" at dissolution? How do the New York and California approaches differ?

2. Which approach to the treatment of professional training do you find most compelling? Is there another approach that would be more appropriate? What do you base your assessment upon?

3. Suppose a spouse decides not to pursue the career path for which he or she acquired training during the marriage. Alternatively, what if the spouse decided upon a career path—*e.g.*, public defender—that did not maximize his or her earning capacity? How would this be treated in New York? California? Should a spouse be held to his or her earning capacity, even if he or she does not live up to it?

4. Only a few states have considered professional training to be marital property. *See, e.g., In re Marriage of McManama*, 272 Ind. 483, 399 N.E.2d 371 (1980). *See generally* Krauskopf, Recompense for Financing Spouse's Education: Legal Protection for the Marital Investor in Human Capital, 28 Kan. L. Rev. 379 (1980). Most states reject the notion of education or professional enhancement as property. *See* Kay, Equality and Difference: A Perspective on No–Fault Divorce and Its Aftermath, 56 U. Cin. L. Rev. 1, 74 n.368 (1987). A report by the California Law Review

Commission, which considered and rejected a proposal to give the working spouse a property interest in the other spouse's increased earnings, probably reflects the attitude of many state legislatures:

> to give the working spouse an interest in half the student spouse's increased earnings for the remainder of the student spouse's life because of the relatively brief period of education and training received during marriage is not only a windfall to the working spouse but in effect a permanent mortgage on the student spouse's future.

Recommendation Relating to Reimbursement of Educational Expenses, 17 Cal. L. Revision Comm. Rep. 233, 234 (1983).

Some of the jurisdictions that reject the property approach nevertheless require the newly educated spouse to reimburse the supporting spouse for all educational expenses. *See, e.g., Mahoney v. Mahoney,* 91 N.J. 488, 453 A.2d 527 (1982); *Hubbard v. Hubbard,* 603 P.2d 747 (Okl.1979). Note that California requires only that the student-spouse reimburse the *community* for educational expenses.

The majority of states reject both the property and reimbursement approaches and require only that the court take into account financial contributions to the other spouse's education as one of many factors in making an equitable division of marital property and an award of spousal support.

5. *Other "Career Assets."* How should career assets other than professional training—such as the goodwill of a business, remarkable success in professional sports, partnership in a law firm or an investment bank, nonvested pension assets—be addressed at dissolution? *See generally* Blumberg, Identifying and Valuing Goodwill at Divorce, 56 L. & Contemp. Prob. 217 (Spring 1993); Blumberg, Marital Property Treatment of Pensions, Disability Pay, Workers' Compensation and Other Wage Substitutes: An Insurance, or Replacement, Analysis, 33 UCLA L. Rev. 1250 (1986).

6. *Intellectual Property as Marital Property.* Should a copyright obtained by the efforts of one spouse during the marriage be considered community property? In other words, should the non-author spouse be entitled not only to ½ of the income derived from the copyright, but also authority to license or transfer the copyright under the federal Copyright Act of 1976, 17 U.S.C. §§ 101–702? The Act generally permits each co-owner to license the copyright independent of the other co-owners. *See In re Marriage of Worth,* 195 Cal.App.3d 768, 241 Cal.Rptr. 135 (1987); Comment, Worthy of Rejection: Copyright as Community Property, 100 Yale L.J. 1053 (1991).

Problem

Sonia and Robert met in 1983 at the Weston School of Business where they were both MBA students. They completed their MBAs in 1985. Sonia, who had accumulated significant debts while in college and graduate school ($60,000), went on the job market. Robert had become more interested in the academic life and decided to enroll in the Ph.D. program in finance. The couple decided to get married following their MBA graduation. Robert borrowed $10,000 from his parents to buy Sonia a beautiful engagement ring. They were married in June 1985. Following graduation, Sonia took a high paying job ($75,000 per year) in Cosmopolitan City and the couple rented a nice house in the suburbs. Robert remained in graduate school. In 1990, Robert inherited $30,000 from his uncle. By that point in time, the couple had saved $40,000 and they decided to pay off Sonia's school debts. Robert's dissertation research went slowly and he did not complete the Ph.D. program until 1992. During this time, he had some scholarship support and a teaching assistant stipend that covered his tuition and other school expenses. Sonia's income paid for most of the couple's living expenses.

Upon graduating from the Ph.D. program, Robert had difficulty finding an academic job. The only academic job available to him was at Boonesville State University. There were some private sector jobs in Cosmopolitan City available to him, but he did not want to leave the academic world. Sonia was on the fast track at her firm and did not want to leave at that time. In addition, there were few decent job opportunities for her in Boonesville. The couple had already been experiencing marital difficulty and the location discord brought these difficulties to a head. Robert moved out of the family residence in October 1992. After a brief effort at marriage counseling, Robert and Sonia decided to go their separate ways. They both sought counsel to figure out how to divide the marital estate. At the time of the separation, they had a joint checking account with $10,000, shares in a mutual fund worth $20,000, a 1987 Honda Accord (bluebook value of $2,500), and assorted furniture, clothing, and household furnishings. Robert had not yet repaid $5,000 of the loan from his parents. In addition, Sonia had contributions to a pension fund (paid by her employer) worth $35,000.

What is their marital property and how would it be divided in Colorado? New York? California?

---

d.   PRE–MARITAL AGREEMENTS

Most of the marital property rules governing management during marriage and distribution after death or dissolution are default rules. That is, the parties may make an agreement before marriage that specifies each spouse's rights to assets when the marriage ends.

Historically, courts have been hostile to pre-marital agreements that change the default rules in the event of dissolution on the ground that they encouraged divorce. Even agreements allocating property in the event of one spouse's death were upheld only if the court found the agreement fair and reasonable to the surviving spouse. In other words, the courts limited couples' ability to contract around the default rules.

In recent decades, however, numerous commentators have argued that couples should be free to make their own arrangements. *See, e.g.,* Shultz, Contractual Ordering of Marriage: A New Model for State Policy, 70 Cal. L. Rev. 204 (1982) (advocating greater use of pre-marital agreements). Courts have begun to uphold such agreements, but more importantly state legislatures have begun to specify the conditions for the creation of valid pre-marital agreements. Many state statutes now explicitly permit pre-marital agreements governing the distribution of assets upon dissolution.

Arizona Revised Statutes[85]

§ 25–201. **Definitions**.

In this article, unless the context otherwise requires:

1. "Premarital agreement" means an agreement between prospective spouses that is made in contemplation of marriage and that is effective on marriage.

2. "Property" means an interest, present or future, legal or equitable, vested or contingent, in real or personal property, including income and earnings.

§ 25–202. **Enforcement of premarital agreements; exception**.

A. A premarital agreement must be in writing and signed by both parties. The agreement is enforceable without consideration.

B. The agreement becomes effective on marriage of the parties.

C. The agreement is not enforceable if the person against whom enforcement is sought proves either of the following:

1. The person did not execute the agreement voluntarily.

2. The agreement was unconscionable when it was executed and before execution of the agreement that person:

(a) Was not provided a fair and reasonable disclosure of the property or financial obligations of the other party.

(b) Did not voluntarily and expressly waive, in writing, any right to disclosure of the property or financial obligations of the other party beyond the disclosure provided.

(c) Did not have, or reasonably could not have had, an adequate knowledge of the property or financial obligations of the other party.

---

85. This statute is taken from the Uniform Premarital Agreement Act (1983), which has been adopted in more than 20 states.

D. If a provision of a premarital agreement modifies or eliminates spousal support and that modification or elimination causes one party to the agreement to be eligible for support under a program of public assistance at the time of separation or marital dissolution, a court, notwithstanding the terms of the agreement, may require the other party to provide support to the extent necessary to avoid that eligibility.

E. An issue of unconscionability of a premarital agreement shall be decided by the court as a matter of law.

F. If a marriage is determined to be void, an agreement that would otherwise have been a premarital agreement is enforceable only to the extent necessary to avoid an inequitable result.

§ 25–203. **Scope of the agreement**

A. Parties to a premarital agreement may contract with respect to:

1. The rights and obligations of each of the parties in any of the property of either or both of them whenever and wherever acquired or located.

2. The right to buy, sell, use, transfer, exchange, abandon, lease, consume, expend, assign or create a security interest in, mortgage, encumber, dispose of or otherwise manage and control property.

3. The disposition of property on separation, marital dissolution, death or the occurrence or nonoccurrence of any other event.

4. The modification or elimination of spousal support.

5. The making of a will, trust or other arrangement to carry out the provisions of the agreement.

6. The ownership rights in and disposition of the death benefit from a life insurance policy.

7. The choice of law governing the construction of the agreement.

8. Any other matter, including their personal rights and obligations, not in violation of public policy or a statute imposing a criminal penalty.

B. The right of a child to support may not be adversely affected by a premarital agreement.

§ 25–204. **Amendment or revocation of agreement**.

After marriage, a premarital agreement may be amended or revoked only by a written agreement signed by the parties. The amendment agreement or the revocation is enforceable without consideration.

§ 25–205. **Limitation of actions**

A statute of limitations applicable to an action asserting a claim for relief under a premarital agreement is tolled during the marriage of the parties to the agreement. However, equitable defenses limiting the time for enforcement, including laches and estoppel, are available to either party.

———————

1. Should courts and legislatures enforce premarital agreements? Should parties be allowed to opt out of the basic marital property rules— such as equitable sharing or community property with regard to income earned during a marriage—through premarital agreements? Should the parties be able to eliminate the statutory right to support? How does the Arizona statute handle this issue?

2. Should courts and legislatures encourage such agreements? If so, how should the law be changed to encourage greater use of premarital agreements?

3. Would it be a good idea to eliminate the default marital property rules and require the soon-to-be-spouses to choose a system of property allocation?

4. What does the Arizona statute provide to reduce the risk of overreaching? How difficult will it be for a plaintiff/spouse to prove the agreement is invalid?

5. Will broader legislative approval of pre-marital agreements increase the number of pre-marital agreements executed?

———————

Problem

When they met in 1973, Linda was a respiratory technician with a high school education and Richard was an emergency room physician. After he completed an ophthalmology residency and set up a private practice in 1977, they became engaged to be married.

During their engagement, they discussed the possibility of executing a premarital agreement, although they did not discuss any specific terms. Richard told Linda he would not marry her unless she signed a premarital agreement.

Richard's attorney prepared a draft agreement, which Linda reviewed briefly. She did not request, nor was she given, a copy of the agreement so she could review it more carefully. A few days later, at Richard's attorney's office, the attorney suggested that Linda could seek the advice of counsel, but she chose not to do so. She signed the agreement. Linda later testified (without contradiction) that she had believed the agreement applied only to Richard's assets accumulated before the marriage, which were negligible.

The agreement provided that each party's separate property would remain that person's separate property, that all of the money each person earned during the marriage would be that person's separate property, even if normally classified as community property, and that neither party would make a claim for spousal support. The agreement also provided that if the parties divorced after 10 years of marriage, Richard would convey to Linda all rights to any vehicles she principally used and one-third the net equity in their residence.

In 1989, when Linda filed for dissolution, Richard had accumulated assets of $2,000,000 and was drawing a salary of $400,000. Linda, who stopped working to raise her children by a previous marriage, had acquired virtually no assets. At the time of their divorce, there were no minor children. Pending the divorce, Linda found a job as a lab technician.

Linda challenges the validity of the premarital agreement. She does not claim (and there is no evidence) that the agreement was entered fraudulently or under coercion. You are Linda's attorney. Construct an argument that the agreement is invalid under Arizona law.

---

e. UNMARRIED COHABITANTS

Virtually all of the rules described in this chapter assume that the parties have a valid marriage. In most states, marriage is ceremonial (*i.e.*, licensed, witnessed, and registered), although a few states recognize "common law" marriages (*i.e.*, a non-ceremonial marriage in which the parties co-habitate and hold themselves out as married). At present, no jurisdiction recognizes common law or ceremonial marriages between gay men or lesbians.[86]

Absent a valid marriage, in general neither member of a couple can take advantage of the marital property rules governing the control and

---

86. There has been litigation challenging the legality of the prohibition on same-sex marriages. The most prominent case is *Baehr v. Lewin*, 74 Haw. 530, 852 P.2d 44 (1993), in which several individuals sued the state, claiming that the state prohibition on same-sex marriages violated state constitutional rights to due process, equal protection, and privacy. A plurality of the Hawaii Supreme Court rejected the privacy and due process claims, *Id.* at 550–57, 852 P.2d at 54–58, but the court remanded the case for an evidentiary hearing on the equal protection claim. *Id.* at 557–80, 852 P.2d at 58–67. In particular, the court held that a state prohibition on same-sex marriages would be unconstitutional unless the state could show a compelling state interest for the prohibition and that the prohibition is narrowly drawn to avoid unnecessary abridgments of individual rights. *Id.* at 580, 852 P.2d at 67. In late 1996, the trial court held that the state's refusal to recognize same-sex marriages violated equal protection. *Baehr v. Mike,* 1996 WL 694235 (Haw.Cir.Ct.1996). The case is pending appeal before the state supreme court.

In 1994, the state legislature took up the issue, and reaffirmed that "Hawaii's marriage licensing laws were originally and are presently intended to apply only to male-female couples, not same-sex couples." 1994 Haw. Sess. Laws, Act 217, § 1. *See also* Haw. Rev. Stat. § 572–1 (1994 amendment in opening sentence limits marriages to same-sex couples). This legislative assertion, of course, does not moot the more fundamental state constitutional claim. In an effort to derail the litigation, the legislature enacted a bill to ensure that registered same-sex couples could receive certain benefits, such as medical insurance and survivorship rights, and another bill placing a state constitutional amendment on the November 1998 ballot that would allow the legislature to permit only heterosexual marriages. L.A. Times, at 3

disposition of property (or of any other tax, pension, social security benefits accorded married people). The precondition of marriage poses a serious limitation for the large number of unmarried couples living together. Such couples, no differently than married couples, acquire property during the relationship and need to divide that property when the relationship ends, either by dissolution or death. Unmarried couples, like married couples, usually neglect before co-habitating to make express agreements to divide property, and frequently neglect to write wills. Moreover, the legislatures' reasons for adopting "equitable distribution" rules, or rules defining income as "community property" to be divided equally—to recognize the value of a spouse's noneconomic contributions to the marriage—seem equally applicable to unmarried couples.

Some states have a property rights doctrine for "putative spouses"—persons who wrongly, but in good faith, believed that their marriage was valid. States that recognize putative spouses frequently extend the protections of marital property to innocent parties. *See, e.g.*, 750 Ill. Comp. Stat. Ann. 5/305 (a person "having gone through a marriage ceremony, who has cohabitated with another to whom he is not legally married in the good faith belief that he was married to that person is a putative spouse [and] acquires the rights conferred upon a legal spouse"); West's Ann. Cal. Fam. Code § 2251 ("if the division of property is in issue," the court shall divide property acquired "during the union" as if it were community or quasi-community property); *In re Estate of Sax,* 214 Cal.App.3d 1300, 263 Cal.Rptr. 190 (1989) (permitting surviving putative spouse to take surviving spouse's statutory share of the community property despite the existence of a valid will leaving the decedent's entire estate to his former wife). The rules for putative spouses, however, apply to relatively few unmarried couples.

Where the law of putative spouses does not apply, courts frequently have applied theories of contract or restitution to divide the property when the parties split up.

Marvin v. Marvin[87]

Supreme Court of California, 1976.
18 Cal.3d 660, 134 Cal.Rptr. 815, 557 P.2d 106.

■ TOBRINER, JUSTICE.

During the past 15 years, there has been a substantial increase in the number of couples living together without marrying. Such nonmarital relationships lead to legal controversy when one partner dies or the couple separates. Courts of Appeal, faced with the task of determining property rights in such cases, have arrived at conflicting positions: two cases (*In re Marriage of Cary* (1973) 34 Cal.App.3d 345, 109 Cal.Rptr. 862; *Estate of*

(Apr. 30, 1997). *See generally* W. Eskridge, The Case for Same–Sex Marriage (1996).

87. The plaintiff, Michelle Triola, had her name legally changed to Michelle Marvin a few days before her separation from the defendant, Lee Marvin.

Atherley (1975) 44 Cal.App.3d 758, 119 Cal.Rptr. 41) have held that the Family Law Act (Civ.Code, § 4000 *et seq.*) requires division of the property according to community property principles, and one decision (*Beckman v. Mayhew* (1974) 49 Cal.App.3d 529, 122 Cal.Rptr. 604) has rejected that holding. We take this opportunity to resolve that controversy and to declare the principles which should govern distribution of property acquired in a nonmarital relationship.

We conclude: (1) The provisions of the Family Law Act do not govern the distribution of property acquired during a nonmarital relationship; such a relationship remains subject solely to judicial decision. (2) The courts should enforce express contracts between nonmarital partners except to the extent that the contract is explicitly founded on the consideration of meretricious sexual services. (3) In the absence of an express contract, the courts should inquire into the conduct of the parties to determine whether that conduct demonstrates an implied contract, agreement of partnership or joint venture, or some other tacit understanding between the parties. The courts may also employ the doctrine of quantum meruit, or equitable remedies such as constructive or resulting trusts, when warranted by the facts of the case.

In the instant case plaintiff and defendant lived together for seven years without marrying; all property acquired during this period was taken in defendant's name. When plaintiff sued to enforce a contract under which she was entitled to half the property and to support payments, the trial court granted judgment on the pleadings for defendant, thus leaving him with all property accumulated by the couple during their relationship. Since the trial court denied plaintiff a trial on the merits of her claim, its decision conflicts with the principles stated above, and must be reversed.

1. *The factual setting of this appeal.*

Since the trial court rendered judgment for defendant on the pleadings, we must accept the allegations of plaintiff's complaint as true, determining whether such allegations state, or can be amended to state, a cause of action. We turn therefore to the specific allegations of the complaint.

Plaintiff avers that in October of 1964 she and defendant "entered into an oral agreement" that while "the parties lived together they would combine their efforts and earnings and would share equally any and all property accumulated as a result of their efforts whether individual or combined." Furthermore, they agreed to "hold themselves out to the general public as husband and wife" and that "plaintiff would further render her services as a companion, homemaker, housekeeper and cook to . . . defendant."

Shortly thereafter plaintiff agreed to "give up her lucrative career as an entertainer [and] singer" in order to "devote her full time to defendant . . . as a companion, homemaker, housekeeper and cook;" in return defendant agreed to "provide for all of plaintiff's financial support and needs for the rest of her life."

Plaintiff alleges that she lived with defendant from October of 1964 through May of 1970 and fulfilled her obligations under the agreement. During this period the parties as a result of their efforts and earnings acquired in defendant's name substantial real and personal property, including motion picture rights worth over $1 million. In May of 1970, however, defendant compelled plaintiff to leave his household. He continued to support plaintiff until November of 1971, but thereafter refused to provide further support.

On the basis of these allegations plaintiff asserts two causes of action. The first, for declaratory relief, asks the court to determine her contract and property rights; the second seeks to impose a constructive trust upon one half of the property acquired during the course of the relationship.

Defendant demurred unsuccessfully, and then answered the complaint. Following extensive discovery and pretrial proceedings, the case came to trial. Defendant renewed his attack on the complaint by a motion to dismiss. * * *

After hearing argument the court granted defendant's motion and entered judgment for defendant. * * *

2. *Plaintiff's complaint states a cause of action for breach of an express contract.*

In *Trutalli v. Meraviglia* (1932) 215 Cal. 698, 12 P.2d 430 we established the principle that nonmarital partners may lawfully contract concerning the ownership of property acquired during the relationship. We reaffirmed this principle in *Vallera v. Vallera* (1943) 21 Cal.2d 681, 685, 134 P.2d 761, 763, stating that "If a man and woman [who are not married] live together as husband and wife under an agreement to pool their earnings and share equally in their joint accumulations, equity will protect the interests of each in such property."

In the case before us plaintiff, basing her cause of action in contract upon these precedents, maintains that the trial court erred in denying her a trial on the merits of her contention. Although that court did not specify the ground for its conclusion that plaintiff's contractual allegations stated no cause of action, defendant offers some four theories to sustain the ruling; we proceed to examine them.

Defendant first and principally relies on the contention that the alleged contract is so closely related to the supposed "immoral" character of the relationship between plaintiff and himself that the enforcement of the contract would violate public policy. He points to cases asserting that a contract between nonmarital partners is unenforceable if it is "involved in" an illicit relationship or made in "contemplation" of such a relationship. A review of the numerous California decisions concerning contracts between nonmarital partners, however, reveals that the courts have not employed such broad and uncertain standards to strike down contracts. The decisions instead disclose a narrower and more precise standard: a contract between nonmarital partners is unenforceable only *to the extent* that it *explicitly* rests upon the immoral and illicit consideration of meretricious sexual services. * * *

Although the past decisions hover over the issue in the somewhat wispy form of the figures of a Chagall painting, we can abstract from those decisions a clear and simple rule. The fact that a man and woman live together without marriage, and engage in a sexual relationship, does not in itself invalidate agreements between them relating to their earnings, property, or expenses. Neither is such an agreement invalid merely because the parties may have contemplated the creation or continuation of a nonmarital relationship when they entered into it. Agreements between nonmarital partners fail only to the extent that they rest upon a consideration of meretricious sexual services. * * *

In summary, we base our opinion on the principle that adults who voluntarily live together and engage in sexual relations are nonetheless as competent as any other persons to contract respecting their earnings and property rights. Of course, they cannot lawfully contract to pay for the performance of sexual services, for such a contract is, in essence, an agreement for prostitution and unlawful for that reason. But they may agree to pool their earnings and to hold all property acquired during the relationship in accord with the law governing community property; conversely they may agree that each partner's earnings and the property acquired from those earnings remains the separate property of the earning partner.[88] So long as the agreement does not rest upon illicit meretricious consideration, the parties may order their economic affairs as they choose, and no policy precludes the courts from enforcing such agreements.

In the present instance, plaintiff alleges that the parties agreed to pool their earnings, that they contracted to share equally in all property acquired, and that defendant agreed to support plaintiff. The terms of the contract as alleged do not rest upon any unlawful consideration. We therefore conclude that the complaint furnishes a suitable basis upon which the trial court can render declaratory relief. The trial court consequently erred in granting defendant's motion for judgment on the pleadings.

3. *Plaintiff's complaint can be amended to state a cause of action founded upon theories of implied contract or equitable relief.*

As we have noted, both causes of action in plaintiff's complaint allege an express contract; neither assert any basis for relief independent from the contract. In *In re Marriage of Cary, supra,* 34 Cal.App.3d 345, 109 Cal.Rptr. 862, however, the Court of Appeal held that, in view of the policy of the Family Law Act, property accumulated by nonmarital partners in an actual family relationship should be divided equally. Upon examining the

---

88. A great variety of other arrangements are possible. The parties might keep their earnings and property separate, but agree to compensate one party for services which benefit the other. They may choose to pool only part of their earnings and property, to form a partnership or joint venture, or to hold property acquired as joint tenants or tenants in common, or agree to any other such arrangement. (*See generally* Weitzman, Legal Regulation of Marriage: Tradition and Change (1974) 62 Cal.L.Rev. 1169.)

Cary opinion, the parties to the present case realized that plaintiff's alleged relationship with defendant might arguably support a cause of action independent of any express contract between the parties. The parties have therefore briefed and discussed the issue of the property rights of a nonmarital partner in the absence of an express contract. Although our conclusion that plaintiff's complaint states a cause of action based on an express contract alone compels us to reverse the judgment for defendant, resolution of the *Cary* issue will serve both to guide the parties upon retrial and to resolve a conflict presently manifest in published Court of Appeal decisions.

Both plaintiff and defendant stand in broad agreement that the law should be fashioned to carry out the reasonable expectations of the parties. Plaintiff, however, presents the following contentions: that the decisions prior to *Cary* rest upon implicit and erroneous notions of punishing a party for his or her guilt in entering into a nonmarital relationship, that such decisions result in an inequitable distribution of property accumulated during the relationship, and that *Cary* correctly held that the enactment of the Family Law Act in 1970 overturned those prior decisions. Defendant in response maintains that the prior decisions merely applied common law principles of contract and property to persons who have deliberately elected to remain outside the bounds of the community property system. *Cary*, defendant contends, erred in holding that the Family Law Act vitiated the force of the prior precedents.

As we shall see from examination of the pre-*Cary* decisions, the truth lies somewhere between the positions of plaintiff and defendant. The classic opinion on this subject is *Vallera v. Vallera, supra,* 21 Cal.2d 681, 134 P.2d 761. Speaking for a four-member majority, Justice Traynor posed the question: "whether a woman living with a man as his wife but with no genuine belief that she is legally married to him acquires by reason of cohabitation alone the rights of a co-tenant in his earnings and accumulations during the period of their relationship." (21 Cal.2d at p. 684, 134 P.2d at p. 762.) Citing *Flanagan v. Capital Nat. Bank* (1931) 213 Cal. 664, 3 P.2d 307, which held that a nonmarital "wife" could not claim that her husband's estate was community property, the majority answered that question "in the negative." (21 Cal.2d pp. 684–685, 134 P.2d 761.) *Vallera* explains that "Equitable considerations arising from the reasonable expectation of the continuation of benefits attending the status of marriage entered into in good faith are not present in such a case." (P. 685, 134 P.2d p. 763.) In the absence of express contract, *Vallera* concluded, the woman is entitled to share in property jointly accumulated only "in the proportion that her funds contributed toward its acquisition." (P. 685, 134 P.2d p. 763.) Justice Curtis, dissenting, argued that the evidence showed an implied contract under which each party owned an equal interest in property acquired during the relationship.

The majority opinion in *Vallera* did not expressly bar recovery based upon an implied contract, nor preclude resort to equitable remedies. But *Vallera*'s broad assertion that equitable considerations "are not present" in the case of a nonmarital relationship (21 Cal.2d at p. 685, 134 P.2d 761) led the Courts of Appeal to interpret the language to preclude recovery based on such theories. (*See Lazzarevich v. Lazzarevich* (1948) 88 Cal.App.2d 708, 719, 200 P.2d 49; *Oakley v. Oakley* (1947) 82 Cal.App.2d 188, 191–192, 185 P.2d 848.) * * *

This failure of the courts to recognize an action by a nonmarital partner based upon implied contract, or to grant an equitable remedy, contrasts with the judicial treatment of the putative spouse. Prior to the enactment of the Family Law Act, no statute granted rights to a putative spouse. The courts accordingly fashioned a variety of remedies by judicial decision. Some cases permitted the putative spouse to recover half the property on a theory that the conduct of the parties implied an agreement of partnership of joint venture. Others permitted the spouse to recover the reasonable value of rendered services, less the value of support received. Finally, decisions affirmed the power of a court to employ equitable principles to achieve a fair division of property acquired during putative marriage.[89]

Thus in summary, the cases prior to *Cary* exhibited a schizophrenic inconsistency. By enforcing an express contract between nonmarital partners unless it rested upon an unlawful consideration, the courts applied a common law principle as to contracts. Yet the courts disregarded the common law principle that holds that implied contracts can arise from the conduct of the parties. Refusing to enforce such contracts, the courts spoke of leaving the parties "in the position in which they had placed themselves" (*Oakley v. Oakley, supra,* 82 Cal.App.2d 188, 192, 185 P.2d 848, 850), just as if they were guilty parties "in pari delicto." * * *

Still another inconsistency in the prior cases arises from their treatment of property accumulated through joint effort. To the extent that a partner had contributed *funds* or *property,* the cases held that the partner obtains a proportionate share in the acquisition, despite the lack of legal standing of the relationship. (*Vallera v. Vallera, supra,* 21 Cal.2d at p. 685, 134 P.2d at 761; *see Weak v. Weak, supra,* 202 Cal.App.2d 632, 639, 21 Cal.Rptr. 9.) Yet courts have refused to recognize just such an interest based upon the contribution of *services.* As Justice Curtis points out "Unless it can be argued that a woman's services as cook, housekeeper, and homemaker are valueless, it would seem logical that if, when she contributes money to the purchase of property, her interest will be protected, then when she contributes her services in the home, her interest in property accumulated should be protected." (*Vallera v. Vallera, supra,* 21 Cal.2d 681, 686–687, 134 P.2d 761, 764 (diss. opn.); *see* Bruch, op. cit. *supra,* 10 Family

---

89. The contrast between principles governing nonmarital and putative relationships appears most strikingly in *Lazzarevich v. Lazzarevich, supra,* 88 Cal.App.2d 708, 200 P.2d 49. When Mrs. Lazzarevich sued her husband for divorce in 1945, she discovered to her surprise that she was not lawfully married to him. She nevertheless reconciled with him, and the Lazzareviches lived together for another year before they finally separated. The court awarded her recovery for the reasonable value of services rendered, less the value of support received, until she discovered the invalidity of the marriage, but denied recovery for the same services rendered after that date.

L.Q. 101, 110–114; Article, *Illicit Cohabitation: The Impact of the Vallera and Keene Cases on the Rights of the Meretricious Spouse* (1973) 6 U.C. Davis L.Rev. 354, 369–370; Comment (1972) 48 Wash.L.Rev. 635, 641.)

Thus as of 1973, the time of the filing of *In re Marriage of Cary, supra,* 34 Cal.App.3d 345, 109 Cal.Rptr. 862, the cases apparently held that a nonmarital partner who rendered services in the absence of express contract could assert no right to property acquired during the relationship. The facts of *Cary* demonstrated the unfairness of that rule.

Janet and Paul Cary had lived together, unmarried, for more than eight years. They held themselves out to friends and family as husband and wife, reared four children, purchased a home and other property, obtained credit, filed joint income tax returns, and otherwise conducted themselves as though they were married. Paul worked outside the home, and Janet generally cared for the house and children.

In 1971 Paul petitioned for "nullity of the marriage." Following a hearing on that petition, the trial court awarded Janet half the property acquired during the relationship, although all such property was traceable to Paul's earnings. The Court of Appeal affirmed the award.

Reviewing the prior decisions which had denied relief to the homemaking partner, the Court of Appeal reasoned that those decisions rested upon a policy of punishing persons guilty of cohabitation without marriage. The Family Law Act, the court observed, aimed to eliminate fault or guilt as a basis for dividing marital property. But once fault or guilt is excluded, the court reasoned, nothing distinguishes the property rights of a nonmarital "spouse" from those of a putative spouse. Since the latter is entitled to half the "quasi marital property" (Civ.Code, § 4452), the Court of Appeal concluded that, giving effect to the policy of the Family Law Act, a nonmarital cohabitator should also be entitled to half the property accumulated during an "actual family relationship." (34 Cal.App.3d at p. 353, 109 Cal.Rptr. 862.)

Cary met with a mixed reception in other appellate districts. In *Estate of Atherley, supra,* 44 Cal.App.3d 758, 119 Cal.Rptr. 41, the Fourth District agreed with *Cary* that under the Family Law Act a nonmarital partner in an actual family relationship enjoys the same right to an equal division of property as a putative spouse. In *Beckman v. Mayhew, supra,* 49 Cal.App.3d 529, 122 Cal.Rptr. 604, however, the Third District rejected *Cary* on the ground that the Family Law Act was not intended to change California law dealing with nonmarital relationships.

If *Cary* is interpreted as holding that the Family Law Act requires an equal division of property accumulated in nonmarital "actual family relationships," then we agree with *Beckman v. Mayhew* that *Cary* distends the act. No language in the Family Law Act addresses the property rights of nonmarital partners, and nothing in the legislative history of the act suggests that the Legislature considered that subject. The delineation of the rights of nonmarital partners before 1970 had been fixed entirely by judicial decision; we see no reason to believe that the Legislature, by enacting the Family Law Act, intended to change that state of affairs.

But although we reject the reasoning of *Cary* and *Atherley*, we share the perception of the *Cary* and *Atherley* courts that the application of former precedent in the factual setting of those cases would work an unfair distribution of the property accumulated by the couple. Justice Friedman in *Beckman v. Mayhew, supra,* 49 Cal.App.3d 529, 535, 122 Cal.Rptr. 604, also questioned the continued viability of our decisions in *Vallera* and *Keene*; commentators have argued the need to reconsider those precedents. We should not, therefore, reject the authority of *Cary* and *Atherley* without also examining the deficiencies in the former law which led to those decisions.

The principal reason why the pre-*Cary* decisions result in an unfair distribution of property inheres in the court's refusal to permit a nonmarital partner to assert rights based upon accepted principles of implied contract or equity. We have examined the reasons advanced to justify this denial of relief, and find that none have merit.

First, we note that the cases denying relief do not rest their refusal upon any theory of "punishing" a "guilty" partner. Indeed, to the extent that denial of relief "punishes" one partner, it necessarily rewards the other by permitting him to retain a disproportionate amount of the property. Concepts of "guilt" thus cannot justify an unequal division of property between two equally "guilty" persons.

Other reasons advanced in the decisions fare no better. The principal argument seems to be that "[e]quitable considerations arising from the reasonable expectation of . . . benefits attending the status of marriage . . . are not present [in a nonmarital relationship]." (*Vallera v. Vallera, supra,* 21 Cal.2d at p. 685, 134 P.2d 761, 763.) But, although parties to a nonmarital relationship obviously cannot have based any expectations upon the belief that they were married, other expectations and equitable considerations remain. The parties may well expect that property will be divided in accord with the parties' own tacit understanding and that in the absence of such understanding the courts will fairly apportion property accumulated through mutual effort. We need not treat nonmarital partners as putatively married persons in order to apply principles of implied contract, or extend equitable remedies; we need to treat them only as we do any other unmarried persons.[90]

The remaining arguments advanced from time to time to deny remedies to the nonmarital partners are of less moment. There is no more reason to presume that services are contributed as a gift than to presume that funds are contributed as a gift; in any event the better approach is to presume, as Justice Peters suggested, "that the parties intend to deal fairly with each other." (*Keene v. Keene, supra,* 57 Cal.2d 657, 674, 21 Cal.Rptr.

90. In some instances a confidential relationship may arise between nonmarital partners, and economic transactions between them should be governed by the principles applicable to such relationships.

593, 603, 371 P.2d 329, 339 (dissenting opn.); *see* Bruch, op. cit., *supra,* 10 Family L.Q. 101, 113.)

The argument that granting remedies to the nonmarital partners would discourage marriage must fail; as *Cary* pointed out, "with equal or greater force the point might be made that the pre–1970 rule was calculated to cause the income producing partner to avoid marriage and thus retain the benefit of all of his or her accumulated earnings." (34 Cal.App.3d at p. 353, 109 Cal.Rptr. at p. 866.) Although we recognize the well-established public policy to foster and promote the institution of marriage (*see Deyoe v. Superior Court* (1903) 140 Cal. 476, 482, 74 P. 28), perpetuation of judicial rules which result in an inequitable distribution of property accumulated during a nonmarital relationship is neither a just nor an effective way of carrying out that policy.

In summary, we believe that the prevalence of nonmarital relationships in modern society and the social acceptance of them, marks this as a time when our courts should by no means apply the doctrine of the unlawfulness of the so-called meretricious relationship to the instant case. As we have explained, the nonenforceability of agreements expressly providing for meretricious conduct rested upon the fact that such conduct, as the word suggests, pertained to and encompassed prostitution. To equate the nonmarital relationship of today to such a subject matter is to do violence to an accepted and wholly different practice. * * *

The mores of the society have indeed changed so radically in regard to cohabitation that we cannot impose a standard based on alleged moral considerations that have apparently been so widely abandoned by so many. Lest we be misunderstood, however, we take this occasion to point out that the structure of society itself largely depends upon the institution of marriage, and nothing we have said in this opinion should be taken to derogate from that institution. The joining of the man and woman in marriage is at once the most socially productive and individually fulfilling relationship that one can enjoy in the course of a lifetime.

We conclude that the judicial barriers that may stand in the way of a policy based upon the fulfillment of the reasonable expectations of the parties to a nonmarital relationship should be removed. As we have explained, the courts now hold that express agreements will be enforced unless they rest on an unlawful meretricious consideration. We add that in the absence of an express agreement, the courts may look to a variety of other remedies in order to protect the parties' lawful expectations.

The courts may inquire into the conduct of the parties to determine whether that conduct demonstrates an implied contract or implied agreement of partnership or joint venture (*see Estate of Thornton* (1972) 81 Wash.2d 72, 499 P.2d 864), or some other tacit understanding between the parties. The courts may, when appropriate, employ principles of constructive trust (*see Omer v. Omer* (1974) 11 Wash.App. 386, 523 P.2d 957) or resulting trust (*see Hyman v. Hyman* (Tex.Civ.App.1954) 275 S.W.2d 149). Finally, a nonmarital partner may recover in *quantum meruit* for the reasonable value of household services rendered less the reasonable value of support received if he can show that he rendered services with the expectation of monetary reward. (*See Hill v. Estate of Westbrook, supra,* 39 Cal.2d 458, 462, 247 P.2d 19.)[91]

Since we have determined that plaintiff's complaint states a cause of action for breach of an express contract, and, as we have explained, can be amended to state a cause of action independent of allegations of express contract,[92] we must conclude that the trial court erred in granting defendant a judgment on the pleadings.

The judgment is reversed and the cause remanded for further proceedings consistent with the views expressed herein.

————————

On remand, the trial court found that the parties had no express or implied agreement to divide the property, and that Triola had not been damaged, but instead had benefited economically from the relationship. Thus, the court denied the claim for a division of the property, but nonetheless awarded Triola, who was unemployed, $104,000 for "economic rehabilitation." The court of appeal reversed the award, holding that on the facts of this case there was no basis in equity for such an award. *Marvin v. Marvin,* 122 Cal.App.3d 871, 176 Cal. Rptr. 555 (1981).

————————

A few other states have followed *Marvin*'s lead. *See, e.g., Watts v. Watts,* 137 Wis.2d 506, 521–34, 405 N.W.2d 303, 309–14 (1987) (permitting recovery on theories of contract and unjust enrichment); *Morone v. Morone,* 50 N.Y.2d 481, 429 N.Y.S.2d 592, 413 N.E.2d 1154 (1980) (holding that an express contract, but not an implied contract, to share earnings is enforceable); *Glasgo v. Glasgo,* 410 N.E.2d 1325 (Ind.App.1980) (holding that a court may divide property based on contract and principles of equity); *Carroll v. Lee,* 148 Ariz. 10, 712 P.2d 923 (1986) (upholding division of the property under principles of implied contract); *In re Marriage of Lindsey,* 101 Wash.2d 299, 304, 678 P.2d 328, 331 (1984) (requiring the court to "make a just and equitable disposition of the property"); *Kozlowski v. Kozlowski,* 80 N.J. 378, 387, 403 A.2d 902, 907 (1979). *But see Hewitt v. Hewitt,* 77 Ill.2d 49, 31 Ill.Dec. 827, 394 N.E.2d 1204 (1979) (rejecting

91. Our opinion does not preclude the evolution of additional equitable remedies to protect the expectations of the parties to a nonmarital relationship in cases in which existing remedies prove inadequate; the suitability of such remedies may be determined in later cases in light of the factual setting in which they arise.

92. We do not pass upon the question whether, in the absence of an express or implied contractual obligation, a party to a nonmarital relationship is entitled to support payments from the other party after the relationship terminates.

Marvin v. Marvin on the ground that it revived common law marriages). These courts have rejected arguments that any contract would be unenforceable because the couples were engaged in illegal or immoral relationships. So long as sexual services were not a consideration in the contract, the contracts are enforceable.

Although a valid marriage remains a prerequisite for many important kinds of rights, *see, e.g., Hinman v. Dep't of Personnel Admin.,* 167 Cal.App.3d 516, 213 Cal. Rptr. 410 (1985) (upholding marriage requirement for eligibility in state family dental plan), *Marvin* and other cases have helped to address the needs of unmarried couples to divide property at the end of the relationship. For example, in *Whorton v. Dillingham,* 202 Cal.App.3d 447, 248 Cal. Rptr. 405 (1988), the court did not pause in applying the *Marvin* principles to a case involving two gay men. *See also Crooke v. Gilden,* 262 Ga. 122, 414 S.E.2d 645 (1992) (enforcing express contract between lesbian couple). *See generally* Kay & Amyx, *Marvin v. Marvin*: Preserving the Options, 65 Cal. L. Rev. 937 (1977); Comment, Property Rights Upon Termination of Unmarried Cohabitation: *Marvin v. Marvin,* 90 Harv. L. Rev. 1708 (1977); Prince, Public Policy Limitations in Cohabitation Agreements: Unruly Horse or Circus Pony?, 70 Minn. L. Rev. 163 (1985).

Problem

Terry and Leslie began living together shortly after they met. Terry, who was unemployed before the relationship began, did not have regular employment during their relationship, but rather undertook all the household duties, such as cooking, cleaning, and shopping. Leslie worked as a manager in a manufacturing company. Five years later, the couple separated.

During the relationship, the parties kept a joint checking account. The couple purchased a house in Leslie's name for $100,000 (the mortgage was also in Leslie's name). Leslie provided the entire downpayment of $20,000. The house, however, required significant work, including electrical work, plumbing, drywall, and painting. Terry alone did this work, although Leslie paid for all the supplies (about $10,000). The repairs increased the value of the house by $50,000. In addition, the joint bank account had $10,000, all of which was accumulated since the relationship began. The couple had no express agreement regarding division of property in the event they would split up.

When the relationship ended, Leslie forced Terry out of the house, took all the money in the joint account, and changed the locks. Terry has hired you to file a claim for some of the assets that Leslie now controls. What claims can Terry assert? How good are those claims?

C.   RIGHTS AND LIMITATIONS OF PROPERTY OWNERS

1.   THE MODEL OF ABSOLUTE RIGHTS

Blackstone's Commentaries

Book 2 *2; Book 1 *134–35; Book 3 *209.[1]

Origin of Property. There is nothing which so generally strikes the imagination, and engages the affections of mankind, as the right of property or that sole and despotic dominion which one man claims and exercises over the external things of the world, in total exclusion of the right of any other individual in the universe. * * *

The third absolute right, inherent in every Englishman, is that of property: which consists in the free use, enjoyment, and disposal of all acquisitions, without any control or diminution, save only by the laws of the land. The origin of private property is probably founded in nature. * * *

So great moreover is the regard of the law for private property, that it will not authorize the least violation of it; no, not even for the general good of the whole community.

* * * [T]he right of *meum* and *tuum* (mine and thine) or property, in lands once being established, it follows, as a necessary consequence, that this right must be exclusive; that is, that the owner may retain to himself the sole use and occupation of his soil: every entry, therefore, thereon without the owner's leave, and especially if contrary to his express order, is a trespass or transgression.[2]

Morris Cohen, Property and Sovereignty

41 (1933).

The classical view of property as a right over things resolves it into component rights such as the *jus utendi, jus disponendi,* etc. But the essence of private property is always the right to exclude others. If * * * somebody else wants to use the food, the house, the land, or the plough that the law calls mine, he has to get my consent.

1. Sir William Blackstone's Commentaries on the Laws of England, published between 1765 and 1769, were recognized as the first widely accepted legal treatise on English law. They were influential in both England and the United States.

2. For an argument that Blackstone did not hold as absolute a view of property rights as these excerpts suggest, see Burns, Blackstone's Theory of the "Absolute" Rights of Property, 54 U.Cin. L. Rev. 67 (1985).

2. THE COASE THEOREM AND THE ECONOMICS OF PROPERTY RIGHTS

Externalities prevent the market from achieving an efficient allocation of resources. From the economist's perspective, legal rules and institutions should be structured to account for the impact of externalities.

In a seminal article, The Problem of Social Cost, 3 J. of Law & Econ. 1 (1960), Professor Ronald Coase argued that the efficiency problems associated with externalities would solve themselves if people could bargain costlessly. Coase showed that regardless of whether polluters (or other externality creators) initially have the right to pollute or victims have the right to be free from pollution, an efficient allocation of resources will obtain if transaction costs—the costs of negotiating, broadly defined—are zero. The allocation of rights affects only the final distribution of resources, not the efficiency of resource allocation. This proposition has come to be known as the Coase Theorem.

Zero Transaction Costs Model. To demonstrate the Coase Theorem, consider the dispute between Custom Bicycle Works (CBW) and its neighbors. Ten homes are directly across the street and downwind from CBW's factory. Over the past 20 years, CBW has developed an international reputation for building the highest quality bicycle wheels. Professional bicycle racers from the world over have purchased their wheels and related components from CBW. In the past year, CBW has patented a new technique for fusing bicycle and wheel components. The technique creates a pungent, although non-toxic, odor. The ten neighbors in the block adjacent to the factory have complained that this odor forces them to keep their windows shut, which makes their houses particularly unpleasant during the hot summer months.

It would cost CBW $100,000 to install a fume control system that would eliminate the odor problem. It would cost $250,000 for CBW to relocate its factory to another location. CBW earns in excess of $500,000 in annual profits. It would cost the neighbors $15,000 each to install air conditioning systems. (This includes the capitalized cost of operating and maintaining the systems.) Such systems balance out the adverse odors by enabling the neighbors to keep their windows shut and to control their indoor temperatures. The residents are indifferent between having air conditioning and being able to keep their windows open (without the disagreeable odor).

The efficient allocation of resources in this example is for CBW to install the fume abatement technology. The total cost to CBW is $100,000. By contrast, the cost of installing individual air conditioners is $150,000 (and relocating CBW or shutting it down would be far more costly).

Coase asked whether the parties—the bicycle factory or the residential neighbors—would efficiently allocate resources regardless of who has the effective entitlement[3] to the air. Let's first assume that the bicycle factory effectively has the right to pollute, *i.e.*, its air emissions violate neither the common law of nuisance, environmental regulatory controls established by statute, nor zoning restrictions. What allocation of resources would obtain? Since CBW is free to pollute, the onus is on the residents to deal with the pollution. They have four options: (1) do nothing and endure the odor (or the sweltering summer heat); (2) install air conditioners, costing them $15,000 each ($150,000 total); (3) offer CBW the cost of installing a fume abatement system ($100,000); and (4) offer CBW the cost of relocation ($250,000). Clearly the least costly option for the residents is to negotiate with CBW to install fume abatement technology. Under the assumption that transaction costs (including the costs of bargaining) are zero, the parties will reach a satisfactory agreement to install the fume abatement technology at the source of the pollution. The cost to the residents will be no more than $150,000 (which is what they would have had to pay to solve the problem unilaterally). Thus, an efficient allocation of resources obtains if the entitlement is initially allocated to the factory.

What allocation of resources will obtain if the residents are allotted the legal entitlement to be free from the type of odor being emitted by CBW? If CBW does nothing, the residences will be legally entitled to shut down the operation. Hence, the onus will be on CBW to come up with a solution to the problem. It has three options: (1) install the fume abatement technology at a cost of $100,000; (2) install air conditioners in the homes of each of the neighbors (at a cost of at least $150,000) in exchange for their promise not to enjoin CBW's operation[4]; and (3) relocate, at a cost of $250,000. CBW would, as a matter of self-interest, install the fume abatement technology, which is the efficient allocation of resources.

This example illustrates the Coase Theorem: In the absence of transaction costs, an efficient allocation of resources will obtain regardless of how the legal entitlement is initially allotted. Recognizing their potential mutual advantage from achieving an efficient allocation of resources, the parties will write a contract that brings about efficient resource use and that shares the benefits of this improvement in social welfare according to their respective bargaining power.

So why worry about externalities? It is important to remember that the Coase Theorem is premised upon the heroic assumption that transactions are costless. The world in which the Coase Theorem operates is analogous to the frictionless surface of the theoretical physicist. In the real world, of course, there is friction and the cost of negotiating a settlement is far from zero. To appreciate more fully Coase's insight, therefore, it is important to understand what is meant by the concept of "transaction costs" and the implications of transaction costs for resource allocation.

3. By effective entitlement, we mean a legal right and a feasible means to enforce that right.

4. What else would CBW want such an agreement to provide?

Positive Transaction Costs Model. Many factors impede the efficient resolution of property disputes in the real world. It is useful to think of four distinct types of transaction cost problems preventing or at least inhibiting efficient, bargained resolutions of such disputes: (1) negotiation and litigation costs; (2) free-rider problems; (3) hold-out problems; and (4) opportunism problems.

Negotiation and litigation costs consist of the time and effort associated with hammering out an agreement and enforcing it. Even if the factory and the neighbors are willing to resolve their dispute through bargaining, the costs of drawing up a contract that specifies all possible contingencies—*e.g.*, gathering the information about what to bargain about, deciding who owns the fume abatement device, deciding who is responsible for repairs should it break—and enforcing the agreement should one party default—*e.g.*, hiring lawyers, court costs—might outweigh the benefits of an agreement.

The *free-rider problem* arises in the following manner. Suppose that residents are entitled under the law to be free from odor pollution, but that it is costly to bring a lawsuit enforcing this entitlement. Each of the neighbors, therefore, would prefer for someone else to sue CBW to enforce the entitlement. Such a lawsuit would have the effect of abating the odor, at no cost to those neighbors who did not get involved in the lawsuit. Such neighbors could in effect *free ride* upon the efforts of others. If all neighbors think this way, none will make the investment necessary to enforce their rights.[5] As a result of the free-rider problem, CBW could continue to pollute with impunity. Although in theory the free-rider problem can occur in any bargaining situation in which more than one party has a common interest, the free-rider problem is most likely to occur when there are large numbers of parties who must get together to obtain the benefits of cooperation.

A related impediment to negotiation is the *hold-out problem*. To illustrate this form of transaction cost, we need to modify our example. Suppose that the cost of installing a fume abatement device were $200,000. In this case, the efficient solution is to install air conditioning systems in each of the ten neighboring homes (at a cost of $150,000). If residents are entitled under the law to be free from odor pollution and transaction costs are zero, CBW would arrange to install air conditioners in the homes of all of the neighbors in exchange for the neighbors' relinquishing the right to enforce their entitlements. In a more complicated world, however, the following bargaining dynamic might occur. CBW negotiates with neighbor #1 and arranges to pay her $15,000 to cover the cost of an air conditioner. Neighbor #2 realizes that CBW would probably be willing to pay even more to avoid being sued. Through savvy negotiation, she arranges for a payment of $20,000 per year. Neighbor #3, hearing of the payments to his neighbors, holds out for $25,000. CBW, realizing the potential for extortion from

---

5. If the costs of bringing a lawsuit exceeded the cost of installing an air conditioner, some neighbors might opt for the air conditioner solution, even though it is collectively less efficient than bringing a lawsuit.

For further elaboration of the implications of costly litigation, see Menell, A Note on Private Versus Social Incentives to Sue in a Costly Legal System, 12 J. Leg. Stud. 41 (1983).

the remaining neighbors, might decide that it is less costly simply to install the fume abatement device. Thus, the potential for hold-outs can lead to an inefficient allocation of resources.

The fourth type of transaction cost results from *opportunism* on the part of the parties. Opportunism occurs when a party attempts to extract a higher price for her entitlement by threatening behavior that would reduce her bargaining adversary's wealth, thus raising the adversary's willingness to buy the entitlement to avoid such a threat. As an example of opportunism, suppose that the factory has the initial entitlement to emit fumes and that the cost of installing a fume abatement device is $100,000. In negotiations with the neighbors, the factory could threaten to increase emissions unless the neighbors paid significantly more than $100,000. Although this threat is clearly inefficient, the factory nonetheless might carry it out in order to establish its credibility to extort a good settlement in future years. On the other hand, the neighbors might install air conditioners to establish their credibility in future negotiations. The net result of such behavior, however, is clearly inefficient for society.

As this discussion indicates, transaction costs can undermine the efficient allocation of resources in a variety of ways. This does not mean, however, that Coase's analysis is unhelpful in addressing these more complex problems. Even where transaction costs are significant, the Coase Theorem provides a useful insight into how to allocate entitlements to achieve an efficient allocation of resources: entitlements should be allocated to the party or parties that would have bargained for them in the absence of transaction costs. Thus, in our odor externality example, society is most likely to achieve the efficient allocation of resources by giving the entitlement to the neighbors (although this may depend on the costs of enforcing the entitlement[6]). As a general proposition, entitlements should be allocated so that the party who could solve the problem at lowest cost bears the onus of addressing the problem. This is commonly referred to as the "least cost avoider" principle. *See* G. Calabresi, The Costs of Accidents (1970). In practice, however, determining which party is the least cost avoider is often difficult (and hence costly). Furthermore, this method of allocating entitlements may ignore important considerations such as distributional and moral bases for assigning entitlements. Nonetheless, the Coase analysis in the presence of transaction costs poses the correct question for those wishing to achieve an efficient allocation of resources.

A second important implication of Coase's analysis is that externalities are, at least from an efficiency standpoint, *reciprocal* in nature. Policy analysts have traditionally viewed our externality example as one in which the factory inflicts harm on the neighbors and the question to be decided is: how should society restrain the factory? Coase's analysis shows, however, that the harm is reciprocal. The reciprocal nature of the harm arises from the potential interference between bicycle production (and jobs) and enjoyment of a residential neighborhood. By avoiding the harm to the neighbors,

6. This problem could be remedied by enabling the neighbors to recover their litigation costs in legal actions to enforce their entitlement.

we "harm" (*i.e.*, impose costs upon) the factory (and, in effect, the factory's investors, employees, and customers). Coase's analysis reveals that from an efficiency standpoint, the real social policy question is: should the factory be allowed to harm the neighbors or should the neighbors be allowed to harm the factory? As Coase noted, "[t]he problem is to avoid the more serious harm." In a world in which transactions are costless, society avoids the more serious harm no matter how initial entitlements are allocated. When transactions are costly, however, an analysis of transaction costs will enable social decisionmakers to determine how to allocate entitlements to avoid the more serious harm.

The following problem will test your understanding of and ability to apply the analytical tools developed in this section.

Problem: The Coase Theorem and Noise Pollution

Pacifica Restaurant offers a relaxing and tranquil setting for its patrons to enjoy sumptuous seafood cuisine on Pier 37. The warehouse next door was recently sold to Slam Dance. Slam Dance features high impact aerobics classes by day (performed to a pounding beat) and raucous live entertainment and dancing by night (also to a pounding beat). Since Slam Dance's opening, Pacifica has watched its business decline. Pacifica's customers frequently complain that they can no longer enjoy serene business lunches because of the noon time aerobic sessions. The romantic dinner atmosphere has been disrupted by the unrelenting banging from rock music and pounding feet on the dance floor.

Before the arrival of Slam Dance, Pacifica earned profits of $300,000.[7] Pacifica estimates that its profits will decline to $50,000 if nothing is done about the noise problem. Slam Dance expects to earn $200,000 under present circumstances. The noise problem can be abated in a number of ways: (A) if Slam Dance installs wall insulation (at an annual cost of $30,000[8]), then Pacifica's profits will be $150,000, and Slam Dance's profits will fall by the cost of insulation; (B) if Pacifica installs wall insulation (at an annual cost of $30,000), then its profits will be $150,000 (less the cost of insulation); (C) if both enterprises install wall insulation, then Pacifica's profits will be $200,000 (less the costs of insulation) and Slam Dance's profits will fall by its cost of insulation; (D) if Slam Dance installs floor and wall insulation (at an annual cost of $70,000), then Pacifica's profits will be $250,000 and Slam Dance's profits will fall by the cost of insulation; (E) if Slam Dance installs floor and wall insulation (annual cost of $70,000) and Pacifica installs wall insulation (annual cost of $30,000), then Pacifica's

---

7. To simplify the problem, assume that there are no external costs other than those explicitly addressed.

8. We have expressed the costs of improvements as annualized amounts so that the comparison of alternatives can be done on the basis of one year's profits and costs. You can think of this way of expressing the costs of improvements as the annual cost of paying off a loan.

profits will be $270,00; and (F) if Slam Dance sells out (at zero return) to Windham Hills, a chain of "fern" bars playing soft instrumental music and offering a variety of entrees featuring alfalfa sprouts, which would earn profits of $80,000 and reduce Pacifica's profits to $250,000 (because of increased competition).

Assume transaction costs are zero.

1. What is the efficient allocation of resources?

2. What will be the ultimate allocation of resources if Pacifica Restaurant is entitled to be free from noise pollution?

3. What will be the ultimate allocation of resources if Slam Dance is entitled to conduct aerobics classes and nightly entertainment as it would like?

4. What if Slam Dance could relocate to an equally good site for $75,000? What outcome would obtain? What additional information do you need to assess this option?

Relax the assumption about transaction costs.

5. What result obtains if instead of a single restaurant, there are five restaurants adjacent to the warehouse purchased by Slam Dance (each has ⅕th the profits and abatement costs of Pacifica), it is costly for them to reach agreements, and Slam Dance has the right to operate as it would like?

6. Same facts as #5 except that the restaurants have the right to be free from noise. What result would obtain?

---

1. Re-read pages 44–47 of the Cronon excerpt. Do you find any examples reflecting Coase's insights?

2. Does the assignment of entitlements affect the long-run allocation of resources? In our odor-externality example, would assignment of the entitlement to the factory favor long-run bicycle production more than would assignment of the entitlement to the residential neighbors? *See* Demsetz, When Does the Rule of Liability Matter? 1 J. Legal Stud. 13 (1972).

3. Even in a world of zero or low transaction costs, doesn't the assignment of entitlements affect the ultimate allocation of resources to the extent that a person's wealth affects his or her willingness to pay? But does this phenomenon make the allocation of resources less "efficient"? Does this mean that entitlements should (must) be assigned with income distribution in mind?

In a related vein, doesn't the assignment of entitlements affect the valuation of resources by the parties? Substantial empirical evidence indicates a significant divergence between consumers' willingness to pay for natural resources and their willingness to accept compensation for such resources. This phenomenon, often referred to as the endowment effect, suggests that the utility people derive from the use of resources depends upon their perception of the allocation of entitlements. One survey found that hunters were willing to pay an average of $247 to preserve a wetland hunting area but would require more than four times that amount to give up an entitlement to the same area. *See* J. Hammaker & D. Brown, Jr., Waterfowl and Wetlands: Toward Bioeconomic Analysis (1974); *see generally*, Menell, Institutional Fantasylands: From Scientific Management to Free Market Environmentalism, 15 Harv. J. L. & Pub. Pol'y 489, 496–97 (1992); Sunstein, Endogenous Preferences, Environmental Law, 22 J. Legal Studies 217 (1993).

What are the implications of the endowment effect for our odor-externality problem? If the entitlement to the air resource is initially assigned to the factory, then the neighbors' decision about whether to acquire the entitlement turns on how much they are *willing to pay*. But if they have the entitlement initially, then the ultimate allocation of the resource will turn on how much the neighbors will demand for the entitlement, *i.e.*, how much they are *willing to be paid*. If the neighbors' willingness to pay is not the same as their willingness to be paid, what are the implications for efficiency? What does it mean for the Coase Theorem?

4. Does Coase's analysis—which relies upon bargaining to reassign entitlements to the highest bidder—in effect encourage bribery and extortion? More generally, does the Coasean mode of analysis reduce all moral issues relating to the allocation of resources in society to the question of who is the least cost avoider? What important questions does this framework overlook?

Should society protect those activities or land uses that were first in time—*e.g.*, the neighbors in the odor example, or the restaurant in the noise problem? Why or why not? Does the Coase Theorem adequately address this question?

5. The Coase Theorem suggests that externality problems might well be solved through private means. In fact, we do see such efforts in many contexts. Isn't the environmental movement based in part on this notion? For example, the Nature Conservancy was formed in 1950 for the purpose of conserving the natural environment. As of 1981, the Nature Conservancy had preserved almost two million acres of forests, marshes, and other important and sensitive ecosystems entirely through voluntary contributions. These reserves have been donated to appropriate government agencies or maintained by the Nature Conservancy.

Does this effort suggest that the externality problem is not significant with regard to nature conservation? Alternatively, might some contributions to the Nature Conservancy be motivated by private gain?[9] What types

---

9. Contributions of assets afford high-income individuals charitable deductions equal to the appreciated value of the donations without having to realize any capital gains. Changes in the tax laws in the 1980s, however, significantly reduced this tax benefit.

of communities are most likely to be able to resolve externality problems through negotiation? Can you think of any other social institutions that have traditionally addressed the tragedy of the commons? *See* Ellickson, Order Without Law (1992); Rose, The Comedy of the Commons: Custom, Commerce, and Inherently Public Property, 53 U. Chi. L. Rev. 711 (1986).

----

3.   AN ANALYTIC FRAMEWORK FOR COMMON LAW DOCTRINES

Guido Calabresi and A. Douglas Melamed, Property Rules, Liability Rules, and Inalienability: One View of the Cathedral

85 Harvard Law Review 1089, 1090, 1092–98, 1105–08, 1110 (1972).

I.   Introduction

* * *

The first issue which must be faced by any legal system is one we call the problem of "entitlement." Whenever a state is presented with the conflicting interests of two or more people, or two or more groups of people, it must decide which side to favor. Absent such a decision, access to goods, services, and life itself will be decided on the basis of "might makes right"—whoever is stronger or shrewder will win. Hence the fundamental thing that law does is to decide which of the conflicting parties will be entitled to prevail. The entitlement to make noise versus the entitlement to have silence, the entitlement to pollute versus the entitlement to breathe clean air, the entitlement to have children versus the entitlement to forbid them—these are the first order of legal decisions.

* * *

The state not only has to decide whom to entitle, but it must also simultaneously make a series of equally difficult second order decisions. These decisions go to the manner in which entitlements are protected and to whether an individual is allowed to sell or trade the entitlement. In any given dispute, for example, the state must decide not only which side wins but also the kind of protection to grant. * * * We shall consider three types of entitlements—entitlements protected by property rules, entitlements protected by liability rules, and inalienable entitlements. The categories are not, of course, absolutely distinct; but the categorization is useful since it reveals some of the reasons which lead us to protect certain entitlements in certain ways.

An entitlement is protected by a property rule to the extent that someone who wishes to remove the entitlement from its holder must buy it from him in a voluntary transaction in which the value of the entitlement is agreed upon by the seller. It is the form of entitlement which gives rise to the least amount of state intervention: once the original entitlement is decided upon, the state does not try to decide its value.[10] It lets each of the parties say how much the entitlement is worth to him, and gives the seller a veto if the buyer does not offer enough. Property rules involve a collective decision as to who is to be given an initial entitlement but not as to the value of the entitlement.

Whenever someone may destroy the initial entitlement if he is willing to pay an objectively determined value for it, an entitlement is protected by a liability rule. This value may be what it is thought the original holder of the entitlement would have sold it for. But the holder's complaint that he would have demanded more will not avail him once the objectively determined value is set. Obviously, liability rules involve an additional stage of intervention; not only are entitlements protected, but their transfer or destruction is allowed on the basis of a value determined by some organ of the state rather than by the parties themselves.

An entitlement is inalienable to the extent that its transfer is not permitted between a willing buyer and a willing seller. The state intervenes not only to determine who is initially entitled and to determine the compensation that must be paid if the entitlement is taken or destroyed, but also to forbid its sale under some or all circumstances. Inalienability rules are thus quite different from property and liability rules. Unlike those rules, rules of inalienability not only "protect" the entitlement; they may also be viewed as limiting or regulating the grant of the entitlement itself.

It should be clear that most entitlements to most goods are mixed. Taney's house may be protected by a property rule in situations where Marshall wishes to purchase it, by a liability rule where the government decides to take it by eminent domain, and by a rule of inalienability in situations where Taney is drunk or incompetent. This article will explore two primary questions: (1) In what circumstances should we grant a particular entitlement? and (2) In what circumstances should we decide to protect that entitlement by using a property, liability, or inalienability rule?

II.   The Setting of Entitlements

What are the reasons for deciding to entitle people to pollute or to entitle people to forbid pollution, to have children freely or to limit procreation, to own property or to share property? They can be grouped under three headings: economic efficiency, distributional preferences, and other justice considerations.

10. A property rule requires less state intervention only in the sense that intervention is needed to decide upon and enforce the initial entitlement but not for the separate problem of determining the value of the entitlement. Thus, if a particular property entitlement is especially difficult to en-force—for example, the right to personal security in urban areas—the actual amount of state intervention can be very high and could, perhaps, exceed that needed for some entitlements protected by easily administered liability rules.

A. Economic Efficiency

* * * Economic efficiency asks that we choose the set of entitlements which would lead to that allocation of resources which could not be improved in the sense that a further change would not so improve the condition of those who gained by it that they could compensate those who lost from it and still be better off than before. * * * To give two examples, economic efficiency asks for that combination of entitlements to engage in risky activities and to be free from harm from risky activities which will most likely lead to the lowest sum of accident costs and of costs of avoiding accidents. It asks for that form of property, private or communal, which leads to the highest product for the effort of producing.

[The authors summarize Coase's result that economic efficiency will obtain if transactions are costless.]

Such a result would not mean, however, that the *same* allocation of resources would exist regardless of the initial set of entitlements. Taney's willingness to pay for the right to make noise may depend on how rich he is; Marshall's willingness to pay for silence may depend on his wealth. In a society which entitles Taney to make noise and which forces Marshall to buy silence from Taney, Taney is wealthier and Marshall poorer than each would be in a society which had the converse set of entitlements. Depending on how Marshall's desire for silence and Taney's for noise vary with their wealth, an entitlement to noise will result in negotiations which will lead to a different quantum of noise than would an entitlement to silence. This variation in the quantity of noise and silence can be viewed as no more than an instance of the well accepted proposition that what is * * * economically efficient * * * varies with the starting distribution of wealth. * * *

All this suggests why distributions of wealth may affect a society's choice of entitlements. It does not suggest why *economic efficiency* should affect the choice, if we assume an absence of any transaction costs. But no one makes an assumption of no transaction costs in practice. Like the physicist's assumption of no friction or Say's law in macro-economics, the assumption of no transaction costs may be a useful starting point, a device which helps us see how, as different elements which may be termed transaction costs become important, the goal of economic efficiency starts to prefer one allocation of entitlements over another.

Since one of us has written at length on how in the presence of various types of transaction costs a society would go about deciding on a set of entitlements in the field of accident law,[11] it is enough to say here: (1) that economic efficiency standing alone would dictate that set of entitlements which favors knowledgeable choices between social benefits and the social costs of obtaining them, and between social costs and the social costs of avoiding them; (2) that this implies, in the absence of certainty as to whether a benefit is worth its costs to society, that the cost should be put on the party or activity best located to make such a cost-benefit analysis;

___

11. [G. Calabresi, The Costs of Accidents (1970).]

(3) that in particular contexts like accidents or pollution this suggests putting costs on the party or activity which can most cheaply avoid them; (4) that in the absence of certainty as to who that party or activity is, the costs should be put on the party or activity which can with the lowest transaction costs act in the market to correct an error in entitlements by inducing the party who can avoid social costs most cheaply to do so; and (5) that since we are in an area where by hypothesis markets do not work perfectly—there are transaction costs—a decision will often have to be made on whether market transactions or collective fiat is most likely to bring us closer to the [economically efficient] result the "perfect" market would reach.

* * *

B.   Distributional Goals

There are, we would suggest, at least two types of distributional concerns which may affect the choice of entitlements. These involve distribution of wealth itself and distribution of certain specific goods, which have sometimes been called merit goods.

All societies have wealth distribution preferences. They are, nonetheless, harder to talk about than are efficiency goals. * * * Distributional preferences * * * cannot usefully be discussed in a single conceptual framework. There are some fairly broadly accepted preferences—caste preferences in one society, more rather than less equality in another society. There are also preferences which are linked to dynamic efficiency concepts—producers ought to be rewarded since they will cause everyone to be better off in the end. Finally, there are a myriad of highly individualized preferences as to who should be richer and who poorer which need not have anything to do with either equality or efficiency—silence lovers should be richer than noise lovers because they are worthier.

* * *

III.   Rules for Protecting and Regulating Entitlements

Whenever society chooses an initial entitlement it must also determine whether to protect the entitlement by property rules, by liability rules, or by rules of inalienability. In our framework, much of what is generally called private property can be viewed as an entitlement which is protected by a property rule. No one can take the entitlement to private property from the holder unless the holder sells it willingly and at the price at which he subjectively values the property. Yet a nuisance with sufficient public utility to avoid injunction has, in effect, the right to take property with compensation. In such a circumstance the entitlement to the property is protected only by what we call a liability rule: an external, objective standard of value is used to facilitate the transfer of the entitlement from the holder to the nuisance. Finally, in some instances we will not allow the sale of the property at all, that is, we will occasionally make the entitlement inalienable.

This section will consider the circumstances in which society will employ these three rules to solve situations of conflict. Because the property rule and the liability rule are closely related and depend for their application on the shortcomings of each other, we treat them together. We discuss inalienability separately.

A. Property and Liability Rules

Why cannot a society simply decide on the basis of the already mentioned criteria who should receive any given entitlement, and then let its transfer occur only through a voluntary negotiation? Why, in other words, cannot society limit itself to the property rule? To do this it would need only to protect and enforce the initial entitlements from all attacks, perhaps through criminal sanctions, and to enforce voluntary contracts for their transfer. Why do we need liability rules at all?

In terms of economic efficiency the reason is easy enough to see. Often the cost of establishing the value of an initial entitlement by negotiation is so great that even though a transfer of the entitlement would benefit all concerned, such a transfer will not occur. If a collective determination of the value were available instead, the beneficial transfer would quickly come about.

Eminent domain is a good example. A park where Guidacres, a tract of land owned by 1,000 owners in 1,000 parcels, now sits would, let us assume, benefit a neighboring town enough so that the 100,000 citizens of the town would each be willing to pay an average of $100 to have it. The park is * * * desirable [from an economic perspective] if the owners of the tracts of land in Guidacres actually value their entitlements at less than $10,000,000 or an average of $10,000 a tract. Let us assume that in fact the parcels are all the same and all the owners value them at $8,000. On this assumption, the park is, in economic efficiency terms, desirable—in values foregone it costs $8,000,000 and is worth $10,000,000 to the buyers. And yet it may well not be established. If enough of the owners hold-out for more than $10,000 in order to get a share of the $2,000,000 that they guess the buyers are willing to pay over the value which the sellers in actuality attach, the price demanded will be more than $10,000,000 and no park will result. The sellers have an incentive to hide their true valuation and the market will not succeed in establishing it.

An equally valid example could be made on the buying side. Suppose the sellers of Guidacres have agreed to a sales price of $8,000,000 (they are all relatives and at a family banquet decided that trying to hold-out would leave them all losers). It does not follow that the buyers can raise that much even though each of 100,000 citizens *in fact* values the park at $100. Some citizens may try to free-load and say the park is only worth $50 or even nothing to them, hoping that enough others will admit to a higher desire and make up the $8,000,000 price. Again there is no reason to believe that a market, a decentralized system of valuing, will cause people to express their true valuations and hence yield results which all would *in fact* agree are desirable.

Whenever this is the case an argument can readily be made for moving from a property rule to a liability rule. If society can remove from the market the valuation of each tract of land, decide the value collectively, and impose it, then the holdout problem is gone. Similarly, if society can value collectively each individual citizen's desire to have a park and charge him a "benefits" tax based upon it, the freeloader problem is gone. If the sum of the taxes is greater than the sum of the compensation awards, the park will result.

Of course, one can conceive of situations where it might be cheap to exclude all the freeloaders from the park, or to ration the park's use in accordance with original willingness to pay. In such cases the incentive to free-load might be eliminated. But such exclusions, even if possible, are usually not cheap. And the same may be the case for market methods which might avoid the holdout problem on the seller side.

Moreover, even if holdout and freeloader problems can be met feasibly by the market, an argument may remain for employing a liability rule. Assume that in our hypothetical, freeloaders can be excluded at the cost of $1,000,000 and that all owners of tracts in Guidacres can be convinced, by the use of $500,000 worth of advertising and cocktail parties, that a sale will only occur if they reveal their true land valuations. Since $8,000,000 plus $1,500,000 is less than $10,000,000, the park will be established. But if collective valuation of the tracts and of the benefits of the prospective park would have cost less than $1,500,000, it would have been inefficient to establish the park through the market—a market which was not worth having would have been paid for.

Of course, the problems with liability rules are equally real. We cannot be at all sure that landowner Taney is lying or holding out when he says his land is worth $12,000 to him. The fact that several neighbors sold identical tracts for $10,000 does not help us very much; Taney may be sentimentally attached to his land. As a result, eminent domain may grossly undervalue what Taney would actually sell for, even if it sought to give him his true valuation of his tract. In practice, it is so hard to determine Taney's true valuation that eminent domain simply gives him what the land is worth "objectively," in the full knowledge that this may result in over or under compensation. The same is true on the buyer side. "Benefits" taxes rarely attempt, let alone succeed, in gauging the individual citizen's relative desire for the alleged benefit. They are justified because, even if they do not accurately measure each individual's desire for the benefit, the market alternative seems worse. For example, fifty different households may place different values on a new sidewalk that is to abut all the properties. Nevertheless, because it is too difficult, even if possible, to gauge each household's valuation, we usually tax each household an equal amount.

* * *

We should also recognize that efficiency is not the sole ground for employing liability rules rather than property rules. Just as the initial entitlement is often decided upon for distributional reasons, so too the choice of a liability rule is often made because it facilitates a combination of efficiency and distributive results which would be difficult to achieve under a property rule. * * *

For further discussions of property rules and liability rules, *see* Symposium: Property Rules, Liability Rules, and Inalienability: A Twenty–Five Year Retrospective, 106 Yale L.J. 2083 (1997). Ayres & Talley, Solomonic Bargaining: Dividing a Legal Entitlement to Facilitate Coasean Trade, 104 Yale L.J. 1027 (1995); Kaplow & Shavell, Do Liability Rules Facilitate Bargaining: A Reply to Ayres and Talley, 105 Yale L.J. 221 (1995), Ayres & Talley, Distinguishing Between Consensual and Nonconsensual Advantages of Liability Rules, 105 Yale L.J. 235 (1995); Kaplow & Shavell, Property Rules Versus Liability Rules: An Economic Analysis, 109 Harv. L. Rev. 713 (1996); Merges, Contracting into Liability Rules: Intellectual Property and Collective Rights Organizations, 84 Cal.L.Rev. 1293 (1996), infra pp. 502–08.

---

4. The Right to Exclude: Trespass and Nuisance Law[12]

As Blackstone emphasized in the eighteenth century, and as our Supreme Court reiterated in *Kaiser Aetna v. United States*, 444 U.S. 164, 176, 100 S.Ct. 383, 391, 62 L.Ed.2d 332 (1979) and *Loretto v. Teleprompter Manhattan CATV Corp.*, 458 U.S. 419, 435, 102 S.Ct. 3164, 3176, 73 L.Ed.2d 868 (1982), the right to exclude is the most basic entitlement in the bundle of property rights. This right is most clearly violated when a person enters another's land without permission; using a shortcut across a neighbor's land, erecting a structure that encroaches on a neighbor's land, or even emitting air pollution that crosses the property line all violate the right to exclude. Such direct violations are covered by the law of trespass. *See, e.g., Martin v. Reynolds Metals Co.*, 221 Or. 86, 342 P.2d 790 (1959), *cert. denied*, 362 U.S. 918, 80 S.Ct. 672, 4 L.Ed.2d 739 (1960) (air pollution that crosses the property line constitutes a trespass); *Borland v. Sanders Lead Co.*, 369 So.2d 523 (Ala.1979).

Property law also protects owners from indirect invasions—*e.g.*, noise, odors, vibration—that interfere with the plaintiff's use and enjoyment of her land. In *William Aldred's Case*, 9 Co. Rep. 57, 77 Eng. Rep. 816 (1611), an English court held that a landowner could recover damages from injuries resulting from the stench of a nearby hog sty. Although the precise criteria to establish a violation have changed since the seventeenth century,

---

12. For a richer description of the origins, evolution, and details of the common law doctrines, see W. Rodgers, Environmental Law: Air and Water §§ 2.1–2.20 (2d ed. 1986); Developments in the Law—Toxic Waste Litigation, 99 Harv. L. Rev. 1458, 1602–31 (1986); W. Prosser & W. Keeton, Prosser and Keeton on Torts (5th ed. 1984).

the basic principles remain intact. These indirect violations come under the law of nuisance.[13]

a. TRESPASS

Under the common law, trespassers are strictly liable for intentional physical invasions of another's interest in the exclusive possession of land.[14] As you read the following cases, consider the advantages and disadvantages of the common law rule and ask whether the modern reforms adequately deal with the shortcomings of the older cases.

Pile v. Pedrick

Supreme Court of Pennsylvania, 1895.
167 Pa. 296, 31 A. 646.

■ WILLIAMS, J. The learned judge of the court below was right in holding that the wall in controversy was not a party wall. It was not intended to be. The defendants were building a factory, and, under the advice of their architect, decided to build within their own lines, in order to avoid the danger of injury to others from vibration which might result from the use of their machinery. They called upon the district surveyor to locate their line, and built within it, as so ascertained. Subsequent surveys by city surveyors have determined that the line was not accurately located at first, but was about [1.5] inches over on the plaintiffs'. This leaves the ends of the stones used in the foundation wall projecting into the plaintiffs' lands, below the surface, 1⅜ inches. This unintentional intrusion into the plaintiffs' close is the narrow foundation on which this bill in equity rests. The wall resting on the stone foundation is conceded to be within the defendants' line. The defendants offered, nevertheless, to make it a party wall, by agreement, and give to plaintiffs the free use of it, as such, on condition that the windows on the third and fourth floors should remain open until the plaintiffs should desire to use the wall. This offer was declined. The trespass was then to be remedied in one of two ways: It could be treated, with the plaintiffs' consent, as a permanent trespass, and compensated for in damages, or the defendants could be compelled to remove the offending ends of the stones to the other side of the line. The plaintiffs insisted upon the latter course, and the court below has, by its decree, ordered that this should be done. The defendants then sought permission to go on the

---

13. The distinction between trespass and nuisance grew out of the now-abandoned procedural forms of action: the action of trespass alleged a direct physical invasion of the plaintiff's land, *e.g.*, the casting of water or stones onto the land; the action of case (from which nuisance is derived) alleged an indirect invasion, *e.g.*, where the defendant built a spout which caused water to seep onto the plaintiff's land.

14. In the case of unintentional invasions, which is treated in essentially the same way as accidental invasions of the person, *see* Prosser & Keeton on Torts, *supra* at 69–70, liability is imposed only if harm results and the defendant's conduct was negligent, reckless, or abnormally dangerous. *Restatement (Second) of Torts* §§ 157–66.

plaintiffs' side of the line and chip off the projecting ends, offering to pay for all inconvenience or injury the plaintiffs or their tenants might suffer by their so doing. This they refused. Nothing remained but to take down and rebuild the entire wall from the defendants' side, and with their building resting on it. This the decree requires. * * *

The decree is affirmed; the costs of this appeal to be paid by the appellants.

Pile v. Pedrick

Supreme Court of Pennsylvania, 1895.
167 Pa. 296, 31 A. 647.

■ WILLIAMS, J. This is an appeal from the same decree just considered in *Pile v. Pedrick*, 31 Atl. 646. It is not denied that the foundation wall on which the appellant has built was located under a mistake made by the district surveyor, and does in fact project slightly into the plaintiffs' land. For one inch and three-eighths, the ends of the stones in the wall are said to project beyond the division line. The defendants have no right, at law or in equity, to occupy land that does not belong to them, and we do not see how the court below could have done otherwise than recognize and act upon this principle. They must remove their wall, so that it shall be upon their land. This the court directed should be done within a reasonable time. To avoid further controversy over this subject, we will so far modify the decree as to permit such removal to be made within one year from the date of filing hereof. In all other respects the decree is affirmed; the appellants to pay all costs made by them upon this appeal.

---

1. How would you classify the rule in *Pile v. Pedrick* within the Calabresi and Melamed framework? To whom does the court allocate the legal entitlement? How may the holder of the entitlement enforce it?

2. Does the rule in *Pile v. Pedrick* promote an efficient use of resources? Is the rule equitable?

3. Would you choose this rule? If not, what alternative rule would you prefer?

Geragosian v. Union Realty Co.

Supreme Judicial Court of Massachusetts, 1935.
289 Mass. 104, 193 N.E. 726.

■ LUMMUS, JUSTICE.

In 1927 one Vartigian built a theatre in Somerville on land the rear of which adjoined the rear of land of one Aaronian. * * * The plaintiff, now owning the Aaronian land, seeks an injunction against the present owners of the theatre, for the removal of trespassing structures.

* * *

The theatre encroaches upon the Aaronian land itself in two respects. First, the platform of the fire escape on the theatre, at the third level, far above the ground, overhangs a piece of the Aaronian land eleven inches wide and three feet long, but causes no interference with the present use of that land. Second, a drain from the theatre runs, at a depth of eight or nine feet below the surface, about fifty-three feet through the unoccupied rear part of the Aaronian land, and a further distance * * * where it empties into a sewer * * *. This drain does not interfere with the use of the right of way over Sewall court, and does not interfere with the present use of the Aaronian land, upon the front of which a block of thirteen one-story garage is maintained for hire.

The defendant Union Realty Company took from Vartigian two mortgages covering the theatre * * *. In 1928 Vartigian conveyed his [interest in the theatre] to Sidney Realty Company, in which Union Realty Company held three-fourths of the stock and Vartigian's wife held the rest. A dispute arose as early as 1929 between Union Realty Company and Vartigian over a candy stand which Vartigian or his wife maintained in the theatre. On January 28, 1930, Union Realty Company, controlling Sidney Realty Company, prevented the further maintenance of the stand.

On January 30, 1930, Vartigian induced his wife's step-brother, the plaintiff Geragosian, to buy the Aaronian land for $3,400. * * * Title passed to him on February 4, 1930. Vartigian then knew of the encroachments, and his purpose in inducing the plaintiff to buy the land was to control it and to make trouble for Union Realty Company. But when the theatre was built, the encroachments were unintentional on the part of Vartigian. The master does not find that Geragosian shared in the purpose of Vartigian, or is under the control of Vartigian. On June 12, 1931, Union Realty Company foreclosed its second mortgage on the theatre, and bought in the theatre at the foreclosure sale. The land and buildings of the plaintiff Geragosian are worth about $2,800. The theatre, with its land, is worth about $250,000. The cost of a new drain which would not trespass on the plaintiff's land would be $4,300. The small part of the fire escape platform that overhangs the plaintiff's land, it is found, "could be removed without much difficulty and without materially interfering with the defendant's use of its fire escapes."

This bill was filed on October 26, 1932, although the controversy had existed since early in 1932, and the fact of encroachment had been called to the attention of Union Realty Company in 1930 or 1931.

The right of property which the plaintiff seeks to protect is legal, not merely equitable. * * *

The protection by injunction of property rights against continuing trespasses by encroaching structures has sometimes been based upon the danger that a continuance of the wrong may ripen into title by adverse possession or a right of prescription. Other cases point out that, since trespassing structures constitute a nuisance, and a plaintiff obtaining a second judgment for nuisance has a right to have the nuisance abated by warrant of the court, the denial of an injunction would only drive the plaintiff to a more dilatory remedy to obtain removal or abatement. But the basic reason lies deeper. It is the same reason "which lies at the foundation of the jurisdiction for decreeing specific performance of contracts for the sale of real estate. A particular piece of real estate cannot be replaced by any sum of money, however large; and one who wants a particular estate for a specific use, if deprived of his rights, cannot be said to receive an exact equivalent or complete indemnity by the payment of a sum of money. A title to real estate, therefore, will be protected in a court of equity by a decree which will preserve to the owner the property itself, instead of a sum of money which represents its value." Knowlton, J., in *Lynch v. Union Institution for Savings*, 159 Mass. 306, 308, 34 N. E. 364, 20 L. R. A. 842. Leaving an aggrieved landowner to remove a trespassing structure at his own expense and risk, would amount in practice to a denial of all remedy, except damages, in most cases. If the landowner should attempt to right his own wrongs, a breach of the peace would be likely to result.

The facts that the aggrieved owner suffers little or no damage from the trespass, that the wrongdoer acted in good faith and would be put to disproportionate expense by removal of the trespassing structures, and that neighborly conduct as well as business judgment would require acceptance of compensation in money for the land appropriated, are ordinarily no reasons for denying an injunction. Rights in real property cannot ordinarily be taken from the owner at a valuation, except under the power of eminent domain. Only when there is some estoppel or laches on the part of the plaintiff, or a refusal on his part to consent to acts necessary to the removal or abatement which he demands, will an injunction ordinarily be refused. It is true that in *Methodist Episcopal Society v. Akers*, 167 Mass. 560, 46 N. E. 381, the court refused an injunction for the removal of a building from a small piece of rough rural land; that in *Harrington v. McCarthy*, 169 Mass. 492, 48 N. E. 278, 61 Am. St. Rep. 298 (compare *Tramonte v. Colarusso*, 256 Mass. 299, 152 N. E. 90; *Crosby v. Blomerth*, 258 Mass. 221, 154 N. E. 763), a slight encroachment of a foundation under ground was held not to require an injunction; that in *Loughlin v. Wright Machine Company*, 273 Mass. 310, 173 N. E. 534, the court refused an injunction against the maintenance of a sewer across a useless six-inch strip owned by the plaintiff; and that in *Malinoski v. D. S. McGrath, Inc.*, 283 Mass. 1, 11, 186 N. E. 225, and cases cited, the right of the court to refuse an injunction because of hardship was stated. But such cases are exceptional. The general rule is that the owner of land is entitled to an injunction for the removal of trespassing structures.

Nothing takes this case out of the general rule. No estoppel nor laches is shown. The motives of Vartigian cannot impair the property rights of Aaronian or his grantee Geragosian. The final decree rightly restrained the further use of the drain across the plaintiff's land, and ordered the removal of the fire escape platform so far as it overhangs said land. * * *

Ordered accordingly.

----

1. How would you classify the rule in *Geragosian v. Union Realty Co.* within the Calabresi and Melamed framework? To whom does the court allocate the legal entitlement? How does it differ from the rule in *Pile*? What showing must the defendant make to avoid an injunction? Do you find the court's rationale for protecting property rights with injunctive relief persuasive? Is the loss of use of a property interest irreplaceable by "any sum of money"?

2. Does the rule in *Geragosian* promote an efficient use of resources? Is the rule equitable?

3. Would you choose this rule? If not, what alternative rule would you prefer?

Raab v. Casper

Court of Appeal of California, 1975.
51 Cal.App.3d 866, 124 Cal.Rptr. 590.

■ FRIEDMAN, ACTING PRESIDING JUSTICE.

Plaintiffs and defendants own adjoining foothill tracts acquired through a common grantor. Plaintiffs' parcel, about 20 acres in size, is longitudinally shaped, with its narrow dimension at the north and south ends. Mr. and Mrs. Casper, the defendants, own two separate parcels, immediately to the west, one of three and one-half acres adjoining the northern portion of plaintiffs' tract, another of four and one-half acres adjoining the southern portion. Plaintiffs' amended complaint sought a mandatory injunction and damages; it alleged in effect two separate, continuing trespasses by defendants; defendants had built a 25 by 35-foot cabin entirely on plaintiffs' land, at its northwest corner near the northerly end of the common boundary; toward the southerly end of the common boundary, defendants had built a family home, approximately one-third of the premises being located on plaintiffs' land.

According to the findings, the common north-south boundary had never been surveyed or marked; the true boundary had been established through a survey by Harvey Butler filed for record in April 1972;[15] commencing in January 1970, defendants started building a small house (*i.e.*, cabin), which was actually located across the boundary, at the north-west corner of plaintiffs' land. The court also found that in September 1970 plaintiffs complained to defendants that they believed the cabin was located on plaintiffs' property; at that time Casper had completed the foundation, exterior walls, roofs and interior partitions, septic tank and leachline, but

----

15. Plaintiffs had bought and paid for this survey after the dispute arose.

not the interior work; Casper continued with construction of the cabin and completed it; defendants did not take the cabin site by adverse possession; defendants had not acted maliciously or willfully, but believed in good faith that they were building the cabin on their own property.

As to the cabin built at the northwestern corner of plaintiffs' land, the court concluded that defendants were good faith improvers. (*See* Code Civ.Proc., §§ 871.1–871.7.) Its judgment realigned the northerly common boundary to give defendants the .287 acres where their cabin was situated; awarded plaintiffs $700 as compensation for the reasonable value of the land, $500 for the cost of a survey, $750 attorney's fee and $70 per year rent until entry of judgment (slightly less than three years). Plaintiffs appeal.

* * *

The good-faith-improver legislation was enacted in 1968. A "good faith improver" is defined as one who makes an improvement to land in good faith and under a mistaken belief that he is the landowner. (Code Civ.Proc., § 871.1.) Such an improver may seek judicial relief but has the burden of establishing his entitlement to relief; the "degree of [his] negligence" should be taken into account in determining his good faith and in determining what belief is consistent with substantial justice. (Code Civ.Proc., § 871.3.)[16] The court may not grant relief if a setoff or right of removal would accomplish substantial justice. (Code Civ.Proc., § 871.4.) Subject to this limitation, the court may effect such adjustments in the parties' positions as are consistent with substantial justice under the circumstances; the relief shall protect the injured owner against pecuniary losses (including litigation expense) but avoid his unjust enrichment; in shaping relief, the court may consider the injured owner's future plans and his need for the land. (§ 871.5.)

We find no case law construing this legislation. It possesses decisional ancestry in the equity doctrine which grants damages but denies injunctive relief against an innocent encroachment which could be removed only at heavy cost and which does not cause irreparable damage to the injured landowner. It may, on occasion, be tied to the law which permits removal of fixtures erroneously and in good faith attached to the land of another. (Civ.Code, § 1013.5.)

The 1968 law adds a synthetic, somewhat alien ingredient to the concept of good faith. In its traditional sense good faith connotes a moral quality; it is equated with honesty of purpose, freedom from fraudulent intent and faithfulness to duty or obligation. Code of Civil Procedure

---

16. We quote section 871.3 in full: "A good faith improver may bring an action in the superior court or, * * * may file a cross-complaint in a pending action in the superior or municipal court for relief under this chapter. In every case, the burden is on the good faith improver to establish that he is entitled to relief under this chapter, and the degree of negligence of the good faith improver should be taken into account by the court in determining whether the improver acted in good faith and in determining the relief, if any, that is consistent with substantial justice to the parties under the circumstances of the particular case."

section 871.3 declares that the improver's "degree of negligence" should be taken into account in determining his good faith and in shaping the relief. Thus, in applying this particular legislation, good faith becomes an artificial attribute, calling for a measure of care as well as honesty. Lack of care as well as dishonesty may negate or diminish good faith. Moreover, section 871.3 calls for consideration of the degree of negligence. Without evoking conventional choices between ordinary and gross negligence, the statute invites consideration of varying intensities of negligence.

* * *

Here the trial court found that defendants "did not act maliciously, intentionally or willfully in constructing the small house [cabin], but acted in the good-faith belief that they were constructing said house on their property." The lack of any reference to negligence arouses appellate suspicion that negligence may have been neglected.

The suspicion is confirmed by evidence supporting an inference of negligence on the part of Mr. Casper, who built the cabin. Some ten years earlier he had indulged in assumptions regarding the boundary line to the south; these assumptions had led him to install part of the yard around his home, part of his driveway and utility lines on the land of plaintiffs. He admitted on the witness stand that he had never known or ascertained the location of the property corners. He had extrapolated his easterly boundary from a line between a jack pine and a manzanita tree; he based this belief on an oral statement made by the seller when he bought the land in 1959. In September 1970 plaintiffs first observed Mr. Casper's partially completed cabin and warned him that he was building on their property. Up to that point he had spent $1,956.28 on the cabin. He disregarded the warning and spent an additional $2,206.85 to complete the cabin. He did so without a survey and without offering to share in the cost of a survey. Plaintiffs spent $1,757.20 for the survey, which the trial court later accepted as the true boundary line.

There is an analogy here to the encroachment decisions which point out that continuation of the offending construction in defiance of the injured owner's opposition is inconsistent with good faith. (*Brown Derby Hollywood Corp. v. Hatson, supra,* 61 Cal.2d at p. 859, 40 Cal.Rptr. 848, 395 P.2d 896; *City of Dunsmuir v. Silva,* 154 Cal.App.2d 825, 828, 317 P.2d 653.) The good-faith-improver legislation of 1968 was drafted and submitted by the California Law Revision Commission, which accompanied section 871.1 with a comment fully consistent with the good faith concept described in the encroachment decisions. We append the Law Revision Commission's comment in the margin.[17]

---

17. "Under this section, a person is not a 'good faith improver' as to any improvement made after he becomes aware of facts that preclude him from acting in good faith. For example, a person who builds a house on a lot owned by another may obtain relief under this chapter if he acted in good faith under the erroneous belief, because of a mistake of law or fact, that he was the owner of the land. However, if the same person makes an additional improvement after he has discovered that he is not the owner of the land, he would not be entitled to relief under this

At this juncture of the case the findings declare: "That at the time of commencement of the construction of the small house, Defendant reasonably believed he was building the same on his land and had made reasonable effort to confirm that fact." The declaration is pregnant with an admission that at some later time defendants no longer possessed that reasonable belief. Whatever defendant Casper's good faith and whatever his reasonable care preceding the warning of September 1970, these elements underwent a transformation after he received that warning.

This appeal presents the precise situation described in the Law Revision Commission's comment, that is, a project characterized by good faith at its inception (according to the trial court findings) but suffering a shift in that characteristic when a warning of possible trespass or encroachment is received before completion. In choosing to proceed with his project in the face of the owner's warning, the improver exposes the owner to injury not measurable in dollars alone. The owner may ultimately receive the reasonable value of his lost land. His injury lies not so much in financial loss as in deprivation of a choice inherent in ownership. Ownership of land includes the freedom not to dispose of it. The good-faith-improver legislation gives the improver something akin to a private power of eminent domain. (*See Donnell v. Bisso Brothers, supra*, 10 Cal.App.3d at p. 46, 88 Cal.Rptr. 645.) The greater the improver's investment, the greater his potential appeal to the court's conscience. The law should not permit him to worsen the true owner's position after the latter has warned him of a possible trespass. Hence, deliberate augmentation of an initial investment after a warning of trespass is a legally significant factor, one which a trial court should not ignore.

In weighing the grant, denial or apportionment of relief, a trial court should consider any interim warning, the character and relative cost of the improvements made before and after the warning and the unitary or separable character of the improvements. As did Solomon, the law should recognize that a unitary improvement cannot be chopped in half—one part entitled to statutory relief, the other not. Despite the comment of the Law Revision Commission, it is not practical to fasten separate findings of good and bad faith upon separate physical parts of an indivisible physical project. The court may conclude that the improver's intransigence equates with negligence rather than dishonesty. In view of the record, the trial court's failure to make a finding on negligence is reversible error.

* * *

1. How would you classify the rule in *Raab v. Casper* within the Calabresi and Melamed framework? To whom does the court allocate the legal entitlement? How is that entitlement enforced? How do the statutory rights differ from the rules in *Pile* and *Geragosian*?

chapter with respect to the additional improvement."

2. If the problem in *Pile* is that the landowner might hold out for an extortionate payment, does the statute in *Raab* solve that problem?

3. In what way does the good faith improver statute change the parties' incentives in monitoring their property and developing land?

4. What additional administrative or litigation costs does the good faith improver statute create? Does the good faith improver statute result in a more efficient allocation of resources than the rules in *Pile* or *Geragosian*? Would you recommend a different rule?

----

b. NUISANCE

Traditionally, a nuisance is an activity that substantially interferes with another's use and enjoyment of his land. Typical examples include pollution that crosses property lines, *see, e.g., Boomer v. Atlantic Cement Co.*, 26 N.Y.2d 219, 309 N.Y.S.2d 312, 257 N.E.2d 870 (1970) (smoke and vibration from cement plant), and hazardous conditions that threaten neighboring property, *see, e.g., People v. Oliver*, 86 Cal.App.2d 885, 195 P.2d 926 (1948) (fire hazard).

Nuisance law is divided into private nuisance and public nuisance.

Private Nuisance. The Restatement defines a private nuisance as a substantial invasion of another's use and enjoyment of land that is either (1) "intentional and unreasonable" or (2) "unintentional and otherwise actionable under the rules controlling liability for negligent or reckless conduct, or for abnormally dangerous conditions or activities." *Restatement (Second) of Torts* § 822. Thus, under the *Restatement*, ownership of a property interest in land is a prerequisite to maintain a private nuisance action.[18] Some courts have used the "substantial invasion"[19] requirement to deny recovery for environmental degradation, such as aesthetic impairment, that does not result in tangible physical changes in land or easily measured economic harm.

Conduct is intentional if it is undertaken to cause the harm in question or if it is substantially certain to cause such harm. Intentional conduct is unreasonable if the "gravity of the harm" to the plaintiff outweighs the "utility of the actor's conduct." *Restatement (Second) of Torts* § 826(a). Section 827 identifies the following factors to be considered to determine the "gravity of harm":

(a) the extent of the harm involved;

(b) the character of the harm involved;

----

18. Some states, however, have expanded the basis for nuisance liability to include threats to health. *See* Cal. Civ. Code § 3479 (defining a nuisance as an injurious activity that "interferes with the comfortable enjoyment of life or property").

19. This requirement distinguishes private nuisance from trespass which makes *any* physical invasion of one's interest in exclusive possession of land actionable, even a trivial invasion.

(c) the social value which the law attaches to the type of use or enjoyment invaded;

(d) the suitability of the particular use or enjoyment invaded to the character of the locality;

(e) the burden on the person harmed of avoiding the harm.

Section 828 lists the following factors to be considered to assess the utility of the defendant's conduct:

(a) the social value which the law attaches to the primary purpose of the conduct;

(b) the suitability of the conduct to the character of the locality;

(c) whether it is impracticable to prevent or avoid the invasion, if the activity is maintained;

(d) whether it is impracticable to maintain the activity if it is required to bear the cost of compensating for the invasion.

Even if the utility of the defendant's conduct outweighs the gravity of the harm, the conduct is "unreasonable" if the harm "is serious and the financial burden of compensating for this and similar harm to others would not make the continuation of the conduct not feasible." *Restatement (Second) of Torts* § 826(b). Thus, in an action for damages, activities that are socially beneficial (under § 826(a)), but that nevertheless cause serious harm, are "unreasonable" unless compensation makes continuation of the activity infeasible. Can you think of other activities that fit into the latter category? What attributes characterize such activities?

Unintentional conduct is actionable if it is negligent or reckless, or involves "abnormally dangerous conditions or activities." A defendant is negligent if he does not conform to a standard of conduct that protects others from unreasonable risks; reasonableness turns on a balancing of the probability and gravity of the risk against the social utility of the conduct generating it. A defendant is strictly liable for harm resulting from abnormally dangerous activities. This doctrine traces its origin to *Rylands v. Fletcher*, 3 H.L. 330 (1868), where the court imposed strict liability for the escape of large quantities of water stored in a reservoir on defendant's land.

Public Nuisance. A public nuisance is "an unreasonable interference with a right common to the public." *Restatement (Second) of Torts* § 821B. Traditionally, public nuisance comprised an eclectic group of actions that disturbed the welfare of a broad segment of the community; many such actions also constituted common law crimes. Examples include obstruction of a public highway, maintenance of houses of prostitution, and public obscenity, as well as pollution. Section 821B(2) has identified several circumstances that normally create a public nuisance:

(a) whether the conduct involves significant interference with the public health, the public safety, the public peace, the public comfort or the public convenience,

(b) whether the conduct is proscribed by a statute, ordinance or administrative regulation, or

(c) whether the conduct is of a continuing nature or has produced a permanent or long-lasting effect, and, as the actor knows or has reason to know, has a significant effect upon the public right.

Generally, public nuisance suits may be brought only by a public official, such as the city attorney. A private individual has standing to bring such a suit only if he can show that his injury was different in kind (not merely in degree) from the injury suffered by the rest of the community. The rationale for this restriction is suggested in 4 W. Blackstone, Commentaries *167: "[I]t would be unreasonable to multiply suits by giving every man a separate right of action for what damnifies him in common only with the rest of his fellow subjects." *See generally* Rothstein, Private Actions for Public Nuisance—The Standing Problem, 76 W. Va. L. Rev. 453 (1976); Bryson & Macbeth, Public Nuisance, The Restatement (Second) of Torts, and Environmental Law, 2 Ecology L.Q. 241, 250–52, 255 (1972).

Sometimes (but not always) a plaintiff can establish standing on the ground that land is unique. The *Restatement* has adopted a more liberal test in actions to *enjoin* or *abate* a public nuisance,[20] extending it to persons having "standing to sue as a representative of the general public or as a member of a class action." *Restatement (Second) of Torts* § 821C(2)(c). This language reflects an awareness that public officials may not always have the resources or incentive to bring public nuisance actions, and that it is desirable to permit private plaintiffs to vindicate the rights of the public as a whole.

Waschak v. Moffat

Supreme Court of Pennsylvania, 1954.
379 Pa. 441, 109 A.2d 310.

■ ALLEN M. STEARNE, JUSTICE. The appeal is from a judgment of the Superior Court refusing to enter judgment *non obstante veredicto* for defendants in an action in trespass and affirming the judgment of the Court of Common Pleas of Lackawanna County in favor of plaintiffs.

Gas or fumes from culm banks, the refuse of a coal breaker, damaged the paint on plaintiffs' dwelling. In this action for damages the applicable legal principles are technical and controversial. Considerable confusion appears in the many cases. The field is that of *liability without fault for escape of substances from land*.

Plaintiffs are owners of a dwelling in the Borough of Taylor which is in the center of Pennsylvania's anthracite coal lands. An action in trespass

---

20. The *Restatement* has retained the standing requirement for damage actions. *Restatement (Second) of Torts* § 821C(1).

was instituted against two partners, operators of a coal breaker in that Borough. Without fault on the part of defendants, gas known as *hydrogen sulfide* was emitted from two of defendants' culm banks. This caused discoloration of the white paint (with lead base) which had been used in painting plaintiffs' dwelling. The painted surface became dark or black. The sole proven damage was the cost of restoring the surface with a white paint, having a titanium and zinc base, which will not discolor. There was no other injury either to the building or occupants. The verdict was for $1,250.

While the verdict is in a relatively modest amount, the principles of law involved, and their application, are extremely important and far reaching. Twenty-five other cases are at issue awaiting the decision in this case. The impact of this decision will affect the entire coal interests—anthracite and bituminous—as well as other industries. Application of appropriate legal principles is of vital concern to coal miners and to other labor.

The pivotal facts are undisputed. To mine anthracite coal, either by deep or strip mining, requires processing in a coal breaker before marketing. Usable coal, broken to various sizes, must first be separated from its by-products of minerals, rock, etc. The by-products are deposited in piles known as culm banks, portions of which may be reclaimed, while other parts are presently regarded as waste. The mining and processing in the present case are conceded to have been conducted by defendants without fault. Fires frequently appear in the culm banks long after the accumulation. Defendants neither committed any negligent act nor omitted any known method to prevent combustion, fires or the emission of gases. In addition to *hydrogen sulfide* two other gases, *carbon monoxide* and *sulfur dioxide* were shown to have also been emitted, but it is not contended that either of these two gases affected the paint in question. *Hydrogen sulfide* was conceded to have been the gas which caused the damage. The emission of this gas is not ordinarily found in the operation of coal mining and processing. *Defendants did not know and had no reason to anticipate the emission of this gas and the results which might follow*. Of the five culm banks only two of them, the Washington Street bank and the settling basin were shown to have emitted *hydrogen sulfide*.

In the court below the case was tried on the theory of *absolute liability* for the maintenance of a nuisance. The jury was instructed that it should determine, as a *matter of fact*, whether or not what the defendants did and the conditions resulting therefrom constituted a "reasonable and natural use" of defendants' land.

[The court then discussed potential rules for liability without fault for an invasion of private interests in land, rejecting, in the circumstances of this case, the rule of *Rylands v. Fletcher*, 3 H.L. 330 (1868), and also declined to follow a somewhat vaguely defined "Absolute Nuisance Doctrine."]

The Rule of the Restatement [of Torts] which unquestionably is accurate and most comprehensive, is as follows:

Section 822. General Rule.

The actor is liable in an action for damages for a nontrespassory invasion of another's interest in the private use and enjoyment of land if,

(a) the other has property rights and privileges in respect to the use or enjoyment interfered with; and

(b) the invasion is substantial; and

(c) the actor's conduct is a legal cause of the invasion; and

√ (d) the invasion is either

(i) intentional and unreasonable; or

(ii) unintentional and otherwise actionable under the rules governing liability for negligent, reckless or ultrahazardous conduct.

This rule we adopt. * * *

Prior to the year 1934 the Glen Alden Coal Company, owners, had ceased to mine coal in this area. The colliery in question was idle, the breaker was dismantled and [miners] in Taylor Borough were out of work. A committee of citizens of the Borough called upon the Glen Alden Coal Company requesting that the mines be reopened in order to aid the citizens. The Glen Alden Company agreed to this and leased coal lands comprising a continuous area of coal veins running from Taylor to Dickson City. When the defendants, in 1934, first began to operate the breaker a large culm bank close to the breaker was in existence and was then burning. In 1937 a new culm bank was started because of the fire in the old one and a conveyor was used to carry the culm to the new location. This was the Main Street bank and was used from 1937 to 1944. A new bank was then started known as the Washington Street bank, which was used from 1944 until October 1948. This bank was the same distance from the breaker as the Main Street bank, but in the opposite direction. In 1948 defendants commenced the construction of a settling basin in compliance with the State law concerning pollution of streams. During the construction the State inspectors approved. In 1949, six months after the Washington Street culm bank was discontinued, fire was discovered and defendants ceased using this breaker material for the settling basin. In the spring of 1949 walls in the settling basin ignited.

It is significant that plaintiffs purchased their home on June 23, 1948. It was close to the breaker, near the Washington Street bank.

Of the various gases emitted from the five culm banks, *hydrogen sulfide* was the gas which caused the damage. The record shows that this was emitted only from the Washington Street bank and the settling basin and from no others. Defendants did not know, and had no reason to be aware, that this particular gas would be so emitted and would have the effect upon the painted house. The record shows that the defendants were guilty of no negligence and used every known means to prevent damage or injury to adjoining properties.

Even if the reasonableness of the defendants' use of their property had been the *sole* consideration, there could be no recovery here. * * *

The dwelling in question had been formerly used by a mine inspector who doubtless desired to be close to the breaker. When plaintiffs purchased the dwelling they were fully aware of the surrounding situation.

In *Versailles Borough v. McKeesport Coal & Coke Co.*, 83 Pittsb.Leg.J. 379, Mr. Justice Musmanno, when a county judge, accurately encompassed the problem when he said:

> The plaintiffs are subject to an annoyance. This we accept, but it is an annoyance they have freely assumed. Because they desired and needed a residential proximity to their places of employment, they chose to found their abode here. It is not for them to repine; and it is probable that upon reflection they will, in spite of the annoyance which they suffer, still conclude that, after all, one's bread is more important than landscape or clear skies.
>
> Without smoke, Pittsburgh would have remained a very pretty *village.* * * *

* * *

In applying the rule of the Restatement, Torts, Sec. 822(d), it is evident the invasion of plaintiffs' land was clearly *not intentional*. And even if it were, for the reasons above stated, it was not unreasonable. On the contrary, since the emission of gases was not caused by any act of defendants and arose merely from the normal and customary use of their land without negligence, recklessness or ultrahazardous conduct, it was wholly *unintentional*, and no liability may therefore be imposed upon defendants.

The judgment is reversed and is here entered in favor of defendants *non obstante veredicto.* * * *

■ MUSMANNO, JUSTICE (dissenting).

The plaintiffs in this case, Joseph J. Waschak and Agnes Waschak, brother and sister, own a modest home in Taylor, Pennsylvania, a town of 7,000 inhabitants in the anthracite region of the northeastern part of the State. * * *

In 1948 the plaintiffs painted their house with a white paint. Some time later the paint began to turn to a light colored brown, then it changed to a grayish tint, once it burst into a silvery sheen, and then, as if this were its last dying gasp, the house suddenly assumed a blackish cast, the blackness deepened and intensified until now it is a "scorched black." The plaintiffs attribute this chameleon performance of their house to the hydrogen sulfide emanating from the defendants' culm deposits in the town—all in residential areas. The hydrogen sulfide, according to the plaintiffs, not only assaults the paint of the house but it snipes at the silverware, bath tub fixtures and the bronze handles of the doors, forcing them, respectively, into black, yellowish-brown and "tarnished-looking" tints.

* * *

The jury by their verdict decided that the defendants did not make a reasonable, lawful and natural use of their land. Reading the record in the case, I am satisfied that the jury was amply justified in their conclusion and I see no warrant for disturbing that verdict. When a property owner so uses his land that it injures his neighbor's the burden is on him to show that he did use his land naturally, reasonably and legally. The defendants in this case failed to meet the burden put on them by the law. * * *

The evidence here does not show any *necessity* on the part of the defendants to locate the culm banks in the very midst of the residential areas of Taylor.

* * * The poisonous gases lifting from the defendants' culm banks were destructive of property, detrimental to health and disruptive of the social life of the town.

There was evidence that the poisonous hydrogen sulfide was of such intensity that the inhabitants compelled to breathe it suffered from headaches, throat irritation, inability to sleep, coughing, lightheadedness, nausea and stomach ailments. These grave effects of the escaping gas reached such proportions that the citizens of Taylor held protest meetings and demanded that the municipal authorities take positive action to curb the gaseous invasion.

Did the release of the gases from the defendants' culm banks constitute under the law a nuisance? Nearly every witness testifying for the plaintiff as to the nature of the gas rising from the culm banks declared that it had the odor of rotten eggs.

Several of the witnesses testified that because of the rotten egg smell which entered their parlors and sitting rooms, it was difficult to entertain visitors. This statement could well qualify as the prize understatement of the case.

It must always be kept in mind that these culm banks were not mole hills. The Main Street dump measured 1,100 feet in length, 650 feet in width and 40 feet in height. If these dimensions were applied to a ship, one can visualize the size of the vessel and what would be the state of its odoriferousness if it was loaded stem to stern with rotten eggs. And that is only one of the dumps. There is another dump at Washington Street and, consequently, another ship of rotten eggs. Its dimensions are 800 feet by 750 feet by 50 feet. A third dump measures 500 feet by 500 feet by 40 feet. Then the defendants constructed a silt dam with the same rotten-egg-smelling materials.

I do not think that there can be any doubt that the constant smell of rotten eggs constitutes a nuisance. If such a condition is not recognized by the law, then the law is the only body that does not so recognize it.

Although the defendants sought to belittle the testimony adduced by the plaintiffs with regard to the intolerable conditions in Taylor caused by the defendants' gaseous banks, it is interesting to note that defendant Robert Y. Moffatt found it convenient and desirable to live outside the Borough of Taylor and, in all the years that he has been operating the coal business which is the subject of this litigation, he never found it profitable to spend a single night in Taylor. Even so, neither he nor his partner can successfully argue that they were unaware of the deleterious fumes rising from the coal refuse which they distributed through the town. * * *

Whether the facts in the case at bar constitute an actionable nuisance is not a question of law. It is one of fact for a jury to determine. * * *

There is a golden rule in law as well as in morals and it reads: "*Sic utere tuo ut alienum non laedas.*" The defendants oppose this maxim with the one that every person has the right to a lawful, reasonable and natural use of this land. But it is entirely possible and in fact desirable that these two maxims live together in peace and harmony. The plaintiffs in this case do not question that the defendants have the right to mine coal and process it, but is it a natural and reasonable use of land to deposit poisonous refuse in residential areas when it can be deposited elsewhere? Certainly the defendants may lawfully operate a breaker in Taylor, and whatever noises, dust and commotion result from the breaker operation are inconveniences which the plaintiff and other Taylor inhabitants must accept as part of the life of a mining community. But the disposition of the poisonous refuse of a mining operation does not fall within the definition of lawful and normal use of land. * * *

The majority states that the "emission of offensive odors, noises, fumes, violations, etc., must be weighed against the utility of the operation." In this respect, the Majority Opinion does me the honor of quoting from an Opinion I wrote when I was a member of the distinguished Court of Common Pleas of Allegheny County. *Versailles Borough v. McKeesport Coal & Coke Co.*, 83 Pittsb.Leg.J. 379. That was an equity case where the plaintiffs sought an injunction against the defendant coal company for maintaining a burning gob pile which emitted smoke. The coal mine was located in the very heart of an industrialized area which contained factories, mills, garbage dumps, incinerators and railroads, all producing their own individualized smoke and vapors so that it could not be said that the discomforts of the inhabitants were due exclusively to the operation of the coal mine. Furthermore, after hearings lasting one month I found that the operation of the mine in no way jeopardized the health of the inhabitants:

> Of course, if the continued operation of this mine were a serious menace to the health or lives of those who reside in its vicinity, there would be another question before us, but there is no evidence in this case to warrant the assumption that the health of anyone is being imperiled.

In the instant case the exact contrary is true. The health of the town of Taylor *is* being imperiled. And then also, as well stated by the lower Court in the present litigation, "Many factors may lead a chancellor to grant or deny injunctive relief which are not properly involved in an action brought to recompense one for injury to his land. * * * A denial of relief by a court of equity is not always precedent for denying redress by way of damages."

Even so, there is a vast difference between smoke which beclouds the skies and gas which is so strong that it peels the paint from houses. I did say in the *Versailles* case, "One's bread is more important than landscape or clear skies." But in the preservation of human life, even bread is preceded by water, and even water must give way to breathable air. Experimentation and observation reveal that one can live as long as 60 or 70 days without food; one can keep the lamp of life burning 3 or 4 days without water, but the wick is snuffed out in a minute or two in the absence of breathable air. For decades Pittsburgh was known as the "Smoky City" and without that smoke in its early days Pittsburgh indeed would have remained a "pretty village." But with scientific progress in the development of smoke-consuming devices, added to the use of smokeless fuel, Pittsburgh's skies have cleared, its progress has been phenomenal and the bread of its workers is whiter, cleaner, and sweeter. * * *

Even if the rights of the plaintiffs were to be considered by Restatement Rules they would still be entitled to recover under the proposition that the defendants were so well informed of the probable harmful effects of their operation that their actions could only be regarded as an intentional invasion of the rights of the plaintiff. Section 825 of the Restatement of Torts declares:

An invasion of another's interest in the use and enjoyment of land is intentional when the actor

(a) acts for the purpose of causing it; or

(b) knows that it is resulting or is substantially certain to result from his conduct.

The record amply proves that the defendants were at least "substantially certain" that their burning culm deposits would invade the plaintiffs' interest in the use and enjoyment of their land.

If there were no other way of disposing of the coal refuse, a different question might have been presented here, but the defendants produced no evidence that they could not have deposited the debris in places removed from the residential districts in Taylor. Certainly, many of the strip-mining craters which uglify the countryside in the areas close to Taylor could have been utilized by the defendants. They chose, however, to use the residential sections of Taylor because it was cheaper to pile the culm there than to haul it away into less populous territory.

This was certainly an unreasonable and selfish act in no way indispensably associated with the operation of the breaker. It brought greater profits to the defendants but at the expense of the health and the comfort of the other landowners in the town who are also entitled to the pursuit of happiness. * * *

It is because of the many fluctuating factors in the cases themselves that the decisions do not seem to be uniform. In point of juridical history, however, they do follow a pattern of wisdom and justice. No one will deny that the defendants are entitled to earn profits in the operation of their breaker, but is it reasonable that they shall so conduct that business as to poison the very lifestream of existence? Is it not reasonable to suppose that if hydrogen sulfide emanating from culm banks can strip paint from wood and steel that it will also deleteriously affect the delicate membranes of the throat and lungs?

The defendants have made much of a case of *Pennsylvania Coal Company v. Sanderson*, 113 Pa. 126, 6 A. 453, 459, where this Court did say that: "To encourage the development of the great natural resources of a country trifling inconveniences to particular persons must sometimes give way to the necessities of a great community." But here we are not dealing with trifling inconveniences. We are dealing with a situation where in effect an inhabitant of Taylor, Pennsylvania, awakens each morning with a basket of rotten eggs on his doorstep, and then, on his way to work finds that some of those eggs have been put into his pocket. No matter how often he may remove them, an invisible hand replaces them. This can scarcely be placed in the category of "trifling inconveniences."

The decision of the Superior Court in this case is logical, fair and in keeping with the philosophy and the pragmatics of the law. It does no violence to the precedents. It applies them in the light of the facts so clearly established in the 600 printed pages of testimony.

I would affirm the decision of the Superior Court.

-----

1.   Do you think this case would have been decided differently under the *Restatement (Second) of Torts*?

2.   *The Definition of "Fault" as Negligence or Unreasonableness.* Under nuisance law, intentional invasions are actionable if unreasonable, and unintentional invasions are actionable if negligent.[21] Both unreasonableness and negligence are measured by weighing the harm caused by defendant's conduct with the social utility of that conduct. In economic terms, a polluter acts unreasonably or is negligent whenever the marginal damages caused by pollution exceed the marginal costs of controlling pollution. An award of damages in such cases should give the defendant an incentive to reduce pollution up to the point where the costs of additional controls just equals the damage avoided. Do you see why the damage award based on "fault" should have this effect?

21. Should the analysis depend on whether the defendant's conduct is "intentional" or "unintentional"? How useful are the concepts of "intention" and "knowledge" in the context of pollution, which normally results from ongoing activities and, in many cases, the polluter is a corporation? How well do the majority and dissenting opinions in *Waschak* deal with these issues?

If this analysis is accepted, is there still a basis to conclude that the defendant in *Waschak* should not be liable?

3. *The Case for Strict Liability*. A rule of strict liability imposes damages upon the polluter regardless of fault. By internalizing the full costs of externality-producing activities, strict liability discourages polluters from operating beyond the point at which marginal social harm exceeds marginal social utility.

There is an active debate over the desirability and consequences of strict liability and fault regimes. *See* Epstein, A Theory of Strict Liability, 2 J. Leg. Studies, 151 (1973); Shavell, Strict Liability Versus Negligence, 9 J. Leg. Studies 1 (1981); Schwartz, The Case Against Strict Liability, 60 Fordham L. Rev. 819 (1992); Kornhauser and Revesz, Sharing Damages Among Multiple Tortfeasors, 98 Yale L.J. 831 (1989). Consider the following arguments for imposing strict liability

Reflecting Pollution Costs in Product Prices. Absent strict liability, residual spillover costs will not be reflected in the price of commodities produced by polluting activities. Such commodities will be underpriced relative to commodities whose production causes no pollution, resulting in resource misallocation. If the price of commodities reflected all of the social costs involved in their production, consumers would purchase fewer of such commodities, thereby reducing pollution and increasing global efficiency. Strict liability thus penalizes pollution in an amount equal to its external cost.[22]

Dynamic Incentives for "Technology–Forcing." Damages from a single injury or incident give a polluter no incentive to impose more pollution controls if it is already operating at or beyond the efficient level of control, given current control technology. The prospect of long-term, repeated damage payments based on strict liability, however, may give a polluter substantial incentive to develop (or purchase from others) environmentally superior technologies that permit a greater level of pollution control at lower cost.

Loss Spreading. Damage awards based on strict liability can spread the entire cost of pollution among the consumers of a polluting company's products to the extent that product prices reflect damage awards. Spillover costs may be spread even more widely because companies can purchase liability insurance. To some extent, the benefits of cost-spreading may be off-set by substantial administrative costs—the costs of tort litigation and processing liability insurance claims. Moreover, some pollution damage is already spread among large numbers of people. Would it be better if potential pollution victims purchased first-party insurance?[23]

---

22. Recall Coase's insight about the reciprocal nature of externalities. In assuming that it is the polluter who is imposing damage on victims, and that the polluter therefore has a responsibility to make good the damage, are we not begging an important question?

23. One potential obstacle to private, first-party insurance might be the lack of resources available to buy insurance.

Moral Rights to a Healthy Environment and Compensation. Strict liability, enforced through injunctive relief, protects individuals from exposure to unhealthy living conditions. Does justice require polluters, and ultimately consumers of the polluters' products, to use some of the profits or benefits of their activities to compensate others for the costs inflicted on them? *See* Epstein, Nuisance Law, Corrective Justice, and Its Utilitarian Constraints, 8 J. Legal Stud. 49 (1979); Epstein, A Theory of Strict Liability, 2 J. Legal Stud. 151 (1973).

Reducing the Judicial Burden. Strict liability avoids the substantial transaction costs in determining liability under a negligence or unreasonableness standard; a court can simply award damages in all cases where the defendant caused harm (of course, proving causation may be difficult and expensive.) Defendants would reduce pollution to the efficient control point (assuming perfect information), and would pay damages for the balance. Over the longer run, the polluter may modify its behavior for the various reasons already discussed.

4. *The Case Against Strict Liability*. What arguments could be mounted against strict liability? Consider the following four arguments:

Plaintiff Can More Cheaply Reduce Pollution Damages. In many cases, the pollution receptor is the "least cost avoider." In such cases, requiring the defendant to compensate the plaintiff would reduce or destroy the plaintiff's incentive to avoid harm. Does it follow that the plaintiff must prove she *cannot* reduce damages more cheaply, or should the defendant bear the burden of proof? Consider the nature of the information needed to decide who can more cheaply reduce damages, the access of the parties to that information, their ability to bear the costs of collecting information and taking appropriate measures, and the resulting incentives.[24]

Even if the plaintiff can reduce damages more cheaply, should she be denied any remedy? In *Waschak* some of the damage might have been avoided by using non-lead paint. Should the defendant have been required to compensate the plaintiff for the cost of using such paint? *Cf. Restatement (Second) of Torts* § 463 (contributory negligence is conduct "which falls below the standard to which he should conform for his own protection"); § 481 (plaintiff's contributory negligence does not bar recovery where infliction of harm by defendant was "intended"); § 918 (plaintiff cannot recover for harm that could have been avoided by "reasonable effort or expenditure" after injury has occurred); § 919 (plaintiff can recover for expenditures made as part of a "reasonable effort" to avoid or reduce harm.).

External Benefits From Polluting Activity. Polluting activities may provide benefits, such as employment and taxes, to the local communi-

---

24. Consider also the possibility that the market could correct judicial error. Which assignment of the burden would maximize the chances that decisions resulting in economic inefficiency would be corrected by private negotiation?

ty. Compensation for damages may cause a pollution source to close or reduce its operations.

Ideally, a polluter should bear its external costs, while those enjoying external benefits should contribute to ensure the polluter remains in business. Although courts traditionally have not attempted to make such benefits assessments, shouldn't they do so in the same way as they assess external costs? Are such benefits inherently more difficult to measure than external costs (remembering that to an economist, the damage caused by pollution is measured by the willingness to pay of those adversely affected)? Is assessment of external costs facilitated because those who suffer such costs voluntarily come into court as plaintiffs seeking redress? Does benefits assessment too closely resemble taxation for a court to undertake it without legislative authorization? *See generally* Calabresi & Melamed, Property Rules, Liability Rules and Inalienability: One View of the Cathedral, 85 Harv. L. Rev. 1089, 1116–23 (1972).

Given the difficulties of assessing and collecting contributions from those enjoying external benefits, a court might well conclude that it is better to permit a polluting activity to continue rather than to impose damage liability and thereby force a reduction or even shutdown of the polluter. One explanation for the development of doctrines limiting the liability of transportation and other industries in the nineteenth century is that courts were trying to protect emerging industries. *See generally* M. Horwitz, The Transformation of American Law 63–108 (1977). *But see* Schwartz, Tort Law and the Economy in Nineteenth–Century America: A Reinterpretation, 90 Yale L.J. 1717 (1981). Does this analysis justify the result in *Waschak*? How should the burdens of proof on the relevant issues be allocated?

Moral Objections to Strict Liability. The judicial development in the nineteenth century of "fault" as a basis for liability was viewed as a product of moral enlightenment. Professor George Fletcher has argued that defendants should be held liable for "disproportionate, excessive risk[s] of harm, relative to the victim's risk-creating activity. For example, a pilot or an airplane owner subjects those beneath the path of flight to nonreciprocal risks of harm. Conversely, cases of nonliability are those of reciprocal risks, namely those in which the victim and the defendant subject each other to roughly the same degree of risk. For example, two airplanes flying in the same vicinity subject each other to reciprocal risks of midair collision." Fletcher, Fairness and Utility in Tort Theory, 85 Harv. L. Rev. 537 (1972). Does Fletcher's analysis suggest that it would be unjust to permit one of two adjacent polluting factories to recover against the other for pollution damage?

Moral objections to strict polluter liability may be strongest if the plaintiff "came to the nuisance." In *Waschak*, the plaintiffs purchased their house with full knowledge that it was in a highly polluted area. Should this knowledge bar their recovery, either in a system requiring proof of "fault" or one based on strict liability?

Consider possible justifications for a "coming to the nuisance" defense. Is it needed to prevent windfall recoveries to plaintiffs, whose purchase prices already Had been discounted to reflect pollution damage? Or does this rationale beg the question? If property owners had a right to recover for pollution damage, would the market have discounted the property price?

Is the "coming to the nuisance" doctrine justified to prevent economically inefficient patterns of land use? Physical separation of polluters and those suffering from pollution is a potential alternative to technological controls. If would-be plaintiffs are free to locate near a pollution source and recover full damages, won't potential incentives for efficient land use patterns be undercut? On the other hand, would denial of damage provide an effective incentive to locate elsewhere? Consider the economic status of many of the people who live in heavily polluted areas. Even if the "coming to the nuisance" doctrine were justified by considerations of economic efficiency, would its adoption be contrary to principles of distributive justice?

Does "coming to the nuisance" justify the decision in *Waschak* on efficiency grounds? Two authors have suggested that some cases invoking the "coming to nuisance" defense are really justified on a "homogeneous community" principle governing cases where all members of the community participate in activities (such as using fossil fuel for home heating) that pose reciprocal burdens, or benefit from a central activity (such as pollution by an industrial plant that provides a town's economic livelihood) that spreads reciprocal costs (such as pollution) across everyone in the community. In these situations, external costs may be roughly matched or offset by benefits. The transaction costs involved in shifting damage may be largely wasted motion, and may not be justified by cost spreading considerations. Bryson & Macbeth, Public Nuisance, the Restatement (Second) of Torts, and Environmental Law, 2 Ecology L.Q. 241, 266–71 (1972).

Once plaintiffs have moved into an area and are unlikely to relocate, isn't denial of relief likely to yield an inefficient outcome? Should the government intervene to pay for pollution control? *See* Ellickson, Alternatives to Zoning: Covenants, Nuisance Rules and Fines as Land Use Controls, 40 U. Chi. L. Rev. 681, 760 (1973). Does this analysis suggest an appropriate judicial strategy for developing and applying damage liability doctrine in pollution cases?

The Transaction Costs of Imposing Strict Liability. Strict liability may involve substantial costs for courts and litigants. The resources saved by not proving "fault" might be swamped by the influx of new cases. Moreover, the resources saved by abandoning the fault requirement may be relatively modest. Plaintiffs must still show causation and damages; in environmental cases, causation is often an important issue involving extensive evidentiary submissions.

The social costs of insurance may be even more significant. In a system imposing liability on the polluter, the polluter will normally obtain third-party liability insurance. Under a system imposing liability upon the receptor, the receptor either bears the injuries or obtains first-party insur-ance. The direct and administrative costs of third-party insurance are estimated to be higher than the costs for first-party insurance coverage for the same set of injuries. *See* Priest, The Current Insurance Crisis and Modern Tort Law, 96 Yale L.J. 1521, 1550–60 (1987). However, first-party insurance dulls receptors' incentives to take preventative care if, as is often true, the insurance company does not classify insureds into sufficiently narrow risk pools and monitoring receptor conduct is costly. *See* Hanson and Logue, The First–Party Insurance Externality: An Economic Justifica-tion for Enterprise Liability, 76 Cornell L. Rev. 129, 131–32 (1990). Finally, some members of our society cannot afford or otherwise lack access to insurance.

How do the foregoing arguments aid your assessment of *Waschak*? Is *Waschak* a strong case to impose strict liability?

5. *An Emerging Trend Toward Strict Liability*. In part pushed by legal scholars, there has been a discernible and growing trend to apply strict liability in cases involving releases of toxic pollutants. The adoption of *Restatement (Second) of Torts* § 826(b) by the American Law Institute is one clear indication of this trend. *See* W. Rodgers, Environmental Law: Air and Water § 2.4 (1986). In addition, some state courts have adopted a rule of strict liability for harm caused by escaping substances, *e.g.*, *State v. Ventron*, 94 N.J. 473, 468 A.2d 150 (1983), and a number of legislatures—state and federal—have so provided by statute, *e.g.*, Minn. Stat. § 115B.04(1); 42 U.S.C. §§ 9601(32), 9607.

Is strict liability for environmental degradation capable of addressing the major environmental problems facing society? Consider the problems of urban air pollution, acid deposition, groundwater contamination, oil spills, and climate change.

Although the successful plaintiff always may recover damages, courts sometimes decline to award injunctive relief. In studying the following materials, consider how the choice between injunctive and damage relief (property and liability rules) might affect the efficiency of resource use. Recall the discussion of the Coase Theorem (and particularly the implica-tions of transaction costs) as well as the insights of Calabresi & Melamed's framework. In the frequent case of one or a few polluters and many victims, what would be the likely impact of a rule awarding victims damages for pollution injuries? What about a rule awarding any victim an injunction against any emissions?

If legal rules are or should be based on considerations other than economic efficiency, would it still be valuable to distinguish alternative forms of relief? For example, if environmental entitlements were grounded on moral principles, might it be appropriate to protect some such entitle-ments by property rules and others by liability rules? What role, if any, is there for rules of inalienability? *See generally* Polinsky, Resolving Nuisance

Disputes: The Simple Economics of Injunctive and Damages Remedies, 32 Stan. L. Rev. 1075 (1980).

Boomer v. Atlantic Cement Co.

Court of Appeals of New York, 1970.
26 N.Y.2d 219, 309 N.Y.S.2d 312, 257 N.E.2d 870.

■ BERGAN, J. Defendant operates a large cement plant near Albany. These are actions for injunction and damages by neighboring land owners alleging injury to property from dirt, smoke and vibration emanating from the plant. A nuisance has been found after trial, temporary damages have been allowed; but an injunction has been denied.

The public concern with air pollution arising from many sources in industry and in transportation is currently accorded ever wider recognition accompanied by a growing sense of responsibility in State and Federal Governments to control it. Cement plants are obvious sources of air pollution in the neighborhoods where they operate.

But there is now before the court private litigation in which individual property owners have sought specific relief from a single plant operation. The threshold question raised by the division of view on this appeal is whether the court should resolve the litigation between the parties now before it as equitably as seems possible; or whether, seeking promotion of the general public welfare, it should channel private litigation into broad public objectives.

A court performs its essential function when it decides the rights of parties before it. Its decision of private controversies may sometimes greatly affect public issues. Large questions of law are often resolved by the manner in which private litigation is decided. But this is normally an incident to the court's main function to settle controversy. It is a rare exercise of judicial power to use a decision in private litigation as a purposeful mechanism to achieve direct public objectives greatly beyond the rights and interests before the court.

Effective control of air pollution is a problem presently far from solution even with the full public financial powers of government. In large measure adequate technical procedures are yet to be developed and some that appear possible may be economically impracticable.

It seems apparent that the amelioration of air pollution will depend on technical research in great depth; on a carefully balanced consideration of the economic impact of close regulation; and of the actual effect on public health. It is likely to require massive public expenditure and to demand more than any local community can accomplish and to depend on regional and interstate controls.

A court should not try to do this on its own as a by-product of private litigation and it seems manifested that the judicial establishment is neither equipped in the limited nature of any judgment it can pronounce nor prepared to lay down and implement an effective policy for the elimination of air pollution. This is an area beyond the circumference of one private lawsuit. It is a direct responsibility for government and should not thus be undertaken as an incident to solving a dispute between property owners and a single cement plant—one of many—in the Hudson River valley.

The cement making operations of defendant have been found by the court at Special Term to have damaged the nearby properties of plaintiffs in these two actions. That court, as it has been noted, accordingly found defendant maintained a nuisance and this has been affirmed at the Appellate Division. The total damage to plaintiffs' properties is, however, relatively small in comparison with the value of defendant's operation and with the consequences of the injunction which plaintiffs seek.

The ground for the denial of injunction, notwithstanding the finding both that there is a nuisance and that plaintiffs have been damaged substantially, is the large disparity in economic consequences of the nuisance and of the injunction. This theory cannot, however, be sustained without overruling a doctrine which has been consistently reaffirmed in several leading cases in this court and which has never been disavowed here, namely that where a nuisance has been found and where there has been any substantial damage shown by the party complaining an injunction will be granted.

The rule in New York has been that such a nuisance will be enjoined although marked disparity be shown in economic consequence between the effect of the injunction and the effect of the nuisance. * * * Thus [under prior cases] if * * * the damage to plaintiffs in these present cases from defendant's cement plant is "not unsubstantial," an injunction should follow.

Although the court at Special Term and the Appellate Division held that injunction should be denied, it was found that plaintiffs had been damaged in various specific amounts up to the time of the trial and damages to the respective plaintiffs were awarded for those amounts. The effect of this was, injunction having been denied, plaintiffs could maintain successive actions at law for damages thereafter as further damage was incurred.

The court at Special Term also found the amount of permanent damage attributable to each plaintiff, for the guidance of the parties in the event both sides stipulated to the payment and acceptance of such permanent damage as a settlement of all the controversies among the parties. The total of permanent damages to all plaintiffs thus found was $185,000. This basis of adjustments has not resulted in any stipulation by the parties.

This result at Special Term and at the Appellate Division is a departure from a rule that has become settled; but to follow that rule literally in these cases would be to close down the plant at once. This court is fully agreed to avoid that immediately drastic remedy; the difference in view is how best to avoid it.[25]

One alternative is to grant the injunction but postpone its effect to a specified future date to give opportunity for technical advances to permit defendant to eliminate the nuisance; another is to grant the injunction conditioned on the payment of permanent damages to plaintiffs which would compensate them for the total economic loss to their property present and future caused by defendant's operations. For reasons which will be developed the court chooses the latter alternative.

If the injunction were to be granted unless within a short period—*e.g.*, 18 months—the nuisance be abated by improved methods, there would be no assurance that any significant technical improvement would occur.

The parties could settle this private litigation at any time if defendant paid enough money and the imminent threat of closing the plant would build up the pressure on defendant. If there were no improved techniques found, there would inevitably be applications to the court at Special Term for extensions of time to perform on showing of good faith efforts to find such techniques.

Moreover, techniques to eliminate dust and other annoying by-products of cement making are unlikely to be developed by any research the defendant can undertake within any short period, but will depend on the total resources of the cement industry Nationwide and throughout the world. The problem is universal wherever cement is made.

For obvious reasons the rate of the research is beyond control of defendant. If at the end of 18 months the whole industry has not found a technical solution a court would be hard put to close down this one cement plant if due regard be given to equitable principles.

On the other hand, to grant the injunction unless defendant pays plaintiffs such permanent damages as may be fixed by the court seems to do justice between the contending parties. All of the attributions of economic loss to the properties on which plaintiffs' complaints are based will have been redressed.

* * *

It seems reasonable to think that the risk of being required to pay permanent damages to injured property owners by cement plant owners would itself be a reasonable effective spur to research for improved techniques to minimize nuisance.

The power of the court to condition on equitable grounds the continuance of an injunction on the payment of permanent damages seems undoubted.* * *

25. Respondent's investment in the plant is in excess of $45,000,000. There are over 300 people employed there.

■ JASEN, J. (dissenting). I agree with the majority that a reversal is required here, but I do not subscribe to the newly enunciated doctrine of assessment of permanent damages, in lieu of an injunction, where substantial property rights have been impaired by the creation of a nuisance.

It has long been the rule in this State, as the majority acknowledges, that a nuisance which results in substantial continuing damage to neighbors must be enjoined. (*Whalen v. Union Bag & Paper Co.*, 208 N.Y. 1; *Campbell v. Seaman*, 63 N.Y. 568; *see also, Kennedy v. Moog Servocontrols*, 21 N.Y.2d 966.) To now change the rule to permit the cement company to continue polluting the air indefinitely upon the payment of permanent damages is, in my opinion, compounding the magnitude of a very serious problem in our State and Nation today.

In recognition of this problem, the Legislature of this State has enacted the Air Pollution Control Act (Public Health Law, §§ 1264–1299–m) declaring that it is the State policy to require the use of all available and reasonable methods to prevent and control air pollution (Public Health Law, § 1275). * * * We have [here] a nuisance which not only is damaging to the plaintiffs, but also is decidedly harmful to the general public. * * *

I see grave dangers in overruling our long-established rule of granting an injunction where a nuisance results in substantial continuing damage. In permitting the injunction to become inoperative upon the payment of permanent damages, the majority is, in effect, licensing a continuing wrong. It is the same as saying to the cement company, you may continue to do harm to your neighbors so long as you pay a fee for it. Furthermore, once such permanent damages are assessed and paid, the incentive to alleviate the wrong would be eliminated, thereby continuing air pollution of an area without abatement.

It is true that some courts have sanctioned the remedy here proposed by the majority in a number of cases, but none of the authorities relied upon by the majority are analogous to the situation before us. In those cases, the courts, in denying an injunction and awarding money damages, grounded their decision on a showing that the use to which the property was intended to be put was primarily for the public benefit. Here, on the other hand, it is clearly established that the cement company is creating a continuing air pollution nuisance primarily for its own private interest with no public benefit. * * *

I would enjoin the defendant cement company from continuing the discharge of dust particles upon its neighbors' properties unless, within 18 months, the cement company abated this nuisance.

It is not my intention to cause the removal of the cement plant from the Albany area, but to recognize the urgency of the problem stemming from this stationary source of air pollution, and to allow the company a specified period of time to develop a means to alleviate this nuisance.

I am aware that the trial court found that the most modern dust control devices available have been installed in defendant's plant, but, I submit, this does not mean that *better* and more effective dust control devices could not be developed within the time allowed to abate the pollution. * * *

———————

1. *Inadequacy of Liability Rules and the Need for Injunctive Relief.* Why shouldn't defendant's enterprise be required only to pay for the damages it caused? If it can pay damages and remain in business, the market has signaled that the benefits derived from the enterprise exceed its costs. If the enterprise cannot pay the damages and remain in business, the costs exceed the benefits, and an award of damages is equivalent to an injunction. What are counter-arguments to this position? *See* Calabresi, Some Thoughts on Risk Distribution and the Law of Torts, 70 Yale L.J. 499, 534–35 (1961); Polinsky, Resolving Nuisance Disputes: The Simple Economics of Injunctive and Damage Remedies, 32 Stan. L. Rev. 1075 (1980); Farber, Reassessing *Boomer*: Justice, Efficiency, and Nuisance Law, in Property Law and Legal Education: Essays in Honor of John E. Cribbet 7 (P. Hay & M. Hoeflich eds., 1988).

Is injunctive relief necessary to avoid the costs of repeated lawsuits to recover future damages as they accrue? Can't this difficulty be resolved by awarding permanent damages, as in *Boomer*? Will permanent damage awards necessarily deprive defendants of any incentive to modify their behavior to cause less pollution damage in the future? Could the terms of a permanent damage award be modified to restore this incentive?

Does *Boomer* affect incentives for industrial siting? Does it provide incentives to negotiate in advance for pollution easements? *See* Goldberg, Relational Exchange, Contract Law, and the *Boomer* Problem, in Readings in the Economics of Contract Law (V. Goldberg ed., 1989).

Could damage awards be inadequate because they fail to include all of the adverse effects of environmental degradation? For example, how could damage awards deal with an uncertain risk of future health damage from current pollution exposure? *See Potter v. Firestone Tire & Rubber Co.,* 6 Cal.4th 965, 25 Cal.Rptr.2d 550, 863 P.2d 795 (1993) (absent present physical injury, recovery for damages for fear of cancer is permitted only if the plaintiff proves that it is more likely than not that the plaintiff will develop cancer from the toxic exposure). Is a damage remedy appropriate for harms with a large psychic component, or those that inflict an individually small amount of damage on many individuals? Is injunctive relief better in these circumstances?

The dissent argues that the use of a liability rule is tantamount to "licensing" pollution. Is this argument persuasive? Does it comport with the principles underlying nuisance law generally?

2. *Right to an Absolute Injunction.* Should the plaintiff automatically be entitled to an injunction prohibiting any discharges by a polluter? Doesn't a rule limiting relief to damages effectively empower a polluter to "take" the plaintiff's property or health without plaintiff's consent upon

payment of compensation in an amount determined by third parties (judge and jury)? Should courts distinguish between pollution adversely affecting health and pollution injuring only property? Does this line of reasoning simply beg the question? Doesn't an injunction also take the defendant's property—an uncompensated taking at that?

Consider also the practical implications of automatically granting a prohibitory injunction. Wouldn't it lead to unjust enrichment by plaintiffs who could extort settlement payments in amounts far exceeding plaintiffs' damages? Moreover, where many potential plaintiffs are involved, doesn't the possibility that each one could obtain a prohibitory injunction threaten serious resource misallocation? *See* Polinsky, Resolving Nuisance Disputes: The Simple Economics of Injunctive and Damage Remedies, 32 Stan. L. Rev. 1075 (1980).

3. *Judicial Balancing of the Equities.* Courts today rarely grant prohibitory injunctions for nuisance on the simple theory that the plaintiff is entitled to prohibit an invasion of his property rights. Instead, courts will normally "balance the equities" to determine whether a damage award is inadequate or otherwise inappropriate. If it decides that injunctive relief is appropriate, it will further "balance the equities" to determine the appropriate form of injunctive relief; among the possibilities are an absolute prohibition, land use accommodations, technological requirements (*e.g.*, installation of new control technologies); and operational controls (*e.g.*, limitations on level or hours of operation). *See* W. Rodgers, Environmental Law: Air and Water § 2.13 (1986). For example, the dissenting judge in *Boomer* would have given defendant an 18–month "variance" to install superior controls.

How well equipped are courts to gather information on and assess the factors involved in framing an injunction that will achieve the socially optimal result? *See* Menell, The Limitations of Legal Institutions in Addressing Environmental Risks, 5 J. Econ. Persp., Summer 1991, at 93. Even if economic efficiency were the sole objective, what factors should a court consider in a case like *Boomer* to frame a decree that would provide an economically efficient solution? Shouldn't the court also consider the effects of the form of relief on the community at large? The court in *Boomer* seemed to believe it was not "channel[ing] private litigation into broad public objectives." Do you agree?

4. *Injunctions as a Spur to Technological Change.* We have already seen that the award of damages without regard to fault might provide an incentive to develop environmentally superior technologies. How could a court use injunctive relief to promote the development of new technologies? What is the likely success of severe measures, such as those contemplated by the *Boomer* dissent? Should the court instead require the defendant to undertake a specified program of research and development? Where a court awards injunctive relief that does not require a complete cessation of emissions, should it require defendant to pay, periodically, damages equal to the harm caused by its remaining emissions?

Problems

1. OK Ranch has operated a large cattle feedlot since the 1950's at its present location. When the cattle ranch was established, the neighboring area was rural with other cattle ranches in the vicinity. In the early 1960's, Smith Development Company acquired three large ranches in the area to develop a retirement community. Smith built a golf course and condominiums. The first units were more than 3 miles from OK Ranch. The retirement community gradually expanded until newer units were within half a mile of the ranch. Despite the use of good feedlot management, the stench and flies from the OK Ranch often made it uncomfortable if not unhealthy for residents of the retirement community to enjoy the outdoor living that attracted them to the area. Smith Development Company sues to enjoin operation of OK Ranch. How should this case be resolved? Who should get the entitlement? How should it be enforced? What if the residents were to sue as individuals? *See Spur Industries, Inc. v. Del E. Webb Development Co.*, 108 Ariz. 178, 494 P.2d 700 (1972).

2. Lake Tahoe, located high in the Sierra Nevada Mountains, has numerous hotels and vacation homes along its shores. Residents and visitors have panoramic views of the surrounding mountain peaks and they enjoy fishing and water sports at the lake and along the streams running to the lake. Sylvia Creek, the largest of the streams flowing to Lake Tahoe, is fed by high mountain streams that flow through Beltran Valley. There are also several ski resorts in the general vicinity of the lake.

Ronco Corp. owns a large tract of land on the western side of Beltran Valley. Maximus Corp. owns a large tract of land on the eastern side. These tracts hold beautiful old growth forests up to the tree line and pristine snow-covered peaks above. These tracts are largely inaccessible, except by foot on steep mountain trails.

Ronco Corp. plans to develop its land as a large ski resort. Under the plans, Ronco Corp. would clear the trees from the south-easterly slopes of the mountain (which drain to Sylvia Creek) to make room for a large-scale ski resort, including a hotel, two restaurants, multiple lifts, snowmaking equipment, and lighting for night skiing. Ronco Corp. also plans to build a roadway up through the remaining forest to reach a restaurant at the top of the mountain.

Maximus Corp., which has accumulated massive debt in recent years, plans to clear-cut large portions of its tract in Beltran Valley to generate cash. Given the remoteness of and harsh weather conditions in the eastern Beltran Valley, there are no non-timber economic uses of this land. In addition, clear-cutting is the only economically feasible way to harvest trees on this tract.

Local environmental groups object to Ronco Corp.'s proposed ski resort development and Maximus Corp.'s plans to clear-cut its tract because it would destroy the last pristine wilderness in this portion of the Sierra Nevada Mountains. The Lake Tahoe Chamber of Commerce believes that a ski resort would destroy the beautiful view from the lake and would compete with existing hotels and ski resorts. The Lake Tahoe Angler's Club is concerned that the ski resort and the clear-cutting on the Maximus Corp. tract will pollute Sylvia Creek and impair the bountiful trout run. Each of these groups also fear that the ski resort will lead to development of the entire Beltran Valley, which could destroy the watershed through erosion.

Which, if any of these groups, can bring a common law claim in trespass or nuisance against Ronco Corp. or Maximus Corp.? What is the likely outcome of such litigation?

---

5.   PROTECTION AGAINST GOVERNMENTAL TAKINGS

Government regulation of land use is widely seen as useful to prevent spillovers and to capture the benefits of coordinated development that may be lost in a private market. (We examine land use regulation in detail in Chapter V.) Unconstrained use of private property can result in serious conflicts among property owners and the public at large. Factories in a residential area can be unsightly, malodorous, and even dangerous. Spillovers from activities on one parcel may adversely affect common resources such as air, groundwater, or even entire ecosystems. For example, clearing trees on one parcel of land can disturb the watershed, thereby altering aquatic and forest ecosystems on adjacent and downstream parcels of land. Similarly, filling a wetland for a development project may threaten the survival of migratory waterfowl. Although nuisance law is available to address such spillovers, litigation is expensive, causation is often difficult or impossible to prove, and the remedy is backward-looking rather than preventive. Government regulation of land use may be the only practical means to prevent land-use conflicts and conserve common resources.

In addition to producing uncompensated spillovers, private ordering may fail to capture benefits, such as economies of scale, that can result from coordinated land use. Construction of infrastructure (*e.g.*, roads, sewer lines) may proceed more efficiently because the government can require uniform health and safety standards, anticipate and coordinate future growth, and eliminate wasteful duplication, whereas private development may be relatively inefficient because of freerider problems. Thus, there are substantial reasons for the government to regulate private land use.

At the same time, government regulation can go "too far." The Takings Clause of the Fifth Amendment[26] provides some protection against government overreaching. It states that the government may "take" private property only for "public use" and that the government must pay the owner "just compensation" for any such taking. The Takings Clause is an important component of any political and economic system that relies on

---

26. The Takings Clause is applicable to the states through the operation of the Fourteenth Amendment. *See Chicago, B. & Q. R. Co. v. Chicago*, 166 U.S. 226, 239, 17 S.Ct. 581, 585, 41 L.Ed. 979 (1897). In addition, state constitutions have takings clauses.

private property. It provides the security and predictability necessary for a market economy. Moreover, it reduces the temptation to finance government projects "off-budget." Thus, it both "bar[s] the Government from forcing some people alone to bear public burdens which, in all fairness and justice, should be borne by the public as a whole," *Armstrong v. United States*, 364 U.S. 40, 49, 80 S.Ct. 1563, 1569, 4 L.Ed.2d 1554 (1960), and, by forcing the government to rely on taxes rather than individual seizures, it promotes greater accountability in government decisionmaking. Finally, the Takings Clause, by protecting private property, protects individual autonomy from government intrusion.

Eminent Domain. The most obvious application of taking doctrine arises when the government decides to acquire title to land to build some public works, like a highway or a city park. In practice, taking doctrine is rarely if ever invoked in these circumstances because the government uses statutory "eminent domain" (also called "condemnation") procedures to acquire title and pay just compensation. The statutory procedures and compensation requirements provide at least as much protection for property owners as the constitutional doctrine. *See generally* J.L. Sackman, Nichols' The Law of Eminent Domain (1964).

Eminent domain procedures are government-initiated. The government entity typically will make an offer of compensation based on its assessment of fair market value, as well as its estimate of other costs (*e.g.*, relocation costs) if required by statute or ordinance.[27] Should the parties reach an impasse, the government may then initiate a judicial condemnation proceeding in which a court determines the reasonable market value of the condemned property interest and other legally compensable costs. The government may take the entire bundle of sticks—an entire parcel (or group of parcels)—or one or a few sticks—*e.g.*, by condemning a right of way for utility service—if done for a public purpose.[28] There is litigation

---

27. The Constitution requires compensation only for the market value of the property; additional compensation, if any, is paid under statutory authority.

28. The Takings Clause requires that government takings be for "public use." The Supreme Court has taken a highly deferential view of this requirement. For example, in *Berman v. Parker*, 348 U.S. 26 (1954), a landowner sought to enjoin a public redevelopment project under which his land was to be transferred (with compensation) to a private developer. He argued that the taking was not for "public use," both because the land would be developed and used privately and because it was being redeveloped for largely aesthetic reasons. The Court upheld the condemnation as constitutional. Viewing public use as defined by the government's traditional police power to regulate public

health, safety, welfare and morals, the Court held that it should defer to the legislature's judgment. "The concepts of the public welfare [which is part of the police power] is broad and inclusive.... The values it represents are spiritual as well as physical, aesthetic as well as monetary. It is within the power of the legislature to determine that the community should be beautiful as well as healthy, spacious as well as clean, well-balanced as well as carefully patrolled." *Id.* at 33. Thirty years later, in *Hawaii Housing Authority v. Midkiff*, 467 U.S. 229 (1984), the Court considered a challenge to a state law that authorized condemnation and redistribution of private land (with compensation). The purpose of the law was to achieve a more equitable distribution of residential land. The Court rejected the argument that a law which took private property and gave it to another private party was not for public use. Rather,

under the eminent domain statutes, but the usual question is the amount of compensation, not whether a taking has occurred.

Takings Cases. The question whether a taking has occurred arises more commonly not when the government has acquired title, but when it has done something—taken a physical action or adopted a regulation—that reduces the value of the property or that takes away some of the sticks in the bundle of rights. For example, government airplane flights over a residential area or over a farm might be a basis for "inverse condemnation," a property-owner initiated suit for damages under the Fifth Amendment. *See, e.g., United States v. Causby*, 328 U.S. 256, 261–66, 66 S.Ct. 1062, 1065–68, 90 L.Ed. 1206 (1946) (frequent, low-flying military flights, which destroyed the use of the property as a farm and which disrupted the property owner's use and enjoyment of the land appropriated an easement and thus required compensation under the Fifth Amendment). *See also Loretto v. Teleprompter Manhattan CATV Corp.*, 458 U.S. 419, 435–38, 102 S.Ct. 3164, 3176–78, 73 L.Ed.2d 868 (1982) (law requiring landlords to permit cable companies to place cables and other equipment on apartment buildings is a taking). Another example would be an environmental regulation that prevented the landowner from making any use of his property to protect barrier islands from erosion caused by construction. *See, e.g., Lucas v. South Carolina*, 505 U.S. 1003, 112 S.Ct. 2886, 120 L.Ed.2d 798 (1992) (state law barring construction of residence on beachfront property is a taking if it denied the landowner all "economically viable use of his land"). Takings cases are more difficult when the deprivation of rights is not complete and the public interest in the regulation is significant. *See, e.g., Penn Central Transportation Co. v. City of New York*, 438 U.S. 104, 98 S.Ct. 2646, 57 L.Ed.2d 631 (1978) (finding no taking as a result of a municipal historic preservation law that cost the landowner millions of dollars in foregone development opportunities).

Takings cases are notoriously difficult to decide.[29] The Supreme Court has not helped matters by pursuing an ad hoc, case-by-case approach. Carol

---

the public use requirement is "coterminous with the scope of the sovereign's police powers." *Id.* at 240, 104 S.Ct. 2321.

State courts, however, are free to impose a more restrictive definition of public use under state constitutional doctrines or statutes. *See, e.g., Petition of City of Seattle*, 96 Wash.2d 616, 628, 638 P.2d 549, 556 (1981) (holding that the city's transfer of private land to a private developer primarily for retail stores but also for a public park, a parking garage, and an art museum did not constitute public use since only a part of the property condemned was "devote[d] ... to truly public uses").

29. Perhaps because it is one of the most difficult areas of the law, takings doctrine has produced an enormous volume of

literature. Some of the important works include: Sax, Takings and the Police Power, 74 Yale L.J. 36 (1964); Michelman, Property, Utility, and Fairness: Comments on the Ethical Foundations of "Just Compensation Law," 80 Harv. L. Rev. 1165 (1967); Sax, Takings, Private Property and Public Rights, 81 Yale L.J. 149 (1971); B. Ackerman, Private Property and the Constitution, 67–113 (1977); Rose, *Mahon* Reconstructed: Why the Takings Issue is Still a Muddle, 57 S. Cal. L. Rev. 561 (1984); Blume & Rubinfeld, Compensation for Takings: An Economic Analysis, 72 Cal. L. Rev. 569 (1984); R. Epstein, Takings: Private Property and the Power of Eminent Domain (1985); Symposium, The Jurisprudence of Takings, 88 Colum. L. Rev. 1581 (1988); Peterson, The Takings Clause:

Rose traces this "muddle" in takings doctrine to two conflicting traditions supporting private property. One is the familiar utilitarian argument that "a country will accumulate wealth if it protects the ability to acquire, but that ability flourishes only where the laws assure some continuity in property expectations." Rose, *Mahon* Reconstructed: Why the Takings Issue is Still a Muddle, 57 S. Cal. L. Rev. 561, 586 (1984). A vigorously enforced Takings Clause would promote this purpose of private property.

The second tradition maintains that private property will "foster the independence and civic participation of a morally committed citizenry."

> The civic property tradition is significant, however, in that its argument for protection of property focused not on accumulating wealth, but rather on maintaining the liberty of a self-governing nation. The implication of this view is that property is to be protected only up to the bounds of some conception of civic and social responsibility.

Id. at 592. This argument recognizes the limits to private ordering, calling for a balancing approach to the interpretation of the Takings Clause.

Takings doctrine has divided into two principal lines of cases: those involving a permanent physical invasion, in which the Takings Clause is rigidly applied to require compensation (although the doctrine is more complicated if the invasion is a required dedication in exchange for a building permit), and those government actions which regulate land use ("regulatory takings"), in which compensation frequently is not required.

Physical Invasion. In permanent physical invasion cases, the government has seized private land for some government purpose. In the leading case, *Loretto v. Teleprompter Manhattan CATV Corp.*, 458 U.S. 419, 102 S.Ct. 3164, 73 L.Ed.2d 868 (1982), a state statute required residential landlords to permit cable television companies to install cables and other equipment on apartment buildings. Although the use of the landlord's property was quite small—consisting of cables on the roof and side of the building and two small boxes on the roof—the Court held that such a permanent physical invasion was a taking regardless of the importance of the government interests served or the economic impact on the landowner. *Id.* at 434–35, 102 S.Ct. at 3175–76.

In Search of Underlying Principles—Part I: A Critique of Current Takings Clause Doctrine, 77 Cal. L. Rev. 1301 (1990); Peterson, The Takings Clause: In Search of Underlying Principles—Part II: Takings As Intentional Deprivations of Property Without Moral Justification, 78 Cal. L. Rev. 53 (1990); Treanor, The Original Understanding of the Takings Clause and the Political Process, 95 Colum. L. Rev. 782 (1995); W. Fischel, Regulatory Takings: Law, Economics, and Politics (1995).

For articles that look at the historical origins and development of takings law, see Ely, "That due satisfaction may be made": The Fifth Amendment and the Origin of the Compensation Principle, 36 Am. J. Leg. Hist. 1 (1992); Comment, The Origins and Original Significance of the Just Compensation Clause of the Fifth Amendment, 94 Yale L.J. 694 (1985); Reznick, Land Use Regulation and the Concept of Takings in Nineteenth Century America, 40 U. Chi. L. Rev. 854 (1973).

The Court identified several reasons for its holding. First, the Court emphasized that of all the rights that collectively describe property, the right to possess and the right to exclude are the most significant; a permanent physical invasion destroys those rights. *Id.* at 435, 102 S.Ct. at 3176. Second, a permanent physical occupation "is qualitatively more severe than a regulation of the use of property, even a regulation that imposes affirmative duties on the owner, since the owner may have no control over the timing, extent, or nature of the invasion." *Id.* at 436, 102 S.Ct. at 3176. Third, the Court believed that the bright-line rule announced in this decision would be relatively easy to administer. *Id.* at 436–38, 102 S.Ct. at 3176–78. Although it did not say so, the Court may also have been influenced by the course of regulatory takings doctrine (discussed below), which has been unable to establish clear criteria and which consequently has tolerated substantial government control of private property.

Loretto contained a strongly worded dissent, which pointed out the incoherence of the Court's holding: any permanent physical occupation, no matter how small, is always deemed a taking, whereas a regulatory devaluation of millions of dollars is not necessarily a taking. *See, e.g., Penn Central Transportation Co. v. City of New York*, 438 U.S. 104, 98 S.Ct. 2646, 57 L.Ed.2d 631 (1978).

A related set of takings cases involve mandatory dedications–requirements that landowners (typically developers) dedicate some property interest, such as an easement or even a fee simple absolute, in exchange for building permits. In such cases, the government does not just demand physical access to the land (as in *Loretto*), but also legal title to the property. Mandatory dedications are quite common in large-scale residential and commercial developments; municipalities, routinely demand development and dedication of streets, sidewalks, and even parks, schools, and sewage treatment facilities. *See* Chapter V, *infra*, pp. 1032–65.

In *Nollan v. California Coastal Comm'n*, 483 U.S. 825, 107 S.Ct. 3141, 97 L.Ed.2d 677 (1987), the state Coastal Commission demanded that a homeowner, who wanted to build a larger house in a specially protected coastal zone, dedicate a public easement across his beachfront property in exchange for a building permit. The Court first observed that the required dedication was closely related to a permanent physical invasion. Citing *Loretto*, the Court stated "We think a 'permanent physical occupation' has occurred * * * where individuals are given a permanent and continuous right to pass to and fro." *Id.* at 832, 107 S.Ct. at 3146. Nonetheless, the Court noted that the dedication might not constitute a taking if it served some legitimate police power purpose.

> Although such a requirement, constituting a permanent grant of continuous access to property, would have to be considered a taking if it were not attached to a development permit, the Commission's assumed power to forbid construction of the house in order to protect the public's view of the beach must surely include the power to condition construction upon some concession of property rights, that serves the same end.

Id. at 836, 107 S.Ct. at 3148. The Court, however, found that the dedication (which would allow the public to walk across the beach) did not substantially advance the (presumed) legitimate purpose of protecting public views from the road. *Id.* at 838–41, 107 S.Ct. at 3149–51.

In *Dolan v. City of Tigard*, 512 U.S. 374, 114 S.Ct. 2309, 129 L.Ed.2d 304 (1994), *infra*, pp. 1049–63, the landowner wanted to expand her hardware store. In exchange for the necessary building permit, the city demanded dedication of adjacent land as open space and dedication of other land for a bicycle path. The city's express concerns were that the adjacent land was subject to flooding and should not be developed, and that the expanded hardware store would generate additional traffic, which the bicycle path would help alleviate. After finding the "essential nexus" between the required dedications and the legitimate state interest, as required under *Nollan*, *id.* at 386–88, 114 S.Ct. at 2317–18, the Court then asked whether the proposed dedications bore a "rough proportionality," in their nature and extent, to the impact of the proposed development. Placing the burden of proof on the municipality, *id.* at 391–95, 114 S.Ct. at 2319–21, the Court held that while the city could restrict development in the flood zone without effecting a taking, the dedication of the fee simple absolute—which would require the landowner to surrender her right to exclude and permit the public to use the land as a park—was disproportionate to city's interest in preventing damage from flooding. Regarding the dedication for the bicycle path, the Court held that "the city has not met its burden of demonstrating that the additional number of vehicle and bicycle trips generated by the [proposed hardware store] reasonably relate to the city's requirement for a dedication of the pedestrian/bicycle pathway easement." *Id.* at 395, 114 S.Ct. at 2321. Although it struck down both of these dedications, the Court made clear that it would uphold dedications in many circumstances. "Dedications for streets, sidewalks, and other public ways are generally reasonable exactions to avoid excessive congestion from a proposed property use." *Id.* at ___, 114 S.Ct. at 2321.

---

1. Are you persuaded by the *Loretto* majority's reasons for the rule it adopts in permanent physical invasion cases? Why should the Court be unwilling to weigh the type or degree of public interest when deciding whether there has been a taking in such cases?

2. Does *Loretto* mean that the government cannot require landlords to install various features for the safety and comfort of tenants, such as mailboxes, appropriate lighting, door locks, and utilities?

3. How is *Loretto*, which seems to draw a bright line rule declaring all permanent physical invasions to be a taking, consonant with *Nollan v. California Coastal Comm'n*, 483 U.S. 825, 107 S.Ct. 3141, 97 L.Ed.2d 677 (1987), and *Dolan v. City of Tigard*, 512 U.S. 374, 114 S.Ct. 2309, 129 L.Ed.2d 304 (1994), where the Court indicated that it would uphold mandatory dedications in certain circumstances?

4.   How difficult will it be to show the "essential nexus" required in *Nollan*? Through what sort of evidence will the government demonstrate the nexus? Why did the Court place the burden of proving rough proportionality on the government? How significant is the *Dolan* criterion? We return to these issues in Chapter V, *infra*, pp. 1032–65.

———————

Regulatory Takings. Regulatory takings arise when the government has restricted the use of privately owned land (but not acquired permanent possession or title, as in a permanent physical invasion case or in eminent domain) to such an extent that compensation is required. Of course, every land use regulation "takes" some right and therefore devalues the property to some extent. Although Justice Holmes decried "the petty larceny of the police power," 1 Holmes-Laski Letters 457 (M. Howe ed., 1953), he also noted that deeming every regulation a taking is unacceptable if only because the government in a complex, densely populated industrial society "could hardly go on if to some extent values incident to property could not be diminished without paying for every such change in the general law." *Pennsylvania Coal Co. v. Mahon*, 260 U.S. 393, 413, 43 S.Ct. 158, 159, 67 L.Ed. 322 (1922). Thus, the principal legal problem in regulatory takings cases is where to draw the line between government regulations requiring compensation and those that may proceed without compensation.

One of the first regulatory takings cases was *Hadacheck v. Sebastian*, 239 U.S. 394, 36 S.Ct. 143, 60 L.Ed. 348 (1915), which upheld a municipal ordinance barring the operation of an existing brick mill in a residential area. The Court was unsympathetic to the fact that the brick mill was in operation before nearby residences were built. "To so hold [in favor of the brick mill] would preclude development and fix a city forever in its primitive condition. There must be progress and if in its march private interests are in the way they must yield to the good of the community." *Id.* at 410, 36 S.Ct. at 145.

A few years later, in *Pennsylvania Coal Co. v. Mahon*, 260 U.S. 393, 43 S.Ct. 158, 67 L.Ed. 322 (1922), the Court struck down a state statute that barred the underground mining of coal if the mining would cause subsidence of land underneath residences on the surface. In *Mahon*, the coal company owned only the subsurface rights to remove the coal; according to the Court, the statute went "too far" and effectively terminated those subsurface rights.[30] The Court, however, did not give much guidance as to when a regulation went "too far."

The Court did not undertake a detailed reexamination of regulatory takings doctrine in land use cases until the *Penn Central* case in 1978. In the meantime, of course, the Court had decided *Euclid v. Ambler Realty Co.*, 272 U.S. 365, 47 S.Ct. 114, 71 L.Ed. 303 (1926) (upholding significant

---

30. Today, such a statute would be readily upheld. *See Keystone Bituminous Coal Ass'n v. DeBenedictis*, 480 U.S. 470, 107 S.Ct. 1232, 94 L.Ed.2d 472 (1987) (upholding a strikingly similar statute against a takings challenge).

restrictions on land use as part of a municipal zoning plan)[31] and *Berman v. Parker*, 348 U.S. 26, 75 S.Ct. 98, 99 L.Ed. 27 (1954) (upholding aesthetic zoning). Although *Euclid* and *Berman* were substantive due process cases and not takings cases, they stood for the proposition that the police powers to regulate land were quite broad and they signaled the Court's growing deference to intrusive land-use regulation.

Penn Central Transportation Co. v. City of New York

Supreme Court of the United States, 1978.
438 U.S. 104, 98 S.Ct. 2646, 57 L.Ed.2d 631.

■ MR. JUSTICE BRENNAN delivered the opinion of the Court.

The question presented is whether a city may, as part of a comprehensive program to preserve historic landmarks and historic districts, place restrictions on the development of individual historic landmarks—in addition to those imposed by applicable zoning ordinances—without effecting a "taking" requiring the payment of "just compensation." Specifically, we must decide whether the application of New York City's Landmarks Preservation Law to the parcel of land occupied by Grand Central Terminal has "taken" its owners' property in violation of the Fifth and Fourteenth Amendments.

I

A

Over the past 50 years, all 50 States and over 500 municipalities have enacted laws to encourage or require the preservation of buildings and areas with historic or aesthetic importance.[32] These nationwide legislative efforts have been precipitated by two concerns. The first is recognition that, in recent years, large numbers of historic structures, landmarks, and areas have been destroyed without adequate consideration of either the values represented therein or the possibility of preserving the destroyed properties for use in economically productive ways. The second is a widely shared belief that structures with special historic, cultural, or architectural significance enhance the quality of life for all. Not only do these buildings and their workmanship represent the lessons of the past and embody precious features of our heritage, they serve as examples of quality for today. "[H]istoric conservation is but one aspect of the much larger problem,

---

31.   *See* Chapter V at pp. 901–08.

32.   *See* National Trust for Historic Preservation, A Guide to State Historic Preservation Programs (1976); National Trust for Historic Preservation, Directory of Landmark and Historic District Commissions (1976). In addition to these state and municipal legislative efforts, Congress has determined that "the historical and cultural foundations of the Nation should be preserved as a living part of our community life and development in order to give a sense of orientation to the American people," National Historic Preservation Act of 1966, 80 Stat. 915, 16 U.S.C. § 470(b) (1976 ed.), and has enacted a series of measures designed to encourage preservation of sites and structures of historic, architectural, or cultural significance. *See generally* Gray, The Response of Federal Legislation to Historic Preservation, 36 Law & Contemp. Prob. 314 (1971).

basically an environmental one, of enhancing—or perhaps developing for the first time—the quality of life for people.''

New York City, responding to similar concerns and acting pursuant to a New York State enabling Act,[33] adopted its Landmarks Preservation Law in 1965. *See* N.Y.C. Admin. Code, ch. 8–A, § 205–1.0 et seq. (1976). The city acted from the conviction that "the standing of [New York City] as a worldwide tourist center and world capital of business, culture and government" would be threatened if legislation were not enacted to protect historic landmarks and neighborhoods from precipitate decisions to destroy or fundamentally alter their character. § 205–1.0(a). The city believed that comprehensive measures to safeguard desirable features of the existing urban fabric would benefit its citizens in a variety of ways: *e.g.*, fostering "civic pride in the beauty and noble accomplishments of the past"; protecting and enhancing "the city's attractions to tourists and visitors"; "support[ing] and stimul[ating] business and industry"; "strengthen[ing] the economy of the city"; and promoting "the use of historic districts, landmarks, interior landmarks and scenic landmarks for the education, pleasure and welfare of the people of the city." § 205–1.0(b).

The New York City law is typical of many urban landmark laws in that its primary method of achieving its goals is not by acquisitions of historic properties,[34] but rather by involving public entities in land-use decisions affecting these properties and providing services, standards, controls, and incentives that will encourage preservation by private owners and users. While the law does place special restrictions on landmark properties as a necessary feature to the attainment of its larger objectives, the major theme of the law is to ensure the owners of any such properties both a "reasonable return" on their investments and maximum latitude to use their parcels for purposes not inconsistent with the preservation goals.

The operation of the law can be briefly summarized. The primary responsibility for administering the law is vested in the Landmarks Preservation Commission (Commission), a broad based, 11–member agency[35]

33. *See* N.Y. Gen. Mun.Law § 96–a (McKinney 1977). It declares that it is the public policy of the State of New York to preserve structures and areas with special historical or aesthetic interest or value and authorizes local governments to impose reasonable restrictions to perpetuate such structures and areas.

34. The consensus is that widespread public ownership of historic properties in urban settings is neither feasible nor wise. Public ownership reduces the tax base, burdens the public budget with costs of acquisitions and maintenance, and results in the preservation of public buildings as museums and similar facilities, rather than as economically productive features of the urban scene. *See* Wilson & Winkler, The Response of State Legislation to Historic Preservation, 36 Law

& Contemp. Prob. 329, 330–331, 339–340 (1971).

35. The ordinance creating the Commission requires that it include at least three architects, one historian qualified in the field, one city planner or landscape architect, one realtor, and at least one resident of each of the city's five boroughs. N.Y.C. Charter § 534 (1976). In addition to the ordinance's requirements concerning the composition of the Commission, there is, according to a former chairman, a "prudent tradition" that the Commission include one or two lawyers, preferably with experience in municipal government, and several laymen with no specialized qualifications other than concern for the good of the city. Goldstone, Aesthetics in Historic Districts, 36 Law & Contemp. Prob. 379, 384–385 (1971).

assisted by a technical staff. The Commission first performs the function, critical to any landmark preservation effort, of identifying properties and areas that have "a special character or special historical or aesthetic interest or value as part of the development, heritage or cultural characteristics of the city, state or nation." § 207–1.0(n); *see* § 207–1.0(h). If the Commission determines, after giving all interested parties an opportunity to be heard, that a building or area satisfies the ordinance's criteria, it will designate a building to be a "landmark," § 207–1.0(n), situated on a particular "landmark site," § 207–1.0(*o*), or will designate an area to be a "historic district," § 207–1.0(h). After the Commission makes a designation, New York City's Board of Estimate, after considering the relationship of the designated property "to the master plan, the zoning resolution, projected public improvements and any plans for the renewal of the area involved," § 207–2.0(g)(1), may modify or disapprove the designation, and the owner may seek judicial review of the final designation decision. Thus far, 31 historic districts and over 400 individual landmarks have been finally designated, and the process is a continuing one.

Final designation as a landmark results in restrictions upon the property owner's options concerning use of the landmark site. First, the law imposes a duty upon the owner to keep the exterior features of the building "in good repair" to assure that the law's objectives not be defeated by the landmark's falling into a state of irremediable disrepair. *See* § 207–10.0(a). Second, the Commission must approve in advance any proposal to alter the exterior architectural features of the landmark or to construct any exterior improvement on the landmark site, thus ensuring that decisions concerning construction on the landmark site are made with due consideration of both the public interest in the maintenance of the structure and the landowner's interest in use of the property. *See* §§ 207–4.0 to 207–9.0.

In the event an owner wishes to alter a landmark site, three separate procedures are available through which administrative approval may be obtained. First, the owner may apply to the Commission for a "certificate of no effect on protected architectural features": that is, for an order approving the improvement or alteration on the ground that it will not change or affect any architectural feature of the landmark and will be in harmony therewith. *See* § 207–5.0. Denial of the certificate is subject to judicial review.

Second, the owner may apply to the Commission for a certificate of "appropriateness." *See* § 207–6.0. Such certificates will be granted if the Commission concludes—focusing upon aesthetic, historical, and architectural values—that the proposed construction on the landmark site would not unduly hinder the protection, enhancement, perpetuation, and use of the landmark. Again, denial of the certificate is subject to judicial review. Moreover, the owner who is denied either a certificate of no exterior effect or a certificate of appropriateness may submit an alternative or modified plan for approval. The final procedure—seeking a certificate of appropriateness on the ground of "insufficient return," *see* § 207–8.0—provides special mechanisms, which vary depending on whether or not the landmark enjoys a tax exemption,[36] to ensure that designation does not cause economic hardship.

Although the designation of a landmark and landmark site restricts the owner's control over the parcel, designation also enhances the economic position of the landmark owner in one significant respect. Under New York City's zoning laws, owners of real property who have not developed their property to the full extent permitted by the applicable zoning laws are allowed to transfer development rights to contiguous parcels on the same city block. *See* New York City, Zoning Resolution Art. I, ch. 2, § 12–10 (1978) (definition of "zoning lot"). A 1968 ordinance gave the owners of landmark sites additional opportunities to transfer development rights to other parcels. Subject to a restriction that the floor area of the transferee lot may not be increased by more than 20% above its authorized level, the ordinance permitted transfers from a landmark parcel to property across the street or across a street intersection. In 1969, the law governing the conditions under which transfers from landmark parcels could occur was liberalized, *see* New York City Zoning Resolutions 74–79 to 74–793, apparently to ensure that the Landmarks Law would not unduly restrict the development options of the owners of Grand Central Terminal. *See* Marcus, Air Rights Transfers in New York City, 36 Law & Contemp. Prob. 372, 375

---

36. If the owner of a non-tax-exempt parcel has been denied certificates of appropriateness for a proposed alteration and shows that he is not earning a reasonable return on the property in its present state, the Commission and other city agencies must assume the burden of developing a plan that will enable the landmark owner to earn a reasonable return on the landmark site. The plan may include, but need not be limited to, partial or complete tax exemption, remission of taxes, and authorizations for alterations, construction, or reconstruction appropriate for and not inconsistent with the purposes of the law. § 207–8.0(c). The owner is free to accept or reject a plan devised by the Commission and approved by the other city agencies. If he accepts the plan, he proceeds to operate the property pursuant to the plan. If he rejects the plan, the Commission may recommend that the city proceed by eminent domain to acquire a protective interest in the landmark, but if the city does not do so within a specified time period, the Commission must issue a notice allowing the property owner to proceed with the alteration or improvement as originally proposed in his application for a certificate of appropriateness. Tax-exempt structures are treated somewhat differently. They become eligible for special treatment only if four preconditions are satisfied: (1) the owner previously entered into an agreement to sell the parcel that was contingent upon the issuance of a certificate of approval; (2) the property, as it exists at the time of the request, is not capable of earning a reasonable return; (3) the structure is no longer suitable to its past or present purposes; and (4) the prospective buyer intends to alter the landmark structure. In the event the owner demonstrates that the property in its present state is not earning a reasonable return, the Commission must either find another buyer for it or allow the sale and construction to proceed. But this is not the only remedy available for owners of tax-exempt landmarks. As the case at bar illustrates, if an owner files suit and establishes that he is incapable of earning a "reasonable return" on the site in its present state, he can be afforded judicial relief. Similarly, where a landmark owner who enjoys a tax exemption has demonstrated that the landmark structure, as restricted, is totally inadequate for the owner's "legitimate needs," the law has been held invalid as applied to that parcel. *See Lutheran Church v. City of New York*, 35 N.Y.2d 121, 359 N.Y.S.2d 7, 316 N.E.2d 305 (1974).

(1971). The class of recipient lots was expanded to include lots "across a street and opposite to another lot or lots which except for the intervention of streets or street intersections f[or]m a series extending to the lot occupied by the landmark building[, provided that] all lots [are] in the same ownership." New York City Zoning Resolution 74–79 (emphasis deleted).[37] In addition, the 1969 amendment permits, in highly commercialized areas like midtown Manhattan, the transfer of all unused development rights to a single parcel. *Ibid.*

B

This case involves the application of New York City's Landmarks Preservation Law to Grand Central Terminal (Terminal). The Terminal, which is owned by the Penn Central Transportation Co. and its affiliates (Penn Central), is one of New York City's most famous buildings. Opened in 1913, it is regarded not only as providing an ingenious engineering solution to the problems presented by urban railroad stations, but also as a magnificent example of the French beaux-arts style.

The Terminal is located in midtown Manhattan. Its south facade faces 42d Street and that street's intersection with Park Avenue. At street level, the Terminal is bounded on the west by Vanderbilt Avenue, on the east by the Commodore Hotel, and on the north by the Pan–American Building. Although a 20–story office tower, to have been located above the Terminal, was part of the original design, the planned tower was never constructed.[38] The Terminal itself is an eight-story structure which Penn Central uses as a railroad station and in which it rents space not needed for railroad purposes to a variety of commercial interests. The Terminal is one of a number of properties owned by appellant Penn Central in this area of midtown Manhattan. The others include the Barclay, Biltmore, Commodore, Roosevelt, and Waldorf–Astoria Hotels, the Pan–American Building and other office buildings along Park Avenue, and the Yale Club. At least eight of these are eligible to be recipients of development rights afforded the Terminal by virtue of landmark designation.

On August 2, 1967, following a public hearing, the Commission designated the Terminal a "landmark" and designated the "city tax block" it occupies a "landmark site."[39] The Board of Estimate confirmed this action

37. To obtain approval for a proposed transfer, the landmark owner must follow the following procedure. First, he must obtain the permission of the Commission which will examine the plans for the development of the transferee lot to determine whether the planned construction would be compatible with the landmark. Second, he must obtain the approbation of New York City's Planning Commission which will focus on the effects of the transfer on occupants of the buildings in the vicinity of the transferee lot and whether the landmark owner will preserve the landmark. Finally, the matter goes to the Board of Estimate, which has final authority to grant or deny the application. *See also* Costonis, The Chicago Plan: Incentive Zoning and the Preservation of Urban Landmarks, 85 Harv. L. Rev. 574, 585–586 (1972).

38. The Terminal's present foundation includes columns, which were built into it for the express purpose of supporting the proposed 20–story tower.

39. The Commission's report stated:

Grand Central Station, one of the great buildings of America, evokes a spirit that is unique in this City. It combines distin-

on September 21, 1967. Although appellant Penn Central had opposed the designation before the Commission, it did not seek judicial review of the final designation decision.

On January 22, 1968, appellant Penn Central, to increase its income, entered into a renewable 50–year lease and sublease agreement with appellant UGP Properties, Inc. (UGP), a wholly owned subsidiary of Union General Properties, Ltd., a United Kingdom corporation. Under the terms of the agreement, UGP was to construct a multistory office building above the Terminal. UGP promised to pay Penn Central $1 million annually during construction and at least $3 million annually thereafter. The rentals would be offset in part by a loss of some $700,000 to $1 million in net rentals presently received from concessionaires displaced by the new building.

Appellants UGP and Penn Central then applied to the Commission for permission to construct an office building atop the Terminal. Two separate plans, both designed by architect Marcel Breuer and both apparently satisfying the terms of the applicable zoning ordinance, were submitted to the Commission for approval. The first, Breuer I, provided for the construction of a 55–story office building, to be cantilevered above the existing facade and to rest on the roof of the Terminal. The second, Breuer II Revised, called for tearing down a portion of the Terminal that included the 42d Street facade, stripping off some of the remaining features of the Terminal's facade, and constructing a 53–story office building. The Commission denied a certificate of no exterior effect on September 20, 1968. Appellants then applied for a certificate of "appropriateness" as to both proposals. After four days of hearings at which over 80 witnesses testified, the Commission denied this application as to both proposals.

The Commission's reasons for rejecting certificates respecting Breuer II Revised are summarized in the following statement: "To protect a Landmark, one does not tear it down. To perpetuate its architectural features, one does not strip them off." Breuer I, which would have preserved the existing vertical facades of the present structure, received more sympathetic consideration. The Commission first focused on the effect that the proposed tower would have on one desirable feature created by the present structure and its surroundings: the dramatic view of the Terminal from Park Avenue South. Although appellants had contended that the Pan–American Building had already destroyed the silhouette of the south facade and that one additional tower could do no further damage and might even provide a better background for the facade, the Commission disagreed, stating that it found the majestic approach from the south to be still unique in the city and that a 55–story tower atop the Terminal would be far more detrimental to its south facade than the Pan–American Building 375 feet away. Moreover, the Commission found that from closer vantage points the

guished architecture with a brilliant engineering solution, wedded to one of the most fabulous railroad terminals of our time. Monumental in scale, this great building functions as well today as it did when built. In style, it represents the best of the French Beaux Arts.

Pan Am Building and the other towers were largely cut off from view, which would not be the case of the mass on top of the Terminal planned under Breuer I. In conclusion, the Commission stated:

> [We have] no fixed rule against making additions to designated buildings—it all depends on how they are done * * * But to balance a 55–story office tower above a flamboyant Beaux–Arts facade seems nothing more than an aesthetic joke. Quite simply, the tower would overwhelm the Terminal by its sheer mass. The "addition" would be four times as high as the existing structure and would reduce the Landmark itself to the status of a curiosity.

> Landmarks cannot be divorced from their settings—particularly when the setting is a dramatic and integral part of the original concept. The Terminal, in its setting, is a great example of urban design. Such examples are not so plentiful in New York City that we can afford to lose any of the few we have. And we must preserve them in a meaningful way—with alterations and additions of such character, scale, materials and mass as will protect, enhance and perpetuate the original design rather than overwhelm it.

Appellants did not seek judicial review of the denial of either certificate. Because the Terminal site enjoyed a tax exemption, remained suitable for its present and future uses, and was not the subject of a contract of sale, there were no further administrative remedies available to appellants as to the Breuer I and Breuer II Revised plans. Further, appellants did not avail themselves of the opportunity to develop and submit other plans for the Commission's consideration and approval. Instead, appellants filed suit in New York Supreme Court, Trial Term, claiming, *inter alia*, that the application of the Landmarks Preservation Law had "taken" their property without just compensation in violation of the Fifth and Fourteenth Amendments and arbitrarily deprived them of their property without due process of law in violation of the Fourteenth Amendment. Appellants sought a declaratory judgment, injunctive relief barring the city from using the Landmarks Law to impede the construction of any structure that might otherwise lawfully be constructed on the Terminal site, and damages for the "temporary taking" that occurred between August 2, 1967, the designation date, and the date when the restrictions arising from the Landmarks Law would be lifted. The trial court granted the injunctive and declaratory relief, but severed the question of damages for a "temporary taking."

     * * *

II

The issues presented by appellants are (1) whether the restrictions imposed by New York City's law upon appellants' exploitation of the Terminal site effect a "taking" of appellants' property for a public use within the meaning of the Fifth Amendment, which of course is made applicable to the States through the Fourteenth Amendment, *see Chicago, B. & Q. R. Co. v. Chicago*, 166 U.S. 226, 239 (1897), and, (2), if so, whether the transferable development rights afforded appellants constitute "just compensation" within the meaning of the Fifth Amendment. We need only address the question whether a "taking" has occurred.[40]

Before considering appellants' specific contentions, it will be useful to review the factors that have shaped the jurisprudence of the Fifth Amendment injunction "nor shall private property be taken for public use, without just compensation." The question of what constitutes a "taking" for purposes of the Fifth Amendment has proved to be a problem of considerable difficulty. While this Court has recognized that the "Fifth Amendment's guarantee . . . [is] designed to bar Government from forcing some people alone to bear public burdens which, in all fairness and justice, should be borne by the public as a whole," *Armstrong v. United States*, 364 U.S. 40, 49 (1960), this Court, quite simply, has been unable to develop any "set formula" for determining when "justice and fairness" require that economic injuries caused by public action be compensated by the government, rather than remain disproportionately concentrated on a few persons. *See Goldblatt v. Hempstead*, 369 U.S. 590, 594 (1962). Indeed, we have frequently observed that whether a particular restriction will be rendered invalid by the government's failure to pay for any losses proximately caused by it depends largely "upon the particular circumstances [in that] case." *United States v. Central Eureka Mining Co.*, 357 U.S. 155, 168 (1958); *see United States v. Caltex, Inc.*, 344 U.S. 149, 156 (1952).

In engaging in these essentially ad hoc, factual inquiries, the Court's decisions have identified several factors that have particular significance. The economic impact of the regulation on the claimant and, particularly, the extent to which the regulation has interfered with distinct investment-backed expectations are, of course, relevant considerations. *See Goldblatt v. Hempstead, supra*, 369 U.S., at 594. So, too, is the character of the governmental action. A "taking" may more readily be found when the interference with property can be characterized as a physical invasion by government, *see, e.g., United States v. Causby*, 328 U.S. 256 (1946), than when interference arises from some public program adjusting the benefits and burdens of economic life to promote the common good.

"Government hardly could go on if to some extent values incident to property could not be diminished without paying for every such change in the general law," *Pennsylvania Coal Co. v. Mahon*, 260 U.S. 393, 413 (1922), and this Court has accordingly recognized, in a wide variety of contexts, that government may execute laws or programs that adversely affect recognized economic values. Exercises of the taxing power are one obvious example. A second are the decisions in which this Court has dismissed "taking" challenges on the ground that, while the challenged government action caused economic harm, it did not interfere with interests that were sufficiently bound up with the reasonable expectations of the claimant to constitute "property" for Fifth Amendment purposes. *See, e.g.*,

---

40. As is implicit in our opinion, we do not embrace the proposition that a "taking" can never occur unless government has transferred physical control over a portion of a parcel.

United States v. Willow River Power Co., 324 U.S. 499 (1945) (interest in high-water level of river for runoff for tailwaters to maintain power head is not property); *United States v. Chandler–Dunbar Water Power Co.*, 229 U.S. 53 (1913) (no property interest can exist in navigable waters); *see also Demorest v. City Bank Co.*, 321 U.S. 36 (1944); *Muhlker v. New York & Harlem R. Co.*, 197 U.S. 544 (1905); Sax, Takings and the Police Power, 74 Yale L.J. 36, 61–62 (1964).

More importantly for the present case, in instances in which a state tribunal reasonably concluded that "the health, safety, morals, or general welfare" would be promoted by prohibiting particular contemplated uses of land, this Court has upheld land-use regulations that destroyed or adversely affected recognized real property interests. *See Nectow v. Cambridge*, 277 U.S. 183, 188 (1928). Zoning laws are, of course, the classic example, *see Euclid v. Ambler Realty Co.*, 272 U.S. 365 (1926) (prohibition of industrial use); *Gorieb v. Fox*, 274 U.S. 603, 608 (1927) (requirement that portions of parcels be left unbuilt); *Welch v. Swasey*, 214 U.S. 91 (1909) (height restriction), which have been viewed as permissible governmental action even when prohibiting the most beneficial use of the property. *See Goldblatt v. Hempstead, supra*, 369 U.S., at 592–593, and cases cited; *see also Eastlake v. Forest City Enterprises, Inc.*, 426 U.S. 668, 674, n. 8 (1976).

Zoning laws generally do not affect existing uses of real property, but "taking" challenges have also been held to be without merit in a wide variety of situations when the challenged governmental actions prohibited a beneficial use to which individual parcels had previously been devoted and thus caused substantial individualized harm. *Miller v. Schoene*, 276 U.S. 272 (1928), is illustrative. In that case, a state entomologist, acting pursuant to a state statute, ordered the claimants to cut down a large number of ornamental red cedar trees because they produced cedar rust fatal to apple trees cultivated nearby. Although the statute provided for recovery of any expense incurred in removing the cedars, and permitted claimants to use the felled trees, it did not provide compensation for the value of the standing trees or for the resulting decrease in market value of the properties as a whole. A unanimous Court held that this latter omission did not render the statute invalid. The Court held that the State might properly make "a choice between the preservation of one class of property and that of the other" and since the apple industry was important in the State involved, concluded that the State had not exceeded "its constitutional powers by deciding upon the destruction of one class of property [without compensation] in order to save another which, in the judgment of the legislature, is of greater value to the public." *Id.*, at 279.

Again, *Hadacheck v. Sebastian*, 239 U.S. 394 (1915), upheld a law prohibiting the claimant from continuing his otherwise lawful business of operating a brickyard in a particular physical community on the ground that the legislature had reasonably concluded that the presence of the brickyard was inconsistent with neighboring uses. *See also United States v. Central Eureka Mining Co., supra* (Government order closing gold mines so that skilled miners would be available for other mining work held not a taking); *Atchison, T. & S. F. R. Co. v. Public Utilities Comm'n*, 346 U.S. 346 (1953) (railroad may be required to share cost of constructing railroad grade improvement); *Walls v. Midland Carbon Co.*, 254 U.S. 300 (1920) (law prohibiting manufacture of carbon black upheld); *Reinman v. Little Rock*, 237 U.S. 171 (1915) (law prohibiting livery stable upheld); *Mugler v. Kansas*, 123 U.S. 623 (1887) (law prohibiting liquor business upheld).

Goldblatt v. Hempstead, supra, is a recent example. There, a 1958 city safety ordinance banned any excavations below the water table and effectively prohibited the claimant from continuing a sand and gravel mining business that had been operated on the particular parcel since 1927. The Court upheld the ordinance against a "taking" challenge, although the ordinance prohibited the present and presumably most beneficial use of the property and had, like the regulations in *Miller* and *Hadacheck*, severely affected a particular owner. The Court assumed that the ordinance did not prevent the owner's reasonable use of the property since the owner made no showing of an adverse effect on the value of the land. Because the restriction served a substantial public purpose, the Court thus held no taking had occurred. It is, of course, implicit in *Goldblatt* that a use restriction on real property may constitute a "taking" if not reasonably necessary to the effectuation of a substantial public purpose, *see Nectow v. Cambridge, supra*; *cf. Moore v. East Cleveland*, 431 U.S. 494 (1977) (STE-VENS, J., concurring), or perhaps if it has an unduly harsh impact upon the owner's use of the property.

Pennsylvania Coal Co. v. Mahon, 260 U.S. 393 (1922), is the leading case for the proposition that a state statute that substantially furthers important public policies may so frustrate distinct investment-backed expectations as to amount to a "taking." There the claimant had sold the surface rights to particular parcels of property, but expressly reserved the right to remove the coal thereunder. A Pennsylvania statute, enacted after the transactions, forbade any mining of coal that caused the subsidence of any house, unless the house was the property of the owner of the underlying coal and was more than 150 feet from the improved property of another. Because the statute made it commercially impracticable to mine the coal, *id.*, at 414, and thus had nearly the same effect as the complete destruction of rights claimant had reserved from the owners of the surface land, *see id.*, at 414–415, the Court held that the statute was invalid as effecting a "taking" without just compensation. *See also Armstrong v. United States*, 364 U.S. 40 (1960) (Government's complete destruction of a materialman's lien in certain property held a "taking"); *Hudson County Water Co. v. McCarter*, 209 U.S. 349, 355 (1908) (if height restriction makes property wholly useless "the rights of property ... prevail over the other public interest" and compensation is required). *See generally* Michelman, Property, Utility, and Fairness: Comments on the Ethical Foundations of "Just Compensation" Law, 80 Harv.L.Rev. 1165, 1229–1234 (1967).

Finally, government actions that may be characterized as acquisitions of resources to permit or facilitate uniquely public functions have often been held to constitute "takings." *United States v. Causby*, 328 U.S. 256

(1946), is illustrative. In holding that direct overflights above the claimant's land, that destroyed the present use of the land as a chicken farm, constituted a "taking," Causby emphasized that Government had not "merely destroyed property [but was] using a part of it for the flight of its planes." *Id.*, 328 U.S., at 262–263, n. 7. *See also Griggs v. Allegheny County*, 369 U.S. 84, (1962) (overflights held a taking); *Portsmouth Co. v. United States*, 260 U.S. 327 (1922) (United States military installations' repeated firing of guns over claimant's land is a taking); *United States v. Cress*, 243 U.S. 316 (1917) (repeated floodings of land caused by water project is taking); *but see National Board of YMCA v. United States*, 395 U.S. 85, 89 (1969) (damage caused to building when federal officers who were seeking to protect building were attacked by rioters held not a taking). *See generally* Michelman, *supra*, at 1226–1229; Sax, Takings and the Police Power, 74 Yale L.J. 36 (1964).

B

In contending that the New York City law has "taken" their property in violation of the Fifth and Fourteenth Amendments, appellants make a series of arguments, which, while tailored to the facts of this case, essentially urge that any substantial restriction imposed pursuant to a landmark law must be accompanied by just compensation if it is to be constitutional. Before considering these, we emphasize what is not in dispute. Because this Court has recognized, in a number of settings, that States and cities may enact land-use restrictions or controls to enhance the quality of life by preserving the character and desirable aesthetic features of a city, *see New Orleans v. Dukes*, 427 U.S. 297 (1976); *Young v. American Mini Theatres, Inc.*, 427 U.S. 50 (1976); *Village of Belle Terre v. Boraas*, 416 U.S. 1, 9–10 (1974); *Berman v. Parker*, 348 U.S. 26, 33 (1954); *Welch v. Swasey*, 214 U.S., at 108, appellants do not contest that New York City's objective of preserving structures and areas with special historic, architectural, or cultural significance is an entirely permissible governmental goal. They also do not dispute that the restrictions imposed on its parcel are appropriate means of securing the purposes of the New York City law. Finally, appellants do not challenge any of the specific factual premises of the decision below. They accept for present purposes both that the parcel of land occupied by Grand Central Terminal must, in its present state, be regarded as capable of earning a reasonable return, and that the transferable development rights afforded appellants by virtue of the Terminal's designation as a landmark are valuable, even if not as valuable as the rights to construct above the Terminal. In appellants' view none of these factors derogate from their claim that New York City's law has effected a "taking."

They first observe that the airspace above the Terminal is a valuable property interest, citing *United States v. Causby, supra.* They urge that the Landmarks Law has deprived them of any gainful use of their "air rights" above the Terminal and that, irrespective of the value of the remainder of their parcel, the city has "taken" their right to this superadjacent airspace, thus entitling them to "just compensation" measured by the fair market value of these air rights.

Apart from our own disagreement with appellants' characterization of the effect of the New York City law, the submission that appellants may establish a "taking" simply by showing that they have been denied the ability to exploit a property interest that they heretofore had believed was available for development is quite simply untenable. Were this the rule, this Court would have erred not only in upholding laws restricting the development of air rights, *see Welch v. Swasey, supra, but also* in approving those prohibiting both the subjacent, *see Goldblatt v. Hempstead*, 369 U.S. 590 (1962), and the lateral, *see Gorieb v. Fox*, 274 U.S. 603 (1927), development of particular parcels.[41] "Taking" jurisprudence does not divide a single parcel into discrete segments and attempt to determine whether rights in a particular segment have been entirely abrogated. In deciding whether a particular governmental action has effected a taking, this Court focuses rather both on the character of the action and on the nature and extent of the interference with rights in the parcel as a whole—here, the city tax block designated as the "landmark site."

Secondly, appellants, focusing on the character and impact of the New York City law, argue that it effects a "taking" because its operation has significantly diminished the value of the Terminal site. Appellants concede that the decisions sustaining other land-use regulations, which, like the New York City law, are reasonably related to the promotion of the general welfare, uniformly reject the proposition that diminution in property value, standing alone, can establish a "taking," *see Euclid v. Ambler Realty Co.*, 272 U.S. 365 (1926) (75% diminution in value caused by zoning law); *Hadacheck v. Sebastian*, 239 U.S. 394 (1915) (87 ½% diminution in value); *cf. Eastlake v. Forest City Enterprises, Inc.*, 426 U.S., at 674 n. 8, and that the "taking" issue in these contexts is resolved by focusing on the uses the regulations permit. *See also Goldblatt v. Hempstead, supra.* Appellants, moreover, also do not dispute that a showing of diminution in property value would not establish a taking if the restriction had been imposed as a result of historic-district legislation, *see generally Maher v. New Orleans*, 516 F.2d 1051 (CA5 1975), but appellants argue that New York City's regulation of individual landmarks is fundamentally different from zoning or from historic-district legislation because the controls imposed by New York City's law apply only to individuals who own selected properties.

Stated baldly, appellants' position appears to be that the only means of ensuring that selected owners are not singled out to endure financial hardship for no reason is to hold that any restriction imposed on individual

41. These cases dispose of any contention that might be based on *Pennsylvania Coal Co. v. Mahon*, 260 U.S. 393 (1922), that full use of air rights is so bound up with the investment-backed expectations of appellants that governmental deprivation of these rights invariably—*i.e.*, irrespective of the impact of the restriction on the value of the parcel as a whole—constitutes a "taking." Similarly, *Welch*, *Goldblatt*, and *Gorieb* illustrate the fallacy of appellants' related contention that a "taking" must be found to have occurred whenever the land-use restriction may be characterized as imposing a "servitude" on the claimant's parcel.

landmarks pursuant to the New York City scheme is a "taking" requiring the payment of "just compensation." Agreement with this argument would, of course, invalidate not just New York City's law, but all comparable landmark legislation in the Nation. We find no merit in it.

It is true, as appellants emphasize, that both historic-district legislation and zoning laws regulate all properties within given physical communities whereas landmark laws apply only to selected parcels. But, contrary to appellants' suggestions, landmark laws are not like discriminatory, or "reverse spot," zoning: that is, a land-use decision which arbitrarily singles out a particular parcel for different, less favorable treatment than the neighboring ones. *See* 2 A. Rathkopf, The Law of Zoning and Planning 26–4, and n. 6 (4th ed. 1978). In contrast to discriminatory zoning, which is the antithesis of land-use control as part of some comprehensive plan, the New York City law embodies a comprehensive plan to preserve structures of historic or aesthetic interest wherever they might be found in the city, and as noted, over 400 landmarks and 31 historic districts have been designated pursuant to this plan.

[The Court rejected the argument that the restrictions in question were arbitrary or unduly subjective on the ground that designations were subject to judicial review.]

Next, appellants observe that New York City's law differs from zoning laws and historic-district ordinances in that the Landmarks Law does not impose identical or similar restrictions on all structures located in particular physical communities. It follows, they argue, that New York City's law is inherently incapable of producing the fair and equitable distribution of benefits and burdens of governmental action which is characteristic of zoning laws and historic-district legislation and which they maintain is a constitutional requirement if "just compensation" is not to be afforded. It is, of course, true that the Landmarks Law has a more severe impact on some landowners than on others, but that in itself does not mean that the law effects a "taking." Legislation designed to promote the general welfare commonly burdens some more than others. The owners of the brickyard in *Hadacheck*, of the cedar trees in *Miller v. Schoene*, and of the gravel and sand mine in *Goldblatt v. Hempstead*, were uniquely burdened by the legislation sustained in those cases.[42] Similarly, zoning laws often affect some property owners more severely than others but have not been held to be invalid on that account. For example, the property owner in *Euclid* who

---

42. Appellants attempt to distinguish these cases on the ground that, in each, government was prohibiting a "noxious" use of land and that in the present case, in contrast, appellants' proposed construction above the Terminal would be beneficial. We observe that the uses in issue in *Hadacheck, Miller,* and *Goldblatt* were perfectly lawful in themselves. They involved no "blameworthiness, . . . moral wrongdoing or conscious act of dangerous risk-taking which induce[d soci-

ety] to shift the cost to a pa[rt]icular individual." Sax, Takings and the Police Power, 74 Yale L.J. 36, 50 (1964). These cases are better understood as resting not on any supposed "noxious" quality of the prohibited uses but rather on the ground that the restrictions were reasonably related to the implementation of a policy—not unlike historic preservation—expected to produce a widespread public benefit and applicable to all similarly situated property. * * *

wished to use its property for industrial purposes was affected far more severely by the ordinance than its neighbors who wished to use their land for residences.

In any event, appellants' repeated suggestions that they are solely burdened and unbenefited is factually inaccurate. This contention overlooks the fact that the New York City law applies to vast numbers of structures in the city in addition to the Terminal—all the structures contained in the 31 historic districts and over 400 individual landmarks, many of which are close to the Terminal.[43] Unless we are to reject the judgment of the New York City Council that the preservation of landmarks benefits all New York citizens and all structures, both economically and by improving the quality of life in the city as a whole—which we are unwilling to do—we cannot conclude that the owners of the Terminal have in no sense been benefited by the Landmarks Law. Doubtless appellants believe they are more burdened than benefited by the law, but that must have been true, too, of the property owners in *Miller, Hadacheck, Euclid, and Goldblatt.* * * *

C

Rejection of appellants' broad arguments is not, however, the end of our inquiry, for all we thus far have established is that the New York City law is not rendered invalid by its failure to provide "just compensation" whenever a landmark owner is restricted in the exploitation of property interests, such as air rights, to a greater extent than provided for under applicable zoning laws. We now must consider whether the interference with appellants' property is of such a magnitude that "there must be an exercise of eminent domain and compensation to sustain [it]." *Pennsylvania Coal Co. v. Mahon*, 260 U.S., at 413. That inquiry may be narrowed to the question of the severity of the impact of the law on appellants' parcel, and its resolution in turn requires a careful assessment of the impact of the regulation on the Terminal site.

Unlike the governmental acts in *Goldblatt, Miller, Causby, Griggs,* and *Hadacheck*, the New York City law does not interfere in any way with the present uses of the Terminal. Its designation as a landmark not only permits but contemplates that appellants may continue to use the property precisely as it has been used for the past 65 years: as a railroad terminal containing office space and concessions. So the law does not interfere with what must be regarded as *Penn Central*'s primary expectation concerning the use of the parcel. More importantly, on this record, we must regard the New York City law as permitting *Penn Central* not only to profit from the Terminal but also to obtain a "reasonable return" on its investment.

Appellants, moreover, exaggerate the effect of the law on their ability to make use of the air rights above the Terminal in two respects. First, it simply cannot be maintained, on this record, that appellants have been

---

43. There are some 53 designated landmarks and 5 historic districts or scenic landmarks in Manhattan between 14th and 59th Streets. *See* Landmarks Preservation Commission, Landmarks and Historic Districts (1977).

prohibited from occupying any portion of the airspace above the Terminal. While the Commission's actions in denying applications to construct an office building in excess of 50 stories above the Terminal may indicate that it will refuse to issue a certificate of appropriateness for any comparably sized structure, nothing the Commission has said or done suggests an intention to prohibit any construction above the Terminal. The Commission's report emphasized that whether any construction would be allowed depended upon whether the proposed addition "would harmonize in scale, material and character with [the Terminal]." Since appellants have not sought approval for the construction of a smaller structure, we do not know that appellants will be denied any use of any portion of the airspace above the Terminal.

Second, to the extent appellants have been denied the right to build above the Terminal, it is not literally accurate to say that they have been denied all use of even those pre-existing air rights. Their ability to use these rights has not been abrogated; they are made transferable to at least eight parcels in the vicinity of the Terminal, one or two of which have been found suitable for the construction of new office buildings. Although appellants and others have argued that New York City's transferable development-rights program is far from ideal, the New York courts here supportably found that, at least in the case of the Terminal, the rights afforded are valuable. While these rights may well not have constituted "just compensation" if a "taking" had occurred, the rights nevertheless undoubtedly mitigate whatever financial burdens the law has imposed on appellants and, for that reason, are to be taken into account in considering the impact of regulation. *Cf. Goldblatt v. Hempstead*, 369 U.S., at 594 n. 3.

On this record, we conclude that the application of New York City's Landmarks Law has not effected a "taking" of appellants' property. The restrictions imposed are substantially related to the promotion of the general welfare and not only permit reasonable beneficial use of the landmark site but also afford appellants opportunities further to enhance not only the Terminal site proper but also other properties.

Affirmed.

■ MR. JUSTICE REHNQUIST, with whom THE CHIEF JUSTICE and MR. JUSTICE STEVENS join, dissenting.

Of the over one million buildings and structures in the city of New York, appellees have singled out 400 for designation as official landmarks.[44] The owner of a building might initially be pleased that his property has been chosen by a distinguished committee of architects, historians, and city planners for such a singular distinction. But he may well discover, as appellant Penn Central Transportation Co. did here, that the landmark designation imposes upon him a substantial cost, with little or no offsetting benefit except for the honor of the designation. The question in this case is

---

44. A large percentage of the designated landmarks are public structures (such as the Brooklyn Bridge, City Hall, the Statute of Liberty and the Municipal Asphalt Plant) and thus do not raise Fifth Amendment taking questions. * * *

whether the cost associated with the city of New York's desire to preserve a limited number of "landmarks" within its borders must be borne by all of its taxpayers or whether it can instead be imposed entirely on the owners of the individual properties.

Only in the most superficial sense of the word can this case be said to involve "zoning." Typical zoning restrictions may, it is true, so limit the prospective uses of a piece of property as to diminish the value of that property in the abstract because it may not be used for the forbidden purposes. But any such abstract decrease in value will more than likely be at least partially offset by an increase in value which flows from similar restrictions as to use on neighboring properties. All property owners in a designated area are placed under the same restrictions, not only for the benefit of the municipality as a whole but also for the common benefit of one another. In the words of Mr. Justice Holmes, speaking for the Court in *Pennsylvania Coal Co. v. Mahon*, 260 U.S. 393, 415 (1922), there is "an average reciprocity of advantage."

Where a relatively few individual buildings, all separated from one another, are singled out and treated differently from surrounding buildings, no such reciprocity exists. The cost to the property owner which results from the imposition of restrictions applicable only to his property and not that of his neighbors may be substantial—in this case, several million dollars—with no comparable reciprocal benefits. And the cost associated with landmark legislation is likely to be of a completely different order of magnitude than that which results from the imposition of normal zoning restrictions. Unlike the regime affected by the latter, the landowner is not simply prohibited from using his property for certain purposes, while allowed to use it for all other purposes. Under the historic-landmark preservation scheme adopted by New York, the property owner is under an affirmative duty to preserve his property as a landmark at his own expense. To suggest that because traditional zoning results in some limitation of use of the property zoned, the New York City landmark preservation scheme should likewise be upheld, represents the ultimate in treating as alike things which are different. The rubric of "zoning" has not yet sufficed to avoid the well-established proposition that the Fifth Amendment bars the "Government from forcing some people alone to bear public burdens which, in all fairness and justice, should be borne by the public as a whole." *Armstrong v. United States*, 364 U.S. 40, 49 (1960).

* * *

I

The Fifth Amendment provides in part: "nor shall private property be taken for public use, without just compensation." In a very literal sense, the actions of appellees violated this constitutional prohibition. Before the city of New York declared Grand Central Terminal to be a landmark, *Penn Central* could have used its "air rights" over the Terminal to build a multistory office building, at an apparent value of several million dollars per year. Today, the Terminal cannot be modified in any form, including the erection of additional stories, without the permission of the Landmark Preservation Commission, a permission which appellants, despite good-faith attempts, have so far been unable to obtain. Because the Taking Clause of the Fifth Amendment has not always been read literally, however, the constitutionality of appellees' actions requires a closer scrutiny of this Court's interpretation of the three key words in the Taking Clause— "property," "taken," and "just compensation."

A

Appellees do not dispute that valuable property rights have been destroyed. And the Court has frequently emphasized that the term "property" as used in the Taking Clause includes the entire "group of rights inhering in the citizen's [ownership]." *United States v. General Motors Corp.*, 323 U.S. 373 (1945). The term is not used in the

> vulgar and untechnical sense of the physical thing with respect to which the citizen exercises rights recognized by law. [Instead, it] ... denote [s] the group of rights inhering in the citizen's relation to the physical *thing, as the right to possess, use and dispose of it.* * * * the constitutional provision is addressed to every sort of interest the citizen may possess. *Id.*, at 377–378 (emphasis added).

While neighboring landowners are free to use their land and "air rights" in any way consistent with the broad boundaries of New York zoning, Penn Central, absent the permission of appellees, must forever maintain its property in its present state. The property has been thus subjected to a nonconsensual servitude not borne by any neighboring or similar properties.

B

Appellees have thus destroyed—in a literal sense, "taken"—substantial property rights of Penn Central. While the term "taken" might have been narrowly interpreted to include only physical seizures of property rights, "the construction of the phrase has not been so narrow. The courts have held that the deprivation of the former owner rather than the accretion of a right or interest to the sovereign constitutes the taking." *Id.*, at 378. *See also United States v. Lynah*, 188 U.S. 445, 469 (1903);[45] *Dugan v. Rank*, 372 U.S. 609, 625 (1963). Because "not every destruction or injury to property by governmental action has been held to be a 'taking' in the constitutional sense," *Armstrong v. United States*, 364 U.S., at 48, however, this does not end our inquiry. But an examination of the two exceptions where the destruction of property does not constitute a taking demonstrates that a compensable taking has occurred here.

---

45. "Such a construction would pervert the constitutional provision into a restriction upon the rights of the citizen, as those rights stood at the common law, instead of the government, and make it an authority for invasion of private right under the pretext of the public good, which had no warrant in the laws or practices of our ancestors." 188 U.S., at 470.

1

As early as 1887, the Court recognized that the government can prevent a property owner from using his property to injure others without having to compensate the owner for the value of the forbidden use.

> A prohibition simply upon the use of property for purposes that are declared, by valid legislation, to be *injurious to the health, morals, or safety of the community*, cannot, in any just sense, be deemed a taking or an appropriation of property for the public benefit. Such legislation does not disturb the owner in the control or use of his property for lawful purposes, nor restrict his right to dispose of it, but is only a declaration by the State that its use by any one, for certain forbidden purposes, is prejudicial to the public interests.... The power which the States have of prohibiting such use by individuals of their property as will be prejudicial to the health, the morals, or the safety of the public, is not—and, consistently with the existence and safety of organized society, cannot be—burdened with the condition that the State must compensate such individual owners for pecuniary losses they may sustain, by reason of their not being permitted, by a noxious use of their property, to inflict injury upon the community. *Mugler v. Kansas,* 123 U.S. 623, 668–669.

Thus, there is no "taking" where a city prohibits the operation of a brickyard within a residential area, *see Hadacheck v. Sebastian,* 239 U.S. 394 (1915), or forbids excavation for sand and gravel below the water line, *see Goldblatt v. Hempstead,* 369 U.S. 590 (1962). Nor is it relevant, where the government is merely prohibiting a noxious use of property, that the government would seem to be singling out a particular property owner. *Hadacheck, supra,* at 413.[46]

The nuisance exception to the taking guarantee is not coterminous with the police power itself. The question is whether the forbidden use is dangerous to the safety, health, or welfare of others. Thus, in *Curtin v. Benson,* 222 U.S. 78 (1911), the Court held that the Government, in prohibiting the owner of property within the boundaries of Yosemite National Park from grazing cattle on his property, had taken the owner's property. The Court assumed that the Government could constitutionally require the owner to fence his land or take other action to prevent his cattle from straying onto others' land without compensating him. "Such laws might be considered as strictly regulations of the use of property, of so using it that no injury could result to others. They would have the effect of making the owner of land herd his cattle on his own land and of making him responsible for a neglect of it." *Id.,* at 86. The prohibition in question, however, was "not a prevention of a misuse or illegal use but the prevention of a legal and essential use, an attribute of its ownership." *Ibid.*

---

46. Each of the cases cited by the Court for the proposition that legislation which severely affects some landowners but not others does not effect a "taking" involved noxious uses of property. *See Hadacheck; Miller v. Schoene,* 276 U.S. 272 (1928); *Goldblatt.*

Appellees are not prohibiting a nuisance. The record is clear that the proposed addition to the Grand Central Terminal would be in full compliance with zoning, height limitations, and other health and safety requirements. Instead, appellees are seeking to preserve what they believe to be an outstanding example of beaux-arts architecture. Penn Central is prevented from further developing its property basically because too good a job was done in designing and building it. The city of New York, because of its unadorned admiration for the design, has decided that the owners of the building must preserve it unchanged for the benefit of sightseeing New Yorkers and tourists.

Unlike land-use regulations, appellees' actions do not merely prohibit Penn Central from using its property in a narrow set of noxious ways. Instead, appellees have placed an affirmative duty on Penn Central to maintain the Terminal in its present state and in "good repair." Appellants are not free to use their property as they see fit within broad outer boundaries but must strictly adhere to their past use except where appellees conclude that alternative uses would not detract from the landmark. While Penn Central may continue to use the Terminal as it is presently designed, appellees otherwise "exercise complete dominion and control over the surface of the land," *United States v. Causby*, 328 U.S. 256, 262 (1946), and must compensate the owner for his loss. *Ibid.* "Property is taken in the constitutional sense when inroads are made upon an owner's use of it to an extent that, as between private parties, a servitude has been acquired." *United States v. Dickinson*, 331 U.S. 745, 748 (1947). *See also Dugan v. Rank, supra,* 372 U.S., at 625.

2

Even where the government prohibits a noninjurious use, the Court has ruled that a taking does not take place if the prohibition applies over a broad cross section of land and thereby "secure[s] an average reciprocity of advantage." *Pennsylvania Coal Co. v. Mahon*, 260 U.S., at 415. It is for this reason that zoning does not constitute a "taking." While zoning at times reduces individual property values, the burden is shared relatively evenly and it is reasonable to conclude that on the whole an individual who is harmed by one aspect of the zoning will be benefited by another.

Here, however, a multimillion dollar loss has been imposed on appellants; it is uniquely felt and is not offset by any benefits flowing from the preservation of some 400 other "landmarks" in New York City. Appellees have imposed a substantial cost on less than one one-tenth of one percent of the buildings in New York City for the general benefit of all its people. * * *

II

Over 50 years ago, Mr. Justice Holmes, speaking for the Court, warned that the courts were "in danger of forgetting that a strong public desire to improve the public condition is not enough to warrant achieving the desire by a shorter cut than the constitutional way of paying for the change."

Pennsylvania Coal Co. v. Mahon, 260 U.S., at 416. The Court's opinion in this case demonstrates that the danger thus foreseen has not abated. The city of New York is in a precarious financial state, and some may believe that the costs of landmark preservation will be more easily borne by corporations such as Penn Central than the overburdened individual tax-payers of New York. But these concerns do not allow us to ignore past precedents construing the Eminent Domain Clause to the end that the desire to improve the public condition is, indeed, achieved by a shorter cut than the constitutional way of paying for the change.

Joseph L. Sax, Some Thoughts on the Decline of Private Property

58 Washington Law Review 481, 481–89, 491–94 (1983).

A case could be made for the proposition that property rights have been in a state of more-or-less continuous decline for many decades, and that there is nothing to report on that front but more of the same. I do not agree. I believe that we have moved in recent years from a situation (characterized by conventional urban zoning) in which we generally encourage developmental rights, though recognizing they must from time to time be restrained, to one in which developmental activity has itself become suspect. As a result, we are in the midst of a major transformation in which property rights are being fundamentally redefined to the disadvantage of property owners.

Because this transition is, by and large, taking place without compensation, it has become commonplace for courts to describe what is occurring in conventional terms. The proliferation of recent historic preservation laws is routinely characterized, for example, as if it were nothing but a continuation of long-accepted zoning practices. In fact, I submit, such laws and many others—wetlands and coastal protection, open space zoning, growth control and the resurgent public trust doctrine—mark a transition the full effects of which have hardly begun to be recognized or felt.

As good an example as any is the recent decision of the United States Supreme Court in *Penn Central Transportation Co. v. City of New York*. After dutifully reciting all the conventional cases in which regulation without compensation was sustained, the majority in effect concluded that the city's refusal to allow Penn Central to build a high-rise above Grand Central Station, which had been designated an architectural landmark, was indistinguishable from a half-century's land regulation and zoning cases. Justice Rehnquist, in dissent, insisted that something importantly different was happening in *Penn Central*. He was right, but he too failed to recognize the full significance of the majority's decision: Rejection of the very claim that there existed a private property right capable of being taken.

What made *Penn Central* an unconventional case? For one thing, the owner in that case was denied the opportunity to pursue an established business expectation, though the majority opinion denied it. Building on air rights had become a conventional economic activity, and one in which many owners had invested great sums of money.

Moreover, the case cannot be justified on the conventional "external harm" theory which is the source of most traditional property regulation. It cannot be said, for example, that the proposed use was a nuisance-like activity that would intrude on the uses others were making of their property. Unlike the case in which an owner wishes to build a factory or to maintain a quarry in a residential neighborhood, Penn Central only asked to be allowed to do what its neighbors had already done, to construct a high-rise building. Neither can it be said—beyond the limits of so-called noxious uses or nuisances—that there was even a conflict between the uses Penn Central wanted to make of its property and those that its neighbors wanted to make of theirs. Thus, *Penn Central* was not a case like *Miller v. Schoene*, in which some choice had to be made between competing and incompatible uses, neither of which could be viewed as wrongful. This illustrates the distinctiveness of the *Penn Central* decision, because *Miller v. Schoene* has long been viewed as at the outer limit of permissible regulation.

Moreover, as Justice Rehnquist emphasized in his dissent, there was no plausible reciprocity of advantage in the case, a feature common to much traditional zoning. Indeed, *Penn Central* is precisely the opposite of a reciprocity case; one landowner was prevented from doing something that all his neighbors had been permitted to do. And he was prevented not because he had done something wrongful or intrusive, but because he had done something admirable—he had built an architecturally distinguished building.

The most accurate way of looking at *Penn Central* is to say that the owner was required to continue conferring a benefit on his neighbors. The owner's situation in *Penn Central* resembles the situation of a landowner who has, up to the present time, refrained from building on his lot, thereby providing his neighbors a scenic amenity. Now he wishes to stop providing that benefit, and to use his property as his neighbors have already used their adjoining tracts. Yet the law requires him to continue bestowing amenity value upon his neighbors even though they have no similar obligation. How can such a result be explained or justified? That is the question Justice Rehnquist raised, and the majority opinion in the case provides no satisfactory answer.

In the pages that follow I propose an explanation of why cases like *Penn Central* are being decided as they are. I argue that *Penn Central* and its companions do not turn on the compensation/no compensation issue, which has traditionally dominated legal thinking about property. Instead, they address the allocational function of property. Put as bluntly as possible my thesis is this: We have endowed individuals and enterprises with property because we assume that the private ownership system will allocate and reallocate the property resource to socially desirable uses. Any such allocational system will, of course, fail from time to time. But when the system regularly fails to allocate property to "correct" uses, we begin to lose faith in the system itself. Just as older systems of property, like feudal tenures, declined as they became nonfunctional, so our own system is declining to the extent it is perceived as a functional failure. Since such failures are becoming increasingly common, the property rights that lead to such failures are increasingly ceasing to be recognized. Thus, the interesting question in the *Penn Central* case is not why the owner failed to receive compensation, but why private ownership of Grand Central Station did not lead to the correct allocation, that is, to maintaining the property as an unobstructed, architecturally distinctive railroad station.

In speaking of the "correct" allocation, I mean to suggest no omniscience either on my part or that of the New York Landmarks Preservation Commission. Rather, I intend only to observe that in cases like *Penn Central* and many other modern situations such as open space preservation or coastal protection, there is widespread agreement that nondevelopment is the correct result, and widespread recognition that conventional bargaining between the owner and potential users of the property is not bringing about that result. I also mean to contrast the outcome in such cases with an earlier belief that demolishing old structures so as to allow vigorous new development was the right result. It is this difference rather than the question whether the owner is being compensated or not that is generating disillusionment with private developmental rights.

Before turning to the reasons for the perceived allocational failure of traditional property, however, I want to comment briefly on the relationship between compensation and allocation. One might say that the ability of the public to avoid compensation significantly affects the allocation decision, for the simple reason that the public will want something (preservation of an historic structure, for example) much more if it is free than if it costs it millions of dollars. But the choice is not always that simple. For example, if a high-rise is not built above Grand Central Station, the public—whether or not it pays compensation to the owner—is foregoing the benefits that come from development. As the employer and welfare provider of last resort, it risks the loss of economic activity, of jobs and of housing, losses not significantly felt by any individual. The public does not casually eschew the benefits of economic development. For this reason, one must view laws constraining development, such as historic preservation ordinances, as allocational choices that are not "free" to the community even when no compensation is paid the owner. Such decisions reflect changing public values, and not simply public avidity for obtaining free benefits.

Why are values changing, and why does the property system not automatically adapt to them? One important explanation may lie in the difference between the different kinds of benefits flowing from property— "exclusive" and "nonexclusive" consumption benefits. In a case of exclusive consumption (a residence or a shopping center, for example), virtually all benefits flow exclusively to those who occupy and use the land. In such a case, where there are no significant externalities, one expects the direct users to be able to organize, calculate and bid for the opportunity to enjoy those benefits. In general, the community as a whole is content to have the property allocated to whomever among such competing exclusive use bidders is willing to make the highest bid. The conventional property system is organized to facilitate such allocations, and such allocations only.

If, however, the "competitors" include those who benefit from maintenance of an existing historic building, the consumption is nonexclusive. That is to say, the number of people who will potentially benefit is much greater: Benefits are not limited to actual occupants; the nature of the benefits will differ among various people in the group; they are likely to be quite small as to any individual; and there is no way of assuring that every beneficiary will contribute, for benefits will flow to all potential beneficiaries whether or not they have contributed (the so-called free-rider problem).

Moreover, it is often particularly difficult for any individual to calculate the value of nonexclusive benefits to him. Such benefits often have a substantial uncertainty or "option element" to them. One may be confident that he will benefit from the presence of the building in some way (just as he benefits from the existence of many as-yet-unread books in the public library), but it is much more difficult to put a price tag on that value than to put such a price tag on his apartment or on a hamburger he consumes.

For all these reasons—diffuseness, smallness of individual interest, imperfect knowledge, differential values to a large number of people, and difficulty of pricing—the likelihood that nonexclusive consumers will organize to bid, and to bid the "right" price for such benefits, is doubtful.

Of course these very uncertainties also suggest reasons to lack confidence in the intervention of government to allocate the land to a given nonexclusive consumptive use through a legal mandate. What I have said to this point seeks to demonstrate not that allocation through law, rather than through bidding, is necessarily right, but only that allocation through conventional bidding—whereby the maximization of profit to the owner is assumed to produce the correct allocation—is fraught with difficulties.

When nonexclusive consumption benefits are very small by comparison to exclusive consumption values, the traditional system of allocation functions well. But as nonexclusive benefits rise in importance, the capacity of traditional private property transactions to allocate satisfactorily diminishes, and in such circumstances one should not be surprised to see diminishing confidence in the property system as an engine of allocation.

    * * *

As nonexclusive consumption values rise in importance, and the capacity of the property system to make correct allocations thereby diminishes, it seems inevitable that we begin to ask ourselves why we allow those private property rights to exist which increasingly produce unwanted results. At least as to land, where property rights are assigned by the public in the first instance (and putting aside those things that are more or less entirely the product of an individual's own creative efforts, such as a symphony or a poem), the assignment of property rights presupposes that private owner-ship would routinely produce socially desirable use allocations.

We assigned property to private owners in the undeveloped West, for example, because we assumed that the uses they would make of the property—settlement, security of the frontier, development of railroads, farms and mines—would maximize net social benefits. Had we not believed that the allocations brought about by private ownership would produce such results, it hardly seems likely that such rights would have been created. The application of a new kind of water right for the arid West in place of traditional riparian rights pointedly illustrates this assumption.
* * *

* * * As the need for nonexclusive uses of the lands rose in the last decade, and as the availability of such lands shrank, we witnessed some remarkable judicial pyrotechnics. For instance, recent California Supreme Court decisions have redefined the nature of the grants made by the legislature in the 1860's, questioned longstanding property rights in water, and explicitly reversed previous decisions holding that absolute private rights had been granted, thereby reinstating the public right of nonexclu-sive use on the inventive theory of implicit reservations in grants made more than a century ago.

However shocking such results may be to conventional legal sensibili-ties, they reveal a trend that is equally obvious in a range of other areas. That trend is exemplified not only by *Penn Central* but also by contempo-rary decisions upholding open space, coastal and wetland zoning.

Nonexclusive consumption benefits have always existed. Why should they be less in harmony with the property system now than they were in the past? The reasons, I suggest, are two, both related to the developmental use of property. First, the more development proceeds, the more the stock of such benefits (coastal access, historic structures, wilderness) declines. Second, and even more important, values are changing, so that the quan-tum of benefits from developmental activity (both exclusive and nonexclu-sive consumption benefits) is perceived as being less than it formerly was, while simultaneously the perceived benefits flowing from nondevelopmen-tal, nonexclusive consumption are sharply increasing.

The building of the railroads, the irrigation of the arid West, the electrification of rural areas, the growth of great cities, even the belching steel mills of Pittsburgh or Gary, idealized America on the march, putting the world on wheels, serving as the breadbasket and the arsenal of democracy. Such images were at least as powerful as the current imagery of the wilderness or of our historic heritage. The nonexclusive consumption benefits of a symbolic sort that flowed from these activities were in harmony with conventional exclusive consumption benefits that flowed to users and builders. The profits that came to landowners in allocating property to development automatically brought in their wake a sense of common purpose to a public enlivened by an idea of progress tied to development. The developmental rights of property owners were truly an engine pulling us where we wanted to go.

Plainly, that animating sense of progress has declined. The change might best be analogized to the mining of a valuable mineral. At first, the richest lodes are mined, and the productive output is very great per acre of land disturbed. As time goes on, the miner must move on to less and less concentrated ores, more and more land must be disrupted, and more energy must be expended to get the same level of output. Over time the benefits of developmental activity diminish, while the costs increase. Our sense of progress diminishes.

[Sax argues that natural resources are important symbols of our nation's history and identity. He relies upon Supreme Court decisions upholding aesthetic zoning and land use regulations generally to argue that nuisance is not the principal basis for the prohibition on uncompensated takings.]

Movement away form the nuisance justification for zoning in favor of concern about neighborhood character, seeing the community as a common, reflects a shift from primary concern with exclusive consumption (with its connotations of individualization and privatization) to nonexclusive consumption (with its connotations of community and shared values). * * *

I want finally to say something about the question that has traditionally most concerned lawyers: the problem of compensation. If owners are to lose developmental rights, should they not be compensated for that loss? At one level, there is an easy, descriptive answer. They are losing such rights and, as the various categories of cases to which I have been referring demonstrate, they usually are not compensated. Obviously, a number of such owners are being sharply disappointed, by conventional standards, in their expectations. Legislatures are alert to the problem, and in many cases (such as historic preservation and inclusionary zoning) mitigating benefits are being provided, though they fall short of full compensation. Among these are tax abatements, density bonuses, and transferable development rights. We are in a transitional state and legislatures are using these devices to ease the pains of transition.

It also has to be recognized that the unwillingness to compensate property owners reflects a desire to bring about some redistribution, though it is redistribution of a peculiar sort. In withdrawing developmental rights (as opposed to existing uses), the legislatures and the courts are in fact leaving in place some long-existing uses, such as open space, coastal access, recreational opportunities, and historic structures. What is changing is not the quantum of de facto nonexclusive benefits, but the quantum of rights to destroy those benefits. Public privileges, long enjoyed, are becoming public rights.

* * *

Finally, it is worth noting—and this may explain why the Supreme Court in *Penn Central* rejected the claim of investment-backed expectations—that we are already so far along in diminishing developmental rights that owners are viewed, in important respects, as already on notice. Anyone today who holds, or wishes to buy, historical properties, wet-lands, or coastal lands, or who plans developments in developing suburbs (to take but the most obvious examples), knows or should know that his opportunities for old-fashioned development are far from clear. * * *

———————

1. What is the efficient allocation of resources in the *Penn Central* case? Will it obtain if the landowner has the entitlement to develop the land?

2. What protection do landowners have from an overzealous Landmarks Preservation Commission? Is the Commission itself constituted so as to be sensitive to landowners' concerns? Is judicial review of the Commission's decisions by a state court likely to provide significant protection?

3. What sort of duties and restrictions does the New York City Landmarks Preservation Law impose on landowners of sites designated as historical landmarks? What are the legal bases by which an owner can alter designated property under New York law? What other statutory provisions mitigate the economic harm to the landowner?

4. What set of factors does the *Penn Central* Court adopt in deciding whether there has been a taking? How does the Court address the landowner's argument that the Landmarks Preservation Law singles out a few landowners to provide substantial public benefits? Doesn't the New York law in fact "forc[e] some people alone to bear public burdens which, in all fairness and justice, should be borne by the public as a whole? " Does the law provide adequate assurances against arbitrariness?

5. Are you persuaded by the *Penn Central* Court's assertion that the landowners have benefited from the Landmarks Preservation Law? Is the law really the same as any other zoning law that prohibits all landowners within the zone from developing their land in particular ways? Isn't Rehnquist right that zoning laws (in contrast to the New York Landmark law) generally impose community-wide burdens and benefits, so that a "decrease in value will more than likely be at least partially offset by an increase in value which flows from similar restrictions" on other parcels? Isn't this what Holmes meant when he spoke of an "average reciprocity of advantage" in the *Mahon* case?

6. Note Justice Rehnquist's argument that many previous cases finding no takings involved prohibitions on uses that would injure the public, somewhat akin to nuisances. Assuming that he is correct, hasn't he (and Sax) been more candid than Justice Brennan in acknowledging that the majority has approved a law that compels the landowner to provide a benefit to the public? Indeed, if the original owner had built an ugly building that no one wanted to preserve, wouldn't the current owner be free from the restrictions of the Landmarks Law? If that is so, why shouldn't the public at large bear the burden of paying for these benefits? Indeed, isn't one purpose of the Takings Clause "to bar Government from

forcing some people alone to bear burdens which, in all fairness and justice, should be borne by the public as a whole?''

7. Is there any real bite to the "investment-backed expectations" criterion? Isn't almost every business under notice that the government might impose further regulations? *Cf.* Kaplow, An Economic Analysis of Legal Transitions, 99 Harv. L. Rev. 509, 602–07 (1986) (arguing that the payment of compensation for takings undermines economic efficiency). Doesn't every owner take a chance that the government will impose additional regulation after the owner purchases property?

8. *Penn Central* held that in a regulatory taking case a court must decide a taking claim by reference to the "whole parcel"; it was not enough to show that part of the landowner's parcel had been adversely affected. *See also Keystone Bituminous Coal Ass'n v. DeBenedictis*, 480 U.S. 470, 496–97, 107 S.Ct. 1232, 1248, 94 L.Ed.2d 472 (1987) (in evaluating the coal company's claim that state regulations prevented it from mining the last 2% of coal in the ground, the court must consider not just the affected segment of property, but the property as a whole). Should the size of the parcel matter?

9. How does Sax explain the Court's decision in *Penn Central*? In what respects does he think that the existing private property system has "failed"? Is it true that the unorganized public has no means to "bid" for the nondevelopmental or nonexclusive benefits that Sax sees as properly protected in a variety of laws, such as landmarks or wetlands preservation statutes? After all, hasn't the public been able to organize sufficiently to create a landmarks preservation law? Or is it just that the public would prefer not to pay for these benefits, and indeed would not pay for them if taking doctrine prohibited such regulation? Don't such regulations put the real social costs "off budget," where they cannot be properly taken into account in setting public policy?

10. Sax does not focus on the compensation issue principally, but on the changing conceptions of property. In what respects does he see those conceptions changing? Is it fair to say that he believes that the bundle of rights that constitute ownership has been depleted, or at least reallocated to other "owners?" Do you think that Sax would agree with the following comment:

> [Property law] will increasingly exist as a collection of use-rights, rights defined in specific contexts and in terms of similar rights held by other people. Property use entitlements will be phrased in terms of responsibilities and accommodations rather than rights and autonomy.

Freyfogle, Context and Accommodation in Modern Property Law, 41 Stan. L. Rev. 1529, 1531 (1989). Are you persuaded by Sax's justifications for not providing compensation in many circumstances in which property values are significantly reduced as a result of property restrictions? How about in the *Penn Central* case?

Problems

1.   In 1958, Loveladies Harbor, Inc. acquired a 250 acre tract on Long Beach Island in New Jersey. Before 1972, when Congress adopted the federal Clean Water Act regulating the development of wetlands, Loveladies had developed 199 acres of the tract with homes (all but 6.4 acres had been sold to individual owners). After 1972, Loveladies sought to develop the remaining 51 acres. After years of negotiations with state officials, Loveladies agreed to develop only 12.5 acres by building 35 homes. Because the project would requiring filling 11.5 acres, Loveladies needed a federal "dredge and fill" permit under § 404 of the Clean Water Act. The Army Corps of Engineers denied the permit in 1982.

Loveladies sued, claiming a taking. In deciding the taking issue, what is the appropriate size of property to be considered? The 250–acre tract? The 51–acre tract? Or the 12.5–acre tract? *See Loveladies Harbor, Inc. v. United States*, 28 F.3d 1171 (Fed.Cir.1994). *See generally* Lisker, Regulatory Takings and the Denominator Problem, 27 Rutgers L. Rev. 663 (1996); Fee, Unearthing the Denominator in Regulatory Takings, 61 U. Chi. L. Rev. 1535 (1994).

2.   The annual development costs for a typical pesticide range from $5 to 15 million. Development of a single product typically takes more than a decade and occasionally takes over 20 years, during which time the company has no return on its investment. For every pesticide that reaches the market, a company may have screened and tested 20,000 other chemicals. For these reasons, pesticide companies believe that the information they develop in the course of product development is extremely valuable, and they take extraordinary steps to ensure that the data remain secret.

In 1978, Congress granted applicants seeking to register new pesticides a 10–year period during which the applicant would have exclusive use of data for new active ingredients in the pesticides (in other words, for 10 years EPA may not disclose or use the data to evaluate another company's application). EPA may use all other data to evaluate another company's application for a similar chemical, but for the first 15 years after the initial submission, the applicant would have to compensate the original submitter. Finally, except for information that would reveal "manufacturing or quality control processes" EPA may at any time publicly disclose health, safety, and environmental data.

A pesticide company has brought suit seeking a declaratory judgment that the pesticide statute constitutes a taking.

Data as Property. Are the health, safety and environmental data property? How would you decide that question? Consider the following statement from a taking case: "Property interests * * * are not created by the Constitution. Rather, they are created and their dimensions are defined by existing rules or understandings that stem from an independent source such as state law." *Webb's Fabulous Pharmacies, Inc. v. Beckwith*, 449 U.S. 155, 161, 101 S.Ct. 446, 450, 66 L.Ed.2d 358 (1980). Are there any characteristics of trade secrets that would cause you to think of them as property or not as property?

Taking. Assuming that the data are property, has there been a taking of any data submitted after adoption of the 1978 law? Is there a taking of the active ingredient data after expiration of the 10–year period? Is there a taking of the other data before expiration of the 15–year compensation period? Is there a taking after expiration of that period? Is there a taking of health, safety, and environmental data disclosed under the public disclosure provision? If you find there is not a taking, is there any constitutional limit to the government's ability to disclose these data?

See Ruckelshaus v. Monsanto Co., 467 U.S. 986, 104 S.Ct. 2862, 81 L.Ed.2d 815 (1984).

Takings Doctrine Since *Penn Central*. The doctrinal muddle that *Penn Central* exemplifies was further compounded in *Agins v. City of Tiburon*, 447 U.S. 255, 100 S.Ct. 2138, 65 L.Ed.2d 106 (1980) and *Keystone Bituminous Coal Ass'n v. DeBenedictis*, 480 U.S. 470, 107 S.Ct. 1232, 94 L.Ed.2d 472 (1987). In *Agins* the city zoned some undeveloped land as open space. The zoning ordinance prevented the landowners from building as many houses as they had originally intended. The Court held that the regulation was not a taking so long as it "substantially advance[s] legitimate state interests" and does not "den[y] an owner economically viable use of his land." 447 U.S. at 260, 100 S.Ct. at 2141. The municipality's interest in conserving open space easily met the first criterion; regarding the second criterion, the Court wrote that since the landowners could build some houses on the land, they were "free to pursue their reasonable investment expectations by submitting a development plan to local officials." 447 U.S. at 262, 100 S.Ct. at 2142. The greatest significance of *Agins* may be that it increased the standard from "reasonably effectuates" a state interest (*Penn Central*) to "substantially advances" a state interest (*Agins*).

In *Keystone*, the Court was faced with a statute remarkably similar to the statute struck down in *Mahon*. Relying on *Agins* and *Penn Central*, however, the Court found that the statute advanced legitimate government interests in public health, environment, and the fiscal integrity of the region. Although the statute denied the company some use of its property, the Court held that viewing the company's property as a whole, the statute did not deny the company economically viable use of its property. "[T]here is no showing that petitioners' reasonable 'investment-backed expectations' have been materially affected by the additional duty to retain the small percentage [of coal] that must be used to support the structures protected" by the Act. 480 U.S. at 499, 107 S.Ct. at 1249.

At present *Penn Central* is probably the outer limit of takings doctrine. After *Penn Central*, the Court decided a series of cases giving landowners somewhat greater constitutional rights against government takings. *See Nollan v. California Coastal Comm'n*, 483 U.S. 825, 107 S.Ct. 3141, 97

L.Ed.2d 677 (1987) (a land use agency must demonstrate a sufficient nexus between an exaction demanded in exchange for a building permit and the legitimate government interest served by the exaction); *Dolan v. City of Tigard*, 512 U.S. 374, 114 S.Ct. 2309, 129 L.Ed.2d 304 (1994) (the government must demonstrate at least a "rough proportionality" between an exaction and the problem it addresses); *First English Evangelical Lutheran Church of Glendale v. County of Los Angeles*, 482 U.S. 304, 107 S.Ct. 2378, 96 L.Ed.2d 250 (1987) (where the government has taken property through a land use regulation, the landowner is entitled to compensation from the moment his land is restricted, not just from the time the regulation is determined to be a taking). Then, in *Lucas v. South Carolina Coastal Council*, the Court reintroduced state nuisance law as a basis to decide whether a taking has occurred.[47]

Lucas v. South Carolina Coastal Council

505 U.S. 1003, 112 S.Ct. 2886, 120 L.Ed.2d 798 (1992).

■ JUSTICE SCALIA delivered the opinion of the Court.

In 1986, petitioner David H. Lucas paid $975,000 for two residential lots on the Isle of Palms in Charleston County, South Carolina, on which he intended to build single-family homes. In 1988, however, the South Carolina Legislature enacted the Beachfront Management Act, S.C. Code § 48–39–250 *et seq.* (Supp. 1990) (Act), which had the direct effect of barring petitioner from erecting any permanent habitable structures on his two parcels. *See* § 48–39–290(A). A state trial court found that this prohibition rendered Lucas's parcels "valueless." This case requires us to decide

---

47. As the Court developed takings doctrine over the last two decades, it also developed a ripeness doctrine that has kept most "as-applied" takings claims in state court. *See Agins v. City of Tiburon*, 447 U.S. 255, 262, 100 S.Ct. 2138, 2142, 65 L.Ed.2d 106 (1980) (because the landowner had not submitted a development plan as required by the ordinance, federal courts could not consider the landowner's claim that the ordinance as applied to that land constituted a taking); *San Diego Gas & Electric Co. v. City of San Diego*, 450 U.S. 621, 101 S.Ct. 1287, 67 L.Ed.2d 551 (1981) (because the state court had ruled only that damages was not an available remedy under state law, but had not ruled either whether there was a taking or whether other remedies were available, the state court's decision was not final and was not yet subject to Supreme Court review); *Williamson County Regional Planning*

Comm'n v. Hamilton Bank, 473 U.S. 172, 186–97, 105 S.Ct. 3108, 3116–22, 87 L.Ed.2d 126 (1985) (a regulatory taking claim was not ripe because the landowner had not sought variances that would have allowed it to develop the property, and because it did not use state procedures, including state judicial procedures, to seek compensation for the alleged taking); *Executive 100, Inc. v. Martin County*, 922 F.2d 1536, 1540–41 (11th Cir.1991) (dismissing claim that denial of rezoning was a taking; claim was not ripe because plaintiffs had not yet sought variances); *Bateson v. Geisse*, 857 F.2d 1300, 1306 (9th Cir.1988) (dismissing claim that withholding building permit was a taking; claim was not ripe since plaintiff had not yet sought compensation in state court for inverse condemnation). *But see Suitum v. Tahoe Regional Planning Agency*, ___ U.S. ___, 117 S.Ct. 1659, ___ L.Ed.2d ___ (1997) (A landowner may chal-

whether the Act's dramatic effect on the economic value of Lucas's lots accomplished a taking of private property under the Fifth and Fourteenth Amendments requiring the payment of "just compensation."

I

A

South Carolina's expressed interest in intensively managing development activities in the so-called "coastal zone" dates from 1977 when, in the aftermath of Congress's passage of the federal Coastal Zone Management Act of 1972, 86 Stat. 1280, as amended, 16 U. S. C. § 1451 *et seq.*, the legislature enacted a Coastal Zone Management Act of its own. *See* S.C. Code § 48–39–10 *et seq.* (1987). In its original form, the South Carolina Act required owners of coastal zone land that qualified as a "critical area" (defined in the legislation to include beaches and immediately adjacent sand dunes, § 48–39–10(J)) to obtain a permit from the newly created South Carolina Coastal Council (respondent here) prior to committing the land to a "use other than the use the critical area was devoted to on [September 28, 1977]." § 48–39–130(A).

In the late 1970's, Lucas and others began extensive residential development of the Isle of Palms, a barrier island situated eastward of the City of Charleston. Toward the close of the development cycle for one residential subdivision known as "Beachwood East," Lucas in 1986 purchased the two lots at issue in this litigation for his own account. No portion of the lots, which were located approximately 300 feet from the beach, qualified as a "critical area" under the 1977 Act; accordingly, at the time Lucas acquired these parcels, he was not legally obliged to obtain a permit from the Council in advance of any development activity. His intention with respect to the lots was to do what the owners of the immediately adjacent parcels had already done: erect single-family residences. He commissioned architectural drawings for this purpose.

The Beachfront Management Act brought Lucas's plans to an abrupt end. Under that 1988 legislation, the Council was directed to establish a "baseline" connecting the landward-most "point[s] of erosion . . . during the past forty years" in the region of the Isle of Palms that includes Lucas's lots. § 48–39–280(A)(2) (Supp. 1988). In action not challenged here, the Council fixed this baseline landward of Lucas's parcels. That was significant, for under the Act construction of occupiable improvements[48] was flatly prohibited seaward of a line drawn 20 feet landward of, and parallel to, the baseline, § 48–39–290(A) (Supp. 1988). The Act provided no exceptions.

B

Lucas promptly filed suit in the South Carolina Court of Common Pleas, contending that the Beachfront Management Act's construction bar

---

lenge a final agency decision prohibiting development without first attempting to sell "transferable development rights" to reduce the impact of the restriction.)

48. The Act did allow the construction of certain nonhabitable improvements, *e.g.*, "wooden walkways no larger in width than six feet," and small wooden decks no larger than one hundred forty-four square feet." §§ 48–39–290(A)(1) and (2) (Supp. 1988).

effected a taking of his property without just compensation. Lucas did not take issue with the validity of the Act as a lawful exercise of South Carolina's police power, but contended that the Act's complete extinguishment of his property's value entitled him to compensation regardless of whether the legislature had acted in furtherance of legitimate police power objectives. Following a bench trial, the court agreed. Among its factual determinations was the finding that "at the time Lucas purchased the two lots, both were zoned for single-family residential construction and * * * there were no restrictions imposed upon such use of the property by either the State of South Carolina, the County of Charleston, or the Town of the Isle of Palms." The trial court further found that the Beachfront Management Act decreed a permanent ban on construction insofar as Lucas's lots were concerned, and that this prohibition "deprive[d] Lucas of any reasonable economic use of the lots, * * * eliminated the unrestricted right of use, and render[ed] them valueless." *Id.*, at 37. The court thus concluded that Lucas's properties had been "taken" by operation of the Act, and it ordered respondent to pay "just compensation" in the amount of $1,232,-387.50. *Id.*, at 40.

The Supreme Court of South Carolina reversed. It found dispositive what it described as Lucas's concession "that the Beachfront Management Act [was] properly and validly designed to preserve ... South Carolina's beaches." 304 S. C. 376, 379, 404 S. E. 2d 895, 896 (1991). Failing an attack on the validity of the statute as such, the court believed itself bound to accept the "uncontested ... findings" of the South Carolina legislature that new construction in the coastal zone—such as petitioner intended—threatened this public resource. *Id.*, at 383, 404 S. E. 2d, at 898. The Court ruled that when a regulation respecting the use of property is designed "to prevent serious public harm," *id.*, at 383, 404 S. E. 2d, at 899 (citing, *inter alia*, *Mugler v. Kansas*, 123 U. S. 623 (1887)), no compensation is owing under the Takings Clause regardless of the regulation's effect on the property's value. * * *

II

[The majority dismissed the argument that this case was inappropriate for plenary review on ripeness grounds. After briefing and argument but prior to the issuance of the South Carolina Supreme Court's decision, South Carolina amended the Beachfront Management Act to authorize the Council, in certain circumstances, to issue "special permits" for the construction or reconstruction of habitable structures seaward of the baseline. Despite the fact that Lucas may have been able to obtain such a permit, the majority concluded that the case was ripe because the South Carolina Supreme Court did not rest its decision on ripeness grounds, thereby precluding Lucas from any remedy for his alleged deprivation up to the time of the 1990 amendment. *See First English Evangelical Lutheran Church of Glendale v. County of Los Angeles*, 482 U.S. 304 (1987) (holding that temporary deprivations of use are compensable under the Takings Clause).]

III

A

Prior to Justice Holmes' exposition in *Pennsylvania Coal Co. v. Mahon*, 260 U. S. 393 (1922), it was generally thought that the Takings Clause reached only a "direct appropriation" of property, *Legal Tender Cases*, 12 Wall. 457, 551 (1871), or the functional equivalent of a "practical ouster of [the owner's] possession." *Northern Transportation Co. v. Chicago*, 99 U.S. 635, 642 (1879). *See also Gibson v. United States*, 166 U. S. 269, 275–276 (1897). Justice Holmes recognized in *Mahon*, however, that if the protection against physical appropriations of private property was to be meaningfully enforced, the government's power to redefine the range of interests included in the ownership of property was necessarily constrained by constitutional limits. 260 U. S., at 414–415. If, instead, the uses of private property were subject to unbridled, uncompensated qualification under the police power, "the natural tendency of human nature [would be] to extend the qualification more and more until at last private property disappear[ed]." *Id.*, at 415. These considerations gave birth in that case to the oft-cited maxim that, "while property may be regulated to a certain extent, if regulation goes too far it will be recognized as a taking." *Ibid.*

Nevertheless, our decision in *Mahon* offered little insight into when, and under what circumstances, a given regulation would be seen as going "too far" for purposes of the Fifth Amendment. In 70–odd years of succeeding "regulatory takings" jurisprudence, we have generally eschewed any "'set formula'" for determining how far is too far, preferring to "engag[e] in * * * essentially ad hoc, factual inquiries," *Penn Central Transportation Co. v. New York City*, 438 U. S. 104, 124 (1978) (quoting *Goldblatt v. Hempstead*, 369 U. S. 590, 594 (1962)). *See* Epstein, Takings: Descent and Resurrection, 1987 Sup. Ct. Rev. 1, 4. We have, however, described at least two discrete categories of regulatory action as compensable without case-specific inquiry into the public interest advanced in support of the restraint. The first encompasses regulations that compel the property owner to suffer a physical "invasion" of his property. In general (at least with regard to permanent invasions), no matter how minute the intrusion, and no matter how weighty the public purpose behind it, we have required compensation. For example, in *Loretto v. Teleprompter Manhattan CATV Corp.*, 458 U. S. 419 (1982), we determined that New York's law requiring landlords to allow television cable companies to emplace cable facilities in their apartment buildings constituted a taking, *id.*, at 435–440, even though the facilities occupied at most only [1.5] cubic feet of the landlords' property, *see id.*, at 438, n. 16. *See also United States v. Causby*, 328 U. S. 256, 265, and n. 10 (1946) (physical invasions of airspace); *cf. Kaiser Aetna v. United States*, 444 U. S. 164 (1979) (imposition of navigational servitude upon private marina).

The second situation in which we have found categorical treatment appropriate is where regulation denies all economically beneficial or productive use of land. *See Agins*, 447 U. S., at 260; *see also Nollan v. California Coastal Comm'n*, 483 U. S. 825, 834 (1987); *Keystone Bitumi-*

nous Coal Assn. v. DeBenedictis, 480 U. S. 470, 495 (1987); *Hodel v. Virginia Surface Mining & Reclamation Assn., Inc.*, 452 U. S. 264, 295–296 (1981). As we have said on numerous occasions, the Fifth Amendment is violated when land-use regulation "does not substantially advance legitimate state interests or *denies an owner economically viable use of his land.*" *Agins, supra*, at 260 (citations omitted) (emphasis added).[49]

We have never set forth the justification for this rule. Perhaps it is simply, as Justice Brennan suggested, that total deprivation of beneficial use is, from the landowner's point of view, the equivalent of a physical appropriation. *See San Diego Gas & Electric Co. v. San Diego*, 450 U. S., at 652 (Brennan, J., dissenting). "[F]or what is the land but the profits thereof [?]" 1 E. Coke, Institutes ch. 1, § 1 (1st Am. ed. 1812). Surely, at least, in the extraordinary circumstance when no productive or economically beneficial use of land is permitted, it is less realistic to indulge our usual assumption that the legislature is simply "adjusting the benefits and burdens of economic life," *Penn Central Transportation Co.*, 438 U. S., at 124, in a manner that secures an "average reciprocity of advantage" to everyone concerned. *Pennsylvania Coal Co. v. Mahon*, 260 U. S., at 415. And the functional basis for permitting the government, by regulation, to affect property values without compensation—that "Government hardly could go on if to some extent values incident to property could not be diminished without paying for every such change in the general law," *id.*, at 413—does not apply to the relatively rare situations where the government has deprived a landowner of all economically beneficial uses.

49. Regrettably, the rhetorical force of our "deprivation of all economically feasible use" rule is greater than its precision, since the rule does not make clear the "property interest" against which the loss of value is to be measured. When, for example, a regulation requires a developer to leave 90% of a rural tract in its natural state, it is unclear whether we would analyze the situation as one in which the owner has been deprived of all economically beneficial use of the burdened portion of the tract, or as one in which the owner has suffered a mere diminution in value of the tract as a whole. (For an extreme—and, we think, unsupportable—view of the relevant calculus, *see Penn Central Transportation Co. v. New York City*, 42 N. Y. 2d 324, 333–334, 366 N. E. 2d 1271, 1276–1277 (1977), *aff'd*, 438 U. S. 104 (1978), where the state court examined the diminution in a particular parcel's value produced by a municipal ordinance in light of total value of the taking claimant's other holdings in the vicinity.) Unsurprisingly, this uncertainty regarding the composition of the denominator in our "deprivation" fraction has produced inconsistent pronouncements by the Court. Compare *Pennsylvania Coal Co. v. Mahon*, 260 U.S. 393, 414 (1922) (law restricting subsurface extraction of coal held to effect a taking), with *Keystone Bituminous Coal Assn. v. DeBenedictis*, 480 U.S. 470, 497–502 (1987) (nearly identical law held not to effect a taking); *see also id.*, at 515–520 (Rehnquist, C.J., dissenting); Rose, *Mahon* Reconstructed: Why the Takings Issue is Still a Muddle, 57 S. Cal. L. Rev. 561, 566–569 (1984). The answer to this difficult question may lie in how the owner's reasonable expectations have been shaped by the State's law of property—*i.e.*, whether and to what degree the State's law has accorded legal recognition and protection to the particular interest in land with respect to which the takings claimant alleges a diminution in (or elimination of) value. In any event, we avoid this difficulty in the present case, since the "interest in land" that Lucas has pleaded (a fee simple interest) is an estate with a rich tradition of protection at common law, and since the South Carolina Court of Common Pleas found that the Beachfront Management Act left each of Lucas's beachfront lots without economic value.

On the other side of the balance, affirmatively supporting a compensation requirement, is the fact that regulations that leave the owner of land without economically beneficial or productive options for its use—typically, as here, by requiring land to be left substantially in its natural state—carry with them a heightened risk that private property is being pressed into some form of public service under the guise of mitigating serious public harm. *See, e.g., Annicelli v. South Kingstown,* 463 A. 2d 133, 140–141 (R.I.1983) (prohibition on construction adjacent to beach justified on twin grounds of safety and "conservation of open space"); *Morris County Land Improvement Co. v. Parsippany–Troy Hills Township,* 40 N. J. 539, 552–553, 193 A. 2d 232, 240 (1963) (prohibition on filling marshlands imposed in order to preserve region as water detention basin and create wildlife refuge). As Justice Brennan explained: "From the government's point of view, the benefits flowing to the public from preservation of open space through regulation may be equally great as from creating a wildlife refuge through formal condemnation or increasing electricity production through a dam project that floods private property." *San Diego Gas & Elec. Co., supra,* at 652 (Brennan, J., dissenting). The many statutes on the books, both state and federal, that provide for the use of eminent domain to impose servitudes on private scenic lands preventing developmental uses, or to acquire such lands altogether, suggest the practical equivalence in this setting of negative regulation and appropriation. *See, e.g.,* 16 U. S. C. § 410ff–1(a) (authorizing acquisition of "lands, waters, or interests [within Channel Islands National Park] (including but not limited to scenic easements)"); § 460aa–2(a) (authorizing acquisition of "any lands, or lesser interests therein, including mineral interests and scenic easements" within Sawtooth National Recreation Area); §§ 3921–3923 (authorizing acquisition of wetlands); N. C. Gen. Stat. § 113A–38 (1990) (authorizing acquisition of, inter alia, "scenic easements" within the North Carolina natural and scenic rivers system); Tenn. Code Ann. §§ 11–15–101 to 11–15–108 (1987) (authorizing acquisition of "protective easements" and other rights in real property adjacent to State's historic, architectural, archaeological, or cultural resources).

We think, in short, that there are good reasons for our frequently expressed belief that when the owner of real property has been called upon to sacrifice *all* economically beneficial uses in the name of the common good, that is, to leave his property economically idle, he has suffered a taking.[50]

---

50. Justice Stevens criticizes the "deprivation of all economically beneficial use" rule as "wholly arbitrary," in that "[the] landowner whose property is diminished in value 95% recovers nothing," while the landowner who suffers a complete elimination of value "recovers the land's full value." This analysis errs in its assumption that the landowner whose deprivation is one step short of complete is not entitled to compensation. Such an owner might not be able to claim the benefit of our categorical formulation, but, as we have acknowledged time and again, "[t]he economic impact of the regulation on the claimant and * * * the extent to which the regulation has interfered with distinct investment-backed expectations" are keenly relevant to takings analysis generally. *Penn Central Transportation Co. v. New York City,* 438 U. S. 104, 124 (1978). It is true that in at

B

The trial court found Lucas's two beachfront lots to have been rendered valueless by respondent's enforcement of the coastal-zone construction ban. Under Lucas's theory of the case, which rested upon our "no economically viable use" statements, that finding entitled him to compensation. Lucas believed it unnecessary to take issue with either the purposes behind the Beachfront Management Act, or the means chosen by the South Carolina Legislature to effectuate those purposes. The South Carolina Supreme Court, however, thought otherwise. In its view, the Beachfront Management Act was no ordinary enactment, but involved an exercise of South Carolina's "police powers" to mitigate the harm to the public interest that petitioner's use of his land might occasion. 304 S.C., at 384, 404 S.E.2d, at 899. By neglecting to dispute the findings enumerated in the Act[51] or otherwise to challenge the legislature's purposes, petitioner "con-

least some cases the landowner with 95% loss will get nothing, while the landowner with total loss will recover in full. But that occasional result is no more strange than the gross disparity between the landowner whose premises are taken for a highway (who recovers in full) and the landowner whose property is reduced to 5% of its former value by the highway (who recovers nothing). Takings law is full of these "all-or-nothing" situations.

Justice Stevens similarly misinterprets our focus on "developmental" uses of property (the uses proscribed by the Beachfront Management Act) as betraying an "assumption that the only uses of property cognizable under the Constitution are developmental uses." We make no such assumption. Though our prior takings cases evince an abiding concern for the productive use of, and economic investment in, land, there are plainly a number of noneconomic interests in land whose impairment will invite exceedingly close scrutiny under the Takings Clause. *See, e.g., Loretto v. Teleprompter Manhattan CATV Corp.*, 458 U.S. 419, 436 (1982) (interest in excluding strangers from one's land).

51. The legislature's express findings include the following: "The General Assembly finds that:

"(1) The beach/dune system along the coast of South Carolina is extremely important to the people of this State and serves the following functions:

"(a) protects life and property by serving as a storm barrier which dissipates wave energy and contributes to shoreline stability in an economical and effective manner;

"(b) provides the basis for a tourism industry that generates approximately two-thirds of South Carolina's annual tourism industry revenue which constitutes a significant portion of the state's economy. The tourists who come to the South Carolina coast to enjoy the ocean and dry sand beach contribute significantly to state and local tax revenues;

"(c) provides habitat for numerous species of plants and animals, several of which are threatened or endangered. Waters adjacent to the beach/dune system also provide habitat for many other marine species;

"(d) provides a natural health environment for the citizens of South Carolina to spend leisure time which serves their physical and mental well-being.

"(2) Beach/dune system vegetation is unique and extremely important to the vitality and preservation of the system.

"(3) Many miles of South Carolina's beaches have been identified as critically eroding.

"(4) * * * [D]evelopment unwisely has been sited too close to the [beach/dune] system. This type of development has jeopardized the stability of the beach/dune system, accelerated erosion, and endangered adjacent property. It is in both the public and private interests to protect the system from this unwise development.

"(5) The use of armoring in the form of hard erosion control devices such as seawalls, bulkheads, and rip-rap to protect erosion-threatened structures adjacent to the beach

cede[d] that the beach/dune area of South Carolina's shores is an extremely valuable public resource; that the erection of new construction, *inter alia*, contributes to the erosion and destruction of this public resource; and that discouraging new construction in close proximity to the beach/dune area is necessary to prevent a great public harm." *Id.*, at 382–383, 404 S. E. 2d, at 898. In the court's view, these concessions brought petitioner's challenge within a long line of this Court's cases sustaining against Due Process and Takings Clause challenges the State's use of its "police powers" to enjoin a property owner from activities akin to public nuisances. *See Mugler v. Kansas*, 123 U. S. 623 (1887) (law prohibiting manufacture of alcoholic beverages); *Hadacheck v. Sebastian*, 239 U. S. 394 (1915) (law barring operation of brick mill in residential area); *Miller v. Schoene*, 276 U. S. 272 (1928) (order to destroy diseased cedar trees to prevent infection of nearby orchards); *Goldblatt v. Hempstead*, 369 U. S. 590 (1962) (law effectively preventing continued operation of quarry in residential area).

It is correct that many of our prior opinions have suggested that "harmful or noxious uses" of property may be proscribed by government regulation without the requirement of compensation. For a number of reasons, however, we think the South Carolina Supreme Court was too quick to conclude that that principle decides the present case. The "harmful or noxious uses" principle was the Court's early attempt to describe in theoretical terms why government may, consistent with the Takings Clause, affect property values by regulation without incurring an obligation to compensate—a reality we nowadays acknowledge explicitly with respect to the full scope of the State's police power. *See, e.g., Penn Central Transportation Co.*, 438 U. S., at 125 (where State "reasonably conclude[s] that 'the health, safety, morals, or general welfare' would be promoted by prohibiting particular contemplated uses of land," compensation need not accompany prohibition); *see also Nollan v. California Coastal Commission*, 483 U. S., at 834–835 ("Our cases have not elaborated on the standards for determining what constitutes a 'legitimate state interest[,]' [but][t]hey have made clear ... that a broad range of governmental purposes and regulations satisfy these requirements"). We made this very point in *Penn Central Transportation Co.*, where, in the course of sustaining New York City's landmarks preservation program against a takings challenge, we rejected the petitioner's suggestion that *Mugler* and the cases following it

has not proven effective. These armoring devices have given a false sense of security to beachfront property owners. In reality, these hard structures, in many instances, have increased the vulnerability of beachfront property to damage from wind and waves while contributing to the deterioration and loss of the dry sand beach which is so important to the tourism industry.

"(6) Erosion is a natural process which becomes a significant problem for man only when structures are erected in close proximity to the beach/dune system. It is in both the public and private interests to afford the beach/dune system space to accrete and erode in its natural cycle. This space can be provided only by discouraging new construction in close proximity to the beach/dune system and encouraging those who have erected structures too close to the system to retreat from it. * * *

"(8) It is in the state's best interest to protect and to promote increased public access to South Carolina's beaches for out-of-state tourists and South Carolina residents alike." S. C. Code § 48–39–250 (Supp. 1991).

were premised on, and thus limited by, some objective conception of "noxiousness":

> [T]he uses in issue in *Hadacheck, Miller*, and *Goldblatt* were perfectly lawful in themselves. They involved no "blameworthiness, * * * moral wrongdoing or conscious act of dangerous risk-taking which induce[d society] to shift the cost to a pa[rt]icular individual." Sax, Takings and the Police Power, 74 Yale L. J. 36, 50 (1964). These cases are better understood as resting not on any supposed "noxious" quality of the prohibited uses but rather on the ground that the restrictions were reasonably related to the implementation of a policy—not unlike historic preservation—expected to produce a widespread public benefit and applicable to all similarly situated property. 438 U.S., at 133–134, n. 30.

"Harmful or noxious use" analysis was, in other words, simply the progenitor of our more contemporary statements that "land-use regulation does not effect a taking if it 'substantially advance[s] legitimate state interests.' ...'" *Nollan, supra,* at 834 (quoting *Agins v. Tiburon,* 447 U. S., at 260); *see also Penn Central Transportation Co., supra,* at 127; *Euclid v. Ambler Realty Co.,* 272 U. S. 365, 387–388 (1926).

The transition from our early focus on control of "noxious" uses to our contemporary understanding of the broad realm within which government may regulate without compensation was an easy one, since the distinction between "harm-preventing" and "benefit-conferring" regulation is often in the eye of the beholder. It is quite possible, for example, to describe in either fashion the ecological, economic, and aesthetic concerns that inspired the South Carolina legislature in the present case. One could say that imposing a servitude on Lucas's land is necessary in order to prevent his use of it from "harming" South Carolina's ecological resources; or, instead, in order to achieve the "benefits" of an ecological preserve.[52] *Compare, e.g., Claridge v. New Hampshire Wetlands Board,* 125 N.H. 745, 752, 485 A.2d 287, 292 (1984) (owner may, without compensation, be barred from filling wetlands because landfilling would deprive adjacent coastal habitats and marine fisheries of ecological support), *with, e.g., Bartlett v. Zoning Comm'n of Old Lyme,* 161 Conn. 24, 30, 282 A. 2d 907, 910 (1971) (owner barred from filling tidal marshland must be compensated, despite municipality's "laudable" goal of "preserv[ing] marshlands from encroachment or

52. In the present case, in fact, some of the "[South Carolina] legislature's 'findings'" to which the South Carolina Supreme Court purported to defer in characterizing the purpose of the Act as "harm-preventing," 304 S. C. 376, 385, 404 S. E. 2d 895, 900 (1991), seem to us phrased in "benefit-conferring" language instead. For example, they describe the importance of a construction ban in enhancing "South Carolina's annual tourism industry revenue," S. C. Code § 48–39–250(1)(b) (Supp. 1991), in "provid[ing] habitat for numerous species of plants and animals, several of which are threatened or endangered," § 48–39–250(1)(c), and in "provid[ing] a natural healthy environment for the citizens of South Carolina to spend leisure time which serves their physical and mental well-being." § 48–39–250(1)(d). It would be pointless to make the outcome of this case hang upon this terminology, since the same interests could readily be described in "harm-preventing" fashion. * * *

destruction"). Whether one or the other of the competing characterizations will come to one's lips in a particular case depends primarily upon one's evaluation of the worth of competing uses of real estate. *See* Restatement (Second) of Torts § 822, Comment g, p. 112 (1979) ("[p]ractically all human activities unless carried on in a wilderness interfere to some extent with others or involve some risk of interference"). A given restraint will be seen as mitigating "harm" to the adjacent parcels or securing a "benefit" for them, depending upon the observer's evaluation of the relative importance of the use that the restraint favors. *See* Sax, Takings and the Police Power, 74 Yale L. J. 36, 49 (1964) ("[T]he problem [in this area] is not one of noxiousness or harm-creating activity at all; rather it is a problem of inconsistency between perfectly innocent and independently desirable uses"). Whether Lucas's construction of single-family residences on his parcels should be described as bringing "harm" to South Carolina's adjacent ecological resources thus depends principally upon whether the describer believes that the State's use interest in nurturing those resources is so important that any competing adjacent use must yield.

When it is understood that "prevention of harmful use" was merely our early formulation of the police power justification necessary to sustain (without compensation) any regulatory diminution in value; and that the distinction between regulation that "prevents harmful use" and that which "confers benefits" is difficult, if not impossible, to discern on an objective, value-free basis; it becomes self-evident that noxious-use logic cannot serve as a touchstone to distinguish regulatory "takings"—which require compensation—from regulatory deprivations that do not require compensation. *A fortiori* the legislature's recitation of a noxious-use justification cannot be the basis for departing from our categorical rule that total regulatory takings must be compensated. If it were, departure would virtually always be allowed. The South Carolina Supreme Court's approach would essentially nullify *Mahon*'s affirmation of limits to the noncompensable exercise of the police power. Our cases provide no support for this: None of them that employed the logic of "harmful use" prevention to sustain a regulation involved an allegation that the regulation wholly eliminated the value of the claimant's land. *See Keystone Bituminous Coal Assn.*, 480 U. S., at 513–514 (Rehnquist, C.J., dissenting).[53]

Where the State seeks to sustain regulation that deprives land of all economically beneficial use, we think it may resist compensation only if the logically antecedent inquiry into the nature of the owner's estate shows that the proscribed use interests were not part of his title to begin with. This accords, we think, with our "takings" jurisprudence, which has

53. *E.g., Mugler v. Kansas*, 123 U. S. 623 (1887) (prohibition upon use of a building as a brewery; other uses permitted); *Plymouth Coal Co. v. Pennsylvania*, 232 U. S. 531 (1914) (requirement that "pillar" of coal be left in ground to safeguard mine workers; mineral rights could otherwise be exploited); *Reinman v. Little Rock*, 237 U. S. 171 (1915) (declaration that livery stable constituted a public nuisance; other uses of the property permitted); *Hadacheck v. Sebastian*, 239 U. S. 394 (1915) (prohibition of brick manufacturing in residential area; other uses permitted); *Goldblatt v. Hempstead*, 369 U. S. 590 (1962) (prohibition on excavation; other uses permitted).

traditionally been guided by the understandings of our citizens regarding the content of, and the State's power over, the "bundle of rights" that they acquire when they obtain title to property. It seems to us that the property owner necessarily expects the uses of his property to be restricted, from time to time, by various measures newly enacted by the State in legitimate exercise of its police powers; "[a]s long recognized, some values are enjoyed under an implied limitation and must yield to the police power." *Pennsylvania Coal Co. v. Mahon*, 260 U.S., at 413. And in the case of personal property, by reason of the State's traditionally high degree of control over commercial dealings, he ought to be aware of the possibility that new regulation might even render his property economically worthless (at least if the property's only economically productive use is sale or manufacture for sale). *See Andrus v. Allard*, 444 U.S. 51, 66–67 (1979) (prohibition on sale of eagle feathers). In the case of land, however, we think the notion pressed by the Council that title is somehow held subject to the "implied limitation" that the State may subsequently eliminate all economically valuable use is inconsistent with the historical compact recorded in the Takings Clause that has become part of our constitutional culture.

Where "permanent physical occupation" of land is concerned, we have refused to allow the government to decree it anew (without compensation), no matter how weighty the asserted "public interests" involved, *Loretto v. Teleprompter Manhattan CATV Corp.*, 458 U.S., at 426—though we assuredly would permit the government to assert a permanent easement that was a pre-existing limitation upon the landowner's title. *Compare Scranton v. Wheeler*, 179 U.S. 141, 163 (1900) (interests of "riparian owner in the submerged lands * * * bordering on a public navigable water" held subject to Government's navigational servitude), *with Kaiser Aetna v. United States*, 444 U. S., at 178–180 (imposition of navigational servitude on marina created and rendered navigable at private expense held to constitute a taking). We believe similar treatment must be accorded confiscatory regulations, *i.e.*, regulations that prohibit all economically beneficial use of land: Any limitation so severe cannot be newly legislated or decreed (without compensation), but must inhere in the title itself, in the restrictions that background principles of the State's law of property and nuisance already place upon land ownership. A law or decree with such an effect must, in other words, do no more than duplicate the result that could have been achieved in the courts by adjacent landowners (or other uniquely affected persons) under the State's law of private nuisance, or by the State under its complementary power to abate nuisances that affect the public generally, or otherwise.

On this analysis, the owner of a lake bed, for example, would not be entitled to compensation when he is denied the requisite permit to engage in a landfilling operation that would have the effect of flooding others' land. Nor the corporate owner of a nuclear generating plant, when it is directed to remove all improvements from its land upon discovery that the plant sits astride an earthquake fault. Such regulatory action may well have the effect of eliminating the land's only economically productive use, but it does not proscribe a productive use that was previously permissible under relevant property and nuisance principles. The use of these properties for what are now expressly prohibited purposes was *always* unlawful, and (subject to other constitutional limitations) it was open to the State at any point to make the implication of those background principles of nuisance and property law explicit. *See* Michelman, Property, Utility, and Fairness, Comments on the Ethical Foundations of "Just Compensation" Law, 80 Harv. L. Rev. 1165, 1239–1241 (1967). In light of our traditional resort to "existing rules or understandings that stem from an independent source such as state law" to define the range of interests that qualify for protection as "property" under the Fifth and Fourteenth amendments, *Board of Regents of State Colleges v. Roth*, 408 U. S. 564, 577 (1972); *see, e.g., Ruckelshaus v. Monsanto Co.*, 467 U. S. 986, 1011–1012 (1984); *Hughes v. Washington*, 389 U. S. 290, 295 (1967) (Stewart, J., concurring), this recognition that the Takings Clause does not require compensation when an owner is barred from putting land to a use that is proscribed by those "existing rules or understandings" is surely unexceptional. When, however, a regulation that declares "off-limits" all economically productive or beneficial uses of land goes beyond what the relevant background principles would dictate, compensation must be paid to sustain it.

The "total taking" inquiry we require today will ordinarily entail (as the application of state nuisance law ordinarily entails) analysis of, among other things, the degree of harm to public lands and resources, or adjacent private property, posed by the claimant's proposed activities, *see, e.g.,* Restatement (Second) of Torts §§ 826, 827, the social value of the claimant's activities and their suitability to the locality in question, *see, e.g., id.,* §§ 828(a) and (b), 831, and the relative ease with which the alleged harm can be avoided through measures taken by the claimant and the government (or adjacent private landowners) alike, *see, e.g., id.,* §§ 827(e), 828(c), 830. The fact that a particular use has long been engaged in by similarly situated owners ordinarily imports a lack of any common-law prohibition (though changed circumstances or new knowledge may make what was previously permissible no longer so, *see* Restatement (Second) of Torts, *supra,* § 827, comment g). So also does the fact that other landowners, similarly situated, are permitted to continue the use denied to the claimant.

It seems unlikely that common-law principles would have prevented the erection of any habitable or productive improvements on petitioner's land; they rarely support prohibition of the "essential use" of land, *Curtin v. Benson*, 222 U. S. 78, 86 (1911). The question, however, is one of state law to be dealt with on remand. We emphasize that to win its case South Carolina must do more than proffer the legislature's declaration that the uses Lucas desires are inconsistent with the public interest, or the conclusory assertion that they violate a common-law maxim such as *sic utere tuo ut alienum non laedas*. As we have said, a "State, by *ipse dixit*, may not transform private property into public property without compensation. * * *" *Webb's Fabulous Pharmacies, Inc. v. Beckwith*, 449 U. S. 155, 164 (1980). Instead, as it would be required to do if it sought to restrain Lucas in a common-law action for public nuisance, South Carolina must identify background principles of nuisance and property law that prohibit the uses he now intends in the circumstances in which the property is presently found. Only on this showing can the State fairly claim that, in proscribing all such beneficial uses, the Beachfront Management Act is taking nothing.

* * *

The judgment is reversed and the cause remanded for proceedings not inconsistent with this opinion.

So ordered.

In a concurring opinion, Justice Kennedy argued that he would not have applied such a narrow view of a property owner's "reasonable, investment-backed expectations." In his view, such expectations "must be understood in light of the whole of our legal tradition," not merely nuisance law.

Justice Blackmun dissented, arguing that Takings Clause precedent allows the State to prohibit land uses that are injurious to public health, safety, or welfare without compensation "no matter how adverse the financial effect on the owner." Justice Stevens also dissented, arguing that the Court's categorical rule is without foundation in Supreme Court jurisprudence, is prone to abuse, and will "freeze the common law." Justice Souter would dismiss the writ of certiorari as having been improvidently granted on the ground that the trial court's determination that the state regulation had deprived the owner of his entire economic interest in the subject property is highly questionable.

Epilogue

On remand, the South Carolina Supreme Court concluded that there was no basis under state common law to find that Lucas' proposed use of his land was not part of the "bundle of sticks" that he acquired when be obtained title to his property. The state supreme court instructed the trial court to calculate damages for the temporary taking—the period of time from the enactment of the 1988 Act until the court's order. *Lucas v. South Carolina Coastal Council*, 309 S.C. 424, 424 S.E.2d 484 (1992).

---

1.   Under *Lucas*, must the government pay compensation only when a regulation that goes beyond background nuisance principles eliminates the entire remaining economic value of a parcel of land?

Lucas holds that the state's power to eliminate substantially all economic value without paying compensation depends on the background principles of nuisance law. Justice Kennedy would expand this reference point to include "all reasonable expectations," which would include "new regulatory initiatives in response to changing conditions." What problems do you foresee in applying the two approaches?

2. What model of the legislative/regulatory process underlies the analysis in *Lucas*? What is the role of the judiciary and the legislature in protecting ecosystems and private property rights? Do these roles accord with their institutional advantages and disadvantages?

3. Will *Lucas* likely yield an efficient allocation of resources? Is *Lucas* fair? By what criteria?

4. Does state nuisance law provide a secure mooring for takings law?

5. In his dissent, Justice Stevens warns that the majority's approach will "greatly hamper the efforts of local officials and planners who must deal with increasingly complex problems in land-use and environmental regulation." Justice Scalia, however, argues that the majority's approach will not significantly affect the government's ability to "go on" because of "the relatively rare situations where the government has deprived a landowner of all economically beneficial uses." Do you find Justice Scalia's assurance convincing? What are the implications of *Lucas* for the protection of ecosystems and natural resources?

6. Reconsider Professor Sax's analysis of compensation for takings following the *Penn Central* decision, *supra* pp. 344–50. Does the Supreme Court in *Lucas* appear to be following the course he charted? Professor Sax interprets *Lucas* as conveying the message that "[s]tates may not regulate land use solely by requiring landowners to maintain their property in a natural state as part of a functioning ecosystem, even though those natural functions may be important to the ecosystem." Sax, Property Rights and the Economy of Nature: Understanding *Lucas v. South Carolina Coastal Council*, 45 Stan. L. Rev. 1433, 1438 (1993). He identifies two fundamentally different views of property. The conventional Lockean view "builds on the idea of property as a discrete entity that can be made one's own by working on it and transforming it into a human artifact." An ecological view of property, on the other hand, does not conceptualize land as "a passive entity waiting to be transformed by its landowner." Rather, the land "is already at work, performing important services in its unaltered state." Forests, for example, "regulate the global climate [and] marshes sustain marine fisheries." *Id.* at 1442.

Professor Sax welcomes the Court's recognition of the emerging view of land as a part of an ecosystem, as opposed to merely private property, but criticizes the Court's effort to limit the legal foundation for an ecosystem conception. He offers an alternative conception of private property, designed to accommodate both economic considerations and the needs of nature's economy. He suggests that it would have the following features:

1. Less focus on individual dominion, and the abandonment of the traditional "island" and "castle-and-moat" images of ownership.

2. More public decisions, because use would be determined ecosystemically, rather than tract by tract; or more decisions made on a broad, system-wide scale.

3. Increased ecological planning, because different kinds of lands have different roles.

4. Affirmative obligations by owners to protect natural services, with owners functioning as custodians as well as self-benefiting entrepreneurs.

45 Stan. L. Rev. at 1451. Professor Sax cites as an appropriate model the system of rights to navigable rivers that has developed in this country. "[O]ne may own private property rights in a navigable river to use the water, but those rights are subordinate to the community's transportation needs [and] may be entirely eliminated where the community's navigation needs so require." *Id.* at 1452. Essentially, "private property interests should be subject to some public claim or servitude, both limiting full privatization and demanding that any private benefits be compatible with public goals." *Id.* at 1453.

Could the Takings Clause embrace Professor Sax's ecological conception of private property? How would it work in practice? Would the *Lucas* case come out differently under this conception? What would be the effect of Sax's approach upon the pattern of land development?

7. *Takings versus Givings.* Protection against takings highlights an asymmetry within the background legal rules of our society. Whereas there is an express constitutional provision requiring the government to pay just compensation to those whose property is condemned for public use, we do not have a comparable principle requiring those who benefit from government projects to share their windfall with society at large. Consider the case of a new subway station. Those property owners who live directly on the land where the new station will be constructed will be compensated for the fair market value of the land taken (measured at the time of the taking—*i.e.*, presumably without consideration of price changes that would result from the project). Those who live nearby will reap large increases in property value as a result of the project. What principles might justify the asymmetry of requiring compensation for the losers but not exacting some of these gains from the winners?

Problems

1. At the urging of General Motors Corporation, the City of Detroit exercises its power of eminent domain to condemn part of a closely knit neighborhood to acquire land for the construction of a new automobile assembly plant. The plant will enhance job opportunities and expand the tax base. Is this a valid exercise of the police power? *See Poletown Neighborhood Council v. City of Detroit*, 410 Mich. 616, 304 N.W.2d 455 (1981).

2. A developer, suspecting that the city will soon amend the zoning law to limit development to single-family dwellings, purchases a lot zoned to permit multi-family housing (a more valuable zoning classification for

the developer). When the City later rezones the area for single-family housing, the developer claims a taking. Would it make any difference to your analysis that the developer knew that the zoning change was imminent when he purchased the land?

3. Recent scientific studies have shown an alarming loss of wetlands throughout the United States. This loss threatens the survival of waterfowl and other important levels of the ecological pyramid. Based upon these studies, the Wisconsin legislature enacts the "No Net Loss of Wetlands Act." The law does not preclude the development of any particular plot of land. Rather it requires that any land developer who wishes to fill a wetland to acquire and donate to the Wisconsin Department of Natural Resources for preservation an equivalent amount of wetland elsewhere in the state. For example, a developer could purchase a converted, diked wetland and reconvert it to its natural state by opening the dikes to permit tidal flow over the land. A developer who owns a wetland sues to enjoin enforcement of the Act. Will he prevail?

4. Re-read the Ronco Corp. and Maximus Corp. problem on pp. 317–18. Assume that a member of the state legislature has proposed the following bill:

Beltran Valley Conservation Act

§ 1 **Purpose**—To preserve the natural beauty of the Beltran Valley, protect the aquatic and wildlife ecosystems in the vicinity, and protect the picturesque scenery of the Lake Tahoe Basin.

§ 2 **Land Use Regulations**—Clear-cutting of trees shall be prohibited in the watershed region of the Beltran Valley extending five miles on either side of Sylvia Creek.

The bill's prohibition on clear-cutting would bar clear-cutting on 10% of the Maximus Corp. tract. It would also require the Ronco Corp. to scale back its ski resort to about half the present proposed size. Finally, the bill would bar clear-cutting on 100% of a third tract, the "Little" tract. The Little tract, which straddles the Sylvia Creek and sits between the Ronco Corp. and Maximus Corp. tracts, has no economic value apart from timber harvesting. The owner, Sam Little, wants to sell the tract to Maximus Corp.

The Judiciary Committee has asked you to assess the constitutionality of this bill. You are asked in particular to decide whether this legislation must include a provision to pay compensation to any of the landowners in Beltran Valley.

5. Notwithstanding the *Lucas* decision, South Carolina remains intent on protecting coastal areas from the erosive forces of the ocean. It enacts the "Critical Coastal Area Construction Code Upgrade Act" which requires that all new buildings constructed in inlet areas along the coast be stabilized by heavily reinforced jetties, terminal groins, and heavily reinforced foundations. The cost of meeting these new code requirements will make the development of many parcels economically infeasible, although

the code is carefully tailored to ensure that it would be technologically feasible to develop all coastal properties. In addition, existing structures must be upgraded to code requirements as a condition of any sales contract. Moreover, all owners of structures in critical areas are subject to a special annual assessment of 3% of the assessed value of improvements to their property. This supplemental property tax will be used by the South Carolina Coastal Council to stabilize the coastal ecosystem. A landowner who owns undeveloped land and a landowner who wants to sell his developed land sue to enjoin enforcement of these provisions. What results would you predict?

6. Although the Takings Clause is self-executing—a court may enforce it without implementing legislation—nothing prevents the government from adopting rules and statutes even more protective of property rights. The non-constitutional efforts follow two main approaches: informational and compensatory.

The informational approach is exemplified by Executive Order 12630, 3 CFR § 554 (1988). The Order—which applies to proposed regulations, proposed legislation, and permits—requires all federal executive departments and agencies to

(a) ensure that permit conditions (1) "[s]erve the same purpose that would have been served by a prohibition of the use or action; and (2) substantially advance that purpose";

(b) ensure that restrictions on the use of property are "not * * * disproportionate to the extent to which the use contributes to the overall problem that the restriction is imposed to redress";

(c) ensure that the permitting process is "kept to the minimum necessary";

(d) prepare documents that (1) "identify clearly * * * the public health or safety risk"; (2) establish that the proposed government action "substantially advances the purpose of protecting public health and safety against the specifically identified risk"; (3) establish that "the restrictions imposed on the private property are not disproportionate" to the risk; (4) estimate the cost to the government in the event that the government action is later deemed a taking.

Exec. Order § 4. Pursuant to § 1(c) of the Order, the Attorney General adopted Guidelines to assist departments and agencies in meeting their obligations under the Order.

Proposals in Congress take the compensatory approach. For example, a House bill would require the federal government to compensate property owners whose property was reduced in value by at least 33% by actions taken under the Endangered Species Act, 16 U.S.C.A. §§ 1531–1544, and the wetlands program of the Clean Water Act, 33 U.S.C.A. § 1344. The bill would deny compensation where the use restriction was proscribed by state law (including nuisance law) and where the federal action was designed to prevent an imminent and identifiable hazard to public health and safety or damage to other property. The property owner would receive not only compensation for devaluation, but also attorney and appraisal fees. The compensation would come out of the operating budget of the agency responsible for the reduction in property value. *See* H.R. 925, 104th Cong. 1st Sess. (Feb. 14, 1995).

A Senate bill was broader; it would cover all "agency and State" actions that reduced the value of private property by at least 33%. It also had an informational component: federal agencies were required to prepare a "takings impact analysis" for proposed actions. *See* S. 605, 104th Cong. 1st Sess. (Dec. 22, 1995). By the end of 1996, Congress had not enacted the proposed bills. *See generally* Sax, Takings Legislation: Where It Stands and What Is Next, 23 Ecology L.Q. 509 (1996); Rose, A Dozen Propositions on Private Property, Public Rights, and the New Takings Legislation, 53 Wash. & Lee L. Rev. 265 (1996); Walsh, Achieving the Proper Balance Between the Public and Private Property Interests: Closely Tailored Legislation as a Remedy, 19 Wm. & Mary Envt'l L. & Pol'y Rev. 317 (1995).

To what extent does the Executive Order go beyond the constitutional requirements as expressed in *Lucas*? What impact do you think the Executive Order has had? How valuable are commands requiring agencies to keep delays "to a minimum" or to ensure that restrictions are not disproportionate? What is the purpose of the documents the agency must prepare? Would the Order be more effective if the agencies had to release the information prepared pursuant to the Order?

How does the House bill differ from the constitutional takings doctrine, as expressed in *Lucas* and *Penn Central*? What would be the impact of the House bill on federal regulation? What is the purpose of the attorney fees provision? What is the purpose of the provision requiring compensation to be paid from the agency's annual appropriations? What would be the impact of the provisions in the Senate bill requiring a "takings impact analysis?"

Although the bills were motivated by allegations that environmental regulation was too burdensome for property owners, the Senate bill would sweep more broadly. What other types of legislation would be affected by the bill?

On balance, do the bills or does the Constitution strike a better balance between private property rights and societal needs to regulate property? What are your criteria?

---

6. LIMITATIONS ON THE RIGHTS OF PROPERTY OWNERS

The cases that follow illustrate conflicts between the rights of property owners and fundamental civil rights and interests of others. As you consider these cases, try to develop a framework to determine the point at which private property rights give way to competing societal interests.

State v. Shack

Supreme Court of New Jersey, 1971.
58 N.J. 297, 277 A.2d 369.

■ WEINTRAUB, C.J.

Defendants entered upon private property to aid migrant farmworkers employed and housed there. Having refused to depart upon the demand of the owner, defendants were charged with violating N.J.S.A. 2A:170–31 which provides that "[a]ny person who trespasses on any lands * * * after being forbidden so to trespass by the owner * * * is a disorderly person and shall be punished by a fine of not more than $50." Defendants were convicted in the Municipal Court of Deerfield Township and again on appeal in the County Court of Cumberland County on a trial *de novo.* * * *

Complainant, Tedesco, a farmer, employs migrant workers for his seasonal needs. As part of their compensation, these workers are housed at a camp on his property.

Defendant Tejeras is a field worker for the Farm Workers Division of the Southwest Citizens Organization for Poverty Elimination, known by the acronym SCOPE, a nonprofit corporation funded by the Office of Economic Opportunity pursuant to an act of Congress, 42 U.S.C. §§ 2861–2864. The role of SCOPE includes providing for the "health services of the migrant farm worker."

Defendant Shack is a staff attorney with the Farm Workers Division of Camden Regional Legal Services, Inc., known as "CRLS," also a nonprofit corporation funded by the Office of Economic Opportunity pursuant to an act of Congress, 42 U.S.C. § 2809(a)(3). The mission of CRLS includes legal advice and representation for these workers.

Differences had developed between Tedesco and these defendants prior to the events which led to the trespass charges now before us. Hence when defendant Tejeras wanted to go upon Tedesco's farm to find a migrant worker who needed medical aid for the removal of 28 sutures, he called upon defendant Shack for his help with respect to the legalities involved. Shack, too, had a mission to perform on Tedesco's farm; he wanted to discuss a legal problem with another migrant worker there employed and housed. Defendants arranged to go to the farm together. Shack carried literature to inform the migrant farmworkers of the assistance available to them under federal statutes, but no mention seems to have been made of that literature when Shack was later confronted by Tedesco.

Defendants entered upon Tedesco's property and as they neared the camp site where the farmworkers were housed, they were confronted by Tedesco who inquired of their purpose. Tejeras and Shack stated their missions. In response, Tedesco offered to find the injured worker, and as to the worker who needed legal advice, Tedesco also offered to locate the man but insisted that the consultation would have to take place in Tedesco's office and in his presence. Defendants declined, saying they had the right to see the men in the privacy of their living quarters and without Tedesco's supervision. Tedesco thereupon summoned a State Trooper who, however, refused to remove defendants except upon Tedesco's written complaint. Tedesco then executed the formal complaints charging violations of the trespass statute.

I.

[The court declined to consider the validity of federal constitutional claims, including an alleged violation of the First Amendment].

* * * We think it unnecessary to explore their validity. The reason is that we are satisfied that under our State law the ownership of real property does not include the right to bar access to governmental services available to migrant workers and hence there was no trespass within the meaning of the penal statute. The policy considerations which underlie that conclusion may be much the same as those which would be weighed with respect to one or more of the constitutional challenges, but a decision in nonconstitutional terms is more satisfactory, because the interests of migrant workers are more expansively served in that way than they would be if they had no more freedom than these constitutional concepts could be found to mandate if indeed they apply at all.

II.

Property rights serve human values. They are recognized to that end, and are limited by it. Title to real property cannot include dominion over the destiny of persons the owner permits to come upon the premises. Their well-being must remain the paramount concern of a system of law. Indeed the needs of the occupants may be so imperative and their strength so weak, that the law will deny the occupants the power to contract away what is deemed essential to their health, welfare, or dignity.

Here we are concerned with a highly disadvantaged segment of our society. We are told that every year farmworkers and their families numbering more than one million leave their home areas to fill the seasonal demand for farm labor in the United States. The Migratory Farm Labor Problem in the United States (1969 Report of Subcommittee on Migratory Labor of the United States Senate Committee on Labor and Public Welfare), p. 1. The migrant farmworkers come to New Jersey in substantial numbers. The report just cited places at 55,700 the number of man-months of such employment in our State in 1968 (p. 7). The numbers of workers so employed here in that year are estimated at 1,300 in April; 6,500 in May; 9,800 in June; 10,600 in July; 12,100 in August; 9,600 in September; and 5,500 in October (p. 9).

The migrant farmworkers are a community within but apart from the local scene. They are rootless and isolated. Although the need for their labors is evident, they are unorganized and without economic or political power. It is their plight alone that summoned government to their aid. In response, Congress provided under Title III–B of the Economic Opportunity Act of 1964 (42 U.S.C. § 2701 *et seq.*) for "assistance for migrant and other seasonally employed farmworkers and their families." Section 2861 states "the purpose of this part is to assist migrant and seasonal farmworkers and their families to improve their living conditions and develop skills necessary for a productive and self-sufficient life in an increasingly complex and technological society." Section 2862(b)(1) provides for funding of programs "to meet the immediate needs of migrant and seasonal farmworkers and their families, such as day care for children, education, health services, improved housing and sanitation (including the provision and maintenance of emergency and temporary housing and sanitation facilities), legal advice and representation, and consumer training and counseling." As we have said, SCOPE is engaged in a program funded under this section, and CRLS also pursues the objectives of this section although, we gather, it is funded under § 2809(a)(3), which is not limited in its concern to the migrant and other seasonally employed farmworkers and seeks "to further the cause of justice among persons living in poverty by mobilizing the assistance of lawyers and legal institutions and by providing legal advice, legal representation, counseling, education, and other appropriate services."

These ends would not be gained if the intended beneficiaries could be insulated from efforts to reach them. It is in this framework that we must decide whether the camp operator's rights in his lands may stand between the migrant workers and those who would aid them. The key to that aid is communication. Since the migrant workers are outside the mainstream of the communities in which they are housed and are unaware of their rights and opportunities and of the services available to them, they can be reached only by positive efforts tailored to that end. The Report of the Governor's Task Force on Migrant Farm Labor (1968) noted that "One of the major problems related to seasonal farm labor is the lack of adequate direct information with regard to the availability of public services," and that "there is a dire need to provide the workers with basic educational and informational material in a language and style that can be readily understood by the migrant" (pp. 101–102). The report stressed the problem of access and deplored the notion that property rights may stand as a barrier, saying "In our judgment, 'no trespass' signs represent the last dying remnants of paternalistic behavior" (p. 63).

A man's right in his real property of course is not absolute. It was a maxim of the common law that one should so use his property as not to injure the rights of others. Broom, Legal Maxims (10th ed. Kersley 1939), p. 238; 39 Words and Phrases, "Sic Utere Tuo ut Alienum Non Laedas," p. 335. Although hardly a precise solvent of actual controversies, the maxim does express the inevitable proposition that rights are relative and there must be an accommodation when they meet. Hence it has long been true that necessity, private or public, may justify entry upon the lands of another. For a catalogue of such situations, *see* Prosser, Torts (3d ed. 1964), § 24, pp. 127–129; 6A American Law of Property (A. J. Casner ed. 1954) § 28.10, p. 31; 52 Am.Jur., "Trespass," §§ 40–41, pp. 867–869. *See also* Restatement, Second, Torts (1965) §§ 197–211; *Krauth v. Geller*, 31 N.J. 270, 272–273, 157 A.2d 129 (1960).

The subject is not static. As pointed out in 5 Powell, Real Property (Rohan 1970) § 745, pp. 493–494, while society will protect the owner in his permissible interests in land, yet

* * * [s]uch an owner must expect to find the absoluteness of his property rights curtailed by the organs of society, for the promotion of the best interests of others for whom these organs also operate as protective agencies. The necessity for such curtailments is greater in a modern industrialized and urbanized society than it was in the relatively simple American society of fifty, 100, or 200 years ago. The current balance between individualism and dominance of the social interest depends not only upon political and social ideologies, but also upon the physical and social facts of the time and place under discussion.

Professor Powell added in § 746, pp. 494–496:

As one looks back along the historic road traversed by the law of land in England and in America, one sees a change from the viewpoint that he who owns may do as he pleases with what he owns, to a position which hesitatingly embodies an ingredient of stewardship; which grudgingly, but steadily, broadens the recognized scope of social interests in the utilization of things. * * *

The process involves not only the accommodation between the right of the owner and the interests of the general public in his use of this property, but involves also an accommodation between the right of the owner and the right of individuals who are parties with him in consensual transactions relating to the use of the property. Accordingly substantial alterations have been made as between a landlord and his tenant. *See Reste Realty Corp. v. Cooper*, 53 N.J. 444, 451–453, 251 A.2d 268 (1969); *Marini v. Ireland*, 56 N.J. 130, 141–143, 265 A.2d 526 (1970).

The argument in this case understandably included the question whether the migrant worker should be deemed to be a tenant and thus entitled to the tenant's right to receive visitors, *Williams v. Lubbering*, 73 N.J.L. 317, 319–320, 63 A. 90 (Sup.Ct.1906), or whether his residence on the employer's property should be deemed to be merely incidental and in aid of his employment, and hence to involve no possessory interest in the realty. *See Scottish Rite Co. v. Salkowitz*, 119 N.J.L. 558, 197 A. 43 (E. & A. 1938); *New Jersey Midland Ry. Co. v. Van Syckle*, 37 N.J.L. 496, 506 (E. & A. 1874); *Gray v. Reynolds*, 67 N.J.L. 169, 50 A. 670 (Sup.Ct.1901); *McQuade v. Emmons*, 38 N.J.L. 397 (Sup.Ct.1876); *Morris Canal & Banking Co. v. Mitchell*, 31 N.J.L. 99 (Sup.Ct.1864); *Schuman v. Zurawell*, 24 N.J.Misc. 180, 47 A.2d 560 (Cir.Ct.1946). These cases did not reach employment situations at all comparable with the one before us. Nor did they involve the question whether an employee who is not a tenant may have visitors notwithstanding the employer's prohibition. Rather they were concerned with whether notice must be given to end the employee's right to remain upon the premises, with whether the employer may remove the discharged employee without court order, and with the availability of a particular judicial remedy to achieve his removal by process. We of course are not concerned here with the right of a migrant worker to remain on the employer's property after the employment is ended.

We see no profit in trying to decide upon a conventional category and then forcing the present subject into it. That approach would be artificial and distorting. The quest is for a fair adjustment of the competing needs of the parties, in the light of the realities of the relationship between the migrant worker and the operator of the housing facility.

Thus approaching the case, we find it unthinkable that the farmer-employer can assert a right to isolate the migrant worker in any respect significant for the worker's well-being. The farmer, of course, is entitled to pursue his farming activities without interference, and this defendants readily concede. But we see no legitimate need for a right in the farmer to deny the worker the opportunity for aid available from federal, State, or local services, or from recognized charitable groups seeking to assist him. Hence representatives of these agencies and organizations may enter upon the premises to seek out the worker at his living quarters. So, too, the migrant worker must be allowed to receive visitors there of his own choice, so long as there is no behavior hurtful to others, and members of the press may not be denied reasonable access to workers who do not object to seeing them.

It is not our purpose to open the employer's premises to the general public if in fact the employer himself has not done so. We do not say, for example, that solicitors or peddlers of all kinds may enter on their own; we may assume for the present that the employer may regulate their entry or bar them, at least if the employer's purpose is not to gain a commercial advantage for himself or if the regulation does not deprive the migrant worker of practical access to things he needs.

And we are mindful of the employer's interest in his own and in his employees' security. Hence he may reasonably require a visitor to identify himself, and also to state his general purpose if the migrant worker has not already informed him that the visitor is expected. But the employer may not deny the worker his privacy or interfere with his opportunity to live with dignity and to enjoy associations customary among our citizens. These rights are too fundamental to be denied on the basis of an interest in real property and too fragile to be left to the unequal bargaining strength of the parties. *See Henningsen v. Bloomfield Motors, Inc.*, 32 N.J. 358, 403–404, 161 A.2d 69 (1960); *Ellsworth Dobbs, Inc. v. Johnson*, 50 N.J. 528, 555, 236 A.2d 843 (1967).

It follows that defendants here invaded no possessory right of the farmer-employer. Their conduct was therefore beyond the reach of the trespass statute. The judgments are accordingly reversed and the matters remanded to the County Court with directions to enter judgments of acquittal.

----

1.   What is the legal basis in *State v. Shack* to override Tedesco's right to exclude? Are there any other legal bases (federal or state) that might also limit a property owner's right to exclude?

2. What is the philosophical basis underlying the court's reasoning? Does the court apply a rights-based approach or a balancing standard to determine who may come onto another's property without the owner's consent?

3. Does *State v. Shack* seriously undermine the right to exclude? To what extent are the advantages of a private property system compromised by the *State v. Shack* holding? Alternatively, is the holding in *State v. Shack* merely a caveat that can be largely circumvented by not allowing workers to reside on the farmer's land?

Problems

1. Anna Martinez, a sister of Hector Martinez, one of the migrant farm workers at Tedesco's farm, arrives for a weekend visit midway through the harvest season. Tedesco allows workers to have weekend visitors so long as they register for one of the available beds. While staying with her brother, Anna learns that her job at a neighboring farm has been eliminated due to an early frost. Anna has nowhere else to stay and there are no job openings at the Tedesco farm. She immediately begins to look for a job. One of Tedesco's work supervisors notices that Anna has been staying over beyond the period for which she is registered. As Tedesco's lawyer, what advice would you give about whether Anna can be prosecuted under trespass laws? As an attorney for CRLS, what advice would you give Anna and Hector?

2. Alex Linwood is a computer programmer at MBI Corporation's industrial park in Greenacres, New Jersey. MBI operates a large cafeteria on the bottom floor of Alex's building. Because the food is fairly "institutional," Alex and his buddies have begun to order pizzas from Pizza Express, a local pizza delivery outlet. Word has spread to other departments and there has been a marked increase in the amount of food delivered to the MBI complex. MBI has instructed the security personnel to turn away all food delivery services at the facility's gate other than those expressly authorized by MBI's executive offices. MBI's president has circulated a memorandum to all personnel extolling the gustatory virtues of the MBI cafeteria and prohibiting employees from ordering food delivered to their offices. What would you advise Alex about his lunch options? What would you advise Pizza Express about whether their activities violate trespass law?

PruneYard Shopping Center v. Robins

Supreme Court of the United States, 1980.
447 U.S. 74, 100 S.Ct. 2035, 64 L.Ed.2d 741..

■ Mr. Justice Rehnquist delivered the opinion of the Court.

We postponed jurisdiction of this appeal from the Supreme Court of California to decide the important federal constitutional questions it presented. Those are whether state constitutional provisions, which permit individuals to exercise free speech and petition rights on the property of a privately owned shopping center to which the public is invited, violate the shopping center owner's property rights under the Fifth and Fourteenth Amendments or his free speech rights under the First and Fourteenth Amendments.

I

Appellant PruneYard is a privately owned shopping center in the city of Campbell, Cal. It covers approximately 21 acres—5 devoted to parking and 16 occupied by walkways, plazas, sidewalks, and buildings that contain more than 65 specialty shops, 10 restaurants, and a movie theater. The PruneYard is open to the public for the purpose of encouraging the patronizing of its commercial establishments. It has a policy not to permit any visitor or tenant to engage in any publicly expressive activity, including the circulation of petitions, that is not directly related to its commercial purposes. This policy has been strictly enforced in a nondiscriminatory fashion. The PruneYard is owned by appellant Fred Sahadi.

Appellees are high school students who sought to solicit support for their opposition to a United Nations resolution against "Zionism." On a Saturday afternoon they set up a card table in a corner of PruneYard's central courtyard. They distributed pamphlets and asked passersby to sign petitions, which were to be sent to the President and Members of Congress. Their activity was peaceful and orderly and so far as the record indicates was not objected to by PruneYard's patrons.

Soon after appellees had begun soliciting signatures, a security guard informed them that they would have to leave because their activity violated PruneYard regulations. The guard suggested that they move to the public sidewalk at the PruneYard's perimeter. Appellees immediately left the premises and later filed this lawsuit in the California Superior Court of Santa Clara County. They sought to enjoin appellants from denying them access to the PruneYard for the purpose of circulating their petitions.

The Superior Court held that appellees were not entitled under either the Federal or California Constitution to exercise their asserted rights on the shopping center property. It concluded that there were "adequate, effective channels of communication for [appellees] other than soliciting on the private property of the [PruneYard]." The California Court of Appeal affirmed.

The California Supreme Court reversed, holding that the California Constitution protects "speech and petitioning, reasonably exercised, in shopping centers even when the centers are privately owned." 23 Cal.3d 899, 910, 153 Cal.Rptr. 854, 860, 592 P.2d 341, 347 (1979).[54] It concluded

---

54. [Ed. Note: Article I, § 2 of the California Constitution provides "Every person may freely speak, write and publish his or her sentiments on all subjects, being respon-

that appellees were entitled to conduct their activity on PruneYard property. In rejecting appellants' contention that such a result infringed property rights protected by the Federal Constitution, the California Supreme Court observed:

> It bears repeated emphasis that we do not have under consideration the property or privacy rights of an individual homeowner or the proprietor of a modest retail establishment. As a result of advertising and the lure of a congenial environment, 25,000 persons are induced to congregate daily to take advantage of the numerous amenities offered by the [shopping center there]. A handful of additional orderly persons soliciting signatures and distributing handbills in connection therewith, under reasonable regulations adopted by defendant to assure that these activities do not interfere with normal business operations * * * would not markedly dilute defendant's property rights.

Before this Court, appellants contend that their constitutionally established rights under the Fourteenth Amendment to exclude appellees from adverse use of appellants' private property cannot be denied by invocation of a state constitutional provision or by judicial reconstruction of a State's laws of private property. * * *

III

Appellants first contend that *Lloyd Corp. v. Tanner*, 407 U.S. 551 (1972), prevents the State from requiring a private shopping center owner to provide access to persons exercising their state constitutional rights of free speech and petition when adequate alternative avenues of communication are available. *Lloyd* dealt with the question whether under the Federal Constitution a privately owned shopping center may prohibit the distribution of handbills on its property when the handbilling is unrelated to the shopping center's operations. *Id.*, at 552. The shopping center had adopted a strict policy against the distribution of handbills within the building complex and its malls, and it made no exceptions to this rule. *Id.*, at 555.[55] Respondents in *Lloyd* argued that because the shopping center was open to the public, the First Amendment prevents the private owner from enforcing the handbilling restriction on shopping center premises. *Id.*, at 564.[56] In rejecting this claim we substantially repudiated the rationale of *Food*

---

sible for the abuse of this right. A law may not restrain or abridge liberty of speech or press."]

55. The center had banned handbilling because it "was considered likely to annoy customers, to create litter, potentially to create disorders, and generally to be incompatible with the purpose of the Center and the atmosphere sought to be preserved." 407 U.S., at 555–556.

56. Respondents relied on *Marsh v. Alabama*, 326 U.S. 501 (1946), and *Food Em-*

ployees v. Logan Valley Plaza, 391 U.S. 308 (1968), in support of their claim that the shopping center's permission to the public to enter its property for the purpose of shopping caused its property to lose its private character, thereby permitting members of the public to exercise the same free speech rights as they would have on similar public facilities or the streets of a city or town. Both of those cases, however, involved no state law authorizing the conduct of the solicitors or handbillers.

Employees v. Logan Valley Plaza, 391 U.S. 308 (1968), which was later overruled in *Hudgens v. NLRB*, 424 U.S. 507 (1976). We stated that property does not "lose its private character merely because the public is generally invited to use it for designated purposes," and that "[t]he essentially private character of a store and its privately owned abutting property does not change by virtue of being large or clustered with other stores in a modern shopping center." 407 U.S., at 569.

Our reasoning in *Lloyd*, however, does not *ex proprio vigore* limit the authority of the State to exercise its police power or its sovereign right to adopt in its own Constitution individual liberties more expansive than those conferred by the Federal Constitution. *Cooper v. California*, 386 U.S. 58, 62 (1967). *See also* 407 U.S., at 569–570. In *Lloyd, supra*, there was no state constitutional or statutory provision that had been construed to create rights to the use of private property by strangers, comparable to those found to exist by the California Supreme Court here. It is, of course, well established that a State in the exercise of its police power may adopt reasonable restrictions on private property so long as the restrictions do not amount to a taking without just compensation or contravene any other federal constitutional provision. *See, e. g., Euclid v. Ambler Realty Co.*, 272 U.S. 365 (1926); *Young v. American Mini Theatres, Inc.*, 427 U.S. 50 (1976). *Lloyd* held that when a shopping center owner opens his private property to the public for the purpose of shopping, the First Amendment to the United States Constitution does not thereby create individual rights in expression beyond those already existing under applicable law. *See also Hudgens v. NLRB, supra*, at 517–521.

IV

Appellants next contend that a right to exclude others underlies the Fifth Amendment guarantee against the taking of property without just compensation and the Fourteenth Amendment guarantee against the deprivation of property without due process of law.

It is true that one of the essential sticks in the bundle of property rights is the right to exclude others. *Kaiser Aetna v. United States*, 444 U.S. 164, 179–180 (1979). And here there has literally been a "taking" of that right to the extent that the California Supreme Court has interpreted the State Constitution to entitle its citizens to exercise free expression and petition rights on shopping center property.[57] But it is well established that "not every destruction or injury to property by governmental action has been held to be a 'taking' in the constitutional sense." *Armstrong v. United States*, 364 U.S. 40, 48 (1960). Rather, the determination whether a state law unlawfully infringes a landowner's property in violation of the Taking

---

57. The term "property" as used in the Taking Clause includes the entire "group of rights inhering in the citizen's [ownership]." *United States v. General Motors Corp.*, 323 U.S. 373 (1945). It is not used in the "vulgar and untechnical sense of the physical thing with respect to which the citizen exercises rights recognized by law. [Instead, it] denote[s] the group of rights inhering in the citizen's relation to the physical thing, as the right to possess, use and dispose of it. * * * The constitutional provision is addressed to every sort of interest the citizen may possess." *Id.*, at 377–378.

Clause requires an examination of whether the restriction on private property "forc[es] some people alone to bear public burdens which, in all fairness and justice, should be borne by the public as a whole." *Id.*, at 49. This examination entails inquiry into such factors as the character of the governmental action, its economic impact, and its interference with reasonable investment-backed expectations. *Kaiser Aetna v. United States, supra,* at 175. When "regulation goes too far it will be recognized as a taking." *Pennsylvania Coal Co. v. Mahon*, 260 U.S. 393, 415 (1922).

Here the requirement that appellants permit appellees to exercise state-protected rights of free expression and petition on shopping center property clearly does not amount to an unconstitutional infringement of appellants' property rights under the Taking Clause. There is nothing to suggest that preventing appellants from prohibiting this sort of activity will unreasonably impair the value or use of their property as a shopping center. The PruneYard is a large commercial complex that covers several city blocks, contains numerous separate business establishments, and is open to the public at large. The decision of the California Supreme Court makes it clear that the PruneYard may restrict expressive activity by adopting time, place, and manner regulations that will minimize any interference with its commercial functions. Appellees were orderly, and they limited their activity to the common areas of the shopping center. In these circumstances, the fact that they may have "physically invaded" appellants' property cannot be viewed as determinative.

This case is quite different from *Kaiser Aetna v. United States, supra. Kaiser Aetna* was a case in which the owners of a private pond had invested substantial amounts of money in dredging the pond, developing it into an exclusive marina, and building a surrounding marina community. The marina was open only to fee-paying members, and the fees were paid in part to "maintain the privacy and security of the pond." *Id.*, at 168. The Federal Government sought to compel free public use of the private marina on the ground that the marina became subject to the federal navigational servitude because the owners had dredged a channel connecting it to "navigable water."

The Government's attempt to create a public right of access to the improved pond interfered with Kaiser Aetna's "reasonable investment backed expectations." We held that it went "so far beyond ordinary regulation or improvement for navigation as to amount to a taking. * * *" *Id.*, at 178. Nor as a general proposition is the United States, as opposed to the several States, possessed of residual authority that enables it to define "property" in the first instance. A State is, of course, bound by the Just Compensation Clause of the Fifth Amendment, *Chicago, B. & Q. R. Co. v. Chicago*, 166 U.S. 226, 233, 236–237 (1897), but here appellants have failed to demonstrate that the "right to exclude others" is so essential to the use or economic value of their property that the state-authorized limitation of it amounted to a "taking." * * *

V

Appellants finally contend that a private property owner has a First Amendment right not to be forced by the State to use his property as a forum for the speech of others. They state that in *Wooley v. Maynard*, 430 U.S. 705 (1977), this Court concluded that a State may not constitutionally require an individual to participate in the dissemination of an ideological message by displaying it on his private property in a manner and for the express purpose that it be observed and read by the public. This rationale applies here, they argue, because the message of *Wooley* is that the State may not force an individual to display any message at all.

Wooley, however, was a case in which the government itself prescribed the message, required it to be displayed openly on appellee's personal property that was used "as part of his daily life," and refused to permit him to take any measures to cover up the motto even though the Court found that the display of the motto served no important state interest. Here, by contrast, there are a number of distinguishing factors. Most important, the shopping center by choice of its owner is not limited to the personal use of appellants. It is instead a business establishment that is open to the public to come and go as they please. The views expressed by members of the public in passing out pamphlets or seeking signatures for a petition thus will not likely be identified with those of the owner. Second, no specific message is dictated by the State to be displayed on appellants' property. There consequently is no danger of governmental discrimination for or against a particular message. Finally, as far as appears here appellants can expressly disavow any connection with the message by simply posting signs in the area where the speakers or handbillers stand. Such signs, for example, could disclaim any sponsorship of the message and could explain that the persons are communicating their own messages by virtue of state law.

---

1. Does the U.S. Constitution protect the high school students' activities at issue in *PruneYard*? If the students attempt to conduct their petitioning activities at a mall in another state (without any specific statutory or state constitutional protection beyond the federal provisions), could the mall operator evict them as trespassers?

2. What test does the Supreme Court set forth to determine when state limitations on the right to exclude amount to a taking? Is this analysis convincing? Does it comport with the *Lucas* decision?

Problems

1. Berkford University, a large private university in California, has received a request from a local chapter of the Freemen Society to conduct a rally in front of the student union. The Freemen Society is an organization

committed to the abolition of the U.S. government. Its members believe that Americans should be allowed to band together and form their own independent communities and militias. The organization does not include any current or former students. The university president does not believe that the group's message will be of particular interest to Berkford students and she is concerned that the demonstration will sully the university's reputation. You have been consulted in your capacity as general counsel to the university. Can the university prohibit such a rally on its campus?

2. The Ku Klux Klan is organizing a parade through the town of Leesburg, South Carolina. Its planned route would cut through Stephens College, a private traditionally black college. College administrators and students are outraged by this plan. You are counsel to the College. Assuming that the group adheres to the College's traditional limits on the time, place, and manner of parades, can the college prevent the Ku Klux Klan from marching across its property (as a matter of trespass or nuisance law)?

3. The Women's Clinic of Greater Hartford performs abortions. Its clinic director and a number of the doctors working there have received death threats in the past year. Activists have begun to picket the clinic. The Sheriff has been called to enforce the trespass laws. Not knowing what to do, he turns to you as county counsel for legal advice. Can the clinic prevent anti-abortion protesters from picketing the entrance to the clinic? See *Schenck v. Pro-Choice Network of Western New York*, ___ U.S. ___, 117 S.Ct. 855, 137 L.Ed.2d 1 (1997).

4. The corporate headquarters for Macrosoft Corporation located in Silicon, California, is the size of a small city, with dozens of buildings, recreation areas, restaurants, a convenience store, and its own mass transportation system. Due to the large number of employees at the facility, an increasing number of organizations have sought to come on to the grounds for various political, civic, professional, and commercial purposes. In the past year, the League of Women Voters set up a voter registration table at the main cafeteria, the Red Cross operated a blood bank, various political candidates held forums, and some professional societies (*e.g.*, computer programmer groups) organized events. Thus far, Macrosoft accommodated all of these requests, although recent events have raised concerns among some of the corporate executives. For example, a panel for a software engineers' symposium featured a speaker who advocated the abolition of copyright law. (Macrosoft is a strong advocate of strengthening copyright protection.) Some programmer meetings have featured speakers from competing companies. Upper management is concerned that such meetings may facilitate the recruiting of key employees from Macrosoft by its competitors. In addition, the proliferation of visitors appears to be distracting Macrosoft employees from their work. The company would like you to draft a coherent (and legally defensible) policy to

address these and foreseeable concerns about access to the corporate campus.

Eyerman v. Mercantile Trust Co.

Missouri Court of Appeals, 1975.
524 S.W.2d 210..

■ RENDLEN, JUDGE.

Plaintiffs appeal from denial of their petition seeking injunction to prevent demolition of a house at #4 Kingsbury Place in the City of St. Louis. The action is brought by individual neighboring property owners and certain trustees for the Kingsbury Place Subdivision. We reverse.

Louise Woodruff Johnston, owner of the property in question, died January 14, 1973, and by her will directed the executor "... to cause our home at 4 Kingsbury Place ... to be razed and to sell the land upon which it is located ... and to transfer the proceeds of the sale ... to the residue of my estate." Plaintiffs assert that razing the home will adversely affect their property rights, violate the terms of the subdivision trust indenture for Kingsbury Place, produce an actionable private nuisance and is contrary to public policy.

The area involved is a "private place" established in 1902 by trust indenture which provides that Kingsbury Place and Kingsbury Terrace will be so maintained, improved, protected and managed as to be desirable for private residences. The trustees are empowered to protect and preserve "Kingsbury Place" from encroachment, trespass, nuisance or injury, and it is "the intention of these presents, forming a general scheme of improving and maintaining said property as desirable residence property of the highest class." The covenants run with the land and the indenture empowers lot owners or the trustees to bring suit to enforce them.

Except for one vacant lot, the subdivision is occupied by handsome, spacious two and three-story homes, and all must be used exclusively as private residences. The indenture generally regulates location, costs and similar features for any structures in the subdivision, and limits construction of subsidiary structures except those that may beautify the property, for example, private stables, flower houses, conservatories, play houses or buildings of similar character.

On trial the temporary restraining order was dissolved and all issues found against the plaintiffs.

* * *

Whether #4 Kingsbury Place should be razed is an issue of public policy involving individual property rights and the community at large. The plaintiffs have pleaded and proved facts sufficient to show a personal, legally protectible interest.

Demolition of the dwelling will result in an unwarranted loss to this estate, the plaintiffs and the public. The uncontradicted testimony was that the current value of the house and land is $40,000.00; yet the estate could expect no more than $5,000.00 for the empty lot, less the cost of demolition at $4,350.00, making a grand loss of $39,350.33 if the unexplained and capricious direction to the executor is effected. Only $650.00 of the $40,-000.00 asset would remain.

Kingsbury Place is an area of high architectural significance, representing excellence in urban space utilization. Razing the home will depreciate adjoining property values by an estimated $10,000.00 and effect corresponding losses for other neighborhood homes. The cost of constructing a house of comparable size and architectural exquisiteness would approach $200,000.00.

The importance of this house to its neighborhood and the community is reflected in the action of the St. Louis Commission on Landmarks and Urban Design designating Kingsbury Place as a landmark of the City of St. Louis. This designation, under consideration prior to the institution of this suit, points up the aesthetic and historical qualities of the area and assists in stabilizing Central West End St. Louis. It was testified by the Landmarks Commission chairman that the private place concept, once unique to St. Louis, fosters higher home maintenance standards and is among the most effective methods for stabilizing otherwise deteriorating neighborhoods. The executive director of Heritage St. Louis, an organization operating to preserve the architecture of the city, testified to the importance of preserving Kingsbury Place intact:[58]

> The reasons [sic] for making Kingsbury Place a landmark is that it is a definite piece of urban design and architecture. It starts out with monumental gates on Union. There is a long corridor of space, furnished with a parkway in the center, with houses on either side of the street, ... The existence of this piece of architecture depends on the continuity of the [sic] both sides. Breaks in this continuity would be as holes in this wall, and would detract from the urban design qualities of the streets. And the richness of the street is this belt of green lot on either side, with rich tapestry of the individual houses along the sides. Many of these houses are landmarks in themselves, but they add up to much more ... I would say Kingsbury Place, as a whole, with its design, with its important houses ... is a most significant piece of urban design by any standard.

To remove #4 Kingsbury from the street was described as having the effect of a missing front tooth. The space created would permit direct access to Kingsbury Place from the adjacent alley, increasing the likelihood the lot will be subject to uses detrimental to the health, safety and beauty of the neighborhood. The mere possibility that a future owner might build a new

---

58. #4 Kingsbury Place was rated as being "highly architecturally significant."

home with the inherent architectural significance of the present dwelling offers little support to sustain the condition for destruction.

We are constrained to take judicial notice of the pressing need of the community for dwelling units as demonstrated by recent U.S. Census Bureau figures showing a decrease of more than 14% in St. Louis City housing units during the decade of the 60's. This decrease occurs in the face of housing growth in the remainder of the metropolitan area. It becomes apparent that no individual, group of individuals nor the community generally benefits from the senseless destruction of the house; instead, all are harmed and only the caprice of the dead testatrix is served. Destruction of the house harms the neighbors, detrimentally affects the community, causes monetary loss in excess of $39,000.00 to the estate and is without benefit to the dead woman. No reason, good or bad, is suggested by the will or record for the eccentric condition. This is not a living person who seeks to exercise a right to reshape or dispose of her property; instead, it is an attempt by will to confer the power to destroy upon an executor who is given no other interest in the property. To allow an executor to exercise such power stemming from apparent whim and caprice of the testatrix contravenes public policy.

The Missouri Supreme Court held in State ex rel. *McClintock v. Guinotte*, 275 Mo. 298, 204 S.W. 806, 808 (banc 1918), that the taking of property by inheritance or will is not an absolute or natural right but one created by the laws of the sovereign power. The court points out the state "may foreclose the right absolutely, or it may grant the right upon conditions precedent, which conditions, if not otherwise violative of our Constitution, will have to be complied with before the right of descent and distribution (whether under the law or by will) can exist." Further, this power of the state is one of inherent sovereignty which allows the state to "say what becomes of the property of a person, when death forecloses his right to control it." *McClintock v. Guinotte, supra* at 808, 809. While living, a person may manage, use or dispose of his money or property with fewer restraints than a decedent by will. One is generally restrained from wasteful expenditure or destructive inclinations by the natural desire to enjoy his property or to accumulate it during his lifetime. Such considerations however have not tempered the extravagance or eccentricity of the testamentary disposition here on which there is no check except the courts.

In the early English case of *Egerton v. Brownlow*, 10 Eng.Rep. 359, 417 (H.L.C. it is stated: "The owner of an estate may himself do many things which he could not (by a condition) compel his successor to do. One example is sufficient. He may leave his land uncultivated, but he cannot by a condition compel his successor to do so. The law does not interfere with the owner and compel him to cultivate his land, (though it may be for the public good that land should be cultivated) so far the law respects ownership; but when, by a condition, he attempts to compel his successor to do what is against the public good, the law steps in and pronounces the condition void and allows the devisee to enjoy the estate free from the condition." A more recent application of this principle is found in *M'Caig's*

Trustees v. Kirk–Session of the United Free Church of Lismore, et al., 1915 Sess.Cas. 426 (Scot.). There, by codicil to her will, testatrix ordered certain statues erected to honor her family in a tower built in the form of an amphitheater on a hill. Balustrades were to be erected so that even the public would have no access inside the tower. Special provision was made for keeping out the public and the ground enclosed was expressly declared to be a private enclosure. There were no living descendants of any member of the family who might, if so permitted, take pleasure in contemplating the proposed statutes. The court states at 434: "If a bequest such as in Miss M'Ciag's codicil were held good, money would require to be expended in perpetuity merely gratifying an absurd whim which has neither reason nor public sentiment in its favor." In striking down the provisions of the codicil, the court further notes that there is indeed a "difference between what a man, uncognosed, may do at his own hand, and what the law will support under the provisions of his will ... therefore, without being illegal in the sense of being contrary to any express rule of the common law or contrary to any statute, the principle of public policy will prevent such post-mortem expenditure. Whether the act is sufficiently contrary to public policy to warrant the court's interference must depend on the degree to which it is against public policy." The court further observed that the erection of the eleven statues "would be of no benefit to anyone except those connected with the carrying out of the work, for whose interest she expresses no concern." *M'Caig's Trustees v. Kirk–Session of the United Free Church of Lismore, et al., supra* at 438. In the case *sub judice*, testatrix similarly expressed no such concern; nothing in the will or record indicates an intent to benefit any razing company called upon to destroy her beautiful home.

 * * *

In *Colonial Trust Co. v. Brown et al.*, 105 Conn. 261, 135 A. 555 (1926) the court invalidated, as against public policy, the provisions of a will restricting erection of buildings more than three stories in height and forbidding leases of more than one year on property known as "The Exchange Place" in the heart of the City of Waterbury. The court stated:

> As a general rule, a testator has the right to impose such conditions as he pleases upon a beneficiary as conditions precedent to the vesting of an estate in him, or to the enjoyment of a trust estate by him as cestui que trust. He may not, however, impose one that is uncertain, unlawful or opposed to public policy.

 * * *

In the instant case, the length of time during which the testator directed that the property should remain in the trust, and the complete uncertainty as to the individuals to whom it would ultimately go, preclude any thought of an intent on his part to forbid the cumbering of the property by long leases or the burdening of it with large buildings, lest the beneficiaries be embarrassed in the development of it along such lines as they might themselves prefer. The only other purpose which can be reasonably attributed to him is to compel the trustee to follow his own peculiar ideas as to the proper and advantageous way to manage such properties. That the restrictions are opposed to the interests of the beneficiaries of the trust and that they are imprudent and unwise is made clear by the statement of agreed facts, but that is not all, for their effect is not confined to the beneficiaries. The Exchange Place property is located at a corner of the public square in the very center of the city of Waterbury, in the heart of the financial and retail business district, is as valuable as any land in the city, and is most favorably adapted for a large building containing stores and offices, and the homestead is located in the region of changing character, so that its most available use cannot now be determined. To impress the restrictions in question upon these properties, as the statement of agreed facts makes clear, makes it impossible to obtain from them a proper income return or to secure the most desirable and stable class of tenants, requires for the maintenance of the buildings a proportion of income greatly in excess of that usual in the case of such properties, and will be likely to preclude their proper development and natural use. The effect of such conditions cannot but react disadvantageously upon neighboring properties, and to continue them, as the testator intended, for perhaps 75 years or even more, would carry a serious threat against the proper growth and development of the parts of the city in which the lands in question are situated. *The restrictions militate too strongly against the interests of the beneficiaries and the public welfare to be sustained, particularly when it is remembered that they are designed to benefit no one, and are harmful to all persons interested, and we hold them invalid as against public policy.* l.c. 564. (Emphasis ours.)

See also Restatement, Second, Trusts § 166(b), pp. 348–349, and illustration at p. 349.

The term "public policy" cannot be comprehensively defined in specific terms but the phrase "against public policy" has been characterized as that which conflicts with the morals of the time and contravenes any established interest of society. Acts are said to be against public policy "when the law refuses to enforce or recognize them, on the ground that they have a mischievous tendency, so as to be injurious to the interests of the state, apart from illegality or immorality." *Dille v. St. Luke's Hospital*, 355 Mo. 436, 196 S.W.2d 615, 620 (1946); *Brawner v. Brawner*, 327 S.W.2d 808, 812 (Mo. banc 1959).

* * *

Although public policy may evade precise, objective definition, it is evident from the authorities cited that this senseless destruction serving no apparent good purpose is to be held in disfavor. A well-ordered society cannot tolerate the waste and destruction of resources when such acts directly affect important interests of other members of that society. It is clear that property owners in the neighborhood of #4 Kingsbury, the St. Louis Community as a whole and the beneficiaries of testatrix's estate will be severely injured should the provisions of the will be followed. No benefits are present to balance against this injury and we hold that to allow the condition in the will would be in violation of the public policy of this state.

Having thus decided, we do not reach the plaintiffs' contentions regarding enforcement of the restrictions in the Kingsbury Place trust indenture and actionable private nuisance, though these contentions may have merit.

The judgment is reversed and the cause remanded to the Circuit Court to enter judgment as prayed.

■ CLEMENS, JUDGE (dissenting).

        * * *

The simple issue in this case is whether the trial court erred by refusing to enjoin a trustee from carrying out an explicit testamentary directive. In an emotional opinion, the majority assumes a psychic knowledge of the testatrix' reasons for directing her home be razed; her testamentary disposition is characterized as "capricious," "unwarranted," "senseless," and "eccentric." But the record is utterly silent as to her motives.

The majority's reversal of the trial court here spawns bizarre and legally untenable results. By its decision, the court officiously confers a "benefit" upon testamentary beneficiaries who have never litigated or protested against the razing. The majority opinion further proclaims that public policy demands we enjoin the razing of this private residence in order to prevent land misuse in the City of St. Louis. But the City, like the beneficiaries, is not a party to this lawsuit. The fact is the majority's holding is based upon wispy, self-proclaimed public policy grounds that were only vaguely pleaded, were not in evidence, and were only sketchily briefed by the plaintiffs.

The only plaintiffs in this case are residents of Kingsbury Place and trustees under its indenture. In seeking to enjoin the removal of testatrix' home at #4 Kingsbury Place, these plaintiffs claim they are entitled to an injunction first, by virtue of language in the trust indenture; secondly, because the razing would constitute a nuisance; and thirdly on the ground of public policy. But plaintiffs have not shown the indenture bars razing testatrix' home or that the razing would create a nuisance. And no grounds exist for ruling that the razing is contrary to public policy.

The Trust Indenture. Kingsbury Place is a "private place" established in 1902 by trust indenture. Except for one well-tended vacant lot (whose existence the majority ignores in saying the street minus #4 Kingsbury Place would be like "a missing front tooth") the trust indenture generally regulates size, constructions and cost of structures to be built on Kingsbury

Place. It empowers the trustees to maintain vacant lots and to protect the street from "encroachment, trespass, nuisance and injury." The indenture's acknowledgment that vacant lots did and would exist shows that such lots were not to be considered an "injury." The fact the indenture empowers the trustees to maintain vacant lots is neither an express nor an implied ban against razing residences. The indenture simply recognizes that Kingsbury Place may have vacant lots from time to time—as it now has—and that the trustees may maintain them—as they now do. The indenture itself affords plaintiffs no basis for injunctive relief.

Nuisance. Plaintiffs contend the non-existence of the Johnston dwelling would create a nuisance. Plaintiffs opined the home's removal would be detrimental to neighbors' health and safety, would lower property values in the area and would be undesirable aesthetically, architecturally, socially and historically. These opinions were based upon conjecture rather than upon a reasonable degree of certainty; hence, they were not binding on the trial court. *Kinzel v. West Park Investment Corp.*, 330 S.W.2d 792 (Mo. 1959); *Abernathy v. Coca–Cola Bottling Co. of Jackson*, 370 S.W.2d 175 (Mo.App.1963). Plaintiffs' witnesses made questionable comparisons with other neighborhoods and speculated a nuisance would arise if the dwelling were removed. These witnesses concluded the lot would thereafter remain vacant, because the trustees would breach their duty under the indenture to maintain the lot, and because the existing private police patrol would no longer function. None of these conclusions have bases in fact. The record reveals the one existing vacant lot on Kingsbury Place is well-maintained by the trustees; it does not constitute a nuisance. There is no reason to presume a second vacant lot would be left untended or that private police would cease patrolling. The facts do not support an inference that plaintiffs' rights in the use of their own lands would be invaded by removing the Johnston home. They are not entitled to injunctive relief on the basis of imagined possibilities.

Public Policy. The majority opinion bases its reversal on public policy. But plaintiffs themselves did not substantially rely upon this nebulous concept. Plaintiffs' brief contends merely that an "agency of the City of St. Louis has recently [?] designated Kingsbury Place as a landmark," citing § 24.070, Revised Code of the City of St. Louis. Plaintiffs argue removal of the Johnston home would be "intentional * * * destruction of a landmark of historical interest." Neither the ordinance cited in the brief nor any action taken under it were in evidence. Indeed, the Chairman of the Landmarks and Urban Design Commission testified the Commission did not declare the street a landmark until after Mrs. Johnston died. A month after Mrs. Johnston's death, several residents of the street apparently sensed the impending razing of the Johnston home and applied to have the street declared a landmark. The Commissioner testified it was the Commission's "civic duty to help those people."

The majority opinion goes far beyond the public-policy argument briefed by plaintiffs. If suggests the court may declare certain land uses, which are not illegal, to be in violation of the City's public policy. And the majority so finds although the City itself is not a litigant claiming injury to its interests. The majority's public-policy conclusions are based not upon evidence in the lower court, but upon incidents which may have happened thereafter.

The court has resorted to public policy in order to vitiate Mrs. Johnston's valid testamentary direction. But this is not a proper case for court-defined public policy.

In *Asel v. Order of United Commercial Travelers*, 355 Mo. 658, 197 S.W.2d 639 (banc 1946), the court viewed as contrary to public policy any act that is inherently vicious and contrary to natural justice. The *Asel* court further cited as the definitive statement of public policy "the principle which declares that no one can lawfully do that which has a tendency to be injurious to the public welfare." 12 Am.Jur., § 666, now 12 Am.Jur.2d, § 175. But plaintiffs' theory below was that only the plaintiffs, not the public, were injured by the imminent demolition of the Johnston home.

The leading Missouri case on public policy as that doctrine applies to a testator's right to dispose of property is *In re Rahn's Estate*, 316 Mo. 492, 291 S.W. 120 (banc 1927), *cert. den.* 274 U.S. 745. There, an executor refused to pay a bequest on the ground the beneficiary was an enemy alien, and the bequest was therefore against public policy. The court denied that contention: "We may say, at the outset, that the policy of the law favors freedom in the testamentary disposition of property and that it is the duty of the courts to give effect to the intention of the testator, as expressed in his will, provided such intention does not contravene an established rule of law." And the court wisely added, "it is not the function of the judiciary to create or announce a public policy of its own, but solely to determine and declare what is the public policy of the state or nation as such policy is found to be expressed in the Constitution, statutes, and judicial decisions of the state or nation, * * * not by the varying opinions of laymen, lawyers, or judges[59] as to the demands or the interests of the public." And, in cautioning against judges declaring public policy the court stated: "Judicial tribunals hold themselves bound to the observance of rules of extreme caution when invoked to declare a transaction void on grounds of public policy, and prejudice to the public interest must clearly appear before the court would be warranted in pronouncing a transaction void on this account." In resting its decision on public-policy grounds, the majority opinion has transgressed the limitations declared by our Supreme Court in *Rahn's Estate*.

The right of these plaintiffs to injunctive relief is by no means clear and injunction is "a harsh remedy, granted only in clear cases." *American Pamcor, Inc. v. Klote*, 438 S.W.2d 287 (Mo.App.1969). It requires judicial

---

59. In his treatise on The Nature of the Judicial Process, p. 141, Mr. Justice Benjamin Cardozo discussed the role of the judge as a legislator and warned: "The judge, even when he is free, is still not wholly free. He is not to innovate at pleasure. He is not a knight-errant, roaming at will in pursuit of his own ideal of beauty or of goodness. He is to draw his inspiration from consecrated principles. He is not to yield to spasmodic sentiment, to vague and unregulated benevolence."

imagination to hold, as the majority does, that the mere presence of a second vacant lot on Kingsbury Place violates public policy.

As much as our aesthetic sympathies might lie with neighbors near a house to be razed, those sympathies should not so interfere with our considered legal judgment as to create a questionable legal precedent. Mrs. Johnston had the right during her lifetime to have her house razed, and I find nothing which precludes her right to order her executor to raze the house upon her death. It is clear that "the law favors the free and untrammeled use of real property." *Gibbs v. Cass*, 431 S.W.2d 662 (Mo.App. 1968). This applies to testamentary dispositions. *Mississippi Valley Trust Co. v. Ruhland*, 359 Mo. 616, 222 S.W.2d 750 (1949). An owner has exclusive control over the use of his property subject only to the limitation that such use may not substantially impair another's right to peaceably enjoy his property. *City of Fredericktown v. Osborn*, 429 S.W.2d 17 (Mo. App.1968), *Reutner v. Vouga*, 367 S.W.2d 34 (Mo.App.1963). Plaintiffs have not shown that such impairment will arise from the mere presence of another vacant lot on Kingsbury Place.

I find no plain error in the trial court's denial of injunctive relief, and on the merits I would affirm the trial court's judgment. * * *

---

1.   Under what circumstances should the public-at-large, neighbors, or other non-property owners be able to limit or prevent a property owner from destroying his or her own property? Should it matter whether the owner makes this decision while living or through testamentary means?

2.   Isn't the state's ability to condemn property for public use an adequate limitation on the right to destroy? To what extent should the government be able to "regulate" historic preservation at the expense of property owners' loss of the right to destroy or alter their property?

3.   Can you imagine situations where a living homeowner should be prevented from razing his or her own home?

D.   REAL ESTATE TRANSACTIONS

The *inter vivos* transfer of interests in land—including fee simple, life estates, easements, and future interests—ordinarily is achieved in three stages.[1] In the first stage, the buyer and seller *execute a contract* for the sale of property. During the second stage, called the *escrow period*, the buyer has the opportunity to use the *recording acts* and other means to

---

1. Real property, personal property, and intellectual property can also be transferred through *inter vivos* gifts, wills, trusts, or intestate succession. Real property can also be transferred through adverse possession and by eminent domain. Intellectual property, such as trademarks, copyrights, and patents, are normally transferred through licensing agreements and contracts.

investigate the validity of the seller's title, inspect the property, and secure financing (*e.g.*, through a mortgage or a deed of trust). The seller has an opportunity to clear up any defects in the title and to address other problems with the property (*e.g.*, a defective roof) as provided in the contract. The parties often negotiate further during this period. The escrow agent may undertake a number of administrative duties during the escrow period; he may determine the amounts due on taxes and liens, arrange for recordation of the deed and other documents, and arrange for the release of encumbrances.

The third stage, called the *closing* (or *close of escrow*), typically takes place a month or more after the contract is signed. At the closing, the seller *delivers* the deed to the property and the buyer gives the seller the purchase price. Normally, the buyer *records* the deed immediately after the closing. Occasionally, there is a fourth stage, in which a lender holding a *security interest* in the property *forecloses* on the property to satisfy a debt on which the landowner/borrower has defaulted.

The following materials are designed to provide you with basic information about real estate contracts, recording acts, delivery of deeds, and security interests and foreclosure proceedings.

1.   STAGE 1: CONTRACT FOR THE SALE OF LAND

The sale of land begins with negotiations over the terms of the real estate contract. The final contract not only contains the price, but also normally discloses existing encumbrances and lists conditions that the buyer must waive before the sale can go forward. When signing the contract, the buyer frequently gives the escrow agent earnest money— several percent of the purchase price—which will be credited to the sale price if the contract is completed or may be forfeited if the buyer breaches the contract.

a.   CAVEAT EMPTOR

Nearly all real estate contracts are conditioned on the buyer's receiving and approving satisfactory inspection reports. Such conditions are critical because the doctrine of *caveat emptor* ("let the buyer beware") broadly places on the buyer the burdens of finding physical defects, such as a leaky roof, inadequate heating or plumbing, or an infestation of termites, and negotiating with the seller to correct them. *See generally* M. Friedman, Contracts and Conveyances of Real Property, § 1.2(n) (5th ed. 1991 & 1995 Cum. Supp.). Absent contract conditions that allow the buyer to renegotiate or rescind the contract, the buyer must accept the property "as is."

Although the doctrine of *caveat emptor* continues to apply in most states, it is not an absolute bar to recovery. First, the buyer's deed usually contains "covenants of title" (described in more detail below). These covenants, however, normally deal with the grantor's liability from competing claims to title, not physical defects in the property.

Second, many states have created an implied warranty of fitness for new houses, especially if the builder is also the seller. *See, e.g.,* Conn. Gen. Stat. § 47–121 (issuance of a certificate of occupancy for a newly constructed single-family dwelling creates an implied warranty for three years that that builder has complied with the building code); Minn. Stat. § 327A.02 (establishing a series of warranties for a new house sold by the builder: (1) a 1–year warrant for faulty workmanship and defective materials; (2) a 2–year warranty for faulty installation of plumbing, electrical, heating, and cooling; and (3) a 10–year warranty for major construction defects); *McDonald v. Mianecki,* 79 N.J. 275, 398 A.2d 1283 (1979) (replacing the doctrine of *caveat emptor* with an implied warranty of habitability for new houses sold by the builder). Court have not been willing to extend this warranty to the sale of existing houses. In *Stevens v. Bouchard,* 532 A.2d 1028, 1030 (Me.1987), the court noted that "[t]he owner of an older house stands in a much different relation to that property than does the builder vendor of a new residence. In the latter case, the vendor has ultimate control over the habitability of the premises. To hold a homeowner who had no part in the construction of the residence to the same level of accountability offends considerations of fairness and common sense."

Third, buyers may sue under the tort of misrepresentation. The buyer must show both a material misrepresentation and his detrimental reliance on the misrepresentation. *See, e.g., Brooks v. Bankson,* 248 Va. 197, 206, 445 S.E.2d 473, 478 (1994) (*caveat emptor* does not apply when a seller makes a false representation of a material fact that induced the buyer to enter the contract); *Stambovsky v. Ackley,* 169 A.D.2d 254, 257–59, 572 N.Y.S.2d 672, 675–76 (1991) (although the seller has no duty to disclose defects under the doctrine of *caveat emptor*, the doctrine does not apply to active concealment, which normally requires an affirmative misrepresentation).

Fourth, the buyer may claim fraud based on failure to disclose material facts. *See, e.g., Karoutas v. HomeFed Bank,* 232 Cal.App.3d 767, 283 Cal.Rptr. 809 (1991) (seller has a duty to disclose "known facts materially affecting the value of the property"). Some courts, however, afford the buyer no relief if he should have discovered the defect. *Marshall v. Crocker,* 387 So.2d 176, 179 (Ala.1980) (since the buyer could by ordinary diligence have discovered evidence of a past fire in the attic, there could be no claim of fraud by misconduct); *Rumford v. Valley Pest Control,* 629 So.2d 623, 629 (Ala.1993) (seller has a duty to disclose known material defects that affect health and safety, not known or readily observable by buyer). *See also* Campbell, Annotation, Liability of Vendor or Real–Estate Broker for Failure to Disclose Information Concerning Off–Site Conditions Affecting Value of Property, 41 A.L.R. 5th 157 (1996).

Problems

1.   Seller contracted with Buyer to sell Seller's house. Before executing the contract, Seller did not tell Buyer that many people in the

neighborhood believed the house to be haunted. Before the close of escrow, Buyer heard that the house was haunted and now wants to rescind the contract. Does Buyer have a good claim for rescission? Would it make a difference to your analysis if the Seller had to some extent promoted the idea that the house was haunted by giving interviews to newspapers and conducting "haunted house" tours? *See Stambovsky v. Ackley*, 169 A.D.2d 254, 572 N.Y.S.2d 672 (1991).

2.   Seller contracted with Buyer to sell Seller's house. Seller did not tell Buyer that some people in the neighborhood, including Seller, felt that one family on the block was too noisy at night. Does the Seller have an affirmative obligation to disclose that some people are disturbed by the noise? *See* West's Ann.Cal. Civ. Code § 1102.6. Would it make a difference to your analysis if Seller was not disturbed by the noise, but knew that other neighbors were?

3.   Suppose that Seller contracted with Buyer to sell Seller's house. Seller did not disclose that a murder had been committed in the house several years earlier. During the escrow period, Buyer learned of the murder and now wants to rescind the contract. Does he have a right to rescind? Would it make a difference to your analysis if the fact of the murder did not affect the market value of the house, but made the buyer uncomfortable. *See Reed v. King*, 145 Cal.App.3d 261, 193 Cal.Rptr. 130 (1983).

4.   You are counsel to a legislative committee that wants to consider a new statute that would discard the doctrine of *caveat emptor* in favor of an obligation of full disclosure of material defects. How should the statute define "material defects"? Should the seller have an obligation to discover material defects? Should the statute limit the disclosure obligation to residential sales, or should it include commercial properties as well? Should the obligation extend to real estate brokers? Would you support this type of statute?

––––––––––

b.   STATUTE OF FRAUDS

A real estate contract must comply with the applicable statute of frauds[2]; the agreement is unenforceable unless it is memorialized by a sufficient writing signed by the party to be charged in a suit based on the contract. The writing need not be a formal contract, but it must contain all essential terms—it must identify the parties, describe both the land and the interest to be conveyed with reasonable certainty, state the purchase price, and provide any other essential terms or conditions. *See, e.g.,* N.J. Stat. Ann. 25:1–11. The contract *should* (but need not) also specify other

---

2.   The statute of frauds was originally adopted in England in 1677 as "An Act for the Prevention of Frauds and Perjuries." *See generally* Hamburger, The Conveyancing Purposes of the Statute of Frauds, 27 Am. J. Legal Hist. 354 (1983). Every state has a statute of frauds, although the precise details and requirements vary.

important rights and obligations, such as the parties' rights to the earnest money in the event of rescission, their rights if the property is damaged or destroyed during the escrow period, their rights to personal property on the land (*e.g.*, carpets, curtains, appliances), circumstances under which the contract is automatically terminated or under which one of the parties may elect to terminate it (*e.g.*, failure to obtain financing or to receive a satisfactory inspection report for the property), and the method of dispute resolution (*e.g.*, arbitration).

––––––––––

Estate of Younge v. Huysmans

Supreme Court of New Hampshire, 1985.
127 N.H. 461, 506 A.2d 282.

■ PER CURIAM.

The issues on this appeal are whether writings between the parties evidenced a meeting of the minds sufficient to create a contract for the purchase and sale of real estate and whether the superior court correctly determined the remedies for breach of the contract. The [trial court] approved the recommendations of the Master, who (1) found that a contract existed between the parties and was breached, and awarded damages to the Huysmanses for aggravation and harassment in addition to costs, and (2) denied the Huysmanses' request for specific performance of the contract. * * *

The Bank of New England (the Bank) is the duly appointed executor of the Estate of Louise C. D. Younge, which owned two tracts of real estate on Governor's Island in Gilford. * * *

John and Carole Huysmans were residents of Governor's Island. They learned of the availability of the Younge Estate property and dealt directly with the Bank, without the assistance of a real estate agent or an attorney. On August 10, 1981, John Huysmans submitted a written purchase and sale agreement to the Bank along with a check for $10,000. The initial offer was $160,000, which was increased to $170,000 following a conversation between Mr. Huysmans and the Bank's Assistant Trust Officer, Jeffrey D. Ross. This offer was increased by Mr. Huysmans to $172,000 after subsequent conversations with Mr. Ross. At the Bank's request, Mr. Huysmans confirmed the offer of $172,000 by a memo on August 22, 1981. The Bank subsequently took the Younge property off the market.

On August 31, 1981, the Bank, through Mr. Ross, mailed a letter containing the following to Mr. Huysmans:

> This is a short note to confirm that we have accepted your offer of $172,000.00 for the Younge property on Governor's Island in Gilford, New Hampshire. We are in the process of drawing up a Purchase and Sale Agreement, which we will forward to you shortly.

The Bank instructed its attorney, Robert H. Hurd, Esq., to prepare a purchase and sale agreement, and continued to hold the Huysmanses' $10,000 check, although it did not negotiate the check.

On September 8, 1981, the Huysmanses recorded the Bank's letter of August 31, 1981, in the Belknap County Registry of Deeds. They signed a purchase and sale agreement for the sale of their own property on the same date. On September 9, 1981, the Huysmanses met with Mr. Hurd, and requested that they receive two separate deeds to the Younge property and have the right of assignment. Near the end of October, the Huysmanses received a copy of the purchase and sale agreement drafted by attorney Hurd. Mr. Huysmans noted on the agreement various problems he had with it: the rights of the Huysmanses could not be assigned to others, no provision was made for transfer of the property in two deeds, and the agreement contained a "fiduciary clause" providing that the Bank was not required to sell to the Huysmanses at the stated price if a higher offer were received. Mr. Huysmans wrote a letter to the Bank on October 29, 1981, in which he stated his concern because the Bank had not followed through on commitments it had made in August regarding assignment of the Huysmanses' rights and transfer of the property in two deeds.

In November 1981, the Bank discovered that Mr. Huysmans had recorded its letter of August 31, 1981. The Bank advised the Huysmanses that it would not proceed with the agreement unless the letter was released from recording at the Registry of Deeds. On November 18th or 19th, Mr. Ross informed Mr. Hurd that "the deal was off," and the Bank returned the uncashed $10,000 deposit check to the Huysmanses on November 25, 1981. After November 1981, the Huysmanses made no further attempt to complete the purchase of the Younge property. The Bank placed the property back on the market. Between December 1981, and April 1982, the Bank repeatedly attempted to obtain releases from the Huysmanses to discharge the recorded letter. On April 8, 1982, the Huysmanses signed and delivered to Mr. Hurd an unwitnessed signed release.

In September 1982, the Bank sold the Younge property to the Cuccis, who took possession and made extensive and costly improvements. In October 1982, the Bank and the Cuccis filed a petition to quiet title, seeking to force the Huysmanses to execute releases of the letter recorded in the Belknap County Registry of Deeds. The Huysmanses answered, alleging that the Bank's August 31, 1981 letter constituted a binding contract between the parties which the Bank had breached, and requesting damages. The Huysmanses did not file a bill in equity for specific performance of the real estate contract until December 27, 1983. The two cases were then consolidated for trial by the superior court.

After a hearing, the master found that the Bank's August 31, 1981 letter to the Huysmanses, along with the tender of $10,000 by the Huysmanses to the Bank, constituted adequate evidence that a contract existed between the parties. The master found that the Bank had breached the contract and awarded $1,175 damages to the Huysmanses. In addition, the

Huysmanses were awarded $15,000 in damages for aggravation and harassment due to the Bank's conduct.

The master determined that the release executed by the Huysmanses was the result of duress, and thus of no effect. The fact that they took no further steps either to set the release aside or to enforce the contract, coupled with the fact that good faith improvements were made to the property by the Cuccis, led the master to deny specific performance to the Huysmanses on the basis of laches. The master recommended that the Bank's letter of August 31, recorded by the Huysmanses, be removed to clear title to the Younge property, decreed to be owned solely by the Cuccis.

I. Meeting of the Minds

The first issue before this court is whether the writings between the parties evidenced a meeting of the minds sufficient to constitute a contract. The master found that a contract existed between the parties. We agree.

"We will uphold a master's findings 'unless they are unsupported by the evidence or are erroneous as a matter of law.' " [citing cases]. A meeting of the minds must occur before a contract is formed. *Turcotte v. Griffin*, 120 N.H. 292, 294, 415 A.2d 668, 669 (1980). The intent of the parties is determined by an objective standard, and not by actual mental assent. *Kilroe v. Troast*, 117 N.H. 598, 600–01, 376 A.2d 131, 133 (1977). The writing is given the meaning which a reasonable person would attach to it. *Id*. In view of the evidence taken as a whole, the writings between the Bank and the Huysmanses constitute sufficient evidence to support the master's finding that a contract existed between the parties.

In order for a memorandum to constitute sufficient evidence of a contract for the sale of land, it must be in writing, signed by the party to be charged, and must identify the parties, state the price, and describe the land. *Cunningham v. Singer*, 111 N.H. 159, 160, 277 A.2d 318, 319 (1971). In *Cunningham*, this court held that a written memorandum signed by both the plaintiff and the defendant was sufficient evidence of a contract for the purchase of land; reasonable certainty that a meeting of the minds occurred is all that is necessary to evidence a contract. *Id*. In the case before us, the Bank's August 31, 1981 letter explicitly accepts the Huysmanses' offer to buy the real estate, and the Bank accepted a check for $10,000 as a deposit from the Huysmanses. We may reasonably assume that the forthcoming purchase and sale agreement mentioned in the Bank's August 31 letter would supplement terms otherwise specified by the exchange of letters.

Although the master did not acknowledge that the second sentence of the Bank's letter, which stated that a purchase and sale agreement would be forthcoming, created an ambiguity as to whether the letter created a valid contract, the record provides a basis on which any ambiguity could be resolved to find a contract between the parties. The purchase and sale agreement and $10,000 check originally sent by the Huysmanses, the Bank's letter of August 31, 1981, and the fact that the Bank took the property off the market, all combine to provide adequate evidence to support the master's finding that the minds of the parties had met. * * *

---

1.   Why did the buyers record the confirming letter from the Bank?

2.   How could there be a meeting of the minds when so many crucial terms were missing, *e.g.*, whether there would be one or two deeds for the two lots, whether the buyers could assign their rights, and whether the seller could sell the property to a higher bidder?

3.   Suppose the Bank had not written a confirming note, but had cashed the check. Would the Bank have a good defense under the Statute of Frauds?

The statute of frauds is designed to reduce evidentiary questions about the existence and content of any agreement and to lessen opportunities for perjury. However, it can be a harsh rule that can defeat the parties' intentions and expectations and that can allow one party to take advantage of the other. To mitigate this harshness, courts have developed two exceptions that give the injured party the right to specific performance of the oral contract.[3]

Doctrine of Part Performance. Under the doctrine of part performance—typically when the buyer has taken possession of the property and either paid a substantial portion of the purchase price or made substantial improvements on the property—some courts will order specific performance of the contract on the ground that part performance removes the evidentiary uncertainties surrounding oral contract. *See, e.g., Shaughnessy v. Eidsmo*, 222 Minn. 141, 147–52, 23 N.W.2d 362, 366–69 (1946) (taking possession plus partial payment in reliance upon the oral agreement, is enough to satisfy the doctrine of part performance without any need to show detrimental reliance). Either party—the buyer or the seller—may invoke the doctrine based on the buyer's part performance.

Equitable Estoppel. Although often using the term "part performance," some courts enforce oral real estate contracts under a theory of equitable estoppel. If one party to the agreement reasonably and detrimentally relied on the oral contract—for example, if the buyer gave up another significant opportunity—the court may order specific performance of the oral contract. In *Hickey v. Green*, 14 Mass.App.Ct. 671, 442 N.E.2d 37 (1982), the Hickeys and Green orally agreed that Green would sell the Hickeys a vacant lot. The Hickeys gave Green a small down payment and promptly contracted to sell their own house to a third person. A short while later, Green told the Hickeys that she did not intend to sell the lot because she had found another buyer offering a higher price. Quoting the *Restatement (Second) of*

---

3.   This remedy is an alternative to the remedy of rescission and restitution.

Contracts § 129, the court made clear that payment of the purchase price alone was not enough to avoid the statute of frauds, for the buyer could be made whole through restitution. *Id.* at 673 n.6, 442 N.E.2d at 38 n.6. The court also made clear that the remedy of specific performance was available only so long as the party relied on the oral promise. Had Green repudiated the agreement before the Hickeys contracted to sell their house, the court likely would not have enforced the oral agreement. *Id.* at 675–76, 442 N.E.2d at 39. The Hickeys' detrimental reliance on the agreement was sufficient to justify an order of specific performance.

A court may also use estoppel where one party would be unjustly enriched from the other party's performance while refusing to fulfill her part of the oral bargain—for example, when the buyer paid the purchase price. In *Baliles v. Cities Service Co.*, 578 S.W.2d 621 (Tenn.1979), the seller orally agreed to sell a lot to the buyer. Relying on that promise, the buyer took possession of the lot, began construction of a house, and, with the seller's help, secured a loan to cover the cost of construction. The court held that to allow the seller to invoke the statute of frauds to bar enforcement of the agreement and to keep the improvements would be a "gross injustice"; as such, equitable estoppel permitted the court to enforce the oral agreement. *Id.* at 624.[4]

---

1. Reconsider *Estate of Younge*. If the court had found that the contract violated the statute of frauds, could it have found an exception under the doctrine of part performance? If not, what additional facts would bring the contract under the exception?

2. Recall that in *Estate of Younge* the buyers contracted to sell their own house. Is that contract an adequate basis to invoke the doctrine of equitable estoppel if the court had found a statute of frauds violation for the Younge Estate contract?

---

c. MARKETABLE TITLE

Real estate contracts normally contain an implied warranty that the seller will deliver *marketable title* (sometimes called merchantable title) to the buyer *at the close of escrow*.[5] Marketable title is legal title that a prudent purchaser would accept because its validity is reasonably free from doubt. *See Peatling v. Baird*, 168 Kan. 528, 528, 213 P.2d 1015, 1016 (1950) ("[a] marketable title to real estate is one which is free from reasonable

---

4. The court resorted to equitable estoppel because the state did not recognize the doctrine of part performance as an exception to the statute of frauds.

5. The contract does not contain an implied warranty of marketable title if the contract states that the seller will convey "insurable title"; in that case the seller need only provide title that is insured by a title company.

doubt, and a title is doubtful and unmarketable if it exposes the party holding it to the hazard of litigation"). Title need not be absolutely perfect to be marketable, and it need not be actually defective to be unmarketable; the test is whether it creates an *unreasonable risk* of litigation. *See Norwegian Evangelical Free Church v. Milhauser*, 252 N.Y. 186, 190, 169 N.E. 134, 135 (1929). Thus, many states hold that title by adverse possession may be marketable title if the evidence of adverse possession is sufficiently clear. *See, e.g., Schlosser v. Creamer*, 263 Md. 583, 284 A.2d 220 (1971) (so long as the seller can satisfy the elements of adverse possession, the buyer must complete the sale); *Sales Int'l Ltd. v. Black River Farms, Inc.*, 270 S.C. 391, 242 S.E.2d 432 (1978) (title by adverse possession is marketable title).

Title is not marketable if, for example, there is a gap in the seller's chain of title, the property violates a zoning ordinance, a neighbor's building encroaches on the property, the property is encumbered (*e.g.*, by a lease, an easement, a real covenant, tax lien, judgment lien, or a mortgage) and the seller has not disclosed the encumbrance in the contract,[6] other persons hold mineral or oil rights, or a spouse has a dower or curtesy interest. *See, e.g., Lohmeyer v. Bower*, 170 Kan. 442, 227 P.2d 102 (1951) (buyer may rescind the contract because the house on the lot was 18 inches from the lot line, in violation of a 3–foot setback requirement in the zoning ordinance, and the house was only one story tall, in violation of an equitable servitude requiring all residences to be two stories).

Risk of loss during the escrow period. The warranty of marketable title is of no use, however, if the property is destroyed or seriously damaged during the escrow period. Under the *doctrine of equitable conversion*, after the parties have executed a valid contract for an interest to which the seller has good legal title, the buyer holds *equitable title*.[7] One consequence of having equitable title is that absent a contrary contract provision, the risk of loss or damage during escrow is on the buyer, so long as the damage is not caused by the seller's negligence. *See, e.g., Bleckley v. Langston*, 112 Ga.App. 63, 65–67, 143 S.E.2d 671, 672–74 (1965) (even though an ice storm destroyed pecan trees and reduced value of property by 27%, seller could enforce contract).[8] Although long criticized, *see* Stone, *Equitable*

6. Title is marketable if the seller will satisfy the lien out of the proceeds from the sale and will have the lien released at the close of escrow. *See generally* Shaw, Annotation, Marketability of Title as Affected by Lien Dischargeable Out of Funds to Be Received from Purchaser at Closing, 53 A.L.R. 3d 678 (1973).

7. The buyer does not yet have legal title, for the seller has not yet delivered the deed to the buyer; the seller retains legal title only as security for payment of the purchase price at closing. But after the parties execute

the contract, the buyer has equitable title, for either party could seek equitable relief (*i.e.*, specific performance) to enforce the contract.

8. For the same reason, the seller's death or mental incompetence during the escrow period is not a basis to rescind the contract; the buyer already has equitable title and may seek specific performance to obtain legal title. Similarly, if the government condemns the property during the escrow period, the purchaser is entitled to the condemnation proceeds.

Conversion by Contract, 13 Colum. L. Rev. 369 (1913), it remains the rule in a majority of states.

Judicial decisions in a significant minority of states put the risk of loss on the seller if the damaged portion of the property, such as a building, was an important part of the contract and if the damage was significant. *See, e.g., Libman v. Levenson*, 236 Mass. 221, 128 N.E. 13 (1920) (after a retaining wall collapsed and caused severe damage to a 4–story building on the property, the court ordered rescission of the contract); *Skelly Oil Co. v. Ashmore*, 365 S.W.2d 582, 587–89 (Mo.1963) (after a building on the property was destroyed by fire, the court required the sellers to reduce the purchase price by the amount of the money they had received from the insurance company). These courts take the position that the buyer's equitable title has no relevance as to which party should bear the risk of loss; indeed, substantial damage to the property during the escrow period would weigh against equitable enforcement of the contract since the seller could not, in a practical sense, perform his half of the bargain.

Still a third approach is followed in the dozen states that have adopted the Uniform Vendor and Purchaser Risk Act (1935). The Act provides:

Any contract hereafter made in this State for the purchase and sale of real property shall be interpreted as including an agreement that the parties shall have the following rights and duties, unless the contract expressly provides otherwise:

(a) If, when neither the legal title nor the possession of the subject matter of the contract has been transferred, all or a material part thereof is destroyed without fault of the purchaser or is taken by eminent domain, the vendor cannot enforce the contract, and the purchaser is entitled to recover any portion of the price that he has paid;

(b) If, when either the legal title or the possession of the subject matter of the contract has been transferred, all or any part thereof is destroyed without fault of the vendor or is taken by eminent domain, the purchaser is not thereby relieved from a duty to pay the price, nor is he entitled to recover any portion thereof that he has paid.

See, e.g., West's Ann. Cal. Civ. Code § 1662.

Where the risk of loss is on the buyer, the buyer must complete the contract, and the seller can obtain specific performance if the buyer refuses. Where the risk of loss is on the seller, some states permit the buyer to rescind the contract and get a refund of the earnest money. *See, e.g., Libman v. Levenson*, 236 Mass. 221, 128 N.E. 13 (1920) (rescission of contract where property is destroyed); *Bryant v. Willison Real Estate Co.*, 177 W.Va. 120, 124–25, 350 S.E.2d 748, 752–53 (1986) (where damage is not substantial, the buyer has a right to rescission and refund if seller refuses to abate purchase price); *Dixon v. Salvation Army*, 142 Cal.App.3d 463, 467, 191 Cal.Rptr. 111, 114 (1983) (interpreting the Uniform Act to permit the buyer to rescind and obtain a refund, but not to permit the buyer to obtain specific performance with abatement of purchase price where a material part is destroyed). Other states permit the buyer also to compel the seller to go forward with the transaction at a reduced purchase price. *See, e.g., Lucenti v. Cayuga Apartments, Inc.*, 48 N.Y.2d 530, 423 N.Y.S.2d 886, 399 N.E.2d 918 (1979) (buyers have either a right of rescission with refund or a right to specific performance with abatement of purchase price, even if the property is materially destroyed).

———————

1.   What are the comparative advantages and disadvantages of the different rules governing the risk of loss?

2.   Would you recommend amending the Uniform Act to provide that the buyer may have the remedy of specific performance with abatement of purchase price?

———————

Problem

Buyer contracts with Seller to buy a vacant lot on which Buyer intends to build an apartment building. Buyer discovers during the escrow period that the utility district has an easement across the property for a sewer line; in the event the lot was developed, the lot owner would hook into the sewer line. Two weeks later, the city rezones the property for single family housing only. The zoning restriction and the easement continue to exist at the closing. Buyer seeks your advice about rescinding the contract. What advice would you give?

———————

d.   BREACH OF CONTRACT AND REMEDIES

Tender of Performance. Real estate contracts normally set a specific closing date. Because the parties need not tender performance until the closing, generally neither party may claim anticipatory breach of the warranty of marketable title; an important exception is where one party has repudiated the contract, in which case the aggrieved party must still demonstrate a willingness and ability to tender performance. *Sirkin v. Hutchcraft*, 507 So.2d 765, 767 (Fla.App.1987) (if the buyer repudiates the contract before closing, the seller may rescind the contract, keep the earnest money as liquidated damages, and sell the property to another party); *Wooten v. DeMean*, 788 S.W.2d 522, 526 (Mo.App.1990) (repudiation must be unequivocal; a request for further negotiations is not repudiation of the contract). Even if one party does not tender performance on the closing date, the contract is still enforceable in equity if the tardy party tenders performance within a reasonable time. If the seller is in breach because of a violation of the warranty of marketable title, in most states the buyer must give the seller a reasonable time to cure the defect (unless it would be futile to do so). *See, e.g., O'Hara Group Denver, Ltd. v. Marcor Housing Systems, Inc.*, 197 Colo. 530, 537–38, 595 P.2d 679, 684–85 (1979) (buyer has the burden of showing that the seller could not cure within a reasonable time). Finally, the buyer's promise to pay the purchase price and the seller's promise to deliver marketable title are normally dependent promises; neither party may bring an action for breach until she has performed her side of the bargain.

If, however, the contract also specifies that *time is of the essence*, a party is in breach if he or she fails to tender performance (*i.e.*, tender marketable title or the purchase price) at the close of escrow. In *Doctorman v. Schroeder*, 92 N.J. Eq. 676, 114 A. 810 (1921), the parties agreed that the buyer would tender the purchase price by 2:30 p.m. on December 20. The contract provided that "It is further distinctly understood and agreed that time shall be the essence of this receipt [of payment]." Doctorman arrived 30 minutes late, and the Schroeders refused to accept payment. The court denied Doctorman's request for specific performance. "[I]n the absence of a waiver [the court held that the fact that the Schroeders waited for a while after 2:30 did not constitute waiver] * * * a court of equity is powerless to come to the relief of a purchaser of property who has failed to pay at the time specified in the agreement, when the agreement distinctly and clearly provides that the time is essential." *Id.* at 810.

Remedies. The remedies for breach include (1) rescission and restitution (including refund of any earnest money if the seller is in breach and return of property if the buyer had taken possession), (2) damages, or (3) specific performance (with abatement of the purchase price if the seller is in breach).

The measure of damages for buyer's breach is *benefit of the bargain*, determined at the time of breach, *incidental damages* (*i.e.*, out-of-pocket expenses, such as attorney fees), and *consequential damages* (*i.e.*, foreseeable losses, such as interest).[9] *Duncan v. Rossuck*, 621 So.2d 1313, 1315–16 (Ala.1993); *Macal v. Stinson*, 468 N.W.2d 34, 35–36 (Iowa 1991).

In some states, the measure of damages for seller's breach is also benefit of the bargain and consequential and incidental damages (the so-called American Rule), *Brouillard v. Allen*, 619 A.2d 988, 991 (Me.1993); *Johnson v. Brado*, 56 Wash.App. 163, 168–69, 783 P.2d 92, 95 (1989), but in other states, if the seller breached because of defective title and if he was acting in good faith when he signed the contract—he reasonably believed he had good title—he is liable only for incidental and consequential damages (the so-called English Rule). *Large v. Gregory*, 417 N.E.2d 1160, 1163–64 (Ind.App.1981); West's Ann.Cal. Civ. Code § 3306; Okla. Stat. tit. 23, § 27.

---

9. The parties may contractually provide instead for liquidated damages (for buyer's breach, typically the earnest money) so long as the amount is reasonable at the time the parties executed the contract.

Estate of Younge v. Huysmans

Supreme Court of New Hampshire, 1985.
127 N.H. 461, 506 A.2d 282.

[In an earlier portion of the opinion, *see supra,* pp. 396–99, the court upheld the trial court's conclusion that the parties had entered a binding contract for the sale of two lots from the Younge Estate].

II.   Specific Performance

The second issue before us is whether the master was correct in finding that the Huysmanses' request for specific performance was barred by the doctrine of laches. We uphold the master's finding.

Specific performance is ordinarily granted to enforce a contract for the sale of real property, unless circumstances make it inequitable or impossible to do so. Failure to act may create such inequity. The issue of laches is "a question of fact for the trier of fact." The question of whether or not laches bars a particular claim is determined not only by the length of time involved, but also by the inequity of permitting a cause of action because of a change in the conditions of the property or the parties involved.

The Huysmanses made no attempt to enforce their agreement with the Bank after November 1981. In September 1982, the Cuccis purchased the Younge property and recorded their purchase. After they purchased the property, the Cuccis made extensive, good faith improvements at substantial expense. The Huysmanses made no claim for specific performance until December 1983. As full-time residents of Governor's Island and interested potential purchasers of the Younge property, they knew or should have known of the open and visible improvements made by the Cuccis to the property.

The master found that the Huysmanses were induced to enter into a release by duress. We need not address this issue because the Huysmanses took no steps to set the release aside during the time they knew or should have known that the Bank had put the property back on the market. Unreasonable delay and prejudice to the opposing party are required for a finding of laches. *State Employees' Ass'n of N.H. v. Belknap County,* 122 N.H. 614, 622, 448 A.2d 969, 973 (1982). The failure of the Huysmanses to bring their action for specific performance until two years after negotiations with the Bank had come to a standstill, and over a year after the Younge property was sold to the Cuccis, constitutes an unreasonable delay. This delay, coupled with the prejudice to the Cuccis that would result from a grant of specific performance, requires that we affirm the master's finding of laches and consequent denial of specific performance.

[The court reversed the $15,000 damages award for "aggravation and harassment" for lacking evidentiary support, but suggested that on remand they may be entitled to benefit of the bargain damages].

1. Why did the court deny specific performance? Would the result have been different if the Cuccis had not made costly improvements to the property?

2. In general, contract remedies are rescission or damages; courts do not routinely grant specific performance unless the legal remedy is inadequate. Why is specific performance routinely available for breach of a real estate contract? *See* Kronman, Specific Performance, 45 U. Chi. L. Rev. 351 (1978).

3. What is the justification for the English and American rules for damages for seller's breach? Which rule do you prefer? Why is the seller's good faith relevant under the English Rule?

---

e. SPECIAL CONSIDERATIONS RELATING TO COMMERCIAL CONTRACTS

Existing Leases and Contracts. Commercial property is often leased to third parties, and it may be subject to ongoing service contracts (*e.g.*, building maintenance services). Because a buyer may be bound by the terms of existing contracts and leases (*i.e.*, the buyer may take title subject to preexisting leases), the buyer should find out about the property owner's preexisting obligations and take those obligations into account in negotiating the sale price.

Personal Property Associated with the Real Property. The sale of commercial property frequently involves the transfer of more than just land and attached buildings (which are considered part of the real estate); it may include personal property, such as furniture, lighting, machinery, and equipment used to maintain or repair the property. Generally, an item deemed to be a *fixture* automatically passes by the deed, but the law of fixtures normally involves a balancing of several factors on an item-by-item basis. To avoid disputes after the close of escrow, the contract should catalog the items included in the transfer.

Environmental Contamination. The presence of hazardous substances presents a serious problem for potential purchasers. Federal and state environmental laws frequently impose liability for the cost of remediation on the present owner, whether or not the present owner created the environmental problem. *See, e.g.*, Comprehensive Environmental Response, Compensation and Liability Act, 42 U.S.C. § 9607(a). An owner may also be liable under state nuisance law. While there are some defenses to liability, *see, e.g.*, 42 U.S.C. §§ 9601(35), 9607(b)(3) ("innocent purchaser defense"), the risk of substantial liability, the expense of litigation, the legal obstacles to using or developing contaminated property, and the practical inability to market contaminated property strongly counsel that the potential purchaser should avoid such problems rather than rely on legal defenses to liability. *See generally* P. Menell and R. Stewart, Environmental Law and Policy Ch. 6 (1994).

Buyers can reduce the risk of liability two ways. First, a buyer can make a careful investigation during the escrow period, including a site history, review of relevant public records held by environmental or public health agencies, on-site visual inspection, and soil and groundwater testing. The real estate contract should include a clause permitting rescission in the event that the property is contaminated.[10] This investigation, in which lawyers as well as environmental engineers and scientists may play a prominent role, is part of a real estate lawyer's obligation to perform "due diligence." A lawyer helping to structure the transaction may be liable for malpractice if she fails to undertake appropriate due diligence.

Second, the buyer can negotiate an indemnity agreement under which the seller promises to indemnify the buyer for remediation costs or other environmental liability. A contractual right of indemnity does not, however, eliminate the buyer's liability. *See* 42 U.S.C. § 9607(e)(1). Rather, it only provides a source of funding in the event the buyer is later found liable. If the seller is judgment-proof, however, the buyer's indemnity clause is worthless.

Problem

Claire Williams owned a house in fee simple absolute at 100 Sunnyvale Lane. Johanna Goldman wanted to buy the house and orally suggested a purchase price of $100,000. After thinking about the offer for a few days, Claire called Johanna and told her that she would accept the offer, with a close in 30 days (to give Johanna a chance to arrange a bank loan). Claire asked for a $5000 deposit in escrow of earnest money. Claire made no express promises concerning the property. Johanna promptly gave Claire a personal check for the earnest money. Johanna had written on the check that it was a "deposit to purchase Claire Williams' house at 100 Sunnyvale; total price $100,000."

Two weeks before the close of escrow, Johanna discovered that the house was infested with termites, to the point of causing structural damage to the house. As a result, the house was worth only $60,000. The termite inspector told Johanna that the infestation must have been obvious to the owner. Another inspector informed Johanna that a child's sand box in the backyard encroaches on the neighbor's property by about 4 inches.

The house is located in a state that follows the Uniform Vendor and Purchaser Risk Act.

10. Most, if not all, lending institutions will not finance the purchase of commercial property, including adjacent property, without an environmental inspection, particularly if the property is near an existing or former industrial site. If the inspection reveals contamination, the lender may demand that the property be cleaned up before making the loan, and it may demand indemnification in the event that the lender is held liable. *Cf.* 42 U.S.C. § 9601(20)(E)-(F) (defining the scope of lender liability for cleanup costs). Modern loan agreements usually require the borrower to comply with all environmental laws.

Johanna comes to you for advice. She thinks that she would like to get out of the agreement. What are her options? What advice would you provide?

---

2.   STAGE 2: ESTABLISHING GOOD TITLE

A private property system must have clear rules to resolve conflicting claims to property and to allow prospective purchasers to determine easily and accurately the existence and validity of preexisting claims to property (and correlatively, to protect purchasers from prior, secret transactions).

Under English common law, the first person to acquire an interest in land was deemed to have a valid interest. Thus, if the grantor conveyed a fee simple absolute to two different people, the first grantee was deemed to have title. Under early English common law, when families stayed in the same area for generations and when property was transferred with great public ceremony—enfeoffment with livery of seisin—potential grantees probably received adequate notice of any preexisting claims. Thorne, Livery of Seisin, 52 Law Q. Rev. 345 (1936); Payne, The English Theory of Conveyancing Prior to the Land Registration Acts, 7 Ala. L. Rev. 227 (1955). However, as the population became more mobile, communal memories faded. More importantly, when transfers by deed became possible in the mid-sixteenth century and as commercial transactions between strangers became common, it became more difficult for a potential purchaser to identify prior claimants before the sale or to verify the validity of their claims in subsequent litigation.

In 1925, England adopted a relatively simple land registration system to establish the validity of title. In the United States, by contrast, colonial and later state legislatures adopted a much more complicated system of public recording of deeds. If a deed to a prior claimant is properly recorded, a *subsequent purchaser* is deemed to have constructive ("record") notice of the prior claim to the property.[11] Such notice is a critical factor—in about half of the states it is the only factor—to determine whether the subsequent purchaser or the prior claimant has superior title.

Recording systems have been repeatedly criticized as "wasteful, unreasonably expensive, archaic, and worst of all, uncertain to achieve that which they purportedly intend to accomplish: certainty in land ownership." Bostick, Land Title Registration: An English Solution to an American Problem, 63 Ind. L.J. 55, 57 (1987).

The records that constitute notice under the recording system are themselves widely scattered. Usually they are county-based. If

---

11. Purchasers do not rely solely on the recording acts. Rather, they also normally buy title insurance from title companies. Title companies do not insure against defects in the property (such as the presence of hazard-ous substances) or against unrecordable claims, such as adverse possession, implied easements, or implied equitable servitudes. *See generally* Powell on Real Property ch. 92.

the land is spread over several counties, a search of the records of each county is required. Pertinent records may be found in a county clerk's office, in a Federal Building, in a City Hall, in a zoning office, in state and federal environmental offices, and throughout the records of courts of all jurisdictions. The possibilities are extraordinary. The level of competence and accuracy in record keeping is wide ranging as well, with presentation running from handwriting to computer cards. Officials and their staffs vary from incompetent to highly trained and motivated professionals. Regrettably, the custodial office is often political, with no prescribed qualifications, and the result is an officeholder whose personal popularity may exceed professional competence.

Against this backdrop of myriad complexity and uncertainty, two additional problems confound the effort to provide a proper title assurance, and both contribute to the overburdening of the recording system. The first problem concerns substantive American property law. The intricate nature of the various means by which and by whom title to realty may be held aggravates and complicates any effort to improve the existing creaky system. The second problem involves the vastly complicated procedures [under the recording act] which must be followed to identify and evaluate the substantive property law interests.

Id. at 68–69.

a.   THE MECHANICS OF MODERN RECORDING SYSTEMS

Any document evidencing an interest in land—*e.g.*, fee simple, mortgage, or easement—may be recorded (often, short term interests, such as a lease for less than a year, may not be recorded). The grantee or his agent presents the document (in most states, the document must be witnessed or acknowledged) to the county recorder, who stamps the date and time of recording on the document and makes a copy of the document. The recorder files the copy of the recorded document among other property records from the county and indexes it under the grantor's and grantee's names or, in some jurisdictions, by tract.

Chain of title. Someone (*e.g.*, a prospective purchaser) making a title search consults these indices to establish a "chain of title" to the property. The chain is the chronological series of conveyances, from grantor to grantee, from sometime in the past until the present. By establishing a chain of title, the prospective purchaser can find out if there are any preexisting grantees with competing claims to the property. Litigants also may construct a chain of title as a basis to determine who has superior title.

Title searches for property indexed by tract are usually straightforward since all of the documents for a given parcel are referenced in a single location. If, as is more common, documents are indexed alphabetically by the names of the grantor and grantee, the searcher must first consult the grantee index to determine the previous owners in the chain of title. In other words, the searcher looks for the name of the current owner— Gamma. Listed with Gamma's name will be the name of his grantor, Beta. Since Beta was also a grantee, the searcher now looks for Beta's name in the grantee index. Next to Beta's name will be the name of her grantor, Alpha, and so forth.

The searcher will then look up the names of each of these owners in the grantor index, beginning with the earliest one. In a majority of states, the searcher need only search for a given owner's name (*e.g.*, Alpha) from the time the owner first acquired the property until he conveyed it to the next person in the chain (*e.g.*, Beta). That is, a searcher has record notice arising from the owner's conveyance only for transactions that occurred during the window of ownership. A minority of states impose the much more onerous requirement that the purchaser search for each name from the beginning of the records until the present. *See generally* Cross, The Record "Chain of Title Hypocrisy", 57 Colo. L. Rev. 787 (1957). As we will see, whether a court applies the majority or the minority rule for title searches affects whether a document is recorded in the chain of title; that is, under certain circumstances, under the majority rule a document may be recorded but still not give record notice (*see* especially Problem 5, *infra*).

Marketable title statutes. It is not clear how far back in time a search should go. A title search can be costly, and the farther back in time the more expensive the search. At the same time, failure to search back far enough subjects a potential purchaser to the risk that she will lose her interest to a preexisting claimant. At a minimum, a title search should exceed the statute of limitations for adverse possession. But given the possibility of disabilities that may toll the statute, it is necessary to go back even further.

Many states have adopted "marketable title" legislation designed to limit the burden of title searches. One common approach seeks to eliminate old reversionary interests, such as power of termination or possibilities of reverter (recall that in most states these interests are not subject to the Rule Against Perpetuities or termination by equitable defenses). Several statutes declare certain future interests invalid after a fixed period of time or if they are obsolete, and others declare them invalid unless they are periodically re-recorded (*i.e.*, every 30 years). *See, e.g.,* Conn. Gen. Stat. § 45a–505 (possibilities of reverter and powers of termination void 30 years after creation unless they are already possessory); Ariz. Rev. Stat. § 33–436 (conditions that provide no actual and substantial benefit are unenforceable); West's Ann. Cal. Civ. Code §§ 885.010–885.070 (converting possibilities of reverter to powers of termination, eliminating power of termination after 30 years unless re-recorded, and terminating obsolete powers of termination). *See also Texaco, Inc. v. Short*, 454 U.S. 516 (1982) (a statute declaring that an unused mineral interest lapses and reverts to the surface owner unless re-recorded every 20 years does not violate due process and is not an unconstitutional taking).

More than a dozen states have adopted another (in some cases, an additional) approach. Under these statutes, the searcher need only go back to the "root title"; any claims that arose before the root title are void. The root title is the most recent recorded transaction that is at least 40 years old. That transaction must be of the same type of interest (*e.g.*, fee simple) held by the person claiming benefit of the act. If a person can show an unbroken chain of title back to the root title, the person has legal title free of all other claims. *See, e.g.,* Iowa Code Ann. §§ 614.29–614.38.

There are some exceptions to this general description. First, title is subject to claims of adverse possession that occurred at least in part after root title. Second, title is subject to an observable easement, even if the easement was granted before root title. Third, a landlord's reversionary interest is not cut off by the statute (this issue arises only with leases longer than 40 years). Claims arising before the root of title can be preserved by filing a notice of preservation within 40 years before the title search.

b.   TYPES OF RECORDING ACTS

There are three types of recording acts in the United States: (1) race statutes, (2) notice statutes, and (3) race-notice statutes. As you look at these statutes, there are several points to keep in mind. First, the recording statutes protect only *subsequent purchasers* (which includes persons who acquire a fee, a mortgage, a lease, or an easement for more than nominal consideration); subsequent donees, such as heirs or devisees, are subject to the common law rule that the first to acquire prevails. It is still important for donees to review recorded documents to assure themselves they have good title before they make significant improvements, but they receive no protection from the recording acts. Second, the recording statutes provide protection only against *recordable documents*. Thus, they provide no protection against prior interests held by adverse possession, under short-term leases (which are not recordable in many states), or under a constructive trust. Disputes involving such claims are resolved under the common law. Third, the recording acts do not affect the grantor's liability under tort law or covenants of title. Nor do they affect the validity of delivery (unless recordation provides some evidence of the grantor's intent to deliver). Rather, the recording acts offer a means to resolve disputes between grantees who have competing claims to the same property.

Race Statutes. In a race jurisdiction, a subsequent purchaser prevails over a prior grantee if he is the first to record. It is irrelevant which of the grantees acquired the land first or whether either of them had notice that the grantor had conveyed the property to more than one grantee. *See* La. Rev. Stat. Ann. § 9:2721; N.C. Gen. Stat. § 47–18(a). Once widespread, race statutes are now quite rare.

Notice Statutes. In a notice jurisdiction, a subsequent grantee prevails over a prior grantee if and only if she is a "bona fide purchaser for value" (BFP). The Florida statute is typical:

> No conveyance, transfer, or mortgage of real property, or of any interest therein, nor any lease for a term of 1 year or longer, shall

be good and effectual in law or equity against creditors or subsequent purchasers for a valuable consideration and without notice, unless the same be recorded according to the law . . . .

Fla. Stat. ch. 695.01. That is, between competing claimants, the subsequent grantee prevails if (1) at the time of purchase she had no notice—actual, inquiry,[12] or record (often called "constructive") notice—of the prior claim ("bona fide") and (2) she gave valuable consideration for the interest ("purchaser for value"). Thus, in some circumstances, the prior claimant may record first, but still lose. For example, suppose O sells the property to A, who does not record. O then sells the same property to B, who does not record. A records, and then B records. Assume that B had no actual or inquiry notice of the prior claim when she purchased the property. Because A recorded after B's purchase, B, the subsequent purchaser, had no notice *at the time of the purchase*; she is a BFP and thus prevails over the prior claim. Approximately half of the states have notice statutes.

Race-notice statutes. In a race-notice jurisdiction, a subsequent purchaser has superior title only if she is both a bona fide purchaser *and* she records her instrument before the prior purchaser. The California statute is typical:

> Every conveyance of real property or an estate for years therein, other than a lease for a term not exceeding one year, is void as against any subsequent purchaser or mortgagee of the same property, or any part thereof, in good faith and for a valuable consideration, whose conveyance is first duly recorded, and as against any judgment affecting the title, unless the conveyance shall have been duly recorded prior to the record of notice of action.

West's Ann. Cal. Civ. Code § 1214. As in a notice jurisdiction, a prior grantee will always prevail if the subsequent purchaser had notice of the prior conveyance. Where the subsequent purchaser had no notice, however, whichever purchaser records first prevails. This type of recording statute is somewhat more protective of the prior grantee than the notice statute.

Miller v. Green

Supreme Court of Wisconsin, 1953.
264 Wis. 159, 58 N.W.2d 704.

■ CURRIE, JUSTICE.

Defendants Hines claim that their title under their deed is superior to the land-contract interest of the plaintiffs inasmuch as their deed was recorded first. Sec. 235.49, Stats., provides as follows:

12. If the buyer's inspection of the property would reveal evidence of possibly competing claims (*e.g.*, people other than that seller's family occupying part of the property; a utility line on the property; a private road running from one lot to another), the buyer has an obligation to investigate further. If that subsequent investigation would reveal other claims to the property, then the buyer is on inquiry notice of such claims. *Leffler v. Smith*, 388 So.2d 261, 263 (Fla.App.1980) (inspection would have shown longstanding, continuous use of the property by the neighbors, thereby giving adequate notice of the easement).

Every conveyance of real estate within this state hereafter made * * * which shall not be recorded as provided by law shall be void as against any subsequent purchaser in good faith and for a valuable consideration of the same real estate or any portion thereof whose conveyance shall first be duly recorded.

The question at issue on this appeal is whether the defendants Hines qualify under the foregoing statute as subsequent purchasers *"in good faith."* Plaintiffs contend that the defendants Hines do not so qualify because the plaintiffs were in possession of the premises on November 29, 1950, when the defendant W. E. Hines paid Mrs. Green $500 toward the purchase price of the farm, and that such possession constituted constructive notice of the plaintiffs' rights under their land contract. This makes it necessary to review the evidence bearing on such possession by the plaintiffs, or either of them.

Approximately 40 acres of the 63–acre tract was cultivated land and the remainder was pasture and woods. The buildings on the farm consisted of a small log house, a barn, and some sheds, which were in a dilapidated condition; the house was unlivable; and such buildings had not been used for many years. The plaintiff Eugene M. Miller had leased the entire 63–acre tract for the crop season of 1950 and had grown crops on the cultivated 40 acres and had grazed livestock on the remaining portion. The crop had been harvested prior to November, 1950, and the livestock had been removed when cold weather came about November 22, 1950. However, starting November 4, 1950 (the date that the Millers contracted to purchase this farm tract), Miller's father, in behalf of the Millers, hauled between 50 and 60 loads of manure to the farm. First the manure was spread over the land, but then after a snowstorm came it was piled on a pile about 100 feet from the road, such pile being about 60 feet long and several feet high. Such hauling of manure was taking place on November 29, 1950 (the date that the defendants Hines made the $500 down payment on the purchase price), and continued until about December 8 or 9, 1950. Also in November, prior to the snowstorm, approximately two acres of land had been plowed by Miller, which plowed land was plainly visible from the abutting highway before the snowstorm.

The Hines farm was located about one-half mile from this 63–acre tract, although the distance by highway was about one and one-half miles. Part of the tract was visible from the Hines home. The defendant W. E. Hines testified that he knew that the plaintiff Eugene M. Miller had leased the tract for the crop season of 1950, but denied that he drove past the tract on the abutting highway during November, 1950, and denied having seen the plowing of the land, the hauling of the manure, or the manure pile on the land, although he admitted finding the manure pile there the following spring.

The general rule is that possession of land is notice to the world of whatever rights the possessor may have in the premises. The reason underlying this rule is well stated in *Pippin v. Boyer* (1911), 146 Wis. 69, 74, 130 N. W. 872:

> The theory of the law is that the person in possession may be asked to disclose the right or title which he has in the premises, and the purchaser will be chargeable with the actual notice he would have received had he made inquiry. * * * In *Frame v. Frame*, 32 W. Va. 463, 478, the court said:

> "The earth has been described as that universal manuscript, open to the eyes of all. When therefore a man proposes to buy or deal with realty, his first duty is to read this public manuscript, that is, to look and see who is there upon it, and what are his rights there. And, if the person in possession has an equitable title to it, he is as much bound to respect it, as if it was a perfect legal title evidenced by a deed duly recorded."

An apt statement of this general principle of possession being constructive notice is stated in *State v. Jewell* (1947), 250 Wis. 165, 171, 26 N.W. (2d) 825, 28 N.W. (2d) 314:

> The possession of real estate is generally considered constructive notice of rights of the possessor, whether the possession is sought to be used for the purpose of charging a purchaser with notice of an outstanding equity, or whether it is sought to charge a subsequent purchaser with notice of an unrecorded instrument and thereby defeat his right to protection under the recording acts. * * *

The authorities generally hold that in order that possession may constitute constructive notice such possession must be "open, visible, exclusive, and unambiguous." *Ely v. Wilcox* (1866), 20 Wis. *523; *Wickes v. Lake* (1869), 25 Wis. 71; and 55 Am. Jur., Vendor and Purchaser, p. 1090, sec. 716. It will thus be seen that the requirements as to the type of possession that will constitute constructive notice are practically identical with the requirements of the type of possession necessary to constitute adverse possession. In view of the fact that the farm buildings were unusable, the plowing of the two acres of land after November 4, 1950, and the hauling of the manure practically every day throughout November were acts which not only were "open and visible," but also "exclusive and unambiguous." They were the customary acts of possession which could be exercised as to unoccupied farmlands at such time of year. Surely they would have been sufficient to have constituted acts of adverse possession, and it would appear that the rule as to acts of possession necessary to constitute constructive notice to a purchaser is no more strict. *Wickes v. Lake, supra*, is authority for the principle that actual residence on the land is not required in order to have sufficient possession to constitute constructive notice.

In *George v. Stansbury* (1922), 90 W.Va. 593, 111 S.E. 598, both the plaintiff and defendants claimed title to a city lot. The plaintiff, during 1919, had maintained a garden on the lot, and the following year, although he did not have a garden there, he permitted the owner of a near-by lot who was excavating for a building to haul a large quantity of dirt from the excavation and dump it on the lot so as to fill a low place. It was during this second year that the defendants purchased the premises and obtained a deed which they recorded, while the plaintiff's title was not recorded. The West Virginia court held that the gardening during the one season, followed by the permitting of the dirt to be hauled in and dumped the second year, constituted sufficient possession to be constructive notice to the defendants of plaintiff's rights, and plaintiff was held to have the superior title. If hauling dirt onto a vacant lot constitutes sufficient possession to be constructive notice to a subsequent purchaser, surely hauling manure onto farmland, as in the instant case, should be held to be equally effective to constitute constructive notice.

. . . .

The learned trial court in the instant case apparently was of the opinion that, in order for the plaintiff Eugene M. Miller's possession of the premises to have been constructive notice to the defendants Hines that Miller claimed rights of ownership therein, there must have been some change in the type of his possession after November 4, 1950 (the date the Millers entered into the contract to purchase). * * *

In other words the trial court found that there was possession of the premises by Miller from November 4, 1950, through to the end of that month, but there was no change in the type of possession. Apparently it was the theory of the trial court that the defendants Hines could assume, because of such lack of change in the character of possession, that the possession after November 4, 1950, was that of a tenant and not of a purchaser. The authorities, however, clearly establish that no such change in the character of possession is necessary.

* * *

[In] *Brinser v. Anderson* (1889), 129 Pa. 376, 404, 18 A. 520, 521, wherein the Pennsylvania court stated:

> Knowledge of the existence of a lease will, of course, give constructive notice of all its provisions; but, the possession, apart from the lease, we think should be treated as notice of the possessor's claim of title, whatever that claim may be, for the lease may be but the first of two or more successive rights acquired by the tenant. While in the occupancy under a lease for years, the tenant * * * may have purchased the legal estate in fee and failed to record his deed. Would it be supposed that a knowledge of the precedent lease would dispense with the duty of inquiry, and entitle a subsequent grantee to the protection of an innocent purchaser? * * *

It is our considered judgment that the acts of possession on the part of the plaintiff Eugene M. Miller throughout the remainder of the month of

November, 1950, following the purchase of the tract by the Millers on November 4, 1950, constituted constructive notice to all the world which required a subsequent purchaser to make inquiry as to what rights, if any, the plaintiff Eugene M. Miller claimed to have in the premises. Subsequent purchasers could not safely assume, without inquiry, as did the defendants Hines, that, because Miller had theretofore been a tenant for the season, there had been no subsequent change in his rights from that of a tenant to that of a purchaser.

■ GEHL, J. (DISSENTING).

The majority say in effect that as a matter of law any entry upon land and its occupation, no matter that the acts of entry may be infrequent and the occupation may be for short interrupted periods, constitutes such possession as to put a purchaser upon inquiry as to the rights of the person so occupying; that possession, regardless of its nature or extent, serves as notice to put the prospective buyer upon inquiry.

That is erroneous. Possession to constitute notice is that which is *required* by law, and is defined in *Ely v. Wilcox*, 20 Wis. 523, 531: "The next question is, whether there was such possession by Ely at the date of the deed to the appellant as to be constructive notice to him of the plaintiff's title. The burden of proof was on the plaintiff to prove such possession. He has failed to prove that either he or any one under him was in actual possession of the premises or any part of them at the date of the deed. The rule is, that possession, to be notice, must be open, visible, exclusive, and unambiguous; not liable to be misunderstood or misconstrued. * * * "

　　　* * *

It was the burden of the plaintiffs to establish that Hines was not a *bona fide* purchaser. The court found that they had not met the burden. The fact that some of the land had been plowed, that a water tank and a pile of manure were left upon the farm (neither of which circumstances is evidence of possession inconsistent with the right of possession of Mrs. Green, and neither of which is a circumstance which would necessarily suggest that Miller rather than Mrs. Green or someone else acting for or under her had left the tank and manure upon the premises and had plowed the land), considered with the fact that the buildings were unoccupied and that the crop season for which period Miller had rented the farm had ended, are not such as to permit us to hold that the court's findings are contrary to the great weight and clear preponderance of the evidence. Certainly we should not say that under those circumstances the court erred in its finding that plaintiffs had failed to meet the burden to establish that their possession of the farm was "open, visible, exclusive, and unambiguous; not liable to be misunderstood or misconstrued."

　　　* * *

1.   What type of recording act did Wisconsin have? What are the elements for a subsequent purchaser to have superior title?

2.   In what respect was Hines not a bona fide purchaser for value? Assuming that he promptly recorded his interest, and that the Millers had not, in what respect did he have notice of the Millers' interest? Was it the prior lease? Was it the limited agricultural activity? Would either alone have been enough to give notice? What else could Hines have done to investigate?

3.   What is the difference between the tests used by the majority and the dissent? Which test resolves the competing claims more equitably?

c.   TITLE REGISTRATION

Fewer than a dozen states also use a title registration system, known as the Torrens system.[13] *See, e.g.,* Colo. Rev. Stat. §§ 38–36–101 to 199; *see generally,* Bostick, Land Title Registration: An English Solution to an American Problem, 63 Ind. L. J. 55 (1987). Under the title registration system, the title registrant initiates a judicial proceeding to adjudicate the validity of all claims to the property. After a court-appointed title searcher investigates available records, the court issues a "certificate of title" declaring who has valid interests in the parcel, including encumbrances such as mortgages, covenants, and easements. The certificate is then indexed in a tract index. Subsequent conveyances are marked on the certificate.

Although the title registration process was designed to simplify title searches and recordation, it is not widely used and some states have repealed it. Where it is available, registration is voluntary, and potential registrants are often deterred by the significant cost and delay involved in the initial judicial proceeding. In addition, some states exempt certain kinds of claims, such as liens, which significantly reduces the value of the system. *See generally* McCormack, Torrens and Recording: Land Title Assurance in the Computer Age, 18 Wm. Mitchell L. Rev. 61 (1992); M. Friedman, Contracts and Conveyances of Real Property § 3.12 (5th ed. 1991 & Cum. Supp. 1995).

1.   Who is advantaged and disadvantaged under each of the three types of recording acts? Which act is the most fair to the parties?

2.   Which system is the easiest to administer? Which one(s) will be more likely to raise difficult factual questions that must be resolved

13.   The system is named after Richard Torrens who introduced it in Australia in the mid-nineteenth century.

through litigation? How is administrative convenience and the need to minimize litigation costs to be balanced against fairness?

Problems

1. O sold Blackacre to A on January 1, and A recorded the deed on July 1. In the meantime, on March 1, O sold Blackacre to B, a bona fide purchaser for value, who recorded a month later on April 1. Who would win the lawsuit *A v. B* under each type of recording act (consider the effect of the majority and minority rule regarding title searches)?

2. O sold Blackacre to A on January 1, and A recorded the deed on July 1. In the meantime, on March 1, O sold Blackacre to B, who was aware of the prior transfer to A. B recorded the deed on April 1. Who would win the lawsuit *A v. B* under each type of recording act (consider the effect of the majority and minority rule regarding title searches)?

3. O sold Blackacre to A on January 1, and A recorded the deed on February 1. One month later, O sold Blackacre to B, who recorded on April 1. B had no actual or inquiry notice at the time he purchased his interest in Blackacre. Who would win the lawsuit *A v. B* under each type of recording act (consider the effect of the majority and minority rule regarding title searches)?

4. O sold Blackacre to A on January 1, and A recorded the deed on March 1. O sold Blackacre to B, a bona fide purchaser for value, on February 1, and B recorded on April 1. Who would win lawsuit *A v. B* under each type of recording act (consider the effect of the majority and minority rule regarding title searches)?

5. O sold Blackacre to A on January 1. A never recorded. On March 1, A sold Blackacre to B, who promptly recorded, and on June 1, B sold Blackacre to C, who promptly recorded. On August 1, O sold Blackacre to X, who promptly recorded. X had no actual or inquiry notice of the other grantees. Who would win the lawsuit *X v. C* under each type of recording act (consider the effect of the majority and minority rule regarding title searches)?

6. O sold Blackacre to A on January 1. A never recorded. On March 1, O sold Blackacre to B, who had actual notice of the prior conveyance. B promptly recorded. On June 1, B sold Blackacre to C, who promptly recorded, and who had no actual or inquiry notice of A's claim. Who would win the lawsuit *C v. A* under each type of recording act (consider the effect of the majority and minority rule regarding title searches)?

7. O sold Blackacre to A on January 1. A never recorded. On March 1, O gave Blackacre to B, who promptly recorded and who had no actual or inquiry notice of A's claim. On June 1, B sold Blackacre to C, who promptly recorded and who had no actual or inquiry notice of A's claim. If A had brought suit to quiet title against B before June 1, who would win the lawsuit *A v. B* in each of the three types of jurisdictions? If A brought suit

against C after June 1, who would win the lawsuit *A v. C* under each type of recording act (consider the effect of the majority and minority rule regarding title searches)?

8.   O sold Blackacre to A on January 1. A never recorded. On March 1, O sold Blackacre to B, who promptly recorded and who had no actual or inquiry notice of A's claim. When A discovered B on the land, A promptly told everyone in town that Blackacre belonged to him. On June 1, B sold Blackacre to C, who had actual notice of A's claim. C promptly recorded. Who would win the lawsuit *A v. C* under each type of recording act (consider the effect of the majority and minority rule regarding title searches)?

9.   In 1959, Johnson sold Blackacre, an unimproved tract, to Omega for $5000 cash. Johnson had good record title, and Omega promptly recorded the general warranty deed in the grantor/grantee indices.

In 1991, Omega sold the still unimproved Blackacre to Alpha for $20,000 cash in exchange for a general warranty deed. Alpha's lawyer, Thompson, told Alpha that he had carefully checked title to the land and that he had promptly recorded the deed. In fact, he had done neither.

In early April 1994, Omega met Beta at a party. Beta mentioned that she was in the market for some unimproved land. Omega described Blackacre, but failed to tell her that he already had sold it to Alpha. When, after inspecting the unimproved land and conducting a careful title search, Beta offered $30,000 for the land, Omega could not resist temptation. On the evening of Friday April 10, he took the money and gave Beta a general warranty deed for the property. As the transaction took place after business hours, Beta could not record the deed immediately. Over the weekend, her father fell ill. Beta left to take care of him (500 miles away).

Meanwhile, on April 11, Thompson ran off with Alpha's spouse. Fearing the worst, Alpha had another lawyer, Sullivan, check all of the matters that Thompson had handled. Sullivan soon discovered that Thompson had not recorded the Blackacre deed. Alpha had the deed recorded first thing Monday April 13.

Beta returned home on April 15, and recorded her deed that day.

In late 1997, Beta sold Blackacre to Chi for $25,000 (nearby development had driven down the market price). Chi promptly recorded her general warranty deed. A few months later, Alpha began construction on Blackacre. Chi promptly sued to quiet title.

In the lawsuit *Chi v. Alpha*, who wins under each type of recording act (consider the effect of the majority and minority rule regarding title searches)?

----

d.   REGISTRATION AND NOTICE OF INTELLECTUAL PROPERTY INTERESTS

Public registration and notice requirements traditionally have played significant roles in the creation, validity, and exercise of intellectual property rights. The importance of these requirements vary significantly across the different types of interests. *See generally* R. Merges, P. Menell, M. Lemley & T. Jorde, Intellectual Property in the New Technological Age (1997).

Patents. Inventors may, but are not required to, seek a patent to protect their claims for their inventions. An inventor who does not file a timely patent application with the Patent and Trademark Office (PTO) risks losing her rights to the invention. *See, e.g.,* 35 U.S.C. § 102(b) (an inventor, whose invention is described in a publication, has one year to file a patent application; otherwise the invention is deemed to be in the public domain). The patent application must clearly disclose the inventor's claims and how the invention works. 35 U.S.C. § 112. Disclosure both reveals the ''boundaries'' of the claimed invention (analogous to the description of land in a real estate contract and a deed) and promotes technological advancement by enabling other inventors to learn from it.

The United States applies a ''first-to-invent'' standard to resolve competing claims to inventions. Thus, even if inventor B files a patent application first, the PTO will award the patent to inventor A if she can establish, by a laboratory journal or other credible source of evidence, that she was the first to discover the invention. By contrast, nearly every other nation awards the patent to the ''first-to-file.''

The patent law also encourages patent owners to provide notice of their patents. To obtain damages for patent infringement, an inventor must first give notice of her patent, either directly on the invention or by filing a patent infringement suit. Since damages do not begin to accrue until notice is given, providing notice of a preexisting patent on a patented product (*e.g.,* ''U.S. Patent No. ...'') ensures that no damage claims are lost.

Trademarks. A common law trademark owner acquires important federal statutory protections by registering the mark with the PTO. Registration establishes *prima facie* evidence of the validity of the trademark, 15 U.S.C. § 1057(b), gives others constructive notice of the registrant's claim of ownership of the mark, 15 U.S.C. § 1072, nationwide constructive use of the mark as of the date of the application, 15 U.S.C. § 1057(c), confers federal jurisdiction over trademark disputes, 15 U.S.C. § 1121, makes the mark incontestable after five years of continuous use, 15 U.S.C. § 1065, and authorizes treble damages and the award of attorney fees, 15 U.S.C. §§ 1116–1120.

Copyrights. Under the 1909 Copyright Act, authors had to register their works with the U.S. Copyright Office both to renew their copyright for an additional 28–year term and to bring an infringement suit. The 1976 Copyright Act creates a longer unified term of copyright protection and thereby eliminates one of the major reasons to register a work. The 1976 Act retains the registration requirement as a prerequisite for an infringement suit. It also encourages registration by according registered copyrights *prima facie* evidence of validity, 17 U.S.C. § 411, and by authorizing statutory damages and attorney fees for infringements that occurred after registration, 17 U.S.C. § 412.

When Congress subsequently amended the 1976 Act to conform to the Berne Convention for the Protection of Literary and Artistic Works, which provides that copyright shall "not be subject to any formality," Congress eliminated the requirement that copyright owners register their works before instituting suits for works whose country of origin is another Berne member nation. Congress, however, retained the registration requirement for domestic works. The Copyright Act no longer requires a notice of copyright (©, followed by date and author), but the Act encourages authors to give notice through provisions precluding a defense of innocent infringement if the infringer used a copy with a proper notice. 17 U.S.C. § 401(d).

———

1.   Should the United States move toward a first-to-file regime to determine patent priority? How would such a system affect the incentives of inventors? In what ways are the considerations similar to those that arise in real property transactions? In what ways are they different?

2.   What factors explain the difference in formal registration/notice across the different modes of intellectual property protection?

———

3.   STAGE 3: DELIVERY OF THE DEED

Under the *doctrine of merger*, when the buyer accepts a deed to an interest in land, the parties' obligations under the contract (including the implied warranty of marketable title) related to the conveyance are discharged and the grantee may only sue under tort law (*e.g.*, misrepresentation, fraud) or under the covenants that may be in the deed. *See, e.g., Knudson v. Weeks*, 394 F.Supp. 963, 976 (W.D.Okl.1975) (subject to exceptions for fraud or mistake, the real estate contract is "merged" into the deed, such that the grantee may only bring claims under covenants in the deed); *Bakken v. Price*, 613 P.2d 1222, 1227–29 (Wyo.1980) (absent fraud, a buyer who has accepted a deed is not entitled to rescind the contract and recover the monies paid). Thus, if the purchaser wants to invoke her contract rights, she should do so before accepting the deed. Many states, however, have abandoned the doctrine of merger, and others refuse to apply it to contract provisions that are collateral to the conveyance.

a.   FORMALITIES OF A VALID DEED

Although the legal requirements for a deed vary from state to state, there are several common elements.

Deed must be in writing. Under the statute of frauds all conveyances of real property must be memorialized in a writing signed by the grantor. *See, e.g.,* Ariz. Rev. Stat. § 33–401 (conveyance must be by a signed and acknowledged deed). Some courts have held that informal documents, such as letters, meet this requirement if those documents evidence the grantor's *present intent to convey* title to the grantee. *See, e.g., Metzger v. Miller*, 291 Fed. 780, 783–84 (N.D.Cal.1923) (interpreting state law, the court held that a series of letters showed a mother's present intent to convey a fee simple interest to her son).

Courts occasionally enforce oral gifts of land notwithstanding the statute of frauds under a theory of *equitable estoppel*, such as where the grantee took possession of the property and made significant improvements in reasonable reliance on the grantor's oral indications that she was making a gift, or where the grantor would be unjustly enriched by invoking the statute of frauds. In *Monarco v. Lo Greco*, 35 Cal.2d 621, 220 P.2d 737 (1950), Natale orally promised his child, Christie, that if Christie lived and worked on the farm, the father would leave the farm to Christie at the parents' deaths. Christie worked the farm for twenty years, helping to increase the value of the property from $4000 to $100,000. Toward the end of his life, however, Natale decided to give the farm to another relative who lived in another state. The court found both that Christie had detrimentally relied on the promise (by giving up any opportunity to obtain further education and accumulate wealth) and that someone else (the geographically distant relative) would be unjustly enriched, and consequently enforced the oral promise. Other courts will enforce an oral conveyance under the doctrine of part performance. *Cf. Binninger v. Hutchinson*, 355 So.2d 863, 865 (Fla.App.1978) (taking possession, without the owner's acquiescence, is not enough to invoke the doctrine of part performance).

Deed must identify the grantor and grantee. To be valid, a deed must identify the grantor and grantee with certainty, either by name or by an adequate description (*e.g.*, grantor's "oldest living child" or "husband").

Deed must contain words of conveyance. A deed must contain language indicating that the grantor has the intent presently to convey the property, *e.g.*, "give," "grant," "bargain and sell," "convey," or "assign." Deeds commonly but needlessly contain an entire string of such words; in most states, any words indicating some sort of conveyance will suffice. Certain words, however, may imply certain covenants in the deed (described in more detail below). In some states, use of the word "grant" or "convey" implies a limited number of specified covenants, such as freedom from encumbrances. In all states, use of the word "quitclaim" signals that there are no covenants.

Deed must describe the property. A deed will only convey land that is specifically described in the document. A deed should therefore contain a metes and bounds (measures and boundaries) description, refer to a government survey, contain a street and number system, or refer to the name of the property. A deed need not explicitly identify or describe improvements, buildings, mineral rights, and air rights; normally they will be transferred unless the deed expressly excludes them.

The deed must also contain a description of the estate transferred, *e.g.*, life estate, fee simple with any conditions. Traditionally, this description is in the "habendum clause" of the grant, although it is now often found in the granting clause.

Grantor must be competent. A deed signed by a minor is voidable (that is, may be declared void at the grantor's option), and a deed signed by a mentally incompetent person is usually void. Because of the legal obstacles to transferring property owned by persons who are not legally competent, courts appoint conservators and guardians (often, but not always, relatives of the incompetent person) with legal authority to make the transfers subject to fiduciary duties.

Consideration. Consideration is not required to transfer land. Even if the grantor is selling the land, most states do not require the deed to contain the purchase price, although some states do. Iowa Code Ann. § 428A.4 (requiring either a declaration of value or a recorded real estate contract).

Witnessing/Acknowledgment. Several states require the grantor's signature to be witnessed (or acknowledged) by a notary public or other disinterested witness before the deed can be recorded. The conveyance is valid even though the deed is not witnessed or acknowledged, but if the deed cannot be recorded, the grantee loses the protections of the recording acts.

Delivery. The title to land is not transferred until the deed is delivered to the grantee or an agent of the grantee. The delivery requirements are discussed in greater detail below.

b.   COVENANTS OF TITLE

Under the doctrine of *caveat emptor*, after delivery a grantee is only protected from title defects—essentially competing claims to the land—by covenants of title in the deed (or by tort claims). Traditionally, there are six types of somewhat overlapping covenants of title, although the buyer and seller are free to modify, delete, or create new covenants.

i.   *Present Covenants*

There are three present covenants—seisin, right to convey, and freedom from encumbrances. In most states, the benefit of present covenants does not "run with the land"—that is, only the original grantee, and not his successors, can rely on the present covenant. *But see* Colo. Rev. Stat. § 38–30–121 (covenants of seisin and freedom from encumbrances run with the land for the benefit of all successors); Ga. Code Ann. § 44–5–60(a) (covenant of freedom from encumbrances runs with the land unless deed expressly provides otherwise).

Seisin: In most states, seisin is a promise that the grantor has title and possession of the land. In some states, it is only a promise that the grantor has possession of the land.

Right to Convey: With this covenant the grantor promises that she has the right to transfer the property. A grantor who is a trustee or an agent for the true owner does not breach this covenant upon transferring the property.

Freedom from Encumbrances: The covenant of freedom from encumbrances is a promise that the land is free from undisclosed encumbrances—such as a mortgage, a lease, a real covenant, an equitable servitude, an easement, a lien, or outstanding taxes. In many states, the buyer's independent knowledge of the easement, absent express disclosure in the deed, is not a defense to seller's breach.

ii.   *Future Covenants*

There are three *future* covenants—quiet enjoyment, warranty, and further assurances. Because the benefit of future covenants runs with the land, successors to the original grantee, as well as the original grantee, may invoke them against any prior grantor who made the covenant. *See, e.g., Smith v. Smith*, 129 Ga.App. 618, 200 S.E.2d 504 (1973) ("Where there has been a breach of the warranty of title to land the last grantee has a right of action against and may sue his immediate warrantor, the remote or original warrantor, or any intermediate warrantor, or any or all of them in one action.").

Warranty: Under this covenant, the grantor promises to defend the grantee from any lawful third party claims to the property. The grantor also covenants to compensate the grantee for losses sustained.

Quiet Enjoyment: Quiet enjoyment is a promise that no third party will assert lawful title to the transferred property. In many states, it is identical to the covenant of warranty.

Further Assurances: Further assurances is a promise that the grantor will take necessary steps to perfect title. This covenant is often omitted from deeds in the United States. It is the only covenant that may be specifically enforced.

c.   TYPE OF DEEDS

There are three main types of deeds used in the United States—general warranty, special warranty, and quitclaim—which are defined by the covenants they contain.

General Warranty Deed. A general warranty deed includes all or several of the traditional covenants of title. *See* 21 Pa.Cons.Stat.Ann. § 5 (a covenant that a grantor will "warrant generally" the property is a promise that the grantor and his successors will defend against all lawful claims to the property). General warranty deeds are rarely used in the West, where special warranty deeds are common, but general warranty deeds are more commonly used in eastern and midwestern states.

Special Warranty Deed. A special warranty deed contains covenants, usually specified by statute, that protect the grantee from certain *acts of the grantor*. *See, e.g., See* 21 Pa.Cons.Stat.Ann. § 6 (a covenant to "specially warrant" is a promise to defend against the lawful demands of the grantor or persons claiming through him). For example, if a special warranty deed contained a covenant of freedom from encumbrances, the grantor would be liable only if she had placed an encumbrance on the property. The grantor would not be liable if the easement already existed on the land when grantor herself received title.

In many states, the covenants for a special warranty deed need not be expressly listed in the deed. For example, if a special warranty deed in California stated that the grantor *"grants* to [the grantee] the land in San Francisco County, State of California, described as follows: ..." the deed impliedly includes (unless expressly excluded) covenants that the grantor has not previously conveyed any interest in the property to another person, and that the property is free from encumbrances imposed by the grantor. *See* West's Ann. Cal. Civ. Code § 1113. *See also* Ala. Code § 35–4–271 (use of "grant," "bargain," or "sell" presumptively creates covenants of seisin, freedom from encumbrances created by the grantor, and quiet enjoyment against the grantor); Ariz. Rev. Stat. § 33–435 (use of "grant" or "convey" presumptively creates covenants of freedom from encumbrances and that the grantor has not previously conveyed any interest in the property to anyone else); Mo. Rev. Stat. § 442.420 (use of the phrase "grant, bargain and sell" presumptively creates covenants of seisin, freedom from encumbrances created by the grantor, and further assurances). In some states, there are no implied covenants. *See, e.g.,* Mass. Gen. Laws Ann. ch. 183, § 12 (use of the word "grant" does not result in any implied covenants).

Quitclaim Deed. A quitclaim deed contains no promises. A quitclaim deed might state that the grantor *"quitclaims* to [the grantee] the land in San Francisco County, State of California, described as follows: ...; together with all appurtenances, rents, issues, and profits, if any." With the use of the word "quitclaims" in the deed, the grantee has no rights against the grantor for defects of title. The grantor only grants whatever interest in the property she may have.

d.   BREACH AND REMEDIES FOR BREACH

In most states, the *present* covenants are breached, if at all, only at the moment of transfer. *See, e.g., Brown v. Lober,* 75 Ill.2d 547, 552, 27 Ill.Dec. 780, 783, 389 N.E.2d 1188, 1191 (1979) (the covenant of seisin is breached only if at the time of conveyance the grantor does not have title). Consequently, the statute of limitations (typically between four and six years) begins to run at the time of the transfer. A few state statutes hold that a breach can occur after the transfer, such as when a third party makes a claim to the property. *See, e.g.,* N.Y.—McKinney's C.P.L.R. 206(c) (actions for breach of the covenants of seisin and freedom from encumbrances accrue upon eviction by a third party).

The *future* covenants are breached, if at all, after the conveyance, when a third party has made a claim to the property. In *Brown v. Lober,* 75 Ill.2d at 547, 552–55, 75 Ill.2d 547, 27 Ill.Dec. 780, 783–85, 389 N.E.2d 1188, 1191–93 (1979), the court rejected the landowner's claim of a breach of the covenant of quiet enjoyment; although a third party had a valid claim to the property, because that person had not yet "interfere[d] with the right of possession"—that is, had not yet made the claim or exercised his rights—there was no breach. The future covenant could be breached only when "there is an actual or constructive eviction of the covenantee by the paramount titleholder." *Id.* at 553, 27 Ill.Dec. at 783, 389 N.E.2d at 1191. The grantee's inability to invoke the future covenants until the third party makes a claim can be problematic if the grantor dies or becomes judgment proof.

Damages for Breach. With the exception of the rarely used covenant of further assurances, breach of a covenant of title gives rise to a claim for damages, not specific performance. *See, e.g., Tropico Land and Improvement Co. v. Lambourn*, 170 Cal. 33, 38–39, 148 P. 206, 208 (1915). Most states cap the grantor's liability at an amount equal to the consideration she received for the property when she sold it. This limitation has its greatest impact when the property substantially appreciated after the conveyance. For example, even though a grantee made large investments in and improvements to the property, he can receive only the purchase price if he later discovers the grantor violated the covenant of seisin. The cap thus protects the grantor, who has no control over the extent to which the grantee (or the market) increased the value of the property. The cap also protects grantors who received relatively little or nothing for the property.

For most covenants, if the title to the entire property failed, the grantee may recover the purchase price, and consequential damages. If the title failed for only part of the property, the damages are in proportion to the value of the land for which the title failed. If the grantor breached the present covenant of freedom from encumbrances, the amount of damages depends on whether the encumbrance can be removed. If the grantee can remove it (*e.g.*, a mortgage), her damages are the cost of removing the encumbrance (capped by the total consideration paid). If the encumbrance is not removable, damages are the difference between the value of the property at the time of the transfer with and without the encumbrance.

Estoppel by Deed. Although the doctrine of estoppel by deed (also called estoppel by after-acquired title) is not a remedy for breach, we mention it here because it may be invoked to perfect the grantee's title. The doctrine applies where the grantor does not own the property he is purporting to convey. If the grantor subsequently acquires title, that title is treated as passing directly to the grantee under the original deed. The grantor is estopped from arguing that the grantee received nothing under the deed because the grantor did not have legal title at the time of the original transfer. Traditionally, this doctrine applied only to warranty deeds, *see, e.g., Tuttle v. Burrows*, 852 P.2d 1314, 1316–17 (Colo.App.1992); *Webster Oil Co., Inc. v. McLean Hotels, Inc.*, 878 S.W.2d 892, 893–95 (Mo.App.1994), although an increasing number of cases apply it to quitclaim deeds that purport to convey a fee simple absolute. *E.g., Turner v. Miller*, 276 So.2d 690, 693–95 (Miss.1973).

Problem

Claire and Johanna (remember them?) finally worked out their differences over the termite infested house; Johanna paid $70,000 for the house, and Claire had the sand box moved so that it did not encroach on the neighbor's property. Claire delivered and Johanna accepted a general warranty deed for the property that included covenants of seisin, freedom from encumbrances, quiet enjoyment, and warranty.

[margin note: general warranty]

Since the conveyance, Johanna spent $40,000 to repair the termite damage, and invested another $100,000 to add two new rooms on the side of the house.

Six years after taking possession, Johanna received a letter from an attorney stating that a neighbor's lot line was eight feet closer to Johanna's house than anyone had previously thought. The correct property line goes through the new rooms that Johanna had just built. The neighbor has demanded that Johanna tear down the encroaching rooms. The neighbor has made clear that he will go to court soon to enforce his rights. Johanna hired a surveyor who confirmed the neighbor's claim about the property line.

In investigating the matter, Johanna discovered that Claire bought the house from Bob 10 years ago for $120,000, and that Bob had bought the house from Alice 18 years ago for $80,000. Apparently, the encroachment first occurred 19 years ago when Alice began to use the additional eight feet of land without the neighbor's permission. Her deed to Bob, and each subsequent deed, describes the lot as including the eight-foot strip. Each grantor is still alive, and each gave his or her grantee a general warranty deed with the same covenants that Johanna received.

The statute of limitations for the present and future covenants is five years, and the period for adverse possession is 20 years.

Johanna again comes to you for advice. What are her rights and remedies against Alice, Bob, and Claire? What course of action do you recommend?

––––––

e.   DELIVERY

Property is not conveyed until the grantor has *delivered* the deed, and the grantee has *accepted* it. Although delivery frequently involves physical transmission of the deed, a valid delivery turns on the grantor's intent— whether the grantor intended, as evidenced by words or actions, to convey an interest in property. For example, in *McMahon v. Dorsey*, 353 Mich. 623, 627–28, 91 N.W.2d 893, 895 (1958), the grantor placed an executed deed for the family farm in a safe deposit box leased to both the grantor and the grantee. After the grantor died, and the grantee discovered the deed, the grantor's heirs challenged the validity of the delivery. At trial, a neighbor testified that the grantor had told him that he (the grantor) had deeded the farm to the grantee. On this testimony alone, which made clear the grantor's intent that execution of the deed transferred property, the court held there was a sufficient basis to find that the deed had been delivered.

The conveyance is not completed until the grantee accepts the deed. If, as in most cases, the conveyance is to the grantee's benefit, his acceptance is presumed.

i. Delivery Directly to a Grantee

Courts presume that a grantor has delivered a deed to the grantee when he physically gives the deed to the grantee, acknowledges the deed in the presence of a notary, or records the deed. *Sweeney v. Sweeney*, 126 Conn. 391, 394–95, 11 A.2d 806, 807–08 (1940). Courts presume that the grantor has not delivered the deed if none of these conditions is met (*e.g.*, he retains an unacknowledged, unrecorded deed). *See, e.g., Jones v. Jones*, 470 So.2d 1207 (Ala.1985) (upholding trial court's conclusion that the deed was not delivered when the grantor retained it in a trunk in his bedroom); *Hans v. Hans*, 482 So.2d 1117, 1119 (Miss.1986) (grantor's retention of the deed raises a presumption that the deed was not delivered). These presumptions can be rebutted by the grantor's words or actions.

Conditions. Deeds commonly contain conditions,[14] and a court must decide whether the condition means that there is no delivery until the condition is met, or whether the interest transferred is subject to a condition. If the former, delivery has failed; the grantee holds no interest. If the latter, the grantor delivered an executory interest to the grantee; the interest becomes a present interest only when the condition is satisfied.

This issue most commonly arises when a grantor executes but retains a deed with the intention that a present interest will pass on his death. If the grantor intended to retain a life estate and transfer a remainder to the grantee, the grantor validly delivered a future interest. *See, e.g., Morelos v. Morelos*, 129 Ariz. 354, 356, 631 P.2d 136, 138 (App.1981) (the court held that there could be a valid delivery of a future interest when the grantor executed a deed, which he gave to the grantee's older sister for safekeeping with the express intent that the grantee should have possession after the grantor's death). However, if the grantor postponed delivery until his death, the delivery would be invalid. Often courts look to what the grantor said when he executed the deed, whether the grantor retained control over the property and the deed, whether the grantor kept the deed in a place to which the grantee had access, and whether the conveyance fit rationally into the grantor's larger estate plan.

Reservations. Often a grantor executes a deed conveying a future interest, but also reserving power to revoke the future interest. The question arises whether there has been a valid delivery. Many though not all courts take the position that reservation of the right to revoke a deed does not prevent a valid delivery. In *St. Louis County National Bank v. Fielder*, 364 Mo. 207, 260 S.W.2d 483 (1953), the grantor retained a life

---

14. In most states, conditions must be express in the deed; parol evidence is not admissible to prove conditions not contained in the deed.

estate and conveyed a remainder subject to the express reservation of the "power to sell, rent, lease, mortgage, or otherwise dispose" of the property during his lifetime. After the grantor's death, his executor challenged the deed as an invalid testamentary gift. The court held that such a reservation was valid and that consequently the grantor had delivered a defeasible fee subject to a life estate.

Problem

The grantor executed a quitclaim deed for a farm to three persons who had helped her during an extended illness. The grantor retained the deed in a strong box in her closet, and instructed another friend to mail the deed to the grantees after her death. The grantor had told others that she had deeded the property to her friends. Although she was completely bedridden during the balance of her life, the grantor continued to collect the rents from and control the operation of the property. In her will, the grantor bequeathed a proportional amount of different property to a fourth friend, who also had helped during her illness. The beneficiary under the will challenged the delivery of the deed (if there was no delivery, she would get the farm under the residuary clause of the will).

1. Should it make any difference to the question of delivery that the grantees were the grantor's friends who had helped her? Should it make any difference that the grantor left a proportional amount of property to a fourth friend?

2. Who bears the burden of proof—the ostensible grantees or the person challenging the delivery?

3. What was the grantor's intent when she executed the deed? How should this case be decided in light of *Morelos v. Morelos* and *McMahon v. Dorsey*?

4. If there was a valid delivery, what interest did the grantor convey? *See Ferrell v. Stinson*, 233 Iowa 1331, 11 N.W.2d 701 (1943).

Bona Fide Purchaser for Value. As noted above, if the grantor gave an executed deed to the grantee, but with no intent to deliver, the grantor did not deliver the undelivered deed; the grantee has no claim to the property. However, if the grantee recorded the undelivered deed and subsequently *sold* the property to someone who had *no actual or constructive notice* of the grantor's claim to the property—a so-called *bona fide purchaser for value (BFP)*—the purchaser would take free of the grantor's claim. That is, between the grantor and the grantee, the grantor has the superior claim to the property. But as between the grantor and the BFP, the BFP has superior title.

ii. *Delivery via a Third Party*

When a grantor sells property through a real estate contract, the parties normally employ an *escrow agent* to hold the deed and other documents during the escrow period. The escrow agent has instructions to give the deed to the grantee if and when the grantee gives the agent a cashier's check covering the purchase price on or before the closing date. When the grantor gives the deed to the escrow agent, the deed is conditionally delivered, *e.g.*, conditional on payment of the purchase price at the closing (this is different than the interest being subject to a condition, *i.e.*, a future interest). If the grantee never satisfies the specified conditions, the deed is returned to the grantor.

When the conveyance is donative, physical transmission of the deed to a third party normally results in a valid delivery. If the grantor gave the deed to his own agent, however, a court would presume no delivery. *Chapman v. Chapman*, 473 So.2d 467, 469 (Miss.1985) (giving deed to grantor's attorney does not constitute delivery). Even if there are conditions on the conveyance (*e.g.*, when the grantor dies), the delivery is not conditional; rather, the grantee has received a springing executory interest, which the grantor cannot take back. *Ferrell v. Stinson*, 233 Iowa 1331, 1336, 11 N.W.2d 701, 704 (1943) (a deed is delivered if the grantor gives it to a third person without reserving the right to recall the deed and with instructions to give it to the grantee after the grantor's death). Sometimes a grantor reserves a right to recall the deed.

Rosengrant v. Rosengrant

Court of Appeals of Oklahoma, 1981.
629 P.2d 800.

■ BOYDSTON, JUDGE.

This is an appeal by J. W. (Jay) Rosengrant from the trial court's decision to cancel and set aside a warranty deed which attempted to vest title in him to certain property owned by his aunt and uncle, Mildred and Harold Rosengrant. The trial court held the deed was invalid for want of legal delivery. We affirm that decision.

Harold and Mildred were a retired couple living on a farm southeast of Tecumseh, Oklahoma. They had no children of their own but had six nieces and nephews through Harold's deceased brother. One of these nephews was Jay Rosengrant. He and his wife lived a short distance from Harold and Mildred and helped the elderly couple from time to time with their chores.

In 1971, it was discovered that Mildred had cancer. In July, 1972 Mildred and Harold went to Mexico to obtain laetrile treatments accompanied by Jay's wife. Jay remained behind to care for the farm.

Shortly before this trip, on June 23, 1972, Mildred had called Jay and asked him to meet her and Harold at Farmers and Merchants Bank in

Tecumseh. Upon arriving at the bank, Harold introduced Jay to his banker J. E. Vanlandengham who presented Harold and Mildred with a deed to their farm which he had prepared according to their instructions. Both Harold and Mildred signed the deed and informed Jay that they were going to give him "the place," but that they wanted Jay to leave the deed at the bank with Mr. Vanlandengham and when "something happened" to them,[15] he was to take it to Shawnee and record it and "it" would be theirs. Harold personally handed the deed to Jay to "make this legal." Jay accepted the deed and then handed it back to the banker who told him he would put it in an envelope and keep it in the vault until he called for it.

In July, 1974, when Mildred's death was imminent, Jay and Harold conferred with an attorney concerning the legality of the transaction. The attorney advised them it should be sufficient but if Harold anticipated problems he should draw up a will.

In 1976, Harold discovered he had lung cancer. In August and December 1977, Harold put $10,000 into two certificates of deposit in joint tenancy with Jay.

Harold died January 28, 1978. On February 2, Jay and his wife went to the bank to inventory the contents of the safety deposit box. They also requested the envelope containing the deed which was retrieved from the collection file of the bank.

Jay went to Shawnee the next day and recorded the deed.

The petition to cancel and set aside the deed was filed February 22, 1978, alleging that the deed was void in that it was never legally delivered and alternatively that since it was to be operative only upon recordation after the death of the grantors it was a testamentary instrument and was void for failure to comply with the Statute of Wills.

The trial court found the deed was null and void for failure of legal delivery. The dispositive issue raised on appeal is whether the trial court erred in so ruling. We hold it did not and affirm the judgment.

The facts surrounding the transaction which took place at the bank were uncontroverted. It is the interpretation of the meaning and legal result of the transaction which is the issue to be determined by this court on appeal.

In cases involving attempted transfers such as this, it is the grantor's intent at the time the deed is delivered which is of primary and controlling importance. It is the function of this court to weigh the evidence presented at trial as to grantor's intent and unless the trial court's decision is clearly against the weight of the evidence, to uphold that finding.

The grantor and banker were both dead at the time of trial. Consequently, the only testimony regarding the transaction was supplied by the grantee, Jay. The pertinent part of his testimony is as follows:

15. Common euphemism meaning their deaths.

A.   And was going to hand it back to Mr. Vanlandingham [sic], and he wouldn't take it.

Q.   What did Mr. Vanlandingham [sic] say?

A.   Well, he laughed then and said that "We got to make this legal," or something like that. And said, "You'll have to give it to Jay and let Jay give it back to me."

Q.   And what did Harold do with the document?

A.   He gave it to me.

Q.   Did you hold it?

A.   Yes.

Q.   Then what did you do with it?

A.   Mr. Vanlandingham [sic], I believe, told me I ought to look at it.

Q.   And you looked at it?

A.   Yes.

Q.   And then what did you do with it?

A.   I handed it to Mr. Vanlandingham [sic].

Q.   And what did he do with the document?

A.   He had it in his hand, I believe, when we left.

Q.   Do you recall seeing the envelope at any time during this transaction?

A.   I never saw the envelope. But Mr. Vanlandingham [sic] told me when I handed it to him, said, "Jay, I'll put this in an envelope and keep it in a vault for you until you call for it."

* * *

A.   Well, Harold told me while Mildred was signing the deed that they were going to deed me the farm, but they wanted me to leave the deed at the bank with Van, and that when something happened to them that I would go by the bank and pick it up and take it to Shawnee to the court house and record it, and it would be mine.

When the deed was retrieved, it was contained in an envelope on which was typed: "J. W. Rosengrant—or Harold H. Rosengrant."

The import of the writing on the envelope is clear. It creates an inescapable conclusion that the deed was, in fact, retrievable at any time by Harold before his death. The bank teller's testimony as to the custom and usage of the bank leaves no other conclusion but that at any time Harold was free to retrieve the deed. There was, if not an expressed, an implied agreement between the banker and Harold that the grant was not to take effect until two conditions occurred—the death of both grantors and the recordation of the deed.

In support of this conclusion conduct relative to the property is significant and was correctly considered by the court. Evidence was presented to show that after the deed was filed Harold continued to farm, use and control the property. Further, he continued to pay taxes on it until his death and claimed it as his homestead.

Grantee confuses the issues involved herein by relying upon grantors' goodwill toward him and his wife as if it were a controlling factor. From a fair review of the record it is apparent Jay and his wife were very attentive, kind and helpful to this elderly couple. The donative intent on the part of grantors is undeniable. We believe they fully intended to reward Jay and his wife for their kindness. Nevertheless, where a grantor delivers a deed under which he reserves a right of retrieval and attaches to that delivery the condition that the deed is to become operative only after the death of grantors and further continues to use the property as if no transfer had occurred, grantor's actions are nothing more than an attempt to employ the deed as if it were a will. Under Oklahoma law this cannot be done. The ritualistic "delivery of the deed" to the grantee and his redelivery of it to the third party for safe keeping created under these circumstances only a symbolic delivery. It amounted to a pro forma attempt to comply with the legal aspects of delivery. Based on all the facts and circumstances the true intent of the parties is expressed by the notation on the envelope and by the later conduct of the parties in relation to the land. Legal delivery is not just a symbolic gesture. It necessarily carries all the force and consequence of absolute, outright ownership at the time of delivery or it is no delivery at all.

The trial court interpreted the envelope literally. The clear implication is that grantor intended to continue to exercise control and that the grant was not to take effect until such time as both he and his wife had died and the deed had been recorded. From a complete review of the record and weighing of the evidence we find the trial court's judgment is not clearly against the weight of the evidence. Costs of appeal are taxed to appellant.

■ BRIGHTMIRE, J., concurring specially.

In a dispute of this kind dealing with the issue of whether an unrecorded deed placed in the custody of a third party is a valid conveyance to the named grantee at that time or is deposited for some other reason, such as in trust or for a testamentary purpose, the fact finder often has a particularly tough job trying to determine what the true facts are.

The law, on the other hand, is relatively clear. A valid *in praesenti* conveyance requires two things: (1) actual or constructive delivery of the deed to the grantee or to a third party; and (2) an intention by the grantor to divest himself of the conveyed interest. Here the trial judge found there was no delivery despite the testimony of Jay Rosengrant to the contrary that one of the grantors handed the deed to him at the suggestion of banker J. E. Vanlandengham.

So the question is, was the trial court bound to find the facts to be as Rosengrant stated? In my opinion he was not for several reasons. Of the four persons present at the bank meeting in question only Rosengrant survives which, when coupled with the self-serving nature of the nephew's statements, served to cast a suspicious cloud over his testimony. And this, when considered along with other circumstances detailed in the majority opinion, would have justified the fact finder in disbelieving it. I personally have trouble with the delivery testimony in spite of the apparent "corroboration" of the lawyer, Jeff Diamond. The only reason I can see for Vanlandengham suggesting such a physical delivery would be to assure the accomplishment of a valid conveyance of the property at that time. But if the grantors intended that then why did they simply give it to the named grantee and tell him to record it? Why did they go through the delivery motion in the presence of Vanlandengham and then give the deed to the banker? Why did the banker write on the envelope containing the deed that it was to be given to either the grantee "or" a grantor? The fact that the grantors continued to occupy the land, paid taxes on it, offered to sell it once and otherwise treated it as their own justifies an inference that they did not make an actual delivery of the deed to the named grantee. Or, if they did, they directed that it be left in the custody of the banker with the intent of reserving a de facto life estate or of retaining a power of revocation by instructing the banker to return it to them if they requested it during their lifetimes or to give it to the named grantee upon their deaths. In either case, the deed failed as a valid conveyance.

---

1. Why was the physical transmission to the nephew inadequate for delivery? How persuasive is the court's argument that it was just a "symbolic" delivery? Aren't all forms of delivery symbolic?

2. What facts most strongly support the appellate court's conclusion that there had been no delivery? Was the grantee misguided, as the appellate court suggested, when he argued that the conveyance was in return for his earlier kindness? If the grantors' donative intent was clear, as the court acknowledges, shouldn't the court have found delivery?

3. Why does a reservation of the power to revoke the interest defeat the grantors' delivery? Is there some concern that the grantors are really writing a will? Or that creditors' rights might be defeated by such an arrangement?

4. Lawyers, like other professionals, may be liable for malpractice if their breach of the duty to use the knowledge, skill and care ordinarily possessed and exercised by members of the profession in good standing proximately causes damage. *See generally* Prosser and Keeton on the Law of Torts 185–87 (5th ed. 1984). Does the grantee have a cause of action against the grantor's lawyer for malpractice?

Bona Fide Purchaser for Value. If the grantee obtained the deed before the close of escrow, he would have no claim to the property since the deed was not yet fully delivered. If, however, the grantee then sold the deed to a *bona purchaser for value*, some courts would estop the grantor from asserting title. Others, however, would hold for the grantor.

4.   STAGE 4: FORECLOSURE OF SECURITY INTERESTS

Many if not most purchases of real property are made with borrowed money. At a minimum, a lender will require the borrower to sign a promissory note, which specifies the terms of repayment. As a hedge against the borrower's default on the promissory note, a lender normally requires a borrower to give a *security interest* in the property. Under the loan agreement, if the borrower defaults, the lender has recourse against the secured property to satisfy the unpaid debt.

a.   TYPES OF SECURITY INTERESTS

There are two basic types of security interests: a mortgage and a deed of trust.[16] With each, the borrower has possession of the secured property so long as he makes loan payments and meets other requirements in the loan agreement, such as maintaining insurance.

With a *mortgage*, the mortgagor (the borrower) gives the mortgagee (the lender) a lien[17] on the property until the loan is repaid. If the borrower defaults, the lender may foreclose on the property and use the proceeds from the foreclosure sale to satisfy the debt (more on foreclosure below).

With a *deed of trust*, the borrower conveys title to a trustee, who holds the property in trust for the benefit of the lender until the debt is repaid. If the borrower defaults, the trustee must follow the lender's instructions, which are usually to sell the property and use the proceeds from the sale to repay the debt. If, on the other hand, the borrower repays the loan in due course, the trustee conveys title back to the borrower.

b.   FORECLOSURE

When the debtor is unwilling or unable to repay the balance of the loan, the lender may foreclose against the secured property. Under most loan agreements, the lender may also foreclose if the debtor has failed to insure the property, failed to pay taxes on the property, or neglected to maintain the property in good repair. In a foreclosure proceeding, the

16. Another important type of security interest is the installment land contract. With this instrument, the buyer takes possession of the land and pays the purchase price in installments. The seller retains the deed until the last payment. Contracts typically provide that if the buyer defaults, the seller may keep the proceeds and eject the buyer from the property. To mitigate the harshness of this arrangement, many courts treat a land installment contract like a mortgage for purposes of foreclosure. *Bean v. Walker*, 95 A.D.2d 70, 73–74, 464 N.Y.S.2d 895, 897–98

(1983) (requiring the seller to use mortgage foreclosure proceedings against the defaulting buyer). Other courts readily find waiver if the seller has accepted late payments previously. *See generally* Freyfogle, Vagueness and the Rule of Law: Reconsidering Installment Land Contract Forfeitures, 1988 Duke L.J. 609; Powell on Real Property, ch. 84D.

17. A minority of states consider giving a mortgage to be a transfer of legal title to the mortgagee, leaving the mortgagor with equitable title.

property is sold at a public auction. The sale proceeds are used to pay the costs of the sale, then unpaid principal and interest accrued to date, and then junior liens. The surplus, if any, goes to the borrower (if there was a surplus, it is likely the borrower would have sold the property at the market price rather than lose it through foreclosure).

There are two distinct types of foreclosures: judicial and private. To initiate a *judicial foreclosure*, the lender must file a lawsuit against the debtor alleging that she is in default and that the debt is secured by real property. If the court finds for the lender, it orders the property sold at a public auction (usually by a public official such as the sheriff) after giving public notice of the sale. Normally, the borrower has a right of *equitable redemption* before the sale, which allows the borrower to stop the foreclosure proceedings by paying the principal balance, accrued interest, penalties, and costs.

Because the judicial foreclosure procedure is time consuming and costly, lenders prefer to exercise a nonjudicial *power of sale foreclosure*, which is normally available with deeds of trust, although about half of the states also allow mortgages to include an explicit power of sale. *See, e.g.*, Ark. Code. Ann. §§ 18–50–101 to –116; West's Ann. Cal.Civ.Code § 2932. Under a power of sale foreclosure, the lender may hold a public sale of real property almost immediately after the borrower defaults and without first having to file a lawsuit.

Right of Redemption Statutes. Roughly half of the states have created a statutory right of redemption. Under these statutes, the borrower (and other persons with an interest in the property, such as the borrower's heirs or junior lienors) may redeem the property for a specified period after the foreclosure sale (the period ranges from three months to two years). Normally, borrowers may remain in possession of the property during the redemption period. When redeeming the property, borrowers normally must pay the costs of the foreclosure sale, the foreclosure sale price, and the entire balance of the principal if the mortgage or deed of trust contains an enforceable acceleration clause. *See, e.g.*, Iowa Code Ann. § 628.11 (allowing foreclosed property owners to redeem the property by paying the foreclosure purchase price and the costs of the sale, all with interest); Wyo. Stat. Ann. § 1–18–103(a) (allowing foreclosed property owners three months to redeem the property by paying the foreclosure purchase price, taxes, assessments, and prior liens the foreclosure purchaser paid, all with interest at the statutory rate). Many states prohibit the borrower from waiving his statutory redemption rights in the original loan agreement. *See, e.g.*, Kan. Stat. Ann. § 60–2414(a) (no waiver for mortgages for agricultural lands or for land with single or two-family dwellings). Some states limit the availability of the right of redemption. *See, e.g.*, Idaho Code § 45–1508 (no right of redemption with a deed of trust); West's Ann. Cal. Code Civ. Proc. § 729.010 (property is subject to a right of redemption if the security interest holder may obtain a deficiency judgment).

Many scholars have criticized redemption statutes as increasing costs that are passed on to all borrowers (*e.g.*, through interest rates) without significant offsetting benefits. Platt, Deficiency Judgments on Oregon Loans Secured by Land: Growing Disparity Among Functional Equivalents, 23 Willamette L. Rev. 37, 49 (1987) (right of redemption increases lender costs without significant benefits to borrowers); Meador, The Effects of Mortgage Laws on Home Mortgage Rates, 34 J. Econ. & Bus. 143 (1982) (estimating that the right of redemption increases interest rates by 0.17%); Clauretie, State Foreclosure Laws, Risk Shifting, and the Private Mortgage Insurance Industry, 56 J. Risk & Ins. 544, 551 (1989) (estimating that the right of redemption increases interest rates by 0.21%). Other scholars argue that a statutory right of redemption may promote efficiency. Schill, An Economic Analysis of Mortgagor Protection Laws, 77 Va. L. Rev. 489 (1991) (arguing that the impact of the statutory right of redemption on interest rates is quite small, and that such statutes may be efficient).

c.   DEFICIENCY JUDGMENT

When the foreclosure sale proceeds do not cover the balance of the loan or junior liens,[18] as is often the case, the lender may seek a *deficiency judgment* against the borrower equal to the difference between the amount owed and the net amount realized in the foreclosure sale. With a deficiency judgment, the borrower may be required to satisfy this judgment with personal assets other than the property on which the mortgage or deed of trust was originally taken.

Anti-deficiency Statutes. During the Great Depression, many states enacted legislation to protect borrowers from deficiency judgments; state legislatures felt that during times of severe economic distress, it would be unfair for property owners not only to lose their property in foreclosure, but then also to have an additional money judgment against them because the value of the property had dropped as a result of general economic conditions. Anti-deficiency statutes vary widely in their scope. Some statutes forbid deficiency judgments for foreclosures on purchase money mortgages[19] or on deeds of trust used to secure the balance of the purchase price, particularly if the real estate contains a residence. *See, e.g.*, Ariz. Rev. Stat. §§ 33–729, 33–814(G) (barring deficiency judgments for purchase money mortgages and deeds of trust for single or two-family residences,

---

18. Foreclosure sales do not generate enough money for many reasons. In some cases, the market value of the property has dropped, or the initial mortgage was too big for the property. In addition, however, foreclosure sales rarely maximize the sale price of the property: the land is sold quickly without any effort to market it to buyers, the land usually is not made available for inspection prior to sale, and buyers are required to pay cash soon after the auction. *See* Schill, An Economic Analysis of Mortgagor Protection Laws, 77 Va. L. Rev. 489, 493 (1991) (giving reasons why foreclosure sales under-value property). For these reasons, mortgagees are likely to purchase the property at the foreclosure sale. Wechsler, Through the Looking Glass: Foreclosure by Sale as De Facto Strict Foreclosure—An Empirical Study of Mortgage Foreclosure and Subsequent Resale, 70 Cornell L. Rev. 850, 870 (1985) (empirical study of one county showing that mortgagees bought the foreclosed property in 78% of the cases).

19. A *purchase money mortgage* is a mortgage under which the loan is secured by the very property purchased with the loan proceeds.

unless the value of the property was diminished by the mortgagor's voluntary waste); West's Ann.Cal.Code Civ.Proc. § 580b (barring deficiency judgments for purchase money mortgages if the property is used as a dwelling); *Merritt v. Ridge*, 323 N.C. 330, 372 S.E.2d 559 (1988) (interpreting North Carolina's anti-deficiency statute to bar actions to recover the costs of the sale, taxes, and attorney fees). Other states forbid deficiency judgments where the lender used a power of sale foreclosure, thereby giving the lender an incentive to maximize the sale price at the non-judicial sale. *See, e.g.*, Alaska Stat. § 34.20.100 (barring deficiency judgment following non-judicial sale); West's Ann.Cal. Code Civ. Proc. § 580d (barring deficiency judgment following non-judicial sale).

Some states allow deficiency judgments, but permit mortgagees to recover an amount equal to only the difference between the unpaid principal and the property's fair market value at the time of foreclosure (instead of what was actually paid at the foreclosure sale). *See, e.g.*, Official Code Ga. Ann. § 44–14–161(a) (barring deficiency judgment following exercise of a power of sale, unless the lender subsequently receives a judicial finding that the sale was at market value); N.Y.—McKinney's Real Prop. Acts. Law § 1371 (deficiency judgment is for the difference between the amount owed and the market value of the property, as determined by the court, at the time of the foreclosure sale).

In general, mortgagors cannot waive these protections in the initial mortgage agreement. *See, e.g., Merritt v. Ridge, supra*, 323 N.C. at 336, 372 S.E.2d at 563; *Valinda Builders, Inc. v. Bissner*, 230 Cal.App.2d 106, 112, 40 Cal.Rptr. 735 738–39 (1964) (anti-deficiency provisions were enacted "in the interests of the general public" and may not be waived in advance of foreclosure).

Some critics have argued that the anti-deficiency statutes, like the statutory right of redemption, are costly, inefficient, and inequitable. In essence, mortgagors as a class pay more for their mortgages (through higher interest rates) to cover the deficiencies. Meador, The Effects of Mortgage Laws on Home Mortgage Rates, 34 J. Econ. & Bus. 143 (1982) (estimating that anti-deficiency statutes increase mortgage interest rates by 0.14%); Clauretie, State Foreclosure Laws, Risk Shifting, and the Private Mortgage Insurance Industry, 56 J. Risk & Ins. 544, 551 (1989) (estimating that anti-deficiency laws increase mortgage interest rates by 0.36%). Other scholars maintain that anti-deficiency statutes may promote efficiency. Mixon & Shepard, Antideficiency Relief for Foreclosed Homeowners: ULSIA Section 551(b), 27 Wake Forest L. Rev. 455 (1992) (arguing that without anti-deficiency protection, many former homeowners would be forced into personal bankruptcy); Schill, An Economic Analysis of Mortgagor Protection Laws, 77 Va. L. Rev. 489 (1991) (arguing that the impact of the anti-deficiency statutes on interest rates is quite small, and that such statutes, working as a form of insurance, may be efficient).

d.   SALES OF PROPERTY SUBJECT TO MORTGAGE

A person who acquires secured property normally takes the property subject to the security interest,[20] unless the security interest has a due-on-sale clause.[21] The grantee is not personally liable for the debt, unless he agreed to assume it, but since he holds subject to the security interest he will lose the property in foreclosure if he fails to make the loan payments. *See, e.g., Braun v. Crew*, 183 Cal. 728, 731, 192 P. 531, 533 (1920). The original borrower remains liable on the promissory note unless the lender releases him. The original borrower remains liable because this person—not the new landowner—is the person on whose credit the lender relied in making the loan.

20. Persons who purchase property at a foreclosure sale do not take the property subject to the foreclosed security interest or to any junior liens; those interests are wiped out by the foreclosure. The purchaser, however, does take subject to any liens that are "senior," or of higher priority, to the foreclosed lien.

21. A due-on-sale clause does not permit a grantee to assume the security interest; rather, it requires the borrower to pay the entire principal at or prior to conveyance. A 1982 federal statute preempted state laws restricting enforcement of due-on-sale clauses. *See* Garn–St. Germain Depository Institutions Act of 1982, 12 U.S.C.A. § 1701j–3.

CHAPTER III

SOCIAL NORMS AND INSTITUTIONS

The set of background legal rules and institutions provide an important part of the governance structure pertaining to a society's property, yet they by no means tell the entire story. "Most people do not take their disputes to lawyers or judges. Norms, rather than laws, provide the rules of conduct; friends, relatives, and coworkers, rather than juries, make findings of fact; shame and ostracism, rather than imprisonment or legal damages, punish the wrongdoer. Court is held not in a courthouse, but in homes, workplaces, and neighborhoods, among networks of kin, friends, and associates. In a sufficiently close-knit group, where norms are well defined and nonlegal sanctions are effective, the law has little impact on behavior."[1]

This chapter explores the role of social norms and institutions in defining and governing property. In some contexts, such processes augment and shape the operation of formal legal rules and institutions. In others, they operate significantly apart from the background legal rules and institutions. In addition, as we will see in later chapters, markets and political institutions play important roles in the determination of property interests by enabling parties to contract around background rules or to alter the background rules and institutions directly through democratic processes. Social norms influence the operation of these institutions as well.

Social norms govern property rights in a variety of ways. They may influence the operation of formal legal rules by affecting the propensity of members of the society to make use of formal legal recourse. Sociologists have found, for example, that many businesspeople involved in long-term relationships will use formal legal sanctions only as a last resort. *See, e.g.,* Macauley, Non–Contractual Relations in Business: A Preliminary Study, 28 Am. Soc. Rev. 55, 64 (1963). Social norms also operate within families, firms, organizations, and religious and social communities to control social behavior and allocate property interests directly. Social norms may form the basis for wholly informal (*i.e.,* non-judicial and non-governmental) institutions to allocate resources and enforce property interests, as was described in the lobster industry in Chapter I, *supra* pages 63–66.

Social norms, therefore, can be at least or more important than formal legal rules and institutions in understanding the governance of resources, creating the structure in which people live and work and resolving disputes. More generally, lawyers and policymakers need to appreciate the operation

---

1. Posner, The Regulation of Groups: The Influence of Legal and Nonlegal Sanc- tions on Collective Action, 63 U. Chi. L. Rev. 133, 133 (1996).

of social norms to assess the range of factors bearing upon the governance of property interests.

Unlike the study of formal law, the study of the manner in which social norms operate cannot focus upon statutory codes or court opinions. By definition, social norms operate in a less formal context and therefore the principles underlying their operation must be gleaned from the study of the range of contexts in which social norms and institutions have developed. We begin with Professor Robert Ellickson's pathbreaking study of the manner in which trespass disputes are handled in a rural ranching community. We then turn to Professor Elinor Ostrom's seminal work on how voluntary organizations have evolved to address the tragedy of the commons in a wide variety of "open access" settings. The next two case studies look at the manner in which social norms have addressed the appropriability problems posed by intellectual property, and how formal legal rules have evolved in response to such social institutions. The last case study looks inside the operation of law firms to understand the role social norms play in structuring incentives in the workplace. As you examine these various case studies, pay special attention to the conditions fostering the formation and operation of social norms and institutions, how such norms and institutions evolve, how they interact with formal legal institutions, and their desirability as a means to govern the allocation of property in a particular community or society.

A. SOCIAL NORMS AS PROPERTY INSTITUTIONS: TRESPASS RULES IN A RURAL SETTING

Robert C. Ellickson, Order Without Law: How Neighbors Settle Disputes

15–64 (1991).

Chapter 1

Shasta County and Its Cattle Industry

Shasta County journalists sometimes refer to their region as "Superior California," a prideful designation that, unlike "Northern California," distinguishes the state's northernmost counties from the San Francisco Bay Area. As Figure 1.1 indicates, the county lies at the northern end of the four-hundred-mile-long Central Valley of California, not far from the Oregon border. The Sacramento River, which drains the northern half of the Central Valley, bisects the county. Redding, Shasta County's county seat and largest city, is situated at an elevation of five hundred feet at the spot where the Sacramento River emerges from the mountains north of the valley to begin a two-hundred-mile trip south toward San Francisco Bay.

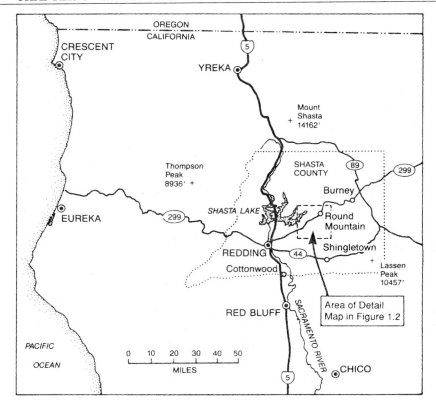

Figure 1.1   Northwestern California

Physical Environment

High mountain peaks lie within sight of Redding in all directions except south. The Trinity Mountains lie to the west; the towering cone of Mount Shasta, actually in Siskiyou County, stands fifty miles due north; and to the east lie other peaks of the volcanic Cascade Range—notably Mount Lassen, which sits in Shasta County's southeastern corner. To the east, north, and west of Redding, foothills rise irregularly toward these distant mountain peaks.

Weather dictates Shasta County's ranching practices. Like the rest of California, the county has a wet season and a dry season. Redding receives an average annual rainfall of 38.74 inches, most of it concentrated in the winter months. Little rain falls between mid-May and November. During the summer months intense sunlight bakes Redding, and the surrounding mountains block cooling winds. The city's average daily high temperature in July is 98 degrees. In the spring the grasslands near Redding are lush and green from the heavy winter rains; by summer, the extreme heat has turned the ground cover brown.

Most of Shasta County's terrain is too mountainous and its soils too poor to support significant agricultural activity. The majority of the land area in the county is commercial-quality forest, most of which the United States Forest Service and a handful of private timber companies own.

Census data describe 16 percent of the county as "land in farms." The bulk of this agricultural land is unirrigated and used only as seasonal pasture for livestock—principally cattle, the county's major agricultural product. Only 1 percent of the county's land is used for raising harvested crops, and a majority of this field-crop acreage is devoted to alfalfa or other hay grown as feed for livestock.

In 1973, the Shasta County Board of Supervisors voted to "close the range" in a fifty-six-square-mile rectangle of territory around Round Mountain, a rural hamlet thirty miles northeast of Redding. This ordinance, which county cattlemen later called "Caton's Folly" to embarrass a supervisor who helped pass it, provided the best opportunity in Shasta County to test the effects of an *actual* change in the rule of liability for cattle trespass. Nine years later, in 1982, the Board of Supervisors considered, but rejected, a petition to close the range in the Oak Run area immediately southwest of Caton's Folly. The Oak Run controversy promised to reveal the effects of a *threatened* change in liability rules. Residents of the Oak Run and Round Mountain areas were interviewed to shed more light on these effects. The general area northeast of Redding—referred to here as the Northeastern Sector—thus warrants closer description.

The Northeastern Sector consists of three ecological zones: grassy plains, foothills, and mountain forest. The elevation of the land largely determines the boundaries of these zones; the higher the terrain, the more rain it receives, and the cooler its summer weather.

The zone between 500 and 1500 feet in elevation, which is the zone closest to Redding, consists of grassy plains. This idyllic, oak-dotted country provides natural pasture during the spring and, if irrigated, can support a herd year-round. A water supply adequate for irrigation is available, however, only near the streams that flow through the area. Moreover, the soil in much of the grassy plains is infertile hardpan. Because of these natural constraints, a full-time rancher who operates in this zone typically needs at least several square miles of pasture for his herds.

The foothills lie roughly between 1500 and 3500 feet in elevation. As Figure 1.2 indicates, both Caton's Folly and the Oak Run area fall within this transition zone. Much of the foothill area has a mixed natural tree cover of pine and oak. In open areas the natural ground cover is less likely to be grass than an unpalatable chaparral of manzanita, buckbrush, and like shrubs. To foothill ranchers this brush is almost as repulsive a thought as the importation of Argentine beef; the more enterprising of them spend much of their energies killing brush to enable forage grasses to grow.

Mountain forest, the third zone, starts at about 3500 feet. Ponderosa pine, Douglas fir, and other conifers that have supplanted the deciduous oaks cover the mountainsides at this elevation. The mountain forests remain green year-round, but most are too cold in winter and too hard to clear to be suitable sites for cattlemen's base ranches. The Roseburg Lumber Company owns much of the mountain forest in the Northeastern Sector. Like other private timber companies in the county, Roseburg has not shown any interest in subdividing its lands for development. For many decades, however, Roseburg and its predecessors in ownership have leased their forests to Shasta County cattlemen for summer range.

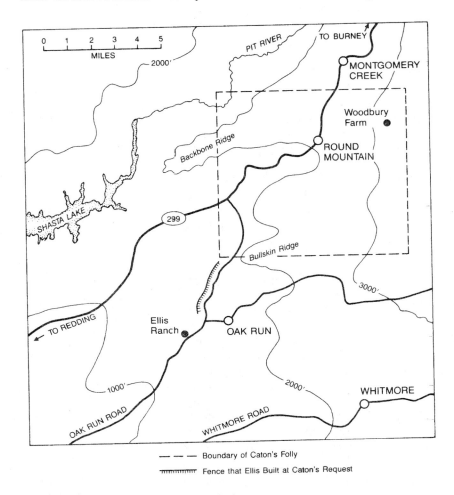

Figure 1.2   The Oak Run–Round Mountain Area

Social Environment

Shasta County has experienced rapid population growth. Redding's location at the northern end of the Central Valley makes it a natural transportation hub. It serves as the gateway to mountain recreation areas lying in three directions, and has emerged as the major regional center on Interstate 5 between Sacramento, California, and Eugene, Oregon. Between 1930 and 1980, the number of county residents increased ninefold, and in the decade from 1970 to 1980, total county population rose from 78,000 to 116,000. The county's population growth rate of 49.0 percent in the 1970s was substantially higher than the overall state rate (18.5 percent) and was somewhat higher than the aggregate rate for California's nonmetropolitan counties (36.4 percent). Indications of social instability have accompanied the influx of migrants. In 1981, Shasta had the highest divorce rate of any county in California, and in 1980, the county's unemployment rate was twice that of the state as a whole.

Precise figures on population trends within the Northeastern Sector are not available. It appears, however, that during the 1970s, the sector's population grew by an even larger percentage than did the county's. Not surprisingly, the demographic histories of the three ecological zones within the sector are rather different.

Residential patterns in the grassy plains have not changed much in recent years. The first pioneers to settle east and northeast of Redding used the grasslands and lower foothills to raise livestock. The descendants of the nineteenth-century pioneer families, such as the Coombses, Donaldsons, and Wagoners, still hold a special place in rural Shasta County society. Oldtimers are quick to identify their roots in the county, and sometimes refer to families who arrived a generation ago as "people who haven't been here very long." Prior to the 1920s, the Southern Pacific Railroad owned alternate sections of the grassy plains—a reward from the United States for laying track to Redding. During the 1920s, Southern Pacific sold off most of its grassland sections at the then market price of $2.50 to $5.00 per acre, thereby enabling the pioneer ranching families to consolidate their hold-ings. Abandoning their prior practice of running their herds at large, these families erected fences around their multithousand-acre spreads, cleared patches of brush, and began to irrigate their better pastures.

Beyond the suburbs of Redding most of the acreage in the grasslands and lower foothills remains divided into ranches at least several square miles in size. Approximately half of these ranches are owned by descen-dants of families that have been in the county for several generations. Although many of these ranches have a current market value of $1 million or more, the ranchers typically have modest annual incomes. For decades, ranchlands in Shasta County have generated an annual cash return of only 1 or 2 percent of their market value. The cattlemen who own and operate the large family ranches tend to follow self-imposed seven-day-a-week work schedules and live in houses less imposing than those one would find in an average American suburb. When estate taxes or property taxes have squeezed a ranching family financially, the family may sell its entire holding to another rancher or to investors seeking tax shelters or, more commonly, may deal off tree-covered pieces of its ranch to developers for subdivision into ranchettes.

The foothills have seen more subdivision activity and absolute popula-tion growth than have the grassy plains. Both supply and demand condi-tions explain this pattern. Because the foothills are somewhat less suited than the grasslands for agriculture, foothill landowners are more likely to subdivide their holdings. Most home buyers would also prefer the foothills to the grasslands as a residential location because the higher elevations are cooler in summer and offer more tree cover. As a result, the foothills within commuting distance of Redding have experienced a multifold increase in population over the past twenty years.

Many of the recent settlers in the foothills are either retirees or younger migrants from California's major urban areas. These newcomers tend to live on minimally improved lots of from five to forty acres, either in owner-built houses or in mobile homes. Many of these ranchettes have sprung up near hamlets, such as Oak Run and Round Mountain, that contain a general store, a post office, an elementary school, and other basic community facilities. Despite these clusters of growth, development in the foothills has been rather diffuse. Especially since the mid–1960s, small-scale developers have subdivided forested areas in every sector of the foothills. Thus virtually all foothill ranchers have some ranchette owners as neighbors. Ranchette owners may keep a farm animal or two as a hobby, but few of them make significant income from agriculture The ranchette owners nevertheless admire both the cattlemen and the folkways traditionally associated with rural Shasta County.

Work Environment: Modes of Cattle Ranching

Most Shasta County ranchers are men. Although women own, manage, and provide most of the physical labor on a number of ranches, rural culture generally supports the differentiation of sex roles. Thus a woman rancher who wishes to be active in the county Cattlemen's Association is likely to participate only in the CowBelles, the women's auxiliary. (In 1985 the National Cattlemen's Association elected its first woman president, JoAnn Smith, but she had come to prominence by serving as president of the Florida CowBelles.)

Despite their long hours of work, few ranchers in Shasta County find raising beef cattle a road to prosperity. The typical rancher runs a cow and calf operation. When his calves are seven to twelve months old, he trucks them a dozen miles south of Redding to the Shasta County auction yard at Cottonwood, where each Friday some three thousand head change hands. Agents for feedlot operators and pasture owners buy the calves, take them to feedlots and pastures outside the county, and feed and fatten them for a few months to prepare them for slaughter. Beginning in the 1970s per capita consumption of beef in the United States began to fall. In 1982, a six-hundred-pound yearling auctioned in Cottonwood brought about $375, compared with about $500 in 1979. Shasta County is at best marginal terrain for cattle ranching. In the early 1980s some cattlemen there were understandably fearful that they would be casualties in a shakeout of their beleaguered industry.

The Traditionalists

Shasta County cattlemen may be loosely grouped into two categories: the traditionalists and the modernists. Traditionalists tend to be more marginal economically, and to have a greater stake in fighting closed-range ordinances.

Traditional cattlemen continue to follow the husbandry practices that were nearly universal in the county as late as the 1920s. A traditionalist's trademark is that he lets his cattle roam, essentially untended, in unfenced mountain areas during the summer. This customary practice evolved in response to the severity of Shasta County's dry season. In the area northeast of Redding, a rancher lacking irrigated pasture needs about ten to twenty acres per animal unit[2] for winter and spring pasture. Thus, to support two hundred cattle—a substantial herd by Shasta County standards—a rancher without irrigated pasture needs at least two thousand acres, or just over three square miles of land. During the dry season the brutal heat makes unirrigated grasslands almost worthless. To feed his animals during the summer, a lowland cattleman must therefore either have access to irrigated pasture or be able to move his animals to the high foothills and mountains, where cooler dry season temperatures enable natural forage to survive. The traditionalist solution is a summer grazing lease on a large tract of mountain forest.

The United States Forest Service, the Bureau of Land Management, and the major private timber companies have all regularly entered into grazing leases with county cattlemen. Although the timber-company grazing leases typically have only a one-year term, the companies have allowed cattlemen to renew them as a matter of course. Federal leases may run for any period up to ten years and they also tend to be automatically renewable. A cattleman who has been leasing a tract of forest for summer range thus tends to regard that leasehold as a part of his normal operations. Although the forest areas remain green in summer, they contain too few open meadows to support many cattle. Traditionalists may have to lease three hundred acres of forest per animal unit. Consequently, a traditionalist with a herd of only a hundred animals may have a summer lease on a forest equal in area to the city of San Francisco.

The fencing of remote forest leaseholds has never been cost-justified in the eyes of either the timber owners or their traditionalist lessees. To reduce the risk that livestock will trespass on contiguous lands, natural barriers such as ridges and gulches are commonly picked as boundaries for grazing leaseholds. But adroit boundary drawing is hardly a foolproof method for controlling strays. Mountain cattle tend to drift down drainage areas to lower elevations, especially after the weather has turned cold or a drought has dried upland creeks. Lessees occasionally erect drift fences across mountain valleys to block the most obvious of these migration routes. Because drift fences are easily destroyed by winter snows, however, many traditionalists let their animals roam in unfenced mountain range. As a result, even a forest lessee who has ridden his leasehold periodically during the summer may be unable to find part of the herd when he gathers his livestock in mid-October. After the October gathering, a traditionalist returns his animals to a base ranch at a lower elevation, and feeds them

2. An "animal unit" is a mature cow plus calf, or the equivalent in terms of forage consumption. A horse converts to 1.25 animal units, a sheep to 0.2 animal units, and so on.
* * *

hay or other stored feed for a few months until the winter rains revive the natural grasses on the base-ranch pastures.[3]

The Modernists

Modernists among the Shasta County cattlemen keep their livestock behind fences at all times in order to increase their control over their herds. To satisfy the need for summer forage that originally caused traditionalist cattlemen to enter into forest leases, modernists install ditches and sprinklers to irrigate base-ranch pastures. One acre of irrigated pasture can support a cow and calf for an entire summer. A modernist who can irrigate about 10 percent of his lands is usually able to run a year-round, fenced operation.

Modernists are more active than traditionalists in managing ranchland vegetation. If not controlled, the native brush that thrives in the foothill zone would consume much of the scarce ground water and soil nutrients that competing grasses need. Modernist foothill ranchers fight the brush by setting controlled burns, spreading herbicides, and dragging chains from tractors to uproot the larger plants. Using these clearing techniques, leading modernist cattlemen have transformed unproductive foothill areas into valuable pasturelands.

Modernists tend to be younger than traditionalists, have more formal education, and be more active in the Cattlemen's Association. Some modernists view the traditionalists as old-fashioned and primitive. Traditionalists, however, see themselves as the "real" cattlemen—the ones who can recognize one of their cows at half a mile and sleep out under the stars in the tradition of the nineteenth-century cowboy.

Despite their stylistic differences, modernists and traditionalists have much in common. Members of both groups believe that the life of the cattleman is the best possible in western America. They enjoy riding horses and wearing blue jeans, cowboy hats, and cowboy boots. They are inclined to decorate their living rooms with an antique rifle above the door and a portrait of John Wayne on the wall. Although traditionalists have a much greater stake than modernists do in keeping the Board of Supervisors from closing the range, modernist cattlemen typically join the traditionalists in opposing proposed legal changes that would increase the liabilities of owners of stray cattle.

The Benefits and Costs of Boundary Fences

The study of cattle trespass incidents is inevitably a study of fencing. A fence demarcates boundaries, keeps out human and animal trespassers, and keeps in the fencebuilder's own animals. In the Farmer–Rancher Parable, Coase perceived the sole benefit of a fence to be the reduction of trespass

---

3. Untimely grazing may damage rangeland. If grazing occurs too early, it may kill immature grass. If it occurs too late, the livestock may eat seeds necessary for the following year's forage. Even though a long-term lessee might consider these risks on his own, grazing leases nevertheless typically specify entry and exit dates.

damages to crops.[4] In fact, cattlemen enclose their lands largely to prevent damage to their own livestock. Predators, rustlers, winter snows, and poisonous plants such as larkspur all pose potentially lethal threats to cattle roaming unfenced countryside. Cattlemen also worry that a bull of worthless pedigree will impregnate a wandering cow. By enclosing his lands, a cattleman can more easily provide salt and other useful dietary supplements and prevent the weight loss that occurs when cattle walk long distances.

The prices of grazing leases reflect the value that ranchers place on fences. In 1982, fenced land in the Northeastern Sector rented for about $10 per animal unit month, whereas unfenced land rented for about $3. Because both arrangements yield the same quantity of forage, the rent differential provides a rough measure of how much ranchers value the protection and control that boundary fences provide.

Since 1874, the year J. F. Glidden took out the first patent on barbed wire, the barbed-wire fence has been the standard American technology for enclosing livestock. California's statutory standard for a "lawful fence" was set at the turn of the century. It calls for three tightly stretched strands of barbed wire stapled to posts situated 16½ feet (one rod) apart. Today, Shasta County ranchers tend to use at least four strands of barbed wire in boundary fences.

Instead of the cedar posts that were customary earlier in the century, fencebuilders now typically use steel posts, which are less expensive, easier to drive into rocky soil, and more likely to survive a controlled burn. (Wooden posts are still essential at corners, gates, stretch panels, and other places where extra strength is needed.)

In 1982, the materials for a new four-strand, barbed-wire fence in Shasta County cost about $2000 per mile. Fence contractors charge at least as much for labor and overhead.[5] Both ranchers and ranchette owners customarily build their own fences and thereby drastically reduce out-of-pocket labor expenditures. I found only one rancher, and no ranchette owner, who admitted having contracted out fencing work.

Barbed-wire fences require periodic maintenance, especially in Shasta County, where many natural forces conspire against fence wire. The extreme summer heat loosens the wire; the winter cold pulls it taut. The deer that migrate through the foothills during the wet season are generally able to jump cattle fences; but when a jumping deer fails to clear a fence cleanly, its hoof may break a tightly stretched top wire. Heavy winter rains, rotting posts, downed trees, unruly bulls, or wayward automobiles may also create a breach. A rancher or his hand therefore must spend a few days each spring, either on horseback or in a pickup truck, riding fence. A conscientious rancher also inspects his fences in the fall after the deer

---

4. *See* Coase, "The Problem of Social Cost," 3 *J.L. & Econ.* 1,3,5 (1960).

5. * * * Technological advances—particularly the invention of barbed wire—have made fencing much less expensive relative to land and labor than it in Abraham Lincoln's log-splitting days. * * *

season, in part to see what damage trespassing hunters may have inflicted. With emergency repairs needed frequently, fence maintenance chores weigh constantly on a rancher's mind.

Ranchers believe that the many benefits of perimeter barriers outweigh fence construction and maintenance costs. Cattlemen with permanent ranches in either the grasslands or foothills almost invariably have perimeter fences, as well as cross fences to divide their spreads into separate pastures. A ranchette owner, however, is unlikely to fence the boundary of his land unless he has livestock. In forest pastures one observes either no fencing or only an occasional drift fence.

Traditionalists running herds in unfenced mountain forests have provoked most of the closed-range political movements in Shasta County. During the summer months mountain cattle may wander onto rural highways or ravage hay fields and gardens in the settled parts of the foothills. Since 1960, the proliferation of ranchettes in the foothills has aggravated these two risks and heightened opposition to the practice of running cattle at large. At times the rural political pot comes to a boil over these issues.

Chapter 2

The Politics of Cattle Trespass

Loose cattle often cause political flaps in Shasta County. Many rural residents know that the Board of Supervisors has the power to adopt closed-range ordinances. They believe that these ordinances increase the civil liabilities of owners of stray livestock not only for trespass damages but also, and more significantly, for damages stemming from highway collisions between vehicles and domestic animals. When residents and motorists in a particular area of the county suffer a rash of cattle-related incidents, they are likely to report their grievances to their local supervisor, whom they ask to mediate the conflict or to support a closed-range ordinance designed to cure the problem. If adopted, a closure indeed serves to reduce the number of loose cattle because fear of liability to motorists makes traditionalists reluctant to run cattle at large in closed range.

At least since 1970, the Board of Supervisors has required constituents who propose adoption of a closed-range ordinance to follow a special procedure. The complainants must draw up a petition that identifies a specific territory for closure, gather signatures on copies of the petition, and forward the signed petition to the board. Although the board does not insist upon the submission of a particular minimum number of signatures, closure proponents gather as many as possible. Upon receiving a petition, the board's staff drafts an ordinance that will implement the closure and publicizes a hearing on the proposed measure. In practice, opponents usually receive sufficient notice of an upcoming hearing to gather signatures on a counterpetition. At the public hearing, the board hears statements from proponents and opponents and then votes on the measure. Over the years, cattlemen have been quite successful in defeating proposed closures. Between 1946 and 1972, the board approved sixteen closures in various parts of Shasta County, but most of those ordinances only involved lands on Redding's urban fringe.

Prior to the 1973 Caton's Folly ordinance that closed an area near Round Mountain, the Board of Supervisors approved only one closure that affected a significant amount of rural territory east of the Sacramento River. In the early 1960s, mountain cattle began to appear in number along a stretch of State Highway 44 in the Shingletown–Viola area, thirty miles east of Redding. Highway 44 is the major route between Redding and Mount Lassen National Park. In 1965 the board voted to close the range in a three-mile-wide strip of land straddling Highway 44 for a distance of twelve and a half miles. This closure affected an area topographically similar to, but south of, the foothills of the Northeastern Sector. The entire sector remained open until the Caton's Folly closure. The history of that ordinance and of the board's rejection of the Oak Run closure petition in 1982 helps reveal the role of elected local officials in cattle trespass disputes.

Caton's Folly: The Closing of the Range at Round Mountain

The hamlet of Round Mountain lies thirty miles northeast of Redding. Scattered along State Highway 299, the main thoroughfare through the settlement, are a general store, an elementary school, and a substation in Pacific Gas & Electric's hydroelectric power grid. The hamlet is 2000 feet in elevation and is surrounded by higher foothills, the most prominent of which has given the place its name. During the 1960s, the area around Round Mountain, like the rest of the Shasta County foothills, became increasingly dotted with ranchettes. The frustration of these ranchette owners over the perceived misdeeds of three traditionalists, Paul Totten, Bob Moquet, and Ward Kearney, helped spawn the Caton's Folly ordinance of 1973. The particular activities of these three deserve brief description.

In the early 1970s, Totten, a small-scale traditionalist with a base ranch west of Redding, leased some thirty square miles of Roseburg Lumber Company forest lands for summer range. The western boundary of Totten's leasehold was three miles east of the hamlet of Round Mountain and at a higher elevation. Just west of the boundary was an aging foothill farm with a sixty-acre irrigated field. John Woodbury had acquired this farm in 1966 and over a period of years had converted the irrigated field from natural grass to alfalfa. During the early 1970s Totten's mountain cattle found and repeatedly used a path that led from the meager offerings of the Roseburg forest to the banquet of Woodbury's unfenced alfalfa field. Whenever Woodbury telephoned him to complain about a trespass, Totten would eventually drive the cattle back up into the forest, but neither as promptly nor as irreversibly as Woodbury would have liked.

Bob Moquet's cattle were a more pervasive and longstanding nuisance. A tough and independent leader of a pioneer clan long settled in the Round Mountain area, Moquet aroused particular hostility because he was repeatedly unresponsive to his neighbors' complaints. He seemed to believe that a cattleman had a divine right to let his cattle loose in the mountains during the summer. Steve Mattingly, a modernist cattleman who raised registered Galloway cattle on a fenced ranch on Buzzard Roost Road, became particularly concerned that Moquet's hybrid bulls might impregnate his cows.

In the early 1970s, Dr. Arthur Cooley, a Redding physician, obtained a summer grazing lease on a large tract of United States Forest Service land situated a few miles west of Round Mountain, on Backbone Ridge. To manage his mountain herd of several hundred animals, Cooley hired Ward Kearney, a traditionalist cowboy of exceptional ability. Kearney shared Moquet's view that people who object to stray cattle should fence them out. Consequently, after driving Cooley's cattle to Backbone Ridge, Kearney would allow them to drift down into the ranchette areas and heavily traveled stretches of Highway 299 near Round Mountain.

The mountain cattle owned by Cooley, Moquet, and Totten tipped the political balance in Round Mountain in favor of closure. In early 1973, Mattingly, Woodbury, and a few longtime area residents began meeting to discuss the problem of stray mountain cattle. These antitraditionalists eventually drafted and gathered signatures on a petition that asked the Board of Supervisors to convert from open to closed range a seven by eight mile rectangle of territory centered on Round Mountain. It is not clear who drew the exact boundaries of this rectangle. Not surprisingly, all of the activists' lands fell within its perimeter. In the end, seventy-two people, mostly Round Mountain residents, signed the closed-range petition.

On March 10, 1973, Mattingly mailed the signed petition to John Caton, the newly elected board member for the supervisorial district that included the foothills in the Northeastern Sector. Caton lived on a ranchette in Montgomery Creek, a hamlet situated three miles northeast of Round Mountain on Highway 299. Caton shared many of the cattlemen's values, yet he was aware that mountain cattle had been endangering both residents and motorists. The deepening conflict between traditionalist cattlemen and the residents of the Round Mountain area placed him in a delicate political position. He offered to help mediate and asked Mattingly and the other petitioners to wait a few months to see whether the problem would abate. It did not. During the summer of 1973, mountain cattle entered Woodbury's alfalfa field on over a dozen occasions. Woodbury said he telephoned Caton to complain each time.

On December 3, 1973, the Board of Supervisors finally held its hearing on the antitraditionalists' petition to close the fifty-six-square-mile rectangle. The hearing was lightly attended. John Woodbury, pasture owner Phil Ritchie, and ranchette owner Ted Plomeson spoke in favor of the closure. The only significant speaker in opposition was Dr. Cooley, whose protestations of economic hardship elicited little sympathy. The official minutes of the board's meeting contain no indication that a representative of the Shasta County Cattlemen's Association was present. At the end of the session, the board voted by a margin of 4 to 1, with Caton in the majority, to declare that the rectangle outlined in the March petition had "ceased to be devoted chiefly to grazing"—the legal language necessary to convert the area from open range to closed range.

With the exception of a few modernists such as Mattingly, Shasta County cattlemen soon came to rue their failure to fight the Round Mountain closure. To chide Caton for supporting what they regarded as a lamentable precedent, they referred to the affected area as "Caton's Folly" or "Caton's Acres." Caton got the point. During the next decade, he successfully persuaded the Board of Supervisors to reject all petitions that would have closed additional territories in foothill areas of his district.

Caton's Repentance: The Defeat of the Oak Run Closure Petition

Caton's change of heart is best illustrated by his handling of a 1981 petition that asked the board to close ninety-six square miles of range in the Oak Run area just southwest of Caton's Folly. The hamlet of Oak Run sits only three miles south of the southwestern corner of Caton's Folly. The hamlet's elevation is 1600 feet, a level where the grassy plains blend with the tangle of brush and trees that typify the foothills. During 1981–82, only a few months before I conducted most of my interviews, the Oak Run area had been the site of perhaps the most heated closed-range battle in the history of Shasta County. Frank Ellis, a recent entrant into the big-time cattle business, had single-handedly provoked the circulation of a petition that sought to triple the area of closed range in the foothills of the Northeastern Sector.

Frank Ellis

Ellis, accompanied by his wife and school-age children, moved to Shasta County in about 1973. A rancher and real estate broker by profession, Ellis was then in his late fifties. He immediately acquired a functioning 2500–acre ranch astride the Oak Run Road two miles west of Oak Run and just south of an area sprouting ranchettes. The size and prominent location of Ellis' base ranch helped to make him a conspicuous personality in the Northeastern Sector. Ellis, who declined my request for an interview, was by all reports a man capable of great charm. According to his neighbors, however, beneath this appealing surface lay a ruthless ambition for wealth and power. Many who dealt with Ellis came to regard him as capricious, spiteful, and not always good for his word. He became the target of numerous lawsuits, and for a time even had an attorney on retainer. Although Ellis' aggressive and colorful personality won him some admirers, his more upstanding neighbors came to view him as an untrustworthy bully.

During the late 1970s, Ellis built up the largest ranching empire in the Northeastern Sector. He started by obtaining a grazing lease on a section of Bureau of Land Management land to the west of his base ranch. Then in 1978 he persuaded the absentee owners of the largest ranching estate in the area to hire him to manage their scattered grasslands and foothills. By this one stroke, Ellis won control over another twenty square miles of pasture. Ellis eventually purchased hundreds of cattle on credit and hired a band of Mexican farmworkers, braceros, to tend them.

The various components of Ellis' ranching empire were not physically connected. Ellis knew that all his holdings were within open range, but he erroneously interpreted this to mean that he could legally herd his livestock onto any intervening land that was not fenced. When moving his livestock about, Ellis' cowboys not only deliberately crossed the unfenced private lands of others but also used those lands as free pasture. By 1981 Ellis' drovers were aggressively running a herd of two to three thousand cattle at large in the grasslands and lower foothills northeast of Redding, an area where virtually all other cattlemen were modernists who kept their animals behind fences.

Ellis' Antagonists

Most of the lands that Ellis' livestock invaded were uncultivated and uninhabited tracts held by speculators, who, if anything, appreciated a herd coming through to beat back the brush. Yet in some areas, particularly those near Oak Run itself, the victims of Ellis' trespasses were ranchette owners who had recently moved to the foothills in search of a pastoral life. Ellis' marauding herds quickly became the bane of these ranchette owners. At least eight built fences at their own expense specifically to keep Ellis' animals off their lands. Although at least two of these ranchette owners saw Ellis as acting within his rights, most of them—particularly Doug Heinz—did not.

Heinz, a skilled craftsman from southern California, moved to Shasta County in 1978 with his wife and small children. The Heinzes acquired a house on a twenty-acre ranchette situated in open range west of Oak Run and about one mile from Ellis' base ranch. As a hobby, Heinz started to raise a few horses and cows on a twelve-acre portion of his ranchette that was enclosed by a five-strand barbed wire fence. The frequent passage of Ellis' herds punctured Heinz's dreams of small-scale squiredom.

According to Heinz, he and Ellis started off on polite terms. On three or four occasions in 1979, several of Ellis' cattle jumped over or broke through Heinz's fence. Heinz reacted to these early trespasses by telephoning Ellis. Ellis' response was to send his drovers to chase the cows within Heinz's field to tire them so they could then be coaxed through the fence. This method of retrieval battered Heinz's fences, and Ellis' drovers never repaired the damage. Heinz's patience ran out one snowy day when he discovered that Ellis' hands had dropped hay for two hundred cattle in the narrow snowplowed driveway leading to his ranchette. The milling herd that flocked to the hay included cows that had just calved, and these skittish new mothers frightened Heinz's small children.

Although most of Heinz's ranchette-owning neighbors had passively endured indignities from Ellis' livestock, Heinz was relatively short-tempered. He purchased a shotgun and called the county sheriff to protest Ellis' activities. According to what Ellis later told acquaintances, Heinz also began to threaten that Ellis might find "dead cattle." On the next occasion that Ellis' cattle broke the fence, Heinz seized three animals and held them for three months without notifying Ellis. This incident eventually led to a lawsuit by Heinz to recover boarding costs and to a countersuit by Ellis for mistreatment of Ellis' animals.

In early 1981, while his lawsuit against Ellis was still pending, Heinz began a political crusade to stop Ellis' at-large grazing practices. Heinz anticipated recruiting a host of allies, and not just among his fellow ranchette owners. During 1978–1981, virtually every foothill motorist had reason to be annoyed at Ellis' failure to keep his livestock off the foothill roads. When Ellis' stock were being moved along the highways, motorists were often delayed for up to an hour. On at least six occasions vehicles collided with Ellis' animals on the Oak Run Road. Heinz succeeded in rallying to the anti-Ellis cause dozens of ranchette-owning newcomers, as well as members of at least one respected and long-established ranching family in the Oak Run area.

Caton's Mediation and the Battle of Petitions

During 1981 Heinz and his allies peppered their local supervisor, John Caton, with complaints about Ellis' herds. Since his christening in the Round Mountain incidents eight years earlier, Caton had become a veteran of political disputes over trespassing cattle. He knew that if he supported a closed-range ordinance for the Oak Run area, he would further alienate the powerful cattlemen's lobby, a group that had never forgiven him for supporting the Caton's Folly ordinance. If he opposed the closure, however, he would offend a potentially more numerous, if less organized, group, the ranchette owners and motorists that Ellis' herds endangered. Caton sought to defuse the controversy before a formal closure petition surfaced. Working in the spring of 1981 with the county animal control officer Brad Bogue, Caton threatened to support a closed-range ordinance for the Oak Run area if Ellis failed to build a fence along a three-mile stretch of the Oak Run Road that his herds made particularly dangerous. In response, Ellis promised Caton that he would build the fence. As the summer of 1981 dragged on without any sign of the fence, Caton began to regard circulation of a closed-range petition as inevitable.

Caton's political instincts proved to be accurate. Some members of the anti-Ellis group preferred to postpone circulating a petition until they had exhausted other types of mediation; this faction, for example, wanted to ask the Shasta County Cattlemen's Association to request Ellis to manage his herds more responsibly. But Heinz decided to force the issue. In the fall of 1981, without consulting some of his leading allies, he drafted and began to circulate a petition designed to close the range in a ninety-six-square-mile area southwest of, and abutting, Caton's Folly. Heinz drew the boundaries broadly in an effort to cast the entire Ellis empire into closed range. The petition did not mention Ellis by name, but it did state that "Our reasons for this stem mostly from the inconsideration and abuse of the open range law of one rancher."[6] Heinz and his allies gathered 42 signatures—an

---

6. The petition continued:
Our reasons to list a few are:

1. Unsafe roadways due to poorly maintained fences, cows are continu-

unimpressive total—and delivered their petition to John Caton in late November 1981.

The Board of Supervisors was scheduled to hold its next hearing on closure petitions three months later, in February 1982. The interval enabled Caton to minimize the political risks posed by the Heinz petition. He immediately publicized receipt of the petition, thereby helping the opposition to organize a countercampaign. Caton showed the Heinz petition to Wayne Thompson, a small-scale sheep rancher who lived on the Oak Run Road. Thompson enlisted his neighbor Larry Brennan, a college graduate who as a hobby raised horses on a large ranchette nearby, to draft a counterpetition urging the board to keep the area open. Brennan began the counterpetition with the following language: "We feel that the 'open range' system serves many purposes for the large and small rancher: 1. Limits of liability...."[7] Thompson tirelessly circulated the counterpetition in the vicinity of Oak Run. Prior to the February hearing, Thompson and his associates submitted to the board the names of 146 individuals, mostly residents of the Oak Run area, who had signed their counterpetition. Heinz's temperamental personality and lack of roots in the area limited his own success and aided Thompson, who outsolicited him by a margin of more than three to one.

The board also received a second counterpetition. Following standard procedures adopted after the Round Mountain controversy, the board's staff had automatically informed the Shasta County Cattlemen's Association that the board had received Heinz's closed-range petition. The association's leaders then circulated a petition on their own. Their petition to keep the range open attracted only 24 signers, but many were members of well-known ranching families operating northeast of Redding.

Caton's last major step after the Heinz petition surfaced was to remind Ellis that Caton's decision on the closure petition would rest largely on whether Ellis kept his promise to build the three miles of fence along Oak Run Road. Ellis finally responded, but grudgingly. By the time of the board's hearing on February 2, 1982, Ellis' employees had erected three miles of five-strand barbed-wire fence (shown in Figure 1.2), a project that probably cost Ellis $5,000 to $10,000. The fence was positioned on private lands (mostly owned by speculators) on which Ellis had grazed his herds without fee. Because the new fence helped to reassure motorists, it became

ally on the roads and jepardizing [sic] the safety of school children.

2. Property destruction of the trespassing cows on private property.

3. Cutting of fences on private property to herd the cows with more ease to areas of private property.

4. Interference of range cows with private herds.

7. The counterpetition continued:

2. Fire protection—through grazing, keeping the grass down.

3. Biological control—through natural fertilization of soil of rangeland, timber production, fuel-wood production.

4. Natural predator control.

5. Prevention of soil erosion due to stronger root systems with annual grasses.

a conspicuous monument to Caton's effectiveness. The fence offered no relief, however, to ranchette owners such as Heinz whose lands lay between Ellis' ranch and the new fence.

The Hearing and Its Aftermath

At the board's February 2 hearing, Caton kept his part of his bargain with Ellis. Caton's decision to oppose the closure had become an easy one. Not only had Thompson's counterpetition attracted far more signatories than the Heinz petition had, but Thompson and the cattlemen were also more successful than the Heinz group in turning out supporters at the board meeting. As Jeff Marotta, a ranchette owner and Heinz ally, stated, "When I saw all those cowboy hats [in the hearing room] I knew we were going to lose." At the hearing six speakers, including Doug Heinz, spoke in favor of the closure, but thirteen, including Bob Bosworth, president of the Shasta County Cattlemen's Association, spoke against it. Although the hall was packed, Ellis himself was not present. As someone said that night, "He wouldn't dare to be."

Caton was also the beneficiary of an unexpected development: by early 1982 the Ellis ranching empire had begun to crumble. Ellis had bought hundreds of cattle on credit in anticipation that beef prices would rise. Instead, prices had fallen. This setback, arriving on top of a variety of other financial reverses, left Ellis without funds to pay creditors. A week or two before the board's hearing, Ellis' banks had begun repossessing his cattle. This juicy bit of news had spread quickly through the gossip mills of the Northeastern Sector foothills.

When the testimony at the hearing came to a close, the other supervisors stated that they would defer to John Caton, the supervisor in whose district the proposed closure lay. Caton recommended that the area remain as open range but added that, if the problem continued, the board should consider closing four sections of land where Heinz and most of the other complaining ranchette owners lived. The board promptly voted unanimously to deny the Heinz petition. To smooth the waters, Dan Gover, the board's chairman and a rancher himself, asked Bob Bosworth to meet with Ellis, Heinz, and county animal control officials to see what could be done to control Ellis' herds. Caton had repented for Caton's Folly.

Within a few months of the hearing, both Heinz and Ellis were gone from the Oak Run area. At least as early as 1980 Heinz had planned to build a house in Redding for his family. Only a few days after the board rejected his petition, he moved out of the Oak Run ranchette and into his newly completed Redding house. Ellis' stay in Oak Run lasted only three months longer than Heinz's. The banks seized Ellis' cattle, and creditors lined up with claims on his ranch. In May 1982 Ellis moved his family one hundred miles south to a farm in another California county in the Central Valley. As his parting shot to Shasta County, Ellis ordered his hands to destroy the three miles of fence along the Oak Run Road that he had had built just six months before. On the day the Board of Supervisors held its hearing, the two leading players in the Oak Run closure fight both knew that they were about to depart from the stage.[8]

Chapter 3

The Resolution of Cattle–Trespass Disputes

Trespass by cattle, the subject of Coase's Parable of the Farmer and the Rancher, is a common event in ranching country. A complex body of law, much of it of unusually ancient lineage, formally applies to these occurrences. In Shasta County, the rules of trespass law vary between open-and closed-range districts, and the location of district boundaries has been the focus of intense political controversy. Nevertheless, it turns out, perhaps counterintuitively, that legal rules hardly ever influence the settlement of cattle-trespass disputes in Shasta County.

Animal Trespass Incidents

Each of the twenty-eight landowners interviewed, including each of the thirteen ranchette owners, reported at least one instance in which his lands had been invaded by someone else's livestock. Hay farmers grow what cattle especially like to eat and can thus expect frequent trespasses. For example, John Woodbury, an alfalfa grower, suffered almost weekly incursions in 1973. Woodbury's situation later improved when many traditionalist cattlemen declined to renew their grazing leases on mountain forest, but he was still experiencing a couple of cattle trespasses a year in the early 1980s. Another hay farmer, Phil Ritchie, could identify six neighbors whose cattle had trespassed on his lands in recent years. Owners of large ranches are also frequent trespass victims because they cannot keep their many miles of aging perimeter fence cattle-tight. Thus, when a rancher gathers his animals on his fenced pastures each spring, he is hardly startled to find a few head carrying a neighbor's brand.

Because beef cattle eat feed equal to about 2½ percent of their body weight each day, a trespass victim's vegetation is always at risk. Nevertheless, a victim usually regards the loss of grass as trivial, provided that the animals are easy to corral and the owner removes them within a day or two. Trespassing livestock occasionally do cause more than nominal damage. Several ranchette owners reported incidents in which wayward cattle had damaged their fences and vegetable gardens; one farmer told of the ravaging of some of his ornamental trees.

The most serious trespasses reported were ones involving at-large cattle or bulls. A ranchette owner described how mountain cattle had once invaded his house construction site, broken the windows, and contaminated the creek. The part-time horsebreeder Larry Brennan told of buying seven tons of hay and stacking it on an unfenced portion of his fifty-acre

---

8. This fact is consistent with the theoretical proposition * * * that the lack of a prospective long-term relationship makes disputants less likely to resolve their differences without the help of third parties, and hence more likely to resort to legal and political action.

ranchette, where it was then eaten by cattle that Frank Ellis had let roam free.

Rural residents especially fear trespasses by bulls. In a modern beef cattle herd, roughly one animal in twenty-five is a bull, whose principal function is to impregnate cows during their brief periods in heat. Bulls are not only much more ornery but also much larger than other herd animals. A Hereford bull has a mature weight of 2000 pounds. By contrast, a mature Hereford cow weighs only 1100–1200 pounds, and Hereford steers (castrated males) are typically slaughtered when they weigh between 1000 and 1150 pounds. Several ranchers who were interviewed had vivid memories of bull trespasses. A farmer who owned irrigated pasture was amazed at the depth of the hoof marks that an entering bull had made. A ranchette owner and a rancher told of barely escaping goring while attempting to corral invading bulls. Because an alien bull often enters in pursuit of cows in heat, owners of female animals fear illicit couplings that might produce offspring of an undesired pedigree. Although no cow owner reported actual damages from misbreeding, several mentioned that this risk especially worried them.

Animal Trespass Law

One of the most venerable English common law rules of strict liability in tort is the rule that an owner of domestic livestock is liable, even in the absence of negligence, for property damage that his animals cause while trespassing. In the memorable words of Judge Blackburn:

> The case that has most commonly occurred, and which is most frequently to be found in the books, is as to the obligation of the owner of cattle which he has brought on his land, to prevent their escaping and doing mischief. The law as to them seems to be perfectly settled from early times; the owner must keep them in at his peril, or he will be answerable for the natural consequences of their escape; that is with regard to tame beasts, for the grass they eat and trample upon, though not for any injury to the person of others, for our ancestors have settled that it is not the general nature of horses to kick, or bulls to gore; but if the owner knows that the beast has a vicious propensity to attack man, he will be answerable for that too.[9]

This traditional English rule formally prevails in the closed-range areas of Shasta County.[10] In the open-range areas of the county—that is, in the great bulk of its rural territory—the English rule has been rejected in favor of the pro-cattleman "fencing-out" rule that many grazing states adopted during the nineteenth century.

9. *Fletcher v. Rylands*, 1 L.R.-Ex.265, 280 (1866) (dictum). *See also* 3 William Blackstone, *Commentaries* *211 ("A man is answerable for not only his own trespass, but that of his cattle also"). * * *

10. *See e.g., Montezuma Improvement Co. v. Simmerly*, 181 Cal. 722, 724, 189 P. 100, 101 (1919). A trespass victim's own misconduct, such as failing to close a cattle gate or breaching a contractual duty to build a fence, may diminish or bar his recovery. *See* Glanville L. Williams, *Liability for Animals* 178–181 (1939). * * *

In 1850, just after California attained statehood, an open-range rule was adopted for the entire state. In that year the legislature enacted a statute that entitled a victim of animal trespass to recover damages only when the victim had protected his lands with a "lawful fence." This pro-cattleman policy grew increasingly controversial as California became more settled and field crops became more common. During the latter part of the nineteenth century, the California legislature enacted a series of statutes effectively closing the range in designated counties, thereby granting more protection to farmers who had not built fences.

The closed-range exceptions eventually began to swamp California's traditional open-range rule and triggered a comprehensive legislative response. In the Estray Act of 1915, the legislature adopted for most of California the traditional English rule that the owner of livestock is strictly liable for trespass damage. This statute, however, retained the open-range rule in six counties in the lightly populated northern part of the state, where the tradition of running cattle at large remained strong. The six counties were Shasta, Del Norte, Lassen, Modoc, Siskiyou, and Trinity.

In 1945 the legislature enacted two amendments that dealt exclusively with Shasta County, the least rural of the six exempt counties. The first stated that a prime agricultural area just south of Redding was "not ... devoted chiefly to grazing"—a declaration that the legislature had decided to close the range in that small area of the county. The second amendment empowered the Board of Supervisors of Shasta County to adopt ordinances designating additional areas of the county as places no longer devoted chiefly to grazing. A board action of this sort would make cattlemen strictly liable for trespass damage occurring in those locations. Between 1945 and 1974 Shasta was the only California county to possess this special authority. As a result Shasta County today has a crazy quilt of open-and closed-range areas that no other California county can match.

The distinction between open range and closed range has formal legal significance in Shasta County trespass disputes. In closed range, the English rule governs and an animal owner is strictly liable for trespass damage to property. In open-range areas, by contrast, even a livestock owner who has negligently managed his animals is generally not liable for trespass damage to the lands of a neighbor.

Even in open range in Shasta County, however, an animal owner is legally liable for animal-trespass damages of three significant sorts. First, owners of goats, swine, and vicious dogs are strictly liable for trespass throughout Shasta County. Second, when a cattleman's livestock have trespassed in the face of a "lawful fence" that entirely enclosed the victim's open-range premises, the cattleman is also strictly liable. (A California statute, unamended since 1915, defines the technological standard that a fence must meet to be "lawful.")[11] Third, common law decisions make a

11. "A lawful fence is any fence which is good, strong, substantial, and sufficient to prevent the ingress and egress of livestock. No wire fence is a good and substantial fence within the meaning of this article unless it has three tightly stretched barbed wires se-

livestock owner liable for *intentional* open-range trespasses. Thus when Frank Ellis actively herded his cattle across the unfenced lands of his neighbors, he was legally liable for trespass. According to some precedents, he would also have been liable had he merely placed his cattle on his own lands in a way that would make it substantially certain that they would venture onto his neighbors' pastures.

When the law of either open or closed range entitles a trespass victim to relief, the standard legal remedy is an award of compensatory damages. (In part because evidence of damage to forage is fleeting, some states, although currently not California, authorize the appointment of disinterested residents of the area to serve as "fence viewers" to assess the amount of the damages.) A plaintiff who has suffered from continuing wrongful trespasses may also be entitled to an injunction against future incursions. California's Estray Act additionally entitles a landowner whose premises have been wrongly invaded by cattle to seize the animals as security for a claim to recover boarding costs and other damages. A trespass victim who invokes this procedure must provide proper notice to the state director of agriculture; if certain statutory requirements are met, the animals can be sold to satisfy the claim.

The formal law provides trespass victims with only limited self-help remedies. A victim can use reasonable force to drive the animals off his land, and is arguably privileged to herd them to a remote location he knows is inconvenient for their owner. In addition, as just noted, a trespass victim willing to give the animals proper care can seize strays and bill the costs of their care to their owner. But a victim is generally not entitled to kill or wound the offending animals. For example, a fruit grower in Mendocino County (a closed-range county) was convicted in 1973 for malicious maiming of animals when, without prior warning to the livestock owner, he shot and killed livestock trespassing in his unfenced orchard. In this respect, as we shall see, Shasta County mores diverge from the formal law.

The distinction between open range and closed range has formal relevance in public as well as private trespass law. Shasta County's law enforcement officials are entitled to impound cattle found running at large in closed range, but not those found in open range. Brad Bogue, the county animal control officer, relies primarily on warnings when responding to reports of loose animals. Regardless of whether a trespass has occurred in open or closed range, Bogue's prime goal is to locate the owner of the livestock and urge the prompt removal of the offending animals. When talking to animal owners, he stresses that it is in the owner's self-interest to take better care of the livestock. When talking to ranchette owners living in open range who have called to complain about trespassing mountain cattle, Bogue informs them of the cattleman's open-range rights. He asserts

curely fastened to posts of reasonable strength, firmly set in the ground not more than one rod [16½ feet] apart, one of which wires shall be at least four feet above the surface of the ground. Any kind of wire or other fence of height, strength and capacity equal to or greater than the wire fence herein described is a good and substantial fence within the meaning of this article. . . ." Cal. Agric. Code § 17121 (West 1968). * * *

that this sort of mediation is all that is required in the usual case. In most years, Bogue's office does not impound a single head of cattle or issue a single criminal citation for failure to prevent cattle trespass.

Knowledge of Animal Trespass Law

The Shasta County landowners interviewed were quizzed about their knowledge of the complex legal rules of animal trespass law reviewed above. The extent of their knowledge is relevant for at least two reasons. First, Coase's parable is set in a world of zero transaction costs, where everyone has perfect knowledge of legal rules. In reality, legal knowledge is imperfect because legal research is costly and human cognitive capacities are limited. The following overview of the working legal knowledge of Shasta County residents provides a glimpse of people's behavior in the face of these constraints. Data of this sort have implications for the design of legal rules to achieve specific instrumental goals, because rules cannot have instrumental effects unless they are communicated to the relevant actors. Second, my research revealed that most residents resolve trespass disputes not according to formal law but rather according to workaday norms that are consistent with an overarching norm of cooperation among neighbors. How notable this finding is depends in part on how many residents know that their trespass norms might be inconsistent with formal legal rules.

Lay Knowledge of Trespass Law

To apply formal legal rules to a specific trespass incident, a Shasta County resident would first have to know whether it had occurred in an open-range or closed-range area of the county. Ideally, the resident would either have or know how to locate the map of closed-range areas published by the county's Department of Public Works. Second, a legally sophisticated person would have a working command of the rules of trespass law, including how they vary from open to closed range.

I found no one in Shasta County—whether an ordinary person or a legal specialist such as an attorney, judge, or insurance adjuster—with a complete working knowledge of the formal trespass rules just described. The persons best informed are, interestingly enough, two public officials without legal training: Brad Bogue, the animal control officer, and Bruce Jordan, the brand inspector. Their jobs require them to deal with stray livestock on almost a daily basis. Both have striven to learn applicable legal rules, and both sometimes invoke formal law when mediating disputes between county residents. Both Bogue and Jordan possess copies of the closed-range map and relevant provisions of the California Code. What they do *not* know is the decisional law; for example, neither is aware of the rule that an intentional trespass is always tortious, even in open range. Nevertheless, Bogue and Jordan, both familiar figures to the cattlemen and (to a lesser extent) to the ranchette owners of rural Shasta County, have done more than anyone else to educate the populace about formal trespass law.

What do ordinary rural residents know of that law? To a remarkable degree the landowners interviewed *did* know whether their own lands were within open or closed range. Of the twenty-five landowners asked to identify whether they lived in open or closed range, twenty-one provided the correct answer, including two who were fully aware that they owned land in both. This level of knowledge is probably atypically high. Most of the landowner interviews were conducted in the Round Mountain and Oak Run areas. The former was the site in 1973 of the Caton's Folly closed-range battle. More important, Frank Ellis' aggressive herding had provoked a furious closed-range battle in the Oak Run area just six months before the landowner interviews were conducted. Two well-placed sources—the Oak Run postmaster and the proprietor of the Oak Run general store—estimated that this political storm had caught the attention of perhaps 80 percent of the area's adult residents. In the summer of 1982, probably no populace in the United States was more alert to the legal distinction between open and closed range than were the inhabitants of the Oak Run area.

What do laymen know of the substantive rules of trespass law? In particular, what do they know of how the rules vary from open to closed range? Individuals who are not legal specialists tend to conceive of these legal rules in black-and-white terms: either the livestock owners or the trespass victims "have the rights." We have seen, however, that the law of animal trespass is quite esoteric. An animal owner in open range, for example, is liable for intentional trespass, trespass through a lawful fence, or trespass by a goat. Only a few rural residents of Shasta County know anything of these subtleties. "Estray" and "lawful fence," central terms in the law of animal trespass, are not words in the cattlemen's everyday vocabulary. Neither of the two most sophisticated open-range ranchers interviewed was aware that enclosure by a lawful fence elevates a farmer's rights to recover for trespass. A traditionalist, whose cattle had often caused mischief in the Northeastern Sector foothills, thought strays could never be seized in open range, although a lawful fence gives a trespass victim exactly that entitlement. No interviewee was aware that Ellis' intentional herding on his neighbors' lands in open range had been in excess of his legal rights.

As most laymen in rural Shasta County see it, trespass law is clear and simple. In closed range, an animal owner is strictly liable for trespass damages. (They of course never used, and would not recognize, the phrase "strict liability," which in the law of torts denotes liability even in the absence of negligence.) In open range, their basic premise is that an animal owner is never liable. When I posed hypothetical fact situations designed to put their rules under stress, the lay respondents sometimes backpedaled a bit, but they ultimately stuck to the notion that cattlemen have the rights in open range and trespass victims the rights in closed range.

Legal Specialists' Knowledge of Trespass Law

The laymen's penchant for simplicity enabled them to identify correctly the substance of the English strict-liability rule on cattle trespass that formally applies in closed range. In that regard, the laymen outperformed the judges, attorneys, and insurance adjusters who were interviewed. In two important respects the legal specialists had a poorer working knowledge of trespass and estray rules in Shasta County than did the lay landowners. First, in contrast to the landowners, the legal specialists immediately invoked *negligence* principles when asked to analyze rights in trespass cases. In general, they thought that a cattleman would not be liable for trespass in open range (although about half seemed aware that this result would be affected by the presence of a lawful fence), and that he would be liable in closed range only *when negligent.* The negligence approach has so dominated American tort law during this century that legal specialists—insurance adjusters in particular—may fail to identify narrow pockets where strict liability rules, such as the English rule on cattle trespass, formally apply.

Second, unlike the lay rural residents, the legal specialists knew almost nothing about the location of the closed-range districts in the county. For example, two lawyers who lived in rural Shasta County and raised livestock as a sideline were ignorant of these boundaries; one incorrectly identified the kind of range in which he lived, and the other admitted he did not know what areas were open or closed. The latter added that this did not concern him because he would fence his lands under either legal regime.

Four insurance adjusters who settle trespass-damage claims in Shasta County were interviewed. These adjusters had little working knowledge of the location of closed-range and open-range areas or of the legal significance of those designations. One incorrectly identified Shasta County as an entirely closed-range jurisdiction. Another confused the legal designation "closed range" with the husbandry technique of keeping livestock behind fences; he stated that he did not keep up with the closed-range situation because the fence situation changes too rapidly to be worth following. The other two adjusters knew a bit more about the legal situation. Although neither possessed a closed-range map, each was able to guess how to locate one. However, both implied that they would not bother to find out whether a trespass incident had occurred in open or closed range before settling a claim. The liability rules that these adjusters apply to routine trespass claims seemed largely independent of formal law.

The Settlement of Trespass Disputes

If Shasta County residents were to act like the farmer and the rancher in Coase's parable, they would settle their trespass problems in the following way. First, they would look to the formal law to determine who had what entitlements. They would regard those substantive rules as beyond their influence (as "exogenous," to use the economists' adjective). When they faced a potentially costly interaction, such as a trespass risk to crops, they would resolve it "in the shadow of" the formal legal rules. Because transactions would be costless, enforcement would be complete: no violation of an entitlement would be ignored. For the same reason, two neighbors who interacted on a number of fronts would resolve their disputes front by front, rather than globally.

The field evidence casts doubt on the realism of each of these literal features of the parable. Because Coase himself was fully aware that transactions are costly and thus that the parable was no more than an abstraction, the contrary evidence in no way diminishes his monumental contribution in "The Problem of Social Cost." Indeed the evidence is fully consistent with Coase's central idea that, regardless of the content of law, people tend to structure their affairs to their mutual advantage. Nevertheless, the findings reported here may serve as a caution to law-and-economics scholars who have underestimated the impact of transaction costs on how the world works.

Norms, Not Legal Rules, Are the Basic Sources of Entitlements

In rural Shasta County, where transaction costs are assuredly not zero, trespass conflicts are generally resolved not *in* "the shadow of the law" but, rather, *beyond* that shadow. Most rural residents are consciously committed to an overarching norm of cooperation among neighbors. In trespass situations, their applicable particularized norm, adhered to by all but a few deviants, is that an owner of livestock is responsible for the acts of his animals. Allegiance to this norm seems wholly independent of formal legal entitlements. Most cattlemen believe that a rancher should keep his animals from eating a neighbor's grass, regardless of whether the range is open or closed. Cattlemen typically couch their justifications for the norm in moral terms. Marty Fancher: "Suppose I sat down [uninvited] to a dinner your wife had cooked?" Dick Coombs: It "isn't right" to get free pasturage at the expense of one's neighbors. Owen Shellworth: "[My cattle] don't belong [in my neighbor's field]." Attorney-rancher Pete Schultz: A cattleman is "morally obligated to fence" to protect his neighbor's crops, even in open range.

The remainder of this chapter describes in greater detail how the norms of neighborliness operate and how deviants who violate these norms are informally controlled. The discussion also identifies another set of deviants: trespass victims who actually invoke their formal legal rights.

Incomplete Enforcement: The Live-and-Let-Live Philosophy

The norm that an animal owner should control his stock is modified by another norm that holds that a rural resident should put up with ("lump") minor damage stemming from isolated trespass incidents. The neighborly response to an isolated infraction is an exchange of civilities. A trespass victim should notify the animal owner that the trespass has occurred and assist the owner in retrieving the stray stock. Virtually all residents have telephones, the standard means of communication. A telephone report is usually couched not as a complaint but rather as a service to the animal owner, who, after all, has a valuable asset on the loose. Upon receiving a telephone report, a cattleman who is a good neighbor will quickly retrieve the animals (by truck if necessary), apologize for the occurrence, and thank the caller. The Mortons and the Shellworths, two ranching families in the Oak Run area particularly esteemed for their neighborliness, have a policy of promptly and apologetically responding to their neighbors' notifications of trespass.

Several realities of country life in Shasta County help explain why residents are expected to put up with trespass losses. First, it is common for a rural landowner to lose a bit of forage or to suffer minor fence damage. The area northeast of Redding lies on a deer migration route. During the late winter and early spring thousands of deer and elk move through the area, easily jumping the barbed-wire fences. Because wild animals trespass so often, most rural residents come to regard minor damage from alien animals not as an injurious event but as an inevitable part of life.

Second, most residents expect to be on both the giving and the receiving ends of trespass incidents. Even the ranchette owners have, if not a few hobby livestock, at least several dogs, which they keep for companionship, security, and pest control. Unlike cattle, dogs that trespass may harass, or even kill, other farm animals. If trespass risks are symmetrical, and if victims bear all trespass losses, accounts balance in the long run. Under these conditions, the advantage of reciprocal lumping is that no one has to expend time or money to settle disputes.

The norm of reciprocal restraint that underlies the "live-and-let-live" philosophy also calls for ranchers to swallow the costs of boarding another person's animal, even for months at a time. A cattleman often finds in his herd an animal wearing someone else's brand. If he recognizes the brand he will customarily inform its owner, but the two will often agree that the simplest solution is for the animal to stay put until the trespass victim next gathers his animals, an event that may be weeks or months away. The cost of "cutting" a single animal from a larger herd seems to underlie this custom. Thus, ranchers often consciously provide other people's cattle with feed worth perhaps as much as $10 to $100 per animal. Although Shasta County ranchers tend to regard themselves as financially pinched, even ranchers who know that they are legally entitled to recover feeding costs virtually never seek monetary compensation for boarding estrays. The largest ranchers northeast of Redding who were interviewed reported that they had never charged anyone or been charged by anyone for costs of that sort. Even when they do not know to whom a stray animal belongs, they put the animal in their truck the next time they take a load of animals to the auction yard at Cottonwood and drop it off without charge so that the brand inspector can locate the owner.

Mental Accounting of Interneighbor Debts

Residents who own only a few animals may of course be unable to see any average reciprocity of advantage in a live-and-let-live approach to animal trespass incidents. This would be true, for example, of a farmer whose fields frequently suffered minor damage from incursions by a particular rancher's livestock. Shasta County norms entitle a farmer in that situation to keep track of those minor losses in a mental account, and eventually to act to remedy the imbalance.

A fundamental feature of rural society makes this enforcement system feasible: Rural residents deal with one another on a large number of fronts, and most residents expect those interactions to continue far into the future. In sociological terms, their relationships are "multiplex" not "simplex." In game-theoretic terms, they are engaged in iterated, not single-shot, play.

They interact on water supply, controlled burns, fence repairs, social events, staffing the volunteer fire department, and so on. Where population densities are low, each neighbor looms larger. Thus any trespass dispute with a neighbor is almost certain to be but one thread in the rich fabric of a continuing relationship.

A person in a multiplex relationship can keep a rough mental account of the outstanding credits and debits in each aspect of that relationship. Should the aggregate account fall out of balance, tension may mount because the net creditor may begin to perceive the net debtor as an overreacher. But as long as the aggregate account is in balance, neither party need be concerned that particular subaccounts are not. For example, if a rancher were to owe a farmer in the trespass subaccount, the farmer could be expected to remain content if that imbalance were to be offset by a debt he owed the rancher in, say, the water-supply subaccount.

The live-and-let-live norm also suggests that neighbors should put up with minor imbalances in their aggregate accounts, especially when they perceive that their future interactions will provide adequate opportunities for settling old scores. Creditors may actually prefer having others in their debt. For example, when Larry Brennan lost seven tons of baled hay to Frank Ellis' cattle in open range, Brennan (although he did not know it) had a strong legal claim against Ellis for intentional trespass. Brennan estimated his loss at between $300 and $500, hardly a trivial amount. When Ellis learned of Brennan's loss he told Brennan to "come down and take some hay" from Ellis' barn. Brennan reported that he declined this offer of compensation, partly because he thought he should not have piled the bales in an unfenced area, but also because he would rather have Ellis in debt to him than be in debt to Ellis. Brennan was willing to let Ellis run up a deficit in their aggregate interpersonal accounts because he thought that as a creditor he would have more leverage over Ellis' future behavior.

The Control of Deviants: The Key Role of Self–Help

The rural Shasta County population includes deviants who do not adequately control their livestock and run up excessive debts in their informal accounts with their neighbors. Frank Ellis, for example, was notoriously indifferent about his reputation among his neighbors. In general, the traditionalists who let their animals loose in the mountains during the summer are less scrupulous than the modernists are in honoring the norms of neighborliness. This is likely due to the fact that traditionalists have less complex, and shorter-lived, interrelationships with the individuals who encounter their range cattle.

To discipline deviants, the residents of rural Shasta County use the following four types of countermeasures, listed in escalating order of seriousness: (1) self-help retaliation; (2) reports to county authorities; (3) claims for compensation informally submitted without the help of attorneys; and (4) attorney-assisted claims for compensation. The law starts to gain bite as one moves down this list.

Self-help. Not only are most trespass disputes in Shasta County resolved according to extralegal rules, but most enforcement actions are also extralegal. A measured amount of self-help—an amount that would serve to even up accounts—is the predominant and ethically preferred response to someone who has not taken adequate steps to prevent his animals from trespassing.

The mildest form of self-help is truthful negative gossip. This usually works because only the extreme deviants are immune from the general obsession with neighborliness. Although the Oak Run–Round Mountain area is undergoing a rapid increase in population, it remains distinctly rural in atmosphere. People tend to know one another, and they value their reputations in the community. Some ranching families have lived in the area for several generations and include members who plan to stay indefinitely. Members of these families seem particularly intent on maintaining their reputations as good neighbors. Should one of them not promptly and courteously retrieve a stray, he might fear that any resulting gossip would permanently besmirch the family name.

Residents of the Northeastern Sector foothills seem quite conscious of the role of gossip in their system of social control. One longtime resident, who had also lived for many years in a suburb of a major California urban area, observed that people in the Oak Run area "gossip all the time," much more than in the urban area. Another reported intentionally using gossip to sanction a traditionalist who had been "impolite" when coming to pick up some stray mountain cattle; he reported that application of this self-help device produced an apology, an outcome itself presumably circulated through the gossip system.

The furor over Frank Ellis' loose cattle in the Oak Run area induced area residents to try a sophisticated variation of the gossip sanction. The ranchette residents who were particularly bothered by Ellis' cattle could see that he was utterly indifferent to his reputation among them. They thought, however, that as a major rancher, Ellis would worry about his reputation among the large cattle operators in the county. They therefore reported Ellis' activities to the Board of Directors of the Shasta County Cattlemen's Association. This move proved unrewarding, for Ellis was also surprisingly indifferent to his reputation among the cattlemen.

When milder measures such as gossip fail, a person is regarded as being justified in threatening to use, and perhaps even actually using, tougher self-help sanctions. Particularly in unfenced country, a victim may respond to repeated cattle trespasses by herding the offending animals to a location extremely inconvenient for their owner. Another common response to repeated trespasses is to threaten to kill a responsible animal should it ever enter again. Although the killing of trespassing livestock is a crime in California, six landowners—not noticeably less civilized than the others—unhesitatingly volunteered that they had issued death threats of this sort. These threats are credible in Shasta County because victims of recurring trespasses, particularly if they have first issued a warning, feel justified in killing or injuring the mischievous animals. Despite the criminality of the conduct (a fact not necessarily known to the respondents), I learned the identity of two persons who had shot trespassing cattle. Another landowner told of running the steer of an uncooperative neighbor into a fence. The most intriguing report came from a rancher who had had recurrent problems with a trespassing bull many years before. This rancher told a key law enforcement official that he wanted to castrate the bull—"to turn it into a steer." The official replied that he would turn a deaf ear if that were to occur. The rancher asserted that he then carried out his threat.

It is difficult to estimate how frequently rural residents actually resort to violent self-help. Nevertheless, fear of physical retaliation is undoubtedly one of the major incentives for order in rural Shasta County. Ranchers who run herds at large freely admit that they worry that their trespassing cattle might meet with violence. One traditionalist reported that he is responsive to complaints from ranchette owners because he fears they will poison or shoot his stock. A judge for a rural district of the county asserted that a vicious animal is likely to "disappear" if its owner does not control it. A resident of the Oak Run area stated that some area residents responded to Frank Ellis' practice of running herds at large by rustling Ellis' cattle. He suggested that Ellis print tee shirts with the inscription: "Eat Ellis Beef. Everyone in Oak Run Does!"

Complaints to public officials. The longtime ranchers of Shasta County pride themselves on being able to resolve their problems on their own. Except when they lose animals to rustlers, they do not seek help from public officials. Although ranchette owners also use the self-help remedies of gossip and violence, they, unlike the cattlemen, sometimes respond to a trespass incident by contacting a county official who they think will remedy the problem. These calls are usually funneled to the animal control officer or brand inspector, who both report that most callers are ranchette owners with limited rural experience. As already discussed, these calls do produce results. The county officials typically contact the owner of the animal, who then arranges for its removal. Brad Bogue, the animal control officer, reported that in half the cases the caller knows whose animal it is. This suggests that callers often think that requests for removal have more effect when issued by someone in authority.

Mere removal of an animal may provide only temporary relief when its owner is a mountain lessee whose cattle have repeatedly descended upon the ranchettes. County officials therefore use mild threats to caution repeat offenders. In closed range, they may mention both their power to impound the estrays and the risk of criminal prosecution. These threats appear to be bluffs; as noted, the county never impounds stray cattle when it can locate an owner, and it rarely prosecutes cattlemen (and then only when their animals have posed risks to motorists). In open range, county officials may deliver a more subtle threat: not that they will initiate a prosecution, but that, if the owner does not mend his ways, the Board of Supervisors may face insuperable pressure to close the range in the relevant area. Because cattlemen perceive that a closure significantly diminishes their legal entitlements in situations where motorists have collided with their livestock, this threat can catch their attention.

A trespass victim's most effective official protest is one delivered directly to his elected county supervisor—the person best situated to change stray-cattle liability rules. Many Shasta County residents are aware that traditionalist cattlemen fear the supervisors more than they fear law enforcement authorities. Thus in 1973 the alfalfa farmer John Woodbury made his repeated phone calls about mountain cattle not to Brad Bogue but to Supervisor John Caton. When a supervisor receives many calls from trespass victims, his first instinct is to mediate the crisis. Supervisor Norman Wagoner's standard procedure was to assemble the ranchers in the area and advise them to put pressure on the offender or else risk the closure of the range. Wagoner's successor, Supervisor John Caton, similarly told Frank Ellis that he would support a closure at Oak Run unless Ellis built three miles of fence along the Oak Run Road. If a supervisor is not responsive to a constituent's complaint, the constituent may respond by circulating a closure petition, as Doug Heinz eventually did in Oak Run.

The rarity of claims for monetary relief. Because Shasta County residents tend to settle their trespass disputes beyond the shadow of the law, one might suspect that the norms of neighborliness include a norm against the invocation of formal legal rights. And this norm is indeed entrenched. Owen Shellworth: "I don't believe in lawyers [because there are] always hard feelings [when you litigate]." Tony Morton: "[I never press a monetary claim because] I try to be a good neighbor." Norman Wagoner: "Being good neighbors means no lawsuits." Although trespasses are frequent, Shasta County's rural residents virtually never file formal trespass actions against one another. John Woodbury, for example, made dozens of phone calls to Supervisor John Caton, but never sought monetary compensation from the traditionalists whose cattle had repeatedly marauded his alfalfa field. Court records and conversations with court clerks indicate that in most years not a single private lawsuit seeking damages for either trespass by livestock or the expense of boarding estrays is filed in the county's courts. Not only do the residents of the Northeastern Sector foothills refrain from filing formal lawsuits, but they are also strongly disinclined to submit informal monetary claims to the owners of trespassing animals.

The landowners who were interviewed clearly regard their restraint in seeking monetary relief as a mark of virtue. When asked why they did not pursue meritorious legal claims arising from trespass or fence-finance disputes, various landowners replied: "I'm not that kind of guy"; "I don't believe in it"; "I don't like to create a stink"; "I try to get along." The landowners who attempted to provide a rationale for this forbearance all implied the same one, a long-term reciprocity of advantage. Ann Kershaw: "The only one that makes money [when you litigate] is the lawyer." Al Levitt: "I figure it will balance out in the long run." Pete Schultz: "I hope they'll do the same for me." Phil Ritchie: "My family believes in 'live and let live.'"

Mutual restraint saves parties in a long-term relationship the costs of going through the formal claims process. Adjoining landowners who practice the live-and-let-live approach are both better off whenever the negative externalities from their activities are roughly in equipoise. Equipoise is as likely in closed range as in open. Landowners with property in closed range—the ones with the greatest formal legal rights—were the source of half of the quotations in the prior two paragraphs.

When a transfer *is* necessary to square unbalanced accounts, rural neighbors prefer to use in-kind payments, not cash. Shasta County landowners regard a monetary settlement as an arms' length transaction that symbolizes an unneighborly relationship. Should your goat happen to eat your neighbor's tomatoes, the neighborly thing for you to do would be to help replant the tomatoes; a transfer of money would be too cold and too impersonal. When Kevin O'Hara's cattle went through a break in a fence and destroyed his neighbor's corn crop (a loss of less than $100), O'Hara had to work hard to persuade the neighbor to accept his offer of money to compensate for the damages. O'Hara insisted on making this payment because he "felt responsible" for his neighbor's loss, a feeling that would not have been in the least affected had the event occurred in open instead of closed range. There can also be social pressure against offering monetary settlements. Bob Bosworth's father agreed many decades ago to pay damages to a trespass victim in a closed-range area just south of Shasta County; other cattlemen then rebuked him for setting an unfortunate precedent. The junior Bosworth, in 1982 the president of the Shasta County Cattlemen's Association, could recall no other out-of-pocket settlement in a trespass case.

Trespass victims who sustain an unusually large loss are more likely to take the potentially deviant step of making a claim for monetary relief. Among those interviewed were adjusters for the two insurance companies whose liability policies would be most likely to cover losses from animal trespass. The adjusters' responses suggest that in a typical year these companies receive fewer than ten trespass damage claims originating in Shasta County. In the paradigmatic case, the insured is not a rancher but rather a ranchette owner, whose family's horse has escaped and trampled a neighboring homeowner's shrubbery. The claimant is typically not represented by an attorney, a type of professional these adjusters rarely encounter. The adjusters also settle each year two or three trespass claims that homeowners or ranchette owners have brought against ranchers. Ranchers who suffer trespasses virtually never file claims against others' insurance companies. An adjuster for the company that insures most Shasta County ranchers stated that he could not recall, in his twenty years of adjusting, a single claim by a rancher for compensation for trespass damage.

Attorney-assisted claims. The landowners, particularly the ranchers, express a strong aversion to hiring an attorney to fight one's battles. To hire an attorney is to escalate a conflict. A good neighbor does not do such a thing because the "natural working order" calls for two neighbors to work out their problems between themselves. The files in the Shasta

County courthouses reveal that the ranchers who honor norms of neighbor-liness—the vast majority—are not involved in cattle-related litigation of any kind.

I did uncover two instances in which animal-trespass victims in the Oak Run–Round Mountain area had turned to attorneys. In one of these cases the victim actually filed a formal complaint. Because lawyer-backed claims are so unusual, these two disputes, both of them bitter, deserve elaboration.

The first involved Tom Hailey and Curtis McCall. For three genera-tions, Hailey's family has owned a large tract of foothill forest in an open-range area near Oak Run. In 1978 Hailey discovered McCall's cattle grazing on some of Hailey's partially fenced land. Hailey suspected that McCall had brought the animals in through a gate in Hailey's fence. When Hailey confronted him, McCall, who lived about a mile away, acted as if the incursion had been accidental. Hailey subsequently found a salt block on the tract—an object he could fairly assume that McCall had put there to service his trespassing herd. Hailey thus concluded that McCall had not only deliberately trespassed but had also aggravated the offense by un-truthfully denying the charge. Hailey seized the salt block and consulted an attorney, who advised him to seek compensation from McCall. The two principals eventually agreed to a small monetary settlement.

Hailey is a semi-retired government employee who spends much of his time outside of Shasta County; he is regarded as reclusive and eccentric—certainly someone outside the mainstream of Oak Run society. McCall, a retired engineer with a hard-driving style, moved to Shasta County in the late 1970s to run a small livestock ranch. The Haileys refer to him as a "Texan"—a term that in Shasta County connotes someone who is both an outsider and lacks neighborly instincts.

The second dispute involved Doug Heinz and Frank Ellis. As described in Chapter 2, Heinz had the misfortune of owning a ranchette near Ellis' ranch. After experiencing repeated problems with Ellis' giant cattle herds, Heinz unilaterally seized three animals that had broken through his fence. Heinz boarded these animals for three months without notifying Ellis. Heinz later asserted he intended to return them when Ellis next held a roundup. According to Heinz, Ellis eventually found out that Heinz had the animals and asked for their return. Heinz agreed to return them if Ellis would pay pasturage costs. When Ellis replied, "You know I'm good for it," Heinz released the animals and sent Ellis a bill. Ellis refused to pay the bill, and further infuriated Heinz by calling him "boy" whenever Heinz brought up the debt.

On January 8, 1981, Heinz filed a small-claims action against Ellis to recover $750 "for property damage, hay and grain ate [sic] by defendant's cattle, boarding of animals." Acting through the attorney he kept on retainer, Ellis responded eight days later with a separate civil suit against Heinz. Ellis' complaint sought $1,500 compensatory and $10,000 punitive damages from Heinz for the shooting deaths of two Black Brangus cows that Ellis had pastured on Bureau of Land Management lands; it also sought compensation for the weight loss Ellis' three live animals had sustained during the months Heinz had been feeding them. The two legal actions were later consolidated. Heinz, who called Ellis' allegation that he had killed two cows "100 percent lies" and "scare tactics," hired an attorney based in Redding to represent him. This attorney threatened to pursue a malicious prosecution action against Ellis if Ellis persisted in asserting that Heinz had slain the Black Brangus cows. In December 1981, the parties agreed to a settlement under the terms of which Ellis paid Heinz $300 in damages and $100 for attorney fees. Ellis' insurance company picked up the tab. By that time Heinz was spearheading a political campaign to close the range Ellis had been using.

The Heinz–Ellis and Hailey–McCall disputes share several characteristics. Although both arose in open range, in each instance legal authority favored the trespass victim: Hailey, because McCall's trespass had been intentional; and Heinz, because Ellis' animals had broken through an apparently lawful fence. In both instances the victim, before consulting an attorney, had attempted to obtain informal satisfaction but had been rebuffed. Each victim came to believe that the animal owner had not been honest with him. Each dispute was ultimately settled in the victim's favor. In both instances, neither the trespass victim nor the cattle owner was a practiced follower of rural Shasta County norms. Thus other respondents tended to refer to the four individuals involved in these two claims as "bad apples," "odd ducks," or otherwise as people not aware of the natural working order. Ordinary people, it seems, do not often turn to attorneys to help resolve disputes.

---

1.   What are the background legal entitlements regarding trespass liability? What is the standard for liability on open-range? closed-range? How are these entitlements enforced?

2.   What are the social norms regarding trespass liability? How do these norms vary between open and closed range lands?

3.   What are the salient features of the resources at issue in Shasta County? What are the salient features of the culture in Shasta County? Do the social norms promote the beneficial use of resources in Shasta County?

4.   Why do social norms tend to predominate in the resolution of trespass disputes? Are they more efficient than reliance upon the background legal rules and institutions? Why don't we see many examples of ranchers using the background legal rules to their own private maximal advantage? How do the informal governance mechanisms affect the operation of formal governance institutions—background legal rules and political institutions?

5.   What conditions favor the establishment and operation of social norms as the dominant governance regime for trespass? Are these social norms likely to play a comparable role in different settings—*e.g.*, suburban,

urban, commercial, family? *Cf.* Merges, Among the Tribes of Shasta County, 18 Law & Soc. Inquiry 299 (1993).

6.   Under what circumstances should courts defer to social norms of a community? *Cf. Pierson v. Post, supra* pages 97–99 (dissent). What factors favor a court's deference to community norms? What factors caution against a court's deference to social norms?

7.   What factors potentially threaten the stability of social norms as the dominant governance regime for trespass in Shasta County? Under what circumstances are social norms responsive to changes in underlying conditions? How does their responsiveness compare to the responsiveness of legal, market, and political institutions?

8.   What light does Ellickson's case study shed upon the relevance of the Coase Theorem? *Cf.* Merges, Among the Tribes of Shasta County, 18 Law & Soc. Inquiry 299, 302–04 (1993); Cooter, The Cost of Coase, 11 J. Legal Stud. 1, 23 (1982).

The social norms reflected in Shasta County are by no means universally adhered to. Consider the following disputes:

Schild v. Rubin

District Court of Appeal, California, 1991.
232 Cal.App.3d 755, 283 Cal.Rptr. 533.

■ BOREN, J.

Two neighbors, who happen to be lawyers, have bounced their unfortunate dispute from a basketball court into the courts of law. Respondent Michael Rubin successfully applied to the trial court for a permanent injunction to prohibit his neighbors, appellant Kenneth Schild and his wife (appellant Gail Schild), and any other person from playing basketball on the Schilds' property except during specified hours of the day. The trial court issued the injunction pursuant to the statute authorizing injunctive relief from willful harassment. (Code Civ.Proc., § 527.6.)[12] Because we find the evidence in the present case does not establish all the requisite

12.   Code of Civil Procedure section 527.6 provides, in pertinent part, as follows:

(a) A person who has suffered harassment as defined in subdivision (b) may seek a temporary restraining order, and an injunction prohibiting harassment provided in this section.

(b) For the purposes of this section, "harassment" is a knowing and willful course of conduct directed at a specific person which seriously alarms, annoys, or harasses the person, and which serves no legitimate purpose. The course of conduct must be such as would cause a reasonable person to suffer substantial emotional distress and must actually cause substantial emotional distress to the plaintiff. "Course of conduct" is a pattern of conduct composed of a series of acts over a period of time, however short, evidencing a continuity of purpose. Constitutionally protected activity is not included within the meaning of "course of conduct."

elements of section 527.6, we reverse and dissolve the injunction issued against the Schilds on July 23, 1990.

FACTS

Kenneth and Gail Schild reside with their two children, 13–year-old Jonathan and 11–year-old Deborah, at their home on Alginet Drive in Encino. Michael and Yifat Rubin reside with their infant child at their home which is adjacent to the rear half of the Schilds' lot. An approximately six-foot-high solid adobe wall separates the two adjacent lots.

In December of 1987, the Schilds installed in the rear of their lot a basketball play area consisting of a metal pole and a standard backboard. The pole was set in a semicircular concrete area with a radius of approximately 15 feet from the pole. The pole and basketball backboard are approximately 55 to 60 feet from the wall which separates the two properties, and the Rubins' residence is at its closest point approximately six to eight feet from the wall.

In January of 1988, Michael Rubin complained to the Schilds about the noise created by Jonathan Schild when he played basketball in the Schilds' backyard. The Rubins complained that the basketball playing interrupted Saturday and Sunday afternoon naps and, in general, interfered with their ability to rest and relax in their own home. The Schilds then poured additional concrete into the hollow cylindrical steel pole supporting the backboard and added four inches of foam rubber with plywood backing to the back of the backboard to deaden the sound of the basketball. Rubin admitted that the "sound projection was diminished somewhat by [those] corrective measures" but deemed the noise from basketball play still at "an unacceptable level."

According to Rubin, the Schilds, their children or guests played basketball or hardball catch on the basketball play area "3 to 5 times per week." A neighbor, Bradley Smith, who supported Rubin's claim of excessive noise stated that the area was used "two to three times per week." It was undisputed that the ball playing occurred for as short a period of time as five minutes to occasionally as long as thirty minutes. The basketball play area was not used before 9 a.m. or after 8 p.m. and was not used on school days prior to 3:30 p.m. The basketball play area was used for varying lengths of time between 3:30 and 6:30 p.m. on weekdays and 12 p.m. to 12:30 p.m. and 4 p.m. to 6:30 p.m. on weekends. Usually, Jonathan Schild played basketball alone when he arrived home from school or played with his father upon his father's return home from work. The nearest public park is two and a half miles from the Schilds' residence.

On March 9, 1989, Rubin again complained of the noise from basketball playing and asked Jonathan to stop playing. Schild advised Jonathan that he could continue playing for another 10 minutes until dinner was ready because it would be dark and impossible to play later. Rubin demanded that Schild stop his son from playing basketball, became enraged, and then sprayed the basketball area with a garden hose. Rubin admitted that he directed the spray onto the basketball court area, claimed that no person was ever "directly sprayed," and deemed the spraying the exercise of his right to abate a "private nuisance." Schild and his son apparently got wet and considered the spraying an assault upon them.

On March 22, 1989, the Schilds filed a complaint against Rubin for assault, battery, trespass, nuisance and intentional infliction of emotional distress, and sought a permanent injunction. Rubin then cross-complained against the Schilds for nuisance and intentional infliction of emotional distress and also sought a permanent injunction. The actions were consolidated and are apparently still pending trial as of the date of this opinion.

According to the Schilds and a neighbor, Joseph Burton, on several occasions between March 9 and March 31, 1990, unusually loud rock music emanated from the Rubins' residence and was directed at the Schilds' residence. During the times when the radio was on, the Schilds did not observe anyone in the Rubins' backyard or any cars in their driveway. The Rubins admitted playing the radio in their home but claimed it was not unusually loud. Neighbor Bradley Smith asserted that he never heard any music of any kind from the Rubins' residence while he was inside his own home across the street from the Rubins' residence.

On April 1, 1990, at approximately 12:30 p.m., a second basketball and hose spraying incident occurred. On April 2, 1990, the Schilds obtained a temporary restraining order against the Rubins. The order was thereafter modified and then followed by a petition for an injunction prohibiting harassment. On May 17, 1990, the court enjoined the Rubins from alarming, annoying or harassing the Schilds and their children and ordered that the Rubins "not direct communication of any kind, either oral, telephone, written or otherwise" to the Schilds or their children or guests and "not interfere in any way with the peaceful use and enjoyment of [the Schilds' residence], including the full and appropriate use of the basketball play area." Rubin did not appeal the issuance of this injunction.

On June 7, 1990, Rubin obtained a temporary restraining order against the Schilds under authority of the willful harassment statute (Code Civ. Proc., § 527.6). Rubin sought a total ban on basketball play (as well as baseball catch). The court ordered the Schilds not to alarm, annoy or harass the Rubins and ordered that neither the Schilds "nor any persons on their property are to engage in any basketball playing or hardball catch activities except from 11 a.m. to 3:30 p.m. and from 4:30 p.m. to 6:30 p.m. daily." At the time of the temporary restraining order, Rubin's wife was pregnant and due to give birth on June 26, 1990. Rubin's wife's pregnancy was a major factor in Rubin's argument in support of a temporary restraining order.

On July 19, 1990, the court held a hearing on Rubin's application for a permanent injunction. The evidence before the court consisted of numerous documents submitted by counsel and limited supplemental testimony from Rubin. In addition to the facts as previously discussed herein, the documents submitted by counsel indicated the results of a study by Bruce Davy, an acoustical engineer retained by Rubin who tested several areas on the Rubins' property for ambient noise levels. Although Davy recorded no violation of the Los Angeles Municipal Code's noise regulations, he projected that based upon his findings, if three people played basketball on the play area, violations of the code noise level "would probably occur." Noise levels recorded near the center of the Rubins' bedroom were recorded with the window open approximately five inches. Rubin also submitted an unsworn real estate appraisal which alleged that the basketball playing on the Schilds' property devalued the Rubins' property 15 percent, reducing its value from $720,000 to $612,000.

The evidence submitted by the Schilds at the hearing included declarations from Clarence Massar, head of the Los Angeles Police Department's noise abatement team, Norman Simon, an architect, and T.C. Chung, an acoustical engineer. Massar criticized Davy's sound testing because of microphone placement and the briefness of his testing and set forth the results of his own sound tests, which found no code violations. Massar also questioned Davy's interpretation of the Los Angeles Municipal Code's noise regulations.

The declaration by Chung indicated that the noise levels inside the Rubins' bedroom could be substantially reduced by closing the windows. According to Simon, the noise levels could be further substantially reduced by installing thermal pane or dual glazed windows which "are not expensive to install and represent an economic[al] solution to noise problems while improving the overall insulation of a structure."

After the court reviewed the evidence submitted at the July 19, 1990, hearing and heard the arguments of counsel, it granted Rubin's petition for an injunction prohibiting harassment, pursuant to Code of Civil Procedure section 527.6. The court ordered that the Schilds not alarm, annoy or harass the Rubins and that neither the Schilds "nor any other persons on their property, are to engage in basketball playing on their property of any kind except between 10:00 a.m. and 12:00 p.m.; between 2:30 p.m. and 5:30 p.m.; and between 7:30 p.m. and 8:30 p.m. daily."[13] The Schilds appeal.

---

13. The court also made the following apt observations:

It is the Court's conclusion that what is involved here is simply spiteful conduct on the part of the parties involved, that there is no and has not been an attempt to find a basis for neighborly accommodation between people living in relatively close quarters to each other as exists throughout the community. Instead what we have [are] lawyers utilizing their own unlimited resources to accelerate petty neighborhood squabbles into a community war. You have even involved your neighbors, and you have in that manner disturbed the tranquility of a whole neighborhood, people taking sides, one against the other. Families with children, who are raising children,

should not really deal with each other in that fashion, especially when we have people who are educated, who are experienced in life, and who are faced with a situation where they recognize that everybody had rights to enjoy their home and their property with their family.

I know that the Court has attempted on many occasions to bring you people to a point where the matter is resolved without taking advantage of the court system and using all of the time that you have used in this court. It appears to the Court and to the community ... that the lawyers here are abusing the limited resources of the Court, which has a myriad of truly difficult matters pending before it crying out for resolution. These matters go back five years or longer, some of

[The Court of Appeal reversed the lower court's decision on the ground that the evidence of Rubin's "substantial emotional distress" was insufficient and that the conduct in question would not "cause a reasonable person to suffer substantial emotional distress." Cal. Code Civ. Proc. § 527.6(b). In rejecting Rubin's characterization of the Schild's basketball playing as a nuisance, the Court noted with approval the observation of another Court that "([p]eople who live in organized communities must of necessity suffer some inconvenience and annoyance from their neighbors and must submit to annoyances consequent upon the reasonable use of property by others.)" Rubin subsequently appealed to the California Supreme Court, which denied review.]

Roddenberry v. Roddenberry

District Court of Appeal, California, 1996.
44 Cal.App.4th 634, 51 Cal.Rptr.2d 907.

■ ZEBROWSKI, J.

* * *

The plaintiff is Eileen Roddenberry ("the first Mrs. Roddenberry"). Until his death shortly before trial, the primary defendant was her former husband, Gene Roddenberry. Gene Roddenberry created the "Star Trek" television series, movies, animations, and other Star Trek properties. Majel Roddenberry ("the second Mrs. Roddenberry") is now a defendant in her capacity as an executor of Gene Roddenberry's estate. Gene Roddenberry's loan-out corporation "Norway" is also a defendant. * * *

FACTUAL SUMMARY

The original "Star Trek" television series.

In the 1960s, during his marriage to the first Mrs. Roddenberry, Gene Roddenberry developed a television series entitled *Star Trek. Star Trek* (hereafter Star Trek 1) appeared on NBC for three seasons from 1966 to 1969.

By the time Gene Roddenberry and the first Mrs. Roddenberry divorced in 1969, Star Trek 1 had rated third in its time slot for each of its

---

them, because they do not have court facilities to get to trial.

Your situation, because you know how to do it, calls for priority treatment by the Court. And therefore, everything else that is before the Court is set aside to deal with your problems. Apparently you people have unlimited resources.... The lawyer's costs, the expert witnesses, the engineers, the fancy testing equipment, it is mind boggling that that kind

of effort and that kind of money should be expended by all of you in this matter.

You have by your conduct and by your position as lawyers embarrassed the Bar and the judicial system as a whole. You have subjected the whole system to ridicule and to public scorn. And many people, [including] your fellow practitioners, I believe would find this kind of conduct intolerable.

three seasons, had amassed a multi-million dollar production deficit, was considered a commercial failure, and had been canceled by NBC. Efforts were underway to syndicate Star Trek 1 for rerun on local television stations. Norway's contract with the Star Trek 1 production company provided that Norway was entitled to several types of income from syndications, including a set payment per rerun and "Profit Participation" payments if reruns ever yielded profits according to the contractual formula.[14]

The divorce settlement agreement and judgment.

In mid–1969, Gene Roddenberry and the first Mrs. Roddenberry agreed to a divorce settlement covering the typical numerous issues and resulting from the typical numerous trade-offs. Among the many community assets distributed was Norway, which held the rerun payment and profit participation rights in "Star Trek." Norway also owned a copyright interest in Star Trek. The settlement agreement allocated Norway to Gene Roddenberry; the first Mrs. Roddenberry received other marital property. The settlement agreement thus allocated to Gene Roddenberry all the previous community property rights in Star Trek, including the marital copyright interests, with only one exception: The first Mrs. Roddenberry was allocated a "one-half interest in all future profit participation income from 'Star Trek' to which [the first Mrs. Roddenberry] and/or [Gene Roddenberry] are entitled."

The agreement was handwritten (mostly by the first Mrs. Roddenberry's attorney), read into the court record (by the first Mrs. Roddenberry's attorney), and entered as a judgment in 1969. The judgment provided that subject to its provisions, "all future income of each party is that party's separate property." Thus except for whatever was included in the category of "profit participation income from Star Trek," the first Mrs. Roddenberry had bargained away all property interests she might have had in Gene Roddenberry's post-divorce income.[15]

The terms "profit participation" and "Star Trek" used in the 1969 settlement agreement and resulting judgment were not expressly defined. The current dispute was possible because of this lack of express definition.

Post-divorce Star Trek projects.

After these events, Gene Roddenberry devoted the remaining twenty-one years of his life to various Star Trek projects. He married the second Mrs. Roddenberry within days of his divorce and remained married to her until his death in 1991. The second Mrs. Roddenberry assisted in his post-divorce Star Trek efforts.

---

14. In Norway's contract with the Star Trek 1 production company, the term "Profit Participation" captioned a section defining Norway's rights to profits from syndications. The contract provided that Star Trek 1 had to repay a large and growing production cost deficit before any syndication profits would be payable to Norway.

15. She was entitled to, and for many years received, alimony. The issue here is whether she retained a property interest in his post-divorce income, as opposed to a family law right to alimony.

These post-divorce efforts gradually bore fruit. From 1973 to 1975, a Star Trek animation series was broadcast on NBC. It won an Emmy and was rerun in syndication. In 1979, "Star Trek: The Motion Picture" was released. Five sequels followed. A new Star Trek television series, "Star Trek: The Next Generation" (hereafter "Star Trek 2") appeared in 1987. Additional projects included television specials, merchandising, music, etc. In January 1993, after Gene Roddenberry's death, a spin-off television series entitled "Star Trek: Deep Space Nine" (hereafter "Star Trek 3") began.

Star Trek 1 goes into profits, suit is filed.

By 1984, 15 years after its cancellation as a financial failure, Star Trek 1 had recouped its production deficit, and Norway began to receive "profit participation" payments. Norway began making payments to the first Mrs. Roddenberry.

Near the end of 1987, the first Mrs. Roddenberry filed suit claiming—correctly, it was later determined—to have been shorted. Initially, she claimed only half of Norway's profit participation in Star Trek 1. Later, she expanded her claim to half of all income from all of Gene Roddenberry's post-divorce Star Trek efforts. She also sued Norway and Gene Roddenberry for fraud in connection with Norway's handling of payments to her.

THE TRIAL COURT JUDGMENT

After trial in part to the court and in part to a jury, and subject to adjustments and qualifications not necessary to detail here, the trial court entered a multi-part judgment.

The Star Trek 1 "profit participation" interest.

The trial court found that the first Mrs. Roddenberry was entitled to half the profit participation payments from Star Trek 1. Offsets claimed by Norway and the estate were disallowed. (This portion of the judgment has not been appealed, and would be affirmed in any event.)[16]

The fraud claim.

The trial court also entered judgment on a jury verdict against Norway for $900,000 in punitive damages for fraud in Norway's handling of profit participation payments to the first Mrs. Roddenberry.

The post-divorce Star Trek projects.

On the first Mrs. Roddenberry's claim to half of all income generated by Gene Roddenberry's post-divorce Star Trek projects, the trial court rendered a split and inconsistent decision.

Preliminarily, the trial court simply ignored the first Mrs. Roddenberry's testimony that she was entitled to half of all post-divorce Star Trek income. This testimony was contrary to the express language of the

---

16. According to the first Mrs. Roddenberry's brief filed in March of 1995, "[t]hus far, she has received only *$13.8 million.*" (Emphasis in original.) She continues to receive disbursements every six months.

settlement agreement and resulting judgment, and was inconsistent with all other evidence. The trial court properly ignored it and focused on the issue of profit participation.

In evaluating the profit participation issue, the trial court identified six categories of Star Trek projects, five of which (all except Star Trek 1) post-dated the 1969 divorce: (1) Star Trek 1, (2) the Star Trek animations in 1973 through 1975, (3) the six motion pictures from 1979 to 1991, (4) the Star Trek 2 television series beginning in 1987, (5) the Star Trek 3 television series beginning in 1993, and (6) various merchandising ventures on an ongoing basis.

With regard to the post-divorce projects designated as (2) the Star Trek animations, (3) the six Star Trek movies, and (6) the merchandising ventures, * * * the trial court found no contractual intent that the first Mrs. Roddenberry would receive any profits generated by these post-divorce projects. As to animations, movies and merchandising, judgment was therefore for defendants.

With regard to Star Trek 2 and 3, the trial court employed a markedly different analysis. Instead of applying the same traditional contractual intent analysis which resulted in a defense verdict on animations, movies and merchandising, the court instead inquired whether Star Trek 2 and 3 were "continuations" of Star Trek 1. Finding that both Star Trek 2 and 3 were "continuations" of Star Trek 1, the trial court awarded the first Mrs. Roddenberry half the profits from Star Trek 2 and 3.

THIS APPEAL

The first Mrs. Roddenberry appeals the ruling that she is not entitled to profits from the animations, movies, and merchandising, on the grounds that this ruling is not supported by substantial evidence.

Norway and the estate appeal the award of half the Star Trek 2 and 3 profits to the first Mrs. Roddenberry on the grounds that this award is not supported by substantial evidence. Norway also appeals the punitive damage award on several grounds. * * *

THE EVIDENCE AND CONTENTIONS REGARDING CONTRACT INTERPRETATION

[The court summarized the voluminous record resulting from more than 15 days of trial, which "ranged far afield and is more notable for its bulk than its relevance."]

The circumstances at the time of contract.

At the time of contract in 1969, the only "Star Trek" property in existence was Star Trek 1. By the time it was canceled shortly before the settlement negotiations, it had amassed a production deficit of $3 million. No further Star Trek projects were in development or contemplated.

The negotiation of the settlement agreement.

Gene Roddenberry would not agree to allow the first Mrs. Roddenberry to share in his post-divorce income except by way of alimony. The first Mrs. Roddenberry would not part with certain items of marital property. The negotiations therefore considered various scenarios, and one asset ultimately allocated to Gene Roddenberry was Norway. The first Mrs. Roddenberry received only the half interest in profit participation from Star Trek.

In a handwritten proposal by the first Mrs. Roddenberry's attorney Jerry Edelman early in the negotiations, he proposed that the first Mrs. Roddenberry be allocated "any income directly or indirectly generated by 'STAR TREK', whether in the form of royalties, rerun fees, profit participation, or otherwise." Gene Roddenberry would not agree, and the allocation to the first Mrs. Roddenberry was limited by negotiation to the "profit participation" item only. Both sides had copies of Norway's contract with the Star Trek 1 production company in which "Profit Participation" was a specific category of revenue.

During their negotiations, the parties regularly defined the profit participation interest as a 30 percent interest. When attorney Edelman read the parties' settlement agreement into the record, Mr. Edelman referred to the first Mrs. Roddenberry's share of the profit participation income from Star Trek as "one-half of 30 percent—15 percent." Thirty percent was the figure both sides believed to be Norway's profit participation interest in Star Trek 1 syndications. Later, because of doubt about the precise percentage figure (which was subject to calculation because of competing interests) the 30 percent figure was not included in the judgment.[17]

The evidence thus showed, and the trial court found, that in their negotiations the parties specifically discussed only profit participation in Star Trek 1. There was no evidence that the parties discussed any post-divorce Star Trek project, or any Star Trek project other than Star Trek 1.
* * *

The first Mrs. Roddenberry's testimony.

The first Mrs. Roddenberry claimed to have been unaware of the Star Trek animations, movies, and merchandising until the litigation. The evidence was strongly against her claim of unawareness, and the trial court found that she was aware of these developments as they occurred. Nevertheless, she did not claim a share of income from the post-divorce Star Trek projects until many years after the divorce, and then only as an addition to a lawsuit initially seeking only profits from Star Trek 1.

The first Mrs. Roddenberry testified that she was present in the courthouse during the entire three days in 1969 on which the settlement agreement was negotiated, but did not directly participate in the negotiations. Instead, the negotiations were conducted by attorney Edelman and

---

17. It was later calculated that after proper allowance for Star Trek star William Shatner's interest, Norway's actual share was 26⅔ percent.

Gene Roddenberry's advisers outside her immediate presence. She did not read the stipulation handwritten by Mr. Edelman before Mr. Edelman read it into the court record. She did not remember any of the terms and conditions which he read to the court. Her testimony demonstrated continuing unfamiliarity with the terms of the settlement agreement and resulting judgment.

She nevertheless claimed half of all of Gene Roddenberry's post-divorce Star Trek income, including income from post-divorce rendition of personal services (expressly excluded by the judgment), rerun royalties (the same argument rejected on the new trial motion in 1970), and all other Star Trek income of every kind. It was the type of baseless demand that would cause all prudent observers to check for their wallet. Her testimony was more in the genre of wishful thinking than factual testimony based on personal knowledge. The trial court ignored or rejected most of her testimony.

The uniqueness of Star Trek's resurgence.

The evidence was uncontradicted that Star Trek's post-divorce resurgence was unprecedented in entertainment industry history. Never before had a financially failed television series enjoyed such subsequent popularity, attracted subsequent investment, and inspired subsequent ventures.

Even though the first Mrs. Roddenberry was unfamiliar with the terms of the settlement agreement, she claimed to have anticipated the post-divorce Star Trek projects and their unprecedented success, and to have intended to obtain an interest in them via the settlement agreement with which she was unfamiliar.

CONTENTIONS ON APPEAL REGARDING PROFIT PARTICIPATION

* * *

After reviewing the record for substantial evidence, we find ample evidence to support the denial of animation, movie and merchandising profits to the first Mrs. Roddenberry. We find no substantial evidence to support the award of half the Star Trek 2 and 3 profits to the first Mrs. Roddenberry. * * *

THE SUBSTANTIAL EVIDENCE TEST AND STAR TREK 2 AND 3

The lack of foundation for the "continuation" theory.

The award of Star Trek 2 and 3 profits to the first Mrs. Roddenberry was not based on evidence of contractual intent, but rather on plaintiff's theory that Star Trek 2 and 3 are "continuations" of Star Trek 1. * * * However, this is merely an example of an old adage: "Ask the wrong question, and you will get the wrong answer."

Whether or not Star Trek 2 and 3 are "continuations" of Star Trek 1 is irrelevant. In order to be relevant, the "continuation" question would have to be the second step of a two-step analysis. The foundational step would be proof of contractual intent that the first Mrs. Roddenberry receive profits from post-divorce "continuations" of Star Trek 1. The second step would be proof that Star Trek 2 and 3 are in fact "continuations" of Star Trek 1. The record here might arguably contain step 2, but it certainly does not contain step 1.

* * *

The "literary property" argument.

On appeal, the first Mrs. Roddenberry raises a new argument in support of her claim to Star Trek 2 and 3 profits (as well as half of all other profits): she claims that she "retained" a profit participation interest in the generic "literary property" entitled Star Trek. While imaginative, this is merely another example of a semantical possibility unsupported by evidence. As discussed below, there was no evidence of "retention" by her of an interest in Norway's "literary property" or copyright. The theory also ignores the contrary avalanche of evidence in the record, and the trial court's finding, that the parties discussed only a division of profits from Star Trek 1, rather than some generic literary property concept. Additionally, it conflicts with the evidence that all copyright interests became the separate property of Gene Roddenberry through his ownership of Norway.

During the settlement negotiations, the first Mrs. Roddenberry proposed that an interest in Norway's Star Trek "royalties" be allocated to her, but she later bargained away that claim. * * *

The first Mrs. Roddenberry nevertheless contends that she "retained" a right to be paid for exploitations of the Star Trek concept. While she does not appear to claim an actual copyright interest, it is clear that she claims the exact equivalent of a copyright interest. * * *

Since she cannot claim an actual copyright interest after bargaining away all royalty claims and transferring Norway and its copyrights to Gene Roddenberry, the first Mrs. Roddenberry instead claims some form of non-copyright "literary property" entitlement to payment when Norway exploits the copyrights. The right she claims would place her in the position of an owner and licensor of a copyright interest, entitled to be paid by her putative licensee, Norway, upon Norway's receipt of profits from exploitation of the copyrighted material. But it is Norway that owns the copyright. * * * Abraham Lincoln once said: "You can call a horse a cow if you want to, but it's still a horse." That applies here. * * *

THE PUNITIVE AWARD FOR FRAUD

The facts.

When Norway began receiving profit participation payments in 1984 for Star Trek 1 syndications, Norway initially forwarded a full half to the first Mrs. Roddenberry. Gene Roddenberry, however, felt that he should receive compensation from her for his post-divorce promotional efforts. It was a plausible claim. His post-divorce efforts arguably created a common fund in which she was sharing. For her to share in such a fund without contributing to the expenses of its creation could constitute unjust enrichment. Gene Roddenberry and his advisers therefore concluded that Norway would not pay a full half to the first Mrs. Roddenberry, but instead only one-third.

Although the unjust enrichment theory was plausible in the abstract, it was flawed in both conception and implementation. First, it was directly contrary to the express terms of the 1969 settlement agreement and judgment, both of which provided for the first Mrs. Roddenberry to receive her half "without deduction or offset of any kind." Second, when Norway began remitting only one-third rather than one-half to the first Mrs. Roddenberry, Norway misrepresented or at least concealed that fact. The initial letter from Norway's accountant advised the first Mrs. Roddenberry that she was receiving "one-half of the gross monies received," and a second told her that she was receiving "fifty percent." The first letter stated that "no deduction" had been made for Gene Roddenberry's post-divorce efforts, nor for "legal, accounting or other expenses incurred," and that "no attempt has been made at this time to seek compensation or reimbursement to Mr. Roddenberry for his personal efforts and expenditures over the years." Later, when the portion being paid was reduced to one-third, the accountant's letters stated only that a check was enclosed "[a]s per my prior correspondence." No advice was given that the amount of the check was only one-third of the profit participation payments made to Norway. Only shortly before trial did Norway pay the withheld sums plus interest.

Liability.

These facts support the finding of liability on at least a theory of concealment, if not affirmative misrepresentation as well. Civil Code sections 1572 and 1710. * * *

CONCLUSION

This is a case that should never have been. It was clear from the outset that the first Mrs. Roddenberry was entitled to half the profit participation payments on Star Trek 1 "without deduction or offset of any kind." It was equally clear that she had no interest in other Star Trek projects and "was not to participate" in income from Gene Roddenberry's post-divorce efforts. It is now clear that she is additionally entitled to the jury's award for fraud. Each side to bear its own costs on appeal.[18]

---

1. Professor Ellickson hypothesizes that welfare-maximizing norms will tend to emerge in the governance of repeat-play, multiplex relationships. Yet we see an utter breakdown in these two cases, one involving neighbors and the other involving people in another relational setting. What factors explain the contentiousness of these disputes? Why didn't a norm of neighborliness prevail in these circumstances? In what other contexts do we tend to see breakdowns of civility and cooperativeness in

18. [Ed. Note: Beam me up Scotty! There's no intelligent life in this sector.]

our society? What explains the disintegrations of social accommodation and harmony in these other contexts?

2.   Are the expert witnesses and evidence presented in the *Schild* case credible? What norms govern the truthfulness of expert witnesses?

3.   The lower court in *Schild* chided the parties for involving neighbors in the dispute. It appears that the neighbors split regarding who was in the right. Suppose that neighbors or mutual friends side with one party and the only support for the other party comes from personal friends of that party alone and paid experts. Should the court take that into consideration? Might such an alignment reflect that the complex social dynamics and cultural norms surrounding a neighborhood or family dispute favor the party with whom the community sides? Under what circumstances is such a reflection of the social norms particularly reliable? Suspect?

4.   To what extent have the greater mobility of families, suburbanization, and the break-up and assimilation of ethnically and culturally homogeneous communities affected the maintenance and enforcement of social norms?

5.   Does the adversarial nature of our legal system undermine norms of neighborliness? *Cf.* Kagan, Do Lawyers Cause Adversarial Legalism? 19 Law & Soc. Inquiry 1 (1994).

B.   THE EVOLUTION OF SOCIAL ORGANIZATIONS TO ADDRESS THE TRAGEDY OF THE COMMONS: WATER ALLOCATION IN THE ARID WEST

A second way in which social processes solve externality and collective action problems is through the development of hybrid property rights consortia. These organizations can exist wholly apart from the formal legal, market, and political institutions as well as become a part of the formal institutional structure.

Elinor Ostrom, Governing the Commons: The Evolution of Institutions For Collective Action

104–114, 125–26, 136–39 (1990).

THE COMPETITIVE PUMPING RACE

The setting

In an earlier geologic era, rivers and streams draining the mountains surrounding what has now become the Los Angeles metropolitan area laid down wide and deep bands of sand and gravel that were then partially overlaid by hard layers of clay. The former streambeds are now deep, water-bearing strata that can be thought of as underground reservoirs. These reservoirs are replenished by the rains that fall in the foothills and upper valleys and, to a more limited extent, by precipitation and drainage on the flat coastal plain itself.

Analyzing institutional change

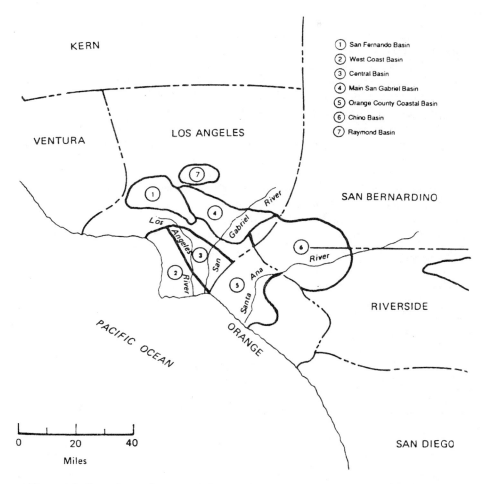

Figure 4.1. Groundwater basins underlying the south coastal plain in California. (Adapted from Lipson 1978.)

In a semiarid region such as Los Angeles, groundwater basins are extremely valuable when used in conjunction with surface supply systems. First, they are sources of inexpensive and high-quality water, as compared with the cost of importing water from long distances. In 1985, the Metropolitan Water District charged $240 per acre-foot (the volume of water that would cover one acre of land with one foot of water) as the wholesale price for imported water from northern California and from the Colorado River. The cost of pumping groundwater in the Los Angeles area averaged around

$134 per acre-foot—a saving of more than $100 per acre-foot. If the 282,458 acre-feet of groundwater that were pumped in 1985 from the three basins discussed in this chapter had been replaced with surface water, it would have cost the industrial users, the urban households, and the irrigators at least $28 million more per year.

The value of the basins as sources of water supply is overshadowed, however, by their even greater value as natural storage vessels that can retain water for use during periods of peak demand. Every surface-water system must have available some type of short-term storage so that it can rapidly meet the accelerated demands of water users that occur at regular intervals during each day and each week, and during the course of a year. The current construction costs for a water tower in the Los Angeles area average around $57,500 per acre-foot. The minimum amount of short-term storage recommended by the relevant engineering standards is 16% of the total water used in an area. In the area of the West Basin, with an annual demand for water of 327,435 acre-feet, storage reservoirs that could hold 52,400 acre-feet would be required if the basin were not available for this purpose. The replacement costs for this single basin would be about $3.01 billion. The loss of all the groundwater basins underlying the Los Angeles metropolitan area would be an economic disaster of major proportions.

Groundwater basins can be destroyed by overextraction and/or pollution. If more water is withdrawn per year than the average level of replenishment (referred to as the safe yield of a basin), eventually the gravel and sand in the water-bearing strata will compact so that they cannot hold as much water as they formerly did. If a groundwater basin is located near the ocean, and its water level is drawn down below sea level, saltwater intrusion will occur along the coast. Wells along the coastline must be abandoned. If intrusion is not halted, eventually the entire basin will no longer be usable as a source of supply of for its storage capacity. Over-extraction threatened all of the groundwater basins in this region until institutional changes were initiated by those most affected.

The logic of the water-rights game

Overextraction was the logical outcome of the way groundwater rights were defined prior to the institutional changes described in this chapter. Water rights in California had been defined on the basis of whether a producer owned the overlying land and used the water on that land (an overlying landowner) or used the water to serve areas other than land owned by the water producer (an appropriator). Under the common law, an overlying landowner held a riparian right to the "full flow" of the water supply underlying his or her land. In a region of extreme scarcity of water, the common law does not provide secure rights for an overlying landowner. Water underlying any parcel of land (e.g., parcel A) can be siphoned to a neighbor's land if the neighbor withdraws water more rapidly than does the owner of parcel A. In *Katz v. Walkinshaw* [141 Cal. 116, 74 P. 766 (1903)], the doctrine of "correlative rights" was developed to replace the strict interpretation of riparian rights. That doctrine held that in times of shortage, if the court was called on to adjudicate among competing interests, the court would treat all overlying owners as correlative and coequal owners. In times of scarcity, each would gain a *proportionate* share of the water rather than an *absolute* share of the water. That doctrine was modified somewhat in *San Bernardino v. Riverside* [186 Cal. 7 (1921)], in which overlying landowners were limited to taking only water that they could put to "beneficial" use.

Thus, overlying landowners facing only other overlying landowners knew that if they went to court to settle a dispute over water rights during a time of shortage, they would all share proportionately in any cutback in the total water available to them. In most groundwater basins, however, overlying landowners faced other water users called "appropriators," whose claim to water was on a different basis than that of an overlying landowner. Appropriators pumped groundwater to be used on land not owned by those withdrawing the water. Most private and public water companies were legally classified as appropriators, because the water they pumped was used by their customers, not by the water companies themselves. Nonoverlying landowners were allowed, if not encouraged, by the appropriative-rights doctrines made part of the statutory law in 1872 to withdraw "surplus water" or water that was not being put to beneficial use by the overlying landowners. The key elements in defining the rights of an appropriator had to do with

1. when the appropriator began to withdraw water from the source,
2. how much water was actually put to beneficial use, and
3. whether or not the use was continuous.

Under the doctrine of "first in time, first in right," appropriators acquired rights depending on their history of use. Among appropriators, a court-resolved conflict over a scarce supply would exclude use by the most junior appropriator, and then the next most junior appropriator, and so forth. The most senior appropriators would be fully protected against encroachment on their rights by more junior appropriators. However, the rights of the most senior appropriators were potentially subordinate to those of overlying landowners.

The simultaneous existence of the doctrines of correlative and appropriative rights in the same state introduced considerable uncertainty about the relative rights of one groundwater producer against others. The uncertainty was compounded by the presence of a third common-law doctrine that enabled groundwater producers to gain rights through "adverse use" or prescription. In regard to land, prescriptive rights are relatively straightforward: If one person occupied someone else's land in an open, notorious, and continuous manner for a set period of time (five years in California), and the owner makes no effort to eject the occupier, the original owner loses the right to the land.

In regard to groundwater, possession of water was not enough to establish open and *adverse* use. Any junior appropriator could legally use any water that was surplus water. Surplus water was defined as a part of the "safe yield" of a basin that was not of beneficial use to overlying landowners or senior appropriators. The safe yield of a basin is the average, long-term supply of water to the basin. If that quantity of water was put to beneficial use, no surplus was available to others. An appropriator had to take nonsurplus water openly and continuously for more than five years to perfect prescriptive rights. Once perfected, prescriptive rights were superior to those of overlying owners and appropriators. The same actions of an appropriator—openly taking water continuously from a basin—could lead to the acquisition of rights *superior* to those of overlying landowners or, alternatively, to the *inferior* rights of a junior appropriator relative to an overlying landowner in time of scarcity. The key difference between these outcomes was whether the court ruled that a surplus did or did not exist for the five-year period prior to litigation. Given that all producers suffered from lack of information concerning the safe yield of a basin and the pumping rates of other producers, no one knew at the time of making such decisions what the pumping rates were or whether or not a surplus existed.

The situation in these basins can be characterized as an open-access CPR [common pool resource] for which clear limits have not been established regarding who can withdraw how much water. In such situations, two strong pressures encourage pumpers to adopt inefficient strategies. The first is a pumping-cost externality. The second is a strategic externality. Pumping costs increase as the pumping lift increases, because of falling water levels, and therefore each person's withdrawals increase the pumping costs for others. No one bears the full cost of personal actions. Each pumper is consequently led toward overexploitation. The strategic externality involved in an open-access groundwater basin is aptly described by Negri.

> With property rights undefined and access nonexclusive, the "rule of capture" governs the "ownership" of the reserve stock. The rule of capture grants [pumpers] exclusive rights to that portion of the groundwater that they pump. What an operator does not withdraw today will be withdrawn, at least in part, by rival[s]. The fear that [pumpers] cannot capture tomorrow what they do not pump today undermines their incentive to forgo current pumping for future pumping.

The two incentives reinforce one another to aggravate the intensity of the pumping race. Without a change of institutions, pumpers in such a situation acting independently will severely overexploit the resource. Overexploitation can lead to destruction of the resource itself.

Current institutions affect not only the intensity of a pumping race but also the relative incentives of different participants to initiate institutional change. Given the legal structure of rights in California, overlying landowners were more motivated than appropriators to launch court action so as to keep appropriators from obtaining prescriptive rights. The decision about when to start litigation, however, involved high risks of being too soon or too late. The overlying owner faced two possibilities:

(1) If he went to court before all "surplus" water had been appropriated, and the court ruled that the water being diverted by the defendant was indeed surplus water, the overlying owner would suffer the costs of the litigation and receive no remedy;

(2) If he waited too long to go to court, the overlying owner might find that the defendant had perfected a prescriptive right if the court ruled that the water being diverted was non-surplus water. There was, in other words, no way for the overlying owner, on whom the burden of initiating litigation rested, to succeed in protecting his right until it had been invaded, and yet within a short time after the right had been invaded, the overlying owner would have lost the right he sought to protect due to prescription.

The uncertainty of the competing water doctrines was compounded by the uncertainty shared by all water producers about the actual supply of water to a basin and the quantity of water withdrawn by all of the parties. It was essential to know the quantities supplied and demanded from a basin to determine the presence or absence of a surplus. Both types of information were costly to obtain. Both could be obtained at the time of litigation by asking the court to appoint a watermaster to make a geologic survey of the basin and determine its water supply and to obtain information about the past water uses of all producers. When determined in this manner, the cost would be shared by all producers involved in the litigation. But that did not solve the problem of uncertainty prior to the initiation of litigation. In past cases, signs of potential problems—such as falling water tables—had not been accepted by the court as sufficient evidence of a water shortage to declare a lack of surplus and uphold the rights of overlying owners as against junior appropriators [*San Bernardino v. Riverside*, 186 Cal. 7 (1921)].

Given these compound uncertainties, it is easy to explain the behavior of groundwater pumpers in the Los Angeles metropolitan area during the first 50 years of this century. To obtain any kind of water right, one needed to show continuous withdrawal of water and application to beneficial use. In that environment of legal uncertainty, attorneys advised producers to pump as much as they needed and to defend later. A pumping race occurred in each of the groundwater basins underlying the Los Angeles area.

Given those incentives, many water producers and local government officials during the 1940s and 1950s worried that all of the basins would be severely overdrawn and that those basins located adjacent to the ocean— West Basin and Central Basin—would be lost to the sea. By the 1960s, however, the pumping race had been halted in all of the coastal basins. Water rights were eventually established in all the basins, except in Orange County, which continues to rely on a pump tax for regulations.

Special water districts have been established throughout the area to obtain surface water, to levy pump taxes on water productions, and to replenish the basins through a variety of artificial means. A series of injection wells has been constructed along the coast to create a barrier of fresh water against the sea, enabling the coastal districts to regulate the use of their basins in a manner similar to the use of a surface reservoir. In other words, diverse private and public actors have extricated themselves from the perversity of the pumping race and transformed the entire structure of the incentives they face. Public arenas were involved in many stages of these developments. The initial steps were taken in the shadow of a court order. Elections and public hearings were held at key stages. The solutions to the pumping race, however, were not imposed on the participants by external authorities. Rather, the participants used public arenas to *impose constraints on themselves*. Because litigation to gain defined water rights was involved in all of the basins, except in Orange County, we first discuss this strategy to transform the pumping race.

THE LITIGATION GAME

The Raymond Basin negotiations

The Raymond Basin is a small basin, with a surface area of 40 square miles, located inland and thus protected from saltwater intrusion. The area was already highly developed by the turn of the century. Later studies have revealed that the safe yield of the basin was steadily exceeded from 1913 onward. The cities of Pasadena, Sierra Madre, Arcadia, Altadena, La Cañada-Flintridge, South Pasadena, San Marino, and Monrovia are located on the surface of the basin. The city of Alhambra lies on its borders and appropriates water from the basin for use within its boundaries. The city of Pasadena was by far the largest producer of water from the basin—its production equaled the production of the other 30 producers combined.
* * *

The city of Pasadena for some years adopted the strategy of the dominant player in a privileged group. From 1914 to 1923, for example, the city replenished the basin by capturing floodwaters and spreading them on the gravel areas located at the feet of the San Gabriel Mountains. The water that percolated into the basin was then available for capture by the city of Pasadena as well as by other groundwater producers. In the late 1920s, the city of Pasadena was a leading participant in the formation of the Metropolitan Water District of Southern California, which would eventually construct an aqueduct to bring water 250 miles to the Los Angeles area from the Colorado River.

During the 1930s, however, the city of Pasadena was no longer willing to undertake independent actions that were substantially benefiting others who were not contributing to the costs. The city tried unsuccessfully to negotiate a voluntary settlement with the other producers whereby all producers would jointly reduce the amounts of water they were withdrawing from the basin. In 1937 Pasadena initiated legal proceedings against the city of Alhambra and 30 other producers. The case was referred to the Division of Water Resources of the California Department of Public Works for determination of the geologic structure of the basin, the safe yield of the basin, and whether or not there was a surplus.

That referral procedure was time-consuming and costly. The draft report of the referee was not completed until March of 1943 and cost about $53,000. The referee found that the yearly withdrawals from the basin were 29,400 acre-feet, whereas the safe yield of the basin was 21,900, leading to an annual overdraft of 7,500 acre-feet per year. The referee recommended that the parties curtail their pumping to the safe yield of the basin.

The parties then shared a single, authoritative "image" of the problem they faced. They also would confront a new "default condition" if they could not agree on their own solution. Prior to litigation, the failure to agree would simply mean a return to the pumping race. Once the court took jurisdiction, an absence of agreement would mean that the judge would decide which parties had to bear the brunt of the cutback. It was not at all clear what the judge would decide. The judge might, for example, assign preeminent rights to the overlying owners and then assign the remainder of the 21,900 acre-feet as a "surplus" to the appropriators to be apportioned according to their seniority. Or the judge might decide that there was no surplus. In that case, senior appropriators might be granted prescriptive rights, and overlying landowners would bear the major brunt of the cutback.

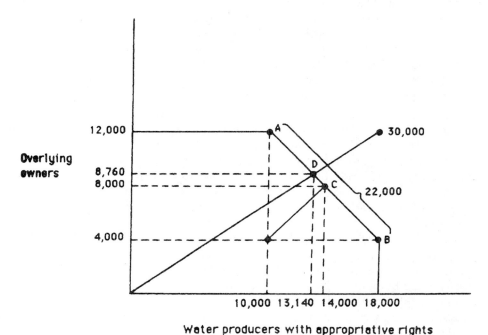

Figure 4.2. The bargaining situation faced by overlying owners and appropriators.

A simplified picture of the bargaining problem that the producers faced is shown in Figure 4.2. If we assume that the overlying owners were withdrawing 12,000 acre-feet and the appropriators (who might become prescriptors) were withdrawing 18,000 acre-feet, the total withdrawals prior to a decision would be 30,000 acre-feet. Everyone accepted the fact that a cutback to 22,000 acre-feet would occur. A worst-case analysis done by the overlying landowners would assume that the judge would declare that there had been no surplus for more than five years prior to litigation. Thus, the appropriators would be given superior rights to all that they had withdrawn. They would be assigned 18,000 acre-feet, leaving only 4,000 acre-feet for the overlying landowners. Point B marks the worst possible solution that the overlying owners could face.

Similarly, the appropriators could do a worst-case analysis and assume that the judge would assign firm rights of 12,000 acre-feet to the overlying landowners and then assign the "surplus" of 10,000 acre-feet to the appropriators according to their seniority. Point A is the worst possible solution from the perspective of the appropriators. For all participants, the range of variation between complete protection and major loss (the line connecting A and B) would be considerable. Further, a fully contested trial would last a long time, given the conflicting legal doctrines, and the costs of litigation would be extremely high.

At the instigation of the city of Pasadena, the parties held some serious negotiations in the shadow of the court. Within the six months they had drafted a stipulated agreement signed by all but 2 of the 32 parties involved in the litigation. The negotiation process was furthered in that instance by the unusual fact that one attorney, Kenneth Wright, represented 16 of the parties. After another six months, one of the holdouts also agreed to the stipulation. The other—the California–Michigan Land and Water Company—never agreed to the stipulation and challenged the final court decision based on the stipulation.

The signatories agreed that the safe yield had been exceeded for a long time and that it was necessary to cut back to the safe yield of the basin. They stated that each producer's withdrawal of groundwater had been open, continuous, and notorious and was, because of the overdraft, adverse to the claims of all of the others. Thus, each producer had prescribed against all of the others. The term "mutual prescription" has been used to describe the concept used by these parties as the foundation for their negotiated settlement. The signatory parties agreed to *share the cutback proportionately* instead of pursuing further legal procedures to determine whose rights took precedence. The proportional division of the cutback is represented by point D in Figure 4.2. They further guaranteed each other's proportional shares of the safe yield (if it were to change in the future) and established an arrangement to enable those most adversely affected by the cutback to obtain exchange rights from others willing to sell their rights on an annual basis.

A short trial was held to hear the objections of the California–Michigan Land and Water Company and to assign the Division of Water Resources of

the California Department of Public Works to serve as the watermaster—
an official monitor—to supervise the agreement. Rather than imposing his
own solution, the judge, after considerable reflection, issued a final judgment on December 23, 1944, based on the stipulated agreement. The final
judgment declared all of the decreed rights to be of equal standing in any
future dispute and enjoined all parties from taking more than their decreed
rights. The judgment continued the role of the watermaster to enforce the
provisions of the judgment and to supervise the exchange pool they had
developed. In addition to the leasing arrangements of the exchange pool,
decreed rights could be leased or sold outright so long as the transfers were
recorded by the watermaster. Two-third of the costs of the watermaster
were to be paid for by the parties, and the state of California would pay for
the remaining costs of monitoring the agreement. The case was appealed to
the California Supreme Court, and the decision was upheld. The United
States Supreme Court declined to review the case.

By negotiating their own agreement, the parties had ended the pumping race faster and at a lower cost than they could have through a court
proceeding. They also had gained firm and marketable rights to defined
shares of the safe yield of the basin. A market for those water rights
developed, and most of the smaller right-holders have sold their rights to
the water companies, for whom the rights have a higher value. There are
now 17 active producers from the basin, and they are almost all municipal
or private water companies. Only three overlying landowners continue to
produce water from the basin. The areas within the basin that did not have
access to imported water formed a municipal water corporation in 1953 and
started receiving imported water in 1955.

      * * *

Conformance of parties to negotiated settlements

Forty-five years have passed since the judgment was entered in the
Raymond Basin case, and 35 and 27 years have passed since the interim
agreements were signed in West Basin and in Central Basin. Thus, the
parties to these three agreements have had many occasions to decide
whether or not to comply. Given the value of groundwater, the temptation
not to comply must have been relatively great for all producers at one time
or another in the combined 107 years of water use that have elapsed.
However, the level of infractions has been insignificant during that time.

The watermaster in each basin has extensive monitoring and sanction-
ing authority. Monitoring activities are obvious and public. Every year,
each party reports total groundwater extractions and receives a report
listing the groundwater extractions of all other parties (or anyone else who
has started to pump). The reliability of these records is high. Several
agencies cross-check the records. The watermaster is authorized to cali-
brate all meters, thereby reducing the probability of one form of cheating.
Given the accuracy of the information and its ease of access, each pumper
knows what everyone else is doing, and each knows that his or her own
groundwater extractions will be known by all others. Thus, the information

available to the parties closely approximates "common knowledge," so frequently a necessary assumption for solutions to [repeat player situations].

Instead of perceiving itself as an active policing agency, the watermaster service tries to be a neutral, monitoring agency. Because anyone who possesses a legal water right can initiate a court action to enforce compliance to the judgments, the watermaster does not need to initiate punitive actions against nonconformers. As expressed by an official of the watermaster service in 1960,

> it is our policy not to take any affirmative actions against any party since this would place us in the position of being an active party in the action. Our policy has been to inform the active parties of any infringements and leave affirmative action up to them. We want to stay as neutral as possible in order to gain as much voluntary cooperation as possible.

In the early years of the West Basin agreement, for example, the Moneta Water Company began to withdraw more than its allocation. After a couple of years, it was obvious that the overextractions were not accidental. In addition to listing Moneta's annual withdrawals in the tabular material included in all reports, the watermaster devoted several pages in an annual report to the recent activities of the company. The company began to comply with the judgment soon after the publication of those facts. Other than a few isolated incidents, handled in the same manner, the original litigants have complied with the curtailments without formal sanctions being imposed. Even the city of Hawthorne has curtailed its withdrawals to the stipulated amounts of the final judgment. It was been necessary, however, to initiate legal action against new pumpers who have attempted to withdraw groundwater without first purchasing water rights. Charges have been filed and defendants enjoined from groundwater production other than under the rights they eventually acquired by purchase.

The levels of quasi-voluntary compliance with the final judgments in all of these court decisions have been extremely high. Although each pumper might be tempted from time to time to withdraw more water than legally allowed, each pumper wants total withdrawals from the basin constrained so that access to the storage and flow values of the resource will be continued over the long run. Given the active, reliable, and neutral monitoring of the watermaster service, no pumper can expect to overextract without everyone else learning about any noncompliance at the end of the next water year. Because everyone is organized and communicating with one another about joint strategies, continued noncompliance is likely to bring legal sanctions, as well as loss of reputation and the application of informal sanctions. Because a pumper is constrained, and almost all pumpers voluntarily agreed to the initial allocation of rights, the basic system is perceived to be fair by most participants. Further, participants continue to have control over the monitoring system to ensure that it continues to be active, fair and reliable. Two-thirds of the watermaster's budget is paid for by those possessing water rights, and they can petition the court to appoint a different watermaster if they are not satisfied with performance.

    * * *

THE ANALYSIS OF INSTITUTIONAL SUPPLY

[I] have described several efforts to solve second-order collective dilemmas. A pumping race is the first-order dilemma facing pumpers from a groundwater basin where legal rights to withdraw water are not limited. Each pumper has a dominant strategy to pump as much water as is privately profitable and to ignore the long-term consequences on water levels and quality. The experience in all of these groundwater basins illustrates how a pumping race can continue for many years, even though water levels fall (raising everyone's costs of lifting water) and salt water intrudes (threatening the long-run survival of the basin itself). Overdraft conditions continued for several decades in these basins. The best explanation for the actions and outcomes during that period is that individuals caught in a pumping race will select their dominant strategy to pump as much as is privately profitable and ignore the consequence for themselves and others.

Given the initial empirical support for this prediction, it is easy to see why theorists would also predict that individuals caught in such situations would refrain from investing resources in designing, negotiating, and supplying new institutions. If pumpers will not limit their groundwater production, why should they invest in the provision of new institutions? The effort to supply institutions is described as simply a second-order dilemma that is no more solvable than the first-order dilemma. The prediction that appropriators will not expend resources to supply new institutions is, however not supported by these case studies.

These groundwater pumpers invested heavily in the supply of institutions. They created new private associations. They paid for costly litigation to allocate water rights. They drafted legislation, had it introduced to the state legislature, and gained sufficient support from other water enterprises to get the legislation passed. They created special districts to tax all the water they withdrew from the basins, as well as the property overlying the area. They spent seemingly endless hours informing themselves abut the structures of their basins, the various concerns and intentions of all parties, and future possibilities.

Incremental, sequential, and self-transforming institutional change in a facilitative political regime

The substantial investments that these groundwater pumpers made in providing new institutions occurred in an incremental and sequential process in the state of California—a home-rule state—where many state-wide institutional facilities are provided to reduce the costs of local institutional supply. The investment in institutional change was not made in a single step. Rather, the process of institutional change in all basins involved many small steps that had low initial costs. Rarely was it necessary for participants to move simultaneously without knowing what others were doing. Because the process was incremental and sequential and early successes were achieved, intermediate benefits from the initial investments were realized before anyone needed to make larger investments. Each institutional change transformed the structure of incentives within which future strategic decisions would be made.

Further, because the appropriators from several neighboring basins were all involved in similar problems, participants in one setting could learn from the experiences of those in similar settings. Sufficient overlap existed among participants across basins to ensure communication about results. Interbasin coordinating arenas were created at several junctures to enhance the ability to exchange information about agreements reached within and across basin boundaries.

In each basin, a voluntary association was established to provide a forum for face-to-face discussions about joint problems and potential joint strategies. Given the uncertain legal structure, attorneys advising water companies and public utilities had consistently advised their clients to pump as much water as they could profitably use and worry about defending their water rights later. The provision of a forum for discussion transformed the structure of the situation from one in which decisions were made independently without knowing what others were doing to a situation in which individuals discussed their options with one another. Discussion by itself was not sufficient to change the pumping strategies of the participants, but discussion did lead to the initiation of litigation, which enabled the participants to reach an enforceable agreement to limit their water withdrawals. Further, the voluntary associations provided a mechanism for obtaining information about the physical structure of the basins to be made available to all pumpers simultaneously. Prior to that investment in information, no one had a clear picture of the boundaries, demand patterns, and water levels throughout the basin. One knew only that the water levels in one's own wells were falling. No one knew the extent of saltwater intrusion or the total quantity of water withdrawn from the basin. The private associations provided a mechanism for sharing the costs and the results of expensive technical studies. By voluntarily sharing the costs of providing information—a public good—participants learned that it was possible to accomplish some joint objectives by voluntary, cooperative action. The membership dues for the associations were modest and were allocated in rough proportion to the amount of water an enterprise withdrew from a basin. By spending time to attend meetings, members gained considerable information about the condition of their basins and the likelihood that others would commit themselves to follow different strategies in the future.

Whereas the voluntary associations provide a mechanism for sharing costs, the state of California provides facilities that help reduce the level of those costs. Maintaining a court system in which individuals have standing to initiate litigation in order to develop firm and transferable rights to a defined quantity of water is one such contribution. The state of California goes even further and subsidizes one-third of the cost of such litigation in order to encourage full exploitation of water resources and settle disputes over water rights when necessary. The Department of Water Resources has provided technical assistance throughout the period, as has the U.S. Geological Survey.

The general home-rule tradition that is built into the state constitution and legislative practices in the state also helps reduce the costs of transforming existing rule systems. It is relatively easy for a group of individuals to introduce new organic legislation authorizing a new type of special district, but state legislators will rarely support such proposed legislation when there is substantial opposition to it in the state. But when individuals in one area have discussed such proposals with others who are likely to be affected, organic laws frequently are passed with close to unanimous support.

---

1. How would you characterize the nature of the resource in this case study? How would you characterize the culture of the surrounding communities?

2. Recall Hardin's description of the "tragedy of the commons," *supra* pp. 17–19. Why didn't Hardin's dire predictions of overuse destroy the common property resource at issue in this case study? Are the informal allocation rules that developed in the Los Angeles area reasonably efficient? Would a more formal system of rules be more efficient? Is it likely that a court or formal political institutions would produce a more efficient rule in practice? What factors might impair these institutions in addressing the commons problem? *Cf.* Menell, Institutional Fantasylands: From Scientific Management to Free Market Environmentalism, 15 Harv. J. L. & Pub. Pol'y 489 (1992); Menell, The Limitations of Legal Institutions for Addressing Environmental Risks, 5 J. Econ. Persp., Summer 1991, at 93.

3. What are the key factors enabling social communities to solve commons problems without the need for formal legal rules? Ostrom describes numerous case studies—addressing in-shore fisheries, surface water irrigation institutions, and mountain pastures—in which communities have banded together to address common resource problems. On the basis of these studies, she offers the following set of design principles for sustainable voluntary allocation organizations:

1. *Clearly Defined Boundaries*—Individuals or households who have rights to withdraw resource units from the CPR [common pool resource] must be clearly defined, as must the boundaries of the CPR itself.

2. *Congruence Between Appropriation and Provision Rules and Local Conditions*—Appropriation rules restricting time, place, technology, and/or quantity of resource units are related to local conditions and to provision rules requiring labor, material, and/or money.

3. *Collective–Choice Arrangements*—Most individuals affected by the operational rules can participate in modifying the operational rules.

4. *Monitoring*—Monitors, who actively audit CPR conditions and appropriator behavior, are accountable to the appropriators or are the appropriators.

5. *Graduated Sanctions*—Appropriators who violate operational rules are likely to be assessed graduated sanctions (depending on the seriousness and context of the offense) by other appropriators, by officials accountable to these appropriators, or both.

6. *Conflict–Resolution Mechanisms*—Appropriators and their officials have rapid access to low-cost local arenas to resolve conflicts among appropriators or between appropriators and officials.

7. *Minimal Recognition of Rights to Organize*—The rights of appropriators to devise their own institutions are not challenged by external governmental authorities.

Ostrom, Governing the Commons 90 (1990). How well do these principles apply to the groundwater case study? Cattle range in Shasta County?

4.   Under what circumstances will social groups produce norms that maximize the society's well-being? What factors might undermine the development of efficient norms in practice? Compare R. Ellickson, Order Without Law 167–83 (1991) (arguing that efficient norms emerge in closely-knit groups); R. Ellickson, Property in Land, 102 Yale L.J. 1315, 1320–21 (1993) (same) with Posner, Law, Economics, and Inefficient Norms, 144 U. Penn. L. Rev. 1697 (1996) (questioning the efficiency of norms emanating from closely knit groups).

―――――――――

Many informal governance structures develop on the basis of geographical considerations. The commons problem associated with the subsurface water in the Los Angeles area formed a common bond for those affected by that resource, *i.e.,* those residing in areas affected by the resource problem. Other social forces serve to bring together social groups, including ethnic background, migration patterns, and economic relations. Consider the following description of the range of informal economic/social groups in society and how they are brought together:

Eric Posner, The Regulation of Groups: The Influence of Legal and Nonlegal Sanctions on Collective Action

63 University of Chicago Law Review 133, 165–168 (1996).

"Informal economic groups" or "trade groups" are solidary groups, sometimes but not always based on ethnicity, devoted to obtaining economic or commercial benefits for their members. I use the term broadly to include all sorts of loosely structured associations, such as networks of ongoing business relationships governed by their own norms.

An example comes from the experience of Japanese immigrants and their descendants on the west coast of the United States. When the first immigrants from Japan arrived in the nineteenth century,

> [t]heir opportunities for employment were severely restricted. Japanese immigrants were denied citizenship rights and therefore could not lodge complaints against discrimination. New immigrants were forced to take jobs wherever they could get them, and the fact that fellow ethnics offered them an opportunity to establish themselves was bound to produce loyalty. Societal hostility and concentration in small business thus mutually reinforced one another.

These immigrants thus formed solidary associations to protect themselves against discrimination by natives; when the natives reacted by hostilely accusing immigrants of being clannish, the immigrants responded by withdrawing even more. Because these immigrants depended heavily on each other for mutual protection, opportunism was very rare. As a result,

> [the] immigrant businesses, dependent upon precapitalist-type bonds of ethnic loyalty, were not only able to survive but could actually thrive within capitalist society. This paradox is resolved by the fact that under certain circumstances, notably in marginal fields of endeavor, noncontractual relations can be less expensive and more efficient than formal contractual ones.

Numerous kin-based networks and ethnicity-based organizations provided contacts, rooms, credit, aid, dispute mediation, and other advantages that ultimately allowed more recent Japanese immigrants and their immediate descendants to dominate certain sectors of the economy—farming, laundries, and grocery stores—and attain an above-average standard of living. In this way a solidary group, because of discrimination against its members, can obtain transactional economies that offset the economic cost of the discrimination.

Other relations besides ethnicity and other hurdles besides social hostility provide incentives to join solidary associations. All economic actors who have continuing relations develop informal methods to monitor behavior, mediate disputes, and apply nonlegal sanctions. Macaulay's well known study, for example, addresses the relations of manufacturers and their customers. Other studies analyze the relations—some related to ethnicity, some not—among actors in the garment industry; consumers and manufacturers of automobiles; residents of cattle country; diamond traders; domestic workers; commercial landlords and tenants; contractors and subcontractors; and members of trade associations. Indeed, the relational contract literature focuses on the continuing relations among economic actors on the ground that such relations are far more common than the one-shot deals assumed by traditional contract law analysis and neoclassical economics.

Other less explicitly business-oriented groups provide members with insurance, contacts, training, political power, capital, and other advantages. These groups allow members to achieve economic success despite the hostility of the larger population. Although recent studies have concentrated on voluntary economic and social associations among blacks, Japanese, Koreans, Chinese, Indians, and other minority ethnic groups, these groups are simply the modern versions of the mutual aid and other voluntary societies created by Polish, Jewish, German, Swedish, Italian, and Irish immigrants (as well as blacks) in the nineteenth century and (sometimes) poorer versions of the social clubs and old boys' networks that continue to facilitate business relations among the mostly white, Protestant, upper-middle class today.

In all of these groups, solidarity creates relatively effective methods for disciplining members who engage in bad-faith conduct. The ubiquity of these groups supports the commonplace notion that group membership is an important element of economic success. It also raises the intriguing possibility that * * * state intervention to promote these groups could have socially beneficial effects.

———————

1.   To what extent should the formal law foster the formation, empowerment, and development of tightly knit communities? What laws and policies would further this objective?

2.   What drawbacks do you see to the pursuit of such an objective? What limitations should be placed on such efforts?

C.   THE EMERGENCE OF STABLE INSTITUTIONS IN THE FACE OF MINIMAL FORMAL PROPERTY RIGHTS: THE CREATION AND ENFORCEMENT OF NON-STATUTORY INTELLECTUAL PROPERTY RIGHTS

As reflected in the prior case study, social processes can, under the proper conditions, solve externality and collective action problems through the development of hybrid property rights consortia. These consortia deal with the establishment of informal entitlements and the enforcement of such rights. Enforcement of rights is often critical to the success of informal means of addressing the problems created by common property resources. The power of collective action can be particularly important in addressing enforcement problems. The following materials describe the evolution of hybrid social institutions that developed to protect areas of intellectual creativity that do not fall squarely within statutory forms of intellectual property.

Robert P. Merges, Contracting Into Liability Rules: Intellectual Property Rights and Collective Rights Organizations

84 California Law Review 1293, 1361–71 (1996).

* * *

III.   Emergence of Exchange Institutions in the Absence of Property Rights

* * * I have identified five private IPR [intellectual property rights] systems: the Hollywood "script registry" run by the Writers Guild of America, employee idea submission/compensation (*i.e.*, "suggestion box") programs, informal know-how trading among certain manufacturing firms, the voluntary fashion design protection schemes initiated by several women's fashion industries in the 1930s (subsequently struck down by the Supreme Court), and computer shareware [computer software which "sellers" make available through catalogues and over the Internet for free, in exchange for payment on the honor system if the user finds it useful].* * * There are undoubtedly other institutions that perform a similar function * * *

A.   Fashion Guilds of the 1930s

In 1932, fifteen manufacturers of expensive women's dresses [those selling for $22.50 and up] organized the Fashion Originators' Guild of America. Guild members agreed to register original designs, which were (and are) *not* protected by patent or copyright law, with the Guild's "Registration bureau," and to refrain from copying other members' designs. Moreover, each Guild members agreed to impose a "declaration of cooperation" on all retailers who sold the member's dresses. In the declaration retailers agreed not to sell copies of any clothing designs registered by the Guild. The agreements signed by retailers also called for an elaborate system of arbitrated dispute resolution, administered by industry insiders, which included a right of appeal. The Guild engaged in extensive policing activities, sending "detectives" to retail stores throughout the country. When a violation was detected and duly prosecuted, the Guild assessed fines, which appeared to be substantial in some cases.

By 1936 the Guild had extended its range considerably. Eligibility was expanded to include all firms selling dresses at $3.75 and up; membership grew from the original fifteen manufacturers to 176, and about 12,000 retailers had signed up. In 1936 Guild members sold over 38% of all women's garments wholesaling for $6.75 or more, and more than 60% of those at $10.75 and above. A parallel set of agreements with producers of textiles was put in place, under which textile producers agreed to sell their products only to manufacturers in the Guild. The Guild was so successful it spawned a copy of its own: Millinery Creators' Guild, Inc., organized to protect women's hat designs.

In addition to protecting members against the copying of their original designs, the Guild restricted members' advertising, prohibited door-to-door sales, coordinated days for special sales, and, most damaging from the antitrust perspective, put a ceiling on members' discounts to retailers. In 1941 the Supreme Court found that the Guild violated the Sherman Act by restricting competition in the women's garment industry.

Putting aside its anticompetitive practices, especially price fixing, the organization in *Fashion Originators' Guild* encouraged originality, eliminated copied items from retail shelves, and raised the price to consumers. The only differences between the Guild and a formal IPR were (1) the fact that the Guild was based on an informal, inter-industry quasi-property right, rather than a formal statutory right; (2) the Guild required concerted action to achieve *any* appropriability, as opposed to the institutions described earlier, which were formed to *enhance* the appropriability of right holders; and (3) the Guild concentrated its enforcement efforts at the retail level, by requiring retailers to sign contracts and by policing retailers rather than targeting competing manufacturers.

Despite its similarity to formal IPR systems, the Guild was condemned out of hand by the Supreme Court. Yet some recent theory on optimal property rights suggests that, at times, enforcement via "internal" governance can be more cost-effective than granting or clarifying formal property rights.

Arguably, then, the Court should have bifurcated the issues in the *Fashion Guild* case, condemning practices such as price fixing, but remanding the case with instructions to find facts regarding the efficacy and economic impact of the basic anti-copying arrangement. * * *

The Guild did not restrict entry in either manufacturing or retailing. It did not dominate the industry: non-members sold 62% of the dresses that sold for $6.75 or more, and 40% of those that sold for $10.75 or more. Presumably non-members also sold the vast bulk of dresses selling for *less than* $6.75. The Guild had sewn up (so to speak) exclusive outlets in the retail market, but this merely formalized the market segmentation that presumably existed to some degree already. Indeed, the same pattern of retail affiliation could easily be achieved by alternative, and arguably legal, vertical restraints. One might even characterize Guild membership as serving a "group trademark" or product quality-designation function, making the retail agreements look somewhat like franchise contracts. By the same token, individual trademarks (in the form of designer "labels") no doubt allowed at least well-established designers some added appropriability beyond that offered by Guild membership. To the same effect is the fact that lead-time advantages can also be effective as a way to appropriate returns in faddish industries. These features do not argue against the need for the Guild; indeed, the fact that firms invested in its creation suggests the opposite.

The Guild reflected a rare mixture of collective action and alternative appropriability mechanisms, which, taken together, obviated the need for formal property rights. The singularity of the conditions under which the Guild flourished refutes the argument that we should expect similar alliances to substitute for all formal intellectual property rights.

B. The Hollywood Script Market

Television and movie scripts are often written by freelancers not under contract with a studio or production company. These writers must submit the scripts if they are to be evaluated for purchase. Submission of scripts, however, is fraught with peril. Copyright protection does not extend to many basic elements of plot and character. Additionally, although numerous common law doctrines occasionally supply an effective theory of recovery for "idea theft," they are applied too unevenly to give much comfort to the professional scriptwriter. Consequently, it is difficult (and of course, expensive) to enforce rights in these aspects of a script, which creates a serious risk of illicit misappropriation. Firms receiving unsolicited scripts face the opposite problem: the risk of a lawsuit every time a movie or TV show bears even a passing resemblance to an unsolicited script which was received sometime in the past.

The Writer's Guild of America, West (WGA), developed a "Script Registry" to lower both these risks. For a fee, writers can deposit a copy of a script they are going to submit with the Registry, which date-stamps it and stores it for five years. The system protects script writers when they submit the manuscript to others: the WGA will testify, if necessary, as to the date of submission, thereby preventing script theft. The WGA receives 30,000 submissions annually and has 150,000 or more scripts on file at any time. The Registry also operates a proven arbitration service that resolves more than 300 cases each year; very few cases go beyond this tribunal to court.

The enhanced enforcement function of the Registry obviously broadens the market for scripts. For certain scripts whose *ex ante* value is low, and which therefore could not justify the higher transaction costs which would attend an individually-negotiated submission contract, the Registry actually *creates* a market. The writers see the advantage of the system:

> "You get a little sense of security that your ideas are somewhat protected," said [one] writer who estimated this was his 20th trip to the registration office. "At least it provides a bit of ammunition in case questions of authorship come up."

> John Bowton ... was at the guild's offices to register an episode for Fox TV's "The Simpsons" that he wrote in the hope of selling to the cartoon's producers.

> "I always feel that if I put the WGA [Registration] number on it, it's like a little shield, like the sign of the cross keeping the vampire away.... This way, they know it's on record and it's the best thing to prove that you came up with the story."

In addition, it should be noted that scriptwriters are part of a fairly close-knit industry with many repeat-play features. These, factors make informal dispute resolution, and the Registry institution itself, run more smoothly. Indeed, WGA membership requirements are structured so as to screen out non-repeat players. To join, a writer must either be employed by a film or television studio that subscribes to the Guild's standard agreement, or have sold at least one script of substantial value. Many producers and studios go further, requiring that all scripts be submitted through literary agents who are themselves WGA members. Another telltale sign that script writers form a close-knit community is that informal sanctions—of the form "you'll never eat lunch in this town again"—are quite effective. Finally, the widespread acceptance of expert arbitration panels in the industry bolsters the impression of a system of shared information and norms.

One alternative to the script registry, "vertical integration" in the form of hiring script writers as employees, is hardly a perfect substitute. Many writers almost surely produce better work as freelancers, a situation that provides them complete freedom to shape their work environment and creative process. It is also no doubt very difficult to pre-identify potentially productive script writers, manage them, and monitor their output. Finally, the "personal service" contracts necessary to bind employee-writers would face serious enforcement problems in the courts. If an employee scriptwriter thought she had hit upon a "blockbuster," she would almost surely quit the company and claim to have developed the idea on her own, rather than allow the employer to reap the lion's share of profits. For all these reasons the script registry may be said to add value by conserving on transaction costs.

C.   Weak (or Absent) Property Rights and the New Institutionalism

[In a series of articles,[19] economists Avner Greif, Paul Milgrom and Barry Weingast describe the Maghribi traders, a tightknit group of Jewish overseas agents who represented Mediterranean merchants in eleventh century trade. In their telling, these traders were more than an ethnic group with a common occupation; they were an economic institution for facilitating trade:

> To reap the benefit of employing overseas agents, an institution was required to enable the agents to commit to act on behalf of the merchants.... [T]he "Maghribi traders" managed their agency relations by forming a coalition whose membership ostracized and retaliated against agents who violated their commercial code. Interrelated contractual arrangements motivated merchants to participate in the collective retaliation against agents who had cheated, and close community ties assured that each member had the necessary information to participate in sanctions when necessary.]

Both the Maghribi guild and the Fashion Originators' Guild were organized to overcome opportunism and high enforcement costs. Because both institutions were organized to reduce transaction costs, we should not be surprised to discover that the two organizations share many common

---

19. [Avner Greif, Reputation and Coalitions in Medieval Trade: Evidence on the Maghribi Traders, 49 J. Econ. Hist. 857 (1989); Paul R. Milgrom, Douglass C. North, and Barry Weingast, The Role of Institutions in the Revival of Trade: The Medieval Law Merchant, Private Judges, and the Champagne Fairs, 2 Econ. And Politics 1 (1990); Avner Greig, Contract Enforceability and Economic Institutions in Early Trade: The Maghribi Traders Coalition, 83 Am. Econ. Rev. 525 (1993); Avner Greif, Paul Milgrom, and Barry R. Weingast, Coordination, Commitment, and Enforcement: The Case of the Merchant Guild, 102 J. Pol. Econ. 745 (1994).]

features in their internal logic and operation. Most importantly for our purposes, both employed *group* boycotts to enforce their rules. Collective enforcement was necessary in the context of Medieval trade where "the maximum punishment imposed by an individual merchant is not sufficient to enable the agent to commit himself. . . ."

It is not incidental that informal norms * * * function best where they are run by a close-knit group of experts with shared understandings of the technology, industry, and entitlements structure. The same story can be told about the Fashion Guild: withholding from a retailer an individual line of dresses, sold by a single manufacturer, was an insufficient sanction because the market provided plenty of good substitutes. An individual line was unlikely to be so profitable that a retailer would agree not to sell copies. But the *collective* threat—to cut off access to the entire "high end" of the dress market—was a far greater sanction. The threat of exclusion from a significant portion of a substantial market segment would increase the likelihood of compliance. The Fashion Guild was apparently successful in resolving this problem: witness that 12,000 retailers had joined the Fashion Guild by the mid–1930s.

There are other similarities between the trading and fashion guilds: (1) a private code of conduct, with informal but escalating sanctions; (2) initial operation within a relatively small social unit; and (3) the ability to enforce the code of conduct effectively due to tractable monitoring conditions and shared access to information.

Finally, monopoly rents may have figured significantly in the Maghribi trade guilds, serving as an incentive for members to remain in the coalition. These rents made credible the coalition's promises to stick together in protecting foreign merchants against expropriation by local political rulers.

The above comparison of these two institutions—widely separated in time and space demonstrates that there are common dynamics that encourage the formation and successful operation of institutions. Institutions for IPR transactions are simply one modern variant on a very old theme.

Recognizing the relationship of IPR institutions to a whole family of institutions, we can draw on Robert Cooter's theory that describes when the state should codify or ratify norms that have emerged organically from repeated interactions in a commercial community:

> The court can benefit business and improve its efficiency by enforcing its norms against violators. The role of the state in a decentralized legal system is to elevate appropriate social norms to the level of law. Elevating a social norm to the level of law involves issuing an authoritative statement of the norm and backing it with the state's coercive power. The "adjudication of social norms" describes the process by which officials decide which social norms to elevate to the level of law.
>
> I envision three steps in adjudicating business norms. First, lawmakers should identify the actual norms that have arisen in business communities. A norm exists in a community when there

is a consensus about what its members ought to do ... Second, lawmakers should identify the incentive structures that produced the norms. Identifying the incentive structure requires constructing a model that characterizes the norm as an equilibrium in a game and testing the model against the facts. Third, the efficiency of the incentive structure should be evaluated using analytical tools from economics. When the incentive structure is efficient, the social norm imposes an obligation to follow a cooperative strategy that results in repeated transactions. Furthermore, the payoff sets are convex, and the effects of the obligatory strategy do not spill over beyond the community in which the norm arose. Those business norms that arise from an efficient incentive structure should be enforced by the state.[20]

1. What conditions favor the formation and stability of informal groups and trade associations to address the appropriability problems associated with creative intellectual work?

2. Do these case studies argue for less intellectual property protection through formal legal institutions? In a 1970 law review article, Professor (now Justice) Stephen Breyer questioned the need for formal legal protection for many works protected by copyright law on the grounds that such protection had monopoly costs and that alternative means of appropriating returns existed. Breyer, The Uneasy Case for Copyright: A Study of Copyright in Books, Photocopies, and Computer Programs, 84 Harv. L. Rev. 281 (1970). He argued that lead time advantages and the role of book clubs, which sponsor authors by disseminating special early-release editions to club members, would address the appropriation problem faced by authors. Would such advantages, without formal legal protection, be sufficient to protect authors' intellectual efforts in writing books today? *See* Merges, Contracting into Liability Rules: Intellectual Property Rights and Collective Rights Organizations, 84 Cal. L. Rev. 1293, 1371–73 (1996); Tyerman, The Economic Rationale for Copyright Protection for Published Books: A Reply to Professor Breyer, 18 UCLA L. Rev. 1100 (1971).

3. To what extent should courts and legislatures defer to informal intellectual property rights institutions in recognizing and adjudicating intellectual property rights? To the contrary, should courts recognize only those forms of intellectual property expressly created by federal statute? *Cf. Bonito Boats v. Thunder Craft Boats*, 489 U.S. 141, 109 S.Ct. 971, 103 L.Ed.2d 118 (1989) (striking down a state-created intellectual property regime for protecting the design of ship hulls as preempted by federal patent law). *See generally* R. Merges, P. Menell, M. Lemley, & T. Jorde, Intellectual Property in the New Technological Age, Ch. 6 (1997).

20. Robert D. Cooter, Structural Adjudication and the New Law Merchant: A Model of Decentralized Law, 14 Int'l Rev. L. & Econ. 215, 226 (1994).

D.   The Interaction of Social Norms and Formal Legal Rules: Photocopying of Copyrighted Materials

Social norms and institutions interact in important and interesting ways with formal legal institutions. They play significant roles in defining the social problems to be addressed and in supplying solutions for courts, legislatures, and regulatory agencies. This case study looks at how the social norms that have developed around a common practice—photocopying of scholarly articles for research purposes—ultimately played a critical role in the interpretation of copyright law.

Williams & Wilkins Company v. United States

United States Court of Claims, 1973.
203 Ct.Cl. 74, 487 F.2d 1345 (en banc), *aff'd by equally divided Court*, 420 U.S. 376, 95 S.Ct. 1344, 43 L.Ed.2d 264 (1975).

■ Davis, Judge:

* * * Plaintiff Williams & Wilkins Company, a medical publisher, charges that the Department of Health, Education, and Welfare, through the National Institutes of Health (NIH) and the National Library of Medicine (NLM), has infringed plaintiff's copyrights in certain of its medical journals by making unauthorized photocopies of articles from those periodicals. Modern photocopying in its relation to copyright spins off troublesome problems.* * *

I

Plaintiff, though a relatively small company, is a major publisher of medical journals and books. It publishes 37 journals, dealing with various medical specialties. The four journals in suit are *Medicine, Journal of Immunology, Gastroenterology,* and *Pharmacological Reviews. Medicine* is published by plaintiff for profit and for its own benefit. The other three journals are published in conjunction with specialty medical societies which, by contract, share the journals' profits with plaintiff. The articles published in the journals stem from manuscripts submitted to plaintiff (or one of the medical societies) by physicians or other scientists engaged in medical research. The journals are widely disseminated throughout the United States (and the world) in libraries, schools, physicians' offices, and the like. Annual subscription prices range from about $12 to $44; and, due to the esoteric nature of the journals' subject matter, the number of annual subscriptions is relatively small, ranging from about 3,100 (*Pharmacological Reviews*) to about 7,000 (*Gastroenterology*). Most of the revenue derived from the journals comes from subscription sales, though a small part comes from advertising. * * *

NIH, the Government's principal medical research organization, is a conglomerate of institutes located on a multiacre campus at Bethesda, Maryland. Each institute is concerned with a particular medical specialty, and the institutes conduct their activities by way of both intramural research and grants-in-aid to private individuals and organizations. NIH employs over 12,000 persons—4,000 are science professionals and 2,000 have doctoral degrees. To assist its intramural programs, NIH maintains a technical library. The library houses about 150,000 volumes, of which about 30,000 are books and the balance scientific (principally medical) journals. The library is open to the public, but is used mostly by NIH in-house research personnel. The library's budget for 1970 was $1.1 million; of this about $85,000 was for the purchase of journal materials.

The NIH library subscribes to about 3,000 different journal titles, four of which are the journals in suit. The library subscribes to two copies of each of the journals involved. As a general rule, one copy stays in the library reading room and the other copy circulates among interested NIH personnel. Demand by NIH research workers for access to plaintiff's journals (as well as other journals to which the library subscribes) is usually not met by in-house subscription copies. Consequently, as an integral part of its operation, the library runs a photocopy service for the benefit of its research staff. On request, a researcher can obtain a photocopy of an article from any of the journals in the library's collection. Usually, researchers request photocopies of articles to assist them in their on-going projects; sometimes photocopies are requested simply for background reading. The library does not monitor the reason for requests or the use to which the photocopies are put. The photocopies are not returned to the library; and the record shows that, in most instances, researchers keep them in their private files for future reference.

The library's policy is that, as a rule, only a single copy of a journal article will be made per request and each request is limited to about 40 to 50 pages, though exceptions may be, and have been, made in the case of long articles, upon approval of the Assistant Chief of the library branch. Also, as a general rule, requests for photocopying are limited to only a single article from a journal issue. Exceptions to this rule are routinely made, so long as substantially less than an entire journal is photocopied, *i.e.*, less than about half of the journal. Coworkers can, and frequently do, request single copies of the same article and such requests are honored.

Four regularly assigned employees operate the NIH photocopy equipment. The equipment consists of microfilm cameras and Xerox copying machines. In 1970, the library photocopy budget was $86,000 and the library filled 85,744 requests for photocopies of journal articles (including plaintiff's journals), constituting about 930,000 pages. On the average, a journal article is 10 pages long, so that, in 1970, the library made about 93,000 photocopies of articles.

NLM, located on the Bethesda campus of NIH, was formerly the Armed Forces Medical Library. In 1956, Congress transferred the library from the Department of Defense to the Public Health Service (renaming it the National Library of Medicine), and declared its purpose to be "* * * to aid the dissemination and exchange of scientific and other information important to the progress of medicine and to the public health * * *." 42 U.S.C. § 275 (1970). NLM is a repository of much of the world's medical literature, in essence a "librarians' library." As part of its operation, NLM cooperates with other libraries and like research-and-education-oriented institutions (both public and private) in a so-called "interlibrary loan" program. Upon request, NLM will loan to such institutions, for a limited time, books and other materials in its collection. In the case of journals, the "loans" usually take the form of photocopies of journal articles which are supplied by NLM free of charge and on a no-return basis. NLM's "loan" policies are fashioned after the General Interlibrary Loan Code, which is a statement of self-imposed regulations to be followed by all libraries which cooperate in interlibrary loaning. The Code provides that each library, upon request for a loan of materials, shall decide whether to loan the original or provide a photoduplicate. The Code notes that photoduplication of copyrighted materials may raise copyright infringement problems, particularly with regard to "photographing *whole issues* of periodicals or books with *current copyrights*, or in making *multiple copies* of a publication." [Emphasis in original text.] NLM, therefore, will provide only one photocopy of a particular article, per request, and will not photocopy on any given request an entire journal issue. Each photocopy reproduced by NLM contains a statement in the margin, "This is a single photostatic copy made by the National Library of Medicine for purposes of study or research in lieu of lending the original."

In recent years NLM's stated policy has been not to fill requests for copies of articles from any of 104 journals which are included in a so-called "widely-available list." Rather, the requester is furnished a copy of the "widely-available list" and the names of the regional medical libraries which are presumed to have the journals listed. Exceptions are sometimes made to the policy, particularly if the requester has been unsuccessful in obtaining the journal elsewhere. The four journals involved in this suit are listed on the "widely-available list." A rejection on the basis of the "widely-available list" is made only if the article requested was published during the preceding 5 years, but requests from Government libraries are not refused on the basis of the "widely-available list."

Also, NLM's policy is not to honor an excessive number of requests from an individual or an institution. As a general rule, not more than 20 requests from an individual, or not more than 30 requests from an institution, within a month, will be honored. In 1968, NLM adopted the policy that no more than one article from a single journal issue, or three from a journal volume, would be copied. * * *

In 1968, a representative year, NLM received about 127,000 requests for interlibrary loans. Requests were received, for the most part, from other libraries or Government agencies. However, about 12 percent of the requests came from private of commercial organizations, particularly drug companies. Some requests were for books, in which event the book itself was loaned. Most requests were for journals or journal articles; and about 120,000 of the requests were filled by photocopying single articles from journals, including plaintiff's journals. Usually, the library seeking an interlibrary loan from NLM did so at the request of one of its patrons. If the "loan" was made by photocopy, the photocopy was given to the patron who was free to dispose of it as he wished. * * *

II

We assume, for the purposes of the case, but without deciding, that plaintiff is the proper copyright owner and entitled to sue here, and we agree with plaintiff that, on that assumption, it can sue for infringement of the eight separate articles. This faces us squarely with the issue of infringement.

Perhaps the main reason why determination of the question is so difficult is that the text of the Copyright Act of 1909, which governs the case, does not supply, by itself, a clear or satisfactory answer. Section 1 of the Act, 17 U.S.C. § 1, declares that the copyright owner "shall have the exclusive right: (a) To print, reprint, publish, copy, and vend the copyrighted work; * * *." Read with blinders, this language might seem on its surface to be all-comprehensive—especially the term "copy"—but we are convinced, for several reasons, that "copy" is not to be taken in its full literal sweep. In this instance, as in so many others in copyright, "[T]he statute is hardly unambiguous * * * and presents problems of interpretation not solved by literal application of words as they are 'normally' used * * *." *DeSylva v. Ballentine*, 351 U.S. 570, 573 (1956).

The court-created doctrine of "fair use" is alone enough to demonstrate that Section 1 does not cover all copying (in the literal sense). Some forms of copying, at the very least of portions of a work, are universally deemed immune from liability, although the very words are reproduced in more than *de minimis* quantity. Furthermore, it is almost unanimously accepted that a scholar can make a handwritten copy of an entire copyrighted article for his own use, and in the era before photoduplication it was not uncommon (and not seriously questioned) that he could have his secretary make a typed copy for his personal use and files. These customary facts of copyright-life are among our givens. The issue we now have is the complex one of whether photocopying, in the form done by NIH and NLM, should be accorded the same treatment—not the ministerial lexicographic task of deciding that photoduplication necessarily involves "copying" (as of course it does in dictionary terms). * * *

III

In the fifty-odd years since the 1909 Act, the major tool for probing what physical copying amounts to unlawful "copying" (as well as what is unlawful "printing," "reprinting" and "publishing") has been the gloss of "fair use" which the courts have put upon the words of the statute. Precisely because a determination that a use is "fair," or "unfair," depends on an evaluation of the complex of individual and varying factors bearing upon the particular use (*see* H.R.Rep. No. 83, 90th Cong., 1st Sess., p. 29), there has been no exact or detailed definition of the doctrine. The courts, congressional committees, and scholars have had to be content with a general listing of the main considerations—together with the example of specific instances ruled "fair" or "unfair." These overall factors are now said to be: (a) the purpose and character of the use, (b) the nature of the copyrighted work, (c) the amount and substantiality of the material used in relation to the copyrighted work as a whole, and (d) the effect of the use on a copyright owner's potential market for and value of his work.

In addition, the development of "fair use" has been influenced by some tension between the direct aim of the copyright privilege to grant the owner a right from which he can reap financial benefit and the more fundamental purpose of the protection "To promote the Progress of Science and the useful Arts." U.S.Const., art. 1, § 8. The House committee which recommended the 1909 Act said that copyright was "[n]ot primarily for the benefit of the author, but primarily for the benefit of the public." H.R.Rep. No. 2222, 60th Cong., 2d Sess., p. 7. The Supreme Court has stated that "The copyright law, like the patent statutes, makes reward to the owner a secondary consideration." *Mazer v. Stein*, 347 U.S. 201, 219 (1954). To serve the constitutional purpose, "'courts in passing upon particular claims of infringement must occasionally subordinate the copyright holder's interest in a maximum financial return to the greater public interest in the development of art, science and industry.' *Berlin v. E. C. Publications, Inc.*, 329 F.2d 541, 544 (2d Cir.1964). Whether the privilege may justifiably be applied to particular materials turns initially on the nature of the materials, *e.g.*, whether their distribution would serve the public interest in the free dissemination of information and whether their preparation requires some use of prior materials dealing with the same subject matter. Consequently, the privilege has been applied to works in the fields of science, law, medicine, history and biography." *Rosemont Enterprises, Inc. v. Random House, Inc.*, 366 F.2d 303, 307 (C.A.2, 1966).

It has sometimes been suggested that the copying of an entire copyrighted work, any such work, cannot ever be "fair use," but this is an overbroad generalization, unsupported by the decisions and rejected by years of accepted practice. The handwritten or typed copy of an article, for personal use, is one illustration, let alone the thousands of copies of poems, songs, or such items which have long been made by individuals, and sometimes given to lovers and others. Trial Judge James F. Davis, who considered the use now in dispute not to be "fair," nevertheless agreed that a library could supply single photocopies of entire copyrighted works to attorneys or courts for use in litigation. It is, of course, common for courts to be given photocopies of recent decisions, with the publishing company's headnotes and arrangement, and sometimes its annotations. There are other examples from everyday legal and personal life. We cannot believe, for instance, that a judge who makes and gives to a colleague a photocopy of a law review article, in one of the smaller or less available journals, which bears directly on a problem both judges are then considering in a case before them is infringing the copyright, rather than making "fair use" of his issue of that journal. Similarly with the photocopies of particular newspaper items and articles which are frequently given or sent by one friend to another. There is, in short, no inflexible rule excluding an entire copyrighted work from the area of "fair use." Instead, the extent of the copying is one important factor, but only one, to be taken into account, along with several others.

Under these over-all standards, we have weighed the multiplicity of factors converging on the particular use of plaintiff's material made by NIH and NLM, as shown by this record. There is no prior decision which is dispositive and hardly any that can be called even close; we have had to make our own appraisal. The majority of the court has concluded that, on this record, the challenged use should be designated "fair," not "unfair." In the rest of this part of our opinion, we discuss *seriatim* the various considerations which merge to that conclusion. But we can help focus on what is probably the core of our evaluation by stating summarily, in advance, three propositions we shall consider at greater length: First, plaintiff has not in our view shown, and there is inadequate reason to believe, that it is being or will be harmed substantially by these specific practices of NIH and NLM; second, we are convinced that medicine and medical research will be injured by holding these particular practices to be an infringement; and, third, since the problem of accommodating the interests of science with those of the publishers (and authors) calls fundamentally for legislative solution or guidance, which has not yet been given, we should not, during the period before congressional action is forthcoming, place such a risk of harm upon science and medicine.

1. We start by emphasizing that (a) NIH and NLM are non-profit institutions, devoted solely to the advancement and dissemination of medical knowledge which they seek to further by the challenged practices, and are not attempting to profit or gain financially by the photocopying; (b) the medical researchers who have asked these libraries for the photocopies are in this particular case (and ordinarily) scientific researchers and practitioners who need the articles for personal use in their scientific work and have no purpose to reduplicate them for sale or other general distribution; and (c) the copied articles are scientific studies useful to the requesters in their work. On both sides—library and requester—scientific progress, untainted by any commercial gain from the reproduction, is the hallmark of the whole enterprise of duplication. There has been no attempt to misappropriate the work of earlier scientific writers for forbidden ends, but rather an effort to gain easier access to the material for study and research. This is important because it is settled that, in general, the law gives copying for scientific purposes a wide scope. *See, e.g., Rosemont Enterprises, Inc. v. Random House, Inc., supra*, 366 F.2d at 306–307.

2. Both libraries have declared and enforced reasonably strict limitations which, to our mind, keep the duplication within appropriate confines.
* * *

3. We also think it significant, in assessing the recent and current practices of the two libraries, that library photocopying, though not of

course to the extent of the modern development, has been going on ever since the 1909 Act was adopted. * * * In fact, photocopying seems to have been done in the Library at least from the beginning of this century. Can Copyright Law Respond to the New Technology? 61 Law.Lib.J., 387, 400 (1968) (comments of V. Clapp). In 1935 there was a so-called "gentlemen's agreement" between the National Association of Book Publishers (since defunct) and the Joint Committee on Materials for Research (representing the libraries), stating in part: "A library * * * owning books or periodical volumes in which copyright still subsists may make and deliver a single photographic reproduction * * * of a part thereof to a scholar representing in writing that he desires such reproduction in lieu of loan of such publication or in place of manual transcription and solely for the purposes of research * * *." Though this understanding discountenanced photoduplication of an entire book it was regularly construed as allowing copying of articles. There have been criticisms of this pact, and we cite it, not as binding in any way on plaintiff or any other publisher, or as showing universal recognition of "single" photocopying, but as representing a very widely held view, almost 40 years ago, of what was permissible under the 1909 statute. * * *

The fact that photocopying by libraries of entire articles was done with hardly any (and at most very minor) complaint, until about 10 or 15 years ago, goes a long way to show both that photoduplication cannot be designated as infringement *per se,* and that there was at least a time when photocopying, as then carried on, was "fair use." There have been, of course, considerable changes in the ease and extent of such reproduction, and these developments bear on "fair use" as of today, but the libraries can properly stand on the proposition that they photocopied articles for many years, without significant protest, and that such copying was generally accepted until the proliferation of inexpensive and improved copying machines, less than two decades ago, led to the surge in such duplication. The question then becomes whether this marked increase in volume changes a use which was generally accepted as "fair" into one which has now become "unfair."

4.   There is no doubt in our minds that medical science would be seriously hurt if such library photocopying were stopped. We do not spend time and space demonstrating this proposition. It is admitted by plaintiff and conceded on all sides. * * *

5.   Plaintiff insists that it has been financially hurt by the photocopying practices of NLM and NIH, and of other libraries. The trial judge thought that it was reasonable to infer that the extensive photocopying has resulted in some loss of revenue to plaintiff and that plaintiff has lost, or failed to get, "some undetermined and indeterminable number of journal subscriptions (perhaps small)" by virtue of the photocopying. He thought that the persons requesting photocopies constituted plaintiff's market and that each photocopy user is a potential subscriber "or at least a potential source of royalty income for licensed copying."

The record made in this case does not sustain that assumption. Defendant made a thorough effort to try to ascertain, so far as possible, the effect of photoduplication on plaintiff's business, including the presentation of an expert witness. The unrefuted evidence shows that (a) between 1958 and 1969 annual subscriptions to the four medical journals involved increased substantially (for three of them, very much so), annual subscription sales likewise increased substantially, and total annual income also grew; (b) between 1959 and 1966, plaintiff's annual taxable income increased from $272,000 to $726,000, fell to $589,000 in 1967, and in 1968 to $451,000; (c) but the four journals in suit account for a relatively small percentage of plaintiff's total business and over the years each has been profitable (though 3 of them show losses in particular years and in all years the profits have not been large, varying from less than $1,000 to about $15,000, some of which has been shared with the sponsoring medical societies); and (d) plaintiff's business appears to have been growing faster than the gross national product or of the rate of growth of manpower working in the field of science. Defendant's expert concluded that the photocopying shown here had not damaged plaintiff, and may actually have helped it. The record is also barren of solid evidence that photocopying has caused economic harm to any other publisher of medical journals.

Plaintiff has never made a detailed study of the actual effect of photocopying on its business, nor has it refuted defendant's figures. It has relied for its assumption (in the words of the chairman of its board) on "general business common sense and things that you hear from subscribers, librarians and so forth." Its argument—and that of the other supporters of its position—is that there "must" be an effect because photocopies supplant the original articles, and if there were no photocopying those who now get the copies would necessarily buy the journals or issues. But this untested hypothesis, reminiscent of the abstract theorems beloved of the "pure" classical economics of 70 or 80 years ago, is neither obvious nor self-proving. One need not enter the semantic debate over whether the photocopy supplants the original article itself or is merely in substitution for the library's loan of the original issue to recognize, as we have already pointed out, that there are other possibilities. If photocopying were forbidden, the researchers, instead of subscribing to more journals or trying to obtain or buy back-issues or reprints (usually unavailable), might expend extra time in note-taking or waiting their turn for the library's copies of the original issues—or they might very well cut down their reading and do without much of the information they now get through NLM's and NIH's copying system. The record shows that each of the individual requesters in this case already subscribed, personally, to a number of medical journals, and it is very questionable how many more, if any, they would add. The great problems with reprints and back-issues have already been noted. In the absence of photocopying, the financial, time-wasting, and other difficulties of obtaining the material could well lead, if human experience is a guide, to a simple but drastic reduction in the use of the many articles (now sought and read) which are not absolutely crucial to the individual's work but are merely stimulating or helpful. The probable effect on scientific progress goes without saying, but for this part of our discussion the significant element is that plaintiff, as publisher and copyright owner, would not be better off. * * *

In this connection it is worth noting that plaintiff does not have to concern itself, with respect to these journals, with authors or medical societies who are interested in a financial return. The authors, with rare exceptions, are not paid for their contributions, and those societies which share profits do not press for greater financial benefits. Indeed, some of the authors of the copied articles involved in this case testified at the trial that they favored photocopying as an aid to the advancement of science and knowledge. * * *

IV

Fusing these elements together, we conclude that plaintiff has failed to show that the defendant's use of the copyrighted material has been "unfair," and conversely we find that these practices have up to now been "fair." There has been no infringement. As Professor (now Mr. Justice) Kaplan observed, it is "fundamental that 'use' is not the same as 'infringement' [and] that use short of infringement is to be encouraged * * *." Kaplan, An Unhurried View of Copyright 57 (1967). * * *

■ COWEN, CHIEF JUDGE (dissenting):

　　* * *

II

The Photocopying of Plaintiff's Copyrighted Articles Was Not Fair Use

1.   Realizing the necessity for showing that the defendant's unauthorized copying of plaintiff's articles was both reasonable and insubstantial, the court relies heavily on policies which were adopted by the libraries in 1965. Although these policies were designed to limit the extent of copying that had been done in prior years, the trial judge's opinion and the findings of fact show the exceptions are routinely granted by the defendant's libraries, that there is no way to enforce most of the limitations, and that defendant is operating a reprint service which supplants the need for journal subscriptions.

In particular, the trial judge has, I think, clearly demonstrated that the claimed "single-copy-per-request" limitation is both illusory and unrealistic. He has found, and it is not disputed, that the libraries will duplicate the same article over and over again, even for the same user, within a short space of time. NLM will supply requesters photocopies of the same article, one after another, on consecutive days, even with knowledge of such facts. I find great difficulty in detecting any difference between the furnishing by defendant's libraries of ten copies of one article to one patron, which he then distributes, and giving each of ten patrons one copy of the same article. The damage to the copyright proprietor is the same in either case.

　　* * *

3.   I recognize that the doctrine of fair use permits writers of scholarly works to make reasonable use of previously copyrighted material by quotation or paraphrase, at least where the amount of copying is small and reliance on other sources is demonstrated. *See, e.g., Rosemont Enterprises, Inc. v. Random House, Inc.,* 366 F.2d 303 (2d Cir.1966), *cert. denied,* 385 U.S. 1009 (1967); *Simms v. Stanton,* 75 F. 6, 13–14 (C.C.N.D.Cal.1896). However, I think the basic error in the court's decision is its holding that the fair use privilege usually granted to such writers should be extended to cover the massive copying and distribution operation conducted by defendant's libraries. The articles are not reproduced by the libraries to enable them to write other articles in the same field. * * *

4.   The trial judge found that it is reasonable to infer from the evidence that the extensive unauthorized copying of plaintiff's journal has resulted in some loss of revenue and serves to diminish plaintiff's potential market for the original articles. Since the inferences made by the trial judge may reasonably be drawn from the facts and circumstances in evidence, they are presumptively as correct as his findings of fact. Accordingly, under the standards which we employ for reviewing the findings of our trial judges, I would adopt these findings.

Although the court states that it rejects the trial determinations as to both actual and potential damage to plaintiff, I think the opinion shows that the court's conclusion is based primarily on its finding that plaintiff failed to prove actual damages. In so doing, the majority relies heavily on evidence that the plaintiff's profits have grown faster than the gross national product and that plaintiff's annual taxable income has increased. This evidence is irrelevant to the economic effects of photocopying the journals in this case, because these periodicals account for a relatively small percent of plaintiff's total business. Moreover, the extent of plaintiff's taxable income for the years mentioned does not reflect the effect of defendant's photocopying of plaintiff's journals, and particularly the effect it will have on the prospects for continued publication in the future.

By the very nature of an action for infringement, the copyright proprietor often has a difficult burden of proving the degree of injury. It is well established, however, that proof of actual damages is not required, and the defense of fair use may be overcome where potential injury is shown. *See, e.g., Henry Holt & Co., Inc. v. Liggett & Myers Tobacco Co.,* 23 F.Supp. 302, 304 (E.D.Pa.1938). As Professor Nimmer has stated, the courts look to see whether defendant's work "tends to diminish or prejudice the potential sale of the plaintiff's work." M. Nimmer, Nimmer on Copyright § 145 at 646 (1973 ed.).

The problem posed by library photocopying of copyrighted material has long been a subject of controversy. Several studies of this problem have pointed out that extensive photocopying by libraries is unfair because of its potential damage to the copyright owner. The trial judge has quoted from the reports of several of these studies.

In a thorough and thoughtful discussion of the effects of reprography, prepared at the University of California, Los Angeles, and funded by the National Endowment for the Arts, it is stated:

> It has long been argued that copying by hand "for the purpose of private study and review" would be a fair use. Users are now asserting that machine copying is merely a substitute for hand copying and is, therefore, a fair use. But this argument ignores the economic differences between the two types of copying. Copying by hand is extremely time consuming and costly, and is not an economic threat to authors. *Viewing reprography as though it were hand copying, however, overlooks the effect of the total number of machine copies made. Few people hand copy, but millions find machine copying economical and convenient. Allowing individual users to decide that their machine copying will not injure the author and will thus be a fair use fails to take into account the true economic effect when thousands of such individual decisions are aggregated.* * * * Project, New Technology and the Law of Copyright: Reprography and Computers, 15 U.C.L.A.L.Rev. 931, 951 (1968).

* * *

Subscription sales provide most of the revenue derived from the marketing of plaintiff's journals. It is important to remember that each of plaintiff's journals caters to and serves a limited market. Plaintiff's share of the profits from these journals has varied from less than $1,000 to about $7,000 annually. In the context of rising costs of publication, an inability to attract new customers, and the loss of even a small number of old subscribers may have a large detrimental effect on the journals. A representative of Williams & Wilkins Company testified that in recent years there have been journals that have failed, and in the opinion of those at Williams & Wilkins, photocopying has played a role in these failures. * * * There is no evidence to show specifically whether any particular instance or instances of unauthorized photocopying of plaintiff's journals has or has not resulted in the loss of revenue to plaintiff. However, I think the record, as a whole, supports the determination of the trial judge that the photocopying in this case has had a tendency to diminish plaintiff's markets in the past.
* * *

IV

A Judgment for Plaintiff Will Not Injure Medicine and Medical Research

The court has bottomed its decision to a very large extent on its finding, which is not disputed, that medical science would be seriously hurt if the photocopying by defendant's libraries is entirely stopped. But the court goes further and concludes that a judgment for plaintiff would lead to this result. It is not altogether clear to me how the court arrives at the second conclusion, and I think it is based on unwarranted assumptions.

The plaintiff does not propose to stop such photocopying and does not desire that result. What plaintiff seeks is a reasonable royalty for such photocopying and, in this case, a recovery of reasonable compensation for the infringement of its copyrights. Plaintiff has established a licensing system to cover various methods of reproducing its journal articles, including reproduction by photocopying. One of the licensees is a Government agency, and on several occasions plaintiff has granted requests from Government agencies and others for licenses to make multiple copies (Finding 36). In May 1967, the photocopying of plaintiff's journal articles was monitored by NLM for a 90–day period which was judged to be a representative sample. As the trial judge has shown, NLM found it would have paid plaintiff from $250 to $300 if it had granted plaintiff's request for royalty payments. The Director of NLM testified that this was, in his opinion, a surprisingly small sum. He also testified (Part III, trial judge's opinion) that the payment of a royalty to plaintiff for photocopying "has nothing to do with the operation of the library in the fulfillment of * * * [its] function. It is an economic and budgetary consideration and not a service-oriented kind of thing." This is the only direct testimony that I have found on how the payment of royalties for photocopying will affect the functions of the library, and it gives no indication or intimation that the payment of royalties to plaintiff will force NLM to cease the photocopying.

The court has laid heavy emphasis on the public interest in maintaining a free flow of information to doctors and scientists, and on the injury that might result if this flow should be stopped. However, there is another facet to the public interest question which is presented in this case. The trial judge put it well in his statement:

> The issues raised by this case are but part of a larger problem which continues to plague our institutions with ever-increasing complexity—how best to reconcile, on the one hand, the rights of authors and publishers under the copyright laws with, on the other hand, the technological improvements in copying techniques and the legitimate public need for rapid dissemination of scientific and technical literature.

In enacting the 1909 Act, the House Committee said:

> The enactment of copyright legislation by Congress under the terms of the Constitution is not based upon any natural right that the author has in his writings * * * but upon the ground that the welfare of the public will be served and progress of science and useful arts will be promoted by securing to authors for limited periods the exclusive rights to their writings. H.R.Rep.No.2222, 60th Cong., 2d Sess. 7 (1909).

In *Mazer v. Stein*, 347 U.S. 201, 219 (1954), the Supreme Court emphasized that the copyright protection given to authors and publishers is designed to advance public welfare, stating:

> "The copyright law, like the patent statutes, makes reward to the owner a secondary consideration. * * *" However, it is "in-

tended definitely to grant valuable, enforceable rights to authors, publishers, etc. * * *''

The economic philosophy behind the clause empowering Congress to grant patents and copyrights is the conviction that encouragement of individual effort by personal gain is the best way to advance public welfare through the talents of authors and inventors in "Science and useful Arts."

In order to promote the progress of science, not only must authors be induced to write new works, but also publishers must be induced to disseminate those works to the public. This philosophy has guided our country, with limited exceptions, since its beginning, and I am of the opinion that if there is to be a fundamental policy change in this system, such as a blanket exception for library photocopying, it is for the Congress to determine, not for the courts. The courts simply cannot draw the distinctions so obviously necessary in this area. * * *

American Geophysical Union v. Texaco Inc.

United States District Court, Southern District of New York, 1992.
802 F.Supp. 1, *aff'd,* 60 F.3d 913 (2d Cir.1994).

OPINION AND ORDER

Findings of Fact and Conclusions of Law

■ LEVAL, DISTRICT JUDGE.

I.

This class action tests the question whether it is lawful under the U.S. Copyright Act, 17 U.S.C. § 101, *et seq.,* for a profit-seeking company to make unauthorized copies of copyrighted articles published in scientific and technical journals for use by the company's scientists employed in scientific research. The plaintiffs are publishers of scientific and technical journals that publish copyrighted material under assignment from the authors. The defendant is Texaco Inc., one of the largest corporations in the United States, which engages in all aspects of the petroleum business from exploration through transportation and refining to retail marketing. This opinion decides the limited issue whether the making of single copies from plaintiffs' journals by a Texaco scientist is fair use under Section 107 of the Copyright Act of 1976. 17 U.S.C. § 107. Many of the facts are not seriously disputed.

Texaco's Scientific Research. Texaco engages in substantial scientific research directed toward improving Texaco's products and developing new products and processes. Texaco employs between 400 and 500 scientists and engineers at six research centers in the United States, including one in Beacon, New York. It spends in excess of $80 million annually in carrying on scientific and technical research, including an average of approximately $37 million a year from 1985 to 1987 at the Beacon facility.

To support its research activities, Texaco subscribes to numerous scientific and technical journals, some published by various of the plaintiffs, and maintains large libraries of such materials. Texaco scientists, on learning of an article that may be helpful or important to their research, regularly make (or cause to be made by Texaco's research libraries) a photocopy to be read, kept in their personal files and used in the laboratory in the course of their research work.

Use of Journals in Research: Photocopying. Learned journals play an important part in scientific research. They serve to disseminate broadly and with reasonable rapidity the results of scientific research being conducted in many places. It is of great importance for scientists doing research to keep abreast of the publication of such articles for many reasons. The reasons include awareness of new learning, suggestion of new ideas and approaches, avoidance of duplication of experimentation that has already been done, avoidance of avenues of experimentation that have been demonstrated to be fruitless, adoption for productive research of findings that have resulted from the research of others, and other valuable uses too numerous and varied to mention.

Because it is important for scientists to remain abreast of such publications, industrial corporations that engage in research use a variety of methods to keep their scientists aware. Among the methods used are purchasing subscriptions to such journals and routing of the newly published issues among the scientists, circulating summaries or indices of recently published studies, circulating photocopies of tables of contents of recently published issues of journals, and simple word of mouth by which scientific co-workers mention to one another recent publications of interest.

It is commonplace for scientists employed at Texaco, and in industry generally, to make for themselves (or to request from the company library) photocopies of particular articles that are expected to be useful in their work. There are numerous reasons for the use of such photocopies. Most importantly, it frees the original journal to circulate among colleagues or to return to the library and permits numerous scientists to keep copies of the same material, or of material bound in the same volume. Photocopying also permits scientists to make and maintain easily referenced personal files of pertinent articles, instead of surrounding themselves with bulky original volumes that include much material that is not relevant for the particular researcher. It avoids the need for repeated trips to the library. It eliminates the risk of error that enters into transcription; it permits a scientist initially to simply file the copy in an appropriate subject file for later review instead of immediately studying the article in detail and taking notes; copies of the article can be taken into the laboratory for use in conducting or evaluating experiments without the risks of errors in transcription and in the misapplication of equations or data; when used in the laboratory, copies eliminate the risk that chemicals or equipment might destroy the original; copies are more conveniently taken home to be read; the reader can make marginal notes directly on copies without defacing the original.

Plaintiffs contend that by this photocopying Texaco infringes the plaintiffs' copyrights. In answer to the complaint, Texaco raises the defense, among others, of "fair use." It contends that such photocopying by scientists in industry is a reasonable and customary practice, necessary to the conduct of scientific research, and that it does not infringe the publishers' copyrights. * * *

Donald Chickering, II, Ph.D. For convenience and to avoid untoward discovery expenses with respect to largely duplicative matters, the stipulation provides that the trial of the issue of fair use be conducted with respect to eight photocopies found in the files of an arbitrarily selected one of Texaco's several hundred scientific researchers.[21] The lot fell on one Donald H. Chickering, II, Ph.D., employed at the Texaco research center at Beacon, New York. Chickering's files were found to contain a number of photocopies of numerous items from various scientific and technical journals. As the subject of this limited issue trial, plaintiffs selected eight copies of complete pieces that appeared in the *Journal of Catalysis*, a monthly publication of Academic Press, Inc., which is one of the plaintiffs in this action.

Chickering is a Ph.D. in chemical engineering who specializes in the study of catalysts and catalysis. Catalysis is "the change in the rate of a chemical reaction brought about by often small amounts of a substance that is unchanged chemically at the end of the reaction." *Webster's Third New International Dictionary* 350 (1976). Chickering has been employed at the Beacon research facility since January 1981 as a "technical man at the bench," that is, a professionally degreed scientist who designs and performs experiments and other work in the laboratory. Chickering's laboratory experiments have involved basic research on catalysis, including investigating various ways of analyzing catalysts, designing, building and operating chemical reactors, using catalysts to make usable products out of previously wasted hydrogen and carbon monoxide, and upgrading the quality of fuels through catalysis. At the time of his testimony, Chickering was the group leader of the "Automation Design and Construction Group," which provided engineering and automation research to support catalysis research, new technology research, and advanced research.

Shortly after Chickering joined Texaco, he had the library at Beacon put his name on the routing lists for the scientific and technical journals that he believed would be of professional interest. Consistent with what Texaco contends is reasonable and customary for scientists employed by for-profit companies, Chickering often photocopied, or had the library photocopy for him, copyrighted articles in scientific and technical journals.

As noted, plaintiffs selected from Chickering's files eight copies of material from Academic Press' *Catalysis*. These included four "articles," two "notes" and two "letters to the editor." Each of them was published

---

21. This fair use "test case" trial is potentially dispositive of plaintiffs' entire case because the parties agreed that (after all appeals and certiorari or all opportunities to appeal or seek certiorari are exhausted) if Texaco's claims of fair use are sustained as to each of the eight articles specified, then all of the claims of copyright infringement shall be dismissed with prejudice. * * *

with a copyright notice showing Academic Press as the owner of the copyright and reserving all reproduction rights. It is assumed for purposes of the trial of the fair use issue that each was indeed copyrighted matter and that the copyright had been validly assigned by the authors to Academic Press.

In each case Chickering photocopied the entirety of the particular article, note or letter. He selected those pieces because the discussion was pertinent to research that he was conducting or expected to conduct in the future and because he expected that the discussion and the information conveyed would be helpful to him in conducting research for Texaco. * * *

Academic Press and the Journal of Catalysis. Academic Press, the publisher of *Catalysis*, is a major publisher of scholarly scientific, technical and medical journals, monographs and books. Academic Press is a wholly-owned subsidiary of Harcourt Brace Jovanovich, Inc., the nation's largest scientific and medical book and journal publisher. Currently, Academic Press publishes 105 scientific, medical and technical journals covering a wide range of specialties in the physical, life and behavioral sciences.

Catalysis first appeared in 1962. It is published monthly. It includes three classes of items: articles, notes and letters to the editor. They vary in form and size, articles being the longest, letters to the editor the shortest. (Because there is no functional distinction between the three for purposes of this inquiry, they are all referred to here as "articles.") All articles in the journal are devoted to scientific and technical matters. Each monthly issue is around 200 pages long and contains approximately 20–25 articles.

Every article published in *Catalysis* is unsolicited; none is written by Academic Press employees. Academic Press does not pay authors for the right to publish an article. Authors interested in publishing in *Catalysis* are directed to submit their articles directly to one of the journal's two editors. Authors are informed that if their manuscript is accepted for publication, the copyright in the article, including the right to reproduce the article in all forms and media, shall be assigned to Academic Press.

The editors are not employees of Academic Press, and, like the authors, they receive no pay. Academic Press reimburses the editors for secretarial support, postage, telephone charges and some travel expenses. The editors have complete editorial control and sole discretion over the content of *Catalysis*. Articles they deem worthy of publication are submitted to peer review for a recommendation as to whether the article should be published, and if so, whether and how the article should be revised. The peer reviewers are not paid by Academic Press.

Academic Press sells two types of subscriptions to *Catalysis*: an institutional rate, which is charged to both profit and nonprofit institutions, and an individual rate. In 1989, an institutional subscription to *Catalysis* cost $828. The individual rate is half the institutional rate. The subscription rates have increased since 1972 at a rate more than three times the increase in the Consumer Price Index.

Texaco's Beacon facility, which pays the institutional rate, had purchased one subscription to *Catalysis* until 1983, when it doubled its subscriptions. In 1988, the Beacon facility increased its subscriptions to three, the number it continues to purchase to date.

In addition to yearly subscriptions, Academic Press offers back issues of *Catalysis* for sale. Back issues are available separately for three years following publication. Thereafter, they are bound together as annual volumes and are offered only in that form. In addition, reprints are available, with the author's prior approval, but only on a minimum order of 100 copies. Each order for reprints is printed separately and takes an average of three weeks to be filled.

The Copyright Clearance Center: Authorizations to Copy. Academic Press also offers users authorization to photocopy pieces from *Catalysis* through the mechanism of the Copyright Clearance Center Inc. ("CCC"). The CCC is a nonprofit, central clearing-house established in 1977 by publishers, authors and photocopy users which, as agent for publishers, grants blanket advance permission for a fee to photocopy copyrighted material registered with CCC, and forwards the fees collected to copyright owners, net of service charge. CCC was formed in response to a Congressional recommendation that an efficient mechanism be established to license photocopying. *See* S.Rep. No. 983, 93d Cong.2d Sess., at 122 (1974); H.R.Rep. No. 83, 90th Cong., 1st Sess., at 33 (1968); S.Rep. No. 94–473, 94th Cong., 1st Sess., at 70–71 (1975); *see generally* A.F. Spilhaus, *The Copyright Clearance Center*, 9 Scholarly Pub. 143 (1978). CCC's Board of Directors is comprised of representatives from the publishing, author and photocopy-user communities. As of 1990, approximately 8,000 domestic and foreign publishers had registered approximately 1.5 million publications with CCC.

Currently, CCC offers two principal services for obtaining advance permission to photocopy copyrighted material that publishers have registered with the CCC. The first method, inaugurated in 1978, is called the Transactional Reporting Service ("TRS"). TRS provides photocopy users with blanket permission to photocopy from any CCC-registered publication, provided the user subsequently reports the making of the photocopy and pays the fees required by the copyright owner. The fee is printed on the first page of each article. The fee for each copy of an article in *Catalysis* has been $2 from 1978 through 1982 and $3 thereafter.[22] Under TRS, users originally reported their photocopying to CCC either by (1) submitting an extra copy of the first page of the article or journal that was photocopied, with certain information marked on it; or (2) by submitting log sheets containing the same information; or (3) by providing such information in computer printout form or magnetic tape. Users, however, objected to identifying the articles they copied because they feared this could give information to their competition as to where their research efforts were being concentrated. Accordingly, CCC eliminated the need to identify the

22. CCC's standard service charge per reported article is 25 cents for articles published prior to January 1, 1983, and 50 cents for articles published after January 1, 1983.

item copied. Since January 1, 1983, the information provided to CCC has been reduced to the journal's standard International Standard Serial Number ("ISSN"), publication year, and the photocopy permissions fee set by the publisher (multiplied by the number of copies made). (The necessary information is set forth at a lower corner of the first page of each article in the journal.)[23] To comply with TRS, a user company might place log sheets at photocopy machines. Whenever company personnel made copies of material covered by CCC, they would make a log entry noting the journal number and year, the numbers of pages and of copies, and the fees prescribed. Library personnel would collect these logs and submit them monthly to CCC with payment.

Some major corporate users objected to the administrative costs of training personnel and setting up recordkeeping necessary for full compliance with TRS. Jane C. Ginsburg, *Reproduction of Protected Works for University Research or Teaching*, 39 J. Copyright Soc'y 181, 209 (1992) (hereinafter "Ginsburg, *Reproduction of Protected Works*").[24] In response, in 1983, CCC inaugurated a second service for obtaining advance permission to photocopy that eliminated the TRS's reporting requirements. This was the Annual Authorization Service ("AAS"). AAS was designed by two econometricians working with the cooperation of major corporate users. Under the AAS, the corporate user is granted a blanket annual license to make photocopies for internal use of any copyrighted material contained in any of the journals and books registered with the CCC. The annual license fee is determined on the basis of a limited photocopying survey, factored by the licensee's employee population and the copying fees for the journals regularly copied by that user. Upon payment of an annual license fee, the AAS licensee is authorized to make unlimited numbers of photocopies from CCC registered publications for internal use. The license is for one year, renewable for an additional year at the licensee's option. At the end of a two-year period a new license can be obtained.

23. Each issue of *Catalysis* also contains a masthead statement asserting:

> No part of this publication may be reproduced or transmitted in any form or by any means, electronic or mechanical, including photocopy, recording, or any information storage and retrieval system, without permission in writing from the copyright owner. The appearance of the code at the bottom of the first page of an article in this journal indicates the copyright owner's consent that copies of the article may be made for personal or internal use, or for the personal or internal use of specific clients. This consent is given on the condition, however, that the copier pay the stated, per copy fee through the Copyright Clearance Center,

Inc. . . . , for copying beyond that permitted by Sections 107 or 108 of the U.S. Copyright Law. This consent does not extend to other kinds of copying, such as copying for general distribution, for creating new collective works, or for resale. Copy fees for pre–1982 articles are the same as those shown for current articles.

24. Few large corporations have employed the TRS. *See* Joseph F. Alen, *New Photocopying License Service Announced*, 6 CBE Views 5 (1983). The TRS service is used primarily by document delivery services and small businesses. Stanley M. Bensen and Sheila Nataraj Kirby, *Compensating Creators of Intellectual Property: Collectives That Collect* 49 (1989) (hereinafter "*Collectives That Collect* ").

The revenue derived from the TRS and the AAS is allocated among the publishers that have registered publications with the CCC, net of CCC's service charges, in accordance with the users' photocopying of their material. The basic fee for photocopying per unit of material is not set by CCC but rather by the individual publishers.

As of January 1991, there were approximately 400 users reporting under the TRS method, and over 100 corporate licensees under the AAS method. The AAS licensees include eleven major petroleum companies (Exxon, Mobil Oil, Amoco, Ashland Oil, BP America, Chevron, Marathon Oil, Atlantic Richfield, Occidental Petroleum, Phillips Petroleum, and Sun Refining and Marketing) as well as other major research-oriented corporations including Allied Signal, Ciba–Geigy, AT & T and its Bell Labs Division, Dupont, Eastman Kodak, Dow Corning, General Electric, IBM, Monsanto, Olin, PPG, Polaroid, Texas Instruments, 3M, Union Carbide, United Technologies and USX. As of December 31, 1989, total permission fees paid to CCC under the TRS program from its inception have amounted to approximately $9 million. Total fees paid by licensees under the AAS program from its inception to December 31, 1989 have amounted to about $18 million. CCC's combined TRS and AAS revenue and distributions have increased each year.[25]

II.

Copyright Protection and the Doctrine of Fair Use

The copyright entered the law of England through the Statute of Anne of 1710. 8 Anne, ch. 19 (1710). Its caption declared it to be "An Act For the Encouragement of Learning by Vesting the Copies of Printed Books in the Authors...." The preamble declares the statute's purpose to be "for the Encouragement of Learned Men to Compose and write useful Books." The act conferred the exclusive right (for 14 years) to the making of copies upon the authors and noted that the practice of pirated publications "too often [causes] the Ruin of [authors] and their Families."

Following a similar line of reasoning the United States Constitution conferred the power on Congress "To promote the progress of science and useful arts by securing for a limited time to authors and inventors the exclusive right to their respective writings and discoveries." U.S. Const. art 1, § 8, cl. 8. The stated objective was "to promote the progress of science

---

25. CCC has entered into bilateral agreements with foreign "Reproduction Rights Organizations" in the United Kingdom (Copyright Licensing Agency Ltd.), Germany (VG Wort), France (Centre Francais du Copyright), Spain (Centro Espanol de Derechos Reprograficos), New Zealand (Copyright Licensing Limited), Norway (KOPINOR), Switzerland (Pro Litteris), Australia (Copyright Agency Limited) and the former U.S.S.R. (Vsesojuznoje Agentstvo Po Avtroskim Pravam). Under these agreements, CCC has the right to grant permission to photocopy users registered under the TRS and licensees under AAS to photocopy, in the United States, copyrighted material for which the Reproduction Rights Organizations have the right to grant such permissions. CCC's surveys of photocopying at corporations in the United States have shown that, on average, approximately twenty-five percent of the photocopying of published copyrighted materials is from foreign publications.

[*i.e.*, knowledge]''; the means by which this was to be accomplished was the granting to authors of exclusive rights with respect to their writings. The theory espoused by this constitutional provision is that the advancement of public good, through growth of knowledge and learning, is to be obtained by securing the private commercial interests of authors. *See Mazer v. Stein*, 347 U.S. 201, 219, 74 S.Ct. 460, 471, 98 L.Ed. 630 (1954). If authors are guaranteed the opportunity to profit from their writings, they will have an incentive to create, and the public will ultimately reap the resulting expansion of human knowledge. In contrast, if no copyright protection were granted and others were permitted to copy freely works of authorship, authors would find it difficult to earn a living from their writings; their energies would be diverted to other pursuits by the need to feed their families; consequently, the public's right to appropriate the works of authors would make the public poorer through loss of the benefit of authors' endeavors. This led James Madison to observe, ''the utility of [the power conferred by the patent and copyright clause] will scarcely be questioned.... The public good fully coincides in both cases with the claims of individuals.'' The Federalist No. 43, at 186 (J. Madison) (C. Beard ed. 1959). Congress promptly acted on the Constitutional grant of authority, passing the first Copyright Act, modeled on the Statute of Anne, in 1790.

Not long after the creation of statutory copyright, courts developed doctrines that limited the scope of the exclusive rights of authors. Although the copyright acts (pre–1976) ostensibly established absolute rights, the ''courts simply refused to read the statute literally in every situation.'' *Sony Corp. of America v. Universal Studios, Inc.*, 464 U.S. 417, 447 n. 29, 104 S.Ct. 774, 791 n. 29, 78 L.Ed.2d 574 (1984) (referring to the 1909 Act). It was recognized for example that the copyright did not confer upon the author any ownership of the *facts* set forth in the author's writings, or even of the ideas.

Another limitation on authors' absolute ownership has come to be known as the doctrine of ''fair use.'' The need for it was explained by Lord Ellenborough's assertion that ''while I shall think myself bound to secure every man in the enjoyment of his copyright, one must not put manacles upon science.'' *Carey v. Kearsley*, 170 Eng.Rep. 679, 681, 4 Esp. 168, 170 (1803). Thus the doctrine recognized that the advancement of knowledge and learning required some reasonable tolerance within which scholars and authors might freely use or quote from the writings of others for comment, criticism, debate, history, etc., without which the ''progress of science'' might be retarded rather than advanced by the authors' ownership. In its early days, the doctrine related primarily to abridgements and was known as the rule of ''fair abridgement.'' *See* William F. Patry, *The Fair Use Privilege in Copyright Law* 6–7 (1985) (hereinafter ''Patry, *Fair Use*''). The contours of the rule are vague. No judicial opinion ever undertook to define clear standards for fair use. In the United States' law, the classic opaque statement was articulated in 1841 by Justice Story in *Folsom v. Marsh*, 9

F.Cas. at 342 (C.C.D.Mass.1841) (No. 4,901).[26] Instructing as to how to approach the question of fair use, Story wrote, "In short, we must often . . . look to the nature and objects of the selections made, the quantity and value of the materials used and the degree in which the use may prejudice the sale or diminish the profits or supersede the objects of the original work." 9 F.Cas. 342, 348.

The fair use doctrine was not expressly incorporated into statute until the Copyright Act of 1976, which largely adopts the formulation of Justice Story, and purports, according to the legislative commentary, merely to "restate the present judicial doctrine of fair use, not to change, narrow, or enlarge it in any way." House Rep. No. 94–1476, 94th Cong., 2d Sess., 66, U.S.Code Cong. & Admin.News 1976, 5659, 5679. *But see* Patry, *Fair Use* at 362. Section 107 of the 1976 Act (which is quoted in full in the margin)[27] instructs that "fair use of a copyrighted work . . . for purposes such as criticism, comment, news reporting, teaching (including multiple copies for classroom use), scholarship or research, is not an infringement of copyright." Although the statute does not attempt to define fair use, it instructs that four factors be considered. The four factors, each of which can be found in Justice Story's 1841 summary, are (i) the purpose and character of the use, (ii) the nature of the copyrighted work, (iii) the amount and substantiality of the portion used, and (iv) the effect of the use on the potential market for the copyright. As vague, broad and far reaching as these factors are, the Supreme Court has noted that they are not exclusive and that the fair use doctrine is an " 'equitable rule of reason.' " *Stewart v. Abend*, 495 U.S. 207, 236, 110 S.Ct. 1750, 1768, 109 L.Ed.2d 184 (1990) (quoting *Sony*, 464 U.S. at 448, 104 S.Ct. at 792). Courts and commentators have repeatedly observed that a fair use inquiry is highly fact-specific and does not readily admit of bright line generalizations. *See, e.g., Harper & Row Publishers, Inc. v. Nation Enters.*, 471 U.S. 539, 560, 105 S.Ct. 2218, 2230, 85 L.Ed.2d 588 (1985) (" 'no generally applicable definition [of fair use] is possible, and each case raising the question must be decided on its own facts' "(citation omitted)); *Wright v. Warner Books, Inc.*, 953 F.2d 731, 740 (2d Cir.1991) ("The fair use test remains a totality inquiry, tailored to the particular facts of each case").

26. The appellation "fair use" did not, however, appear until *Lawrence v. Dana*, 15 F.Cas. 26 (C.C.D.Mass.1869) (No. 8,136). *See* Alan Latman, Robert Gorman and Jane C. Ginsburg, *Copyright for the Nineties* 579 (1989); Patry, *Fair Use* at 27.

27. § 107. *Limitations on Exclusive rights: Fair use.* Notwithstanding the provisions of section 106, the fair use of a copyrighted work, including such use by reproduction in copies or phonorecords or by any other means specified by that section, for purposes such as criticism, comment, news reporting, teaching (including multiple copies for classroom use), scholarship, or research, is not an infringement of copyright. In determining whether the use made of a work in any particular case is a fair use the factors to be considered shall include—(1) the purpose and character of the use, including whether such use is of a commercial nature or is for nonprofit educational purposes; (2) the nature of the copyrighted work; (3) the amount and substantiality of the portion used in relation to the copyrighted work as a whole; and (4) the effect of the use upon the potential market for or value of the copyrighted work. 17 U.S.C. § 107.

First Factor—The Purpose and Character of the Secondary Use

Throughout the development of the fair use doctrine, courts consistently expressed preference for secondary uses that did not merely copy and offer themselves as substitutes for the original copyrighted text, but that used the matter taken from the copyrighted work for some new objective or purpose. In Story's classic *Folsom* formulation, this preference was expressed in the focus on "the objects of the selections made . . . and the degree to which the use . . . may *supersede* the objects of the original work." 9 Fed.Cas. at 348 (emphasis added). Story added

> [N]o one can doubt that a reviewer may fairly cite [quote] largely from the original work, if . . . [its design be] . . . criticism. On the other hand, it is as clear, that if he thus [quotes] the most important parts of the work, with a view, not to criticise, but to *supersede the use of the original work*, [infringement will be found]. 9 F.Cas. at 344–45 (emphasis supplied).

An example of this thinking was set forth in 1740 in one of the earliest fair use cases, *Gyles v. Wilcox*, 26 Eng.Rep. 489, 2 Atk. 141 (1740) (No. 130), relating to abridgements, which stated, "Where books are colourably shortened only, they are undoubtedly infringement within the meaning of the [Statute of Anne]. . . . But this must not be carried so far as to restrain persons from making a real and fair abridgment, for abridgments may with great propriety be called a new book, because . . . the invention, learning, and judgment of the [secondary] author is shewn in them. . . ." Rulings and explanations of this sort led courts eventually to generalize that under the first factor "productive" uses were favored. *Sony*, 464 U.S. 417, 478–479 (Blackmun, J., dissenting). (The word "productive" was not necessarily an ideal description of the line of authorities because it risked the misconception that it encompassed any copying for a socially useful purpose. In fact, as illustrated by the quotations above from *Gyles* and *Folsom*, what the early authorities had meant was a secondary use that was productive in that it produced a new purpose or result, different from the original—in other words, a secondary use that transformed, rather than superseded, the original.) * * *

What has emerged * * * seems to be a two-track pattern of interpretation of the first factor: Secondary users have succeeded in winning the first factor by reason of either (1) transformative (or productive) nonsuperseding use of the original, or (2) noncommercial use, generally for a socially beneficial or widely accepted purpose. * * *

I conclude that on either branch of the analysis plaintiffs win the first factor, as Texaco's copying is neither transformative nor noncommercial.

Texaco's copying is not transformative or productive but is superseding. Texaco's copying is not of the transformative, nonsuperseding type that has historically been favored under the fair use doctrine. Texaco simply makes mechanical photocopies of the entirety of relevant articles. Nor is the copy of the original employed as part of a larger whole, for some new purpose. The dimensions of the original and of the copy are identical. The principal purpose of Texaco's copies is to supersede the original and permit duplication, indeed, multiplication. A scientist can make a copy, to be read subsequently and kept for future reference, without preventing the circulation of the journal among co-workers. This kind of copying contributes nothing new or different to the original copyrighted work. It multiplies the number of copies. This is the type of superseding copying that has been disfavored since the earliest discussions of the doctrine and was thought by many to preclude a finding of fair use prior to the Supreme Court's decision in *Sony*.

Texaco argues that this copying should be considered "productive" because its purpose is to advance scientific discovery. The argument fails for several reasons. That is not the kind of productivity that was intended by the discussions and holdings. As noted above, what was meant was that the copying should produce something new and different from the original, and not that a superseding copy would qualify, so long as it was made in pursuit of a beneficial cause. If the latter were the meaning of the doctrine, precious little would be left of the copyright protection as applied to scholarly or scientific writing. For scholarly and scientific writing has no readership except among those who use it in scholarly and productive or educational undertakings. If that fact alone were sufficient to justify the making of superseding copies, the authors and publishers of scholarly, scientific and educational materials could not protect their copyrights and could not survive as against inexpensive copier technology.

Texaco argues also that its copies should be considered transformative because it is important for scientists like Chickering to work with a photocopy and not with the original. It argues that the original is in many ways not useful to a scientist. Chickering testified that he needs a photocopy, in preference to an original, because he wishes to write notes in the margin and to take it into the lab where it may be exposed to corrosive chemicals, without damaging the original. He also needs a photocopy because it is less bulky; its slender 8–10 pages can be conveniently taken home to read or stored in a file, in preference to a 200–page complete issue, much less a complete annual volume.

This argument has some merit. In some circumstances, photocopying for the purpose of transferring text onto material of different character or shape could be a convincing transformation. Thus if the original were copied onto plastic paper so that it could be used in a wet environment, onto metal so that it would resist extreme heat, onto durable archival paper to prevent deterioration, or onto microfilm to conserve space, this might be a persuasive transformative use. Indeed, if Chickering were the subscriber and sole user of the subscription to *Catalysis*, and he made an extra copy of an article for use in the lab or for marking with scratch notes, the argument might have considerable force.

Here, however, where three subscriptions to *Catalysis* are serving the needs of hundreds of scientists, the principal feature of the photocopying is its capacity to give numerous Texaco scientists their own copy based on Texaco's purchase of an original. The most prominent feature of this copying is that the copies supersede the original and multiply its presence. Thus even if some transformative purpose was present in transferring the article from its journal into a slender photocopy, that use is overshadowed by the primary aspect of the copying, which is to multiply copies. * * *

Texaco's copying is for commercial gain. Nor does this come within the class of copying that has prevailed under the first factor because of its nonprofit educational or social value.

Texaco contends its copying should be considered comparable to that in *Williams & Wilkins*—copying done by scientists for the purpose of advancing science, rather than for commercial gain. Texaco emphasizes the social good to be derived from its research, including the development of cleaner burning, more efficient fuels to benefit the earth's ecology and resources. Texaco points out that its scientists and engineers are encouraged by Texaco to participate in scientific meetings and symposia and to publish papers of scientific merit. From 1986 to 1991 Texaco scientists have published more than 130 papers. In addition, Texaco scientists work with members of the academic community to exchange results of research. And Texaco finances research at universities in areas of common interest. Texaco contends it shares the results of its research with the scientific community at large by encouraging its scientists to write and publish articles and make presentations at scientific symposia.

Notwithstanding all this, I cannot accept Texaco's argument. Granted, the copiers are scientists, they are using their copies to assist in socially valuable scientific research, and they do not resell the copies. Nonetheless their research is being conducted for commercial gain. Its purpose is to create new products and processes for Texaco that will improve its competitiveness and profitability. Chickering testified that he selected articles to copy because they related to the research that he was doing in the course of his employment at Texaco. The purpose of this research was in each case to improve Texaco's commercial performance.

In sum, because the secondary use in question was copying of a superseding nature (done to create additional copies of the original) and was not transformative (or productive in the fair use sense), and because it was carried on in a commercial context for the purpose of producing profits, I find that plaintiffs easily prevail on the first factor inquiring into the purpose and character of the use.

Second Factor—The Nature of the Copyrighted Work

The second factor under § 107 looks to the "nature of the copyrighted work." Although there is an aspect of the facts that favor plaintiffs, I conclude that this factor favors Texaco.

The aspect that favors the plaintiffs is that the articles and materials published in *Catalysis* are created for publication with the purpose and intention of benefitting from the protection of the copyright law. These are the kinds of exercises of authorship that the copyright law was designed to protect in its objective "to promote the progress of science." * * *

Copyright protection is vitally necessary to the dissemination of scientific articles of the sort that are at issue. This is not because the authors insist on being compensated. To the contrary, such articles are written and published without direct payment to the authors. But copyright protection is essential to finance the publications that distribute them. Circulation of such material is small, so that subscriptions must be sold at very high prices. If cheap photoduplications could be freely made and sold at a fraction of the subscription price, *Catalysis* would not sell many subscriptions; it could not sustain itself, and articles of this sort would simply not be published. And without publishers prepared to take the financial risk of publishing and disseminating such articles, there would be no reason for authors to write them; even if they did, the articles would fail to achieve distribution that promoted the progress of science. * * *

On the other hand, courts have often observed that "the scope of fair use is greater with respect to factual than nonfactual works." *New Era Publications Int'l ApS v. Carol Publishing Group,* 904 F.2d 152, 157 (2d Cir.), *cert. denied,* 498 U.S. 921, 111 S.Ct. 297, 112 L.Ed.2d 251 (1990); *Rogers,* 960 F.2d at 310; *see generally* Gorman, *Fact or Fancy? The Implications for Copyright,* 29 J. Copyright Soc'y 560 (1982). It is difficult to tell whether such a judicial assertion about fair use is intended as prescriptive or descriptive. This may be nothing more than the logical consequence of two other principles: First, that facts are not subject to copyright ownership, *Feist Publications,* 111 S.Ct. at 1287; *Hoehling,* 618 F.2d 972, and second, the principle, discussed above, that quotation when done for the purpose of reporting facts accurately has a high claim for recognition as a favored purpose under the first fair use factor. Regardless whether the statement is a prescriptive utterance of a rule creating for factual material a special vulnerability to fair use, or merely a description of the inevitable consequence of the application of other rules about factual writing, it is unquestionably true that fair use is more easily found where the copyrighted material is of a factual nature rather than a fictional type. The material here being copied by Texaco's scientists is "essentially factual in nature," *Maxtone-Graham,* 803 F.2d at 1263, consisting of reports on scientific experimental research. The texts describe procedures followed and characterize the results found. Results are expressed largely in tables and graphs. I therefore conclude that the second factor favors Texaco.

Third Factor—Amount and Substantiality of Portion Used

The third factor looks to "the amount and substantiality of the portion used in relation to the copyrighted work as a whole." This factor clearly favors the plaintiffs, as Chickering has copied the entirety of the copyrighted articles in question. The Supreme Court acknowledged in *Sony* that the reproduction of an entire copyrighted work ordinarily "militat[es] against a finding of fair use." *Sony,* 464 U.S. at 450, 104 S.Ct. 792. * * *

Fourth Factor—Effect on the Market for the Copyrighted Work

The fourth factor looks at "the effect of the use upon the potential market for or value of the copyrighted work."

Plaintiffs contend that were it not for the photocopying practiced by Texaco's scientists, Texaco would need to provide its scientists additional copies through any one or more of a number of different routes, all of which would substantially supplement the revenues of the copyright owning publishers: Plaintiffs argue Texaco could purchase additional subscriptions; it could purchase back issues or back volumes; it could order tear sheets from document delivery services that purchase subscriptions; it could order photocopies from document services that make copies under license agreements with the plaintiff-publishers and pay royalties to the publishers for all copies made; it could negotiate a license directly with a particular publisher to pay a blanket fee for the right to make photocopies at will; or, alternatively, Texaco could photocopy articles as needed for its scientists by operating under the TRS or AAS license services offered by the CCC.

I find that plaintiffs have powerfully demonstrated entitlement to prevail as to the fourth factor. * * *

Texaco seeks unsuccessfully to show that Academic Press would not receive substantial additional revenues if Texaco (and similarly situated photocopiers) ceased to make unauthorized photocopies. While Texaco makes valid points on certain issues, its contentions do not undermine the strength of the publishers' proof of loss of revenue. First, in response to the publishers' contention that Texaco would buy additional subscriptions, back issues or back volumes, Texaco argues that what a scientist needs is a *photocopy*, and that need would not be served by additional subscriptions, back issues or back volumes. A scientist wants a *photocopy* on which to scribble notes in the margin without defacing an original; the photocopy also will be taken into the laboratory where corrosive chemicals may spill on it without fear of damaging the original. Furthermore, complete issues (or, *a fortiori*, complete volumes) are far too bulky to be kept in scientist's files or even used conveniently. All of this makes complete issues of the journal impracticable. Texaco shows, furthermore, that Academic Press does not offer reprints on terms convenient to the needs of Texaco's individual scientists as reprints may be purchased only with a minimum order of 100 copies. Thus, Texaco argues, if Texaco stopped making photocopies for Chickering and his colleagues, Texaco would not replace those photocopies by purchasing numerous additional subscriptions or by purchasing back issues and back volumes. Such purchases would not serve the necessary ends. I find that Texaco's contentions are substantially correct (although perhaps slightly overstated). I accept as correct that Texaco would not ordinarily fill the need now being supplied by photocopies through the purchase of back issues or back volumes. I accept also that Texaco would not fill this need by enormously enlarging the number of its subscriptions. Nonetheless, this does not significantly undermine the plaintiffs' position.

The plaintiffs have shown that there are a variety of other avenues Texaco could and would follow to provide its scientists promptly and relatively inexpensively with working copies of articles for their files (which would produce revenues for the publishers). These include the ordering of photocopies from document delivery services that would pay royalties to the publishers, the negotiation of blanket licenses with individual publishers, and the use of a CCC license under either the TRS or the AAS.

Moreover, although I accept Texaco's contention that it would not replace its scientists' individual copies by vastly increasing the number of subscriptions, the evidence supports the inference that, if Texaco stopped photocopying, it would increase the number of subscriptions somewhat. * * * Nor does Texaco's evidence contradict the probability that, if it stopped photocopying, its scientists would place orders for photocopies with document delivery services; such document services would promptly make and deliver photocopies, bill Texaco a modest fee, and pay royalties to the publisher under a private license agreement.

Finally, as noted above, the publishers have shown that the copying licenses offered by CCC would also satisfy the needs of Texaco's scientists for photocopies at a reasonable cost and burden to Texaco. This would provide significant additional revenue to the publishers and add value to their copyrights. * * *

In view of the fact that the publishers have demonstrated a substantial harm to the value of their copyrights through such copying, the fourth factor gives strong support to the conclusion that this copying is not a fair use.

Equitable Rule of Reason

The Supreme Court in *Sony* characterized the fair use doctrine as an "equitable rule of reason." *Sony*, 464 U.S. at 448 & n. 31, 104 S.Ct. at 792 & n. 31 (quoting H.Rep. No. 94–1476, at 66–66, U.S.Code Cong. & Admin.News 1976 at 5680), and explained in *Stewart* that the fair use doctrine " 'permits courts to avoid rigid application of the copyright statute when, on occasion, it would stifle the very creativity which that law is designed to foster.' " *Stewart*, 495 U.S. at 236, 110 S.Ct. at 1768 (quoting *Iowa State University Research Foundation, Inc. v. American Broadcasting Cos.*, 621 F.2d 57, 60 (2d Cir.1980)); *see generally*, Lloyd L. Weinreb, *Fair's Fair: A Comment on the Fair Use Doctrine*, 103 Harv.L.Rev. 1137 (1990). The statute, furthermore, does not characterize the four listed factors as exclusive. Thus, although I find that analysis under the four enumerated factors strongly favors the plaintiffs, I go on to consider a number of equitable arguments proffered by Texaco that do not fit neatly into the four-factor analysis.

Texaco contends its photocopying should come within the principles of * * * *Williams & Wilkins* and should be found a fair use.

[*Williams & Wilkins* is] easily distinguishable from the present facts. Taking its own holding at face value, it strongly suggests that Texaco's use should be considered infringing.

The first argument considered by the *Williams & Wilkins* court as favoring a finding of fair use was that the 1909 Copyright Act left it unclear whether photocopying was among the exclusive rights of the copyright owner. 487 F.2d at 1350–1352, 1359. If the Court of Claims was correct in that observation, it is certainly no longer available, as the 1976 Act clearly specifies in § 106(1) that "the owner of the copyright has the exclusive rights . . . (i) to reproduce the copyrighted work in copies. . . ."

The Court of Claims went on (in Part III of the opinion) to specify numerous factors that supported its conclusion that the photocopying by NIH and NML constituted a fair use. 487 F.2d at 1354, *et seq.* Most of these factors are not available to Texaco. The list included (i) that the plaintiff-publishers were not being economically harmed by the defendant's photocopying practices; (ii) that medicine and medical research would be "seriously hurt" by holding the practices of NIH and NML to be an infringement; (iii) that if infringement were found, the court could not devise a remedy (in the nature of a compulsory license) that would protect defendants' ability to make copies without exceeding judicial authority and trespassing into areas reserved to a legislature; (iv) that the defendants were "non-profit institutions, devoted solely to the advancement and dissemination of medical knowledge," and were not attempting to profit or gain financially by the photocopying; (v) that the researchers for whom the photocopies were made needed them for scientific work and had no purpose to reduplicate them for sale or other distribution; and (vi) "scientific progress, untainted by any commercial gain from the reproduction is the hallmark of the whole enterprise of duplication." The court stated that its conclusion of fair use "rests upon all of the elements discussed in Part III *supra* and not upon any one, or on any combination less than all." 487 F.2d at 1362.

Only one of those factors is present in this case—that being the use of the copies for scientific research without resale. All the rest are notably absent. The absence of most of them from the present facts is so apparent it requires little discussion. For example, that court found no harm to the copyright owners; this court finds that the copyright owners suffer a substantial loss of revenue. Also, while the duplication in *Williams & Wilkins* was devoted solely to scientific progress, untainted by any commercial gain, here it is commercial profit that is the hallmark of the enterprise.

Some of the differences call for comment. Those are the Court of Claims' conclusion that medicine and medical research would be "seriously hurt" if NIH and NML were forbidden from engaging in the copying practice, *see* 487 F.2d at 1356; and that a solution to the problem was beyond the court's power. *See* 487 F.2d at 1359–1360. Since the time of that decision, circumstances have substantially changed; such findings are no longer justified.

A problem that has bedeviled the application of the copyright laws to the making of copies has been the transaction costs of arriving at a license agreement, when a small number of photocopies is made. An honest user, who would be happy to pay a reasonable royalty, faces the problem of the enormous administrative difficulty and expense of making an agreement with the copyright owner for a license to make a single copy. Notwithstanding that the transaction might ultimately involve a fee of no more than a few dollars, enormous time, expense and burden may be involved for both sides in reaching such an agreement. The would-be copier would need to write to the copyright owner (assuming the name and current address can be readily found in the publication), propose a license and ask what the fee would be. The copyright owner would need to set a fee for the proposed transaction (if it did not have standardized rates) and to write back to the copier, who might then accept the proposed royalty fee (or make a counter offer). Eventually, through an exchange of correspondence involving a minimum of three letters, agreement could be reached, the copier would send a check for a few dollars to cover the royalty, and proceed to make a copy. A two-dollar royalty might easily engender hundreds of dollars of transaction costs, consuming many wasted hours. It might also delay the making of the copy for weeks.

Because of the outlandishly wasteful delay, expense, and inconvenience involved in negotiating such a transaction, virtually no user has been willing to do it. It therefore became a widespread practice that universities, foundations, research institutes and business companies simply photocopied without authorization. In *Williams & Wilkins* the court noted that during 1970 NIH's library made about 93,000 photocopies, aggregating nearly 1,000,000 pages. Since that time the volume of publications and the practice of photocopying have so proliferated, it is likely that today's numbers are vastly higher. It is clear that scientists at the NIH could not reasonably have entered into negotiations with medical publishers every time their work called for the making of a photocopy of a journal article. The *Williams & Wilkins* court therefore had considerable basis for concluding that medical research would have been substantially harmed by a ruling forbidding such unauthorized copying. Researchers might have been forced to do without photocopies, which would have been a substantial impediment to their research, or would have needed to engage in absurdly inefficient negotiations. The Court of Claims contemplated that the problem might conceivably be solved by the establishment of compulsory license fees, but concluded that this was beyond the court's power.

The monumental change since the decision of *Williams & Wilkins* in 1973 has been the cooperation of users and publishers to create workable solutions to the problem. *See generally Collectives That Collect* at 45–53. Most notable has been the creation of the CCC, and its establishment of efficient licensing systems—the TRS, established in 1978, followed by the AAS, established in 1983. Because some large users found that the TRS imposed administrative and recordkeeping burdens more onerous than they were eager to assume, the TRS was less successful than had been hoped. In response to the request of users for a system that would free them from TRS' recordkeeping burdens, the CCC developed the Annual Authorization Service. Upon the payment of a single global fee based on an audit of the user's photocopying practice, AAS permits free copying without any administrative burden of recordkeeping or reporting. As noted above, many of the largest corporations involved in research have become licensees under a CCC Annual Authorization.[28]

In addition to the framework created by the CCC, publishers and individual users have also, since *Williams & Wilkins*, developed private annual licensing agreements. For example, AT & T Bell Labs, in addition to its membership in the CCC, has over 200 agreements with publishers covering photocopying with respect to some 350 journals that are not registered with the CCC. Furthermore, publishers have extended photocopying licenses to document delivery services.

In this manner, private cooperative ingenuity has found practical solutions to what had seemed unsurmountable problems. Texaco can no longer make the same claims as were successfully advanced by the NIH to the Court of Claims in 1973. A finding that such unauthorized copying is an infringement would no longer impede the progress of science. Texaco could conveniently, and without undue administrative burden, retain the benefits of photocopying at will, simply by complying with one of the CCC's licensing systems.

* * * I do not accept Texaco's contention that CCC's TRS is too burdensome to qualify as a solution to the licensing problem. Texaco relies on the fact that the TRS has not attracted a large corporate following and that a number of users advised CCC they were unwilling to assume the administrative and reporting burdens required by TRS. * * *

Considering the features of the TRS objectively, Texaco has failed to show that they are so burdensome as to be unacceptable. To the contrary, the TRS represents a reasonable practicable solution for the industrial user community. The evidence shows that the administrative burdens for a user complying with TRS are modest and manageable.[29] Texaco has certainly failed to show otherwise.

The availability of a TRS or AAS license from the CCC renders moot the argument that so influenced *Williams & Wilkins* that a finding of

---

28. Two other CCC licensing programs are illustrative of the ways in which mechanisms have evolved in the age of photocopying to protect the copyrights of authors and publishers without imposing impracticable burdens on photocopy users. First, the CCC has established the Academic Pilot Licensing Program with several universities to develop a blanket licensing program modeled on the AAS for university photocopying. It is expected that the blanket license will cover individual and collective research or administrative reprography, but not "course packets," which are expected to continue to be licensed on a transactional basis. *See* Ginsburg, *Reproduction of Protected Works*, at 210 and Appendix C. Second, following this court's decision in *Basic Books, Inc. v. Kinko's Graphics Corp.*, 758 F.Supp. 1522 (S.D.N.Y.1991) (finding

that photocopy business' unauthorized copying of excerpts from books for compilation into university course packets was not a fair use), the CCC received between 1200 to 2000 daily requests for permissions from photocopy businesses. In response, the CCC started the Academic Permissions Service ("APS"). APS is a transactional license program for the purpose of creating course packets and anthologies that is available to copy shops, as well as university copy centers and departments. *See* Ginsburg, *Reproduction of Protected Works* at 210–211.

29. Law firms routinely keep a log of all photocopying done and bill clients for such copying on a per-page basis to a specific client-matter code. The recording and reporting requirements of the TRS are scarcely more burdensome.

infringement would harm science. The acceptance and use of CCC services by large research-oriented business corporations, including eleven major petroleum companies, undermines Texaco's reliance on the contention that unauthorized photocopying is customary and reasonable in private industrial research laboratories.

     * * *

Conclusion

The court finds that Texaco's photocopying of eight articles from the *Journal of Catalysis* for use by Donald H. Chickering, II, was not fair use under § 107 of the Copyright Act of 1976.[30] As to those articles, judgment is awarded to the plaintiffs on Texaco's affirmative defense of fair use.

———————

1. How have changes in technology affected the institutions and legal rules relating to the copying of articles from scholarly journals?

2. Do you find Judge Leval's reliance upon the emergence of the Copyright Clearance Center to be a convincing basis to reject Texaco's claim as to the fourth fair use factor? Consider the following argument by Judge Jacobs, in his dissent to the Second Circuit's affirmance:

> The majority holds that photocopying journal articles without a license is an infringement. Yet it is stipulated that (1) institutions such as Texaco subscribe to numerous journals, only 30 percent of which are covered by a CCC license; (b) not all publications of each CCC member are covered by CCC licenses; and (c) not all articles in publications covered by the CCC are copyrighted. It follows that no CCC license can assure a scientist that photocopying any given article is legal. * * *
>
> Under a transactional license, the user must undertake copyright research every time an article is photocopied. First, one must consult a directory to determine whether or not the publisher of the journal is a member of the CCC. If it is, one must ascertain whether the particular publication is one that is covered by the CCC arrangement, because not all publications of participating publishers are covered. Then one must somehow determine whether the actual article is one in which the publisher actually holds a copyright, since there are many articles that, for such reasons as government sponsorship of the research, are not subject to copyright. The production director of plaintiff Springer–Verlag testified at trial that it is almost impossible to tell which articles might be covered by a copyright. Since even an expert has difficulty making such a determination, the transactional scheme would seem to require that an intellectual property lawyer be posted at each copy

---

30. The parties disagree as to which side bears the burden of proof of fair use. I do not rule on the question as my findings and conclusions would be the same in either case.

machine. Finally, once it is determined that the specific article is covered, the copyist will need to record in a log the date, name of publication, publisher, title and author of article, and number of pages copied.

It may be easier to hand copy the material. The transactions costs alone would compel users to purchase a blanket license. However, if (as the majority holds) three of the fair use factors tip in favor of the publishers even without considering the market for license fees, a blanket license offers Texaco no safe harbor. Individual publishers remain free to stand upon the rights conferred in this Court's opinion, and negotiate separate licenses with separate terms, or sell offprints and refuse any license at all. Unless each publisher's licensing rights are made to depend upon whether or not that publisher participates in the CCC, we have the beginnings of a total market failure: with many thousands of scientific publications in circulation, a user cannot negotiate licensing fees individually with numerous publishers—unless it does nothing else. For many publications, licenses are simply not available. As to those, Dr. Chickering has the choice of hand copying, typescript, or the photocopying of selected pages only.

The blanket license fares no better. The CCC license cannot confer absolution for the photocopying of articles published by non-members of the CCC. Nor can the participating publishers properly collect fees for the photocopying of articles for which they do not hold the copyright. The district court found that there is currently a viable market for licensing, chiefly for the following reasons: (a) "[M]any of the largest corporations involved in research have become licensees under a CCC Annual Authorization." 802 F.Supp. at 24. However, until this case is decided, companies have had little choice but to become licensees or defendants. (b) The CCC has developed an Annual Authorization arrangement that "permits free copying without any administrative burden of recordkeeping or reporting." *Id.* That system works, however, only if one ignores the rights of publishers who are non-members of the CCC. (c) "[P]ublishers and individual users have ... developed private annual licensing agreements. For example, AT & T Bell Labs, in addition to its membership in the CCC, has over 200 agreements with publishers covering photocopying with respect to some 350 journals that are not registered with the CCC. Furthermore, publishers have extended photocopying licenses to document delivery services." *Id.* at 24–25. These developments "(and the other parallel steps taken by the owner-user communities)", satisfy the district court that "[r]easonably priced, administratively tolerable licensing procedures are available...." *Id.* at 25.

It is hard to escape the conclusion that the existence of the CCC—or the perception that the CCC and other schemes for collecting license fees are or may become "administratively tolerable"—is the chief support for the idea that photocopying scholarly articles is unfair in the first place. The majority finds it "sensible" that a use "should be considered 'less fair' when there is a ready market or means to pay for the use." 60 F.3d at 931. That view is sensible only to a point. There is no technological or commercial impediment to imposing a fee for use of a work in a parody, or for the quotation of a paragraph in a review or biography. Many publishers could probably unite to fund a bureaucracy that would collect such fees. The majority is sensitive to this problem, but concludes that "[t]he vice of circular reasoning arises only if the availability of payment is conclusive against fair use." 60 F.3d at 931. That vice is not avoided here. The majority expressly declines to "decide how the fair use balance would be resolved if a photocopying license for Catalysis articles were not currently available." 60 F.3d at 931. Moreover, the "important" fourth factor, 60 F.3d at 931, tips in favor of the publishers (according to the majority) "[p]rimarily because of lost licensing revenue" and only "to a minor extent" on the basis of journal sales and subscriptions. 60 F.3d at 931.

I do not agree with the majority that the publishers "have created, primarily through the CCC, a workable market for institutional users to obtain licenses for the right to produce their own copies of individual articles via photocopying." 60 F.3d at 930. By the CCC's admission, in its correspondence with the Antitrust Division of the Justice Department, "the mechanism for the negotiation of a photocopy license fee is often not even in place.... Nor can it be said that CCC's current licensing programs have adequately met the market's needs." There is nothing workable, and there is no market.

Even if the CCC is or becomes workable, the holder of a CCC blanket license is not thereby privileged to photocopy journal articles published by non-members of the CCC, as to which articles there is no "ready market or means to pay for the fair use". *See* 60 F.3d at 931. This Court has ended fair-use photocopying with respect to a large population of journals, but the CCC mechanism allows fair-use photocopying only of some of them. The facts before us demonstrate that the holder of a blanket license must still deal separately with CCC-member Bell Labs as to certain hundreds of its publications. With respect to the journals for which the publishers do not market licenses, users will either (a) research which publications are in this category and copy them longhand, in typescript or in partial photocopy, or (b) ignore our fair-use doctrine as unworkable. Neither option serves scientific inquiry or respect for copyright. In any event, it seems to me that when a journal is used in a customary way—a way that the authors uniformly intend and wish—the user should not be subjected on a day to day basis to burdens that cannot be satisfied without a team of intellectual property lawyers and researchers.

The fourth factor tips decidedly in Texaco's favor because there is no appreciable impairment of the publishing revenue from journal subscriptions and sales; because the publisher captures additional revenue from institutional users by charging a double subscription price (and can presumably charge any price the users will pay); and because the market for licensing is cumbersome and unrealized.

60 F.3d at 937–39. Which view—Judge Leval's or Judge Jacobs'—do you find more persuasive?

Even though Judge Jacobs' line of reasoning did not prevail in *American Geophysical*, would it change the result in a case in which a publisher's works were not available through CCC? Another collective rights agency? Where the licensing fee was particularly high and the copyright holder refused to negotiate?

Is the problem to which Judge Jacobs refers simply a transitional issue, that will be an anachronism 5 or 10 years from now? Should courts engage in predictions about technological progress?

3.   Should courts rely so heavily upon social norms and institutions in making decisions about formal legal rights? Recall the framework put forth by Professor Robert Cooter, *supra* pp. 507–08 in Merges, *supra* pp. 502–08. Is the court's reliance upon the CCC a good application of Cooter's thesis? In what circumstances are socially evolved norms more likely to be more efficiency-enhancing than rules promulgated on the basis of "expert" agency deliberation?

4.   Custom and industry practice play important roles in many other areas of the law, including the analysis of negligence, contractual performance, and environmental regulation.   Do these applications of social norms in the implementation of formal law make sense?

5.   In a series of cases brought by academic publishers against photocopying services regarding whether copyright permissions are needed for university course readers, *see, e.g., Basic Books v. Kinko's Graphics Corp.*, 758 F.Supp. 1522 (S.D.N.Y.1991), the courts rejected photocopiers' fair-use defense, largely on the ground that the copy shop is a for-profit operation. Whereas professors largely ignored the copyright law in assembling course readers prior to the early 1990s, *see* R. Ellickson, Order without Law 258–64 (1991), the combination of greater oversight by universities since these copyright decisions and the greater ease of obtaining copyright permissions as a result of the growth of the CCC and similar institutions have brought a large segment of the academic community into compliance with the law. What features of academic institutions enabled such a rapid adherence to the new legal order?

6.   In the aftermath of *American Geophysical*, do you think that businesses will likely fall into line relatively quickly? What factors come into play? In what ways is the university course reader context instructive? What are the principal impediments to adherence to the law? What are the

principal impediments to enforcement of the law? What strategies might publishers use to enforce the law or to change social norms?

7. The Internet has spawned a strong social norm favoring the free flow of ideas and information. This body of thought is not yet fully formed, but it has a number of articulate adherents in the computer community. It is essentially libertarian in nature, and is often summed up in the computer hacker credo "information wants to be free." *See* Barlow, The Economy of Ideas: A Framework for Rethinking Patents and Copyrights in the Digital Age, Wired, Mar. 1994, at 84.

Consider the following story. The San Francisco Chronicle disseminates via its Web Page an electronic version of key stories from its daily edition. A story about AIDS treatment was copied onto a bulletin board by an AIDS activist without obtaining copyright permission from the Chronicle. One of the users of the bulletin board, who happened to be knowledgeable about copyright law, disseminated a message calling into question unauthorized reproduction of the copyrighted article. The user was promptly "flamed," an Internet term referring to criticism and ostracization, by many users of the bulletin board. These users felt that the copyright law should not in any way inhibit the rapid dissemination of information about treatment for this dreaded disease. What does this anecdote indicate about cultural norms regarding copyright protection?

8. Notwithstanding the concerns raised by many Internet users, other information distributors (*e.g.*, libraries), and information consumers generally, the principal content-producing industries—book publishers, music publishers, motion picture studios—have lobbied for strong protection of copyright interests on the Internet and everywhere else. What does this conflict suggest for the evolution of governance regimes for digital content? What vision is most likely to prevail? *Cf.* Samuelson, The Copyright Grab, Wired, Jan. 1996, at 134; Lehman, Intellectual Property and the National Information Infrastructure: The Report of the Working Group on Intellectual Property Rights (1995); Menell, The Challenges of Reforming Intellectual Property Protection for Computer Software, 94 Colum. L. Rev. 2644 (1994); Goldstein, Copyright's Highway: From Gutenberg to the Celestial Jukebox (1994); Litman, Copyright Legislation and Technological Change, 68 Or. L. Rev. 275 (1989).

Problem: Policies to Foster the Creation of Multi–Media Works

The advent of low-cost widely distributed networked computers has spawned a new industry creating "multi-media works," compilations of photographic, graphic, dramatic, audiovisual, text, sound, and other works such as an interactive encyclopedia or golf course video game. The technology allows users to move quickly from one part of the work to another, zoom in for more detail, search the database effortlessly, and create their own works. One of the major challenges to this nascent industry is negotiating for the many types of rights to "digital content" needed to create the new works. The transaction costs of acquiring such rights can be staggering. Anecdotal evidence suggests that many ventures are not feasible because of the costs of acquiring rights.

A consortium of user groups, libraries, and small companies designing multi-media products has called for significant revision of the fair use doctrine so as to foster creation and dissemination of new works. Their proposals range from relaxing the standards for finding copyright infringement in complex multi-media works (*e.g.*, compiling large ranges of content) to broader protections for non-profit ventures. Educational organizations have called for expanding the domain of fair use to cover course readers and multi-media works used in the classroom. Some copyright professors have called for the promulgation of a governmental compulsory licensing system for multimedia works. Other professors have suggested that any governmental regime is likely to be obsolete before it can be created and will not be as capable of moving with the technology. They feel that strong intellectual property rights will promote the evolution of new institutions to address the needs of this area. They cite the success of private collective rights associations—like ASCAP and BMI for music licensing, the CCC for photocopying, and the Hollywood Script Registry—which developed to address other problems in intellectual property rights licensing, and they feel that similar hybrid organizations will develop for the new markets created by computer and network technologies if given the chance. The "content" producers—music publishers, motion picture producers, book publishers, *etc.*—call for strengthening of intellectual property rights (smaller scope for fair use, larger sanctions for copyright violations, no compulsory licensing) so as to enable them to better enforce their rights in the information age. They are concerned that the Internet will make "digital piracy" easier and more difficult to detect.

You have been appointed Special Counsel to the Senate Judiciary Committee, which has jurisdiction over the intellectual property laws. The Committee has requested your analysis of what steps Congress should take to address this issue. Analyze the various proposals within the Calabresi & Melamed framework. What policy or policies would you recommend? What role will the Internet likely play in addressing the negotiation problems associated with multi-media works? *See* Merges, Contracting into Liability Rules: Intellectual Property Rights and Collective Rights Organizations, 84 Cal. L. Rev. 1293, 1373–91 (1996); Reichman, Legal Hybrids Between the Patent and Copyright Paradigms, 94 Colum. L. Rev. 2432, 2504 (1995); D. Karjala, Comment on the IIP Report Exposure '94, (Japan) Institute of Intellectual Property, International Intellectual Property Symposium: A Proposal of the New Rule on Intellectual Property for Multimedia, English Text, April 7, 1994, at 18.

E.   THE ROLE OF SOCIAL NORMS IN STRUCTURING PROPERTY INTERESTS IN ORGANIZATIONS: THE CASE OF LAW FIRMS

Social and economic organizations come in a large variety of forms in our society, from families, small businesses, and other closely-knit groups

to large law firms, multi-national corporations, universities, health maintenance organizations (HMOs), public agencies, residential communities,
non-profit organizations, labor unions, and trade associations. The internal
structure of these organizations—the implicit rights of members or employees to use the resources of the organization, the rules governing membership and tenure in the organization, the relationships among different
parts of the organization, and the rules governing the division of profits
from the venture—determines their productivity and the distribution and
management of vast amounts of resources and wealth in our society.

Managing an organization is a lot like managing the commons. The
principal purpose of most group enterprises is to create value—financial
and psychic—for their members. This inevitably involves a tension—rules
that promote sharing of the resources and product within an organization
promote teamwork but they also discourage individual effort because each
member cannot fully enjoy the product of his or her labor; rules that allow
individual members to claim their full contribution to the enterprise may
discourage teamwork.

Every venture can be structured in a variety of ways. For example, a
restaurant company can own all of the means of production from growing
food through the many stages of distribution and production to serving the
final product. Alternatively, it can contract out for many of the services
involved in serving food. At the extreme, it can be a franchisor which does
not operate any restaurants, but merely establishes the model for operating
a restaurant and enters into long-term contracts with suppliers and owner-
operators who actually implement the concept. Similarly, the practice of
law can be structured in a broad variety of ways, from in-house counsel to
specialty law firms to large full-service firms. Within a firm, there are a
large range of options for structuring the partnership:

- partnership size: large or small

- ratio of partners to associates: high or low

- promotion system: up and out versus possibility of associates passed
  over for partner remaining on as permanent associates

- frequency of partnership meetings: frequent or infrequent

- compensation: based on productivity (business brought in and billable hours) or lock-step (*i.e.*, years with firm)

- breadth of compensation range: high or low

- sharing of information about partner salaries and financial data:
  fully shared or known only by compensation committee

- hierarchy within partnership: equal status versus caste system

- percentage of partnership vote required to promote an associate to
  partnership: 50%—100%

- percentage of partnership vote required to hire a partner laterally:
  50%—100%

- percentage of partnership vote required to fire a partner: managing partner decision or 50%—100% vote of partnership

This section examines the evolution of the large law firm in the past century. As background to this case study, it is useful to have some familiarity with the field of "transaction cost economics." Transaction cost economics explains the choice of organizational form for particular ventures using the tools of economics. *See generally* O.E. Williamson, The Mechanisms of Governance (1995); O.E. Williamson, The Economic Institutions of Capitalism (1985). A recent article summarizes the field in the following manner:

> Transaction cost economics ["TCE"] studies how trading partners protect themselves from the hazards associated with exchange relationships. * * * TCE maintains that in a complex world, contracts are typically incomplete. Because of this incompleteness, parties who invest in relationship-specific assets expose themselves to a hazard: If circumstances change, their trading partners may try to expropriate the rents accruing to the specific assets. One way to safeguard those rents is through integration, where the parties merge and eliminate adversarial interests. Less extreme options include reciprocal buying arrangements, in which each party exposes itself to form a mutual exchange of "hostages," and partial ownership agreements. In general, a variety of such "governance structures" may be employed; the appropriate one depends on the particular characteristics of the relationship. In this way, TCE may be considered the study of alternative institutions of governance. Its working hypothesis, as expressed by Williamson, is that economic organization is really an effort to "align transactions, which differ in their attributes, with governance structures, which differ in their costs and competencies, in a discriminating (mainly, transaction cost economizing) way." Simply put, TCE tries to explain how trading partners choose, from the set of feasible institutional alternatives, the arrangement that offers protection for their relationship-specific investments at the lowest total cost.
>
> Transactions differ in a variety of ways: the degree to which relationship-specific assets are involved, the amount of uncertainty about the future and about other parties' actions, the complexity of the trading arrangement, and the frequency with which the transaction occurs. Each matters in determining the preferred institution of governance, although the first—asset specificity—is held to be particularly important. Williamson defines asset specificity as "durable investments that are undertaken in support of particular transactions, the opportunity cost of which investments is much lower in best alternative uses or by alternative users should the original transaction be prematurely terminated." This could describe a variety of relationship-specific investments, including both specialized physical and human capital, along with

intangibles such as R & D and firm-specific knowledge or "capabilities."

Governance structures can be described along a spectrum. At one end lies the pure, anonymous spot market, which suffices for simple transactions such as basic commodity sales. Market prices provide powerful incentives for the exploitation of profit opportunities, and market participants are quick to adapt to changing circumstances as information is revealed through prices. When specialized assets are at stake, however, and when product or input markets are thin, bilateral coordination of investment decisions may be desirable, and combined ownership may be efficient. At the other end of the spectrum from the simple, anonymous spot market thus lies the fully integrated firm, where trading parties are under unified ownership and control. TCE posits that such hierarchies offer greater protection for specific investments and provide relatively efficient mechanisms for responding to change where coordinated adaptation is necessary. Compared to decentralized structures, however, hierarchies provide managers weaker incentives to maximize profits and normally incur additional bureaucratic costs. Between the two poles of market and hierarchy are a variety of "hybrid" modes, such as complex contracts and partial ownership arrangements. The movement from market to hierarchy thus entails a trade-off between the high-powered incentives and adaptive properties of the market, and the safeguards and central coordinating properties of the firm.

Implicit in TCE is a notion that market forces work to bring about an "efficient sort" between transactions and governance structures, so that exchange relationships observed in practice can be explained in terms of transaction cost economizing.

Shelanski & Klein, Empirical Research in Transaction Cost Economics: A Review and Assessment, 11 J. L. Econ. & Org. 325, 336–38 (1995). TCE is subject to various criticisms, including its narrowly economic or efficiency-oriented view of the world. Nonetheless, it provides a valuable lens through which to view and understand the structure of organizations. Since one of the key roles of lawyers is advising corporate and organizational entities, it is essential that they understand the ways in which organizations may be internally governed.

The structure of law firms provides but one revealing exploration into this growing field. It is of particular relevance to law students for obvious reasons. As you study these materials, think about how the structure of law firms, in terms of both ownership and control, encourages the creation of value for law firm partners and the realization of other personal and professional aspirations of lawyers. You should also seek to glean the key factors in resolving the ubiquitous organizational tension between encouraging teamwork among members of an organization and discouraging individuals from shirking responsibilities, grabbing disproportionate profits of the venture, and leaving the enterprise. At the end of this case study, we will apply the lessons of this example to another context—the challenge of structuring a new high technology venture.

Robert T. Swaine, The Cravath Firm and Its Predecessors: 1819–1947

Vol. II, 1–12 (1947).

The dominant personality of this volume is Paul D. Cravath. He was the authoritative head of the firm until his death in 1940, and his conceptions of the management of a law office still control its operations. * * *

The firm's practice, even in litigation, has dealt primarily with corporate and financial problems, and the character of the work from year to year has been increasingly determined by national economic conditions. Cycles of security issues in boom times have been followed by cycles of receiverships and reorganizations in times of depression, while, without letup, problems arising from the constantly heavier impact on business of Federal taxation and regulation have pre-empted more and more of the time of partners and staff.

        * * *

Cravath had a definite philosophy about the organization of his law firm, its partners, its practice and its relation to its associates.

As to recruiting the legal staff:

Cravath believed that a staff trained within the office would be better adapted to its methods of work than a staff recruited from older men who, in practice elsewhere, might have acquired habits inconsistent with Cravath methods, and hence he insisted that the staff should be recruited, so far as possible, from men just out of the law schools.

He believed that these men should have had a thorough preliminary education in the arts as well as in the theory of the law. Cravath believed that disciplined minds are more likely to be found among college graduates than among men lacking in formal education; that mastery of the fundamental theories of the common law is a *sine qua non* of legal competence; and that such mastery can better be taught in the law schools than by practitioners in a busy office. The best men, too, are most likely to be found in the law schools which have established reputations by reason of their distinguished faculties and rigorous curricula, and which, by that very fact, attract the more scholarly college graduates.

Cravath believed in seriousness of purpose—a man with a competent mind, adaptable to practicing law according to Cravath standards, should have made a good scholastic record at college. But he recognized, without full approval, the tradition of the early decades of this century—that "gentlemen" went to college primarily to have a good time and make friends. Hence, while a good college record was always a factor in favor of an applicant, lack of such a record was not necessarily an excluding factor. Cravath himself had not made an unusually distinguished college record. As the playboy traditions of college life became obsolete in the stern realities of the depression for the '30s, however, college records of applicants came to have added importance. For a poor law school record Cravath never had tolerance. * * *

The scholastic standards of the "Cravath system" thus made a Phi Beta Kappa man from a good college who had become a law review editor at Harvard, Columbia or Yale the first choice. * * *

Cravath did not, however, want colorless, narrow-minded bookworms. From applicants who met his standards of scholarship, he wanted those who also had warmth and force of personality and physical stamina adequate to the pressure to which they would often be subject because of the rugged character of the work. * * *

As to training associates:

Cravath preferred that men should not specialize in such branches of the law as real estate or administration of estates or, later, taxation, until they had attained a general experience over several years. This objective required that a man should not be confined to the work of one client or even be assigned to one partner for any undue length of time.

At the outset of their practice Cravath men are not thrown into deep water and told to swim; rather, they are taken into shallow water and carefully taught strokes. The Cravath office does not follow the practice of many other offices of leaving small routine matters entirely to young men fresh from law school without much supervision, on the theory that a man best learns how to handle cases by actually handling them. Under the "Cravath system" a young man watches his senior break a large problem down into its component parts, is given one of the small parts and does thoroughly and exhaustively the part assigned to him—a process impracticable in the handling of small routine matters. Cravath believed that the man who learns to analyze the component parts of a large problem involving complicated facts, and to do each detailed part well, becomes a better lawyer faster than the man who is not taught in such detail. Matters involving small amounts often involve difficult, complicated law problems, and a man may be misled, perhaps made careless, by being allowed to handle such a matter without adequate analysis and supervision.

Cravath's insistence that the legal staff be recruited from men just graduating from the law schools, rather than from older, experienced lawyers, was based not only upon his desire for a Cravath-trained staff but also upon his belief that the office and its clients would get the best service from men confident of unimpeded opportunity for advancement. When a former associate asked him, in 1916, whether there might be an opportunity for him to return to the office and make it his career, Cravath referred to the "office policy of filling advanced positions from the ranks of the young men who enter the office as beginners," and added: "I feel that if our office has been successful it is very largely because of our adherence to this plan, which has enabled young men to feel that if they remain with us during the years of preparation they will have the first chance when opportunities for responsible positions from time to time develop."

It is a fundamental part of the Cravath training that a man's responsibility shall be increased as his growing competency permits. * * *

As the men grow in professional stature, those who evidence capacity for delegation are given opportunity to expand their own activities by the use of younger assistants to whom they can in turn give the same kind of training they have enjoyed. The art of delegation in the practice of the law is difficult, requiring nicety of balance which many men with fine minds and excellent judgment are unable to attain. There have been many cases— some even among the partners—of inability to find the happy medium between doing all of a job personally and turning it over completely to an assistant. The more nearly he attains the right compromise between these two extremes, the greater the amount of effective work a man can turn out, and hence the greater his value to the firm.

As to compensation:

Before Cravath came to the firm, law students in the office and several of the admitted associates received no compensation. Those associates made their living by doing what business they could develop for themselves and paid for desk room by assisting in office business. Cravath could not tolerate the inefficiency and divided loyalty implicit in such an arrangement. He abolished the study of law within the office, and every associate, including the man fresh from law school, was put on a salary. Because its demands in time, energy and competence are heavy, the Cravath office tries to keep annual advancements and ultimate compensation at least as high as those of any other office in the City.

Adoption by other city offices of many of the same principles on which the "Cravath system" is based led, about 1910, to competitive bidding for the highest-ranking men of the leading law schools. This gave a few men inordinately high beginning salaries, sometimes double those of the generally applicable scale. The discrimination among the men just coming out of law school became unfair and made the initial salary offered too important a criterion in the choice of offices. Within a few years the evils of the practice were admitted by the offices and strongly objected to by the faculties of the law schools; on their suggestion it was abandoned after World War I, following a conference among the managing partners of the larger offices. Beginning salaries thereafter tended to become uniform, and at increasing rates, until the disruption of education during World War II and elimination of the regular annual crop of law school graduates made it impossible to apply uniform standards to men of widely varying ages who had spent years in Government service.

As to tenure:

Every lawyer who enters the Cravath office has a right to aspire to find his life career there—but only by attaining partnership.

Men who are willing to stay only a year or two are not desired, for the "Cravath system" cannot train a man in that short time. They are expected to remain as long, but only as long, as they are growing in responsibility. Cravath used to say that, except for a few research scholars and specialists, no one should be permitted to stay in the office more than six years unless the partners had determined to admit him into the partnership. Most of the partners admitted up to 1926 had been in the office for five or six years. As the work of the office, the complexity of the problems, the number of partners and the size of the staff increased rapidly during the '30s, the period of apprenticeship for the partners admitted in 1940 lengthened to about eight years. The dislocations due to World War II further lengthened the period; the partners admitted in 1946 all graduated from law school before 1936.

Ten years is too long for a man to remain a Cravath associate under normal conditions unless he has been told that the chances of his being made a partner are still good. A man who is not growing professionally creates a barrier to the progress of the younger men within the organization and, himself, tends to sink into a mental rut—to lose ambition; and loss of ambition induces carelessness. It is much better for the man, for the office and for the clients that he leave while he still has self-confidence and determination to advance. The frustrated man will not be happy, and the unhappy man will not do a good job.

Under the "Cravath system" of taking a substantial number of men annually and keeping a current constantly moving up in the office, and its philosophy of tenure, men are constantly leaving. Where do they go? Associates with good records have no difficulty in finding promising and profitable opportunities if they do not stay too long, causing potential connections to question their success and hesitate to gamble on advanced age or salary levels. The firm constantly has requests from clients and other leading industrial and financial organizations to supply men for legal and executive positions. Other high-ranking law firms of the City and elsewhere have taken Cravath men as partners; many Cravath men have formed successful law firms of their own; and quite a number have become members of law school faculties. It is often difficult to keep the best men long enough to determine whether they shall be made partners, for Cravath-trained men are always in demand, usually at premium salaries. Because among the many called to the staff only a few can be chosen as partners, even good men are likely to feel that the odds against them are so great that they should accept flattering offers from others.

Almost without exception, the relations between the Cravath partners and the men who have left the office to compete professionally have remained friendly, and often intimate. Cravath partners take great pride in the success of the alumni. Business which such men have been doing while with the firm has frequently been encouraged to continue with them; new business is often referred to former associates.

As to choosing partners:

The "Cravath system" has given the firm a multiplicity of talent from which to choose its partners. While recognizing the risks of too much inbreeding, Cravath insisted that new partners should be chosen from within the office, unless special requirements otherwise compelled. Young partners and young associates are seldom subjected to the discouragement of seeing someone come in over them from the outside. * * *

Obviously not all the men competent to be partners can be taken into the firm—for that would make the firm unwieldy. The choice is difficult; factors which control ultimate decisions are intangible; admittedly they are affected by the idiosyncrasies of the existing partners. Mental ability there must be, but in addition, personality, judgment, character. No pretense is made that the ultimate decisions are infallible. Only infrequently have mistakes been made in taking men into the firm; more often, mistakes not so easily remedied have been made in not admitting others.

As to interests outside the firm:

Probably the most rigid feature of the "Cravath system" has been insistence that for every man in the office, from the senior partner to the neophyte law clerk, the practice of law must be the primary interest and that that practice shall be solely as a member of the Cravath team.

This is not to say that the great advantages of interests outside the law are not recognized. On the contrary, Cravath himself gave much time to charitable, educational and artistic activities. He wanted his partners and associates to have such interests, and believed that the few who allowed office work to pre-empt all their energies were harming themselves and the firm. Neither partners nor associates, however, are encouraged to have outside business interests, and they may not have any such interest which would impair their work at the office. There are no half-time partners or associates. Nor is there any such thing as the business of individual partners or associates: all the business in the office must be firm business. This means that there is no division of fees between the firm and its associates, as there is in many other offices. The problem of the firm is to do effectively the business which comes to it; by so doing that business, more comes in. Hence, business-getting ability is not a factor in the advancement of a man within the office at any level, except in so far as that ability arises out of competence in doing law work, as contrasted with family or social connections.

Cravath early came to believe that in most cases the client is best advised by a lawyer who maintains an objective point of view and that such objectivity may be impeded by any financial interest in the client's business or any participation in its management. Accordingly, he made it the policy of the firm that neither its partners nor its associates should hold equity securities of any client, or serve as a director of a corporate client, or have a financial interest, direct or indirect, in any transaction in which the firm was acting as counsel. Occasionally, more frequently in recent years, clients have insisted upon exceptions permitting partners to occupy directorships and own qualifying equity securities, but the exceptions have been few.

As to the relations of the partners inter se:

Every partner is expected to cooperate with every other in the firm's business, through whichever partner originating, and to contribute to all the work of the firm to the maximum of his ability. The formation among the partners of cliques practicing independently of each other, which developed under Guthrie, would not be allowed today.

Attainment of partnership does not mark either the limit of potential growth or accession to any automatic hierarchy. The younger partner who evidences capacity to win the confidence of clients with whom he works so that they continue with the firm, who impresses others who come into contact with his work so that other business comes to the firm through him, and who takes responsibility for a number of varied matters, at the same time supervising the work of members of the staff and sometimes of other partners, may well rise, and indeed often has risen, within the firm more rapidly than some of his seniors. The partners are judged *inter se* just as are the associates, and adjustments are made to reflect the evaluation of the younger partners by their seniors.[31] Complete objectivity in such appraisals is not easy, for the most companionable man is not always the best, or most effective, lawyer.

* * *

As to the firm's management:

Cravath believed that a law firm, like any other successful organization, must have strong executive direction, and until the mid–1930s his firm was under a dictatorship in his person. Details of office management were, of course, left to the conventional managing clerk, and there has always been a managing partner, chosen from the younger partners, charged with supervision of managerial detail and, in effect, the liaison between the senior partner and the staff.

Cravath never completely delegated to anyone ultimate determination of office policy or evaluation of associates and partners. However, as the legal and clerical staffs began to increase rapidly after world War I, he relied more on the judgments of his partners. Weekly firm meetings started about 1923, where matters of general policy and of management, as well as current law problems, are discussed. Today every partner has a voice in the decision of every important question, as well as the benefit of the views of all his partners.

---

31.   Cravath partners are true partners, not salaried associates given the nominal title of partner.

1. In what ways is the problem of structuring a law firm like the problem of managing the commons? How does the "Cravath system" address the tragedy of the commons? How does it discourage shirking and promote teamwork among the firm's members?

2. What are the drawbacks to the Cravath system? *See, e.g.*, Wilkins & Gulati, Why Are There So Few Black Lawyers in Corporate Law Firms? 84 Cal. L. Rev. 493 (1996). Would you want to work in an organization structured in this way?

Steven Brill, Bye, Bye, Finley, Kumble: The Firm Everyone Loves to Hate Is Falling Apart

The American Lawyer, September, 1987, at 3.*

It was a grand experiment. Take 198 restless, disgruntled, money-conscious, hard-driving partners from around the country. Free them from stuffy old firms that insist on paying for seniority or pedigree rather than productivity. Give them 450 associates, 17 offices, huge bounties for bringing in business, and ceaseless harangues from on high about billing and realization. And see what happens.

What happened for the last half decade was the fastest growing, most lavishly paying, most reviled (especially by those at firms whose partners or clients had been raided), most talked about law firm ever. What's happening now is $76 million of debt that's growing, name partners not talking to each other, at least one key client afraid to send new business, and partner and associate resumes flooding the mails from Beverly Hills to Park Avenue.

Three years ago, name partner and just-anointed co-managing partner Marshall Manley of the firm currently called Finley, Kumble, Wagner, Heine, Underberg, Manley, Myerson & Casey told me, "Come back in a few years and see if this system isn't working. If it doesn't work . . . we'll all be gone. Our partners came here by voting with their feet, and they'll leave the same way."

Co-managing partner Steven Kumble added, during an interview for the same 1984 article, that the firm would have seven hundred lawyers in a year or two, and be an entirely new kind of legal institution: a "total meritocracy."

The total meritocracy, it turned out, was at its core not much more than a commission-for-fees operation, soon to fall under the weight of that commission structure. Lawyers got paid the most for bringing in business, not for legal work, and certainly not for their contribution to building any kind of long-term institution.

* Steven Brill is Chairman and CEO of American Lawyer Media. This article is republished with permission from the September 1987 issue of *The American Lawyer.* © 1987 *American Lawyer Media, L.P.*

And when some of these rainmakers didn't bring in the business they promised—or when the business declined or evaporated because of the firm's aggressive billing practices—their incomes were nonetheless not cut. For their support was too important to either Kumble or Manley or others in what by 1985 had become an incessant power struggle that made the firm letterhead more a fight card than a law partnership. * * *

1. Declining Revenue

For all its spending ($11.5 million for remodeled offices in New York and a $500,000 art collection) and lavish, much-heralded bidding for rainmakers and pseudo-rainmakers ($800,000 for former senator Paul Laxalt, who reportedly is doing about as well so far as a client getter as a presidential candidate), Finely, Kumble's revenue per lawyer actually dropped from $226,000 in fiscal 1985 to $219,000 in fiscal 1987.

And that declining revenue-per-lawyer calculation generously takes into account the addition of new lawyers by calculating a weighted average number of lawyer-years each year.

Meantime expenses are skyrocketing. For example, rent jumped to $11.6 million from $8.2 million in fiscal 1987 over fiscal 1986. That's a 41 percent increase at a time when the number of lawyers increased about 10 percent. And "promotion expense," as the firm's profit and loss statement describes it, reached $5.3 million, up from an already incredible $4.1 million in fiscal 1986. Insurance costs, apparently because of an escalating number of seemingly insignificant but persistent malpractice suits in a firm that perhaps cares too much about taking in business and suing to collect on it rather than doing quality work, went from $2.9 million to $5.4 million. This, despite a deductible of $1 million per case. * * *

VOTING WITH THEIR FEET

Finley, Kumble began in 1968 with a group of five partners, led by Kumble. They had a vision that they could build a bigger, richer firm by being more aggressive, more merit-oriented, and just plain more business-like than any firm had ever been. By 1979, they were 70 lawyers, all in New York and all there for one thing: money. They had come because they could make more of it there than anywhere else.

Some tried too hard to make it; one partner got nailed for stock fraud, another was cited by the court for conflict of interest in a bankruptcy fee-splitting arrangement.

In 1978 Marshall Manley signed on. A brash New Yorker then transplanted to Los Angeles, Manley had been bounced from Manatt, Phelps, Rothenberg, Manley & Tunney, which he'd helped build, because he'd given what was then thought to be an intemperate, self-puffing interview to me in Esquire magazine. Now he was ready to build a second firm.

Manley is a brilliant businessman and an indescribably alluring business getter. And by 1984 he'd built the Finley, Kumble California operation from nothing to 150 prospering lawyers, many with glittering credentials that far outshone their New York partners.

By 1984 the Washington, D.C., office under the leadership of Robert Washington, Jr., had also grown dramatically. What had been the product of a merger with a small-time firm had blossomed into an 80–lawyer powerhouse specializing in municipal finance and international trade, among other areas. Florida, too, was flourishing, having been built after several false starts by the ever-persistent, ever-focused Kumble, a charming, articulate business getter whose style and business acumen matched or beat the Wall Street partners he was now challenging.

New Yorkers Andrew Heine, a sophisticated, Yale-educated, corporate lawyer, and Neil Underberg, a well-respected real estate specialist, rounded out the Finley, Kumble leadership group—five tough, cocky partners on the make.

It was an exciting place to be in 1984. As Jerold Miles, a former managing partner at Los Angeles's Agnew, Miller & Carlson, said at the time in explaining his 1981 decision to join Manley's new team, "When I decided to leave ... I had eighteen offers. One night I went home and started describing all of them to my wife, and after I went through them, I told her I thought I was going to take Finley, Kumble. And she said she knew I was going to, because when I had described that opportunity to her it was the only time my eyes sparkled. Here was the chance to leave a top-heavy firm and go to the only pure meritocracy anywhere, where whatever I did and whatever I built I would benefit from."

The competition saw it differently. The firm became a hated symbol of all the new market forces that were making the profession so much less comfortable.

Manley, Washington, and Kumble traveled the country, making pitches to new clients, exhorting partners and associates to keep their billings up, and signing on new lawyers whom they judged to be "charismatic" enough (a favorite word for client getters) to keep the steamroller going.

It all seemed to be working, for the firm had indeed found a market niche among up-and-coming midsize businesses eager to make it to the Fortune 500 and just as eager to sign on with a group of lawyers who were also challenging those at the top. These clients were less likely to have large in-house departments and less likely to be wedded already to any large firm. They were, therefore, more susceptible than others with large legal budgets to Finley, Kumble's we'll-win-for-you, we'll-handle-your-work-everywhere pitches.

Yet clouds were also visible. The firm's only culture was money. Even the youngest associate learned that a "bulls—t" partner was one who perhaps did good legal work but wasn't charismatic enough to attract new business. Thus, the ratio between highest earning and lowest earning partners was as much as 10:1. For the short term, Manley, Kumble, and the others at the top did fabulously with this setup; by paying partners who simply did client work no more and sometimes less than senior associates were paid at other firms, the top partners were leveraging these partners the way other firms leverage associates.

But how could the most talented lawyers who lacked "charisma" be attracted to such a firm? And how, then, could clients be served well in that environment?

And if associates were exhorted to bill at least 2,000 hours a year—and given bonuses for doing more—wouldn't realization rates go down and client dissatisfaction rise? Similarly, with the firm paying such a premium for work brought in, wouldn't bills be higher than they'd be at other firms? For example, if Manley got a cut of 10 percent, and didn't bill a dime's worth of time, the client was, in effect, paying a 10 percent finder's fee on top of the cost and profit conventionally attached to the partners and associates who did his work. With the firm employing lots of high-priced partners like Manley, and also making straight referral deals with many of the three dozen people it calls "counsel" but who similarly do little or no legal work, wouldn't those costs start to turn off clients?

Worse, with other firms awakening to what Kumble and his partners had been the first to see—that in the modern age of law as a business, partners need to be paid for their productivity and not their seniority or they'll leave—wouldn't the firm's recruiting advantage be dissipated? Wouldn't those partners who were prone to vote with their feet now be satisfied at home or find other eager firms with whom to cast their votes?

There was another problem, too. It didn't have to do with money but rather with the only factor that often overrides money in business deals gone sour: clashing egos.

William Horne, Hale and Dorr's Velvet Purge

The American Lawyer, December, 1990, at 15.*

If Hale and Dorr managing partner John Hamilton, Jr., were writing a book, the latest chapter might be titled "Eliminating Partners By Negotiation." Over the past nine months Hamilton and a handful of department heads at the 319–lawyer Boston firm have quietly orchestrated a tidy, almost bloodless purge of eight of the firm's 96 equity partners. * * *

Except for litigator Blair Perry, 61, those departing say they are leaving of their own volition. "It was sort of a mutual decision," says litigator David Mortensen, 48, the spokesman for several partners planning to spin off their own firm.

But a former partner with close ties to the firm says Hale and Dorr made a "purely commercial decision" in encouraging these partners to leave—not surprising, given the state of the economy in New England. Litigation chief John Fabiano, the firm spokesman on the departures, concedes that these partners' practices no longer fit in at Hale and Dorr.

* William Horne is a Senior Writer for The American Lawyer. This article is republished with permission from the December 1990 issue of *The American Lawyer.* © 1990 *American Lawyer Media, L.P.*

"Some of the areas these guys are in are areas where the firm is not making money," he says. Another litigation partner puts it more bluntly: "They were cases of square pegs in round holes." * * *

Perhaps the most striking "early retirement," however, is Perry's. Perry has worked at Hale and Dorr since graduating cum laude from Harvard Law School 33 years ago. On March 1 he was asked to leave. "You can assume it was for economic reasons, but I've been there thirty-three years and all of a sudden [Hamilton] said, 'We'd like you to leave. We think you would be happier somewhere else,' " says Perry.

At his last litigation department meeting Perry announced that he wanted to dispel rumors that he was leaving voluntarily. "That's not true," he recalls saying.

Perry is known as an excellent trial lawyer; the former Hale and Dorr partner calls him a "genius at strategy and tactics."

"I consider Blair a friend," Fabiano says, "but he's consistently refused to change his practice in the direction the firm is going. He works alone and at his own pace. We gave him a golden parachute early retirement.

All the upcoming departures are the result of a management initiative that began in November 1989. Hamilton asked all equity partners to draw up individual business plans for their practice in 1990—not in response to any economic problems, he says, but merely as a planning tool. After reviewing the plans Hamilton and the department heads were able to determine which partners' plans didn't mesh with the firm's.

Hale and Dorr's articles of partnership require a two-thirds vote by the partnership to expel a partner. But the firm apparently gave the departing partners a monetary incentive to move on and move on quietly. * * *

Partners remaining at the firm express mixed feelings about the departures. "I think the feeling of all was one of sadness," says one partner. But another partner espouses a view one might expect at what is widely known as a tightly managed, bottom-line firm: "There's no mutiny on the ship. I don't believe *I* should be kept on when my partners view me as not contributing value. We can't afford to have mediocre partners or superior partners that do mediocre work. We have to be viewed as excellent, outstanding, superior. In the long term, being a good lawyer is not good enough."

---

1.   What were the causes for the failure of Finley, Kumble? How did the "Cravath system" avoid these problems? Does this example imply that sharing norms must take precedence over compensation schemes based upon what an attorney brings in or produces if a firm is to be sustainable? What other factors may have been at work in undermining the Finley, Kumble partnership?

2. Do the "early retirements" at Hale & Dorr suggest that a partnership is not sustainable unless partners are rewarded in some reasonable proportion to their productivity? How might the downturn in the New England economy preceding the "early retirements" have played a role in these decisions? Why was the firm willing to provide "golden parachutes" to the departing partners?

3. Review the list on pp. 545-46 of options for law firm structures. What firm structures are most likely to best militate between the dual and potentially inconsistent objectives of promoting productivity and maintaining stability within a modern law firm? *Cf.* Brill, The Changing Meaning of Partnership: A Survey on Partnership and Governance at Major Firms, The American Lawyer (Mar. 1990) (supplement) (surveying how aspects of law firm governance changed at 75 of the largest 100 law firms in the United States between 1980 and 1990).

Marc Galanter and Thomas Palay, The Transformation of the Big Law Firm

In Lawyers' Ideals/Lawyers' Practices: Transformations in the American Legal Profession 31, 33-61 (R.L. Nelson, et al., eds. 1992).

The big law firm has been with us for almost a century. It is, in a Darwinian sense, a success story. Big firms are flourishing. There are more of them, they are bigger, they command a bigger share of an expanding legal market. The big law firm is also a success in a deeper sense, as a social form for organizing the delivery of comprehensive, continuous, high-quality legal services. Like the hospital in the practice of medicine, the big firm established the standard format for delivering complex services in the practice of law. Many features of its style—specialization, teamwork, continuous monitoring on behalf of clients, representation in many forums—have been emulated in other vehicles for delivering legal services. The specialized boutique firm, the public-interest law firm, the corporate law department—all model themselves on the style of practice developed in the large firm. Even legal professions in other countries are emulating the American big firm.

* * *

The Emergence of the Big Firm

The big firm and its distinctive style of practice emerged around the turn of the century. The break from earlier law practice can be discussed under the six headings; (1) partners, (2) other lawyers, (3) relations to clients, (4) work, (5) support systems, and (6) new kinds of knowledge. Any of these indicia of the big firm can be found apart from the whole cluster, but it is the clustering of all six that gave the big firm its distinctive institutional character—a character that is changing as these features are rearranged.

Partners: In the big law firm the loose affiliation of lawyers, sharing offices and occasionally sharing work for clients, is replaced by the office in which clients "belong to" the firm rather than to an individual lawyer. The entire practice of these lawyers is shared by the firm. The proceeds, after salaries and expenses, are divided among the partners pursuant to some agreed upon formula.

Other lawyers: Unpaid clerks and permanent assistants are replaced by salaried "associates" (as we have come to call them) who are expected to devote their full efforts to the firm's clients. A select group of academically qualified associates, chosen on grounds of potential qualification for partnership, are given a prospect of eventual promotion to partnership after an extended probationary period during which they work under the supervision of their seniors, receive training, and exercise increasing responsibility.

Clients: Firms represent large corporate enterprises, organizations, or entrepreneurs with a need for continuous (or recurrent) and specialized legal services that could be supplied only by a team of lawyers. The client "belongs to" the firm, not to a particular lawyer. Relations with clients tend to be enduring. Such repeat clients are able to reap benefits from the continuity and from the economies of scale enjoyed by the firm.

Work: The work involves specialization in the problems of particular kinds of clients. It involves not only representation in court, but services in other settings and forums. The emergence of the firm represents the ascendancy of the office lawyer and the displacement of the advocate as the paradigmatic professional figure. The preference for office work is displayed in the advice of a partner to a young lawyer aspiring to join the predecessor to the Cravath firm: "New York is not a very good field for one who desires to make a specialty of court practice or litigation work. The business connected with corporations and general office practice is much more profitable and satisfactory and you will find that the better class of men at our Bar prefer work in that line."

Litigation no longer commanded the energies of the most eminent lawyers. By 1900, Robert Swaine concludes, "the great corporate lawyers of the day drew their reputations more from their abilities in the conference room and facility in drafting documents than from their persuasiveness before the courts." In 1908 Roscoe Pound remarked this shift and apprised its consequences for reform: "The leaders of the American bars are not primarily practitioners in the courts. They are chiefly client caretakers.... Their best work is done in the office, not in the forum. They devote themselves to study of the interests of particular clients, urging and defending those interests in all their varying forms, before legislatures, councils, administrative boards and commissions quite as much as in the courts. Their interest centers wholly in an individual client or set of clients, not in the general administration of justice."

Support Systems: The emergence of the big firm is associated with the introduction of new office technologies. The displacement of copying, clerks, and messengers by the typewriter, stenography, and the telephone greatly increased the productivity of lawyers.

New Kinds of Knowledge: The proliferation of printed materials—reporters, digests, treatises—rendered obsolete the earlier style of legal research and required mastery of new areas of specialized knowledge. The acquisition of legal skills changed too. Between 1870 and 1910 the portion of those admitted to the bar who were law school graduates rose from one-quarter to two-thirds.

The blending of these features into the big law firm as we know it is commonly credited to Paul D. Cravath, who in the first decade of this century established the "Cravath system" of hiring outstanding graduates straight out of law school on an understanding that they might progress to partnership after an extended probationary period, requiring them to work for the firm only, eschewing practices of their own, paying them salaries, providing training and a "graduated increase in responsibility." * * *

The core of the big firm, we submit, is the "promotion to partnership." This is our shorthand for the organization of the firm around the expectation that the junior lawyer can cross the line by promotion and become a partner. Partners and juniors are not equals, but form a hierarchy with command and supervision exercised by partners. But the junior lawyers are neither transient apprentices nor permanent employees. They are peers, fellow professionals of presently immature powers, who have the potential to achieve full and equal stature.

Firms can offer this promise only when they are confident that they will attract sufficient work to keep these young lawyers busy. That is, the senior lawyers must have either clients who produce more work than the senior lawyers can handle themselves or a reputation that will attract such clients. Typically, association with a corporation or "super-capitalist" provided the necessary stream of work and "the publicity from serving such clients and the expansive contacts of these clients result[ed] in a growing network of contacts for the emergent firm."

The big law firm—and with it, the organization of law practice around the promotion to partnership pattern—became the industry standard. Gradually, the older patterns of fluid partnerships, casual apprenticeship, and nepotism were displaced. Law firms grew. In every city, the number of big firms (as big was then defined) increased at an accelerating rate, and over time there were ever-bigger firms. First in New York, then in other large cities, then in smaller cities throughout the county there were more, bigger law firms. This can be seen in Wayne Hobson's compilation of the number of firms with four or more lawyers, which grew from 17 in 1872, to 39 in 1882, to 87 in 1892, to 210 in 1903, to 445 in 1914, to "well over 1000" in 1924. As firms grew, the lawyers in them became more specialized and firms began to departmentalize.

Though ascendant in the profession, these successful lawyers were subservient to and dependent on their business clients. From its origins the big firm was haunted by a sense that the profession had compromised its identity and had itself become a branch of business.

By the 1930s, the scale and stability of these firms was recognized in the pejorative term "law factory." The phrase captures not only the instrumentalism, but the systematization, division of labor, and coordination of effort introduced by the large firm.[32] The frenetic pace and intense specialization of the large firm repelled many established lawyers. The factory metaphor was felt to identify something about these offices that was profoundly at odds with professional traditions of autonomy and public service.

Circa 1960: The Golden Age of the Big Law Firm

Before the Second World War the big firm had become the dominant kind of law practice. It was the kind of lawyering consumed by the major economic actors. It commanded the highest prestige. It attracted many of the most highly talented entrants to the profession. It was regarded as the "state of the art," embodying the highest technical standards. In the postwar years this dominance was solidified.

To get a reading on the changes over the past generation, we will develop as a baseline a portrait of the big firm in its "golden age" before the transformation that it is now undergoing. This golden age of the big firm, the late 1950s and the early 1960s, was a time of stable relations with clients, of steady but manageable growth, of comfortable assurance that an equally bright future lay ahead—which is not to say that its inhabitants did not look back fondly to an earlier time when professionalism was unalloyed.

New York firms loom disproportionately large in studies of the golden age. New York City was home to a much larger share of big-firm practice then than it is now. In the early 1960s, there were twenty-one firms in New York with fifty or more lawyers and only seventeen firms of that size in the rest of the country. * * *

Hiring: Firms were built by "promotion to partnership." Lateral hiring was almost unheard of, and big firms did not hire from one another. Partners might leave and firms might split up, but it didn't happen very often. Hiring of top law graduates soon after their graduation was one of the building blocks of the big firm. Most hiring was from a handful of law schools, and walk-in interviews during the Christmas break were the norm. Starting salaries at the largest New York firms were uniform—$4000 in 1953, rising to $7500 in 1963. The "going rate" was fixed at a luncheon, attended by managing partners of prominent firms, held annually for this purpose.

---

32. Some sought to wring further parallels, attributing to large firms the standardization, "robotization," and monotony thought characteristic of factories. In 1939, muckraking journalist Fernand Lundberg entitled the last of his series of *Harper's* articles on lawyers, "The Law Factories: Brains of the Status Quo." Lundberg explains that the "term 'law factories,' widely used in the legal profession, may be derisive, but it is accurate. The great law firms are organized on factory principles and grind out standardized legal advice, documents and services as systematically as General Motors turns out automobiles."

Historically, the big firms had confined hiring to white Christian males. Few African-Americans and women had the educational admission tickets to contend for these jobs. But there were numerous Jews who did and, with a few exceptions, they too were excluded. This exclusion began to break down slowly after the Second World War. Jewish associates were hired, and some moved up the ladder to partner. The lowering of barriers to Jews was part of a general lessening of social exclusiveness. In 1957, 28 percent of the partners in the eighteen firms studied by Erwin Smigel were listed in the Social Register. By 1968, the percentage had dropped to 20 percent. But African–Americans and other minorities of color were still hardly visible in the world of big law firms. In 1956 there were approximately eighteen women working in large New York firms—something less than one percent of the total complement of lawyers. As late as 1968, Cynthia Fuchs Epstein estimates, "only forty women were working in Wall Street firms or had some Wall Street experience."

Promotion and Partnership: Only a small minority of those hired as associates achieved partnership. Of 454 associates hired by the Cravath firm between 1906 and 1948, only 36 (just under 8 percent) were made partners. Cravath may have been the most selective but it was not that different from other firms. * * *

The time it took to become a partner varied from firm to firm and associate to associate. For the New York lawyers becoming partners around 1960 the average time seems to have been just under ten years. Outside New York the time to partnership was closer to seven years. Throughout the 1960s the time to partnership dropped.

One of the basic elements of the structure of the big firm is the up or out rule that prescribes that after a probationary period, the young lawyer will either be admitted to the partnership or will leave the firm. In this model, there can be no permanent connection other than as a partner. It is easy to overestimate the rigor with which the up or out rule was in fact applied. In his 1958 study, Klaw observed that "[f]ew Wall Street firms have an absolutely rigid up-or-out policy, but most of them discourage men from staying on indefinitely as associates." Many firms had an explicit up or out rule—in some cases quite recently minted—but there was at work a competing and powerful norm that it was not nice to fire a lawyer. * * *

For associates who did not make partner, firms undertook outplacement, recommending them for jobs with client corporations and with smaller firms.[33] Ties might be maintained as the firm referred legal work to them or served as outside counsel to the corporation.

* * *

Partners were chosen by proficiency, hard work, and ability to relate to clients. In many cases there was some consideration of the candidate's

33. In our "circa 1960" period, corporate legal work in many cases paid better than law firms.

ability to attract business. And selection depended on the perceived ability of the firm to support additional partners.

Achieving partnership, the "strongest reward," meant not only status but security and assurance of further advancement: "[T]hey ... know that they will advance up the partnership ladder." There was certainly pressure to keep up with one's peers, but competition between partners was restrained. In this environment, "[a]dmission to the partnership of a leading firm was a virtual guarantee not only of tenured employment but of a lifetime of steadily increasing earnings unmatched by a lawyer's counterparts in the other learned professions."

But this should not lead one to conclude that the classic pattern of dividing the proceeds of the big-firm partnership was some approximation of giving each partner an equal share—or a share by seniority (the so-called lockstep system). If this was ever true, by circa 1960 the prevailing practice was to divide profits by individualized shares rather than by a norm of equal participation.

Work and Clients: The work of the big firm was primarily office work in corporate law, securities, banking, and tax with some estate work for wealthy clients. Divorces, automobile accidents, and minor real estate matters would be farmed out or referred to other lawyers. Litigation was not prestigious, and it was not seen as a money-maker. Mayer estimates that "litigation occupies less than one-tenth the time of large law firm" and reports that"[s]ome firms avoid it entirely." He describes large-firm litigation in the early 1960s as involving taxes, contracts, personal injury defense, and defense of corporations and directors from shareholder suits. "But to most large law firms, the word 'litigation' connotes an antitrust suit, not because the number of such cases is large but because each of them represents so enormous a quantity of work." The surge of antitrust litigation tended to elevate the standing of litigators, who had been "overshadowed by office-lawyer partners ... who seldom, if ever, went near a courtroom." Where big firms were involved in litigation, it was typically on the side of the defendant. Big firms usually represented dominant actors who could structure transactions to get what they wanted; it was the other side that had to seek the help of courts to disturb the status quo. Disdain of litigation reflected the prevailing attitude among the corporate establishment that it was not quite nice to sue.

As they grew, many firms broadened their client bases, becoming less dependent on a single main client. Relations with clients tended to be enduring. "A partner in one Wall Street firm estimate[d] its turnover in dollar volume at 5 per cent a year, mostly in one-shot litigation." Corporations had strong ties to "their" law firms. Many partners sat on the boards of their clients—a practice that had been viewed as unprofessional earlier in the century—and would lose favor again later. * * *

Circa 1960, New York still dominated the world of big-time law practice. Large firms elsewhere were constructed along the same "promotion to partnership" lines, but tended to operate a bit differently. Firms outside New York tended to be more recently founded. There was also less departmentalization, specialization, and supervision. The organization was less formal, with fewer rules about meetings, training, conflicts of interest, and so on. The turnover of associates was lower, and there was less up or out pressure. Partnership was also easier to attain and came earlier. There was more use of such intermediate classifications as junior or limited partners. There was more lateral hiring. Outside New York, firms were less highly leveraged. The ration of associates to partners in the nineteen New York firms Smigel studied was two to one; in the firms outside New York, it was, in some instances, as low as one to one. A lawyer from a big firm in Chicago observed that New York firms "frequently employ two or three or even more associates per partner. In Chicago these ratios are lower; and there has been a well-defined trend in recent years, toward increasing the number of partners in the larger firms as compared with the number of associates."

For big firms, circa 1960 was a time of prosperity, stable relations with clients, steady but manageable growth, and a comfortable assumption that this kind of law practice was a permanent fixture of American life. Notwithstanding their comfortable situation may inhabitants and observers regarded the world of the big firm as sadly declined from an earlier day when lawyers were statesmen and served as the conscience of business. Echoing laments that have recurred since the last century, partners complained to Smigel that law had turned into a business. No longer, Mayer reflects, do young associates regard themselves as servants of the law and holders of a public trust: "[T]hey are too busy fitting themselves for existence in the 1950s, when efficiency, accuracy, and intelligence are the only values to be sought."

Big law firms enjoyed an enviable autonomy. They were relatively independent vis-à-vis their clients; they exercised considerable control over how they did their work; and they were infused with a sense of being in control of their destinies. A sharp contrast with present practices and perspectives is implicit in the retrospective glance of a contemporary author:

> [C]ompetition was very much a gentlemanly affair. With the banks and manufacturing corporations pacing America's industrial expansion—and with the Securities Acts and New Deal legislation complicating business transactions—the workload grew faster than the firms' ability to service it. Protected by their captive relationships, the established practices had no reason to fear competitive assaults and were not, in turn, moved to encroach on their competitors' turf. Blessed with virtual monopolies in their respective markets, they focused instead on practice standards, on establishing self-indulgent compensation systems, and on perfecting the mystique and the mannerisms of elite professionals. How cases were staffed and billed, how partners were selected and paid, and how new partners were admitted to the ranks were issues based on internal considerations rather than market factors. Free to conduct their affairs as they saw fit, the established practices could all

but ignore such boorish concerns as efficiency, productivity, marketing and competition.[34]

The Transformation of the Big Firm

The more numerous and more diverse lawyers of the late 1980s were arrayed in a very different structure of practice than their counterparts a generation earlier. There has been a general shift to larger units of practice. The number of lawyers working in sizable aggregations, capable of massive and coordinated legal undertakings has multiplied many times over. One estimate is that in 1988, there were 35,000 lawyers at 115 firms with more than 200 lawyers and a total of 105,000 lawyers in 2000 firms larger than 20 lawyers.

Growth: In the late 1950s there were only 38 law firms in the United States with more than fifty lawyers—and more than half of these were in New York City. In 1985, there were 508 firms with fifty-one or more lawyers.

Not only were there more big firms, but they were growing faster.* * *

In 1960 big law firms were clearly identified with a specific locality, as they had been since the origin of the big firm. But by 1980, of the 100 largest firms, 87 had branches.* * *

In the 1980s the home office and branch pattern was joined by the genuine multi-city law firm.* * *

Not only did the number of branches increase, but so did their size. The average size of each branch of a NY firm went from eight lawyers in 1980 to seventeen in 1987.* * *

Increasingly, large firms operate on an international basis.* * *

Over the past thirty years, there has been a marked movement away from New York City as the nation's legal center.* * *

Work and Clients: The kinds of work big firms do have changed. The mix of work coming into big firms has been changed by a surge of corporate litigation since the 1970s and by the increase in the number, size, and responsibility of in-house legal departments. Long-term retainer relations have given way to comparison shopping for lawyers on an *ad hoc* transactional basis. Corporations that view legal expenses as ordinary costs of doing business rather than singular emergencies have monitored legal costs, set litigation budgets, required periodic reporting, and awarded new business on the basis of competitive presentations from competing outside firms.

The practice of law has become more specialized. Within large firms, specialization has become more intense and the work of various levels more differentiated. Much routine work has been retracted into corporate law departments, shifting the work of large outside firms away from office practice toward litigation and deals. With more deals, higher stakes, more

34. Stevens, Mark, 1987, *Power of Attorney: The Rise of the Giant Law Firms.*

regulation to take into account, and more volatile fluctuations of interest and exchange rates there is greater demand for intensive lawyering. The large contested and/or risk-prone one-of-a-kind, "bet your company" transactions—litigations, takeovers, bankruptcies, and such—make up a larger portion of what big law firms do. Since few clients provide a steady stream of such matters and those that have them increasingly shop for specialists to handle them, firms are under ever greater pressure to generate a steady (or increasing) supply of such matters, by retaining the favors of old clients and securing new ones.

Competitiveness: The new aggressiveness of in-house counsel, the breakdown of retainer relationships, and the shift to discrete transactions has made conditions more competitive. The practice of law has become more openly commercial and profit-oriented, "more like a business." Firms rationalize their operations; they engage professional managers and consultants; their leaders worry about billable hours, profit centers, and marketing strategies. "Eat what you kill" compensation formulas emphasize rewards for productivity and business-getting over "equal shares" or seniority. There is more differentiation in the power partners wield and the rewards they receive; standing within the firm depends increasingly on how much business a partner brings in. Rising overhead costs and associate salaries put pressure on partners. In many firms, partners work more hours, but their income has not increased correspondingly.

The need to find new business has led to aggressive marketing. Some firms have taken on marketing directors, a position that did not exist in 1980. In 1985, there were forty such positions. By 1989 "almost 200 law firms ha[d] hired their own marketing directors." The push for new business also brought about increased emphasis on "rainmaking" by more of the firm's lawyers. Those lawyers who are responsible for bringing in business enjoy a new ascendancy over their colleagues. The need to find new business has shaken the traditional structure of the big firm. A description of big firms in the Southeast reports that the "shift from a traditional reliance upon a small number of rainmakers to the aggressive stance that everyone must make rain has resulted in a reduction in numbers of associates receiving a vote for partnership as well as—in many cases—a redivision of partners' profit pie. Many firms also go a step further by eliminating non-producing partners and restructuring or jettisoning non-productive departments".

The search for new business has been directed not only toward would-be clients, but to existing ones. In a setting where corporations are more inclined to divide their custom among several law firms, firms engage in "cross-selling" to induce the purchaser of services from one department to avail itself of the services offered by other departments.

Lateral Hiring and Mergers: In the classical big firm, almost all hiring was at the entry level. Partners were promoted from the ranks of associates. Those who left went to corporations of smaller firms, not to similar large firms since these adhered to the same no lateral hiring norm. But starting in the 1970s, lateral movement became more frequent. At first, firms made an occasional lateral hire to meet a need for litigators or to fill some other niche. But soon lateral hiring developed into a means of systematically upgrading or enlarging the specialities and localities they could service and of acquiring rainmakers who might bring or attract new clients. As lateral movement increased, a whole industry of "headhunter" firms emerged, gaining respectability as it grew. The number of legal search firms grew rapidly from 83 in 1984 to 167 in 1987 to 244 in 1989.

The flow of lateral movement widened from individual lawyers to whole departments and groups within firms and to whole firms. Mass defections and mergers became common, enabling firms at a stroke to add new departments and expand to new locations. A casual search of the legal press from 1985 to 1989 produced a list of seventy-one mergers involving eighty-three firms with more than fifty lawyers; in fifty-eight of these mergers, at least one of the merging firms had one hundred lawyers—a sizable portion of the whole population of firms of that size. Mergers were not only a way to grow; they also provided a convenient device to shake out or renegotiate terms with less productive partners.

Firms hired laterally not only by mergers but by inducing specific lawyers to change firms, "cherry picking" as it came to be called in the late 1980s. A 1988 survey of the five hundred largest law firms found that over a quarter reported that more than half of their new partners were not promoted from within but came from other firms. Lateral movement was not confined to the partner level. The same survey found that one quarter of the responding firms reported that more than half their associates were hired laterally. Increasingly, associates move from one big firm to another. A recent survey of promotions at thirty-five large firms in seven localities reveals thirty-three of the thirty-five firms hired some associates laterally and that of 2227 associates who entered in the late 1970s, 500 (22 percent) had not come to those firms directly from law school, but "arrived at their current firm later in their careers". A recent *New York Law Journal* survey found that at twenty-three of the thirty largest firms in New York, an average of 24 percent of the associates being considered for partnership were lateral hires.

The other side of this movement was splits and dissolutions of firms. As firms grew larger the task of maintaining an adequate flow of business often became more difficult. Firms were more vulnerable to defections by valued clients or the lawyers to whom those clients are attached. Size multiplies the possibility of conflicts of interests resulting in tension between partners who tend old clients and those who propose new ones that can induce a breakaway. Surrounded by other firms attempting to grow by attracting partners with special skills or desirable clients, firms are vulnerable to the loss of crucial assets. So dissolution may be catalyzed by lateral movement and merger activity and such break-up in turn stimulates a new round of lateral movement.

Hiring: As firms grew, thus requiring larger numbers of qualified associates, recruitment activity intensified. Recruiting visits to an increasing roster of law schools, extensive summer programs, brochures, and expense-paid "call-backs" of candidates have become familiar parts of the big law firm scene. Starting salaries have increased dramatically, beginning with a great contraction of the supply of associates in the late 1960s. The Vietnam War draft diverted law graduates to occupations in which they could obtain deferments, just when 1960s activism inspired a disdain for corporate practice among students seeking work in poverty law and public-interest law. The percentage of elite law graduates entering private practice dropped precipitously. Confronted by criticism that their work was unful-filling and inimical to the public interest, many firms acceded to demands that recruits be able to spend time on "pro bono publico" activities. The *Wall Street Journal* reported that "now it's common for [the big corporate law firms] to permit their attorneys to spend substantial portions of their time in noncommercial work."

Firms responded to their supply problem not only by accommodating their recruits' public-interest impulses but by sharply increasing their compensation. In 1967, the starting salary for associates at elite firms in New York was $10,000; scheduled to increase to $10,500 for 1968 recruits. In February 1968, the Cravath firm, breaking with the "going rate" cartel, raised the salaries for incoming associates to $15,000, setting in motion a new competitive system of bidding for top prospects. Firms that wanted to be considered in the top stratum had to match the Cravath rate. The change in New York starting salaries reverberated throughout the upper reaches of the profession. The salaries of more senior associates had to be raised to preserve differentials; the take of junior partners had to be adjusted accordingly; firms outside New York, though paying less, had to give corresponding raises to maintain parity with their New York rivals. Unlike later increases in compensation, the one in the late 1960s was not accompanied by pressure to bill more hours. In fact, it appears that hourly billings were dropping during this period.

In 1986, when the highest-paid beginning associates were getting $53,000, Cravath administered a second shock by unilaterally raising salaries to $65,000. At the time of the first "Cravath shock" the big-firm "going rate" referred primarily to a few dozen firms, most which were located in New York; by the time the second occurred the big-firm world consisted of several hundred geographically dispersed firms, many national in scope. Long-accepted city differentials have been eroded by branching, especially by recent moves by New York firms into other legal markets, causing some firms in those localities to match the higher New York salaries.

As the number and size of large firms has increased, recruitment has become more competitive and more meritocratic, leading to changes in the social composition of the new recruits. The range of law schools from which the big firms recruit has widened, and recruitment has gone "deeper" into each graduation class. Religious, racial, and gender barriers have been swept away. The social exclusiveness in hiring that was still a feature of the world of elite law practice in 1960 has receded into insignificance. Performance in law school and in the office counts for more; social connections for less.

By the late 1980s the population of lawyers in big firms included a significant number of women and members of minority groups. A 1989 survey of the 250 largest firms found that 24 percent of their lawyers were women: 9.2 percent of the partners and 33 percent of the associates. A 1987 survey of these firms reported that women were "40 percent of the associates hired in the last two years, the same percentage as women in law school". The percentage of women partners increased at almost one percent a year throughout the 1980s. These numerical gains took place even as many women have expressed dissatisfaction with working conditions and career lines in large firms, especially as these obstruct and penalize child-rearing. Women have been less satisfied than their male counterparts with law practice in general and with practice in large firms specifically.

African–Americans remained underrepresented in the world of large law firms. In 1989 they composed 2.2 percent of associates and less than one percent of partners. The ratio of partners had doubled since 1981, but the percentage of African–American associates declined slightly after 1981 (from 2.3 percent to 2.2 percent), while the percentages of other minorities rose.

Leverage: Firms have become more highly leveraged—that is, the ratio of associates to partners has risen.* * *

Promotion and Partnership: Over the two decades preceding 1980 the period during which lawyers served as associates before becoming partners became shorter. Robert Nelson found that the average time spent as an associate by those promoted to partnership in large Chicago firms during the 1950s was 7.5 years; this fell to 7.21 in the 1960s; to 6.19 for those promoted between 1970 and 1975; to 5.64 for those promoted between 1976 and 1980. But in the 1980s time to partner seems to be stretching out. A study of five large new England firms found that associates had to wait eight or nine years instead of seven. A *National Law Journal* survey of thirty-five firms in seven localities found that some two-thirds of associates hired in the late 1970s had spent seven to eight "years to partner". Many partners anticipated further increases.

Generally, increases in leverage suggest that a smaller percentage of associates will be promoted to partner. Nelson studied associates hired by nineteen large Chicago firms from 1971 to 1983 and determined which of them were still with these firms in 1984. If we assume that anyone who was there after nine years had become a partner, we see that fewer than half of those hired before 1975 had departed by 1984, so that more than half had become partners. But Nelson suggests that "if we project current annual rates [of departure] over a six-year period [the normal period to partnership in Chicago], little more than one-quarter of the lawyers starting with firms would be expected to make partner". * * *

Firms have also increased the use of personnel who are not eligible to be partners. This is most evident in the increasing delegation of work to paralegals—that is, lower-salaried nonlawyer employees performing routine legal tasks under the supervision of lawyers.* * *

The search for leverage without "the pressure created by regular associates eager to make partner" is also evident in the hiring of associates on a lower-paid nonpartnership track.* * *

Another device for enlarging capacity without engaging new associates is the use of "temporary" lawyers. These "legal temps" are not employees of the firm, but are supplied by agencies who screen and certify them.* * *

In these ways the classic big-firm notion of "promotion to partnership"—that all the lawyers were potentially members of a fraternity of peers—is attenuated. But if all lawyers are no longer potential peers, some nonlawyers are being invited into the core of the firm's operations. We have noted the drive to cover more specialities and more locations. The movement to build on successful relations with clients to sell them new kinds of services is not limited to legal services. Since legal services are often consumed in conjunction with other services, some firms have adopted strategies of hiring non-lawyer professionals. "Firms have brought in engineers, teachers, lobbyists, regulatory economists, banking regulators, nurses, doctors, and business managers (MBAs) to help provide client services". Other firms have established coordinate "nonlegal" businesses (investment advice, economic consulting, real estate development, consulting on personnel management, marketing newsletters, etc.) Others project a grander vision of the evolution of law firms into diversified knowledge conglomerates: "If the railroads had asked themselves what business they were in and had answered 'Transportation,' they might be in the airline business [today] . . . We realized we were in the business of selling knowledge, whether we were advising legal clients, giving seminars, doing investment banking, making video tapes, or publishing newsletters."

A partner at Arnold & Porter, which has established three consulting subsidiaries, anticipates that

> by the end of the century . . . large firms will become immensely more diversified in the services they offer. They will become more oriented toward problem-solving than traditional law firms, assemble teams of experts—lawyers and non-lawyers—and offer their clients "one stop shopping." . . . By the end of the century, legal services will be provided broadly in the context of a diversified service firm that will draw upon the talents of many disciplines with financial, economic and scientific resources available within a single institution.

In the meantime it is clear that the notion of the law firm as an exclusive and specialized repository of distinctively legal knowledge and skills has been loosened, if not abandoned.

As the firm copes with the exigencies of its new competitive environment, the situation of the junior lawyer is more precarious and more pressured, although it is also more lucrative. But the partnership core is even more affected. Partners are under mounting pressure to maintain a high level of performance—and performance that fits the business strategy of the firm. Many new features of the law firm world such as mergers and lateral movement amplify the power of dominant lawyers within a firm to sanction their errant colleagues—and the prevalent culture endorses such sanctions. So partners worry about having their prerogatives of shares reduced or even being "pushed off the iceberg" or "de-partnerized." There are now real possibilities of downward movement. "[W]ith profits being squeezed and competition on the rise," reported one consultant, "many firms can no longer afford to support these [unproductive or disaffected] partners. Firms are trying to 'rehabilitate' these partners, decreasing some partners' incomes and asking others to leave." Thus a long-established 87 lawyer Seattle firm recently dismissed eight partners and six associates, on the grounds that "the firings were necessary to increase profitability and keep talented attorneys from being hired away." The unassailable security of partnership is no longer assured. "Partnership used to be forever, but it is no longer."

---

1.   Galanter and Palay describe a three-phase evolution of law partnerships from gentlemanly organizations that operated like selective private clubs to the much larger and more open entities of the 1960s to the much more competitive and diverse membership entities of today. What were the principal factors driving these transformations?

2.   Why has the "up or out" promotion system been such a mainstay of law firm organization? *See* M. Galanter & T.M. Palay, Tournament of Lawyers: The Transformation of the Big Law Firm (1991); Galanter & Palay, Why the Big Get Bigger: The Promotion-to-Partner Tournament and the Growth of Large Law Firms, 76 Va. L. Rev. 747 (1990); Kordana, Law Firms and Associate Careers: Tournament Theory Versus the Production–Imperative Model, 104 Yale L.J. 1907 (1995). Why has it begun to deteriorate in recent years?

3.   The Code of Professional Responsibility prohibits non-lawyers from being partners within law firms. C.W. Wolfram, Modern Legal Ethics 885 (1986). What might explain the creation and persistence of this rule? How have law firms effectively worked around this rule?

4.   To what extent have the transformations that have occurred in large law firms manifested in other law practices—*e.g.*, small firms, government, non-profit organizations?

Ronald J. Gilson & Robert H. Mnookin, Sharing Among the Human Capitalists: An Economic Inquiry into the Corporate Law Firm and How Partners Split Profits

37 Stanford Law Review 313, 339, 341–43, 345–46, 349–52, 354–56, 376–79 (1985).

I.   The Central Framework: The Law Firm Through the Lens of Portfolio and Agency Theory

[The authors use economic analysis to posit that the structure of law firms reflects the inherent tension between the gains from diversification of risk and the losses from diminished work incentives. Portfolio theory suggests that owners of valuable but risky assets (such as lawyers who possess specialized skills—*i.e.*, human capital) will pool their resources to together so as to diversify their risks. Agency theory predicts that workers whose compensation is less than their marginal product will tend to shirk responsibilities, grab as large a share of the "pie" as possible, or leave with valuable clients.]

II.   The Importance of Income Division: Alternative Methods of Dividing the Partnership Pie

Analysis of both portfolio and agency theory directs attention to precisely the same subject: the manner in which firm income is divided. Diversification, the core recommendation of portfolio theory, is achievable only by means of an agreement specifying how future income will be shared. Agency theory, in turn, highlights the likelihood that those lawyers who turn out to be more successful than their peers will threaten to leave the firm unless they receive their real value—a demand for a quite different manner of dividing firm income. * * *

The puzzle becomes more complicated upon examination of the experts' claim that a seniority system is inconsistent with firm success. Several of the most successful large firms, including Cravath, Swaine & Moore, Covington & Burling, and Wilmer, Cutler & Pickering, remain committed to essentially 'lockstep,' seniority-based compensation systems and yet seem to be more profitable than ever. These examples pose the problem directly: Why are some prosperous and stable large firms able to divide the pie according to a sharing bargain that appears to be at odds with the self-interest of the most productive partners? What curtails grabbing or leaving? * * *

A.   *The Sharing Model: Achieving Diversification or "A Mutual Fund for the Benefit of the Retired and Disabled"?*

Many established corporate law firms traditionally have divided profits on the basis of a seniority system. Under such a system, lawyers are typically grouped into classes based on their year of admission to the partnership and their income will depend upon the seniority of their class. For our purposes, the pure case would have the following elements:

(1) each partner's share of profits depends entirely upon his seniority, which is itself determined on the basis of the class to which he has been assigned;

(2) a partner's class depends only upon the year he was admitted to the partnership and cannot be changed;

(3) all partners in a single class earn the same income;

(4) in any given year, the relationship between the incomes of partners in different classes is based upon a fixed, predetermined ratio; and

(5) the members of each class march 'lockstep' down the compensation path until after a fixed number of years they all become 'full share' partners.

This model is best understood as a means of capturing the gains available from diversification. Under a lockstep seniority system, an individual lawyer, upon being admitted to the partnership, is quite literally exchanging his human capital for participation in a portfolio of human capital diversified both with respect to the personal characteristics of the lawyers and with respect to specialty. Indeed, it is striking just how well diversified the portfolios of established firms are. New partners in such firms in essence "buy into" mutual funds through which they are able to share not only in the future income of their contemporaries, but also in the future income of lawyers who offer differing levels of expertise and experience and who span two or even three generations. In other words, "buying into" a lockstep traditional firm offers a more diversified portfolio than that available in a partnership made up of lawyers in a single age cohort. * * *

[A] sharing model designed to capture the gains from diversification will, if successful, create its own problems—shirking, grabbing, and leaving. * * *

The challenge of the sharing model is thus to provide diversification without giving rise to shirking, grabbing, or leaving.

B. *The Marginal Product Approach: The Problems of Measuring Productivity*

In order to give lawyers an incentive to be productive—*i.e.*, to avoid the risk of shirking posed by seniority systems—the new conventional wisdom is that a firm should divide the pie on the basis of productivity, rather than seniority. Each year firms should attempt to determine each partner's relative contribution to firm productivity and then divide income in accordance with this determination. As an abstract proposition, paying each partner in proportion to his contribution to firm profitability sounds straightforward enough, albeit coming at the expense of diversification. In actual operation, however, it is a very complicated task that is impossible to accomplish with complete accuracy. Not only is there likely to be a gap between actual productivity and the firm's approximation of productivity, but the use of some formula to make this approximation also leaves the firm vulnerable to a new set of agency problems: Partners are given an incentive to maximize their own income by maximizing the factors measured by the formula, rather than by actually maximizing their productivity. * * *

3. *The difficulty of creating a formula: the example of client generation.*

It may seem as if there is an easy response to the previous section's observations: Devise a carefully crafted formula that is sufficiently refined to avoid the problems that we have identified. * * *

[O]nce again we confront the problem that any formula will always create incentives to maximize the factors that it weighs, to the detriment of the goal whose attainment is its purpose. For example, suppose we decide to reward client generation with a one-time bonus when the client first employs the firm. This creates an incentive to attract the client in the first place, but creates no incentive for the lawyer who initially attracts the client to assure that the client remains satisfied and therefore willing to provide the firm with additional work in the future. Firms can mitigate this problem by giving the lawyer who generates business a continued bonus determined by the volume of work that the client provides in any period. This refinement, however, hardly solves the general problem. If a significant part of the lawyer's earning depends on the amount of work generated by particular clients, an incentive is created for the lawyer to resist efforts by others to get to know the client because his livelihood is put at the risk of performance of others. Moreover, one would also want to control not only for attracting the work, by also for its profitability. If the lawyer's client-generation bonus depends only on the number of hours that he works for the client, an incentive is created to bill the client at a lower rate in order to encourage a greater amount of work, notwithstanding the fact that the firm's overall profit might be reduced as a result: One partner may well be better off with a larger piece of a smaller pie. A formula thus does not prevent the interests of the individual lawyer and those of the firm from diverging.

Finally, a formula that rewards client generation may also create incentives to grab or leave. It would hardly be surprising were a client's loyalty to shift from its original contact to the lawyer who actually does its work. If the formula does not reflect this shift in role, it does not reflect the productivity of the client's current lawyer. That lawyer is then in the same position as a more productive lawyer in a sharing firm—his income does not reflect his actual productivity—and he has the same incentives to grab and leave. * * *

III.   Individual Capital Versus Firm–Specific Capital: Constraints on Grabbing and Leaving in a Sharing Model

* * *

A.   *The Distinction Between Individual Capital and Firm–Specific Capital*

As we stressed earlier, every lawyer in a firm has made an investment in his or her individual human capital. For the purposes of this analysis, we can measure the value of this investment as the capitalized value of the amount of money that the lawyer would expect to earn by leaving the firm and taking alternative employment—either by joining a different law firm or by forming a new law firm. By way of contrast, the value of firm-specific capital is the capitalized value of the difference between a firm's earnings as an ongoing institution and the combined value of the human capital of its individual partners, if this human capital were deployed outside the firm in its next most productive use. Because firm-specific capital can be neither easily removed from the firm nor duplicated outside the firm, the return on this capital is available to lawyers within the firm but is lost to lawyers who leave the firm. Examples of this phenomenon readily come to mind. Having IBM as a client is valuable to Cravath, Swaine & Moore, but if there is no individual partner who upon leaving the firm, can take IBM with him, then the client relationship with IBM is an asset of the firm.[35] Returns on this asset are available to individual lawyers only so long as they remain within the firm.

Our basic thesis is that firm specific capital, by constraining grabbing and leaving, provides the glue that holds together an organization committed to the sharing model. Without firm capital, the ex ante sharing bargain is subject to ex post cheating: More productive partners may claim, after the fact, a larger share than they are entitled to under the original sharing bargain. The strength of their claim, however, depends not on the accuracy of their belief about their relative productivity within the firm, but on whether they can earn a greater return on their individual capital in its next best deployment if they leave the firm. Without a realistic threat of leaving for more money, an attempt to grab is likely to be ineffective. In this regard, the Cravath firm again provides a very instructive example. According to a recent article, the full-share partners in Cravath each earned $855,000 in 1983, while the youngest partners enjoyed annual earnings of $285,000—a three-to-one ratio. While firms all around it split up, merge, or oust partners, Cravath continues to employ a pie-division system that approximates our pure sharing model, does no lateral hiring, has no written partnership agreement, and apparently suffers no defections. And the explanation for so stable a sharing model seems clear. If the earnings figures are correct, it seems unlikely that very many of the Cravath partners could make more money elsewhere. In other words, there is plenty of firm-specific capital to 'glue' the partnership together. * * *

IV.   The Missing Constraint on Shirking: Simple Formulas and the Enigma of Firm Culture

* * *

Our inquiry, then, is into the process by which lawyers are socialized: What social mechanisms serve to instill the nonshirking values that their

35. Covington & Burling, another prestigious sharing firm, also seems to possess firm-specific capital in ample amounts:

Now in its 63d year, Covington indeed retains the reputation of being not just the biggest but also the best firm in town. Peculiarly, that reputation is an institutional one; Covington & Burling seems greater than the sum of its parts. It cannot count among its 212 attorneys a single "rainmaker," or a superstar lawyer with an instantly recognizable name, in the mold of Clark Clifford, Lloyd Cutler or Edward Bennett Williams. "Covington gets business because of its trademark, not because

somebody played tiddledywinks with Daniel Gribbon when they were in prep school," says one former Covington associate, referring to the chairman of the firm's five-member management committee....

When the time comes to divvy up the profits at Covington, a former partner says, "the firm never lets partners claim they brought in business. The firm did, with its reputation over the long term."

Marcus, [Covington Challenge: To Stay on Top, Nat'l L.J., May 4, 1981], at 1, col. 4, at 28, col. 1, at 30, col. 3.

internal monitor helps to enforce? And while related questions have commanded substantial attention from sociologists and lawyers employing sociological analysis, we think our emphasis on agency and portfolio theory allows us to identify some different areas of inquiry and pose some testable hypotheses that may warrant further attention.

As an initial matter, it is obvious that the socialization of lawyers does not begin when the lawyer starts work with a firm. The concept of being a "professional"—that there is a positive personal, as opposed to economic, value to meeting the standards of one's craft—begins at least in law school. Consider, for example, the implicit message that the elite law schools transmit. Traditionally, the highest embodiment of student achievement is the law review note, an article on a legal subject, published in a professional journal and characterized by exhaustive research by the author. The piece often includes hundreds of footnotes, each of which typically contains citations of multiple authorities that support the proposition asserted in the text. Moreover, before the note is published and despite the exhaustive research undertaken by the author, the elite law reviews read literally every authority cited in order to ensure "complete" accuracy, regardless of the importance of any particular point or the likelihood that an inaccuracy would be noticed. No one who has participated in a law review cite check would contend that the cite check is motivated by any form of tangible cost-benefit analysis.

The point is reinforced by a familiar refrain on the part of law firm recruiters when they claim that their firm does only high quality work: Once the firm undertakes a task, it expends the time necessary to produce a "professional" product even if it cannot bill the client for it. This lesson—that professional quality is determined without regard to economic reward—seems to us an important part of the antishirking culture necessary to perpetuate a sharing model. It suggests, in turn, that sharing firms would more highly value graduates of elite law schools and, in particular, law review editors at those schools, than would firms that follow a productivity approach.

The socialization of antishirking norms may well begin long before the potential attorney enters law school. The elite law schools select only high achievers, many of whom have already demonstrated a willingness to work more than the amount simply required to achieve high grades. And it may be that particular social or ethnic environments are more effective at instilling these values than are others. If certain background attributes are signals of antishirking values, we would expect sharing firms to place greater emphasis on these characteristics, especially if the firm is unable to hire law school graduates with the highest credentials. A sharing firm's commitment to other values typically associated with emphasis on academic achievement—a commitment to meritocracy—would complicate an empirical test of this hypothesis. It would thus be interesting to know whether sharing firms that successfully recruit law school graduates with outstanding credentials place less emphasis on social characteristics than do sharing firms whose hiring programs are less successful.

To this point we have emphasized that screening techniques can be means by which sharing firms reduce the risks of shirking. We would also expect sharing firms to employ training techniques intended to reinforce the earlier socialization of those whom their screening has identified. This may help explain the lengthy period necessary to attain partnership in firms committed to the sharing model, as well as the historical pattern of "up and out," pursuant to which associates who are not made partners are forced to leave the firm even though they may still be able to play an economically valuable role. The values of a sharing model may not allow for a second class of law firm citizen. From a training perspective, the length of time required to attain partner status may facilitate a mentor approach to legal training. This may in turn have the advantage of exposing a young lawyer not only to the techniques of legal practice, but to the attitudes of the mentor as well. * * *

V.   The Changing Legal Environment

* * *

A.   *The Changing Market for Legal Services—*
The Role of General Counsel

The marketplace for corporate legal services is undergoing substantial change. While some of these changes relate to the structure of the firms providing services in the marketplace, the most significant changes are occurring on the demand side. Buyers are becoming much more sophisticated. General counsel for major corporations are creating a revolution and are the primary agents of change.

A variety of anecdotal evidence supports the observation that general counsel are substantially affecting the marketplace for services provided by corporate law firms. The status of house counsel is rising in the process. The traditional perception was that only routine legal work was done in-house, and the important and interesting legal problems were necessarily referred to outside counsel. Today, however, the size of the in-house corporate legal staffs of many companies is growing very rapidly. Some corporations in fact now do nearly all their legal work in-house.

It is not only the size of in-house legal staffs that has changed. Twenty years ago, the chief in-house lawyer for a corporation was commonly viewed as a competent professional who probably would not quite measure up to partnership quality in a major law firm. Indeed, corporations quite commonly hired as general counsels senior associates who were unlikely to become partners in their law firms. Today, however, corporations regularly persuade important partners in major law firms to resign from the partnership to become general counsel.

General counsel and other top corporate executives are becoming much more sophisticated about the process of buying legal services. * * *

---

1.   To what extent do Professors Gilson and Mnookin shed light on the analogy between the incentives within a law firm and the incentives reflected in the tragedy of the commons? How do "sharing" law firms divide up the bundle of sticks? How about "marginal product" firms?

2.   What is "firm-specific" capital? What type of resource is it? Is it a private good or a public good? Which type of firm, sharing or marginal product, is more likely to foster the creation of firm-specific capital? What are the incentives to create such capital?

3.   Which type of firm, sharing or marginal product, is more efficient? On what factors does this depend?

4.   What is meant by the concept "law firm culture"? In what ways does it help to overcome the problems of shirking, grabbing, and leaving?

5.   Which type of law firm, sharing or marginal product, is more likely to be welcoming of persons of diverse backgrounds and ethnicity? Why?

6.   At which type of firm is the partnership hurdle likely to be higher? Why?

7.   What are the implications of the changes in the demand for legal services for the structure of law firms? What societal changes have affected the structure of law firms?

8.   In 1992, a new legal services organization called Legal Research Network, Inc. was formed. It operates upon a clearinghouse/independent contractor model. Corporate clients and law firms propose projects to LRN—such as a memorandum on a specialized area of law. LRN then identifies a specialist from its "rolodex" of pre-screened experts, many of whom are law school professors who have written academic papers or worked in a particular area. The "expert" and LRN negotiate a price for the work, which LRN presents to the client (with a surcharge for LRN overhead). What changes in the market for legal services created a niche for this organization? What organizational benefits does it offer? What risks does this service engender? Does LRN pose a serious threat to traditional law practice? *See* Osbourne, Should You Be Afraid of this Man? Am. Law., June 1995, at 70.

9.   What light does this case study shed upon advising clients about structuring other ventures, such as small businesses, large businesses, hospitals, health maintenance organizations, university governance, government agencies? Consider the following problem.

Problem: Advising a High–Technology Client

To: Associate

From: Senior Partner

Re: HEALTHWARE Inc.

Janet Peterson called me yesterday about a new venture that she plans to try to get off the ground. As you may know, Janet is a computer programmer. She has an interesting idea for a new venture and would like our advice on how she might structure the business so as have the best potential for success.

The proposed venture will be called HEALTHWARE. Janet believes that she can tap into the current diet/health/environmental/personal computer craze by developing a user-friendly computer program that would monitor the user's diet and fitness activity. The user would input information on his or her health (*e.g.*, age, weight, medical history, dietary restrictions). Each day, the user would input information on diet and physical exercise. The program would have simple "pull down" menus for making this quick and easy; nutritional information on all foods would be stored in the program. The computer would periodically provide an analysis of the user's health, as well as suggestions for achieving the user's goals, whether weight reduction, better fitness, or general health. In addition, the program would compile a record of the user's activities which could be brought to annual physicals. Other sub-routines would be available for pregnant and lactating women, children, the elderly, diabetics, vegetarians, triatheletes, etc.

Janet thinks that she could attract the diverse people necessary to pull this project off: programmers, a nutritionist, a physician, a fitness consultant. She is concerned, however, that any one of these people could, after becoming familiar with the product, develop a competing product.

What are the options for structuring HEALTHWARE? What problems do you foresee in structuring this venture? Assuming that the product is popular, what are the major risks to HEALTHWARE's success? How can we structure HEALTHWARE so as to overcome these problems? To what extent can the allocation of property rights—in both the product and the enterprise—address these problems?

CHAPTER IV

MARKET INSTITUTIONS

The United States has operated as a market-based economy since colonization. In contrast to background property rules, markets operate on the basis of mutual consent through private, contractual agreements to allocate rights to material resources. Such agreements range from simple sales of goods to complex long-term relationships governing the use of land or intellectual property. In light of the potential for contractual arrangements, background legal rules are most usefully seen as a set of default rules that contracting parties usually may vary and override to serve their mutual interests. Because a market system promotes productive uses of resources, see *supra* pp. 14–20, production, commerce, and land development most commonly occur within the market domain. The market system can also serve other important social functions as well, including providing property owners with some independence and autonomy from other private actors and government.

The traditional view of market institutions emphasizes freedom of contract: the legal ability of parties to bind themselves voluntarily in exchange for commitments from the other contracting party or parties. Nonetheless, as we have seen, property law does not always give market institutions such free reign. For example, grantors may not create contingent future interests that could potentially vest after expiration of the perpetuities period; nor may they impose certain restraints on the alienation of land. As we will see in this Chapter, property law limits the types of contractual arrangements that are enforceable and the ways in which such agreements may be enforced. Although the property doctrines have significant parallels to traditional contract law, the application of these principles to property interests has led to important distinctions, some which are outmoded and some of which have continuing economic and social significance.

Prior chapters have introduced market institutions by emphasizing the importance of alienability, in discussing the distinctive rules governing real estate transactions, and through the theoretical construct of the Coase Theorem. This Chapter focuses more generally on the operation of market institutions in allocating property. It examines landlord-tenant law, the law of non-possessory interests and law governing common interest communities (*e.g.*, condominiums, cooperatives, and gated communities)—three areas of property law in which contractual instruments are widely if not universally used to reorder the bundle of property rights, and where common law and statutes have significantly constrained types, content, and enforcement of agreements. Landlord-tenant law covers an interesting and evolving mix of estate law (non-freehold estates) and social policy governing landlords' and tenants' rights and duties regarding both commercial property and one of the most common forms of housing in the United States—rental property. We will examine how well the various landlord-tenant doctrines respond to market failures and felt social needs. The law of non-possessory interests concerns the ways in which neighbors can reach and enforce agreements regarding the use and enjoyment of each other's land. Such agreements range from a simple right-of-way for a sewer line to the highly structured agreements governing modern homeowner associations. The law of common interest communities is perhaps the most extensive form of contractual property governance, in which individuals create a quasi-democratic system through contractual agreement and live within a hybrid form of governance. Such communities are increasingly common and present novel and difficult challenges to traditional doctrines.

A. LANDLORD-TENANT LAW

1. INTRODUCTION

a. EVOLUTION OF LEASEHOLD INTERESTS

The freehold estates—fee simple, fee tail, and life estate—were the only possessory interests recognized and protected by the early common law courts. The rights associated with these estates roughly correspond with the rights we now associate with ownership—alienability, exclusive possession and use, and in the case of a fee simple, inheritability.

At early common law, nonfreehold interests (also called villeinage tenure) were reserved for a class of people—called villeins—who were allowed to work the land so long as they paid for the privilege in crops or services. In many cases, villeins were no more than serfs who were obligated to obey the freehold tenants. Because the villeins' interests in the land were not recognized at common law, they could assert their rights only in the manorial courts.[1] Thus, the villeinage tenant had neither property nor contract rights under common law, but only a status with certain perquisites that other people generally observed.

---

1. Manorial law was separate from the common law and usually was based on the customary practices of the manor. For example, the manorial custom that the villeinage tenant could be evicted only for specific enumerated causes (*e.g.*, disloyalty) was enforceable as law before the manorial court.

There are several possible explanations why the common law courts were unwilling to protect nonfreehold tenants. The courts probably were reluctant to invent or recognize new forms of legal interests that might disrupt existing arrangements and expecta-

tions of the dominant classes. In addition, many leases violated the spirit of the prohibition of usury. But an additional explanation may be that the concept of a nonfreehold estate violated a basic tenet of property in feudal England. Property was not viewed as an object of commerce, but as the source of a family's wealth, political power, and social status. Indeed, from the word "estate" we derive the word "status." A lease for a term of years, creating a solely commercial relationship, was at odds with these traditional social arrangements.

Two developments strengthened the nonfreehold tenants' position by transforming the source of their obligations and rights from customary arrangements to negotiated agreements, or leases. First, many wealthy freehold tenants regularly had difficulty producing cash on short notice, a problem that was exacerbated by the Church's prohibition on usury. To acquire the necessary money and avoid the religious prohibition, the freeholder would surrender his possession and use of the land for a term of years to a proto-capitalist, who hoped to recover the principal of the loan and some profit from the revenues of the land.[2]

Second, the scourge of the bubonic plague in the mid-fourteenth century sharply reduced the number of laborers. As a result, the bargaining power of villeins increased, and many villeins left their manors (and their status as serfs) in search of better work. Where once landholders could effectively keep laborers in villeinage tenure as serfs, they were now forced to hire workers and negotiate leases.

Nonfreehold tenants gradually gained legal (*i.e.*, common law) rights as social practices changed. The first remedies were contractual—either damages or specific performance for breach of lease provisions.[3] The original contractual remedy, however, was limited, for it was available only against the contracting party—the landlord. The tenant had no remedy against eviction by third party trespassers or the landlord's successors.

From the early thirteenth to the late fifteenth centuries, the courts relaxed these rules and gave tenants additional rights and remedies, including an injunctive remedy against the landlord's successors, a damages remedy against third-party trespassers, and eventually an injunctive remedy against all trespassers. Because these actions were not against the original contracting party, they were grounded in property rather than contract. *See generally* Lesar, The Landlord–Tenant Relation in Perspective: From Status to Contract and Back in 900 Years?, 9 Kan. L. Rev. 369 (1961); Hicks, The Contractual Nature of Real Property Leases, 24 Baylor L. Rev. 443 (1972).

As England evolved into an industrial society in the nineteenth century, tenants became less concerned with trespass and more concerned with services, such as heat, lighting, plumbing, garbage removal, and security. In addition, urban tenants were often less able than their rural cousins to make needed repairs, and thus depended on the landlord to maintain the premises. As a result, urban leases carefully allocated a variety of responsibilities between the tenant and the landlord. The lease once again was

2. Eventually, the mortgage came to replace the lease as a means of securing a debt.

3. Early leases contained few express covenants, and courts at first implied no additional obligations. Later, common law courts imposed on landlords an obligation to deliver possession at the beginning of the term and to refrain from interfering with the tenant's quiet enjoyment of the premises. Courts, however, steadfastly refused to impose an implied obligation to ensure suitability for use. If the premises were destroyed without the landlord's fault, the tenant was still liable for the rent. In addition, the doctrine of waste effectively required tenants to make necessary repairs.

viewed more as a contract than a property interest; legal disputes typically did not involve trespass by a third party, but rather a claimed breach of a covenant by the landlord or the tenant.

The contract/property distinction continues to have important legal consequences. Whether a lease is viewed as a contract or as property determines whether the tenant still owes rent when the premises are destroyed or the purpose of the lease is made impossible by changes in the law; whether the doctrine of unconscionability applies[4]; whether breach of a material covenant allows the injured party to rescind (*i.e.*, whether covenants are mutually dependent); whether the landlord can sue immediately for the remaining rent after the tenant has abandoned the premises; and whether the landlord must mitigate damages by finding a substitute tenant following the tenant's abandonment. In addition, overlying every lease is a set of statutes and regulations (such as the local housing code) controlling the conduct of the parties and allocating obligations that the parties often cannot waive or renegotiate. Thus, modern landlord-tenant law is not only based on property and contract doctrines, but also is governed by modern regulatory concerns.

b. COMMON LAW NONFREEHOLD ESTATES

When a landowner leases real property, two interests are created: the tenant's present possessory interest in the land (*i.e.*, the leasehold) and the landlord's reversion, typically in a fee simple, although it could be in a life estate or even in another leasehold. The lease is distinguished from other interests described in the second part of this Chapter—easements, real covenants, equitable servitudes, and licenses—in that the latter only give the grantee a limited right of use, whereas a leasehold gives the lessee full and exclusive possession. At the margins, there are cases where it may be difficult to distinguish one from the other, such as an exclusive easement for a fixed period of time, but the distinction is usually clear.[5]

i. *Types of Leasehold Interests*

There are four basic types of leasehold interests: a term of years, a periodic tenancy, a tenancy at will, and an occupancy at sufferance.

A *term of years* is a tenancy for a definite period of time, with an ascertainable beginning and ending date (although the lease may also be

---

4. Some states have enacted provisions specifically authorizing courts to apply the unconscionability doctrine to rental agreements. *See, e.g.*, Ala. Code § 7–2A–108; Colo. Rev. Stat. § 4–2.5–108; Md. Code Ann., Com. Law § 2A–108; Ohio Rev. Code Ann. § 5321.14. Other states have a general unconscionability provision governing all contracts, including leases. *See, e.g.*, Cal. Civ. Code § 1670.5(a); *Ilkhchooyi v. Best*, 37 Cal.

App.4th 395, 45 Cal.Rptr.2d 766 (1995) (upholding a trial court finding that a commercial lease provision requiring a tenant to pay the landlord part of the sales price for a lease assignment was unconscionable).

5. Normally, a lodger in a hotel or motel is not a tenant. The lodger has a right of occupancy, but has none of the other rights normally associated with possession.

determinable). It is created by express agreement of the parties.[6] At common law, and in some states, there is no upper limit on the duration of a term of years lease. Most states, however, limit the duration of leases. *See, e.g.,* Cal. Civ. Code § 717 (51 years for agricultural leases); Cal. Civ. Code § 718 (99 years for private city lots, 55 years for government land, 35 years for oil and gas leases, and 66 years for tidelands); Tenn. Code Ann. § 66–7–103 (10 years for oil and gas leases); La. Rev. Stat. Ann. § 41:1292 (99 years for leases of public lands). A term of years ends automatically on the last day of the lease; neither party need give notice of termination.

The *periodic tenancy* developed four centuries ago from the *tenancy at will* (described below); indeed, some states continue to refer to a periodic tenancy as a tenancy at will. *See, e.g.,* Fla. Stat. ch. 83.03.

A periodic tenancy is renewed automatically at the end of each lease period (*e.g.,* at the end of each month in a month-to-month tenancy) unless one party gives timely, written notice of termination. At common law, notice must be given one period prior to termination for leases less than a year, and notice must be given 6 months in advance of termination for leases greater than or equal to a year. State statutes frequently alter the common law notice requirements. *See, e.g.,* 735 Ill. Comp. Stat. 5/9–205 to – 207 (60–day notice to terminate periodic leases with a period of at least a year; 4–month notice for a periodic agricultural lease with a period of at least one year; 30–day notice for periodic leases less than a year); Fla. Stat. ch. 83.03 (for non-residential tenancies, 3–month notice for a year-to-year lease; 15–day notice for a month-to-month lease; and 7–day notice for a week-to-week lease). Failure to give timely and adequate notice binds the parties for another term.

Periodic tenancies are frequently created by an express agreement for a periodic lease,[7] although courts will also find an implied periodic lease based on the conduct of the parties. An implied periodic lease may arise, for example, when the parties do not have a valid lease, but the tenant paid, and the landlord accepted, periodic rental payments. *See Harry's Village, Inc. v. Egg Harbor Twp.,* 89 N.J. 576, 583, 446 A.2d 862, 865 (1982) (although the parties lease violated the statute of frauds, tenant's monthly payment of rent created a month-to-month tenancy); *Hill v. Turley,* 218

6. In general, if the lease term is longer than one year, the statute of frauds requires that the lease be in writing and signed by the person to be charged. *See* 740 Ill. Comp. Stat. § 8½; Cal. Civ. Code §§ 1091, 1624(c). Many states have modified the traditional rule. *See* Tenn. Code Ann. § 66–7–101 (written lease required if term is longer than 3 years). Violation of the statute of frauds usually means that the agreement is void. However, the doctrines of part performance and equitable estoppel may be available to avoid the statute of frauds. For example, the *Restatement (Second) of Property (Landlord and Tenant)* § 2.3 provides that if the tenant has gone into possession the court should recognize a tenancy at will; if the tenant has gone into possession and paid rent, the court should recognize a periodic tenancy; and if the parties have undertaken "substantial performances which are clearly referable to the terms of the lease," the court should give full effect to the oral agreement.

7. A periodic lease must satisfy the applicable statute of frauds; if the period is longer than a year, the lease must be in writing.

Mont. 511, 516–17, 710 P.2d 50, 53–54 (1985) (although the oral lease for three years violated the statute of frauds, the parties had a year-to-year periodic lease because agreed reserved rent was annual, even though the tenant made monthly installment payments); *Restatement (Second) of Property (Landlord and Tenant)* § 2.3; *but see Kent v. Humphries*, 50 N.C.App. 580, 586–87, 275 S.E.2d 176, 181 (1981) (treating invalid oral lease as a tenancy at will, even though tenant paid monthly rent).

A majority of courts will also imply a periodic lease when the tenant has held over after the expiration of a lease, and the landlord accepted rental payments rather than exercise the right to evict the tenant. *See Mississippi State Dep't of Public Welfare v. Howie*, 449 So.2d 772, 778–79 (Miss. 1984) (in accepting rent checks from the holdover tenant, the landlord created a month-to-month tenancy and waived his right to eviction); Cal. Civ. Code § 1945 (with the landlord's acceptance of the holdover tenant's rental payments, the parties are presumed to create a periodic lease); Fla. Stat. chs. 83.02–83.04 (accepting payments from a non-residential holdover tenant only creates an occupancy at sufferance, unless the landlord gave written consent to the continued occupancy, in which case a periodic tenancy is created). Still other courts will imply a periodic lease where the tenancy is of no specific duration but the rental payments are periodic. *See, e.g., Wright v. Vickaryous*, 598 P.2d 490, 497–98 (Alaska 1979).

A *tenancy at will* is a lease that is terminable by the landlord or the tenant at any time, the death of either party, the execution of a new lease to a third party, or the conveyance of the fee. In most states, an attempt to create a tenancy terminable at will by only the landlord results in a tenancy at will terminable by either party; courts are split when the agreement is terminable at will only by the tenant. While no notice of termination was required at common law, many states now require notice before termination. *See, e.g.,* Cal. Civ. Code § 789 (the landlord must give 30–day written notice); D.C. Code Ann. § 45–1403 (either party may terminate a tenancy at will with 30–day written notice); Ga. Code Ann. § 44–7–7 (to terminate a tenancy at will, the tenant must give 30–day notice, or the landlord must give 60–day notice).

A tenancy at will may be the product of an express agreement. For example, in *Day v. Kolar*, 216 Neb. 47, 49, 341 N.W.2d 598, 599 (1983), where the lease provided that the leasehold was to last from September 30, 1981 to September 30, 1982, but also provided that the lease was terminable by either party with no notice, the court held that the leasehold was not a term of years but a tenancy at will. More commonly, a tenancy at will results when the parties have no lease—they failed to execute a lease or the agreement is void—but the tenant nevertheless took possession with the landlord's permission. *See, e.g., Swart v. Western Union Telegraph Co.*, 142 Mich. 21, 105 N.W. 74 (1905) (even though the parties never completed their negotiations, because the tenant took possession, the court implied a tenancy at will); *Restatement (Second) of Property (Landlord and Tenant)*

§ 2.3 (tenant's taking possession, with landlord's acquiescence but without payment of rent, constitutes a tenancy at will).

A special case arises where an employer provides an employee with a residence. For example, in *Covina Manor, Inc. v. Hatch*, 133 Cal.App.2d Supp. 790, 284 P.2d 580 (1955), Hatch was employed by Covina Manor. During his employment, Covina Manor gave him oral permission to occupy a house on the property. Some time later, Hatch was fired and Covina Manor demanded that he vacate the house.

> whether we accept the [plaintiff's] testimony * * * to the effect that defendants were granted oral permission to occupy the premises without specification as to time and absent any agreement for the payment of rent, or whether we accept defendants' version that they entered into possession of the property under a verbal agreement—invalid under the statute of frauds—that the property was to be conveyed to them in consideration of services rendered or to be rendered by defendants, the status of defendants was that of tenants at will.

Id. at 793, 284 P.2d at 582. The court rejected Covina Manor's argument that Hatch was only a licensee. As a licensor, Covina Manor could obtain trespass damages from the moment the license was orally revoked; if the parties had a lease, Covina Manor could only obtain damages from the time it properly terminated the lease, which was much later in time in this case. The test for a lease, as opposed to a license, according to this court, was whether the agreement gave the defendant "exclusive possession of the premises against all the world, including the owner." *Id.* at 793, 284 P.2d at 583. The facts of the case showed that Hatch had a lease, not a license. *See also Lasher v. Allegheny County Redevelopment Auth.*, 211 Pa.Super. 408, 412, 236 A.2d 831, 833 (1967) (where grantor stayed on the property after conveyance, with grantee's permission, the parties created a tenancy at will); *Townsend v. Singleton*, 257 S.C. 1, 6, 183 S.E.2d 893, 897 (1971) (where tenant holds over after expiration of term of years, the parties are bound by a tenancy at will, with the damages measured by the reasonable rental value). Some other courts have found a license in similar circumstances, especially where occupancy of the residence was a necessary part of the job.

An *occupancy at sufferance* exists when the tenant, who was once in rightful possession, remains in possession after his possessory rights have ended, typically when the landlord lawfully terminated the tenancy. *See, e.g., Rivera v. Santiago*, 4 Conn.App. 608, 610, 495 A.2d 1122, 1124 (1985) (tenant holding over after the termination of a lease is an occupant at sufferance). The occupant is not a true trespasser (although many courts conclude that the holdover tenant is a trespasser) because he did not enter the property wrongfully.

An occupancy at sufferance is a temporary situation. In most states, the landlord may either elect to hold the occupant at sufferance for another lease term, or evict the tenant and collect the reasonable rental value (often measured by rent reserved in the terminated lease) for the period during which the occupant was in unlawful possession. *See, e.g., Cusumano v. Outdoors Today, Inc.*, 608 S.W.2d 136, 139–40 (Mo.Ct.App.1980) (if the landlord accepts rent from a holdover tenant, the parties have created a month-to-month tenancy; otherwise, the landlord may evict the holdover tenant without notice).

ii. Termination of Leases

As mentioned earlier, a lease for a term of years ends without notice on the last day of the lease. A periodic tenancy (and in many states a tenancy at will) ends only after the landlord or the tenant has given appropriate notice of termination. A few other circumstances may also terminate a lease.

Mutual Agreement. The parties may mutually consent to early termination of the lease. Since mutual consent to terminate the lease amounts to a reconveyance of the leasehold to the landlord, the parties must comply with the statute of frauds if the remaining time on the lease is in excess of the statutory limit (*e.g.*, 1 year).

Destruction of the Premises. At common law, physical destruction of the premises did not terminate a lease. *See, e.g., Gade v. National Creamery Co.*, 324 Mass. 515, 87 N.E.2d 180 (1949) (even though the first floor of the building collapsed through no fault of the tenant, the tenant had to continue to pay rent and the landlord was not liable for damages absent proof of either misrepresentation by the landlord or an express provision permitting termination of the lease). In the nineteenth century, courts began to hold that if the lease was only for the building, destruction of the building through no fault of the tenant would terminate the lease. *See, e.g., Graves v. Berdan*, 26 N.Y. 498 (1863) (rejecting the common law rule that the tenant was obliged to continue to pay rent even though the building burned down; because the tenant's interest was in the building, not the land, the rent should be completely abated); *Crow Lumber and Building Materials Co. v. Washington County Library Board*, 428 S.W.2d 758, 764 (Mo.App.1968) (the lease was terminated after destruction of the building since the lease was only for part of a building as library space and not for any portion of the land); *Gonzalez v. Cavazos*, 601 S.W.2d 202, 203–04 (Tex.Civ.App.1980) ("lessee of lands (rather than of the improvements alone) upon which the improvements are destroyed * * * cannot be relieved from an express covenant to pay rent unless is it so stipulated in the contract, or the lessor has covenanted to rebuild").

Some state statutes have modified the common law rule to provide that a lease is terminated when the premises are destroyed, so long as the tenant is not responsible for the destruction. *See, e.g.*, Cal. Civ. Code § 1933(4) (destruction of the premises terminates a lease); Tenn. Code Ann. § 66–7–102 (lease is terminated if building is rendered untenantable through no fault of the tenant).

Eminent Domain. If the government takes the entire parcel of leased land by eminent domain, the lease is terminated and the tenant's obligation to pay rent ceases. Pursuant to the Fifth Amendment (and corresponding provisions in state constitutions and statutes), the government must pay "just compensation" for the property taken. The general rule is that the landlord and tenant split the compensation award. Despite strong criticism to the contrary, *see Restatement (Second) of Property (Landlord and Tenant)* §§ 8.1(2)(b), 8.2(2)(b), 11.1, if the government does not take all of the land, but only part of it, the tenant's obligation to pay the full rent remains intact, even though the tenant can use only the remaining portion of the premises. The tenant will receive part of the compensation award—which presumably will compensate for having to pay full rent.

Death. At common law and in virtually all states today, a party's death terminates a tenancy at will. *See, e.g., Dean v. Simpson*, 235 Miss. 162, 171, 108 So.2d 546, 549 (1959); *Ferrigno v. O'Connell*, 315 Mass. 536, 537, 53 N.E.2d 384, 384 (1944). However, in most states death of one party does not terminate other types of leases. *See, e.g., Joost v. Castel*, 33 Cal.App.2d 138, 141, 91 P.2d 172, 174 (1939) (tenant's death does not terminate a term of years); *Israel v. Beale*, 270 Mass. 61, 64, 169 N.E. 777, 778 (1930) (tenant's death does not terminate a year-to-year lease, absent an express or implied condition to the contrary); *State Bank of Loretto v. Dixon*, 214 Minn. 39, 43, 7 N.W.2d 351, 353 (1943) (tenant's death does not terminate periodic lease). *See generally* Donaldson, Annotation, Death of Lessee as Terminating Lease, 42 A.L.R. 4th 963 (1985). A few states have altered these rules by statute. *See, e.g.,* N.J. Stat. Ann. § 46:8–9.1 (the executor may terminate a residential lease for more than one year after the lessee has died). A few states have altered that rule by statute or decisional law for periodic leases. *See, e.g.,* Cal. Civ. Code § 1934.

Substantial Breach of a Material Covenant. At common law, lease provisions were considered to be *independent*; one party's breach—even the tenant's breach of the covenant to pay rent—did not give the other party a right to terminate the lease (although the injured party would have a right to damages and perhaps injunctive relief). Thus, even though contract law considered some non-lease contract provisions *mutually dependent*, and thus allowed the remedy of rescission, because a lease was considered a conveyance of property the remedy of rescission was unavailable. The one exception was the implied covenant of quiet enjoyment (described *infra,* pp. 623–29, which was a promise that the landlord would not disrupt the tenant's quiet enjoyment of the premises; if there was a breach, the tenant could rescind the lease. In more modern times, statutes and cases provide that the tenant's breach of the covenant to pay rent is a basis for the landlord to rescind. However, well into modern times, breach of other important covenants, including the covenant to repair, a covenant not to assign or sublet, and non-competition agreements, was not a basis for rescission in many states; the property doctrine of independent covenants continued to prevail.

Medico–Dental Bldg. Co. v. Horton & Converse

Supreme Court of California, 1942.
21 Cal.2d 411, 132 P.2d 457.

■ CURTIS, JUSTICE.

Plaintiff brought this suit for rent alleged to be due under a lease, for the amount of an electricity charge against defendant during the last month of its occupancy of the premises, and for money expended for renovation following the defendant's removal. A trial was had before the court without a jury, and findings were made in favor of the defendant pursuant to its claim that plaintiff's breach of a restrictive covenant in the lease, which violation was not waived by the defendant, prevented the maintenance of this action except as to the expenditure for electricity as alleged in the complaint and admitted in the answer. * * *

On July 1, 1934, defendant, Horton & Converse, as lessee, entered into a written lease covering certain space on the ground floor of the Medico–Dental Building at Eighth and Francisco Streets, Los Angeles, for a term of sixteen years and four months, at a minimum monthly rental of $600 for the part of the term concerned herein, and a fixed percentage of the gross sales. At the time the lease was made, defendant was in possession of the premises, having occupied them since 1925 under a prior lease. As successor in interest by virtue of an assignment of the lease involved herein, plaintiff, Medico–Dental Building Company stands in the position of the original lessor.

The lease provided that the premises should be "used and occupied by lessee as a drug store and for no other business or purpose, without the written consent of lessor." It also contained the following stipulation: "Lessor agrees not to lease or sublease any part or portion of the Medico–Dental Building to any other person, firm or corporation for the purpose of maintaining a drug store or selling drugs or ampoules, or for the purpose of maintaining a cafe, restaurant or lunch counter therein during the term of this lease."

On December 30, 1937, plaintiff leased the entire ninth floor of the same building to one Dr. Boonshaft, a physician, for a term of three years commencing April 15, 1938. This lease contained the following provisions: "The premises demised hereby are to be used solely as offices for the practice of medicine and dentistry, and lessee agrees that he will not maintain therein or thereon, nor permit to be maintained therein or thereon, a drug store or drug dispensary, nor will lessee compound or dispense, or permit to be compounded or dispensed, drugs or ampoules except in connection with the regular course of treatment of lessee's own patients. Lessee agrees not to display any sign or advertisement on the inside or outside of the demised premises, or the building of which the demised premises are a part embodying the words 'Pharmacy,' 'Drug Store,' 'Dispensary' or words of like import. Lessee understands that lessor has heretofore executed a lease to Horton & Converse granting to said Horton & Converse the exclusive privilege of conducting a drug store business on the ground floor of said Medico–Dental Building, and lessee agrees that he will not do, or permit to be done, anything in connection with the premises demised hereby which would in any way conflict with or constitute a breach by the lessor therein of said Horton & Converse lease.''

Dr. Boonshaft went into possession under his lease on April 15, 1938, and occupied the entire ninth floor of the building, where he had from thirty-two to thirty-six treatment rooms and had six to eight doctors associated with him in an organization known as the Boonshaft Medical Group. Independent of this staff but subject to frequent call to the premises in the course of the work of this enterprise were some thirty consultant doctors. The plan of operation of the medical organization was to register groups of employees and lodge members and their families for medical treatment on the basis of a monthly charge per family; registration and payment of the fixed sum entitled the patient to receive, among other things, certain drugs, but additional charges were made for other medicines. Dr. Boonshaft maintained a drug room wherein drugs were sold and prescriptions filled per the order of the regular staff or the consultant doctors in the treatment of patients of the Medical Group. He obtained a pharmacy license on May 10, 1938. Until June 25 of that year he bought his drugs from defendant's store *in the building*. However, he objected to the sales tax charged in connection with such purchases, and on June 25, 1938, he commenced buying wholesale from defendant's wholesale department at another location, which source of supply he continued to patronize to the time of trial.

The order of pertinent events as set forth in the trial court's findings may be summarized as follows: During the month of May, 1938, a drug store in charge of a registered pharmacist was opened and maintained on the ninth floor of the Medico–Dental Building, which said drug store was registered as a pharmacy with the California State Board of Pharmacy; there drugs were sold, and prescriptions were compounded and filled, and a charge was made therefor. On July 8, 1938, a sales tax permit was issued to Dr. Boonshaft. During the last week of July, 1938, defendant learned of these facts as to the operation of the drug store, and on August 3, 1938, it notified plaintiff in writing of its discovery of these matters and charged that such practice constituted a breach of its lease (an express demand being made in the letter that plaintiff take immediate steps to stop the objectionable selling of drugs and the compounding and filling of prescriptions). During the time between August 3 and August 31, 1938, the drug store continued to operate as before. Agents of plaintiff had conferences relative to defendant's objection, but such discussions were not communicated to defendant and defendant had no knowledge of plaintiff's disposition regarding its complaint except as manifested at a meeting held in defendant's office on August 8, 1938, at which time plaintiff advised defendant that it would take the matter up further and see what it could do about it and advise defendant. Defendant did not have any further communication from plaintiff concerning the objection to the drug store until August 19, 1938, when the attorney for plaintiff informed defendant that no arrangements could be made with Dr. Boonshaft and plaintiff could not do anything with him; in reply on that occasion defendant, through its president, said that it was going to vacate the premises in order to avoid a waiver of its exclusive right to maintain a drug store and sell drugs in the building. (The record shows that plaintiff's attorney then responded: "Well, use your own judgment about that.") Plaintiff failed thereafter to take any further action. (The next day defendant closed its store, placed a sign on the door announcing service was available at one of its other locations, and piled empty packing boxes at the entrance and on the main part of the floor of its leased premises in the Medico–Dental Building for the purpose of impressing plaintiff with its intention to move.) On August 24, 1938, defendant sent plaintiff a written notice of rescission and vacated the store on August 31, 1938.

In line with this chronology the trial court found that plaintiff by executing the lease with Dr. Boonshaft did demise a part of the Medico–Dental Building to a tenant other than defendant for the purpose of maintaining a drug store and selling drugs on the premises, and that the making of the lease with Dr. Boonshaft was a breach of defendant's lease; that plaintiff in not taking immediate action to abate the drug store on the ninth floor of the building violated its lease with defendant; that plaintiff breached its lease with defendant on August 19, 1938, when it advised defendant that it could make no arrangements with Dr. Boonshaft and could not do anything with him regarding the selling of drugs and the maintaining of the drug store; and that such breaches of the lease were in material respects and were not waived by defendant.

The court also found that a material part of the consideration which induced defendant to enter into the lease with plaintiff was the right to be protected against competition, and that a material part of the consideration failed as the result of plaintiff's execution of the Boonshaft lease.

* * *

On this appeal from the judgment rendered for defendant in consequence of the above findings, plaintiff advances the following propositions: (1) Covenants in leases are independent and performance of a covenant by the landlord is not a condition precedent to an action for rent against the tenant; (2) a covenant "not to lease" for a restricted purpose is breached only by actual leasing for such purpose, or by acquiescence in the conduct of the second lessee which is in violation of the restriction, neither of which appears in this case; (3) even if the covenants are dependent and there was a breach of the covenant involved herein, the breach was not so substantial as to go to the whole of the consideration; and (4) there was a waiver by the defendant of the alleged violation. Consideration of the legal aspect of these respective contentions in conjunction with the factual situation which confronted the trial court will demonstrate the propriety of the judgment entered.

The first controversial point is whether the covenants "not to lease" and "to pay rent" are mutually independent or dependent. It is plaintiff's position that a lease is a conveyance as distinguished from a contract, so that any covenant on the part of the lessor is independent of the lessee's obligation to pay rent and each party has his remedy for breach of covenant in an action for damages. While it is true that a lease is primarily a conveyance in that it transfers an estate to the lessee, it also presents the aspect of a contract. This dual character serves to create two distinct sets of rights and obligations—"one comprising those growing out of the relation of landlord and tenant, and said to be based on the 'privity of estate,' and the other comprising those growing out of the express stipulations of the lease, and so said to be based on 'privity of contract.'" *Samuels v. Ottinger*, 169 Cal. 209, 211, 146 P. 638. Those features of the lease which are strictly contractual in their nature should be construed according to the rules for the interpretation of contracts generally and in conformity with the fundamental principle that the intentions of the parties should be given effect as far as possible. In line with this concept is the authoritative observation in 32 Am.Jur. § 144, p. 145, that "covenants and stipulations on the part of the lessor and lessee are to be construed to be dependent upon each other or independent of each other, according to the intention of the parties and the good sense of the case, and technical words should give way to such intention."

Noteworthy here are the several provisions of the lease itself plainly indicating the intention and understanding of the parties as to the interbalancing considerations existing between the respective covenants. The agreement by the lessor "not to lease" any other part of the building to any other person for the purpose of its use as a drug store or for the sale of drugs, and the agreement by the lessee "to pay rent" appear in a rider attached to and made a part of the lease, a circumstance of incorporation not to be overlooked in the measure of the parties' comprehension of the reciprocal nature of the specified promises. Moreover, the lessee was limited by the terms of the lease to maintaining a drug store, a restriction emphasizing the import of the lessor's duty in negotiating future demises of other portions of the building. Finally to be noted is the express language of the lease manifesting the conditional character of the stipulations therein contained: "Time is of the essence of this lease and all of the terms and covenants hereof are conditions, and upon the breach by lessee of any of the same lessor may, at lessor's option, terminate this lease ..." Thus, the parties recognized in plain terms the essential interdependence of their obligations.

It is an established rule that those covenants which run to the entire consideration of a contract are mutual and dependent. Undoubtedly the restrictive covenant in defendant's lease was of such a nature. The exclusive right to conduct a drug store in the building was vital to defendant's successful operation of its business under the circumstances which prevailed in this case. Defendant's pharmacy was of a distinctive type in that it catered principally to doctors and dentists for reference of prescription work, did not carry the general line of merchandise found in the ordinary drug store, and did not rely upon transient trade. Defendant was and had been maintaining a chain of exclusive prescription pharmacies in Los Angeles for eighteen years. The fact that the Medico–Dental Building was tenanted for the most part by practitioners of the medical and dental professions motivated defendant to select that location for the establishment of one of its retail units. Defendant had occupied the same premises since 1925, and depended upon the tenants of the building and their patients for the major portion of its business. In fact, when vacancies occurred defendant's income from the store suffered to such an extent that the rent was temporarily reduced, and restoration to the former monthly rental level was made contingent upon a material increase in the occupancy of the building. Thus plaintiff knew, as appears from its letter granting the rent concession to defendant, that the "chief source" of defendant's business on the premises was the tenants in the building, and that it was therefore of prime importance that no competitor be rented quarters there. The correlation of these facts with the express provisions of the lease above noted compels the conclusion that the restrictive covenant was not incidental or subordinate to the main object of the lease, but went to the whole of the consideration, and that as such it must be deemed a dependent covenant.

[The court discussed two cases in other jurisdictions holding that non-competition clauses were dependent with the covenant to pay rent].

The second question is whether the restrictive covenant was breached by leasing for the prohibited purpose or by the lessor's acquiescence in the conduct of the other lessee amounting to a violation of the restriction.

As to the first part of this question, relative to leasing for the forbidden purpose, the trial court found that plaintiff did lease *a portion* of the Medico–Dental Building to Dr. Boonshaft for the purpose of maintaining a drug store and selling drugs on the premises so demised; that, by executing such lease, plaintiff breached its agreement with defendant; and that, by virtue of one of the provisions of the lease with Dr. Boonshaft, plaintiff intended to and did give such tenant the right and privilege of maintaining a drug store, selling drugs and compounding prescriptions on the premises, and by so doing failed to protect the defendant against competition.

This finding, as to the purpose of plaintiff's demise to Dr. Boonshaft, was based undoubtedly upon inferences drawn from the provisions of that tenant's lease; inferences that plaintiff knew at the time such lease was executed that the Boonshaft Medical Group contemplated the conduct of a type of medical business which would require a large stock of drugs, and that a drug store would be operated in connection therewith; that Dr. Boonshaft regarded the privilege of maintaining a drug store as a material part of the consideration in support of his lease; and inferences drawn from the conduct of plaintiff and Dr. Boonshaft following the latter's entry into possession of the demised premises.

[The appellate court then described in detail the factual bases for the trial court's conclusions. In particular, the trial court found that (1) Dr. Boonshaft and the building manager had stated that Boonshaft's drugstore was permitted under the lease; (2) Boonshaft's drugstore was operated and stocked substantially the same as any other drugstore, according to its pharmacist and three pharmacy inspectors; and (3) the lease provision permitting Boonshaft to dispense drugs specified that Boonshaft would not post a sign or advertisement with the words "pharmacy," "drugstore," or "dispensary," suggesting that the lessor anticipated an objection from the defendant about Boonshaft's operation.]

As to the second part of the second question—whether the restrictive covenant was breached by the plaintiff's acquiescence in the conduct of Dr. Boonshaft amounting to a violation of the restriction—the trial court found that the plaintiff in not taking immediate action to abate the drug store on the ninth floor and in advising defendant that it could not do anything with Dr. Boonshaft with respect to the objectionable activity, breached its lease with defendant.

Bearing on this feature of the case is the following evidence. The drug store on the ninth floor was opened in May, 1938. In the latter part of July, 1938, defendant learned that Dr. Boonshaft was maintaining a pharmacy on the premises, and on August 3, 1938, it wrote a letter to plaintiff protesting against the competing activity and demanding that plaintiff immediately put a stop to such objectionable practice. All of the parties concerned met in conference in defendant's office five days later, with the result that plaintiff promised to see what arrangements could be made and to advise defendant. Communications were thereupon had between plaintiff and Dr. Boonshaft, but defendant did not hear further from plaintiff until August 19, 1938, when plaintiff's attorney advised Mr. Horton, defendant's president, by telephone that he had been unable to do anything with Dr. Boonshaft, that "there could not be any arrangements made," and Mr. Horton then said that he thought the premises would be vacated, to which the attorney replied: "Use your own judgment about that."

[The court concluded that the landlord's position "was uncompromising in form," thereby forcing the tenant to continue with the lease and risk waiver, or vacate the premises].

The foregoing observations from the record demonstrate that the findings of the trial court relative to acquiescence have ample support in the evidence, and the conclusion is required that plaintiff concurred in Dr. Boonshaft's maintenance of his drug store in the building.

The third point, that even if there was a breach of the restrictive covenant, it was not so substantial as to go to the whole of the consideration, was discussed in part in connection with the treatment of the first proposition concerning the interdependence of the parties' covenants under the terms of the lease. As was there stated, various special circumstances such as the exclusive nature of defendant's pharmacy, the limited source of its patronage, and the many years of its tenancy in the building establish the materiality of plaintiff's breach of its obligation to protect defendant against a rival business. Another factor substantiating this view is the record's disclosure that the Horton & Converse lease here involved would not have been executed had it not been for the insertion of the restrictive covenant in accordance with the request of Mr. Horton, defendant's president, that plaintiff's assignor incorporate in the instrument the same rights as to freedom from competition that defendant enjoyed under its previous lease of the same quarters in the Medico–Dental Building. Thus, it is apparent that the exclusive right to engage in a specified business in a particular building was the essence of the consideration for defendant's payment of rent during its many years of occupancy of the premises. It is reasonable to infer from the fact that an entire floor was leased "as offices for the practice of medicine and dentistry" that a substantial amount of business would be created by the various doctors occupying the several rooms on that floor, and that a drug store operated on that floor in connection with such practice would deprive defendant of a considerable source of revenue within the normal range of expectation. Plaintiff complains of defendant's failure to prove as a ground of rescission the prejudicial effect of Dr. Boonshaft's drug business and the exact pecuniary detriment sustained because of such competing activity. While consistent with practical considerations, it is said that a breach of a contractual right in a trivial or inappreciable respect will not justify rescission of the agreement by the party entitled to the benefit in question, a default in performance will not be tolerated if it is so dominant or pervasive as in any real or substantial measure to frustrate the purpose of the undertaking. See discussion by Justice Cardozo in *Jacob & Youngs v. Kent*, 230 N.Y. 239, 129 N.E. 889, 23 A.L.R. 1429. But where, as here, the covenant of the lessor is of such character that its breach will defeat the entire object of the lessee in entering into the lease, such as rendering his further occupancy of the premises a source of continuing financial loss incapable of satisfactory measurement in damages, it must be held that the covenant goes to the root of the consideration for the lease upon the lessee's part. Commensurate with this principle, it is plain that the defendant's loss of potential business on account of the competing drug store was not a matter easily susceptible of monetary estimate, and proof of this element was not required of defendant under its presentation of the rights and duties of the parties in the circumstances of this case. A contrary view would authorize plaintiff to execute instruments similar to the Boonshaft lease for every floor of its building and thus render the restrictive covenant in defendant's lease valueless insofar as the protection of its essential source of income was concerned.

[The court rejected the plaintiff's fourth argument that the defendant waived the restrictive covenant by selling drugs wholesale to Boonshaft in June and July. The court concluded that the defendant did not knowingly waive the breach because (1) Boonshaft was one of the many customers serviced from the defendant's wholesale sales office located elsewhere; and (2) the defendant promptly objected when it discovered that Boonshaft sold drugs in violation of the lease.]

---

1.   Does the court in *Medico-Dental* treat the lease as a conveyance or a contract? What is the significance of the distinction? What criteria does the court use to decide whether lease covenants are independent or dependent?

2. How did the landlord breach the lease? When did the breach occur? Assuming that the breach did not occur until Boonshaft opened the pharmacy, what could the landlord have done to cure the breach?

3. What are the tenant's remedies for breach of the lease? If the tenant chooses to rescind the lease, may he do so immediately upon discovering a breach? Or must the tenant give the landlord some opportunity to cure the breach? Does the tenant run any risk by waiting for the landlord to cure the breach? What facts in this case establish the breach as "substantial," and thus entitle the tenant to rescind the lease?

———————

To overcome the traditional property rule of independent covenants, or to expand effectively the list of clauses that are considered dependent, many leases specifically state that breach of any covenant gives the injured party a right to terminate the lease. Nonetheless, because termination is an extreme remedy, many courts have limited the parties' power to terminate a lease. For example, courts have denied forfeiture on grounds that the landlord did not act unequivocally to terminate the lease, *Padilla v. Sais*, 76 N.M. 247, 251, 414 P.2d 223, 226 (1966) (lease remains in effect after breach of the covenant to pay rent until landlord unequivocally acts to terminate the lease), the landlord waived the breach by accepting rent, *EDC Associates, Ltd. v. Gutierrez*, 153 Cal.App.3d 167, 170–71, 200 Cal. Rptr. 333, 335 (1984) (right to assert forfeiture for violation of covenant to pay rent waived by accepting rent); *C & A Land Co. v. Rudolf Inv. Corp.*, 163 Ga. App. 832, 834, 296 S.E.2d 149, 150 (1982) (landlord waived right to terminate for breach of covenant to pay rent by accepting rental checks, even though it never cashed the checks),[8] and the landlord acted unconscionably in seeking forfeiture, *see, e.g., Bethlehem Steel Corp. v. Shonk Land Co.*, 169 W. Va. 310, 288 S.E.2d 139 (1982) (because the landlord failed to seek forfeiture after a breach early in the lease term, the later attempt to seek forfeiture was unconscionable).

———————

c. BARGAINING POWER

As you go through the landlord-tenant materials, consider the fairness and efficacy of particular allocations of rights. One thing to think about is the notion of "bargaining power."

8. A court, however, may rely on an anti-waiver clause to find that the landlord's actions did not constitute waiver. *See, e.g., Karbelnig v. Brothwell*, 244 Cal.App.2d 333, 341–43, 53 Cal.Rptr. 335, 340–41 (1966) (because of an anti-waiver clause in the lease, acceptance of rent could not be deemed as a waiver of tenant's breach of a provision barring assignment); *Riverside Development Co. v. Ritchie*, 103 Idaho 515, 521, 650 P.2d 657, 663 (1982) (because of provision requiring waiver to be in writing, landlord's cashing rent checks after breach of failure to pay rent by a certain date does not constitute waiver).

The actual distribution of bargaining power depends substantially on local market conditions, the state of the economy, interest rates, the sophistication and shrewdness of the parties, and so forth. A local recession, for example, may make it is difficult for landlords to find tenants; the vacancy rate is high and rents are depressed. These conditions magnify the tenants' bargaining power. Where, by contrast, the vacancy rate is quite low, the competition for rental space is stiff and landlords have a substantial edge in bargaining.

Bargaining power involves more than just market conditions. To anticipate all possible contingencies, leases contain all sorts of provisions allocating rights and obligations between the parties. Many of the clauses are never invoked, but they are put in the lease "just in case."

The natural product of frequently occurring, complex relationships is a form document. Form leases are especially common in residential leaseholds. Because landlords generally are more sophisticated in business dealings and more organized as a group than are residential tenants, it is almost always the landlord, and not the tenant, who offers the form lease as the starting, and often final, bargaining position.

There is nothing necessarily wrong with form leases. Many form lease provisions fairly balance obligations between the parties. In addition, there is in principle nothing preventing the tenant from negotiating the provisions in the form lease, or from declining to accept the lease.

Nonetheless, many form residential leases are one-sided. A lease commonly used in Oakland, California states that the tenant must pay the landlord's attorney fees in any action for eviction, irrespective of whether the landlord wins. Another provision waives all claims against the landlord for damages or injuries, "from any cause whatsoever." The lease requires all guests staying over two days to be registered. And it waives the tenant's right to a refund of deposits if the tenant abandons the premises before the term has expired, regardless of the reasons. To put it mildly, some form leases are more attentive to the landlords' interests than the tenants' interests.

The prospective residential tenant may face several obstacles when attempting to negotiate the terms of a form lease. A tight housing market can severely undercut the tenant's ability to bargain. Because other prospective tenants are lined up to take the apartment without reviewing the lease, landlords may offer a lease on a "take it or leave it" basis. If the vacancy rate is sufficiently low, the tenant who insists on negotiating the lease terms runs the risk of having no housing.

Moreover, printed leases look official. Tenants who do not know their legal rights (and do not have ready access to legal advice before signing the lease) may think that it is fruitless to try to change the printed form, which usually has no space for modifications. There is also the usual psychological advantage of having your agenda in writing; it is a tenet of negotiating that the party who comes to the meeting with a written proposal gets most of what he wants.

To make matters worse, some leases are long and written in "legalese," not readily understood by many tenants. A 1970 study found that only half of tenants read their leases carefully, and that among that half there was a wide range of understanding. Most tenants did not even try to negotiate any lease provisions, and those that did generally had the skills and educational background to negotiate. Mueller, Residential Tenants and Their Leases: An Empirical Study, 69 Mich. L. Rev. 247 (1970). The results of this study raise difficult questions regarding how much the law should protect knowledgeable people who do not read documents that they sign, and whether legal doctrines should presume that people have carefully negotiated their leases.

The picture is not completely bleak for tenants. One reason that form leases seem so weighted in favor of the landlord is that the tenant's rights are defined elsewhere: in state statutes, local ordinances, and case law. Because many of those rights cannot be bargained away (especially in residential leases), there is hardly any need to put them in the lease. *See, e.g.,* Cal. Civ. Code § 1953 (declaring "void as contrary to public policy" lease provisions that purport to waive the tenant's statutory rights to a notice or hearing, the right to assert a cause of action that may arise in the future, procedural rights in litigation, rights involving security deposits, and the right to have the landlord exercise any duty of care imposed by law); Cal. Civ. Code § 1942.5(d) (declaring void any provision purporting to waive the tenant's rights to be protected from retaliatory eviction); S.D. Codified Laws § 43–32–8 (parties may not agree in the lease to waive the warranty of habitability); *Lloyd v. Service Corp. of Alabama, Inc.,* 453 So.2d 735, 741 (Ala.1984) (creating a presumption that exculpatory clauses in leases are unenforceable, unless the landlord can show that "the provisions were explained to the lessee * * * and that there was in fact a real and voluntary meeting of the minds and not merely an objective meeting"); *Galligan v. Arovitch,* 421 Pa. 301, 304, 219 A.2d 463, 465 (1966) (holding exculpatory clauses in a residential lease invalid since tenants are not permitted to bargain them away).

The emergence of these and other statutory and judge-made tenants' rights in the 1970s signaled a revolutionary change in landlord-tenant law. *See generally* Rabin, The Revolution in Residential Landlord–Tenant Law: Causes and Consequences, 69 Cornell L. Rev. 517 (1984). A tenant's right to protection against retaliatory eviction has evolved into a statutory right to a lease renewal except upon a showing of good cause. The landlord's traditional tort immunity from failure to disclose defects has been replaced in many states with a general duty of "reasonable care." The landlord's right to withdraw from the rental market, while not entirely eliminated, has been severely restricted in some states and cities by laws that make it difficult to convert rental units to condominiums. And the landlord's common law right to refuse prospective tenants arbitrarily has been restricted by federal and state laws barring discrimination. *See, e.g.,* Fair Housing Act, 42 U.S.C. §§ 3601–3631 (barring discrimination based on "race, color, religion, sex, handicap, familial status, or national origin").

The following sections delineate the rights of landlords and tenants and discuss corresponding remedies. In many cases, these rights and remedies are default rules; the parties may bargain for a different set of rules in their contract (lease). In others, however, the law not only sets the default rules but also prohibits contractual reordering; in essence, the rights and remedies are inalienable. As you study these materials, think about the application of these rules in both residential and commercial settings, and ask whether and to what extent parties should be free to negotiate for rights and obligations different from the default rules.

2.   LANDLORD'S RIGHTS AND REMEDIES

Tenants have three types of duties: a duty to fulfill the express obligations in the lease (*e.g.*, to pay rent), implied duties not to commit waste or maintain a nuisance, and a duty to vacate the premises at the end of the lease term. Stated slightly differently, tenants are liable for breaching express and implied covenants in the lease and for holding over after the expiration of a lease.

a.   REMEDIES FOR TENANT'S BREACH AND FOR HOLDING OVER

The tenant's failure to vacate after a lease has expired or has been terminated precipitates a substantial portion of landlord-tenant litigation, especially in residential leaseholds. Often, the landlord's primary goal is to evict the tenant; in many cases collecting damages is at best a secondary consideration.

Forcible Entry and Forcible Detainer. A landlord may be tempted to use "self-help" after the tenant's breach, especially when the tenant owes back rent or another tenant is ready to move in. A landlord may want to seize the tenant's belongings, cut off utilities, change the locks, or enter the premises to retake possession, all in an effort to force the tenant to leave. Frequently, leases contain provisions expressly authorizing the landlord to enter and physically retake possession.

As a general (although not universal) rule, however, landlords may not use self-help. Indeed, two types of self-help, forcible entry and forcible detainer, have been illegal for almost as long as there has been an English landlord tenant law.[9] Consider the following provisions.

---

9. Before 1166, there were no English laws protecting possessors (including lessees) from forceful dispossession. That year, Henry II instituted the assize of novel disseisen, which provided a summary remedy for dispossession, to eliminate the violence that frequently accompanied land disputes. This remedy eventually became more elaborate and fell into disuse, which led to the Forcible Entry Act in 1381. *See* Comment, Defects in the Current Forcible Entry and Detainer Laws of the United States and England, 25 UCLA L. Rev. 1067, 1068–70 (1978).

California Civil Code

789.3. Utility services; prevention of access to property; removal of doors, windows or personalty; intent to terminate occupancy; liability of landlord; injunctive relief.

(a) A landlord shall not with intent to terminate the occupancy under any lease or other tenancy or estate at will, however created, of property used by a tenant as his residence willfully cause, directly or indirectly, the interruption or termination of any utility service furnished the tenant, including, but not limited to, water, heat, light, electricity, gas, telephone, elevator, or refrigeration, whether or not the utility service is under the control of the landlord.

(b) In addition, a landlord shall not, with intent to terminate the occupancy under any lease or other tenancy or estate at will, however created, of property used by a tenant as his or her residence, willfully:

(1) Prevent the tenant from gaining reasonable access to the property by changing the locks or using a bootlock or by any other similar method or device;

(2) Remove outside doors or windows; or

(3) Remove from the premises the tenant's personal property, the furnishings, or any other items without the prior written consent of the tenant. * * *

(c) Any landlord who violates this section shall be liable to the tenant in a civil action for all of the following:

(1) Actual damages of the tenant.

(2) An amount not to exceed [$100] for each day or part thereof the landlord remains in violation of this section. * * * [I]n no event shall less than [$250] be awarded for each separate cause of action. * * *

(d) In any action under subdivision (c) the court shall award reasonable attorney's fees to the prevailing party. In any such action the tenant may seek appropriate injunctive relief to prevent continuing or further violation of the provisions of this section during the pendency of this action. * * *

California Code of Civil Procedure

1159. Forcible entry; party in possession.

Every person is guilty of a forcible entry who either:

1. By breaking open doors, windows, or other parts of a house, or by any kind of violence or circumstances of terror enters upon or into any real property; or,

2. Who, after entering peaceably upon real property, turns out by force, threats, or menacing conduct, the party in possession. * * *

1160. **Forcible detainer defined.**

Every person is guilty of a forcible detainer who either:

1.   By force, or by menaces and threats of violence, unlawfully holds and keeps the possession of any real property, whether the same was acquired peaceably or otherwise; or,

2.   Who, in the night-time, or during the absence of the occupant of any lands, unlawfully enters upon real property, and who, after demand made for the surrender thereof, for the period of five days, refuses to surrender the same to such former occupant.

A landlord who violates §§ 1159–1160 is liable for treble actual damages, Cal. Code Civ. Proc. § 735, and statutory damages of $600. Cal. Code Civ. Proc. § 1174(b). *See also* Fla. Stat. ch. 83.67 (landlord cannot shut off utilities, change the locks, remove doors, roof, walls, or windows; tenant's remedy includes damages or 3 months' rent); N.J. Stat. Ann. §§ 2A:39–1 to 2A:39–3 (no one may enter a residence "in any manner without the consent" of the tenant, except pursuant to legal procedures); Tex. Prop. Code Ann. § 24.001 (defining forcible entry and detainer as "an entry without the consent of the person in actual possession of the property"). *Cf.* Ariz. Rev. Stat. § 33–1368(D)–(E) (authorizing landlord to disconnect utilities, change locks, remove and store tenant's property after giving notice and obtaining a writ).[10]

Jordan v. Talbot

Supreme Court of California, 1961.
55 Cal.2d 597, 361 P.2d 20, 12 Cal.Rptr. 488.

■ TRAYNOR, JUSTICE.

Plaintiff was a tenant in defendant's apartment house. The lease provided that the lessor had a right of re-entry upon the breach of any condition in the lease and a lien upon all personal effects, furniture, and baggage in the tenant's apartment to secure the rents and other charges.

---

10. Some states, either by common law or statute, permit the landlord to seize or "distrain" the tenant's belongings to satisfy the rent when the tenant is in default. *See, e.g.,* Ga. Code Ann. § 44–7–70 ("The landlord shall have power to distrain for rent as soon as the same is due if the tenant is seeking to remove his property from the premises"). Most statutes permitting distraint limit the types of tenant's goods that the landlord can seize, and others have abolished or modified this remedy significantly. *See, e.g.,* Del. Code Ann. tit. 25, §§ 6301–6310 (abolishing distraint for rent for non-commercial leaseholds, but setting up a system of court-administered distraint for commercial leaseholds). Most of these statutes have survived due process challenges on the ground that they do not involve state action. *Davis v. Richmond,* 512 F.2d 201 (1st Cir.1975) (finding no state action); *Greco v. Guss,* 775 F.2d 161 (7th Cir. 1985) (rejecting a due process challenge on the ground that the tenant had an adequate post-seizure remedy).

One of the conditions was the payment of $132.50 rent on the first of each month. Plaintiff paid the rent for eight months. After she was two months in arrears in rent, defendant, without her consent and during her temporary absence, unlocked the door of her apartment, entered and removed her furniture to a warehouse, and refused to allow her to re-occupy the apartment. Thereupon plaintiff filed this action for forcible entry and detainer and for conversion of her furniture and other personal property.

The jury returned a verdict of $6,500 for forcible entry and detainer and for conversion and $3,000 punitive damages. * * *

Defendant contends that there is no evidence that he violated either section 1159 or 1160 of the Code of Civil Procedure and that the evidence is therefore insufficient as a matter of law to sustain a verdict for forcible entry and detainer. * * *

Defendant's Right of Re-entry Is Not a Defense to an Action for Forcible Entry

In defining forcible entry section 1159 of the Code of Civil Procedure refers to "every person," thereby including owners as well as strangers to the title. Under section 1172 of the Code of Civil Procedure the plaintiff "shall only be required to show, in addition to the forcible entry or forcible detainer complained of, that he was peaceably in the actual possession at the time of the forcible entry, or was entitled to the possession at the time of the forcible detainer. The defendant may show in his defense that he or his ancestors, or those whose interest in such premises he claims, have been in the quiet possession thereof for the space of one whole year together next before the commencement of the proceedings, and that his interest therein is not ended or determined; and such showing is a bar to the proceedings." Nowhere is it stated that a right of re-entry is a defense to an action for forcible entry or detainer.

Nor can such a defense be implied from the historical background or purpose of the statute.[11]

Both before and after the enactment of the present forcible entry and detainer statutes this court held that ownership or right of possession to the property was not a defense to an action for forcible entry. In *McCauley v. Weller*, 1859, 12 Cal. 500, 524 (decided before the enactment of sections 1159–1179a of the Code of Civil Procedure) and in *Voll v. Hollis*, 1882, 60 Cal. 569, 573 (decided after the enactment of the foregoing sections) it was held that evidence of defendant's ownership of the land was irrelevant to the question of liability for a forcible entry and detainer. "[T]he action of forcible entry and detainer is a summary proceeding to recover possession

11. The original forcible entry and detainer statute, enacted in England in 1381 (5 Richard II c. 7; *see Dickinson v. Maguire*, 9 Cal. 46, 50–51), provided only criminal sanctions for its breach. The purpose of the statute was to preserve the peace by preventing disturbances that frequently accompanied struggles for the possession of land. *See* 2 Taylor, Landlord and Tenant 412 (9th ed.); *Dickinson v. Maguire, supra.* This early prohibition against self-help extended to persons having a right to possession and thus fostered recourse to orderly court process. *See* 1 Harper and James, The Law of Torts, 260.

of premises forcibly or unlawfully detained. The inquiry in such cases is confined to the actual peaceable possession of the plaintiff and the unlawful or forcible ouster or detention by defendant the object of the law being to prevent the disturbance of the public peace, by the forcible assertion of a private right. Questions of title or right of possession cannot arise; a forcible entry upon the actual possession of plaintiff being proven, he would be entitled to restitution, though the fee simple title and present right of possession are shown to be in the defendant. The authorities on this point are numerous and uniform." *Voll v. Hollis, supra,* 60 Cal. 569, 573; *accord*: *Giddings v. 76 Land and Water Co.,* 1890, 83 Cal. 96, 100–101, 23 P. 196; *Mitchell v. Davis,* 1863, 23 Cal. 381, 384, 385; *Davis v. Mitchell,* 1865, 1 Cal.Unrep. 206, 207–208; *Lasserot v. Gamble,* 1896, 5 Cal.Unrep. 510, 515, 46 P. 917; *Kerr v. O'Keefe,* 1903, 138 Cal. 415, 421, 71 P. 447; *California Products, Inc. v. Mitchell,* 1921, 52 Cal.App. 312, 314, 198 P. 646; *Eichhorn v. De La Cantera,* 1953, 117 Cal.App.2d 50, 54–55, 255 P.2d 70; *Martin v. Cassidy,* 1957, 149 Cal.App.2d 106, 110, 307 P.2d 981.

In *Lasserot v. Gamble, supra*; *Kerr v. O'Keefe, supra*; *California Products, Inc. v. Mitchell, supra,* and *Martin v. Cassidy, supra,* the landlord entered pursuant to a lease granting him a right of re-entry similar to defendant's right of re-entry in the present case. In each case the court held that absent a voluntary surrender of the premises by the tenant, the landlord could enforce his right of re-entry only by judicial process, not by self-help. Under section 1161 of the Code of Civil Procedure a lessor may summarily obtain possession of his real property within three days. This remedy is a complete answer to any claim that self-help is necessary.

As in the foregoing cases, the lease herein is silent as to the method of enforcing the right of re-entry. In any event a provision in the lease expressly permitting a forcible entry would be void as contrary to the public policy set forth in section 1159. *Spencer v. Commercial Co.,* 30 Wash. 520, 71 P. 53, 55 (involving forcible entry and detainer statutes identical with section 1159); *cf. California Products Inc. v. Mitchell, supra,* 52 Cal.App. 312, 314–315, 198 P. 646. Regardless of who has the right to possession, orderly procedure and preservation of the peace require that the actual possession shall not be disturbed except by legal process.

Defendant Was Guilty of Forcible Entry

Section 1159 Subdivision 1 prohibits an entry by means of breaking open doors or windows. Defendant violated this section when he unlocked plaintiff's apartment without her consent and entered with the storage company employees to remove her furniture, even though there was no physical damage to the premises or actual violence.

It is true that before 1872 several cases held that actual force or violence was a necessary element in an action for forcible entry. * * * It is also true that some cases subsequent to the adoption of section 1159 have stated that only an entry accompanied by force or violence constitutes a violation of section 1159, subdivision 1. In most of these cases, however, the statements were unnecessary to the decision. * * *

Many other decisions of this court and the district courts of appeal have implied force in an entry made upon land in the possession of another without his consent, despite the absence of either violence or physical damage. * * *

Even if we were to interpret the first subdivision of section 1159 as being inapplicable unless a door or window was physically damaged or threats of violence actually occurred, the evidence in the instant case would nevertheless support a finding of forcible entry as defined by subdivision 2 of section 1159. Under that subdivision a forcible entry is completed if, after a peaceable entry, the occupant is excluded from possession by force or threats of violence. The removal of plaintiff's furniture without her consent rendered the apartment unsuitable for residence and forced her to seek shelter elsewhere. Moreover, when plaintiff returned to her apartment at 1:30 a.m. and inquired about her belongings defendant's employee ordered her to "Get the hell out of here. You're out of this place. Don't talk to me about it. Call Mr. Talbot." The jury could reasonably conclude that plaintiff was justified in believing that any attempt on her part to reinstall her furniture would be met by force. It has long been settled that there is a forcible entry under subdivision 2 if a show of force is made that causes the occupant to refrain from re-entering. * * *

"The statute was intended to prevent bloodshed, violence and breaches of the peace, too likely to result from wrongful entries into the possession of others; and it would be absurd to say, that to enable a party to avail himself of its provisions, there must have occurred precisely the evil which it was the object of the law to prevent." *McCauley v. Weller, supra,* 12 Cal. 500, 527. "Although the entry was peaceably made, the subsequent exclusion of plaintiff by force and threats constituted a forcible entry under the statute." *Kerr v. O'Keefe, supra,* 138 Cal. 415, 421, 71 P. 447, 450.

      * * *

Defendant Was Guilty of a Forcible Detainer

Subdivision 1 of section 1160 of the Code of Civil Procedure provides that a person is guilty of a forcible detainer if he "[b]y force or by menaces and threats of violence unlawfully holds and keeps the possession of any real property, whether the same was acquired peaceably or otherwise." In the present case there is evidence that the apartment was withheld by force and menace and that such withholding was unlawful.

Force and menace can be implied from defendant's agent's removal of plaintiff's furniture and his admonishment to "Get the hell out of here. You're out . . ."

The detention was unlawful, for a person who obtains possession to property by a forcible entry does not have the right to retain possession. *Lasserot v. Gamble,* 515, 46 P. 917. Moreover, defendant did not properly serve a three-day notice as required by section 791 of the Civil Code. It is settled that no immediate right to possession can be obtained under a right of re-entry until a proper three-day notice has been served on the lessee or grantee. Civ.Code, § 791.

Section 791 provides that a lessor having a right to re-entry may re-enter after the right has accrued upon three days notice as provided in sections 1161 and 1162 of Code of Civil Procedure. Defendant testified that he posted a three-day notice under plaintiff's door. There is no evidence that plaintiff was personally served or that a copy of the three-day notice was mailed to her home. The mere act of posting the notice under the door does not comply with section 1162.

Defendant Was Not Authorized to Enforce His Lien by Entering Plaintiff's Home

The provision in the lease granting defendant a lien does not specify a means of enforcement. In *Childs Real Estate Co. v. Shelburne Realty Co.,* 23 Cal.2d 263, 268, 143 P.2d 697, 699, where the lessor had a similar lien, we stated "in the absence of provisions in the lease for enforcement, equitable action would be necessary to make the lien operative." Even if the lease had authorized a forcible entry it would be invalid as violating the policy of the forcible entry and detainer statutes.

* * *

We conclude therefore that the evidence supports the verdict of forcible entry and detainer. There was evidence that defendant entered plaintiff's apartment without her consent. Such an entry violates section 1159 of the Code of Civil Procedure. There was evidence that defendant refused to allow plaintiff to re-enter her apartment. Such conduct violates section 1160 of the Code of Civil Procedure. Since the policy of these sections is the preservation of the peace, the rights thereunder may not be contracted away; thus defendant's right of re-entry and his lien on personal property in the apartment did not justify his entry into the apartment. * * *

■ SCHAUER, JUSTICE (dissenting).

* * *

The record, viewed favorably to plaintiff, shows also that on May 14, 1958, plaintiff by her own admission was two months in arrears in rent and had previously given defendant a rent check for one of such months which had not been honored by her bank. Her possession was under a written lease which provided, among other things, that

> In the event of any violation of said terms and conditions by the tenants the lessor shall have the right to take possession forthwith and terminate this tenancy returning to tenants any unused portion of rent paid, after deducting necessary closing charges....

> Lessor shall have a lien upon all personal effects, furniture and baggage contained in tenants' apartment for all unpaid charges.

On May 10, 1958, defendant served upon plaintiff a three-day notice to quit. Then on May 14, 1958, in plaintiff's absence defendant's manager entered the premises by means of a key (undisputedly without any breach of the peace) and had plaintiff's furniture and other possessions removed by a storage company and stored for plaintiff's account. When plaintiff returned to the apartment and entered it some time after 1:30 a.m. on May 15, 1958, she discovered the absence of her furnishings and made inquiry of the manager. He said to her, "Get the hell out of here. You're out of this place. Don't talk to me about it. Call Mr. Talbot [defendant]." Later the same day she telephoned to defendant's attorney who told her her furniture was at the storage company if she wanted to pick it up. Still later in the day she filed this action for forcible entry and detainer and for conversion. * * *

I believe that the above-quoted terms of the lease gave defendant a contractual right to enter the apartment and to remove the furnishings, and provide a complete defense to this action.

In *Baxley v. Western Loan & Bldg. Co.* (1933), 135 Cal.App. 426, 27 P.2d 387, as in the case at bench, plaintiff charged forcible entry and detainer under the provisions of sections 1159 and 1160 of the Code of Civil Procedure. There, defendant was vendor under an installment contract of sale of an apartment house which gave the vendee the right of possession "until a breach or a default by the vendee" and gave the vendor the right upon any breach or default to "reenter upon the premises and resume possession thereof." After the vendee fell in arrears on several payments defendant's employee informed the manager of the apartment that he was going to take possession and remain on the premises for defendant. The manager admitted him, installed him in one of the apartments, and agreed to continue as manager for defendant. The next day plaintiff appeared at the building and demanded that defendant's representative leave the premises, which was refused. During the discussion which followed either force or threats of force were used by both parties. Plaintiff then left the premises. It was held (135 Cal.App. at page 429 (2), 27 P.2d at page 388) that no forcible entry was shown under subdivision 1 of section 1159 because the actual entry by defendant was not accompanied "by any kind of violence or circumstances of terror," that subdivision 2 was intended to cover situations where one who had gained peaceable access thereafter evicted the occupant by force or the like, and that no such circumstance had occurred. With respect to forcible detainer under the provisions of section 1160, the court, citing various cases, recognized the rule to be that (135 Cal.App. at page 430 (3), 27 P.2d at page 389) "When contractual relations exist between the parties whereby the right to possession has been given to the one taking possession by means of the peaceable entry, then neither the entry nor detention of the property is 'unlawful' within the meaning of said section 1160 dealing with *forcible detainer*," and held that neither defendant's entry upon nor its detention of the premises was "unlawful" under the provisions of section 1160.

More specifically, as to the contractual rights of the owner, Mr. Justice Spence spoke for a unanimous court as follows: "Upon default in the payments, respondent was entitled to possession under the contract between the parties and could take possession if it could be done peaceably. We are of the opinion that when respondent, acting under its right conferred upon it by the contract between the parties, obtained possession of the premises by means of a peaceable entry, neither the entry upon nor the detention of the premises was 'unlawful' within the meaning of the subdivisions of said section 1160 relating to *forcible detainer*."

And in *Moldovan v. Fischer* (1957), 149 Cal.App.2d 600, 308 P.2d 844, in which defendants had made a non-forcible entry during the absence of the occupant, the rule was again declared, in reliance upon *Baxley v. Western Loan & Bldg. Co.* (1933), *supra*, 135 Cal.App. 426, 430, 27 P.2d 387, that (149 Cal.App.2d at pages 608–609 (9, 10), 308 P.2d at page 850) "where there is no force involved in the entry, and where the entry is pursuant to a contract between the parties, the entry is lawful," no unlawful entry or detainer has occurred and any "subsequent force and threats of force did not make the entry forcible." * * *

Plaintiff, however, relies upon *California Products, Inc. v. Mitchell* (1921), 52 Cal.App. 312, 198 P. 646, in which defendants, lessors of premises on which plaintiff was five months in arrears in the payment of rent, removed a lock from the door and entered during plaintiff's absence. The lease provided that at any time the rent was unpaid it should be lawful for the lessors "without previous notice or demand, to reenter the demised premises and the same peaceably to hold and enjoy thenceforth as if this lease had not been made." The court, in seemingly mistaken reliance upon *Winchester v. Becker* (1906), 4 Cal.App. 382, 88 P. 296, held that defendants' entry had been forcible, and was consequently not protected by the quoted lease provision. In the latter case (*Winchester v. Becker, supra*) defendant had first entered plaintiff's house by means of a key which was secreted over the back door. Plaintiff thereafter recovered this key and ordered defendant's agent off the premises. Defendant the[n], claiming "under a *pretended agreement for a sale of the land* on which a deposit of $100 had been paid" (italics added) *but which contained no authority for defendant to enter*, again entered the premises through the front door by means of a "false key." The finding was that defendant entered "fraudulently and without right" and the reviewing court held that the second entry was forcible within the provisions of subdivision 1 of section 1159 of the Code of the Civil Procedure ("breaking open doors, windows, or other parts of a house").

I believe the better view, and one more in keeping with the general weight of authority in other jurisdictions, is that stated and followed in the first cited cases (*Baxley v. Western Loan & Bldg. Co.* (1933), *supra*, 135 Cal.App. 426, 27 P.2d 387, and *Moldovan v. Fischer* (1957), *supra*, 149 Cal.App.2d 600, 308 P.2d 844), and that where, as here, entry is authorized by contract and is made by means of a key only, which is, after all, the same means as used by the tenant to enter, and where no actual force, violence, menace, threats or "circumstances of terror" are shown, no forcible entry has been established. Further, since defendant here, as in *Baxley* and *Moldovan*, had a contractual right to possession of the premises, his detention of them following peaceable entry was lawful and did not constitute forcible detainer. The holding of the majority, "that the evidence supports the verdict of forcible entry and detainer. There was evidence that defendant entered plaintiff's apartment without her consent," appears to me, on the whole record, to merit no more persuasive effect than that which the drawee bank accorded plaintiff's rent check the check with which plaintiff, during the period relevant to this lawsuit, purportedly "paid" for the right to use and occupy that portion of defendant's premises which the majority refer to as "plaintiff's apartment."

It should be recognized that it is still presumably lawful for adult persons, not convicted of felony, to own real property, contract for its rental, require the tenant to pay the agreed value of occupancy, and provide for security therefor, including a right of peaceful reentry upon any default of the tenant. Tenants and property owners may agree that the latter shall have some rights as against defaulting tenants, short of the time and expense required by court proceedings, and where such rights can be exercised peaceably, as was done here, it seems to me only common and elementary justice that the courts uphold them. * * *

Finally, and most distressing in my view, is the seeming alignment of the court on the side of the person who not only breached a contract but, according to the undisputed evidence, appears to have compounded the civil wrong by issuing and passing a check without sufficient funds or credit, to the end of extending her unlawful taking of the owner's property (the use and occupation of his premises) for a further period without compensation. To reward such a person for such conduct at the expense of the innocent party to the contract (whose only wrong consisted in believing that a contract, admittedly executed by competent parties with a lawful object and for a valuable consideration, would be upheld) appears to me to pervert law and subvert justice.

In the circumstances I would hold that as a matter of law plaintiff is not entitled to judgment against defendant for forcible entry and detainer.

---

1.   Are you persuaded that the court in *Jordan v. Talbot* properly read § 1159(1) to hold the landlord guilty of forcible entry? Did the landlord break open anything? Did he use violence or "circumstance of terror"?

2.   Why was the lease provision not an adequate waiver of the tenant's rights? Does the court effectively hold that tenants are not competent to waive their rights? What would be wrong with a knowing and intelligent waiver?

Note that the inalienability rule that the court adopts is a property rule. Had the court employed contract doctrine, the tenant would have been required to show that the waiver provision in the lease was unconscionable. Is the waiver provision unconscionable on its face? What criteria should a court use to determine unconscionability?

3.   What is the policy basis for the court's broad definition of forcible entry and detainer? Is it necessary? Would it be sufficient to hold the landlord strictly liable for damages resulting from violence, but otherwise allow entry and re-possession according to the terms of the lease? Many states find a forcible entry and detainer only when the landlord has used unreasonable force; "peaceable" entry and detainer, typically in the tenant's absence, are permitted. Which interpretation of forcible entry and detainer is preferable?

4.   Suppose that the county sheriff's deputy enters an apartment and evicts the tenants under an invalid writ of execution. Is the sheriff guilty of forcible entry and detainer? Should it matter that the sheriff's deputy did not know the writ was invalid? *See Bedi v. McMullan*, 160 Cal.App.3d 272, 206 Cal.Rptr. 578 (1984).

5.   Does the holding in *Jordan v. Talbot* mean that if a homeowner returns from vacation to find a squatter in possession of his home he cannot throw the person out? Is self-help unlawful if your landlord rented your apartment to another tenant in your absence? If so, what is your remedy?

––––––––

Unlawful Detainer. Recognizing that landlords have a legitimate need for prompt repossession when the tenant breaches certain lease provisions, maintains a nuisance, commits waste, or holds over after expiration of a lease, courts and legislatures have created a summary proceeding for eviction, usually called an unlawful detainer action. *See Restatement (Second) of Property (Landlord and Tenant)*, § 12.1 Statutory Note 1 (listing state summary eviction procedures). *See generally* Comment, No Easy Way Out: Making the Summary Eviction Process a Fairer and More Efficient Alternative to Landlord Self–Help, 41 UCLA L. Rev. 759 (1994). In contrast to the provisions for conventional civil remedies, summary proceedings provide shorter periods for giving notice, filing pleadings, and setting a trial date, and limit the substantive claims and defenses that can be raised.

The precise details vary significantly from state to state, but the basic procedure is as follows: The summary eviction process begins when the landlord serves the tenant with a notice (the period of notice varies from three to ten days) demanding that the tenant either perform an affirmative covenant (such as pay rent) or quit the premises; notice is not required if the action is brought after expiration of the lease or if it is not possible to cure the breach. In many states, if the tenant performs the obligation during the notice period, or if the landlord waives the breach, the landlord cannot pursue eviction. The lease is considered terminated either when the tenant vacates the premises or when (after the notice period) the landlord files an unlawful detainer action seeking possession (assuming that the landlord ultimately prevails in the action).

A trial date is set as soon as there is room on the summary calendar, which may mean 3–8 weeks. In many jurisdictions, the court may order the tenant to pay the rent into a court-managed escrow account pending trial. *See, e.g.,* Cal. Code Civ. Proc. § 1170.5(c) (requiring payments if trial is not held within 20 days and court finds there is a "reasonable probability" that the landlord will prevail at trial). As discussed later in this chapter, the tenant may raise a number of affirmative defenses, including that: he did not breach the lease; the eviction notice was defective; the landlord waived the breach[12]; the landlord violated the local rent control ordinance; the tenant owed no (or reduced) rent because of the landlord's breach of the warranty of habitability; the tenant lawfully used some of the rent to make repairs; or the landlord's termination of the lease was retaliatory. The tenant may not file a cross-complaint if he remains in possession. If the tenant loses on the merits or by default, the court will award the landlord a judgment for possession, forfeiture of the lease, unpaid rent, and any damages caused by the unlawful detainer (*i.e.,* rental value for the tenant's possession after termination of the lease and before the court judgment); other kinds of damages may be recovered in a civil action.

With the judgment for possession, the landlord can then get the sheriff to evict the tenant upon a few days notice to the tenant (assuming that the tenant did not voluntarily leave upon receiving notice of the judgment). Although the tenant may appeal, the judgment normally is not stayed pending appeal. *See, e.g.,* Cal. Code Civ. Proc. § 1176(a) (permitting a stay only on showing that the tenant will suffer "extreme hardship in the absence of a stay and that the [landlord] will not be irreparably injured by its issuance").

Damages. Unlawful detainer statutes often exclude many damages claims and counter-claims; the parties may pursue such claims in a separate civil action. In most states, the landlord may recover past rent due, the value of the tenant's use of the property during the holdover period (which is not necessarily the same as the reserved rent), and in some states an additional penalty. *See, e.g.,* Ala. Code § 6–6–314 (double annual rent plus consequential damages); Nev. Rev. Stat. § 40.360(2) (rent plus triple damages); Utah Code Ann. § 78–36–8 (rent due plus damages for use and waste).

Holding Tenant to Another Term. If the tenant has held over after the expiration of the lease,[13] the landlord has two remedies: (1) he may

---

12. For example, if the landlord brought the unlawful detainer action because the tenant held over after the termination of the lease, the landlord's acceptance of rent presumptively creates a new periodic tenancy based on the frequency of the payments (*e.g.,* monthly payments would create a month-to-month tenancy).

13. A court will not find that a tenant has held over if he is only a few hours late in vacating the premises, or if he left only a few inconsequential items in the premises. A court will also not find that a tenant has held over if there are circumstances beyond the tenant's control that prevent him from leaving on time. *See, e.g., Herter v. Mullen,* 159

terminate the lease and regain possession through the unlawful detainer procedure described above, or (2) he may hold the tenant for a new lease, under the same conditions as the original lease. The choice of remedies is entirely the landlord's election. *See generally* Powell on Property ¶ 250. In some states, the landlord can hold the tenant for another term (*e.g.*, one year lease), but in other states, the landlord can hold the tenant only for a periodic lease. *See, e.g., Moudry v. Parkos*, 217 Neb. 521, 349 N.W.2d 387 (1984).

In some cases the tenant has held over because the parties were negotiating for a new lease, but negotiations broke down. The tenant's liability in these circumstances depends in part on the negotiations and actions of the parties. In *Donnelly Advertising Corp. v. Flaccomio*, 216 Md. 113, 140 A.2d 165 (1958), the tenant offered to renew the lease, but with a lower rent. The landlord did not accept this offer or even pursue negotiations. Rather, after the tenant remained in possession after expiration of the lease, the landlord sued the tenant for rent under the old agreement. The court held for the landlord.

> [T]he general rule is that a tenant who has remained after the expiration of the term is not a tenant holding over, and thus liable for a full year's rent, if such tenant has remained with the express or tacit consent of the landlord while the parties negotiate for a new lease. But the mere existence of negotiations is not sufficient to relieve the tenant from liability if the landlord has not actually consented to the holding over.

Id. at 121, 140 A.2d at 169. Since the landlord had not consented to the tenant's continued occupation during negotiations, the landlord could hold the tenant for a new lease.

In *Cowell v. Snyder*, 15 Cal.App. 634, 115 P. 961 (1911), the landlord began negotiating for a higher rent as the first lease came to an end. The tenant expressly rejected the landlord's proposal, and continued to occupy the property after the lease expired. The landlord did not terminate the lease; rather the parties continued to negotiate over the rent, and the landlord accepted rent as provided in the expired lease. Finally, the landlord sued for rent, claiming that the tenant should have paid the higher rent.

> [W]here a landlord seasonably gives notice to his tenant for years that the terms of the lease with respect to the amount of rental will be changed in the event the tenant continues to occupy the property beyond the expiration of his term, and the tenant does so continue to occupy the property, and does not manifest his refusal to be bound by such new terms, that by his silence he will be deemed to have acquiesced in the changed contract and become bound by it. But the cases also hold that where a tenant, holding

N.Y. 28, 53 N.E. 700 (1899) (tenant's illness); *Feiges v. Racine Dry Goods Co.*, 231 Wis. 270, 285 N.W. 799 (1939) (tenant's employees went on strike). In such cases, the court will hold that the tenant is a tenant at will until he is able to leave.

over beyond the expiration of his term, announces that he will not accept the new terms proposed by his landlord, no agreement results, and therefore no contract by which the new terms become operative between the parties.

> In such a case, where the landlord does not receive the rental from the tenant, the tenant becomes, in effect, a trespasser and liable to the landlord for the reasonable rental value of the premises so occupied by him to be collected as damages.

Id. at 637, 115 P. at 963. Since the landlord had accepted rent and since the tenant had not acquiesced in the higher rent, the court held that the landlord had tacitly elected to hold the tenant for a new term, under the original rent, and thus could not sue for the higher rent, or even seek damages measured by the reasonable rental value for the occupation.

b.   REMEDIES FOR TENANT'S ABANDONMENT

In most jurisdictions, the tenant has *abandoned* the premises when she has left the premises and has not paid the rent when due. *See, e.g.,* Ariz. Rev. Stat. § 33–1370(H) (a leasehold is abandoned if the tenant has been absent for 7 days after the rent has been outstanding for 10 days, or the tenant has been absent for 5 days and the rent has been outstanding for 5 days and none of the tenant's personal property remains on the premises); R.I. Gen. Laws § 34–18–11 (a leasehold is abandoned if the rent is in default for more than 15 days and the tenant has removed substantially all possessions from the premises). *See also* Cal. Civ. Code § 1951.3 (a lease is deemed abandoned if, after lessee fails to pay rent, the lessor gives notice of belief of abandonment and the lessee does not give notice of intent not to abandon).

At common law, the landlord had three principal remedies after the tenant abandoned the premises. The landlord could (1) terminate the lease by accepting surrender; (2) sue the tenant for the rent as it becomes due; or (3) retake possession to relet the premises on the tenant's account.

Accepting Surrender. The landlord can terminate the lease and the tenant's liability (except for rents already due) by treating the abandonment as an offer of surrender and accepting surrender (because abandonment and surrender are considered a form of estoppel, the landlord's acceptance of surrender need not satisfy the statute of frauds).

A landlord's acceptance of surrender usually is a deliberate choice, but it may also occur inadvertently. Generally speaking, a court will find surrender when the landlord uses the property in a manner that is inconsistent with the tenant's right to possession. *See, e.g., Coffin v. Fowler,* 483 P.2d 693 (Alaska 1971) (placing caretakers in possession of the abandoned premises was not acceptance of surrender since the landlord is entitled to protect the property); *Bove v. Transcom Electronics, Inc.,* 116 R.I. 210, 214, 353 A.2d 613, 615 (1976) (upholding a trial court finding that the landlord accepted surrender when the landlord's agent accepted the keys from the tenant). Particularly difficult problems arise where the landlord attempts to relet the premises on the tenant's account (see below).

Periodic Suits for Rent. If the landlord does not wish to accept surrender, he can either sue for rent as it becomes due (*e.g.,* each month) or wait until the lease expires and then sue for the entire amount of unpaid past rent. *See, e.g., Williams v. Aeroland Oil Co.,* 155 Fla. 114, 118, 20 So.2d 346, 348 (1944). Although the traditional rule did not require mitigation, today a majority of jurisdictions treat the lease as a contract in this respect and require the landlord to mitigate damages by making reasonable efforts to relet the premises.

Sommer v. Kridel

Supreme Court of New Jersey, 1977.
74 N.J. 446, 378 A.2d 767.

■ PASHMAN, J.

We granted certification in these cases to consider whether a landlord seeking damages from a defaulting tenant is under a duty to mitigate damages by making reasonable efforts to re-let an apartment wrongfully vacated by the tenant. * * *

I

A.

Sommer v. Kridel

* * * On March 10, 1972 the defendant, James Kridel, entered into a lease with the plaintiff, Abraham Sommer, owner of the "Pierre Apartments" in Hackensack, to rent apartment 6–L in that building.[14] The term of the lease was from May 1, 1972 until April 30, 1974, with a rent concession for the first six weeks, so that the first month's rent was not due until June 15, 1972.

One week after signing the agreement, Kridel paid Sommer $690. Half of that sum was used to satisfy the first month's rent. The remainder was paid under the lease provision requiring a security deposit of $345. Although defendant had expected to begin occupancy around May 1, his plans were changed. He wrote to Sommer on May 19, 1972, explaining

> I was to be married on June 3, 1972. Unhappily the engagement was broken and the wedding plans cancelled. Both parents were to assume responsibility for the rent after our marriage. I was discharged from the U.S. Army in October 1971 and am now a

---

14. Among other provisions, the lease prohibited the tenant from assigning or transferring the lease without the consent of the landlord. If the tenant defaulted, the lease gave the landlord the option of re-entering or re-letting, but stipulated that failure to re-let or to recover the full rental would not discharge the tenant's liability for rent.

student. I have no funds of my own, and am supported by my stepfather.

In view of the above, I cannot take possession of the apartment and am surrendering all rights to it. Never having received a key, I cannot return same to you.

I beg your understanding and compassion in releasing me from the lease, and will of course, in consideration thereof, forfeit the 2 month's rent already paid.

Please notify me at your earliest convenience.

Plaintiff did not answer the letter.

Subsequently, a third party went to the apartment house and inquired about renting apartment 6–L. Although the parties agreed that she was ready, willing and able to rent the apartment, the person in charge told her that the apartment was not being shown since it was already rented to Kridel. In fact, the landlord did not re-enter the apartment or exhibit it to anyone until August 1, 1973. At that time it was rented to a new tenant for a term beginning on September 1, 1973. The new rental was for $345 per month with a six week concession similar to that granted Kridel.

Prior to re-letting the new premises, plaintiff sued Kridel in August 1972, demanding $7,590, the total amount due for the full two-year term of the lease. Following a mistrial, plaintiff filed an amended complaint asking for $5,865, the amount due between May 1, 1972 and September 1, 1973. The amended complaint included no reduction in the claim to reflect the six week concession provided for in the lease or the $690 payment made to plaintiff after signing the agreement. Defendant filed an amended answer to the complaint, alleging that plaintiff breached the contract, failed to mitigate damages and accepted defendant's surrender of the premises. He also counterclaimed to demand repayment of the $345 paid as a security deposit.

The trial judge ruled in favor of defendant. Despite his conclusion that the lease had been drawn to reflect "the 'settled law' of this state," he found that "justice and fair dealing" imposed upon the landlord the duty to attempt to re-let the premises and thereby mitigate damages. He also held that plaintiff's failure to make any response to defendant's unequivocal offer of surrender was tantamount to an acceptance, thereby terminating the tenancy and any obligation to pay rent. As a result, he dismissed both the complaint and the counterclaim. The Appellate Division reversed in a *per curiam* opinion, and we granted certification.

B.

Riverview Realty Co. v. Perosio

This controversy arose in a similar manner. On December 27, 1972, Carlos Perosio entered into a written lease with plaintiff Riverview Realty Co. The agreement covered the rental of apartment 5–G in a building owned by the realty company at 2175 Hudson Terrace in Fort Lee. As in the companion case, the lease prohibited the tenant from subletting or assigning the apartment without the consent of the landlord. It was to run for a two-year term, from February 1, 1973 until January 31, 1975, and provided for a monthly rental of $450. The defendant took possession of the apartment and occupied it until February 1974. At that time he vacated the premises, after having paid the rent through January 31, 1974.

The landlord filed a complaint on October 31, 1974, demanding $4,500 in payment for the monthly rental from February 1, 1974 through October 31, 1974. Defendant answered the complaint by alleging that there had been a valid surrender of the premises and that plaintiff failed to mitigate damages. The trial court granted the landlord's motion for summary judgment against the defendant, fixing the damages at $4,050 plus $182.25 interest.

The Appellate Division affirmed the trial court, holding that it was bound by prior precedents, including *Joyce v. Bauman, supra*, 138 N.J.Super. 270, 350 A.2d 517 (App.Div.1976). Nevertheless, it freely criticized the rule which it found itself obliged to follow:

> There appears to be no reason in equity or justice to perpetuate such an unrealistic and uneconomic rule of law which encourages an owner to let valuable rented space lie fallow because he is assured of full recovery from a defaulting tenant. Since courts in New Jersey and elsewhere have abandoned ancient real property concepts and applied ordinary contract principles in other conflicts between landlord and tenant there is no sound reason for a continuation of a special real property rule to the issue of mitigation. * * *

We granted certification.

II

As the lower courts in both appeals found, the weight of authority in this State supports the rule that a landlord is under no duty to mitigate damages caused by a defaulting tenant. This rule has been followed in a majority of states, Annot. 21 A.L.R.3d 534, § 2(a) at 541 (1968), and has been tentatively adopted in the American Law Institute's Restatement of Property. *Restatement (Second) of Property*, § 11.1(3) (Tent. Draft No. 3, 1975).

Nevertheless, while there is still a split of authority over this question, the trend among recent cases appears to be in favor of a mitigation requirement.

The majority rule is based on principles of property law which equate a lease with a transfer of a property interest in the owner's estate. Under this rationale the lease conveys to a tenant an interest in the property which forecloses any control by the landlord; thus, it would be anomalous to require the landlord to concern himself with the tenant's abandonment of his own property.

For instance, in *Muller v. Beck, supra*, where essentially the same issue was posed, the court clearly treated the lease as governed by property, as opposed to contract, precepts.[15] The court there observed that the "tenant had an estate for years, but it was an estate qualified by this right of the landlord to prevent its transfer," 94 N.J.L. at 313, 110 A. at 832, and that "the tenant has an estate with which the landlord may not interfere." *Id.* at 314, 110 A. at 832. Similarly, in *Heckel v. Griese, supra*, the court noted the absolute nature of the tenant's interest in the property while the lease was in effect, stating that "when the tenant vacated, . . . no one, in the circumstances, had any right to interfere with the defendant's possession of the premises." 12 N.J.Misc. at 213, 171 A. 148, 149. * * *

Yet the distinction between a lease for ordinary residential purposes and an ordinary contract can no longer be considered viable. As Professor Powell observed, evolving "social factors have exerted increasing influence on the law of estates for years." 2 Powell on Real Property (1977 ed.), § 221[1] at 180–81. The result has been that

> [t]he complexities of city life, and the proliferated problems of modern society in general, have created new problems for lessors and lessees and these have been commonly handled by specific clauses in leases. This growth in the number and detail of specific lease covenants has reintroduced into the law of estates for years a predominantly contractual ingredient.

Thus in 6 Williston on Contracts (3d ed. 1962), § 890A at 592, it is stated:

> There is a clearly discernible tendency on the part of courts to cast aside technicalities in the interpretation of leases and to concentrate their attention, as in the case of other contracts, on the intention of the parties, * * *.

See also Javins v. First National Realty Corp., 138 U.S.App.D.C. 369, 373, 428 F.2d 1071, 1075 (D.C.Cir.1970), *cert. denied,* 400 U.S. 925 (1970) ("the trend toward treating leases as contracts is wise and well considered") * * *

This Court has taken the lead in requiring that landlords provide housing services to tenants in accordance with implied duties which are hardly consistent with the property notions expressed in *Muller v. Beck, supra*, and *Heckel v. Griese, supra. See Braitman v. Overlook Terrace Corp.*, 68 N.J. 368, 346 A.2d 76 (1975) (liability for failure to repair defective apartment door lock); *Berzito v. Gambino*, 63 N.J. 460, 308 A.2d 17 (1973) (construing implied warranty of habitability and covenant to pay rent as mutually dependent); *Marini v. Ireland*, 56 N.J. 130, 265 A.2d 526 (1970) (implied covenant to repair); *Reste Realty Corp. v. Cooper*, 53 N.J. 444, 251 A.2d 268 (1969) (implied warranty of fitness of premises for leased purpose). In fact, in *Reste Realty Corp. v. Cooper, supra*, we specifically noted that the rule which we announced there did not comport with the historical

---

15. It is well settled that a party claiming damages for a breach of contract has a duty to mitigate his loss.

notion of a lease as an estate for years. 53 N.J. at 451–52, 251 A.2d 268. And in *Marini v. Ireland, supra,* we found that the "guidelines employed to construe contracts have been modernly applied to the construction of leases." 56 N.J. at 141, 265 A.2d at 532.

Application of the contract rule requiring mitigation of damages to a residential lease may be justified as a matter of basic fairness. Professor McCormick first commented upon the inequity under the majority rule when he predicted in 1925 that eventually

> the logic, inescapable according to the standards of a "jurispru- dence of conceptions" which permits the landlord to stand idly by the vacant, abandoned premises and treat them as the property of the tenant and recover full rent, will yield to the more realistic notions of social advantage which in other fields of the law have forbidden a recovery for damages which the plaintiff by reasonable efforts could have avoided. [McCormick, *The Rights of the Land- lord Upon Abandonment of the Premises by the Tenant,* 23 Mich. L.Rev. 211, 221–22 (1925)]

Various courts have adopted this position. *See* Annot., *supra,* § 7(a) at 565.

The pre-existing rule cannot be predicated upon the possibility that a landlord may lose the opportunity to rent another empty apartment be- cause he must first rent the apartment vacated by the defaulting tenant. Even where the breach occurs in a multi-dwelling building, each apartment may have unique qualities which make it attractive to certain individuals. Significantly, in *Sommer v. Kridel,* there was a specific request to rent the apartment vacated by the defendant; there is no reason to believe that absent this vacancy the landlord could have succeeded in renting a different apartment to this individual.

We therefore hold that antiquated real property concepts which served as the basis for the pre-existing rule, shall no longer be controlling where there is a claim for damages under a residential lease. Such claims must be governed by more modern notions of fairness and equity. A landlord has a duty to mitigate damages where he seeks to recover rents due from a defaulting tenant.

If the landlord has other vacant apartments besides the one which the tenant has abandoned, the landlord's duty to mitigate consists of making reasonable efforts to re-let the apartment. In such cases he must treat the apartment in question as if it was one of his vacant stock.

As part of his cause of action, the landlord shall be required to carry the burden of proving that he used reasonable diligence in attempting to re-let the premises. We note that there has been a divergence of opinion concerning the allocation of the burden of proof on this issue. *See* Annot., *supra,* § 12 at 577. While generally in contract actions the breaching party has the burden of proving that damages are capable of mitigation, here the landlord will be in a better position to demonstrate whether he exercised reasonable diligence in attempting to re-let the premises. *Cf. Kulm v.*

Coast-to-Coast Stores Central Org., 248 Or. 436, 432 P.2d 1006 (1967) (burden on lessor in contract to renew a lease).

III

The *Sommer v. Kridel* case presents a classic example of the unfairness which occurs when a landlord has no responsibility to minimize damages. Sommer waited 15 months and allowed $4658.50 in damages to accrue before attempting to re-let the apartment. Despite the availability of a tenant who was ready, willing and able to rent the apartment, the landlord needlessly increased the damages by turning her away. While a tenant will not necessarily be excused from his obligations under a lease simply by finding another person who is willing to rent the vacated premises, *see, e.g., Reget v. Dempsey–Tegler & Co.*, 70 Ill.App.2d 32, 216 N.E.2d 500 (Ill.App. 1966) (new tenant insisted on leasing the premises under different terms); *Edmands v. Rust & Richardson Drug Co.*, 191 Mass. 123, 77 N.E. 713 (1906) (landlord need not accept insolvent tenant), here there has been no showing that the new tenant would not have been suitable. We therefore find that plaintiff could have avoided the damages which eventually accrued, and that the defendant was relieved of his duty to continue paying rent. Ordinarily we would require the tenant to bear the cost of any reasonable expenses incurred by a landlord in attempting to re-let the premises, but no such expenses were incurred in this case.

In *Riverview Realty Co. v. Perosio*, no factual determination was made regarding the landlord's efforts to mitigate damages, and defendant contends that plaintiff never answered his interrogatories. Consequently, the judgment is reversed and the case remanded for a new trial. Upon remand and after discovery has been completed, the trial court shall determine whether plaintiff attempted to mitigate damages with reasonable diligence, *see Wilson v. Ruhl, supra*, 356 A.2d at 546, and if so, the extent of damages remaining and assessable to the tenant. As we have held above, the burden of proving that reasonable diligence was used to re-let the premises shall be upon the plaintiff.

In assessing whether the landlord has satisfactorily carried his burden, the trial court shall consider, among other factors, whether the landlord, either personally or through an agency, offered or showed the apartment to any prospective tenants, or advertised it in local newspapers. Additionally, the tenant may attempt to rebut such evidence by showing that he proffered suitable tenants who were rejected. However, there is no standard formula for measuring whether the landlord has utilized satisfactory efforts in attempting to mitigate damages, and each case must be judged upon its own facts. *Compare Hershorin v. La Vista, Inc.*, 110 Ga.App. 435, 138 S.E.2d 703 (App.1964) ("reasonable effort" of landlord by showing the apartment to all prospective tenants); *Carpenter v. Wisniewski*, 139 Ind. App. 325, 215 N.E.2d 882 (App.1966) (duty satisfied where landlord advertised the premises through a newspaper, placed a sign in the window, and employed a realtor); *Re Garment Center Capitol, Inc.*, 93 F.2d 667, 115 A.L.R. 202 (2d Cir. 1938) (landlord's duty not breached where higher rental was asked since it was known that this was merely a basis for negotiations); *Foggia v. Dix*, 265 Or. 315, 509 P.2d 412, 414 (1973) (in mitigating damages, landlord need not accept less than fair market value or "substantially alter his obligations as established in the pre-existing lease"); *with Anderson v. Andy Darling Pontiac, Inc.*, 257 Wis. 371, 43 N.W.2d 362 (1950) (reasonable diligence not established where newspaper advertisement placed in one issue of local paper by a broker); *Scheinfeld v. Muntz T. V., Inc.*, 67 Ill.App.2d 8, 214 N.E.2d 506 (Ill.App.1966) (duty breached where landlord refused to accept suitable subtenant); *Consolidated Sun Ray, Inc. v. Oppenstein*, 335 F.2d 801, 811 (8th Cir.1964) (dictum) (demand for rent which is "far greater than the provisions of the lease called for" negates landlord's assertion that he acted in good faith in seeking a new tenant).

IV

The judgment in *Sommer v. Kridel* is reversed. In *Riverview Realty Co. v. Perosio*, the judgment is reversed and the case is remanded to the trial court for proceedings in accordance with this opinion.

----

1.   What is the purpose of the requirement that the landlord mitigate damages upon the tenant's abandonment? Is it unfair to impose on landlords an obligation to mitigate? Is a lease provision waiving the landlord's obligation to mitigate damages enforceable? Or is the obligation inalienable? Is it unconscionable? Should the mitigation rule apply to both residential and commercial leases?

2.   Courts are divided as to whether a landlord may sue immediately upon abandonment for the entire balance of future rents on a contract theory of anticipatory breach. *See, e.g., Williams v. Aeroland Oil Co.*, 155 Fla. 114, 117–18, 20 So.2d 346, 348 (1944) (rejecting anticipatory breach claim); *Szabo Associates, Inc. v. Peachtree–Piedmont Associates*, 141 Ga. App. 654, 234 S.E.2d 119 (1977) (landlord may sue for the difference between the reserved rent and the rental value); Cal. Civ. Code § 1951.2 (landlord may collect unpaid rent at termination (plus interest), benefit of the bargain for the time between termination and the judgment (plus interest), and the amount by which the reserved rent exceeds the rental loss that could have been reasonably avoided for the balance of the lease (reduced to present value), if the lease permitted this remedy or landlord relet the premises in a reasonable and good faith effort to mitigate damages); Cal. Civ. Code § 1951.4 (landlord may recover rent as it becomes due so long as the landlord does not terminate the lease and the tenant has the right to sublet or assign the leasehold).

Should landlords be allowed to sue under a contract theory of anticipatory breach? In what sense, if any, is a suit for anticipatory breach unfair?

3.   In states that do not permit suits for anticipatory breach, some landlords bargain for an express rent acceleration clause, which allows the

landlord to sue for the entire amount of rent remaining on the lease. Nonetheless, some courts do not permit enforcement of such clauses. *See, e.g., Fifty States Management Corp. v. Pioneer Auto Parks, Inc.*, 46 N.Y.2d 573, 389 N.E.2d 113, 415 N.Y.S.2d 800 (1979) (stating that enforcement of an acceleration clause would be unconscionable for a minor breach, but upholding enforcement for non-payment of rent); *Triple C. Leasing, Inc. v. All–American Mobile Wash*, 64 Cal.App.3d 244, 251, 134 Cal.Rptr. 328, 331 (1976) (holding an acceleration clause unenforceable as liquidated damages). Should courts (or legislatures) permit enforcement of acceleration clauses?

Reletting on the Tenant's Account. This common law remedy permits the landlord (often only after providing proper notice to the tenant) to find a substitute tenant and use the rents to offset the original tenant's obligations. This remedy now exists only in the minority of states that do not already require the landlord to mitigate his damages by seeking a substitute tenant. Normally, the landlord either must have expressly retained in the lease the right to relet on the tenant's account or must have informed the tenant that he was reletting to mitigate damages. In *Kanter v. Safran*, 68 So.2d 553 (Fla.1953), the Supreme Court of Florida indicated that the landlord's reletting following the tenant's abandonment would raise a close question about the landlord's accepting surrender. But the court made clear that there would be no acceptance of surrender if the landlord relet the premises pursuant to an express lease provision permitting reletting or if the landlord so informed the tenant before reletting the premises. *Id.* at 557.

Under this remedy, if the new rent does not cover the old obligations, or the new tenant leaves, the old tenant remains liable. *See Lawrence Barker, Inc. v. Briggs*, 39 Cal.2d 654, 664–65, 248 P.2d 897, 902–03 (1952); *Kanter v. Safran*, 68 So.2d 553, 557 (Fla.1953). A nice issue arises when the landlord finds a substitute tenant willing to pay a higher rent. Several jurisdictions require the landlord to credit the "excess" rent to offset past rents due. *See generally* Payne, Landlord and Tenant: Respective Rights in Excess Rent When Landlord Relets at Higher Rent During Lessee's Term, 50 A.L.R. 4th 403 (1986). At least one case has held that if surplus rents remain after accounting for past rents due, the old tenant is entitled to them. *See Centurian Development, Ltd. v. Kenford Co.*, 60 App. Div.2d 96, 400 N.Y.S.2d 263 (1977).

---

3.   TENANT'S RIGHTS AND REMEDIES

a.   IMPLIED COVENANT TO DELIVER POSSESSION

Every lease has an implied covenant that the landlord will deliver possession at the beginning of a lease term.

There are two different lines of cases defining the tenant's right to possession at the beginning of the lease. Under the "American Rule,"[16] the landlord is required only to put the tenant in "legal possession"; the landlord has fulfilled this obligation if the landlord has legal authority to lease the premises and has given no one else permission to occupy the premises. *See, e.g., Snider v. Deban*, 249 Mass. 59, 65, 144 N.E. 69, 71 (1924) (where a former tenant remained in possession after expiration of the lease, "[t]he lessor makes no covenant [with the new tenant] against such a wrongdoer any more than against a wrongdoer who * * * expels the tenant after the [lease] has begun").

The "English Rule" implies a covenant to place the tenant in actual possession of the entire premises at the beginning of the lease. *Adrian v. Rabinowitz*, 116 N.J.L. 586, 590, 186 A. 29, 31 (1936) (the lease contains an implied provision that the "premises [will be] open to the entry and exclusive possession of the lessee"); *Cheshire v. Thurston*, 70 Ariz. 299, 219 P.2d 1043 (1950) (the lease contains an implied provision to put the tenant in actual possession).

The difference between the two rules is manifested in the treatment of holdovers and trespassers. *See generally* Weissenberger, The Landlord's Duty to Deliver Possession: The Overlooked Reform, 46 U. Cin. L. Rev. 937 (1977). Under the American Rule, breach occurs only if either (1) the landlord, (2) someone with paramount title, or (3) someone with the landlord's consent (*e.g.,* under a lease) is in possession when the tenant is first entitled to possession. Under the English Rule, breach occurs whenever anyone else is in possession, regardless of the circumstances, at the beginning of the tenant's lease.

The arguments in favor of the English Rule are substantial: (1) the landlord should know better than the tenant the status of possession of the premises before the date the tenant is entitled to possession; (2) the landlord is the only one who can evict someone improperly in possession before the tenant is entitled to possession; (3) the landlord is the only one who can get some assurance that the current tenant will not holdover; and (4) often (particularly in residential leases) the landlord has greater resources and experience to proceed quickly with eviction. In short, the landlord should bear the risk because the landlord is in the best position to evict holdovers and trespassers and deliver actual possession. For these reasons, the English Rule is the majority rule in the United States. *See generally* Karnezis, Annotation, Implied Covenant or Obligation to Provide Lessee with Actual Possession, 96 A.L.R. 3d 1155 (1980).

Under either rule, when the landlord does not deliver possession within a reasonable time, the tenant may terminate the lease and recover consequential damages (*e.g.,* additional moving costs). *See, e.g.,* Cal. Civ. Code § 1932(1); *Draper Machine Works v. Hagberg*, 34 Wash. App. 483,

---

16. The American Rule for delivery of possession is based on an early doctrinal error. Courts that follow this rule erroneously presume that it derives from the common law covenant of quiet enjoyment. In England, however, these two types of covenants always have been distinct.

486–87, 663 P.2d 141, 143 (1983) (tenant may rescind for breach of the covenant to deliver); Md. Code Ann., Real Prop. § 8–204 (tenant may rescind the lease, obtain a refund of all deposits, and obtain consequential damages).

Many states following the English Rule provide the tenant with an alternative remedy; the tenant may stand on the lease, but fully abate the rent until the landlord physically delivers the leasehold, and recover general damages measured by the difference between the agreed rent and the rental value of the premises during the lease term and consequential damages, such as relocation costs. *See, e.g., Draper Machine Works v. Hagberg*, 34 Wash. App. 483, 487, 663 P.2d 141, 143 (1983) (if tenant does not rescind, he must pay rent but may claim consequential damages "for the reasonable rental of temporary premises while awaiting possession"); Md. Code Ann., Real Prop. § 8–204 (tenant may keep the lease with full abatement of the rent until the premises is delivered and obtain consequential damages); *Foreman & Clark Corp. v. Fallon*, 3 Cal.3d 875, 884, 92 Cal.Rptr. 162, 168, 479 P.2d 362, 368 (1971) (abatement of the rent and consequential damages). Some states permit recovery of lost profits as part of consequential damages, although since the tenant is not in possession, such damages are often difficult to prove.

———

1. What criteria should a court use to decide whether a tenant can rescind for a breach of this covenant? How much delay of delivery is required until the tenant may rescind? A few hours? A week?

2. Suppose that the parties signed a lease waiving the tenant's remedies for breach of the right to deliver possession. Would the waiver be valid?

Tenants Rights and Remedies

b.   IMPLIED COVENANT OF QUIET ENJOYMENT

Every lease contains an implied covenant of quiet enjoyment that neither the landlord, someone with paramount title (*e.g.*, a mortgagee), nor someone acting with the landlord's consent will disrupt the tenant's possession of the premises. *See, e.g.*, Cal. Civ. Code § 1927 (the landlord has an implied duty to ensure quiet possession "against all persons lawfully claiming" the premises); N.D. Cent. Code § 47–16–08 (same); *Andrews & Knowles Produce Co. v. Currin*, 243 N.C. 131, 135, 90 S.E.2d 228, 230 (1955) (absent a contrary lease provision, each lease has an implied covenant that the lessee shall enjoy quiet possession during the lease term; unauthorized entry and repossession by the landlords or others acting under them is a breach of this covenant). Most commonly, tenants raise breach of the covenant of quiet enjoyment as a defense to a landlord's suit for rent after the tenant has relinquished the leasehold, but many states also allow the tenant to remain in possession of the premises and sue for damages for breach of the covenant (the tenant may also have other claims, such as trespass and forcible entry and detainer).

In most states, the implied covenant of quiet enjoyment does not cover the disruptive behavior of third parties, such as neighbors. If a third party unlawfully took possession of the tenant's property, or if a neighbor disrupted the tenant's quiet enjoyment of the leasehold, the tenant would have no action against the landlord for breach of the covenant of quiet enjoyment. *See, e.g., Stewart v. Lawson*, 199 Mich. 497, 165 N.W. 716 (1917). Increasingly, however, courts have been willing to modify the general rule by making, in effect, the landlord responsible for the activities of other tenants. *See, e.g., Colonial Court Apartments, Inc. v. Kern*, 282 Minn. 533, 534–35, 163 N.W.2d 770, 771–72 (1968) (holding that the acts of a tenant can breach another tenant's covenant of quiet enjoyment if they "materially disturb the latter tenant in the use, occupancy, and enjoyment" of the premises); *Cohen v. Werner*, 85 Misc.2d 341, 378 N.Y.S.2d 868 (1975) (upholding a tenant's claim for breach of the covenant of quiet enjoyment where the landlord knew about the loud, continuous noise from the upstairs tenant but did nothing to abate it); *Gottdiener v. Mailhot*, 179 N.J.Super. 286, 291–92, 431 A.2d 851, 854–55 (1981) (excessive noise and harassing behavior from neighboring tenants was a basis to claim constructive eviction since the landlord had the authority to evict the neighboring tenants). These cases focus less on whether the landlord is responsible for or approved the disrupting tenant's conduct than whether the landlord is legally able to remedy the problem. Some of the cases also emphasize that lease provisions prohibiting excessive noise are generally included for the benefit of other tenants; that is, the injured tenant is a third-party beneficiary of the lease between the landlord and the disrupting tenant.

Actual Eviction. The most obvious type of breach of the covenant of quiet enjoyment occurs when the landlord physically ousts the tenant from the entire premises; in such circumstances the ousted tenant can affirm the lease, cease payment of rent (until possession is restored), and recover consequential damages, or the tenant can terminate the lease and sue for general damages (difference between fair rental value and reserved rent) and special damages (*e.g.*, cost of relocation).[17] A more complicated circumstance arises when the ouster is only partial. Consider the following problem:

Problem: Partial Actual Eviction

The tenant leased a piece of property that fronted a highway and on which he operated a gasoline service station. The federal government wanted to widen the highway, and negotiated with the landlord to purchase half of the tenant's leasehold, leaving the tenant with a narrow strip of

---

17. Under the right circumstances, a tenant would also be entitled to damages for forcible entry and forcible detainer.

land. The tenant did not consent to the sale. The tenant retained possession of the narrow strip, but refused to pay any rent for the portion retained. The landlord filed an unlawful detainer action on the ground that the tenant had breached the covenant to pay rent, and the tenant defended on the ground that because of the landlord's breach of the covenant of quiet enjoyment, he had no obligation to pay rent.

1. Is the landlord's sale of part of the land in fee simple to the government a breach of the covenant of quiet enjoyment?

2. If so, should the tenant be relieved of the entire obligation to pay rent (until the premises are restored), or only in proportion to the value of the land sold? Should there be a threshold requirement that the partial eviction be substantial? What are the arguments supporting a rule of complete abatement for partial eviction? *Cf.* N.Y. Real Prop. Acts Law § 853 (providing for treble damages for partial or actual eviction). Would it make a difference to you if the eviction had come, not from the landlord, but from the landlord's landlord (*i.e.*, a person with paramount title)? What rule would you suggest in that case?

3. Regardless of the rule for abatement of rent, should the tenant be relieved of other obligations under the lease (*e.g.*, an express covenant to repair or maintain the premises)? That is, should the entire lease be suspended until the landlord restores the premises?

4. Suppose instead that the government had taken part of the land by eminent domain. In such a proceeding, the government would take free of any encumbrances (including the lease), but it would be required by the Constitution to pay property owners "just compensation" for the taking. Is the tenant still relieved of the obligation to pay rent? Is the tenant entitled to a share of the compensation award?

See Giraud v. Milovich, 29 Cal.App.2d 543, 85 P.2d 182 (1938).

Constructive Eviction. Actual eviction cases rarely arise today. More commonly, the breach of the covenant of quiet enjoyment arises in "constructive eviction" cases; the landlord does something, or fails to perform some obligation in the lease or possibly under a statute, that substantially interferes with a tenant's use of the premises—*i.e.*, renders the premises uninhabitable or unsuitable for the tenant's intended use. In *Dyett v. Pendleton*, 8 Cow. 727 (N.Y.1826), perhaps the first case to find constructive eviction, the landlord

> introduced into the house, (two rooms upon the second floor and two rooms upon the third floor whereof had been leased to the defendant,) divers lewd women or prostitutes, and kept and detained them in the said house all night, for the purpose of prostitution; that the said lewd women or prostitutes would frequently enter the said house in the day time, and after staying all night, would leave the same by day-light in the morning; * * *

> [the landlord] and said lewd women or prostitutes * * * were
> accustomed to make a great deal of indecent noise and distur-
> bance, the said women or prostitutes often screaming extravagant-
> ly, and so as to be heard throughout the house, and by the
> neighbors, and frequently using obscene and vulgar language so
> loud as to be understood at a considerable distance; that such
> noise and riotous proceedings, being from time to time continued
> all night, greatly disturbed the rest of persons sleeping in other
> parts of the said house, and particularly in those parts thereof
> demised to the defendant; that the practices aforesaid were mat-
> ters of conversation and reproach in the neighborhood, and were of
> a nature to draw, and did draw, odium and infamy upon the said
> house, as being a place of ill fame, so that it was no longer
> respectable for moral and decent persons to dwell or enter therein;
> that all the said immoral, indecent and unlawful practices and
> proceedings were by the procurement or with the permission and
> concurrence of the plaintiff; that the defendant, being a person of
> good and respectable character, was compelled, by the repetition of
> the said indecent practices and proceedings, to leave the said
> premises * * *

Id. at 735–36. After abandoning the premises, the tenant refused to pay further rent, and the landlord sued for the rent.

Several appellate judges rejected the tenant's defense that the landlord had breached the covenant of quiet enjoyment, thereby relieving the tenant of the obligation to pay further rent. One judge wrote:

> [Tenant's claim] would * * * introduce a new and very exten-
> sive chapter in the law of landlord and tenant; for if the encour-
> agement or practice of lewdness on premises under the same roof
> with the tenements leased, would warrant an abdication by the
> tenant, and release him from his covenant to pay rent, there is no
> reason why, if the landlord should by any other means render the
> occupation of the premises inconvenient or uncomfortable, the
> same consequences should not ensue. * * * If the lessor illegally
> interferes with his lessee's enjoyment of the demised premises,
> otherwise than by an entry and eviction, the tenant has his
> remedy by civil suit or public prosecution.

Id. 739–40. But the majority held otherwise. "The total failure of the consideration, especially when produced by the act of the [landlord], is a valid defence to an action * * *. This is the great and fundamental principle which led the courts to deny the lessor's right to recover rent where he had deprived the tenant of the consideration of his covenant, by turning him out of the possession of the demised premises. It must be wholly immaterial by what acts that failure of consideration has been produced; the only inquiry being, has it failed by the conduct of the lessor?" *Id.* at 733.

In most states, a tenant may use constructive eviction as a basis to terminate the lease—and raise the breach of the implied covenant as a defense to a suit for rent—only if the tenant abandons the premises within a reasonable period of time. For example, in *Clark v. Spiegel*, 22 Cal.App.3d 74, 79, 99 Cal.Rptr. 86, 89 (1971), the court explained that "during that four-year period of time [following the landlords' breach, the plaintiff] gambled that his business would prosper. He cannot now place [the landlords] in the position of insurers of that gamble by the simple expedient of suing upon breach of the covenant of quiet enjoyment." *See also McNally v. Moser*, 210 Md. 127, 122 A.2d 555 (1956) (tenant may not terminate lease based on constructive eviction where he did not abandon until one year after notice of breach); *Maki v. Nikula*, 224 Or. 180, 187–88, 355 P.2d 770, 773 (1960) (tenant who waited 26 months to claim constructive eviction lost his claim because his efforts were not "prompt and energetic enough to justify such a long delay").

Alternatively, a tenant may remain in possession and sue for breach of contract damages. *Guntert v. City of Stockton*, 55 Cal.App.3d 131, 126 Cal.Rptr. 690 (1976).

---

1. What is the purpose of requiring the tenant to vacate the premises within a reasonable amount of time to claim constructive eviction as a defense to a suit for rent? What sort of factors might be considered in deciding what is "reasonable"? What are the potential disadvantages to the tenant who might invoke this remedy?

2. Could the tenant abandon part of the premises (the part made unusable) and claim a partial constructive eviction? What would be the remedy in that case?

3. Suppose that the landlord cured the breach before the tenant vacated the premises. Has the tenant failed to vacate within "a reasonable time"? What circumstances might affect your answer?

4. If the tenant elected to keep the lease and sue for damages, must the breach be as substantial as a breach that a tenant would assert as a defense in a suit for rent? What are the advantages and disadvantages of a damages remedy compared to the remedy of abandonment and rescission?

5. What criteria would you use to decide what constitutes a sufficient interference to justify a claim of constructive eviction? Would a tenant's hypersensitivity to noise or dust be a relevant factor? Does the answer depend on whether the landlord knew of the hypersensitivity? Is the landlord's good faith a relevant consideration in deciding whether there has been a breach?

6. Does the landlord have to do something for there to be a breach of the covenant of quiet enjoyment? Can failure to do something be sufficient? Or can failure to act constitute a breach only when there already exists a separate affirmative duty (such as a lease covenant to repair or to remove the garbage)? Note that if constructive eviction is available for the landlord's failure to act when there is no corresponding affirmative duty, the

doctrine has been extended to create a separate substantive right of tenantability.

7. Should a residential tenant be able to waive the right to quiet enjoyment in the lease? *See, e.g.,* Cal. Civ. Code § 1953(a)(2) (declaring void as against public policy a lease provision waiving the covenant of quiet enjoyment in a residential lease). What about non-residential leases? *See Lee v. Placer Title Co.,* 28 Cal.App.4th 503, 512–14, 33 Cal.Rptr.2d 572, 577–78 (1994) (upholding provision in a commercial lease modifying remedies for breach of the covenant of quiet enjoyment); *Johnson v. Missouri–Kansas–Texas Railroad Co.,* 216 S.W.2d 499, 505 (Mo.1949) (upholding a provision in a commercial lease waiving the covenant of quiet enjoyment). Why should there be a difference?

Problem: Landlord's and Tenant's Rights

For over thirty years, Al Perez has been the resident janitor at the Home for Women, a private, non-profit nursing home in Grayville, California ("Home"). Perez lived in an apartment in a small ground-floor addition to the Home. Perez has never signed an agreement formally giving him possession of the apartment, but on January 1st of each year he signed a document, entitled "Annual Contract of Employment," which set out his obligations, monthly wages, and employment benefits. Perez's residence in the apartment and around-the-clock availability to perform janitorial and maintenance work have always been express conditions of his employment. The document makes no mention of a rental payment, and in fact Perez has never made such a payment or paid for utilities. Instead, he and the Director of the Home have considered the market value of his apartment in their annual negotiations over his wages. The apartment is largely self-contained, with its own cooking facilities, fireplace, washer and dryer, entrance, and mailing address, although its water, heat, and electricity come from the main part of the Home's building. No staff member has ever sought access to "Al's apartment" (as everyone called it) without first obtaining Perez's permission, although the Director has always retained a key.

In July, Steven Adams, the long-time Director, retired and a new Director, Richard Headstrong, took over. The Board of Governors of the Home was concerned that the out-going Director had not kept the Home's expenses low enough, and so in hiring Headstrong they gave him a firm mandate to bring costs under control and increase revenues where possible.

On Headstrong's first day of work, Perez presented him with a list of needed repairs, including the replacement of the Home's furnace, which Perez thought dangerously unsafe. Headstrong ignored Perez's list.

In October, Perez was surprised to see his apartment advertised in the "For Rent" column of the local newspaper. A few days later, Perez returned to his apartment to find Headstrong showing the place to Tanya and Thomas Tenant. When Perez demanded an explanation, Headstrong informed Perez that he did not plan to renew Perez's employment contract for the coming year, having determined that a janitorial service would be cheaper and that renting the apartment would produce much-needed income.

Perez became enraged and promised himself to get back at Headstrong. The next week, Perez informed Grayville's Office of Building Inspection that the Home's furnace was unsafe. On October 28th, a building inspector examined the furnace, determined that it violated the housing code, and mailed the Home an order to replace the furnace immediately. Headstrong ignored the order.

In the meantime, the Tenants signed a lease for the apartment for one year commencing January 1. The form lease expressly provided that "Landlord covenants to deliver to Tenant the right to Possess said apartment. Landlord does not covenant to place Tenant in actual possession of the apartment." The rent was set at $500 per month, to be paid on the 1st of each month. The lease required a $500 security deposit payable upon the signing of the lease. The lease had no provision governing the destruction of the premises, although it did state that the Landlord would provide utilities.

On December 25th, during one of Grayville's coldest winters on record, the Home's furnace exploded, causing extensive damage and leaving the Home without heat but injuring no one. The residents were temporarily placed in nearby nursing homes. Perez stayed in possession of his apartment by keeping a roaring fire going at all times in the fireplace.

On the morning of January 1, the Tenants drove up to the Home with all their worldly possessions, only to find their apartment without heat, Perez in defiant possession, and Headstrong nowhere to be found. They left Headstrong a letter stating that they considered the lease terminated and demanded their security deposit back. They promptly found another apartment, signed a year's lease, and moved in.

On January 10, Headstrong comes to you to make sense of this mess. He wants to evict Perez and hold Tenants to the lease for the remainder of the term. What advice would you provide?

------

c. TENANT'S RIGHT TO HABITABLE PREMISES

The common law did not provide tenants with an implied covenant of habitability or suitability for use. Because a lease was considered primarily a conveyance of land—most leases were for agricultural lands—the value of the lease was in the land itself. The tenant's interest in any buildings on the land was considered secondary, or perhaps a small fraction of the value of the leasehold. In addition, the enduring principle of *caveat emptor*, or in this case *caveat lessee*, gave the lessee the burden of inspecting the leasehold before agreeing to the lease. Under the doctrine of waste, repairs were considered to be the tenant's responsibility.

The covenant of quiet enjoyment was an unsatisfactory remedy for residential tenants. First, it did not establish any affirmative obligations; it only provided remedies in the event the landlord physically evicted the tenant or violated an express covenant that led to a constructive eviction. Second, a tenant who abandoned the tenancy after a claimed constructive eviction ran the dual risks that he had not abandoned soon enough and that the breach was not substantial and thus that he would owe rent. Third, in a tight housing market abandonment is not a realistic option.

Early Statutes and Decisions Leading to the Implied Warranty of Habitability. In the late nineteenth and early twentieth centuries, a few legislatures and courts began to undermine the pervasive authority of *caveat lessee.* In the late nineteenth century several states adopting the Field Civil Code imposed a duty on the landlord to keep the premises in habitable condition (although the parties could agree in the lease to waive this duty). The remedies for breach included damages and a self-help remedy whereby the tenant could use the rent to make the repairs if the landlord refused to do so. In the early decades of the twentieth century Connecticut, Iowa, and New York adopted statutes providing a tenant-initiated remedy of rent withholding for serious housing code violations. *See* R. Cunningham, W. Stoebuck & D. Whitman, The Law of Property § 6.37 (2nd ed. 1993). These statutes established a new remedy for violations of existing substantive standards.

Courts also began to question the suitability of *caveat lessee* in urban, residential dwellings. In *Ingalls v. Hobbs,* 156 Mass. 348, 31 N.E. 286 (1892), the court implied a covenant for suitability of use in extremely narrow circumstances—a short-term residential lease of furnished premises—on the grounds that the tenant was not interested in the land but in the house for a particular use; the tenant intended to use the property immediately without the need for repairs; and the tenant had no real opportunity to inspect the premises for defects. In 1931, the Minnesota Supreme Court rejected *caveat lessee* in a broader context. In *Delamater v. Foreman,* 184 Minn. 428, 239 N.W. 148 (1931), the tenant had rented an apartment in a "modern" building; the apartment was infested with bedbugs, and the tenants sued for damages.

> The written lease was silent as to any provision as to who should be charged with the responsibility of waging any necessary war on vermin. The rule at common law was that the law did not impliedly impose any such duty upon the landlord. * * * But such rule, like many of the rules of law, is not inflexible, but to some degree elastic, and must be construed to meet conditions unknown at common law. There is much in and about such an apartment building far beyond the control of a tenant in one of the apartments. He cannot interfere with the walls, partitions, floors, and ceilings wherein the verminous enemy may propagate; nor can he interfere with the cracks and openings affording an opportunity of

access from such walls, partitions, floors, and ceilings into the apartment. If the attack is sufficiently serious and comes from this source, it violates the landlord's implied covenant that the premises will be habitable.

Id. at 429–30, 239 N.W. at 149.

Three decades later, the Wisconsin Supreme Court implied a warranty of habitability in every residential lease. In *Pines v. Perssion,* 14 Wis.2d 590, 111 N.W.2d 409 (1961), the court wrote:

> Legislation and administrative rules, such as the safeplace statute, building codes, and health regulations, all impose certain duties on a property owner with respect to the condition of his premises. Thus, the legislature has made a policy judgment—that it is socially (and politically) desirable to impose these duties on a property owner—which has rendered the old common-law rule obsolete. To follow the old rule of no implied warranty of habitability in leases would, in our opinion, be inconsistent with the current legislative policy concerning housing standards. The need and social desirability of adequate housing for people in this era of rapid population increases is too important to be rebuffed by that obnoxious legal cliché, *caveat emptor.* Permitting landlords to rent "tumble-down" houses is at least a contributing cause of such problems as urban blight, juvenile delinquency, and high property taxes for conscientious landowners.

Id. at 595–96, 111 N.W.2d at 412–13. Since the landlord had breached the implied warranty, the tenants were relieved of the mutually dependent covenant to pay rent; they were liable only for reasonable rental value during their occupation. 14 Wis.2d at 596–97, 111 N.W. at 413.

The Evolution of Housing Codes and the Failure of Administrative Enforcement. Perhaps the most important specific reason behind the creation of legislative and judicial doctrines of implied warranty of habitability was the ineffectiveness of municipal and state-wide housing codes. *See generally* Abbott, Housing Policy, Housing Codes and Tenant Remedies: An Integration, 56 B.U.L. Rev. 1 (1976); *see also* Sax & Hiestand, Slumlordism as a Tort, 65 Mich. L. Rev. 869 (1967) (arguing that because of the ineffectiveness of administrative enforcement of housing codes courts should create a new tort for the injury that tenants suffer in living in substandard housing).

The first important housing codes in this country were the 1867 New York Tenement House Law and a similar Massachusetts statute for Boston in 1868. Applicable only to New York City dwellings with three or more families, the New York statute was a public health measure designed to lessen the risk of cholera epidemics that originated in the extraordinarily crowded New York City tenements. The 1901 New York Tenement House Law expanded the number of minimum standards. By 1920, 12 states and 40 cities had some form of housing codes, usually applicable only to multi-unit buildings. Housing codes were much more widely adopted after World

War II, however, when the federal government required housing codes as a condition for federal slum clearance funds. *See generally* Note, Municipal Housing Codes, 69 Harv. L. Rev. 1115 (1956). The impact of the 1954 federal statute was dramatic; in 1956 only 56 communities had housing codes; by 1968, almost 5000 communities had such codes.

Modern housing codes are remarkably detailed. They create a statutory duty to provide and maintain decent housing by imposing standards for: building structure (*e.g.*, walls, floors); facilities (*e.g.*, toilets, sinks, radiators); services (*e.g.*, heat, running water, electricity); and occupancy (*e.g.*, number of people per dwelling). Some codes contain qualitative standards. *See, e.g.,* Wash. Rev. Code § 59.18.060 ("reasonably good repair"); Vermont Stat. Ann. tit. 9, § 4457 ("safe, clean, and fit for human habitation"). Other codes are quantitative. *See, e.g.,* N.Y. Mult. Dwell. Law § 30 (specifying types of rooms that must have windows and the minimum required ratio between the size of those windows and the total floor space); Me. Rev. Stat. Ann. tit. 14, § 6021 (if the lease requires the landlord to provide heat, the heating facilities must be "capable of maintaining a minimum temperature of at least 68 degrees Fahrenheit at a distance of 3 feet from the exterior wall, 5 feet above the floor level at an outside temperature of minus 20 degrees Fahrenheit").

Local administrative agencies frequently have a range of judicial and administrative enforcement mechanisms—including civil penalties, injunctive relief, and criminal penalties—to remedy housing code violations. Some state laws authorize municipalities to make emergency repairs and then put a lien on the property to recover the cost of the repairs. In other jurisdictions, municipalities may petition a court to appoint a receiver to take over the building, collect rents, and make the repairs before returning the building to the owner. *See* Hirsch, Hirsch & Margolis, Regression Analysis of the Effects of Habitability Laws Upon Rent: An Empirical Observation on the Ackerman–Komesar Debate, 63 Cal. L. Rev. 1098, 1111–12 nn. 55 & 58 (1975) (citing statutes).[18]

Despite the array of available remedies, several studies in the late 1960s and early 1970s found housing agencies to be generally ineffective in ensuring a minimum quality of housing for low-income renters. *See generally* M. Teitz & S. Rosenthal, Housing Code Enforcement in New York City (1971); B. Lieberman, Local Administration and Enforcement of Housing Codes: A Survey of 39 Cities (1969). In practice civil penalties tended to be small, except in the most egregious cases. Injunctions were relatively rare, perhaps because of the difficulty of supervising repairs. Criminal prosecu-

---

18. For a number of years, New York City took title to apartment buildings whose owners had defaulted on their property taxes; typically such buildings were also in serious violation of housing codes. Rather than putting the buildings back on the market after a tax foreclosure sale, the city assumed the role of the landlord. The result was disastrous.

"Several billion dollars later, * * * New York has become the largest slumlord in the country, with 33,000 units of some of the worst housing in the city on its hands. None of the buildings pays taxes. By one recent survey, 58% have rat problems and 30% have holes in the floor." Gladwell, From Savior to Slumlord, Wash. Post, Mar. 27, 1994, at A1.

tions were also rare, perhaps because of the large burden of proof (beyond a reasonable doubt) and other procedural protections for defendants, the unwillingness of prosecutors to pursue these cases (convictions in these "small" cases do not advance a prosecutor's career), and the unwillingness of judges to impose jail sentences or serious fines. Repair and lien statutes were usually ineffective because substandard housing often was so heavily encumbered by existing mortgages and liens (*e.g.*, for back taxes) that the city rarely recovered any money to pay for the repairs. Receivership statutes were also unsuccessful because the receiver usually had insufficient capital to make repairs until it had collected rent for a few years.

In many cities housing agencies were underfunded and understaffed, and inspections were rarely carried out. *See* Note, Enforcement of Municipal Housing Codes, 78 Harv. L. Rev. 801 (1965); Gribetz & Grad, Housing Code Enforcement: Sanctions and Remedies, 66 Colum. L. Rev. 1254 (1966).[19] Studies showed that many housing inspection offices were rife with corruption. Moreover, housing agencies may have been "captured" by landlords. For example, most codes have a variance process through which the owner can demand a hearing to present evidence that enforcing the code would result in "manifest injustice." One study in Philadelphia showed that the housing agency granted two-thirds of the requested variances. *See* Abbott, Housing Policy, Housing Codes and Tenant Remedies: An Integration, 56 B.U.L. Rev. 1, 53 (1976). Under these circumstances it would difficult for even the best enforcement personnel to remain enthusiastic.

Judicial and Legislative Reform. As the inadequacy of the covenant of quiet enjoyment and housing codes became evident in the 1960s, the pace of reform quickened. Not only were courts widely viewed as appropriate vehicles for social change,[20] but state and local legislatures enacted a range of new laws specifically aimed at making tenants more secure in their tenure. Statutes and ordinances were enacted to regulate rent increases, to require evictions to be based on "just cause," and to hold various waiver clauses unconscionable or void as against public policy. Other statutes were designed to prevent "retaliatory eviction." There was a powerful sense that substandard housing—along with racism, inadequate education, and limited employment opportunities—contributed to the serious social malaise in many parts of the nation. In an early warranty of habitability case, the

---

19. Underfunded agencies tend to adopt a triage policy that focuses on middle income housing to ensure neighborhood preservation rather than to cure health and safety violations in more depressed areas. *See* Quinn, Urban Triage and Municipal Housing Code Enforcement: An Analysis of the St. Louis Case, in Administrative Discretion and Public Policy Implementation (D. Shumavon & H.K. Hibbeln eds. 1986).

20. The widespread use of courts in the civil rights movement led people to view courts as a forum in which to assert rights for relatively powerless groups. Tenants, particularly poor tenants, were a natural constituency for civil rights lawyers. In addition, President Johnson's Great Society programs provided funding for legal services. The lawyers in these programs not only represented tenants in conventional disputes with landlords, but they also sought to change the law through both class action and other types of impact litigation and legislation.

Supreme Court of Washington wrote: "A disadvantaged tenant should not be placed in a position of agreeing to live in an uninhabitable premises. [Uninhabitable] [h]ousing conditions * * * are a health hazard, not only to the individual tenant, but to the community * * *. [S]uch housing conditions are at least a contributing cause of such problems as urban blight, juvenile delinquency and high property taxes for the conscientious landowners." *Foisy v. Wyman,* 83 Wash.2d 22, 515 P.2d 160, 164–165 (1973), citing *Pines v. Perssion* 14 Wis.2d 590, 595–96, 111 N.W.2d 409, 412–13 (1961). The warranty of habitability was thus part of a broader political and legal movement to address the problems of society at large.

Javins v. First National Realty Corp.

United States Court of Appeals for the District of Columbia Circuit, 1970.
428 F.2d 1071.

■ SKELLY WRIGHT, CIRCUIT JUDGE.

These cases present the question whether housing code violations which arise during the term of a lease have any effect upon the tenant's obligation to pay rent. * * *

* * * We now reverse and hold that a warranty of habitability, measured by the standards set out in the Housing Regulations for the District of Columbia, is implied by operation of law into leases of urban dwelling units covered by those Regulations and that breach of this warranty gives rise to the usual remedies for breach of contract.

I

The facts revealed by the record are simple. By separate written leases, each of the appellants rented an apartment in a three-building apartment complex in Northwest Washington known as Clifton Terrace. The landlord, First National Realty Corporation, filed separate actions in the Landlord and Tenant Branch of the Court of General Sessions on April 8, 1966, seeking possession on the ground that each of the appellants had defaulted in the payment of rent due for the month of April. The tenants, appellants here, admitted that they had not paid the landlord any rent for April. However, they alleged numerous violations of the Housing Regulations as "an equitable defense or [a] claim by way of recoupment or set-off in an amount equal to the rent claim," as provided in the rules of the Court of General Sessions. They offered to prove

> that there are approximately 1500 violations of the Housing Regulations of the District of Columbia in the building at Clifton Terrace, where Defendant resides some affecting the premises of this Defendant directly, others indirectly, and all tending to establish a course of conduct of violation of the Housing Regulations to the damage of Defendants....

Appellants conceded at trial, however, that this offer of proof reached only violations which had arisen since the term of the lease had commenced. The Court of General Sessions refused appellants' offer of proof and entered judgment for the landlord. The District of Columbia Court of Appeals affirmed, rejecting the argument made by appellants that the landlord was under a contractual duty to maintain the premises in compliance with the Housing Regulations.

II

Since, in traditional analysis, a lease was the conveyance of an interest in land, courts have usually utilized the special rules governing real property transactions to resolve controversies involving leases. However, as the Supreme Court has noted in another context, "the body of private property law ..., more than almost any other branch of law, has been shaped by distinctions whose validity is largely historical." Courts have a duty to reappraise old doctrines in the light of the facts and values of contemporary life—particularly old common law doctrines which the courts themselves created and developed. As we have said before, "The continued vitality of the common law ... depends upon its ability to reflect contemporary community values and ethics."

The assumption of landlord-tenant law, derived from feudal property law, that a lease primarily conveyed to the tenant an interest in land may have been reasonable in a rural, agrarian society; it may continue to be reasonable in some leases involving farming or commercial land. In these cases, the value of the lease to the tenant is the land itself. But in the case of the modern apartment dweller, the value of the lease is that it gives him a place to live. The city dweller who seeks to lease an apartment on the third floor of a tenement has little interest in the land 30 or 40 feet below, or even in the bare right to possession within the four walls of his apartment. When American city dwellers, both rich and poor, seek "shelter" today, they seek a well known package of goods and services—a package which includes not merely walls and ceilings, but also adequate heat, light and ventilation, serviceable plumbing facilities, secure windows and doors, proper sanitation, and proper maintenance.

Professor Powell summarizes the present state of the law:

> ... The complexities of city life, and the proliferated problems of modern society in general, have created new problems for lessors and lessees and these have been commonly handled by specific clauses inserted in leases. This growth in the number and detail of specific lease covenants has reintroduced into the law of estates for years a predominantly contractual ingredient. In practice, the law today concerning estates for years consists chiefly of rules determining the construction and effect of lease covenants.... 2 R. Powell, Real Property ¶ 221(1) at 179 (1967).

Ironically, however, the rules governing the construction and interpretation of "predominantly contractual" obligations in leases have too often remained rooted in old property law.

Some courts have realized that certain of the old rules of property law governing leases are inappropriate for today's transactions. In order to reach results more in accord with the legitimate expectations of the parties and the standards of the community, courts have been gradually introducing more modern precepts of contract law in interpreting leases. Proceeding piecemeal has, however, led to confusion where "decisions are frequently conflicting, not because of a healthy disagreement on social policy, but because of the lingering impact of rules whose policies are long since dead."

In our judgment the trend toward treating leases as contracts is wise and well considered. Our holding in this case reflects a belief that leases of urban dwelling units should be interpreted and construed like any other contract.

III

Modern contract law has recognized that the buyer of goods and services in an industrialized society must rely upon the skill and honesty of the supplier to assure that goods and services purchased are of adequate quality. In interpreting most contracts, courts have sought to protect the legitimate expectations of the buyer and have steadily widened the seller's responsibility for the quality of goods and services through implied warranties of fitness and merchantability. * * *

The rigid doctrines of real property law have tended to inhibit the application of implied warranties to transactions involving real estate. Now, however, courts have begun to hold sellers and developers of real property responsible for the quality of their product. For example, builders of new homes have recently been held liable to purchasers for improper construction on the ground that the builders had breached an implied warranty of fitness. In other cases courts have held builders of new homes liable for breach of an implied warranty that all local building regulations had been complied with. And following the developments in other areas, very recent decisions and commentary suggest the possible extension of liability to parties other than the immediate seller for improper construction of residential real estate.

Despite this trend in the sale of real estate, many courts have been unwilling to imply warranties of quality, specifically a warranty of habitability, into leases of apartments. Recent decisions have offered no convincing explanation for their refusal; rather they have relied without discussion upon the old common law rule that the lessor is not obligated to repair unless he covenants to do so in the written lease contract. However, the Supreme Courts of at least two states, in recent and well reasoned opinions, have held landlords to implied warranties of quality in housing leases. *Lemle v. Breeden*, S.Ct.Hawaii, 462 P.2d 470 (1969); *Reste Realty Corp. v. Cooper*, 53 N.J. 444, 251 A.2d 268 (1969). In our judgment, the old no-repair rule cannot coexist with the obligations imposed on the landlord by a typical modern housing code, and must be abandoned in favor of an implied warranty of habitability. In the District of Columbia, the standards of this warranty are set out in the Housing Regulations.

IV

A. In our judgment the common law itself must recognize the landlord's obligation to keep his premises in a habitable condition. This conclusion is compelled by three separate considerations. First, we believe that the old rule was based on certain factual assumptions which are no longer true; on its own terms, it can no longer be justified. Second, we believe that the consumer protection cases discussed above require that the old rule be abandoned in order to bring residential landlord-tenant law into harmony with the principles on which those cases rest. Third, we think that the nature of today's urban housing market also dictates abandonment of the old rule.

The common law rule absolving the lessor of all obligation to repair originated in the early Middle Ages. Such a rule was perhaps well suited to an agrarian economy; the land was more important than whatever small living structure was included in the leasehold, and the tenant farmer was fully capable of making repairs himself. These historical facts were the basis on which the common law constructed its rule; they also provided the necessary prerequisites for its application.

Court decisions in the late 1800's began to recognize that the factual assumptions of the common law were no longer accurate in some cases. For example, the common law, since it assumed that the land was the most important part of the leasehold, required a tenant to pay rent even if any building on the land was destroyed. Faced with such a rule and the ludicrous results it produced, in 1863 the New York Court of Appeals declined to hold that an upper story tenant was obliged to continue paying rent after his apartment building burned down. The court simply pointed out that the urban tenant had no interest in the land, only in the attached building. * * *

These as well as other similar cases demonstrate that some courts began some time ago to question the common law's assumptions that the land was the most important feature of a leasehold and that the tenant could feasibly make any necessary repairs himself. Where those assumptions no longer reflect contemporary housing patterns, the courts have created exceptions to the general rule that landlords have no duty to keep their premises in repair.

It is overdue for courts to admit that these assumptions are no longer true with regard to all urban housing. Today's urban tenants, the vast majority of whom live in multiple dwelling houses, are interested, not in the land, but solely in "a house suitable for occupation." Furthermore, today's city dweller usually has a single, specialized skill unrelated to maintenance work; he is unable to make repairs like the 'jack-of-all-trades' farmer who was the common law's model of the lessee. Further, unlike his agrarian predecessor who often remained on one piece of land for his entire life, urban tenants today are more mobile than ever before. A tenant's tenure in a specific apartment will often not be sufficient to justify efforts at repairs. In addition, the increasing complexity of today's dwellings renders them much more difficult to repair than the structures of earlier times. In a multiple dwelling repair may require access to equipment and areas in the control of the landlord. Low and middle income tenants, even if they were interested in making repairs, would be unable to obtain any financing for major repairs since they have no long-term interest in the property.

Our approach to the common law of landlord and tenant ought to be aided by principles derived from the consumer protection cases referred to above. In a lease contract, a tenant seeks to purchase from his landlord shelter for a specified period of time. The landlord sells housing as a commercial businessman and has much greater opportunity, incentive and capacity to inspect and maintain the condition of his building. Moreover, the tenant must rely upon the skill and *bona fides* of his landlord at least as much as a car buyer must rely upon the car manufacturer. In dealing with major problems, such as heating, plumbing, electrical or structural defects, the tenant's position corresponds precisely with "the ordinary consumer who cannot be expected to have the knowledge or capacity or even the opportunity to make adequate inspection of mechanical instrumentalities, like automobiles, and to decide for himself whether they are reasonably fit for the designed purpose." *Henningsen v. Bloomfield Motors, Inc.*, 32 N.J. 358, 375, 161 A.2d 69, 78 (1960).[21]

Since a lease contract specifies a particular period of time during which the tenant has a right to use his apartment for shelter, he may legitimately expect that the apartment will be fit for habitation for the time period for which it is rented. We point out that in the present cases there is no allegation that appellants' apartments were in poor condition or in violation of the housing code at the commencement of the leases. Since the lessees continue to pay the same rent, they were entitled to expect that the landlord would continue to keep the premises in their beginning condition during the lease term. It is precisely such expectations that the law now recognizes as deserving of formal, legal protection.

Even beyond the rationale of traditional products liability law, the relationship of landlord and tenant suggests further compelling reasons for the law's protection of the tenants' legitimate expectations of quality. The inequality in bargaining power between landlord and tenant has been well documented. Tenants have very little leverage to enforce demands for better housing. Various impediments to competition in the rental housing market, such as racial and class discrimination and standardized form leases, mean that landlords place tenants in a take it or leave it situation. The increasingly severe shortage of adequate housing further increases the landlord's bargaining power and escalates the need for maintaining and improving the existing stock. Finally, the findings by various studies of the social impact of bad housing has led to the realization that poor housing is

---

21. Nor should the average tenant be thought capable of 'inspecting' plaster, floorboards, roofing, kitchen appliances, etc. To the extent, however, that some defects are obvious, the law must take note of the present housing shortage. Tenants may have no real alternative but to accept such housing with the expectation that the landlord will make necessary repairs. Where this is so, *caveat emptor* must of necessity be rejected.

detrimental to the whole society, not merely to the unlucky ones who must suffer the daily indignity of living in a slum.

Thus we are led by our inspection of the relevant legal principles and precedents to the conclusion that the old common law rule imposing an obligation upon the lessee to repair during the lease term was really never intended to apply to residential urban leaseholds. Contract principles established in other areas of the law provide a more rational framework for the apportionment of landlord-tenant responsibilities; they strongly suggest that a warranty of habitability be implied into all contracts for urban dwellings.

B. We believe, in any event, that the District's housing code requires that a warranty of habitability be implied in the leases of all housing that it covers. The housing code—formally designated the Housing Regulations of the District of Columbia—was established and authorized by the Commissioners of the District of Columbia on August 11, 1955. Since that time, the code has been updated by numerous orders of the Commissioners. The 75 pages of the Regulations provide a comprehensive regulatory scheme setting forth in some detail: (a) the standards which housing in the District of Columbia must meet; (b) which party, the lessor or the lessee, must meet each standard; and (c) a system of inspections, notifications and criminal penalties. The Regulations themselves are silent on the question of private remedies.

Two previous decisions of this court, however, have held that the Housing Regulations create legal rights and duties enforceable in tort by private parties. * * *

The District of Columbia Court of Appeals gave further effect to the Housing Regulations in *Brown v. Southall Realty Co.*, 237 A.2d 834 (1968). There the landlord knew at the time the lease was signed that housing code violations existed which rendered the apartment "unsafe and unsanitary." Viewing the lease as a contract, the District of Columbia Court of Appeals held that the premises were let in violation of Sections 2304 and 2501 of the Regulations and that the lease, therefore, was void as an illegal contract. In the light of *Brown*, it is clear not only that the housing code creates privately enforceable duties as held in *Whetzel*, but that the basic validity of every housing contract depends upon substantial compliance with the housing code at the beginning of the lease term. The *Brown* court relied particularly upon Section 2501 of the Regulations which provides:

> Every premises accommodating one or more habitations shall be maintained and kept in repair so as to provide decent living accommodations for the occupants. This part of this Code contemplates more than mere basic repairs and maintenance to keep out the elements; its purpose is to include repairs and maintenance designed to make a premises or neighborhood healthy and safe.

By its terms, this section applies to maintenance and repair during the lease term. Under the *Brown* holding, serious failure to comply with this section before the lease term begins renders the contract void. We think it untenable to find that this section has no effect on the contract after it has been signed. To the contrary, by signing the lease the landlord has undertaken a continuing obligation to the tenant to maintain the premises in accordance with all applicable law.

This principle of implied warranty is well established. Courts often imply relevant law into contracts to provide a remedy for any damage caused by one party's illegal conduct.[22] * * *

[T]he housing code must be read into housing contracts—a holding also required by the purposes and the structure of the code itself. The duties imposed by the Housing Regulations may not be waived or shifted by agreement if the Regulations specifically place the duty upon the lessor. Criminal penalties are provided if these duties are ignored. This regulatory structure was established by the Commissioners because, in their judgment, the grave conditions in the housing market required serious action. Yet official enforcement of the housing code has been far from uniformly effective. Innumerable studies have documented the desperate condition of rental housing in the District of Columbia and in the nation. In view of these circumstances, we think the conclusion reached by the Supreme Court of Wisconsin as to the effect of a housing code on the old common law rule cannot be avoided:

> The legislature has made a policy judgment—that it is socially (and politically) desirable to impose these duties on a property owner—which has rendered the old common law rule obsolete. To follow the old rule of no implied warranty of habitability in leases would, in our opinion, be inconsistent with the current legislative policy concerning housing standards. *Pines v. Perssion*, 14 Wis.2d 590, 596, 111 N.W.2d 409, 412–413 (1961).

We therefore hold that the Housing Regulations imply a warranty of habitability, measured by the standards which they set out, into leases of all housing that they cover.

V

In the present cases, the landlord sued for possession for nonpayment of rent. Under contract principles,[23] however, the tenant's obligation to pay rent is dependent upon the landlord's performance of his obligations, including his warranty to maintain the premises in habitable condition. In

---

22. As a general proposition, it is undoubtedly true that parties to a contract intend that applicable law will be complied with by both sides. We recognize, however, that reading statutory provisions into private contracts may have little factual support in the intentions of the particular parties now before us. But, for reasons of public policy, warranties are often implied into contracts by operation of law in order to meet generally prevailing standards of honesty and fair deal-ing. When the public policy has been enacted into law like the housing code, that policy will usually have deep roots in the expectations and intentions of most people. *See* Costigan, Implied-in-Fact Contracts and Mutual Assent, 33 Harv.L.Rev. 376, 383–385 (1920).

23. In extending all contract remedies for breach to the parties to a lease, we include an action for specific performance of the landlord's implied warranty of habitability.

order to determine whether any rent is owed to the landlord, the tenants must be given an opportunity to prove the housing code violations alleged as breach of the landlord's warranty.[24]

At trial, the finder of fact must make two findings: (1) whether the alleged violations[25] existed during the period for which past due rent is claimed, and (2) what portion, if any or all, of the tenant's obligation to pay rent was suspended by the landlord's breach. If no part of the tenant's rental obligation is found to have been suspended, then a judgment for possession may issue forthwith. On the other hand, if the jury determines that the entire rental obligation has been extinguished by the landlord's total breach, then the action for possession on the ground of nonpayment must fail.[26]

The jury may find that part of the tenant's rental obligation has been suspended but that part of the unpaid back rent is indeed owed to the landlord. In these circumstances, no judgment for possession should issue if the tenant agrees to pay the partial rent found to be due. If the tenant refuses to pay the partial amount, a judgment for possession may then be entered. * * *

In just a few years—by the mid–1970s—the process of reform was largely completed. Statutes and court decisions in most states established an implied warranty of habitability for residential leases and created new tenant-initiated remedies for enforcement. *See, e.g., Green v. Superior Court*, 10 Cal.3d 616, 111 Cal.Rptr. 704, 517 P.2d 1168 (1974); *Boston Housing Authority v. Hemingway* 363 Mass. 184, 293 N.E.2d 831, 843 (1973); *Fair v. Negley* 257 Pa.Super. 50, 54–58, 390 A.2d 240, 243–245 (1978); *Teller v. McCoy*, 162 W.Va. 367, 394–95, 253 S.E.2d 114, 130–131 (1978); Fla. Stat. ch. 83.201; S.D. Codified Laws § 43–32–9. *See generally* Cunningham, The New Implied and Statutory Warranties of Habitability in Residential Leases: From Contract to Status, 16 Urb. L. Rev. 3 (1979). Although the procedures to enforce the warranty vary from state to state, the substantive right is pretty much the same: the landlord impliedly

---

24. To be relevant, of course, the violations must affect the tenant's apartment or common areas which the tenant uses. Moreover, the contract principle that no one may benefit from his own wrong will allow the landlord to defend by proving the damage was caused by the tenant's wrongful action. However, violations resulting from inadequate repairs or materials which disintegrate under normal use would not be assignable to the tenant. Also we agree with the District of Columbia Court of Appeals that the tenant's private rights do not depend on official inspection or official finding of violation by the city government. *Diamond Housing Corp. v. Robinson*, 257 A.2d 492, 494 (1969).

25. The jury should be instructed that one or two minor violations standing alone which do not affect habitability are *de minimis* and would not entitle the tenant to a reduction in rent.

26. As soon as the landlord made the necessary repairs rent would again become due. Our holding, of course, affects only eviction for nonpayment of rent. The landlord is free to seek eviction at the termination of the lease or on any other legal ground.

warrants to maintain the residential property in a habitable condition as measured by the local housing code. *See Green v. Superior Court,* 10 Cal.3d at 637, 111 Cal.Rptr. at 719, 517 P.2d at 1183 ("In most cases substantial compliance with those applicable building and housing code standards which materially affect health and safety will suffice to meet the landlord's obligations under the common law implied warranty of habitability."); *Park West Management Corp. v. Mitchell,* 47 N.Y.2d 316, 328, 418 N.Y.S.2d 310, 316, 391 N.E.2d 1288, 1294 (1979) ("while certainly a factor in the measurement of the landlord's obligation, violation of a housing code or sanitary regulation is not the exclusive determinant of whether there has been a breach").

---

1. The *Javins* court claims that its decision moves landlord-tenant law away from anachronistic property law to contract law. Does this mean that the landlord and tenant should be able to bargain over the precise obligations under the warranty? Should residential tenants be allowed to waive the implied warranty?

The *Javins* court argues that modern contract law creates implied warranties for merchantability of goods. Is this a sound analogy? A warranty for merchantability usually applies to new, not used, goods; used goods may be sold "as is." Moreover, in most real estate transactions, including sales of homes, *caveat emptor* (subject to disclosure obligations in many states) continues to apply. Why should leases be different?

2. What is different about "today's urban housing market," to use the court's language, that compels the rule announced in *Javins*? What is different about modern tenants?

Is there an economic justification for the rule announced in *Javins*?

3. Why did the court hold that the housing code should be read into each lease? Since the landlord is already bound by the housing code, what difference does it make that it is made an implied part of each lease?

4. *Javins* and other cases creating an implied warranty of habitability are widely hailed as important milestones in reform of landlord-tenant law. Is it appropriate for courts to engage is non-constitutional policymaking when the legislature could (and in many states did) undertake similar reforms? Shouldn't courts leave such questions to the legislature? And if the legislature declines to act, shouldn't the courts respect that decision? Or are courts obligated to act if the legislature does not undertake reform?

Are courts institutionally capable of delineating the contours of the tenants' substantive rights and intricate remedies? Are they better able than legislatures to make such rules?

Tenant-Initiated Remedies to Enforce Habitability Requirements. The hallmark of the warranty of habitability, whether adopted in legislation or established in judge-made doctrines, is that tenants could use self-help— either spending part of the rent on repairs or withholding rent payments— to obtain its remedies without facing eviction for nonpayment. In other words, the implied warranty and the covenant to pay rent are mutually dependent. Although the substantive criteria and procedures vary significantly from state to state, in general the implied warranty is breached only when the defect has a substantial impact on health or safety (thus minor housing code violations are not a basis to claim breach) and only after the landlord has had a reasonable opportunity to cure the defect.[27]

Although tenants usually may seek damages, injunctive relief, or rescission for breach of the warranty, *see, e.g., Quevedo v. Braga*, 72 Cal.App.3d Supp. 1, 140 Cal.Rptr. 143 (1977) (permitting damages), *Lemle v. Breeden*, 51 Haw. 426, 436, 462 P.2d 470, 475 (1969) (permitting damages and rescission)[28] the main emphasis is on the newly created self-help remedies. The remedies generally fall into one of three categories: *rent application*, *rent withholding*, or *rent abatement*. Many states permit more than one of these remedies.

About half of the states have adopted *rent application* statutes, sometimes called "repair and deduct" statutes. Under this approach, the tenant can use some of the rent money to make repairs if the residence is substantially untenantable. If the tenant meets the procedural and substantive criteria for rent application, he can successfully defend an unlawful detainer action or a suit for back rent. *See, e.g.*, Cal. Civ. Code § 1942 (tenant may use rent to make repairs if the property is untenantable, after giving the landlord notice of the need for the repairs and a reasonable time to make the repairs); Tex. Prop. Code Ann. §§ 92.056–92.0561 (tenant may use rent to make certain repairs after giving the landlord both notice of the need for the repairs and subsequent notice of the tenant's intent to make the repairs himself); Wash. Rev. Code § 59.18.100 (tenant may make repairs after giving the landlord specified notice and an opportunity to make the repairs). Although the remedy is relatively easy for tenants to use, it is limited in many states by the number of times a tenant can invoke it annually or the amount of rent a tenant can spend on repairs. *See, e.g.*, Cal. Civ. Code § 1942 (tenant may use this remedy up to twice in any 12– month period; each time the tenant may spend up to one month's rent);

---

27. Significant variations in the warranty include its scope (most jurisdictions include all rental housing; some states restrict it to multi-unit or urban apartments); the definition of "habitable" (usually, though not always, some variant of the housing code); whether tenants can waive the warranty for defects they were aware of at the time they signed the lease (most jurisdictions say no); and the method of measuring damages or offsets.

28. Of course, tenants may also have causes of action based on tort law. *See, e.g., Stoiber v. Honeychuck*, 101 Cal.App.3d 903, 162 Cal.Rptr. 194 (1980) (tenant may sue not only for damages on contractual claim of warranty of habitability, but also for damages based on negligence, nuisance, and intentional infliction of emotional distress).

Wash. Rev. Code § 59.18.100 (tenant may spend only two months' rent annually).

Rent-withholding statutes permit the tenant to withhold rent until the landlord corrects health-threatening defects or otherwise makes the premises "habitable." _See, e.g.,_ Fla. Stat. ch. 83.201 (if premises are "wholly untenantable" the tenant may withhold rent after giving the landlord notice and 20 days to make repairs). In some states, the tenant cannot invoke this remedy without a prior judicial determination that the premises are uninhabitable. _See, e.g.,_ N.C. Gen. Stat. § 42–44(c). Most rent-withholding statutes require (or authorize the court to require) the tenant to pay the rent into a court-administered escrow account. _See, e.g.,_ Conn. Gen. Stat. § 47a–14h (the tenant must pay the withheld rent to the local housing agency, to be held in escrow until the landlord complies with the housing code); S.D. Codified Laws § 43–32–9 (if the cost of repairs exceeds one month's rent, the tenant can withhold rent if she places it in a separate bank account maintained expressly for this purpose). In some jurisdictions, the landlord may withdraw money from the court's account to pay for repairs. Once the repairs are completed, all of the money in the account is turned over to the landlord. _See, e.g.,_ Fla. Stat. ch. 83.201 (tenant must pay withheld funds); Ohio Rev. Code Ann. §§ 5321.09–5321.10 (court may release withheld funds under specified conditions). To provide additional incentive to improve conditions, a few statutes require that the money be returned to the tenant if the landlord does not complete the repairs within a specified period. _See, e.g.,_ Md. Code Ann., Real Prop. § 8–211(n)(5) (6 months).

Under _rent-abatement_ statutes and decisions, the tenant simply stops paying rent. When the landlord files an unlawful detainer action for possession and back rent, the tenant defends on the ground that the landlord breached the warranty of habitability. In many states, a court will enter a protective order requiring tenants to pay the rent into a court escrow account pending judgment. If the court finds that the landlord breached the warranty of habitability, it will enter judgment for the tenant, reduce the rent, and deny the landlord possession. The judgment is commonly conditional, however, on the tenant paying the reduced back rent within a few days of the judgment. _See, e.g.,_ Cal. Code Civ. Proc. § 1174.2 (5 days). If the court finds that the landlord did not breach the warranty, it will give the landlord a judgment for back rent and possession. The tenant's good faith belief that the premises were not inhabitable is not a defense.

There are three principal ways to determine the amount of rent reduction (essentially a set-off of the tenant's damages for breach) under the rent abatement statutes. Some jurisdictions provide that the reduction is the difference between the reserved rent and the actual rental value of the premises during the period of the breach. _See, e.g.,_ Wash. Rev. Code § 59.18.110. Other states calculate abatement as the difference between the fair rental value of the premises as warranted and the fair rental value of the premises in their present condition. _See, e.g., Green v. Superior_

Court, 10 Cal.3d 616, 638, 111 Cal.Rptr. 704, 719, 517 P.2d 1168, 1183 (1974). A third method reduces the rent by a percentage equal to the percentage reduction in value resulting from the breach. *See, e.g., Academy Spires, Inc. v. Brown*, 111 N.J. Super. 477, 268 A.2d 556 (1970); *Restatement (Second) of Property (Landlord and Tenant)*, § 11.1.

---

1. Most repair and deduct statutes place significant restrictions on this remedy. Most importantly, the amount of money a tenant can spend annually on repairs is usually capped by one or two months' rent. What is the purpose of this restriction? If the landlord has had notice and an opportunity to make the repairs, why should there be any restrictions on the amount of money a tenant can deduct?

2. What are the advantages and disadvantages of relying on the local housing codes to define the substantive standards for the common law warranty of habitability? Should any housing code violation constitute a breach of the warranty of habitability?

3. Should the landlord's good faith make a difference in deciding whether the landlord has breached the warranty of habitability? What if the breach is due to a garbage strike by city employees? Or by the landlord's maintenance workers? What if a boiler in the building unexpectedly broke down in the middle of winter? Would it make a difference if the landlord warned the tenant upon moving in that the boiler might break down? Is the warranty breached if the apartment has no gas or electricity for three months following an earthquake? *Cf. Peterson v. Superior Court*, 10 Cal.4th 1185, 1205, 43 Cal.Rptr.2d 836, 899 P.2d 905, 917 (1995) (in holding that the warranty of habitability was not a basis to hold landlords strictly liable for torts in the rented premises, the court wrote "The tenant further reasonably can expect that the landlord will maintain the property in a habitable condition by repairing promptly any conditions, of which the landlord has actual or constructive notice, that arise during the tenancy and render the dwelling uninhabitable").

4. Suppose that a tenant successfully defends an unlawful detainer action on the ground that the landlord violated the warranty. How should the court determine the proper rent abatement? From the tenant's point of view, what are the advantages and disadvantages of the different measures of rent abatement for a breach of the warranty of habitability? Is it possible, under any methods of measuring rent abatement, that the landlord would have to let the tenant live rent-free and still pay the tenant damages? *See McKenna v. Begin*, 3 Mass. App. Ct. 168, 173–74, 325 N.E.2d 587, 592 (1975).

5. Suppose the tenant incorrectly, but in good faith, withholds rent on the ground that the residential leasehold is uninhabitable. Is the tenant protected from eviction following a judgment for the landlord by paying the entire rent promptly following the adverse judgment? *Should* the tenant acting in good faith be protected from eviction?

6.   Why shouldn't the tenant be allowed to make a knowing waiver of the warranty in the lease? Wouldn't a waiver be most justifiable when the defect exists at the beginning of the leasehold and the tenant has explicitly and specifically waived his rights to claim a breach for those defects? What if the tenant wanted a reduced rent and bargained to make some of the repairs himself? What if the tenant just wanted a reduced rent? Is "inadequate bargaining power" a sufficient justification in all cases? Moreover, can't a tenant later waive his rights under the warranty by simply not invoking them? How, if at all, is that different from a waiver in the lease?

7.   Should the warranty of habitability be extended to a more general warranty for suitability for use for all—residential and commercial—leases? What are the relevant differences between residential and commercial leases? Are there significant differences in the parties' relative bargaining power or sophistication? Are there differences in the tenants' ability to make repairs or spread costs? *See Schulman v. Vera*, 108 Cal.App.3d 552, 558–63, 166 Cal.Rptr. 620, 623–26 (1980) (rejecting an implied warranty of suitability for use for commercial leases); *Davidow v. Inwood N. Professional Group—Phase I*, 747 S.W.2d 373, 377 (Tex.1988) (creating an implied warranty for suitability of use in commercial leases). *See also* Comment, An Economic Analysis of Implied Warranties of Fitness in Commercial Leases, 94 Colum. L. Rev. 658 (1994) (arguing that it would be economically efficient for lawmakers to establish an implied warranty for general fitness in commercial leases in all cases, and an implied warranty for particular fitness in special cases).

Efficacy of the Warranty of Habitability. Despite the strong arguments favoring the implied warranty in residential leases, there are some serious doubts that the warranty of habitability can achieve one of the primary goals that prompted its adoption—ensuring decent housing for poor tenants—and serious concerns that vigorous enforcement might do low-income tenants more harm than good. Consider the following assessment.

Charles J. Meyers, The Covenant of Habitability and the American Law Institute

27 Stanford Law Review 879, 889–893 (1975).*

Let us consider the probable economic consequences of the *Restatement* rules [providing for an inalienable warranty of habitability in residential leases].

Four categories of rental housing may be identified, one of which is unaffected by the covenant of habitability and therefore need not be considered further. That category consists of dwellings that substantially

* © 1975 the Board of Trustees of The Leland Stanford Junior University.

comply with the housing code and are considered "suitable" for residential purposes.

The other three categories of housing will be affected by the covenant and consist of:

1) dwellings that do not comply with the housing code and are considered unsuitable for residential use, but that can be brought up to code standards by additional investment that can be recovered through higher rents.

2) dwellings that do not comply with the housing code and are considered unsuitable for residential use but that can be brought up to code standards by an expenditure that will reduce the landlord's rate of return (because rents cannot be raised sufficiently to cover repair costs) but will not eliminate a positive return on sunk capital.

3) dwellings that do not comply with the housing code and are considered unsuitable for residential use, for which the costs of repair to meet code standards (together with other expenses) will result in a negative return on sunk capital.

No one knows how the nation's substandard housing stock is divided among these three categories, and the proportions are likely to vary from city to city. Whatever those proportions may be, some portion of the housing stock will fall into category (3) and will be withdrawn from the market because of the imposition of the duty of habitability. To the extent such withdrawal occurs, low-income tenants as a class are hurt, not helped, by the *Restatement* rules. It is the further contention here that application of the *Restatement* rules to the other two categories of slum housing will also adversely affect the interests of low-income tenants, certainly in the long run.

As to rental housing in category (1), housing that can be profitably improved, the *Restatement* says, in effect, that such housing cannot be rented in substandard condition. Therefore, the landlord will improve the property and charge higher rents. The class of tenants theretofore occupying the premises will either lose occupancy because they cannot afford the new rents or will remain in possession and have less disposable income for other goods and services. In the latter case, the *Restatement* makes a judgment for the tenant, that he should (must) spend more money on housing and less on clothes, food, recreation, and other items, even though left to his own devices he would and previously did make the opposite choice. Where courts derive the authority to make this choice for tenants and why it is a better choice than the tenants' own is not apparent.

Rental housing in category (2)—housing that can be improved by expenditures reducing, although not eliminating, the landlord's return—presents different considerations. Here low-income tenants as a class are initially benefited by the *Restatement* rules. As long as the landlord recovers from rents all of his out-of-pocket expenses, including the cost of repairs plus interest on the investment in repairs, he is likely to make the repairs in order to protect his equity in the property. Even if his equity is zero (because no one will buy the property), he may still invest in repairs if the rents cover all costs, including as costs the return the landlord would have received by investing the repair money in some other venture. * * *

* * * In the long run, however, unless rents fully reflect the costs of the additional repairs required by the *Restatement*, the quantity of category (2) property will decline. First, because of the lower profit position, the operating costs associated with increasing building age will take their toll faster than normal and the building will be prematurely forced into a deficit position and removed from the market. Second, no new category (2) property will be built; while present owners need only cover their operating costs, potential owners must be able to cover their initial capital expenses.

Category (3) consists of housing unsuitable for residential use (under the *Restatement* rules) for which the cost of repairs (when added to other operating expenses) exceeds the rental income that may be obtained from the property. This housing will be abandoned sooner or later, the timing depending on the landlord's perceptions and the financing arrangements for the property.

If the property is not mortgaged, the property will be abandoned as soon as the landlord concludes that his deficit position is irreversible. Once the property starts to lose money, the only reason for holding onto it is the expectation that sometime in the near future, the situation will turn around, and by an amount in excess of the losses previously suffered. For this reversal to occur it is probably necessary for rents to rise, which by hypothesis cannot happen for property in category (3).

If the property is mortgaged, the mortgagor will default, leaving the lending institution to take over. The lending institution will operate the property as long as rental income exceeds costs (including the cost of *Restatement* mandated repairs plus interest), thereby reducing the bad-debt loss the lender would otherwise suffer. The lender can afford to operate the property when the mortgagor-landlord could not, because the lender obviously does not have to pay himself interest. All the lender requires is a positive return on irretrievably sunk capital so as to reduce the unpaid balance on principal.

When neither the landlord without a mortgage nor the foreclosing mortgagee can break even on the property, the residuary legatee is the state. The state can take over the property for taxes, remove it from the tax rolls, and in theory pay for the *Restatement* repairs out of rental income not reduced by taxes. The state's ability to continue operation of the property depends, of course, on its ability either to divert public funds from former objects of support or to increase taxes to subsidize low-rent housing. Empirical evidence of what actually happens to slum housing after the state takes it over for taxes is lacking, but the prospects are probably poor that the properties will remain in the housing stock, for central city expenses are rising faster than tax revenues. Moreover, as cities increase the tax rate more rental properties slip into a deficit position, with landlords refusing to invest in repairs and ultimately abandoning the property to the city for taxes. Thus tax foreclosures tend to result in a vicious circle unless substandard structures are demolished after the city acquires them; city expenses rise, real estate taxes rise, and more structures are abandoned for taxes, to start the process all over again.

---

1. According to Professor Meyers, what adverse consequences does the warranty of habitability produce for landlords? For tenants? What are the premises of his argument that lead to these unhappy results? Are they valid? What are the weaknesses in his arguments?

2. Even if Meyers is correct about the economic consequences of the warranty, are there other justifications for it? To put the matter somewhat differently, why are poor tenants barred in most cases from bargaining with landlords to live in substandard housing if some landlords (and their buildings) are forced out of business? Is it because, as Justice Cardozo wrote, that "unless repairs in the rooms of the poor were made by the landlord, they would not be made by anyone," *Altz v. Leiberson*, 233 N.Y. 16, 19, 134 N.E. 703, 704 (1922)? Or is the warranty popular with legislators and judges because it "has the * * * attraction of * * * seeming to enable a principal manifestation of poverty to be eliminated without any expenditure by the government," R. Posner, Economic Analysis of the Law 259 (1973)?

3. If vigorous enforcement of the warranty leads to unpalatable secondary consequences (such as higher rents or a tighter housing market), what policy alternatives would you suggest?

4. Many other scholars agree with the gist of Meyers' analysis. *See* R. Posner, Economic Analysis of Law 470–74 (4th ed. 1994); Sax & Hiestand, Slumlordism as a Tort, 65 Mich. L. Rev. 869, 873–74 (1967); Note, Landlord's Violation of Housing Code During Lease Term is Breach of Implied Warranty of Habitability Constituting Partial or Total Defense to an Eviction Action Based on Nonpayment of Rent, 84 Harv. L. Rev. 729, 733–36 (1971); Comment, Rent Withholding Won't Work: The Need for a Realistic Rehabilitation Policy, 7 Loy. (L.A.) L. Rev. 66, 83 (1974). While some authors have argued that under the right conditions the warranty will not harm tenants, *see, e.g.,* Ackerman, Regulating Slum Housing Markets on Behalf of the Poor: Of Housing Codes, Housing Subsidies and Income Redistribution Policy, 80 Yale L.J. 1093 (1971); Kennedy, The Effect of the Warranty of Habitability on Low Income Housing: "Milking" and Class Violence, 15 Fla. State U.L. Rev. 485 (1987), those arguments have been cogently criticized for their unrealistic assumptions about housing markets for the poor. *See, e.g.,* Komesar, Return to Slumville: A Critique of the Ackerman Analysis of Housing Code Enforcement and the Poor, 82 Yale L.J. 1175 (1973); Hirsch, Hirsch & Margolis, Regression Analysis of the Effects of Habitability Laws Upon Rent: An Empirical Observation on the Ackerman–Komesar Debate, 63 Cal. L. Rev. 1098 (1975).

Relationship of Tort Law to the Warranty of Habitability. The warranty of habitability bumps up against tort law. Historically, and perhaps still in a majority of jurisdictions today, landlords were not liable in tort for their tenants' injuries from defects in the leased premises. There are several exceptions to this general rule. Landlords are liable for injuries that resulted from failing to disclose latent defects about which the landlord had actual or constructive knowledge, *City of Yuma v. Evans*, 85 Ariz. 229, 235, 336 P.2d 135, 139 (1959) (landlord city is liable for injuries from electric shock when evidence showed that city had actual knowledge of the hidden defect or the defect existed long enough to infer that the city should have known of the defect), from defects in common areas, *Paul v. Sharpe*, 181 Ga. App. 443, 444–45, 352 S.E.2d 626, 627–28 (1987) (landlord violated duty of reasonable care in a common area when a tenant's guest was injured after a railing collapsed), from negligent repairs, *Janofsky v. Garland*, 42 Cal.App.2d 655, 109 P.2d 750 (1941) (landlord liable for negligent repair of a ceiling, which fell on the tenant), and from breach of an express covenant to repair, *Williams v. Davis*, 188 Kan. 385, 362 P.2d 641 (1961) (landlord liable for injuries resulting from defects that the landlord had previously promised to repair). Some courts have expanded this last exception to include injuries from breach of the implied warranty of habitability. *See, e.g., Dwyer v. Skyline Apartments, Inc.*, 123 N.J. Super. 48, 51–53, 301 A.2d 463, 464–65 (1973) (tenant must show not only breach of the warranty but also breach of duty to exercise reasonable care, which includes some actual or constructive notice of the defect). Nevertheless, the common law rule exempted landlords from many negligence claims on the leased premises. *See generally* Browder, The Taming of a Duty—The Tort Liability of Landlords, 81 Mich. L. Rev. 99 (1982).

Increasingly, however, courts have moved away from a general immunity with exceptions toward a generalized duty of "reasonable care." *See, e.g., Sargent v. Ross*, 113 N.H. 388, 308 A.2d 528 (1973) (rejecting common law rule of landlord's tort immunity with exceptions and replacing it with a general rule of liability based on negligence); *Peterson v. Superior Court*, 10 Cal.4th 1185, 43 Cal.Rptr.2d 836, 899 P.2d 905 (1995) (holding that a landlord may be liable in negligence, but not strict liability, for injury from latent defect). *See also Henrioulle v. Marin Ventures, Inc.*, 20 Cal.3d 512, 143 Cal.Rptr. 247, 573 P.2d 465 (1978) (holding invalid lease clauses purporting to exculpate the landlord for his negligence).

Historically, courts held landlords immune from tort liability for injuries caused by the criminal acts of others on the leased property. Increasingly, however, courts have held landlords liable for negligently failing to protect tenants from the criminal acts of third parties if the criminal acts were foreseeable. Sometimes the landlord's duty arises from an express promise, sometimes from having voluntarily undertaken to install security measures, and sometimes from the warranty of habitability (*e.g.*, the warranty includes an obligation to install secure locks). *See, e.g., Kline v. 1500 Massachusetts Avenue Apartment Corp.*, 439 F.2d 477, 481–85 (D.C.Cir.1970) (a landlord has a tort duty under the implied warranty of habitability to take protective measures to guard the common areas from criminal activity); *Trentacost v. Brussel*, 82 N.J. 214, 228, 412 A.2d 436, 443 (1980) (a landlord has a tort duty under the implied warranty of habitability "to furnish reasonable safeguards to protect tenants from foreseeable criminal activity on the premises"); *Ann M. v. Pacific Plaza Shopping Center*, 6 Cal.4th 666, 679, 25 Cal. Rptr.2d 137, 863 P.2d 207, 215 (1993) (a landlord is liable for not providing security guards, who might have prevented a rape, only if the plaintiff can demonstrate a "high degree of foreseeability" of violent crime, which usually requires evidence of "prior similar incidents of violent crime on the landowner's premises"). Note that if the duty arises from the court's view of tort law generally, and not from the warranty of habitability, the duty extends to commercial leaseholds as well. *See generally* Comment, The Landlord's Liability for Criminal Injuries—The Duty to Protect, 24 Tulsa L.J. 261 (1988); Markatos, Property Law: The Growing Accountability of Landlords for Third–Party Criminal Attacks, 1991 Annual Survey of American Law 501.

d. TENANT'S RIGHT AGAINST RETALIATORY EVICTION

At common law, the landlord could refuse to renew a lease for any reason. Today, however, that power is substantially restricted. Civil rights laws, for example, generally prohibit landlords from refusing to renew a lease for certain discriminatory reasons. *See infra* pp. 656–75. Some statutes and local ordinances go even further and require the landlord to show good cause for refusal to renew a residential lease. In these jurisdictions, tenants effectively have defeasible life estates. Perhaps the most extreme limitation is in New York, where state regulations make the nearly 200,000 rent-controlled apartments and the 900,000 rent-stabilized apartments in New York City inheritable by family members under certain circumstances.[29]

Another important restriction on the landlord's authority to refuse to renew a lease is the doctrine barring "retaliatory eviction." In the leading case, *Edwards v. Habib*, 397 F.2d 687 (D.C.Cir.1968), the landlord gave the residential tenant a 30–day notice to terminate the periodic lease after the tenant complained to the local housing authorities about the condition of the apartment. When the tenant did not vacate the premises at the end of the lease, the landlord filed an unlawful detainer action. The court held that under these circumstances the tenant could raise retaliatory eviction as an affirmative defense to eviction. The court reasoned that a doctrine of retaliatory eviction was necessary to avoid undermining housing codes, and

29. *See* N.Y. Comp. Codes R. & Regs. tit. 9, §§ 2204.6(d) (rent-controlled units) and 2520.6(n)-(o), 2523.5(b)(2) (rent-stabilized units). *See also Braschi v. Stahl Associates Co.*, 74 N.Y.2d 201, 543 N.E.2d 49, 544 N.Y.S.2d 784 (1989) (holding that a gay couple may fall within the statutory definition of family, and thus that the surviving member of the couple may have a right to continued occupation of the apartment at the rent-controlled price); *East 10th Street Associates v. Goldstein Estate*, 154 A.D.2d 142, 552 N.Y.S.2d 257 (1990) (extending *Braschi* to rent-stabilized units).

to assist the investigation and enforcement of housing code violations, which depend largely on private initiative.

Protected Activities and Prohibited Actions. State courts and legislatures have expanded the doctrine beyond the reasoning and holding in *Habib. See* Hirsch, Hirsch & Margolis, Regression Analysis of the Effects of Habitability Laws Upon Rent: An Empirical Observation on the Ackerman–Komesar Debate, 63 Cal. L. Rev. 1098, 1113 n.62 (1975) (listing statutes). Many statutes and ordinances, for example, list protected activities. *See, e.g.,* Alaska Stat. § 34.03.310 (complaints to the landlord, efforts to enforce tenant's rights, complaints to government agencies, and formation of a tenants' union); R.I. Gen. Laws § 34–18–46 (complaints to housing agency, complaints to landlord about housing conditions, joining a tenants' union, or "availed himself or herself of any other lawful rights and remedies''); Tex. Prop. Code Ann. § 92.331 (protecting similar activities, but requiring that the tenant be acting in good faith); Cal. Civ. Code § 1942.5 (protected activities include "any rights under the law'').

Many statutes also prohibit particular landlord actions in addition to non-renewal—such as raising the rent—designed to punish the tenant for undertaking a protected activity. *See, e.g.,* Md. Code Ann., Real Prop. § 8–208.1 (prohibiting the landlord from evicting the tenant, arbitrarily increasing the rent, or decreasing services in retaliation); Wash. Rev. Code § 59.18.240 (landlord cannot evict the tenant, increase the rent, reduce services, or increase tenant's obligations in retaliation); *E & E Newman, Inc. v. Hallock*, 116 N.J.Super. 220, 281 A.2d 544 (1971) (holding that a steep increase in the rent following the tenant's complaints was, under the circumstances, an illegal retaliatory rent increase).

Commercial Leaseholds. Some state courts and legislatures have applied the doctrine to commercial leases as well as residential leases. *See, e.g., Windward Partners v. De los Santos*, 59 Haw. 104, 117, 577 P.2d 326, 334 (1978) (extending defense of retaliatory eviction to non-residential leases); *Custom Parking, Inc. v. Superior Court*, 138 Cal.App.3d 90, 101, 187 Cal.Rptr. 674, 681–82 (1982) (the doctrine applies to commercial leases where the landlord evicted the tenant for testifying truthfully at trial). Some courts, however, do not see the same compelling need for the doctrine in non-residential leases. In *Espenschied v. Mallick*, 633 A.2d 388, 394 (D.C.App.1993), the court wrote: "appellant has failed to adduce any evidence indicating there exists the commercial analogue of the comprehensive findings which inspired *Edwards, i.e.,* 'appalling condition[s] and shortage[s]' and 'the inequality of bargaining power between tenant and landlord.' '' *See also William C. Cornitius, Inc. v. Wheeler*, 276 Or. 747, 556 P.2d 666 (1976) (declining to extend the doctrine to commercial leases absent specific endorsement from the legislature).

Remedies. Tenants usually invoke the protections against retaliatory eviction as a defense in an unlawful detainer action. Many states also permit tenants to bring a private cause of action for damages, including punitive damages. *See, e.g., Aweeka v. Bonds*, 20 Cal.App.3d 278, 97 Cal.Rptr. 650 (1971).

Elements. Whether asserted as an affirmative defense in an unlawful detainer action or as a cause of action for damages, the tenant bears the burden of proving the requisite elements: the tenant undertook a protected activity and the landlord subsequently declined to renew the lease (or took some other action) for retaliatory reasons. In some jurisdictions, it is enough for the tenant to establish a *prima facie* case, at which point the burden shifts to the landlord to show absence of improper motive (presumably because the landlord has the best evidence of his motives). *See, e.g.,* R.I. Gen. Laws § 34–18–46(b) (rebuttable presumption of retaliatory eviction if landlord takes action against tenant within 6 months of protected activity); N.Y. Real Prop. Law § 223–b(5) (rebuttable presumption of retaliatory eviction if landlord proceeds against tenant within 6 months of protected activity). In most jurisdictions, the tenant must also establish that there is no unpaid rent. *See, e.g.,* Alaska Stat. § 34.03.310(c) (notwithstanding the retaliatory eviction provision, the landlord may bring an unlawful detainer action if the tenant is in default of rent); Ariz. Rev. Stat. § 33–1381(c)(2) (regardless of prohibition on retaliatory eviction, landlord may bring an action for possession if tenant is in default of the rent).

---

1. In many cases, the landlord will have mixed motives for raising the rent or moving to evict the tenant. That is, in addition to the retaliatory motive, the landlord may also have substantial, legitimate motives for evicting the tenant. How is a court to decide such cases? Which party has the burden of proof over which issues?

2. Would it be retaliatory eviction if a landlord terminated a lease because the tenant reported to the police that the landlord was engaged in criminal activity? Would it make a difference to your analysis if the accusation was false? Under what circumstances, if any, would you permit termination for a false criminal accusation?

3. The most obvious retaliatory action is the termination of a periodic lease. With a lease for a term of years, by contrast, there is no automatic renewal—the term ends automatically. If the landlord refused to enter into a new lease, could a holdover tenant raise retaliatory eviction as a defense? *See Van Buren Apartments v. Adams,* 145 Ariz. 325, 701 P.2d 583 (App. 1984).

4. Is a tenant bound by a lease purporting to waive his right to raise this defense or sue for damages? Are those rights effectively waived if the parties engage (or agree to engage) in binding arbitration?

Problems: Retaliatory Eviction

1. Reconsider the *Perez* problem on pp. 628–29. Does Mr. Perez have a good claim for retaliatory eviction?

2. Alice Barela rented a house from Leonardo Valdez on a month-to-month lease. She and her 9–year old daughter had lived in the house for four years.

When Barela found out that Valdez had sexually molested her daughter, she called the police. The police arrested Valdez, and he later pled guilty to lewd conduct in public. In the meantime, after Barela's police report, Valdez gave Barela a written 30–day notice of termination. When Barela did not vacate the house at the end of the lease, Valdez filed an unlawful detainer action.

Barela comes to you for advice. Does she have a good defense based on retaliatory eviction?

How would your analysis change if Barela had falsely accused Valdez of the crime? Would it make a difference if Barela had called the police in good faith? Or if she had acted with a genuine belief, but a bit recklessly (*e.g.*, she called the police after receiving information from her daughter's friend but before speaking to her daughter)? If you would impose a "good faith" or similar requirement, who should bear the burden of proof? *See Barela v. Superior Court*, 30 Cal.3d 244, 178 Cal.Rptr. 618, 636 P.2d 582 (1981).

3. Tenant operates a small grocery store under a year-to-year lease. In the middle of the lease, Tenant applied for and received a permit to sell alcohol. Landlord, who strongly opposes the use of alcohol on moral and religious grounds, was deeply upset when he learned that Tenant had begun to sell alcohol at the store. Following appropriate procedures, Landlord gave Tenant a written notice that he would not renew the lease. Tenant refuses to vacate (or stop selling alcohol) and defends the subsequent unlawful detainer action on the grounds of retaliatory eviction. Tenant argues that Landlord has sought to evict him for exercising his rights.

Is the landlord's refusal to renew the lease because he opposes the sale of alcohol retaliatory eviction? If so, could the landlord have avoided the defense by insisting on a covenant in the original lease that the tenant will not sell alcohol on the premises? Would such a covenant be an impermissible waiver of the tenant's rights? If not, would a provision generally waiving the tenant's rights to retaliatory eviction be upheld?

Review Problem

The Stevens Company owns and manages three apartment buildings in an economically depressed section of Oakland. Joe Dumont manages the Parkwood, a 4-story pre-war building, on Mathews Street. Most of the tenants pay their rent on time and the halls and grounds of the building are usually neat. The Parkwood is across the street from a vacant lot that often attracts drug dealers.

In 1992, Joe Dumont advertised to let a vacant apartment on the ground floor. Juditha Crowley answered the advertisement. She had two young children and was single. On her tenancy application, she listed as sources of income a low paying job, AFDC, and child support from the father of her children. In the interview, she acknowledged that the father of the children was often delinquent on the support payments. Joe expressed some concern about Juditha's ability to pay the $650/month rent for the unfurnished apartment. Juditha very much wanted the apartment and she noted that she had recently received a worker's compensation award of $2500. Joe said he would get back to her.

A few days later, Joe Dumont sent Juditha a rental lease agreement offering the apartment to Juditha for a one-year term. In addition to standard rental provisions regarding payment of rent, the agreement contained the following terms: a security deposit of $2500; a requirement that all guests staying over 2 days must be registered in the rental office; a requirement that the tenant pay the landlord's attorney fees should any matter be taken to court, mediation, or arbitration; and a provision stating that the security deposit would be automatically forfeited upon failure to pay the rent within 10 days of the first of the month. Juditha considered the terms onerous, but because she had encountered difficulty finding an apartment, she reluctantly signed the lease and turned over her worker's compensation check as security.

During the first few years of the tenancy, Juditha usually paid her rent by the first of the month. On two occasions, she was more than 10 days late, but she notified Joe of the lateness in advance and was never more than 20 days late. She accompanied her late payments with a pecan pie. Joe Dumont was reasonably attentive to problems in the apartment. He repaired some leaky pipes within a few days and replaced the refrigerator after it broke down.

In early 1997, Juditha's sister, Daria, had a falling out with her husband and began spending increasing amounts of time staying with Juditha. On March 19th, Daria's husband, Charles, became violent and Daria arrived at Juditha's apartment in the middle of the night with bruises and a suitcase. With no money and no job, she had no place else to go. Juditha did not formally inform Joe of her sister's extended visit, but Joe was often wandering the halls and it was clear to him what was going on.

On March 23, 1997, Charles came looking for Daria. He arrived at Juditha's home and demanded to come in. When Juditha refused, he kicked in the door, found Daria, and demanded that she return with him. Daria refused and Juditha dialed the police. As soon as Juditha began describing the situation to the 911 operator, Charles left, but not before kicking some of the furniture.

Juditha contacted Joe Dumont and asked him to repair the door. Joe looked at the damage and asked how it happened. After Juditha explained, Joe said that Juditha was responsible for the cost of replacing the door. Juditha complained, saying that it was the landlord's responsibility. Joe said he would call for an estimate, but reiterated that Juditha would be paying the cost. Juditha contacted her friend Michael, who came over with a tool kit and got the door back together, although it could be easily broken into again.

The next day, while Juditha and Daria were out, someone broke into the apartment and stole some of the personal effects of Juditha and Daria. That evening, someone threw a rock through one of the windows. Juditha called Joe and insisted that a new door be installed, that the window be replaced, and that bars be installed around the window frames. Joe said that he was not going to get involved in a domestic dispute and that Juditha was responsible for the repairs. Juditha, fearing for her family, hired Michael to replace the window and replace the door. Juditha deducted these costs from her April 1 rent check.

Upon receiving the check, Joe wrote to Juditha demanding the full rent and stating that he would be applying the security deposit until the full rent was received. Juditha was incensed by Joe's response. She threw a paperweight through the new window, packed up many of her more valuable belongings (other than furniture), and left with her children and Daria to stay with her mother in San Jose. That evening, vandals entered through the broken window and stole Juditha's stereo and the refrigerator. They also trashed the apartment.

1. Your firm represents the Stevens Company. What is your assessment of the Company's rights?

2. You are a poverty lawyer in Oakland. Juditha comes to you for advice. What is your assessment of her situation?

---

e. TENANT'S RIGHT AGAINST DISCRIMINATION

The Fair Housing Act of 1968, as amended in 1974 and 1988, prohibits discrimination in the sale or leasing of housing on the basis of race, color, religion, sex, handicap, familial status, or national origin. 42 U.S.C. §§ 3601–3619, 3631. It contains limited exemptions for single-family homes sold or rented by the owner (without the use of any sales or rental agent or advertisement), § 3404(b), religious organizations, private clubs, and housing for the elderly (for which the prohibition of discrimination on the basis of familial status does not apply), § 3607. The Americans with Disabilities Act, 42 U.S.C. § 12183, requires all new construction to be designed to provide access to and accommodate persons with disabilities, but generally does not apply to private residential construction. *See generally* Comment, The Americans with Disabilities Act "Readily Achievable" Requirement for Barrier Removal: A Proposal for the Allocation of Responsibility Between Landlord and Tenant, 15 Cardozo L. Rev. 569 (1993). Many states have statutes that reinforce and expand upon these federal protections. *See, e.g.,* Iowa Code § 216.8 (prohibiting discrimination in leasing on the basis of "race, color, creed, sex, religion, national origin, disability, or familial status''); Mich. Comp. Laws § 37.2502 (barring discrimination in real estate transactions on the basis of "religion, race, color, national origin, age, sex, height, weight, familial status, or marital status"); Unruh Civil Rights Act, Cal. Civ. Code § 51 (barring businesses from discriminating on the basis of "race, sex, color, religion, ancestry, national origin, or blindness or other physical disability").[30]

Notwithstanding the clarity of these prohibitions, proving discrimination in housing rental markets is often difficult in practice given the range of legitimate factors that landlords may consider in selecting tenants (*e.g.*, income, references, credit history), the fact that vacancies typically occur episodically, and that word of mouth and friendships often are significant factors in leasing decisions. In addition, as the following case illustrates, the application of these laws to address the roots of discrimination within our society has itself been complex and controversial.

United States v. Starrett City Associates

United States Court of Appeals for the Second Circuit, 1988.
840 F.2d 1096.

■ MINER, CIRCUIT JUDGE:

The United States Attorney General, on behalf of the United States ("the government"), commenced this action under Title VIII of the Civil Rights Act of 1968 ("Fair Housing Act" or "the Act") against defendants-appellants Starrett City Associates, Starrett City, Inc. and Delmar Management Company (collectively, "Starrett") in the United States District Court for the Eastern District of New York (Neaher, J.). The government maintained that Starrett's practices of renting apartments in its Brooklyn housing complex solely on the basis of applicants' race or national origin, and of making apartments unavailable to black and hispanic applicants that are then made available to white applicants, violate section 804(a), (b), (c) and (d) of the Act, 42 U.S.C. § 3604(a)-(d) (1982).

The parties made cross-motions for summary judgment based on extensive documentary submissions. The district court granted summary judgment in favor of the government and permanently enjoined appellants

30. Courts often expand upon the statutory provisions. *See, e.g., Marina Point, Ltd. v. Wolfson*, 30 Cal.3d 721, 180 Cal.Rptr. 496, 640 P.2d 115 (1982) (holding that Act bars discrimination against potential tenants with children); *Smith v. Fair Employment and Housing Comm'n*, 12 Cal.4th 1143, 51 Cal. Rptr.2d 700, 913 P.2d 909 (1996) (rejecting a constitutional challenge to a statutory provision prohibiting housing discrimination based on marital status, even though the landlord had a genuine religious belief that it was sinful to rent an apartment to an unmarried couple). The courts have, however, recognized limited exceptions. *See, e.g., Roth v. Rhodes*, 25 Cal.App.4th 530, 537–39, 30 Cal. Rptr.2d 706, 709–10 (1994) (allowing landlord to rent office space only to medical doctors, and not podiatrists); *Harris v. Capital Growth Investors XIV*, 52 Cal.3d 1142, 278 Cal.Rptr. 614, 805 P.2d 873 (1991) (landlord's minimum income policy for tenants did not violate the Unruh Act because it involved an economic status rather than a personal characteristic).

from discriminating on the basis of race in the rental of apartments. Starrett appeals from this judgment.

BACKGROUND

Appellants constructed, own and operate "Starrett City," the largest housing development in the nation, consisting of 46 high-rise buildings containing 5,881 apartments in Brooklyn, New York. The complex's rental office opened in December 1973. Starrett has made capital contributions of $19,091,000 to the project, the New York State Housing Finance Agency has made $362,720,000 in mortgage loans, and the U.S. Department of Housing and Urban Development subsidizes Starrett's monthly mortgage interest payments. The United Housing Foundation abandoned a project to build a development of cooperative apartments at the Starrett City site in 1971. Starrett proposed to construct rental units on the site on the condition that the New York City Board of Estimate approve a transfer to Starrett of the city real estate tax abatement granted to the original project. The transfer created "substantial community opposition" because "the neighborhood surrounding the project and past experience with subsidized housing" created fear that "the conversion to rental apartments would result in Starrett City's becoming an overwhelmingly minority development." *United States v. Starrett City Assocs.*, 660 F.Supp. 668, 670 (E.D.N.Y.1987). The transfer was approved, however, "upon the assurance of Starrett City's developer that it was intended to create a racially integrated community."

Starrett has sought to maintain a racial distribution by apartment of 64% white, 22% black and 8% hispanic at Starrett City. Starrett claims that these racial quotas are necessary to prevent the loss of white tenants, which would transform Starrett City into a predominantly minority complex. Starrett points to the difficulty it has had in attracting an integrated applicant pool from the time Starrett City opened, despite extensive advertising and promotional efforts. Because of these purported difficulties, Starrett adopted a tenanting procedure to promote and maintain the desired racial balance. This procedure has resulted in relatively stable percentages of whites and minorities living at Starrett City between 1975 and the present.

The tenanting procedure requires completion of a preliminary information card stating, *inter alia*, the applicant's race or national origin, family composition, income and employment. The rental office at Starrett City receives and reviews these applications. Those that are found preliminarily eligible, based on family composition, income, employment and size of apartment sought, are placed in "the active file," in which separate records by race are maintained for apartment sizes and income levels. Applicants are told in an acknowledgment letter that no apartments are presently available, but that their applications have been placed in the active file and that they will be notified when a unit becomes available for them. When an apartment becomes available, applicants are selected from the active file for final processing, creating a processed applicant pool. As vacancies arise, applicants of a race or national origin similar to that of the departing tenants are selected from the pool and offered apartments.

In December 1979, a group of black applicants brought an action against Starrett in the United States District Court for the Eastern District of New York. The district court certified the plaintiff class in June 1983. *Arthur v. Starrett City Assocs.*, 98 F.R.D. 500 (E.D.N.Y.1983). Plaintiffs alleged that Starrett's tenanting procedures violated federal and state law by discriminating against them on the basis of race. The parties stipulated to a settlement in May 1984, and a consent decree was entered subsequently, *see Arthur v. Starrett City Assocs.*, No. 79–CV–3096, slip op. at 1 (E.D.N.Y. April 2, 1985). The decree provided that Starrett would, depending on apartment availability, make an additional 35 units available each year for a five-year period to black and minority applicants.

The government commenced the present action against Starrett in June 1984, "to place before the [c]ourt the issue joined but left expressly unresolved" in the *Arthur* consent decree: the "legality of defendants' policy and practice of limiting the number of apartments available to minorities in order to maintain a prescribed degree of racial balance." *United States v. Starrett City Assocs.*, 605 F.Supp. 262, 263 (E.D.N.Y.1985). The complaint alleged that Starrett, through its tenanting policies, discriminated in violation of the Fair Housing Act. Specifically, the government maintained that Starrett violated the Act by making apartments unavailable to blacks solely because of race, 42 U.S.C. § 3604(a); by forcing black applicants to wait significantly longer for apartments than whites solely because of race, *id.* § 3604(b); by enforcing a policy that prefers white applicants while limiting the numbers of minority applicants accepted, *id.* § 3604(c); and by representing in an acknowledgment letter that no apartments are available for rental when in fact units are available, *id.* § 3604(d). * * *

Starrett maintained that the tenanting procedures "were adopted at the behest of the [s]tate solely to achieve and maintain integration and were not motivated by racial animus." To support their position, appellants submitted the written testimony of three housing experts. They described the "white flight" and "tipping" phenomena, in which white residents migrate out of a community as the community becomes poor and the minority population increases, resulting in the transition to a predominantly minority community. Acknowledging that " 'the tipping point for a particular housing development, depending as it does on numerous factors and the uncertainties of human behavior, is difficult to predict with precision,' " one expert stated that the point at which tipping occurs has been estimated at from 1% to 60% minority population, but that the consensus ranged between 10% and 20%. Another expert, who had prepared a report in 1980 on integration at Starrett City for the New York State Division of Housing and Community Renewal, estimated the complex's tipping point at approximately 40% black on a population basis. A third expert, who had been involved in integrated housing ventures since the 1950's, found that a 2:1 white-minority ratio produced successful integration.

The court, however, accepted the government's contention that Starrett's practices of making apartments unavailable for blacks, while reserving them for whites, and conditioning rental to minorities based on a "tipping formula" derived only from race or national origin are clear violations of the Fair Housing Act. The district court found that apartment opportunities for blacks and hispanics were far fewer "than would be expected if race and national origin were not taken into account," while opportunities for whites were substantially greater than what their application rates projected. Minority applicants waited up to ten times longer than the average white applicant before they were offered an apartment. Starrett City's active file was 21.9% white in October 1985, but whites occupied 64.7% of the apartments in January 1984. Although the file was 53.7% black and 18% hispanic in October 1985, blacks and hispanics, respectively, occupied only 20.8% and 7.9% of the apartments as of January 1984. Appellants did not dispute this. Further, the court found that appellants' tipping argument was undercut by the "wide elasticity of that standard" and the lack of difficulty they had in increasing their black quota from 21% to 35% "when it became necessary to avoid litigating the private *Arthur* lawsuit which threatened their unlawful rental practices." The court also found that Starrett violated the Act by making untrue representations of apartment unavailability to qualified minority applicants in order to reserve units for whites. Finally, the court rejected Starrett's claim that the duty imposed upon government to achieve housing integration justified its actions, stating that "[d]efendants cannot arrogate to themselves the powers" of a public housing authority.

The court concluded that Starrett's obligation was "simply and solely to comply with the Fair Housing Act" by treating "black and other minority applicants ... on the same basis as whites in seeking available housing at Starrett City." The court noted that Starrett did not dispute any of the operative facts alleged to show violations of the Fair Housing Act. Accordingly, Judge Neaher granted summary judgment for the government, enjoining Starrett from discriminating against applicants on the basis of race and "[r]equiring [them] to adopt written, objective, uniform, nondiscriminatory tenant selection standards and procedures" subject to the court's approval. The court retained jurisdiction over the parties for three years.

On appeal, Starrett presses arguments similar to those it made before the district court. We affirm the district court's judgment.

DISCUSSION

Title VIII of the Civil Rights Act of 1968 ("Fair Housing Act" or "the Act"), 42 U.S.C. §§ 3601–3631 (1982), was enacted pursuant to Congress' thirteenth amendment powers "to provide, within constitutional limitations, for fair housing throughout the United States." 42 U.S.C. § 3601. Section 3604 of the statute prohibits discrimination because of race, color or national origin in the sale or rental of housing by, *inter alia*: (1) refusing to rent or make available any dwelling, *id.* § 3604(a); (2) offering discriminatory "terms, conditions or privileges" of rental, *id.* § 3604(b); (3) making, printing or publishing "any notice, statement, or advertisement . . . that indicates any preference, limitation, or discrimination based on race, color . . . or national origin," *id.* § 3604(c); and (4) representing to any person "that any dwelling is not available for . . . rental when such dwelling is in fact so available," *id.* § 3604(d).

Housing practices unlawful under Title VIII include not only those motivated by a racially discriminatory purpose, but also those that disproportionately affect minorities. Section 3604 "is designed to ensure that no one is denied the right to live where they choose for discriminatory reasons." *See Southend Neighborhood Improv. Ass'n v. County of St. Clair,* 743 F.2d 1207, 1210 (7th Cir.1984). Although "not every denial, especially a temporary denial, of low-income public housing has a discriminatory impact on racial minorities" in violation of Title VIII, *see Arthur v. City of Toledo,* 782 F.2d 565, 577 (6th Cir.1986), an action leading to discriminatory effects on the availability of housing violates the Act, *see Southend Neighborhood Improv. Ass'n,* 743 F.2d at 1209–10.

Starrett's allocation of public housing facilities on the basis of racial quotas, by denying an applicant access to a unit otherwise available solely because of race, produces a "discriminatory effect . . . [that] could hardly be clearer," *Burney v. Housing Auth.,* 551 F.Supp. 746, 770 (W.D.Pa.1982). Appellants do not contend that the plain language of section 3604 does not proscribe their practices. Rather, they claim to be "clothed with governmental authority" and thus obligated, under *Otero v. New York City Housing Auth.,* 484 F.2d 1122 (2d Cir.1973), to effectuate the purpose of the Fair Housing Act by affirmatively promoting integration and preventing "the reghettoization of a model integrated community." We need not decide whether Starrett is a state actor, however. Even if Starrett were a state actor with such a duty, the racial quotas and related practices employed at Starrett City to maintain integration violate the antidiscrimination provisions of the Act.

Both Starrett and the government cite to the legislative history of the Fair Housing Act in support of their positions. This history consists solely of statements from the floor of Congress. These statements reveal "that at the time that Title VIII was enacted, Congress believed that strict adherence to the anti-discrimination provisions of the [A]ct" would eliminate "racially discriminatory housing practices [and] ultimately would result in residential integration." *Burney,* 551 F.Supp. at 769. Thus, Congress saw the antidiscrimination policy as the means to effect the antisegregation-integration policy. While quotas promote Title VIII's integration policy, they contravene its antidiscrimination policy, bringing the dual goals of the Act into conflict. The legislative history provides no further guidance for resolving this conflict.

We therefore look to analogous provisions of federal law enacted to prohibit segregation and discrimination as guides in determining to what extent racial criteria may be used to maintain integration. Both the thirteenth amendment, pursuant to which Title VIII was enacted, and the fourteenth amendment empower Congress to act in eradicating racial discrimination and both the fourteenth amendment and Title VIII are informed by the congressional goal of eradicating racial discrimination through the principle of antidiscrimination. Further, the parallel between the antidiscrimination objectives of Title VIII and Title VII of the Civil Rights Act of 1964, 42 U.S.C. §§ 2000e–2000e–17 (1982), has been recognized. Thus, the Supreme Court's analysis of what constitutes permissible race-conscious affirmative action under provisions of federal law with goals similar to those of Title VIII provides a framework for examining the affirmative use of racial quotas under the Fair Housing Act.

Although any racial classification is presumptively discriminatory, a race-conscious affirmative action plan does not necessarily violate federal constitutional or statutory provisions. However, a race-conscious plan cannot be "ageless in [its] reach into the past, and timeless in [its] ability to affect the future." *Wygant v. Jackson Bd. of Educ.*, 476 U.S. 267 (1986) (plurality opinion). A plan employing racial distinctions must be temporary in nature with a defined goal as its termination point. *See, e.g., Johnson v. Transportation Agency*, 107 S.Ct. 1442, 1456 (1987). Moreover, we observe that societal discrimination alone seems "insufficient and over expansive" as the basis for adopting so-called "benign" practices with discriminatory effects "that work against innocent people," *Wygant*, 106 S.Ct. at 1848, in the drastic and burdensome way that rigid racial quotas do. Furthermore, the use of quotas generally should be based on some history of racial discrimination within the entity seeking to employ them. Finally, measures designed to increase or ensure minority participation, such as "access" quotas, *see Burney*, 551 F.Supp. at 763, have generally been upheld, *see, e.g., Johnson*, 107 S.Ct. at 1456–57. However, programs designed to maintain integration by limiting minority participation, such as ceiling quotas, *see Burney*, 551 F.Supp. at 763, are of doubtful validity, *see Jaimes*, 833 F.2d at 1207 (invalidating public housing authority integration plan to the extent it acts as strict racial quota), because they " 'single[ ] out those least well represented in the political process to bear the brunt of a benign program,' " *Fullilove*, 448 U.S. at 519, 100 S.Ct. at 2796 (Marshall, J., concurring) (quoting *Regents v. Bakke*, 438 U.S. 265, 361, 98 S.Ct. 2733, 2784, 57 L.Ed.2d 750 (1978) (Brennan, J., concurring in part and dissenting in part)).

Starrett's use of ceiling quotas to maintain integration at Starrett City lacks each of these characteristics. First, Starrett City's practices have only the goal of integration maintenance. The quotas already have been in effect for ten years. Appellants predict that their race-conscious tenanting practices must continue for at least fifteen more years, but fail to explain adequately how that approximation was reached. In any event, these practices are far from temporary. Since the goal of integration maintenance is purportedly threatened by the potential for "white flight" on a continuing basis, no definite termination date for Starrett's quotas is perceivable. Second, appellants do not assert, and there is no evidence to show, the existence of prior racial discrimination or discriminatory imbalance adversely affecting whites within Starrett City or appellants' other complexes. On the contrary, Starrett City was initiated as an integrated complex, and Starrett's avowed purpose for employing race-based tenanting practices is to maintain that initial integration. Finally, Starrett's quotas do not provide minorities with access to Starrett City, but rather act as a ceiling to their access. Thus, the impact of appellants' practices falls squarely on minorities, for whom Title VIII was intended to open up housing opportunities. Starrett claims that its use of quotas serves to keep the numbers of minorities entering Starrett City low enough to avoid setting off a wave of "white flight." Although the "white flight" phenomenon may be a factor "take[n] into account in the integration equation," *Parent Ass'n of Andrew Jackson High School v. Ambach*, 598 F.2d 705, 720 (2d Cir.1979), it cannot serve to justify attempts to maintain integration at Starrett City through inflexible racial quotas that are neither temporary in nature nor used to remedy past racial discrimination or imbalance within the complex.

Appellants' reliance on *Otero* is misplaced. In *Otero* the New York City Housing Authority ("NYCHA") relocated over 1800 families in the Lower East Side of Manhattan to make way for the construction of new apartment buildings. 484 F.2d at 1125. Pursuant to its regulations, NYCHA offered the former site occupants first priority of returning to any housing built within the urban renewal area. However, because the response by the largely minority former site residents seeking to return was nearly seven times greater than expected, NYCHA declined to follow its regulation in order to avoid creating a "pocket ghetto" that would "tip" an integrated community towards a predominantly minority community. It instead rented up half of these apartments to non-former site occupants, 88% of whom were white.

In a suit brought by former site occupants who were denied the promised priority, the district court held as a matter of law that "affirmative action to achieve racially balanced communities was not permitted where it would result in depriving minority groups" of public housing, and thus granted summary judgment in favor of plaintiffs. This court reversed the grant of summary judgment, stating that public housing authorities had a federal constitutional and statutory duty "to fulfill, as much as possible, the goal of open, integrated residential housing patterns and to prevent the increase of segregation, in ghettos," but we recognized that "the effect in some instances might be to prevent some members of a racial minority from residing in publicly assisted housing in a particular location."

Otero does not, however, control in this case. The challenge in *Otero* did not involve procedures for the long-term maintenance of specified levels of integration, but rather, the rental of 171 of 360 new apartments to non-former site occupants, predominantly white, although former site residents, largely minority, sought those apartments and were entitled to priority under NYCHA's own regulation. The *Otero* court did not delineate the statutory or constitutional limits on permissible means of integration, but held only that NYCHA's rent-up practice could not be declared invalid as a matter of law under those limits. In fact, the court in *Otero* observed that the use of race-conscious tenanting practices might allow landlords "to engage in social engineering, subject only to general undefined control through judicial supervision" and could "constitute a form of unlawful racial discrimination."

It is particularly important to note that the NYCHA action challenged in *Otero* only applied to a single event—the initial rent up of the new complexes—and determined tenancy in the first instance alone. NYCHA sought only to prevent the immediate creation of a "pocket ghetto" in the Lower East Side, which had experienced a steady loss of white population, that would tip the precarious racial balance there, resulting in increased white flight and inevitable "non-white ghettoization of the community." *Id.* at 1124. Further, the suspension of NYCHA's regulation did not operate as a strict racial quota, because the former site residents entitled to a rental priority were approximately 40% white, *id.* at 1128. As a one-time measure in response to the special circumstances of the Lower East Side in the early 1970's, the action challenged in *Otero* had an impact on non-whites as a group far less burdensome or discriminatory than Starrett City's continuing practices.

CONCLUSION

We do not intend to imply that race is always an inappropriate consideration under Title VIII in efforts to promote integrated housing. We hold only that Title VIII does not allow appellants to use rigid racial quotas of indefinite duration to maintain a fixed level of integration at Starrett City by restricting minority access to scarce and desirable rental accommodations otherwise available to them. We therefore affirm the judgment of the district court.

■ Jon O. Newman, Circuit Judge, dissenting:

Congress enacted the Fair Housing Act to prohibit racial segregation in housing. Starrett City is one of the most successful examples in the nation of racial integration in housing. I respectfully dissent because I do not believe that Congress intended the Fair Housing Act to prohibit the maintenance of racial integration in private housing.

I.

Starrett City is a privately owned apartment complex in Brooklyn. It consists of 46 high-rise buildings containing 5,881 rental units. Nearly 17,000 people live there. From its inception Starrett City has been planned and operated to achieve and maintain racial integration.

The complex was originally to have been built as a cooperatively owned housing development by the sponsor of Co–Op City in the Bronx. When financing was not obtained, the project was taken over by the current owner, whose business was rental housing. Because New York City had given the previous developer substantial tax abatements, the City's approval was necessary if Starrett City was to have the benefit of these tax abatements. The prospect of a large, low-income rental housing complex generated considerable political opposition within the City from those who feared that the project would attract only minority tenants. The new owner and the New York State Division of Housing and Community Renewal (DHCR) gave assurances that affirmative steps would be taken to maintain Starrett City as an integrated community. On these assurances, the New York City Board of Estimate approved the construction of Starrett City as a rental development.

At that time, DHCR policy called for an integration goal of 70% majority and 30% minority tenants in state-sponsored projects. The defendants adopted this goal for Starrett City. Since the size of tenants' families varied, the target percentages reflected the anticipated racial distribution of rental units, rather than of persons living in the complex. To reach its target of racial balance, Starrett City explicitly declined to rent on a first-come, first-served basis. Instead, reacting to the fact that Blacks and other minorities applied for apartments at Starrett City in far greater numbers than Whites, the management imposed ceilings on the number of apartments of various sizes that would be rented to Blacks and other minorities. As the number of tenants of each minority reached the ceiling for a particular size of apartment, subsequent applicants from that minority were placed on a waiting list until sufficient vacancies occurred to permit a rental to a member of that minority without exceeding the established ceiling.

As experience with this rental policy developed, Starrett City decided that it would permit the percentage of apartments rented to minorities to move above 30% and to reach approximately 35%. The components of this aggregate figure are 21% Black, 8% Hispanic, 4.5% Oriental, and 2% other or mixed. These figures have been fairly constant since 1976. During that period the minority percentage of the Starrett City *population* has been approximately 45%. In 1984, Starrett City agreed, as part of a settlement of a lawsuit brought by a class of Black applicants, to raise the minority rental unit percentage to 38% over five years.

The consequence of Starrett's policy of maintaining racial balance has been that Black applicants constitute a disproportionately larger share of the waiting list for apartments than do Whites, and remain on the list for considerably longer periods of time than do Whites. As of November 1985, Blacks made up approximately 54% of the waiting list while Whites filled approximately 22% of the places on the list. For a two-bedroom apartment, the average waiting time on the list for qualified applicants was twenty months for Blacks and two months for Whites; for a one-bedroom apartment, the comparable figures were eleven months and four months.

The development of Starrett City as an apartment complex committed to a deliberate policy of maintained racial integration has at all times occurred with the knowledge, encouragement, and financial support of the agency of the United States directly concerned with housing, the Department of Housing and Urban Development (HUD). Under a contract between HUD and Starrett City, the federal government pays all but one percent of the debt service of the mortgage loan extended to Starrett City by the New York State Housing Finance Agency (HFA). By March 1986 HUD had paid HFA more than $211 million on Starrett City's behalf. In exchange for this interest subsidy, Starrett City agreed to limit the rent for eligible tenants to a monthly figure specified by HUD or to a stated percentage of the tenant's monthly income (initially 25%, now 30%), whichever is greater. In addition, HUD has provided rental subsidies for tenants with low incomes. Since 1981 these rental subsidies have been nearly $22 million a year.

Despite its close cooperation in the development of Starrett City as an integrated housing complex, the United States now sues Starrett City to force it to abandon the rental policies that have enabled it to maintain racial integration. The bringing of the suit raises a substantial question as to the Government's commitment to integrated housing. The timing of the suit puts that commitment further in doubt. In 1979 a class of Black applicants for housing at Starrett City brought suit to challenge on federal statutory and constitutional grounds the same tenant selection policies at issue in this case. *Arthur v. Starrett City Associates*, 79 Civ. 3096 (ERN) (E.D.N.Y.1979). With the federal government observing from the sidelines, the parties to the *Arthur* litigation engaged in protracted settlement negotiations. More than four years later, a mutually advantageous settlement was reached. Starrett City was permitted to continue its policy of maintaining integration through its tenant selection policies. In return, Starrett City agreed to increase by three percent over five years the proportion of rental units occupied by minority tenants. At the same time, DHCR, the state housing agency, which was also a defendant in the *Arthur* litigation, agreed to take affirmative steps to promote housing opportunities for minorities in DHCR-supervised housing projects in New York City. Specifically, the State agency agreed to give a priority in other projects to minority applicants on the Starrett City waiting list. No member of the class of minority applicants for housing at Starrett City objected to the settlement. Thus, the needs of the minority class for whose benefit the suit had been brought were met to their satisfaction by providing for more rental opportunities both at Starrett City and elsewhere. Just one month after that settlement was reached, the United States filed this suit, ostensibly concerned with vindication of the rights of the same minority applicants for housing who had just settled their dispute on favorable terms.

II.

The only issue in this case is whether Starrett City's rental policies violate Title VIII of the Civil Rights Act of 1968, 42 U.S.C. §§ 3601–3631 (1982 & Supp. III 1985), generally known as the "Fair Housing Act." The United States has explicitly declined to assert any claim of a constitutional violation.

The defendants do not dispute that their rental policies fall within the literal language of Title VIII's prohibition on discriminatory housing practices. *See* 42 U.S.C. § 3604. Instead they contend that they are state actors for purposes of the Fourteenth Amendment, that their policies are to be tested under both the Fourteenth Amendment and the Fair Housing Act by the strict scrutiny standard of *Regents of the University of California v. Bakke*, 438 U.S. 265 (1978), and that they meet this test because their race-conscious policies further the compelling state interest of promoting integrated housing and are narrowly tailored to achieve that interest. At a minimum, they contend, they are entitled to a trial on the merits to prove their claim.

In my view, the defendants are entitled to prevail simply on the statutory issue to which the Government has limited its lawsuit. Though the terms of the statute literally encompass the defendants' actions, the statute was never intended to apply to such actions. This statute was intended to bar perpetuation of segregation. To apply it to bar maintenance of integration is precisely contrary to the congressional policy "to provide, within constitutional limitations, for fair housing throughout the United States." 42 U.S.C. § 3601.

We have been wisely cautioned by Learned Hand that "[t]here is no surer way to misread a document than to read it literally." *Guiseppi v. Walling*, 144 F.2d 608, 624 (2d Cir.1944) (concurring opinion), *aff'd sub nom. Gemsco, Inc. v. Walling*, 324 U.S. 244 (1945). That aphorism is not always true with respect to statutes, whose text is always the starting point for analysis and sometimes the ending point. But literalism is not always the appropriate approach even with statutes, as the Supreme Court long ago recognized: "It is a familiar rule, that a thing may be within the letter of the statute and yet not within the statute, because not within its spirit, nor within the intent of its makers." *Church of the Holy Trinity v. United States*, 143 U.S. 457, 459 (1892).

Title VIII bars discriminatory housing practices in order to end segregated housing. Starrett City is not promoting segregated housing. On the contrary, it is maintaining integrated housing. It is surely not within the spirit of the Fair Housing Act to enlist the Act to bar integrated housing. Nor is there any indication that application of the statute toward such a perverse end was within the intent of those who enacted the statute. It is true that there are some statements in the legislative history that broadly condemn discrimination for "any" reason. Senator Mondale, the principal sponsor of Title VIII, said that "we do not see any good reason or justification, in the first place, for permitting discrimination in the sale or rental of housing." 114 Cong.Rec. 5642 (1968). But his context, like that in which the entire debate occurred,[31] concerned maintenance of segregation, not integration. His point was that there was no reason for discriminating against a Black who wished to live in a previously all-White housing project. He explicitly decried the prospect that "we are going to live separately in white ghettos and Negro ghettos." *Id.* at 2276. The purpose of Title VIII, he said, was to replace the ghettos "by truly integrated and

---

31.   Because Title VIII was offered as a floor amendment in the Senate, there are no committee reports.

balanced living patterns." *Id.* at 3422. As he pointed out, "[O]ne of the biggest problems we face is the lack of experience in actually living next to Negroes." *Id.* at 2275. Starrett City is committed to the proposition that Blacks and Whites shall live next to each other. A law enacted to enhance the opportunity for people of all races to live next to each other should not be interpreted to prevent a landlord from maintaining one of the most successful integrated housing projects in America.

None of the legislators who enacted Title VIII ever expressed a view on whether they wished to prevent the maintenance of racially balanced housing. Most of those who passed this statute in 1968 probably could not even contemplate a private real estate owner who would deliberately set out to achieve a racially balanced tenant population. Had they thought of such an eventuality, there is not the slightest reason to believe that they would have raised their legislative hands against it.

This Circuit has previously ruled that Title VIII does not apply literally to prohibit racially based rental policies adopted to promote integration. *Otero v. New York City Housing Authority*, 484 F.2d 1122 (2d Cir.1973). In that case a public housing authority had committed itself by regulation to give first priority for rental housing to applicants who had been displaced by construction of the project. The housing authority then disregarded its own regulation, based on its apprehension that giving first priority to the class of those displaced from the site, most of whom were non-White, would cause the project to pass the so-called "tipping point" and become predominantly non-White. The first question in *Otero* was whether the authority's deliberate decision not to honor its priority policy because the benefitted class was predominantly non-White violated Title VIII. The Court held that the Act was not violated simply because a race-conscious decision had been made in connection with rental policy:

> Congress' desire in providing fair housing throughout the United States was to stem the spread of urban ghettos and to promote open, integrated housing, even though the effect in some instances might be to prevent some members of a racial minority from residing in publicly assisted housing in a particular location.

Id. at 1134.

Once the Court decided that a race-conscious rental policy did not necessarily violate the Act, it then faced the difficult issue in the case— whether the Act imposed an affirmative duty to promote integration of sufficient force to permit the authority to violate its own regulation. On that issue, the Court also ruled in favor of the authority, remanding for a trial at which the defendant could establish that its apprehension concerning a "tipping point" was well founded and that abandonment of its priority policy was necessary to promote integration.

Our case is much easier than *Otero*. Starrett City is not seeking to be released from a commitment it has previously made to any of the applicants for housing. To prevail it need not find in Title VIII some affirmative obligation compelling it to promote integration. It has freely chosen to promote integration and is entitled to prevail unless something in Title VIII forbids its voluntary policy. If anything in Title VIII prohibited race-conscious rental policies adopted to promote integration, *Otero* would have been summarily decided against the defendant.

Acknowledging the significance of the ruling in *Otero*, the Court distinguishes it essentially on the ground that *Otero* involved a policy of limited duration, applicable only to the period in which those displaced from the site were applying for housing in the new project, whereas Starrett City seeks to pursue a long-term policy of maintaining integration. I see nothing in the text or legislative history of Title VIII that supports such a distinction. If, as the Court holds, Title VIII bars Starrett City's race-conscious rental policy, even though adopted to promote and maintain integration, then it would bar such policies whether adopted on a short-term or a long-term basis. Since the Act makes no distinction among the durations of rental policies alleged to violate its terms, *Otero*'s upholding of a race-conscious rental policy adopted to promote integration cannot be ignored simply because the policy was of limited duration.[32]

But even if Title VIII can somehow be construed to make the lawfulness of a race-conscious rental policy that promotes integration turn on the duration of the policy, Starrett City is entitled to a trial so that it can prove its contention that its policy is still needed to maintain integration. * * *

Whether integration of private housing complexes should be maintained through the use of race-conscious rental policies that deny minorities an equal opportunity to rent is a highly controversial issue of social policy. There is a substantial argument against imposing any artificial burdens on minorities in their quest for housing. On the other hand, there is a substantial argument against forcing an integrated housing complex to become segregated, even if current conditions make integration feasible only by means of imposing some extra delay on minority applicants for housing. Officials of the Department of Justice are entitled to urge the former policy. Respected civil rights advocates like the noted psychologist, Dr. Kenneth Clark, are entitled to urge the latter policy, as he has done in an affidavit filed in this suit. That policy choice should be left to the

32. The Court, drawing a parallel between Title VIII and Title VII, which bars discrimination in employment, 42 U.S.C. § 2000e (1982), supports its view of Title VIII with Supreme Court decisions approving only limited use of race-conscious remedies under statutory and constitutional standards in the employment context. Though Titles VIII and VII share a common objective of combating discrimination, their differing contexts preclude the assumption that the law of affirmative action developed for employment is readily applicable to housing. The Title VII cases have not been concerned with a "tipping point" beyond which a work force might become segregated. Yet that is a demonstrated fact of life in the context of housing. *Cf. Parent Ass'n of Andrew Jackson High School v. Ambach*, 598 F.2d 705, 718–20 (2d Cir. 1979) (recognizing validity of a "tipping point" concern in the public school context in the course of framing a remedial desegregation decree). The statutory issue arising under Title VIII should be decided on the basis of what practices Congress was proscribing when it enacted this provision. Whether the constitutional standards for affirmative action differ between the employment and housing contexts need not be considered since the Government has explicitly declined in this litigation to advance any claim of unconstitutional action.

individual decisions of private property owners unless and until Congress or the New York legislature decides for the Nation or for New York that it prefers to outlaw maintenance of integration. I do not believe Congress made that decision in 1968, and it is a substantial question whether it would make such a decision today. Until Congress acts, we should not lend our authority to the result this lawsuit will surely bring about. In the words of Dr. Clark:

> [I]t would be a tragedy of the highest magnitude if this litigation were to lead to the destruction of one of the model integrated communities in the United States.

Because the Fair Housing Act does not require this tragedy to occur, I respectfully dissent.

---

1. *Traditional Statutory Interpretation.* The traditional role of courts in statutory interpretation is to determine what the legislature intended when it enacted the statute. The two opinions in *Starrett City* nicely illustrate the different approaches to this task. The majority opinion emphasizes the language of the statute. The dissent also considers the language of the statute but concludes that it is not necessarily determinative (recall Learned Hand's cautionary aphorism). The dissent emphasizes the purpose of the statute and its historical backdrop. Which opinion provides a more persuasive account of what Congress intended? Which provides a better method of statutory interpretation? *See* Ehrman, Integration versus Antidiscrimination: Which Policy Should Prevail When Applying the Fair Housing Act? 24 Mem. St. U. L. Rev. 33 (1993); Kushner, The Fair Housing Amendments Act of 1988: The Second Generation of Fair Housing, 42 Vand. L. Rev. 1049, 1116–17 (1989); Note, The Legality of Integration Maintenance Quotas: Fair Housing or Forced Housing?, 55 Brooklyn L. Rev. 197 (1989).

2. *Dynamic Statutory Interpretation.* Should it matter that a statute is twenty-years old and that the underlying issues, social dynamics, and societal attitudes have changed? To what extent should a court interpreting such a statute go further than the enacting legislature expressly intended? To what extent should a court change or shape its interpretation with the times?

Is it legitimate, within our constitutional structure, for courts to play such an active role in statutory interpretation? Is it unwise for the court to go beyond the text of the statute? Not only are legislative statements and reports unreliable indicators of legislative intentions (never having been enacted into law, they did not receive explicit majority support), but the courts' use of such documents invites interest groups to manipulate the legislative history. In addition, restricting interpretation to legislative text may force the legislature to deal more openly with controversial issues, rather than leave them to the "policy lottery" of subsequent judicial interpretation. On the other hand, given the demands on a modern legislature, is it realistic to expect the legislature to revisit the issues in a timely fashion? Can the legislature implicitly leave to the courts the authority to develop new interpretations as the circumstances warrant? In light of these questions, which opinion in *Starrett City* is the more "activist"? *See generally* Macey, Promoting Public–Regarding Legislation Through Statutory Interpretation, An Interest Group Model, 86 Colum. L. Rev. 223 (1986); Eskridge, Public Values in Statutory Interpretation, 137 U. Pa. L. Rev. 1007 (1989); Sunstein, Interpreting Statutes in the Regulatory State, 103 Harv. L. Rev. 405 (1989); W.K. Eskridge, Jr., Dynamic Statutory Interpretation (1994); Eskridge & Frickey, Statutory Interpretation as Practical Reasoning, 42 Stan. L. Rev. 321 (1990); Rodriguez, The Substance of the New Legal Process, 77 Cal. L. Rev. 919 (1989); Scalia, Judicial Deference to Administrative Interpretations of Law, 1989 Duke L.J. 511.

3. *Neighborhood Tipping.* As reflected in Judge Newman's opinion, a powerful rationale for the tenant selection system developed by Starrett City is to prevent the residential community from becoming segregated. Social scientists in the 1950s and 1960s found strong evidence that many neighborhoods underwent a systematic process whereby racial segregation becomes inevitable after the percentage of non-whites in a community rises above a certain point, what has been called the tipping point. Morton Grodzins concluded that many white residents will exit a neighborhood after the percentage of non-white residents reaches 20 percent of that neighborhood's population. Grodzins, Metropolitan Segregation, 197 Sci. Amer. 24 (1957). Grodzins concludes that "[t]he tip-point phenomenon is so universal that it constitutes strong evidence in favor of control. Without control, there has been a total failure to achieve interracial communities."

Under the assumptions that Congress did, as Judge Newman argues, intend to "bar perpetuation of segregation" in the enactment of the Fair Housing Act and that Starrett City would become increasingly non-white in its racial make-up without its tenant selection system, does the Fair Housing Act prohibit the rental practices in question in this case?

Is the tipping phenomenon "universal" today? Has America moved beyond the point at which we can expect neighborhoods to become irreversibly segregated once the percentage of non-whites exceeds some percentage? Or does this phenomenon remain potent in many, even if not all, contexts?

A more recent survey reveals that a majority of white Americans do not object to living in integrated neighborhoods and that 30 to 50% say they prefer integrated neighborhoods to all-white neighborhoods. Comment, Individual Rights and Democratic Realities: The Problem of Fair Housing, 82 Nw. U.L. Rev. 874, 896 (1988). Studies also show that once the racial barrier in a neighborhood is broken, "black demand [for housing] grows rapidly given the high value placed on integrated housing," stabilizes when African Americans comprise 50–70% of a neighborhood, and declines above that point. D.S. Massey & N.A. Denton, American Apartheid: Segregation and the Making of the Underclass 95–96 (1993). What are the implications of these findings for the issues raised in *Starrett City*?

4. *Affirmative Action in Housing.* Even if the tipping phenomenon continues to operate, should the government institute or permit "affirmative action" to prevent it? *See* Kushner, The Fair Housing Amendments Act of 1988: The Second Generation of Fair Housing, 42 Vand. L. Rev. 1049, 1115 (1989) (noting that "the House rejected an amendment designed to prohibit affirmative action"); D. Bell, And We Are Not Saved: The Elusive Quest for Racial Justice 153 (1989) ("A so-called benign housing quota seems invidious to the blacks excluded by its operation. They are no less victims of housing bias than are those excluded from neighborhoods by restrictive covenants."). Is a policy favoring the rental of apartments to whites for the purpose of maintaining racial balance a valid form of affirmative action? *See* Goel, Maintaining Integration Against Minority Interests: An Anti–Subjugation Theory for Equality in Housing, 22 Urb. Law. 369 (1990). Does the majority in *Starrett City* allow any use of race-conscious policies to prevent segregation? *Cf. South-Suburban Housing Center v. Greater South Suburban Board of Realtors*, 935 F.2d 868 (7th Cir.1991) (authorizing landlord to actively solicit white tenants in order to promote integration). Should the government seek to stabilize racial diversity within communities?

5. *Social Construction of Race.* Critical race scholars view race as a social construction. *See generally* Haney Lopez, The Social Construction of Race: Some Observations on Illusion, Fabrication, and Choice, 29 Harv. C.R.–C.L. L. Rev. 1 (1994); Harris, Whiteness as Property, 106 Harv. L. Rev. 1709 (1993); Bell, Xerces and the Affirmative Action Mystique, 57 Geo. Wash. L. Rev. 1595 (1989). They call for a transformation of this social construction in order to combat racial oppression. Professor Martha Mahoney has argued that

> race derives much of its power from seeming to be a natural or biological phenomenon or, at the very least, a coherent social category. For whites, residential segregation is one of the forces giving race a "natural" appearance: "good" neighborhoods are equated with whiteness, and "black" neighborhoods are equated with joblessness.

Segregation, Whiteness, and Transformation, 143 U. Pa. L. Rev. 1659, 1661 (1995). What are the implications of this perspective for the issues presented in *Starrett City*? Does the very concept of a tipping point legitimate a derogatory and hence counter-productive construction of race? Are policies aimed at integration and assimilation, as opposed to non-discrimination, empowerment of underrepresented minorities, and respect for distinct communities, a source of racial problems?

6. One curious feature of *Starrett City* is that the United States, which was the plaintiff, limited its attack on Starrett City's system for selecting tenants to violations of the federal Fair Housing Act and did not allege that these practices violated the equal protection clause of the 14th Amendment. This case was brought during the Reagan administration. It is fair to say that the Department of Justice at that time did not wish to see federal constitutional protections against racial discrimination expanded.

But why did the Department of Justice pursue this case at all, especially in light of the successful settlement (without opposition) of the *Arthur* litigation just a few months prior to the filing by the federal government? Is it clear that the outcome in this case served the interests of African Americans? Will the African Americans who ultimately gain access to Starrett City in less time, because of the prohibition upon multiple waiting lists, be served by the court's decision? What about the existing residents of Starrett City? The surrounding community? If the ultimate outcome of this controversy is to undermine the racial balance of Starrett City, will the purposes of the Fair Housing Act have been served?

7. *Epilogue.* Four years after the *Starrett City* decision, the percentage of white residents of Starrett City had declined from 62 percent to 50 percent. The chairman of the management company predicted that Starrett City would likely become a "totally minority community" within the decade if the trend continued. *See* Sam Roberts, White Tilt to Balance a Project in Canarsie, N.Y. Times, Aug. 4, 1992, at B3.

The prediction has not proven to be accurate, although for reasons that could not have been anticipated at the time that the prediction was made. During the early 1990s, the New York City area saw a large influx of Russian émigrés resulting from the liberalization of immigration policies following the break-up of the Soviet Union. At the same time, the federal government implemented a preference program that gave priority to this group (among others). Starrett City already had a sizable Russian émigré community, and hence may of the newer émigrés were attracted to Starrett City. Because of the federal preference program, these applicants skipped over the waiting list, which had the effect of stabilizing the size of the white population at about half. Starrett City currently (as of 1997) has a population that is 53% Caucasian and 47% minority. Although the preference program is no longer in effect, it is likely that Starrett City will remain racially integrated well into the future, if for no other reason than that the turnover rate is low.

* * *

Problems

1. In 1974, Congress created the Section 8 Housing Assistance Payments Program which provides low-income and minority households with housing certificates to rent privately owned apartments that rent at or below fair market rent. The Department of Housing and Urban Development, though local agencies, subsidizes participating landlords by paying the difference between the tenants' contribution (30 percent of their income) and the actual rental price. Hence the vouchers vary in value, but their effect is the same—enabling low income households to keep their total housing cost down to 30 percent of their income.

Anita and Gregory Phillips, an African American couple with three children, qualified for the Section 8 program. With the assistance of the local housing agency, they answered an advertisement offering to rent a three-bedroom house in a predominantly white, middle-class suburb. After showing them the house, the landlord suggested that it was not large enough for them and he suggested that they see another house he had available that might be more suitable. That house, however, which was located in a predominantly African American neighborhood, had only two bedrooms. The landlord later acknowledged to an official of the local housing agency responsible for implementing Section 8 that he disliked the Section 8 program and that he would prefer that the agency not refer Section 8 certificate holders to his properties.

Is a landlord's unwillingness to rent to Section 8 participants, a significant percentage of whom are African American, a violation of the federal anti-discrimination law? What if the landlord based his policy on concerns about prospective tenants' ability to afford his housing? *See* Beck, Fighting Section 8 Discrimination: The Fair Housing Act's New Frontier, 31 Harv. C.R.–C.L. L. Rev. 155 (1996).

2.   Alex and Kim Gonzales, a young professional couple, were looking for a larger apartment in San Francisco in anticipation of the birth of their first child. Alex is a lawyer working for a well-known public interest organization. Kim is a social worker. They answered the following advertisement in a local newspaper: "Lovely three bedroom apartment overlooking the park. $1600/month. Call John Clancy at 594–6023." After seeing the apartment and meeting with John Clancy, the building manager, Alex and Kim indicated that they would like to take the rental. John invited them to his office to complete a rental application, which asked about their housing history, employment, financial circumstances, and references. Alex and Kim filled out the application on the spot. John quickly looked it over and commented that everything looked fine. He shook their hands and said he would send them a lease agreement the next day.

Alex received the application two days later. It looked fine to him, although he thought that the provision regarding the resolution of disputes seemed a bit one-sided. He left a message on John's answering machine stating that he wanted the apartment, explaining his concerns about the dispute resolution provision, and asking John to return his call as soon as possible. When Alex returned home that evening, he was surprised to hear a return message from John stating that the apartment was no longer available. Alex called John immediately to find out what had happened. The following conversation ensued:

John: "I am sorry but the apartment is no longer available."

Alex: "That doesn't make any sense. Three days ago you indicated that we could have the apartment. The only things that have happened since that time are that you sent us a rental agreement, I left you a message asking to discuss one of the terms, and I gave notice to my current landlord that we would be moving out in a month. What gives?"

John: "Well, I have had trouble renting to lawyers in the past, and I didn't want to get into hassles. Someone else who wasn't a lawyer answered the ad and I decided to go with her instead."

Do Alex and Kim have a valid discrimination claim? Should they? Suppose that the advertisement had stated the following: "Lovely three bedroom apartment overlooking the park. $1600/month. Call John Clancy at 594–6023. Lawyers should not apply." Would this advertisement be actionable?

---

4. TRANSFERABILITY OF LEASES

An important issue in many leases is whether the tenant may transfer—assign or sublet—the lease before expiration of the leasehold.[33] Tenants want to preserve some flexibility to transfer the lease if their financial circumstances have changed (*e.g.*, the tenant's business is no longer profitable) or if the leasing market has changed (*e.g.*, the leasehold has become more valuable and the tenant wants to capture the appreciation). Landlords, on the other hand, want to ensure that the rent checks will arrive without interruption, that the other lease covenants will be fulfilled, and that the person in possession will take reasonably good care of the premises. In short, the landlord wants to control who might become an assignee or subtenant, and may also want to capture any appreciation.

Before getting into the details of assignment and subleasing, we must begin with some basic terminology describing the relationship of the landlord and the original tenant. When the landlord conveys a leasehold to the tenant, he has conveyed a property interest. The landlord holds the reversion; if, for some reason, the leasehold came to an end, the leasehold would revert to the landlord. This ongoing property relationship between the landlord and tenant is called *privity of estate*. Privity is just a word for relationship.

The lease, however, is also a contract. It is a set of agreements by the landlord and tenant to fulfill specified (and sometimes implied) obligations. This ongoing contractual relationship is called *privity of contract*.

When the original parties initially agree to the lease, both types of privity exist, and they form the basis for the parties' legal obligations, such as the obligation to pay rent. The key point is that as long as either privity exists, the original tenant remains liable for all of the lease covenants.

a. ASSIGNMENT

Absent a release (*i.e.*, acceptance of surrender) from the landlord, a tenant usually cannot unilaterally abandon the leasehold without incurring

33. A tenant may transfer only a term of years or a periodic tenancy; a tenancy at will is not transferable. *See, e.g., Hunnicutt v. Head*, 179 Ala. 567, 60 So. 831 (1912).

substantial liability for the rent. In those circumstances, the tenant may assign her lease to another person.

Because an assignee takes the entire property interest that the landlord originally conveyed (and because the landlord still retains the reversion), the landlord and assignee are in privity of estate. The privity of estate between the landlord and the original tenant is dissolved. The landlord and assignee, however, are not in privity of contract; absent a new contract between the landlord and assignee, and absent the assignee's express assumption of the covenants in the original lease, there is no contractual relationship between them. *See, e.g., Shaffer v. George*, 64 Colo. 47, 50–51, 171 P. 881, 882 (1917); *Realty and Rebuilding Co. v. Rea*, 184 Cal. 565, 569, 194 P. 1024, 1026 (1920).

Because of privity of estate, during his occupancy the assignee is liable for covenants that "run with the land." A lease covenant runs with the land—*i.e.*, is binding on a successor without his express agreement—if the lease expresses the parties' intent that the covenant run with the land ("the tenant promises for himself and his assigns to pay rent in the amount of . . .") and the covenant "touches and concerns" the land (*i.e.*, affects the use or enjoyment of the land, including payment of rent). *See, e.g., Shaffer v. George*, 64 Colo. 47, 51, 171 P. 881, 882 (1917) (the assignee is liable for covenants that run with the land, such as the covenant to pay rent, the covenant to pay taxes, and the covenant to yield up the premises in good condition). However, because there is no contractual relationship between the assignee and the landlord, his obligations cease when he assigns his property interest to another assignee. *See, e.g., Bonfils v. McDonald*, 84 Colo. 325, 335, 270 P. 650, 654 (1928); *Kelly v. Tri–Cities Broadcasting, Inc.*, 147 Cal.App.3d 666, 676–78, 195 Cal.Rptr. 303, 308–10 (1983).

If the assignee expressly assumed the covenants in the lease, however, he would be in privity of contract with the landlord, and would be contractually obligated to fulfill all provisions until the privity of contract ended. *See, e.g., Broida v. Hayashi*, 51 Haw. 493, 497, 464 P.2d 285, 288 (1970) ("An assignee who covenants with the lessee to perform all the obligations in the original lease is liable to the lessee on privity of contract."); *Hartman Ranch Co. v. Associated Oil Co.*, 10 Cal.2d 232, 244–45, 73 P.2d 1163, 1169 (1937) (by assuming the lease, the assignee is bound by express and implied covenants in the original lease).

Although assignment breaks the privity of estate between the landlord and the original tenant, they continue to be in privity of contract. Neither the landlord's consent to assignment, nor even the assignee's express assumption of the lease provisions will break the original privity of contract. *See, e.g., Broida v. Hayashi*, 51 Haw. 493, 496–97, 464 P.2d 285, 288 (1970) (assignee's express assumption of the lease does not break the tenant's privity of contract with the landlord); *Sanford v. Sallan*, 263 Mich. 299, 300, 248 N.W. 628, 628–29 (1933) (absent a release, an assignment does not break the privity of contract); *De Hart v. Allen*, 26 Cal.2d 829, 832, 161 P.2d 453, 455 (1945). As a result, unless the landlord expressly or impliedly releases the original tenant from the contract, the tenant remains liable under the covenant to pay rent, even though she assigned the leasehold to someone else. The original tenant's liability, however, is as a surety; if the landlord successfully sues him for breach of a covenant that ran with the land, the original tenant may seek indemnity from the assignee. *McKee's Cash Store v. Otero*, 19 Ariz. 418, 424, 171 P. 910, 912 (1918) (assignee is liable to the original tenant for amounts the tenant paid to the landlord in damages).

b. SUBLEASE

A tenant may not want to assign the lease, but only transfer, or sublet, part of the leasehold. In a sublease, in contrast to an assignment, the original tenant retains a reversion in the leasehold. For example, in *Haynes v. Eagle–Picher Co.*, 295 F.2d 761 (10th Cir.1961), the assignee executed an agreement with Eagle–Picher, under which Eagle–Picher took possession of the property to operate it as a mine. The agreement provided that the property would revert to the assignee if, by a particular date, the mine was not producing a specified amount of mined material. On the agreed date, the mine was meeting the minimum production provision. The court held that before the agreed date, Eagle–Picher had only a sublease, because the original assignee retained a reversionary interest, even though it was contingent. After the agreed date, however, when the mine met the productivity criterion and the property did not revert, the agreement became an assignment. *Id.* at 763–64. *See also Bostonian Shoe Co. v. Wulwick Associates*, 119 A.D.2d 717, 719, 501 N.Y.S.2d 393, 394 (1986) (because the agreement required the leasehold to revert to the original tenant one day before expiration of the lease, the agreement was a sublease). In a minority of jurisdictions, even a reservation of a right of entry in the event of a broken condition creates a sublease rather than an assignment. *Hartman Ranch Co. v. Associated Oil Co.*, 10 Cal.2d 232, 243, 73 P.2d 1163, 1168 (1937).

The legal relationship between the landlord and the original tenant is not changed by a sublease. The landlord and the tenant remain in privity of estate *and* privity of contract, and thus the original tenant remains liable to the landlord for all covenants in the lease (and the landlord remains liable to the tenant). Because the subtenant has neither privity of estate nor privity of contract with the landlord, he is not liable to the landlord and the landlord is not liable to the subtenant for breach of any of the express or implied lease provisions. *Haynes v. Eagle–Picher Co.*, 295 F.2d 761, 763 (10th Cir.1961) (landlord has no cause of action against the subtenant, even though there is language in the original lease that sublessees would be bound by the terms of the master lease); *Davis v. Vidal*, 105 Tex. 444, 446, 151 S.W. 290, 291 (1912) (because the agreement was a sublease, the landlord had no cause of action against the subtenant).[34] The subtenant is

---

34. Conceivably, the landlord and subtenant are liable to each other in equity for covenants that run with the land. R. Cunningham, W. Stoebuck, D. Whitman, The Law of Property § 6.70 (2d ed. 1993).

liable only to the original tenant pursuant to the terms of their separate agreement.[35]

However, if the subtenant expressly assumed the obligations under the original lease, the landlord may hold the subtenant to the terms of the lease under a theory of third-party beneficiary. *Hartman Ranch Co. v. Associated Oil Co.*, 10 Cal.2d 232, 244–46, 73 P.2d 1163, 1169–70 (1937). Conversely, if the landlord expressly agreed to the sublease, the subtenant would be a third-party beneficiary who may sue the landlord for breach of the covenant of quiet enjoyment. *Marchese v. Standard Realty & Dev. Co.*, 74 Cal.App.3d 142, 147, 141 Cal.Rptr. 370, 373 (1977).

On occasion, the sublessor (*i.e.*, the original tenant) may voluntarily surrender his leasehold to the landlord. Even though the landlord accepts surrender (and he is under no obligation to do so), the subtenant's interest is unaffected. Because there is no privity of estate or contract between the landlord and the sublessee, the landlord has no authority to collect rent from the sublessee (or even sue for the value of the sublessee's use of the property) unless the landlord was careful to have the sublessor assign the landlord the right to receive rental payments as part of the surrender agreement. *Warnert v. MGM Properties*, 362 N.W.2d 364, 368 (Minn.Ct. App.1985) (the tenant's voluntary surrender of its leasehold did not entitle the landlord to possession of the property because the surrender did not extinguish the subtenant's interest under the sublease). If, however, the landlord terminated the sublessor's lease because of the sublessor's breach, the entire interest—including the sublessee's interest—would be forfeited to the landlord. *See, e.g., V.O.B. Co. v. Hang It Up, Inc.*, 691 P.2d 1157, 1159 (Colo.Ct.App.1984).

c.   LIMITATIONS ON ASSIGNMENT AND SUBLEASE

At common law, there were no restrictions on the tenant's right to assign or sublet his leasehold. At the same time, nothing prohibited the landlord from seeking and enforcing an explicit lease provision barring the tenant from assigning or subletting the leasehold. In a majority of jurisdictions today, such prohibitions on subleasing and assignment are valid. *See, e.g., Coulos v. Desimone*, 34 Wash.2d 87, 98, 208 P.2d 105, 111 (1949) (the landlord may refuse consent to an assignment "irrespective of the character of the proposed assignee and although [the landlord] is actuated by mere caprice or whim," quoting 32 Am. Jur. 305, 343); *Dress Shirt Sales, Inc. v. Hotel Martinique Assocs.*, 12 N.Y.2d 339, 342, 190 N.E.2d 10, 11, 239 N.Y.S.2d 660, 662 (1963) ("unless the lease provides that the lessor's consent shall not be unreasonably withheld," the lessor may "refuse arbitrarily for any reason or no reason").

---

35.   One exception is where the original tenant becomes insolvent. In that circumstance a court may order the subtenant to pay rent (under the terms of the sublease) directly to the landlord. *City Inv. Co. v. Pringle*, 73 Cal.App. 782, 788, 239 P. 302, 304 (1925).

In many states, however, courts readily find such provisions waived. If, for example, the landlord knowingly accepted rent from the assignee or sublessee, the landlord has waived his right to terminate the lease for breach. *Weisman v. Clark*, 232 Cal.App.2d 764, 768–69, 43 Cal.Rptr. 108, 111 (1965). Courts also strictly construe restrictions on subleasing and assignments against the landlord. For example, in *Drake v. Eggleston*, 123 Ind.App. 306, 313, 108 N.E.2d 67, 70 (1952), the court held that subletting only a portion of the residence did not violate the covenant not to sublet the premises without the landlord's consent. In *Willenbrock v. Latulippe*, 125 Wash. 168, 171, 215 P. 330, 331 (1923), the court held that a lease provision prohibiting subleasing did not prohibit assignment. *See also 24 Broad Street Corp. v. Quinn*, 19 N.J.Super. 21, 30, 87 A.2d 759, 763 (1952) (prohibition on transfer or assignment does not prohibit sublease). Moreover, even when the tenant breaches a covenant prohibiting subleasing or assignment, the transfer is not automatically void but rather "voidable" at the landlord's election; the assignment or sublease remains valid until the landlord seeks forfeiture. *Woods v. North Pier Terminal Co.*, 131 Ill.App.3d 21, 23–24, 86 Ill.Dec. 354, 356, 475 N.E.2d 568, 570 (1985) (assignment is valid, despite covenant restricting assignment, since landlord never objected to assignment).

More than a dozen states—by decision or by legislative reform—now hold that the landlord may not arbitrarily deny permission to sublet or assign. Rather, landlords must use "reasonable commercial standards" when deciding whether to accept or reject a subtenant or assignee. *See, e.g., Campbell v. Westdahl*, 148 Ariz. 432, 436–37, 715 P.2d 288, 292–93 (App. 1985); *Homa-Goff Interiors, Inc. v. Cowden*, 350 So.2d 1035, 1037–38 (Ala.1977); *Restatement (Second) of Property (Landlord and Tenant)* § 15.2.

Kendall v. Pestana

Supreme Court of California, 1985.
40 Cal.3d 488, 709 P.2d 837, 220 Cal.Rptr. 818.

■ BROUSSARD, JUSTICE.

This case concerns the effect of a provision in a commercial lease[36] that the lessee may not assign the lease or sublet the premises without the lessor's prior written consent. The question we address is whether, in the absence of a provision that such consent will not be unreasonably withheld, a lessor may unreasonably and arbitrarily withhold his or her consent to an assignment.[37] This is a question of first impression in this court.

36. We are presented only with a commercial lease and therefore do not address the question whether residential leases are controlled by the principles articulated in this opinion.

37. Since the present case involves an assignment rather than a sublease, we will speak primarily in terms of assignments. However, our holding applies equally to subleases. * * *

I.

* * *

The allegations of the complaint may be summarized as follows. The lease at issue is for 14,400 square feet of hangar space at the San Jose Municipal Airport. The City of San Jose, as owner of the property, leased it to Irving and Janice Perlitch, who in turn assigned their interest to respondent Ernest Pestana, Inc. Prior to assigning their interest to respondent, the Perlitches entered into a 25–year sublease with one Robert Bixler commencing on January 1, 1970. The sublease covered an original five-year term plus four 5–year options to renew. The rental rate was to be increased every 10 years in the same proportion as rents increased on the master lease from the City of San Jose. The premises were to be used by Bixler for the purpose of conducting an airplane maintenance business.

Bixler conducted such a business under the name "Flight Services" until, in 1981, he agreed to sell the business to appellants Jack Kendall, Grady O'Hara and Vicki O'Hara. The proposed sale included the business and the equipment, inventory and improvements on the property, together with the existing lease. The proposed assignees had a stronger financial statement and greater net worth than the current lessee, Bixler, and they were willing to be bound by the terms of the lease.

The lease provided that written consent of the lessor was required before the lessee could assign his interest, and that failure to obtain such consent rendered the lease voidable at the option of the lessor.[38] Accordingly, Bixler requested consent from the Perlitches' successor-in-interest, respondent Ernest Pestana, Inc. Respondent refused to consent to the assignment and maintained that it had an absolute right arbitrarily to refuse any such request. The complaint recites that respondent demanded "increased rent and other more onerous terms" as a condition of consenting to Bixler's transfer of interest.

The proposed assignees brought suit for declaratory and injunctive relief and damages seeking, inter alia, a declaration "that the refusal of ERNEST PESTANA, INC. to consent to the assignment of the lease is unreasonable and is an unlawful restraint on the freedom of alienation. . . ." * * *

II.

The law generally favors free alienability of property, and California follows the common law rule that a leasehold interest is freely alienable.

---

38. Paragraph 13 of the sublease between the Perlitches and Bixler provides: "Lessee shall not assign this lease, or any interest therein, and shall not sublet the said premises or any part thereof, or any right or privilege appurtenant thereto, or suffer any other person (the agents and servants of Lessee excepted) to occupy or use said premises, or any portion thereof, without written consent of Lessor first had and obtained, and a consent to one assignment, subletting, occu- pation or use by any other person, shall not be deemed to be a consent to any subsequent assignment, subletting, occupation or use by another person. Any such assignment or sub- letting without this consent shall be void, and shall, at the option of Lessor, terminate this lease. This lease shall not, nor shall any interest therein, be assignable, as to the in- terest of lessee, by operation of alaw [sic], without the written consent of Lessor."

Contractual restrictions on the alienability of leasehold interests are, however, permitted. "Such restrictions are justified as reasonable protection of
the interests of the lessor as to who shall possess and manage property in
which he has a reversionary interest and from which he is deriving
income." (Schoshinski, American Law of Landlord and Tenant (1980)
§ 8:15, at pp. 578–579. *See also* 2 Powell on Real Property, ¶ 246[1], at p.
372.97.)

The common law's hostility toward restraints on alienation has caused
such restraints on leasehold interests to be strictly construed against the
lessor. * * * This is particularly true where the restraint in question is a
"forfeiture restraint," under which the lessor has the option to terminate
the lease if an assignment is made without his or her consent.

Nevertheless, a majority of jurisdictions have long adhered to the rule
that where a lease contains an approval clause (a clause stating that the
lease cannot be assigned without the prior consent of the lessor), the lessor
may arbitrarily refuse to approve a proposed assignee no matter how
suitable the assignee appears to be and no matter how unreasonable the
lessor's objection. The harsh consequences of this rule have often been
avoided through application of the doctrines of waiver and estoppel, under
which the lessor may be found to have waived (or be estopped from
asserting) the right to refuse consent to assignment.

The traditional majority rule has come under steady attack in recent
years. A growing minority of jurisdictions now hold that where a lease
provides for assignment only with the prior consent of the lessor, such
consent may be withheld *only where the lessor has a commercially reasonable objection to the assignment*, even in the absence of a provision in the
lease stating that consent to assignment will not be unreasonably withheld.

For the reasons discussed below, we conclude that the minority rule is
the preferable position. * * *

III.

The impetus for change in the majority rule has come from two
directions, reflecting the dual nature of a lease as a conveyance of a
leasehold interest and a contract. *See Medico–Dental etc. Co. v. Horton &
Converse* (1942) 21 Cal.2d 411, 418, 132 P.2d 457. The policy against
restraints on alienation pertains to leases in their nature as *conveyances.*
Numerous courts and commentators have recognized that "[i]n recent
times the necessity of permitting reasonable alienation of commercial space
has become paramount in our increasingly urban society." *Schweiso v.
Williams, supra,* 150 Cal.App.3d at p. 887, 198 Cal.Rptr. 238.

Civil Code section 711 provides: "Conditions restraining alienation,
when repugnant to the interest created, are void." It is well settled that
this rule is not absolute in its application, but forbids only *unreasonable*
restraints on alienation. Reasonableness is determined by comparing the
justification for a particular restraint on alienation with the quantum of
restraint actually imposed by it. "[T]he greater the quantum of restraint

that results from enforcement of a given clause, the greater must be the justification for that enforcement." *Wellenkamp v. Bank of America*, 582 P.2d 970. In *Cohen v. Ratinoff, supra,* the court examined the reasonableness of the restraint created by an approval clause in a lease: "Because the lessor has an interest in the character of the proposed commercial assignee, we cannot say that an assignment provision requiring the lessor's consent to an assignment is inherently repugnant to the leasehold interest created. We do conclude, however, that *if such an assignment provision is implemented in such a manner that its underlying purpose is perverted by the arbitrary or unreasonable withholding of consent, an unreasonable restraint on alienation is established.*" (*Id.,* 147 Cal.App.3d at p. 329, 195 Cal.Rptr. 84, italics added.)

One commentator explains as follows: "The common-law hostility to restraints on alienation had a large exception with respect to estates for years. A lessor could prohibit the lessee from transferring the estate for years to whatever extent he might desire. It was believed that the objectives served by allowing such restraints outweighed the social evils implicit in the restraints, in that they gave to the lessor a needed control over the person entrusted with the lessor's property and to whom he must look for the performance of the covenants contained in the lease. Whether this reasoning retains full validity can well be doubted. Relationships between lessor and lessee have tended to become more and more impersonal. Courts have considerably lessened the effectiveness of restraint clauses by strict construction and liberal applications of the doctrine of waiver. With the shortage of housing and, in many places, of commercial space as well, the allowance of lease clauses forbidding assignments and subleases is beginning to be curtailed by statutes." (2 Powell, *supra,* ¶ 246[1], at pp. 372.97– 372.98, fns. omitted.)

The Restatement Second of Property adopts the minority rule on the validity of approval clauses in leases: "A restraint on alienation without the consent of the landlord of a tenant's interest in leased property is valid, *but the landlord's consent to an alienation by the tenant cannot be withheld unreasonably*, unless a freely negotiated provision in the lease gives the landlord an absolute right to withhold consent." (*Rest.2d Property*, § 15.2(2) (1977), italics added.)[39] A comment to the section explains: "The landlord may have an understandable concern about certain personal qualities of a tenant, particularly his reputation for meeting his financial obligations. The preservation of the values that go into the personal selection of the tenant justifies upholding a provision in the lease that curtails the right of the tenant to put anyone else in his place by transferring his interest, but this justification does not go to the point of allowing the landlord arbitrarily and without reason to refuse to allow the tenant to transfer an interest in leased property." (*Id.*, com. a.) Under the Restatement rule, the lessor's interest in the character of his or her tenant is

---

39. This case does not present the question of the validity of a clause absolutely prohibiting assignment, or granting absolute discretion over assignment to the lessor. We note that under the Restatement rule such a provision would be valid if freely negotiated.

protected by the lessor's right to object to a proposed assignee on reasonable commercial grounds. (*See id.*, reporter's note 7 at pp. 112–113.) The lessor's interests are also protected by the fact that the original lessee remains liable to the lessor as a surety even if the lessor consents to the assignment and the assignee expressly assumes the obligations of the lease.

The second impetus for change in the majority rule comes from the nature of a lease as a *contract*. As the Court of Appeal observed in *Cohen v. Ratinoff, supra*, "[s]ince *Richard v. Degan & Brody, Inc.* [espousing the majority rule] was decided, . . . there has been an increased recognition of and emphasis on the duty of good faith and fair dealing inherent in every contract." (*Id.*, 147 Cal.App.3d at p. 329, 195 Cal.Rptr. 84.) Thus, "[i]n every contract there is an implied covenant that neither party shall do anything which will have the effect of destroying or injuring the right of the other party to receive the fruits of the contract. . . ." *Universal Sales Corp. v. Cal. etc. Mfg. Co.* (1942) 20 Cal.2d 751, 771, 128 P.2d 665. "[W]here a contract confers on one party a discretionary power affecting the rights of the other, a duty is imposed to exercise that discretion in good faith and in accordance with fair dealing." *Cal. Lettuce Growers v. Union Sugar Co.* (1955) 45 Cal.2d 474, 484, 289 P.2d 785. Here the lessor retains the discretionary power to approve or disapprove an assignee proposed by the other party to the contract; this discretionary power should therefore be exercised in accordance with commercially reasonable standards. "Where a lessee is entitled to sublet under common law, but has agreed to limit that right by first acquiring the consent of the landlord, we believe the lessee has a right to expect that consent will not be unreasonably withheld." *Fernandez v. Vazquez, supra*, 397 So.2d at p. 1174; *accord, Boss Barbara, Inc. v. Newbill, supra*, 638 P.2d at p. 1086.[40]

Under the minority rule, the determination whether a lessor's refusal to consent was reasonable is a question of fact. Some of the factors that the trier of fact may properly consider in applying the standards of good faith and commercial reasonableness are: financial responsibility of the proposed assignee; suitability of the use for the particular property; legality of the proposed use; need for alteration of the premises; and nature of the occupancy, *i.e.*, office, factory, clinic, etc.

Denying consent solely on the basis of personal taste, convenience or sensibility is not commercially reasonable. Nor is it reasonable to deny consent "in order that the landlord may charge a higher rent than originally contracted for." *Schweiso v. Williams, supra*, 150 Cal.App.3d at p. 886. This is because the lessor's desire for a better bargain than contracted for has nothing to do with the permissible purposes of the restraint on alienation—to protect the lessor's interest in the preservation of the property and the performance of the lease covenants. " '[T]he clause is for the protection of the landlord *in its ownership and operation of the particular property*—not for its general economic protection.' "(*Ringwood*

---

40. Some commentators have drawn an analogy between this situation and the duties of good faith and reasonableness implied in all transactions under the Uniform Commercial Code.

Associates v. Jack's of Route 23, Inc., supra, 379 A.2d at p. 512, quoting *Krieger v. Helmsley–Spear, Inc.* (1973) 62 N.J. 423, 302 A.2d 129, italics added.)

In contrast to the policy reasons advanced in favor of the minority rule, the majority rule has traditionally been justified on three grounds. Respondent raises a fourth argument in its favor as well. None of these do we find compelling.

First, it is said that a lease is a conveyance of an interest in real property, and that the lessor, having exercised a personal choice in the selection of a tenant and provided that no substitute shall be acceptable without prior consent, is under no obligation to look to anyone but the lessee for the rent. This argument is based on traditional rules of conveyancing and on concepts of freedom of ownership and control over one's property.

A lessor's freedom at common law to look to no one but the lessee for the rent has, however, been undermined by the adoption in California of a rule that lessors—like all other contracting parties—have a duty to mitigate damages upon the lessee's abandonment of the property by seeking a substitute lessee. Furthermore, the values that go into the personal selection of a lessee are preserved under the minority rule in the lessor's right to refuse consent to assignment on any commercially reasonable grounds. Such grounds include not only the obvious objections to an assignee's financial stability or proposed use of the premises, but a variety of other commercially reasonable objections as well. (*See, e.g., Arrington v. Walter E. Heller Int'l Corp.* (1975) 30 Ill.App.3d 631, 333 N.E.2d 50 (desire to have only one "lead tenant" in order to preserve "image of the building" as tenant's international headquarters); *Warmack v. Merchants Nat'l Bank of Fort Smith* (Ark.1981) 612 S.W.2d 733 (desire for good "tenant mix" in shopping center); *List v. Dahnke* (Colo.App.1981) 638 P.2d 824 (lessor's refusal to consent to assignment of lease by one restaurateur to another was reasonable where lessor believed proposed specialty restaurant would not succeed at that location).) The lessor's interests are further protected by the fact that the original lessee remains a guarantor of the performance of the assignee.

The second justification advanced in support of the majority rule is that an approval clause is an unambiguous reservation of absolute discretion in the lessor over assignments of the lease. The lessee could have bargained for the addition of a reasonableness clause to the lease (*i.e.,* "consent to assignment will not be unreasonably withheld"). The lessee having failed to do so, the law should not rewrite the parties' contract for them.

Numerous authorities have taken a different view of the meaning and effect of an approval clause in a lease, indicating that the clause is not "clear and unambiguous," as respondent suggests. As early as 1940, the court in *Granite Trust Bldg. Corp. v. Great Atlantic & Pacific Tea Co.*, 36 F.Supp. 77, examined a standard approval clause and stated: "It would seem to be the better law that when a lease restricts a lessee's rights by requiring consent before these rights can be exercised, *it must have been in the contemplation of the parties that the lessor be required to give some reason for withholding consent.*" (*Id.*, at p. 78, italics added.) * * *

In light of th[is and other] interpretations given to approval clauses * * *, and in light of the increasing number of jurisdictions that have adopted the minority rule in the last 15 years, the assertion that an approval clause "clearly and unambiguously" grants the lessor absolute discretion over assignments is untenable. It is not a rewriting of a contract, as respondent suggests, to recognize the obligations imposed by the duty of good faith and fair dealing, which duty is implied by law in every contract.

The third justification advanced in support of the majority rule is essentially based on the doctrine of stare decisis. It is argued that the courts should not depart from the common law majority rule because "many leases now in effect covering a substantial amount of real property and creating valuable property rights were carefully prepared by competent counsel in reliance upon the majority viewpoint." *Gruman v. Investors Diversified Services*, 78 N.W.2d at p. 381. As pointed out above, however, the majority viewpoint has been far from universally held and has never been adopted by this court. Moreover, the trend in favor of the minority rule should come as no surprise to observers of the changing state of real property law in the 20th century. The minority rule is part of an increasing recognition of the contractual nature of leases and the implications in terms of contractual duties that flow therefrom. We would be remiss in our duty if we declined to question a view held by the majority of jurisdictions simply because it is held by a majority. As we stated in *Rodriguez v. Bethlehem Steel Corp.* (1974) 12 Cal.3d 382, 115 Cal.Rptr. 765, 525 P.2d 669, the "vitality [of the common law] can flourish only so long as the courts remain alert to their obligation and opportunity to change the common law when reason and equity demand it."

A final argument in favor of the majority rule is advanced by respondent and stated as follows: "Both tradition and sound public policy dictate that the lessor has a right, under circumstances such as these, to realize the increased value of his property." Respondent essentially argues that any increase in the market value of real property during the term of a lease properly belongs to the lessor, not the lessee. We reject this assertion. One California commentator has written: "[W]hen the lessee executed the lease he acquired the contractual right for the exclusive use of the premises, and all of the benefits and detriment attendant to possession, for the term of the contract. He took the downside risk that he would be paying too much rent if there should be a depression in the rental market. . . . Why should he be deprived of the contractual benefits of the lease because of the fortuitous inflation in the marketplace[?] By reaping the benefits he does not deprive the landlord of anything to which the landlord was otherwise entitled. The landlord agreed to dispose of possession for the limited term and he could not reasonably anticipate any more than what was given to him by the terms of the lease. His reversionary estate will benefit from the increased value from the inflation in any event, at least upon the expiration of the lease." (4 Miller & Starr, Current Law of Cal. Real Estate (1977) 1984 supp., § 27:92 at p. 321.)

Respondent here is trying to get *more* than it bargained for in the lease. A lessor is free to build periodic rent increases into a lease, as the lessor did here. Any increased value of the property beyond this "belongs" to the lessor only in the sense, as explained above, that the lessor's reversionary estate will benefit from it upon the expiration of the lease. We must therefore reject respondent's argument in this regard. * * *

■ LUCAS, JUSTICE, dissenting.

I respectfully dissent. In my view we should follow the weight of authority which, as acknowledged by the majority herein, allows the commercial lessor to withhold his consent to an assignment or sublease arbitrarily or without reasonable cause. The majority's contrary ruling, requiring a "commercially reasonable objection" to the assignment, can only result in a proliferation of unnecessary litigation.

The correct analysis is contained in the opinion of Justice Carl Anderson for the Court of Appeal in this case. I adopt the following portion of his opinion as my dissent:

" * * * The plain language of the lease provides that the lessee shall not assign the lease 'without written consent of Lessor first had and obtained. . . . Any such assignment or subletting without this consent shall be void, and shall, at the option of Lessor, terminate this lease.' The lease does not require that 'consent may not unreasonably be withheld'; the lease does not provide that 'the lessor may refuse consent only where he has a good faith reasonable objection to the assignment.' Neither have the parties so contracted, nor has the Legislature so required. Absent such legislative direction, the parties should be free to contract as they see fit.

"Appellant urges this court to rewrite the contract by adding a limitation on the lessor's withholding of consent—'that such consent may not be unreasonably withheld.' He urges that such must be implied in the term 'without written consent of lessor first had and obtained'; and he places the burden on the lessor to add language to negate that, if such be his intent—language such as 'such consent may be arbitrarily, capriciously and/or unreasonably withheld.'

"However, it is obvious that the attorney for the lessor agreeing to such a term was entitled to rely upon the state of the law then existing in California. And at such time (Dec. 12, 1969), it is clear that California followed the 'weight of authority' in these United States and allowed such consent to be arbitrarily or unreasonably withheld absent a provision to the contrary. (*Richard v. Degen & Brody, Inc.* (1960) 181 Cal.App.2d 289.) The *Richard v. Degen & Brody* court clearly held that the weight of authority as expressed in 51 Corpus Juris Secundum § 36 was the law of California: '. . . where a subletting or assignment of the leased premises without the consent of the lessor is prohibited, he [lessor] may withhold his assent arbitrarily and without regard to the qualifications of the proposed assignee, unless . . . the lease provides that consent shall not be arbitrarily or unreasonably withheld, and in granting his assent may impose such conditions as he sees fit.' " (*Id.* at p. 299.)

"Even those few jurisdictions and authorities which have rejected the 'arbitrary and capricious' rule have forthrightly recognized that in doing so, they depart from the majority * * *

"To rewrite this contract (as appellant would have us do) for the benefit of one who was not an original party thereto, and to the detriment of one who stands in privity with one who was, and to hold that there is a triable issue of fact concerning whether respondents unreasonably withheld their consent when they had already contracted for that right, creates only mischief by breeding further uncertainty in the interpretation of otherwise unambiguously written contracts. To so hold only encourages needless future litigation.

"We respectfully suggest that if California is to adopt the minority rule and reject the majority rule which recognizes the current proviso as valid, unambiguous and enforceable, that it do so by clear affirmative legislative action. To so defer to the legislative branch, protects not only this contract but 'those tens of thousands of landlords, tenants and lawyers who have relied on our unbroken line of judicial precedent.' "

I would affirm the judgment.

———

Following the *Kendall* decision, the state legislature enacted Cal. Civ. Code §§ 1995.010–1995.270, which both codified and amended the *Kendall* holding. Section 1995.010 restricts the new provisions to non-residential leases and § 1995.220 provides that any ambiguity in a restriction must be construed in favor of transferability. The other key provisions are:

California Civil Code

1995.230. **Prohibition on Transfer**. A restriction on transfer of a tenant's interest in a lease may absolutely prohibit transfer.

1995.240. **Standard or condition of transfer**. A restriction on transfer of a tenant's interest in a lease may provide that the transfer is subject to any express standard or condition, including, but not limited to, a provision that the landlord is entitled to some or all of any consideration the tenant receives from a transferee in excess of the rent under the lease.

1995.250. **Requirement of landlord's consent**. A restriction on transfer of a tenant's interest in a lease may require the landlord's consent for transfer subject to any express standard or condition for giving or withholding consent, including, but not limited to, either of the following:

(a) The landlord's consent may not be unreasonably withheld.

(b) The landlord's consent may be withheld subject to express standards or conditions.

1995.260. **Standard for giving or withholding consent**. If a restriction on transfer of the tenant's interest in a lease requires the landlord's consent for transfer but provides no standard for giving or withholding consent, the restriction on transfer shall be construed to include an implied standard that the landlord's consent may not be unreasonably withheld. Whether the landlord's consent has been unreasonably withheld in a particular case is a question of fact on which the tenant has the burden of proof. The tenant may satisfy the burden of proof by showing that, in response to the tenant's written request for a statement of reasons for withholding consent, the landlord has failed, within a reasonable time, to state in writing a reasonable objection to the transfer.

---

1.   Why do landlords commonly try to restrict alienability of leaseholds?

2.   The *Kendall* court adopted the rule, accepted in about 15 jurisdictions, that the lessor must use "reasonable commercial standards" when approving a subtenant or assignee. Is such a rule necessary in a commercial lease, where the parties are presumed to be able to bargain? Do you find persuasive the argument that such a rule is necessary to promote free alienability of property? How is alienability unreasonably restricted by a provision barring subleasing or assignment?

3.   Does the *Kendall* case reinforce or undermine freedom of contract in landlord-tenant relationships? What is there to prevent landlords from simply including a clause in leases prohibiting subleases and assignments altogether?

4.   Under what circumstances may a landlord be deemed to have withheld consent unreasonably?

5.   How does the subsequent legislation change the *Kendall* holding? Doesn't § 1995.230 permit the landlord to withhold consent for arbitrary reasons? What, if any, are the advantages of the statutory rules?

6.   The *Kendall* case and the subsequent legislative treatment of this issue are limited to commercial leases. Should this doctrine apply to residential leases? Are the arguments stronger or weaker in that context?

Problems: Limitations on Subleasing and Assignment

1.   Suppose that Landlord and Tenant signed a 10–year lease for office space at $22 per square foot. Upon occupancy, Tenant spent $400,000 on improvements. The lease provided:

> (a) Tenant shall not, without prior written consent of the Landlord, which consent shall not be unreasonably withheld, assign this Lease or any interest herein or sublet the Premises or

any part thereof, or permit the use or occupancy of the Premises by any person other than Tenant.

(b) Before entering into any assignment of this Lease or into a sublease of all or part of the Premises, Tenant shall give written notice to Landlord identifying the intended assignee or sublessee by name and address and specifying the terms of the intended assignment or sublease. For a period of 30 days after such notice is given, Landlord shall have the right by written notice to Tenant to terminate this Lease as of a date specified in such notice, which date shall not be less than 30 days nor more than 60 days after the date such notice is given. If Landlord so terminates this Lease, Landlord may, if it elects, enter into a new lease covering the Premises with the intended assignee or sublessee on such terms as Landlord and such person may agree, or enter into a new lease covering the Premises with any other person; in such event, Tenant shall not be entitled to any portion of the profit, if any, which Landlord may realize on account of such termination by reletting.

Three and one-half years later, Tenant requested Landlord's consent to sublease part of the office space at $33 per square foot. Landlord wrote that it was terminating the lease in 45 days; it intended to negotiate a separate lease with the proposed subtenant. Tenant vacated the premises and sued for breach of covenant not to withhold consent unreasonably.

Does the "recapture" clause in this lease violate the judicial prohibition of unreasonable restraints on alienation? In other words, is the landlord's effort to capture the appreciated value of the leasehold "unreasonable"? Does the recapture clause violate the implied covenant of good faith and fair dealing? Or is it a rational and reasonable business decision? *See Carma Developers (California), Inc. v. Marathon Development California, Inc.*, 2 Cal.4th 342, 6 Cal.Rptr.2d 467, 826 P.2d 710 (1992). What is the result under the Civil Code?

2. Can a court analyze a lease using other doctrines, such as doctrines of unconscionability or of adhesion contracts?

Consider the following lease provision:

If in connection with the transaction involving the proposed assignment or sublease, tenant receives rent or other consideration for tenant's business, business opportunity, good will, a covenant not to compete and/or the like, either initially or over the term of the assignment or sublease, in excess of all sums then payable hereunder, whether as minimum rent, percentage rent, or otherwise, * * * tenant shall pay to landlord as additional rent hereunder three-quarters of the excess of each such payment of rent or other consideration received by tenant promptly after its receipt.

The tenant, who ran a drycleaning business, wanted to sell his business and assign his lease. The sales agreement specifically allocated $40,000 of the total price to the value of a covenant not to compete in the lease and nothing to the value of the lease. The lessor demanded payment of $30,000 (pursuant to the master lease) before giving its written consent to the assignment (the lease provided that a proposed lease assignment or sublease required the landlord's prior written approval, "which shall not be unreasonably withheld").

Is the lease provision unconscionable? *See Ilkhchooyi v. Best*, 37 Cal.App.4th 395, 45 Cal.Rptr.2d 766 (1995).

3. Landlord is a deeply religious person who owns a small commercial building. He leased a storefront in the building to a couple who planned to open a small take-out business. The lease is for five years and contains a clause requiring the landlord's permission for assignment or sublet, but also includes another clause that the landlord will not "unreasonably refuse permission to sublet or assign." After a year, the tenants' business was losing money, and they began to look for an assignee. After considerable effort, they found a local chain of video stores that was looking for a new location. The chain had excellent credit and good references from its landlords in other locations.

Landlord was impressed with the proposed assignee's credentials. However, when he also found out that the outlet would rent x-rated videos (less than 10% of its rentals), he refused permission for the assignment. Tenant challenged this refusal in court. Landlord claimed that under the Free Exercise of Religion Clause of the First Amendment the state can not force him to rent to a tenant whose activities on the landlord's property would violate the landlord's religious principles. *Cf.* Religious Freedom Restoration Act, 42 U.S.C. §§ 2000bb to 2000bb–4 (the government may not "substantially burden a person's exercise of religion" unless the burden furthers a "compelling governmental interest" and the burden is the "least restrictive means" of furthering that interest); *City of Boerne v. Flores*, ___ U.S. ___, ___ S.Ct. ___, ___ L.Ed.2d ___, 1997 WL 345322 (1997) (RFRA exceeds Congress' power because it violates the standards of the Free Exercise Clause and improperly intrudes on state prerogatives to regulate health and safety). How should the case be decided?

---

5. RENT CONTROL

a. BACKGROUND

State-wide residential rent control first became popular as a result of the housing shortage and rapidly rising housing prices that existed after World War I. Most of these controls expired by the mid–1920s, but were reimposed during World War II.

Richard Arnott, Time for Revisionism on Rent Control?
Journal of Economic Perspectives, Winter 1995, at 99, 100–02.

The History of Rent Control

Rent controls were imposed in the United States shortly after the country's entry into World War II. Putting the country on a war footing required massive relocation of labor, with consequent pressure on many local housing markets. Controls were imposed to ensure affordable housing and to prevent profiteering. The appropriateness of imposing controls in wartime seems to be virtually undisputed. The form of controls was a freeze on nominal rents.

The rent freeze continued after the end of the war in the belief that the return of soldiers would otherwise cause a rapid and disruptive rise in rents, at least in certain markets. However, there was a housing boom in the late 1940s and early 1950s, which lowered market-clearing rents and permitted almost painless decontrol. The only jurisdiction to retain wartime controls was New York City, and these were applied only to pre–1947 housing.

European countries imposed wartime rent freezes, too. In fact, controls in several countries had lingered on from the First World War. The postwar experience of the European countries was less fortunate. Housing reconstruction took much longer because of their war-ravaged economies and extensive destruction of their housing stocks. As a result, many European jurisdictions retained a rent freeze on at least prewar housing long after World War II. While the nominal rent freezes were typically not absolute— intermittent adjustments were made—controlled rents fell significantly in real terms, to only a fraction of the rents in the uncontrolled housing that was constructed after the war.

* * * The type of controls imposed in this period has come to be termed "hard" or "first-generation" rent control.

Since the early 1950s, the pattern of rent regulation has been significantly different in Europe than in North America. In much of Europe, the legacy of first-generation controls is still keenly felt. In some jurisdictions, controls gave rise to housing problems that prompted increasingly intrusive government intervention. In others, the uncontrolled rental housing sector grew healthily, while the older, controlled housing in the downtown areas deteriorated, but remained keenly sought after due to the wide disparity in (quality-adjusted) rents between the controlled and uncontrolled sectors. Over the last 15 years, largely as a result of the perceived failure of socialism and renewed faith in the market, European governments have been eliminating or relaxing controls.

In North America, only the experience of New York City has been similar to that of the European countries. In all other jurisdictions, rent controls were absent from the early 1950s to the early 1970s. In the '70s, however, rent control ordinances were passed in Boston, Washington, D.C., Los Angeles, and San Francisco, as well as in a host of towns in California, Connecticut, Massachusetts, New Jersey, and New York state. Also, all the Canadian provinces introduced some form of rent control in the mid-'70s, in conjunction with that nation's federal wage and price control program. While each jurisdiction has had its own political history with respect to rent control, broadly speaking the reimposition of controls in the 1970s came about as a result of both the radicalism of the period and the unnerving inflation in the wake of the oil crisis.

Very few U.S. cities that did not introduce rent controls during this period have introduced them since, and most U.S. cities that did introduce controls have retained them, though in many cases with substantial modification. Only four of the ten Canadian provinces have retained controls. Estimates of the proportion of the U.S. rental housing stock currently subject to rent control range from 10–15 percent.

The controls imposed during the 1970s differed significantly from the first-generation rent control programs. They have been termed variously "soft" rent control, "second-generation" rent control, rent review, and rent regulation. They entail a complex set of regulations governing not only allowable rent increases, but also conversion, maintenance, and landlord-tenant relations.

Second-generation rent controls commonly permit automatic percentage rent increases related to the rate of inflation. They also often contain provisions for other rent increases: cost pass-through provisions which permit landlords to apply for rent increases above the automatic rent increase, if justified by cost increases; hardship provisions, which allow discretionary increases to assure that landlords do not have cash-flow problems; and rate-of-return provisions, which permit discretionary rent increases to ensure landlords a "fair" or "reasonable" rate of return. Second-generation controls commonly exempt rental housing constructed after the application of controls, although new housing may be brought under the controls at a later time.

In some jurisdictions, second-generation rent control has permitted full vacancy decontrol, whereby the unit becomes completely decontrolled when it is vacated. Other jurisdictions' programs permit inter-tenancy decontrol, whereby controls apply during successive tenancies but no restrictions are placed on inter-tenancy rent increases. Others contain alternative decontrol mechanisms; probably the most common has been rent level decontrol, whereby a unit is decontrolled when its controlled rent rises above a certain level. Yet others have no decontrol provisions.

Such rent regulation often contains provisions which accord tenants improved security of tenure—rent increase appeal procedures, eviction procedures more favorable to the tenant, and so on—and it often includes restrictions to prevent cutbacks in maintenance, and on the conversion of controlled rental housing to owner-occupied housing.

Clearly, second-generation rent controls are very different from a rent freeze. There is considerable flexibility in the design of a second-generation rent control package, in fact so much that it may be inappropriate to generalize broadly about the effects of second-generation controls. Rent review packages can be categorized according to their "hardness," or resemblance to first-generation controls; for example, Santa Monica has a harder set of regulations than Los Angeles. Most of the European control programs currently in effect also fit the above description of second-generation rent controls.

---

b.   PREEMPTION BY STATE LAW

Because municipal corporations are creatures of state law, they are ultimately subservient to overriding state policies. Under the doctrine of preemption, local ordinances that conflict with state law or policy may be declared invalid. In some states, state legislatures have adopted statutes expressly preempting rent control ordinances. *See, e.g.,* Ariz. Rev. Stat. § 33–1329 (rent control "is of statewide concern. Therefore, the power to control rents on private residential property is preempted by the state. [Municipalities] shall not have the power to control rents"); Colo. Rev. Stat. § 38–12–301; Mass. Ann. Laws ch. 40 §§ 1–6; Cal. Civ. Code §§ 1954.25– 1954.31 (forbidding commercial rent control). In other states, constitutional "home rule" provisions protect some areas of law from state preemption unless there is an overriding reason for state-wide law. *See, e.g., Inganamort v. Borough of Fort Lee,* 62 N.J. 521, 303 A.2d 298 (1973) (upholding a municipality's power to enact a rent control ordinance as a valid police power "to deal with the evil of inordinate rent arising out of a housing shortage").

Conflict with state law sometimes arises when cities adopt ordinances designed to prevent landlords from taking their rental units off of the market, usually through "condo conversion."[41] A Berkeley rent control ordinance, for example, required landlords to provide notice to tenants at least six months prior to removing their units from the rental housing market, and to pay tenants $4500 in "relocation assistance" when they moved. In general, the state courts had upheld such restrictions. *See Griffin Development Co. v. City of Oxnard,* 39 Cal.3d 256, 217 Cal.Rptr. 1, 703 P.2d 339 (1985) (holding that local ordinances restricting condo conversion are not preempted by state law); *Kalaydjian v. City of Los Angeles,* 149 Cal.App.3d 690, 197 Cal.Rptr. 149 (1983) (upholding an ordinance requiring relocation assistance of up to $2500 per tenant). Some cities have imposed a moratorium on conversions. *See generally* Snyderman & Morrison, Rental Market Protection Through the Conversion Moratorium: Legal Limits and Alternatives, 29 DePaul L. Rev. 973 (1980). Some legislatures have preempted such local ordinances. *See, e.g.,* Cal. Gov't Code §§ 7060–7060.7 (expressly barring a governmental agency from compelling a landlord "to continue to offer [residential] accommodations * * * for rent"); *Channing Properties v. City of Berkeley,* 11 Cal.App.4th 88, 14 Cal.Rptr.2d 32 (1992) (declaring invalid the Berkeley requirement for six-month's notice, since the state statute required only 60 days notice).

c. CONSTITUTIONAL LITIGATION

Landlords have challenged the constitutionality of rent control on a number of bases. The Supreme Court faced takings attacks on rent controls

---

41. Since 1970, the rate of condo conversion has accelerated dramatically. Where the rental market is already tight, the impact of condo conversion on renters can be substantial. *See generally* Day & Fogel, The Condominium Crisis: A Problem Unresolved, 21 Urb. Law Ann. 3 (1981). Roughly half of the states provide tenants with some protection from the impacts of condo conversion. *See, e.g.,* Cal. Gov't Code § 66427.1 (requiring developers to give tenants adequate notice of intent to convert as well as an option for 90 days to purchase their units).

imposed during both World Wars and in both cases upheld the laws as permissible temporary measures designed to deal with the economic exigencies created by war. *Block v. Hirsh*, 256 U.S. 135 (1921); *Bowles v. Willingham*, 321 U.S. 503 (1944). The Supreme Court addressed the constitutionality of a second-generation rent control regime in 1988.

Pennell v. City of San Jose

Supreme Court of the United States, 1988.
485 U.S. 1, 108 S.Ct. 849, 99 L.Ed.2d 1.

■ CHIEF JUSTICE REHNQUIST delivered the opinion of the Court.

This case involves a challenge to a rent control ordinance enacted by the city of San Jose, California, that allows a hearing officer to consider, among other factors, the "hardship to a tenant" when determining whether to approve a rent increase proposed by a landlord. Appellants Richard Pennell and the Tri–County Apartment House Owners Association sued in the Superior Court of Santa Clara County seeking a declaration that the ordinance, in particular the "tenant hardship" provisions, are "facially unconstitutional and therefore . . . illegal and void." * * *

The city of San Jose enacted its rent control ordinance (Ordinance) in 1979 with the stated purpose of

"alleviat[ing] some of the more immediate needs created by San Jose's housing situation. These needs include but are not limited to the prevention of excessive and unreasonable rent increases, the alleviation of undue hardships upon individual tenants, and the assurance to landlords of a fair and reasonable return on the value of their property." San Jose Municipal Ordinance 19696, § 5701.2.

At the heart of the Ordinance is a mechanism for determining the amount by which landlords subject to its provisions may increase the annual rent which they charge their tenants. A landlord is automatically entitled to raise the rent of a tenant in possession[42] by as much as eight percent; if a tenant objects to an increase greater than eight percent, a hearing is required before a "Mediation Hearing Officer" to determine whether the landlord's proposed increase is "reasonable under the circumstances." The Ordinance sets forth a number of factors to be considered by the hearing officer in making this determination, including "the hardship to a tenant." § 5703.28(c)(7). Because appellants concentrate their attack on the consideration of this factor, we set forth the relevant provision of the Ordinance in full:

5703.29. Hardship to Tenants. In the case of a rent increase or any portion thereof which exceeds the standard set in Section

---

42. Under § 5703.3, the Ordinance does not apply to rent or rent increases for new rental units first rented after the Ordinance takes effect, § 5703.3(a), to the rental of a unit that has been voluntarily vacated, § 5703.3(b)(1), or to the rental of a unit that is vacant as a result of eviction for certain specified acts, § 5703.3(b)(2).

5703.28(a) or (b), then with respect to such excess and whether or not to allow same to be part of the increase allowed under this Chapter, the Hearing Officer shall consider the economic and financial hardship imposed on the present tenant or tenants of the unit or units to which such increases apply. If, on balance, the Hearing Officer determines that the proposed increase constitutes an unreasonably severe financial or economic hardship on a particular tenant, he may order that the excess of the increase which is subject to consideration under subparagraph (c) of Section 5703.28, or any portion thereof, be disallowed. Any tenant whose household income and monthly housing expense meets [certain income requirements] shall be deemed to be suffering under financial and economic hardship which must be weighed in the Hearing Officer's determination. The burden of proof in establishing any other economic hardship shall be on the tenant.

If either a tenant or a landlord is dissatisfied with the decision of the hearing officer, the Ordinance provides for binding arbitration. A landlord who attempts to charge or who receives rent in excess of the maximum rent established as provided in the Ordinance is subject to criminal and civil penalties. * * *

Turning now to the merits, we first address appellants' contention that application of the Ordinance's tenant hardship provisions violates the Fifth and Fourteenth Amendments' prohibition against taking of private property for public use without just compensation. In essence, appellants' claim is as follows: § 5703.28 of the Ordinance establishes the seven factors that a hearing officer is to take into account in determining the reasonable rent increase. The first six of these factors are all objective, and are related either to the landlord's costs of providing an adequate rental unit, or to the condition of the rental market. Application of these six standards results in a rent that is "reasonable" by reference to what appellants contend is the only legitimate purpose of rent control: the elimination of "excessive" rents caused by San Jose's housing shortage. When the hearing officer then takes into account "hardship to a tenant" pursuant to § 5703.28(c)(7) and reduces the rent below the objectively "reasonable" amount established by the first six factors, this additional reduction in the rent increase constitutes a "taking." This taking is impermissible because it does not serve the purpose of eliminating excessive rents—that objective has already been accomplished by considering the first six factors—instead, it serves only the purpose of providing assistance to "hardship tenants." In short, appellants contend, the additional reduction of rent on grounds of hardship accomplishes a transfer of the landlord's property to individual hardship tenants; the Ordinance forces private individuals to shoulder the "public" burden of subsidizing their poor tenants' housing. As appellants point out, "[i]t is axiomatic that the Fifth Amendment's just compensation provision is 'designed to bar Government from forcing some people alone to bear public burdens which, in all fairness and justice, should be borne by the public as a whole.'" *First English Evangelical Lutheran Church of Glendale v.*

County of Los Angeles, 482 U.S. 304, 318–319 (1987) (quoting *Armstrong v. United States*, 364 U.S. 40, 49 (1960)).

We think it would be premature to consider this contention on the present record. As things stand, there simply is no evidence that the "tenant hardship clause" has in fact ever been relied upon by a hearing officer to reduce a rent below the figure it would have been set at on the basis of the other factors set forth in the Ordinance. In addition, there is nothing in the Ordinance requiring that a hearing officer in fact reduce a proposed rent increase on grounds of tenant hardship. Section 5703.29 does make it mandatory that hardship be considered—it states that "the Hearing Officer *shall* consider the economic hardship imposed on the present tenant"—but it then goes on to state that if "the proposed increase constitutes an unreasonably severe financial or economic hardship ... he *may* order that the excess of the increase" be disallowed. § 5703.29 (emphasis added). Given the "essentially ad hoc, factual inquir[y]" involved in the takings analysis, *Kaiser Aetna v. United States*, 444 U.S. 164, 175 (1979), we have found it particularly important in takings cases to adhere to our admonition that "the constitutionality of statutes ought not be decided except in an actual factual setting that makes such a decision necessary." *Hodel v. Virginia Surface Mining & Reclamation Assn., Inc.*, 452 U.S. 264, 294–295, (1981). * * *

Appellants also urge that the mere provision in the Ordinance that a hearing officer may consider the hardship of the tenant in finally fixing a reasonable rent renders the Ordinance "facially invalid" under the Due Process and Equal Protection Clauses, even though no landlord ever has its rent diminished by as much as one dollar because of the application of this provision. The standard for determining whether a state price-control regulation is constitutional under the Due Process Clause is well established: "Price control is 'unconstitutional ... if arbitrary, discriminatory, or demonstrably irrelevant to the policy the legislature is free to adopt....'" *Permian Basin Area Rate Cases*, 390 U.S. 747, 769–770 (1968) (quoting *Nebbia v. New York*, 291 U.S. 502, 539 (1934)). * * * Accordingly, appellants do not dispute that the Ordinance's asserted purpose of "prevent[ing] excessive and unreasonable rent increases" caused by the "growing shortage of and increasing demand for housing in the City of San Jose," § 5701.2, is a legitimate exercise of appellees' police powers. *Cf. Block v. Hirsh*, 256 U.S. 135, 156 (1921) (approving rent control in Washington, D.C., on the basis of Congress' finding that housing in the city was "monopolized"). They do argue, however, that it is "arbitrary, discriminatory, or demonstrably irrelevant," *Permian Basin Area Rate Cases, supra*, 390 U.S., at 769–770, for appellees to attempt to accomplish the additional goal of reducing the burden of housing costs on low-income tenants by requiring that "hardship to a tenant" be considered in determining the amount of excess rent increase that is "reasonable under the circumstances" pursuant to § 5703.28. As appellants put it, "[t]he objective of alleviating individual tenant hardship is ... not a 'policy the legislature is free to adopt' in a rent control ordinance."

We reject this contention, however, because we have long recognized that a legitimate and rational goal of price or rate regulation is the protection of consumer welfare. *See, e.g., Permian Basin Area Rate Cases, supra*, 390 U.S., at 770; *FPC v. Hope Natural Gas Co.*, 320 U.S. 591, 610–612 (1944) ("The primary aim of [the Natural Gas Act] was to protect consumers against exploitation at the hands of natural gas companies"). Indeed, a primary purpose of rent control is the protection of tenants. *See, e.g., Bowles v. Willingham*, 321 U.S. 503, 513, n. 9 (1944) (one purpose of rent control is "to protect persons with relatively fixed and limited incomes, consumers, wage earners ... from undue impairment of their standard of living"). Here, the Ordinance establishes a scheme in which a hearing officer considers a number of factors in determining the reasonableness of a proposed rent increase which exceeds eight percent and which exceeds the amount deemed reasonable under either § 5703.28(a) or § 5703.28(b). The first six factors of § 5703.28(c) focus on the individual landlord—the hearing officer examines the history of the premises, the landlord's costs, and the market for comparable housing. Section 5703.28(c)(5) also allows the landlord to bring forth any other financial evidence—including presumably evidence regarding his own financial status—to be taken into account by the hearing officer. It is in only this context that the Ordinance allows tenant hardship to be considered and, under § 5703.29, "balance[d]" with the other factors set out in § 5703.28(c). Within this scheme, § 5703.28(c) represents a rational attempt to accommodate the conflicting interests of protecting tenants from burdensome rent increases while at the same time ensuring that landlords are guaranteed a fair return on their investment. *Cf. Bowles v. Willingham, supra*, at 517 (considering, but rejecting, the contention that rent control must be established "landlord by landlord, as in the fashion of utility rates"). We accordingly find that the Ordinance, which so carefully considers both the individual circumstances of the landlord and the tenant before determining whether to allow an additional increase in rent over and above certain amounts that are deemed reasonable, does not on its face violate the Fourteenth Amendment's Due Process Clause.[43]

We also find that the Ordinance does not violate the Amendment's Equal Protection Clause. Here again, the standard is deferential; appellees need only show that the classification scheme embodied in the Ordinance is "rationally related to a legitimate state interest." *New Orleans v. Dukes*, 427 U.S. 297, 303 (1976). As we stated in *Vance v. Bradley*, 440 U.S. 93 (1979), "we will not overturn [a statute that does not burden a suspect class or a fundamental interest] unless the varying treatment of different groups or persons is so unrelated to the achievement of any combination of

---

43. The consideration of tenant hardship also serves the additional purpose, not stated on the face of the Ordinance, of reducing the costs of dislocation that might otherwise result if landlords were to charge rents to tenants that they could not afford. Particularly during a housing shortage, the social costs of the dislocation of low-income tenants can be severe. By allowing tenant hardship to be considered under § 5703.28(c), the Ordinance enables appellees to "fine tune" their rent control to take into account the risk that a particular tenant will be forced to relocate as a result of a proposed rent increase.

legitimate purposes that we can only conclude that the legislature's actions were irrational." *Id.*, at 97. In light of our conclusion above that the Ordinance's tenant hardship provisions are designed to serve the legitimate purpose of protecting tenants, we can hardly conclude that it is irrational for the Ordinance to treat certain landlords differently on the basis of whether or not they have hardship tenants. The Ordinance distinguishes between landlords because doing so furthers the purpose of ensuring that individual tenants do not suffer "unreasonable" hardship; it would be inconsistent to state that hardship is a legitimate factor to be considered but then hold that appellees could not tailor the Ordinance so that only legitimate hardship cases are redressed. *Cf. Woods v. Cloyd W. Miller Co.,* 333 U.S. 138, 145 (1948) (Congress "need not control all rents or none. It can select those areas or those classes of property where the need seems the greatest"). We recognize, as appellants point out, that in general it is difficult to say that the landlord "causes" the tenant's hardship. But this is beside the point—if a landlord does have a hardship tenant, regardless of the reason why, it is rational for appellees to take that fact into consideration under § 5703.28 of the Ordinance when establishing a rent that is "reasonable under the circumstances."

For the foregoing reasons, we hold that it is premature to consider appellants' claim under the Takings Clause and we reject their facial challenge to the Ordinance under the Due Process and Equal Protection Clauses of the Fourteenth Amendment.

■ JUSTICE SCALIA, with whom JUSTICE O'CONNOR joins, concurring in part and dissenting in part.

I agree that the tenant hardship provision of the Ordinance does not, on its face, violate either the Due Process Clause or the Equal Protection Clause of the Fourteenth Amendment. I disagree, however, with the Court's conclusion that appellants' takings claim is premature. I would decide that claim on the merits, and would hold that the tenant hardship provision of the Ordinance effects a taking of private property without just compensation in violation of the Fifth and Fourteenth Amendments.

I

Appellants contend that any application of the tenant hardship provision of the San Jose Ordinance would effect an uncompensated taking of private property because that provision does not substantially advance legitimate state interests and because it improperly imposes a public burden on individual landlords. I can understand how such a claim—that a law applicable to the plaintiffs is, root and branch, invalid—can be readily rejected on the merits, by merely noting that at least some of its applications may be lawful. But I do not understand how such a claim can possibly be avoided by considering it "premature." Suppose, for example, that the feature of the rental ordinance under attack was a provision allowing a hearing officer to consider the race of the apartment owner in deciding whether to allow a rent increase. It is inconceivable that we would say judicial challenge must await demonstration that this provision has actually been applied to the detriment of one of the plaintiffs. There is no difference, it seems to me, when the facial, root-and-branch challenge rests upon the Takings Clause rather than the Equal Protection Clause. * * *

II

The Fifth Amendment of the United States Constitution, made applicable to the States through the Fourteenth Amendment, provides that "private property [shall not] be taken for public use, without just compensation." We have repeatedly observed that the purpose of this provision is "to bar Government from forcing some people alone to bear public burdens which, in all fairness and justice, should be borne by the public as a whole." *Armstrong v. United States*, 364 U.S. 40, 49 (1960).

Traditional land-use regulation (short of that which totally destroys the economic value of property) does not violate this principle because there is a cause-and-effect relationship between the property use restricted by the regulation and the social evil that the regulation seeks to remedy. Since the owner's use of the property is (or, but for the regulation, would be) the source of the social problem, it cannot be said that he has been singled out unfairly. Thus, the common zoning regulations requiring subdividers to observe lot-size and set-back restrictions, and to dedicate certain areas to public streets, are in accord with our constitutional traditions because the proposed property use would otherwise be the cause of excessive congestion. The same cause-and-effect relationship is popularly thought to justify emergency price regulation: When commodities have been priced at a level that produces exorbitant returns, the owners of those commodities can be viewed as responsible for the economic hardship that occurs. Whether or not that is an accurate perception of the way a free-market economy operates, it is at least true that the owners reap unique benefits from the situation that produces the economic hardship, and in that respect singling them out to relieve it may not be regarded as "unfair." That justification might apply to the rent regulation in the present case, apart from the single feature under attack here.

Appellants do not contest the validity of rent regulation in general. They acknowledge that the city may constitutionally set a "reasonable rent" according to the statutory minimum and the six other factors that must be considered by the hearing officer (cost of debt servicing, rental history of the unit, physical condition of the unit, changes in housing services, other financial information provided by the landlord, and market value rents for similar units). San Jose Municipal Ordinance 19696, § 5703.28(c) (1979). Appellants' only claim is that a reduction of a rent increase below what would otherwise be a "reasonable rent" under this scheme may not, consistently with the Constitution, be based on consideration of the seventh factor—the hardship to the tenant as defined in § 5703.29. I think they are right.

Once the other six factors of the Ordinance have been applied to a landlord's property, so that he is receiving only a reasonable return, he can no longer be regarded as a "cause" of exorbitantly priced housing; nor is he any longer reaping distinctively high profits from the housing shortage. The seventh factor, the "hardship" provision, is invoked to meet a quite different social problem: the existence of some renters who are too poor to afford even reasonably priced housing. But that problem is no more caused or exploited by landlords than it is by the grocers who sell needy renters their food, or the department stores that sell them their clothes, or the employers who pay them their wages, or the citizens of San Jose holding the higher paying jobs from which they are excluded. And even if the neediness of renters could be regarded as a problem distinctively attributable to landlords in general, it is not remotely attributable to the *particular* landlords that the Ordinance singles out—namely, those who happen to have a "hardship" tenant at the present time, or who may happen to rent to a "hardship" tenant in the future, or whose current or future affluent tenants may happen to decline into the "hardship" category.

The traditional manner in which American government has met the problem of those who cannot pay reasonable prices for privately sold necessities—a problem caused by the society at large—has been the distribution to such persons of funds raised from the public at large through taxes, either in cash (welfare payments) or in goods (public housing, publicly subsidized housing, and food stamps). Unless we are to abandon the guiding principle of the Takings Clause that "public burdens . . . should be borne by the public as a whole," *Armstrong*, 364 U.S., at 49, this is the only manner that our Constitution permits. The fact that government acts through the landlord-tenant relationship does not magically transform general public welfare, which must be supported by all the public, into mere "economic regulation," which can disproportionately burden particular individuals. Here the city is not "regulating" rents in the relevant sense of preventing rents that are excessive; rather, it is using the occasion of rent regulation (accomplished by the rest of the Ordinance) to establish a welfare program privately funded by those landlords who happen to have "hardship" tenants.

Of course all economic regulation effects wealth transfer. When excessive rents are forbidden, for example, landlords as a class become poorer and tenants as a class (or at least incumbent tenants as a class) become richer. Singling out landlords to be the transferors may be within our traditional constitutional notions of fairness, because they can plausibly be regarded as the source or the beneficiary of the high-rent problem. Once such a connection is no longer required, however, there is no end to the social transformations that can be accomplished by so-called "regulation," at great expense to the democratic process.

The politically attractive feature of regulation is not that it permits wealth transfers to be achieved that could not be achieved otherwise; but rather that it permits them to be achieved "off budget," with relative invisibility and thus relative immunity from normal democratic processes. San Jose might, for example, have accomplished something like the result here by simply raising the real estate tax upon rental properties and using the additional revenues thus acquired to pay part of the rents of "hardship" tenants. It seems to me doubtful, however, whether the citizens of San Jose would allow funds in the municipal treasury, from wherever derived, to be distributed to a family of four with income as high as $32,400 a year—the generous maximum necessary to qualify automatically as a "hardship" tenant under the rental Ordinance. The voters might well see other, more pressing, social priorities. And of course what $32,400-a-year renters can acquire through spurious "regulation," other groups can acquire as well. Once the door is opened it is not unreasonable to expect price regulations requiring private businesses to give special discounts to senior citizens (no matter how affluent), or to students, the handicapped, or war veterans. Subsidies for these groups may well be a good idea, but because of the operation of the Takings Clause our governmental system has required them to be applied, in general, through the process of taxing and spending, where both economic effects and competing priorities are more evident.

That fostering of an intelligent democratic process is one of the happy effects of the constitutional prescription—perhaps accidental, perhaps not. Its essence, however, is simply the unfairness of making one citizen pay, in some fashion other than taxes, to remedy a social problem that is none of his creation. As the Supreme Court of New Jersey said in finding unconstitutional a scheme displaying, among other defects, the same vice I find dispositive here:

> "A legislative category of economically needy senior citizens is sound, proper and sustainable as a rational classification. But compelled subsidization by landlords or by tenants who happen to live in an apartment building with senior citizens is an improper and unconstitutional method of solving the problem." *Property Owners Assn. v. North Bergen*, 74 N.J. 327, 339, 378 A.2d 25, 31 (1977).

I would hold that the seventh factor in § 5703.28(c) of the San Jose Ordinance effects a taking of property without just compensation.

---

1. Do you consider San Jose's rationale for imposing rent control to be sincere? Are the concerns cited by the City really transitory? Is it likely that they will abate in the foreseeable future? Why did the municipal legislature emphasize this element?

2. Do you consider San Jose's solution to its housing problems to be sound? Is rent control likely to alleviate or exacerbate such problems? Will it cause other problems? In assessing the constitutional challenge of the rent control ordinance, should the Supreme Court take the City's rationale at its word?

3. Does the majority opinion in *Pennell* adequately respond to Scalia's dissent? Had the majority reached the merits, how do you think it would have come out?

4.   Although facial challenges to rent control have been unsuccessful, state courts have found rent control ordinances to violate the Constitution *as applied* in individual cases. An ordinance may not create unwarranted procedural obstacles to landlords seeking to exercise their statutory rights, *Birkenfeld v. City of Berkeley*, 17 Cal.3d 129, 130 Cal.Rptr. 465, 550 P.2d 1001 (1976) (onerous procedure required for landlords to obtain rent increases for increased costs effectively prevented landlords from seeking and obtaining legitimate rent increases and therefore violated due process), and it must permit landlords a reasonable economic return on their investment. *See, e.g., Fisher v. City of Berkeley*, 37 Cal.3d 644, 686, 209 Cal.Rptr. 682, 693 P.2d 261 (1984); *Apartment Ass'n of Greater Los Angeles v. Santa Monica Rent Control Board*, 24 Cal.App.4th 1730, 30 Cal.Rptr.2d 228 (1994); *Helmsley v. Borough of Fort Lee*, 78 N.J. 200, 228–29, 394 A.2d 65, 78–79 (1978) (ordinance limiting annual rent increases to 2.5% violated due process because it did not provide "adequate administrative relief" for hardship cases).

---

d.   POLICY CONSIDERATIONS

Richard Arnott, Time for Revisionism on Rent Control?

Journal of Economic Perspectives, Winter 1995, at 99, 99, 103–09, 117–18.

Economists have been virtually unanimous in their opposition to rent control. In a survey of economists' opinions, Alston, Kearl, and Vaughan (1992) asked a stratified random sample of 1990 American Economic Association members whether they "generally agree," "agree with provisions," or "generally disagree" with 40 statements related to economic theory and policy. The greatest degree of consensus on any question—93.5 percent—was agreement or qualified agreement with the statement: "A ceiling on rents reduces the quantity and quality of housing available." This is hardly a discriminating question concerning economists' attitudes towards rent control, but is nonetheless suggestive. There has been widespread agreement that rent controls discourage new construction, cause abandonment, retard maintenance, reduce mobility, generate mismatch between housing units and tenants, exacerbate discrimination in rental housing, create black markets, encourage the conversion of rental to owner-occupied housing, and generally short-circuit the market mechanism for housing.

In recent years, however, there has been a wave (or at least a swell) of revisionism among housing economists on the subject of rent control. While few actually advocate controls, most are considerably more muted and qualified in their opposition. Perhaps a majority, at least among the younger generation, would agree with the statement that a well-designed rent control program can be beneficial.

* * *

Textbook Analysis of a Rent Freeze

Just as there have been two generations of controls, so have there been two generations of economic theory applying to rent controls. The first generation, examined in this section, employs standard supply-demand analysis to examine the effects of a rent freeze [*i.e.*, first-generation controls]. The second, to be discussed in the next section employs modern economic theory of imperfect markets to examine second-generation controls.

The textbook analysis of a rent freeze [is well known.] Fixing rent below the market-clearing level has three types of effects. First, tenants who manage to find rent-controlled housing benefit. These are disproportionately long-term residents of the jurisdiction, who benefit at the expense of new residents, most of whom must live in uncontrolled housing or the worst controlled housing. Second, producers forced to charge lower rents see the value of their property fall and react in various ways, like reducing maintenance expenses, trying to convert their buildings from controlled rental housing to owner-occupied housing, and thinking twice before constructing any additional rental housing. Third, the below-market rental prices lead to excess demand for housing, which causes various phenomena: a mismatch of housing units to households (for example, the proverbial elderly widow living in the same large, rent-controlled apartment long after her family has left home, at the same time that there is an acute housing shortage); reduced housing mobility causing reduced labor mobility; an increase in discrimination, since disfavored groups are rationed out; and various gray-or black-market phenomena such as "key money," which is the payment of a "nonrefundable deposit" upon moving in. * * *

Modern Analysis of Second–Generation Rent Controls

No fully articulated modern model of rent controls exists. Rather there are a number of different partial models of housing markets which can be employed to focus on different rent-control phenomena. These can be broadly categorized into perfectly competitive and imperfectly competitive models.

Perfectly Competitive Models

* * *

In a pair of seminal papers, Sweeney presented the first modern model of the rental housing market to treat both dynamics and quality differentiation explicitly. The model focuses on the economic decisions of a landlord who has a durable housing unit of a given quality. Knowing the rent function, which relates rent to quality, and the maintenance technology, which relates the rate at which the housing unit deteriorates in quality to the level of maintenance, the landlord chooses the path of maintenance expenditures to maximize the discounted present value of net revenue from the unit. The other components of the model are construction, abandonment, demand, expectations, and market-clearing. Typically, housing is constructed at the top end of the quality spectrum and then filters downward in quality, at a rate depending on maintenance, until it is eventually abandoned [and possibly razed and/or reconstructed—*e.g.*, gentrification.]

[S]ome valuable insights can be gained from [these models.] For example, Olsen (1988) has pointed out that second-generation rent control packages can be designed to stimulate maintenance. Recall that rent level decontrol allows a housing unit to be decontrolled when its controlled rent rises above a certain level. Since the controlled rent can be increased through upgrading via cost pass-through, it may be profit-maximizing for a landlord to upgrade a unit so as to decontrol it.[44] As well, maintenance can be stimulated by a generous cost pass-through provision, which permits the rent on a unit to be increased by, say, $1.50 for every $1.00 increase in cost.

Imperfectly Competitive Models

If the economy were perfectly competitive, any binding form of rent control would reduce social surplus and models a la Sweeney could be employed to analyze their baleful effects. But the conditions for perfect competition are extremely strong. The housing market does seem somewhat competitive in the sense that it exhibits negligible economies of scale and has insignificant barriers to entry and exit. However, the housing market also seems imperfectly competitive in a number of ways: externalities created by neighbor and neighborhood effects are at least moderately important; housing is highly heterogeneous which, combined with idiosyncratic tastes, renders the market thin; search costs are substantial (as evidenced by real estate agents' fees); futures/insurance markets are virtually nonexistent; and imperfections in capital markets impact the housing market in important ways.

Only in the past decade have housing economic theorists turned their attention to models of the housing market which capture these features. Two classes of models are particularly relevant to the study of rent control: monopolistically competitive models and contract models. Both have been adapted from labor economics.

The monopolistically competitive models of the rental housing market are similar to the search-based matching models of Diamond (1984) and Pissarides (1990). In such models, a household searches among vacant units for a housing unit that suits its tastes. If a household really likes a unit, for its own idiosyncratic reasons, it will take the unit even if the rent is higher than that of units of broadly comparable quality. Since landlords know that their differentiated product gives them market power, they exploit that power by pricing above marginal cost. Free entry and exit drive profits to zero and excess capacity manifests itself as vacant housing units. Igarashi and Arnott (1994) show that in a particular model of this type, moderate rent controls are beneficial, although stringent rent controls are harmful.

---

44. Olsen also pointed out that standard analyses ignore *tenant* maintenance. To the extent that controls transfer property rights from landlords to tenants, they may encourage increased tenant maintenance.

The broad intuition is that rent control restricts the ability of landlords to exploit their market power. * * *

The market imperfection which drives the contract models is asymmetric information. In one such model, there are two groups of tenants, good and bad. A landlord discovers the identity of a tenant only after she has rented an apartment for one period. The economic environment is such that, in the absence of controls, a bad tenant moves every period, even though moving is costly, because she can get a substantially lower rent from a new landlord who does not know her identity. Each landlord realizes that by "economically evicting" his bad tenants, other landlords will be stuck with them. But since he does not pay the associated cost, he ignores it. Thus, there is a bad-tenant turnover externality—a beggar-thy-neighbor policy with respect to bad tenants. Imposing intra-tenancy rent control and prohibiting eviction eliminates the incentive for bad tenants to move, and hence the externality, and can make not only bad tenants but also good tenants better off.

The above arguments indicate that a *well-designed* rent control program can improve on the unrestricted equilibrium of an imperfect market. However, they do not establish that an optimal rent control program is either the best available policy or at least a component of the best policy package. No paper has established either result. On broad theoretical grounds, however, it is likely that some form of rent control would be included in an optimal housing policy package. * * *

The above argument for the potential desirability of second-generation rent controls was based on efficiency considerations. In contrast, the traditional advocates of controls emphasize distributional concerns. Specifically, they argue that controls redistribute from rich to poor and ensure cheap housing. I find little merit in either argument. Whatever redistribution controls achieve is poorly targeted. As well, when there is a broad-based income tax, redistribution by modifying commodity prices is in general unwise. For related reasons, cheap housing, as distinct from a reduction in inequality or poverty, is a dubious goal of social policy.

The Political Economy of Rent Control

As a matter of practical politics, there is more room to doubt the worth of rent control. Even if the optimal rent control package would be beneficial, the actual rent control package thrown up by the political process may be harmful. * * *

Reflections and Conclusions

* * *

Is Revisionism on Rent Control in Order?

Economists' traditional opposition to rent control is based on a combination of ingrained hostility to price controls and the experience with first-generation controls—the type that was imposed in New York City and across much of Europe in the years following World War II. In this paper, my primary theme was that modern, second-generation rent controls are so different that they should be judged largely independently of the experience with first-generation controls. * * * [S]econd-generation controls should be judged on the empirical evidence and, since the programs are so varied, on a case-by-case basis. My reading of the empirical evidence is that many of the claimed effects of second-generation controls are imperceptible. And those effects that are perceptible have ambiguous efficiency and welfare implications. * * *

—————

1. *Empirical Studies of Rent Control.* Anthony Downs summarizes the substantial empirical literature on the effects of rent control. *Residential Rent Controls: An Evaluation* (Urban Land Institute 1988). He finds that second-generation rent controls do not significantly reduce the amount of new construction of multifamily housing and have ambiguous effects on maintenance expenditures. Other factors, such as availability of land, interest rates, income tax policy, and availability of government subsidies may have a much greater impact on construction of new rental housing. These studies also show that middle and upper-income households derive significant benefits from rent control, *i.e.*, the effective subsidy is not targeted to the poor. *See also* Olsen, Is Rent Control Good Social Policy?, 67 Chi.–Kent L. Rev. 931 (1991) (review of empirical studies).

2. *Effects on Mobility.* Rent control creates an incentive for existing tenants to stay in rent controlled housing after their economic situation has improved and even if their jobs have changed to a more distant location. For example, recent law school graduates, who may have relatively high paying jobs in San Francisco or Silicon Valley, stay in Berkeley much longer than if there were no rent control. Thus, rent control creates a bias in favor of existing and more settled tenants and against potential new tenants, who may be more deserving in terms of economic status.

3. *Traditional Arguments for Rent Control.* Does Arnott dismiss the traditional redistributive and protective arguments too quickly? Rent control provides security of tenure to many people who are on fixed incomes. Such tenants have often built a rich social life in their community and derive substantial benefit from maintaining their place in a geographically (and often ethnically) defined community. *See* J.I. Gilderbloom and R.P. Applebaum, Rethinking Rent Housing (1988); Cirace, Housing Market Instability and Rent Stabilization, 54 Brooklyn L. Rev. 1275 (1989); *see also* Note, Reassessing Rent Control: Its Economic Impact in a Gentrifying Housing Market, 101 Harv. L. Rev. 1835 (1988). Does second-generation rent control provide a nice middle ground for serving society's competing concerns? What elements of second-generation rent control are most defensible? What features are least defensible?

4. *The Personhood and Communitarian Justifications for Rent Control.* Professor Peggy Radin tries to answer both the efficiency and to a lesser extent the distributional concerns raised by rent control by offering a

personhood rationale for this form of government intervention in the market. Radin, Residential Rent Control, 15 Phil. & Pub. Aff. 350 (1986). She begins with the proposition that housing is not "an ordinary market commodity." Rather,

> A tenant's interest in continuing to live in an apartment that she has made home for some time seems somehow a stronger or more exigent claim than a commercial landlord's interest in maintaining the same scope of freedom of choice regarding lease terms and in maintaining a high profit margin. * * *

> To the extent there does exist the intuitive appeal for preserving the tenant's home * * *, it can be understood in terms of the distinction between personal and fungible property. * * * Property that is "personal" in the philosophical sense is bound up with one's personhood, and is distinguishable from property that is held merely instrumentally or for investment and exchange and is therefore purely commercial or "fungible."

Id. at 359, 362. Radin extends the argument beyond the individualistic focus of the personhood perspective by suggesting that rent control also serves communitarian values by preserving and stabilizing community structures. *Cf.* Garet, Communality and the Existence of Groups, 56 So. Cal. L. Rev. 1001 (1983). Thus, her arguments would exclude (or minimize) the moral claims of landlords, would-be tenants, and relatively short-term tenants. Her argument provides no basis to oppose vacancy decontrol, or to include new construction under a rent control regime.

Radin sees no moral reason to compensate landlords for their economic loss. From her point of view, residential tenancies (or at least long-term ones) should not be commodified to begin with.

> [I]f part of the wrong is the fact of commodification, the fact of placing the object in the market realm, then to place a market value on the interest even while decommodifying it seems contradictory or equivocal. If this argument is accepted, there is no corrective justice reason to compensate landlords whose wealth is diminished by rent controls.

Id. at 367–68. Do you find this reasoning convincing? Does the personhood and communitarian perspectives provide a sound basis for rent control policy? Does it make a difference that many landlords are small businesspersons who invest little capital but lots of sweat, and who live with or in the same economic circumstances as their tenants? Can Radin's arguments overcome the consequentialist concerns that economists raise about rent controls? *See* Brennan, Rights, Market Failure, and Rent Control, 17 Phil. & Pub. Aff. 66 (1988); Radin, Rent Control and Incomplete Commodification: A Rejoinder, 17 Phil. & Pub. Aff. 80 (1988); M.G. Freed & D.D. Polsby, Personhood, Commodification and the Protection of Incumbency: Toward a Microeconomic Moral Reality (manuscript 1989).

5. *Political Economy of Rent Control.* As noted by Arnott, the political economy of rent control critically affects its efficacy. One commentator has suggested:

> Although rent control is bad for renters taken as a whole, it is good for the particular subgroup of tenants that votes on the measure and bad for the subgroup of tenants that does not vote. Rent control benefits those of the "tenant class" who are now tenants, at the expense of those who will become tenants later. These include nonresidents, those who are too young to establish independent households, and those who are currently homeowners and plan to become tenants.

> [R]ent control is often deceptively portrayed as protection for the poor or as a restraint on exorbitant landlord profits. However, * * * rent control operate[s], in effect if not in intent, against the interests of those who cannot vote and in favor of those who can and do vote. For the current tenant, the immediate and certain advantage of rent control usually outweighs the speculative future disadvantages.

Rabin, The Revolution in Residential Landlord–Tenant Law: Causes and Consequences, 69 Cornell L. Rev. 517, 555–56 (1984). Moreover, the burdens of rent control are highly concentrated on residential landlords, and the benefits are widely spread across a much larger group of long-term tenants, many of whom are financially secure.

Might these political considerations, rather than concerns about the inefficiency of rent control, have driven the evolution toward second-generation controls? To what extent are second-generation controls the predictable outcome of the relative power and mobilization of the different interest groups affected by rent control? These controls tend to benefit incumbents (*i.e.*, those living in controlled units) much more than new entrants into the rental market. This would suggest that second-generation regimes—especially those featuring vacancy decontrol and exemption of new construction—reflect an uneasy compromise between landlords (seeking to eliminate controls entirely over time) and current tenants (who care predominantly about maintaining their present arrangement, or at least being insulated from the vagaries of the market). What explains the fact that Berkeley, California and Cambridge, Massachusetts—two university-centered communities with a high degree of mobility as a result of the high proportions of college students—have had among the most restrictive and persistent rent control regimes in the United States? *See* Navarro, Rent Controls in Cambridge, Massachusetts, 78 The Public Interest 83 (Winter 1985); R.J. Devine, Who Benefits from Rent Control? (Oakland: Center for Community Change 1986). What is the significance of the fact that the California legislature enacted a statute mandating vacancy decontrol in municipal rent control ordinances, Cal. Civ. Code §§ 1954.50–1954.53, and Massachusetts voters adopted a statute banning rent control? Mass. Ann. Laws, ch. 400, §§ 1–6.

6. Low-Income Housing Policy

As discussed above, the use of rent control to address problems of housing affordability is problematic. From both constitutional and moral perspectives, there are serious questions regarding the appropriateness of requiring landlords as a class to subsidize the costs of housing for other members of the society. Even if Justice Scalia's position in *Pennell* is not controlling as a matter of federal takings law, his argument still has moral force. Moreover, there is substantial basis to question the efficacy of rent control in addressing the problem of housing affordability. It is often inefficient and poorly tailored to address the housing problems faced by a substantial proportion of the population.

Because housing is all but essential for human survival, many advocates of the poor have argued that there is, or at least should be, a federal constitutional right to shelter. Since the U.S. Constitution does not expressly provide for such a right, advocates have relied upon the due process and equal protection clauses in the Fifth and Fourteenth Amendments to challenge state and local policies affecting the supply, availability, and quality of housing. *See* Michelman, Welfare Rights in a Constitutional Democracy, 1979 Wash. U. L.Q. 659. The federal courts, however, have rebuffed all such efforts to read a right to housing into the U.S. Constitution. *See, e.g., Lindsey v. Normet*, 405 U.S. 56, 92 S.Ct. 862, 31 L.Ed.2d 36 (1972); *Williams v. Barry*, 708 F.2d 789, 793 (D.C.Cir.1983).

Even if there is no constitutional right to housing, housing is an important aspect of welfare policy generally. Although the United States has no single, comprehensive low-income housing policy, the federal and state governments have over the past 70 years attempted numerous programs to address the housing needs of the poor.

Michael H. Schill, Privatizing Federal Low Income Housing Assistance: The Case of Public Housing

75 Cornell Law Review 878, 894–900 (1990).*

1. A Short History of Public Housing

Since the mid–1930s, the federal government has funded the construction of housing for low income households. New Deal agencies such as the Public Works Administration bought land, cleared slums and built almost 22,000 housing units. Direct federal provision of housing was initially dealt a blow in 1935 when a federal appeals court upheld a lower court ruling that the federal government could not use its power of eminent domain to condemn sites for housing projects because housing was not a "public purpose." In 1937, however, Congress passed the Wagner–Steagall Housing Act of 1937, establishing the public housing program. Under the Act, public housing would be built by local public housing authorities ("PHAs") rather than by the federal government. In addition to concerns of comity, the program utilized PHAs because several state courts had held that cities and states had the power to condemn property for housing. Under the program, a PHA and the federal government execute an Annual Contributions Contract ("ACC") which sets forth the parties' rights and obligations. The PHA funds the purchase of land and the construction of housing by issuing long term bonds, typically with a forty-year maturity. The federal government undertakes an obligation to make all debt service payments on the bonds, effectively subsidizing all capital costs. The PHA, in turn, obligates itself to operate the public housing in a manner consistent with federal statutes and regulations during the term of the ACC. The municipality in which the project is located is required to grant an exemption from real property taxes for the housing development. Unlike housing built by the Public Works Administration, public housing was, from the start, limited to low income households. Due to the onset of World War II, only a modest number of units were built under the 1937 Housing Act. In 1949, however, Congress passed the Housing Act of 1949 which provided federal subsidies for slum clearance and urban redevelopment. As part of the Act, Congress authorized the construction of an additional 810,000 public housing units and established the national housing policy of "[a] decent home and a suitable living environment for every American family...." It was not until 1972, however, that all of the housing units authorized by the 1949 Act were actually completed. Today, approximately 1.3 million units of public housing exist in the United States.

From its inception, public housing was controversial. In the 1930s, the private real estate lobby alleged that the program was socialistic and wasteful. Projects were frequently segregated by race and built in less desirable neighborhoods where their presence would not be "offensive' " to community residents. Public housing was originally created for temporary occupancy by the "submerged middle class." As soon as residents could get themselves on their feet, they were expected to move elsewhere. During the 1950s, however, the socioeconomic character of public housing changed. Federal government policies and programs such as mortgage insurance, tax preferences for homeownership and highway construction subsidized the movement of middle and moderate income households out of the city to the suburbs. At roughly the same time, black migration from the South to northern cities accelerated. As manufacturing jobs followed the migration of households to suburban locations, central cities increasingly became home to low income and black households. Public housing no longer served as a temporary haven for upwardly mobile households, but instead became a permanent home to a very poor and disproportionately nonwhite population.

As the income of public housing residents plummeted and the age of public housing projects increased, the rents charged by PHAs to cover operating expenses became increasingly burdensome. Some PHAs deferred maintenance due to shortages of funds. In 1969, Congress's action to assist tenants by limiting maximum rents chargeable by PHAs further added to PHA burdens. The federal government enacted subsidy programs to help PHAs pay for operating and modernization expenses. Neither of these subsidies, however, was fully funded, and many PHAs further cut back on maintenance which led to structural deterioration and, in some extreme cases, the demolition of uninhabitable buildings.

2.   Public Housing Today

At present, there are over 1.3 million units of public housing in the United States, housing 3.5 million people. Public housing constitutes 1.5% of the nation's housing stock. The average annual income of households is $6,539. Approximately 60% of nonelderly resident households have no one employed and half receive Aid to Families with Dependent Children. Thirty-eight percent of such households are composed of elderly persons. Data from a 1986 survey of PHAs indicate that 60% of all families in public housing are headed by blacks and an additional 24% by hispanics.

Over one-half of public housing developments are comprised of single family homes or garden apartments. In addition, one quarter of all units are located in suburban locations. Although several public housing developments have serious structural and social problems, most studies indicate that public housing is in much better condition than its popular image would indicate. A 1980 study of the physical condition of public housing commissioned by the federal government concluded that while the vast majority of the housing stock was in good condition, seven and two-fifths percent of all units had "chronic problems." Another study that examined social, financial, managerial and physical problems concluded that only fifteen percent of all public housing units were troubled. Furthermore, surveys indicate that residents of public housing are quite satisfied with their living conditions, and that most public housing authorities have extremely long waiting lists.

3.   The Future Role of Public Housing in Federal Housing Assistance

Public housing is only one of several housing programs enacted by the federal government to assist low income households. Since the mid–1970s, the government has increasingly relied on the private sector to deliver housing assistance. One supply-oriented approach initiated by the federal government in 1974 is called the Section 8 New Construction and Substantial Rehabilitation Program. Under this program, the government subsidizes the rents of tenants who live in new or substantially renovated structures owned by non-profit or profit-motivated developers. The subsidy, which is tied to the units in these structures, is guaranteed for a period of twenty to forty years and covers the difference between the amount paid by the tenants (usually thirty percent of adjusted income) and a fair market rent based upon the developer's capital and operating costs. In 1974, Congress also enacted one of a series of demand-oriented subsidy programs called the Section 8 Existing Housing Certificate Program. Under this program, participating households are issued a certificate that enables them to rent dwellings owned by private landlords. Provided that they lease homes that meet minimum quality standards and that do not cost more than the federally prescribed maximum level, households participating in the Section 8 Existing Housing Certificate Program must pay no more than thirty percent of their income for rent. The difference between thirty percent of income and the dwelling's rent is paid for by the federal government.

Curtis Berger, Beyond Homelessness: An Entitlement to Housing

45 University of Miami Law Review 315, 316–26, 334–35 (1991).

* * * While concern for the homeless is both fashionable and correct, to direct our attention only toward the homeless leaves untouched, and may draw attention from, a systemically far deeper national dilemma—that of housing indigency. * * *

II.   STATISTICAL DATA

Our nation once made a commitment to remedy the housing needs of the poor. The following statistics stand in stark contrast to that commitment:

(1) Governmental guidelines say that a family should spend no more than thirty percent of its income on housing, including rent or mortgage payments and utility bills. Most Americans spend less, some far less. Yet, nearly three out of four poor families in rural America pay more for housing than the government states they can afford. In 1985, one study found that seventy-two percent of rural poor homeowners spent more than thirty percent of their income on housing, forty-two percent spent more than half, and twenty-six percent spent more than seventy percent.

(2) In the same year, the typical poor renter household paid sixty-five percent of its income for shelter. Eighty-five percent (5.8 million) of all poor rental households paid at least thirty percent of their income for rent and utilities, sixty-three percent (4.3 million) spent more than half, and forty-five percent (3.1 million) spent at least seventy percent.

(3) Between 1970 and 1985, the number of low-rent units (units renting for less than $250 per month in 1985 dollars) declined by 1.8 million (from 9.7 to 7.9 million). During the same period, the number of low-income renter households (households with income less than $10,000 in 1985 dollars) rose by 3.7 million (from 7.9 to 11.6 million). In all, the number of low-income renter households (11.6 million) outstripped the supply of low-rent units (7.9 million) by 3.7 million households.

(4) Even this one-sided comparison understated the actual shortage of low-rent units. More than ten percent of these low-rent units sat vacant because either they or their neighborhoods were deemed uninhabitable. Additionally, of the remaining 7.1 million occupied low-rent units, only two-thirds were actually tenanted by low-income households; moderate-income households occupied the remainder. In sum, 11.6 million low-income households competed for an available 4.8 million low-rent units.

(5) The median gross rent for unassisted poor households, measured in constant 1989 dollars, rose forty-nine percent, from $253 to $376, between 1974 and 1987. By comparison, the median rent for all rental units during this same time rose by only sixteen percent, from $353 to $411.

(6) Although we have no statistical measure on the extent to which individuals and families are forced to double-up, anecdotal evidence suggests that overcrowding has become rampant. The New York City Housing Authority, for example, estimates that as many as eighty percent of the 150,000 units that it operates contain at least one "illegal" occupant.

(7) Between 1980 and 1987, the home mortgage foreclosure rate nearly tripled. In 1985, almost six percent of all mortgages were in default, a percentage not seen since the mid–1930's. Moreover, elderly homeowners, faced with mounting utility, tax, repair, and medical bills, often found themselves forced to sell in order to convert their equity into cash to pay these bills.

(8) Any improvement since 1985 has been marginal.

In placing these numbers in perspective, one is faced with a paradox. From 1982 to 1989, America experienced the longest peacetime expansion in history, with our gross national product increasing an average of four percent per year. During the same time, housing conditions worsened. A further paradox helps to explain the first: As a nation, we once made a commitment to end housing indigency, a commitment which we have let atrophy in the last two decades. The original commitment stems from Franklin Roosevelt's second inaugural address in 1937. Speaking of his concern for that one-third of our nation that was "ill-housed, ill-clad, and ill-nourished," the President stated, "[t]he test of our progress is not whether we add more to the abundance of those who have too much; it is whether we provide enough for those who have too little." A few months later, Congress enacted the United States Housing Act of 1937, public housing's statutory bedrock. Congress renewed its commitment in 1949 when, in launching the federal urban renewal program, it vowed to realize as soon as feasible "a decent home in a suitable environment for every American [family]." Again in 1968, Congress established a ten-year goal "to meet all of the nation's housing needs and eliminate all of its substandard housing."

Certainly, we made some serious mistakes in all three of these programs. Moreover, in no instance did the performance fully match the rhetoric. But until World War II interrupted the progress made after 1937, and for most of the post-war era until the middle-to-late 1970's, housing conditions significantly improved.

More than twenty years have passed since either Congress or the Executive Branch has declared a universal entitlement to decent housing as a national goal. During much of this period, there has been almost no national will to examine the full dimension of our housing problem. We have directed most of our concern narrowly to the steps that would end our daily discomfort at the sight of the homeless.

What mutes the sense of deeper urgency is the shifting nature of the housing problem. President Roosevelt's "ill-housed" * * * were literally that. Those families had shelter, but the shelter was primitive, unsanitary, unhealthful, and unsafe. Although ill-housing conditions have not disappeared, they have much abated. Governmental data indicate that today less than two percent of the nation's occupied housing units lack basic plumbing, and the term "dilapidation" no longer appears in the nation's Census of Housing. Although on any given day, thousands of housing units in our larger cities bear code violations, housing quality no longer remains the pressing issue that animated both the rhetorical and programmatic commitments of a generation ago.

The systemic housing issue of the 1990's is affordability. Millions of lower-income households can no longer find suitable shelter within their means. Were it not for the literally homeless, however, whose presence we cannot avoid, the issue of affordability would largely escape our notice. The homeless whom we see, unfortunately, are only the *visible* couriers warning us of a far deeper social malady that affects many millions more. Unseen is the four-year-old child going to bed hungry because her welfare mother must spend sixty percent of her monthly stipend for rent, or the young working couple doubled-up in a small apartment with the wife's parents, or the ten-year-long waiting list in many cities for public housing apartments. Some have dubbed these hidden legions the pre-homeless. The pre-homeless, tragically, describes those persons who may soon cross the narrow divide between shelter and the streets, unless we address the deeper issue—that of affordability.

How did we get into this mess? There are explanations. Most are familiar: the virtual end of new public housing starts, neighborhood gentrification and the loss of single room occupancy and other rental units, housing abandonment, the widening of poverty, the shrinkage of all federal outlays for subsidized housing, historically high mortgage interest rates, the failure of welfare and housing allowances to keep pace with rising rental costs, pervasive racial discrimination, the displacement of factory jobs by much lower-paying service jobs, the suppression of the minimum wage level, the shrinkage in household size, and a rapid rise in the number of households headed by single mothers—an especially vulnerable group. A few reasons, like the underfunding of public housing authorities, the Social Security Administration's pervasive (and often illegal) denial of disability insurance benefits, and the sometimes self-defeating role of tax-shelters, may be somewhat less familiar. But, attention to the past is useful only as it illuminates the future. Recriminations, however much deserved, cannot produce a single unit of housing.

We have used the phrase "housing entitlement" as if its meaning were self-evident. For the literally homeless, an entitlement has meant little more than temporary shelter, clean linens, a warm meal, and, in the case of families with school-age children, some educational continuity. Limiting our aspirations to this definition, however, does not bring us very far because apart from the meanness of so limited a goal, we would continue to ignore the deeper problem of homelessness: the pervasive lack of affordable housing. As a humanitarian nation, we need to have a far more concrete commitment to provide housing to our citizens, and a realistic and workable plan to achieve that goal.

III. HOUSING ENTITLEMENT PROPOSALS

I propose that we guarantee to every American household a basic level of housing that meets current federal standards of quality and affordability. Affordable shelter must be seen as a fundamental right, as part of that entitlement to an adequate standard of living that every humane society— certainly one as fortunate as our own—should wish to assure every one of its residents. The phrase "fundamental right" has constitutional overtones, but I am not asserting the need for an entitlement of constitutional dimension. As a constitutional pragmatist, I accept the United States Supreme Court's view that the present Constitution contains no shelter protection. Further, I do not believe that either this reading of the text or the text itself will change within any time soon. Even if the Constitution did embody a shelter guarantee, we have learned from the school and prison cases how difficult, ad hoc, and time-consuming it is for the courts to mandate institutional reform. The entitlement, if there is to be one, requires legislation—and not a single program—but a multi-frontal attack on each dimension of the problem.

In the course of any discussion about entitlements, we cannot avoid the nagging question: How is the entitlement to be paid for? This is a question that must worry us in an era of massive federal deficits, fiscally crippled states and cities, and a flood of other urgent priorities in education, medical care, crime control, and infrastructure repair. We could help to finance a housing entitlement were we to redirect a small part of the current fifty-seven billion dollar annual housing subsidy that chiefly benefits the higher-income homeowners, in the form of the income tax deduction for mortgage interest and property taxes, but that subsidy is a sacred cow we cannot milk. We must assume that new dollars will not come easily and that proposals for spending them must be cost-effective.

The proposals that I make fall into four general categories: preserving the present supply of subsidized units, increasing the supply of low-cost units, strengthening the effective demand of low-income households, and attending to the specialized needs of certain disadvantaged groups. * * *

IV. CONCLUSION

In the United States, we have neither embraced a domestic constitutional right to housing, as have such western democracies as Sweden and the Netherlands, nor do we now profess that our citizens have "the fundamental right, regardless of economic circumstances, to enjoy adequate shelter at reasonable costs," as does our neighbor Canada. Moreover, we have not authorized our government to take "extraordinary steps" to alleviate any housing shortage, as has Germany. In none of these countries, nor in any other western democracy, with the exception of Great Britain (whose current government shares this government's political vision), does the extent of homelessness even begin to approach the dimensions of our own. Homelessness will not begin to recede until our government, the President and the Congress, look beyond the immediate crisis to the systemic problems that have produced and will prolong it. To solve those problems, we must once again regard affordable housing as everyone's right.

Robert C. Ellickson, The Untenable Case for an Unconditional Right to Shelter

15 Harvard Journal of Law and Public Policy 17, 20–28, 32–34 (1992).

As homelessness has become a prominent domestic issue, numerous advocates have called for constitutional recognition of an individual's unconditional right to enjoy a minimum level of shelter. I argue here that these advocates have failed to deal with the fundamental fact that a society must maintain incentives to work. Both theory and data indicate that an unconditional shelter right, presumably coupled with ironclad rights to enjoy other material benefits, could be counterproductive, even for the poor.* * *

II.   Three Approaches to Welfare Rights

* * *

If individuals are in fact partly motivated by material ends, the recognition of unconditional welfare rights might diminish society's aggregate wealth in several ways. First, a person who is guaranteed sustenance has less reason to work. Second, if income taxes or other taxes on labor are used to fund welfare guarantees, welfare programs diminish the marginal material rewards of wage-earners, thereby decreasing their labor incentives. Third, a welfare state invariably gives rise to administrative costs and wasteful rent-seeking efforts. Finally, as more and more individuals and households in an area receive government assistance, neighborhood residents may no longer be able to sustain the traditional informal norm that an employable person has a duty to be in the workforce. Although there is no consensus on the magnitude of the various costs of maintaining a welfare state, even left-liberal social scientists and politicians are concerned about these issues.

To simplify the analysis drastically, assume that a society may adopt one or another of three possible strategies to resolve the inherent tension between providing welfare and encouraging work. The three, which I now briefly outline, are (1) the welfare approach, (2) the conditional-welfare approach, and (3) the unconditional-welfare approach.

In a market economy such as the United States, each individual essentially owns his own labor. This endowment of rights to labor creates direct material incentives to participate either in self employment, household production, or labor markets. In a market economy, each worker serves as the primary monitor against his own shirking. However, some workers will inevitably be mentally or physically incapable of performing marketable tasks, or will simply be unqualified to perform the jobs available in the market. A government that adopts a *no-welfare approach* does little or nothing to relieve an individual of the consequences of being unemployable or unemployed.

Many voters apparently regard the laissez-faire system just described as unacceptably cruel to those who either cannot work or are jobless for reasons largely beyond their control. As a result, over the last century the democratic nations with market economies have all instituted welfare-state programs to supplement (and, perhaps unintentionally, to supplant) more traditional systems of social insurance such as the extended family, the voluntary association, and organized religion.

Policymakers in the United States have generally opted for the second strategy, a *conditional-welfare approach*. Few U.S. programs render all applicants eligible for long-term welfare benefits. Eligibility for benefits is instead typically restricted to limited categories of persons, notably those who either cannot work (because of age or disability), or should not be in the workforce (because they are caretakers of small children). Persons who fall outside these categories are expected to make their way without significant governmental assistance. This approach to welfare is conditional in the sense that applicants for benefits must prove that they should be excused from the presumptive duty to be self-supporting. The welfare benefits that are made more broadly available, such as food stamps and general assistance, typically are conditional in another sense: A beneficiary's entitlement depends on continuing compliance with specified "workfare" obligations. The lawmakers who create these conditional-welfare programs intend to soften the harsh consequences of the laissez-faire system, while at the same time minimizing harm to work incentives.

A society that pursues the third strategy, *the unconditional-welfare approach*, promises all of its members certain minimal material comforts with no questions asked. Most advocates of a right to shelter appear to contemplate an entitlement of this variety. If a society were able to deliver on this set of promises, it would free its members from much of the stress of being personally responsible for providing for themselves. The unconditional-welfare approach inherently places in the hands of central authorities the task of distributing most social largesse. In practice, these same central authorities must also assume great responsibility for policing against shirking—a responsibility that a market economy largely decentralizes to each individual. Because the managers of an unconditional-welfare state have little discretion in distributing material benefits (at least in theory), they are likely to institute elaborate nonmaterial incentives to induce people to work.

Unconditional-welfare systems appear to be most viable within small, closely-knit societies that are capable of administering informal sanctions. For example, a kibbutz that assures housing to each of its members may be able to correlate social status positively with industriousness and to ostracize or even expel able-bodied shirkers. By contrast, experience abroad suggests that a nation-state is too large and too loosely-knit to generate informal social forces that successfully support norms of work. In practice, a state that adopts the unconditional-welfare approach therefore tends to resort to heavy-handed coercion to enforce legal duties to work. Even though the unconditional-welfare approach may eliminate certain stresses that individuals bear when they must be self-sufficient, this approach introduces the new stresses that arise when an individual is monitored by a powerful centralized bureaucracy.

Communist states, of course, provide the crispest examples of the unconditional-welfare approach. Communist bills of rights contain an array of positive rights including, typically, an express right to shelter. These constitutions also set out what might be called "bills of duties," which invariably include an express duty to work. Although the authorities who have managed Communist regimes have tried exhortation and other non-coercive techniques, they have also resorted to criminal prosecutions to enforce duties to work.

III.   Do Shelter Rights Lead to Improved Housing Conditions?

It is theoretically possible that the guarantee of a right to shelter (and related welfare benefits) would, by weakening work incentives, shrink the aggregate social welfare pie so much that everyone, including the poor, would end up materially worse off. This prospect may seem utterly fanciful on its face. In this section, I introduce some evidence that it is not. Poor persons in the United States, who lack a constitutional right to shelter, tend to live in more spacious and better-maintained housing than do poor persons in nations that recognize a right to shelter. Moreover, the housing conditions of poor households in the United States have been steadily improving with time. Although these facts hardly prove that the United States would injure the poor by embracing an unconditional right to shelter, they do demonstrate that our conditional-welfare system has proven to be much more successful than its detractors would have us believe. In general, the United States deserves high commendation for the housing its people enjoy. American housing is much larger, better-equipped, and cheaper than that in Japan, for example.

A.   Housing in Jurisdictions That Recognize a Right to Shelter

Comparative housing data are of poor quality. In addition, an analysis cannot readily control for the many factors, other than the presence or absence of a right to shelter, that might determine a nation's housing success. Despite these difficulties, a brief look at housing conditions in different nations is instructive.

International evidence shows that proclaiming a right to shelter does not magically lead to better housing conditions. It is hardly news that the Communist states that have long espoused a right to housing have done a dreadful job of delivering on that promise. The median household in the Soviet Union lives in two rooms and has about 130 square feet per capita; the median U.S. household occupies five rooms and has nearly 600 square feet per capita; Only 2% of United States households, compared to 76% of Soviet households, live in two rooms or less. To put it bluntly: Americans below the poverty line typically live far more spaciously than do middle-class Soviets.

More pertinent to debates over housing in western democracies are the housing patterns in Sweden and the Netherlands, two nations that Professor Berger praises for having embraced a constitutional right to housing. The scant evidence available suggests that poor households in these nations live in worse housing than do their counterparts in the United States. In the early 1980s, for example, 5% of Swedish housing units and 4.1% of Dutch housing units lacked full plumbing facilities, whereas only 2.7% of U.S. housing units did. At the same time, it is perhaps relevant that 64.4% of United States dwelling units were occupied by homeowners, while only 41.4% of Swedish and 42.7% of Dutch dwelling units were. Despite the legal promises of their nations, observers in Sweden and Holland report shortages of low-rent housing units. Because housing-production costs in Sweden are more than double what they are in the United States, housing affordability is a much more serious problem there.

Because advocates of shelter rights aspire to change current law, they are likely to stress nonlegal theories of American housing triumphs, such as unusually plentiful endowments of land and other resources, or the good fortune of having avoided wartime destruction. These particular hypotheses are weak; Sweden, for example, has a lower population density than does the United States and did not suffer war damage. More credible is the hypothesis that federal income tax incentives have led to greater—some economists would say excessive—investment in U.S. housing.

This tax hypothesis, however, underscores the potential effects of basic legal choices on economic performance. Observers who believe that natural resources and deep-rooted cultural traditions are paramount should heed the divergent trajectories of the economies of East and West Germany, and of North and South Korea. Should not the advocates of unconditional shelter rights be wary of importing the general welfare strategy of nations with inferior housing records?

B.   Trends in Housing Conditions in the United States

Contrary to the commentators' perceptions of a housing "crisis," during this century most poor American households—despite their lack of a right to shelter—have benefited from steadily improving housing conditions. For example, the percentage of black households lacking complete plumbing plunged from 79.6% in 1940 to 6.1% in 1980, and the percentage living with more than one person per room dropped from 28.3% in 1960 to 9.1% in 1980. Contrary to what some advocates might have predicted for the Reagan decade, the available data indicate that these auspicious trends have continued since 1980. The residential situation of the institutionalized poor has also improved as prisons, mental hospitals, and similar accommodations have become much more livable.

The nation's progress in housing is often overlooked because panhandlers and other impoverished people have become increasingly visible in conspicuous downtown locations during the past decade. Although advocates for the homeless tend to link this "homelessness" problem with changes in housing markets, I have argued elsewhere that it is more plausibly attributed to the deinstitutionalization of the mentally ill, the drug epidemic, the loosening of police supervision of street behavior, and the deepening of underclass subcultures. Observers should be cautious about inferring a "housing crisis" from a rise in panhandling. The fragmentary evidence on the subject suggests that many panhandlers dwell permanently in conventional housing. * * *

V.   Conclusion: The Grand Constitutional Design

Why has our political system balked at expressly recognizing "a right to shelter," "a right to a minimum income," and other similar rights, when for more than a century it has guaranteed self-ownership of labor and a right to schooling? The essential reason is both simple and manifest: The proposed entitlements tend to discourage work, while the existing entitlements tend to encourage it.

The current constitutional provisions reject the unconditional-welfare approach. To secure the value of the rights that our constitutions presently confer, a recipient must complement the conferrals with personal labor. Owning one's own labor is valuable only to the extent that one is willing to work. The value of receiving an education depends significantly on one's willingness to apply oneself in school. By increasing the rewards of work, the present constitutional guarantees help induce individuals to contribute to the nation.

Events in several American cities illustrate the drawbacks of establishing unconditional rights to material aid. During the early 1980s, New York City, Philadelphia, and Washington, D.C. each guaranteed their citizens unqualified rights to receive emergency shelter. These open-door shelter policies attracted unexpected numbers of able-bodied entrants, and the shelters apparently fostered dependency. In Philadelphia, housing advocates eventually agreed to allow the city to deny shelter to employable persons who had refused to comply with job-hunting requirements. When the D.C. City Council backtracked from that jurisdiction's right to shelter, D.C. voters declined to reverse that retreat. Many New York City shelter administrators came to favor imposing some sort of workfare obligation on able-bodied members of the shelter population, but encountered resistance from lawyers who represented the homeless.

Remarkably, despite these events and the magnitude of the issue involved, most of the advocates of unconditional shelter rights either ignore the tension between welfare and work, or dismiss its importance. Those who have drafted our constitutions and conditional welfare programs have served us better. They have been attuned to the desirability of having a decentralized system for monitoring against shirking. They have been aware of the inherent tension between positive and negative liberties, and aware that a bill of rights that delivers on promises of unconditional welfare rights would be hard-pressed to deliver on promises to shield the individual from an intrusive state. Moreover, international evidence does not support the proposition that recognition of an unconditional right to shelter actually results in better housing for the poor. Shifting jobs from carpenters to lawyers is not the way to improve housing conditions.

———————

1.   Should the United States recognize a right to shelter? Should such a right be part of the Bill of Rights guaranteed by the U.S. Constitution? Even if you do not support a constitutional right to housing, should the government subsidize the provision of housing for the indigent?

2.   Assuming that the electorate did support programs to assist indigent persons in obtaining habitable housing, what policy or policies should the government undertake? Consider the following options:

- Expansion and improvement of public housing

- Privatizing public housing by selling units at below market prices to qualifying households

- Provision of housing vouchers (or rent certificates) to qualifying households which can be used in lieu of rent

- Changes in zoning laws to promote more construction of lower cost, higher density housing

- Expanded use of linkage requirements under which developers of new commercial and residential real estate projects must provide a designated proportion of new units for lower income households

What are the advantages and disadvantages of these various approaches? What comprehensive program would make most sense?

3.   To what extent is the right to housing distinct from welfare and redistribution policy generally? With limited resources for redistribution to the poor, what should be the relative priorities among the provision of food, education, housing, police, and health care services? Should the government provide such assistance in inalienable forms—such as housing vouchers, food stamps, medical assistance—or through direct cash assistance which poor households could use as they wished? To what extent should such policies be implemented on the federal level, the state level, or the local level?

B.   TRADITIONAL NONPOSSESSORY INTERESTS

Nonpossessory rights in land, known as servitudes, are arrangements between private parties that give one party the right to use or to restrict the use of another's land. In contrast to contractual rights and obligations (which generally relate only to the promisor and promisee), the property rights and obligations created by servitudes pass to successive owners and occupiers without the need expressly to assign these rights and obligations or to renegotiate the arrangement.

By the Industrial Revolution, English law recognized four different types of servitudes, each with its own historical origins: easements (the right to use another's land); profits á prendre (the right to remove natural resources from another's land); real covenants (lease provisions that bind both the lessor's and lessee's successors and that are enforced "at law," *i.e.,* for damages), and equitable servitudes (promises between neighboring landowners that bind their successors and that are enforced in equity). French, Design Proposal for the New Restatement of the Law of Property—Servitudes, 21 U.C. Davis L. Rev. 1213, 1214 (1988). Because there were no significant land use planning or zoning statutes at that time, servitudes provided the only mechanisms for residential and commercial landowners to preserve amenities threatened by urban crowding and congestion.

Although governmental land use planning has become widespread in the twentieth century, the number and variety of servitudes has continued to grow. Increased attention to historic and environmental preservation has contributed to this development. But servitudes remain popular primarily because of their usefulness in designing complex residential, commercial, and industrial projects. They are more flexible, more easily arranged (especially at the beginning stages of a project), and more durable than zoning laws. Properly structured, servitudes restrict the use of individual parcels of land to obtain common benefits. Professor French has noted that the ability to pass rights and obligations to successive owners without renegotiation provides

> the stability needed for investments dependent upon maintenance of particular uses of land. Servitudes promote efficient land use because they allow an investor to purchase only the degree of control needed to maximize the investment, rather than the entire fee.

Id. at 1215. She also noted, however, that

> the permanence of servitudes * * * poses economic and social risks. Servitudes can freeze land uses and distort patterns of development. They can impose burdens that become unreasonable and depress land values. Although the parties are free to renegotiate the terms of the arrangement at any time, transaction costs and free-rider and bilateral monopoly problems may prevent the most efficient use of land. In addition, the existence of servitudes can clog the title and diminish the marketability of the land.

Id. Some authors are enthusiastic about the advantages of servitudes, especially among residential landowners. *See* Epstein, Covenants and Constitutions, 73 Cornell L. Rev. 906 (1988); Ellickson, Cities and Homeowners Associations, 130 U. Pa. L. Rev. 1519 (1982); Sterk, Freedom from Freedom of Contract: The Enduring Value of Servitude Restrictions, 70 Iowa L. Rev. 615 (1985). Other authors are concerned that private arrangements will

impacts, especially for excluded individuals and future gener-
have ne(1982); Alexander, Freedom, Coercion, and the Law of Servi-
atio Cornell L. Rev. 883 (1988).

he law of servitudes is complex, technical, and top-heavy with history.
ough easements, profits, real covenants, and equitable servitudes are
nceptually similar, if not identical in important respects, the rules
governing their creation, durability, and termination vary in important
ways. Numerous scholars have argued that these distinctions serve little or
no purpose and should be replaced by a single nonpossessory interest. *See
generally* Symposium on Servitudes, 55 S. Cal. L. Rev. 1177 (1982). We will
examine these arguments and reform proposals at the end of this section.
Legislatures and courts, however, have not been quick to act on these
criticisms and suggestions, and hence it necessary to understand the
history, structure, and complex logic of the common law.

1. EASEMENTS

An easement gives the holder the right to use or restrict the use of
another person's land.[1] The owner of the servient tenement[2] may not
revoke the easement at will[3] or interfere with the easement holder's use of
the property, and the easement holder may protect his rights from interference by third parties. An easement, however, does not necessarily create an
exclusive right. The easement holder normally cannot prevent the servient
possessor from also using the land involved in the easement, or from
granting another easement on the same piece of land, unless the parties
clearly intend to create an exclusive easement.

a. CLASSIFICATION

Easements are classified along two different axes: *affirmative* or *negative*, and *appurtenant* or *in gross*. An *affirmative easement* privileges the
holder of the easement to use of another's land. For example, it could give
A the right to construct and use a right of way across B's land (otherwise
enjoinable as a trespass).

---

1. At common law there was a conceptually distinct right, called a profit á prendre,
to remove natural resources from someone
else's land. Profits were classified according
to their particular use. For example, a piscary
involved the right to take fish, and estovers
was the right to cut timber for fuel. Today,
the rules governing profits and easements are
substantially identical, and some states make
no distinction between the two interests. *See,
e.g., Costa v. Fawcett*, 202 Cal.App.2d 695,
702, 21 Cal.Rptr. 143, 148 (1962).

2. The land that is "burdened" by the
easement is called the servient tenement or
estate. If the easement holder's land is "ben-

efited" by the easement—for example, if the
land is more easily accessible because of the
easement—it is the dominant tenement or
estate.

3. By contrast, a license is permission—
as opposed to a right—to use another's land,
and thus is revocable at any time. A license,
however, may become irrevocable under an
estoppel theory if the licensee expended money or labor in reasonable reliance on the
continued existence of the license. Such an
irrevocable license is treated like an easement. *See, e.g., Cooke v. Ramponi*, 38 Cal.2d
282, 286–89, 239 P.2d 638, 641–42 (1952).

The holder of a *negative easement* has the right to prevent possessor from using the servient tenement in an otherwise lawful For example, if A has a negative easement for light against B, A cannot B from erecting a building that blocks the light from reaching A's land common law, and in virtually all states today, the only negative easement are for light, air, lateral support, and flow of an artificial stream. American courts, in contrast to their English counterparts, have shown greater flexibility in stretching these categories. *See, e.g., Petersen v. Friedman,* 162 Cal.App.2d 245, 247–48, 328 P.2d 264, 266 (1958) (enforcing a negative easement for an unobstructed view of the San Francisco Bay).

An *easement appurtenant* is an incident of ownership of the dominant tenement, and is not personal to the original holder (where the original parties' intent is ambiguous, most states have a constructional preference for easements appurtenant over easements in gross so long as the holder's land is benefited by the easement). The easement appurtenant passes with the possession of the dominant tenement; a successive owner of the dominant tenement enjoys the benefits of the easement whether or not the deed transferring the dominant tenement specifically mentions the easement. In general, a successor to the servient tenement takes possession of that interest subject to the easement unless he is protected by the recording act, *e.g.*, he is a bona fide purchaser for value without actual, inquiry, or record notice of the easement.[4]

An *easement in gross* is personal to the holder, *i.e.*, independent of his possession of any land. Examples include easements to erect and maintain billboards or to lay utility lines. Because there is no dominant tenement, successors to the holder's land (if any) do not have the easement. Most American (but not English) courts hold that successors to the servient tenement are subject to the easement.

Because an easement in gross is not incident to a particular parcel of land, there is an issue of whether it is alienable, devisable, or inheritable. Historically, in England and this country, an easement in gross that included a power to sever and remove something from the servient tenement (*i.e.*, a profit) was alienable. In England and in a few states, other easements in gross terminated upon attempted transfer.[5] In the United States, only commercial easements in gross are generally assignable. *See*

---

4. As discussed in Chapter II.D.2, in a "notice" jurisdiction, someone who purchases the servient tenement without actual, inquiry, or record notice of the easement (*i.e.*, a bona fide purchaser for value, or BFP) takes free of the easement. In a "race-notice" state, the purchaser of the servient tenement takes free of the easement only if he is both a BFP and records before the easement holder records.

5. Courts holding that easements in gross are not assignable normally state that

such easements are disfavored because they make the underlying fee more difficult to market. It seems unlikely, however, that the assignability of easements in gross will reduce marketability of servient tenements any more than appurtenant easements. Perhaps the real reason is that while both kinds of easements make servient tenements less alienable, only easements appurtenant make the dominant tenement more valuable and thus more marketable.

Restatement of Property §§ 489–491 (presuming that commercial easements are alienable).

———————

1.   Why do we need nonpossessory interests at all? Couldn't a property owner create a right-of-way or other easement using a defeasible fee, *e.g.*, a fee simple subject to a condition subsequent? What are the relative advantages and disadvantages of creating a defeasible fee?

2.   What reasons might justify courts' reluctance to recognize more than a few types of negative easements?

———————

b.   REPAIRS

In general, the terms of the grant creating the easement fix the duty to maintain and repair an easement. Absent controlling language, the owner of the servient tenement has no duty to maintain or repair the easement; that burden rests with the dominant possessor. *See, e.g.,* Cal. Civ. Code § 845.

c.   CREATION OF EASEMENTS

Easements may be created expressly, by operation of law, or by prescription.

i.   *Express Easements*

A grant conveying an easement must conform to the statute of frauds; the conveyance must be in writing and signed by the party to be charged.[6] The creation and conveyance of easements should also be recorded to protect the holder from claims by a subsequent bona fide purchaser for value of the servient tenement.

Easements may be created by grant or by reservation. An easement by grant would be created if "A" conveyed a right-of-way across A's land to "B." Alternatively, an easement by reservation would be created if A conveyed a fee simple to B, but expressly reserved for herself a right-of-way across the land.[7] In some states, a grantor may even reserve an easement in favor of a third party. *See, e.g., Willard v. First Church of Christ, Scientist, Pacifica*, 7 Cal.3d 473, 476–79, 102 Cal.Rptr. 739, 741–44, 498 P.2d 987,

———————

6. Failure to observe the requirements of the statute of frauds will result in a license rather than an easement. Part performance or estoppel may permit enforcement of a grant of an easement that does not meet the statute of frauds.

7. Don't be confused by the two uses of the word "grant." In the previous paragraph, grant referred to the *instrument* for creating an easement. Here, an easement by grant is used in contrast to an easement by reservation. Either an easement by grant or an easement by reservation may be created in a grant instrument.

989–92 (1972) (rejecting the common law rule barring reservations in favor of a third party); *Restatement of Property* § 472 cmt. b.

Scope. The scope of an express easement is determined largely by the terms of the grant. Where the language is ambiguous, courts will look to the parties' contemporaneous treatment of the easement. In general, the owner of an easement cannot "materially" increase or create a new burden on the servient tenement. For example, in *Wall v. Rudolph*, 198 Cal.App.2d 684, 18 Cal.Rptr. 123 (1961), the easement was for "road purposes." When the easement was created around the turn of the century, the parties' predecessors used the road to transport ranch and agricultural supplies. Five decades later, the owner of the dominant tenement developed a waste disposal site on his land, and drove his trucks over the easement to the waste site. Even though the new use fit within the express terms of the easement, the court readily granted the servient owner's request for an injunction because the amount of traffic on the road was now significantly greater than when the easement was created.

Faus v. City of Los Angeles

Supreme Court of California, 1967.
67 Cal.2d 350, 431 P.2d 849, 62 Cal.Rptr. 193.

■ TOBRINER, JUSTICE.

The issue in this case devolves from the fact that in 1955 public motor coach service was substituted for public electric railway service over rights of way in the Los Angeles area that were granted for an electric railway. Plaintiff urges that the conversion of the rights of way conflicts with the terms of the instruments of their creation, causing a destruction of the easements to which the parcels were subject. For the reasons set forth in this opinion we have concluded that the present use of the subject parcels sufficiently complies with the purposes of the grantors to permit survival of the easements. * * *

The seven grants in the present case all date from the period 1901–1911 and involve parcels of land lying in the then outskirts of the expanding Los Angeles area. Although the seven deeds differ in many respects, they typically conveyed rights of way for the construction and operation of a passenger railway running into central Los Angeles. Within the time limits set forth in the deeds the grantee railroads constructed the specified facilities and commenced to render the required services. Thereafter, the original grantors subdivided and sold all of their lands abutting the rights of way except strips along the edges of the rights of way, which they dedicated for public streets.

The grantee railroads and their various successors (ultimately the Los Angeles Transit Lines) maintained streetcar service over the subject parcels until May 1955. At various times between 1924 and 1948 the City of Los Angeles, acting pursuant to deeds from the railroads, paved for street purposes certain portions of the rights of way lying parallel to the tracks. Neither the original grantors nor their heirs urged any objection to this use. Indeed the heirs of the grantors of the parcels involved in the second and third causes of action actually petitioned the city to pave the longitudinal portions of the rights of way.

Pursuant to an order of the California Public Utilities Commission authorizing the cessation of such streetcar services on condition that the Los Angeles Transit Lines provide substitute motor coach service along the same routes, the company, in May 1955, terminated the electric railway services. The order also required the Los Angeles Transit Lines to refrain from alienating the rights of way for 180 days so that the city might acquire this property. During that period the city took the land by condemnation; the heirs of the original grantors were not named in that action. The city later widened the adjoining streets, incorporating into them all of the land which had formerly borne the tracks.

Plaintiff Faus has located the heirs of the original grantors and has obtained from them an assignment of all interest which they might have in the subject parcels. Plaintiff commenced the present action in May 1960, urging that the city's use of the land violated the conditions contained in the original deeds and thus entitles him to an award for the taking of the property. The trial court accepted this contention and entered judgment in plaintiff's favor.

Defendant City of Los Angeles urges that the uses to which the subject parcels are now devoted cannot be deemed inconsistent with the terms of the original grants. It acknowledges that the grantors specified that the property was to be used "for the purposes of an electric railway" or "for an electric railway" and that several of the deeds explicitly state that cessation of railway service for six months shall cause reversion of the land.[8] But defendant contends that the deeds must be construed with reference to the grantor's underlying purpose. That purpose, the city asserts, was to make sure that the inhabitants of the properties which the grantors wished to subdivide would enjoy the best means of interurban public transport which was technologically feasible. The very language of the deeds discloses the concern of the grantors that the vehicles of transportation stop at available places for boarding.[9]

---

8. For instance, the deed set forth as Exhibit A provides: "If said electric railway is not in operation within the time set down above, or if, at any time hereafter, when said railway has been completed, the same shall cease to be operated for a period of six months, constituting a practical abandonment of the same, then this deed shall be null and void * * *."

9. For instance, the deeds set forth as Exhibits A, B, G, and H provide that the railway "shall stop all 'local' or 'suburban' trains for passengers desiring to get on or off the cars, but no stops shall be made by through 'limited', 'express', or 'special' trains." The deed set forth as Exhibit D provides that the railway furnish not less than eight 'local' services each way per day over the route between the hours of 6 a.m. and 10 p.m., in addition to providing for the stopping of local or suburban trains as set forth in the deeds marked Exhibits A and B.

Fifty years of technological change, embracing developments in internal combustion vehicles and techniques of highway construction, have undoubtedly produced a situation in which motor buses have won public preference because of their greater flexibility of route and schedule. Plaintiff acknowledges "the economic and functional obsolescence of the electric street railways." Plaintiff has not suggested that the bus service provided over the roads which now occupy the former railroad right of way affords a less satisfactory means of public transport for the adjacent landowners than that previously supplied by the streetcar network. Moreover, the order of the Public Utilities Commission, coming as it does from the agency authorized to determine and declare the public interest in matters of transportation, affords persuasive evidence that the bus service now provided over the former railroad routes constitutes an adequate substitute.

Because its operation must necessarily be prospective, we make the "assumption * * * in the case of an easement created by conveyance that the conveyance, having by its nature a prospective operation, should be assumed to have been intended to accommodate future needs." (2 American Law of Property, § 8.69, p. 281.) Our courts have been receptive to the contention that changed economic and technological conditions require reevaluation of restrictions placed upon the use of real property and may render legally inoperative certain changes in use which would otherwise require a reversion.

As early as 1894, this court was prepared to rule, contrary to the then prevailing authorities, that land subject to an easement for street purposes could be used for a passenger or freight railway without thereby surcharging the easement. (*Montgomery v. Santa Ana Westminster Railway Co.* (1894) 104 Cal. 186, 37 P. 786.) "The world moves," we noted. "The trend of judicial opinion, except where overshadowed and incrusted with *stare decisis*, is to a broader and more comprehensive view of the rights of the public in and to the streets and highways of [a] city * * * and, while carefully conserving the rights of individuals to their property, the courts have not hesitated to declare the shadowy title which the owner of the fee holds to the land in a public street or highway, during the duration of the easement of the public therein, as being subject to all the varied wants of the public, and essential to its health, enjoyment and progress." (104 Cal. at p. 192, 37 P. p. 788.)

Thus, in *Abbot Kinney Co. v. City of Los Angeles, supra,* 223 Cal.App.2d 668, 36 Cal.Rptr. 113, then Presiding Justice Burke ruled that a conveyance of land for use "as a pleasure park or beach," which expressly provided that use of the premises for "buildings of any kind or character" or for "teaming" would cause a reversion, was nevertheless consistent with the paving of part of the property as a parking lot. In reaching this conclusion the court placed primary stress upon the changes in the prevailing mode of transportation which had occurred since the original dedication of the park. The court noted that at the time of its creation the park was served by an electric railway but that the railway had been abandoned when "the automobile became almost the exclusive means of public transport." (223 Cal.App.2d at p. 671, 36 Cal.Rptr. at p. 115.) Accordingly, the court concluded that realization of the "primary purpose and intent" of the grantors which was "to have said beach used by and open to the public" necessarily required that the concept of "public beach" be expanded to include parking facilities. "Changing conditions, in customs, usages and improvements," the court declared, "must be deemed to have been contemplated by the grantor." (223 Cal.App.2d at p. 675, 36 Cal.Rptr. at p. 118.)

Similarly, in *Griffith v. City of Los Angeles* (1959) 175 Cal.App.2d 331, 346 P.2d 49, the court held that a grant of land to be used "exclusively as a public park and pleasure ground" was consistent with the use of one of the canyons in the park as a rubbish dump which, after being filled, would provide a level recreation area. The court pointed out that "a dedication must be understood and construed with reference to its primary object and purpose. Nothing is improper which conduces to that object. The real question is whether the use in a particular case, and for a designated purpose, is consistent or inconsistent with such primary object." (*Griffith v. City of Los Angeles* (1959) 175 Cal.App.2d 331, 337, 346 P.2d 49, 54.) The court held that, "The dedicator is presumed to have intended the property to be used by the public in such way as will be most convenient and comfortable, and according to not only the proprieties and uses known at the time of the dedication, but also to those justified by lapse of time and change of conditions." (175 Cal.App.2d at p. 337, 346 P.2d at p. 54.)

Most closely in point is *Wattson v. Eldridge, supra*, 207 Cal. 314, 278 P. 236. In that case, "In the year 1905 the Abbot Kinney Company, a corporation, conceived the idea of creating a city to be known as 'Venice of America,' having a system of waterways and canals resembling those of the Old World city." (P. 317, 278 P. p. 237.) Accordingly, the company constructed intercommunicating canals converging into a lagoon, connected with the adjacent ocean. Thereafter the company transferred the canal areas to the City of Venice by an instrument which provided that "the premises herein conveyed shall be used * * * solely and only for permanent waterways, and canals, free to the public forever." (Pp. 317–318, 278 P. p. 237.)

Several years later, this court passed upon the issue whether the deed encompassed a substitute use of the area when the city proposed to close the canals and fill them in for utilization as streets.

In upholding that undertaking this court noted that, "[A] dedication must be understood and construed with reference to its primary object and purpose. * * * While the several intercommunicating canals * * * were used as well for recreation purposes, they must of necessity, and because of the peculiar plan and construction of said city, be held to have been intended by the builder of that city to serve primarily as highways over which persons resident therein and the public generally might pass." (207 Cal. at p. 320, 278 P. at p. 238.) "With changing conditions of travel and use," the court concluded, "a city has the right to adapt and appropriate its highways from time to time such uses as in its judgment would be most conducive to the public good * * *." (207 Cal. at p. 321, 278 P. at p. 239.)

The court finally pointed out that although the parties may not have "actually contemplated" the conversion of the canals to streets, "it may properly be said to have been within the legal contemplation of all that they were to be used for all purposes by which the object of their creation—as public highways or thoroughfares—could be promoted." (*Wattson v. Eldridge, supra,* 207 Cal. 314, 321, 278 P. 236, 239.)

The substitution in the instant case is less extensive than that in *Wattson.* There the obvious objectives of the original provision for the use of the areas as canals were multiple: recreational, including boating and swimming; residential, by inducement to build unusual and appealing houses fronting the canals; and, finally, transportational. The substitution of paved highways eliminated the first two objectives. In the present case, no such liquidation of primary objectives has occurred; here, indeed, the sole and exclusive purpose has merely been to up-date the transportation system so that a modern vehicular means of transport may be utilized in place of an outmoded one.

* * *

The right to substitute modern mechanisms of transportation for old ones under the deeds in the present case must be viewed in the light of its public effect. We deal here with an improvement of public transportation by a public utility for the benefit of the public. We note that in the cases cited, such as *Wattson, Kinney,* and *Griffith,* the courts dealt with matters that affected the public interest. In each of those cases the courts sanctioned a more efficient and publicly beneficial means to achieve the deeds' underlying and main purpose. We fail to see why we should carve an exception in the instant case and hold that the deeds fix forever the means of public transport in the straitjacket of an outmoded method.

* * *

We have concluded that the grantors primarily intended to provide public transportation service across their land. Regular bus transportation along the roads which now encompass the rights of way effectuates this purpose of public service and permits survival of the easements. * * *

The judgment is reversed.

---

1.   How did Faus come into possession of these reversionary interests? Is this analogous to the domain name prospecting problem, *supra* pp. 131–32. Is there any socially redeeming value to this litigation? Or is it simply rent seeking?

2.   The deeds creating the easements in this case were defeasible. That is, upon violation of stated conditions (cessation of use as a railroad), the easement reverted to the grantors. Faus, acting on behalf of all of the property owners, sought only damages and not forfeiture. Why?

3.   The current uses of the land in *Faus* violate the express scope of the easements. How does the court nevertheless find that the easements' conditions are not violated? Is there something special about *dedicated* easements (*i.e.*, grants of easements to governments for public purposes)? Should courts be especially flexible when interpreting dedicated easements?

4.   If a reviewing court should disregard (or at least downplay) the express language of the grant defining the easement's scope or purposes, how should the court discern the "underlying purpose" of the easement? Is there any principle of interpretation? Or do the results depend on the whim of the court? Or is the principle: When the grantee is the government, the scope of the easement should be read as widely as possible to fulfill evolving governmental purposes?

Problems: Express Easements

1.   The plaintiff owns land in the Sierra. Her predecessor granted the state an easement "for highway purposes" across specifically described land. Thirty years after it constructed the road, the state wants to build a "vista point" and "roadside rest" next to the highway on the land that was included (but never used) in the original easement. Is the plaintiff entitled to an injunction on the ground that the proposed use exceeds the scope of the easement? *See Norris v. State*, 261 Cal.App.2d 41, 67 Cal.Rptr. 595 (1968).

2.   Defendant Falcon Cable Television received a franchise from the City of Alhambra to wire the city for cable television. It also received permission from PacTel to use its telephone poles to string the cable. Falcon, however, neglected to obtain permission from Benjamin Salvaty, on whose property one of PacTel's telephone poles sat. When Falcon strung the cable, Salvaty sued for inverse condemnation, trespass, nuisance, unfair business practices, and misrepresentation. Falcon defended on the ground that PacTel had acquired an express easement in 1926 for "the construction, operation, repair and maintenance thereon and thereover of a pole line for the stringing of telephone and electric light and power wires." How should a court resolve this lawsuit? *See Salvaty v. Falcon Cable Television*, 165 Cal.App.3d 798, 212 Cal.Rptr. 31 (1985).

3.   Consider the following grant to a railroad:

in consideration of the covenants on the part of the [railroad] hereinafter contained, subject to the reservations and provisos and upon the conditions hereinafter mentioned and expressed, and for other good and sufficient considerations [the grantor] has granted [certain described property to the railroad and its successors] but upon and subject to the reservations and conditions and for the uses and purposes hereinafter designated and stipulated, and none other, and while devoted to those uses and purposes. The sole uses and purposes for which the said parcels of land are hereby conveyed are as follows, to wit: For the maintenance and operation of a railroad upon and over said lands, in conjunction with the main line of [the railroad], and for the construction and maintenance of a freight shed or sheds or other terminal facilities for railroad purposes, to have and to hold * * * for the uses and purposes aforesaid and none other, and for so long as a railroad shall be maintained and operated thereon and no longer.

Does the railroad have an easement or a fee (subject to a condition subsequent and/or covenants)? What additional facts should a court consider in classifying this interest? *See Tamalpais Land & Water Co. v. Northwestern Pac. RR Co.,* 73 Cal.App.2d 917, 927–30, 167 P.2d 825, 830–31 (1946); *Machado v. Southern Pacific Transportation Co.,* 233 Cal.App.3d 347, 352–61, 284 Cal.Rptr. 560, 562–69 (1991). Should the court presume that a grant of real property is a fee simple or resolve interpretive disputes in favor of the grantee?

------

ii. *Easements by Operation of Law*

Two kinds of easements may be created by operation of law when land is subdivided—an easement by implication and an easement by necessity.[10]

An *easement by implication* arises in the following situation. Suppose that "A" owned a large tract of land and irrigated the northern half. To drain the used irrigation water, A built a drainage ditch that ran from the irrigated land in the north across the southern half of the tract. A later sold the northern half of the tract to "B," keeping the southern half for herself. The grant was silent about an easement to drain used irrigation water across A's southern tract. Does B nevertheless have a drainage easement across the southern tract?

The answer is yes if (1) the two parcels were under single ownership; (2) there was a "permanent" or "continuous" pre-subdivision use (a "quasi-easement") across the allegedly servient tenement; (3) the use was apparent upon reasonable inspection; and (4) the easement is "reasonably necessary." *See Fristoe v. Drapeau,* 35 Cal.2d 5, 8, 215 P.2d 729, 731 (1950); *Romanchuk v. Plotkin,* 215 Minn. 156, 160, 9 N.W.2d 421, 424 (1943). Perhaps the most difficult issue is "apparent upon reasonable inspection," especially where the easement is for underground sewer pipes

------

10. The *Restatement* makes no distinctions among easements created by operation of law. Instead, it identifies eight factors to be used in deciding whether such an easement exists. Those factors are: whether the claimant is the grantor or grantee; the terms of the conveyance; the consideration for the conveyance; whether the claim is made against a simultaneous grantee of a common grant; the extent of necessity of the ease-ment; whether such an easement would create reciprocal benefits in the grantor and grantee; the manner in which the land was used prior to the conveyance; and the extent to which the parties knew of the prior use of the land. *Restatement of Property* § 476. Relying on these factors rather than the relatively clear common law rules undoubtedly would add significant indeterminacy to the law.

or utility lines. In general, courts have emphasized that if an adequate inspection of the utility and sewer connections would reveal the underground lines and pipes, the criterion of "apparent upon reasonable inspection" is satisfied. *See, e.g., Romanchuk v. Plotkin*, 215 Minn. 156, 162, 9 N.W.2d 421, 425 (1943) ("An underground drainpipe * * * connected with and forming the only means of draining waste from plumbing fixtures and appliances of a dwelling house, is apparent, because a plumber could see the fixtures and appliances and readily determine the location and course of the sewer drain"); *Van Sandt v. Royster*, 148 Kan. 495, 83 P.2d 698 (1938).

An *easement by necessity* arises when land is subdivided, and one of the parcels is landlocked from the public road. Because such land normally is unusable without adequate access,[11] courts will consider whether the owner of the landlocked parcel has an easement by necessity. The basic criteria are: (1) that the purported servient and dominant tenements were owned by a single owner at the time of the conveyance giving rise to the necessity; and (2) that an easement is "necessary."

There are multiple definitions of "necessary." Many states have abandoned the common law requirement for "absolute necessity," instead requiring "reasonable necessity," which presumably takes account of the cost of using or building alternate routes. *Restatement of Property* § 476 cmt. g. Other courts use a standard of "strict" necessity, which is considered to be stiffer than "reasonable" necessity. *County of Los Angeles v. Bartlett*, 203 Cal.App.2d 523, 528, 21 Cal.Rptr. 776, 778 (1962) (strict necessity means that the proposed easement is the "only possible means of access").

Scope. It is difficult to determine precisely the scope of easements created by operation of law. Absent a document creating the easement or some other clear expression of intent, courts are left to the metaphysical world of "implied" intent. Courts have held that the scope of an easement by necessity depends on a court's assessment of what is necessary to permit the owner of the dominant tenement to use her land. The prior conduct of the parties and to a lesser extent the foreseeable changes in the dominant tenement's use bear on this determination. *Soltis v. Miller*, 444 Pa. 357, 360–61, 282 A.2d 369, 370–71 (1971) (the scope of an easement by necessity is "coextensive with the reasonable needs, present and future, of the dominant estate * * * and to vary with the necessity, insofar as may be consistent with the full reasonable enjoyment of the servient tenement").

The scope of an easement by implication, which is more directly tied to the actual (although unexpressed) intent of the parties, is limited to the prior use of the "quasi-easement" and foreseeable changes in the use of the dominant tenement. One court wrote:

11. "Without such a finding, the conveyed inner portion would have little use, save by helicopter, and helicopters did not factor into the thinking of legal minds over the centuries during which this law crystallized." Powell on Real Property ¶ 410.

An implied easement is not confined to the precise use at the time of the transfer, *i.e.*, it may have a broader scope than the quasi-easement on which it is based. The test is the intended use reasonably contemplated by the parties. * * * "The [use authorized] is to be measured * * * by such uses as the parties might reasonably have expected from the future uses of the dominant tenement."

George v. Goshgarian, 139 Cal.App.3d 856, 861–62, 189 Cal.Rptr. 94, 98 (1983) (quoting *Fristoe v. Drapeau*, 35 Cal.2d 5, 9, 215 P.2d 729, 732 (1950)).

In *Fristoe*, the implied easement was a road that ran between the dominant and servient parcels. When the easement was created, it was used for access to an orchard. Decades later, the dominant parcel was developed for residential use. The court held that the servient owner was not entitled to an injunction barring residential traffic. "[C]onsideration must be given not only to the actual uses being made at the time of the severance, but also to such uses as the facts and circumstances show were within the reasonable contemplation of the parties at the time" the easement was created. 35 Cal.2d at 10, 215 P.2d at 732.

Reese v. Borghi

District Court of Appeal, California, 1963.
216 Cal.App.2d 324, 30 Cal.Rptr. 868.

■ SULLIVAN, JUSTICE.

Defendants Franzo and Mary Borghi, husband and wife, appeal from a declaratory judgment granting plaintiffs Clyde L. and Marie W. Reese, husband and wife, a right-of-way of necessity over a parcel of land previously conveyed to defendants by plaintiffs. * * *

The principal facts are not in dispute. In 1953 plaintiffs acquired five contiguous parcels of land referred to in the record as Whiteside, B–1, B–2, C and A, together with a nonexclusive perpetual easement and right-of-way appurtenant thereto over and along a private road called Witherly Lane, which ran in a general easterly and westerly direction and connected on the west with a main highway. All of the above parcels are situated on the north side of the above road. Proceeding from west to east, the parcels lie generally as follows: Whiteside, the most westerly, abuts the road on the north; next, parcel B–2 abuts the road on the north with parcel B–1 in the rear and to the north of B–2;[12] next, parcel A abuts the road on the north with parcel C in the rear and to the north of parcel A. Thus, generally speaking and with the exception mentioned in the footnote, parcel B–1 lies

---

12. A finger of land protrudes southerly from the main part of parcel B–1 extending between Whiteside and B–2 and thus abutting the road along 25 feet thereof.

behind parcel B–2 and, immediately to the east of such strip of land, parcel C lies behind parcel A.

In 1955 plaintiffs sold and deeded Whiteside to the grantee bearing that name and also sold and deeded parcel A to one Symes. On April 2, 1956, plaintiffs sold and conveyed to the defendants both parcel B–1 and parcel B–2. As a result of such conveyance parcel C, which was retained by plaintiffs, became landlocked without any means of ingress or egress to or from Witherly Lane.

The record discloses considerable evidence bearing upon the circumstances surrounding the sale made by plaintiffs to defendants. It appears, and the court so found, that for some years prior to the sale plaintiffs used a pathway along and upon the easterly boundary of the strip of land composed of parcels B–2 and B–1 in order to obtain access to parcel C from Witherly Lane. It also appears that when plaintiffs contemplated the sale of this strip of land, they also had in mind that they might buy parcel A from Symes, thus acquiring access to the road. Symes had listed parcel A with a real estate broker for sale and plaintiffs had discussed with Symes the purchase of this parcel after the expiration of the exclusive listing "in order to save the * * * real estate commission * * *." Plaintiffs claimed that they had an understanding with the defendants that if they were unable to buy parcel A from Symes they would continue to have an easement along the pathway customarily used by them which was on the two parcels sold to the defendants.

It developed that plaintiffs were unable to buy Symes' parcel because it was purchased by the secretary of defendants' counsel, who subsequently conveyed the property to the defendants. In view of the conclusion which we reach, it is not necessary to recite the details of this remarkable transaction. Suffice it to say that it effectively thwarted plaintiffs' plans for an access route to the road over the Symes' property.

As already pointed out, plaintiffs claimed an informal agreement with the defendants assuring the former an easement over the property being sold. On this point plaintiffs also introduced evidence to the effect that they proposed that such a provision be included in the written agreement of sale but that defendants' counsel informed plaintiffs it would be unnecessary since they could depend on the defendants to adhere to any understanding between the parties. The record discloses conflicting evidence on this phase of the case.

One significant and crucial occurrence remains to be noted. After the defendants acquired parcels B–1 and B–2 from plaintiffs, they constructed their family residence on the property in such a way as to block and render unusable the pathway which plaintiffs had previously used in order to reach parcel C.

On April 13, 1959, plaintiffs commenced the instant action in declaratory relief. Their complaint set forth four separately stated causes of action: the first sought "a way of necessity from that portion of lot deeded to defendants"; the second sought similar relief on the basis of an estoppel;

the third sought the declaration of an easement by implication; and the fourth sought an easement by implication on the basis that the defendants, knowing that plaintiffs desired to buy the Symes' property, proceeded to purchase it themselves, thus causing the plaintiffs to be landlocked.

The trial court found that the plaintiffs formerly owned all the parcels; that they had an easement appurtenant thereto over Witherly Lane; that they sold parcels B–1 and B–2 to the defendants; that plaintiffs' retained parcel C thereupon was landlocked; that plaintiffs had previously used a pathway over parcels B–1 and B–2 which was blocked and rendered unusable by defendants' residence; that at the time plaintiffs conveyed parcels B–1 and B–2 to defendants "the parties * * * intended that plaintiffs have a temporary right of way ten feet in width for purposes of ingress and egress from parcel C to Witherly Lane along and across the property conveyed to defendants * * * until parcel C was no longer landlocked * * * "; and that the location of such ten foot right-of-way along the eastern boundary of parcel A (*i.e.*, the property purchased by defendants from Symes) was a location best suited for the interests of all parties concerned. The court concluded that plaintiffs were entitled to "a right of way of necessity, ten feet in width," over and along the easterly boundary of parcel A to continue until parcel C is no longer landlocked. Judgment was entered accordingly. * * * [N]o objection is made on this appeal to the validity of the right-of-way granted plaintiffs because of its location on the property conveyed to defendants by Symes rather than on that conveyed by plaintiffs. The location of the right-of-way is therefore not in issue.

Defendants contend before us (1) that the awarding of such right-of-way constitutes a taking of their property without just compensation in violation of their constitutionally guaranteed rights; (2) that in the light of the evidence the court was powerless to declare an easement by implied reservation; and (3) that the court erred in relieving plaintiffs of their failure to file a cost bill within the prescribed statutory period.

Defendants' first contention rests upon the proposition that under section 1001 of the Civil Code "[a]ny person may * * * acquire private property for any use" specified in section 1238 of the Code of Civil Procedure by proceedings in eminent domain as provided in said Code, that one of the uses so specified is for "[b]yroads leading from highways to * * * farms" [Cal. Code Civ. Proc. § 1238(6)], that an easement is a substantial property right and that under established principles of constitutional law no such property can be taken without just compensation. The short answer to this ponderous plea is that the right-of-way in question was sought and acquired as a common law right and not by the exercise of the power of eminent domain. Plaintiffs' common law right to seek a right-of-way of necessity is not affected by the fact that he could have a right-of-way by condemnation. * * *

We turn to defendants' second contention. They claim that "[t]here can be no easement by implied reservation where the evidence clearly shows that the parties were thoroughly acquainted with the absence of access and did not, at the time of the conveyance, intend to create such a servitude." In support of this position they argue that an implied easement must be based upon "obvious, continuous, and pre-existing use" (the gist of the argument being that none existed here) and that the unqualified conveyance made by the plaintiffs precludes, in the absence of any finding of fraud or mistake, any intention of the parties to create an easement at the time of the conveyance.

The defect in the above argument derives from defendants' confusion concerning the basis on which the trial court granted relief. As determined by the court, plaintiffs' rights in the instant case rest on a claim to a right-of-way necessity not to an easement by implication based, to use defendants' language, on an "obvious, continuous, and pre-existing use." * * * In the law on the subject there is a well recognized and long standing distinction between a right-of-way of necessity arising by operation of law and an easement by implication based upon a preexisting use. (3 Powell on Real Property, §§ 410, 411; 2 Thompson on Real Property (1961 Replacement), §§ 355, 358, 362.) * * *

Thus Thompson, *op. cit.*, § 362, page 410, states: "A doctrine closely related to the theory of easements by inference or implication is that of 'ways by necessity.' This rule, however, differs somewhat from the implication theory because whereas an easement may be generally based on the implied intent of the parties at the time of separation, and while necessity may be an operative factor in determining intent, a way of necessity rests on public policy often thwarting the intent of the grantor or grantee. Its philosophy is that the demands of our society prevent any man-made efforts to hold land in perpetual idleness as would result if it were cut off from all access by being completely surrounded by lands privately owned."

* * *

The California rule is settled that a right-of-way of necessity arises by operation of law when it is established that (1) there is a strict necessity for the right-of-way as when the claimants' property is landlocked and (2) the dominant and servient tenements were under the same ownership at the time of the conveyance giving rise to the necessity.

We are satisfied therefore that the record before us supports the court's action. By uncontradicted evidence, indeed by stipulation of the defendants, parcel C was shown to be landlocked. The trial court so found and also found more particularly that as a result of their conveyance to defendants, plaintiffs would have no means of ingress or egress to or from Witherly Lane unless they were given a right-of-way over defendants' land. The court also found that prior to the conveyance both parcels had been under the common ownership of plaintiffs. These findings are sufficient to support the judgment. They are nowhere negated by any express intent of the parties to the contrary. (*County of Los Angeles v. Bartlett* (1962) 203 Cal.App.2d 523, 529, 21 Cal.Rptr. 776.) * * *

1. *Implied Easements.* Many courts are reluctant to find an implied easement by reservation, often imposing a higher degree of necessity than for an implied easement by grant. Why?

Why should courts permit implied easements at all? Why shouldn't courts demand that all easements be expressly created? Should a court find an implied easement if the parties expressed a contrary intent when conveying the underlying parcels? *See Warfield v. Basich*, 161 Cal.App.2d 493, 499, 326 P.2d 942, 945–46 (1958).

2. *Intent.* Is an easement by necessity based on the actual or probable intent of the parties or on some public policy? If the latter, what is the public policy? Must a court refuse to find an easement by necessity if the parties expressly intended not to create an easement? *See County of Los Angeles v. Bartlett*, 203 Cal.App.2d 523, 21 Cal.Rptr. 776 (1962).

3. *Dormant Easement By Necessity.* Must an easement by necessity be "necessary" at the time the landlocked parcel is created? Suppose the grantee had alternative access (*e.g.*, a license across another parcel) to a public road when the parcel was created. If that access was later revoked, would the landlocked grantee now have an easement by necessity? In other words, can there be a "dormant" easement by necessity? *See Leonard v. Bailwitz*, 148 Conn. 8, 166 A.2d 451 (1960); *Othen v. Rosier*, 148 Tex. 485, 226 S.W.2d 622 (1950).

4. *Grantor's Easement By Necessity.* Should a grantor who landlocks himself be able to claim an easement by way of necessity? *See Hewitt v. Meaney*, 181 Cal.App.3d 361, 368, 226 Cal.Rptr. 349, 352 (1986).

If a private grantor who landlocks himself is entitled to an easement by necessity, can the government also claim such an easement under analogous circumstances? Or must the government use eminent domain procedures and pay for the easement? *See Leo Sheep Co. v. United States*, 440 U.S. 668 (1979).

5. *Common Ownership.* What is meant by "common ownership"? Suppose that Clark, who owned parcel A, later signed an installment contract to buy the adjacent parcel B. As is normal with installment contracts, Clark did not receive the deed to parcel B until years later, when the installment payments were completed. Before then, he sold parcel A to Sparling, thereby landlocking parcel B. Does Clark have an easement by necessity? *See Roemer v. Pappas*, 203 Cal.App.3d 201, 249 Cal.Rptr. 743 (1988).

Why should one party be burdened with the easement by necessity on the ground that his parcel was once unified with the landlocked parcel? If there are other landowners whose property contributes to the landlocked circumstances, why shouldn't the easement run across their land? Wouldn't it make most sense to imply the easement across the most convenient right of way? Put slightly differently, what does the fact of common ownership have to do with anything? *Cf. Tenison v. Forehand*, 281 Ala. 379, 202 So.2d 740 (1967) (upholding right of landowner to condemn right of way where necessary).

6. *Private Eminent Domain: Private Ways of Necessity.* The *Reese* court observed that the landlocked plaintiffs could have sought a right-of-way through condemnation. About a dozen states provide statutory procedures for private landowners to condemn a right-of-way of necessity across adjoining properties. Such statutes are particularly important when a landlocked property owner does not satisfy the requirements to establish an easement by necessity under the common law. In some states, the landlocked property owner must petition a public official to condemn a private road across the land of another. *See, e.g.,* Miss. Code Ann. § 65–7–201; Wyo. Stat. Ann. § 24–9–101. Other states allow private landowners to exercise the power of eminent domain directly so long as they meet the statutory requirement of necessity and pay compensation. *See, e.g.,* Wash. Rev. Code §§ 8.24.010–8.24.030. State statutes vary in terms of the degree of necessity a landowner must show. *Compare State ex. rel. Grays Harbor Logging Co. v. Superior Court*, 82 Wash. 503, 144 P. 722 (1914) (reasonable necessity) *with Welch v. Shipman*, 357 Mo. 838, 210 S.W.2d 1008 (1948) (strict necessity). Some statutes limit the condemning of private ways of necessity to particular purposes. *See, e.g.,* Colo. Const. art. 2, § 14 (limited to "agricultural, mining, milling, domestic or sanitary purposes"); Okla. Stat. tit. 27, § 6 ("agriculture, mining, and sanitary purposes"). Some statutes specify the criteria for selecting the location of an easement. *See, e.g.,* Wash. Rev. Code § 8.24.025 (favoring passage over non-agricultural and non-silvicultural land).

Do these statutes violate the Takings Clause by authorizing condemnation and transfer of property for a private purpose? *Compare Estate of Waggoner v. Gleghorn*, 378 S.W.2d 47, 50 (Tex.1964) (striking down state statute authorizing private way of necessity "to the extent that it authorizes the taking of private property for a private purpose") *with Johnston v. Alabama Public Service Comm'n*, 287 Ala. 417, 252 So.2d 75 (1971) (upholding constitutionality of statute authorizing private ways of necessity on ground that such rights of way serve the state's interests in industrial development); *State ex. rel. Mountain Timber Co. v. Superior Court*, 77 Wash. 585, 590, 137 P. 994, 996 (1914) (noting that a private way of necessity is "promotive of the public welfare, in that it prevents a private individual from bottling up a portion of the resources of the state").

Is there any justification for not paying a landowner subjected to an easement by necessity compensation for the fair market value of the encumbrance? Should the common law doctrine of easement by necessity be replaced by private eminent domain legislation (which requires compensation)? Should the common law doctrine of easement by implication be similarly replaced? What would be the advantages and disadvantages of such a reform?

---

iii. *Easements By Prescription*

Prescription is the third method to create an easement. Common law judges justified prescriptive easements on the fiction of the "lost grant."

The courts presumed that continuous use of another's land for the prescriptive period was authorized by some previously granted easement, and that the grant creating this right had been lost. Today most states justify prescriptive rights on the public policy ground of maximizing use of underutilized land.

Establishing prescriptive rights is closely analogous to establishing title by adverse possession. To acquire a prescriptive easement, the use must be (1) actual; (2) adverse; (3) open and notorious; and (4) continuous and uninterrupted for the prescriptive period. *Cleary v. Trimble*, 229 Cal.App.2d 1, 6–7, 39 Cal.Rptr. 776, 779 (1964). In states that require payment of taxes for adverse possession, the prescriptive user need not pay property taxes or assessments to obtain an easement by prescription (unless, in the rare case, they are separately assessed against the easement). As with adverse possession, the claimant's good faith is irrelevant. "Tolling" of the prescriptive period and "tacking" of successive adverse uses follow the adverse possession rules.

The criterion that the easement be "open and notorious" is especially problematic when the easement is for an underground utility or sewer line. In *Field-Escandon v. DeMann*, 204 Cal.App.3d 228, 251 Cal.Rptr. 49 (1988), the court held that although this criterion could be satisfied by constructive notice of the adverse use (which meant that the landowner must have "actual notice of circumstances sufficient to put a prudent person upon inquiry" of the use), there could be no prescriptive easement absent some visible signs of an underground sewer.

The most controverted criterion is adverse use. In many states, adverse use is presumed if the claimant has used another's land, although opinions are inconsistent. *See, e.g., Le Deit v. Ehlert*, 205 Cal.App.2d 154, 159–62, 22 Cal.Rptr. 747, 751–53 (1962) (reluctantly upholding a jury instruction that open, notorious, continuous, and peaceable use gives rise to a presumption of adverse use). Given the presumption of adverse use, many landowners (particularly in commercial districts) run the risk that the public's use of their private sidewalks or parking lots may result in a public easement. To avoid this result, some landowners block access to their property for one day each year, thereby defeating the "continuous use" criterion. Other landowners rely on state statutes to defeat the "adverse use" criterion.

California Civil Code

813. Consent to use of land; recordation of notice; revocation.

The holder of record title to land may record * * * a description of said land and a notice reading substantially as follows: "The right of the public or any person to make any use whatsoever of the above described land or any portion thereof (other than any use expressly allowed by a written or recorded map, agreement, deed or dedication) is by permission, and subject to control, of owner: Section 813, Civil Code."

The recorded notice is conclusive evidence that subsequent use of the land during the time such notice is in effect by the public or any user for any purpose * * * is permissive and with consent in any judicial proceeding involving the issue as to whether * * * any user has a prescriptive right in such land or any portion thereof.

In the event of use by other than the general public, any such notices, to be effective, shall also be served by registered mail on the user.

The recording of a notice pursuant to this section shall not be deemed to affect rights vested at the time of recording. * * *

1008.   Title by prescription; permissive use.

No use by any person or persons, no matter how long continued, of any land, shall ever ripen into an easement by prescription, if the owner of such property posts at each entrance to the property or at intervals of not more than 200 feet along the boundary a sign reading substantially as follows: "Right to pass by permission, and subject to control, of owner: Section 1008, Civil Code."

———

1.   Why should use of another's land create a presumption of adverse use? Does the presumption simply cloud the underlying issue of whether the claimant's use was adverse?

2.   Doesn't the law of prescriptive easements effectively authorize a private condemnation? If so, shouldn't the court order payment for the property taken? *See* Merrill, Property Rules, Liability Rules, and Adverse Possession, 79 Nw. U. L. Rev. 1122 (1984).

3.   Shouldn't every owner, not just owners of commercial property, post signs as specified in Civil Code § 1008 whenever there is any chance that someone might regularly trespass? If that sounds wasteful, wouldn't it be more efficient to change the rules for prescriptive easements to require prescriptive users to give property owners actual notice of their adverse use and claim of right?

———

Finley v. Botto

District Court of Appeal, California, 1958.
161 Cal. App. 2d 614, 327 P.2d 55.

■ SCHOTTKY, JUSTICE.

Plaintiffs commenced an action against defendants in which plaintiffs alleged that they owned an easement in a certain walkway lying between two apartment houses owned by the respective parties. Plaintiffs prayed for judgment quieting their title to said alleged easement and for an injunction compelling defendants to remove a fence constructed by defendants upon said walkway. Defendants in their answer denied that plaintiffs had any right to any easement. Following a trial the court entered judgment denying plaintiffs' right to an easement and to an injunction, one of the findings of the court reading as follows:

> That the predecessors in interest of the parties to this action who owned the respective properties involved in this case when the space between the houses began to be used for walkway purposes by plaintiffs' predecessors were congenial, cooperative neighbors, and such use was permitted by defendants' predecessors as a gesture of good will and neighborly accommodation. That no claim of right was asserted by plaintiffs' predecessors, nor was any indication ever brought to the notice of defendants or their predecessors that such a claim would or might be asserted, until defendants constructed a fence on their north property line in 1955, thus denying to plaintiffs the full use of the walkway, at which time plaintiff, Thomas Finley, did to and in the presence of defendant, Daniel L. Botto, assert such a claim for the first time. This was approximately two months prior to the filing of this action, and therefore the Court concludes and finds that plaintiffs' showing is lacking in essential factors that are necessary to establish by prescription or adverse possession the right claimed by them.

* * *

The appellants and the respondents are adjoining landowners. Appellants' property lies to the north of that of the respondents. Each lot extends from E Street in the city of Marysville to a rear alley, and each contains an apartment building which is constructed close to the common boundary line. On appellants' property, in addition to the apartment house, are three cottages which are in the rear of the apartment house. At the rear of the apartment building is a laundry room which is used by all the tenants of appellants. The distance between the two apartment buildings is four feet. The areaway between the two buildings was used by appellants' tenants to reach the laundry room, and for the tenants of the cottages to reach E Street. In 1955, respondents erected a fence on their side of the boundary line. This fence is one foot south of appellants' building and prevents easy access to the rear of the building. When the fence was constructed appellants voiced an objection and thereafter this suit was brought. It appears that at one time there was a brick wall dividing the properties at the boundary line and when the wall was in place it was impossible to walk from E Street to the rear of appellants' property. The wall disintegrated and by 1939 was in bad shape. In 1941 there was no actual wall between the buildings but evidence remained that there had been one. After 1944 the then owner of respondents' property completed the demolition of the wall and made the brick walkway between the two apartment houses. The then owner of respondents' property testified:

[Mr. Weis] Q. Did anything occur which would indicate or convey to you any knowledge or impression that the Ertmodes were making or asserting a claim to an easement across your property?

A. Of course not, no. It was a matter of we were just being neighborly and we wouldn't have thought of anyone trying to make a legal claim to it. That would have been the last thing we would have expected.

Appellants acquired the legal title to their property in 1949 and respondents acquired the title to theirs in 1950. Appellant Thomas Finley testified that his relations with respondents have always been friendly and that the first indication he gave to respondents that he claimed any easement over respondents' part of the property was when respondents started to build the fence. Respondent Daniel L. Botto testified that the relationship between appellants and respondents after respondents acquired their property have been neighborly and friendly, and that appellants' son had married respondents' daughter.

Appellants first cite the following from a note in 27 A.L.R.2d at page 341:

In the great majority of instances in which a lane, private road, alley, driveway, or passageway lying over and along the boundary between lots or tracts has been used without interruption by the adjoining owners for the full prescriptive period, and for a common purpose, and without any oral agreement therefor being shown, the user of each owner has been regarded as adverse to the other and the claim of prescriptive easement upheld as against any attempt to restrict or deny the use.

Appellants then state that in the case at bar the vital factors thus recognized in the great majority of American jurisdictions as creating an easement are present: (1) There is a passageway lying over and along the boundary between lots; (2) the passageway has been used without interruption between adjoining owners for the full prescriptive period, for a common purpose; and (3) no oral agreement for such use was shown on trial.

Appellants then argue that the user of each owner should be regarded as adverse to the other, and that plaintiff Finley's claim to a prescriptive easement should be upheld as against any attempt to restrict or deny his use.

Appellants rely strongly on the case of *Bernstein v. Dodik*, 129 Cal.App. 454, in which plaintiffs sought to quiet title to an easement and to enjoin defendants from interfering therewith. Plaintiffs and defendants owned adjoining lots in a Los Angeles subdivision. A driveway had been constructed between the two lots, over and along the dividing line; a strip of 4.6 feet of the driveway was on one lot and a strip of 3.1 feet of driveway was on the other lot. Plaintiffs, and their predecessors, had made use of the way without oral agreement for more than five years. Defendants claimed that plaintiffs' use was permissive; that there had not been communicated to defendants any knowledge that plaintiffs' use was under claim of right. The trial court gave judgment in favor of plaintiffs, and appellants quote from the opinion affirming the judgment, at page 458, as follows:

> ... While it is a well-established principle that the use must be adverse, yet it is an equally well-established principle that where the use of the easement is continuous or openly and notoriously adverse to the owner, it creates the presumptive knowledge in him that the person using the easement is doing so under a claim of right.

However, the appellate court also said, at page 457:

> ... The question as to whether or not the use of the driveway was under a claim of right or as a mere matter of neighborly accommodation was a question of fact to be determined by the trial court in the light of the relation of the parties, their conduct, the situation of the property and all the surrounding circumstances. (*Abbott v. Pond*, 142 Cal. 393; *Humphreys v. Blasingame*, 104 Cal. 40.)

Appellants also cite *Murray v. Fuller*, 82 Cal.App.2d 400, in which defendants appealed from a judgment declaring that the plaintiffs were the owners of an easement for right of way over a strip of land approximately 7 feet wide along the west boundary of defendants' lots. A strip had been used as a driveway for ingress to and egress from the rear of plaintiffs' property to the street on which said property fronted. The use had been made for more than five years. The use was made by plaintiffs and their predecessors, without asking or receiving permission of any person and without opposition from defendants or defendants' predecessors. The use had been open, continuous and notorious. In affirming the judgment the appellate court said, at page 406: "The use of the driveway by plaintiffs and their predecessors and their tenants without express permission amounted to trespass and afforded grounds for legal redress from defendants' predecessors, and it was therefore sufficient to initiate a prescriptive title."

Respondents in reply point out that the decisions relied upon by appellants are cases in which judgments that an easement had been established were affirmed upon appeal. Respondents argue that the evidence is sufficient to support the finding that the use of the walkway by appellants and their predecessors in interest was permissive and not adverse. Respondents cite *O'Banion v. Borba*, 32 Cal.2d 145, in which the court said at page 147:

> ... In this connection it is pertinent to observe that whether the use of the easement is adverse and under a claim of right, or permissive and with the owner's consent, and the nature of the user is sufficient to put the owner on notice, are questions of fact.... Also, if there is any substantial evidence to support the judgment, it must be affirmed. All conflicts must be resolved in favor of the prevailing party and the evidence viewed in the light most favorable to him.

. . .

There has been considerable confusion in the cases involving the acquisition of easements by prescription, concerning the presence or absence of a presumption that the use is under a claim of right adverse to the owner of the servient tenement, and of which he has constructive notice, upon the showing of an open, continuous, notorious and peaceable use for the prescriptive period. Some cases hold that from that showing a presumption arises that the use is under a claim of right adverse to the owner. It has been intimated that the presumption does not arise when the easement is over unenclosed and unimproved land. (*See* 28 C.J.S. 736; 4 Tiffany, Real Property (3d ed.), § 1196a.) Other cases hold that there must be specific direct evidence of an adverse claim of right, and in its absence, a presumption of permissive use is indulged. The preferable view is to treat the case the same as any other, that is, the issue is ordinarily one of fact, giving consideration to all the circumstances and the inferences that may be drawn therefrom. * * *

We are unable to agree with appellants that the evidence in the instant case compelled a finding that they were entitled to a boundary line easement. If the judgment had been in favor of appellants we would, as was done in the cases cited by appellants, hold that it was supported by the evidence. But as stated in *Bernstein v. Dodik*, *supra*, the principal case relied upon by appellants, "The question as to whether or not the use of the driveway was under a claim of right or as a mere matter of neighborly accommodation was a question of fact to be determined by the trial court in the light of the relation of the parties, their conduct, the situation of the property and all the surrounding circumstances."

It was for the trial judge, who not only heard the evidence but also, under stipulation of counsel, viewed the premises, to weigh the evidence, and we are convinced that the evidence hereinbefore set forth, together with the inferences that may reasonably be drawn therefrom, support the findings and judgment. We believe that the record supports the following statement in the court's memorandum opinion:

The Court cannot help but feel that this so-called walkway was originally constructed to avoid a muddy condition caused by dripping of eaves which in themselves were very close to the actual property line, and entirely as a neighborly gesture of good will. The court further feels that this construction was so regarded by the families using it and that until the denial of its full and free use became an inconvenience, no claim of right was made.

* * * The relationship between the parties and the surrounding circumstances as shown by the record entitled the trial court to draw the inference that the continued use of the walkway by appellants was permissive and not under claim of right.

The judgment is affirmed.

1.   The Finleys seem to have fulfilled all of the formal requirements for an easement by prescription. Why did they lose the lawsuit? Has the court invoked a "neighborly accommodation" exception to an easement by prescription? Is this a form of implied permission (note that if Botto had given explicit permission, there would have been no need to mention "neighborly accommodation")?

2.   Should there be other circumstances—the relationship of the parties, or the nature of the land itself—in which the court would imply permission? Would it be relevant that many persons used the land?

Negative Easements. American courts uniformly hold that a landowner cannot obtain a negative easement by prescription.[13] That is, conduct that would otherwise create a prescriptive easement for light—receiving light that flows across the landowner's land for the prescriptive period—does not create a cause of action. *See, e.g., Pacifica Homeowners' Ass'n v. Wesley Palms Retirement Community*, 178 Cal.App.3d 1147, 1152, 224 Cal.Rptr. 380, 382 (1986). The reason is that negative easements by prescription pose serious threats to developmental values that underlie much of American land use law.

Negative easements for light or air conceivably could be created by implication under existing statutes. For example, some statutes provide that trees and shrubs blocking solar collectors may be abated as a public nuisance. *See, e.g.,* Solar Shade Control Act, Cal. Pub. Res. Code §§ 25980–25986. Such a statute arguably creates an implied private cause of action by one neighbor against another. Similarly, height limitations in city zoning ordinances could be enforceable by neighboring landowners. The courts, however, have decided otherwise. *See Sher v. Leiderman*, 181 Cal.App.3d 867, 226 Cal.Rptr. 698 (1986) (holding that the Solar Access Act does not create a private right of action for nuisance); *Taliaferro v. Salyer*, 162 Cal.App.2d 685, 689–91, 328 P.2d 799, 801–02 (1958) (holding that municipal ordinances imposing height restrictions do not create easements enforceable by neighbors).

Scope. The scope of a prescriptive easement is determined primarily by the adverse use that led to the creation of the easement. *See Twin Peaks Land Co. v. Briggs*, 130 Cal.App.3d 587, 594–95, 181 Cal.Rptr. 25, 28 (1982).

Problems: Easements by Prescription

1.   Hotel A was constructed in 1925 on Miami Beach. Hotel B was constructed next door several years later. At that time, neither hotel cast a

---

13. In contrast to American law, English common law permitted courts to find, under the proper circumstances, implied and prescriptive easements for light, air and view under the so-called Doctrine of Ancient Lights.

shadow on the other's property. Both hotels became quite profitable, capitalizing on the sunny weather for which Miami is famous. In 1965, Hotel B decided to build an additional 20 stories. When completed, the addition from Hotel B would cast a shadow on much of Hotel A's beach and pool area during much of the afternoon.

What is the policy reason preventing Hotel A from obtaining an order enjoining Hotel B from its construction project? Is the need to maximize development (in this case, adding another 20 stories) so much more important than protecting existing investment and expectations? If the court were to permit a negative easement by prescription, what should be the criteria for an injunction? *See Fontainebleau Hotel Corp. v. Forty–Five Twenty–Five, Inc.*, 114 So.2d 357, 359–60 (Fla.Ct.App.1959).

2. A commercial truck repair business drove trucks across neighboring property (a truck stop) for 22 years without objection from the truck stop owner. The truck stop owner held the property under a 49–year lease. When the truck stop owner tried to move some tanks in a way that would block the truck repair business from driving across the truck stop, the owner of the repair business sought an injunction against both the truck stop owner and his landlord, claiming a prescriptive easement. Who prevails? Can a person obtain a prescriptive easement from a landlord? *See Dieterich Int'l Truck Sales, Inc. v. J.S. & J. Services, Inc.*, 3 Cal.App.4th 1601, 5 Cal.Rptr.2d 388 (1992).

Review Problem

In 1940, Sam Firestone owned lots 1, 2, and 3, and Ben Johnson owned lot 4 of a 4-acre tract in Olive Branch County in the State of West Carolina. Firestone operated a farm on lot 1 and left lots 2 and 3 undeveloped. Path A ran across lot 3 to lot 2. Path B ran the length of lot 4 to the Pala River where it connected to a dock that lay at the boundary between lots 2 and 4.

In 1945, Margaret and Gary Emerson purchased lots 2 and 3 from Sam Firestone and built a house on lot 2. They used path A to enter and exit their property. In 1950, the Emersons had a daughter, Irene.

Irene began dating Chuck Firestone, Sam's son, in the ninth grade. Their love blossomed and they were eventually married in 1972. The Emersons gave the newlyweds lot 3 as a wedding present. Irene and Chuck built a home there and lived happily. Gary and Meg Emerson continued to use path A across lot 3 to enter and exit lot 2.

In 1973, Ben Johnson decided to construct a barn and cattle grazing area toward the northwest corner of his property. This building cut off path B 100 yards from lot 2.

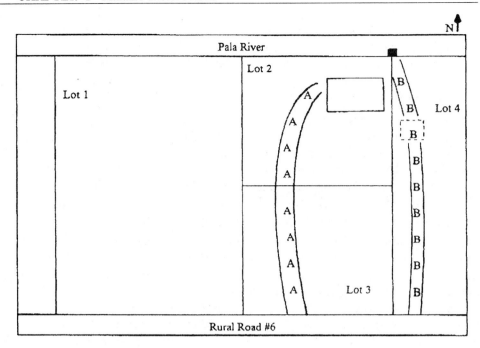

In 1975, Irene died. She left her estate to Chuck. Chuck stayed on lot 3 and continued to get along well with the Emersons.

In 1986, Chuck became ill and died. His will left lot 3 to his father, Sam Firestone.

Since Chuck's death, tension between the Emersons and Sam Firestone has gradually mounted. In 1990, Sam cleared and planted corn rows on the entirety of lot 2. The Emersons, however, continued to use the path. Since that time, Sam has not attempted to plant corn on the path, although the path has become narrower and is sometimes obstructed by farm equipment. Over the past year, Sam has made clear his desire to acquire lot 2. In December 1996, Sam offered the Emersons $400,000 for lot 2, which was about 25% above its appraised value. Sam indicated that he wanted the property to enlarge his farm, but a rumor circulating around town suggested that Sam had been negotiating with a major real estate developer who would like to acquire lots 1—3 to build a gated community along the river. The Emersons, now in their mid–70s and retired, turned Sam down. They are attached to their home and community and do not want to uproot at this stage of their lives. Following this refusal, Sam vowed to force the Emersons off their property by whatever means available. He has threatened to obstruct path A and sue the Emersons for trespass.

The Emersons have come to you for advice. West Carolina has a 7–year statute of limitations applicable to the acquisition of an easement by prescription. In addition, the West Carolina Civil Code contains the following provisions:

28.02 **Condemnation authorized—Private way of necessity defined.** An owner, or one entitled to the beneficial use, of land which is so situated with respect to the land of another that it is necessary for its proper use and enjoyment to have and maintain a private way of necessity or to construct and maintain any drain, flume or ditch, on, across, over or through the land of such other, for agricultural, domestic or sanitary purposes, may condemn and take lands of such other sufficient in area for the construction and maintenance of such private way of necessity, or for the construction and maintenance of such drain, flume or ditch, as the case may be.

28.03. **Selection of route—Criteria.** If it is determined that an owner, or one entitled to the beneficial use of land, is entitled to a private way of necessity and it is determined that there is more than one possible route for the private way of necessity, the selection of the route shall be guided by the following priorities in the following order:

(1) Nonagricultural and nonsilvicultural land shall be used if possible.

(2) The least-productive land shall be used if it is necessary to cross agricultural land.

(3) The relative benefits and burdens of the various possible routes shall be weighed to establish an equitable balance between the benefits to the land for which the private way of necessity is sought and the burdens to the land over which the private way of necessity is to run.

28.04. **Procedures for condemnation—Fees and costs.** Any landowner who satisfies the criteria for establishing a private way of necessity may petition the superior court in the county in which the property is situated to condemn a private way of necessity across adjoining land. The petitioner shall provide 60 days notice of the petition to the owner of the adjoining land. The court shall award the adjoining landowner due compensation, as determined pursuant to the eminent domain authority. The court may award reasonable attorneys' fees and expert witness costs to the condemnee.

What legal options do the Emersons have to maintain access to their property? What arguments could Sam Firestone offer in response? What practical advice would you offer?

---

d. **TERMINATION OF EASEMENTS**

Easements may be terminated in a variety of ways.

i. By Expiration

Easements that are created for the life of the holder or for a term of years expire at the end of the designated period. Similarly, defeasible easements expire on the occurrence of the stated event. Easements by necessity expire when the necessity ends. In states with marketable title acts, an easement may expire after a specified period of non-use, unless re-recorded.

As a general matter, the equitable doctrine of "changed conditions" cannot be invoked to terminate an easement. Even though it may be impossible (or highly inefficient) to achieve the grantor's and grantee's original intent because of changed conditions, the easement remains valid and enforceable. However, an easement that relies on a structure on the servient tenement (*e.g.*, a stairway on or passageway through a building) expires if the structure is destroyed. *See, e.g.*, Cal. Civ. Code § 811(2). Absent language to the contrary in the original grant, such an easement is not revived if the structure is rebuilt. *See, e.g., Rudderham v. Emery Bros.*, 46 R.I. 171, 125 A. 291 (1924) (easement is destroyed when building destroyed, and is not revived when building rebuilt).

ii. By the Easement Holder

The owner of the dominant tenement may terminate the easement by release, abandonment, estoppel, or, in some states, by excessive use.

Release occurs when the easement holder transfers his interest in the easement to the owner of the servient tenement (subject to the statute of frauds).

Abandonment. An easement created in a grant may be abandoned, and thus terminated, when the easement holder stops using the easement and independently manifests an intent to abandon the easement. Non-use alone is not enough to deem such an easement abandoned. *See, e.g., Buechner v. Jonas*, 228 Cal.App.2d 127, 131–32, 39 Cal.Rptr. 298, 300 (1964).[14] The intent to abandon may be demonstrated either by oral statements or by actions that are inconsistent or interfere with the use of the easement. *Lake Merced Golf & Country Club v. Ocean Shore R.R. Co.*, 206 Cal.App.2d 421, 436–42, 23 Cal.Rptr. 881, 889–93 (1962) (cessation of railroad service, lack of maintenance work, and conveyance of other sections of the railroad right of way were sufficient evidence of the railroad company's intent to abandon the easement). Temporary or partial interference is not a sufficient basis to find abandonment. *McCarty v. Walton*, 212 Cal.App.2d 39, 45–46, 27 Cal.Rptr. 792, 795 (1963). Some statutes provide a supplemental procedure to deem an easement abandoned in certain circumstances. *See, e.g.*, Cal. Civ. Code § 887.050 (easement abandoned if not used for 20 years, evidence of its existence has not been recorded in that period (*e.g.*, a deed, a

---

14. Many jurisdictions, however, hold that voluntary non-use alone is a sufficient basis to find abandonment of an easement by prescription. *See, e.g.*, Cal. Civ. Code § 811(4) (an easement by prescription is abandoned after five years of non-use).

document stating an intent to preserve), and no taxes were assessed or paid in that period).

Estoppel. An easement may also be terminated by estoppel if the following criteria are met: (1) the easement holder's words or conduct indicating that she will no longer use the easement; (2) the servient owner's reasonable reliance on the easement holder's representations; and (3) the servient owner's material change in position.

Excessive Use. Only a few courts have held that an easement is terminated by the easement holder's excessive use of the easement. Most states, however, will terminate a profit for excessive use. Excessive use of an easement can be remedied by damages and injunctive relief.

iii. By the Owner of the Servient Tenement

The owner of the servient tenement may terminate an easement through merger, by conveyance in some circumstances, and through prescription.

Merger. The owner of the servient tenement (or the dominant tenement) can terminate the easement by merger. That is, where the servient owner acquires the dominant tenement (or when the owner of the dominant tenement acquires the servient tenement), the easement is permanently terminated and not revived upon subsequent subdivision of the two parcels (unless, say, the criteria for an easement by implication are met).

Sale to a BFP. Sale of the servient tenement to a bona fide purchaser for value will terminate the easement if the grantee meets the requirements of the recording act (*i.e.*, first recorded in a race-notice state). Prescriptive easements, however, are not affected by conveyances of the servient tenement. Since the recording acts "relate only to priorities among instruments affecting land ownership * * * an easement acquired by prescription is effective against a successor of the servient owner, even when such successor is a bona fide purchaser without notice." Powell on Real Property, ¶ 424; *McKeon v. Brammer*, 238 Iowa 1113, 29 N.W.2d 518 (1947). For the same reason, sale of the servient tenement to a BFP probably does not terminate an easement by necessity or an easement by implication. Because implied easements and easements by necessity often are readily apparent, however, it may be difficult for the purchaser of the servient tenement to establish lack of notice.

Prescription. The owner of the servient tenement may acquire the easement by prescription. *See, e.g., Masin v. La Marche*, 136 Cal.App.3d 687, 693–95, 186 Cal.Rptr. 619, 622–23 (1982). Because the servient owner generally may use the easement (so long as that use does not interfere with the easement holder's rights), use alone will not result in acquisition by prescription. Rather, the servient owner must block the easement holder from using the easement, or otherwise demonstrate exclusive control of the land, for the prescriptive period.

iv.   By Third Parties

The most common method of third-party termination is by condemnation, *i.e.*, when a government agency takes the servient tenement by eminent domain. Since the easement is a property interest, the owner of the easement is entitled to compensation under the federal and state constitutions. The value of the easement is measured by the diminution in the value of the dominant tenement. *See, e.g., United States v. Welch*, 217 U.S. 333, 30 S.Ct. 527, 54 L.Ed. 787 (1910).

Some state courts have held that easements are terminated when the servient tenement is sold at a tax sale (*i.e.*, for failure to pay property taxes). This position is difficult to support. Because property is generally assessed according to its market value (which includes a discount for any easements to which the property is subject), seizure and sale of property should have no effect on the existence of an easement. Moreover, property that benefits from an easement generally is assessed for property taxes taking into account the value that the easement adds. For this reason, many other states hold that the purchaser of a servient tenement at a tax sale takes title subject to the easement. *See, e.g., Smith v. Smith*, 21 Cal.App. 378, 131 P. 890 (1913).

A similar issue arises when a mortgagee forecloses on the servient tenement for default in the mortgage payments. The majority rule is that easements that exist before the execution of the mortgage are not terminated upon subsequent foreclosure, but that easements created after execution of the mortgage are terminated. In a sense, a subsequent easement is subject to the mortgagee's prior rights.

e.   CONSERVATION EASEMENTS

Conservation easements were first widely used by governments in the 1930s to preserve the natural scenic views surrounding highways and other areas. The application of the ancient doctrine of easements to the preservation of land was not, however, without its problems. A 1961 congressional study concluded that "such easements breed misunderstandings, administrative difficulties, are difficult to enforce, and cost only a little less than the fee." H.R. Rep. No. 273, 87th Cong., 1st Sess. (1961).

In the 1960s, federal funding to enhance scenic areas around the burgeoning federal highway system, IRS rulings (and subsequent codification) allowing taxpayers to deduct the value of easements donated to charitable organizations, growing acceptance of preservation and conservation, and the enactment of state enabling legislation spurred greater use of conservation easements. *See* Blackie, Conservation Easements and the Doctrine of Changed Circumstances, 40 Hastings L.J. 1187, 1190–95 (1989). More than 40 states now recognize conservation easements.

The 1981 Uniform Conservation Easement Act, which has been adopted in 17 states,[15] defines a conservation easement as:

---

15. Conservation easement enabling statutes vary widely. Even among states adopting the Uniform Act, there is some variation in the precise terms.

a non-possessory interest of a holder in real property imposing limitations or affirmative obligations of which include retaining or protecting natural, scenic, or open-space values or real property, assuring its availability for agricultural, forest, recreational, or open-space use, protecting natural resources, maintaining or enhancing air or water quality, or preserving the historical, architectural, archaeological, or cultural aspects of real property.

UCEA § 1. Thus, conservation easements may contain both affirmative obligations on the servient tenement (such as permitting the public a right-of-way to fish along a stream) and negative restrictions. Such negative restrictions frequently extend well beyond the four categories of negative easements recognized under the common law. The Uniform Act allows any governmental body or a charitable organization concerned with conservation to hold such easements. Conservation easements are, by definition, held in gross. They benefit the public-at-large and not any particular piece of property. Successors to the servient tenement are subject to the conservation easement. UCEA § 4.

———

1. *Competing Social Policies.* The conservation easement runs counter to a longstanding policy of American property law promoting the development of land. The conservation easement also conflicts with traditional property law doctrines disfavoring restrictions on land, especially restrictions that are negative in nature (and hence more difficult for subsequent purchasers to discover) and potentially perpetual in duration. *See* Korngold, Privately Held Conservation Servitudes, A Policy Analysis in the Context of In Gross Real Covenants and Easements, 63 Tex. L. Rev. 433, 455–63 (1984). The unfettered discretion afforded under the UCEA and comparable state legislation to create broad negative easements allows landowners to prevent any further development of their land essentially forever.

Does this discretion present a serious risk to the society-at-large? Alternatively, should the law more affirmatively embrace and foster preservation values? *Cf.* Freyfogle, Ethics, Community, and Private Land, 23 Ecology L.Q. 631 (1996); Sprankling, The Antiwilderness Bias in American Property Law, 63 U. Chi. L. Rev. 519 (1996); R. Nash, Wilderness and the American Mind (3d ed. 1982); A. Leopold, A Sand County Almanac (1949). Should there be a higher threshold or a public process for decisions preserving land in perpetuity, such as the enactment of specific state or federal wilderness legislation or the approval of public officials (*e.g.*, zoning commission)? Should there be a time limit on conservation easements (perhaps subject to renewal)?

2. *Termination and Reformation of Conservation Easements.* Conservation easements may be terminated in the same manner as traditional

easements. Professor Gerald Korngold has argued that conservation easements should also be subject to the doctrine of changed circumstances, *see infra* pp. 767–72, under which courts may invalidate or alter other types of servitudes (but generally not easements) that become obsolete. Korngold, *supra*, at 482–86; *but see* Blackie, Conservation Easements and the Doctrine of Changed Circumstances, 40 Hastings L.J. 1187, 1190–95 (1989) (arguing that courts should be hesitant to extend the doctrine of changed conditions into the domain of conservation easements). Should conservation easements be subject to the equitable doctrine of changed circumstances? Should the legislature custom-tailor a new changed conditions doctrine for conservation easements? What criteria should apply?

Alternatively, a court might apply by analogy the *cy pres* doctrine to alter conservation easements held by a charitable trust. Under this doctrine, courts may reform a trust where the literal terms of the trust become impracticable. The court's aim is to effectuate the grantor's intent as well as possible given the circumstances. W. F. Fratcher, 4A Scott on Trusts § 399 (4th ed. 1986). Would application of this doctrine help to address concerns about conservation easements in perpetuity?

3. *Proliferation of Conservation Easements.* The past decade has seen a remarkable rise in the number of conservation easements and the number of trusts seeking to acquire such easements. In addition, conservation easements are an important instrument in the development of habitat conservation plans under the Endangered Species Act of 1973, 16 U.S.C. §§ 1531–1544. The popularity of conservation easements, however, is sensitive to the availability of tax deductions for such grants.

4. *Enforcement.* It is often difficult and costly for land conservation organizations to monitor adherence to the terms of conservation easements. In addition, it may be too late to enforce a restriction where an ecosystem has been irreversibly altered. Conservation organizations have become more sophisticated in the drafting of conservation easements in order to try to prevent these sorts of problems.

Problem: Conservation Easement

In 1983, the Land Conservation Trust negotiated with a number of large rural wetland owners to establish way-stations for a species of migratory birds that traditionally fly along a particular corridor. Fiedrich, the owner of a large ranch and pond along the flyway, agreed to restrict the use of his land during the migratory season to foster the migratory pattern. Fiedrich received a valuable tax deduction for having entered into the agreement.

Over the years, the number of birds using the Fiedrich way-station gradually declined. More recently, the remaining birds have altered their migratory pattern as a result of numerous factors, including the gradual spread of residential and commercial development to Fiedrich's vicinity.

What was once relatively low-valued rural land is now worth millions of dollars as a suburban development. Fiedrich would like to sell the ranch and retire in the Southwest. As encumbered by the easement, the land is not worth much. As unencumbered land which can be developed into a townhouse community surrounding a picturesque pond, the ranch is worth over $4,000,000.

Should the land-use restriction for the way-station remain enforceable or be terminated? How would you argue this case for each side? Suppose that instead of a restriction preventing interference with the birds' migratory pattern that the easement merely referred to general conservation purposes. How would that change your analysis and advocacy?

The following chart summarizes the doctrinal rules regarding easements.

Easements

Classification   **Affirmative**: holder may use servient tenement

Negative: holder may prevent servient owner from lawful use
- four traditional categories: (1) light; (2) air flow; (3) support; (4) flow of artificial stream
- expanded by conservation easements

Creation   **Express**: written instrument
Implied: prior use; necessity
Prescription

Enforcement

Servient	Dominant
1. any possessor 2. notice (actual, inquiry, record) to satisfy recording act	**Appurtenant**: any possessor may enforce; presumed appurtenant if land benefited **In gross**: personal to original holder (i.e., there is no dominant tenement); not assignable unless commercial

Remedy   damages; injunctive relief

Termination   expiration; release; condemnation; abandonment; estoppel; merger; sale to BFP; marketable title act

2.   REAL COVENANTS

A covenant is a promise to do or refrain from doing something. A covenant that is connected to land in a legally significant way, enforceable by damages, is called a real covenant. In contrast to covenants in most contracts, the burdens and benefits of real covenants pass to successive owners of the underlying estates.[16]

Although they serve similar functions, and sometimes look very much alike, real covenants and easements are different from one another. An affirmative real covenant is a promise to do an affirmative act. Typical examples include a tenant's covenant in the lease to pay rent, a landowner's covenant with her homeowner's association to pay monthly maintenance dues, and a landowner's promise to a neighbor to keep his trees trimmed. An affirmative easement, by contrast, is a right to use another's land. There is no promise to do anything; indeed, the servient owner's usual obligation is to refrain from interfering with the easement holder's rights.

Negative easements and negative real covenants are more closely related. In each case, one landowner has agreed to refrain from some action on his land that he otherwise is legally allowed to do. Negative easements, however, are generally limited to easements for air, light, support, and flow of an artificial stream. All other agreements not to do something are called negative real covenants. Examples of negative real covenants include a tenant's covenant not to make excessive noise late at night and a landowner's covenant with his homeowner's association not to paint his house a garish color.

Easements and real covenants differ in other ways. An easement, for example, creates rights *in rem, i.e.,* against the community or public. If someone has an easement across some property, he can enforce his rights in that easement against anyone who interferes with his rights. A real covenant, by contrast, creates rights *in personam, i.e.,* solely against the covenantor or her successors.

a.   ELEMENTS OF A REAL COVENANT

What follows is a description of the common law requirements for the

---

16. Under traditional common law (but not under modern law), the rights and duties associated with contracts were not readily assignable. *See* Corbin, Assignment of Contract Rights, 74 U. Pa. L. Rev. 207 (1926). Accordingly, the benefits and burdens of the original covenants were not transferred with the interest in the land. Because of the perceived important advantages in having the benefits and burdens of covenants ''run'' with estates in land, particularly to protect existing amenities in residential areas, courts created an elaborate set of requirements to supersede the unhelpful contract theory.

Because under modern contract doctrine an assignee who expressly assumes the obligations in pre-existing covenants becomes liable for those covenants, the law of real covenants is principally concerned with situations where the assignee has not expressly assumed the covenants.

benefits and burdens of a real covenant to run with an estate in land.[17] It assumes that the covenant is enforceable between the original parties under the normal rules of contract. In addition, the covenant must satisfy the statute of frauds provision governing transfers of interests in land (although some jurisdictions hold that the statute of frauds does not apply).

i.   Burden

There are four criteria for the burden of a real covenant to run to successive owners of the covenantor's estate—intent, vertical privity, horizontal privity, and touch and concern. Most states also effectively require a form of notice through the recording statutes, although notice was not a requirement at common law.

Intent. The original parties must have intended to bind the covenantor's successors. As a general matter, the original agreement need not expressly refer to "assigns" or "successors" (although use of these words in the agreement would establish the requisite intent); it is enough if a court can discern that intention from the circumstances surrounding the agreement. In practice, courts conclude that the parties intended a covenant to run if it touches and concerns the land. Stoebuck, Running Covenants: An Analytical Primer, 52 Wash. L. Rev. 861, 875 (1977).

Vertical Privity. Vertical privity describes the required relationship between the covenantor and the subsequent landowner. Vertical privity exists if the covenantor's successor has succeeded to the same estate that the covenantor had. To "succeed," one may acquire the land by devise, intestacy, grant, or judicial sale—any means except adverse possession. In addition, the successor must acquire the same interest (although the successor could acquire a smaller portion of land) than his predecessor had.

Contrast easements, where any *possessor* of the servient tenement must honor the easement. Thus, while a tenant (who has not succeeded to the landlord's entire estate) of the servient tenement must respect an easement created for the benefit of some other parcel, the tenant is free from the burdens of real covenants that the landlord has made with other landowners. *See, e.g., Higgins v. Monckton*, 28 Cal.App.2d 723, 728–30, 83 P.2d 516, 519–20 (1938). Similarly, an adverse possessor (who has succeeded to nothing) takes title subject to easements created prior to his adverse possession, but takes free of his predecessor's real covenants.

Horizontal Privity. Horizontal privity describes the required relationship between the original covenantor and the original covenantee. Unfortunately, jurisdictions in the United States define horizontal privity in a variety of ways. The most restrictive approach requires the covenantor and covenantee to have simultaneous interests in the land that is the subject of the covenant. Thus, the parties are in horizontal privity if they are landlord and tenant, or if they are owners of servient and dominant tenements

---

17. Although courts and lawyers often state that real covenants "run with the land," this expression is inaccurate. It is more accurate to say that real covenants "run with estates in land."

respecting an easement. *Hurd v. Curtis*, 36 Mass. (19 Pick.) 459 (1837) (landlord-tenant); *Morse v. Aldrich*, 36 Mass (19 Pick.) 449 (1837) (easement).

A less restrictive and more commonly adopted definition requires the covenant to be created simultaneously with a transfer of an interest in land. This definition not only includes the circumstances identified in the previous paragraph, but it also includes covenants created in connection with the conveyance of a fee. Thus, if A conveys part of his land to B, and additionally wants B and his assigns to prune the trees on B's lot, A must include that covenant as part of the deed transferring ownership in order to enforce it against B's successors.

The derivation of the horizontal privity requirement is one of the great doctrinal wrong turns of American property law. The first mention of a "privity" requirement in England was in *Spencer's Case*, 77 Eng. Rep. 72 (1583), the original source for much of the law on covenants. The court held that the burden of the lessee's covenant would not run unless the original parties were in "privity as is between lessor and lessee."[18] Two hundred years later, in *Webb v. Russell*, 100 Eng. Rep. 639 (K.B. 1789), the court flatly stated that a covenant would not run unless there was "privity of estate between the parties." A careful reading of *Webb* shows that the court meant that, under English law, the burdens of covenants would run only when the parties had a landlord-tenant relationship. English law did not and still does not permit covenants between landowners to run.

It is apparent why the English courts invented the privity of estate requirement. At common law, contractual duties were not assignable without the assignee's consent since the essence of a contract was the personal promise of the parties. Thus, there was no means to force the covenantor's assignee to accept the burdens of the covenant. This doctrinal result was especially problematic in landlord-tenant law. Consequently, the common law courts held that the landlord and tenant were not only in privity of contract, but also in "privity of estate," since a property interest—a leasehold—had been conveyed. It was a short step to conclude that the landlord and assignee were also in privity of estate, and thus that the assignee must bear the burdens of the covenants that run with the land.

American courts (in contrast to English courts) later concluded that covenants should be enforceable between assignees of fee owners. But in expanding application of the doctrine of real covenants, the American courts uncritically adopted the privity language in *Webb* and held that there could be no real covenants between fee owners unless the original parties were in privity.

The horizontal privity requirement is of little consequence in landlord-tenant relationships; it limits real covenants to those covenants that were created when the lease was executed, which usually covers all relevant

---

18. The Statute of Henry VIII, c. 34 (1540), already provided that the burden of a   covenant ran to the landlord's successors.

covenants. However, horizontal privity sharply restricts the ability of fee owners to create real covenants since fee owners often do not want to transfer an interest in land at the same time that they want to create a real covenant.

If horizontal privity was ever useful in American law, it was because it prevented the ready formation of real covenants at a time when courts believed real covenants unduly restricted the alienability of land. Today, covenants that regulate land use are widely believed to enhance marketability. Consequently, most commentators advocate abolition of the horizontal privity requirement, *see, e.g.,* C. Clark, Real Covenants and Other Interests Which "Run with Land" (2d ed. 1947); Walsh, Covenants Running with the Land, 21 N.Y.U.L.Q. Rev. 28, 41–44 (1946); Newman & Losey, Covenants Running with the Land, and Equitable Servitudes; Two Concepts, or One?, 21 Hastings L.J. 1319, 1331 (1970), and many (although not all) states have followed this suggestion.

Touch and Concern. The touch and concern criterion requires that the real covenant relate to the covenantor's use of his land. This requirement often refers to a physical use or restriction of the covenantor's land. Thus, covenants to repair or maintain the land or structures on the covenantor's land are readily held to touch and concern the land. Although some courts have held to the contrary, it also appears that in most jurisdictions a covenant restricting competing business activity touches and concerns the affected land; such a covenant restricts the owner's use of the land. *Whitinsville Plaza, Inc. v. Kotseas,* 378 Mass. 85, 390 N.E.2d 243 (1979).

Covenants to pay money have created some confusion. On the surface, a promise to pay money seems quite divorced from the covenantor's use of the land. Nevertheless, courts have always held that a tenant's covenant to pay rent touches and concerns the land. And while some older decisions held that other payments, such as payments to purchase insurance, repay a security deposit, or pay homeowner's dues, did not touch and concern the land, the modern trend is to hold otherwise.

It is difficult to give a precise justification for the touch and concern requirement. In a loose sense, it is designed to identify those covenants that a successor ought to be obligated to fulfill simply because he has succeeded to the covenantor's interest in the land. Stated differently, if the covenant is not related to the covenantor's land—*e.g.,* R covenants to give E legal advice about a pending criminal case—there is no good reason to expect the covenantor's successor to fulfill that covenant.

Some courts, however, have used this requirement to advance other goals. *See, e.g., Norcross v. James,* 140 Mass. 188, 2 N.E. 946 (1885) (declaring a covenant not to compete to be unenforceable against successors because it did not touch and concern the land, rather than declaring anti-competitive business agreements void on other public policy grounds).[19]

19. This case was overruled in *Whitins-*   N.E.2d 243 (1979).
ville Plaza, Inc., v. Kotseas, 378 Mass. 85, 390

Because, in addition, there is substantial confusion about how to apply the requirement, some authors have argued that the touch and concern requirement should be eliminated. *See, e.g.*, French, Toward a Modern Law of Servitudes: Reweaving the Ancient Strands, 55 S. Cal. L. Rev. 1261, 1319 (1982); *but see* Stake, Toward an Economic Understanding of Touch and Concern, 1988 Duke L.J. 925. To date, neither courts nor legislatures have fully adopted this suggestion, although some courts have liberalized the requirement in practice.

Notice. The common law of real covenants did not impose a requirement that a successor of the servient estate have notice of the covenant in order to be bound. Although that remains the rule in many jurisdictions, the recording acts—providing that bona fide purchasers for value may not be bound in certain circumstances—effectively impose a notice requirement where the servient owner purchased her interest.

ii.   Benefit

The requirements of touch and concern and intent apply on the benefit side as well as the burden side. In addition, there must be *vertical privity* between the covenantee and his successor. Vertical privity exists when a successor has succeeded to the same interest (*e.g.*, fee simple absolute) as the original covenantee (and any intermediary parties). The *Restatement* would weaken this requirement substantially by allowing the benefit to run to persons who succeed to any possessory interest in the covenantee's property. Thus, under the *Restatement* (and in some states), a subtenant could enforce the tenant's covenants with the landlord. An adverse possessor, however, could not enforce the covenants attached to his land as he has not succeeded to his interest. Few, if any, states require horizontal privity for the benefit to run. Stoebuck, Running Covenants: An Analytical Primer, 52 Wash. L. Rev. 861, 880–81 (1977). Notice is not required.

b.   REMEDY FOR BREACH

Because of one of the many historical accidents that plague property law, real covenants are enforced by a damages remedy only.

Historically, equitable defenses (*e.g.*, unclean hands, estoppel, laches, and waiver) were not available in an action to enforce a real covenant (*i.e.*, damages), although some states have relaxed this rule. Comment, Covenants and Equitable Servitudes in California, 29 Hastings L.J. 545, 581–86 (1978). Traditionally, many states enforced real covenants at law even though changes in the surrounding neighborhood (*e.g.*, industrialization in a residential neighborhood) defeated the original parties' intent or made the purpose of the covenant obsolete. Numerous states, however, now hold that the doctrine of changed conditions is a defense to a claim for damages, and, moreover, may be used to terminate a real covenant. *Hess v. Country Club Park*, 213 Cal. 613, 2 P.2d 782 (1931); *Restatement of Property* § 564; Stoebuck, Running Covenants: An Analytical Primer, 52 Wash. L. Rev. 861, 882–85 (1977).

c. TERMINATION OF REAL COVENANTS

Real covenants, like easements, may be expressly designed to terminate at some fixed point in time, or upon some condition. The parties may agree to terminate a covenant through a formal release (which may have to satisfy the statute of frauds), or the covenantor may effectively waive his right to enforce the covenant. In some states, real covenants automatically expire after a statutorily fixed period of time unless renewed.

Eagle Enterprises, Inc. v. Gross

Court of Appeals of New York, 1976.
39 N.Y.2d 505, 349 N.E.2d 816, 384 N.Y.S.2d 717.

■ GABRIELLI, JUSTICE.

In 1951, Orchard Hill Realties, Inc., a subdivider and developer, conveyed certain property in the subdivision of Orchard Hill in Orange County to William and Pauline Baum. The deed to the Baums contained the following provision:

> The party of the first part shall supply to the party of the second part, seasonably, from May 1st to October 1st, of each year, water for domestic use only, from the well located on other property of the party of the first part, and the party of the second part agrees to take said water and to pay the party of the first part, a fee of Thirty-five ($35.00) dollars per year, for said water so supplied.

In addition, the deed also contained the following:

> It is expressly provided that the covenants herein contained shall run with the land * * * and shall bind and shall enure to the benefit of the heirs, distributees, successors, legal representatives and assigns of the respective parties hereto.

Appellant is the successor in interest of Orchard Hill Realties, Inc., and respondent, after a series of intervening conveyances, is the successor in interest of the Baums. * * *

According to the stipulated facts, respondent has refused to accept and pay for water offered by appellant since he has constructed his own well to service what is now a year-round dwelling. Appellant, therefore, instituted this action to collect the fee specified in the covenant * * * for the supply of water which, appellant contends, respondent is bound to accept. The action was styled as one "for goods sold and delivered" even though respondent did not utilize any of appellant's water. Two of the lower courts found that the covenant "ran" with the land and, hence, was binding upon respondent as successor to the Baums, but the Appellate Division reversed and held that the covenant could not be enforced against respondent. We must now decide whether the promise of the original grantees to accept and make payment for a seasonal water supply from the well of their grantor is enforceable against subsequent grantees and may be said to "run with the land." We agree with the determination of the Appellate Division and affirm its order.

Regardless of the express recital in a deed that a covenant will run with the land, a promise to do an affirmative act contained in a deed is generally not binding upon subsequent grantees of the promisor unless certain well-defined and long-established legal requisites are satisfied. In the landmark *Neponsit* case [reprinted, *infra*, at pp. 777–82], we adopted and clarified the following test, originating in the early English decisions, for the enforceability of affirmative covenants (*cf. Spencer's Case*, 77 Eng. Rep. 72 [1583]), and reaffirmed the requirements that in order for a covenant to run with the land, it must be shown that:

(1) The original grantee and grantor must have intended that the covenant run with the land.

(2) There must exist "privity of estate" between the party claiming the benefit of the covenant and the right to enforce it and the party upon whom the burden of the covenant is to be imposed.

(3) The covenant must be deemed to "touch and concern" the land with which it runs.

Even though the parties to the original deed expressly state in the instrument that the covenant will run with the land, such a recital is insufficient to render the covenant enforceable against subsequent grantees if the other requirements for the running of an affirmative covenant are not met. * * *

It is this third prong of the tripartite rule which presents the obstacle to appellant's position and which was the focus of our decisions in *Neponsit* and *Nicholson v. 300 Broadway Realty Corp.* (7 NY2d 240, 244, *supra*). *Neponsit* first sought to breathe substance and meaning into the ritualistic rubric that an affirmative covenant must "touch and concern" the land in order to be enforceable against subsequent grantees. Observing that it would be difficult to devise a rule which would operate mechanically to resolve all situations which might arise, Judge Lehman observed that "the distinction between covenants which run with land and covenants which are personal, must depend upon the effect of the covenant on the legal rights which otherwise would flow from the ownership of land and which are connected with the land." (*Neponsit, supra*, p. 258). Thus, he posed as the key question whether "the covenant in purpose and effect substantially [alters] these rights" (p. 258). In *Nicholson*, this court reaffirmed the soundness of the reasoning in *Neponsit* as "a more realistic and pragmatic approach" (*supra*, p. 245).

* * *

A close examination of the covenant in the case before us leads to the conclusion that it does not substantially affect the ownership interest of landowners in the Orchard Hill subdivision. The covenant provides for the supplying of water for only six months of the year; no claim has been advanced by appellant that the lands in the subdivision would be waterless without the water it supplies. Indeed, the facts here point to the converse conclusion since respondent has obtained his own source of water. The record, based on and consisting of an agreed stipulation of facts, does not demonstrate that other property owners in the subdivision would be deprived of water from appellant or that the price of water would become prohibitive for other property owners if respondent terminated appellant's service. Thus, the agreement for the seasonal supply of water does not seem to us to relate in any significant degree to the ownership rights of respondent and the other property owners in the subdivision of Orchard Hill. * * * The obligation to receive water from appellant resembles a personal, contractual promise to purchase water rather than a significant interest attaching to respondent's property. It should be emphasized that the question whether a covenant is so closely related to the use of the land that it should be deemed to "run" with the land is one of degree, dependent on the particular circumstances of a case. * * *

Accordingly, the order of the Appellate Division should be affirmed, with costs.

---

1. *Vertical Privity*. What if any purpose is served by the vertical privity requirement? Is it more appropriate for some kinds of covenants than others? For example, should vertical privity be required for negative covenants to run? Should it be required for covenants in short-term leases? Is it less appropriate where the lease is for an extraordinarily long period of time, say 99 years?

Would it be sensible to drop the vertical privity requirement for the benefit to run, but to keep it for the burden to run?

Is there any justification for the rule that an adverse possessor of the servient estate is not bound by the real covenant? Isn't notice enough?

2. Suppose that the covenantee has not assigned his complete interest (*i.e.*, he granted something short of the entire estate). Can the present possessor enforce the covenant? Can the holder of the reversionary interest (the original covenantee) enforce the covenant?

3. *Touch and Concern*. Why did the promise to accept and pay for water in *Eagle Enterprises* not touch and concern Gross' land? Does the quote from the *Neponsit* case help to decide the issue in this case?

If the covenant were to prune trees or maintain a building on the promisor's land (affirmative covenant), or not to cut down certain trees on the promisor's land (negative covenant), there is no doubt that the burden of the covenant would touch and concern the promisor's land. Does a covenant not to engage in a business that competes with the promisee's business touch and concern the land? What about a covenant to give an option to purchase? *See Claremont Terrace Homeowners' Ass'n v. United States*, 146 Cal.App.3d 398, 408, 194 Cal.Rptr. 216, 222 (1983).

Would a tenant's covenant to pay the landlord's property taxes on the leasehold property touch and concern the land? What if the tenant covenanted to pay taxes on some other parcel of land? What about a covenant to engage in binding arbitration?

What is the purpose of the touch and concern requirement? Is it to enforce promises that are "objectively intended to promote land utilization," Reichman, Judicial Supervision of Servitudes, 7 J. Legal Stud. 139, 151–52 (1978)? Even if that is the purpose of the requirement, why have an objective test? Why not leave it to the subjective judgment of the contracting parties? That is, why not eliminate the touch and concern requirement entirely? *See* Epstein, Notice and Freedom of Contract in the Law of Servitudes, 55 S. Cal. L. Rev. 1353 (1982).

Nonpossessive Interests

	Easement	Real Covenant
Classification	**Affirmative**: holder may use servient tenement **Negative**: holder may prevent servient owner from lawful use • four traditional categories: (1) light; (2) air flow; (3) support; (4) flow of artificial stream • expanded by conservation easements	**Affirmative**: promise that servient owner will do something **Negative**: promise that servient owner will abstain from doing something
Creation	**Express**: written instrument **Implied**: prior use; necessity **Prescription**	**Express**: written agreement
Enforcement	**Servient** 1. any possessor 2. notice (actual, inquiry, record) to satisfy recording act **Dominant** **Appurtenant**: any possessor may enforce; presumed appurtenant if land benefited **In gross**: personal to original holder (i.e., there is no dominant tenement); not assignable unless commercial	**Burden** 1. intent 2. vertical privity 3. horizontal privity 4. touch & concern 5. notice **Benefit** 1. intent 2. vertical privity 3. touch & concern
Remedy	damages; injunctive relief	damages
Termination	expiration; release; condemnation; abandonment; estoppel; merger; sale to BFP; marketable title act	release; condemnation; merger; changed conditions; sale to BFP; marketable title act

Horizontal privity: privity of estate between original covenanting parties (lease, easement, or covenant in deed transferring land).

Vertical privity: privity of estate between successive parties; must succeed to same interest.

Touch & concern: promise must affect use and enjoyment of the land.

The preceding chart summarizes the doctrinal rules for real covenants, along with the rules for easements.

---

3.   Equitable Servitudes

Although the development of real covenants was an important doctrinal advance, it did not fully meet the demand for flexible, private land use arrangements in the nineteenth century. First, there was increasing demand for legal machinery to preserve the residential character of neighborhoods. Property owners wanted to protect their investments through equitable remedies, such as injunction. Second, the English law courts refused both to enlarge the class of negative easements (whose obligations passed to successive possessors of the property) and to permit burdens of real covenants to run between fee owners. When the law courts did not respond to the demands for reform, the English equity courts invented the doctrine of equitable servitudes.

The leading English case is *Tulk v. Moxhay*, 41 Eng. Rep. 1143 (1848). That case involved both affirmative covenants (to maintain Leicester Square as a garden for the benefit of surrounding properties) and a negative covenant (not to put any buildings on the square). The purpose of the covenants was to maintain the property as a park. An assignee of the convenantor, Moxhay, had notice of the covenants, although he had not specifically agreed to observe them. Tulk (one of the original covenantees) filed suit to enjoin Moxhay from breaching the negative covenant when Moxhay threatened to construct a building on the vacant land.

The court could not characterize the agreement as a negative easement because it did not fall into one of the four traditional categories. Nor could it deem the agreement to be a negative real covenant whose burden ran with the land, for the parties were adjacent landowners and thus were not in landlord-tenant privity. The court, however, stated that it would be inequitable for a person who bought land with knowledge of the underlying restrictive covenant to disregard that covenant. To avoid this inequity, but fit loosely within existing doctrinal confines, the court suggested that the covenantor's assignee had a contractual obligation to the covenantee. "[F]or if an equity is attached to the property by the owner, no one purchasing with notice of that equity can stand in a different situation from the party from whom he purchases." *Id.* at 1144. Relief was specific performance of the contract (*i.e.*, injunction), a somewhat odd result since it allowed the extraordinary remedy of injunction, but not the more usual remedy of damages. Subsequent decisions abandoned the contract theory and replaced it with a property theory: the original covenant creates an "equitable servitude," an interest in property that passes to successive owners who have knowledge of the restriction.

The *Tulk* case was significant because it simplified the requirements to enforce covenants. The court imposed a new notice requirement, but it implicitly dispensed with privity as the English understood that term; the covenant in *Tulk* was not between a landlord and a tenant.[20] Courts in the United States enthusiastically adopted the concept of equitable servitudes, which have become the primary means of enforcing private land use restrictions. Today, equitable servitudes have substantially replaced real covenants except in landlord-tenant law;[21] they extend to both affirmative and negative obligations. Brower, Running Covenants and Public Policy, 77 Mich. L. Rev. 12, 24–25 (1978).

a.   ELEMENTS OF EQUITABLE SERVITUDES

i.   *Burden*

There are two requirements for the burden of an equitable servitude to run with the land—touch and concern and notice.

Touch and Concern. This requirement is the same as the touch and concern requirement for real covenants.

Intent. Although intent is commonly thought to be required for the burden to run, one author concludes from a review of the cases that it is not required. *See* Stoebuck, Running Covenants: An Analytical Primer, 52 Wash. L. Rev. 861, 895 (1977).

Privity. There is no requirement of horizontal privity. There also appears to be no requirement of vertical privity for restrictive equitable servitudes; anyone with a possessory interest in the land is bound. Thus, the short term tenant, who is not liable at law for the real covenant, is liable in equity for negative covenants.[22]

Notice. In contrast to real covenants, the burden of equitable servitudes do not run unless the party to be held liable had notice of the equitable servitude when he acquired possession. Notice may be actual, constructive, or record. *Mackinder v. OSCA Dev. Co.*, 151 Cal.App.3d 728, 735–37, 198 Cal.Rptr. 864, 869–70 (1984) (holding that the grantees had adequate record notice of a covenant to pay homeowner association dues since the covenant was recorded in each person's chain of title, even though not in each person's deed); *Sanborn v. McLean*, 233 Mich. 227, 206 N.W. 496 (1925) (holding that the uniform appearance of a neighborhood put the

---

20. The court did not discuss the touch and concern requirement (which was easily met in *Tulk*), but subsequent decisions retained the requirement for equitable servitudes.

21. Many covenants qualify as both a real covenant and an equitable servitude.

Most landowners, however, prefer injunctive relief to damages.

22. The *Restatement* concludes that because there is no vertical privity requirement, adverse possessors are also bound by restrictive equitable servitudes. *See Restatement of Property* § 539 cmt. i.

purchaser on constructive notice that all lots were restricted to residential buildings). No notice is required, however, if the person against whom enforcement is sought was a donee, heir, or devisee. *Restatement of Property* § 539; R. Cunningham, W. Stoebuck & D. Whitman, The Law of Property § 8.28 (2d ed. 1993).

ii. *Benefit*

The requirements are touch and concern and intent.

Touch and Concern. This requirement is the same as the touch and concern requirement for real covenants.

Intent. There is limited authority in the case law that the benefit of an equitable servitude will not run unless the parties so intend. *See* Stoebuck, Running Covenants: An Analytical Primer, 52 Wash. L. Rev. 861, 895–97 (1977).

Privity. Most courts have dispensed entirely with the vertical and horizontal privity requirements for the running of the benefit in equity.

Notice. There is no notice requirement for the benefit of an equitable servitude to run with the land.

b. REMEDY

The usual remedy for breach of an equitable servitude is injunctive relief. If, however, the covenant is one to pay money, courts usually will not order payment, but instead will impose a lien on the covenantor's property, thus limiting his liability to the value of the property.

Equitable defenses may be used to prevent enforcement of equitable servitudes. The defenses include waiver, laches, unclean hands, and estoppel. One especially important defense is the doctrine of neighborhood change (sometimes called "changed conditions" or "changed circumstances"). Under this doctrine, a court will not enforce a covenant in equity if, because of changed conditions, it is no longer possible to fulfill the parties' original intent. In addition, a court will refuse enforcement if the underlying covenant violates public policy. *See, e.g., Boughton v. Socony Mobil Oil Co., Inc.*, 231 Cal.App.2d 188, 190–93, 41 Cal.Rptr. 714, 715–17 (1964) (indicating that covenants creating a monopoly or other unreasonable restraint on competition are unenforceable); *Doo v. Packwood*, 265 Cal.App.2d 752, 756, 71 Cal.Rptr. 477, 480 (1968) (restating general principle, but upholding a covenant barring use of the grantee's property as a competing grocery store).

Bolotin v. Rindge

District Court of Appeal, California, 1964.
230 Cal.App.2d 741, 41 Cal.Rptr. 376.

■ FILES, JUSTICE.

This is an action for declaratory relief and to quiet title against tract-wide deed restrictions which limit the use of plaintiffs' property to single family residential purposes. The trial court gave judgment declaring the restrictions to be unenforceable in part. Defendants have appealed. It is necessary to reverse the judgment because of the absence of a finding of fact on an issue which must be resolved before the controversy can be decided.

Plaintiffs own an unimproved lot situated at the northeast corner of Wilshire Boulevard and Hudson Avenue in the City of Los Angeles. This lot is a part of a tract which was subdivided by G. Allen Hancock in 1923 in the area now known as Hancock Park. Defendants are owners of other lots in the same tract. All the lots in the tract are subject to deed restrictions imposed by the original subdivider. These restrictions require, among other things, that each lot shall be used solely for single, private residences and that each residence shall front on a north-south street. These restrictions will expire January 1, 1970. All the lots in the tract except four have been improved with single family residences. The four lots which have never been improved are the northeast and northwest corners of Wilshire and Hudson, and the two lots which are immediately north of the two corner lots.

There is no dispute that the Hancock Park area is one of the most desirable and expensive residential areas in the community. It is also undisputed that the character of Wilshire Boulevard has changed greatly since 1923. A stipulation of facts lists these changes in some detail. Plaintiffs' evidence also includes the testimony of a qualified real estate broker and appraiser who testified that in his opinion plaintiffs' lot was not suitable for single family residential use, that there was no commonsense use to which the property could be put so long as the deed restrictions remained, and that the highest and best use for the property would be a commercial building similar to others which have been built on Wilshire Boulevard, both east and west of the subject property. He expressed the opinion that such a development would have no adverse effect upon either the market values of the residences in the tract or upon the amenities of living there. In his opinion, a building on plaintiffs' lot would help to protect the residences from the noise of the Wilshire traffic. There is an office building on the south side of Wilshire whose parking lot is directly across the street from plaintiff's lot. The witness pointed out that the use of plaintiffs' property for a commercial building would bring the commercial influence only 100 feet closer to the defendants' residences.

Defendants produced the testimony of a real estate broker that an office building on plaintiffs' lot would make the residences in the tract much less desirable as homes. In his opinion, a commercial building would inevitably bring more traffic and more parking, and would shut out sunlight. Defendants' witness was also of the opinion that the market value of the residences would decrease if a commercial building were built on plaintiffs' lot.

The findings of fact made by the trial court consist of these two paragraphs:

> The changes in the uses of property abutting Wilshire Boulevard in the vicinity of lot 212 of tract 6388 in the City of Los Angeles and the increase of vehicular traffic on said boulevard along said lot, have resulted in said lot having no substantial value solely for single family residential purposes, but said lot has a market value in excess of $200,000.00 for business uses.

> The refusal to enforce the single family residence restriction and the prohibition of commercial use of said lot 212, contained in the deeds to said lot and adjacent lots issued in 1923 and subsequent thereto, will not have an adverse effect upon the market value of other lots in said tract or tract 7040.

The only formal conclusion of law made by the trial court was that plaintiffs are entitled to a judgment declaring that the deed restrictions are not enforceable in specified respects.

A court will declare deed restrictions to be unenforceable when, by reason of changed conditions, enforcement of the restrictions would be inequitable and oppressive, and would harass plaintiff without benefiting the adjoining owners. (*Wolff v. Fallon*, 44 Cal.2d 695, 696, 284 P.2d 802.) In that case there was a finding of fact, supported by expert testimony, that the use of the plaintiff's property for commercial purposes would not detrimentally affect the adjoining property or neighborhood. A judgment quieting title against the restrictions was affirmed.

In *Marra v. Aetna Construction Co.*, 15 Cal.2d 375, at pages 378–379, 101 P.2d 490, at pages 492–493, the court said: "Also well recognized is the rule that a building restriction in the nature of a servitude will not be enforced where changed conditions in the neighborhood have rendered the purpose of the restrictions obsolete. But, if the original purpose of the covenant can still be realized, it will be enforced even though the unrestricted use of the property would be more profitable to its owner."

In that case the evidence showed that the lot for whose benefit the restriction had been imposed was no longer being used for residential purposes, and hence the Supreme Court concluded it was no longer equitable to restrict the servient lot to residential purposes.

The difficulty in the present case is that there is no finding that the purposes of the restrictions have become obsolete, or that the enforcement of the restrictions on the plaintiffs' property will no longer benefit the defendants. The trial court's finding as to the effect upon defendants is limited to the statement that there will be no adverse effect upon market value. This is not the test.

The purpose of the deed restrictions, it seems clear enough, was to preserve the tract as a fine residential area by excluding from the tract many of the activities which might be offensive to the residents or which would create noise, traffic, congestion, or other conditions which would lessen the comfort and enjoyment of the residents. Bringing the prohibited activities into the neighborhood might or might not depreciate the market value of the homes. If the restrictions should be broken, and a commercial building erected on the Wilshire frontage, speculators might be willing to pay more for the other parcels in anticipation of future expansion of the commercial development. Thus the intrusion of an office building might increase market values even though it offended the senses of the residents and destroyed the physical conditions which had made their neighborhood a desirable one for them.

In *Miles v. Clark*, 44 Cal.App. 539, at pp. 549–550, 187 P. 167, at p. 172, where a decree enjoining a breach of deed restrictions was affirmed, the court said: "The fact that apart from and surrounding the tract some business has grown up, and that the land has become more valuable in consequence, in no manner entitles defendants to be relieved of the restrictions they have created. This condition is but the natural result of the improvement of the various tracts, and the fact that the property may have become more valuable thereby for business purposes is immaterial. [Citations.] Courts in such cases are not controlled exclusively by money value, but may protect a home."

* * *

The judgment is reversed.

_____

1. The trial court in *Bolotin v. Rindge* expressly found that the proposed new land use would not affect the market value of the remaining lots. Why is that finding not dispositive of plaintiffs' claim that the restrictive covenant is not enforceable?

2. What is the basis for the equitable defense of neighborhood change? Is it that the economic value of the restriction is quite small or even negative? If so, isn't this a societal judgment about the value of the restriction? What if the covenantee sincerely wants the restriction? Moreover, aren't many restrictive covenants of little economic value at their creation? Consider the following:

> Ownership is meant to be a bulwark against the collective preferences of others; it allows one, rich or poor, to stand alone against the world no matter how insistent or intense its collective preferences. To say that ordinary ownership presents a holdout problem is not to identify a defect in the system; it is to identify one of its essential strengths.

Epstein, Notice and Freedom of Contract in the Law of Servitudes, 55 S. Cal. L. Rev. 1366–67 (1982). Or is the basis of the doctrine a justifiable effort to mitigate the inevitable frustration of the intent of the original parties, perhaps as evidenced by drastic change in economic value?

3. *Easements.* Courts refuse to enforce easements if, in very limited circumstances, certain conditions have changed. For example, if the necessity has vanished, a court will not enforce an easement by necessity. If a

structure which contains an easement is destroyed, the court will hold the easement extinguished. Should, therefore, the doctrine of neighborhood change be available as a defense against enforcement of easements? Should the doctrine of neighborhood change be available as a defense to suits to enforce a fee simple subject to a condition subsequent? *Cf.* Cal. Civ. Code §§ 885.030–.040 (declaring powers of termination void after 30 years unless re-recorded or if obsolete).

4. *Restrictions That Violate Constitutional Protections or Public Policy.* Courts refuse to enforce private covenants deemed to violate constitutional protections, such as racially restrictive covenants or covenants restricting speech. *Shelley v. Kraemer*, 334 U.S. 1 (1948) (finding that enforcement by a court of a private agreement prohibiting the occupancy of property by "people of the Negro or Mongolian Race" would constitute state action and would violate the Equal Protection Clause of the 14th Amendment). *See also Gerber v. Longboat Harbour North Condominium*, 757 F.Supp. 1339 (M.D.Fla.1991) (refusing to enforce private covenant prohibiting display of the American flag, which violated the First Amendment). As described at pp. 867–69, *infra*, this line of authority is narrowly restricted by the state action doctrine.

State courts have also refused to enforce covenants that violate other important public policies. In *Crane Neck Ass'n, Inc. v. New York City/Long Island County Services Group*, 61 N.Y.2d 154, 460 N.E.2d 1336 (1984), a state agency leased a private home to establish a group home for eight mentally disabled adults. Neighbors sued, alleging that the group home violated a covenant limiting the neighborhood to "single family dwellings." New York's highest court refused to enforce the covenant in equity on the ground that such a restriction would "contravene [the state's] long-standing public policy favoring the establishment of such residences for the mentally disabled." The court also held that the Contract Clause of the U.S. Constitution, Art. 1, § 10 (providing that "No State shall * * * impair[ ] the Obligation of Contracts"), does not preclude a state from "protecting the general good of the public through social welfare legislation paramount to the interests of parties under private contracts," so long as the means are "reasonably necessary to further an important public purpose and the measures taken that impair the contract are reasonable and appropriate to effectuate that purpose." *Id.* at 167, 472 N.Y.S.2d at 908, 460 N.E.2d at 1343. *Accord Craig v. Bossenbery*, 134 Mich.App. 543, 351 N.W.2d 596 (1984); *but see Clem v. Christole*, 582 N.E.2d 780 (Ind. 1991) (retroactive application of a state statute invalidating covenants restricting group homes is a taking for which just compensation must be paid); *Omega Corp. of Chesterfield v. Malloy*, 228 Va. 12, 319 S.E.2d 728 (1984) (enforcing "single family dwelling" restriction to prevent group home for mentally disabled).

Problems

1. *Changed Conditions.* A housing tract consists of 490 lots, all of which are subject to reciprocal negative covenants barring commercial use of the property. The tract is located between Wilshire Blvd. on the north and Olympic Blvd. on the south, from the eastern border of Beverly Hills to the western edge of Fairfax Avenue. "A" owns lots 14–18 on Wilshire Blvd. and lots 63–68, which are immediately adjacent to the southern borders of lots 14–18. A plans to build a 27 story building on lots 14–18, and a two-story parking garage on lots 63–68.

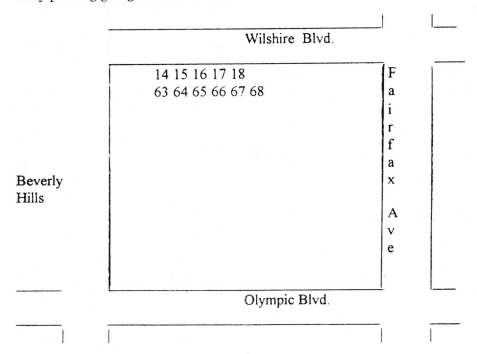

Wilshire Blvd. had long since become a major thoroughfare as well as an important business area. Indeed, in 1938, the lots fronting Wilshire (including lots 14–18) had been relieved of the restrictive covenant on the basis of the doctrine of neighborhood change. The trial judge in the current case specifically found that lots 63–68 were "so impaired by the encroachments of business on Wilshire that it is no longer desirable for first class residential use and is suitable only for business and commercial use as an adjunct to Wilshire Blvd. property, but that enforcement of said restriction upon [the lots in question] will continue to benefit and effectuate the purposes of same as originally imposed with respect to other lots in the tract."

Should the court enter declaratory relief lifting the restriction on lots 63–68? *See Atlas Terminals, Inc. v. Sokol*, 203 Cal.App.2d 191, 21 Cal.Rptr. 293 (1962).

2. *Marketable Title Legislation.* Massachusetts has significantly altered the default rules of the common law through the following legislation.

Massachusetts General Laws, Ch. 184

Section 27. **Restrictions * * *; limitations on enforceability; extension of period.**

No restriction * * * shall be enforceable * * * after thirty years from the imposition of the restriction unless (1) the restriction is imposed as part of a common scheme applicable to four or more parcels * * * and provision is made in the instrument or instruments imposing it for extension for further periods of not more than twenty years at a time by owners of record, at the time of recording of the extension, of fifty per cent or more of the restricted area in which the subject parcel is located, and an extension in accordance with such provision is recorded before the expiration of thirty years * * * or (2) in the case of any other restriction, a notice of restriction is recorded before the expiration of the thirty years, and in case of such recording, twenty years have not expired after the recording of any notice of restriction without the recording of a further notice of restriction.

Section 30. **Enforceability of restrictions; presumptions and prerequisites; temporary injunction.**

No restriction shall be enforced or declared to be enforceable unless it is determined that the restriction is, at the time of the proceeding, of actual and substantial benefit to a person claiming rights of enforcement. Further, even if a restriction is found to be of such benefit, it shall not be enforced except by award of money damages if any of the following conditions are found to exist:

(1) changes in the character of the properties affected or their neighborhood, in available construction materials or techniques, in access, services or facilities, in applicable public controls of land use or construction, or in any other conditions or circumstances, which reduce materially the need for the restriction or the likelihood of the restriction accomplishing its original purposes or render it obsolete or inequitable to enforce except by award of money damages, or

(2) conduct of persons from time to time entitled to enforce the restriction has rendered it inequitable to enforce except by award of money damages, or

(3) in case of a common scheme the land of the person claiming rights of enforcement is for any reason no longer subject to the restriction or the parcel against which rights of enforcement are claimed is not in a group of parcels still subject to the restriction and appropriate for accomplishment of its purpose, or

(4) continuation of the restriction on the parcel against which enforcement is claimed or on parcels remaining in a common

scheme with it or subject to like restrictions would impede reasonable use of land for purposes for which it is most suitable, and would tend to impair the growth of the neighborhood or munici-

Nonpossessory Interests

	Easement	Real Covenant	Equitable Servitude
Classification	**Affirmative**: holder may use servient tenement **Negative**: holder may prevent servient owner from lawful use • four traditional categories: (1) light; (2) air flow; (3) support; (4) flow of artificial stream • expanded by conservation easements	**Affirmative**: promise that servient owner will do something **Negative**: promise that servient owner will abstain from doing something	**Affirmative**: promise that servient owner will do something **Negative**: promise that servient owner will abstain from doing something
Creation	**Express**: written instrument **Implied**: prior use, necessity **Prescription**	**Express**: written agreement	**Express**: written instrument **Implied**: preexisting common plan
Enforcement	**Servient** 1. any possessor 2. notice (actual, inquiry, record) to satisfy recording act **Dominant** **Appurtenant**: any possessor may enforce; presumed appurtenant if land benefited **In gross**: personal to original holder (i.e., there is no dominant tenement); not assignable unless commercial	**Burden** 1. intent 2. vertical privity 3. horizontal privity 4. touch & concern 5. notice **Benefit** 1. intent 2. vertical privity 3. touch & concern	**Burden** 1. intent 2. touch & concern 3. notice (not required for donees) **Benefit** 1. intent 2. touch & concern
Remedy	damages; injunctive relief	damages	injunctive relief
Termination	expiration; release; condemnation; abandonment; estoppel; merger; sale to BFP; marketable title act	release, condemnation; merger; changed conditions; sale to BFP; marketable title act	release; condemnation; merger; unclean hands; estoppel; waiver; changed conditions; laches; sale to BFP; marketable title act

Horizontal privity: privity of estate between original covenanting parties (lease, easement, or covenant in deed transferring land).

Vertical privity: privity of estate between successive parties; must succeed to same interest.

Touch & concern: promise must affect use and enjoyment of the land.

pality in a manner inconsistent with the public interest or to contribute to deterioration of property or to result in decadent or substandard areas or blighted open areas, or

> (5) enforcement, except by award of money damages, is for any other reason inequitable or not in the public interest.

1. Using the Calabresi and Melamed framework, *see supra* pp. 281–87, explain how this remedial regime differs from traditional common law doctrine.

2. Does the Massachusetts statute improve the allocation of resources?

3. What other remedial approaches would you recommend to improve the use of restricted land over time?

The preceding chart on page 774 summarizes the doctrinal rules for equitable servitudes, along with the rules for easements and real covenants.

---

4. SPECIAL PROBLEMS OF HOMEOWNERS' ASSOCIATIONS

English and American courts created the law of real covenants and equitable servitudes long before the widespread use of modern homeowner associations, including condominiums, cooperatives, and gated communities. Although we address these "common interest communities" (CICs) in Section C, below, it is useful to consider here the fit between these longstanding property interests and the new forms of ownership and land use reflected in CICs.

a. ENFORCEMENT BY HOMEOWNERS' ASSOCIATION

Many condominium and other housing developments have a homeowners' association that is responsible for maintenance of the common areas and for enforcement of the covenants in each property owner's deed. The associations are financed through monthly assessments, which each homeowner must pay to the association. Two doctrinal problems arise when homeowners' associations attempt to enforce covenants in homeowners' deeds. First, the association generally owns no property benefited by the covenants; that is, it is not in privity with the original covenantee (*i.e.,* the developer). Second, one of the most important covenants, the covenant to pay monthly assessments, does not seem to "touch and concern" the land.

To illustrate the first problem, consider the following situation: "A" owns a single family house with a magnificent rose garden. A sells the house to "B." Because he is a sentimental sort, A includes (and B accepts) a negative covenant restricting the lot to a single family dwelling, and an affirmative covenant to maintain the garden. A does not own any other property in the neighborhood, and thus the benefit of these covenants is in gross.

In most jurisdictions, A can enforce the covenants against B under a contract theory, but can A enforce them against B's successor? In other words, does the burden of a covenant whose benefit is held in gross run with the land?

The English courts have long held that the burdens of such covenants do not run at law or in equity. The covenant (or equitable servitude) simply expires when the burdened estate is sold to the successor. *See, e.g., London County Council v. Allen*, 3 K.B. 642 (1914).[23] Many American courts follow the English rule, *see, e.g., Stegall v. Housing Auth. of Charlotte*, 278 N.C. 95, 178 S.E.2d 824 (1971),[24] but other American courts permit enforcement of such covenants in equity, *see, e.g., Van Sant v. Rose*, 260 Ill. 401, 103 N.E. 194 (1913) (enjoining a threatened breach of negative covenant). *See generally* Roberts, Promises Respecting Land Use—Can Benefits be Held in Gross?, 51 Mo. L. Rev. 933 (1986).

The English rule may be an acceptable result in the example given above; individuals with no real stake in a dispute—no real injury from breach of the covenant—should not have the right to enforce the covenant against the covenantor's successors. But the English rule is wholly unsatisfactory in the context of homeowners' associations.

Typically, each homeowner in a housing development has covenanted to observe certain restrictive covenants (*e.g.*, to ensure uniformity of appearance) and an affirmative covenant to pay a monthly assessment for maintenance. Although each original homeowner covenanted with the developer, the developer subsequently transferred management authority to the homeowners' association, which often owns no property (the homeowners typically jointly own the common areas). Thus, while the developer may have the right to enforce the covenants against the original purchasers, the developer (and the developer's successor—the homeowner's association) cannot enforce against successive purchasers of residences under the English rule.

---

23. The basis for the English rule is unclear. It may derive from the fact that a covenant in gross does not benefit any land, and thus is to be discouraged. By contrast, if the covenantor was also the grantor, some land would be benefited (the land belonging to the grantee/covenantee) even though the burden would be in gross. Perhaps for this reason most courts allow the benefit to run when the burden is held in gross.

24. The English rule for covenants is consistent with the corresponding rule for easements. In England, subsequent possessors of the servient tenement are not bound by the easement. American courts following the English rule on covenants take an inconsistent position on easements; in virtually all states, subsequent possessors of the servient tenement hold subject to the easement.

Neponsit Property Owners' Ass'n, Inc., v. Emigrant Industrial Savings Bank

Court of Appeals of New York, 1938.
278 N.Y. 248, 15 N.E.2d 793.

■ LEHMAN, JUDGE.

The plaintiff, as assignee of Neponsit Realty Company, has brought this action to foreclose a lien upon land which the defendant owns. The lien, it is alleged, arises from a covenant, condition or charge contained in a deed of conveyance of the land from Neponsit Realty Company to a predecessor in title of the defendant. The defendant purchased the land at a judicial sale. The referee's deed to the defendant and every deed in the defendant's chain of title since the conveyance of the land by Neponsit Realty Company purports to convey the property subject to the covenant, condition or charge contained in the original deed. * * * The defendant moved for judgment on the pleadings * * *. The plaintiff moved to dismiss the counterclaim * * * and to strike out the affirmative defenses * * *. The motion of the plaintiff was granted and the motion of the defendant denied. The Appellate Division unanimously affirmed the order of the Special Term and granted leave to appeal to this court upon certified questions.

* * *

It appears that in January, 1911, Neponsit Realty Company, as owner of a tract of land in Queens county, caused to be filed in the office of the clerk of the county a map of the land. The tract was developed for a strictly residential community, and Neponsit Realty Company conveyed lots in the tract to purchasers, describing such lots by reference to the filed map and to roads and streets shown thereon. In 1917, Neponsit Realty Company conveyed the land now owned by the defendant to Robert Oldner Deyer and his wife by deed which contained the covenant upon which the plaintiff's cause of action is based.

That covenant provides:

And the party of the second part for the party of the second part and the heirs, successors and assigns of the party of the second part further covenants that the property conveyed by this deed shall be subject to an annual charge in such an amount as will be fixed by the party of the first part, its successors and assigns, not, however exceeding in any year the sum of four ($4.00) Dollars per lot 20x100 feet. The assigns of the party of the first part may include a Property Owners' Association which may hereafter be organized for the purposes referred to in this paragraph, and in case such association is organized the sums in this paragraph provided for shall be payable to such association. The party of the second part for the party of the second part and the heirs, successors and assigns of the party of the second part covenants that they will pay this charge to the party of the first part, its successors and assigns on the first day of May in each and every year, and further covenants that said charge shall on said date in each year become a lien on the land and shall continue to be such lien until fully paid. Such charge shall be payable to the party of the first part or its successors or assigns, and shall be devoted to the maintenance of the roads, paths, parks, beach, sewers and such other public purposes as shall from time to time be determined by the party of the first part, its successors or assigns. And the party of the second part by the acceptance of this deed hereby expressly vests in the party of the first part, its successors and assigns, the right and power to bring all actions against the owner of the premises hereby conveyed or any part thereof for the collection of such charge and to enforce the aforesaid lien therefor.

These covenants shall run with the land and shall be construed as real covenants running with the land until January 31st, 1940, when they shall cease and determine.

Every subsequent deed of conveyance of the property in the defendant's chain of title, including the deed from the referee to the defendant, contained, as we have said, a provision that they were made subject to covenants and restrictions of former deeds of record.

There can be no doubt that Neponsit Realty Company intended that the covenant should run with the land and should be enforceable by a property owners association against every owner of property in the residential tract which the realty company was then developing. The language of the covenant admits of no other construction. Regardless of the intention of the parties, a covenant will run with the land and will be enforceable against a subsequent purchaser of the land at the suit of one who claims the benefit of the covenant, only if the covenant complies with certain legal requirements. These requirements rest upon ancient rules and precedents. The age-old essentials of a real covenant, aside from the form of the covenant, may be summarily formulated as follows: (1) It must appear that grantor and grantee intended that the covenant should run with the land; (2) it must appear that the covenant is one "touching" or "concerning" the land with which it runs; (3) it must appear that there is "privity of estate" between the promisee or party claiming the benefit of the covenant and the right to enforce it, and the promisor or party who rests under the burden of the covenant. Clark on Covenants and Interests Running with Land, p. 74. Although the deeds of Neponsit Realty Company conveying lots in the tract it developed "contained a provision to the effect that the covenants ran with the land, such provision in the absence of the other legal requirements is insufficient to accomplish such a purpose." *Morgan Lake Co. v. New York, N. H. & H. R. R. Co.*, 262 N.Y. 234, 238, 186 N.E. 685, 686. * * *

The covenant in this case is intended to create a charge or obligation to pay a fixed sum of money to be "devoted to the maintenance of the roads, paths, parks, beach, sewers and such other public purposes as shall from time to time be determined by the party of the first part [the grantor], its successors or assigns." It is an affirmative covenant to pay money for use in connection with, but not upon, the land which it is said is subject to the burden of the covenant. Does such a covenant "touch" or "concern" the land? These terms are not part of a statutory definition, a limitation placed by the State upon the power of the courts to enforce covenants intended to run with the land by the parties who entered into the covenants. Rather they are words used by courts in England in old cases to describe a limitation which the courts themselves created or to formulate a test which the courts have devised and which the courts voluntarily apply. *Cf. Spencer's Case*, Coke, vol. 3, part 5, 16a; *Mayor of Congleton v. Pattison*, 10 East 130. In truth such a description or test so formulated is too vague to be of much assistance and judges and academic scholars alike have struggled, not with entire success, to formulate a test at once more satisfactory and more accurate. "It has been found impossible to state any absolute tests to determine what covenants touch and concern land and what do not. The question is one for the court to determine in the exercise of its best judgment upon the facts of each case." Clark, *op. cit.* p. 76.

* * * It has been often said that a covenant to pay a sum of money is a personal affirmative covenant which usually does not concern or touch the land. Such statements are based upon English decisions which hold in effect that only covenants, which compel the covenanter to submit to some restriction on the use of his property, touch or concern the land, and that the burden of a covenant which requires the covenanter to do an affirmative act, even on his own land, for the benefit of the owner of a "dominant" estate, does not run with his land. *Miller v. Clary*, 210 N.Y. 127, 103 N.E. 1114, L.R.A.1918E, 222, Ann.Cas.1915B, 872. In that case the court pointed out that in many jurisdictions of this country the narrow English rule has been criticized and a more liberal and flexible rule has been substituted. In this State the courts have not gone so far. We have not abandoned the historic distinction drawn by the English courts. So this court has recently said: "Subject to a few exceptions not important at this time, there is now in this state a settled rule of law that a covenant to do an affirmative act, as distinguished from a covenant merely negative in effect, does not run with the land so as to charge the burden of performance on a subsequent grantee [citing cases]. This is so though the burden of such a covenant is laid upon the very parcel which is the subject-matter of the conveyance." *Guaranty Trust Co. of New York v. New York & Queens County Ry. Co.*, 253 N.Y. 190, 204, 170 N.E. 887, 892, opinion by Cardozo, Ch. J.

Both in that case and in the case of *Miller v. Clary, supra*, the court pointed out that there were some exceptions or limitations in the application of the general rule. * * * It may be difficult to classify these exceptions or to formulate a test of whether a particular covenant to pay money or to perform some other act falls within the general rule that ordinarily an affirmative covenant is a personal and not a real covenant, or falls outside the limitations placed upon the general rule. At least it must "touch" or "concern" the land in a substantial degree, and though it may be inexpedient and perhaps impossible to formulate a rigid test or definition which will be entirely satisfactory or which can be applied mechanically in all cases, we should at least be able to state the problem and find a reasonable method of approach to it. It has been suggested that a covenant which runs with the land must affect the legal relations—the advantages and the burdens—of the parties to the covenant, as owners of particular parcels of land and not merely as members of the community in general, such as taxpayers or owners of other land. Clark, *op. cit.* p. 76. *Cf.* Professor Bigelow's article on *The Contents of Covenants in Leases*, 12 Mich.L.Rev. 639; 30 Law Quarterly Review, 319. That method of approach has the merit of realism. The test is based on the effect of the covenant rather than on technical distinctions. Does the covenant impose, on the one hand, a burden upon an interest in land, which on the other hand increases the value of a different interest in the same or related land?

Even though we accept that approach and test, it still remains true that whether a particular covenant is sufficiently connected with the use of land to run with the land, must be in many cases a question of degree. A promise to pay for something to be done in connection with the promisor's land does not differ essentially from a promise by the promisor to do the thing himself, and both promises constitute, in a substantial sense, a restriction upon the owner's right to use the land, and a burden upon the legal interest of the owner. On the other hand, a covenant to perform or pay for the performance of an affirmative act disconnected with the use of the land cannot ordinarily touch or concern the land in any substantial degree. Thus, unless we exalt technical form over substance, the distinction between covenants which run with land and covenants which are personal, must depend upon the effect of the covenant on the legal rights which otherwise would flow from ownership of land and which are connected with the land. The problem then is: Does the covenant in purpose and effect substantially alter these rights?

       *   *   *

Looking at the problem presented in this case from the same point of view and stressing the intent and substantial effect of the covenant rather than its form, it seems clear that the covenant may properly be said to touch and concern the land of the defendant and its burden should run with the land. True, it calls for payment of a sum of money to be expended for "public purposes" upon land other than the land conveyed by Neponsit Realty Company to plaintiff's predecessor in title. By that conveyance the grantee, however, obtained not only title to particular lots, but an easement or right of common enjoyment with other property owners in roads, beaches, public parks or spaces and improvements in the same tract. For full enjoyment in common by the defendant and other property owners of these easements or rights, the roads and public places must be maintained. In order that the burden of maintaining public improvements should rest upon the land benefited by the improvements, the grantor exacted from the grantee of the land with its appurtenant easement or right of enjoyment a covenant that the burden of paying the cost should be inseparably attached to the land which enjoys the benefit. It is plain that any distinction or definition which would exclude such a covenant from the classification of covenants which "touch" or "concern" the land would be based on form and not on substance.

Another difficulty remains. Though between the grantor and the grantee there was privity of estate, the covenant provides that its benefit shall run to the assigns of the grantor who "may include a Property Owners' Association which may hereafter be organized for the purposes referred to in this paragraph." The plaintiff has been organized to receive the sums payable by the property owners and to expend them for the benefit of such owners. Various definitions have been formulated of "privity of estate" in connection with covenants that run with the land, but none of such definitions seems to cover the relationship between the plaintiff and the defendant in this case. The plaintiff has not succeeded to the ownership of any property of the grantor. It does not appear that it ever had title to the streets or public places upon which charges which are payable to it must be expended. It does not appear that it owns any other property in the residential tract to which any easement or right of enjoyment in such property is appurtenant. It is created solely to act as the assignee of the benefit of the covenant, and it has no interest of its own in the enforcement of the covenant.

The arguments that under such circumstances the plaintiff has no right of action to enforce a covenant running with the land are all based upon a distinction between the corporate property owners association and the property owners for whose benefit the association has been formed. If that distinction may be ignored, then the basis of the arguments is destroyed. How far privity of estate in technical form is necessary to enforce in equity a restrictive covenant upon the use of land, presents an interesting question. Enforcement of such covenants rests upon equitable principles (*Tulk v. Moxhay*, 2 Phillips, 774; *Trustees of Columbia College v. Lynch*, 70 N.Y. 440, 26 Am.Rep. 615; *Korn v. Campbell*, 192 N.Y. 490, 85 N.E. 687, 37 L.R.A.N.S. 1, 127 Am.St.Rep. 925), and at times, at least, the violation "of the restrictive covenant may be restrained at the suit of one who owns property or for whose benefit the restriction was established, irrespective of whether there were privity either of estate or of contract between the parties, or whether an action at law were maintainable." *Chesebro v. Moers*, 233 N.Y. 75, 80, 134 N.E. 842, 843, 21 A.L.R. 1270. The covenant in this case does not fall exactly within any classification of "restrictive" covenants, which have been enforced in this State (*Cf. Korn v. Campbell*, 192 N.Y. 490, 85 N.E. 687, 37 L.R.A.,N.S. 1, 127 Am.St.Rep. 925), and no right to enforce even a restrictive covenant has been sustained in this State where the plaintiff did not own property which would benefit by such enforcement so that some of the elements of an equitable servitude are present. In some jurisdictions it has been held that no action may be maintained without such elements. *But cf. Van Sant v. Rose*, 260 Ill. 401, 103 N.E. 194, 49 L.R.A.N.S. 186. We do not attempt to decide now how far the rule of *Trustees of Columbia College v. Lynch, supra*, will be carried, or to formulate a definite rule as to when, or even whether, covenants in a deed will be enforced, upon equitable principles, against subsequent purchasers with notice, at the suit of a party without privity of contract or estate. *Cf. Equitable Rights and Liabilities of Strangers to a Contract*, by Harlan F. Stone, 18 Columbia Law Review, 291. There is no need to resort to such a rule if the courts may look behind the corporate form of the plaintiff.

The corporate plaintiff has been formed as a convenient instrument by which the property owners may advance their common interests. We do not ignore the corporate form when we recognize that the Neponsit Property Owners' Association, Inc., is acting as the agent or representative of the Neponsit property owners. As we have said in another case: when Neponsit Property Owners' Association, Inc., "was formed, the property owners were expected to, and have looked to that organization as the medium through which enjoyment of their common right might be preserved equally for all." *Matter of City of New York, Public Beach, Borough of Queens*, 269 N.Y. 64, 75, 199 N.E. 5, 9. Under the conditions thus presented we said: "It may be difficult, or even impossible to classify into recognized categories the nature of the interest of the membership corporation and its members in the land. The corporate entity cannot be disregarded, nor can the separate interests of the members of the corporation" (page 73, 199 N.E. page 8). Only blind adherence to an ancient formula devised to meet entirely different conditions could constrain the court to hold that a corporation formed as a medium for the enjoyment of common rights of property owners owns no property which would benefit by enforcement of common rights and has no cause of action in equity to enforce the covenant upon which such common rights depend. Every reason which in other circumstances may justify the ancient formula may be urged in support of the conclusion that the formula should not be applied in this case. In substance if not in form the covenant is a restrictive covenant which touches and concerns the defendant's land, and in substance, if not in form, there is privity of estate between the plaintiff and the defendant.

* * *

The order should be affirmed, with costs, and the certified questions answered in the affirmative.

————————

1.   How does the court deal with the property owner's claim that the covenant to pay assessments does not run with the land because it is an affirmative covenant?

2.   Why does the covenant to pay monthly assessments "touch and concern" the land?

What is the point of the touch and concern requirement? Isn't it just a means to give notice? Is there really much danger that the covenanting parties would intend and agree to have a genuinely personal promise run with the land to successors? Would it be better—*i.e.*, reduce litigation costs and uncertainty—to eliminate the requirement, so long as the promisor's successor had notice of the promise?

3.   All states have resolved the doctrinal problem posed by a requirement to pay monthly assessment to a homeowner association. Some states

have created special statutory rules to permit homeowner associations to enforce covenants against all homeowners. In other states, courts have followed *Neponsit* to hold that homeowner associations are proxies (or trustees) for the collective interests of homeowners. *See, e.g., Merrionette Manor Homes Improvement Ass'n v. Heda*, 11 Ill. App.2d 186, 192, 136 N.E.2d 556, 559 (1956).

Whatever the doctrinal justification, the underlying concern involves the practicality of enforcement. As the court in *B.C.E. Development, Inc. v. Smith*, 215 Cal.App.3d 1142, 1149, 264 Cal.Rptr. 55, 59–60 (1989) stated:

> Typically the interest in enforcing restrictions will be common to most, if not all, members of the community. Requiring individual landowners to shoulder the burden of enforcement litigation would be unreasonable. The administration of the common areas in the development is typically allocated to a homeowners' association, or to some other entity constituted to represent all the owners. * * * It is highly reasonable in these circumstances that the representative association or other central agency undertake, on behalf of all homeowners, such litigation as may be required to enforce the CC&Rs [conditions, covenants, and restrictions]. Where the clear intent of the CC&Rs is to vest enforcement powers in an enforcement agency, there is no reason to further condition such enforcement powers upon the retention by the enforcement agency of land ownership in the development.

Should privity be eliminated for all other cases as well (again, so long as there is notice of the covenant)? Would eliminating touch and concern and privity put too much weight on notice? How reliable is the system for giving notice?

---

b.   NONRECIPROCAL COVENANTS

A developer, "G," grants lot #1 to a purchaser, "P." In the deed, P covenants not to paint his house purple "for the benefit of G and his assigns." G then conveys lot #2 (which is in the same subdivision as lot #1) to a subsequent purchaser, "S," with the identical restriction. At the time of the conveyance, S has actual knowledge of the restriction in P's deed. In neither deed does G covenant to restrict G's remaining land. In other words, the restrictions are non-reciprocal.

May S enforce the restrictive covenant against P? Under traditional common law, and the law of equitable servitudes, the answer is yes; the benefit of the G–P real covenant and equitable servitude runs to G's successor, S, because S purchased after the G–P covenant was made. Since G's property had the benefit of P's covenant, so does S's property.

May P enforce the restriction against S? Under traditional common law, the answer is no. There is nothing in S's covenant with G stating that the G–S covenant is for P's (rather than for G's) benefit. Use of the word "assigns" in the G–S deed does not extend to *previous* assigns like P, but only to persons who acquired from G *after* S. The G–P covenant is not relevant since it only restricted P's behavior, and did not restrict G's (or S's) behavior for P's benefit. *See, e.g., Werner v. Graham*, 181 Cal. 174, 183 P. 945 (1919) (developer and assignee must jointly agree in the deed to create reciprocal equitable servitudes); *King v. Snyder*, 189 Cal.App.2d 482, 11 Cal.Rptr. 328 (1961) (joint agreement must expressly state that restrictions are for the benefit of all other landowners and must "particularly describe" the land benefited and burdened). In other words, because the G–P covenant was nonreciprocal, G's land (some of which S now owns) is not burdened by a covenant for P's benefit. The lesson is that including a nonreciprocal restrictive covenant in each homeowner's deed will only permit subsequent purchasers to enforce against prior purchasers, and not the other way around.

This asymmetry in enforcement power (caused by the nonreciprocity in the original covenants) frequently creates problems when successors of the original parties seek to enforce covenants against each other. One solution would be for the court to read the G–S covenant as burdening S's land for the benefit of P's land (as well as G's remaining land), and thus allow P to enforce the G–S covenant on a third-party beneficiary theory. *See Restatement of Property* § 541; *Rodgers v. Reimann*, 227 Or. 62, 361 P.2d 101 (1961). Courts adopting this approach will do so only if there is a common plan of development reflecting a uniform restriction of which the party to be bound had notice. *Weigman v. Kusel*, 270 Ill. 520, 522–24, 110 N.E. 884, 885–86 (1915).

c. NONUNIFORM REQUIREMENTS

Developers commonly begin projects intending to impose reciprocal restrictions on the lots sold, *e.g.*, restrictions to residential purposes only. To ensure that the restrictions run with the land, the developer will include those restrictions in the deeds to the individual lots. Later on, however, the developer may forget or even purposely decide not to include the restrictions in later sales. Although the developer's initial intent was that all lots would be subject to the restrictions, the more recent purchasers will claim that they are not subject to the restrictions since their deeds do not contain the restrictions. The question is whether the court should imply reciprocal equitable servitudes in those deeds that do not explicitly contain restrictions, thereby allowing property owners to enforce the restrictions against each other.

Turner v. Brocato

Court of Appeals of Maryland, 1955.
206 Md. 336, 111 A.2d 855 (1955).

■ HAMMOND, JUDGE.

The bill of complaint in this case was brought by the appellants, owners of homes in a residential development in the northern suburbs of

Baltimore, whose lots were subject to restrictions against use for business, to obtain a declaration that the lot of the appellees was part of the development and, as such, similarly restricted, although it had been deeded by the developer free of restrictions. Right to relief was based on the claim that the developer, either expressly by deed, or by necessary implication from a course of conduct under the general plan of development, or both, had promised that all of the land retained by him was, and must continue to be, burdened by the same restrictions he had imposed on each lot as he had conveyed it and that in equity those who had become grantees with notice that the promise applied to their grants, were bound by it at the suit of one similarly bound. The chancellor held that the appellants had not met the burden of showing the restrictions which the developer had placed on their lots were for the common benefit and advantage of all those who had bought from him, rather than being personal to him, and that, consequently, he could, if he so desired, convey free of restrictions, any part of the tract which he had retained. The appeal is from the dismissal of the bill.

The facts are not in real dispute. In 1927, Charles G. Fenwick bought a tract of land of some forty-seven acres near the northern limits of Baltimore, bounded on the east by Roland Park, on the west by Falls Road, and on the south by land owned by the Penniman family. The land rises sharply from Falls Road toward Roland Ave. and is divided by Bellemore Road, running east and west between those two thoroughfares. Fenwick bought the land, which he called Poplar Hill, to resell as building sites for expensive residences. He caused to be prepared a plat of the whole tract, designated the Sutton–Britcher plat and dated August 24, 1927. On it was drawn a line roughly parallel to and about three hundred seventy feet east of Falls Road. Seventy-five numbered lots were laid out to the east of this line, thirty-eight comprising Section A and thirty-seven, Section B. The remaining land, to the west of these sections and to the east of Falls Road, was designated as Section C. This was not then subdivided into lots. On August 31, 1927, Fenwick sold his first lot, one in Section A. The deed imposed on the lot what came to be known as Poplar Hill restrictions. With three exceptions, every lot in the entire tract was sold subject to the same restrictions, running in each case, fifty years from the date of the conveyance. Fenwick covenanted in the first deed that the restrictions in it should apply to all lots in Section A "but shall not apply to the other remaining property belonging to the party of the first part". A few days later, a second lot was sold in Section B; in the deed the same restrictions were imposed on the grantee and the grantor promised that they applied to all lots in Section B. It was repeated that they did not apply to his remaining land. In July, 1929, Fenwick sold the first lot in Section C, lot seventy-eight, which is owned now by an appellant and is next to the lot in dispute. In the deed, the restrictions which had been imposed on lots in Sections A and B were incorporated by reference. From then on, all of Poplar Hill was in course of active development. A revision of the Sutton–Britcher plat was prepared, dated February 10, 1930, on which was the legend "This plat supersedes plat dated August 24, 1927''. The revision showed no division into sections but on it were added, to the seventy-five numbered lots in what had been Sections A and B, twelve additional lots in what had been designated Section C, numbered seventy-seven to eighty-eight. It was not recorded but a number of recorded deeds in Section C, and elsewhere, in Poplar Hill refer to it. A reproduction of the revised plat, on which were drawn lines indicating a right-of-way, was recorded with a deed from Fenwick to Baltimore City, granting a right-of-way for sewers. That recorded plat bears the legend "See plat of Poplar Hill dated February 10, 1930''.

Unnumbered on the revised Sutton–Britcher plat was a finger of land on the southeast corner of Falls Road and Bellemore Road, running some five hundred feet along Falls Road south of Bellemore Road, with a depth of approximately one hundred feet. It, like the rest of Section C, had been unnumbered on the first plat. A part of this finger of land is the subject of this controversy. The northern one hundred fifty feet of it is the land owned by the appellees, acquired by them in 1953 from one Bushman, who had acquired it from Fenwick without restrictions and, in turn, had so conveyed it. The appellees' land is contiguous on the east to lot seventy-eight, the first lot sold in Section C. To the south of appellees' lot, Fenwick still owns frontage of one hundred eighty-five feet on Falls Road. Still further to the south along Falls Road is the remainder of the original finger of land, which is now owned by a man named Somers, who purchased it from Fenwick free of restrictions. He uses forty feet of it next to his store, which adjoins it to the south, as a parking space for customers. The residents of Poplar Hill were not aware that the land Somers bought was in the development and, because of its location and topography, feel that its use will not harm them.

Fenwick stopped referring to sections and remaining land early in the development. The first deed which omitted these references was in October, 1929. From then until now, only two deeds out of fifty-eight have mentioned sections or remaining land of the grantor. These were in 1931. Sometimes the same such deed conveyed a lot in Section C and lots in other sections, with the same restrictions binding each. It is agreed that all of the lots in what were originally Sections A and B are restricted. All of the lots in Section C were conveyed subject to restrictions, except lot eighty-six, and the Somers lot, and the lot of the appellees. Unexplained is the exception of lot eighty-six. Its owners, who are appellants, agree it is bound to the same extent as all other lots in the development.

The western gateway to Poplar Hill, where Bellemore Road meets Falls Road, is between the house which was on the tract when Fenwick bought it, the so-called gatehouse on lot eighty-eight, on the north, and the appellees' lot, on the south. Just about the time Fenwick started to open up the lots in Section C in 1929, a large sign was hung on the appellees' lot just across from the gatehouse, which had been the second lot sold in Section C. It stated in conspicuous letters: "Poplar Hill—A Restricted Residential Development—Albert P. Strobel, Jr. Co., Agents''. Such a sign remained there continuously for some twenty years, until March, 1950.

From 1930 on, Strobel has been the exclusive sales agent for Poplar Hill. Almost everyone who was interested in, and all who bought in Poplar Hill, were given a sales plat identical with the revised Sutton–Britcher plat, showing the division of the development into lots numbered one to eighty-eight, with no reference to sections. The standard phrase "subject to Poplar Hill restrictions" was included in all contracts of sale. In addition, Strobel prepared separate lists of restrictions, which did not mention sections or the remaining land of the grantor, and these were distributed to those interested in purchasing lots and to those who did purchase. At the trial, appellees conceded on the record that the lot owners of Poplar Hill, largely those in Section C, who were in the courtroom as witnesses, would testify that they had bought their properties in reliance upon the restrictions being applicable to Poplar Hill, that they had built expensive properties on their lots and that they regard them as now being covered by the restrictions. Strobel testified that the restrictions were a selling point, that the majority of the buyers would not have bought in a high class, residential development like Poplar Hill without such restrictions. * * *

Poplar Hill restrictions * * * forbade the maintenance or operation of a number of specified noxious or offensive trades or businesses on the land conveyed and its restriction to use "for one single one-family residence only, together with a private garage for the sole use of the owner of the lot upon which it is located, and other structures appurtenant to the main residence, to be used in connection therewith and not for the purpose of trade." * * *

The appellees produced evidence that their lot, at the southeast corner of Falls and Bellemore Roads, was a high bluff unsuited for residential use. They showed that to the south of it, opposite the Kelly Avenue bridge at Mt. Washington, is a cluster of business properties, and to the north of it— north of the gatehouse—is a tavern; that there is a tavern across Falls Road to the north, that Jones Falls runs as an open storm drain directly opposite the lot, and that west of Jones Falls, are a group of buildings owned, and used for manufacturing, by the Maryland Nut and Bolt Company. It is suggested that this renders the lot suitable only for commercial or industrial use, and appropriate for the use they intend—a cleaning establishment.

The appellees say further that the evidence shows that they had neither actual knowledge nor constructive notice of any equities claimed by the appellants. They deny that any restriction imposed by Fenwick was intended by him to, or did, bind any land he continued to hold in Section C. Further, they say that if any part of Section C retained by Fenwick was bound by the restrictions, the finger of land, of which they now own a part, was not included because of its unsuitability for residential use and the fact that it was unnumbered. [The court then held "that the finger of land was a part of Poplar Hill and a part of Section C."]

The law of the case seems clear. In *McKenrick v. Savings Bank*, 174 Md. 118, 128, [the court] said:

These cases sufficiently establish as the law of this state these principles: That one owning a tract of land, in granting a part thereof, may validly impose upon the part granted restrictions upon the use thereof for the benefit of the part retained, and upon the part retained for the benefit of the part granted, or upon both for the benefit of both; that, where the covenants in the conveyance are not expressly for or on behalf of the grantor, his heirs and assigns, they are personal and will not run with the land, but that, if in such a case it appears that it was the intention of the grantors that the restrictions were part of a uniform general scheme or plan of development and use which should affect the land granted and the land retained alike, they may be enforced in equity; that covenants creating restrictions are to be construed strictly in favor of the freedom of the land, and against the person in whose favor they are made; and that the burden is upon one seeking to enforce such restrictions, where they are not specifically expressed in a deed, to show by clear and satisfactory proof that the common grantor intended that they should affect the land retained as a part of a uniform general scheme of development.

* * *

The decisions of this Court have long recognized that equity, under appropriate facts, will enforce what variously has been called reciprocal negative easements, implied equitable reciprocal servitudes or merely equities attached to land. In determining whether the facts justified relief, the Maryland cases, early and late, consistently have looked not only to language in deeds, which gratified the requirements of the statute of frauds, but also to matters extrinsic—conduct, conversation and correspondence—to find and give effect in equity to the actual intent. * * *

Where the terms of the deeds show that the covenants are to bind the heirs and assigns of the grantee and the grantor, it may be found that the restrictions were not for the sole benefit of the grantor and binding only on the grantee, but rather were to have the effect of running with the land. * * * We think that there is to be found from all the evidence, including the deeds, an intent by Fenwick to bind all of the land in Poplar Hill by restrictions similar to those imposed, in substantial uniformity on each lot sold. We find, too, that the appellees bought with notice of the right of lot owners to require that this burden remain attached to the land, not only while in Fenwick's hands, but after the sale to one with notice, even though the restrictions were not expressly imposed on the lot so sold.

As a test of whether there is a common plan or scheme of development which permits the inference of intent that the restrictions were not for the personal benefit of the grantor, but rather for the common advantage and benefit of all who purchased from him, this Court has used the language of *Mulligan v. Jordan* (N. J.) 24 A. 543, at p. 544, that this inference is to be confined to cases " * * * where there has been proof of a general plan or scheme for the improvement of the property, and its consequent benefit, and the covenant has been entered into as part of a general plan to be

exacted from all purchasers, and to be for the benefit of each purchaser, and the party has bought with reference to such general plan or scheme, and the covenant has entered into the consideration of his purchase." We find that the evidence in the case before us shows that all of these tests have been fully met. It is admitted that there was a general plan of development of all of Sections A and B from the time sales began. Some eighteen months later, Section C was opened. The same restrictions were imposed on all lots sold and offered for sale there as had been, and continued to be, imposed in the two other sections, and with the opening of Section C, all distinction between the various sections was done away with. The restrictions were of a character used in highgrade, residential subdivisions. The testimony of the owners that they bought believing the restrictions were applicable to all of Poplar Hill, that they would not have bought except for this belief, is convincing. The testimony of the sales agent that restrictions were a selling point, that a majority of the owners would not have bought except for them, and that the price paid was a reflection of the restrictions, has weight. Some of the deeds expressly said that the restrictions were part of the consideration of the purchase. The sign at the entrance to the property on the very lot here involved, that Poplar Hill was a restricted residential development, can only have reflected the belief of the developer that all of the tract was restricted and his intent to induce purchases in reliance on that fact. The use of the phrase "Poplar Hill restrictions" in the contracts of sale and in the conversation of salesmen indicated that all of the area was to be on the same footing. Fenwick himself gave specific reflection of this in writing on at least three occasions.
* * *

This is not a case where the only evidence of a general plan is the imposition of restrictions in each deed, which has been held insufficient. Here, the appellants have met the burden of proof as to a general plan of development by clear and satisfactory evidence. * * * That several lots were conveyed without restrictions does not of itself negative an intent that there should be a general comprehensive plan, nor is it fatal to a finding that there was such a plan.

The appellees argue that even if the evidence supports the finding that there was a general plan of development, from which is to be inferred an intent that the restrictions should bind all of the land, whether sold or retained, this goes no further than to justify a holding that purchasers of restricted lots can enforce the restrictions *inter sese*, * * * and does not justify an extension of the holding to include as restricted land sold without restrictions. * * *

The text writers and cases in England and the other States support the appellants and not the appellees. 3 Tiffany, Real Property, 3rd ed., sec. 860, p. 483, and Sec. 867, p. 503. In II American Law of Property, Sec. 9.30, p. 426, the author discusses the theory of implied reciprocal servitude, arising at the time of purchase of restricted land against the common grantor's remaining land, and said: "This theory is of particular importance where the common grantor, contrary to his understanding with the prior purchaser, fails to insert express restrictions in later sales of the remaining lands." In Sec. 9.33, p. 431, there is discussed the situation of a uniform plan of development with no express promise to earlier purchasers that lots sold later would be restricted, and the sale of lots without restrictions at a later date. It is said: " * * * the courts in several recent cases have recognized the existence of an implied reciprocal servitude against these remaining lots based upon the existence of the general plan." It may be added that this has been done in early as well as recent cases. * * *

On the matter of notice, we think it clear that Bushman, who took from Fenwick, and the appellees, who took from Bushman, both did so with notice, both actual and constructive, of the equity or implied servitude which bound all of Poplar Hill, including that still owned by Fenwick. Bushman was a salesman for Strobel, the general sales agent, and fully familiar with Poplar Hill. As part of the same transaction in which he purchased the lot here involved, he purchased three restricted lots in what had been Section A. His explanation as to why he thought the lot of the appellees could be transferred without restrictions was that it was not in Poplar Hill. This unexplained assumption has already been seen to be unwarranted. One of the appellees had worked for a cleaning establishment on Falls Road, a block or so away from the west entrance to Poplar Hill. He was a driver-salesman for eleven years, from 1940 to 1951. He was familiar with all of the roads in Poplar Hill. He had customers on all of them and knew exactly where the development was. He went in there about four times a week. He must have driven towards and by the sign on the very lot he later purchased, which advertised Poplar Hill as a highly restricted development, several thousand times. He claims he did not ever see it. The other appellee has been in business in the neighborhood near the west entrance of Poplar Hill for about three years. He goes through the development every day going to and from work. A fact which at least arouses the necessity for inquiry was the title company report on the lot involved, which, in the first instance, indicated that it was subject to Poplar Hill restrictions. Subsequently, the title company was persuaded to make its guarantee absolute. Nevertheless, the appellees were put on notice by this action of the title company. Had they inquired, they would have found from the residents of Poplar Hill that all of them considered all of Poplar Hill restricted. As was said in *Sanborn v. McLean, supra*, (p. 498 of 206 N. W.): "Considering the character of use made of all lots open to a view by Mr. McLean when he purchased, we think he was put thereby to inquiry, beyond asking his grantor, whether there were restrictions. * * * He could not avoid noticing the strictly uniform residence character given the lots by the expensive dwellings thereon, and the least inquiry would have quickly developed the fact that lot 86 was subjected to a reciprocal negative easement * * *."

In addition to actual notice, we think that the land records afforded constructive notice of the restrictions applicable to all of Poplar Hill. * * * We think that constructive notice was afforded by the land records which showed: (1) the substantially uniform restrictions placed on each lot sold in the development; (2) the deeds in which Fenwick entered into the covenants for himself, heirs and assigns; (3) the deeds reserving to Fenwick, his heirs and assigns, the power to waive or change certain of the restrictions "as to any part of said tract then owned", from which can be implied a covenant that the remaining restrictions [at issue in this case] could not be waived as to "any part of said tract". The validity of our conclusion on this point is not weakened by the assumption of the title company, in the first instance, that Poplar Hill restrictions covered the lot involved. * * *

1.   The court first implies a reciprocal equitable servitude on all lots in the subdivision, even those lots conveyed without restriction. What is the basis for the court's holding? Does every express restriction create an implied reciprocal restriction in the property retained? Is there an element of reliance that leads to a finding of reciprocal restrictions?

2.   What types of notice did the appellees have of the restriction to residential uses?

3.   What is the significance of the fact that the lots were developed pursuant to a common plan? Is it a basis to infer reciprocal servitudes? Is it a basis for notice? Must the common plan be in effect before the first lot is sold?

5.   Reform of Non–possessory Interest Law

Uriel Reichman, Toward a Unified Concept of Servitudes

55 Southern California Law Review 1177, 1179–80, 1182, 1231–38, 1241–42, 1248–53, 1255–57 (1982).

We have a number of patterns and forms which are regarded as law, and have been so regarded and used for some reason, although I cannot presently recall what that reason is.[25]

Servitudes provide the legal foundation of many of today's comprehensive private planning schemes that determine the physical layout, regulation, and operation of large residential and commercial developments. The market's sophistication is not matched, however, by an adequate analytical process in the courts. The American law of servitudes remains a murky subject burdened with obsolete forms and rules that have caused confusion and uncertainty.

Students of property law are initially confronted with three concepts: easements, real covenants, and equitable servitudes, all of which fit into the generic group of servitudes. Different rules apply to each of these forms. The following examples are illustrative.

25.   36 Hen. 6, 26b–26 (1548).

"Privity of estate" is necessary for the "running" of covenant obligations, but is inapplicable to the other two classes. No servitudes, other than easements, can be acquired by prescription or held "in gross." Rights acquired according to a "general scheme," however, can usually only be enforced under a theory of equitable servitudes. Once created, covenants "run" with the promisor's estate (vertical privity), whereas easements and equitable servitudes are "attached to land" and seem to be enforceable even against a person who acquired title by adverse possession. Only equitable servitudes are enforceable against a subsequent owner who had no notice of the restriction, provided that no value was given for the land. In some cases, an action for breach of covenant can be maintained by the original promisee against the original promisor, notwithstanding the fact that the land was transferred prior to the violation. No such remedy is available to the owner of an easement or an equitable servitude. The doctrine of "change in circumstances" applies to equitable servitudes, and perhaps to covenants, but not to easements. Other defenses, like laches, hardship, and unclean hands, are traditionally only associated with equitable servitudes.

The above rules reflect what seems to be the majority view, but the subject is so marred with disagreement that contradictory authority can be found to refute almost all of the above propositions. * * *

The thesis of this Article is that the three forms of servitudes should be considered as one concept. The normative distinctions * * * would therefore almost entirely disappear. It is unimportant whether the unified concept is entitled a servitude, a land obligation, or any other term. The importance is in understanding that only a single concept is necessary—a concept which primarily partakes the qualities of what is presently described as an easement. In fact, the proposed approach accords with today's practices. All servitudes appear in the same documents and substantially serve the same function. * * *

II. UNIFYING THE SERVITUDES RULES

* * *

A. SURVEYING THE DOMAIN OF SERVITUDES

1. *A Functional Analysis of Servitudes*

The phenomenon of servitudes can be best explained by a functional analysis: The common denominator of most servitudes is the promotion of the efficient utilization of land resources. From the dogmatic perspective, ownership is defined as the freedom to do with a piece of land whatever the owner pleases. That freedom, although restricted by specific rules believed to serve the public interest, manifests itself through a corresponding duty of noninterference imposed on the public at large. However, protection of owners' freedom is essential, but insufficient by itself, to promote the efficient use of land resources; unless voluntary transfers are possible, property could not shift to its best use.

Effective accommodation of sellers' and buyers' utilities requires flexibility in molding transactions. For that reason, not only is title transferable in its entirety, but separate elements are transferable as well. Possession, sometimes without title, can be segmented and sold by reference to physical criteria (*e.g.*, condominium units, air space, and subsurface minerals) or by reference to time (*e.g.*, lease duration, future interests, and time sharing).

Situations arise, however, where even partial possession is not the desired object of a transaction. *Servitudes are used to transfer owners' entitlements, other than possession, for the efficient utilization of land.* "Transfer," as here used, is meant to imply that certain rights, which a person has as an owner of land, could be permanently replaced by a corresponding obligation to do, or not to do, certain specified actions. It follows that the grantor of a servitude cannot defeat it by transferring his title or a conflicting interest. "Owners' entitlements" is used here in a broad sense, namely whatever an owner can do or refrain from doing respecting his land. Finally, "possession" is used in contradistinction to a servitude itself, although the line between the two is not always easily drawn. The distinction is nevertheless important since possession has other functions, and is differently regulated. Exclusivity of use distinguishes possession from servitudes in most cases, but there are varying degrees of exclusivity.

There are three characteristics of servitudes, each of which is important to land use planning: limited scope (not amounting to possession), permanency, and flexibility in structuring the right. Without the ability to purchase non-possessory segments of ownership entitlements, some beneficial transactions will not be concluded and other transactions will result in waste. The theoretically perpetual duration of servitudes encourages reliance and capital investment. Promoting the efficient utilization of land is more than a common characteristic of servitudes, it is the overriding policy governing these rights and carries normative implications. A review of the judicial role in creating and terminating servitudes substantiates this assertion. * * *

In situations where a promise has no bearing on land use regulation, the courts treat the arrangement as a contract between the original parties and exempt the promisor's transferees from liability. In such cases, it is irrelevant whether or not the transacting parties clearly expressed their written intention that the promise would "run with the land," or that the promisor's transferee had actual or constructive notice of the obligation. As a matter of positive law, where land use efficiency gains could not conceivably be accomplished, servitudes are not recognized. By applying the "touch and concern" test, the courts are actually exercising their power to fix the boundaries of servitudes.

This somewhat unusual interventionist theory is justified because the permanent attachment to land of merely personal obligations is likely to frustrate the objectives of a private land holding system.

In the first place, obligations not related to actual property use are highly individualized. They tend, therefore, to become inefficient in the short run following a transfer. Consensual termination of such rights might not occur because of prohibitive transaction costs. The best way to insure efficient termination of such arrangements is to shift the burden of negotiation; instead of making the transferee negotiate for a release, the aspiring beneficiary will have to reach agreement with each new owner. Personal contracts remain the subject of personal bargains.

There is another reason for the "touch and concern" rule. Private property is sanctioned by society not only to promote efficiency, but also to safeguard individual freedom. Servitudes are a kind of private legislation affecting a line of future owners. Limiting such "legislative powers" to an objective purpose of land planning eliminates the possibility of creating modern variations of feudal serfdom. There might be nothing objectionable in personal agreements concerning personal labor, adherence to ideologically prescribed modes of behavior, or promises to buy from a certain supplier. When such obligations, however, become permanently enforced against an ever-changing group of owners, the matter acquires different dimensions. One point needs emphasis: The courts are not involved in measuring efficiency gains; this is clearly the prerogative of the parties. The courts only deny the permanency of agreements clearly unrelated to land use.

Judicial termination of obsolete servitudes also helps to achieve efficiency. An obsolete servitude is of no value to the beneficiary; it could be of great value to the owner of the encumbered land, however, since it prevents the best use of the property. A consensual termination may not be reached if excessive "blackmail" money is demanded or if transaction costs are too high. Instead of waiting for such an agreement to be reached, the courts simply pronounce the death of the servitude. Thus, when the positive utility of the servitudes has ended, the courts do not allow it to become a bare device to collect money.

2.   *The Content of Servitudes*

        * * *

a.   *Accommodations among neighbors*: Most servitudes fall into this category. Through individual bargaining or initial private planning the combined use of several separate units is made more efficient. In short, servitudes are often used to implement the Coase theorem. * * *

Essentially, transacting parties are free to mold whatever types of servitudes they desire, constrained only by the "touch and concern" doctrine. To determine if the arrangement is a "nonrunning" personal obligation or a land use related promise, the transaction must be reviewed as a whole, including its effect on both "dominant" and "servient" estates. For example, where the elimination of a spillover is not the reason for the imposition of a negative duty, a land use function was probably not contemplated. Similarly, where a positive duty is to be performed outside the burdened estate, it is most likely that the intention was a purchase of labor rather than accommodation of the owners' relations. * * *

b. *Sharing the benefits of one piece of land*: The second category, that of sharing the benefits of a single piece of land by the possessor and another person, is marked by far less flexibility. The benefit of these servitudes, by definition, inures only to a given person and does not benefit or attach to land. After a few generations a single beneficiary might be replaced by many heirs. Even where such a servitude is greatly diminished in utility, it is difficult to reach a termination transaction. Transaction costs might be substantial; more troubling is the possibility that not all the beneficiaries could be located. Attempts to judicially terminate the right would be hampered by procedural problems. * * *

If the agreement *in toto*, rather than only the attributes of the burden, is considered, nonprivilege servitudes in gross rarely deserve recognition. A duty to grow only strawberries and sell them to the beneficiary at a fixed price, or to use only materials produced by the beneficiary for fencing, relates to the use of land, insofar as the owner of the encumbered property is concerned. But the primary objects of these agreements are, respectively, the sale of agricultural products and the forced acquisition of certain building materials. The harmful effects of enforcing such promises against a line of owners are clearly evident.

The above discussion indicates that judicial supervision of servitudes in gross is largely justified. This supervision, however, should not take the form of mere adherence to rigid patterns. Accordingly, in addition to active privileges, other "land obligations" could qualify to "run with land." The public's right to view a landmark house or a forest, even from outside a fenced estate, is, in essence, a sharing of land. Negative servitudes purchased for such purposes should therefore be held to be valid servitudes in gross.

3. *Use of the Functional Test To Define Content*

The three forms of servitudes provide very little guidance regarding the permissible content of the rights. The needed guidance, however, can come from the functional test described above: servitudes are transfers of owners' entitlements, other than possession, for the efficient utilization of land. The test corresponds to the prevailing judicial attitude and permits discretion in borderline cases by its reliance upon the overriding policy that governs servitude creation. Though the functional test is somewhat imprecise, it nonetheless enables the courts to be responsive to changing circumstances and needs. * * *

B. CREATION

1. *Explicit Creation*

Every recorded obligation which is intended to "run with the land" and which satisfies the judicial criteria discussed in the previous section, is a valid servitude. This statement reflects the current state of the law, in the event the horizontal privity rule is finally laid to rest. Both the legal and practical reasons for the horizontal privity rule disappeared long ago * * *

2. *Informal Creation*

There are situations in which the courts will recognize the existence of a servitude although the owner of the burdened land never agreed in writing to grant such a right. Five theories support that result: implication, necessity, implied reciprocity, estoppel in rem, and prescription. * * * [T]he forms servitudes may take are not vital to the functioning of these rules.

* * *

C. ENFORCEMENT

1. *Parties Against Whom a Servitude Can Be Enforced*

* * *

a. *Equitable characteristics of equitable servitudes*: It has been argued that since equitable servitudes are equitable interests they may sometimes provide greater protection than other servitudes. For example, a bona fide donee may be bound by an equitable servitude but not by an easement or real covenant. This Article has shown that the concept of equitable servitudes changed from a purely equitable right to a legal right resembling an easement. In the United States the ability to record such rights has rendered them indistinguishable from other servitudes. Equitable servitudes therefore should be treated as legal interests. Equitable theories still have a place in the American law of servitudes, however. Specifically, since servitudes are conceptualized as interests in land, a promise to grant such a right will implicate equitable rules. Equitable servitudes should therefore provide no more and no less protection than other land obligations. The provisions of the recording acts define the position of a grantee who paid no consideration for the land and had no actual or constructive notice of a previously created right. The type of servitude involved is immaterial.

b. *The vertical privity rule*: One of the major deficiencies of real covenants is the vertical privity rule. According to this rule a covenant is enforceable only against a successor to exactly the same interest, or one of corresponding duration, "held by the promisor at the time the promise was made." The *Restatement* explains vertical privity as a measure of "formal identification," justified by the policy of keeping the running of burdens within "narrow formal limits." The *Restatement*'s rationale for the vertical privity is unpersuasive, however. Historically, the rule emerged as an unwarranted extension of lease theories to agreements among neighbors. Yet the threat that the lease might be terminated should alone be sufficient to deter even a sublessee, who owes no duty to the landlord for want of privity, from disregarding the lessee's obligations. No such remedy is available to the beneficiary of a real covenant.

The arbitrariness of the rule can be illustrated by an example. Suppose a community restricts itself to single family homes and imposes on all lots a duty to maintain front lawns. Neighbors should not lose their right to enforce the "covenants" merely because a lessee or adverse possessor occupies the land. Suppose a neighbor wishes to enforce the obligation to maintain front lawns against a noncomplying lessee of the neighboring lot. If the vertical privity rule is enforced, first the neighbor must find the landlord, and even then, enforcement beyond compensation might prove impossible. Similar problems arise when a trespasser takes over the land. Beneficiaries of covenants have no right to control transactions concerning the burdened land. Accordingly, the remedies of covenant beneficiaries should not be affected by the rights granted by the owner of the "servient estate," nor should covenant beneficiaries be penalized for the owner's negligence in keeping out trespassers.

Fortunately, the vertical privity rule is not often applied. By calling the land obligation an equitable servitude or negative easement, the rule is simply avoided. Easements and equitable servitudes are considered attached to land and every possessor, regardless of how he obtained the possession, must comply with the servitudes' obligations. Why then should not the contract-privity analysis be eliminated altogether? Proponents of the rule point out that in certain cases it would be unfair to place substantial liabilities on one who possesses the land for only a short time (as in the case of a lease for a few months). Most examples offered by proponents of the rule relate to monetary obligations, such as community assessments or payments for repair and maintenance of party walls. As previously explained, these obligations should not have been conceptualized as servitudes. Since they are servitudes under current American law, however, the issue cannot be avoided.

The best solution to the problem of monetary obligations is a unified approach entailing a presumption that servitudes apply to all possessors of encumbered land. The defendant-possessor would have the burden of proving that the servitude was not meant to impose a specific obligation upon him. The presumption clearly could not be rebutted where servitudes such as residential restrictions or a duty to keep up a lawn are involved; but, unduly burdensome monetary obligations may cause different results. * * *

The theory of real covenants focuses on the transfer of duties. When possession is taken over by a trespasser, no voluntary transfer can be construed. Thus, a covenant cannot be enforced against a trespasser. A property conceptualization of covenants eliminates these difficulties. The beneficiary of a servitude is considered to be vested with a right in the encumbered land. Consequently, there is no need to deal with a transfer of duty. The beneficiary is merely enforcing his rights with respect to the land of another, and it is immaterial how the defendant obtained possession. The anomaly of providing a trespasser with immunities, when a purchaser is denied such defenses, is therefore resolved. * * *

Acquisition of title by adverse possession would likewise raise no difficulties under a property conceptualization. The elapse of the statutory period eliminates only those interests to which the possession was adverse.

Accordingly, where the trespasser did not violate the servitudes, he would owe the same duties as the owner he replaced. * * *

c.   *The enforceability of benefits*: There are no substantial differences between real covenants, easements, and equitable servitudes regarding the right of enforcement. Where a servitude benefits another's land, a purchaser without notice of the benefit may logically enforce the right. The Restatement recognizes that no horizontal privity is required as a condition to the "running of benefits." Furthermore, instead of strict vertical privity, only succession to "some interest" of the promisee is needed. As a general rule every lawful possessor of the dominant tenement is entitled to demand compliance with a servitude.

Because servitudes are intended to supplement possessory rights, their benefits naturally inure to the possessor. Owners are likewise permitted to enforce servitudes to protect their reversionary interests, and in cases where monetary obligations are involved, one might logically conclude that owners alone are provided with the right of enforcement. But *Neponsit Property Owners' Association v. Emigrant Industrial Savings Bank*, a case which applies to all types of servitudes, permitted a homeowners' association to enforce the benefit as an "agent or representative" of the owners. The effect of the fusion of the forms on the "running of benefits" is therefore minimal. * * *

2.   *Remedies Available to the Beneficiary*
     * * *

Without pretending to exhaust the topic of remedies for servitude violations, this Article suggests a few modifications which could provide the judiciary with greater flexibility. Servitudes tend to be efficient upon creation. Absent significant changes, the right should be specifically enforced. This attitude promotes the expectations of the parties and encourages utilization of private planning. Problems arise, however, as the utility of the servitude fluctuates over time. Changes in patterns of land uses and technological developments often necessitate judicial ingenuity in structuring remedies. Where the utility of the servitude is reduced, the courts have traditionally resorted to one of the two following measures: (1) damages in lieu of specific performance or (2) a declaration that the right is totally extinguished. These attitudes are particularly justified where several owners of burdened lots are involved. Prohibitive transaction costs, including freeloader problems, may prevent the conclusion of a termination transaction. By decreeing damages the courts are actually forcing resale of entitlements. In more extreme cases, where the servitude has lost almost all of its original benefits, the right is judicially abolished to solve the transactions costs and freeloader problems.

There are cases, however, in which the alternative of modification, with or without compensation, would be more appropriate. The servitude could be modified as to its content or location. For example, the need for some commercial activities might be felt in a community several years after its establishment. By permitting these activities, but continuing the ban on other objectionable land uses, and granting compensation to the injured beneficiaries, a more equitable result is reached. Similarly, a court should be allowed to shift a right of way from the center of a lot to one of its corners. When such a decree also provides compensation to cover the costs of constructing a new road and compensation for diminished utility, the interests of both the owner of the servient estate and the holder of the servitude are better treated. * * *

Susan F. French, Toward a Modern Law of Servitudes: Reweaving the Ancient Strands

55 Southern California Law Review 1261, 1304, 1313–17 (1982).

III.   OUTLINES OF A MODERN LAW OF SERVITUDES

The prime functions of the law of servitudes must be to provide property owners with the means to create land use arrangements of indefinite duration as well as the means to terminate them when they are no longer useful or desirable. * * *

C.   Modification and Termination of Servitudes

Simplification of the doctrinal structure of servitudes law hinges on providing an effective means to modify and terminate servitudes when they become obsolete, economically wasteful, or unduly burdensome. In developing means of termination and modification, attention should focus on facilitating private negotiations as well as on providing judicial procedures. The principal procedural obstacles to privately negotiated releases and modifications of servitudes are the difficulty of locating all the parties with interests in servitudes and the need for unanimous consent. Traditional doctrine attempted to use appurtenance, privity, and touch and concern to deal with these problems by limiting the interested parties to those with land in the vicinity. Modern law might retain this approach, at least for use restrictions, by limiting those with enforceable interests to landowners in the immediate area or whose land is described in the creating instrument. Such an approach, however, invalidates servitudes before they become burdensome.

A better approach might be drawn from customary subdivision practice, or from the recent Uniform Planned Community Act,[26] both of which provide for termination of servitudes by less than unanimous agreement of the benefited parties. Standard subdivision conditions, covenants, and restrictions documents provide that after a relatively long initial period, usually twenty-five or thirty years, lot owners may alter or abrogate the covenants by majority or greater assent. Thereafter, lot owners are given this power at shorter intervals, such as every ten years. The Uniform Act permits termination of the planned development arrangements at any time on the assent of unit owners entitled to at least eighty percent of the votes

---

26.   Uniform Planned Community Act, 7A U.L.A. (Supp. 43 1981). The Act was approved by the National Conference of Commissioners on Uniform State Laws in 1980.

in the unit owners association. The advantage of the first approach is that it relieves the benefited parties of the risk of having to mount continual battles against potential redevelopers. The advantage of the Uniform Act is that it provides more flexibility in dealing with obsolete servitudes at the point of obsolescence.

A statute providing a method for modifying or terminating servitudes by a majority or a greater number of persons entitled to enforcement rights would facilitate private resolution of the problems caused by obsolete servitudes. * * *

Because such a modification and termination procedure is designed to avoid the high transaction costs posed by multiple parties, it need not be applied to servitude interests shared by a small number of parties. An appropriate cut-off point might be the twelve-unit line drawn by the Uniform Planned Development Act. This limitation would exempt most traditional easements from modification or termination by less than unanimous consent. Servitudes created in leases also would be normally exempted by such a limitation.

Where private negotiation fails to resolve disputes over continued enforcement of servitudes, the law must provide adequate doctrinal bases for judicial resolution. Modern law can expand the changed conditions doctrine developed in equitable servitudes to deal with obsolescence in servitudes creating affirmative obligations and affirmative rights to use the land of another. The modern law should develop two explicit grounds for relief from servitude obligations in addition to obsolescence: (1) that an affirmative obligation has become unduly burdensome; and (2) that the economic arrangement implemented by the servitude obligation has become obsolete, wasteful, or unreasonable. * * *

Finally, modern law should provide more flexibility in servitude enforcement. Traditionally, the law has generally taken an all-or-nothing position: servitudes were either enforced by injunction or they were not enforced at all. Two intermediate positions should be developed in modern law. One would permit courts to modify servitude obligations to adjust to changing conditions; the other would cause damages to be awarded more frequently, and even permit termination of servitude obligations upon payment of fair compensation in the appropriate cases. * * *

Lawrence Berger, Unification of the Law of Servitudes

55 Southern California Law Review 1339–43 (1982).

At first blush, the notion of unifying the law of servitudes into one coherent whole sounds both attractive and superficially plausible. After all, easements, equitable servitudes, and real covenants all involve the limited rights of one person in the land of another. Specifically, they are respectively rights to use or to control the use of another's land or at least to insist that he perform some land-related affirmative duty. So why not have one body of law to govern them? The answer, I suppose, is that it really does not matter whether one labels the structure as one, two, or three bodies of law. The real issues are whether the rules in the structure make good policy sense and whether they are unnecessarily inconsistent. I say this because it is absolutely clear that the law about the various servitudes cannot be "unified" in the sense that the same rules should always apply to each of them. The rules are different and many of the variances make good sense.

Let me give a number of examples of what I mean. Affirmative easements may be created by prescription. If A wrongfully crosses B's land throughout the statutory period for adverse possession, and A's acts meet the various requirements of being open, notorious, uninterrupted, hostile, and so on, the courts give A a prescriptive easement by analogy to the statutory rules of adverse possession. The theory, of course, is that A is committing a trespass for which B has a cause of action, and if he does not bring a suit within the period of the adverse possession statute, he is barred from doing so later and A's trespass ripens into a permanent legal right. In the United States no analogous rule applies to so-called negative easements or equitable servitudes. For example, if C, as owner of Blackacre, receives air and light from across D's adjacent unimproved land, C cannot get a prescriptive right to have the air and light continue. Analytically, the reason for this is that D has no cause of action against C for receiving the air and light. There is, therefore, no lawsuit that C can claim is barred by the passage of time, and C's receipt of the air and light does not ripen into a prescriptive right. And in policy it should not. No act of C calls D's attention to the fact that D must sue or lose a right to build on his own property. Rights to do acts on someone else's land can be acquired by prescription by actually doing them. Rights that a neighbor not do something on his own land by their nature cannot and should not be so acquired.

* * *

One more illustration of difference in treatment will suffice to show the difficulty of thoroughly integrating all the rules concerning servitudes. This concerns the continuing liability of the originally burdened person after he no longer has an interest in the property. Suppose L conveys an easement over his land to M and later sells the fee simple to N. Thereafter if N tries to interfere with M's right to cross, L is not responsible for his grantee's wrongful act. The same rule is true of restrictive covenants. For example, a promisor-former owner is not liable for his grantee's breach of a covenant against construction of commercial property. Only the breaching party is liable in damages or injunction.

The law is more complex, however, with respect to affirmative covenants at law. On the one hand a tenant who assigns his leasehold interest in land to an assignee is still bound on his promise to pay rent and if the assignee fails to pay, the tenant-assignor must make good, although he has an action over against the assignee. On the other hand, a person buying in fee simple and promising to pay a monthly assessment to an association for maintenance of common areas is not liable for obligations accruing after he sells the property to another. The reason for the difference is clear. In the landlord-tenant situation when the landlord rents the property, he is relying upon the credit of the tenant for the entire lease period, and the tenant should not be able to escape that liability just by assigning the lease. With a fee simple, however, it is well understood that the first buyer will not own the property forever, and it is contemplated that he will pay the assessments only as long as he is an owner. Further, unlike the lease, the assessment is a potentially infinite obligation which, if it were held to bind the original promisor forever, would render the assessment device useless. Nobody would buy property subject to such an onerous personal obligation. The rules on original party liability are not uniform as to the different servitudes, nor should they be. The differences in legal result make good sense. They stem from the fact that, although servitudes of different types may be similar and related to each other, there are enough differences in their origin, economic function, and community expectation concerning them that opposing, yet sound rules about them can appropriately evolve.

That is not to say that some streamlining and simplification of the rules on servitudes is not desirable. As I have pointed out elsewhere,[27] it would undoubtedly serve a useful purpose to get rid of most of the privity of estate requirements as to covenants at law and thereby integrate those rules about servitudes. In general, the possessor of land ought to be responsible for breach of a duty created by servitude whether in the form of a restrictive covenant, affirmative covenant, or affirmative easement. However, even there complete uniformity is not possible. For it is clear that, although a tenant should not be allowed to violate a restrictive covenant agreed to by his landlord (for example, not to operate a commercial establishment), he should not, unless he consents, be personally liable to perform his landlord's affirmative promises (*e.g.*, to pay maintenance association dues). Professor French denominates this a problem of vertical privity but I would prefer to say that the tenant should not be liable because it would not accord with community expectation to hold him so. In any case, no matter what the label, most everyone would agree with the above different rules as they have developed.

In conclusion, I would agree that the law of servitudes should be "unified" (however that word is defined) where that would mean the elimination of unnecessary or irrational differences in the rules (as in privity of estate at law) but the variances should be maintained in those many areas where the law, as it has evolved, is supported by sound policy and community expectation.

Allison Dunham, Statutory Reformation of Land Obligations

55 Southern California Law Review, 1345, 1346–47, 1351–52 (1982).

I. STATUTORY REFORM

The modern trend in reforming property law is to use statutes. * * * The movement toward statutory reform is an indication that private

---

27. *See* Berger, A Policy Analysis of Promises Respecting the Use of Land, 55 Minn. L. Rev. 167, 190–95 (1970).

agreements and common law institutions have not kept pace with the needs of modern society. * * *

III. REQUIREMENT OF CERTAINTY

I agree with Professors Reichman and French to the extent that they argue for substantive integration of the legal rules governing land obligations. Neither Professor Reichman nor Professor French, however, adequately address the impact of their proposal on the recent trend to simplify land transfers. Specifically, they fail to discuss the problem of title examination. Their proposal to extend the doctrine of changed circumstances to cover easements, rights of entry, and the like, fails to provide a solution to the title search problem. The caution of the title examining industry will allow no examiner to conclude that an encumbrance is removed by reason of changed circumstances without an official determination that circumstances have indeed changed.

Thus, given the constraints of the title assuring system, invalidating servitudes through application of the changed circumstances doctrine will have the same effect on marketability as invalidating them through the privity and touch and concern requirements; only complete elimination of the common-law servitude system can achieve title simplification objectives. The recommendations of Professors Reichman and French regarding the termination problem will produce only more judicial supervision and, therefore, more uncertainty.

If this conclusion is correct, as I believe it is, then reform cannot be accomplished by any system short of a means for the elimination of restrictions with absolute certainty. To realize this objective, legislation is necessary; only two types of legislation seem appropriate:

(1) a limit on the duration of restrictions, calculated from the *time* of recordation (a certain point of beginning), or

(2) a provision that, on application by the owner of a servient estate and on payment to the owner of the dominant estate of a sum equal to the loss suffered by reason of the release, the servient estate is released from the restriction.

Carol M. Rose, Servitudes, Security, and Assent: Some Comments on Professors French and Reichman
55 Southern California Law Review 1403, 1413–16 (1982).

Easements and covenants are second only to the "fee tail" or perhaps to "springing uses" as a symbol of the mindless formalism of traditional property law. * * *

II. TOUCHING AND CONCERNING CHANGED CIRCUMSTANCES
* * *

If we are seriously concerned about servitudes that outlast their usefulness for land development, there is a simpler and less unsettling way to limit inefficient servitudes [than the changed circumstances doctrine]. Although our present authors prefer servitudes of potentially infinite duration, other authors have urged that servitudes be limited to some fixed period. Indeed, with the possible exception of servitudes designed to assure permanently the continued duration of our natural or historic heritage, no servitude should be expected to last in perpetuity. Servitudes rather should be geared to the expected life of the development they serve—land development, after all, is the chief reason why we put up with servitudes in the first place. The parties should state a limited length of time that they think the servitude will enhance the development; the legislatures too can state at least a presumptive life span of servitudes for different development purposes. Only thereafter should the courts tell us what a reasonable life expectancy might have been at the time the servitude was created—not what we now think its appropriate life is. Beyond that period, let the servitude be open for renegotiation.[28]

French's and Reichman's papers suggest that a principal reason for nonnegotiated extinguishments of servitudes is that some changes may render negotiation impossible, so that the beneficiaries of a servitude cannot be assembled to agree upon its extinguishment even if they might be amenable. Taken seriously, this suggestion argues that the changed circumstance doctrine should be confined to situations in which the claimants' rights have become too complex for extinguishment through ordinary negotiation.

One approach to this problem is to limit and specify the claimants to servitude rights, so that future negotiation for extinguishment remains possible. This function, Professor French points out, was once served by restraints on easements in gross and by the requirement that servitudes benefit some ascertainable land. No doubt some old doctrines can be improved or expanded, while still limiting the numbers of potential claimants with whom future extinguishment must be negotiated.

No doubt too, given the complexity of modern real estate development, we should expect some matters to become too complex for negotiation. Here, the "changed circumstance" rule might be applied to limit one's remedies to damages, even where there is no inference of acquiescence to the change. But where negotiations are possible, it is hardly compatible

---

28. Limiting the duration of servitudes should lessen the difficulties of interpreting the original intent of the parties as to whether and how long the servitude should endure. If the parties set their own duration, the outside duration might be established by the reasonable life of the property development that is served by the restriction. *Cf.* Homes Association Handbook, at 212 (advocating periodic review of covenants). At the expiration of the agreed upon duration, the servitude may be viewed either as terminated (and renegotiable), or as presumptively renewed unless objected to by some specified percentage of affected property owners. *Id.* at 212, 336. The presumptive-renewal method is undoubtedly preferable where the parties limit the servitude to a period shorter than the expected life of the land development, *e.g.*, condominium upkeep requirements that are set at a mortgage period, or at the first expected complete ownership turnover.

with a property conception of servitudes to use "changed circumstance" as a general defense to servitude obligations, so as effectively to rearrange property rights through a kind of private eminent domain.[29]

A general use of changed circumstance doctrine is not important if servitudes are limited in duration; if they are so limited, then the original parties can count on an appropriate duration that they set themselves, while the rest of us can be assured that the "dead hand" will be removed unless future parties overtly signal its continued usefulness.

For the sake of utilization of land, the parties to a servitude agreement should be able to rely on its duration over the period in which they regard it as land enhancing. But if, as I believe to be the case, we can tolerate lasting servitudes more easily because we can infer the continued voluntary acceptance of successors in interest, then there is no reason why we should not, from time to time, require the successors to make their acceptance explicit. * * *

----

1.   *Unification of Servitude Law.* There is fairly broad agreement that servitude law would benefit from simplification and the discarding of some obsolete terminology and requirements. But should the law be unified? How would Reichman respond to Berger's observations?

29. It is of course true that some current law does just this. *See Blakeley v. Gorin,* 365 Mass. 590, 313 N.E.2d 903 (1974), interpreting Mass. Gen. Laws Ann. ch. 184, § 30 (West 1979). In *Blakeley,* the beneficiary of a covenant for light and air was confined to a damage remedy for a violation of the covenant, on the basis of a statute prohibiting an injunctive remedy where such a remedy was not "in the public interest." The court's discussion of the "public interest" dwelt largely on the point that the restricted hotel property would have much greater market value (and hence taxable value) if the restriction were removed. The decision suggests that servitudes might have little effect as property rights in the face of changing market forces; simply because the market would sufficiently enhance the hotel's value without the restriction, the hotel owners could extinguish the restriction by paying market-value damages to the owner of the benefitted property, rather than that owner's asking price.

As the authors here point out, there are comparable solutions in nuisance law. See the much-discussed *Boomer v. Atlantic Cement Co., Inc.,* 26 N.Y.2d 219, 257 N.E.2d 870, 309 N.Y.S.2d 312 (1970), in which the court held that a cement plant was a nuisance to nearby residents, but confined their remedy to damages. *Id.* at 228, 257 N.E.2d at 875, 309 N.Y.S.2d at 319. The dissent viewed this solution as an unlawful exercise of eminent domain for a private purpose. *Id.* at 230–31; 257 N.E.2d at 876; 309 N.Y.S.2d at 321 (Jasen, J., dissenting). *Boomer,* however, involved multiple claimants, and could be viewed as a solution required by the difficulty of negotiating a voluntary transaction. Moreover, it is at least arguable that "private eminent domain" in the nuisance context is more justifiable than it is in the servitude context, since the parties in nuisance cases have never had any consensual dealings with each other to define their respective property rights, and the courts must settle those often uncertain rights willy-nilly. The parties to a covenant, on the other hand, are at least indirectly related through the consensual arrangements of their respective predecessors in interest—arrangements that defined the very property interests at issue and that presumably were known and accepted by the current parties.

2. *Property Model versus Contract Model.* Reichman observes that "servitudes are often used to implement the Coase theorem," yet he recommends at various places that the law of servitudes would be more efficacious if based on a property rather than a contract model. Is a property approach more in line with promoting Coasian bargaining than a contract approach? What aspects of contract doctrine undermine its efficacy in this sphere? Why is a property approach better able to foster efficiency?

What aspects of a property approach undermine an efficient allocation of resources? What doctrines or types of statutes are available to alleviate these problems? Are these doctrines and statutes adequate?

3. *Horizontal and Vertical Privity.* Reichman recommends, with the support of many other scholars (and no doubt countless first year property students), that the horizontal and vertical privity requirements be abolished. Do you agree with this assessment? How does he recommend dealing with affirmative obligations when a short-term tenant is in possession of the property? Does his solution create more administration and litigation problems than it solves?

4. *Touch and Concern.* Reichman would retain the touch and concern requirement as a means for distinguishing servitudes from purely personal bargains. Other scholars have argued that this requirement is unnecessary. "Insistence upon the touch and concern requirement denies the original parties their contractual freedom by subordinating their desires to the interests of future third parties, who by definition have no proprietary claim to the subject property * * *. If a seller insists that a personal covenant bind the land even though it works to the disadvantage of the immediate or even future purchasers, then the seller will have to accept a reduction in the purchase price to make good his sentiments." Epstein, Notice and Freedom of Contract in the Law of Servitudes, 55 S. Cal. L. Rev. 1353, 1360 (1982). Professor Epstein argues that as long as subsequent purchasers of land receive adequate notice of applicable burdens that run with the land, then there is no persuasive liberty or efficiency basis for invalidating such requirements, even if they do not touch and concern the land itself. Do you agree?

The *Restatement (Third) of Property (Servitudes)* § 3.2 (Tentative Draft No. 2, 1991), provides that "[n]either the burden nor the benefit of a covenant is required to touch or concern land in order for the covenant to be valid as a servitude." The comments note that courts developed this doctrine in the nineteenth and early twentieth centuries as a flexible, although vague, mechanism for policing unwise servitudes. As courts have developed clearer and better reasoned rules for policing servitudes, the touch and concern doctrine has become obsolete and, because of its vague contours, increasingly counterproductive.

> *Modern uses of the touch and concern doctrine.* Today, most of the cases in which failure to touch or concern the land is invoked as the primary basis for refusing to enforce a servitude involve monetary obligations and tying arrangements. Although there are good reasons why some of these servitudes should not be enforced,

they do not apply to all monetary obligations and tying arrangements. The touch and concern doctrine does not provide the means to discriminate between those which should and should not be enforced, which leads to apparently incomprehensible distinctions in cases and to invalidation of some legitimate servitudes. Monetary obligations and tying arrangements that should not be enforced are captured by the rules stated in § 3.5 on indirect restraints on alienation lacking rational justification, § 3.6 on unreasonable restraints of trade, and § 3.7 on unconscionable servitude arrangements.

Comment d, *Restatement (Third) of Property (Servitudes)* § 3.2 (Tentative Draft No. 2, 1991).

5. *Termination and Modification of Nonpossessory Interests.* Professors Reichman, French, Dunham, and Rose suggest a range of options for reforming these doctrines. What are the advantages and disadvantages of these alternative approaches? What overall approach would be most efficacious?

6. *Unifying Servitudes and Defeasible Fees.* Professor Korngold suggests that "the law should integrate defeasible fees involving land use controls and servitudes. These interests serve the same purpose: they create rights and corresponding restrictions related to the use of land. The tensions between freedom of contract rights and the policy disfavoring restrictions on land inhere in both interests." Korngold, For Unifying Servitudes and Defeasible Fees: Property Law's Functional Equivalence, 66 Tex. L. Rev. 533, 535 (1988). Under his unified scheme, the extreme remedy of forfeiture for violating a condition in a defeasible fee would be circumscribed, where appropriate, by the use of damages or injunctive relief. Is this reform needed?

C.   COMMON INTEREST COMMUNITIES (CICs)

The past three decades have witnessed a dramatic rise in the development of "common interest communities" (CICs) throughout the United States. *See generally* E. McKenzie, *PRIVATOPIA*: Homeowner Associations and the Rise of Residential Private Government (1994). They constitute almost one-fifth of residential housing in the United States today and their growth is continuing. CICs cover a broad spectrum of residential housing, from urban high density apartment buildings (condominiums and cooperatives) to suburban gated communities to time-shared resort lodging. The developers of these communities use detailed covenants, conditions, and restrictions to tailor the living environment to a targeted audience, such as retirees, vacationers, or young families, and to create a quasi-democratic governance structure to manage the community and provide it flexibility to evolve over time.

A number of factors have fueled the growth of this form of housing. Large tax subsidies to owner-occupied housing—the failure to include the imputed rental value of owner-occupied housing in taxable personal income[30] and the deferral of capital gains from the sale of a home so long as the proceeds from a sale are reinvested in another home occupied by the owner—have spurred home ownership generally and encouraged developers to innovate in the market for residential housing. *See generally* Hansmann, Condominium and Cooperative Housing: Transactional Efficiency, Tax Subsidies, and Tenure Choice, 20 J. Legal Stud. 25 (1991). Even though detached housing located near good employment opportunities and cultural centers is beyond the reach of many households today, the development of separately owned dwellings in multi-unit structures enables a much broader segment of the population to own their own home. For this reason, condominiums, consisting of vertically stacked and horizontally attached units, provide a substantial proportion of the starter-home market.

CICs have also risen in popularity as a result of the doctrinal and practical limitations of traditional nonpossessory interests. As discussed earlier, easements, real covenants, and equitable servitudes cannot always be counted upon to secure the integrity of a neighborhood. Perhaps more significantly, there are often significant free-rider problems associated with the enforcement of nonpossessory interests. CICs are able to overcome these problems by governing the commons directly and spreading the costs of enforcement over the residents of the community through *ex ante* agreement and periodic assessments. *See* French, The Constitution of a Private Residential Government Should Include a Bill of Rights, 27 Wake Forest L. Rev. 345, 349 (1992).

CICs are also able to provide homeowners with shared amenities without burdening homeowners with the headaches of maintaining these amenities. Many CICs provide swimming pools, community rooms, tennis courts, golf courses, playgrounds, parks, landscaped grounds, and exercise facilities. *See* Community Association Institute, Community Association Factbook 9 (1988). Busy homeowners do not have to spend their weekends mowing the grass or cleaning the pool. The homeowner association maintains these amenities and spreads the costs among the members.

A fourth set of factors promoting the growth of CICs has been dissatisfaction with the provision of services by local governments. CICs are able to supplement and in some cases wholly replace local governments in the provision of road maintenance, utility service, security, fire protection, and other basic services.

---

30. It is commonly thought that the deductibility of mortgage interest and property taxes favors owner-occupied housing over rental housing. As economists have pointed out, however, landlords may also take such deductions, and competition in the market for rental housing should result in this subsidy being passed through to renters. *See* Hansmann, Condominium and Cooperative Housing: Transactional Efficiency, Tax Subsidies, and Tenure Choice, 20 J. Legal Stud. 25, 39–40, n.39 (1991). Hence, the key tax difference between owner-occupied and rental housing is that home owners are not taxed on the imputed rental income of their home whereas landlords are taxed upon rental income (less depreciation and other expenses).

Although CICs have become a major part of residential living in the United States, experience has revealed that CICs are not panaceas for the ills of traditional single-family home ownership and rental housing. While they have ameliorated some of the burdens, responsibilities, and risks of the traditional forms of housing and community structure, they have introduced new problems and challenges.

Although CICs come in a wide variety of forms, their basic structure is the same: exclusive occupancy rights to a dwelling unit; co-ownership of common areas; detailed covenants, conditions, and restrictions governing the use and sometimes transfer of units and the use of common areas; assessment of fees to operate the CIC; and participation by owners in the governance of the CIC. We begin this section with a summary of the predominant forms of CICs, noting their historical development and key attributes. We then discuss legislative constraints on the formation, restrictions, and operation of CICs and the role of courts in overseeing the governance of homeowner associations and the validity of the most significant types of CIC restrictions. We conclude by examining key issues relating to the future of CICs and their governance.

1. PREDOMINANT FORMS

a. COOPERATIVES

The cooperative form first came into use in New York City in the mid- to late-19th century as a device to share ownership among the residents of large, typically luxury, apartment buildings. Co-ops became more important during the housing shortage following World War I, and by the late 1920s, there were over 100 such buildings in New York City and Chicago. Castle, Legal Phases of Cooperative Buildings, 2 S. Cal. L. Rev. 1 (1928). Their popularity increased during World War II as a means to circumvent emergency rent control statutes. R.R. Powell & P.J. Rohan, 4B Powell on Real Property ¶ 632.2[2] (1996).

Changes in the tax laws sustained the popularity of cooperatives following the war. By 1960, cooperatives accounted for about 1 percent of multi-family dwelling units in the United States, with a third of these in New York City. By the mid–1970s, that percentage had grown to about 2 percent of multi-family housing units. U.S. Dep't Housing and Urban Development, Annual Housing Survey: 1983, Part A, General Housing Characteristics (Current Housing Reports ser. H–150–83 (1984)). Since that time, the percentage of cooperative units has fallen, although this drop has been more than offset by increases in the percentage of condominium ownership. *Id.* Together cooperative and condominium ownership is about 10 percent of multi-family housing units, and more than 20 percent of new residential construction. The cooperative form has remained concentrated in larger cities, such as New York, Chicago, and Los Angeles, while the condominium form has proliferated throughout the United States.

Cooperatives often use a corporation or business trust model to structure ownership interests in multi-unit buildings. Under the more common corporate ownership model, the CIC developer forms a corporation and conveys the land to the corporation. The corporation assigns stockholders "proprietary leases" to specific dwelling units. P.J. Rohan & M.A. Reskin, Condominium Law & Practice § 1.04 (1965). Thus, the residents do not hold actual title to their apartment; rather they hold exclusive use and lease renewal rights for as long as they retain their stock in the corporation. Since the corporation holds title, the cooperative is typically financed through a blanket mortgage. The corporation operates under a charter and set of bylaws governing the use of dwelling units and common areas, the sharing of costs to finance and maintain the building, limitations on the transferability of interests, and the structure, procedures, and voting rules governing the management of the corporation. The shareholders of the corporation elect directors who oversee the operation of the building.[31]

b.   CONDOMINIUMS

Condominiums rely on the more traditional land ownership model of freehold interests to structure the rights and responsibilities of residents. Members of a condominium typically own their individual dwelling unit in fee simple.[32] Recognizing the discord between the notion of stacked fee simples and the traditional Anglo–American concept of owning property from the center of the earth to the sky (*ab infimis usque ad coelum*), one observer has aptly defined a condominium as "a freehold interest in a horizontal slice in a vertical column of air." Spahn, in Transcript, The Emerging Profile of Condominium, 12 (Condominium Institute, Third Annual Conference (Berkeley, Cal., 1963)).[33] Condominium owners possess title to the interior spaces of their dwelling units extending to or even part way through exterior and common walls. In addition to their freehold

31.   The trust model is similar to the corporate model, substituting a business trust whose trustees hold title to the property in place of the corporation. A declaration of trust governs the operation of the CIC, including the assignment of beneficial interests or proprietary leases to purchasers, rules governing the use of dwelling units and common areas, obligations to share the costs of operating the CIC, limitations on the transferability of interests, and the creation of a governing board. P.J. Rohan & M.A. Reskin, Condominium Law & Practice § 1.03 (1965). Cooperatives may also be organized under the traditional doctrines of concurrent interests as joint tenancies or tenancies in common, although these forms of ownership are rarely used to structure modern cooperatives. *Id*. at § 1.02.

32.   Although far less common, some developers have created leasehold condominiums in which the residents only acquire unit leases. Under this arrangement, the developer typically will obtain a long-term lease of the land. Leasehold condominiums tend to arise where a condominium form is attractive, but the landowner does not wish to actually sell the land as a result of adverse tax implications, trust restrictions upon the land, or other considerations. *See generally* R.R. Powell & P.J. Rohan, 4B Powell on Real Property § 632.4[2][k] (1996).

33.   The condominium form traces its roots to civil law nations. The separate ownership of floors and rooms began in the Middle Ages in parts of continental Europe. Leyser, The Ownership of Flats—A Comparative Study, 7 Int'l & Comp. L.Q. 31, 33 (1958). The condominium form first came to the attention of American lawyers through its use in Puerto Rico, which adopted a condominium statute in 1958. Within a decade, every state had adopted a condominium enabling act and the use of this form proliferated.

interests, condominium owners are also tenants in common with other unit owners in the underlying land and in the spaces and building parts used in common. These spaces include the exterior shell of the building, the basement, the roof, the lobby, the garage, hallways, elevators, and grounds.

Developers record three types of documents to establish condominiums: the declaration or master deed; the bylaws; and the deeds to individual units. The declaration typically describes the land, dwelling units, and common elements of the building (including detailed floor plans and plats), incorporates applicable covenants and other land use restrictions (including restrictions on occupancy, use, partition, and sometimes even transfer), establishes a homeowner association, and provides for the amendment of the declaration and bylaws.[34] The bylaws set forth the rules and procedures governing the homeowner association and the administration of the condominium development. The deeds to individual units transfer title to the purchaser. Each deed cross-references the declaration for the condominium development.

In most other respects, the operation of cooperatives and condominiums are similar, although the legal and financing formalities can differ significantly. For example, in contrast to shareholders of a cooperative, condominium owners typically finance their ownership interest individually by pledging their fee interest as security.

An important substantive difference arises if the building is destroyed. In a cooperative, the corporation recovers the insurance proceeds and decides whether to rebuild (unless the governing instruments provide otherwise). Residents influence the exercise of this discretion through their shareholder voting rights. By contrast, condominium owners typically have more control in deciding whether a destroyed building will be rebuilt and more direct access to insurance proceeds. In some states, insurance proceeds are distributed *pro rata* to unit owners if the condominium building is substantially destroyed. *See, e.g.,* Conn. Gen. Stat. § 47–84; N.Y. Real Prop. Law § 339–cc (requiring at least three-fourths destruction); Md. Code Ann., Real Prop. § 11–111 (requiring at least two-thirds destruction). In other states, the property is deemed to be owned in common by unit owners (in proportion to their prior undivided interest) if a decision to rebuild is not made within a designated period of time. *See, e.g.,* Iowa Code Ann. § 499B.16 (30 days); Minn. Stat. § 515.26 (180 days); Miss. Code Ann. § 89–9–35 (3 years). Unit owners may then seek partition of the property if they wish to go their separate ways and receive their proportionate share of the net value (sale proceeds and insurance recovery less debts).

The condominium form has become the most common means to create ownership interests in multi-unit residential buildings. It offers a flexible model which has been adapted to a wide range of uses, including time share resorts in which purchasers acquire ownership interests that are limited to a particular time of year, business offices, retail space, silos, horse stalls,

---

34. State condominium enabling acts set forth the particular information that must be disclosed in the declaration. This legislation is discussed in section 2, *infra.*

and boat berths. Natelson, Law of Property Owners Associations 32 (1989). Condominiums have yet to make substantial inroads into the commercial and industrial real estate markets, although some commentators predict that its use in these markets will rise in the coming years. R.R. Powell & P.J. Rohan, 4B Powell on Real Property ¶ 632.2[3] (1996).

c. PLANNED UNIT DEVELOPMENTS AND SUBDIVISIONS WITH MANDATORY MEMBERSHIP HOMEOWNER ASSOCIATIONS

CICs have also been developed to structure communities of single family homes and groupings of mixed housing forms, *e.g.*, single family and attached housing. In these CICs, homeowners own both the dwelling unit and the land on which it is built. In some communities, homeowners' fee interest extends to front and backyards and other surrounding grounds. Developers typically establish a non-profit corporation that owns the common areas, including roads, recreational facilities, clubhouses, and park areas although homeowners may own this property as tenants in common. As with condominiums and cooperatives, homeowner associations of planned unit developments (PUDs) have a quasi-democratic decisionmaking structure, responsibility to manage the common areas, power to assess homeowners for the costs of operating the association, and authority to enforce the covenants, conditions, and restrictions governing the CIC.

State zoning enabling legislation and local zoning authorities establish the structure for PUDs. The basic model by which developers plan and market PUDs is similar to that used in developing condominiums. Prior to selling units, the developer records a declaration of covenants, conditions, and restrictions which provides for the establishment of a homeowner association and the rules governing its decisionmaking process (*e.g.*, rules to select officers and directors, voting rights), responsibilities (*e.g.*, management of common areas), and powers (*e.g.*, collecting assessments, enforcement of covenants). In addition, the developer incorporates the covenants, conditions, and restrictions into the deeds of all properties sold in the development.

The first formal homeowner associations established in the United States date back to the early part of the 19th century, when the communities of Louisburg Square in Boston and Gramercy Park in New York were developed. The early common law did not clearly establish whether the burdens of paying assessments to maintain common areas ran with the land or were merely personal covenants that would not automatically bind subsequent purchasers. As courts became more receptive to homeowner associations, *see, e.g., Neponsit Property Owners Ass'n v. Emigrant Indus. Savings Bank*, 278 N.Y. 248, 15 N.E.2d 793 (1938) (holding that homeowner associations may enforce covenants, conditions, and restrictions and that maintenance assessments may run with the land), *supra*, pp. 777–82, developers increasingly turned to homeowner associations to develop and market homes. The popularity of these developments took off in the 1960s as young families sought suburban living. By the mid–1970s, more than 20,000 homeowner associations had been developed and the number has sky-rocketed since that time. Community Association Institute, Community Association Factbook 9 (1988). The scale of PUDs has also grown dramatically. Entire communities with tens of thousands of residents covering thousands of acres have been developed in Columbia, Maryland, Irvine, California, and elsewhere.

The following document contains excerpts from a standard declaration of protective covenants for a planned unit development.

Declaration of Protective Covenants for Blackacre Community Association[35]

THIS DECLARATION is made on the date hereinafter set forth by _____, Inc., a corporation (hereinafter sometimes called "Declarant").

WITNESSETH

WHEREAS, Declarant desires to subject the real property described in Article II, Section 1, hereof to the provisions of this Declaration to create a residential community of single-family housing and to provide for the subjecting of other real property to the provisions of this Declaration;

NOW, THEREFORE, Declarant hereby declares that the real property described in Article II, Section 1, of this Declaration, including the improvements constructed or to be constructed thereon, is hereby subjected to the provisions of this Declaration and shall be held, sold, transferred, conveyed, used, occupied, and mortgaged or otherwise encumbered subject to the covenants, conditions, restrictions, easements, assessments and liens, hereinafter set forth, which are for the purpose of protecting the value and desirability of, and which shall run with the title to, the real property hereby or hereafter made subject hereto, and shall be binding on all persons having any right, title, or interest in all or any portion of the real property now or hereafter made subject hereto, their respective heirs, legal representatives successors, successors-in-title, and assigns and shall inure to the benefit of each and every owner of all or any portion thereof.

Article I

Definitions

The following words, when used in this Declaration or in any Supplementary Declaration (unless the context shall prohibit), shall have the following meanings:

(a) *"Association"* shall mean and refer to Blackacre Community Association, Inc., a nonprofit corporation, its successors and assigns.

---

35. Adapted from a form declaration obtained from Hyatt & Rhoads, P.C., Atlanta, Georgia.

(b) *"By-Laws"* shall refer to the By–Laws of Blackacre Community Association, Inc., attached to this Declaration as Exhibit "___" and incorporated therein by this reference.

(c) *"Common Property"* shall mean any and all real and personal property and easements and other interests therein, together with the facilities and improvements located thereon, now or hereafter owned by the Association for the common use and enjoyment of the Owners.

(d) *"Community"* shall mean and refer to that certain real property and interests therein described in Exhibit "___", attached hereto, and (i) such additions thereto as may be made by Declarant (or its Mortgagee or transferee, as provided in the Declaration) by Supplementary Declaration of all or any portion of the real property described in Exhibit "___", attached hereto; and (ii) such additions thereto as may be made by the Association by Supplementary Declaration of other real property.

(e) *"Community–Wide Standard"* shall mean the standard of conduct, maintenance, or other activity generally prevailing in the Community. Such standard may be more specifically determined by the Board of Directors of the Association. Such determination however, must be consistent with the Community–Wide Standard originally established by the Declarant.

(f) *"Declarant"* shall mean and refer to [Developer] and the Successor-in-title and assigns of [Developer], provided any such successor-in-title or assign shall acquire for the purpose of development or sale all or any portion of the remaining undeveloped or unsold portions of the real property described in Exhibit "___", attached hereto or in Exhibit "___", attached hereto, and provided further, in the instrument of conveyance to any such successor-in-title or assign, such successor-in-title or assign is designated as the "Declarant" hereunder by the grantor of such conveyance, which grantor shall be the "Declarant" hereunder at the time of such conveyance; provided, further, upon such designation of such successor Declarant, all rights of the former Declarant in and to such status as "Declarant" hereunder shall cease, it being understood that as to all of the property described in Exhibit "___", attached hereto, and in Exhibit "___", attached hereto, which is now or hereafter subjected to this Declaration, there shall be only one person or legal entity entitled to exercise the rights and powers of the "Declarant" hereunder at any one point in time.

(g) *"Lot"* shall mean any plot of land within the Community, whether or not improvements are constructed thereon, which constitutes or will constitute, after the construction of improvements, a single dwelling site as shown on the plat for the Community, or amendments thereto, recorded in the land records of the county where the Community is located. The ownership of each Lot shall include, and there shall pass with each Lot as an appurtenance thereto, whether or not separately described, all of the right title, and interest of an Owner in the Common Property, which shall include, without limitation, membership in the Association.

(h) *"Majority"* means those eligible votes, Owners, or other group as the context may indicate totaling more than fifty (50%) percent of the total eligible number.

(i) *"Mortgage"* means any mortgage, deed to secure debt, and any and all other similar instruments used for the purpose of conveying or encumbering real property as security for the payment or satisfaction of an obligation.

(j) *"Mortgagee"* shall mean the holder of a Mortgage.

(k) *"Owner"* shall mean and refer to the record owner, whether one or more Persons, of the fee simple title to any Lot located within the Community, excluding, however, any Person holding such interest merely as security for the performance or satisfaction of any obligation.

(*l*) *"Person"* means any natural person, as well as a corporation, joint venture, partnership (general or limited), association, trust, or other legal entity.

Article II

Property Subject to this Declaration

Section 1. *Property Hereby Subjected to This Declaration.* The real property which is, by the recording of this Declaration, subject to the covenants and restrictions hereafter set forth and which, by virtue of the recording of this Declaration shall be held, transferred, sold, conveyed, used, occupied and mortgaged or otherwise encumbered subject to this Declaration is the real property described in Exhibit "___", attached hereto and by reference made a part hereof.

Section 2. *Other Property.* Only the real property described in Section 1 of this Article II is hereby made subject to this Declaration; provided, however, by one or more Supplementary Declarations, Declarant and the Association have the right, but not the obligation, to subject other real property to this Declaration, as hereinafter provided.

Article III

Association Membership and Voting Rights

Section 1. *Membership.* Every Person who is the record owner of a fee or undivided fee interest in any Lot that is subject to this Declaration shall be deemed to have a membership in the Association. The foregoing is not intended to include Persons who hold an interest merely as security for the performance of an obligation, and the giving of a security interest shall not terminate the Owner's membership. No Owner, whether one or more Persons, shall have more than one (1) membership per Lot. In the event of multiple Owners of a Lot, votes and rights of use and enjoyment shall be as provided in this Declaration and in the By–Laws. Membership shall be appurtenant to and may not be separated from ownership of any Lot. The rights and privileges of membership, including the right to vote and to hold office, may be exercised by a member or the member's spouse, but in no event shall more than one (1) vote be cast nor office held for each Lot owned.

Section 2. *Voting.* Members shall be entitled to one (1) vote for each Lot owned. When more than one Person holds an ownership interest in any Lot, the vote for such Lot shall be exercised as those Owners themselves determine and advise the Secretary prior to any meeting. In the absence of such advice, the Lot's vote shall be suspended in the event more than one Person seeks to exercise it.

Article IV

Assessments

Section 1. *Purpose of Assessment.* The assessments provided for herein shall be used for the general purposes of promoting the recreation, health, safety, welfare, common benefit, and enjoyment of the Owners and occupants of Lots, including the maintenance of real and personal property, all as may be more specifically authorized from time to time by the Board of Directors.

Section 2. *Creation of the Lien and Personal Obligation for Assessments.* Each Owner of any Lot, by acceptance of a deed therefor, whether or not it shall be so expressed in such deed, covenants and agrees to pay to the Association: (a) annual assessments or charges; (b) special assessments, such assessments to be established and collected as hereinafter provided; and (c) specific assessments against any particular Lot which are established pursuant to the terms of this Declaration, including, but not limited to, reasonable fines as may be imposed in accordance with the terms of this Declaration. All such assessments, together with late charges, interest, not to exceed the maximum legal rate, costs, and reasonable attorney's fees actually incurred, shall be a charge on the land and shall be a continuing lien upon the Lot against which each assessment is made. Each such assessment, together with late charges, interest, costs, and reasonable attorney's fees actually incurred, shall also be the personal obligation of the person who was the Owner of such Lot at the time the assessment fell due. Each Owner shall be personally liable for his or her portion of each assessment coming due while he or she is the Owner of a Lot, and his or her grantee shall be jointly and severally liable for such portion thereof as may be due and payable at the time of conveyance; provided, however, the liability of a grantee for the unpaid assessments of its grantor shall not apply to any first Mortgage holder taking title through foreclosure proceedings or deed in lieu of foreclosure.

Assessments shall be paid at a uniform rate per Lot in such manner and on such dates as may be fixed by the Board of Directors, which may include, without limitation, acceleration, upon ten (10) days' written notice, of the annual assessment for delinquents. Unless otherwise provided by the Board, the assessment shall be paid in annual installments.

Section 3. *Computation.* It shall be the duty of the Board prepare a budget covering the estimated coats of operating the Association during the coming year, which shall include a capital contribution or reserve in accordance with a capital budget separately prepared. The Board shall cause the budget and the assessments to be levied against each Lot for the following year to be delivered to each member at least thirty (30) days prior to the end of the current fiscal year. The budget and the assessment shall become effective unless disapproved at a meeting by a Majority of the Owners. Notwithstanding the foregoing, however, in the event the membership disapproves the proposed budget or the Board fails for any reason so to determine the budget for the succeeding year, then and until such time as a budget shall have been determined, as provided herein, the budget in effect for the then current year shall continue for the succeeding year.

Section 4. *Special Assessments.* In addition to the other assessments authorized herein, the Association may levy special assessments in any year. So long as the total amount of special assessments allocable to each Lot does not exceed _____ Dollars in any one fiscal year, the Board may impose the special assessment. Any special assessment which would cause the amount of special assessments allocable to any Lot to exceed this limitation shall be effective only if approved by a Majority of the Owners and, so long as the Declarant has an option unilaterally to subject additional property to this Declaration as provided in Article IX hereof, the Declarant. Special assessments shall be paid as determined by the Board, and the Board may permit special assessments to be paid in installments extending beyond the fiscal year in which the special assessment is imposed.

Section 5. *Lien for Assessments.* All sums assessed against any Lot pursuant to this Declaration, together with late charges, interest, costs and reasonable attorney's fees actually incurred, as provided herein shall be secured by a lien on such Lot in favor of the Association. Such lien shall be superior to all other liens and encumbrances on such Lot, except for (a) liens of *ad valorem* taxes; or (b) liens for all sums unpaid on a first Mortgage or on any Mortgage to Declarant duly recorded in the land records of the county where the Community is located and all amounts advanced pursuant to such Mortgage and secured thereby in accordance with the terms of such instrument.

All other persons acquiring liens or encumbrances on any Lot after this Declaration shall have been recorded in such records shall be deemed to consent that such liens or encumbrances shall be inferior to future liens for assessments, as provided herein, whether or not prior consent is specifically set forth in the instruments creating such liens or encumbrances.

Section 6. *Effect of Nonpayment of Assessments: Remedies of the Association.* Any assessments which are not paid when due shall be delinquent. Any assessment delinquent for a period of more than ten (10) days shall incur a late charge in an amount as the Board may from time to time determine. The Association shall cause a notice of delinquency to be given to any member who has not paid within ten (10) days following the due date. If the assessment is not paid within thirty (30) days a lien, as herein provided, shall attach and, in addition the lien shall include the late charge, interest, not to exceed the maximum legal rate, on the principal amount due, and all late charges from the date first due and payable, all costs of collection, reasonable attorney's fees actually incurred, and any other amounts provided or permitted by law. In the event that the assessment remains unpaid after sixty (60) days, the Association may, as the Board shall determine, institute suit to collect such amounts and to foreclose its lien. Each Owner, by acceptance of a deed or as a party to any other type of a conveyance, vests in the Association or its agents the right and power to bring all actions against him or her, personally, for the collection of such charges as a debt or to foreclose the aforesaid lien in the same manner as other liens for the improvement of real property. The lien provided for in this Article shall be in favor of the Association and shall be for the benefit of all other Owners. The Association, acting on behalf of the Owners shall have the power to bid on the Lot at any foreclosure sale or to acquire, hold, lease, mortgage, or convey the same. No Owner may waive or otherwise exempt himself from liability for the assessments provided for herein, including, by way of illustration, but not limitation, abandonment of the Lot. No diminution or abatement of assessment shall be claimed or allowed by reason of any alleged failure of the Association to take some action or perform some function required to be taken or performed by the Association under this Declaration or the By–Laws, or for inconvenience or discomfort arising from the making of repairs or improvements which are the responsibility of the Association, or from any action taken by the Association to comply with any law, ordinance, or with any order or directive of any municipal or other governmental authority, the obligation to pay assessments being a separate and independent covenant on the part of each Owner.

All payments shall be applied first to costs and attorney's fees, then to late charges, then interest and then to delinquent assessments.

Section 7. *Date of Commencement of Annual Assessments.* The annual assessments provided for herein shall commence as to all Lots then existing and subject to assessment under this Declaration on the first day of the month following the conveyance of the first Lot by the Declarant to a Person other than Declarant and shall be due and payable in a manner and on a schedule as the Board of Directors may provide. The first annual assessment shall be adjusted according to the number of months then remaining in that fiscal year.

Section 8. *Assessment Obligation of Declarant.*

(a) After the commencement of assessment payments as to any Lot, Declarant, on behalf of itself and its successors and assigns, covenants and agrees to pay the full amount of the assessments provided herein for each Lot it owns containing an occupied residence; provided, however, each Lot owned by Declarant which does not contain an occupied residence shall not be subject to any assessment provided for herein.

(b) Notwithstanding anything to the contrary herein, the Declarant may contribute assessments due from it in services or materials or a combination of services and materials, rather than in money (herein collectively called "in kind contribution"). The amount by which monetary assessments shall be decreased as a result of any in kind contribution shall be the fair market value of the contribution. If the Declarant and the Association agree as to the value of any contribution, the value shall be as agreed. If the Association and the Declarant cannot agree as to the value of any contribution, the Declarant shall supply the Association with a detailed explanation of the service performed and material furnished, and the Association shall acquire bids for performing like services and furnishing like materials from three (3) independent contractors approved by the Declarant who are in the business of providing such services and materials. If the Association and the Declarant are still unable to agree on the value of the contribution. the value shall be deemed to be the average of the bids received from the independent contractors.

Section 9. *Specific Assessments.* The Board shall have the power to specifically assess pursuant to this Section as, in its discretion, it shall deem appropriate. Failure of the Board to exercise its authority under this Section shall not be grounds for any action against the Association or the Board of Directors and shall not constitute a waiver of the Board's right to exercise its authority under this Section in the future with respect to any expenses, including an expense for which the Board has not previously exercised its authority under this Section. The Board may specifically assess Lots for the following Association expenses, except for expenses incurred for maintenance and repair of items which are the maintenance responsibility of the Association as provided herein:

(a) Expenses of the Association which benefit less than all of the Lots may be specifically assessed equitably among all of the Lots which are benefited according to the benefit received.

(b) Expenses of the Association which benefit all Lots, but which do not provide an equal benefit to all Lots, may be assessed equitably among all Lots according to the benefit received.

Article V

Maintenance

Section 1. *Association's Responsibility.* The Association shall maintain and keep in good repair the Common Property. This maintenance shall include, without limitation, maintenance, repair, and replacement, subject to any insurance then in effect, of all landscaping and improvements situated on the Common Property. The Association shall maintain all entry features for the Community. The Association shall also maintain all property outside of Lots located within the Community which was originally maintained by Declarant.

In addition, the Association shall have the right, but not the obligation, to maintain property not owned by the Association where the Board has determined that such maintenance would benefit all Owners.

The foregoing maintenance shall be performed consistent with the Community–Wide Standard.

Section 2. *Owner's Responsibility.* All maintenance of the Lot and all structures, parking areas, and other improvements thereon shall be the sole responsibility of the Owner thereof, who shall maintain such Lot in a manner consistent with the Community–Wide Standard and this Declaration. In the event that the Board of Directors of the Association determines that (a) any Owner has failed or refused to discharge properly his obligations with regard to the maintenance, repair, or replacement of items for which he is responsible hereunder; or (b) that the need for maintenance, repair, or replacement, which is the responsibility of the Association hereunder, is caused through the willful or negligent act of an Owner, his or her family, guests, lessees, or invitees, and is not covered or paid for by insurance, in whole or in part, then, the Association may perform the repair, replacement or maintenance and shall, except in the event of an emergency situation, give the Owner written notice of the Association's intent to provide such necessary maintenance, repair, or replacement, at Owner's sole cost and expense. The notice shall set forth with reasonable particularity the maintenance, repairs, or replacement deemed necessary. The Owner shall have ten (10) days within which to complete such maintenance, repair, or replacement, or, in the event that such maintenance, repair, or replacement is not capable of completion within a ten (10) day period, to commence such work which shall be completed within a reasonable time. If any Owner does not comply with the provisions hereof, the Association may provide any such maintenance, repair, or replacement at Owner's sole cost and expense, and all costs shall be added to and become a part of the assessment to which such Owner is subject and shall become a lien against the Lot.

Section 3. *Party Walls and Party Fences.*

(a) *General Rules of Law to Apply.* Each wall or fence built as a part of the original construction of the Lots which shall serve and separate any two (2) adjoining Lots shall constitute a party wall or fence and, to the extent not inconsistent with the provisions of this Section, the general rules of law regarding party wall. The cost of reasonable repair and maintenance of a party wall or fence shall be shared by the Owners who make use of the wall or fence in equal proportions.

(b) *Sharing of Repair and Maintenance.* The cost of reasonable repair and maintenance of a party wall or fence shall be shared by the Owners who make use of the wall or fence in equal proportions.

(c) *Damage and Destruction.* If a party wall or fence is destroyed or damaged by fire or other casualty, then to the extent that such damage is not covered by insurance and repaired out of the proceeds of insurance, any Owner who has used the wall may restore it, and if the other Owner or Owners thereafter make use of the wall, they shall contribute to the cost of restoration thereof in equal proportions without prejudice, however, to the right of any such Owners to call for a larger contribution from the others under any rule of law regarding liability for negligent or willful acts or omissions.

(d) *Right to Contribution Runs With Land.* The right of any Owner to contribution from any other Owner under this Section shall be appurtenant to the land and shall pass to such Owner's successors-in-title.

(e) *Arbitration.* In the event of any dispute arising concerning a party wall or fence, or under the provisions of this Section, each party shall appoint one (1) arbitrator. Should any party refuse to appoint an arbitrator within ten (10) days after written request therefor by the Board of Directors, the Board shall appoint an arbitrator for the refusing party. The arbitrators thus appointed shall appoint one (1) additional arbitrator and the decision by a majority of all three (3) arbitrators shall be binding upon the parties and shall be a condition precedent to any right of legal action that either party may have against the other.

Article VI

Use Restrictions and Rules

Section 1.   *General.* The Board of Directors may, from time to time, without consent of the members, promulgate, modify, or delete use restrictions and rules and regulations applicable to the Lots and the Common Property. This authority shall include, but shall not be limited to, the right to limit the type and size and to set the maximum and minimum speeds of vehicles within the Community. The Board shall also have the authority to impose all other necessary traffic and parking regulations and to restrict the maximum noise levels of vehicles in the Community. Such regulations and use restrictions shall be binding upon all Owners and occupants until and unless overruled, canceled, or modified in a regular or special meeting by the vote of Owners holding a Majority of the total votes in the Association and by the vote of the Declarant, so long as the Declarant has an option unilaterally to subject additional property to this Declaration as provided in Article IX hereof.

* * *

Section 6.   *Occupants Bound.* All provisions of the Declaration and of any rules and regulations or use restrictions promulgated pursuant thereto which govern the conduct of Owners and which provide for sanctions against Owners shall also apply to all occupants of any Lot.

* * *

Section 10.   *Architectural Standards.* No exterior construction, alteration, addition, or erection of any nature whatsoever (including, without limitation, fences, pools, tennis courts, exterior lighting, treehouses and play equipment) shall be commenced or placed upon any part of the Community, except such as is installed by the Declarant, or as is approved in accordance with this Section, or as is otherwise expressly permitted herein. No exterior construction, addition, erection, or alteration shall be made unless and until the plans and specifications showing the nature, kind shape, height, materials, and location shall have been submitted in writing to and approved by the Board or its designee. The Board or its designee may promulgate written guidelines for the exercise of this review.

The Board or its designee shall be the sole arbiter of such plans and may withhold approval for any reason, including purely aesthetic considerations, and it shall be entitled to stop any construction in violation of these restrictions. Any member of the Board or its representatives shall have the right, during reasonable hours, to enter upon any Lot to inspect any Lot and any improvements thereon for the purpose of ascertaining whether or not these restrictive covenants have been or are being complied with. Such person or persons shall not be deemed guilty of trespass by reason of such entry. In the event the Board or its designee fails to approve or to disapprove such design and location within sixty (60) days after the plans and specifications have been submitted to it, approval will not be required, and this Section will be deemed to have been fully complied with.

* * *

Article XI

Easements

Section 1. *Easements for Encroachment and Overhang.* There shall be reciprocal appurtenant easements for encroachment and overhang as between each Lot and such portion or portions of the Common Property adjacent thereto or as between adjacent Lots due to the unintentional placement or settling or shifting of the improvements constructed, reconstructed, or altered thereon (in accordance with the terms of this Declaration) to a distance of not more than five (5) feet, as measured from any point on the common boundary between each Lot and the adjacent portion of the Common Property or as between adjacent Lots, as the case may be, along a line perpendicular to such boundary at such point; provided, however, in no event shall an easement for encroachment exist if such encroachment occurred due to willful conduct on the part of an Owner, tenant, or the Association.

Section 2. *Easements for Use and Enjoyment.*

(a) Every Owner of a Lot shall have a right and easement of ingress and egress, use and enjoyment in and to the Common Property which shall be appurtenant to and shall pass with the title to his Lot, subject to the following provisions:

> (i) the right of the Association to charge reasonable admission and other fees for the use of any portion of the Common Property, to limit the number of guests of Lot Owners and tenants who may use the Common Property, and to provide for the exclusive use and enjoyment of specific portions thereof at certain designated times by an Owner, his family, tenants, guests, and invitees;

> (ii) the right of the Association to suspend the voting rights of a Lot Owner and the right of an Owner to use the recreational facilities in the Community, if any, for any period during which any assessment against his Lot which is hereby provided for remains unpaid; and, for a reasonable period of time for an infraction of the Declaration, By-Laws, or rules and regulations;

(iii) the right of the Association to borrow money for the purpose of improving the Common Property, or any portion thereof, or for construction, repairing or improving any facilities located or to be located thereon, and give as security for the payment of any such loan a Mortgage conveying all or any portion of the Common Property; provided, however, the lien and encumbrance of any such Mortgage given by the Association shall be subject and subordinate to any rights, interests, options, easements and privileges herein reserved or established for the benefit of Declarant, or any Lot or Lot Owner, or the holder of any Mortgage, irrespective of when executed, given by Declarant or any Lot Owner encumbering any Lot or other property located within the Community (Any provision in this Declaration or in any such Mortgage given by the Association to the contrary notwithstanding, the exercise of any rights therein by the holder thereof in the event of a default thereunder shall not cancel or terminate any rights, easements or privileges herein reserved or established for the benefit of Declarant, or any Lot or Lot Owner, or the holder of any Mortgage, irrespective of when executed, given by Declarant or any Lot Owner encumbering any Lot or other property located within the Community.); and

(iv) the right of the Association to dedicate or transfer all or any portion of the Common Property subject to such conditions as may be agreed to by the members of the Association. No such dedication or transfer shall be effective unless an instrument agreeing to such dedication or transfer has been approved by at least a Majority of the Owners present, or represented by proxy, at a meeting duly called for such purpose and by the Declarant, so long as the Declarant has an option unilaterally to subject additional property to this Declaration as provided in Article IX hereof.

(b) Any Lot Owner may delegate his or her right of use and enjoyment in and to the Common Property and facilities located thereon to the members of his family, his tenants and guests and shall be deemed to have made a delegation of all such rights to the occupants of any leased Lot.

Section 3. *Easements for Utilities.* There is hereby reserved to the Association blanket easements upon, across, above and under all property within the Community for access, ingress egress installation, repairing, replacing, and maintaining all utilities serving the Community or any portion thereof, including but not limited to, gas, water, sanitary sewer, telephone and electricity as well as storm drainage and any other service such as, but not limited to, a master television antenna system, cable television system or security system which the Association might decide to have installed to serve the Community. It shall be expressly permissible for the Association or its designee, as the case may be, to install repair, replace, and maintain or to authorize the installation, repairing, replacing, and maintaining of such wires, conduits, cables and other equipment related to the providing of any such utility or service. Should any party furnishing any such utility or service request a specific license or easement by separate recordable document, the Board shall have the right to grant such easement.

Article XII

General Provisions

Section 1. *Enforcement.* Each Owner and every occupant of a Lot shall comply strictly with the By–Laws, the rules and regulations, the use restrictions, as they may be lawfully amended or modified from time to time, and with the covenants, conditions, and restrictions set forth in this Declaration and in the deed to his or her Lot, if any. The Board of Directors may impose fines or other sanctions, which shall be collected as provided herein for the collection of assessments. Failure to comply with this Declaration, the By–Laws or the rules and regulations shall be grounds for an action to recover sums due for damages or injunctive relief, or both, maintainable by the Board of Directors, on behalf of the Association or, in a proper case, by an aggrieved Owner. Failure by the Association or any Owner to enforce any of the foregoing shall in no event be deemed a waiver of the right to do so thereafter.

Section 2. *Self-Help.* In addition to any other remedies provided for herein, the Association or its duly authorized agent shall have the power to enter upon a Lot or any portion of the Common Property to abate or remove, using such force as may be reasonably necessary, any erection, thing or condition which violates this Declaration, the By–Laws, the rules and regulations, or the use restrictions. Unless an emergency situation exists, the Board shall give the violating Lot Owner ten (10) days' written notice of its intent to exercise self-help. All costs of self-help, including reasonable attorney's fees actually incurred shall be assessed against the violating Lot Owner and shall be collected as provided for herein for the collection of assessments.

Section 3. *Duration.* The provisions of this Declaration shall run with and bind the land and shall be and remain in effect perpetually to the extent permitted by law; provided, however, so long as the law of the state of _____ limits the period during which covenants restricting lands to certain uses may run, any provisions of this Declaration affected thereby shall run with and bind the land so long as permitted by such law, and such provisions may be renewed or extended, in whole or in part, beyond the initial period permitted by such law for successive periods not to exceed the period permitted by such law, provided such renewal or extension is approved by at least a Majority of the Owners present or represented by proxy at a meeting duly called for such purpose. Further, no such renewal or extension shall be effective unless there is filed for record in the Office of the Clerk of the _____ Court of the county where the Community is located on or before the effective date thereof an instrument executed by the President and Secretary of the Association which shall state the terms of such renewal or extension and which shall contain a certification by such Secretary that such extension and renewal was duly approved. Every purchaser or grantee of any interest in any real property subject to this

Declaration, by acceptance of a deed or other conveyance therefor, thereby agrees that such provisions of this Declaration may be extended and renewed as provided in this Section.

Section 4. *Amendment.* This Declaration may be amended unilaterally at any time and from time to time by Declarant (a) if such amendment is necessary to bring any provision hereof into compliance with any applicable governmental statute, rule, or regulation or judicial determination which shall be in conflict therewith; (b) if such amendment is necessary to enable any reputable title insurance company to issue title insurance coverage with respect to the Lots subject to this Declaration; (c) if such amendment is required by an institutional or governmental lender or purchaser of mortgage loans, including, for example, the Federal National Mortgage Association or Federal Home Loan Mortgage Corporation, to enable such lender or purchaser to make or purchase mortgage loans on the Lots subject to this Declaration; or (d) if such amendment is necessary to enable any governmental agency or reputable private insurance company to insure mortgage loans on the Lots subject to this Declaration; provided, however, any such amendment shall not adversely affect the title to any Owner's Lot unless any such Lot Owner shall consent thereto in writing. Further, so long as Declarant has the right unilaterally to subject additional property to this Declaration as provided in Article IX hereof, Declarant may unilaterally amend this Declaration for any other purpose; provided, however, any such amendment shall not materially adversely affect the substantive rights of any Lot Owner hereunder, nor shall it adversely affect title to any Lot without the consent of the affected Lot Owner.

In addition to the above, this Declaration may be amended upon the affirmative vote or written consent, or any combination thereof, of at least a majority of the Owners and the consent of the Declarant, so long as Declarant has an option unilaterally to subject additional property to this Declaration as provided in Article IX hereof. Amendments to this Declaration shall become effective upon recordation, unless a later effective date is specified therein.

Section 5. *Partition.* The Common Property shall remain undivided, and no Lot Owner nor any other Person shall bring any action for partition or division of the whole or any part thereof without the written consent of all Owners of all portions of the property located within the Community and without the written consent of all holders of all Mortgages encumbering any portion of the property, including, but not necessarily limited to, the Lots located within the Community.

* * *

Section 10. *Conveyances of Common Property.* The Association shall accept such conveyances of Common Property as are made from time to time to the Association by Declarant.

1. *Occupancy restrictions.* What restrictions does the Blackacre Declaration place upon occupancy of units within the community? Are such restrictions valid? What doctrines might come into play in assessing their validity?

2. *Aesthetics.* How does the Residential Association govern the aesthetic features of the Blackacre community? By what criteria or processes are "community-wide standards" defined? Do you foresee any potential problems arising from the Association's regulation of aesthetics or enforcement of owners' maintenance obligations?

3. *Governance.* How would you describe the governance structure of this CIC? Is it democratic?

4. *Funding.* How is the Residential Association funded? How are the general and special assessments determined? How does the association ensure that homeowners pay the various assessments?

What, if any, is the developer's obligation to pay assessments as the development is getting started? Who pays the assessments for unoccupied residences?

Are there any potential problems with the Board's power to impose "specific assessments"?

5. *Enforcement.* Who may enforce the covenants, conditions, and restrictions of the CIC? How does enforcement work? How may the homeowners or the Association amend the rules and restrictions?

6. Does this declaration strike you as a good way of governing a residential community? Will it foster a sense of community? Would you want to live in such a community?

---

2.   LEGISLATION GOVERNING CICs

The National Housing Act of 1961 authorized the Federal Housing Administration (FHA) to insure mortgages on single family units in multi-unit projects in those states recognizing title for such units. As a result, all 50 states enacted condominium enabling legislation in the 1960s, typically adopting the general approach and provisions of the FHA Model Act.[36] This legislation enabled the creation of condominium ownership by authorizing ownership of individual apartment units, prescribing procedural, disclosure, and recording requirements for the creation and operation of condominiums (including the creation of a governing homeowner association), entitling apartment owners to undivided interests in common areas, subjecting owners to covenants, bylaws, and administrative provisions, and authorizing the homeowner association to enforce the rules and requirements. As there was no comparable legislation governing cooperatives and planned

---

36. FHA Form No. 3285 (1962; rev. 1973). *See generally* Kenin, Condominium: A Survey of Legal Problems and Proposed Legislation, 17 U. Miami L. Rev. 145 (1962).

unit developments, CICs were created through general state corporate law and common law rules governing nonpossessory interests.

The proliferation of condominium development in the 1960s and early 1970s revealed serious risks associated with this new form of housing ownership. Senator William Proxmire captured these concerns:

> The condominium boom, once confined to vacation spots, is now hitting our Nation's cities with epidemic force. * * *
>
> [D]evelopers and real estate agents are heralding the condominium as the wave of the future. Open the real estate pages of any metropolitan area newspaper and you will be bombarded with advertisements that promise your dreams will come true when you buy your own condominium. Prospective buyers are told that they will have all the advantages of home ownership, without the headaches of maintenance and repair. They are lured with visions of swimming pools and tennis courts—country club living at apartment prices.
>
> Certainly condominiums do represent an attractive housing choice for many people. They offer homeownership and its accompanying tax benefits to people whose incomes are too low to afford conventional housing.
>
> But too often bright promises fade in the face of sad realities, and the condominium owner finds himself faced with unanticipated problems and unexpected expenses.
>
> The monthly condominium fee charged for maintaining common areas and other building expenses doubles or triples, because the developer understated the expenses in the promotional material.
>
> The swimming pool he thought he had bought along with the house turns out to belong instead to the developer, who rents it out to the condominium owners at an exorbitant fee.
>
> The project's owners are locked into a long-term contract with a management company, often one in which the developer has an interest, so they are not free to select the management and negotiate the rates.
>
> In older buildings converted to condominiums, owners are often saddled with expensive repairs, as long-neglected electrical and mechanical systems left untouched by cosmetic renovation fall apart completely.
>
> The owner may find himself paying as much or more for his condominium as he would have to pay for a house. He is disappointed and frustrated; he feels he has been misinformed and misled. And yet willy-nilly he is the owner of his condominium castle, and the law holds that he is responsible for whatever befalls him in it.

120 Cong. Rec. 32704 (1974). In response to these types of problems, many states replaced or supplemented their condominium enabling acts with second generation statutes imposing additional and stricter disclosure requirements and consumer protections. Many of these enactments incorporated aspects of the Uniform Condominium Act (UCA), which was developed in 1977 and amended in 1980. In 1982, the National Conference of Commissioners on Uniform State Laws promulgated the Uniform Common Interest Ownership Act (UCIOA), which deals comprehensively and consistently with all cooperatives and planned developments, as well as with condominiums. The newest state legislation draws upon this model act. *See, e.g.,* Conn. Gen. Stat. §§ 47–68a to –115.

Legislation regulating the creation, operation, and restrictions of CICs today falls into three general categories: requirements mandating the disclosure of information regarding CICs to prospective purchasers; requirements governing the procedures of homeowner associations; and substantive regulation of CIC restrictions.

a.   DISCLOSURE REQUIREMENTS

Reflecting a central premise of market institutions and the freedom of contract paradigm, states have relied principally upon information disclosure requirements to ensure that CICs serve their intended purposes. The underlying assumption is that the substantive provisions of CICs will be fair and efficient and that CIC governance will operate smoothly if consumers voluntarily enter into purchase agreements on the basis of full information.

First generation condominium enabling acts imposed disclosure requirements on all condominium developments.[37] About half of the states have adopted second generation statutes that have tightened and expanded these requirements. *See* UCA art. 4; UCIOA art. 4. Eight of these states— Alaska, California, Colorado, Connecticut, Maryland, Minnesota, Oregon, and West Virginia—have enacted comprehensive CIC statutes extending disclosure and other requirements to all forms of CIC developments. Natelson, Law of Property Owners Associations § 3.2.1 (1989 & 1996 Supp.). Some states require developers to provide warranties of fitness and merchantability and allow buyers a "cooling off" period following the signing of an agreement during which the buyer may back out of the agreement. *See, e.g.,* Fla. Stat. ch. 718.203 (3–year warranty), § 718.503 (cancellation right); UCIOA §§ 4–108, 4–113 to 4–117.

---

37. The federal Securities Act of 1933 imposes additional disclosure requirements upon offerings of resort condominiums sold with an emphasis on investment attributes. *See* Note, Condominium Regulation: Beyond Disclosure, 123 U. Pa. L. Rev. 639, 650–56 (1975). In addition, some state Blue Sky laws, which require investment companies to disclose the terms of their solicitations, impose limited disclosure requirements upon some CIC developments. *See, e.g.,* N.Y. Gen. Bus. Law § 352–e.

1.   How useful are disclosure requirements? Is there a substantial risk that potential buyers will not read lengthy and complex association documents during the escrow period? Or that they will not understand the terms? Or that they will not appreciate the future impact of the restrictions and procedures?

2.   If you think that disclosure requirements are necessary but not sufficient, what additional legal limitations would you impose on homeowner associations?

3.   Who should have the obligation to disclose? The seller of an individual unit? The Association? How should the disclosure obligation be enforced?

———————

b. PROCEDURAL REQUIREMENTS

In view of the complexity of CIC disclosures and the limited capacity of many prospective unit owners to understand the terms and project what they will mean for the future, information disclosure does not guarantee that CICs will adequately protect consumers. In addition, disclosures relating to the creation of a CIC do not ensure that consumers will be protected from rules and practices later promulgated by homeowner associations. As a result, most states impose some procedural requirements upon homeowner associations.[38]

All states provide for the creation of some governing body for condominiums, although the statutes vary significantly in specifying the structure and procedural requirements. The modern uniform acts, which have been adopted in about a third of the states, provide fairly detailed requirements for the structure, procedures, and voting rules of homeowner associations.

———————

Uniform Common Interest Ownership Act (1994)

ARTICLE 2

CREATION, ALTERATION, AND TERMINATION OF COMMON INTEREST COMMUNITIES

§ 2–117. *Amendment of Declaration.*

(a) Except in cases of amendments that may be executed by a declarant under Section 2–109(f) or 2–110, or by the association under Section 1–

———————

38. California, Florida, New York, and a few other states have authorized state agencies to regulate some aspects of CICs.

107, 2–106(d), 2–108(c), 2–112(a), or 2–113, or by certain unit owners under Section 2–108(b), 2–112(a), 2–113(b), or 2–118(b), and except as limited by subsection (d), the declaration, including any plats and plans, may be amended only by vote or agreement of unit owners of units to which at least [67] percent of the votes in the association are allocated, or any larger majority the declaration specifies. The declaration may specify a smaller number only if all of the units are restricted exclusively to nonresidential use.

* * *

(d) Except to the extent expressly permitted or required by other provisions of this [Act], no amendment may create or increase special declarant rights, increase the number of units, change the boundaries of any unit or the allocated interests of a unit, in the absence of unanimous consent of the unit owners.

* * *

(f) By vote or agreement of unit owners of units to which at least 80 percent of the votes in the association are allocated, or any larger percentage specified in the declaration, an amendment to the declaration may prohibit or materially restrict the permitted uses of or behavior in a unit or the number or other qualifications of persons who may occupy units. The amendment must provide reasonable protection for a use or occupancy permitted at the time the amendment was adopted.

* * *

§ 2–118.   *Termination of Common Interest Community.*

(a) Except in the case of a taking of all the units by eminent domain (Section 1–107) or in the case of foreclosure against an entire cooperative of a security interest that has priority over the declaration, a common interest community may be terminated only by agreement of unit owners of units to which at least 80 percent of the votes in the association are allocated, or any larger percentage the declaration specifies. The declaration may specify a smaller percentage only if all of the units are restricted exclusively to nonresidential uses.

* * *

ARTICLE 3

MANAGEMENT OF THE COMMON INTEREST COMMUNITY

§ 3–101.   *Organization of Unit Owners' Association.*

A unit owners' association must be organized no later than the date the first unit in the common interest community is conveyed. The membership of the association at all times consists exclusively of all unit owners or, following termination of the common interest community, of all former unit owners entitled to distributions of proceeds under Section 2–118 or their heirs, successors, or assigns. The association must be organized as a profit or nonprofit corporation, trust, [or] partnership [, or as an unincorporated association].

§ 3–102. *Powers of Unit Owners' Association.*

(a) Except as provided in subsection (b), and subject to the provisions of the declaration, the association [, even if unincorporated,] may:

(1) adopt and amend bylaws and rules and regulations;

(2) adopt and amend budgets for revenues, expenditures, and reserves and collect assessments for common expenses from unit owners;

(3) hire and discharge managing agents and other employees, agents, and independent contractors;

(4) institute, defend, or intervene in litigation or administrative proceedings in its own name on behalf of itself or two or more unit owners on matters affecting the common interest community;

(5) make contracts and incur liabilities;

(6) regulate the use, maintenance, repair, replacement, and modification of common elements;

(7) cause additional improvements to be made as a part of the common elements;

(8) acquire, hold, encumber, and convey in its own name any right, title, or interest to real estate or personal property, but (i) common elements in a condominium or planned community may be conveyed or subjected to a security interest only pursuant to Section 3–112 and (ii) part of a cooperative may be conveyed, or all or part of a cooperative may be subjected to a security interest, only pursuant to Section 3–112;

(9) grant easements, leases, licenses, and concessions through or over the common elements;

(10) impose and receive any payments, fees, or charges for the use, rental, or operation of the common elements, other than limited common elements described in Section 2–102(2) and (4), and for services provided to unit owners;

(11) impose charges for late payment of assessments and, after notice and an opportunity to be heard, levy reasonable fines for violations of the declaration, bylaws, rules, and regulations of the association;

(12) impose reasonable charges for the preparation and recordation of amendments to the declaration, resale certificates required by Section 4–109, or statements of unpaid assessments;

(13) provide for the indemnification of its officers and executive board and maintain directors' and officers' liability insurance;

(14) assign its right to future income, including the right to receive common expense assessments, but only to the extent the declaration expressly so provides;

(15) exercise any other powers conferred by the declaration or bylaws;

(16) exercise all other powers that may be exercised in this State by legal entities of the same type as the association;

(17) exercise any other powers necessary and proper for the governance and operation of the association; and

(18) by regulation, require that disputes between the executive board and unit owners or between two or more unit owners regarding the common interest community must be submitted to nonbinding alternative dispute resolution in the manner described in the regulation as a prerequisite to commencement of a judicial proceeding.

(b) The declaration may not impose limitations on the power of the association to deal with the declarant which are more restrictive than the limitations imposed on the power of the association to deal with other persons.

(c) Unless otherwise permitted by the declaration or this [Act], an association may adopt rules and regulations that affect the use of or behavior in units that may be used for residential purposes only to:

(1) prevent any use of a unit which violates the declaration;

(2) regulate any behavior in or occupancy of a unit which violates the declaration or adversely affects the use and enjoyment of other units or the common elements by other unit owners; or

(3) restrict the leasing of residential units to the extent those rules are reasonably designed to meet underwriting requirements of institutional lenders who regularly lend money secured by first mortgages on units in common interest communities or regularly purchase those mortgages.

Otherwise, the association may not regulate any use of or behavior in units.

(d) If a tenant of a unit owner violates the declaration, bylaws, or rules and regulations of the association, in addition to exercising any of its powers against the unit owner, the association may:

(1) exercise directly against the tenant the powers described in subsection (a)(11);

(2) after giving notice to the tenant and the unit owner and an opportunity to be heard, levy reasonable fines against the tenant for the violation; and

(3) enforce any other rights against the tenant for the violation which the unit owner as landlord could lawfully have exercised under the lease or which the association could lawfully have exercised directly against the unit owner, or both.

(e) The rights granted under subsection (d)(3) may only be exercised if the tenant or unit owner fails to cure the violation within 10 days after the association notifies the tenant and unit owner of that violation.

(f) Unless a lease otherwise provides, this section does not:

(1) affect rights that the unit owner has to enforce the lease or that the association has under other law; or

(2) permit the association to enforce a lease to which it is not a party in the absence of a violation of the declaration, bylaws, or rules and regulations.

§ 3–103. *Executive Board Members and Officers.*

(a) Except as provided in the declaration, the bylaws, subsection (b), or other provisions of this [Act], the executive board may act in all instances on behalf of the association. In the performance of their duties, officers and members of the executive board appointed by the declarant shall exercise the degree of care and loyalty required of a trustee. Officers and members of the executive board not appointed by the declarant shall exercise the degree of care and loyalty required of an officer or director of a corporation organized under [insert reference to state non-profit corporation law].

(b) The executive board may not act on behalf of the association to amend the declaration (Section 2–117), to terminate the common interest community (Section 2–118), or to elect members of the executive board or determine the qualifications, powers and duties, or terms of office of executive board members (Section 3–103(f)), but the executive board may fill vacancies in its membership for the unexpired portion of any term.

(c) Within [30] days after adoption of any proposed budget for the common interest community, the executive board shall provide a summary of the budget to all the unit owners, and shall set a date for a meeting of the unit owners to consider ratification of the budget not less than 14 nor more than 30 days after mailing of the summary. Unless at that meeting a majority of all unit owners or any larger vote specified in the declaration reject the budget, the budget is ratified, whether or not a quorum is present. In the event the proposed budget is rejected, the periodic budget last ratified by the unit owners must be continued until such time as the unit owners ratify a subsequent budget proposed by the executive board.

* * *

§ 3–105. *Termination of Contracts and Leases of Declarant.*

Except as provided in Section 1–207, if entered into before the executive board elected by the unit owners pursuant to Section 3–103(f) takes office, (i) any management contract, employment contract, or lease of recreational or parking areas or facilities, (ii) any other contract or lease between the association and a declarant or an affiliate of a declarant, or (iii) any contract or lease that is not bona fide or was unconscionable to the unit owners at the time entered into under the circumstances then prevailing, may be terminated without penalty by the association at any time after the executive board elected by the unit owners pursuant to Section 3–103(f) takes office upon not less than [90] days' notice to the other party. This section does not apply to: (i) any lease the termination of which would terminate the common interest community or reduce its size, unless the real estate subject to that lease was included in the common interest community for the purpose of avoiding the right of the association to terminate a lease under this section, or (ii) a proprietary lease.

§ 3–106. *Bylaws.*

(a) The bylaws of the association must provide

(1) the number of members of the executive board and the titles of the officers of the association;

(2) election by the executive board of a president, treasurer, secretary, and any other officers of the association the bylaws specify;

(3) the qualifications, powers and duties, terms of office, and manner of electing and removing executive board members and offices and filling vacancies;

(4) which, if any, of its powers the executive board or officers may delegate to other persons or to a managing agent;

(5) which of its officers may prepare, execute, certify, and record amendments to the declaration on behalf of the association; and

(6) a method for amending the bylaws.

(b) Subject to the provisions of the declaration, the bylaws may provide for any other matters the association deems necessary and appropriate.

§ 3–107. *Upkeep of Common Interest Community.*

(a) Except to the extent provided by the declaration, subsection (b), or Section 3–113(h), the association is responsible for maintenance, repair, and replacement of the common elements, and each unit owner is responsible for maintenance, repair, and replacement of his unit. Each unit owner shall afford to the association and the other unit owners, and to their agents or employees, access through his unit reasonably necessary for those purposes. If damage is inflicted on the common elements or on any unit through which access is taken, the unit owner responsible for the damage, or the association if it is responsible, is liable for the prompt repair thereof.

* * *

§ 3–108. *Meetings.*

A meeting of the association must be held at least once each year. Special meetings of the association may be called by the president, a majority of the executive board, or by unit owners having 20 percent, or any lower percentage specified in the bylaws, of the votes in the association. Not less than [10] nor more than [60] days in advance of any meeting, the secretary or other officer specified in the bylaws shall cause notice to be hand-delivered or sent prepaid by United States mail to the mailing address of each unit or to any other mailing address designated in writing by the unit owner. The notice of any meeting must state the time and place of the meeting and the items on the agenda, including the general nature of any proposed amendment to the declaration or bylaws, any budget changes, and any proposal to remove an officer or member of the executive board.

§ 3–109. *Quorums.*

(a) Unless the bylaws provide otherwise, a quorum is present throughout any meeting of the association if persons entitled to cast [20] percent of the votes that may be cast for election of the executive board are present in person or by proxy at the beginning of the meeting.

(b) Unless the bylaws specify a larger percentage, a quorum is deemed present throughout any meeting of the executive board if persons entitled to cast [50] percent of the votes on that board are present at the beginning of the meeting.

§ 3–110. *Voting; Proxies.*

* * *

(c) If the declaration requires that votes on specified matters affecting the common interest community be cast by lessees rather than unit owners of leased units: * * * (ii) unit owners who have leased their units to other persons may not cast votes on those specified matters; and (iii) lessees are entitled to notice of meetings, access to records, and other rights respecting those matters as if they were unit owners. Unit owners must also be given notice, in the manner provided in Section 3–108, of all meetings at which lessees are entitled to vote.

(d) No votes allocated to a unit owned by the association may be cast.

* * *

§ 3–115. *Assessments for Common Expenses.*

(a) Until the association makes a common expense assessment, the declarant shall pay all common expenses. After an assessment has been made by the association, assessments must be made at least annually, based on a budget adopted at least annually by the association.

(b) Except for assessments under subsections (c), (d), and (e), all common expenses must be assessed against all the units in accordance with the allocations set forth in the declaration pursuant to Section 2–107(a) and (b). Any past due common expense assessment or installment thereof bears interest at the rate established by the association not exceeding [18] percent per year.

(c) To the extent required by the declaration:

(1) any common expense associated with the maintenance, repair, or replacement of a limited common element must be assessed against the units to which that limited common element is assigned, equally, or in any other proportion the declaration provides;

(2) any common expense or portion thereof benefiting fewer than all of the units must be assessed exclusively against the units benefited; and

(3) the costs of insurance must be assessed in proportion to risk and the costs of utilities must be assessed in proportion to usage.

(d) Assessments to pay a judgment against the association (Section 3–117(a)) may be made only against the units in the common interest community at the time the judgment was entered, in proportion to their common expense liabilities.

(e) If any common expense is caused by the misconduct of any unit owner, the association may assess that expense exclusively against his unit.

(f) If common expense liabilities are reallocated, common expense assessments and any installment thereof not yet due must be recalculated in accordance with the reallocated common expense liabilities.

§ 3–116. *Lien for Assessments.*

(a) The association has a statutory lien on a unit for any assessment levied against that unit or fines imposed against its unit owner. Unless the declaration otherwise provides, fees, charges, late charges, fines, and interest charged pursuant to Section 3–102(a)(10), (11), and (12) are enforceable as assessments under this section. If an assessment is payable in installments, the lien is for the full amount of the assessment from the time the first installment thereof becomes due.

* * *

§ 3–118. *Association Records.*

The association shall keep financial records sufficiently detailed to enable the association to comply with Section 4–109. All financial and other records must be made reasonably available for examination by any unit owner and his authorized agents.

———————

1. *Amendments.* By what procedures can the Declaration be amended or the CIC terminated under the Uniform Act? Do these procedures adequately protect the expectations of all homeowners? Are these procedures more restrictive than the procedures in the Declaration for the Blackacre Community Association?

2. *Enforcement.* What are the mechanisms for enforcement under the Uniform Act? Does the Association have any enforcement powers against tenants?

3. *Declarant.* What provisions exist to prevent self-dealing by the declarant?

4. *Governance*. Does the Uniform Act specify how officers and other board members are chosen? To what extent does it impose voting requirements and meeting requirements?

5. *Assessments*. What procedures and criteria does the Uniform Act impose for assessments?

6. Where they differ, is the Uniform Act an improvement over the Declaration for the Blackacre Community Association? Overall, does it provide a fair and clear framework to balance and resolve individual and collective homeowner interests?

Comprehensive CIC statutes (such as the UCIOA) also govern the form and operation of homeowner associations in non-condominium CICs as well. In states that have not adopted comprehensive acts, traditional corporate law governs the operation of non-condominium homeowner associations that are incorporated. In most states, however, developers need not incorporate homeowner associations. Thus, there are no specific legal requirements governing the creation and operation of unincorporated homeowner associations in these states, although most developers establish homeowner associations for these developments following the model of other nonprofit membership organizations. Natelson, Law of Property Owners Associations §§ 3.2.1 to 3.2.2 (1989).

c. SUBSTANTIVE LIMITATIONS

A number of states also place substantive limitations on the types of restrictions that developers and homeowner associations may adopt. For example, UCIOA § 2–111 and UCA § 2–111 accord unit owners the right to "make any improvements or alterations" to their units that do not impair the structural integrity of the CIC. Florida protects basic associational and political rights of unit owners, *see* Fla. Stat. Ann. ch. 718.123 (forbidding regulation of the "right to peaceably assemble" or the right "to invite public officers or candidates for public office to appear and speak" in common areas of the condominium), although other states (and the uniform acts) do not specifically protect the civil rights of unit owners against the actions of homeowner associations. *See* Note, The Rule of Law in Residential Associations, 99 Harv. L. Rev. 472, 475 (1985). A few states require that CIC restrictions be "reasonable." *See, e.g.,* Utah Code Ann. § 57–8–10(1).

Most state statutes, however, do not limit the substantive power of CICs or the discretionary authority of homeowner associations so long as developers properly disclose the terms and conditions of their developments and establish minimum procedural safeguards regarding the governance of these communities. As the next section describes, however, courts exercise some authority over the decisions and policies of CICs.

3.   THE JUDICIAL ROLE IN OVERSEEING HOMEOWNER ASSOCIATIONS

When disputes arise, courts sometimes are called upon to review the decisionmaking processes and substantive decisions of homeowner associations and, if valid, enforce their restrictions.[39] A court must first determine the appropriate standard of review. Courts often draw upon the more traditional models of judicial review—such as those applicable to corporate boards, local governments, and administrative agencies—but their standards have reflected the particular contexts and therefore have had an *ad hoc* quality. *See generally* Brower, Communities Within the Community: Consent, Constitutionalism, and Other Failures of Legal Theory in Residential Associations, 7 J. Land Use & Envtl. L. 203 (1992); Note, Judicial Review of Condominium Rulemaking, 94 Harv. L. Rev. 647, 658 (1981) (arguing that most courts have adopted a "loosely defined standard of reasonableness, * * * refusing to enforce regulations that are 'unreasonable' or 'arbitrary and capricious' "). To understand how courts have approached the task of reviewing CIC restrictions and homeowner association decisions, we will first examine the five principal models—contract, local government, administrative agency, corporate board, and trust—that scholars have suggested. We will then survey a range of cases to see how courts in practice have reviewed homeowner association decisions and restrictions.

a.   CONTRACT/CONSENT MODEL

This model assumes that the property owners in CICs purchase their interests with knowledge—either actual or constructive through the recordation of CIC declarations—of the covenants, conditions, and restrictions by which they will be governed. Hence, they voluntarily agree to be governed by the terms and conditions of the community, especially those contained in the initial declaration. *See* Epstein, Notice and Freedom of Contract in the Law of Servitudes, 55 S. Cal. L. Rev. 1353, 1358 (1982); Ellickson, Cities and Homeowner Associations, 130 U. Pa. L. Rev. 1519 (1982). To the extent that a homeowner association merely implements the covenants of the CIC (perhaps limited only at the margins by doctrines such as unconscionability), the owners' prior assent to the terms of the governance structure is enough to legitimate the association's decisions.

This contract/consent model is more problematic when applied to subsequent amendments to the CIC restrictions. Suppose, for example, that the homeowner association votes to amend the CIC covenants to disallow residents from operating businesses out of their home, *i.e.*, a residential use

---

39. CIC declarations increasingly provide for alternative dispute resolution mechanisms—arbitration and mediation—to resolve disputes. *See* Winokur, Reforming Servitude Regimes: Toward Associational Federalism and Community, 1990 Wis. L. Rev. 537, 543 n.35; R.R. Powell & P.J. Rohan, 4B Powell on Real Property ¶ 632.5[11][c] (1996). Even in these circumstances, however, courts must pass judgment upon the determinations of the arbiter, typically with only a limited scope of review.

restriction. If the homeowners unanimously agreed that the restriction should be adopted, the amendment would be valid under the contract/consent model. Suppose, however, that only a simple majority of homeowners is required to impose the restriction and that only 51% of the units approve its adoption. Under a traditional market view of consent, this restriction could not be deemed to have been consented to by the other 49% of unit owners. An expanded notion of consent—what has been called "participatory consent"—"maintains that members of a democratically governed association consent to particular decisions reached by participating in the decisionmaking process, even if their own views do not prevail on particular substantive issues." *See* Note, The Rule of Law in Residential Associations, 99 Harv. L. Rev. 472, 479 (1985). Under this view, all property owners may be deemed to have consented to the new restriction on the ground that their initial assent to be governed by a democratically constituted homeowner association bound them to subsequent decisions of such governing body. *See Kroop v. Caravelle Condominium, Inc.*, 323 So.2d 307, 309 (Fla.Ct.App.1975) ("Plaintiff acquired title to her condominium unit with knowledge that the Declaration of Condominium might thereafter be lawfully amended").

The contract/consent model emphasizes the notion that personal autonomy is the source of obligation and that the views of the larger society outside of the CIC have little or no bearing on the voluntary restrictions of the CIC. Thus, a reviewing court should base its decisions exclusively on the agreements creating and implementing the CIC; the court should ensure that the association has scrupulously implemented such agreements and has followed its own procedures, and the court should defer to the judgment of the homeowner association with regard to any questions within its discretion. A court should not import standards from the larger community outside of the CIC (aside, for example, from unconscionability). *See* Brower, Communities within the Community: Consent, Constitutionalism, and Other Failures of Legal Theory in Residential Associations, 7 J. Land Use & Envtl. L. 203, 245–46 (1992); Ellickson, Cities and Homeowner Associations, 130 U. Pa. L. Rev. 1519, 1526–30 (1982).

The contract/consent model relies heavily on both notice and consent, *i.e.*, that prospective homeowners received notice of restrictions and association procedures, understood those rules (including their prospective application), and consented to them. Professor Brower points out that

> The basic flaw in consent theories is that they are based on unrealistic assumptions about how people actually make home ownership decisions. Despite various state statutes requiring disclosure to potential purchasers of substantive and procedural residential association restrictions, empirical evidence indicates that most purchasers neither read nor understand those documents, nor do they fully comprehend what common ownership entails. Further, most common interest development residents decide to purchase in these communities on grounds other than their shared rights and responsibilities, even if they are aware of

them. * * * [I]t is even more doubtful whether they adequately understand and assign a proper value to possible future modifications of the original documents.

Brower, Communities Within the Community: Consent, Constitutionalism, and Other Failures of Legal Theory in Residential Associations, 7 J. Land Use & Envtl. L. 203, 246–47 (1992). *See also* Alexander, Freedom, Coercion, and the Law of Servitudes, 73 Cornell L. Rev. 883, 892–95 (1988). The evidence regarding lack of meaningful consent, however, is disputed. *See* Natelson, Consent, Coercion, and "Reasonableness" in Private Law: The Special Case of the Property Owners Association, 51 Ohio St. L.J. 41, 58–65 (1990) (discussing a survey showing that most property owners understand and consent to restrictions). Professor Natelson maintains that homeowner association decisionmaking "contains elements of both coercion and consent." *Id.* at 44.

b.   LOCAL GOVERNMENT MODEL

Concerned not only about the lack of meaningful consent, but also about the risk that association rules may curtail basic civil liberties, some authors have championed other, more exacting models of judicial review. *See* Note, The Rule of Law in Residential Associations, 99 Harv. L. Rev. 472, 481–83 (1985); Alexander, Freedom, Coercion, and the Law of Servitudes, 73 Cornell L. Rev. 883, 888–93 (1988). Because many homeowner associations, especially those within large CICs, assume many municipal functions—they provide basic services, regulate land use, and tax residents, and they use democratic processes to make legislative decisions—some authors advocate courts applying an external standard to assess the validity of CIC restrictions. *See* Rosenberry, Condominiums and Homeowner Associations: Should They Be Treated Like "Mini–Governments?" 8 Zoning & Plan. L. Rep. 151, 155 (Oct. 1985).

Under this view, residents of CICs should receive the same constitutional protections against the effective governing authority—the homeowner association—as residents of any publicly constituted government. Moreover, courts should review the decisions of homeowner associations not only on the basis of the associations' own internal values, but on the basis of values that are "widely shared throughout the rest of the polity." Alexander, Dilemmas of Group Autonomy: Residential Associations and Community, 75 Cornell L. Rev. 1, 6 (1989).

Some scholars, however, question the applicability of this model. Residents voluntarily submit to homeowner associations, at least much more than they do to public governments. *See* Ellickson, Cities and Homeowners Associations, 130 U. Pa. L. Rev. 1519, 1520 (1982). Homeowner associations, moreover, usually are much smaller than local governments, wield a much smaller set of regulatory and enforcement powers, and have no authority to redistribute wealth. *See* Natelson, Consent, Coercion, and "Reasonableness" in Private Law: The Special Case of the Property Owners Association, 51 Ohio St. L.J. 41, 49 (1990); Reichman, Residential

Private Governments: An Introductory Survey, 43 U. Chi. L. Rev. 253, 276–78 (1976).

c. ADMINISTRATIVE AGENCY MODEL

A middle ground between the contract/consent model and the local government model is to view homeowner associations as administrative agencies that have been delegated constrained authority to administer a regulatory framework. As part of this authority, agencies have legislative powers to promulgate, interpret, and amend rules, and adjudicatory power to enforce the rules. *See* Note, Judicial Review of Condominium Rulemaking, 94 Harv. L. Rev. 647, 659–63 (1981).

Courts use a process-oriented framework to review decisions of administrative agencies to balance the tension between the need to allow agencies substantial latitude to administer a broad range of functions effectively and the need to ensure that the agency adheres to its legislative mandate and standards of reasonableness. *See generally* Administrative Procedure Act, 5 U.S.C. §§ 551–559, 701–706; K. Davis & R. Pierce, Administrative Law Treatise (3d ed. 1994). Thus, a court using the administrative agency model of judicial review would require the homeowner association to give homeowners proper notice of issues being addressed, a fair opportunity to provide input, and a concise statement of the basis for decisions rendered. *See, e.g.,* UCIOA § 3–108, *supra.* Courts would also assess whether the association's decisions are within its delegated authority and are reasonable (*i.e.*, not arbitrary, capricious, or an abuse of discretion).

d. CORPORATE BOARD MODEL

The modern corporation provides a model that may more closely reflect the specialized contractual nature among members of a CIC. According to this model, the CIC is conceptualized as a "corporation" whose "shareholders"—the property owners—have delegated authority to a "corporate board"—the homeowner association—to manage the affairs of the corporation.[40] A court would judge homeowner association decisions by the same standards applied to more traditional corporate boards: its decisionmaking processes must adhere to the governing rules, the board must act within its delegated authority, and the board members have a fiduciary duty to the members of the CIC. This model thus focuses upon controlling bad faith, fraud, or actions beyond delegated authority. Subject to these limitations, boards have broad discretion to make decisions; so long as the board exercises its authority according to proper procedures and in good faith, a reviewing court will usually uphold its decisions, a standard of review often referred to as the "business judgment rule." *See* R. Clark, Corporate Law 123–25 (1986); Note, Judicial Review of Condominium Rulemaking, 94 Harv. L. Rev. 647, 663–67 (1981).

---

40. As noted above, many cooperatives expressly use the corporate structure. Thus, the standards governing corporate boards are directly applicable to these entities.

The analogy suffers some serious shortcomings. Most corporations are profit-oriented, risk-taking organizations, and the business judgment rule is a rule designed to insulate directors from liability. It is not clear that such a rule should apply to a challenge to the validity of a decision or regulation adopted by non-profit residential associations that typically do not engage in risk-taking activities. R.G. Natelson, Law of Property Owners Associations §§ 3.1, 10.3.3.2 (1989).

e. TRUST MODEL

A similar approach views the CIC as a trust whereby the homeowner association acts as a trustee charged with the fiduciary duties of impartiality, loyalty (which includes prohibitions on self-dealing), reasonable care, and information reporting. *See* Reichman, Residential Private Governments: An Introductory Survey, 43 U. Chi. L. Rev. 253, 296–300 (1976). The trust model would be less deferential to homeowner association decisions than the corporate board model because it does not apply the rather permissive business judgment rule.

One conceptual problem with the trust model is that trusts are normally reserved for persons unable to make their own decisions, such as children. Moreover, trust beneficiaries are less able than homeowners to exercise an exit option if they are unhappy with trust management.

—————

As CICs have proliferated and evolved, courts have sought to develop models of judicial review that accord with the inherent nature and functional characteristics of the governing homeowner associations. To some extent, the decisions have followed each of the models described above, but they also reflect a range of considerations that depend upon the particular context. The following cases are representative of the principal modes of judicial review of homeowner association decisions. As you consider these cases, try to develop a general, coherent framework to determine what standard of review courts will apply in particular circumstances. Under what circumstances will courts invoke one or another model of judicial review? To what extent have courts developed hybrid models? What are the effective judicial limits—substantive and procedural—upon the decisions of homeowner associations?

—————

Hidden Harbour Estates, Inc. v. Norman

District Court of Appeal of Florida, 1975.
309 So.2d 180.

■ DOWNEY, JUDGE.

The question presented on this appeal is whether the board of directors of a condominium association may adopt a rule or regulation prohibiting the use of alcoholic beverages in certain areas of the common elements of the condominium.

Appellant is the condominium association formed, pursuant to a Declaration of Condominium, to operate a 202–unit condominium known as Hidden Harbour. Article 3.3(f) of appellant's articles of incorporation provides, *inter alia*, that the association shall have the power "to make and amend reasonable rules and regulations respecting the use of the condominium property." A similar provision is contained in the Declaration of Condominium.

Among the common elements of the condominium is a club house used for social occasions. Pursuant to the association's rule making power the directors of the association adopted a rule prohibiting the use of alcoholic beverages in the club house and adjacent areas. Appellees, as the owners of one condominium unit, objected to the rule, which incidentally had been approved by the condominium owners voting by a margin of 2 to 1 (126 to 63). Being dissatisfied with the association's action, appellees brought this injunction suit to prohibit the enforcement of the rule. After a trial on the merits at which appellees showed there had been no untoward incidents occurring in the club house during social events when alcoholic beverages were consumed, the trial court granted a permanent injunction against enforcement of said rule. The trial court was of the view that rules and regulations adopted in pursuance of the management and operation of the condominium "must have some reasonable relationship to the protection of life, property or the general welfare of the residents of the condominium in order for it to be valid and enforceable." In its final judgment the trial court further held that any resident of the condominium might engage in any lawful action in the club house or on any common condominium property unless such action was engaged in or carried on in such a manner as to constitute a nuisance.

With all due respect to the veteran trial judge, we disagree. It appears to us that inherent in the condominium concept is the principle that to promote the health, happiness, and peace of mind of the majority of the unit owners since they are living in such close proximity and using facilities in common, each unit owner must give up a certain degree of freedom of choice which he might otherwise enjoy in separate, privately owned property. Condominium unit owners comprise a little democratic sub-society of necessity more restrictive as it pertains to use of condominium property than may be existent outside the condominium organization. The Declaration of Condominium involved herein is replete with examples of the curtailment of individual rights usually associated with the private ownership of property. It provides, for example, that no sale may be effectuated without approval; no minors may be permanent residents; no pets are allowed.

Certainly, the association is not at liberty to adopt arbitrary or capricious rules bearing no relationship to the health, happiness and enjoyment of life of the various unit owners. On the contrary, we believe the test is reasonableness. If a rule is reasonable the association can adopt it; if not, it cannot. It is not necessary that conduct be so offensive as to constitute a nuisance in order to justify regulation thereof. Of course, this means that each case must be considered upon the peculiar facts and circumstances thereto appertaining.

Finally, restrictions on the use of alcoholic beverages are widespread throughout both governmental and private sectors; there is nothing unreasonable or unusual about a group of people electing to prohibit their use in commonly owned areas.

Accordingly, the judgment appealed from is reversed and the cause is remanded with directions to enter judgment for the appellant.

---

1. What model of judicial review did the trial court adopt? What model did the appellate court adopt? How do they differ?

2. Toward the end of its opinion, the appellate court wrote that since restrictions on the use of alcoholic beverages are widespread in society, the association's restriction was reasonable. Did the court confuse "unusual" and "unreasonable"?

3. How is a court to determine what is a reasonable restriction? If "reasonable" refers to some societal standard, why should the court impose that standard on a small group of persons who have voluntarily and democratically decided to adopt another standard?

Hidden Harbour Estates, Inc. v. Basso

District Court of Appeal of Florida, 1981.
393 So.2d 637.

■ MOORE, JUDGE.

Plaintiff, Hidden Harbour Estates, appeals from a final judgment denying its request for injunctive relief. Hidden Harbour had sought to enjoin the appellees from maintaining a shallow water well on their property. We affirm.

Hidden Harbour Estates is a condominium development containing mobile homes situated on lots owned by the individual residents. In 1975, Hidden Harbour's Board of Directors became aware of an increase in the salinity of the two deep well systems which supplied the water for the common usage of the unit owners. In May, 1975, the Board adopted a regulation that restricted lawn watering to one day per week while a member of the Board of Directors, Charles Burtoft, conducted a study of the water-salinity problem. Later in 1975, when the salinity of the well water decreased, the restriction was relaxed.

In November, 1975, the Bassos, who were owners of one of the mobile home units, applied to the Board of Directors for permission to drill a shallow well on their property. Such permission was allegedly required under the use restrictions in Article 13 of the Declaration of Condominium, which stated:

13.1. The use of the condominium will be in accordance with the following provisions, as long as the condominium exists:

a. . . . No temporary or permanent improvements or alterations may be made to any lot, and no lot owner may change the appearance of any portion of the exterior of his mobile home or apartment without the written approval of the Board of Directors of the Association.

A decision on the Bassos' request was not made until March, 1976, at which time it was denied, despite the fact that Burtoft had informed the Board that a shallow well would not affect the condominium water supply. The Board had three basic reasons, not articulated until the trial of this cause, for denying the Bassos' request:

(1) The threat of increased salinity;

(2) Staining of sidewalks and other common areas of the condominium;

(3) The proliferation of more wells by other unit owners.

The Bassos nonetheless drilled a well in early January, 1977. On January 31, 1977, Hidden Harbour brought an action for injunctive relief, alleging that the Bassos were in violation of the use restrictions of the Declaration of Condominium by drilling an unauthorized well. This action resulted in the judgment now appealed.

Before addressing ourselves to the merits of the trial court's decision, we will summarize the law in regard to the enforcement of use restrictions against condominium unit owners. As we opined in *Sterling Village Condominium, Inc. v. Breitenbach*, 251 So.2d 685 (Fla. 4th DCA 1971):

Daily in this state thousands of citizens are investing millions of dollars in condominium property. Chapter 711, F.S.A., 1967, the Florida Condominium Act, and the Articles or Declarations of Condominiums provided for thereunder ought to be construed strictly to assure these investors that what the buyer sees the buyer gets. Every man may justly consider his home his castle and himself as the king thereof; nonetheless his sovereign fiat to use his property as he pleases must yield, at least in degree, where ownership is in common or cooperation with others. The benefits of condominium living and ownership demand no less. The individual ought not be permitted to disrupt the integrity of the common scheme through his desire for change, however laudable that change might be.

Id. at 688. *Breitenbach* involved an attempt by a unit owner to replace a screen enclosure with glass jalousies, even though the declaration of condominium prohibited "material alterations" or "substantial additions" to the common elements of the condominium. The screened enclosures were within the areas defined as common elements. Thus, even though Breitenbach's attempt to replace the screen enclosure was certainly a reasonable one and would have doubtlessly improved their unit, we were impelled to uphold the use restrictions in order to vindicate the condominium association's interest in maintaining a uniform exterior. A similar result occurred in *Pepe v. Whispering Sands Condominium Association*, 351 So.2d 755 (Fla. 2d DCA 1977), wherein the Court expressed the view that the restrictions in the declaration of condominium were of paramount importance in defining the rights and obligations of unit owners. The Court stated:

> A declaration of a condominium is more than a mere contract spelling out mutual rights and obligations of the parties thereto it assumes some of the attributes of a covenant running with the land, circumscribing the extent and limits of the enjoyment and use of real property. Stated otherwise, it spells out the true extent of the purchased, and thus granted, use interest therein. Absent consent, or an amendment of the declaration of condominium as may be provided for in such declaration, or as may be provided by statute in the absence of such a provision, this enjoyment and use cannot be impaired or diminished.

(footnotes omitted) *Id*. at 757–58. *See also, Wilshire Condominium Association, Inc. v. Kohlbrand*, 368 So.2d 629 (Fla. 4th DCA 1979).

Hidden Harbour Estates, Inc. v. Norman, 309 So.2d 180 (Fla. 4th DCA 1975), presented the question of whether a condominium association, through the exercise of its rule making powers, could prohibit the consumption of alcoholic beverages in the common areas of the condominium. In that case, we stated the ''rule of reasonableness'' to be the touchstone by which the validity of a condominium association's actions should be measured.

> Certainly, the association is not at liberty to adopt arbitrary or capricious rules bearing no relationship to the health, happiness and enjoyment of life of the various unit owners. On the contrary, we believe the test is reasonableness. If a rule is reasonable the association can adopt it; if not, it cannot. It is not necessary that conduct be so offensive as to constitute a nuisance in order to justify regulation thereof. Of course, this means that each case must be considered upon the peculiar facts and circumstances thereto appertaining.

Id. at 182. We found that the restriction on consumption of alcoholic beverages was reasonable because it was designed to ''promote the health, happiness, and peace of mind of the majority of the unit owners.'' *Id*. at 182.

There are essentially two categories of cases in which a condominium association attempts to enforce rules of restrictive uses. The first category is that dealing with the validity of restrictions found in the declaration of condominium itself. The second category of cases involves the validity of rules promulgated by the association's board of directors or the refusal of the board of directors to allow a particular use when the board is invested with the power to grant or deny a particular use.

In the first category, the restrictions are clothed with a very strong presumption of validity which arises from the fact that each individual unit owner purchases his unit knowing of and accepting the restrictions to be imposed. Such restrictions are very much in the nature of covenants running with the land and they will not be invalidated absent a showing that they are wholly arbitrary in their application, in violation of public policy, or that they abrogate some fundamental constitutional right. *See, White Egret Condominium, Inc. v. Franklin*, 379 So.2d 346 (Fla.1979). Thus, although case law has applied the word "reasonable" to determine whether such restrictions are valid, this is not the appropriate test, and to the extent that our decisions have been interpreted otherwise, we disagree. Indeed, a use restriction *in a declaration of condominium* may have a certain degree of unreasonableness to it, and yet withstand attack in the courts. If it were otherwise, a unit owner could not rely on the restrictions found in the declaration of condominium, since such restrictions would be in a potential condition of continuous flux.

The rule to be applied in the second category of cases, however, is different. In those cases where a use restriction is not mandated by the declaration of condominium *per se*, but is instead created by the board of directors of the condominium association, the rule of reasonableness comes into vogue. The requirement of "reasonableness" in these instances is designed to somewhat fetter the discretion of the board of directors. By imposing such a standard, the board is required to enact rules and make decisions that are reasonably related to the promotion of the health, happiness and peace of mind of the unit owners. In cases like the present one where the decision to allow a particular use is within the discretion of the board, the board must allow the use unless the use is demonstrably antagonistic to the legitimate objectives of the condominium association, *i.e.*, the health, happiness and peace of mind of the individual unit owners.

In the instant case, Hidden Harbour has articulated three basic reasons for denying the Bassos' request for permission to drill a well. First, the Board felt that such a well would increase the level of salinity in the deeper wells owned by the Hidden Harbour Condominium Association. Secondly, the Board believed the water pumped from the Bassos' well would impose a threat of staining the sidewalks and other common areas of the condominium association. Thirdly, the Board felt that if the Bassos were allowed to drill a well, then there would be a proliferation of other wells.

These reasons for denial were in the best interest of all of the unit owners, since they were legitimate objectives which would have promoted the aesthetic appeal of the condominium development. However, in order for the Board to justify its denial of the Bassos' application to drill a well, it was necessary that the Board be able to demonstrate that its denial was reasonably related to the fulfillment of the desired and laudable objectives mentioned above. This the Board failed to do. The evidence at trial indicated that the Bassos' well had no effect on the increased salinity of the wells owned by Hidden Harbour. In fact, this was known by one of the members of the Board of Directors at the time that the Bassos applied for permission to drill a well. No discoloration of commonly owned property had occurred at the time of trial, even though the Bassos frequently used the "illicit" well for more than a year and a half. Finally, there was not a shred of evidence to support a finding that the Bassos' well precipitated a proliferation of other wells in Hidden Harbour or that a proliferation of wells would be detrimental. Simply stated, Hidden Harbour failed to demonstrate a reasonable relationship between its denial of the Bassos' application and the objectives which the denial sought to achieve.

* * *

We do not hold that, as a matter of law, Hidden Harbour was not entitled to injunctive relief in a situation similar to the one presently before this court. We merely hold that under the facts of this case, as demonstrated by the evidence at trial, such relief would not have been proper.

Accordingly, the judgment of the trial court is affirmed.

-----

1. What model(s) of judicial review did this court apply? In what way does the type of judicial review depend on the type of restriction? Do you consider the court's approach to judicial review to be sound?

2. The court takes the position that restrictions adopted in the initial declaration should be entitled to great deference, even if a little unreasonable, and that restrictions adopted later should be reviewed more closely under a standard of "reasonableness." Should courts apply an even stricter standard of review for some types of subsequently adopted restrictions? Consider less-than-unanimous votes to change voting rights, allocation of expenses, or any other wealth-shifting restrictions. Should such restrictions always be unreasonable absent unanimous consent? *See, e.g.,* Mo. Rev. Stat. § 448.2–117(4) (unanimous consent needed to increase the number of units, to change the boundaries of units, to change the allocated votes, liability for expenses or undivided ownership in the common areas, and to change the use restrictions on units). Or is it possible to use a liability rule to compensate objectors. *See* Ellickson, Cities and Homeowners Associations, 130 U. Pa. L. Rev. 1519, 1530–39 (1982) (suggesting that if the declaration included a taking clause and compulsory arbitration—to reduce adjudication costs—courts could uphold less-than-unanimous decisions to adopt wealth-shifting rules).

3. Did the court find that the association's decision was *per se* unreasonable? On what basis did the court find the decision unreasonable? Suppose that you are counsel for the homeowner association. If another homeowner wants to dig a well, what advice would you give the association in considering its decision?

4. Should a reviewing court require the association to provide the reasons at the time the association makes the decision? Or should an

association be able to offer additional reasons during the course of litigation?

Rhue v. Cheyenne Homes, Inc.

Supreme Court of Colorado, 1969.
168 Colo. 6, 449 P.2d 361.

■ Pringle, Justice.

In the trial court, Cheyenne Homes, Inc., obtained an injunction prohibiting Leonard Rhue and Family Homes, Inc., hereinafter referred to as plaintiffs in error, from moving a thirty year old Spanish style house into a new subdivision which was about 80% improved and which contained only modern ranch style or split level homes.

At the time that the subdivision in which the plaintiffs in error seek to locate this house was platted, the owner placed upon the entire area certain restrictive covenants contained in a "Declaration of Protective Covenants," which was duly recorded. As recited in the document, these protective covenants were for the purpose of "protecting the present and future values of the properties located" in the subdivision. Admittedly, the house which the plaintiffs in error wish to put in the subdivision does not violate any of the few specific restrictions contained in the protective covenants. However, paragraph C–2 of the recorded protective covenants contains the following declaration:

> C–2. No building shall be erected, placed or altered on any lot until the construction plans and specifications and a plan showing the location of the structure shall have been approved by the architectural control committee . . .

Plaintiffs in error contend that restriction C–2 is not enforceable because no specific standards are contained therein to guide the committee in determining the approval or disapproval of plans when submitted. We disagree.

It is no secret that housing today is developed by subdividers who, through the use of restrictive covenants, guarantee to the purchaser that his house will be protected against adjacent construction which will impair its value, and that a general plan of construction will be followed. Modern legal authority recognizes this reality and recognizes also that the approval of plans by an architectural control committee is one method by which guarantees of value and general plan of construction can be accomplished and maintained.

So long as the intention of the covenant is clear (and in the present case it is clearly to protect present and future property values in the subdivision), covenants such as the one before us have been upheld against the contention that they lacked specific restrictions providing a framework within which the architectural committee must act. *Winslette v. Keeler*, 220

Ga. 100, 137 S.E.2d 288; *Kirkley v. Seipelt*, 212 Md. 127, 128 A.2d 430; *Fairfax Community Assoc. v. Boughton*, 127 N.E.2d 641 (Ohio Com.Pl.); *Hannula v. Hacienda Homes*, 34 Cal.2d 442, 211 P.2d 302, 19 A.L.R.2d 1268. In *Kirkley v. Seipelt, supra*, the plaintiff in error argued unsuccessfully that a covenant requiring approval of plans failed in the test of reasonableness because there were no standards to guide the approving party.

* * * While we have here enunciated the proposition that the covenant requiring approval of the architectural committee before erection of a house in the subdivision is enforceable, we point out that there is a corollary to that proposition which affords protection and due process of law to a purchaser of a lot in the subdivision, namely, that a refusal to approve plans must be reasonable and made in good faith and must not be arbitrary or capricious. *Kirkley v. Seipelt, supra; Winslette v. Keeler, supra; Hannula v. Hacienda Homes, supra.*

Since two of the three committee members testified that they would disapprove the plans if they were presented to them, we examine the evidence to determine if such refusal is warranted under the rules we have laid down. There was testimony that the house was about thirty years old, and that the other houses were no older than two years. The house of plaintiffs in error has a stucco exterior and a red tile roof. The other houses are commonly known as ranch style or split level, and are predominantly of brick construction with asphalt shingle roofs. There was further testimony that the style of the house would devalue the surrounding properties because it was "not compatible" with the houses already in place.

One member of the committee expressed concern that the house of plaintiffs in error would devalue surrounding property. The other added that he thought the covenant gave the architectural committee the authority to refuse approval to plans for property which would seriously affect the market value of other homes in the area. Clearly, a judgment of disapproval of the plans by the committee is reasonable and in good faith and in harmony with the purposes declared in the covenant.

The judgment is affirmed.

---

1. What model of judicial review does the court employ? What must the homeowner prove for the court to reverse the association's decision? What are the strengths and weaknesses of this model of judicial review?

2. In light of this model of judicial review, how significant are the dangers that the association will make decisions reflecting the personal whim of individual board members? What are the substantive standards that the association imposes? In this particular case, what was the evidence supporting the review committee's decision? Is it possible for the association to adopt more specific standards?

3. *Political Activities*. To what extent should courts uphold restrictions on important constitutional values, such as freedom of speech or

religion? Even though a court is not likely to find state action in such restrictions (which would have permitted the property owner to raise a constitutional claim), should the court hold that restrictions on speech, political activity, or religious activity are arbitrary and capricious? *Cf.* Fla. Stat. ch. 718.123 (forbidding regulation of the "right to peaceably assemble" or the right "to invite public officers or candidates for public office to appear and speak" in common areas of the condominium). Should a court have a stricter standard of review for such restrictions?

Could a property owner make a viable argument that external aesthetic changes to his residence (such as the color of the exterior walls) are a form of speech and thus should be protected as much as other forms of speech?

4. *Aesthetics Regulation.* Many CICs restrict the architectural and other aesthetic features of the community by requiring unit owners to obtain the approval of an architectural review board of any changes affecting the exterior appearance of their property. As illustrated in *Rhue v. Cheyenne Homes, Inc.,* courts generally uphold and defer to homeowner associations with regard to aesthetic judgments. Should a court uphold such a regulation where the property owner's proposed activity has little or no impact on other owners or the association properties? How should a court measure the degree of impact?

Portola Hills Community Ass'n v. James

Court of Appeal of California, 1992.
4 Cal.App.4th 289, 5 Cal.Rptr.2d 580.

■ CROSBY, ACTING PRESIDING JUSTICE.

Is a private restriction prohibiting a homeowner from installing a satellite dish in his yard unreasonable? * * *

I

The parties stipulated to the following facts: Defendant John James is the owner of a lot in the planned community of Portola Hills. The Portola Hills Community Association enforces a comprehensive set of covenants, conditions and restrictions. The CC&Rs "*completely ban*[ ] the use of satellite dishes in Portola Hills. [¶] 5. Separate architectural guidelines prepared by the Portola Hills Community Association and adopted by the Board of Directors state in pertinent part as follows: [¶] '13. Satellite Dish: *Absolutely no satellite dish of any nature will be acceptable on the exterior of the units* or lots anywhere within the Association. Cable television has been provided for this purpose.'" (Italics added.)

Despite the ban, James asked the association's architectural control committee to approve a landscaping plan that included a backyard satellite dish. The "landscape plans were approved by the [a]rchitectural [c]ontrol [c]ommittee with the exception of the installation of the satellite dish."

James installed the dish anyway. The association sued for a permanent injunction, damages, and attorneys fees. James cross-complained for attorneys fees.

The trial was a fairly abbreviated affair. The court accepted the stipulated facts, and both sides submitted trial briefs. Photographs, the CC&Rs, association by-laws, architectural guidelines, and various correspondence between the parties were received in evidence. * * *

The court acknowledged the "presumption that the[ ] by-laws are valid," but concluded the ban against exterior satellite dishes was unreasonable.[41] James was awarded costs, including more than $14,000 in attorneys fees.

II

Civil Code section 1354 provides, "The covenants and restrictions in the declaration shall be enforceable equitable servitudes, *unless unreasonable*, and shall inure to the benefit of and bind all owners of separate interests in the [project]. Unless the declaration states otherwise, these servitudes may be enforced by any owner of a separate interest or by the association, or by both." (Italics added.) Restrictions are presumed valid, as the trial judge recognized. However, "[w]hether an amendment is reasonable depends on the circumstances of the particular case." (*Ritchey v. Villa*

---

41. "I agree with [the association] that [satellite dishes] can be regulated subject to zoning, but in a reasonable manner. In balancing the intent of the community here or that of the homeowner's association as a whole against that of the [defendant], I don't think it's reasonable to put a total ban on [satellite dishes].

Restrictions that would assure that it had been done in an aesthetically acceptable manner would certainly be appropriate. The facts of this case are very simple. You [have] a two story house, and you have a satellite [dish] sandwiched between the defendant's two story house and a rather high slope in the back.

The [dish], ten feet h[igh], is anchored to the ground level, the first floor or very close to it. You have fences, side fences of 6 feet or so, substantial shrubbery and [an] offer by the defendants to install additional shrubbery.

From the photographs submitted, the [dish is] not observable from adjoining property. And that includes property up the slope to the back of the house because [it is] concealed by other shrubbery there. It's [also] the clear enunciated policy of the federal government to foster the use of [satellite dishes].

I don't think it can be said that providing cable is a sufficient alternative, because satellites as we know it, and I think [I] can almost take judicial notice of it, offers the potential for viewing worldwide events, worldwide and communicated worldwide, and I don't believe—well, cable I suppose has that capacity but they certainly haven't fulfilled it, so anyway, in a nutshell I'm going to rule for defendant[ ].

I think they have a right to install a satellite dish subject to reasonable restrictions by the homeowners and I think some additional landscaping might be accomplished here to make it even less observable, but I think they've substantially complied with it.

They have given a lot of thought to what they installed. In viewing these photographs, the ones you'd have to be concerned with are the neighbors immediately to either side of them or above them and from the evidence submitted they are not complaining.

I don't see how it could affect somebody down the street or down the block. I appreciate the Association's view that they have the total ban restriction. There's a presumption that their by-laws are valid and they did what they could I suppose to enforce it. * * * "

Nueva Condominium Assn. (1978) 81 Cal.App.3d 688, 694, 146 Cal.Rptr. 695.) A homeowner is allowed to prove a particular restriction is unreasonable as applied to his property.

The question of reasonableness is one of law, and we review it *de novo* in light of the trial court's factual findings. (*City of Oceanside v. McKenna* (1989) 215 Cal.App.3d 1420, 1424, 264 Cal.Rptr. 275 [restriction requiring owner occupancy]). Applying this standard, we reach the same conclusion as the trial judge. He made a finding, supported by ample evidence and not challenged on appeal, that James' dish is not visible to other residents or the public. With that established, the question becomes whether the ban against a satellite dish that cannot be seen promotes any legitimate goal of the association. It clearly does not. Accordingly, the restriction is unreasonable as a matter of law. * * *

As an aside, we note the association's only legitimate concern is with "exterior" structures. Those are defined in the CC&R's as structures "which [are] visible to others in the [p]roject and/or to the public." (Declaration, art. IX, § 2.) A dish that cannot be seen by anyone else would not even appear to qualify as an exterior structure under the association's own rules. * * *

[The court then held that the association's appeal was frivolous and imposed a sanction of $3000 and attorney fees against the association and appellate counsel].

———————

1.   What is the model of judicial review in this case?

2.   Did the court strike down the association's decision refusing permission in this case, or did it strike down the CC&R banning satellite dishes? May the association adopt a new CC&R banning satellite dishes that are visible?

3.   On what basis does the court conclude that the Association's only legitimate concern is with "external structures"? Are there no legitimate reasons for a total ban? What about the risk of liability from injury if a neighborhood child gets hurt on the satellite dish? Or the administrative costs of determining in each case whether a satellite dish is visible or not?

4.   Why does the association have to provide any reason given that the total ban was a part of the CC&Rs and that James (presumably) had notice of the ban when he purchased his residence? In other words, why should reasonableness matter if James consented to the restriction?

5.   What message does awarding of sanctions send to homeowner associations? Or to CIC members who don't like particular restrictions?

———————

Problems

1. A condominium declaration of covenants and restrictions states that "No truck, camper, trailer, boat of any kind or other form of recreational vehicle shall be parked on the [Bernardo] Villas 6 project, except temporarily and solely for the purposes of loading and unloading, without the prior approval of the Architectural Committee.   * * * The carports shall be used for parking of passenger automobiles or non-powered vehicles such as bicycles, only * * *."

An owner's tenant bought a new pickup which he parked in the space assigned to his landlord. The pickup had a camper shell, and the tenant used the truck to commute to work. The homeowner's association sued to enjoin the tenant and landlord from parking the pickup in the parking space and to recover fines. How should the court rule?

See Bernardo Villas Management Corp. Number Two v. Black, 190 Cal. App.3d 153, 235 Cal.Rptr. 509 (1987). Would you agree with the following statement?

> The court's impression was that the pickup with its camper shell was the equivalent of a station wagon. Beauty—even with cars—is in the eye of the beholder. In this world where those persons concerned with upwardly mobile status frequently drive off-road vehicles including well-appointed jeeps or pickup trucks, we think the trial court's ruling is eminently sensible. The pickup truck, often both comfortable and economical, has become for many the equivalent of the convertible in earlier years. As times change, cultural perceptions—including society's acceptance of certain types of vehicles—also change. The pickup truck no longer has a pejorative connotation. One person's Bronco II is another's Rolls–Royce.

Id. at 154, 235 Cal.Rptr. at 510.   If this statement is the holding, what limitations (aside from dangerous activities) can the association impose? Under this language, are aesthetic limitations *per se* unreasonable?

2. Suppose that a developer, aware of the holdings in *Portola Hills* and *Bernardo Villas*, included a restriction prohibiting residents from parking their vehicles in driveways or on association-owned streets. Should a court uphold the restriction if a property owner later challenges it as unreasonable? *See Holleman v. Mission Trace Homeowners Ass'n*, 556 S.W.2d 632 (Tex.Civ.App.1977).

Winston Towers 200 Ass'n v. Saverio

District Court of Appeal of Florida, 1978.
360 So.2d 470.

PER CURIAM.

Plaintiff condominium association appeals a final judgment for defendant unit owner in an action seeking to enjoin the keeping of a pet.

Defendant, Joseph Saverio, purchased a unit in the Winston Towers Condominium in December, 1971. He owned a female dog which was properly registered with the plaintiff, Winston Towers 200 Association, Inc. In February, 1974, the members of the association voted to amend the by-laws with respect to the ownership and replacement of pets. The amended by-law provided that all pets, including any pet acquired as a replacement of a prior pet not registered as of February 28, 1973 would not be permitted on the premises. Any unit owner violating this provision would be assessed a fine of $10 per day. In May, 1975 Mr. Saverio's dog gave birth to two pups, one of which he decided to keep. The association informed him that since the pup could not be registered, he was not permitted under the amended by-laws to keep it and unless he removed the pup from the premises he would be fined $10 per day. Mr. Saverio refused to comply and the association brought the instant action seeking to enjoin him from keeping the pup. A hearing was held at which only the attorneys for the parties argued. After argument of counsel, the judge ruled that the by-law in question was invalid and unenforceable in that it attempted to impose a retroactive regulation. He thereupon denied the relief sought by the association and entered judgment for Mr. Saverio. We affirm.

The record supports the trial judge's determination that the subject amendment to the by-laws was void and unenforceable inasmuch as it was an attempt to impose a retroactive regulation. We, therefore, conclude that the judge correctly entered judgment for Mr. Saverio.

---

1.   What is the model of judicial review in this case?

2.   In what respect was the regulation retroactive? Weren't the puppies born after the association adopted the regulation?

3.   Even if the regulation was retroactive, what is wrong with retroactive application of a regulation? Should *all* retroactive regulations be banned? Suppose that the association decided to ban a certain kind of barbecue grill because of recent reports that it posed an unusual threat of fire. Under this case, must the association permit the continued use of dangerous appliances?

4.   *Occupancy Restrictions.* Many CICs restrict occupancy of dwelling units. Many CICs targeting retirees exclude young children (and sometimes younger adults) to create a more peaceful environment and to foster critical mass for "seniors" activities. Some CICs seeking to foster a family neighborhood have restricted occupancy to single family households. Assuming that there is no statutory obstacle to such restrictions, should a court uphold them? *Bellarmine Hills Ass'n v. Residential Sys. Co.*, 84 Mich. App. 554, 269 N.W.2d 673 (1978); *Crane Neck Ass'n v. New York City/Long*

Island County Serv. Group, 61 N.Y.2d 154, 460 N.E.2d 1336, 472 N.Y.S.2d 901, *cert. denied*, 469 U.S. 804, 105 S.Ct. 60, 83 L.Ed.2d 11 (1984).

Before 1988, courts generally upheld age restrictions in covenants if they were fairly and uniformly applied. *See, e.g., Riley v. Stoves*, 22 Ariz. App. 223, 526 P.2d 747 (1974). In 1988, Congress amended the Fair Housing Act of 1968 to prohibit housing discrimination against families except with regard to qualified senior citizen housing. Fair Housing Amendments Act, Pub. L. No. 100–430, § 6, 102 Stat. 1620–23 (1988). *Cf. Massaro v. Mainlands Section 1 & 2 Civic Ass'n*, 3 F.3d 1472 (11th Cir.1993) (holding that the CIC in that case did not qualify for senior citizen community exception); Korngold, Single Family Use Covenants: For Achieving a Balance between Traditional Family Life and Individual Autonomy, 22 U.C. Davis L. Rev. 951 (1989).

Laguna Royale Owners Ass'n v. Darger

Court of Appeal of California, 1981.
119 Cal.App.3d 670, 174 Cal.Rptr. 136.

■ KAUFMAN, ASSOCIATE JUSTICE.

Defendants Stanford P. Darger and Darlene B. Darger (the Dargers) were the owners of a leasehold condominium in Laguna Royale, a 78–unit community apartment complex on the ocean front in South Laguna Beach. The Dargers purported to assign three one-quarter undivided interests in the property to three other couples: Wendell P. Paxton and Daila D. Paxton, Keith I. Gustaveson and Elsie Gustaveson, and Keith C. Brown and Geneva B. Brown (collectively the other defendants) without the approval of Laguna Royale Owners Association (Association). Association instituted this action to obtain a declaration that the assignments from the Dargers to defendants were invalid because they were made in violation of a provision of the instrument by which the Dargers acquired the property, prohibiting assignment or transfer of interests in the property without the consent and approval of Association's predecessor in interest. Following trial to the court judgment was rendered in favor of Association invalidating the assignments from the Dargers to the other defendants. Defendants appeal.

Facts

The Laguna Royale development is built on land leased by the developer from the landowner in a 99–year ground lease executed in 1961. As the units were completed, the developer sold each one by executing a Subassignment and Occupancy Agreement with the purchaser. This document conveyed an undivided ⅟₇₈ interest in the leasehold estate for a term of 99 years, a right to exclusive use of a designated unit and one or more garage spaces and a right to joint use of common areas and facilities; it also contained certain restrictions. The restriction pertinent to this action is paragraph 7, which provides in relevant part: "7. Subassignee (the purchaser) shall not assign or otherwise transfer this agreement, ... nor shall subassignee sublet ... without the consent of and approval of Lessee...."

Upon the sale of all units and completion of the project, the developer entered into an "Assignment Agreement" with the Association, transferring and assigning to the Association all the developer's rights, powers and duties under the Subassignment and Occupancy Agreements, including *inter alia* the "right to approve or disapprove assignments or transfers of interests in Laguna Royale pursuant to Paragraph 7 of the Subassignment and Occupancy Agreements."

In 1965, Ramona G. Sutton acquired unit 41, consisting of some 3,000 square feet, by a Subassignment and Occupancy Agreement with the developer. In 1973 the Dargers purchased unit 41 from the executrix of Mrs. Sutton's estate. As owner of a unit in the project, the Dargers automatically became members of the Association and were bound by the Association's bylaws.

The Dargers reside in Salt Lake City, Utah, where Mr. Darger became a vice president of a large banking chain not long after the Dargers acquired their unit at Laguna Royale. The responsibilities of Mr. Darger's new position made it difficult for them to get away, and they attempted unsuccessfully to lease their unit through real estate agents in Laguna Beach. On October 30, 1973, Mr. Darger wrote to Mr. Yount, then chairman of the board of governors of the Association, in which he stated in part: "It has been suggested that we might sell shares in our apartment to two or three other couples here. These associates would be aware of the restrictions regarding children under 16 living there, as well as the restrictions regarding pets, and would submit themselves to the regular investigation of the Board given prospective purchasers and lessees. I would expect that the apartment will remain vacant most of the time, as now, and not more than one of the families will occupy the apartment at one time."

[In subsequent correspondence, Mr. Yount indicated that the board would reluctantly agree to the sale. Two years later, Mr. Darger had his attorney prepare and submit to the board a draft document that would evidence the board's approval of the sale to a total of four owners, including Mr. Darger.]

Subsequently Mr. Darger received from Mr. Henry [the new chairman of the board] a letter dated January 12, 1976, which read in part: "The matter of multiple ownership of Apt. 41 has been studied in depth and detail with our own attorney, and the ultimate decision being that to do so would be contrary to recorded Lease, Subassignment and Occupancy agreement. In this connection you are respectfully requested to refer to Paragraphs 4 and 7 of such Agreement which limit use of units solely to residential purposes, without exception, and require written consent by your Board of Governors for any assignment thereof."

A few days later Mr. Darger received from Mr. Henry another letter dated January 16, 1976, that read in part: "The Board has determined that the transfer as you requested would create and impose an undue, unreasonable burden and disadvantage on the other owners' and residents' enjoyment of their apartments and the common facilities. Further, your requested transfer would be contrary to and in conflict with the close community living nature of Laguna Royale and would be contrary to the single family character of the private residential purpose to which all apartments are restricted under the recorded Master Lease and the Subassignment and Occupancy Agreement, as well as the By–Laws and House Rules, by which all owners are bound.''

On February 23, 1976, Mr. Darger sent a formal letter request for approval to transfer unit 41 from the Dargers to themselves and the other defendants on condition that "the three new couples subsequently receiv[e] individual approvals after a 'Request For Approval Of Sale Or Lease' form has been filed with the Board for each, and each has submitted to a personal interview by the Board for its consideration." The letter further requested that if approval was not given, "the Board specify its reasons for denial and indicate how the request made herein differs from the situation of the owners of at least two other units where there is multiple ownership between more than one party who have no family or corporate relationship, [and] in light of the written and verbal approvals for such a transfer of apartment #41 that have been extended by the Board to us over the past two and one half years."

By a letter from its attorney to the Dargers dated March 16, 1976, Association advised the Dargers that it would not consent to the requested transfer. It was denied that written and verbal approvals had been given the Dargers in the past, and it was stated in relevant part:

> The reason the Association will not consent to your requested transfer is that the Board feels it is obligated to protect and preserve the private single family residential character of Laguna Royale, together with the use and quiet enjoyment of all apartment owners of their respective apartments and the common facilities, taking into consideration the close community living circumstances of Laguna Royale.

> The Board feels strongly about its power of consent to assignments and other transfers of leasehold interests and considers the protection and preservation of that power to be critical in maintaining the character of Laguna Royale for the benefit of all owners as a whole. A four family ownership of a single apartment, with the guests of each owner potentially involved, would compound the use of the apartment and common facilities well beyond the normal and usual private single family residential character to the detriment of other owners and would frustrate effective controls over general security, guest occupants and rule compliance, as has been the case in the past.

> Provision 7 of the Subassignment and Occupancy Agreement, under which all apartment leasehold interests are held, requires the unqualified consent to any transfer. Provision 10 of said

agreement provides for the termination of the leasehold interest in the event of a violation of Provision 7, or other breach. . . .

No apartments in Laguna Royale are held by multiple families in the manner that you have requested. In any event, any consents given by the Association to transfers in the past cannot be regarded as setting any precedent or in any way limiting or impairing the power of the Association to refuse its consent to any present or future transfer. In this regard, the language of Provision 7 of the Subassignment and Occupancy Agreement provides that consent given to any particular transfer shall not operate as a waiver for any other transfer.

After consultation with legal counsel the Dargers proceeded nevertheless, and on June 11 they executed instruments purporting to assign undivided one-fourth interests in the property to themselves and the other three couples. The instruments were recorded on June 30, and on July 3, 1976, the Dargers informed Association by letter of the transfers enclosing on Association's forms a separate "Request For Approval Of Sale Or Lease" and financial statement prepared and executed by each of the other couples. These papers show that the other defendants all reside in Salt Lake City, Utah. Each executed request form contains a warranty by the purchaser that if the application is approved no child under 16 years of age "will make residency at this property" and an agreement that the purchaser "will abide by and conform to the terms and conditions of the master lease, . . . all amendments described in the Subassignment and Occupancy Agreement . . . and the By–Laws of the Laguna Royale Owners . . . Association."

After unsuccessfully demanding that the other defendants retransfer their purported interests to the Dargers, the Association filed this action.

At trial the testimony confirmed that no more than one family of defendants used the property at a time and, although the matter was not examined in detail, answers to questions by one or more defendants indicated that 13–week periods had been agreed upon for exclusive use by each of the four families. It was also indicated that for substantial periods during the year, no use at all was being made of the unit. The evidence also showed that a number of Laguna Royale units were owned by several unrelated persons, but that in each case the owners used the unit "as a family."

No formal findings were made. However, in its notice of intended decision the court stated in relevant part:

The Court concludes that the Subassignment and Occupancy Agreement, . . . is in law a sublease. . . . Therefore, Civil Code Section 711 does not apply to void the requirement that consent be given to the transfer of defendant Darger's interest. The provisions of Title 10 of the Administrative Code, Section 2792.25, as cited in *Ritchey v. Villa Nueva Condominiums* (1978) 81 Cal. App.3d 688, 146 Cal.Rptr. 695, only govern the restrictions of condominiums by laws, and not restrictions that may exist because of leasehold interests. The plaintiff association had the right to approve any transfer of defendant Darger's interest. The Court finds that the plaintiff association acted reasonably in refusing to grant consent to the proposed transfer by Darger to the other defendants. Plaintiff is entitled to a declaration that the assignments by Darger to the other defendants are invalid. Plaintiff is awarded attorney fees in the amount of $2500.

Judgment was entered accordingly.

Contentions, Issues and Discussion

Defendants contend paragraph 7 of the Subassignment and Occupancy Agreement prohibiting assignments or transfers without the consent of Association is invalid because it is in violation of their constitutional rights to associate with persons of their choosing (U.S. Const., 1st amend.; Cal. Const., art. I, § 1), because it constitutes an unlawful restraint on alienation (Civ. Code, § 711), and because it does not comply with a regulation of the Real Estate Commissioner (Cal. Admin. Code, tit. 10, § 2792.25). Failing those, defendants contend finally that if by its finding that Association acted reasonably in refusing to approve the transfers, the court meant to indicate that Association had the duty to act reasonably in withholding consent and did so, that determination is not supported by substantial evidence and is contrary to law.

Association contends that the prohibition against transfer or assignment without its consent is not invalid on any of the bases urged by defendants. It argues primarily that its right to withhold approval or consent is absolute, that in exercising its power it is not required to adhere to a standard of reasonableness but may withhold approval or consent for any reason or for no reason at all. Secondarily, it argues that the evidence supports the finding it acted reasonably in disapproving the transfers to the other defendants.

We reject Association's contention that its right to give or withhold approval or consent is absolute. We likewise reject defendants' contention that the claimed right to approve or disapprove transfers is an invalid restraint on alienation because it is repugnant to the conveyance of a fee. We hold that in exercising its power to approve or disapprove transfers or assignments Association must act reasonably, exercising its power in a fair and nondiscriminatory manner and withholding approval only for a reason or reasons rationally related to the protection, preservation and proper operation of the property and the purposes of Association as set forth in its governing instruments. We hold that the restriction on transfer contained in paragraph 7 of the Subassignment and Occupancy Agreement (hereafter simply paragraph 7), thus limited, does not violate defendants' constitutional rights of association and is not invalid as an unreasonable restraint on alienation. However, we conclude that in view of the present provisions of Association's bylaws, its refusal to consent to the transfers to defendants was unreasonable as a matter of law. Accordingly, we reverse the judgment with directions to enter judgment for defendants. * * *

As indicated, the initial positions of the parties are at opposite extremes. Association contends that the Subassignment and Occupancy Agreement constitutes a sublease and that under the law applicable to leasehold interests, when a lease contains a provision permitting subletting only upon consent of the lessor, the lessor is under no obligation to give consent and, in fact, may withhold consent arbitrarily. Defendants on the other hand contend that the Subassignment and Occupancy Agreement conveys, in essence, a fee,[42] and that under California law when a fee simple interest is granted, any restriction on the subsequent conveyance of the grantee's interest contained in the original grant is repugnant to the interest conveyed and is therefore void.

We reject the extreme contentions of both parties; the rules of law they propose, borrowed from the law of landlord and tenant developed during the feudal period in English history (*see Green v. Superior Court* (1974) 10 Cal.3d 616, 622, 111 Cal.Rptr. 704, 517 P.2d 1168), are entirely inappropriate tools for use in affecting an accommodation of the competing interests involved in the use and transfer of a condominium. Even assuming the continued vitality of the rule that a lessor may arbitrarily withhold consent to a sublease (*but see* Note, *Effect of Leasehold Provision Requiring the Lessor's Consent to Assignment* (1970) 21 Hast.L.J. 516), there is little or no similarity in the relationship between a condominium owner and his fellow owners and that between lessor and lessee or sublessor and sublessee. Even when the right to the underlying land is no more than an undivided interest in a ground lease or sublease, ownership of a condominium constitutes a statutorily recognized estate in real property (*see* Civ. Code, § 783), and in our society the right freely to use and dispose of one's property is a valued and protected right. (U.S. Const., amends. 5 and 14; Cal. Const., art. I, § 7, subd. (a); *see* 5 Witkin, Summary of Cal. Law (8th ed. 1974) Constitutional Law, § 273, p. 3563.) Ownership and use of condominiums is an increasingly significant form of "home ownership" which has evolved in recent years to meet the desire of our people to own their own dwelling place, in the face of heavy concentrations of population in urban areas, the limited availability of housing, and, thus, the impossibly inflated cost of individual homes in such areas.

On the other hand condominium living involves a certain closeness to and with one's neighbors, and, as stated in *Hidden Harbour Estates, Inc. v. Norman* (Fla.App.1975) 309 So.2d 180, 181–182: "[I]nherent in the condominium concept is the principle that to promote the health, happiness, and

---

42. It is unclear to us how the Subassignment and Occupancy Agreement could convey a fee interest when the entire interest in the land underlying the development is only a 99–year ground lease. It would appear that defendants' argument more appropriately ought to be that once consent was given pursuant to the Subassignment and Occupancy Agreement to the transfer from the estate of Ramona Sutton to the Dargers, the rule in *Dumpor's Case* (1578) 76 Eng.Rep. 1110, became applicable and that thereafter no consent to any further assignment was required. (*See* 3 Witkin, Summary of Cal. Law (8th ed. 1973) Real Property, § 491, p. 2170.)

peace of mind of the majority of the unit owners since they are living in such close proximity and using facilities in common, each unit owner must give up a certain degree of freedom of choice which he might otherwise enjoy in separate, privately owned property." (*See also White Egret Condominium v. Franklin* (Fla.1979) 379 So.2d 346, 350; *Seagate Condominium Association, Inc. v. Duffy* (Fla.App.1976) 330 So.2d 484, 486.) Thus, it is essential to successful condominium living and the maintenance of the value of these increasingly significant property interests that the owners as a group have the authority to regulate reasonably the use and alienation of the condominiums.

Happily, there is no impediment to our adoption of such a rule; indeed, the existing law suggests such a rule. In the only California appellate decision of which we are aware dealing with the problem of restraints on alienation of a condominium, *Ritchey v. Villa Nueva Condominium Assn.*, *supra*, 81 Cal.App.3d 688, 695, 146 Cal.Rptr. 716, the court upheld as a reasonable restriction on an owner's right to sell his unit to families with children, a duly adopted amendment to the condominium bylaws restricting occupancy to persons 18 years and over. And, of course, Civil Code section 1355 pertaining to condominiums expressly authorizes the recordation of a declaration of project restrictions and subsequent amendments thereto, "which restrictions shall be enforceable equitable servitudes where reasonable, and shall inure to and bind all owners of condominiums in the project."

Reasonable restrictions on the alienation of condominiums are entirely consistent with Civil Code section 711 in which the California law on unlawful restraints on alienation has its origins. The day has long since passed when the rule in California was that all restraints on alienation were unlawful under the statute; it is now the settled law in this jurisdiction that only unreasonable restraints on alienation are invalid.

Nor does the right of Association reasonably to approve or disapprove the assignment or transfer of the Dargers' ownership interest violate defendants' constitutional right to associate freely with persons of their choosing. Preliminarily, there is considerable doubt of whether the actions of Association constitute state action so as to bring into play the constitutional guarantees. (*Cf. Moose Lodge No. 107 v. Irvis* (1972) 407 U.S. 163, 173; *Newby v. Alto Riviera Apartments* (1976) 60 Cal.App.3d 288, 293–295, 131 Cal.Rptr. 547; *see generally* 5 Witkin, Summary of Cal. Law (8th ed. 1974) Constitutional Law, § 338, pp. 3631–3632.) In any event, however, the constitutionally guaranteed freedom of association, like most other constitutionally protected rights, is not absolute but is subject to reasonable restriction in the interests of the general welfare. (*Village of Belle Terre v. Boraas* (1974) 416 U.S. 1, 9; *White Egret Condominium v. Franklin, supra*, 379 So.2d at pp. 349–351.) Moreover, it may be persuasively argued that if any constitutional right is at issue it is the due process right of an owner of property to use and dispose of it as he chooses. (*See generally* 5 Witkin, Summary of Cal. Law (8th ed. 1974) Constitutional Law, § 273, p. 3563.) And, of course, property rights are subject to reasonable regulation to promote the general welfare. Finally, any determination of the validity or invalidity of Association's right to approve or disapprove assignments or transfers of the Dargers' interest will of necessity impinge upon someone's constitutional freedom of association. A determination that the power granted the Association is invalid would adversely affect the constitutional right of association of the remaining owners at least as much as a contrary determination would affect the same right of the Dargers. (*Cf. Presbytery of Riverside v. Community Church of Palm Springs* (1979) 89 Cal.App.3d 910, 925, 152 Cal.Rptr. 854.)

Having concluded that a reasonable restriction on the right of alienation of a condominium is lawful, we must now determine whether Association's refusal to approve the transfer of the Dargers' interest to the other defendants was reasonable in the circumstances of the case at bench. The criteria for testing the reasonableness of an exercise of such a power by an owners' association are (1) whether the reason for withholding approval is rationally related to the protection, preservation or proper operation of the property and the purposes of the Association as set forth in its governing instruments and (2) whether the power was exercised in a fair and nondiscriminatory manner. Another consideration might be the nature and severity of the consequences of application of the restriction (*e.g.*, transfer declared void, estate forfeited, action for damages). (*See* 3 Witkin, Summary of Cal. Law (8th ed. 1974) Real Property, § 315, p. 2025; *Rest. Property*, §§ 404–406.)

* * *

To determine whether or not Association's disapproval of the transfers to the other defendants was reasonable it is necessary to isolate the reason or reasons approval was withheld. Aside from the assertion that it had the power to withhold approval arbitrarily, essentially three reasons were given by the Association for its refusal to approve the transfers: (1) the multiple ownership of undivided interests; (2) the use the defendants proposed to make of the unit would violate a bylaw restricting use of all apartments to "single family residential use"; and (3) the use proposed would be inconsistent with "the private single family residential character of Laguna Royale, together with the use and quiet enjoyment of all apartment owners of their respective apartments and the common facilities, taking into consideration the close community living circumstances of Laguna Royale." As to (3) Association asserted: "A four family ownership of a single apartment, with the guests of each owner potentially involved, would compound the use of the apartment and common facilities well beyond the normal and usual private single family residential character to the detriment of other owners and would frustrate effective controls over general security, guest occupants and rule compliance, . . ." We examine each of these reasons in light of the indicia of reasonableness referred to above.

Insofar as approval was withheld based on multiple ownership alone, Association's action was clearly unreasonable. In the first place, multiple ownership has no necessary connection to intensive use. Twenty, yea a hundred, persons could own undivided interests in a condominium for investment purposes and lease the condominium on a long-term basis to a single occupant whose use of the premises would probably be less intense in every respect than that considered "normal and usual." Secondly, the Association bylaws specifically contemplate multiple ownership; in Section 7 of Article III, dealing with voting at meetings, it is stated: "Where there is more than one record owner of a unit, any or all of the record owners may attend [the meeting] but only one vote will be permitted for said unit. In the event of disagreement among the record owners of a unit, the vote for that unit shall be cast by a majority of the record owners." Finally, the evidence is uncontroverted that a number of units are owned by several unrelated persons. Although those owners at the time of trial used their units "as a family," there is nothing in the governing instruments as they presently exist that would prevent them from changing the character of their use.

We turn to the assertion that the use of the premises proposed by defendants would be in violation of section 1 of article VIII of the bylaws which provides: "All apartment unit uses are restricted and limited to single family residential use and shall not be used or occupied for any other purpose" and paragraph 4 of the Subassignment and Occupation Agreement which provides: "The premises covered hereby shall be used solely for residential purposes, ..." The term "single family residential use" is not otherwise defined, and if there is any ambiguity or uncertainty in the meaning of the term it must be resolved most favorably to free alienation. (*Randol v. Scott* (1895) 110 Cal. 590, 595–596, 42 P. 976; *Burns v. McGraw* (1946) 75 Cal.App.2d 481, 485–486, 171 P.2d 148; *Riley v. Stoves* (1974) 22 Ariz.App. 223, 526 P.2d 747, 749.) Actually, there is no evidence that defendants proposed to use the property other than for single family residential purposes. It is uncontroverted that they planned to and did use the property one family at a time for residential purposes. Thus, the proposed use was not in violation of the restriction to single family residential use. (*White Egret Condominium v. Franklin*, *supra*, 379 So.2d at p. 352).

The reasonableness of Association's disapproval of the transfers from the Dargers to the other defendants must stand or fall in the final analysis on the third reason offered by the Association for its action: the prospect that defendants' proposed use of the apartment and common facilities would be so greatly in excess of that considered "usual and normal" as to be inconsistent with the quiet enjoyment of the premises by the other occupants and the maintenance of security.

There can be no doubt that the reason given is rationally related to the proper operation of the property and the purposes of the Association as set forth in its governing instruments. The bylaws provide that "[t]he purpose of the Association is to manage and maintain the community apartment project ... on a non-profit basis for the benefit of all owners of Laguna Royale." By subdivision (M)(6) of section 2 of Article V of the bylaws the Board is empowered to "prescribe reasonable regulations pertaining to ... [r]egulating the purchase and/or lease of an apartment to a buyer or sublessee who has no children under 16 years of age that will occupy the apartment temporarily or full time as a resident." This power is said by the bylaws to be given the Board in recognition of "the prime importance of both security and quiet enjoyment of the Apartments owned by each member, and of the common recreational areas...."

* * *

The difficulty with upholding the Association's disapproval of the transfers by the Dargers to the other defendants is twofold. First, no evidence was introduced to establish that the intensity or nature of the use proposed by defendants would in fact be inconsistent with the peaceful enjoyment of the premises by the other occupants or impair security. We may take judicial notice as a matter of common knowledge that the use of a single apartment by four families for 13 weeks each during the year would create some problems not presented by the use of a single, permanent resident family. The moving in and out would, of course, be more frequent, and it might be that some temporary residents would not be as considerate of their fellow occupants as more permanent residents. However, we are not prepared to take judicial notice that the consecutive use of unit 41 by these four families, one at a time, would be so intense or disruptive as to interfere substantially with the peaceful enjoyment of the premises by the other occupants or the maintenance of building security.

Secondly, and most persuasive, a provision of the bylaws, subdivision (A) of section 1 of article VIII, provides:

> Residential use and purpose, as used herein and as referred to in the lease, sub-assignment and occupancy agreement pertaining to and affecting each apartment unit in LAGUNA ROYALE shall be and is hereby deemed to exclude and prohibit the rental of any apartment unit for a period of time of less than ninety (90) days, as it is deemed and agreed that rentals of apartment units for less than ninety (90) day periods of time are contrary to the close community apartment character of LAGUNA ROYALE; interfere with and complicate the orderly administration and process of the security system and program and maintenance program of LAGU-NA ROYALE, and interfere with the orderly management and administration of the common areas and facilities of LAGUNA ROYALE. Accordingly, no owner shall rent an apartment unit for a period of time of less than ninety (90) days.

The point is self-evident: under the present bylaws the Dargers could effect the same use of the property as is proposed by defendants by simply leasing to each couple for a period of 90 days each year.

Under these circumstances we are constrained to hold that Board's refusal to approve the transfers to the other defendants on the basis of the prospect of intensified use was unreasonable as a matter of law. * * *

■ GARDNER, PRESIDING JUSTICE, DISSENTING.

I dissent.

Stripped to its essentials, this is a case in which the other owners of a condominium are attempting to stop the owner of one unit from embarking on a time sharing enterprise. The majority properly conclude that the owners as a group have the authority to regulate reasonably the use and alienation of the units. The majority then conclude that the Board's refusal to approve this transfer was unreasonable as a matter of law. To the contrary, I would find it to be entirely reasonable and would affirm the judgment of the trial court.

The use of a unit on a time sharing basis is inconsistent with the quiet enjoyment of the premises by the other occupants. Time sharing is a remarkable gimmick. P. T. Barnum would have loved it. It ordinarily brings enormous profits to the seller and in this case would bring chaos to the other residents. Here we have only four occupants but if this transfer is permitted there is nothing to stop a more greedy occupant of a unit from conveying to 52 or 365 other occupants.

If as an occupant of a condominium I must anticipate that my neighbors are going to change with clocklike regularity I might just as well move into a hotel—and get room service.

---

1.   What model of judicial review did the court use?

2.   *Burden of Judicial Oversight.* One risk with close judicial oversight is that it will undermine effective operation of homeowner associations. Whether the association wins or loses, litigation can impose significant litigation costs along with the demoralization costs felt acutely in an association of homeowners. Judicially or legislatively imposed rules may help to transform homeowner associations into bureaucratic, timid mini-municipalities—ironically, the very form of governance that most home-owners were seeking to escape through CICs. *Cf.* Robert G. Natelson, Law of Property Owners Associations 46 n. 38 (Supp. 1996) (citing cases with substantial awards of attorney fees). Are these concerns an adequate reason for a deferential standard of judicial review?

Could the developer avoid judicial review by including a provision in the original declaration that property owners agree to waive their rights to judicial review and instead submit to binding arbitration?

3.   *Transfer Restrictions.* CICs, particularly apartment buildings, have sought to limit the transferability of units so as to maintain a "congenial" living environment. Two general bodies of law limit these types of restrictions: anti-discrimination law and the rule against restraints on alienation.

Anti-Discrimination Law. As mentioned earlier, *Shelley v. Kraemer*, 334 U.S. 1 (1948), held that racially restrictive covenants violated the Fourteenth Amendment and were unenforceable. For reasons described in note 4, below (state action doctrine), the reach of *Shelley v. Kraemer* is quite limited, perhaps limited to racial covenants. Federal and state anti-discrimination law has partly filled this void. Thus, the Fair Housing Act,

42 U.S.C. §§ 3601–3619, prohibits discrimination on the basis of race, color, religion, sex, handicap, familial status, or national origin. Some state laws have gone further. *See, e.g.,* Mich. Comp. Laws § 37.2505 (prohibiting discrimination on the basis of religion, race, color, national origin, age, sex, height, weight, familial status, or marital status).

Rule Against Restraints on Alienation. Transfer restrictions may also be challenged on the ground that they are an unlawful restraint on alienation. Thus, a covenant giving a homeowner association an unrestricted right to disapprove the sale of residential units would very likely be an illegal restraint. *See, e.g., Davis v. Geyer,* 151 Fla. 362, 9 So.2d 727 (1942) (striking down a provision stating that the property could not be sold without the approval of the association).

Many transfer restrictions, however, are not so absolute. In *Chianese v. Culley,* 397 F.Supp. 1344 (S.D.Fla.1975), the Culleys contracted with the Chianeses to sell the Culleys' condominium unit. The Culleys subsequently refused to complete the transaction on the ground that the homeowner association invoked a clause in the Declaration allowing the association to block the sale "in order to secure a community of congenial residents and thus protect the value of the apartments." More specifically, Article XII F of the Declaration provided that the sale or lease of any unit was subject to association approval; the association had 60 days to approve the sale or to disapprove the sale and find another purchaser. The association had found another purchaser. The Chianeses alleged that the clause constituted an unlawful restraint on alienation.

The *Chianese* court noted that Article XII F was not an absolute restraint on alienation; either the property would be sold to the Chianeses or it would be sold to another buyer. Citing the *Restatement of Property* § 413(1) and several cases, the court held that the restriction was valid as "it is confined to a lawful purpose, is within reasonable bounds, and is expressed in clear language." Although the opinion does not address the issue, it is apparent that the rule against restraints on alienation has little to do with the property owner's right to choose a successor, or any rights a potential buyer might have. Rather, subject to very broad limits (*e.g.,* the association's purpose cannot be illegal), the purpose of the rule is to keep the property marketable.

Suppose the restriction was not a right of first refusal, as in *Chianese,* but a substantive standard by which the association could disapprove a sale on the ground that the proposed purchaser was not financially responsible and so might fail to pay required assessments. Would such a restriction be valid? Suppose the restriction imposed a standard that because residents live in close proximity purchasers must be friendly and share common concerns and values about noise, pets, and levels of maintenance. Is the restriction valid? *See Mowatt v. 1540 Lake Shore Drive Corp.,* 385 F.2d 135 (7th Cir.1967).

4. *The State Action Doctrine.* In response to the Dargers' claim that the association had violated their constitutional rights, the court questioned "whether the actions of Association constitute state action so as to

bring into play the constitutional guarantees." The court raises this question because the 14th Amendment guarantees of due process and equal protection apply only to state action; private actors cannot violate the Fourteenth Amendment. Thus, the applicability of federal constitutional guarantees turns upon whether homeowner associations—institutions created solely through private agreements—can be deemed state actors. Two Supreme Court decisions from the 1940s have been suggested as bases to subject the decisions of homeowner associations to constitutional limitations, although both approaches have been severely limited by subsequent cases. *See generally* R.R. Powell & P.J. Rohan, Powell on Property § 632.5[11][e] (1996).

Judicial Enforcement Theory. In *Shelley v. Kraemer*, 334 U.S. 1, 68 S.Ct. 836, 92 L.Ed. 1161 (1948), the Supreme Court refused to enforce a racially restrictive covenant contained in a deed on the ground that state action—the exercise of judicial authority to enforce the deed restriction—would contravene federal constitutional protections against racial discrimination. If taken to its logical extreme, this holding would imply that any covenant or restriction in a CIC declaration—indeed, *any* private agreement—is state action (if it is to be judicially enforced) and hence is subject to federal constitutional law. Although some courts have applied the judicial enforcement theory beyond the context of racially restrictive covenants, *see, e.g., Franklin v. White Egret Condominium, Inc.*, 358 So.2d 1084, 1088 (Fla.Ct.App.1977), *aff'd on other grounds*, 379 So.2d 346 (Fla. 1979) (holding unconstitutional a "no children" restriction); *West Hill Baptist Church v. Abbate*, 24 Ohio Misc. 66, 72–76, 261 N.E.2d 196, 200–02 (1969) (holding unconstitutional a restrictive covenant that limited uses to residential purposes, thereby barring construction of a church), more recent Supreme Court and lower court decisions suggest that the judicial enforcement theory will be narrowly limited to cases involving racial discrimination. *See Rendell–Baker v. Kohn*, 457 U.S. 830, 102 S.Ct. 2764, 73 L.Ed.2d 418 (1982) (a private school receiving public funding and regulated by public authorities did not act under color of state law when it discharged employees, and thus it did not violate the employees' constitutional rights against government interference with free speech); *Lugar v. Edmondson Oil Co.*, 457 U.S. 922, 937, 102 S.Ct. 2744, 2754, 73 L.Ed.2d 482 (1982) (state action exists only when "the conduct allegedly causing the deprivation of a federal right [may] be fairly attributable to the State"); *Flagg Bros., Inc. v. Brooks*, 436 U.S. 149, 98 S.Ct. 1729, 56 L.Ed.2d 185 (1978) (a state statute authorizing a warehouseman to sell stored goods for nonpayment does not constitute state action absent participation by public officials); *Jackson v. Metropolitan Edison Co.*, 419 U.S. 345, 95 S.Ct. 449, 42 L.Ed.2d 477 (1974) (termination of electric service for nonpayment by a publicly regulated private utility does not constitute state action); *Ginsberg v. Yeshiva of Far Rockaway*, 45 A.D.2d 334, 358 N.Y.S.2d 477 (1974) (judicial enforcement of a restrictive covenant preventing a religious school is not state action).

Public Function Theory. In *Marsh v. Alabama*, 326 U.S. 501, 66 S.Ct. 276, 90 L.Ed. 265 (1946), the Supreme Court held that a private company town—which provided police and other traditional governmental services— was the functional equivalent of a municipality, and therefore could not restrict the liberty of press and religion of residents or others inside town boundaries. *Id.* at 506–08, 66 S.Ct. at 278–79. This holding would appear to cover the actions of at least some homeowner associations, particularly those possessing the broad range of powers typically associated with local governments.

The Supreme Court has not yet directly addressed whether federal constitutional law is applicable to residential associations, although the emerging case law strongly suggests that the Court will not subject a privately structured community to the limitations upon public actors. In *Hudgens v. National Labor Relations Board*, 424 U.S. 507, 96 S.Ct. 1029, 47 L.Ed.2d 196 (1976), in which union pickets were forced to leave a shopping mall under threat of arrest for trespass, the Court held that the pickets' First Amendment rights had not been abridged because a self-contained shopping mall was not the functional equivalent of a municipality. In *Ball v. James*, 451 U.S. 355, 366, 101 S.Ct. 1811, 68 L.Ed.2d 150 (1981), the Court held that a private water district was not subject to the federal constitutional requirement of "one person, one vote," on the ground that the entity did not perform the "normal functions of government"; it "cannot impose *ad valorem* property taxes or sales taxes. It cannot enact any laws governing the conduct of citizens, nor does it administer such normal functions of government as the maintenance of streets, the operation of schools, or sanitation, health or welfare services." In *Lugar v. Edmondson Oil Co.*, 457 U.S. 922, 936–37, 102 S.Ct. 2744, 2753–54, 73 L.Ed.2d 482 (1982), which held that there is no state action where a state officer, pursuant to state law, helps to enforce a pre-judgment attachment, the Court wrote:

> Careful adherence to the "state action" requirement preserves an area of individual freedom by limiting the reach of the federal law and federal judicial power. * * * A major consequence is to require the courts to respect the limits of their own power as directed against * * * private interests. Whether this is good or bad policy, it is a fundamental fact of our political order.

See also Jackson v. Metropolitan Edison Co., 419 U.S. 345, 352, 95 S.Ct. 449, 454, 42 L.Ed.2d 477 (1974) (public function theory applies when non-governmental actors exercise authority "traditionally exclusively reserved to the State").

Would according state action status to homeowner associations be good or bad policy? If homeowner associations are not treated as state actors, in what ways can a court subject homeowner associations to the type of scrutiny to which local governments are subject? To what extent can states, through their constitutions, extend protections to residents of homeowner associations? *Cf. PruneYard, supra* pp. 377–82. Should such rights be inalienable?

Montoya v. Barreras

Supreme Court of New Mexico, 1970.
81 N.M. 749, 473 P.2d 363.

■ SISK, JUSTICE.

Twenty of the defendants in a quiet-title action appeal from that portion of the final decree which relieved and excluded from the burden of residential restrictions and covenants one lot owned by plaintiff in a subdivision in Santa Fe, New Mexico in which these defendants also owned lots.

Defendants rely on three points, but because we hold that the second point is controlling and requires reversal the other points need not be discussed. Point II reads as follows:

> The "Declaration of Protective Covenants to the Linda Vista Addition of the City of Santa Fe" does not permit the removal of restrictions on only one lot in the subdivision while retaining the restrictions on all other lots in the subdivision, and therefore, the trial court erred in overruling appellants' legal defense 1(E).

Legal defense 1(E), as it appears in the amended answer of defendants, reads:

> The Covenant (X) does not permit the relinquishment of the restrictions on only one lot or one portion of the subdivision while retaining the restrictions on other lots in the subdivision.

In 1940, the owner of a tract of land in Santa Fe, New Mexico, whom we will refer to as the grantor, executed and recorded an instrument title "Declaration of Protective Covenants for the Linda Vista Addition to the City of Santa Fe, New Mexico," which declared that all of the described tract was encumbered by and subject to twelve paragraphs of restrictions. Paragraph (X) of the restrictive covenants, which contains the language directly in dispute, provides: "These covenants are to run with the land and shall be binding on all the parties and all persons claiming under them until January 1, 1966, at which time said covenants shall be automatically extended for successive periods of ten (10) years unless by a vote of the majority of the then owners of the lots it is agreed to change the said covenants in whole or in part."

All of the evidence before the trial court was documentary. No plat of the addition is included in the transcript. The parties executed a Stipulation Agreement in which they agreed that during December, 1967, and January and February, 1968, a majority of the owners of lots within the residential subdivision had signed a "Consent to Change of Protective Covenants" pertaining to the plaintiff's lot, by which they voted for and consented to the removal of all of the restrictions from that one lot and to its use for commercial purposes.

Plaintiff contends that such removal of the residential restrictions from one lot only was proper because the language of paragraph (X) is ambiguous and must be construed strictly against the grantor and in favor of free use of the land. By such construction they argue that the phrase " * * * change the said covenants in whole or in part" in paragraph (X) is not limited to changing the residential covenants themselves as they affect all of the lots, but permits the complete removal of the covenants from one lot while retaining them on all other lots.

The plaintiff's authorities recite the long-established rules that, if ambiguous, a restriction on property must be construed against its grantor and in favor of free use. But alleging that a restriction is ambiguous does not necessarily make it so. These general rules can have significance only as applied to the particular facts of the individual case. Restrictive covenants must be considered reasonably, though strictly, and an illogical, unnatural, or strained construction must be avoided. *H. J. Griffith Realty Co. v. Hobbs Houses, Inc.*, 68 N.M. 25, 357 P.2d 677 (1960). In the *Griffith* case this court noted that in construing restrictive covenants, perhaps more than in any other field of law, each case must depend on its own particular facts, and an attempt to apply general rules is unsatisfactory.

The issue to be determined is therefore whether, considering the declaration of restrictive covenants as a whole, paragraph (X) can be reasonably and logically construed to permit the residential restrictions to be removed on one lot only, or on a lot-by-lot basis, by a majority of the owners in the subdivision. We do not believe that it can.

Before applying the general rule that restrictive covenants should be construed in favor of the free use of property, the court must recognize that " * * * effect is to be given to the intention of the parties as shown by the language of the whole instrument, considered with the circumstances surrounding the transaction, and the object of the parties in making the restrictions." *Hoover v. Waggoman*, 52 N.M. 371, 199 P.2d 991 (1948).

Considering the entire document, by clear statement and with plain intent, it constitutes a detailed plan for residential development and restriction as to all of the lots in the subdivision. Under the facts and circumstances of this case, we are not faced with the resolution of an ambiguous restriction.

Examination of the entire declaration reveals that the original restrictions were clearly imposed on all of the described property. The declaration describes the property and is then followed by the granting clause which declares that all of the property shall be encumbered by the restrictions. Following this granting clause, twelve paragraphs of restrictive covenants are listed, including the provision in covenant (X) that they may be changed in whole or in part. The phrase "in whole or in part" in covenant (X) clearly modifies the words "to change," and the direct object of "to change" is the word "covenants," not the word "lots." Thus, the covenants may be changed in whole or in part, but we cannot construe this language as permitting any such change or changes to apply to only a portion of the lots on which the restrictions were imposed. Nor is there anything in the covenants themselves which can be construed as either expressly or impliedly modifying or changing the granting clause itself, which expresses the intent and purpose that all of the described property is encumbered by the restrictions, whether they remain as originally stated or are subsequently changed in whole or in part. The original restrictions were clearly imposed on all of the described property, and though the restrictions themselves may be changed in whole or in part, the change or changes which might be made must affect all of the described property.

Historically, restrictive covenants have been used to assure uniformity of development and use of residential area to give the owners of lots within such an area some degree of environmental stability. To permit individual lots within an area to be relieved of the burden of such covenants, in the absence of a clear expression in the instrument so providing, would destroy the right to rely on restrictive covenants which has traditionally been upheld by our law of real property. As in *Gorman v. Boehning*, 55 N.M. 306, 232 P.2d 701, 26 A.L.R.2d 868 (1951), the declaration of the grantor in this case contemplates a plan of development limited to residential purposes. To completely insure a plan of residential development, the grantor must impose reciprocal restrictive covenants on the property for the common benefit of all of his grantees and their assigns.

All of the lots in the subdivision were sold subject to the provisions of the declaration. Restrictions as to the use of land are mutual, reciprocal, equitable easements in the nature of servitudes in favor of owners of other lots within the restricted area, and constitute property rights which run with the land. Where the covenants manifest a general plan of restriction to residential purposes, such covenants constitute valuable property rights of the owners of all lots in the tract. *Gorman v. Boehning, supra.*

* * *

[In *Riley v. Boyle*, 6 Ariz.App. 523, 434 P.2d 525 (1967), the] court * * * held that each owner had the contractual right to have the restrictions enforced against all of the lots unless the partial change in the restrictions voted by 51 per cent of the owners was made equally applicable to all lots in the subdivision and that the attempted exemption of one lot was null and void. Both our case and the *Riley* case, *supra*, deal directly with the partial changing or amending of restrictive covenants, and we agree with the Arizona court that absolution from the restrictions as to only some, but not all, of the lots is not a valid construction where the language of the instrument manifests the intent for orderly residential neighborhood development. In *Cowherd Development Company v. Littick*, 361 Mo. 1001, 238 S.W.2d 346 (1951), in holding that the extension of the restrictions could not apply to part of the lots and not others, the court noted that one of the primary purposes of residential restrictions in a subdivision is to assure purchasers of lots that they may build homes without fear of commercial expansion or encroachment.

The soundness of the reasoning in *Riley v. Boyle, supra*, is evidenced when the results of the interpretation plaintiff would place on paragraph (X) of the restrictions are considered. Plaintiff's interpretation would permit the majority of owners to remove all restrictions from their lots while leaving the burden on the lots of the minority. It would permit the majority of owners, whose lots might not be adversely affected because of their insulated location in the subdivision, to authorize offensive conse-quences for the minority by removing or imposing restrictions only on certain lots within the area. Because the grantor encumbered all of the property with restrictions, we cannot infer from the declaration the inten-tion that any subsequent change or changes in the restrictions could be made applicable to only one lot or a portion of the lots in the residential subdivision.

Our holding that the declaration does not permit the majority of owners to exempt one lot only from the residential restrictions, contrary to the vested rights of the minority of owners, does not necessarily mean that the plaintiff was or is without a remedy. This court has long recognized that individual lots in a subdivision may be relieved of restrictive covenants if there has been such a change in the conditions which existed when the covenants were imposed as to defeat the intended objects and purposes of the covenants and their enforcement is no longer necessary to afford the protection originally contemplated. In the present case, however, no allega-tion of change of conditions was raised by the pleadings nor was any finding concerning change of conditions requested or made.

To the extent that it relieves and excludes the plaintiff's lot from the operation and effect of the restrictive covenants, the decree is reversed with directions to enter a new decree consistent with this opinion.

1. What model of judicial review did the court select?

2. Do you agree with the appellate court that the covenant is unam-biguous; that is, that there is no reasonable doubt that the covenants are to apply to all lots equally?

If the court is right—that under the existing CC&Rs there is no mechanism to lift the restrictions on less than all lots—what could the developer have done to permit some change over time, without losing the uniformity that the homeowners generally desire? Would it be better to leave one lot without restrictions? Or with just a few restrictions? How would the developer know which lot to leave unrestricted?

Would it be better to create a process to relieve one or more lots of the restrictive covenants? What are the dangers of leaving the decision to some sort of homeowner or board vote? Should there be some combination of substantive criteria and voting mechanism? Note that if the restrictions are too easily lifted, many homeowners' expectations about the development will be dashed. On the other hand, if the restrictions could only be lifted by a unanimous vote, there would be substantial risks of a hold-out problem.

3. The *Montoya* opinion suggests that the plaintiffs could use a substantive judicial doctrine—changed conditions. Isn't this approach unde-mocratic, particularly by comparison to the vote actually used in *Montoya*?

4. As reflected in the *Montoya* case, courts are sensitive to whether regulations have a disproportionate impact on certain unit owners. Since

the voting members of a homeowner association board are property owners in the CIC themselves, broad authority to burden or advantage particular units could tempt board members to favor themselves or friends. Even if board members did not engage in self-dealing, there is also a risk that distrust would undermine relations among homeowners and the associations to adopt and enforce rules. What legal rules and mechanisms exist to minimize these risks in local government decisions? Which, if any, of those mechanisms are available in CICs?

Problems

How would you assess the validity of the following regulations?

A.   The association adopted a regulation that increased the monthly parking fee for nonresident owners (but not resident owners) from $25 to $75. The association wanted to prevent nonresident owners from realizing a profit when they rented their parking spaces to their tenants at market rates. *See Thanasoulis v. Winston Towers 200 Ass'n, Inc.*, 110 N.J. 650, 542 A.2d 900 (1988). Suppose that the association's motive was to discourage leasing of parking spaces to persons who did not live in the condominium complex?

B.   The cooperative adopted a regulation establishing a housing safety patrol. Residents could either pay $25 per month to help finance the patrol or participate directly in the patrol for two hours each week. *Garrison Apartments, Inc. v. Sabourin*, 113 Misc.2d 674, 449 N.Y.S.2d 629 (N.Y. Civ. Ct. 1982).

Rywalt v. Writer Corp.

Colorado Court of Appeals, 1974.
34 Colo.App. 334, 526 P.2d 316.

■ VAN CISE, JUDGE.

Defendant The Dam Homeowner's Association (Association) appeals from a judgment entered in favor of plaintiffs Fred and Dorothy Colyer (Colyer) and Lee and Bernice Scott (Scott) enjoining the Association from constructing a tennis court on "common property" of the Association in the vicinity of the Colyer and Scott residences * * *

Plaintiffs Colyer and Scott own adjacent homes on lots in "The Dam," a subdivision developed by defendant The Writer Construction Corporation (Writer). All lot owners in the subdivision are members of the Association. The land to the north rear of the Colyer and Scott lots is "common property," owned by the Association for the use and enjoyment of all of its members. On that common property is a tennis court located close to the north line of the Colyer property and northeast of the Scott property. The Association, through its board of directors, proposed to construct, with funds furnished by Writer, a second tennis court adjacent to the west side of the existing one, close to the north line of both plaintiffs' properties.

Plaintiffs filed suit to enjoin the Association from constructing a tennis court in that location. They alleged that the decision to build the second court and to locate it behind their properties was *ultra vires* and constituted arbitrary and capricious action by the board of the Association. Plaintiffs also alleged that construction of the tennis court would constitute: (1) unreasonable interference with their view, (2) interference with access to other common properties, and (3) an unreasonable invasion of their privacy. The court found insufficient harm to plaintiffs to support injunctive relief on these grounds.

The court did conclude that the Association's board had acted arbitrarily and capriciously, and on that basis entered its order enjoining construction of the tennis court unless and until certain conditions were met. In support of its order, the court made extensive findings as to (1) the incompleteness of minutes of meetings, (2) the use of the annual meeting of members for the sole purpose of electing directors, (3) the practice of holding closed board meetings, (4) the failure to submit the matter of the second tennis court to the architectural control committee, (5) the existence of other matters which, in the opinion of the trial court, should have priority, such as drainage problems and camper and boat parking, (6) the inadequacy of a membership poll taken with regard to the location of the proposed new court, and (7) the failure to poll them at all on whether a new court was needed or required. None of the above support a conclusion that the board acted arbitrarily or capriciously.

Pertinent statutes, the articles of incorporation, the bylaws, and the declaration of covenants and restrictions pertaining to the Association, contain no special provisions with regard to conduct of directors meetings, agenda for membership meetings, or requirements for polling members other than on assessments. The architectural control committee's review function is limited to structures constructed or maintained on lots and not on the common properties. Both the articles and the bylaws specify that "the affairs of this Association shall be managed by a board of six directors." The bylaws provide further that "the board of directors shall have power ... exercise for the Association all powers, duties, and authority vested in or delegated to this Association and not reserved to the membership by other provisions of these bylaws, the articles of incorporation, or the declaration."

The good faith acts of directors of profit or non-profit corporations which are within the powers of the corporation and within the exercise of an honest business judgment are valid. Courts will not, at the instance of stockholders or otherwise, interfere with or regulate the conduct of the directors in the reasonable and honest exercise of their judgment and duties. *Horst v. Traudt*, 43 Colo. 445, 96 P. 259; *Taylor v. Axton–Fisher Tobacco Co.*, 295 Ky. 226, 173 S.W.2d 377, 148 A.L.R. 834; 19 Am.Jur.2d Corporations § 1148; 19 C.J.S. Corporations § 984. There being no evidence that the directors acted in bad faith or in fraud of the rights of the members, the injunction cannot be upheld. * * *

---

1.   What model of judicial review does the appellate court apply?

2.   Notice that the *Rywalt* court used an "internal" standard of review.

> Internal review examines the consistency of the residential association regulation with the specific purposes of the common interest development and the powers granted the governing board by the association documents. External review compares the residential association rules to external public norms such as legislation or custom. * * *

> * * * In an internal review of reasonableness, the residential governance documents determine the result of any balancing of private and public values and any accommodation between stability and flexibility in covenant enforcement. The judge simply lays the residential association rule alongside the powers of the association and ensures that the rules fall within those substantive limits. In contrast, an external review of reasonableness requires that the judge weigh and accommodate the private goals inherent in the residential association regulation with the larger, public interests implicated by that choice.

Brower, Communities Within the Community: Consent, Constitutionalism, and Other Failures of Legal Theory in Residential Associations, 7 J. Land Use & Envtl. L. 203, 232, 234 (1992). Which of the previous cases that you have read use an "external" standard of review? What is the source of the external standard? Which standard is more defensible? Does your answer depend on the type of decision under review?

3.   The *Rywalt* trial court was concerned about a number of practices, including the use of closed board meetings, the absence of meeting minutes, and the failure to use the architectural control committee. Why was the trial court troubled by these practices? Why did the appellate court conclude that these practices were of no legal significance?

4.   How sound is the analogy between homeowner associations and profit-making corporations? Consider that most corporations are risk-taking (that is one of the purposes of limited liability), and that the purpose of the business judgment rule is to insulate directors from liability. How is the charge of the homeowner association different? Are some sorts of homeowner decisions most appropriate for the corporate board model of judicial review?

5.   In *Papalexiou v. Tower West Condominium*, 167 N.J. Super. 516, 401 A.2d 280 (1979), a property owner challenged a special assessment based on a by-law authorizing an assessment grounded on a board finding of an emergency. While the court stated that "[a]bsent a demonstration of

the board's lack of good faith, self-dealing, dishonesty or incompetency, its determination * * * should not be judicially reviewed." *Id.* at 528, 401 A.2d at 286. Nonetheless, the court reviewed the association's decisionmaking procedures, its deliberations, and its reliance on counsel. Has the *Papalexiou* court really followed the corporate model? Or has it adapted the model to review of homeowner associations? Did it properly equate good faith with adequate decisionmaking procedures?

6. *Coherence of Judicial Review.* On the basis of the foregoing cases, is there any coherent general framework or consistent set of principles underlying judicial review of CICs? Notwithstanding the varying contexts, do these cases suggest that courts accord appropriate deference to association decisions? Might the cases be harmonized by reference to the degree of sophistication and procedural safeguards of the governing homeowner association—*i.e.*, those boards that are represented by counsel and follow fair procedures are more likely to be upheld? Should the fact that a CIC has many or few members, a "politically" active membership (*e.g.*, frequent, well-attended meetings), or alternative dispute mechanisms (*e.g.*, mediation) make a difference in the degree of deference accorded homeowner association decisions by a reviewing court? What principle or set of principles should courts apply in reviewing homeowner association decisions?

---

4. THE FUTURE OF CIC GOVERNANCE

The proliferation of common interest communities has evoked concerns about the future of residential neighborhoods and the use of servitudes to create and govern such neighborhoods.

a. DURATION

As residential associations age, their restrictions may be poorly adapted to changing economic conditions, changing values and preferences, and other changing conditions. While some judicial doctrines (*e.g.*, changed conditions) and association rules (*e.g.*, those allowing a majority or super-majority of property owners to amend restrictions) permit some flexibility, it may be quite expensive, time-consuming, or even impossible to change restrictions in practice. Professor James Winokur has written:

> [R]eciprocal residential promissory servitudes confer decidedly mixed blessings on our neighborhoods and on our society as a whole. By so strictly segregating land uses, these servitudes often exclude not only all nonresidential uses, but also residential uses which vary in density, in cost, or in caliber of improvements. Neighborhood servitude restrictions can effectively segregate social classes, isolating residents of one neighborhood from outsiders who neither live, shop nor work with residents of these exclusive districts. In contrast to some uniquely beautiful servitude-restricted neighborhoods, much of the suburban sprawl controlled by

association-administered servitude regimes has become aesthetically undifferentiated and culturally desolate. Servitude regimes have generated growing resident dissatisfaction with "strait jacket" restrictions which invade aspects of home life previously left to personal choice. Conflict among neighbors is often sharp, and litigation between servitude regime residents and their owners associations has mushroomed.

＊ ＊ ＊ [T]he domination of housing markets by potentially perpetual, uniform servitude regimes has begun to undercut both the economic efficiency of these servitudes and the personal liberties of existing residents and potential buyers. Enforcement of all restrictions imposed by servitude regimes, limiting neither the duration nor the content of servitudes, can also undermine the availability of neighborhoods conducive to human flourishing, where each individual's identity can be based on personal control of a unique place in the residential environment.

Winokur, The Mixed Blessings of Promissory Servitudes: Toward Optimizing Economic Utility, Individual Liberty, and Personal Identity, 1989 Wis. L. Rev. 1, 3–5. These problems are exacerbated because many buyers do not really read or understand the complex association rules before they close the real estate deal. *Id.* at 30. Winokur's solution is to moderate the association's enforcement powers.

[B]eyond a statutory initial term of a few decades, large scale promissory servitude regimes should remain enforceable against any given lot by, at most, an enforcement group much smaller than the entire development. Legislative enactment of such a reform would facilitate consensual modification of obsolete servitudes, thus decreasing growing pressures for costly discretionary judicial supervision of servitudes. With modification of older servitudes realistically attainable by the parties themselves, termination of servitudes under the "changed circumstances" doctrine could then be decreed only where unanticipated changes wholly frustrate the servitudes' purposes. ＊ ＊ ＊ Legislation should bar private, quasi-governmental servitude regimes from impinging on several specific individual rights already constitutionally protected from infringement by public governments. Courts should less readily infer an intention that servitudes bind successors and give reasonable notice to those bound.

Id. at 6. *See also id.* at 78–96. After, say, 20 years, all restrictions (except covenants to pay assessments) would be enforceable by only a dozen other neighboring property owners forming a "pod." Do you agree with this assessment and proposal?

Professor Korngold rejects Winokur's argument and opposes his proposal. "Servitudes should be enforced like other contracts for several reasons: efficiency, moral obligation and freedom of choice." Korngold, Resolving the Flaws of Residential Servitudes and Owners Associations: For Reformation Not Termination, 1990 Wis. L. Rev. 513, 516–17. He acknowledges the problems of obsolete restrictions and holdouts, but argues that

> [o]bsolescence of servitudes can be addressed with the "changed conditions" doctrine and a clearly articulated doctrine barring enforcement of covenants that violate public policy. Additionally, holdouts can be reduced by including provisions that allow termination and modification of servitudes with less-than-unanimous consent.

Id. at 518–19. *See also id.* at 520–23. He would also have courts and legislatures impose requirements that associations treat property owners equally, use fair procedures, act within prescribed powers, and make rational decisions. *Id.* at 527–32. Aside from these limits, Korngold would permit little judicial interference.

> In addition to the usual reasons for deference—for example, the expertise of private government compared to the courts and the prohibitive cost of reviewing all determinations—the policies underlying servitude enforcement require that courts exhibit great caution before imposing their judgment. The private government should be sustained in all but the most extraordinary cases, because the efficiencies of delegating decisions to a private government should not be undermined, the owners' free choice to enter into a community relationship should be respected, and the democratic participatory process of the private government should be supported by the courts. The courts should override only those judgments that are clearly irrational, on the theory that such grossly unreasonable and inefficient decisions violate the legitimate expectations of a purchaser.

Id. at 532. Do you think Winokur or Korngold has the better argument?

---

b. INDIVIDUAL RIGHTS

Because of the state action problem discussed earlier (*i.e.*, that homeowner associations are not arms of the state government), most constitutional restrictions do not apply to homeowner associations. There are some notable exceptions, but most of them have to do with outsiders who want in. *See, e.g., Shelley v. Kraemer*, 334 U.S. 1, 68 S.Ct. 836, 92 L.Ed. 1161 (1948) (refusing enforcement of racially restrictive covenants); Fair Housing Act, 42 U.S.C. §§ 3601–3619 (prohibiting discrimination on the basis of race, color, religion, sex, handicap, familial status, or national origin).

Only a very few statutes deal with the civil rights of residents. *See, e.g.,* Fla. Stat. Ann. § 718.123 (forbidding regulation of the "right to peaceably assemble" or the right "to invite public officers or candidates for public office to appear and speak" in common areas of the condominium). Although a "reasonableness" standard of judicial review might invalidate restrictions that violate norms of equal protection or due process, *see, e.g.,*

Montoya v. Barreras, 81 N.M. 749, 473 P.2d 363 (1970) (striking down a change in the CC&Rs that did not treat all property owners equally), *supra*, pp. 870–73, the expense of adjudication and the uncertainty of the standard of review as well as the courts' practice of deferring to many association decisions leave many restrictions untouched. As a result, some scholars have argued that CICs, and possibly legislatures, should adopt a minimum set of rights applicable to all members of property owner associations.

Susan F. French, The Constitution of a Private Residential Government Should Include a Bill of Rights

27 Wake Forest Law Review 345, 346–47, 349–51 (1992).

* * * Beyond required contributions to support the common facilities, [ ]people who buy into common interest developments are often asked to give up significantly greater degrees of freedom to obtain the advantages offered by ownership of property in the community.

The degree of freedom prospective purchasers are asked to give up is determined by the developer, who creates the constitution for the new community in its recorded declaration of servitudes. Although UCIOA regulates many aspects of the community's structure and management, it places no limits on the developer's freedom to impose architectural controls, restraints on alienation of individual units, or use and occupancy restrictions. Nor does the Act limit the developer's ability to grant similar powers to the community association. UCIOA leaves to other areas of law, including the general law of servitudes, the question whether there are substantive limits on the degrees of freedom the developer can require people to give up in order to become members of the common interest community.

Developers probably conceive of the documents they use to create common interest communities as instruments for enhancing the quality of life and promoting property values, rather than as instruments for oppression. Since their primary interest is usually in making money, they draft common interest community constitutions with an eye on what will sell, rather than on the extent to which the law will permit them to deprive community members of their liberty. What will sell depends on a lot of factors, of course, only one of which is the degree of control the community association enjoys over the owners and residents of the community. However, other factors being equal, rational consumers should select a community on the basis of the degree of freedom of choice they wish to give up. Increasingly, Americans have been willing to give up some degree of freedom to secure the advantages of ownership in common interest communities.

* * *

Although there are obvious advantages to be gained by purchasing housing in a common interest community, there are also severe risks. If the developer has created a community with rigid restrictions, the association may not be able to adapt to changing conditions, thus property values may fall. If the developer has created a community with flexible restrictions, the community association may adopt changes that substantially reduce the value of units to their owners or force them to move. Dreams of home-ownership can turn sour for people whose building or landscaping plans are not approved and for people who learn too late that they will not be permitted to put up political signs, for sale signs, or holiday decorations. Dreams can turn to nightmares for homeowners who are forced to a choice of moving or giving up beloved pets, lovers, or even children.

* * * Recognizing the shortcomings in their ability to predict future needs of the community, developers are granting broader and more flexible powers to the community association. The governing documents increasingly look like constitutions rather than civil codes. However, developers have not designed an adequate response to the fears the existence of such powers will inevitably provoke. * * *

The fear of interference with personal freedom to live as one wishes and financial fears of being treated unequally or being prevented from selling or renting the property are likely to surface in many potential purchasers. So, too, is the fear that restraints on alienation will prevent the owner from leasing or selling the property when necessary or convenient. Although there are countervailing reasons why owners might want the community association to have the power to determine life styles and activities within the community and to control resales or prevent rentals, limiting the association's ability to do so will probably result in reassuring more potential buyers than it will frighten. * * *

Problem: Bill of Rights

At the end of her article, Professor French proposed the following Homeowner's Bill of Rights.

1. *Equal Treatment*: Similarly situated owners and residents shall be treated similarly.

2. *Speech*: The rights of residents to display political signs and symbols of the kinds normally displayed in or outside of residences located in single-family residential neighborhoods in their individually owned property shall not be abridged, except that the association may adopt reasonable time, place, and manner restrictions for the purpose of minimizing damage and disturbance to other owners and residents.

3. *Religious and Holiday Displays*: The rights of residents to display religious and holiday signs, symbols, and decorations of the kinds normally displayed in or outside of residences located in single-family residential neighborhoods in their individually owned property shall not be abridged, except that the association may adopt reasonable time, place, and manner

restrictions for the purpose of minimizing damage and disturbance to other owners and residents.

4. *Household Composition*: The association shall make no rule that interferes with the freedom of residents to determine the composition of their households, except that the association shall have the power to require that all occupants be members of a single housekeeping unit, and to limit the total number of occupants permitted in each lot or unit on the basis of size and facilities of the unit and its fair share use of the common facilities, including parking.

5. *Activities Within Individually Owned Property*: The association shall make no rule that interferes with the activities of the residents carried on within the confines of their individually owned properties, except that the association may prohibit activities not normally associated with property restricted to residential use, and it may restrict any activities that impose monetary costs on the association or other owners, that create danger to the health or safety of other residents, that generate excessive noise or traffic, and that create unsightly conditions visible outside the unit, that block the views from other units, or that create a nuisance.

6. *Pets*: Unless the keeping of pets is prohibited at the time of the sale of the first lot or unit, no rule prohibiting the keeping of ordinary household pets shall be adopted thereafter over the objection of any owner expressed in writing to the association. The association may adopt reasonable regulations designed to minimize damage and disturbance to other owners and residents, including regulations requiring damage deposits, waste removal, leash controls, noise controls, occupancy limits based on size and facilities of the unit and fair share use of the common areas. Nothing in this provision shall prevent the association from requiring removal of any animal that presents an actual threat to the health or safety of residents or from requiring abatement of any nuisance.

7. *Allocations of Burdens and Benefits*: The initial allocation of financial burdens and rights to use common facilities among the various lots or units shall not be changed to the detriment of any unit owner over that owner's objection expressed in writing to the association. Nothing in this provision shall prevent the association from changing the common facilities available, from adopting generally applicable rules for use of common facilities, or from denying use privileges to those who abuse the facilities, violate rules for use of common facilities or fail to pay assessments.

8. *Alienation*: The association shall not adopt rules that prohibit transfer of any lot or unit, or require consent of the association for transfer of any lot or unit, for any period of greater than two months. The association shall not impose any fee on transfer of any unit greater than an amount reasonably based on the costs of transfer to the association.

1.   Do you think that states should adopt legislation along the lines of the above Bill of Rights? Do you agree with the specific items in Professor French's proposed list? Would you delete or modify some of these rights? Would you add additional rights?

2.   Should the Bill of Rights include a takings clause to compensate homeowners if the association's actions or decisions reduce the value of their property? What would be the substantive criteria for compensation? What would be the procedures for enforcement? *See* Ellickson, Cities and Homeowner Associations, 130 U. Pa. L. Rev. 1519, 1525, 1535–39 (1982).

3.   Suppose that a state enacted the above Bill of Rights, but included a provision allowing a community to amend or abolish any of the rights by consent of all association members. Would this be an improvement? Should any of the rights be inalienable?

Assuming that new property owners have notice and existing property owners can exit, why shouldn't a group of property owners be permitted to renounce any "rights" they consider destructive, immoral, or simply undesirable? *See* Note, The Rule of Law in Residential Associations, 99 Harv. L. Rev. 472, 483–89 (1992).

4.   Professor Brower suggests a different, more open-ended approach based on judicial review rather than legislative enactment.

> Courts should examine residential association regulations through a two-step system: first, a primarily procedural, ultra vires analysis; second, a public policy review which candidly considers substantive values. The first step is a standard internal consistency examination. The regulation must be tested against the limits on private governments, if any, imposed by state law and by the governing association documents.
>
> * * *
>
> [T]he private, consensual nature of these communities and their counter-societal purposes argue for a relatively cautious conception of the public policy exception. That reading is more consistent with the values of private autonomy and personal liberty implicated by these residential associations and with the maintenance of a boundary between the public and private spheres.

Brower, Communities Within the Community: Consent, Constitutionalism, and Other Failures of Legal Theory in Residential Associations, 7 J. Land Use & Envtl. L. 203, 262–63, 271 (1992).

Which approach do you prefer?

5.   *Rights of Non–Members.* To what extent should non-members of CICs—including prospective members (*i.e.*, applicants), guests, and lessees—be protected against the decisions of homeowner associations? Should they be entitled to due process protections? Protections against discrimination of any kind?

c. COMMUNITY

A number of commentators have emphasized the importance of foster-ing a genuine sense of "community" in residential and civic life. Scholars, however, cannot agree on the definition of community. Professor Alexander has written that community involves "more than an instrumental conver-gence of individual ends—[but rather] reciprocal empathy." Alexander, Dilemmas of Group Autonomy: Residential Associations and Community, 75 Cornell L. Rev. 1, 26 (1990). Professor Winokur is concerned about the possibility of creating community. "[I]n modern American residential neighborhoods, * * * the empathic and congenial qualities of 'community' are often subordinate to its property value implications." Winokur, Reform-ing Servitude Regimes: Toward Association Federalism and Community, 1990 Wis. L. Rev. 537, 540.

Professor Frug maintains that

[t]he reason for the creation of the *polis* [which Frug defines as including homeowner associations as well as cities], Aristotle argued, was not wealth maximization or protection from redistrib-ution, but friendship. * * * Of course, the exact form that a social organization based on friendship would take is uncertain and certainly cannot be determined by deduction. But new possibilities for the structuring of social life will occur to us if we allow ourselves to go beyond the limited possibilities of human relation-ship allowed by the seller/customer relationship * * *.

* * * I favor the enriching process of genuine democratic participation, a process designed to change our ideas about how society can be organized and how people ought to treat each other.

Frug, Cities and Homeowners Associations: A Reply, 130 U. Pa. L. Rev. 1589, 1600–01 (1982).

Professor Brower, on the other hand, sees private residential communi-ties somewhat differently.

By creating distinct community norms and amenities, common interest developments promote the value of private autonomy and personal liberty. * * * The courts have interpreted the Constitu-tion and other laws to safeguard * * * diversity by recognizing that modern society is sometimes harsh and discordant and that a certain amount of discomfort and offense is inevitable. Therefore, the ability to structure one's private environment and to create a shelter form a society which one cannot control becomes particu-larly valuable, especially in and around the home.

Brower, Communities Within the Community: Consent, Constitutionalism, and Other Failures of Legal Theory in Residential Associations, 7 J. Land Use & Envtl. L. 203, 217–18 (1992).

1.   Are the use of formal restrictions and political governance structures of residential association conducive to the encouragement of norms of neighborliness or civic participation? Should they be redrawn to encourage such values? How should they be redrawn?

2.   If neighborliness and civic participation are so valued, why have homeowner associations not taken appropriate steps to restructure themselves? Does Professor Frug's vision resonate with a substantial proportion of Americans? That is, do Americans have a more individualistic ethos in their residential choices? Does Brower have the more accurate vision of why people join such associations, and that people define their communities not geographically, but through networks of friends and family, work, religious communities and/or social activity unconnected to where they live?

Problem

You are an attorney for the Affordable Housing Coalition (AHC), a non-profit entity dedicated to providing affordable housing for low- and moderate-income households. AHC is particularly concerned with fostering stable, safe, and affordable housing in neighborhoods that might otherwise become increasingly undesirable or unavailable to families of low or moderate means. Housing may become undesirable due to the deterioration of existing structures and neighborhoods. Alternatively, housing may become unavailable due to gentrification of a neighborhood—an escalating market that effectively raises the costs of land and homes out of the price range of prospective and existing residents.

AHC is considering acquiring a largely abandoned 6–square-block tract of land in a depressed inner city neighborhood. Many of the buildings have been vacant for a number of years and many of the landowners have defaulted on their property taxes. Hence the city can acquire title to most of the land easily and would undoubtedly be willing to sell the land at a reasonable price to anyone willing to redevelop it. AHC would purchase the area and either rehabilitate the existing structures or construct new homes and apartments. AHC would also build a park and community center that would be open to all neighborhood residents. AHC would be eligible for government, community, and foundation support to assist in renovating the structures and constructing new facilities. AHC has numerous contributors who would volunteer their time, energy, and resources to the effort.

AHC would strive to achieve its goals by establishing a community land association (CLA) to govern the neighborhood. The CLA would have four main components:

(1) *Initial Sale*: AHC would sell the new dwellings for the cost of construction plus land acquisition. (In view of the many subsidies—financial and in kind—it is expected that the units would sell for 30—40% below the cost of comparable dwellings on the open

market.) Prospective residents would be screened by the Residency Committee of the CLA (which is described below) to ensure that their income fell within the income range target sought by AHC. AHC would provide below-market financing to new residents to the extent its resources permitted and participating lenders cooperated.

(2) *Neighborhood Responsibilities*: Each homeowner would agree to donate 2% of their gross household income to support the neighborhood association and activities. In addition, each household would agree to donate 100 hours per year of work to non-governance activities and projects designated by the CLA. (Households could be relieved of this responsibility by donating an extra $5 per hour for each hour missed to the CLA.) Such activities would include, but not be limited to, maintenance of common areas, participation in a neighborhood security patrol, assistance in repairing structures, and maintenance of the CLA community center. Furthermore, each homeowner would agree to obtain the approval of the Renovation Committee before making any significant modifications to their dwelling. Each homeowner would agree to sell his or her dwelling if any resident of the household were convicted of a drug trafficking offense in the CLA vicinity.

(3) *CLA Governance Structure*: The CLA would be governed by democratic principles. Each dwelling unit would have one vote in the CLA governance structure. In addition, AHC would possess 25% of the votes in any decision and upon each committee. Various committees would be established to oversee neighborhood issues (management, security, renovation, maintenance, residency, and social programs). The Residency Committee would apply a means test to ensure that new residents fall within the low- to moderate-income range that AHC seeks to maintain in the community.

(4) *Resale Provisions*: Each homeowner would agree to sell his/her home to other low or moderate income persons at the price he/she paid (plus the cost of any improvements to the land/structures and inflation, less depreciation). The Residency Committee would review the proposed sale price to ensure compliance with these criteria and would also screen prospective purchasers to ensure that prospective purchasers satisfy the low/moderate income standard. The only exception to changes in ownership through the Residency Committee process is upon an owner's death, whereupon the interest could pass through will or intestacy to the owner's spouse, children, or member(s) of the household who resided with the owner for at least one year prior to the owner's death.

AHC would like you to analyze its redevelopment plan and the proposed CLA plan as a means to achieve its goals. Please divide your analysis into the following parts:

I. Analyze any legal impediments to the AHC redevelopment plan and proposed CLA. How would these problems be resolved in court?

II.   Analyze whether the proposed redevelopment plan and CLA would achieve AHC's objectives over the long term. What problems do you foresee over time? How might such problems be addressed in the governance structure or the terms of the CLA?

III.   Do CICs hold much promise as a means to help address inner city housing and poverty problems?

———————

CHAPTER V

POLITICAL INSTITUTIONS

In the preceding chapters we described and analyzed three sets of institutions governing the allocation of resources. Background legal rules, as set forth in common law rules and statutes and administered by the courts, are the set of default rules that govern in the absence of superseding private agreements, shared social understandings, or government regulations. Social norms augment and sometimes trump the background legal rules by providing what is often a less formal, community-derived and administered system to allocate resources and resolve disputes. Markets are a third governance system, in which individuals bargain to achieve a preferred allocation of rights and responsibilities. These bargains, subject to a variety of legal constraints, may alter or supplant the background rules to better serve the interests of the contracting parties. This chapter explores the fourth major institutional structure governing the allocation of resources in society—political institutions—particularly in the context of municipal regulation of property rights in land.

A. THEORIES OF LOCAL POLITICS

There are, broadly speaking, two competing normative theories of democratic governance—pluralism and republicanism—each of which has distinctive implications for municipal land use regulation. In addition, both pluralism and republicanism must contend with the insights of economic theory—in particular public choice theory and the Tiebout Hypothesis—regarding the operation of political institutions.

Pluralism. Pluralism, which is the predominant strain of American political thought, focuses on individual interests. Professor Cass Sunstein has written:

> Under the pluralist view, politics mediates the struggle among self-interested groups for scarce social resources. Only nominally deliberative, politics is a process of conflict and compromise among various social interests. Under the pluralist conception, people come to the political process with preselected interests that they seek to promote through political conflict and compromise. Preferences are not shaped through governance, but enter into the process as exogenous variables.

> * * * The common good consists of uninhibited bargaining among the various participants, so that numbers and intensities of preferences can be reflected in political outcomes. The common

good amounts to an aggregation of individual preferences. Moreover, the efforts to alter or shape preferences—through, for example, * * * education * * *—may assume the status of tyranny.

Sunstein, Interest Groups in American Public Law, 38 Stan. L. Rev. 29, 32–
33 (1985). *See also* R. Dahl, A Preface to Democratic Theory (1956). Thus,
pluralists do not expect government officials to deliberate collectively to
identify the public good. Rather, pluralists view politics as a marketplace in
which legislators advance the goals of their constituents; legislators bargain, trade votes, form coalitions, and compromise with each other to
achieve their constituents' purposes.

One serious problem implied by the pluralist conception of politics is
that a faction may dominate political decisions at the expense of smaller or
less well organized groups. In Federalist No. 10, James Madison argued
that a large republic would be less prone to factions, in part because of the
large number of people and issues, and that a small republic would be more
vulnerable to factions.

The smaller the society, the fewer probably will be the distinct
parties and interests composing it; the fewer probably will be the
distinct parties and interests, the more frequently will a majority
be found of the same party; and the smaller the number of
individuals composing a majority, and the smaller the compass
within which they are placed, the more easily will they concert and
execute their plans of oppression.

The Federalist, No. 10, at 83 (C. Rossiter ed. 1961).

Although he was referring to the dangers of factions in states (in
contrast to the national government), Madison's argument applies with
greater force to municipalities, where the limited number of citizens and
issues (especially in relatively homogeneous communities) and the structure of local government reduce the opportunities for coalitions and bargaining that ameliorate the dangers of faction. *See* R. Dahl & E. Tufte,
Size and Democracy 89–109 (1973).

For example, in many municipalities, especially suburbs, the regulation
of land use is of central concern to residents and the local government. In
such towns the majority of homeowners, concerned about the adverse
consequences of development (*e.g.*, congestion, noise, increased property
taxes), may act in concert politically to use the legal system (*i.e.*, zoning) to
prevent or heavily burden development at the expense of both the minority
of landowners who want to develop their land and future residents who
have no voice at all in the local government. *See generally* Briffault, Our
Localism, Part II—Localism and Legal Theory, 90 Colum. L. Rev. 360
(1990). The problems of factions in municipalities are exacerbated because
most municipalities (in contrast to the state and federal governments) are
unicameral and many of them do not make a clear distinction between
executive and legislative branches. That is, municipal political institutions
are not structured to minimize the probability of a single faction controlling the local government. W.A. Fischel, Regulatory Takings: Law, Econom-

ics, and Politics 277–78 (1995); Levmore, Bicameralism: When Are Two Decisions Better Than One?, 12 Int. Rev. L. & Econ. 145 (1992).

One limitation on factions is judicial review. Judicially enforced constitutional rights for individuals impose substantive and procedural limits on the authority of the legislative and executive branches. *See generally* J. Choper, Judicial Review and the National Political Process 64–70 (1980) (the basic function of judicial review is to prevent constitutional violations that popular majorities would support); Sunstein, Interest Groups in American Public Law, 38 Stan. L. Rev. 29, 49–55 (1985). As we will see later in this chapter, federal and state courts have imposed some constitutional limits on municipal land use authority. Those limits, however, are mostly at the margins and generally do not effectively deal with concerns that municipalities do not take into account the effects of their decisions on non-residents. More significantly, at least in the land-use context, state courts review municipal land use decisions for their reasonableness. This type of judicial review, which has its roots in administrative law rather than constitutional law,[1] seeks to ensure that the municipality has an adequate factual basis for its decision and that it has followed the statutory procedures and criteria in reaching its decision.

The Madisonian critique of small governments does not wholly undermine the argument for municipal land use authority. The existence of numerous municipalities in a metropolitan area permits residents to move, and the very smallness of municipalities that gives rise to the dangers of factions also permits individuals a more direct voice in municipal affairs. A.O. Hirschman, Exit, Voice, and Loyalty (1970); Rose, Planning and Dealing: Piecemeal Land Controls as a Problem of Local Legitimacy, 71 Cal. L. Rev. 837, 882–87 (1983); Gillette, Plebiscites, Participation, and Collective Action in Local Government Law, 86 Mich. L. Rev. 930, 944–45 (1988). Moreover, there are substantial opportunities to change municipal boundaries through annexation, incorporation, and sometimes secession. Briffault, The Local Government Boundary Problem in Metropolitan Areas, 48 Stan. L. Rev. 1115 (1996).

Republicanism. Republicanism rejects the view that individuals are wholly autonomous and that the public interest is just the aggregation of individual preferences. "[C]ommunity describes not just what they *have* as fellow citizens but also what they *are*, not a relationship they choose (as in a voluntary association) but an attachment they discover, not merely an attribute but a constituent of their identity." M. Sandel, Liberalism and the Limits of Justice 150 (1982).

Modern reconstructions of republicanism stress civic virtue. For modern republicans, political life is more than the use of govern-

---

1. To put the matter in perspective, while a federal court could overturn an administrative agency decision that the court found "unreasonable," *see* 5 U.S.C. § 706, it could not overturn an act of Congress that the court deemed unreasonable, absent a determination that the legislature's unreasonableness rose to the level of a constitutional violation. Thus, to some extent, state courts treat municipalities analogously to administrative agencies rather than independent, sovereign bodies of government.

ment to further the ends of private life, as it is in liberalism. Rather, politics is a distinct and in some respects superior sphere. By participating in public life, citizens rise above their merely private interests and enter a public-spirited dialogue about the common good. Once found, the public interest disciplines their private pursuits. Indeed, one of the more important tasks of government is to make the citizenry more virtuous by changing individual preferences.

* * * In republican thought, private preferences are secondary; they are if anything the products of government action rather than its inputs. * * * Rather than mechanically processing preferences, government involves an intellectual search for the morally correct answer.

D.A. Farber & P.P. Frickey, Law and Public Choice: A Critical Introduction 43–44 (1991).

Republicans reject interest group politics in favor of discussion and negotiation. Professor William Simon, for example, emphasizes the importance of collective decisionmaking.

The critique of the private sphere expresses * * * a commitment to public collective decisionmaking over private individual decisionmaking. It tends to see public collective decisionmaking as an expression of virtue and solidarity and hence both intrinsically more satisfying and conducive to better decisions. It tends to see private individual decisionmaking as an expression of corruption and alienation. Although the relations between institutions and attitudes are complex and often obscure, there is one straightforward sense in which collective public decisionmaking is associated with civic virtue and solidarity: it compels the participants to address each other in terms that appeal to common interests.

Simon, Social-Republican Property, 38 UCLA L. Rev. 1335, 1340 (1991). Professor Sunstein focuses on the deliberative aspect of decisionmaking:

The republican conception carries with it a particular view of human nature; it assumes that through discussion people can, in their capacities as citizens, escape private interests and engage in pursuit of the public good. In this respect, political ordering is distinct from market ordering. Moreover, this conception reflects a belief that debate and discussion help to reveal that some values are superior to others. Denying that decisions about values are merely matters of taste, the republican view assumes that "practical reason" can be used to settle social issues.

Sunstein, Interest Groups in American Public Law, 38 Stan. L. Rev. 29, 31–32 (1985). Republicans thus believe that individual political participation not only enhances and enriches individuals' lives but also leads to greater collective discussion, deliberation, and decisionmaking. Frug, Empowering Cities in a Federal System, 19 Urb. Law. 553, 559 (1987) (improved collective deliberation); Frug, The City As a Legal Concept, 93 Harv. L. Rev. 1057, 1068–69, 1071 (1980) (greater personal empowerment).

Not surprisingly, much of the republican focus is on municipal governments, which of all levels of government affords the best opportunity for collective discussion, deliberation, and decisionmaking. Many municipalities have relatively few residents, thereby allowing the possibility of personal participation and interaction, and the residents are more likely to be informed about local issues, to have common interests and values, and to put aside individual interests in favor of the common good. *See generally* Frug, The City As a Legal Concept, 93 Harv. L. Rev. 1057, 1068–73 (1980) (participation in municipal affairs allows individuals to control their own lives and creates a sense of "common venture"); Gillette, Plebiscites, Participation, and Collective Action in Local Government Law, 86 Mich. L. Rev. 930, 964–68, 984–85 (1988) (the small size of the body politic permits repeated interactions and greater commitment to the common good); S.L. Elkin, City and Regime in the American Republic 146–88 (1987) (increasing local authority will enhance individual political participation); J.J. Mansbridge, Beyond Adversary Democracy 270–89 (1983) (municipalities offer a greater possibility of "face-to-face" interactions and of making a commitment to the common good). Municipalities also mediate between individuals and more centralized levels of government.

Some republicans also champion direct democracy—neighborhood meetings, town meetings, referenda, and ballot initiatives—because it may offer some opportunity for direct public dialogue and participation in politics.

> Where municipal residents propose to express themselves on matters of wide-ranging concern that generate neither substantial adverse spillovers nor potential havoc with budgetary or other polycentric issues, * * * there seems little merit to the claim that plebiscites are inappropriate. To the contrary, they may not only provide expressions of public interest as more powerful than what emerges from representative processes, they may also stimulate the conversation and conduct that underlie arguments for more active forms of participation. * * * The more we believe that citizens are motivated by disinterested public spirit, the more we might be willing to delegate decisionmaking to them. The more we believe that such public spiritedness would be fostered by systematically conferring on citizens the responsibility for collective concerns, the more local plebiscites appear to be appropriate mechanisms for encouraging deliberation and overcoming tendencies towards expropriation and obstacles to cooperation.

Gillette, Plebiscites, Participation, and Collective Action in Local Government Law, 86 Mich. L. Rev. 930, 986–87 (1988). *See also* S.L. Elkin, City and Regime in the American Republic 171–74 (1987) (advocating "neighborhood assemblies with significant powers, citywide referenda, and city legislatures, also with significant powers * * * in an attempt to place citizens in a deliberative relationship"); J.J. Mansbridge, Beyond Adversary

Democracy (1983) (a study of town-meeting democracy, arguing that repeated, face-to-face interactions give participants an opportunity to find the common good).

Republicanism, however, may create conditions that allow mistreatment of persons inside as well as outside the community. Some scholars, for example, have argued that the republican vision of governmental decision-making, with its emphasis on consensus and conflict suppression, can be repressive for some of the community's members, especially those who dissent from the collective determination of the "morally correct answer" or of the common good. *See, e.g.*, Gutmann, Communitarian Critics of Liberalism, 14 Phil. & Pub. Aff. 308, 319 (1985). The price of community-wide conformity may be suppression of individualism and difference.

Moreover, the republican vision may inherently foster exclusion. "Historically, the republican commitment to intrapolitical equality has often been accompanied by an exclusiveness that leads to relatively great toleration of extrapolitical inequality." Simon, Social-Republican Property, 38 UCLA L. Rev. 1335, 1404 (1991). In effect, the creation of a cohesive community may require exclusion of people unlikely to subscribe to the community's values or to its commitment to republican decisionmaking. *See also* Briffault, Our Localism: Part II—Localism and Legal Theory, 90 Colum. L. Rev. 346 (1990) (arguing that the republican argument in favor of greater municipal power would produce even greater parochialism in suburbs at the expense of relatively powerless, excluded communities). *But see* Frug, The Geography of Community, 48 Stan. L. Rev. 1047, 1106–07 (1996) (arguing that it may be possible to engage in communitarian negotiation among municipalities to change the rules for zoning, development, taxation, and allocation of tax revenues, and thereby overcome the problems caused by political fragmentation, such as exclusionary zoning, without resort to centralized government).

Public Choice Theory. Public choice theory has challenged the Madisonian vision of representative government as a rational process yielding public-regarding legislation. *See generally* M. Hayes, Lobbyists and Legislators (1981); R. McCormick & R. Tollison, Politicians, Legislation and the Economy (1981); J.Q. Wilson, Political Organizations (1973); Salisbury, An Exchange Theory of Interest Groups, 13 Midwest J. Pol. Sci. 1 (1969); J. Buchanan & G. Tullock, The Calculus of Consent (1962).

> Public choice theorists typically treat legislation as an economic transaction in which interest groups form the demand side, and legislators form the supply side. On the whole, this branch of public choice theory demonstrates that the market for legislation is a badly functioning one. That is, the market systematically yields too few laws that provide "public goods" (*i.e.*, laws that contribute to the overall efficiency of society by providing a collective benefit that would probably not arise from individuals acting separately). And it systematically yields too many laws that are "rent-seeking" (*i.e.*, laws that distribute resources to a designated group without contribution to society's overall efficiency).

The demand for legislation is determined by the incidence and activity of interest groups. The optimistic pluralists believed that interest groups would form in response to true disturbances in the social environment and, hence, normally would press legitimate grievances and would bring a variety of socioeconomic perspectives into the subsequent political debates. Public choice theory suggests, however, that interest groups form more selectively and, therefore, that the demand for legislation is highly biased.

Professor Mancur Olson's "logic of collective action"[2] helps to explain why interest groups form so selectively. He argues that interest group formation involves a classic "free rider problem." Legislation is a "nonexcludable" public good that will benefit all members of the affected group even if they do not contribute to its enactment. Because group members will have incentives to free ride (*i.e.*, collect the benefit without contributing to the effort), not enough members will contribute, and the public good will not be provided. The free rider problem is most acute for large groups in which individual stakes will usually be very small, for there the tendency to rely on others to carry the ball will be quite substantial. The problem is less acute for small groups, especially where the potential gain for each beneficiary is larger, because in those groups there is more opportunity for the members to work out a collective deal, and free riders can more easily be monitored and perhaps excluded from the law's benefits. This is more likely if the small group enjoys consensus about its goals, for consensus substantially reduces the transaction costs of group formation.

The free rider problem means that social and economic difficulties will not always stimulate group formation, especially for large, diffuse groups like consumers and taxpayers, and that (in contrast) small, elite groups might more easily organize, though for no other reason than to raid the public fisc. * * *

* * * Under Olson's theory, one would expect [legislation that produces] concentrated benefits and, especially concentrated costs to stimulate more interest group formation, because the smaller and more focused groups will normally be better able to surmount the free rider problem. Conversely, [legislation that has] distributed costs or benefits will presumably not tend to produce as much organizational activity. * * *

The supply of legislation depends on the responses of legislators to these demand patterns. Optimistic pluralists paid little attention to the incentive structures of elected representatives and generally just assumed that the representatives' policy choices represented some kind of amalgam of constituency preferences and

2. Mancur Olson, The Logic of Collective Action: Public Goods and the Theory of   Groups (1965).

reasonable judgment. Public choice theorists, however, suggest that representatives' supply of legislation is driven by a desire to avoid controversy [so as to maximize the likelihood of being reelected] and, hence, is skewed toward nondecision and rent-seeking. * * *

One can predict what sort of legislative output is likely * * * based on the incidence of costs and benefits. Legislation—whether symbolic or substantive—is unlikely where there is little organized demand (distributed benefits), or where demand is met by strong opposition (because of concentrated costs). * * * In situations of consensual demand patterns (primarily concentrated benefit, distributed cost measures), legislators will tend to distribute benefits to organized groups, or to grant those groups self-regulatory authority. In conflictual demand situations (concentrated cost measures), legislators will often seek to delegate regulation of the group to an agency. If the legislation distributed benefits at the expense of a concentrated group, the cost payers will tend, over time, to organize themselves effectively to influence the agency. This phenomenon, together with natural bureaucratic forces, results in what is often "agency capture," [whereby the agency becomes beholden to the interests most directly and strongly affected by the regulatory program it administers].

Eskridge, Politics Without Romance: Implications of Public Choice Theory for Statutory Interpretation, 74 Va. L. Rev. 275, 285–88 (1988).

Tiebout Hypothesis. Charles Tiebout offered a more optimistic view of the efficacy of local government based upon the efficiency-enhancing effects of interjurisdictional competition and voter mobility. Tiebout, A Pure Theory of Local Expenditures, 64 J. Pol. Econ. 416 (1956). In Tiebout's model, local jurisdictions compete—through their provision of public services (*e.g.*, schools, police), amenities, zoning restrictions, and tax rates—with each other to attract citizens. This interjurisdictional competition tends to produce a broad range of local communities catering to the diverse preferences of a heterogeneous society. Individuals "vote with their feet" by selecting to live in those communities most congenial to their preferences. Communities that fail to provide desired policies shrink while those satisfying the demands of citizens grow. Under a rather strong set of assumptions—(1) a limitless supply of jurisdictions; (2) costless mobility of individuals; (3) full information about the attributes of jurisdictions; and (4) no interjurisdictional externalities—Tiebout showed that competition among local jurisdictions will lead to an optimal allocation of locally produced public goods and policies.

Whether or not the strong form of the Tiebout Hypothesis obtains fully in the real world (which it almost surely does not), the underlying dynamics of the Tiebout model—some degree of citizen mobility and interjurisdictional competition—have important implications for the operation of local politics. There is no question that these forces shape the demographic, social, and political composition of communities and the policies pursued and the "deals" made by local governments to attract and maintain a strong tax base, create jobs, and foster a desirable living environment. Local governments aspire to attract development projects that enhance the welfare of their citizens and attract other citizens who complement the social milieu. *See generally* P.E. Peterson, The Price of Federalism (1995); R. Bish, & V. Ostrom, Understanding Urban Government 53 (1973) (describing how municipalities alter their tax rates and other policies in response to consumer demand). On the other hand, the very mobility of citizens may undermine the possibility of republican decisionmaking and the plausibility of the republican argument for enhanced municipal authority. *See* Briffault, Our Localism: Part II—Localism and Legal Theory, 90 Colum. L. Rev. 346, 404–15 (1990). Citizens who vote with their feet act in narrowly self-interested ways; enhanced municipal authority, allowing greater differentiation among municipal services and policies, may encourage more self-interested behavior.

As you study the materials in this Chapter, keep in mind the pluralist and republican visions of politics as well as the insights of economic theory. Ask yourself which model is most appropriate in particular contexts. Try to form your own normative judgments about the role(s) of political institutions in governing resources, the ways in which political institutions can be made more responsive to social needs, and the relative effectiveness of political institutions among the range of institutions for governing resources.

B.   LEGAL AND POLITICAL INSTITUTIONS REGULATING LAND USE

1.   LEGAL AUTHORITY FOR LAND USE REGULATION

Under the conventional view of municipal formation, municipalities are creatures of the state and thus can exercise only the regulatory authority expressly granted by the state legislature. *See, e.g., City of Worcester v. Worcester Consolidated Street Railway Co.*, 196 U.S. 539, 549, 25 S.Ct. 327, 330, 49 L.Ed. 591 (1905) (describing a city as a "creature of the State" whose powers are subject to state control); J. Dillon, Municipal Corporations 448–55 (5th ed. 1911) (describing "Dillon's Rule"—that municipalities may exercise only the authority expressly granted by the state legislature). Some scholars maintain that municipalities continue to be relatively impotent in the face of state authority. *See* Frug, The City As a Legal Concept, 93 Harv. L. Rev. 1057 (1980); Frug, Empowering Cities in a Federal System, 19 Urban Law. 553 (1987); *see also* G.L. Clark, Judges and the Cities: Interpreting Local Autonomy 60–81 (1985) (describing models of municipal autonomy involving the power to initiate governmental action and immunity from central government review). Professor Frug, in particular, has argued that municipal powerlessness grows not only out of Dillon's Rule, but also from the limited scope of home rule provisions, cities' constrained ability to generate revenues and borrow money, federal constitutional limits on municipal discretion, and conditions on federal and state grants-in-aid. Frug, The City As a Legal Concept, *supra*, 93 Harv. L. Rev. at 1062–67, 1109–17.

Other scholars, however, maintain that municipalities have substantial regulatory authority, especially over land use. Professor Richard Briffault points out that many states have abandoned Dillon's Rule. More importantly, legislative and constitutional "home rule" provisions, adopted in more than 40 states, afford "charter cities" and in some cases all municipalities broad spending and regulatory authority, effectively reversing Dillon's Rule. Briffault, Our Localism: Part I—The Structure of Local Government Law, 90 Colum. L. Rev. 1, 10 (1990). *See generally* D.R. Mandelker, Land Use Law, 121–24 (3d ed. 1993); R.M. Anderson, American Law of Zoning, 49–58 (3d ed. 1986); D. Netsch, P. Salsich & J. Wegner, State and Local Government in a Federal System 110–43 (3d ed. 1990). As Briffault asserts, "Localism as a value is deeply embedded in the American legal and political culture." Briffault, Our Localism: Part I, *supra*, at 10. Although states have the power to override municipal authority, such as municipal land use authority, they rarely do so unless there is some broadly felt state-wide interest, such as environmental protection.

We need not resolve the broader dimensions of this debate here, as it is generally acknowledged that municipalities have substantial discretion over land use regulation. The basis for most municipal land use regulatory authority is the zoning enabling act, which every state has adopted in one form or another. The enabling act authorizes municipalities to adopt and enforce zoning ordinances that segregate land uses. In addition, statutory and constitutional home rule provisions in many states are an independent source of municipal land use authority.

Given the breadth of municipal land use authority under home rule provisions, a key legal issue is whether and to what extent state statutes preempt local land use decisions or ordinances. For example, under some state constitutions, charter cities may exercise their land use powers independently of any state statute, including the state zoning enabling act. In *Thompson v. Cook County Zoning Board of Appeals*, 96 Ill.App.3d 561, 568–69, 51 Ill.Dec. 777, 783–84, 421 N.E.2d 285, 292 (1981), the court held that Cook County, a "home rule" local government, is bound by its own rezoning procedures and not those specified in the state enabling act. "A home-rule unit has the power to enact whatever zoning ordinance it chooses as long as the legislative enactment comports with constitutional requirements." *See also State ex rel. Davis Investment Co. v. City of Columbus*, 175 Ohio St. 337, 341, 194 N.E.2d 859, 862 (1963) (in the course of upholding a zoning ordinance, the court held that a charter city is governed by the terms of the charter, and "statutory provisions relating to subjects covered by the charter are inapplicable").

In some states, state laws may preempt charter provisions, but only if the legislative intent to preempt is clear. *See, e.g., Nelson v. City of Seattle*, 64 Wash.2d 862, 866–67, 395 P.2d 82, 84 (1964) (upholding rezoning even though it did not comply with state procedures; state statutes do not preempt zoning power of first-class cities unless the legislative intent to preempt is "clear and unambiguous"). In other states, municipal land use decisions are preempted if they are simply inconsistent with state statutes. In *Los Angeles v. State of California*, 138 Cal.App.3d 526, 532–33, 187 Cal.Rptr. 893, 896–97 (1982), the court upheld a state statute requiring a charter city to make its zoning scheme consistent with its general plan. "General law prevails over local enactments of a chartered city, even in regard to matters which would otherwise be deemed strictly municipal affairs, where the subject of the general law is of statewide concern."

A few state courts have held that the zoning power is not included in home rule grants. *See, e.g., City of Livonia v. Department of Social Services*, 423 Mich. 466, 493–94, 378 N.W.2d 402, 415 (1985) (a charter city may not alter state-mandated zoning requirements for adult foster care homes; a municipality's zoning power does not derive from home rule provisions but from the state zoning enabling act).

2.   MECHANISMS FOR LAND USE REGULATION

Local governments use four basic mechanisms to regulate land use. First and foremost, they adopt and enforce "zoning ordinances" to impose limits on the size and location of structures, the size and shape of lots, and the use of land and structures. As we will see in more detail below, zoning ordinances may be amended and are subject to "variances" and "conditional use permits." The adoption and adjustment of zoning ordinances are at the core of municipal land use regulation.

Second, local planning commissions develop and use "general plans" to specify the jurisdiction's goals for future development, including distribution of population density and infrastructure. General plans exemplify a form of technocratic rationality that is under constant stress both from the practical limits of knowledge and rationality in a staggeringly complex area like municipal land use and from the rough and tumble of land use politics.

Third, local officials adopt "subdivision controls" for residential developments, especially single-family developments. Subdivision requirements establish specific criteria for the location and design of streets, major utility lines, and other public infrastructure, and they frequently require dedications of land or payments for off-site improvements, such as roads, parks, or even schools. In some states, subdivision controls may also prohibit subdivision (and thus development) of environmentally vulnerable lands, such as wetlands. For example, a California statute requires denial of subdivision approval if "design of the subdivision or the proposed improvements are likely to cause substantial environmental damage or substantially and avoidably injure fish or wildlife or their habitat." Cal. Gov't Code § 66474(e). *See also* Mont. Code Ann. § 76–3–608(3)(a) (requiring governing body to review subdivision proposals for "the effect on agriculture, local services, the natural environment, wildlife and wildlife habitat, and public health and safety'').

Fourth, ''building codes'' dictate building materials, structural elements, minimum habitability standards and in some cases aesthetic elements of new buildings. Building codes may also restrict the owner's right to change designated historic buildings.

3.   DISTRIBUTION OF MUNICIPAL REGULATORY AUTHORITY

Municipalities often employ four different entities, one elected and three appointed, to adopt and implement land use regulations. The local elected legislature (*e.g.*, city council, board of supervisors, or town committee) has authority to adopt and make significant amendments to the zoning ordinance. The appointed planning commission, which frequently has a staff of professional planners, usually has responsibility to prepare general plans and plan amendments, to conduct hearings and make recommendations on zoning amendments, and to process applications for ''conditional use permits.'' The building department has authority to review and grant or deny building permits, and the board of zoning appeals rules on applications for ''variances'' and appeals from building department decisions. In smaller jurisdictions, the functions of these agencies often are combined. *See generally* R.M. Anderson, American Law of Zoning §§ 4.10, 4.17–4.24, 17.02–17.28 (3d ed. 1986).

C.   EUCLIDEAN ZONING: CONSTRAINED DISCRETION

Zoning in the United States is commonly thought to have begun with the enactment of New York City's comprehensive zoning ordinance in 1916.[3] By the early 1900s, the consequences of industrialization rapidly changed the character of New York City, especially lower Manhattan. A coalition of business people and city planners, brought together out of concern that the city was being consumed by industrial development, sought to establish new municipal land use regulations. Apparently inspired by the 1891 ordinance of Frankfurt-on-the-Main, Germany, which divided the city into different districts for different uses, *see* Logan, The Americanization of German Zoning, 42 J. Am. Inst. Planners 377 (1976), the city adopted a zoning ordinance that created three types of districts to

3. Los Angeles had enacted a comprehensive zoning ordinance in 1909, but the better known New York ordinance precipitated the national interest in comprehensive zoning.

There were earlier municipal ordinances regulating building height and locations, which courts often upheld, but these ordinances were designed for a single purpose, such a segregating a particular noxious use

from residential neighborhoods. *See, e.g., In re Hang Kie*, 69 Cal. 149, 152, 10 P. 327, 328–29 (1886) (upholding an ordinance barring laundries in residential neighborhoods); *Shea v. City of Muncie*, 148 Ind. 14, 46 N.E. 138 (1897) (upholding an ordinance barring taverns from residential neighborhoods); *Cronin v. People*, 82 N.Y. 318 (1880) (upholding an ordinance barring slaughter houses from residential neighborhoods).

separate factories from commercial districts and to limit the spread of skyscrapers. *See generally* S.I. Toll, Zoned American 143–87 (1969).

Evidently influenced by the New York ordinance, the U.S. Department of Commerce published a model Standard State Zoning Enabling Act in 1922. Under this influential and widely adopted model act, municipalities could regulate land use to "promot[e] health, safety, morals, or the general welfare of the community." Standard State Zoning Enabling Act § 1 (1926). Enumerated municipal land use powers included authority to restrict the height and number of stories of structures, population density, and the location and use of buildings. Most importantly, the Act barred municipalities from exercising their land use authority through case-by-case decision making. Rather, it required municipalities to adopt land use regulations and establish districts, into which different classes of uses would be segregated. "All such regulations shall be uniform for each class or kind of building throughout each district, but the regulations in one district may differ from those in other districts." Standard State Zoning Enabling Act § 2 (1926). Through mandatory separation—not the play of market forces—each class of land use would be protected from the externalities created by other types of uses.

Zoning caught on quickly. By 1925, 500 cities had zoning ordinances, and by 1930, 35 states had adopted zoning enabling acts. Today every major city except Houston, and 97% of the municipalities with a population over 5000 have zoning laws, and even in Houston voters only narrowly defeated a ballot proposal to adopt zoning. Dyer, Zoning Defeated by Narrow Margin, Houston Chron., Nov. 3, 1993, at A1. *See also* Developments in the Law—Zoning, 91 Harv. L. Rev. 1427, 1434–35 (1978).

As municipalities began to adopt comprehensive zoning ordinances in the 1920s, landowners whose development plans were threatened or derailed challenged the constitutionality of such laws. A few state courts read the municipalities' police powers narrowly; provisions that barred particular uses (*e.g.*, retail stores) in residential districts violated due process unless there was a demonstrated threat to public welfare, safety, or health. *See, e.g., Ignaciunas v. Risley*, 98 N.J.L. 712, 719, 121 A. 783, 786 (1923) (holding invalid an ordinance barring commercial buildings in residential districts because the proposed store posed no threat to the public welfare, safety, or health); *City of St. Louis v. Evraiff*, 301 Mo. 231, 250, 256 S.W. 489, 495 (1923) (striking down an ordinance that proscribed use of property for a junk yard because it did not pose a threat to public health, safety, or morals). Accurately anticipating later doctrinal developments, these opinions declared that a broader reading of the police powers would permit regulation of aesthetics. A somewhat larger number of state courts, however, upheld zoning ordinances as constitutional. Then, in 1926, a case from Euclid, Ohio reached the U.S. Supreme Court. The case, *Village of Euclid v. Ambler Realty Co.*, 272 U.S. 365, 47 S.Ct. 114, 71 L.Ed. 303 (1926), was a due process challenge to Euclid's zoning law, whose very enactment, the landowner claimed, had reduced his property values by 75%.

Euclid framed the sharp conflict between private ownership and public authority to regulate land. Counsel for the village argued that municipal police powers were broad and that unless a regulation was manifestly unreasonable, a court should not substitute its judgment about the wisdom of the regulation for that of the legislature. *Id.* at 367–68, 47 S.Ct. at 115.

Counsel for the landowner maintained that the police power extended only to the regulation of nuisances, and that "courts consistently decline to permit an extension of the police power to uses of property involving mere questions of taste or preference or financial advantage of others." *Id.* at 376, 47 S.Ct. at 79.

> Even if the world could agree by unanimous consent upon what is beautiful and desirable, it could not, under our constitutional theory, enforce its decision by prohibiting a land owner, who refuses to accept the world's view of beauty, from making otherwise safe and innocent uses of his land. * * * The world has not reached a unanimous judgment about beauty, and there are few unlikelier places to look for stable judgments on such subjects than in the changing discretion of legislative bodies, moved this way and that by the conflict of commercial interests on the one hand and the assorted opinions of individuals, moved by purely private concerns, on the other.

Id.

Village of Euclid v. Ambler Realty Co.

Supreme Court of the United States, 1926.
272 U.S. 365, 47 S.Ct. 114, 71 L.Ed. 303.

■ MR. JUSTICE SUTHERLAND delivered the opinion of the Court.

The Village of Euclid is an Ohio municipal corporation. It adjoins and practically is a suburb of the city of Cleveland. Its estimated population is between 5,000 and 10,000, and its area from 12 to 14 square miles, the greater part of which is farm lands or unimproved acreage. It lies, roughly, in the form of a parallelogram measuring approximately 3 ½ miles each way. East and west it is traversed by three principal highways: Euclid avenue, through the southerly border, St. Clair avenue, through the central portion, and Lake Shore boulevard, through the northerly border, in close proximity to the shore of Lake Erie. The Nickel Plate Railroad lies from 1,500 to 1,800 feet north of Euclid avenue, and the Lake Shore Railroad 1,600 feet farther to the north. The three highways and the two railroads are substantially parallel.

Appellee is the owner of a tract of land containing 68 acres, situated in the westerly end of the village, abutting on Euclid avenue to the south and the Nickel Plate Railroad to the north. Adjoining this tract, both on the east and on the west, there have been laid out restricted residential plats upon which residences have been erected.

On November 13, 1922, an ordinance was adopted by the village council, establishing a comprehensive zoning plan for regulating and restricting the location of trades, industries, apartment houses, two-family houses, single family houses, etc., the lot area to be built upon, the size and height of buildings, etc.

The entire area of the village is divided by the ordinance into six classes of use districts, denominated U–1 to U–6, inclusive; three classes of height districts, denominated H–1 to H–3, inclusive; and four classes of area districts, denominated A–1 to A–4, inclusive. The use districts are classified in respect of the buildings which may be erected within their respective limits, as follows: U–1 is restricted to single family dwellings, public parks, water towers and reservoirs, suburban and interurban electric railway passenger stations and rights of way, and farming, non-commercial greenhouse nurseries, and truck gardening; U–2 is extended to include two-family dwellings; U–3 is further extended to include apartment houses, hotels, churches, schools, public libraries, museums, private clubs, community center buildings, hospitals, sanitariums, public playgrounds, and recreation buildings, and a city hall and courthouse; U–4 is further extended to include banks, offices, studios, telephone exchanges, fire and police stations, restaurants, theaters and moving picture shows, retail stores and shops, sales offices, sample rooms, wholesale stores for hardware, drugs, and groceries, stations for gasoline and oil (not exceeding 1,000 gallons storage) and for ice delivery, skating rinks and dance halls, electric substations, job and newspaper printing, public garages for motor vehicles, stables and wagon sheds (not exceeding five horses, wagons or motor trucks), and distributing stations for central store and commercial enterprises; U–5 is further extended to include billboards and advertising signs (if permitted), warehouses, ice and ice cream manufacturing and cold storage plants, bottling works milk bottling and central distribution stations, laundries, carpet cleaning, dry cleaning, and dyeing establishments, blacksmith, horseshoeing, wagon and motor vehicle repair shops, freight stations, street car barns, stables and wagon sheds (for more than five horses, wagons or motor trucks), and wholesale produce markets and salesrooms; U–6 is further extended to include plants for sewage disposal and for producing gas, garbage and refuse incineration, scrap iron, junk, scrap paper, and rag storage, aviation fields, cemeteries, crematories, penal and correctional institutions, insane and feeble-minded institutions, storage of oil and gasoline (not to exceed 25,000 gallons), and manufacturing and industrial operations of any kind other than, and any public utility not included in, a class U–1, U–2, U–3, U–4, or U–5 use. There is a seventh class of uses which is prohibited altogether.

Class U–1 is the only district in which buildings are restricted to those enumerated. In the other classes the uses are cumulative; that is to say, uses in class U–2 include those enumerated in the preceding class U–1; class U–3 includes uses enumerated in the preceding classes, U–2, and U–1; and so on. In addition to the enumerated uses, the ordinance provides for accessory uses; that is, for uses customarily incident to the principal use, such as private garages. Many regulations are provided in respect of such accessory uses.

* * *

A single family dwelling consists of a basement and not less than three rooms and a bathroom. A two-family dwelling consists of a basement and not less than four living rooms and a bathroom for each family, and is further described as a detached dwelling for the occupation of two families, one having its principal living rooms on the first floor and the other on the second floor.

Appellee's tract of land comes under U–2, U–3 and U–6. The first strip of 620 feet immediately north of Euclid avenue falls in class U–2, the next 130 feet to the north, in U–3, and the remainder in U–6. The uses of the first 620 feet, therefore, do not include apartment houses, hotels, churches, schools, or other public and semipublic buildings, or other uses enumerated in respect of U–3 to U–6, inclusive. The uses of the next 130 feet include all of these, but exclude industries, theaters, banks, shops, and the various other uses set forth in respect of U–4 to U–6, inclusive.[4]

* * *

The lands lying between the two railroads for the entire length of the village area and extending some distance on either side to the north and south, having an average width of about 1,600 feet, are left open, with slight exceptions, for industrial and all other uses. This includes the larger part of appellee's tract. Approximately one-sixth of the area of the entire village is included in U–5 and U–6 use districts. That part of the village lying south of Euclid avenue is principally in U–1 districts. The lands lying north of Euclid avenue and bordering on the long strip just described are included in U–1, U–2, U–3, and U–4 districts, principally in U–2.

* * *

The ordinance is assailed on the grounds that it is in derogation of § 1 of the Fourteenth Amendment to the Federal Constitution in that it deprives appellee of liberty and property without due process of law and denies it the equal protection of the law, and that it offends against certain provisions of the Constitution of the state of Ohio. The prayer of the bill is for an injunction restraining the enforcement of the ordinance and all attempts to impose or maintain as to appellee's property any of the restrictions, limitations or conditions. The court below held the ordinance to be unconstitutional and void, and enjoined its enforcement.

---

4. The court below seemed to think that the frontage of this property on Euclid avenue to a depth of 150 feet came under U–1 district and was available only for single family dwellings. An examination of the ordinance and subsequent amendments, and a comparison of their terms with the maps, shows very clearly, however, that this view was incorrect. Appellee's brief correctly interpreted the ordinance: "The northerly 500 feet thereof immediately adjacent to the right of way of the New York, Chicago & St. Louis Railroad Company under the original ordinance was classed as U–6 territory and the rest thereof as U–2 territory. By amendments to the ordinance a strip 630 feet wide north of Euclid avenue is classed as U–2 territory, a strip 130 feet wide next north as U–3 territory and the rest of the parcel to the Nickel Plate right of way as U–6 territory."

Before proceeding to a consideration of the case, it is necessary to determine the scope of the inquiry. The bill alleges that the tract of land in question is vacant and has been held for years for the purpose of selling and developing it for industrial uses, for which it is especially adapted, being immediately in the path or progressive industrial development; that for such uses it has a market value of about $10,000 per acre, but if the use be limited to residential purposes the market value is not in excess of $2,500 per acre; that the first 200 feet of the parcel back from Euclid avenue, if unrestricted in respect of use, has a value of $150 per front foot, but if limited to residential uses, and ordinary mercantile business be excluded therefrom, its value is not in excess of $50 per front foot.

It is specifically averred that the ordinance attempts to restrict and control the lawful uses of appellee's land, so as to confiscate and destroy a great part of its value; that it is being enforced in accordance with its terms; that prospective buyers of land for industrial, commercial, and residential uses in the metropolitan district of Cleveland are deterred from buying any part of this land because of the existence of the ordinance and the necessity thereby entailed of conducting burdensome and expensive litigation in order to vindicate the right to use the land for lawful and legitimate purposes; that the ordinance constitutes a cloud upon the land, reduces and destroys its value, and has the effect of diverting the normal industrial, commercial, and residential development thereof to other and less favorable locations.

The record goes no farther than to show, as the lower court found, that the normal and reasonably to be expected use and development of that part of appellee's land adjoining Euclid avenue is for general trade and commercial purposes, particularly retail stores and like establishments, and that the normal and reasonably to be expected use and development of the residue of the land is for industrial and trade purposes. Whatever injury is inflicted by the mere existence and threatened enforcement of the ordinance is due to restrictions in respect of these and similar uses, to which perhaps should be added—if not included in the foregoing—restrictions in respect of apartment houses. Specifically there is nothing in the record to suggest that any damage results from the presence in the ordinance of those restrictions relating to churches, schools, libraries, and other public and semipublic buildings. It is neither alleged nor proved that there is or may be a demand for any part of appellee's land for any of the last-named uses, and we cannot assume the existence of facts which would justify an injunction upon this record in respect to this class of restrictions. For present purposes the provisions of the ordinance in respect of these uses may therefore be put aside as unnecessary to be considered. It is also unnecessary to consider the effect of the restrictions in respect of U–1 districts, since none of appellee's land falls within that class.

* * *

Building zone laws are of modern origin. They began in this country about twenty-five years ago. Until recent years, urban life was comparatively simple; but, with the great increase and concentration of population, problems have developed, and constantly are developing, which require, and will continue to require, additional restrictions in respect of the use and occupation of private lands in urban communities. Regulations, the wisdom, necessity, and validity of which, as applied to existing conditions, are so apparent that they are now uniformly sustained, a century ago, or even half a century ago, probably would have been rejected as arbitrary and oppressive. Such regulations are sustained, under the complex conditions of our day, for reasons analogous to those which justify traffic regulations, which, before the advent of automobiles and rapid transit street railways, would have been condemned as fatally arbitrary and unreasonable. And in this there is no inconsistency, for, while the meaning of constitutional guaranties never varies, the scope of their application must expand or contract to meet the new and different conditions which are constantly coming within the field of their operation. In a changing world it is impossible that it should be otherwise. But although a degree of elasticity is thus imparted, not to the *meaning*, but to the *application* of constitutional principles, statutes and ordinances, which, after giving due weight to the new conditions, are found clearly not to conform to the Constitution, of course, must fall.

The ordinance now under review, and all similar laws and regulations, must find their justification in some aspect of the police power, asserted for the public welfare. The line which in this field separates the legitimate from the illegitimate assumption of power is not capable of precise delimitation. It varies with circumstances and conditions. A regulatory zoning ordinance, which would be clearly valid as applied to the great cities, might be clearly invalid as applied to rural communities. In solving doubts, the maxim *sic utere tuo ut alienum non laedas*, which lies at the foundation of so much of the common law of nuisances, ordinarily will furnish a fairly helpful clew. And the law of nuisances, likewise, may be consulted, not for the purpose of controlling, but for the helpful aid of its analogies in the process of ascertaining the scope of, the power. Thus the question whether the power exists to forbid the erection of a building of a particular kind or for a particular use, like the question whether a particular thing is a nuisance, is to be determined, not by an abstract consideration of the building or of the thing considered apart, but by considering it in connection with the circumstances and the locality. *Sturgis v. Bridgeman*, L. R. 11 Ch. 852, 865. A nuisance may be merely a right thing in the wrong place, like a pig in the parlor instead of the barnyard. If the validity of the legislative classification for zoning purposes be fairly debatable, the legislative judgment must be allowed to control. *Radice v. New York*, 264 U.S. 292, 294.

There is no serious difference of opinion in respect of the validity of laws and regulations fixing the height of buildings within reasonable limits, the character of materials and methods of construction, and the adjoining area which must be left open, in order to minimize the danger of fire or collapse, the evils of overcrowding and the like, and excluding from residential sections offensive trades, industries and structures likely to create nuisances. *See Welch v. Swasey*, 214 U.S. 91; *Hadacheck v. Los Angeles*, 239

U. S. 394; *Reinman v. Little Rock*, 237 U.S. 171; *Cusack Co. v. City of Chicago*, 242 U.S. 526, 529, 530.

Here, however, the exclusion is in general terms of all industrial establishments, and it may thereby happen that not only offensive or dangerous industries will be excluded, but those which are neither offensive nor dangerous will share the same fate. But this is no more than happens in respect of many practice-forbidding laws which this court has upheld, although drawn in general terms so as to include individual cases that may turn out to be innocuous in themselves. *Hebe Co. v. Shaw*, 248 U.S. 297, 303; *Pierce Oil Corp. v. City of Hope*, 248 U.S. 498, 500. The inclusion of a reasonable margin, to insure effective enforcement, will not put upon a law, otherwise valid, the stamp of invalidity. Such laws may also find their justification in the fact that, in some fields, the bad fades into the good by such insensible degrees that the two are not capable of being readily distinguished and separated in terms of legislation. In the light of these considerations, we are not prepared to say that the end in view was not sufficient to justify the general rule of the ordinance, although some industries of an innocent character might fall within the proscribed class. It cannot be said that the ordinance in this respect "passes the bounds of reason and assumes the character of a merely arbitrary fiat." *Purity Extract Co. v. Lynch*, 226 U.S. 192, 204. Moreover, the restrictive provisions of the ordinance in this particular may be sustained upon the principles applicable to the broader exclusion from residential districts of all business and trade structures, presently to be discussed.

* * *

We find no difficulty in sustaining restrictions of the kind thus far reviewed. The serious question in the case arises over the provisions of the ordinance excluding from residential districts apartment houses, business houses, retail stores and shops, and other like establishments. This question involves the validity of what is really the crux of the more recent zoning legislation, namely, the creation and maintenance of residential districts, from which business and trade of every sort, including hotels and apartment houses, are excluded. Upon that question this court has not thus far spoken. The decisions of the state courts are numerous and conflicting; but those which broadly sustain the power greatly outnumber those which deny it altogether or narrowly limit it, and it is very apparent that there is a constantly increasing tendency in the direction of the broader view. We shall not attempt to review these decisions at length, but content ourselves with citing a few as illustrative of all. [citations omitted]

* * *

The decisions enumerated in the first group cited above agree that the exclusion of buildings devoted to business, trade, etc., from residential districts, bears a rational relation to the health and safety of the community. Some of the grounds for this conclusion are promotion of the health and security from injury of children and others by separating dwelling houses from territory devoted to trade and industry; suppression and prevention of disorder; facilitating the extinguishment of fires, and the enforcement of street traffic regulations and other general welfare ordinances; aiding the health and safety of the community, by excluding from residential areas the confusion and danger of fire, contagion, and disorder, which in greater or less degree attach to the location of stores, shops, and factories. Another ground is that the construction and repair of streets may be rendered easier and less expensive, by confining the greater part of the heavy traffic to the streets where business is carried on.

* * *

The matter of zoning has received much attention at the hands of commissions and experts, and the results of their investigations have been set forth in comprehensive reports. These reports which bear every evidence of painstaking consideration, concur in the view that the segregation of residential, business and industrial buildings will make it easier to provide fire apparatus suitable for the character and intensity of the development in each section; that it will increase the safety and security of home life, greatly tend to prevent street accidents, especially to children, by reducing the traffic and resulting confusion in residential sections, decrease noise and other conditions which produce or intensify nervous disorders, preserve a more favorable environment in which to rear children, etc. With particular reference to apartment houses, it is pointed out that the development of detached house sections is greatly retarded by the coming of apartment houses, which has sometimes resulted in destroying the entire section for private house purposes; that in such sections very often the apartment house is a mere parasite, constructed in order to take advantage of the open spaces and attractive surroundings created by the residential character of the district. Moreover, the coming of one apartment house is followed by others, interfering by their height and bulk with the free circulation of air and monopolizing the rays of the sun which otherwise would fall upon the smaller homes, and bringing, as their necessary accompaniments, the disturbing noises incident to increased traffic and business, and the occupation, by means of moving and parked automobiles, of larger portions of the streets, thus detracting from their safety and depriving children of the privilege of quiet and open spaces for play, enjoyed by those in more favored localities—until, finally, the residential character of the neighborhood and its desirability as a place of detached residences are utterly destroyed. Under these circumstances, apartment houses, which in a different environment would be not only entirely unobjectionable but highly desirable, come very near to being nuisances.

If these reasons, thus summarized, do not demonstrate the wisdom or sound policy in all respects of those restrictions which we have indicated as pertinent to the inquiry, at least, the reasons are sufficiently cogent to preclude us from saying, as it must be said before the ordinance can be declared unconstitutional, that such provisions are clearly arbitrary and unreasonable, having no substantial relation to the public health, safety, morals, or general welfare. *Cusack Co. v. City of Chicago, supra,* pp. 530–531; *Jacobson v. Massachusetts,* 197 U.S. 11, 30–31.

It is true that when, if ever, the provisions set forth in the ordinance in tedious and minute detail, come to be concretely applied to particular premises, including those of the appellee, or to particular conditions, or to be considered in connection with specific complaints, some of them, or even many of them, may be found to be clearly arbitrary and unreasonable. But where the equitable remedy of injunction is sought, as it is here, not upon the ground of a present infringement or denial of a specific right, or of a particular injury in process of actual execution, but upon the broad ground that the mere existence and threatened enforcement of the ordinance, by materially and adversely affecting values and curtailing the opportunities of the market, constitute a present and irreparable injury, the court will not scrutinize its provisions, sentence by sentence, to ascertain by a process of piecemeal dissection whether there may be, here and there, provisions of a minor character, or relating to matters of administration, or not shown to contribute to the injury complained of, which, if attacked separately, might not withstand the test of constitutionality.

* * *

* * * [T]he gravamen of the complaint is that a portion of the land of the appellee cannot be sold for certain enumerated uses because of the general and broad restraints of the ordinance. What would be the effect of a restraint imposed by one or more or the innumerable provisions of the ordinance, considered apart, upon the value or marketability of the lands, is neither disclosed by the bill nor by the evidence, and we are afforded no basis, apart from mere speculation, upon which to rest a conclusion that it or they would have any appreciable effect upon those matters. Under these circumstances, therefore, it is enough for us to determine, as we do, that the ordinance in its general scope and dominant features, so far as its provisions are here involved, is a valid exercise of authority, leaving other provisions to be dealt with as cases arise directly involving them.

* * *

Decree reversed.

---

1. *Nuisances.* How did the Court respond to Ambler Realty's argument that the police power extended only to the regulation of nuisances?

What is the point of the Court's discussion of apartment houses? Note that at one point Sutherland says that an apartment house in a single-family residential neighborhood is "a mere parasite" that "come[s] very near to being [a] nuisance[ ]." 272 U.S. at 394, 395, 47 S.Ct. at 120. Is this simply rank prejudice against apartment dwellers, or does the Court, by focusing on the most difficult case—the segregation of multi-family and single-family residences—also broadly extend the legitimate scope of the legislatively exercised police power?

2. *Judicial Deference.* What role does judicial deference to legislative judgment play in the decision? Where does the Court draw the line between

deference and rejection of legislative judgment? More specifically, what is the standard of review? Who bears the burden of proof?

What is the Court's response to the argument that legislative distinctions are inevitably crude and will unnecessarily restrict businesses that pose no threat to health, safety, morals, or general welfare? Is there a constitutional limit to the errors that the Court will permit?

3. *"Facial" v. "As Applied" Constitutional Violation.* At the end of the opinion, the Court emphasizes that it was asked to decide only whether the ordinance was valid on its face, not in its specific application. What is the importance of this distinction and how does it affect the outcome in this case? Is it possible that Ambler Realty could return to court and successfully claim that the application of the zoning ordinance to its property violates due process? What sort of additional evidence must Ambler Realty produce? Is diminution of value relevant? What sort of evidence would help to show that the zoning ordinance, as applied to Ambler Realty's land, does not bear a substantial relation to the public health, safety, morals, and general welfare?

4. *Nectow v. City of Cambridge.* Less than two years after *Euclid*, zoning returned to the Supreme Court. In *Nectow v. City of Cambridge*, 277 U.S. 172, 48 S.Ct. 447, 72 L.Ed. 842 (1928), Nectow challenged the constitutionality of a zoning ordinance as it applied to him. His land straddled two districts; roughly 80% of the land was in an unrestricted district and 20% of the land was in a district that excluded most businesses and industry. To the north and west of the restricted land (and across a street) were residences; to the south was a Ford auto assembly plant and a soap factory; and to the east was the remaining 80% of Nectow's land. A master appointed by the state court found that "the districting of the plaintiff's land in a residence district would not promote the health, safety, convenience and general welfare of the inhabitants of that part of the defendant City, taking into account the natural development thereof and the character of the district and the resulting benefit to accrue to the whole City." 277 U.S. at 187, 48 S.Ct. at 448. The Court added its own observation that the restricted land "is of comparatively little value for the limited uses permitted by the ordinance." *Id.*

The Supreme Court adhered to the *Euclid* standard of review; the zoning ordinance would be set aside only if it "is clear that [the city council's] action 'has no foundation in reason and is a mere arbitrary or irrational exercise of power having no substantial relation to the public health, the public morals, the public safety or the public welfare in its proper sense.'" *Id.* at 187–88, 48 S.Ct. at 448 (quoting *Euclid*, 272 U.S. at 395, 47 S.Ct. at 121). Nonetheless, the Court held that the master's findings, which the court found supported by the evidence, showed that the "substantial relation" test was not met and thus compelled the conclusion that the zoning classification of Nectow's land violated due process. 277 U.S. at 188, 48 S.Ct. at 448.

Does *Nectow* pose a serious threat to the validity of zoning ordinances? Or is the case merely a sport—a one-time event reflecting the transition to a broad judicial acceptance of legislative judgments about land use regulation?

———————

Daniel R. Mandelker, The Zoning Dilemma

23–24, 32 (1970).

[O]wnership of title to the land continues to rest with the private developer, but the public agency, under the zoning ordinance, regulates the use to which the land is to be put. * * * While the zoning ordinance contains the legislative allocation of land uses on a community scale, the implementation of the development pattern contemplated by the ordinance is left to private initiative. In other words, there is a gap between the adoption of the zoning framework and its execution in the market place. Implementation of the ordinance depends on an appropriate private market response, both at the right place and at the right time.

But why, if we rely on the private market to implement the zoning ordinance, do we need the zoning ordinance in the first place? Cannot the market be trusted to make land use allocations which are appropriate for the community? In the absence of a zoning ordinance, the community land development pattern would be a summation of a series of development decisions made individually by private entrepreneurs, acting to maximize their own opportunity gains and to minimize their own opportunity costs. Why not assume that the sum of these individual development decisions represents a collective public interest which we can legally sanction? The answer lies in whether we perceive the land market as making perfect or imperfect allocations through the pricing system. We might achieve a helpful perspective on this problem by noting, as we have stated, that each entrepreneur in that market need consider only his own opportunity costs and gains. He is not compelled by the private market to consider the externalities which his own development decision may visit on others. * * * A zoning ordinance based on the separation of land use incompatibilities must therefore intervene to prevent the visitation of externalities which the private market cannot prevent. By making district allocations predicated on land use separations, zoning ordinances correct for the externalities which the private market need not consider.

* * *

We were initially willing to concede that the regulation of land use interdependencies, accomplished in part through the ancient nuisance remedy, was based on externally applied objective criteria which did not have a base in value preferences. This assumption must now be questioned. While many land use incompatibilities are a product of physical damage flowing from close proximity, in many cases the conflict is predicated solely on matters of taste and preference rather than on observable physical effect. Regulation of land use separations based on taste must necessarily carry with it the implicit acceptance of value judgments about the order of land development. Certainly this is true of residential zoning, in which the conventional separation of single family dwellings from apartments can only be defended by judgmental preference. Zoning strategies based on this preference carry with them an implicit hierarchical model of residential development in which single family development is favored, and in which upward pressures on these more favored uses are assumed to visit harmful externalities which the legal system should control.

―――――――――

1. *Market Failure.* In the first two paragraphs of this excerpt, Professor Mandelker seems to assume that the only appropriate response to market failure is administrative regulation. Is there a market solution to this market failure?

2. *Property Rules and Liability Rules.* How would Calabresi and Melamed analyze and resolve the problem Mandelker describes?

3. *Scope of the Police Power.* In the third paragraph, Mandelker makes explicit that much of zoning is not about activities that could be characterized as nuisances; instead, it often is about "taste and preference." What, if any, are the implications of this fact for judicial review? Should zoning be restricted to the administrative control of nuisances?

―――――――――

Bradley C. Karkkainen, Zoning: A Reply to the Critics

10 Journal of Land Use and Environmental Law 45, 64–65, 68–70 (1994).

Zoning is only partially about protecting individual property owners against the effects of "spillovers" or negative externalities that adversely affect the market values of their property. Specifically, zoning [also] protects a homeowner's consumer surplus in a home and in the surrounding neighborhood, that lies above the market value of that home. * * *

Neighborhoods are not just made up of individual parcels, but include collective resources comprising a neighborhood commons, and the property rights of an urban neighborhood dweller typically consist both in specified rights in an individual dwelling and inchoate rights in a neighborhood commons. This commons consists of open-access (but use-restricted) communally-owned property, such as streets, sidewalks, parks, playgrounds, and libraries. It also includes restricted-access but communally-owned property, such as public schools, public recreational facilities, and public transportation facilities.

It further includes a privately-owned "quasi-commons" to which the public generally is granted access, but with privately-imposed restrictions as to use, cost, and duration. These generally include restaurants, nightspots, theaters, groceries, and retail establishments. It will include (risking the appearance of an oxymoron) "private commons," like churches, temples, private schools, political organizations, clubs, and fraternal and civil organizations. These are essentially private associations, but are characterized by some substantial degree of open access to members of the community. Finally, the neighborhood commons will include other intangible qualities such as neighborhood ambiance, aesthetics, the physical environment (including air quality and noise), and relative degrees of anonymity or neighborliness.

These features together make up the "character" of a neighborhood. They are what give the neighborhood its distinctive flavor. A purchaser of residential property in an urban neighborhood buys not only a particular parcel of real estate, but also a share in the neighborhood commons. Typically, the differences in the neighborhood may be as crucial to a decision to purchase as differences in individual parcels.

To some extent, differences in the neighborhood commons will be reflected in the market values of individual parcels. * * * But because different people value different features in a neighborhood, not all such neighborhood differences will be reflected in property values.

For many people, a high level of consumer surplus may attach to particular features of a neighborhood commons. * * * These values are highly subjective and may not be widely shared by people who have never lived in the neighborhood, so they may add little or nothing to the market value of the property. Moreover, these resources are for the most part non-fungible and therefore irreplaceable. To me, enjoying the use of these resources is precisely what it means to live in my neighborhood. * * * I will naturally want to protect those collective resources of my neighborhood that I care about most, whether they are reflected in the market value of my property or are part of my consumer surplus. These values can be almost priceless, especially for long-term neighborhood residents. Like one's home, one's neighborhood may be centrally bound up in one's definition of self and sense of his or her place in the world.

———————

1. *Commons v. Private Property.* Does Karkkainen's argument expand the "commons" to include all (or substantially all) property? What is left of private property?

2. *Personhood Theory of Property.* How does this description of consumer surplus in one's home relate to Radin's personhood theory of property, *supra*, pp. 6–9?

3. *Consumer Surplus.* When one buys a home, one may well look to the set of neighborhood characteristics that Karkkainen describes. But his justification of zoning assumes that market prices for residential real estate do not fully reflect the individual (or idiosyncratic) value that a resident places on his or her property, the so-called consumer surplus. But if that consumer surplus is so individualized, how can a uniform zoning restriction capture each individual's distinctive valuation. That is, if the zoning ordinance can be written to reflect the preferences and tastes of thousands

of residents, won't the market substantially or even fully reflect the value of those preferences and tastes since there are probably many outsiders who also would value living in such a neighborhood?

4. *Allocation of Entitlement.* While it is understandable that many residents should want to maintain the *status quo*, aren't there other landowners, not to mention outsiders, who should be able to develop their own "definition of self and sense of * * * place in the world." Why should there be a rule in favor of those who arrived first? Isn't there a substantial risk that the "neighborhood character" argument will permit inadvertent or even intentional exclusion of less affluent people or minorities?

What is to prevent a neighborhood from seeking highly restrictive zoning (in the name of neighborhood character) only later to extract valuable concessions from landowner/developers?

5. *Zoning v. Covenants and Nuisance Law.* Is one implication of the author's argument that zoning may be appropriate for established residential neighborhoods, but that it has little purpose in non-residential neighborhoods or in new residential developments, where private covenants and nuisance law can deal with spillovers effectively?

Richard A. Epstein, A Conceptual Approach to Zoning: What's Wrong With *Euclid*

5 New York University Environmental Law Journal 277, 286, 288–91 (1996).

II

The Constitutional Payoff

* * *

A. *Euclid's Mistake*

* * *

In *Euclid v. Ambler Realty Co.*, the seminal land-use planning decision, the Supreme Court adopted a posture of deference toward a comprehensive land-use ordinance enacted by well-meaning local officials who were grappling with the difficult matters of projected interdependence in future land uses. After all, regulating land-use requires dealing with neighbors, and while neighbors may be able to move away from each other, land will have to remain behind. The Court said that almost anything the government wants to do in order to handle the externality question is acceptable because the idea of nuisance is sufficiently pliable to allow virtually any form of government regulation to fall within its ambit. Moreover, this presumption of deference is bolstered by imprecise common law terms: there is no clear demarcation separating nuisances, for which regulation is appropriate, from ordinary activities, for which it is not. As a result, the Court gave birth to a very powerful system of public planning without asking what risks, if any, might be prevented by the application of stricter scrutiny.

* * *

B.   Euclid Today

The issue in *Euclid* carries over into the modern context. Most of the really pitched battles before zoning boards involve the future direction of undeveloped land. The endless veto powers given to immediate neighbors who suffer only minor financial loss could have powerfully negative consequences for the larger region for which that development is only a part. But political separations can prevent those costs from being registered. Developers have learned that buying land in small communities is a risky business, precisely because extensive negotiations are necessary to bring projects to fruition—projects that were stalled not because of external risks, but because neighbors thought they could extract a pound of flesh from the developer. Just as zoning boards can aggravate externality problems, so too can they aggravate coordination problems as well.

* * *

There is a second odd feature of zoning that is worthy of mention. In many ways the entire zoning process fundamentally misunderstands the way in which individuals wish to integrate and coordinate their activities. The clue to the difficulty lies in the fact that the original meaning of the word "zone" implied that every use inside a single zone was uniform in content. That is why we have industrial zones, commercial zones, single family zones, and multi-family zones. This vision of the world presupposes that identical uses within single zones are wonderful, that mixed uses are to be discouraged, and, as noted, that the problems with the zoned boundaries are to be ignored.

C.   Mixed Uses

This is a monumentally rigid vision of how the world ought to be organized. Although there is perhaps some local disadvantage to having just one deviation from that particular pattern of uses, there is a huge overall advantage. Do you allow one convenience store, for example, to exist within walking distance of a large residential area? Yes. Do you want to have an uneven concentration of homes in a neighborhood so that some space can be reserved for a park land, and so forth? Yes. The same people who support zoning as a way to achieve convergent development have to worry about the question of mixed uses. Given the strong presumptions in favor of zones, the variance looks like an exceptional grant, sought by someone who wants to deviate from the normatively acceptable pattern of uses.

* * *

III

Conclusion: A Return to Laissez–Faire?

We must understand how the alternatives to zoning work before we can decide on its utility as a land-planning device. * * *

The entire interplay of [private law] principles [nuisance law, servitude law, and the Takings Clause], therefore, leads to a sophisticated set of rules whose overall strength is easy to underestimate. The full legal system, as it is fully understood, takes into account initial property rights, multiple uses, externalities, internalities, coordination difficulties, covenants by way of correction, single owners, and forced exchanges. Can zoning provide an improvement to the common-law system in proportion to its increase in costs and delay? I suspect that the answer to this question is negative, and that we should here, as in other areas, seek to find ways to clip the wings of zoning authorities. *Euclid* set the inquiry off on the wrong track.

---

1. *Nuisance and Servitude Law.* Professor Epstein's argument is that nuisance law, servitude law, and takings doctrine together are adequate in most if not all circumstances in which municipalities use zoning. Other authors have echoed this point, but added that market forces also play a role in shaping land use patterns. *See also* Siegan, Non-Zoning in Houston, 13 J.L. & Econ. 71 (1970) (arguing that Houston has land use patterns similar to those in other cities, but through covenants, nuisance law, and market choices); S.B. Warner, Streetcar Suburbs: The Process of Growth in Boston, 1870–1900 (1971) (arguing that Boston suburbs in the late nineteenth century developed residential land use patterns of income segregation in response to market forces, including economies of scale in residential developments and purchasers' preferences to live near people with similar levels of income).

What does Epstein's argument assume about the efficacy of nuisance law? Are there practical reasons why nuisance law may not be an adequate tool for resolving the problem of externalities? Does nuisance law enable property owners to plan for the future?

What are the difficulties of relying on servitude law? Consider the problems facing a group of neighboring property owners in an already-developed area. What sort of coordination problems are likely to arise? Are the coordination problems likely to be serious or easily overcome? Isn't one purpose of a democratically elected government to overcome coordination problems? Are these coordination problems as serious with undeveloped land?

2. *Allocation of Entitlement.* Epstein assumes that the entitlement to make land use decisions should rest with the individual property owner. For a wide range of land use issues, zoning places at least some of the entitlement with the governmental zoning authority. Is there any reason why the entitlement should rest with one or the other?

3. *Municipal Land Use Planning.* Planned unit developments (PUDs), which often involve hundreds of homes in a single development, might be viewed as little municipalities at least with regard to land use planning. Indeed, PUD developers often negotiate with municipalities to not impose Euclidean zoning so that developers can impose their own land

use plan through a system of reciprocal covenants. Shouldn't already developed municipalities have some ability to capture the same benefits of coordinated land use planning? Is zoning the only realistic means to achieve that end? Are their reasons why municipalities will have difficulty achieving that end?

4. *Efficiency.* Professor Ellickson recognizes the need for some land use regulations (he thinks, for example, that the transaction costs of negotiating covenants is too high in established neighborhoods). But he argues that it would be more efficient and equitable to enforce municipal land use regulations through a system of judicially determined nuisance damages and administratively assessed fines for violations of regulations. He would have few mandatory land use standards and he would not permit injunctive relief in nuisance cases except in unusual cases (*e.g.*, uses that threaten personal safety or individual liberty).

> Zoning is * * * an example of what Calabresi terms a system of specific deterrence. Specific deterrence systems impair the efficiency of resource allocation to the extent that they require compliance with a standard even when the prevention costs [the opportunity costs of foregone development and the costs of mitigating nuisance damages] involved in compliance exceed the resulting reduction in nuisance costs. The inadequacies of the information and staff available to existing governmental planning agencies create doubts about their ability to evaluate and weigh prevention and nuisance costs correctly. This element of inefficiency would be lessened if the sanction for a zoning violation were limited to a fine or an award of damages keyed to the amount of nuisance costs resulting from lack of compliance. An enterprise could then choose to violate an inefficient standard, pay the monetary penalty, and escape a higher level of prevention costs. * * *

> The most prevalent systems of land use control in the United States are neither as efficient nor as equitable as available alternatives. Detailed mandatory zoning standards inevitably impair efficient urban growth and discriminate against migrants, lower classes, and landowners with little political influence. The elimination of all mandatory zoning controls on population densities, land use locations, and building bulks is therefore probably desirable. * * *

> Consensual systems of internalization—the merger of adjoining parcels and covenants between their owners—are good mechanisms for handling external costs, particularly in areas where much of the land is still undeveloped. In all locations the wish of landowners to show good manners to their neighbors, essentially a consensual system, operates to limit the incidence of nuisances. Although these voluntary mechanisms should be strengthened, more coercive devices to discourage unneighborly behavior are also needed. * * * [S]ubstantial injuries from nuisances [should be] internalized through private lawsuits by the injured neighbors; a

plaintiff entitled to a remedy would be able to choose between collecting damages and purchasing the termination of the nuisance at the objective cost of that termination to the nuisance maker.

Pervasive but individually trivial harms caused by noxious land uses cannot be efficiently internalized through nuisance suits. These external costs can best be deterred through: (1) fines, often graduated by geographic area, levied against the pervasive damage of nuisances that offer a reasonably stable objective index of noxiousness and (2) selected uniform mandatory standards applicable to the pervasive nuisances that do not present such an index. These fines and mandatory standards should generally apply to both existing and prospective land uses to assure equal treatment of landowners and to create political pressures against excessively strict fines or standards. These internalization devices could be administered by metropolitan Nuisance Boards * * *.

Ellickson, Alternatives to Zoning: Covenants, Nuisance Rules, and Fines in Land Use Controls, 40 U.Chi. L. Rev. 681, 706–07, 779–80 (1973). Is this approach an improvement over Epstein's *laissez-faire* approach? Ellickson identifies three types of costs in zoning—nuisance costs (the costs of harmful spillovers), administrative costs (public costs of administering and enforcing land use regulations and private costs of dealing with land use authorities and with other landowners), and prevention costs (opportunity costs of foregone development and out-of-pocket costs to reduce nuisance costs). The system that minimizes the sum of these three costs is the most efficient. How are these costs affected by the different systems—standard zoning, Epstein's laissez-faire, or Ellickson's hybrid system of nuisance rules and administrative fines?

William A. Fischel, Equity and Efficiency Aspects of Zoning Reform

27 Public Policy 301, 302, 305–07 (1979).

The rationale for zoning, according to received doctrine, is provided by the actual or potential existence of externalities in urban property markets. These externalities give rise to market failure, and zoning is thought of as an attempt by government officials, in league with planners, to allocate resources more efficiently.

The outlook taken in this paper is that zoning should *not* be seen, in either a positive or a normative sense, as attempting to allocate resources efficiently. Zoning is much more usefully viewed as an attempt to redistribute property rights or "entitlements" from those who own undeveloped land (the "landowners") to other community residents (the "community"). It involves the establishment of control over the landowners' property for the enjoyment of those who have political control of the community. This approach does not look at a zoning ordinance and ask whether certain restrictions are efficient. It looks at an ordinance and asks what benefits these controls give to the politically dominant group in the community. Having established these controls within the limits set by enabling laws, court decisions, and internal political pressures, the community *may* then attempt to exchange them with the landowners for other types of benefits.

* * *

The nature of the benefits of [zoning] restriction to the community is a matter of some debate. Among those suggested are prevention of increasing municipal costs, lower tax rates from fiscally profitable housing, direct enjoyment of open land, preservation of community social values, and prevention of environmental disamenities. We are not for the moment interested in the exact nature of these benefits. Two points are important. First, the benefits are those perceived by existing residents who comprise the community, not by potential occupants of additional housing. Second, to the extent that any degree of restriction of development is enforceable, the total benefits will be reflected in the value of existing housing. That is, the more restrictions that are assigned to the community, the more valuable is an existing housing site in the community. Zoning and other local controls are valuable entitlements in the portfolio of community residents' assets.

* * *

Despite its heroic assumptions, the Coase theorem provides two important insights. The first is that the initial entitlement in restriction, which we call zoning, does not have to be at the maximum benefit point. Zoning need not be viewed, either positively or normatively, as a nonmarket groping for efficient allocation of resources. If zoning can be exchanged, there will be some tendency to reach that point. Second, the Coase theorem shows that the fundamental issue in land regulation is not whether regulations are necessary; the problem is not one of "laissez faire versus planning." Some restriction is clearly desirable, regardless of how entitlements are distributed. The issue is seen to devolve to two questions: Of the various initial entitlements in land use restrictions: (1) which is most equitable, and (2) which is most likely to lead to the maximum benefit point?

* * *

There are, however, a number of obvious transaction costs that will not go away even under the best system. Information about benefits to the community must be obtained, differential impacts among neighborhoods must be contended with, and all the problems of collective choice stand in the way, regardless of the initial distribution. Nonetheless some trade clearly does go on, even legally. Landowners who wish to develop their tracts may be willing to pay for various community services and infrastructure. Certain types of land use may help pay local taxes. Developers may dedicate land to public use or playgrounds, parks, or schools.

———————

1. *Efficiency v. Entitlement.* What is the significance of Professor Fischel's point that zoning should not be evaluated in terms of efficiency, but rather viewed as a community entitlement?

2. *Zoning Entitlement Market.* Fischel suggests that a community could "exchange" its zoning entitlement. What sorts of exchanges does he have in mind? Does this approach solve some of the coordination problems that arise with using a system of covenants in a partially developed community?

Fischel acknowledges some obstacles to the market in entitlements, such as inadequate information. How serious are these obstacles to his approach? Does the existence of these obstacles suggest that the initial entitlements should be set with some attention to their efficiency?

3. *Exactions.* Doesn't Fischel's approach give a municipality incentive to impose the strictest possible zoning restrictions in order to extract the greatest concessions from developers that the market will bear? Do you see any dangers in this approach? Who will pay the costs of this exaction—the developer, the landowner who sold the land to the developer, or the future users of the development? Are there any practical limits to the municipality extracting value in this fashion?

4. *Property Rule v. Liability Rule.* In terms of the Calabresi and Melamed framework, *supra*, pp. 281–87, does Fischel contemplate that the zoning entitlements will be governed by a property rule or by a liability rule? Which would you recommend?

D. THE SCOPE OF THE POLICE POWER: COMMUNITY, PROPERTY RIGHTS, AND CIVIL RIGHTS

After the *Euclid* Court held that municipalities could, consistent with due process, invoke the police power to regulate private land use, the balance of power between the community's right to shape land use and individual property and civil rights shifted dramatically in favor of municipal authority. Highly deferential judicial review as well as the underlying logic of *Euclid* quickly led municipalities not only to regulate uses that directly affected health and welfare, but also to regulate or even prohibit uses that reflect individual aesthetic judgment, that involve individual rights of free expression, and that affect personal decisions as to who can live together.

1. ZONING FOR AESTHETICS

Before *Euclid*, most courts held that aesthetics were beyond the scope of the police power and thus constitutionally beyond state or municipal regulatory authority. In *City of Passaic v. Paterson Bill Posting, Advertising & Sign Painting Co.*, 72 N.J.L. 285, 287, 62 A. 267, 268 (1905), the New Jersey Supreme Court declared that "[a]esthetic considerations are a matter of luxury and indulgence rather than necessity," and thus are not subject to the police power. This narrow reading of the police power, however, was eroded to some extent by decisions that accepted transparently false justifications only nominally meeting the health, safety, morals, or general welfare requirement. For example, in *Thomas Cusack Co. v. City of Chicago*, 242 U.S. 526, 529, 37 S.Ct. 190, 191, 61 L.Ed. 472 (1917), the Supreme Court rejected a due process challenge to municipal regulation of billboards on the ground that "offensive and insanitary accumulations are habitually found about them, and that they afford convenient concealment and shield for immoral practices, and for loiterers and criminals." *See also St. Louis Gunning Advertisement Co. v. City of St. Louis*, 235 Mo. 99, 137 S.W. 929 (1911) (upholding a municipal ban on billboards in part on the ground that they provided hiding places for criminals and prostitutes).

Both *Euclid* and the post-*Lochner* shift to greater judicial deference to legislative judgment on most matters greatly expanded the permissible scope of the police power (even though it was still described in terms of public health, safety, and welfare). *Berman v. Parker*, 348 U.S. 26, 75 S.Ct. 98, 99 L.Ed. 27 (1954), exemplified this change. In *Berman* the city wanted to condemn private property, which it would then turn over to a private developer for redevelopment. The condemnation was undertaken pursuant to the city's slum clearance program. The property owners objected on the ground that the condemnation was not for a public purpose and was thus beyond the police power, in violation of due process. The *Berman* Court found no due process violation. First, it emphasized that the state and federal legislatures, not the judiciary, have the principal responsibility to determine the scope of the police power. "Subject to specific constitutional limitations, when the legislature has spoken, the public interest has been declared in terms well-nigh conclusive." *Id.* at 32, 75 S.Ct. at 102. Second, the Court noted that the permissible limits of the police power are quite broad. "The concept of the public welfare is broad and inclusive. The values it represents are spiritual as well as physical, aesthetic as well as monetary. It is within the power of the legislature to determine that the community should be beautiful as well as healthy, spacious as well as clean, well-balanced as well as carefully patrolled." *Id.* at 33, 75 S.Ct. at 102.

It was a short step for federal courts to recognize that cities could also restrict land use to promote a wide variety of municipal interests, such as historic preservation, *Penn Central Transportation Co. v. New York City*, 438 U.S. 104, 129, 98 S.Ct. 2646, 2662, 57 L.Ed.2d 631 (1978) (preserving structures with historic, architectural, or cultural significance is "an entirely permissible governmental goal"), and conservation of open spaces, *Agins v. Tiburon*, 447 U.S. 255, 260–62, 100 S.Ct. 2138, 2141–42, 65 L.Ed.2d 106 (1980) (zoning regulations to conserve open space serve a "legitimate" governmental purpose).

Following *Berman*, state courts began to hold that aesthetic zoning fell within the police power. The New Jersey Supreme Court, which in 1905 soundly rejected the legitimacy of aesthetic considerations, now declared that "[c]onsideration of aesthetics in municipal land use planning is no longer a matter of luxury or indulgence. * * * The development and preservation of natural resources and clean, salubrious neighborhoods contribute to psychological well-being as well as stimulate a sense of civic pride." *State v. Miller*, 83 N.J. 402, 416 A.2d 821, 824 (1980). Courts have upheld "anti-monotony" ordinances, *Novi v. City of Pacifica*, 169 Cal. App.3d 678, 682, 215 Cal.Rptr. 439, 441 (1985) (a zoning ordinance requiring variety in the appearance of certain structures was "reasonably related" to public health and safety), and ordinances requiring the owners of commercial buildings to submit their exterior remodeling plans to the planning agency for review and approval of aesthetic considerations. *Village of Hudson v. Albrecht*, 9 Ohio St.3d 69, 73, 458 N.E.2d 852, 857 (1984).[5] Courts have also recognized as legitimate the government's interest in maintaining property values. *See, e.g., New York v. Stover*, 12 N.Y.2d 462, 466, 240 N.Y.S.2d 734, 736, 191 N.E.2d 272, 274 (1963) (upholding an ordinance proscribing placement of clotheslines in front of residences because the ban helped to preserve property values).

Although now generally recognized as a valid police power, zoning for aesthetics in some circumstances may violate constitutional protections of free speech and equal protection.

a. SIGNS

Much aesthetic zoning legislation and litigation has dealt with the regulation of commercial and political signs, such as billboards and on-premise commercial signs. State courts routinely hold that municipal regulation and even exclusion of signs fall well within the police power. *See, e.g., John Donnelly & Sons, Inc. v. Outdoor Advertising Board*, 369 Mass. 206, 218, 339 N.E.2d 709, 717 (1975) (upholding a zoning ordinance that for aesthetic reasons excluded billboards from a suburban community); *Asselin v. Town of Conway*, 137 N.H. 368, 373, 628 A.2d 247, 251 (1993) (upholding restrictions on sign illumination).

Zoning restrictions of signs, however, may run afoul of the Equal Protection Clause[6] or the First Amendment's protection of free speech.[7]

5. A few states, however, continue to refuse to allow regulation based solely on aesthetics. *See, e.g., Board of Supervisors v. Rowe*, 216 Va. 128, 145, 216 S.E.2d 199, 213 (1975) ("a county cannot limit or restrict the use which a person may make of his property under the guise of its police power where the exercise of such power would be justified solely on aesthetic considerations").

6. The Equal Protection Clause of the Fourteenth Amendment provides that no state shall "deny to any person within its jurisdiction the equal protection of the laws." Essentially, it prohibits discrimination based on legislative classifications absent adequate justification.

7. The First Amendment provides "Congress shall make no law * * * abridging the freedom of the press * * *." It is applicable to the states through the Fourteenth Amendment. *Near v. Minnesota*, 283 U.S. 697, 707, 51 S.Ct. 625, 627, 75 L.Ed. 1357 (1931); *Schneider v. State*, 308 U.S. 147, 160, 60 S.Ct. 146, 150, 84 L.Ed. 155 (1939).

The First Amendment also contains the Establishment and Free Exercise Clauses, which limit government regulation of religion, and which may affect the validity of some zoning and other land use decisions. *See Larkin v. Grendel's Den, Inc.*, 459 U.S. 116, 103 S.Ct. 505, 74 L.Ed.2d 297 (1982) (a state law permitting churches within 500 feet of a business to veto the business's application for a liquor license violated the Establishment Clause); *Church of the Lukumi Babalu Aye, Inc. v. City of Hialeah*, 508 U.S.

The first important Supreme Court case regarding the constitutionality of sign ordinances was *Metromedia, Inc. v. City of San Diego*, 453 U.S. 490, 101 S.Ct. 2882, 69 L.Ed.2d 800 (1981). In that case, an ordinance prohibited off-premise commercial billboards but permitted on-premise commercial signs. In a plurality opinion, the Court upheld the city's aesthetic and traffic safety justifications for the ban on off-premise commercial signs and the exemption for on-premise signs, but struck down the exemption's limitation to commercial signs as a violation of the First Amendment.

Three years later, in *Members of City Council of Los Angeles v. Taxpayers for Vincent*, 466 U.S. 789, 104 S.Ct. 2118, 80 L.Ed.2d 772 (1984), the Court upheld an ordinance that prohibited the posting of any signs on public property. The Court's opinion made clear that aesthetics were a substantial governmental interest that could justify the ordinance's limitation on speech. "The problem addressed by this ordinance—the visual assault on the citizens of Los Angeles presented by an accumulation of signs posted on public property—constitutes a significant substantive evil within the City's power to prohibit." *Id*. at 807, 104 S.Ct. at 2130. "Here, the substantive evil—visual blight—is not merely a possible byproduct of the activity, but is created by the medium of expression itself. * * * The ordinance curtails no more speech than is necessary to accomplish its purpose." *Id*. at 810, 104 S.Ct. at 2131.

City of Ladue v. Gilleo

Supreme Court of the United States, 1994.
512 U.S. 43, 114 S.Ct. 2038, 129 L.Ed.2d 36.

■ JUSTICE STEVENS delivered the opinion of the Court.

An ordinance of the City of Ladue prohibits homeowners from displaying any signs on their property except "residence identification" signs, "for sale" signs, and signs warning of safety hazards. The ordinance permits commercial establishments, churches, and nonprofit organizations to erect

520, 113 S.Ct. 2217, 124 L.Ed.2d 472 (1993) (an ordinance prohibiting animal sacrifices for religious purposes violated the Free Exercise Clause).

In 1993, Congress enacted the Religious Freedom Restoration Act, 42 U.S.C. §§ 2000bb to 2000bb–4. The Act prohibits government actions, including laws of "general applicability," that "substantially burden" the free exercise of religion unless the government can show both that it has a "compelling" governmental interest and that the action is the "least restrictive means" to achieve that interest. 42 U.S.C. § 2000bb–1(a). Under the First Amendment, courts carefully scrutinize statutes whose object is to infringe upon religious practices (as in *Hialeah*), but normally uphold neutral laws of general applicability even if they affect religious practices and even if the government makes no showing of compelling governmental interest (such as height restrictions in zoning laws). In *City of Boerne v. Flores*, ___ U.S. ___, ___ S.Ct. ___, ___ L.Ed.2d ___, 1997 WL 345322 (1997), which involved a church's challenge under the Act to a denial of a building permit, the Court held that the Act violated the standards of the Free Exercise Clause and improperly intruded on state prerogatives to regulate health and safety.

certain signs that are not allowed at residences. The question presented is whether the ordinance violates a Ladue resident's right to free speech.

I

Respondent Margaret P. Gilleo owns one of the 57 single-family homes in the Willow Hill subdivision of Ladue. On December 8, 1990, she placed on her front lawn a 24– by 36–inch sign printed with the words "Say No to War in the Persian Gulf, Call Congress Now." After that sign disappeared, Gilleo put up another but it was knocked to the ground. When Gilleo reported these incidents to the police, they advised her that such signs were prohibited in Ladue. The City Council denied her petition for a variance. Gilleo then filed this action under 42 U.S.C. § 1983 against the City, the Mayor, and members of the City Council, alleging that Ladue's sign ordinance violated her First Amendment right of free speech.

The District Court issued a preliminary injunction against enforcement of the ordinance. Gilleo then placed an 8.5– by 11–inch sign in the second story window of her home stating, "For Peace in the Gulf." The Ladue City Council responded to the injunction by repealing its ordinance and enacting a replacement. Like its predecessor, the new ordinance contains a general prohibition of "signs" and defines that term broadly. The ordinance prohibits all signs except those that fall within one of ten exemptions. Thus, "residential identification signs" no larger than one square foot are allowed, as are signs advertising "that the property is for sale, lease or exchange" and identifying the owner or agent. Also exempted are signs "for churches, religious institutions, and schools," "commercial signs in commercially or industrial zoned districts," and on-site signs advertising "gasoline filling stations." Unlike its predecessor, the new ordinance contains a lengthy "Declaration of Findings, Policies, Interests, and Purposes," part of which recites that the

> "proliferation of an unlimited number of signs in private, residential, commercial, industrial, and public areas of the City of Ladue would create ugliness, visual blight and clutter, tarnish the natural beauty of the landscape as well as the residential and commercial architecture, impair property values, substantially impinge upon the privacy and special ambiance of the community, and may cause safety and traffic hazards to motorists, pedestrians, and children."

Gilleo amended her complaint to challenge the new ordinance, which explicitly prohibits window signs like hers. The District Court held the ordinance unconstitutional, and the Court of Appeals affirmed. * * *

II

While signs are a form of expression protected by the Free Speech Clause, they pose distinctive problems that are subject to municipalities' police powers. Unlike oral speech, signs take up space and may obstruct views, distract motorists, displace alternative uses for land, and pose other problems that legitimately call for regulation. It is common ground that governments may regulate the physical characteristics of signs—just as they can, within reasonable bounds and absent censorial purpose, regulate audible expression in its capacity as noise. *See, e.g.,* *Ward v. Rock Against Racism*, 491 U.S. 781 (1989); *Kovacs v. Cooper*, 336 U.S. 77 (1949). However, because regulation of a medium inevitably affects communication itself, it is not surprising that we have had occasion to review the constitutionality of municipal ordinances prohibiting the display of certain outdoor signs.

In *Linmark Associates, Inc. v. Willingboro*, 431 U.S. 85 (1977), we addressed an ordinance that sought to maintain stable, integrated neighborhoods by prohibiting homeowners from placing "For Sale" or "Sold" signs on their property. Although we recognized the importance of Willingboro's objective, we held that the First Amendment prevented the township from "achieving its goal by restricting the free flow of truthful information." *Id.,* at 95. In some respects *Linmark* is the mirror image of this case. For instead of prohibiting "For Sale" signs without banning any other signs, Ladue has exempted such signs from an otherwise virtually complete ban. Moreover, whereas in *Linmark* we noted that the ordinance was not concerned with the promotion of aesthetic values unrelated to the content of the prohibited speech, *id.,* at 93–94, here Ladue relies squarely on that content-neutral justification for its ordinance.

In *Metromedia*, we reviewed an ordinance imposing substantial prohibitions on outdoor advertising displays within the City of San Diego in the interest of traffic safety and aesthetics. The ordinance generally banned all except those advertising "on-site" activities. The Court concluded that the City's interest in traffic safety and its aesthetic interest in preventing "visual clutter" could justify a prohibition of off-site commercial billboards even though similar on-site signs were allowed. 453 U.S. at 511–512. Nevertheless, the Court's judgment in *Metromedia*, supported by two different lines of reasoning, invalidated the San Diego ordinance in its entirety. According to Justice White's plurality opinion, the ordinance impermissibly discriminated on the basis of content by permitting on-site commercial speech while broadly prohibiting noncommercial messages. *Id.,* at 514–515. On the other hand, Justice Brennan, joined by Justice Blackmun, concluded "that the practical effect of the San Diego ordinance [was] to eliminate the billboard as an effective medium of communication" for noncommercial messages, and that the city had failed to make the strong showing needed to justify such "content-neutral prohibitions of particular media of communication." *Id.,* at 525–527. The three dissenters also viewed San Diego's ordinance as tantamount to a blanket prohibition of billboards, but would have upheld it because they did not perceive "even a hint of bias or censorship in the city's actions" nor "any reason to believe that the overall communications market in San Diego is inadequate." *Id.,* at 552–553 (Stevens, J., dissenting in part). *See also id.,* at 563, 566 (Burger, C. J., dissenting); *id.,* at 569–570 (Rehnquist, J., dissenting).

In *City Council of Los Angeles v. Taxpayers for Vincent*, 466 U.S. 789 (1984), we upheld a Los Angeles ordinance that prohibited the posting of signs on public property. Noting the conclusion shared by seven Justices in

Metromedia that San Diego's "interest in avoiding visual clutter" was sufficient to justify a prohibition of commercial billboards, *id.*, at 806–807, in *Vincent* we upheld the Los Angeles ordinance, which was justified on the same grounds. We rejected the argument that the validity of the City's aesthetic interest had been compromised by failing to extend the ban to private property, reasoning that the "private citizen's interest in controlling the use of his own property justifies the disparate treatment." *Id.*, at 811. We also rejected as "misplaced" respondents' reliance on public forum principles, for they had "failed to demonstrate the existence of a traditional right of access respecting such items as utility poles ... comparable to that recognized for public streets and parks." *Id.*, at 814.

These decisions identify two analytically distinct grounds for challenging the constitutionality of a municipal ordinance regulating the display of signs. One is that the measure in effect restricts too little speech because its exemptions discriminate on the basis of the signs' messages. *See Metromedia*, 453 U.S. at 512–517 (opinion of White, J.). Alternatively, such provisions are subject to attack on the ground that they simply prohibit too much protected speech. *See id.*, at 525–534 (Brennan, J., concurring in judgment). The City of Ladue contends, first, that the Court of Appeals' reliance on the former rationale was misplaced because the City's regulatory purposes are content-neutral, and, second, that those purposes justify the comprehensiveness of the sign prohibition. A comment on the former contention will help explain why we ultimately base our decision on a rejection of the latter.

III

While surprising at first glance, the notion that a regulation of speech may be impermissibly underinclusive is firmly grounded in basic First Amendment principles.[8] Thus, an exemption from an otherwise permissible regulation of speech may represent a governmental "attempt to give one side of a debatable public question an advantage in expressing its views to the people." *First Nat. Bank of Boston v. Bellotti*, 435 U.S. 765, 785–786 (1978). Alternatively, through the combined operation of a general speech restriction and its exemptions, the government might seek to select the "permissible subjects for public debate" and thereby to "control ... the search for political truth." *Consolidated Edison Co. of N.Y. v. Public Service Comm'n of N.Y.* 447 U.S. 530, 538 (1980).[9]

The City argues that its sign ordinance implicates neither of these concerns, and that the Court of Appeals therefore erred in demanding a

8. Like other classifications, regulatory distinctions among different kinds of speech may fall afoul of the Equal Protection Clause. *See, e.g., Carey v. Brown*, 447 U.S. 455, 459–471 (1980) (ordinance that forbade certain kinds of picketing but exempted labor picketing violated Clause); *Police Dept. of Chicago v. Mosley*, 408 U.S. 92, 98–102 (1972) (same).

9. Of course, not every law that turns on the content of speech is invalid. *See generally* Stone, Restrictions of Speech Because of its Content: The Peculiar Case of Subject-Matter Restrictions, 46 U. Chi. L. Rev. 79 (1978). *See also Consolidated Edison Co. of N.Y. v. Public Service Comm'n of N.Y.*, 447 U.S. at 545, and n.2 (Stevens, J., concurring in judgment).

"compelling" justification for the exemptions. The mix of prohibitions and exemptions in the ordinance, Ladue maintains, reflects legitimate differences among the side effects of various kinds of signs. These differences are only adventitiously connected with content, and supply a sufficient justification, unrelated to the City's approval or disapproval of specific messages, for carving out the specified categories from the general ban. Thus, according to the Declaration of Findings, Policies, Interests, and Purposes supporting the ordinance, the permitted signs, unlike the prohibited signs, are unlikely to contribute to the dangers of "unlimited proliferation" associated with categories of signs that are not inherently limited in number. Because only a few residents will need to display "for sale" or "for rent" signs at any given time, permitting one such sign per marketed house does not threaten visual clutter. Because the City has only a few businesses, churches, and schools, the same rationale explains the exemption for on-site commercial and organizational signs. Moreover, some of the exempted categories (*e.g.*, danger signs) respond to unique public needs to permit certain kinds of speech. Even if we assume the validity of these arguments, the exemptions in Ladue's ordinance nevertheless shed light on the separate question of whether the ordinance prohibits too much speech.

Exemptions from an otherwise legitimate regulation of a medium of speech may be noteworthy for a reason quite apart from the risks of viewpoint and content discrimination: they may diminish the credibility of the government's rationale for restricting speech in the first place. *See, e.g., Cincinnati v. Discovery Network, Inc.*, 507 U.S. 410 (1993). In this case, at the very least, the exemptions from Ladue's ordinance demonstrate that Ladue has concluded that the interest in allowing certain messages to be conveyed by means of residential signs outweighs the City's aesthetic interest in eliminating outdoor signs. Ladue has not imposed a flat ban on signs because it has determined that at least some of them are too vital to be banned.

Under the Court of Appeals' content discrimination rationale, the City might theoretically remove the defects in its ordinance by simply repealing all of the exemptions. If, however, the ordinance is also vulnerable because it prohibits too much speech, that solution would not save it. Moreover, if the prohibitions in Ladue's ordinance are impermissible, resting our decision on its exemptions would afford scant relief for respondent Gilleo. She is primarily concerned not with the scope of the exemptions available in other locations, such as commercial areas and on church property. She asserts a constitutional right to display an antiwar sign at her own home. Therefore, we first ask whether Ladue may properly prohibit Gilleo from displaying her sign, and then, only if necessary, consider the separate question whether it was improper for the City simultaneously to permit certain other signs. In examining the propriety of Ladue's near-total prohibition of residential signs, we will assume, *arguendo*, the validity of the City's submission that the various exemptions are free of impermissible content or viewpoint discrimination.

IV

In *Linmark* we held that the City's interest in maintaining a stable, racially integrated neighborhood was not sufficient to support a prohibition of residential "For Sale" signs. We recognized that even such a narrow sign prohibition would have a deleterious effect on residents' ability to convey important information because alternatives were "far from satisfactory." 431 U.S. at 93. Ladue's sign ordinance is supported principally by the City's interest in minimizing the visual clutter associated with signs, an interest that is concededly valid but certainly no more compelling than the interests at stake in *Linmark*. Moreover, whereas the ordinance in *Linmark* applied only to a form of commercial speech, Ladue's ordinance covers even such absolutely pivotal speech as a sign protesting an imminent governmental decision to go to war.

The impact on free communication of Ladue's broad sign prohibition, moreover, is manifestly greater than in *Linmark*. Gilleo and other residents of Ladue are forbidden to display virtually any "sign" on their property. The ordinance defines that term sweepingly. A prohibition is not always invalid merely because it applies to a sizeable category of speech; the sign ban we upheld in *Vincent*, for example, was quite broad. But in *Vincent* we specifically noted that the category of speech in question—signs placed on public property—was not a "uniquely valuable or important mode of communication," and that there was no evidence that "appellees' ability to communicate effectively is threatened by ever-increasing restrictions on expression." 466 U.S. at 812.

Here, in contrast, Ladue has almost completely foreclosed a venerable means of communication that is both unique and important. It has totally foreclosed that medium to political, religious, or personal messages. Signs that react to a local happening or express a view on a controversial issue both reflect and animate change in the life of a community. Often placed on lawns or in windows, residential signs play an important part in political campaigns, during which they are displayed to signal the resident's support for particular candidates, parties, or causes. They may not afford the same opportunities for conveying complex ideas as do other media, but residential signs have long been an important and distinct medium of expression.

Our prior decisions have voiced particular concern with laws that foreclose an entire medium of expression. Thus, we have held invalid ordinances that completely banned the distribution of pamphlets within the municipality, *Lovell v. Griffin*, 303 U.S. 444, 451–452 (1938); handbills on the public streets, *Jamison v. Texas*, 318 U.S. 413, 416 (1943); the door-to-door distribution of literature, *Martin v. Struthers*, 319 U.S. 141, 145–149 (1943); *Schneider v. State*, 308 U.S. 147, 164–165 (1939); and live entertainment, *Schad v. Mount Ephraim*, 452 U.S. 61, 75–76 (1981). *See also Frisby v. Schultz*, 487 U.S. 474, 486 (1988) (picketing focused upon individual residence is "fundamentally different from more generally directed means of communication that may not be completely banned in residential areas"). Although prohibitions foreclosing entire media may be completely free of content or viewpoint discrimination, the danger they pose to the freedom of speech is readily apparent—by eliminating a common means of speaking, such measures can suppress too much speech.

Ladue contends, however, that its ordinance is a mere regulation of the "time, place, or manner" of speech because residents remain free to convey their desired messages by other means, such as *hand-held* signs, "letters, handbills, flyers, telephone calls, newspaper advertisements, bumper stickers, speeches, and neighborhood or community meetings." However, even regulations that do not foreclose an entire medium of expression, but merely shift the time, place, or manner of its use, must "leave open ample alternative channels for communication." *Clark v. Community for Creative Non–Violence,* 468 U.S. 288, 293 (1984). In this case, we are not persuaded that adequate substitutes exist for the important medium of speech that Ladue has closed off.

Displaying a sign from one's own residence often carries a message quite distinct from placing the same sign someplace else, or conveying the same text or picture by other means. Precisely because of their location, such signs provide information about the identity of the "speaker." As an early and eminent student of rhetoric observed, the identity of the speaker is an important component of many attempts to persuade.

Residential signs are an unusually cheap and convenient form of communication. Especially for persons of modest means or limited mobility, a yard or window sign may have no practical substitute. Even for the affluent, the added costs in money or time of taking out a newspaper advertisement, handing out leaflets on the street, or standing in front of one's house with a hand-held sign may make the difference between participating and not participating in some public debate. Furthermore, a person who puts up a sign at her residence often intends to reach *neighbors,* an audience that could not be reached nearly as well by other means.

A special respect for individual liberty in the home has long been part of our culture and our law; that principle has special resonance when the government seeks to constrain a person's ability to speak there. Most Americans would be understandably dismayed, given that tradition, to learn that it was illegal to display from their window an 8–by 11–inch sign expressing their political views. Whereas the government's need to mediate among various competing uses, including expressive ones, for public streets and facilities is constant and unavoidable, its need to regulate temperate speech from the home is surely much less pressing.

Our decision that Ladue's ban on almost all residential signs violates the First Amendment by no means leaves the City powerless to address the ills that may be associated with residential signs.[10] It bears mentioning that individual residents themselves have strong incentives to keep their own

___

10.   Nor do we hold that every kind of sign must be permitted in residential areas. Different considerations might well apply, for example, in the case of signs (whether political or otherwise) displayed by residents for a fee, or in the case of off-site commercial advertisements on residential property. We also are not confronted here with mere regulations short of a ban.

property values up and to prevent "visual clutter" in their own yards and neighborhoods—incentives markedly different from those of persons who erect signs on others' land, in others' neighborhoods, or on public property. Residents' self-interest diminishes the danger of the "unlimited" proliferation of residential signs that concerns the City of Ladue. We are confident that more temperate measures could in large part satisfy Ladue's stated regulatory needs without harm to the First Amendment rights of its citizens. As currently framed, however, the ordinance abridges those rights.

————————

1. *Political v. Commercial Speech.* In an effort to address a First Amendment prohibition on content-based regulation of expression, the city banned virtually all signs. Why did the Court reject this approach?

Is the Court's reasoning and holding limited to political expression? Does the Court's opinion make a distinction, for purposes of the First Amendment, between commercial speech and non-commercial speech? Should it? Are property owners now free to post signs announcing garage sales? What about signs announcing one's availability for work?

2. *Economic Incentives and Social Norms.* At the end of the opinion, the Court states that the city should not worry much about visual clutter because homeowners have a substantial economic incentive to keep their property neat. Do you think that all residents will have the same incentive to reduce clutter? Or is it more likely that some people will disregard their own economic interests because they want to express themselves? Moreover, isn't there a potential collective action problem; some property owners will reap the benefits from other owners keeping their property tidy, but will not make the same efforts themselves? To what extent can social norms be relied upon to regulate aesthetic concerns? What factors will affect the significance of social norms in this setting?

3. *Free Speech and Property Rights. Ladue* teaches that even though the scope of the police power to regulate land use is quite broad, it cannot exceed the limits imposed by individual constitutional rights, such as the First Amendment's protection of fee speech. Why is the police power not similarly limited by the Takings Clause, which requires the government to provide just compensation whenever it takes private property?

Is it possible to square *Ladue* with *State v. Shack, supra* pp. 372–76, which held that a property owner's bundle of rights does not include the right to exclude farmworker organizers? Both cases balance the property owner's rights (in *Shack* the right to exclude, and in *Ladue* the right to post signs) against the rights of others (in *Shack* the rights of resident farmworkers and farmworker organizers, and in *Ladue* the rights of neighbors as represented by the city). Both rights are considered important; in *Loretto* (the physical invasion takings case), for example, the Supreme Court called the right to exclude the most important of property rights. Yet in *Shack* the property owner loses and in *Ladue* the property owner wins. Does the balance shift with the property owner's interest (commercial or political speech) or with the outsiders' interests (tidiness or health and safety)?

How much of the outcome in *Ladue* is due to the property owner's free speech interest and how much is due to the property interest? Recall that in *Members of City Council of Los Angeles v. Taxpayers for Vincent*, 466 U.S. 789, 104 S.Ct. 2118, 80 L.Ed.2d 772 (1984), the Court upheld an ordinance prohibiting posting of signs on public property.

4. *Political Models of Local Government.* What model of local politics—pluralism, republicanism, public choice theory, or the Tiebout Hypothesis—best explains the process by which Ladue adopted the ban on residential signs? Should a court's review of the ordinance turn on its assessment of the nature of the underlying political process? Do you think it did in *Ladue*?

Problems: Regulation of Signs and Aesthetics

1.   You are a Deputy City Attorney of Ladue. Following this opinion, the City Council asks the City Attorney to draft a sign ordinance that is the most restrictive possible, consistent with the holding of the case. The City Attorney asks you to undertake the project and directs your attention to language in the opinion suggesting that a municipality can regulate the "time, place and manner" of speech, and that "more temperate measures" would survive constitutional scrutiny. What would you recommend?

2.   Not long after you complete the draft sign ordinance, the City Attorney asks you to evaluate the constitutionality of a city ordinance that prohibits houses from being painted in a "garish" fashion. The issue arises because one homeowner subject to the ordinance has painted his entire house purple with yellow polka dots. He does not deny that the colors on the house violate the ordinance; rather he claims that he has a First Amendment right to express himself. According to the property owner, the colors express his strong feeling about the need to protect individuality and private ownership of property. The paint job is a type of performance art with a political message. The neighbors uniformly hate the colors and have demanded that the city take legal action. *Cf. People v. Stover*, 12 N.Y.2d 462, 240 N.Y.S.2d 734, 191 N.E.2d 272 (1963) (landowner hung a clothesline with rags to protest local tax policies).

---

b.   ADULT THEATERS

Some of the most controversial land use cases have involved zoning decisions for adult movie theaters or live entertainment. Most residents don't want them in or near residential neighborhoods (or in their towns at all), but theater operators claim a First Amendment right to free expression. In *Young v. American Mini Theatres, Inc.*, 427 U.S. 50, 96 S.Ct. 2440,

49 L.Ed.2d 310 (1976), the city of Detroit had adopted a zoning ordinance that specifically targeted adult movie theaters. Under the ordinance, adult movie theaters could not be located within 1000 feet of each other or within 500 feet of a residential area.

The Court readily declared that the 1000–foot restriction would not violate the First Amendment if it applied to all movie theaters. "The city's interest in planning and regulating the use of property for commercial purposes is clearly adequate to support that kind of restriction applicable to all theaters within the city limits." *Id.* at 62–63, 96 S.Ct. at 2448. In support, the Court cited the doctrine that permits "[r]easonable regulations of the time, place, and manner of protected speech, where those regulations are necessary to further significant government interests." *Id.* at 63, n.18, 96 S.Ct. at 2449, n. 18.

The constitutional difficulty arose because the city subjected only adult theaters to the restriction; the case thus presented a claim of equal protection, with heavy First Amendment overtones. As the plurality pointed out, First Amendment doctrine permits many content-based distinctions. *See, e.g., Lehman v. City of Shaker Heights*, 418 U.S. 298, 94 S.Ct. 2714, 41 L.Ed.2d 770 (1974) (the First Amendment permits a public rapid transit system to accept product advertising but to reject all political advertising). The only question was whether "the line drawn by these ordinances is justified by the city's interest in preserving the character of its neighborhoods." 427 U.S. at 71, 96 S. Ct. at 2452. The plurality answered that question affirmatively. First, the city's interest in preserving the quality of urban life "must be accorded high respect." In addition, the problems of neighborhood decay were "serious," and the city had documented that concentrations of adult theaters contributed to that decay. *Id.* at 71 & n. 34, 96 S.Ct. at 2452 & 2453 n. 34.   Second, the First Amendment concerns were small. The ordinance only limited the location of adult theaters, and it did not suppress or greatly restrict access to adult theaters. *Id.* at 71 & n. 35, 96 S.Ct. at 2452 & 2453 n. 35.

The next case to confront this issue was *Schad v. Borough of Mount Ephraim*, 452 U.S. 61, 101 S.Ct. 2176, 68 L.Ed.2d 671 (1981). The owners of an adult bookstore that also allowed customers to watch live, nude dancing were convicted of violating a zoning ordinance that banned all live entertainment. Conceding that the municipal power to zone is "broad" and "essential [to achieve] a satisfactory quality of life," the Court nevertheless held that "when a zoning law infringes upon a protected liberty, it must be narrowly drawn and must further a sufficiently substantial government interest." *Id.* at 68, 101 S.Ct. at 2182.

The Court distinguished the circumstances in *American Mini Theatres* from the Mount Ephraim ordinance. The Detroit ordinance did not impose a significant burden on speech (it only dispersed certain kinds of theaters and there was no evidence that dispersal restricted access to the theaters), and Detroit had evidence that concentrations of adult theaters led to the deterioration of surrounding neighborhoods. *Id.* at 71–72, 101 S.Ct. at 2184. Mount Ephraim's ordinance, on the other hand banned *all* live entertainment—including concerts and plays—thereby imposing a substantial burden on speech. Moreover, the borough presented no evidence that the broad ban promoted any legitimate municipal interests, such as prevention of traffic congestion. *Id.* at 72–76, 101 S.Ct. at 2184–86. The Court struck down the ordinance.

———————

City of Renton v. Playtime Theatres, Inc.
475 U.S. 41, 106 S.Ct. 925, 89 L.Ed.2d 29 (1986).

■ JUSTICE REHNQUIST delivered the opinion of the Court.

This case involves a constitutional challenge to a zoning ordinance, enacted by appellant city of Renton, Washington, that prohibits adult motion picture theaters from locating within 1,000 feet of any residential zone, single- or multiple-family dwelling, church, park, or school. Appellees, Playtime Theatres, Inc., and Sea–First Properties, Inc., filed an action in the United States District Court for the Western District of Washington seeking a declaratory judgment that the Renton ordinance violated the First and Fourteenth Amendments and a permanent injunction against its enforcement.

* * *

In May 1980, the Mayor of Renton, a city of approximately 32,000 people located just south of Seattle, suggested to the Renton City Council that it consider the advisability of enacting zoning legislation dealing with adult entertainment uses. No such uses existed in the city at that time. Upon the Mayor's suggestion, the City Council referred the matter to the city's Planning and Development Committee. The Committee held public hearings, reviewed the experiences of Seattle and other cities, and received a report from the City Attorney's Office advising as to developments in other cities. The City Council, meanwhile, adopted Resolution No. 2368, which imposed a moratorium on the licensing of "any business ... which ... has as its primary purpose the selling, renting or showing of sexually explicit materials." The resolution contained a clause explaining that such businesses "would have a severe impact upon surrounding businesses and residences."

In April 1981, acting on the basis of the Planning and Development Committee's recommendation, the City Council enacted Ordinance No. 3526. The ordinance prohibited any "adult motion picture theater" from locating within 1,000 feet of any residential zone, single- or multiple-family dwelling, church, or park, and within one mile of any school. The term "adult motion picture theater" was defined as "[a]n enclosed building used for presenting motion picture films, video cassettes, cable television, or any other such visual media, distinguished or characteri[zed] by an emphasis on matter depicting, describing or relating to 'specified sexual activities' or 'specified anatomical areas ... for observation by patrons therein."

In early 1982, respondents acquired two existing theaters in downtown Renton, with the intention of using them to exhibit feature-length adult films. The theaters were located within the area proscribed by Ordinance No. 3526. At about the same time, respondents filed the previously mentioned lawsuit challenging the ordinance on First and Fourteenth Amendment grounds, and seeking declaratory and injunctive relief. While the federal action was pending, the City Council amended the ordinance in several respects, adding a statement of reasons for its enactment and reducing the minimum distance from any school to 1,000 feet.

      * * *

In our view, the resolution of this case is largely dictated by our decision in *Young v. American Mini Theatres, Inc., supra.* There, although five Members of the Court did not agree on a single rationale for the decision, we held that the city of Detroit's zoning ordinance, which prohibited locating an adult theater within 1,000 feet of any two other "regulated uses" or within 500 feet of any residential zone, did not violate the First and Fourteenth Amendments. *Id.,* 427 U.S., at 72–73 (plurality opinion of Stevens, J., joined by Burger, C.J., and White and Rehnquist, JJ.); id., at 84 (Powell, J., concurring). The Renton ordinance, like the one in *American Mini Theatres,* does not ban adult theaters altogether, but merely provides that such theaters may not be located within 1,000 feet of any residential zone, single-or multiple-family dwelling, church, park, or school. The ordinance is therefore properly analyzed as a form of time, place, and manner regulation. *Id.,* at 63, and n. 18; *id.,* at 78–79 (Powell, J., concurring).

Describing the ordinance as a time, place, and manner regulation is, of course, only the first step in our inquiry. This Court has long held that regulations enacted for the purpose of restraining speech on the basis of its content presumptively violate the First Amendment. *See Carey v. Brown,* 447 U.S. 455, 462–463, and n. 7 (1980); *Police Dept. of Chicago v. Mosley,* 408 U.S. 92, 95, 98–99 (1972). On the other hand, so-called "content-neutral" time, place, and manner regulations are acceptable so long as they are designed to serve a substantial governmental interest and do not unreasonably limit alternative avenues of communication. *See Clark v. Community for Creative Non–Violence,* 468 U.S. 288, 293 (1984); *City Council of Los Angeles v. Taxpayers for Vincent,* 466 U.S. 789, 807 (1984); *Heffron v. International Society for Krishna Consciousness, Inc.,* 452 U.S. 640, 647–648 (1981).

At first glance, the Renton ordinance, like the ordinance in *American Mini Theatres,* does not appear to fit neatly into either the "content-based" or the "content-neutral" category. To be sure, the ordinance treats theaters that specialize in adult films differently from other kinds of theaters. Nevertheless, as the District Court concluded, the Renton ordinance is aimed not at the content of the films shown at "adult motion picture theatres," but rather at the secondary effects of such theaters on the surrounding community. The District Court found that the City Council's "predominate concerns" were with the secondary effects of adult theaters, and not with the content of adult films themselves. But the Court of

Appeals, relying on its decision in *Tovar v. Billmeyer*, 721 F.2d 1260, 1266 (CA9 1983), held that this was not enough to sustain the ordinance. According to the Court of Appeals, if *"a motivating factor"* in enacting the ordinance was to restrict respondents' exercise of First Amendment rights the ordinance would be invalid, apparently no matter how small a part this motivating factor may have played in the City Council's decision. 748 F.2d, at 537 (emphasis in original). This view of the law was rejected in *United States v. O'Brien*, 391 U.S., at 382–386, the very case that the Court of Appeals said it was applying:

> It is a familiar principle of constitutional law that this Court will not strike down an otherwise constitutional statute on the basis of an alleged illicit legislative motive. * * *

> * * *

> * * * What motivates one legislator to make a speech about a statute is not necessarily what motivates scores of others to enact it, and the stakes are sufficiently high for us to eschew guesswork. *Id.*, at 383–384.

The District Court's finding as to "predominate" intent, left undisturbed by the Court of Appeals, is more than adequate to establish that the city's pursuit of its zoning interests here was unrelated to the suppression of free expression. The ordinance by its terms is designed to prevent crime, protect the city's retail trade, maintain property values, and generally "protec[t] and preserv[e] the quality of [the city's] neighborhoods, commercial districts, and the quality of urban life," not to suppress the expression of unpopular views. As Justice Powell observed in *American Mini Theatres*, "[i]f [the city] had been concerned with restricting the message purveyed by adult theaters, it would have tried to close them or restrict their number rather than circumscribe their choice as to location." 427 U.S., at 82, n. 4.

In short, the Renton ordinance is completely consistent with our definition of "content-neutral" speech regulations as those that "are *justified* without reference to the content of the regulated speech." *Virginia Pharmacy Board v. Virginia Citizens Consumer Council, Inc.*, 425 U.S. 748, 771 (1976) (emphasis added); *Community for Creative Non–Violence, supra*, 468 U.S., at 293; *International Society for Krishna Consciousness, supra*, 452 U.S., at 648. The ordinance does not contravene the fundamental principle that underlies our concern about "content-based" speech regulations: that "government may not grant the use of a forum to people whose views it finds acceptable, but deny use to those wishing to express less favored or more controversial views." *Mosley, supra*, 408 U.S., at 95–96.

It was with this understanding in mind that, in *American Mini Theatres*, a majority of this Court decided that, at least with respect to businesses that purvey sexually explicit materials,[11] zoning ordinances

---

11. *See American Mini Theatres*, 427 U.S., at 70 (plurality opinion) ("[I]t is manifest that society's interest in protecting this type of expression is of a wholly different, and lesser, magnitude than the interest in untrammeled political debate * * * ").

designed to combat the undesirable secondary effects of such businesses are to be reviewed under the standards applicable to "content-neutral" time, place, and manner regulations. Justice Stevens, writing for the plurality, concluded that the city of Detroit was entitled to draw a distinction between adult theaters and other kinds of theaters "without violating the government's paramount obligation of neutrality in its regulation of protected communication," 427 U.S., at 70, noting that "[i]t is th[e] secondary effect which these zoning ordinances attempt to avoid, not the dissemination of 'offensive' speech," *id.*, at 71, n. 34. Justice Powell, in concurrence, elaborated:

> [The] dissent misconceives the issue in this case by insisting that it involves an impermissible time, place, and manner restriction based on the content of expression. It involves nothing of the kind. We have here merely a decision by the city to treat certain movie theaters differently because they have markedly different effects upon their surroundings. * * * Moreover, even if this were a case involving a special governmental response to the content of one type of movie, it is possible that the result would be supported by a line of cases recognizing that the government can tailor its reaction to different types of speech according to the degree to which its special and overriding interests are implicated. *See, e.g., Tinker v. Des Moines School Dist.*, 393 U.S. 503, 509–511 (1969); *Procunier v. Martinez*, 416 U.S. 396, 413–414 (1974); *Greer v. Spock*, 424 U.S. 828, 842–844 (Powell, J., concurring); *cf. CSC v. Letter Carriers*, 413 U.S. 548 (1973). *Id.*, at 82, n. 6.

The appropriate inquiry in this case, then, is whether the Renton ordinance is designed to serve a substantial governmental interest and allows for reasonable alternative avenues of communication. *See Community for Creative Non–Violence*, 468 U.S., at 293; *International Society for Krishna Consciousness*, 452 U.S., at 649, 654. It is clear that the ordinance meets such a standard. As a majority of this Court recognized in *American Mini Theatres*, a city's "interest in attempting to preserve the quality of urban life is one that must be accorded high respect." 427 U.S., at 71 (plurality opinion); *see id.*, at 80 (Powell, J., concurring) ("Nor is there doubt that the interests furthered by this ordinance are both important and substantial"). Exactly the same vital governmental interests are at stake here.

The Court of Appeals ruled, however, that because the Renton ordinance was enacted without the benefit of studies specifically relating to "the particular problems or needs of Renton," the city's justifications for the ordinance were "conclusory and speculative." 748 F.2d, at 537. We think the Court of Appeals imposed on the city an unnecessarily rigid burden of proof. The record in this case reveals that Renton relied heavily on the experience of, and studies produced by, the city of Seattle. In Seattle, as in Renton, the adult theater zoning ordinance was aimed at preventing the secondary effects caused by the presence of even one such theater in a given neighborhood. *See Northend Cinema, Inc. v. Seattle*, 90

Wash.2d 709, 585 P.2d 1153 (1978). The opinion of the Supreme Court of Washington in *Northend Cinema*, which was before the Renton City Council when it enacted the ordinance in question here, described Seattle's experience as follows:

> The amendments to the City's zoning code which are at issue here are the culmination of a long period of study and discussion of the problems of adult movie theaters in residential areas of the City. ... [T]he City's Department of Community Development made a study of the need for zoning controls of adult theaters.
>
> ... The study analyzed the City's zoning scheme, comprehensive plan, and land uses around existing adult motion picture theaters. ... *Id.*, at 711, 585 P.2d, at 1155.
>
> [T]he [trial] court heard extensive testimony regarding the history and purpose of these ordinances. It heard expert testimony on the adverse effects of the presence of adult motion picture theaters on neighborhood children and community improvement efforts. The court's detailed findings, which include a finding that the location of adult theaters has a harmful effect on the area and contribute to neighborhood blight, are supported by substantial evidence in the record. *Id.*, at 713, 585 P.2d, at 1156.
>
> The record is replete with testimony regarding the effects of adult movie theater locations on residential neighborhoods. *Id.*, at 719, 585 P.2d, at 1159.

We hold that Renton was entitled to rely on the experiences of Seattle and other cities, and in particular on the "detailed findings" summarized in the Washington Supreme Court's *Northend Cinema* opinion, in enacting its adult theater zoning ordinance. The First Amendment does not require a city, before enacting such an ordinance, to conduct new studies or produce evidence independent of that already generated by other cities, so long as whatever evidence the city relies upon is reasonably believed to be relevant to the problem that the city addresses. That was the case here. Nor is our holding affected by the fact that Seattle ultimately chose a different method of adult theater zoning than that chosen by Renton, since Seattle's choice of a different remedy to combat the secondary effects of adult theaters does not call into question either Seattle's identification of those secondary effects or the relevance of Seattle's experience to Renton.

We also find no constitutional defect in the method chosen by Renton to further its substantial interests. Cities may regulate adult theaters by dispersing them, as in Detroit, or by effectively concentrating them, as in Renton. "It is not our function to appraise the wisdom of [the city's] decision to require adult theaters to be separated rather than concentrated in the same areas. ... [T]he city must be allowed a reasonable opportunity to experiment with solutions to admittedly serious problems." *American Mini Theatres*, 427 U.S., at 71 (plurality opinion). Moreover, the Renton ordinance is "narrowly tailored" to affect only that category of theaters shown to produce the unwanted secondary effects, thus avoiding the flaw that proved fatal to the regulations in *Schad v. Mount Ephraim*, 452 U.S. 61 (1981), and *Erznoznik v. City of Jacksonville*, 422 U.S. 205 (1975).

Respondents contend that the Renton ordinance is "under-inclusive," in that it fails to regulate other kinds of adult businesses that are likely to produce secondary effects similar to those produced by adult theaters. On this record the contention must fail. There is no evidence that, at the time the Renton ordinance was enacted, any other adult business was located in, or was contemplating moving into, Renton. In fact, Resolution No. 2368, enacted in October 1980, states that "the City of Renton does not, at the present time, have any business whose primary purpose is the sale, rental, or showing of sexually explicit materials." That Renton chose first to address the potential problems created by one particular kind of adult business in no way suggests that the city has "singled out" adult theaters for discriminatory treatment. We simply have no basis on this record for assuming that Renton will not, in the future, amend its ordinance to include other kinds of adult businesses that have been shown to produce the same kinds of secondary effects as adult theaters. *See Williamson v. Lee Optical Co.*, 348 U.S. 483, 488–489 (1955).

Finally, turning to the question whether the Renton ordinance allows for reasonable alternative avenues of communication, we note that the ordinance leaves some 520 acres, or more than five percent of the entire land area of Renton, open to use as adult theater sites. The District Court found, and the Court of Appeals did not dispute the finding, that the 520 acres of land consists of "[a]mple, accessible real estate," including "acreage in all stages of development from raw land to developed, industrial, warehouse, office, and shopping space that is criss-crossed by freeways, highways, and roads."

Respondents argue, however, that some of the land in question is already occupied by existing businesses, that "practically none" of the undeveloped land is currently for sale or lease, and that in general there are no "commercially viable" adult theater sites within the 520 acres left open by the Renton ordinance. The Court of Appeals accepted these arguments, concluded that the 520 acres was not truly "available" land, and therefore held that the Renton ordinance "would result in a substantial restriction" on speech. 748 F.2d, at 534.

We disagree with both the reasoning and the conclusion of the Court of Appeals. That respondents must fend for themselves in the real estate market, on an equal footing with other prospective purchasers and lessees, does not give rise to a First Amendment violation. And although we have cautioned against the enactment of zoning regulations that have "the effect of suppressing, or greatly restricting access to, lawful speech," *American Mini Theatres*, 427 U.S., at 71, n. 35 (plurality opinion), we have never suggested that the First Amendment compels the Government to ensure that adult theaters, or any other kinds of speech-related businesses for that matter, will be able to obtain sites at bargain prices. *See id.*, at 78 (Powell, J., concurring) ("The inquiry for First Amendment purposes is not concerned with economic impact"). In our view, the First Amendment requires only that Renton refrain from effectively denying respondents a reasonable opportunity to open and operate an adult theater within the city, and the ordinance before us easily meets this requirement.

In sum, we find that the Renton ordinance represents a valid governmental response to the "admittedly serious problems" created by adult theaters. *See id.*, at 71 (plurality opinion). Renton has not used "the power to zone as a pretext for suppressing expression," *id.*, at 84 (Powell, J., concurring), but rather has sought to make some areas available for adult theaters and their patrons, while at the same time preserving the quality of life in the community at large by preventing those theaters from locating in other areas. This, after all, is the essence of zoning. Here, as in *American Mini Theatres*, the city has enacted a zoning ordinance that meets these goals while also satisfying the dictates of the First Amendment.[12] The judgment of the Court of Appeals is therefore.

Reversed.

———

1. *Content–Neutral Regulation.* Why does the Court work so hard to show that the Renton ordinance is "content neutral? " Are you persuaded by the Court's discussion that the ordinance is content neutral?

2. *Legitimate Municipal Interests.* What are the legitimate government interests advanced by this statute? On what information or studies did Renton rely in drafting the ordinance? Are there any limits on the information that a municipality could use?

In a dissenting opinion, Justice Brennan wrote that the "City Council conducted no studies, and heard no expert testimony, on how the protected uses would be affected by the presence of an adult movie theater, and never considered whether residents' concerns could be met by [less intrusive restrictions]. As a result, any 'findings' regarding 'secondary effects' caused by adult movie theaters * * * were not 'findings' at all, but purely speculative conclusions." 475 U.S. at 60. Do you agree or disagree with the dissent's argument?

3. *Opportunity to Operate.* The *Renton* Court held that the First Amendment bars a city from effectively denying adult businesses a "reasonable opportunity" to operate, but also that such businesses must "fend for themselves in the real estate market." How should a court determine whether the business operator has a "reasonable opportunity? " Should a court exclude from its consideration:

---

12. Respondents argue, as an "alternative basis" for affirming the decision of the Court of Appeals, that the Renton ordinance violates their rights under the Equal Protection Clause of the Fourteenth Amendment. As should be apparent from our preceding discussion, respondents can fare no better under the Equal Protection Clause than under the First Amendment itself. *See Young v. American Mini Theatres*, Inc., 427 U.S., at 63–73.

[The Court also held that the ordinance was not unconstitutionally vague or overbroad].

- land that is presently occupied by governmental agencies, such as a sewage treatment plant, a solid waste disposal site, or an airport
- land that is under a long-term lease
- land that has no infrastructure, such as sidewalks, roads, and lighting
- land, such as swamp, that would require large development costs
- land that is rented at prices that the business owner cannot afford
- land that is located in industrial zones and so would be unattractive to customers

See *Topanga Press, Inc. v. City of Los Angeles*, 989 F.2d 1524 (9th Cir.1993); *Woodall v. City of El Paso*, 950 F.2d 255, *modified*, 959 F.2d 1305 (5th Cir. 1992); *Walnut Properties, Inc. v. City of Whittier*, 861 F.2d 1102 (9th Cir.1988).

4. *Political Models of Local Government*. What model of local politics—pluralism, republicanism, public choice theory, or the Tiebout Hypothesis—best explains the process by which Renton adopted the regulation governing the location of adult movie theaters? Should a court's review of the ordinance turn on its assessment of the nature of the underlying political process? Do you think it did in *Renton*?

Problem: Regulation of Adult Businesses

The St. Louis Board of Aldermen adopted a zoning ordinance patterned after the Detroit ordinance (adult business—bookstores, theaters, peep shows, and massage parlors—cannot be located within 1000 feet of each other and cannot be located within 500 feet of a residential zone, school, or church). At a subsequent trial challenging the constitutionality of the ordinance, the evidence showed that the Board did not rely on the advice of experts, conduct any studies, or even review existing studies or other evidence. Rather, the Board relied entirely on the personal opinion of the president of the Board that such an ordinance was necessary to revitalize city neighborhoods. The president testified that he based his opinion on his personal observations that adult businesses tend to attract transients and are not conducive to a stable, growing, vibrant neighborhood. He did not offer any more specific support for his opinion.

After *Renton*, how should the trial court rule on the First Amendment challenge? See *Thames Enterprises v. City of St. Louis*, 851 F.2d 199 (8th Cir.1988).

2. ZONING FOR FAMILIES AND GROUP HOMES

Zoning allows existing landowners to preserve certain amenities (*e.g.*, reduced traffic and noise, uniformity of uses) and enhance property values, or at least reduce the risk that development will erode property values. Zoning often allows residents to preserve the *status quo* more effectively than would either nuisance law or the law of servitudes. Litigation is expensive and nuisance law does not address sub-nuisance externalities, and in developed neighborhoods high coordination costs and holdouts prevent the effective use of servitudes.

Zoning, however, is inherently exclusionary. By permitting only specified uses, it necessarily excludes others. And by excluding certain uses, it frequently excludes certain people. Zoning for single-family housing, for example, excludes people who can afford to live only in apartment buildings or who live in arrangements not legally recognized as families.

a. SINGLE–FAMILY HOUSING

Nearly all municipal zoning ordinances have zones for single-family houses, and many of these ordinances define "family" in terms of the number of unrelated people who may live together. Such ordinances raise important federal and state constitutional questions.

In *Village of Belle Terre v. Boraas*, 416 U.S. 1, 94 S.Ct. 1536, 39 L.Ed.2d 797 (1974), a local zoning ordinance barred two or more unrelated persons from living together in a single household. The Village invoked the ordinance to prevent a group of college students from the State University of New York at Stony Brook from renting a house together. Relying heavily on *Berman*, the Supreme Court rejected a multi-faceted constitutional challenge to a zoning ordinance. The Court emphasized that the "police power is not confined to elimination of filth, stench, and unhealthy places. It is ample to lay out zones where family values, youth values, and the blessings of quiet seclusion and clean air make the area a sanctuary for people." *Id*. at 9, 94 S.Ct. at 1541.

Subsequently, in *Moore v. City of East Cleveland*, 431 U.S. 494, 97 S.Ct. 1932, 52 L.Ed.2d 531 (1977), the Supreme Court held invalid a zoning ordinance whose narrow definition of family prevented a grandmother from living with her two grandchildren, who themselves were cousins. A plurality opinion stated that "[w]hen a city undertakes such intrusive regulation of the family, neither *Belle Terre* nor *Euclid* governs; the usual judicial deference to the legislature is inappropriate." *Id*. at 499, 97 S.Ct. at 1935. Although the plurality invoked due process to limit the scope of the police power in these circumstances, its evident reluctance to extend its due process analysis too broadly[13] signaled that for federal constitutional purposes, municipalities could continue to enact zoning ordinances prohibiting unrelated persons from living together.

State courts—which may interpret their own constitutions more broadly than the federal constitution—are divided over whether *state* law toler-

---

13. "Substantive due process has at times been a treacherous field for this Court. There are risks when the judicial branch gives enhanced protection to certain substan- tive liberties without the guidance of the more specific provisions of the Bill of Rights." 431 U.S. at 502, 97 S.Ct. at 1937.

ates restrictive definitions of "family" in a zoning ordinance. In *Dinan v. Board of Zoning Appeals*, 220 Conn. 61, 595 A.2d 864 (1991), a landlord rented a two-family house to two sets of tenants, each consisting of five unrelated persons. Under the zoning ordinance, each unit was restricted to a single family, which was defined as persons "related by blood, marriage, or adoption, living together as a single housekeeping unit." In upholding the ordinance as rationally related to legitimate governmental purposes, the court wrote:

> The [city council adopting zoning regulations] could reasonably have concluded that roomers or such occupants as the plaintiffs' tenants are less likely to develop the kind of friendly relationships with neighbors that abound in residential districts occupied by traditional families. While the plaintiffs' tenants continue to reside on the property, they are not likely to have children who would become playmates of other children living in the area. Neighbors are not so likely to call upon them to borrow a cup of sugar, provide a ride to the store, mind the family pets, water the plants or perform any of the countless services that families both traditional and nontraditional, provide to each other as a result of longtime acquaintance and mutual self-interest.

Id. at 74, 595 A.2d at 870.[14]

State v. Baker

Supreme Court of New Jersey, 1979.
81 N.J. 99, 405 A.2d 368.

■ JUSTICE PASHMAN.

The issue presented by this appeal is whether a municipality may utilize criteria based upon biological or legal relationships in order to limit the types of groups that may live within its borders. Specifically, we must determine the validity of § 17:3–1(a)(17) of the Plainfield Zoning Ordinance which seeks to preserve the "family" character of the municipality's neighborhoods by prohibiting more than four unrelated individuals from sharing a single housing unit. For the reasons to be given below, we conclude that although the goal sought to be furthered by that provision is entirely legitimate, the means chosen do not bear a substantial relationship to the effectuation of that goal. Hence, the regulation violates N.J.Const. (1947) Art. I, par. 1 and Art. IV, § 6, par. 2, and cannot stand.

14.   Many other courts have reached the same result. *See, e.g., Rademan v. City and County of Denver*, 186 Colo. 250, 253–55, 526 P.2d 1325, 1327–28 (1974) (holding that two married couples and two other individuals claiming to live together as a "communal family" do not qualify as a family under the zoning ordinance and upholding the ordinance as rationally related to a permissible state objective); *Town of Durham v. White Enterprises, Inc.*, 115 N.H. 645, 648–49, 348 A.2d 706, 708–09 (1975) (upholding an ordinance prohibiting more than four unrelated persons from living together while not imposing a similar restriction on persons related by blood, marriage, or adoption).

Defendant Dennis Baker is the owner of a house located at 715 Sheridan Avenue, Plainfield. This dwelling is situated in a zone restricted to single family use. On three separate occasions during the fall of 1976 defendant was charged with allowing more than one family to reside in his home in violation of § 17:11–2 of the Plainfield Zoning Ordinance. "Family" is defined in the ordinance as:

> One (1) or more persons occupying a dwelling unit as a single non-profit housekeeping unit. More than four (4) persons ... not related by blood, marriage, or adoption shall not be considered to constitute a family. (City of Plainfield Zoning Ordinance § 17:3–1(a)(17))

A trial as to all three charges was held in Plainfield Municipal Court. The evidence presented indicated that the home was generally shared by nine individuals: Mr. and Mrs. Baker, their three daughters, Mrs. Conata and her three children. Several other persons also apparently resided within the household for indeterminate periods of time.

The Bakers and Conatas lived together in what defendant termed an "extended family." The two groups view each other as part of one large family and have no desire to reside in separate homes. Defendant, an ordained minister of the Presbyterian Church, testified that the living arrangement arose out of the individuals' religious beliefs and resultant desire to go through life as "brothers and sisters." The Bakers and Conatas ate together, shared common areas and held communal prayer sessions. Each occupant contributed a fixed amount per week to defray household expenses.

Defendant was found guilty of all three charges and fines were imposed. After a trial de novo in the Union County Court—based upon the Municipal Court transcript—defendant was again found in violation of the ordinance. The County Court judge concluded that defendant's religious beliefs regarding his lifestyle were sincere and that the household resembled a traditional extended family, thus constituting a "single non-profit housekeeping unit" within the meaning of the zoning ordinance. Nevertheless, he found both that the living arrangement of the Bakers and Conatas violated the numerical restriction of § 17:3–1(a)(17) and that the provision was a valid exercise of the municipality's police powers. Accordingly, he imposed the same penalties as had the Municipal Court. He ordered, however, that the fines for the first and third violations be suspended.

* * *

I

A municipality's zoning power, although broad, is not without limits. In order to be valid, a zoning regulation must both represent a reasonable exercise of the police power and bear a real and substantial relation to a legitimate municipal goal. Moreover, the regulation may "not exceed the public need or substantially affect uses which do not partake of the offensive character of those which cause the problem sought to be ameliorated." *Kirsch Holding Co. v. Borough of Manasquan*, 59 N.J. 241, 251, 281 A.2d 513, 518 (1971). Under this test the numerical limitations of § 17:3–1(a)(17) must fall.

We have no quarrel with the legitimacy of Plainfield's goal. Local governments are free to designate certain areas as exclusively residential and may act to preserve a family style of living. *See Berger v. State, supra,* 71 N.J. at 223, 364 A.2d 993; *Collins v. Board of Adj. of Margate City,* 3 N.J. 200, 208, 69 A.2d 708 (1949); *Village of Belle Terre v. Boraas,* 416 U.S. 1 (1974). A municipality is validly concerned with maintaining the stability and permanence generally associated with single family occupancy and preventing uses resembling boarding houses or other institutional living arrangements. *See Berger v. State, supra,* 71 N.J. at 225, 364 A.2d 993. Moreover, a municipality has a strong interest in regulating the intensity of land use so as to minimize congestion and overcrowding. As we stated in *Berger,* a municipality may endeavor in every legitimate way to "secure and maintain 'the blessings of quiet seclusion' and to make available to its inhabitants the refreshment of repose and the tranquility of solitude." 71 N.J. at 223, 364 A.2d at 1002.

Nevertheless, the power to attain these goals is not without limits. A municipality may not, for example, zone so as to exclude from its borders the poor or other unwanted minorities. *See, e.g., Oakwood at Madison, Inc. v. Township of Madison,* 72 N.J. 481, 371 A.2d 1192 (1977); *So. Burlington Cty. NAACP v. Twp. of Mt. Laurel,* 67 N.J. 151, 336 A.2d 713, *cert. den. and app. dism.,* 423 U.S. 808 (1975). Nor may zoning be used as a tool to regulate the internal composition of housekeeping units. *Taxpayer's Ass'n of Weymouth Tp. v. Weymouth Tp.,* 80 N.J. 6, 33 (1976), *cert. den. and app. dism.,* 430 U.S. 977 (1977). *See, e.g., Kirsch Holding Co. v. Borough of Manasquan, supra; City of White Plains v. Ferraioli,* 34 N.Y.2d 300, 357 N.Y.S.2d 449, 313 N.E.2d 756 (Ct.App.1974). A municipality must draw a careful balance between preserving family life and prohibiting social diversity.

The fatal flaw in attempting to maintain a stable residential neighborhood through the use of criteria based upon biological or legal relationships is that such classifications operate to prohibit a plethora of uses which pose no threat to the accomplishment of the end sought to be achieved. Moreover, such a classification system legitimizes many uses which defeat that goal. Plainfield's ordinance, for example, would prohibit a group of five unrelated "widows, widowers, older spinsters or bachelors or even of judges" from residing in a single unit within the municipality. *Kirsch Holding Co. v. Borough of Manasquan, supra,* 59 N.J. at 248, 281 A.2d 513. On the other hand, a group consisting of 10 distant cousins could so reside without violating the ordinance. Thus the ordinance distinguishes between acceptable and prohibited uses on grounds which may, in many cases, have no rational relationship to the problem sought to be ameliorated.

Regulations based upon biological traits or legal relationships necessarily reflect generalized assumptions about the stability and social desirability of households comprised of unrelated individuals assumptions which in many cases do not reflect the real world. Justice Schaefer, writing for the Supreme Court of Illinois, has noted that:

> a group of persons bound together only by their common desire to operate a single housekeeping unit, might be thought to have a transient quality that would affect adversely the stability of the neighborhood, * * * And it might be considered that a group of unrelated persons would be more likely to generate traffic and parking problems than would an equal number of related persons. *But none of these observations reflects a universal truth.* Family groups are mobile today, and not all family units are internally stable and well-disciplined. Family groups with two or more cars are not unfamiliar. (*City of Des Plaines v. Trottner*, 34 Ill.2d 432, 437, 216 N.E.2d 116, 119 (Sup.Ct.1966) (emphasis supplied))

Accordingly, that court held a municipality without power to adopt a zoning ordinance which would "penetrate so deeply * * * into the internal composition of a single housekeeping unit." *Id.* at 120.

Nevertheless, despite the inexactitude and overinclusiveness of such regulations, we would be reluctant to condemn them in the absence of less restrictive alternatives. Such options do, however, exist.

The courts of this and other states have often noted that the core concept underlying single family living is not biological or legal relationship but, rather, its character as a single housekeeping unit. As long as a group bears the "generic character of a family unit as a relatively permanent household," it should be equally as entitled to occupy a single family dwelling as its biologically related neighbors.

Plainfield has a legitimate interest in preserving a "family" style of living in certain residential neighborhoods. Such a goal may be achieved, perhaps more sensibly, by the single-housekeeping unit requirement, as well as the exclusion of incompatible residential uses such as commercial residences, non-familial institutional uses, boarding homes and other such occupancies without infringing unnecessarily upon the freedom and privacy of unrelated individuals.[15]

In addition to preserving a "family" style of living, the municipality also defends its ordinance as necessary to prevent overcrowding and congestion. The instant regulation, however, is too tenuously related to these goals to justify its impingement upon the internal makeup of the housekeeping entity. The Plainfield Ordinance is both underinclusive and overinclusive. It is overinclusive because it prohibits single housekeeping units which may not, in fact, be overcrowded or cause congestion; it is

---

15. The dissent suggests that today's opinion will allow multi-family occupancy in single family homes. This ignores the fact that municipalities are empowered to restrict residences to groups which actually constitute bona fide single-housekeeping units the true criterion of single residence dwellings. *Berger v. State, supra,* 71 N.J. at 227, 364 A.2d 993. Municipal officials remain free to define in a reasonable manner what constitutes such a unit. Moreover, space-related occupancy limitations, may be used to preclude the possibility of household groups of "unrestricted" size. Thus, only groups compatible with a residential area will benefit by today's opinion.

underinclusive because it fails to prohibit certain housekeeping units composed of related individuals which do present such problems. Thus, for example, five unrelated retired gentlemen could not share a large eight bedroom estate situated upon five acres of land, whereas a large extended family including aunts, uncles and cousins, could share a small two bedroom apartment without violating this ordinance.

An appropriate method to prevent overcrowding and congestion was suggested by this Court in *Kirsch Holding Co. v. Borough of Manasquan, supra*. We there stated that "[w]hen intensity of use, *i.e.*, overcrowding of dwelling units and facilities, [presents a problem] consideration might quite properly be given to zoning or housing code provisions, which would have to be of general application, limiting the number of occupants in reasonable relation to available sleeping and bathroom facilities or requiring a minimum amount of habitable floor area per occupant." (59 N.J. at 254, 281 A.2d at 520) *See Sente v. Mayor and Mun. Coun. of Clifton*, 66 N.J. 204, 330 A.2d 321 (1974). Area or facility-related ordinances not only bear a much greater relation to the problem of overcrowding than do legal or biologically based classifications, they also do not impact upon the composition of the household. They thus constitute a more reasoned manner of protecting the public health.

Other legitimate municipal concerns can be dealt with similarly. Traffic congestion can appropriately be remedied by reasonable, evenhanded limitations upon the number of cars which may be maintained at a given residence. Moreover, area-related occupancy restrictions will, by decreasing density, tend by themselves to reduce traffic problems. Disruptive behavior which, of course, is not limited to unrelated households may properly be controlled through the use of the general police power. As we stated in *Kirsch v. Borough of Manasquan, supra*: "Ordinarily obnoxious personal behavior can best be dealt with officially by vigorous and persistent enforcement of general police power ordinances and criminal statutes * * *. Zoning ordinances are not intended and cannot be expected to cure or prevent most anti-social conduct in dwelling situations." (59 N.J. at 253–254, 281 A.2d at 520) Restrictions based upon legal or biological relationships such as Plainfield's impact only remotely upon such problems and hence cannot withstand judicial scrutiny.

Plainfield, in attempting to justify its regulation, relies upon *Village of Belle Terre v. Boraas*, 416 U.S. 1 (1974). In that case the United States Supreme Court upheld an ordinance which limited to two the number of unrelated individuals who could reside in a single-family dwelling. *Belle Terre* has been widely criticized by the commentators[16] and its rationale appears to have been undermined in part by the more recent case of *Moore v. City of E. Cleveland*, 431 U.S. 494 (1977). In any event, *Belle Terre* is at

---

16. *See, e.g.*, Williams and Doughty, Studies in Legal Realism: Mount Laurel, Belle Terre and Berman, 29 Rutgers L.Rev. 73, 76–82 (1975); Hartman, Village of Belle Terre v. Boraas: Belle Terre Is a Nice Place to Visit But Only "Families" May Live There, 8 Urb.L.Ann. 193 (1974); Note, Village of Belle Terre v. Boraas: "A Sanctuary for People", 9 U.S.F.L.Rev. 391 (1974).

most dispositive of any federal constitutional question here involved. We, of course, remain free to interpret our constitution and statutes more stringently. * * * *See generally* Brennan, State Constitutions and the Protection of Individual Rights, 90 Harv.L.Rev. 489 (1977). We find the reasoning of *Belle Terre* to be both unpersuasive and inconsistent with the results reached by this Court in *Kirsch Holding Co. v. Borough of Manasquan, supra,* and *Berger v. State, supra.* Hence we do not choose to follow it.

* * *

Accordingly, we hold that zoning regulations which attempt to limit residency based upon the number of unrelated individuals present in a single non-profit housekeeping unit cannot pass constitutional muster. Although we recognize that we are under a constitutional duty to construe municipal powers liberally, *see* N.J.Const. (1947), Art. IV, § 7, par. 11, municipalities cannot enact zoning ordinances which violate due process. *See, e.g., Pascack Ass'n Ltd. v. Mayor & Council of Washington Tp.,* 74 N.J. 470, 483, 379 A.2d 6 (1977); *Berger v. State,* 71 N.J. 206, 223–224, 364 A.2d 993 (1976); N.J.Const. (1947), Art. I, par. 1; Art. IV, § 6, par. 2.[17]

II

Having concluded that Plainfield's numerical requirement is invalid, we must determine whether the Baker household fulfilled the remaining municipal criterion of a "single non-profit housekeeping unit." We conclude that the Baker–Conata alliance was of sufficient permanence so as to resemble a more traditional extended family. Thus, the County Court judge's finding that the Baker household constituted a "single non-profit housekeeping unit" within the intendment of § 17:3–1(a)(17) is adequately based on the record.

Conclusion

Today we hold that municipalities may not condition residence upon the number of unrelated persons present within the household. Given the availability of less restrictive alternatives, such regulations are insufficiently related to the perceived social ills which they were intended to ameliorate. Although we do not doubt Plainfield's good faith, the means it chose

17. Article I, par. 1 of our Constitution ensures the natural and unalienable right of individuals to pursue and obtain safety and happiness. Encompassed within its strictures is the requirement of due process upon which today's analysis is based. In addition, we would be remiss if we did not note that the right of privacy is also included within the protection offered by that provision. *See, e.g., State v. Saunders,* 75 N.J. 200, 381 A.2d 333 (1977). Although this right is not absolute, it may be restricted only when necessary to promote a compelling government interest. Article IV, § 6, par. 2 expressly provides that the power to zone shall be deemed to be within the police power of the State. We have, however, interpreted that provision as mandating that zoning regulations reasonably promote the welfare of the public as a whole. *See So. Burlington Cty. NAACP v. Tp. of Mt. Laurel, supra.* These provisions, when read together, require that zoning restrictions be accomplished in the manner which least impacts upon the right of individuals to order their lives as they see fit. For the reasons contained herein, the Plainfield regulation fails this test. Thus, it violates the right of privacy and due process.

to further its legitimate goals were overreaching in their scope and hence cannot be permitted to stand.

For the foregoing reasons, the judgment of the Appellate Division is affirmed.

■ Mountain, J., dissenting.

* * * The most immediately significant result of this decision is that it deprives homeowners whose properties are located in "one-family residence zones" or in other restricted residential areas of the protection they have hitherto enjoyed against the possibility that other dwellings in the same zone would be used for multi-family purposes or for occupancy by groups of unrelated individuals unrestricted as to size. As of this writing, there is no homeowner in New Jersey who can say with any assurance that his next door neighbor's house, or that of his friend down the street, may not at any time and without warning, either be occupied by two or more families or by a group of unrelated persons indefinite in number. All of this may happen although the properties are located in a Triple–A Residential one-family zone. * * *

The majority argues that Plainfield's definition of "family," as embracing only four unrelated persons while including nuclear families of any size, is both overinclusive and underinclusive. It points to the possibility of ten distant relatives assembling under one roof while five or more jurists or other similar groups are forbidden to cohabit together. The argument proceeds upon the oft-rejected premise that legislation that could have, but did not, exclude or include every person who might properly have been so classified is therefore invalid. Much the same argument was advanced before the Supreme Court in *Belle Terre*:

> It is said, however, that if two unmarried people can constitute a "family," there is no reason why three or four may not. But every line drawn by a legislature leaves some out that might well have been included. That exercise of discretion, however, is a legislative, not a judicial, function. (416 U.S. at 8)

Justice Douglas went on to quote Justice Holmes' famous response to this kind of argument:

> When a legal distinction is determined, as no one doubts that it may be, between night and day, childhood and maturity, or any other extremes, a point has to be fixed or a line has to be drawn, or gradually picked out by successive decisions, to mark where the change takes place. Looked at by itself without regard to the necessity behind it the line or point seems arbitrary. It might as well or nearly as well be a little more to one side or the other. But when it is seen that a line or point there must be, and that there is no mathematical or logical way of fixing it precisely, the decision of the legislature must be accepted unless we can say that it is very wide of any reasonable mark. *Louisville Gas Co. v. Coleman*, 277 U.S. 32, 41 (dissenting opinion). (416 U.S. at 8 n. 5)

Limiting occupancy to single families and to not more than four unrelated individuals, as has been done by the City of Plainfield, is in every sense fair and reasonable and should be sustained. The majority would be better employed in protecting the rights of homeowners grievously threatened by this decision rather than in conjuring up imaginary hobgoblins in the form of nonexistent invasions by swarms of country cousins.

* * * The majority * * * has deplorably denigrated one of the greatest and finest of our institutions—the family. The family should be entitled—as until now it has been—to stand on its own in a distinctly preferred position. There is no support in our mores as there should be none in our law, to justify the elevation of any group of unrelated persons to a position of parity with a family. Justice Brennan, concurring, in *Moore v. East Cleveland*, 431 U.S. 494 (1977), and quoting from the brief filed by the Village of Belle Terre in that earlier case, has expressed the point perhaps as well as it can be stated,

> Whether it be the extended family of a more leisurely age or the nuclear family of today the role of the family in raising and training successive generations of the species makes it more important, we dare say, than any other social or legal institution. . . .
> If any freedom not specifically mentioned in the Bill of Rights enjoys a preferred position in the law it is most certainly the family. (431 U.S. at 511)

Similarly the plurality opinion of Justice Powell in the same case drew a sharp line between judicial solicitude for the family as an institution and its attitude toward unrelated groups. It should be stated that the ordinance in *East Cleveland* defined "family" in such a way that a grandmother could not maintain a common household with two grandchildren who were cousins, although she could have done so had they been brothers. The City of East Cleveland relied on *Belle Terre* to sustain its position. Justice Powell disagreed:

> . . . [O]ne overriding factor sets this case apart from *Belle Terre*. The ordinance there affected only unrelated individuals. It expressly allowed all who were related by "blood, adoption or marriage" to live together, and in sustaining the ordinance we were careful to note that it promoted "family needs" and "family values." 416 U.S. at 9. East Cleveland, in contrast, has chosen to regulate the occupancy of its housing by slicing deeply into the family itself. (431 U.S. at 498)

---

1.   *Definition of "Family."* The majority characterized the municipality's goal as "preserv[ing] a family style of living." 81 N.J. at 105, 405 A.2d at 371. What, precisely, does this mean? What are the characteristics of a family style of living? What aspects of a family style of living are desirable? What are the characteristics of "boarding houses or other institutional arrangements" that the court agrees a municipality may seek to avoid?

The dissent argues that the court's opinion has denigrated the traditional family. In what way does the opinion do so?

Isn't *Baker* and other single-family zoning cases about who—the state legislature, the local community, the courts, or private individuals—may define "family"? Is there an unambiguous meaning to "family" (recall the facts and holding in *Moore v. City of East Cleveland*)? To what extent is "family" socially constructed? Given our constitutional concerns for privacy and autonomy from government intrusion, should the municipal government be able to use zoning laws to determine who may live together?

2. *Standard of Review.* After showing that the definition of "family" in the ordinance was underinclusive (in terms of meeting the municipality's goals), the *Baker* court concluded that the definition has "no rational relationship" to the municipality's goals. 81 N.J. at 107, 405 A.2d at 372. Is this statement accurate? Isn't there some rational relationship? What is the factual basis for the court's rather broad conclusion? Does the court's argument mean that anytime it can find an exception to some legislative classification, the legislation will fail as being underinclusive?

3. *Single Housekeeping Unit.* How is a city to determine whether a group of people living together constitutes a single housekeeping unit? What facts must the city collect to enforce its ordinance? How difficult will it be for the city to collect and prove these facts? Will the city's investigation be intolerably intrusive?

The court criticizes zoning regulations based on biological traits or legal relationships as reflecting generalized assumptions. But are there not also generalized assumptions inherent in the court's substitute definition of "single housekeeping unit"?

Does the court's holding mean that a municipality may not exclude group homes for emotionally disturbed children so long at they function as a "single housekeeping unit"? What about a group home for recovering alcoholics? *See Open Door Alcoholism Program, Inc. v. Board of Adjustment*, 200 N.J.Super. 191, 491 A.2d 17 (1985). What about a half-way house for convicted felons recently released from prison?

4. *Nuisance.* Is the *Baker* court's suggestion that the city can rely on "vigorous and persistent enforcement" of the criminal laws to control obnoxious behavior a constructive suggestion? Isn't one of the advantages of regulation that the local government can prevent problems before they occur? Is criminal enforcement a realistic solution to "obnoxious personal behavior"?

Although the court says that biological and legal relationships "impact only remotely upon such problems," aren't such relationships more likely than a group of unrelated people in a single housekeeping unit to exercise social control over other members and deal with the problems that individuals may be having?

5. *Constitutional Right.* In another part of the opinion, the dissent argues that a constitutional holding undermines basic democratic ideals because it leaves the legislature no recourse. But isn't that the point of

having judicially enforced constitutional rights? *See* J. Choper, Judicial Review and the National Political Process 64–70 (1980) (the basic function of judicial review is to prevent constitutional violations that popular majorities would support).

Or is there an issue as to the *source* of the constitutional right? If there is no explicit textual basis in the state constitution for the court's holding, is there a danger that the court will create new constitutional rights on its own whim? Since the legislature cannot override a constitutional decision, doesn't the *Baker* opinion undermine the democratic process? Recall the discussion at the beginning of this Chapter about the danger of factions, especially in small governments such as municipalities. Does that discussion suggest that the court should scrutinize more carefully *municipal* legislative decisions but review more deferentially state legislative decisions?

6. *Comparison to Common Interest Communities.* Recall the discussion in Chapter IV.C of the exclusionary impacts of common interest communities. Do CICs have more discretion than municipalities in setting occupancy restrictions? Should they have more discretion?

7. *Political Models of Local Government.* What model of local politics—pluralism, republicanism, public choice theory, or the Tiebout Hypothesis—best explains the process by which Plainfield adopted the ordinance defining "family." Should a court's review of the ordinance turn on its assessment of the nature of the underlying political process? Do you think it did in *Baker*?

Problem

Winston is a small semi-rural community. The community is overwhelmingly politically and socially conservative. A substantial majority of the population is church-going. Many residents' families have lived in the community for decades.

A minister at one of the local churches spearheaded a drive to prevent homosexuals from co-habitating in Winston, and one of the town council members introduced a measure to amend the definition of "family" in the zoning ordinance to achieve that end. At subsequent town meetings—which were some of the highest attended in memory—many townspeople and the town's religious leaders openly supported a proposal explicitly to exclude homosexuals from co-habitating on the ground that such people were immoral and that homosexuals should not be in neighborhoods with children. There were no dissenting voices.

The town attorney was aware of *Belle Terre* and *Moore*, as well as of state cases in other jurisdictions, such as *Baker*. The attorney also knew that there was no controlling state legislation or case law governing the definition of "family" in the zoning context. He advised the town council to reframe the proposal so as to ban all living arrangements in the single-family zone (which is the only type of residential zone in Winston) except those between people related by blood, adoption, or marriage. The council's stated reasons were to "preserve the family style of living" in Winston, to "protect property values," and to "protect children from immoral behavior."

Two unrelated women living together in the town come to you for legal advice. Their landlord just informed them that he would not renew their lease when it expired next month. The landlord's action was in direct response to town officials who had threatened the landlord with fines for violating the new ordinance. The women have lived together in Winston for seven years, and each of them has worked in Winston.

What advice would you provide? How would you construct a legal argument on behalf of your clients? How would the town respond? How would a court resolve the controversy?

---

b. GROUP HOMES

Group homes pose special problems for municipal zoning. Often funded and regulated by state law, group homes are designed for persons in need of significant supervision and assistance, such as drug addicts, disturbed children, disabled persons, or juvenile delinquents. Compared to institutional settings, residential neighborhoods may provide highly desirable settings for such people. At the same time, neighborhood residents' fears about crime, safety, congestion, noise, and property values often generate considerable local political and legal opposition to the placement of group homes in residential neighborhoods. As a result, many zoning ordinances exclude group homes from certain residential districts, especially single-family residential zones, and other ordinances permit group homes only under limited conditions.

Municipal restrictions of group homes raise both constitutional and statutory issues under federal and state law. The principal federal constitutional claim raised by differential treatment of group homes is a denial of equal protection.[18]

In *City of Cleburne v. Cleburne Living Center*, 473 U.S. 432, 105 S.Ct. 3249, 87 L.Ed.2d 313 (1985), the zoning ordinance required a conditional

---

18. The Fourteenth Amendment provides that no state shall "deny to any person within its jurisdiction the equal protection of the laws." Courts test the validity of classifications based on race and a few other categories under the "strict scrutiny" test; few such classifications are upheld. L.H. Tribe, American Constitutional Law ch. 16 (2d ed. 1988).

Most other classifications, such as those based on wealth, are tested under the highly deferential "rational basis" test. *See San Antonio Independent School District v. Rodri-* *guez*, 411 U.S. 1, 93 S.Ct. 1278, 36 L.Ed.2d 16 (1973) (upholding under the rational basis test a state-wide system for financing schools that made distinctions on the basis of wealth); *Village of Belle Terre v. Boraas*, 416 U.S. 1, 94 S.Ct. 1536, 39 L.Ed.2d 797 (1974) (upholding under the rational basis test a zoning ordinance that created a classification of unrelated people who live together, *i.e.*, excluding them from the definition of a "family").

use permit for group homes for "insane or feeble-minded" people, for alcoholics, and for drug addicts, but the city did not require such permits for sanitariums, nursing homes, convalescent homes, or group homes for the elderly. Cleburne denied the Living Center a conditional use permit for a proposed group home for retarded adults, and the Living Center claimed a violation of equal protection. Applying the relatively relaxed "rational basis" test to the ordinance, the Supreme Court rejected the city's justifications for the denial—*i.e.*, neighborhood fears of the group home residents, and concerns that junior high school students would harass the group home residents—on the ground that the former justification reflected a "negative attitude" and not a reason, and that the later justification applied equally to other group homes (*e.g.*, nursing homes) that did not require a permit. *Id.* at 448–49.

Some federal courts have applied *Cleburne*'s analysis to invalidate restrictions on group homes for convicted felons and the elderly. *See, e.g., Bannum, Inc. v. City of Louisville*, 958 F.2d 1354 (6th Cir.1992) (striking down a requirement that group homes for convicted criminals, but not other group homes, obtain a conditional use permit; the city presented no evidence showing that ex-offenders posed a threat to safety); *Burstyn v. City of Miami Beach*, 663 F.Supp. 528 (S.D.Fla.1987) (striking down a zoning ordinance that regulated homes for the elderly, but not other buildings, such as apartment buildings, condominiums, or hospitals, which housed elderly persons). *But see Bannum, Inc. v. City of St. Charles*, 2 F.3d 267 (8th Cir.1993) (upholding an ordinance requiring half-way houses for convicted criminals to obtain a conditional use permit, even though such a permit was not required for apartment buildings, convalescent homes, hotels, or hospitals; the city could rationally conclude that some half-way house residents could pose a threat to public welfare).

Shortly after *Cleburne*, Congress amended the federal Housing Act to extend the statutory prohibitions on housing discrimination to disabled persons. *See* 42 U.S.C. § 3604(f). The legislative history of the amendments indicates that Congress intended the amendments to apply to zoning restrictions on group homes for disabled persons. H.R. Rep. No. 711, 100th Cong., 2d Sess. 24 (1988) (the amendment applies to "local land use and health and safety laws, regulations, practices, or decisions" including those "which have their effect of excluding, for example, congregate living arrangements for persons with handicaps"). Although the Act has some exceptions, *see, e.g., Elliott v. City of Athens*, 960 F.2d 975 (11th Cir.1992) (invoking a provision that permits reasonable local restrictions on the total number of occupants to uphold a zoning restriction on the number of families who can live together in a group home for recovering alcoholics), it may well eliminate most of the municipal limitations on group housing for disabled persons. *See City of Edmonds v. Washington State Building Code Council*, 18 F.3d 802 (9th Cir.1994) (a zoning restriction on the number of unrelated persons living together is valid under the Act only if the restriction also applies to the number of related persons who can live together).

In anticipation of or following the federal Housing Act, numerous state statutes explicitly limited municipal authority to bar certain kinds of group homes—especially group homes for mentally or physically disabled persons—in single-family residential districts. A Virginia statute, for example, provides that "for the purposes of locally adopted zoning ordinances, a residential facility in which no more than eight mentally ill, mentally retarded, or developmentally disabled persons reside * * * shall be considered for all purposes residential occupancy by a single family." Va. Code Ann. § 15.1–486.3A. *See also* Ariz. Rev. Stat. Ann. § 36–582 ("[f]or the purpose of all local ordinances, a residential facility which serves six or fewer persons shall not be included within the definition of any term which implies that the residential facility differs in any way from a single family residence"; the "residents and operators of such a facility shall be considered a family"); Ind. Code Ann. § 12–28–4–7 (a zoning ordinance may not exclude a facility for the mentally ill solely because the residents are unrelated, although a city may space such facilities at least 3000 feet apart).[19]

In the absence of such statutes, some state courts have held that state-approved and state-funded group homes are impliedly exempt from municipal zoning restrictions. For example, in *Region 10 Client Mgt., Inc. v. Town of Hampstead*, 120 N.H. 885, 424 A.2d 207 (1980), New Hampshire had adopted a statute promoting the establishment of "community residences" for developmentally disabled persons. Even though the state statute did not expressly override zoning ordinances restricting placement of such homes, the state supreme court held that local zoning ordinances could not frustrate this state policy. Despite a "long tradition of local home rule, plenary authority exists within the legislature to override local control when necessary for the greater good." *Id.* at 888, 434 A.2d at 209. Other state courts, however, have found no implied preemption despite pervasive state licensing and regulation of group homes. *See, e.g., Village of Nyack v. Daytop Village, Inc.*, 78 N.Y.2d 500, 507–08, 577 N.Y.S.2d 215, 218, 583 N.E.2d 928, 931–32 (1991) (because the state regulation of substance abuse facilities and the state's substance abuse policy do not "by their very nature" conflict with local zoning regulations, state licensing and regulation of substance abuse facilities do not preempt local zoning laws absent other evidence of legislative intent to preempt).

Some state courts skirt the preemption issue by interpreting the zoning ordinance definition of "family" liberally to permit group homes in areas zoned for single families. In *City of West Monroe v. Ouachita Ass'n for Retarded Children, Inc.*, 402 So.2d 259 (La.App. 1981), the city sought a declaratory judgment that a state-licensed group home for six mentally disabled adults (and a couple acting as house parents) in a zone for single-

---

19. Several state courts have upheld these statutes against claims that they improperly intrude on home rule prerogatives. *See, e.g., Los Angeles v. State Department of Health*, 63 Cal.App.3d 473, 133 Cal.Rptr. 771 (1976) (holding that the state statute preempts a conflicting charter city ordinance because placement of homes for disabled persons is a matter of statewide concern).

family dwellings did not meet the definition of a family: "one or more persons living together as a single housekeeping unit, which may include not more than four lodgers or boarders." The court found that the group home "falls squarely within the plain and unambiguous language of the ordinance." *Id.* at 263.

> [T]he residents cannot be deemed to be an unrelated group of people occupying only a part or a portion of another's house. The mentally retarded adults have common interests, common goals, common problems, and will be receiving some supervisory attention from the houseparent couple who will also reside in the home. They will not be mere lodgers or boarders, especially in the commercial context in which those terms are used in the ordinance. Rather, the persons residing in the group home constitute a single housekeeping unit composed of persons who are living and working together toward common goals and who will, as nearly as possible, emulate the lifestyle of the traditional family as we know it.

Id. at 265. *See also City of White Plains v. Ferraioli*, 34 N.Y.2d 300, 304–05, 313 N.E.2d 756, 758–59, 357 N.Y.S.2d 449, 451–53 (1974) (a residential foster home for 10 children living with a married couple with two children of their own is a "family" home under the ordinance even though it does not satisfy the literal terms of the ordinance).

Other courts read the legislative definition of "family" more narrowly, and then also proceed to find the definition constitutional. In *Behavioral Health Agency of Central Arizona v. City of Casa Grande*, 147 Ariz. 126, 708 P.2d 1317 (1985), the city denied a conditional use permit to a group home providing elderly foster care for six unrelated persons in an area zoned for single-family houses. The court upheld the denial because the group home did not meet the ordinance's definition of a "family": "Any number of individuals customarily living together as a single housekeeping unit and using common cooking facilities." According to the court, a

> group of unrelated elderly persons, whose composition will constantly be changing upon the death or serious injury of its members, and their attendants or supervisors, whose composition will also be changed when needed, do not "customarily" live together. * * * [W]e do not believe that the city council intended to allow for example a group of prisoners, serving a sentence for life without parole, to live in the single-family residential area just because they happened to be sharing common cooking facilities and living together as a single housekeeping unit. Nor do we believe that the city council intended that the single family residential area could be used by a group of permanently, criminally insane persons who might be living together as a single housekeeping unit and using common cooking facilities.

147 Ariz. at 129, 708 P.2d at 1320. The court then cited *Belle Terre* in rejecting constitutional challenges based on privacy, due process, and equal protection. 147 Ariz. at 131–32, 708 P.2d at 1322–23. *See also Hayward v.*

Gaston, 542 A.2d 760, 770 (Del.1988) (a zoning ordinance barring a residential treatment center for emotionally disturbed juveniles in an area for single family dwellings is rationally related to legitimate goals of controlling noise, traffic, and population density); *Penobscot Area Housing Development Corp. v. City of Brewster*, 434 A.2d 14, 22–25 (Me.1981) (a group of mentally disabled adults and their non-resident caretakers did not meet the zoning ordinance's criteria of "domestic bond" necessary to get an occupancy permit, and the ordinance did not violate either equal protection or due process).

---

1. *Competing Interests.* What are the property owners' concerns about the establishment of group homes? To what extent are these concerns legitimate and adequately based in fact rather than irrational fear? Should the federal Housing Act be extended to prohibit discrimination against all group homes, not just those housing disabled people?

On the other hand, why shouldn't cities and neighborhoods be able to exclude unwanted uses? Whatever else a family might mean, it probably does not mean eight or more unrelated adults who have serious problems, such as a history with drug or alcohol abuse. Because of the risk of potential problems of unknown probability and unknown magnitude, the market value of neighboring properties will probably fall if such a group home is established. As the family home is the largest investment for most families, are not concerns about property values an adequate basis to exclude group homes?

2. *NIMBY.* If a group home cannot be established in a single-family zone, it will likely be placed elsewhere, presumably in a less desirable neighborhood, or in a neighborhood that does not have the political and legal resources to oppose it. Should the courts and state legislatures tolerate the pathological effect of NIMBYism (Not–In–My–Back–Yard)? Or should they seek a more comprehensive, city-wide, or region-wide solution?

3. *Judicial Review.* How should courts approach zoning laws that exclude group homes? Should courts view the issue in utilitarian terms— *i.e.*, find the best result for all concerned? Or should courts undertake a rights-based approach? Whose rights should courts consider? Should courts weigh the rights of the potentially excluded residents to be treated equally (essentially a discrimination claim)? The right of the group home operator to use his property as he sees fit (a property rights claim)? The rights of the neighbors to exclude certain uses from their neighborhood (a collectively held right)?

Problems: Group Homes

1. A state-licensed operator of group homes wants to establish a group home as a half-way house for six convicted adult felons (non-violent

crimes only) in a house in an R–1 zone of the city. The local authorities sued to enjoin the operator from using the house for that purpose on the ground that it violates the zoning ordinance. The municipal ordinance defines an R–1 zone as an area limited to "single-family" homes. The ordinance does not define "family."

The group home residents would participate in training programs to teach them basic living and social skills so they could live successfully in the community. During the day, residents would work at regular jobs. Staff would cook the meals, although residents would participate in some preparation and cleanup. Expenses would be covered by government grants. Residents would stay for 6–12 months. As residents leave, new residents would take their place. There is no permanent authority figure in the house, but rather a rotating set of professional staff who stay for only a few days at a time.

You are the City Attorney. Construct an argument that the group home does not meet the city's zoning requirements. *See Civitans Care, Inc. v. Board of Adjustment*, 437 So.2d 540 (Ala.Civ.App.1983).

2. A state-licensed operator of group homes wants to establish a group home for six adolescents whom the courts have adjudged delinquent and referred for group home placement. Each child would have been found guilty of a crime, such as dealing drugs or burglary. The operator wants to place the group home in a house in the R–1 zone, but the local authorities have sued to enjoin the operator from using the house for that purpose on the ground that it violates the zoning ordinance.

The municipal ordinance defines an R–1 zone as an area limited to "single-family" homes. The ordinance defines "family" as "any number of individuals living together as a single non-profit housekeeping unit and doing their cooking on the premises, excluding, however, occupants of a club, fraternity house, lodge, residential club, or rooming house."

The children would be at all times under the legal jurisdiction of the court and their placement in the group home would be in lieu of commitment to a penal institution. Because the children are referred by the courts, they would not be free to leave until a judge determined that they had been rehabilitated. The children would attend local public schools and would receive group therapy and psychological counseling in the home. They would have chores around the house. They would eat meals together, prepared by the staff. The average length of stay would be less than 18 months. As children leave, other children would replace them. The household would be run by a married couple—houseparents—who are employed by the group home operator (which, in turn, is paid a per diem rate by the state). In addition to the houseparents, there are two residential staff and a psychologist who would work in the home.

You are the lawyer for the group home operator. Construct an argument that the group home is a permitted use under the city's zoning laws. *See Wengert v. Zoning Hearing Board*, 51 Pa.Cmwlth. 79, 414 A.2d 148 (1980).

3. A state-licensed operator of group homes wants to establish a group home for 10 recovering, adult, male alcoholics. The operator wants to place the group home in the single-family R–1 zone, but the local authorities have sued to enjoin operation of the group home on the ground that it violates the zoning ordinance.

The ordinance defines an R–1 zone as an area limited to single family-homes. The ordinance does not define "family." However, in *State v. Baker*, 81 N.J. 99, 405 A.2d 368 (1979), the New Jersey Supreme Court held that zoning ordinances may not define "family" based on blood, marriage, or adoption. Rather, the criterion is whether a group of people living together as a single housekeeping unit "bear the generic character of a family unit as a relatively permanent household." This jurisdiction follows the *Baker* holding.

The group home would not be a treatment facility, but rather a home where residents would live full-time. Certified alcoholism counselors would conduct group therapy in the house, but psychological counseling would not take place on the premises. Residents would share in cooking and living responsibilities, and they would eat together. Residents would have to be employed outside of the group home. Persons with criminal records would not be eligible to live in the group home, and persons who resumed drinking would be required to leave. The average length of stay would be six months. There would be a resident manager to administer the house.

The trial court enjoined the group home operator. In its opinion, the court wrote:

> It is thus evident that in order for a group of unrelated persons living together as a single housekeeping unit to constitute a single family in terms of a zoning regulation, they must exhibit a kind of stability, permanency, and function lifestyle which is equivalent to that of the traditional family unit. In [the court's] view, the residents [of the group home], although comprising a single housekeeping unit, would not bear these generic characteristics of a single family. While the residents would share in the household responsibilities and dine together, their affiliation with one another would be no different than if they were fellow residents of a boarding house. Clearly, their living arrangements would not be the functional equivalent of a family unit. The individual lifestyles of the residents and the transient nature of their residencies would not permit the group to possess the elements of stability and permanency which have long been associated with single-family occupancy.

See *Open Door Alcoholism Program, Inc. v. Board of Adjustment*, 200 N.J.Super. 191, 200, 491 A.2d 17, 22 (1985).

You are the attorney for the group home operator. Construct the argument that you will use in your appeal to the state supreme court.

3.   GROWTH CONTROLS

Some communities want to restrict or stop all residential and commercial development. Their aim may be to preserve certain resources (*e.g.,* the "small-town character" of the local community, environmental amenities (especially open space, but also air and water quality), agricultural land) to prevent over-taxing infrastructure (*e.g.,* sewerage capacity, roads), or to exact from developers benefits (*e.g.,* new infrastructure) to which they are not entitled under the subdivision laws. *See generally* Ellickson, Suburban Growth Controls: An Economic and Legal Analysis, 86 Yale L.J. 385 (1977).

Some states have used tax incentives to slow the pace of development, especially for agricultural lands. For example, California cities and counties may contract with farmers holding land in established agricultural preserves to use the land only for agricultural purposes in exchange for property tax relief. Cal. Gov't Code §§ 51200–51295. *See generally* Dean, The California Land Conservation Act of 1965 and the Fight to Save California's Prime Agricultural Lands, 30 Hast. L.J. 1859 (1979). Some states and localities have issued bonds to pay farmers directly for such agreements. *See* Feder, Sowing Preservation: Towns Are Slowing Invasion of Farms by Bulldozers, N.Y.Times Business, p. 1 (Mar. 20, 1997) (describing one town's use of bonds to pay farmers to surrender development rights).

More commonly, municipalities have imposed moratoria on or strictly limited the number or timing of building permits in certain zones, or have established "greenbelt" zones in which no development is permitted. For example, in *Golden v. Planning Board of the Town of Ramapo*, 30 N.Y.2d 359, 334 N.Y.S.2d 138, 285 N.E.2d 291 (1972), the town prohibited additional residential development unless there were adequate public facilities (*i.e.,* sewers, drainage facilities, parks, schools, roads, and firehouses). The town adopted an 18–year plan to provide these facilities, but also permitted development if the developer provided them earlier. The court held that while it would not tolerate "community efforts at immunization or exclusion," it found the Ramapo ordinance used "sequential development and timed growth, to provide a balanced cohesive community dedicated to the efficient utilization of land." The Ramapo ordinance did not

> impose permanent restrictions on land use, * * * [but was intended] to prevent premature subdivision absent essential municipal facilities. * * *
>
> In sum, where it is clear that the existing physical and financial resources of the community are inadequate to furnish the essential services and facilities which a substantial increase in population requires, there is a rational basis for "phased growth."

Id. at 379, 334 N.Y.S.2d at 152, 285 N.E.2d at 301.

In *Construction Industry Ass'n v. City of Petaluma*, 522 F.2d 897 (9th Cir.1975), Petaluma, a small city north of San Francisco that was rapidly growing in the late 1960s and early 1970s, imposed an annual quota on building permits. The city claimed that the limitation was necessary to ensure that development would "take place in a reasonable, orderly, attractive manner" and "to protect its small town character in surrounding open-space." The Ninth Circuit agreed that that ordinance would exclude some people who wanted to live in Petaluma but it rejected the building association's and landowners' due process claim. Relying on *Euclid* and *Belle Terre*, the court held that the public welfare "is sufficiently broad to uphold Petaluma's desire to preserve its small town character, its open spaces and low density of population, and to grow at an orderly an deliberate pace." *Id.* at 909.

Associated Home Builders of the Greater Eastbay, Inc., v. City of Livermore

Supreme Court of California, 1976.
18 Cal.3d 582; 557 P.2d 473; 135 Cal.Rptr. 41.

■ Tobriner, J.

1. Summary of proceedings.

The initiative ordinance in question was enacted by a majority of the voters at the Livermore municipal election of April 11, 1972, and became effective on April 28, 1972. The ordinance * * * states that it was enacted to further the health, safety, and welfare of the citizens of Livermore and to contribute to the solution of air pollution. Finding that excessive issuance of residential building permits has caused school overcrowding, sewage pollution, and water rationing, the ordinance prohibits issuance of further permits until three standards are met: "1. Educational Facilities—No double sessions in the schools nor overcrowded classrooms as determined by the California Education Code. 2. Sewage—The sewage treatment facilities and capacities meet the standards set by the Regional Water Quality Control Board. 3. Water Supply—No rationing of water with respect to human consumption or irrigation and adequate water reserves for fire protection exist."

[The Court held that the enactment of the zoning ordinance by initiative did not violate the state zoning law and that the zoning ordinance was not void for vagueness].

4. On the limited record before us, plaintiff cannot demonstrate that the Livermore ordinance is not a constitutional exercise of the city's police power.

* * * Plaintiff contends that the ordinance proposes, and will cause, the prevention of nonresidents from migrating to Livermore, and that the ordinance therefore * * * exceeds the police power of the municipality.

The ordinance on its face imposes no absolute prohibition or limitation upon population growth or residential construction. It does provide that no building permits will issue unless standards for educational facilities, water supply and sewage disposal have been met, but plaintiff presented no evidence to show that the ordinance's standards were unreasonable or unrelated to their apparent objectives of protecting the public health and welfare. Thus, we do not here confront the question of the constitutionality of an ordinance which limits or bars population growth either directly in express language or indirectly by the imposition of prohibitory standards; we adjudicate only the validity of an ordinance limiting building permits in accord with standards that reasonably measure the adequacy of public services.

* * * We deal here with a case in which a land use ordinance is challenged solely on the ground that it assertedly exceeds the municipality's authority under the police power; the challenger eschews any claim that the ordinance discriminates on a basis of race or wealth. Under such circumstances, we view the past decisions of this court and the federal courts as establishing the following standard: the land use restriction withstands constitutional attack if it is fairly debatable that the restriction in fact bears a reasonable relation to the general welfare. For the guidance of the trial court we point out that if a restriction significantly affects residents of surrounding communities, the constitutionality of the restriction must be measured by its impact not only upon the welfare of the enacting community, but upon the welfare of the surrounding region. * * *

* * * The constitutional measure by which we judge the validity of a land use ordinance that is assailed as exceeding municipal authority under the police power dates in California from the landmark decision in *Miller v. Board of Public Works* (1925) 195 Cal. 477. Upholding a Los Angeles ordinance which excluded commercial and apartment uses from certain residential zones, we declared that an ordinance restricting land use was valid if it had a "real or substantial relation to the public health, safety, morals or general welfare." (195 Cal. at p. 490.) A year later the United States Supreme Court, in the landmark case of *Euclid v. Ambler Co.* (1926) 272 U.S. 365, adopted the same test, holding that before a zoning ordinance can be held unconstitutional, "it must be said ... that [its] provisions are clearly arbitrary and unreasonable, having no substantial relation to the public health, safety, morals, or general welfare." (272 U.S. at p. 395.) * * *

Recent decisions of the United States Supreme Court and the Court of Appeals for the Ninth Circuit have applied this liberal standard and, deferring to legislative judgment, have upheld ordinances attacked as exclusionary. In *Village of Belle Terre v. Boraas, supra,* 416 U.S. 1, the court sustained an ordinance which banned all multiple family housing. The majority opinion by Justice Douglas found a rational basis for the ordinance in the community's desire to preserve a pleasant environment; "[the] police power," he asserted, "is not confined to the elimination of filth, stench, and unhealthy places. It is ample to lay out zones where family values, youth values, and the blessings of quiet seclusion and clean air make the area a sanctuary for people." (416 U.S. at p. 9.) In dissent, Justice Marshall argued that the village's exclusion of groups of three or more unrelated persons from living in a single residence violated protected rights of privacy and association. He agreed, however, that the village could properly enact ordinances to control population density and restrict uncontrolled growth so long as it did not abridge fundamental rights, and that in reviewing such ordinances the courts should defer to the legislative judgment. (*See* 416 U.S. at pp. 13, 19–20.)

In *Construction Ind. Ass'n, Sonoma Cty. v. City of Petaluma, supra,* 522 F.2d 897, the Ninth Circuit Court of Appeals upheld a city ordinance fixing a housing development growth rate of 500 units per year. Relying largely on *Belle Terre v. Boraas, supra,* 416 U.S. 1, the court concluded that "the concept of public welfare is sufficiently broad to uphold Petaluma's desire to preserve its small town character, its open space and low density of population, and to grow at an orderly and deliberate pace." (522 F.2d at pp. 908–909.) * * *

We conclude from these federal decisions that when an exclusionary ordinance is challenged under the federal due process clause, the standard of constitutional adjudication remains that set forth in *Euclid v. Ambler Co., supra,* 272 U.S. 365: if it is fairly debatable that the ordinance is reasonably related to the public welfare, the ordinance is constitutional. * * *

[The Court emphasized that the Livermore ordinance was different than other ordinances struck down as exclusionary in that the other ordinances prevented low-and moderate-income people from moving to the community but imposed no restrictions on wealthier people].

We therefore reaffirm the established constitutional principle that a local land use ordinance falls within the authority of the police power if it is reasonably related to the public welfare. Most previous decisions applying this test, however, have involved ordinances without substantial effect beyond the municipal boundaries. The present ordinance, in contrast, significantly affects the interests of nonresidents who are not represented in the city legislative body and cannot vote on a city initiative. We therefore believe it desirable for the guidance of the trial court to clarify the application of the traditional police power test to an ordinance which significantly affects nonresidents of the municipality.

When we inquire whether an ordinance reasonably relates to the public welfare, inquiry should begin by asking whose welfare must the ordinance serve. In past cases, when discussing ordinances without significant effect beyond the municipal boundaries, we have been content to assume that the ordinance need only reasonably relate to the welfare of the enacting municipality and its residents. But municipalities are not isolated islands remote from the needs and problems of the area in which they are located; thus an ordinance, superficially reasonable from the limited viewpoint of the municipality, may be disclosed as unreasonable when viewed from a larger perspective.

These considerations impel us to the conclusion that the proper constitutional test is one which inquires whether the ordinance reasonably relates to the welfare of those whom it significantly affects. If its impact is limited to the city boundaries, the inquiry may be limited accordingly; if, as alleged here, the ordinance may strongly influence the supply and distribution of housing for an entire metropolitan region, judicial inquiry must consider the welfare of that region.

As far back as *Euclid v. Ambler Co.*, courts recognized "the possibility of cases where the general public interest would so far outweigh the interest of the municipality that the municipality would not be allowed to stand in the way." (272 U.S. 365, 390.) More recently, in *Scott v. City of Indian Wells* (1972) 6 Cal.3d 541, we stated that "To hold ... that defendant city may zone the land within its border without any concern for [nonresidents] would indeed 'make a fetish out of invisible municipal boundary lines and a mockery of the principles of zoning.' " (p. 548.) The New Jersey Supreme Court summed up the principle and explained its doctrinal basis: "[It] is fundamental and not to be forgotten that the zoning power is a police power of the state and the local authority is acting only as a delegate of that power and is restricted in the same manner as is the state. So, when regulation does have a substantial external impact, the welfare of the state's citizens beyond the borders of the particular municipality cannot be disregarded and must be recognized and served." (*So. Burlington Cty. N.A.A.C.P. v. Tp. of Mt. Laurel, supra*, 336 A.2d 713, 726.)[20]

We explain the process by which a trial court may determine whether a challenged restriction reasonably relates to the regional welfare. The first step in that analysis is to forecast the probable effect and duration of the restriction. In the instant case the Livermore ordinance posits a total ban on residential construction, but one which terminates as soon as public facilities reach specified standards. Thus to evaluate the impact of the restriction, the court must ascertain the extent to which public facilities currently fall short of the specified standards, must inquire whether the city or appropriate regional agencies have undertaken to construct needed improvements, and must determine when the improvements are likely to be completed.

The second step is to identify the competing interests affected by the restriction. We touch in this area deep social antagonisms. We allude to the conflict between the environmental protectionists and the egalitarian humanists; a collision between the forces that would save the benefits of nature and those that would preserve the opportunity of people in general to settle. Suburban residents who seek to overcome problems of inadequate schools and public facilities to secure "the blessing of quiet seclusion and clean air" and to "make the area a sanctuary for people" (*Village of Belle Terre v. Boraas, supra*, 416 U.S. 1, 9) may assert a vital interest in limiting immigration to their community. Outsiders searching for a place to live in the face of a growing shortage of adequate housing, and hoping to share in

20. *See also Golden v. Planning Board of Town of Ramapo* (1972) 30 N.Y.2d 359; Walsh, Are Local Zoning Bodies Required by the Constitution to Consider Regional Needs? (1971) 3 Conn.L.Rev. 244; Williams & Doughty, Studies in Legal Realism: Mount Laurel, Belle Terre and Berman (1975) 29 Rutgers L.Rev. 73; Note *op. cit. supra*, 26 Stan.L.Rev. 585, 606–608; Stanford Environmental Law Society, A Handbook for Controlling Local Growth (1973) page 16.

the perceived benefits of suburban life, may present a countervailing interest opposing barriers to immigration.

Having identified and weighed the competing interests, the final step is to determine whether the ordinance, in light of its probable impact, represents a reasonable accommodation of the competing interests.[21] We do not hold that a court in inquiring whether an ordinance reasonably relates to the regional welfare, cannot defer to the judgment of the municipality's legislative body. But judicial deference is not judicial abdication. The ordinance must have a real and substantial relation to the public welfare. There must be a reasonable basis in fact, not in fancy, to support the legislative determination. Although in many cases it will be "fairly debatable" (*Euclid v. Ambler Co., supra*, 272 U.S. 365, 388) that the ordinance reasonably relates to the regional welfare, it cannot be assumed that a land use ordinance can never be invalidated as an enactment in excess of the police power.

The burden rests with the party challenging the constitutionality of an ordinance to present the evidence and documentation which the court will require in undertaking this constitutional analysis. Plaintiff in the present case has not yet attempted to shoulder that burden. * * * [Because the trial court granted the plaintiffs an injunction based solely on the pleadings, the parties had presented no evidence regarding the "likely duration or effect of the ordinance's restriction upon building permits," whether the city had "undertaken to construct the needed improvements or when such improvements will be completed," the extent of the regional housing shortage or the likely impact of the Livermore ordinance on regional housing needs, or the impact of new housing on air pollution and existing municipal facilities.]

In short, we cannot determine on the pleadings and stipulations alone whether this ordinance reasonably relates to the general welfare of the region it affects. The ordinance carries the presumption of constitutionality; plaintiff cannot overcome that presumption on the limited record before us. Thus the judgment rendered on this limited record cannot be sustained on the ground that the initiative ordinance falls beyond the proper scope of the police power.

[The court then remanded the case for trial on these factual issues].

■ Mosk, J. I dissent.

Limitations on growth may be justified in resort communities, beach and lake and mountain sites, and other rural and recreational areas; such restrictions are generally designed to preserve nature's environment for the

---

21. For example, in upholding a city ordinance requiring a subdivider to dedicate land for park purposes, we stated in *Associated Home Builders etc., Inc. v. City of Walnut Creek* (1971) 4 Cal.3d 633 that the risk that increased development costs could exclude economically depressed persons could be "balanced against the phenomenon of the appallingly rapid disappearance of open areas in and around our cities." (4 Cal.3d at p. 648.)

benefit of all mankind. They fulfill our fiduciary obligation to posterity. As Thomas Jefferson wrote, the earth belongs to the living, but in usufruct.

But there is a vast qualitative difference when a suburban community invokes an elitist concept to construct a mythical moat around its perimeter, not for the benefit of mankind but to exclude all but its fortunate current residents.

The majority, somewhat desultorily, deny that the ordinance imposes an absolute prohibition upon population growth or residential construction. It is true that the measure prohibits the issuance of building permits for single-family residential, multiple residential and trailer residential units until designated public services meet specified standards. But to see such restriction in practicality as something short of total prohibition is to employ ostrich vision.

First of all, the ordinance provides no timetable or dates by which the public services are to be made adequate. Thus the moratorium on permits is likely to continue for decades, or at least until attrition ultimately reduces the present population. Second, it is obvious that no inducement exists for present residents to expend their resources to render facilities adequate for the purpose of accommodating future residents. It would seem more rational, if improved services are really contemplated for any time in the foreseeable future, to admit the new residents and compel them to make their proportionate contribution to the cost of the educational, sewage and water services. Thus it cannot seriously be argued that Livermore maintains anything other than total exclusion.

The trial court found, *inter alia*, that the ordinance prohibited the issuance of building permits for residential purposes until certain conditions are met, but the measure does not provide that any person or agency is required to expend or commence any efforts on behalf of the city to meet the requirements. Nor is the city itself obliged to act within any specified time to cure its own deficiencies. Thus, in these circumstances procrastination produces its own reward: continued exclusion of new residents.

The significant omissions, when noted in relation to the ordinance preamble, reveal that the underlying purpose of the measure is "to control residential building permits in the City of Livermore"—translation: to keep newcomers out of the city—and not to solve the purported inadequacies in municipal educational, sewage and water services. Livermore concedes no building permits are now being issued and it relates no current or prospective schedule designed to correct its defective municipal services.

* * * [M]ay Livermore build a Chinese Wall to insulate itself from growth problems today? And if Livermore may do so, why not every municipality in Alameda County and in all other counties in Northern California? With a patchwork of enclaves the inevitable result will be creation of an aristocracy housed in exclusive suburbs while modest wage earners will be confined to declining neighborhoods, crowded into sterile, monotonous, multifamily projects, or assigned to pockets of marginal housing on the urban fringe. The overriding objective should be to minimize

rather than exacerbate social and economic disparities, to lower barriers rather than raise them, to emphasize heterogeneity rather than homogeneity, to increase choice rather than limit it.

I am aware, of course, of the decision in *Village of Belle Terre v. Boraas* (1974) 416 U.S. 1, in which the Supreme Court, speaking through Justice Douglas, rejected challenges to an ordinance restricting land use to one-family dwellings, with a very narrow definition of "family," excluding lodging houses, boarding houses, fraternity houses, or multiple-dwelling houses. The village sought to assure that it would never grow much larger than 700 persons living in 220 residences. Comparable, although some growth was permitted, was the ordinance approved in *Construction Ind. Ass'n, Sonoma Cty. v. City of Petaluma* (9th Cir.1975) 522 F.2d 897. Also similar, although allowing phased growth, was *Golden v. Planning Board of Town of Ramapo* (1972) 30 N.Y.2d 359.

In *Belle Terre*, Justice Douglas declared, "The police power is not confined to elimination of filth, stench, and unhealthy places.... It is ample to lay out zones where family values, youth values, and the blessings of quiet seclusion and clean air make the area a sanctuary for people.... A quiet place where yards are wide, people few, and motor vehicles restricted are legitimate guidelines in a land-use project addressed to family needs."

This is a comforting environmentalist declaration with which few would disagree, although the result was to allow the village of Belle Terre to remain an affluent island. Nevertheless, "preservation of the character of the community" is a stirring slogan, at least where it is used for nothing more harmful than the exclusion of the six students who rented the large house in Belle Terre. Complications arise when ordinances are employed to exclude not merely student lodgers, but all outsiders. While the affluent may seek a congenial suburban atmosphere other than Belle Terre or Livermore, what are the alternatives for those in megalopolitan areas who cannot afford similar selectivity?

The right of all persons to acquire housing is not a mere esoteric principle; it has commanded recognition in a wide spectrum of aspects. In *Shelley v. Kraemer* (1948) 334 U.S. 1, race restrictive covenants were declared to be constitutionally unenforceable. Chief Justice Vinson noted in his opinion that among the guarantees of the Fourteenth Amendment "are the rights to acquire, enjoy, own and dispose of property." In *Reitman v. Mulkey* (1967) 387 U.S. 369, the Supreme Court upheld our invalidation of a ballot proposition, declaring that "Neither the State nor any subdivision or agency thereof shall deny, limit or abridge, directly or indirectly, the right of any person, who is willing or desires to sell, lease or rent any part or all of his real property, to decline to sell, lease or rent such property to such person or persons as he, in his absolute discretion, chooses." Justice Douglas, in a concurring opinion in *Reitman*, went even further to insist that "housing is clearly marked with the public interest." (*Id.* at p. 385.) Again in *Jones v. Mayer Co.* (1968) 392 U.S. 409, 418, a case involving racial discrimination in housing, Justice Stewart spoke of the right of all citizens " 'to inherit, purchase, lease, sell, hold, and convey real and personal property.' " (*Also see Buchanan v. Warley* (1917) 245 U.S. 60.)

One thing emerges with clarity from the foregoing and from numerous related cases: access to housing is regarded by the Supreme Court as a matter of serious social and constitutional concern. While this interest has generally been manifest in the context of racial discrimination, there is no valid reason for not invoking the principle when persons of all races and of all economic groups are involved. There are no invariable racial or economic characteristics of the goodly numbers of families which seek social mobility, the opportunities for the good life available in a suburban atmosphere, and access to types of housing, education and employment differing from those indigenous to crowded urban centers.

* * *

Communities adopt growth limits from a variety of motives. There may be conservationists genuinely motivated to preserve general or specific environments. There may be others whose motivation is social exclusionism, racial exclusion, racial discrimination, income segregation, fiscal protection, or just fear of any future change; each of these purposes is well served by growth prevention.

Whatever the motivation, total exclusion of people from a community is both immoral and illegal. (Cal. Const., art. I, §§ 1, 7, subds. (a) & (b).) Courts have a duty to prevent such practices, while at the same time recognizing the validity of genuine conservationist efforts.

The problem is not insoluble, nor does it necessarily provoke extreme results. Indeed, the solution can be relatively simple if municipal agencies would consider the aspirations of society as a whole, rather than merely the effect upon their narrow constituency. (*See, e.g.,* A.L.I. Model Land Development Code, art. 7.) Accommodation between environmental preservation and satisfaction of housing needs can be reached through rational guidelines for land-use decision-making. Ours, of course, is not the legislative function. But two legal inhibitions must be the benchmark of any such guidelines. First, any absolute prohibition on housing development is presumptively invalid. And second, local regulations, based on parochialism, that limit population densities in growing suburban areas may be found invalid unless the community is absorbing a reasonable share of the region's population pressures.

Under the foregoing test, the Livermore ordinance is fatally flawed. I would affirm the judgment of the trial court.

———

1. *Judicial Determination of the Public Welfare.* The court specifies the steps that a trial court must undertake in evaluating the validity of a growth control ordinance. The first step requires the court to evaluate the probable effect of the ordinance. What sort of facts or data should the court consider? How difficult will it be for the parties to develop reliable data?

The trial court must then identify and weigh the competing interests. How will the court be able to identify a genuine municipal interest in environmental preservation? Isn't it likely that suburbs considering growth-controls will develop a sudden interest in environmental protection, such as preserving water or air quality, or preserving endangered species?

How, in any event, is the court to weigh the regional need for housing against the municipality's interest in environmental protection (or preservation of small-town character)? What criteria should the court use? Does it help much to know that the court must find a "real and substantial relation to the public welfare"? Who bears the burden of proof? Is that determinative in most cases?

2. *Assignment of the Initial Entitlement.* Professor William Fischel argues that the "growth control" movement has been especially strong in California, and that a primary reason is the California Supreme Court. W.A. Fischel, Regulatory Takings: Law, Economics, and Politics 218–52 (1995). In a range of decisions involving due process, vested rights, attorney fees, and municipal annexation, the state supreme court repeatedly ruled against developers and supported local land-use restrictions that "transfer[red] wealth from one class of people, owners of undeveloped land, to another class of people, owners of already-existing houses." *Id.* at 251. That is, growth controls significantly increased the market value of houses. *See also* Advisory Commission on Regulatory Barriers to Affordable Housing, "Not in My Back Yard": Removing Barriers to Affordable Housing, Report to President Bush and Secretary Kemp (1991) (estimating that building codes, zoning ordinances, and growth controls add 25–30% to the price of housing). Fischel points out that the "absence of a coherent regulatory takings doctrine promotes this transfer of wealth in a majoritarian context," Fischel, Regulatory Takings, at 251, but he maintains that in "California, * * * the judiciary made the regulatory commons problem even worse. It not only encouraged local government regulation; it entitled private parties to join the feeding frenzy." *Id.* at 252. *See also* J.M. Pogodzinski, A Public Choice Perspective on Zoning and Growth Controls: NIMBYism, the Tiebout Mechanism, and Local Democracy, in Readings in Public Policy 154–57 (J.M. Pogodzinski ed., 1995) (largely supporting Fischel's analysis, although with some reservations).

Recall Fischel's earlier article, *supra*, pp. 917–19, in which he suggested that the initial assignment of land use entitlements did not necessarily raise questions of efficiency. Does the experience in California suggest that the initial assignment of entitlements is important or should be constrained in some fashion? What is the appropriate standard by which to constrain the municipality?

3. *Political Models of Local Government.* What model of local politics—pluralism, republicanism, public choice theory, or the Tiebout Hypothesis—best explains the process by which Livermore court adopted the growth controls? Should a court's review of the ordinance turn on its assessment of the nature of the underlying political process? Do you think

the *Livermore* court relied on such considerations? Do you think that the court's deferential standard of review invites communities to exclude?

Robert C. Ellickson, Suburban Growth Controls: An Economic and Legal Analysis

86 Yale Law Journal 385, 400–03, 405–08, 416–19, 468, 500–04 (1977).

I.   The Economic Effects of Various Municipal Strategies to Limit Housing Construction

B.   *The Economic Consequences of Growth Controls*

  2.   *Distributional Effects of Municipal Growth Controls*

  * * *

   a.   *Effects on Owners of Existing Housing: The Homeowner Becomes Monopolist*

Antigrowth measures have one premier class of beneficiaries: Those who already own residential structures in the municipality doing the excluding. If consumer demand for residency in a suburb is not completely elastic, its housing owners can employ growth controls to cartelize housing supply. Current landlords obviously have an interest in barring the entry of competitors. Upon reflection, one can see that suburban homeowners also should be tempted to exert monopoly power. The owner-occupant's gains from that transfer will be increased if construction of new housing units is limited, since the price of all used housing will be raised. * * *

   b.   *Effects on Suppliers of New Housing*

The burdens of antigrowth policies are borne by the owners of factors employed to produce new housing and by housing consumers generally. * * *

Land is usually the most inelastically supplied factor in housing production because it is the only factor that is completely immobile. An owner of vacant land will be unable to escape serious losses from antigrowth ordinances in the common situation where his tract is much more valuable for residential development than, for example, for agriculture, commercial, or industrial use. The costs of exclusion borne by housing suppliers are thus likely to be felt largely by landowners—especially farmers, speculators, homebuilders, and others who own large tracts of undeveloped or underdeveloped real estate.

   c.   *Effects on Housing Consumers*

If demand for housing [in a suburb] is not perfectly elastic, that suburb's exclusionary devices will raise the price of both new and used housing. These price increases will reduce the surplus—*i.e.*, impair the welfare—of four distinct groups of housing consumers. The two groups worst affected (in dollar terms) will be: (1) current tenants who like [the suburb] too much to want to move out (as they will have to pay higher rents when they renew their leases); and (2) all households that move into [the suburb] in the future. These two groups will suffer a loss in surplus equal to the full housing price increase. The two remaining groups will lose less surplus. They will consist of: (1) tenants who subsequently leave the municipality because their rents go up; and (2) potential immigrants [to the suburb] who have decided not to buy or rent there simply because of the price increase caused by the antigrowth policies. * * *

3. *Extraterritorial Effects of Municipal Growth Controls*

* * * Antigrowth policies that raise housing prices within municipal boundaries make housing in competing jurisdictions relatively more attractive to consumers. As a result, the demand for housing in competing areas is enhanced, raising the price of both new and used housing there. * * *

A municipality's particular appeal to consumers may be a product of its locational advantages in its metropolitan area. In that case the major external beneficiaries of its exclusionary policies would be owners of land and dwellings near its boundaries who could offer similar locational advantages. The outsiders most hurt would be tenants living at those locations since the excluded consumers would bid up their rents. * * *

II. **Homeowners v. Landowners: The Politics of Growth Controls**

A. *The Majoritarian Model: The Portrait of an Exclusionary Suburb*

* * *

As Madison warned in a famous *Federalist* paper, a small government confronting a single issue is the surest breeding ground for a majoritarian oppression. The fewer the voters, the easier it is for a majority to establish a common ground for agreement and to monitor the behavior of elected officials. Likewise, an absence of multiple issues reduces the need for candidates to build coalitions by promising favors to minority interests.

Small municipalities combine the majoritarian building blocks of single issues and few voters. Since local public schools in the United States are usually managed by independently elected school boards, the only major discretionary function left to officials of general-purpose units of local government is land-use planning. As a result, this issue often dominates municipal election campaigns.

The demography of small municipalities militates in favor of majoritarianism. In the United States, 70% of suburban households live in owner-occupied housing units. These homeowners have a common interest in exclusion. Prodevelopment interests are far out-numbered and can hope to achieve political influence only if the homeowner majority is splintered on land-use issues. * * *

Thus, the ideal environment for a homeowner majority to work its "plans of oppression," to use Madison's phrase, is a small suburb of mostly well-to-do homeowners who confront the single issue of urban growth. In such a suburb, the political process is stacked against those who benefit from new housing construction.

B.   *The Influence Model: The Conditions for Developer Manipulation*

Under an "influence model" of politics, the strength of an interest group is purely a function of its ability to contribute money, manpower, or other political assets to election campaigns. The more powerful groups are those that can be reorganized to raise campaign contributions and those whose members have the greatest wealth. Madison's analysis suggests that the influence model becomes increasingly more accurate than the majoritarian model as an electorate increases in size and issues become more numerous. As governmental complexity increases, majority sentiment on any single issue is less likely to prevail; organized minorities become ever more able to engage in logrolling and to take advantage of majority disorganization.

* * *

Developer influence should be at its greatest in a large, complex, local government whose voting population includes many tenants and whose homeowners represent a wide range of income classes. Most central cities and many of the older suburban counties have these characteristics. * * *

IV.   When Should Landowners or Municipalities Be Protected by Property Rules?

* * *

A.   *The Meager Scope of a Landowner's Absolute Privilege to Develop*

A landowner protected by a property rule is entitled to prevent a suburb from using eminent domain to acquire his development rights. Under current law the boundary of a landowner's absolute privilege to develop is essentially determined by the "public use" limitation on the exercise of eminent domain. * * * Given the current state of the law, [the landowner] has little hope of prevailing on that issue. As a practical matter, a landowner in the United States today is at the mercy of a municipality willing to acquire his land at market value—a sum that may be less than what the landowner would demand in a voluntary exchange.

This diminution of private property rights is defensible because it facilitates efficient municipal growth controls. A suburb's greenbelt acquisition program, for example, would be efficient where the resulting benefits to its residents of open space, protection of "character," and lower net congestion costs (*e.g.*, less air pollution, less time lost in traffic snarls) would exceed the costs of the program to victimized landowners and housing consumers. If a suburb were entitled to buy up development rights only from consenting sellers, it might be discouraged from embarking on an efficient growth-control program by the fear that some landowners would decide to hold out for the highest possible price. * * * In brief, the efficiency rationale for granting local governments extensive authority to condemn development rights is to reduce the administrative costs of their implementing efficient growth-control programs.

This curtailment of landowner rights also has some appeal from a distributional standpoint. A rule that makes landowners unable to insist on more than the market value of their land in effect gives priority to the surplus current residents have in the existing character of their town over any personal pleasure a landowner might get from development. In particular, its helps channel the efficiency gains resulting from a growth-control program to local residents and away from landowners who successfully pursue holdout strategies.

* * *

B. *The Ample Scope of a Municipality's Absolute Right to Prohibit Nuisances*

A local government should be entitled, moreover, to prevent a large variety of land uses without paying compensation. Property-rule protection, in short, should be provided much more readily to municipalities than to landowners. * * *

1. *Suggested Doctrines for Deciding Whether Municipal Land–Use Controls Constitute Takings*

When a landowner challenges a suburban antigrowth measure as a taking, the trial court's first step should be to decide whether or not the land-use activity regulated can be characterized as being less than normally desirable to neighbors—*i.e.*, as being a nuisance. When the challenged ordinance is one that restricts nuisance activities, a landowner should be able to prevail on a taking claim only when he can prove that the ordinance is grossly inefficient—that is, that its costs vastly exceed its benefits.

On the other hand, when a municipal enactment has prohibited a landowner from carrying out a land-use activity that cannot be characterized as a nuisance, his prima facie case for a taking should be much less onerous; merely proof that that restriction has caused a substantial drop in the market value of his land. * * * [A] local government should be able to defeat his taking claim by successfully [proving] both: (1) that the challenged restriction on nonnuisance activities is efficient; and (2) that the landowner should be able to recognize that as a taxpayer his own long-term self-interest in avoiding the administrative costs of minor compensatory payments makes it fair to deny him compensation.

* * *

VIII. A Comprehensive Legal Approach to Municipal Growth Controls

A. *The Proposed Legal Rules*

When should landowners be absolutely privileged to proceed with their developments? Almost never. A suburb must be entitled to force restrictions (sometimes cushioned by compensation) on landowners or else it will not be able to implement efficient antigrowth programs. Injunctive relief is appropriate, however, against a municipal program motivated by discrimination against ethnic or ideological minorities.

What kinds of development should a municipality be able to stop without paying compensation to landowners? When a government prohibits *subnormal* land uses, a landowner should be required to prove that the prohibition is grossly inefficient in order to recover for any resulting diminution in the value of his land. Most growth controls restrict land uses that are not subnormal. When a suburban restriction that dictates *above-normal* landowner conduct substantially reduces the value of a person's land, that person should receive compensation unless the suburb can affirmatively prove that its restriction is both fair to that landowner and efficient.

* * *

X. The Law of Development Restrictions: Quotas, Moratoria, and the Regulation of Area, Bulk and Use

C. *Application to Other Current Problems*

* * *

1. *Construction Quotas*

In the celebrated case of *Construction Industry Association v. City of Petaluma*, the federal district judge held that Petaluma's plan to limit developers' building permits to 500 housing units per year violated the excluded housing consumers' federal constitutional right to freedom of travel. He decreed the quota program and its related measures to be void.

* * *

The course of the *Petaluma* litigation would have been quite different under the recommended system. Because construction quotas prohibit normal land uses, a landowner who sought damages in a state court proceeding would only have to show that the program substantially diminished his land value. To recover damages for past delays, he would have to prove that he actually would have built earlier had there been no quota. A class action for compensation for past consumer injuries would likely have succeeded; the Petaluma Plan appears to be a textbook example of a homeowner cartel aspiring to monopolize housing supply in the face of nonelastic demand. The city could avoid liability for prospective damages by repealing its program. It could retain the Plan without any liability at all if it could prove that the quota system were efficient and also fair to both consumers and landowners. Not much chance of that.

2. *Development Moratoria*

When a developer challenges a moratorium on building permits (or rezonings, subdivision map approvals, utility hook-ups, etc.), most courts succumb to the * * * fallacy that the dispute must be governed by a property rule. They choose between either mandating that the developer be given the go-ahead he seeks or denying him relief altogether. This approach crates the usual twin problems. If a landowner's remedy against a moratorium is prospective only, the municipality wins by force. Development is delayed without compensation for the period of the litigation. On the other hand, compelling a municipality to provide services to prospective developers is needlessly intrusive into its affairs.

* * *

In general, the courts have been much too tolerant of moratorium measures. Because moratoria usually prevent landowners from pursuing normal land-use activities, they are always suspect from the standpoint of horizontal equity. In addition, many moratoria appear to be inefficient. If the costs of a slowdown were shifted by the courts from landowners and housing consumers with little political power to a suburb's taxpayers generally, probably few suburban officials would choose, for example, to buy time to prepare master plans. If suburbs can delay growth without liability, they may use devices like the Ramapo staged-growth program to help boost housing values to monopoly levels. A moratorium lasting but a few months and aimed at dealing with a true emergency might be defensible under the Michelman fairness test; an 18–year delay (the maximum under the Ramapo Plan) clearly is not. The recommended legal approach would entitle a town like Ramapo to determine its rate of growth but also would sensitize it to the full social costs of its policies.

———

1. *Effects of Growth Controls.* Who are the winners and losers from growth controls? What factors affect the magnitude of the losses and gains? What are the equity considerations?

2. *Models of Growth Control Politics.* Ellickson poses two different models of the politics of land use decisions. What do the models predict about the conditions under which growth controls will be adopted?

3. *Property Rules v. Liability Rules.* In an earlier article, Ellickson argued that in striking down growth controls courts should sometimes apply liability rather than property rules (to use the Calabresi and Melamed framework). Ellickson, Alternatives to Zoning: Covenants, Nuisance Rules, and Fines in Land Use Controls, 40 U.Chi. L. Rev. 681 (1973). That insight informs the article excerpted above. Under what circumstances does Ellickson think that a landowner or a municipality should have rights enforced by a property rule? Ellickson's rule for a taking (and thus the scope of the property and liability rules for municipalities) depends on whether the proposed activity is a "nuisance." How does he define "nuisance"? Will the definition vary from city to city or neighborhood to neighborhood?

Why is the scope of the property rule for municipalities so much broader than the scope of the property rule for landowners?

Why does Ellickson prefer a liability rule in other circumstances?

4. *Market for Zoning Entitlements*. Recall Fischel's article, *supra*, pp. 917–19, viewing zoning as a community entitlement which the community can sell. How, if at all, does Fischel's view of zoning restrictions differ from Ellickson's?

---

4.   EXCLUSIONARY ZONING

An often-voiced concern is that suburban zoning and planning policies promote "exclusionary zoning"—the deliberate exclusion of low- and moderate-income families and individuals. Exclusionary zoning is distinct from zoning specifically intended to achieve racial segregation,[22] although exclusionary zoning often has a disproportionate impact on racial minorities.

The techniques of exclusionary zoning can take many forms. Some of the more commonly used techniques include large-lot zoning, large minimum square footage requirements for houses, prohibitions on apartment buildings and mobile homes, prohibitions on multi-bedroom apartments, expensive architectural or building standards, and overzoning for nonresidential uses (thus reducing the amount of land available for residential development). A key motivation behind these requirements is to keep out residential developments for low-income families that increase the demand for public services (*e.g.*, public schools) but that do not generate a corresponding increase in property tax revenue. Housing for low-income families "is generally less costly (and therefore has a lower taxable value) per household and per capita than the housing of more affluent residents; consequently, ad valorem property tax revenues will be lower per new resident." Karkkainen, Zoning: A Reply to the Critics, 10 J. Land Use & Envt'l L. 45, 51 (1992).

Professor Ellickson explains why suburban communities are especially prone to exclusionary zoning:

> The normal profit-maximizing strategy of a suburb dominated by a homeowner majority is to discourage construction of modest-priced housing suitable for occupancy by families with school-age children and to attract blue-chip fiscal assets like light industrial plants. One should recognize that these particular policies are dictated by two significant constraints on municipal fiscal choices contained in state constitutions: the requirement that children be provided with "free" elementary and secondary education, and the requirement that property taxes be uniformly assessed. These constitutional provisions prohibit alternative fiscal strategies like charging tuition in public schools or imposing heavier property taxes on houses suitable for occupancy by families with many children.

---

22. Municipalities may not base zoning restrictions on race. *Buchanan v. Warley*, 245 U.S. 60, 82 (1917) (invalidating a racially restrictive zoning ordinance as a violation of due process).

Ellickson, Suburban Growth Controls: An Economic and Legal Analysis, 86 Yale L.J. 385, 452 (1977).

Imbedded in the expression "exclusionary zoning" are certain assumptions about the motivations and consequences of strict zoning practices.

> First, strict zoning is motivated by the desire for a low marginal tax rate and high service benefits per family relative to tax rates. This desire is threatened by inclusion in the municipality of poor and minority families requiring a disproportionate share of public revenues, and thereby reducing public and private amenities. Second, strict zoning laws increase local housing prices, which keep the poor out of a community. Third, such strict zoning by upper status suburbs results in residential segregation by income and race, especially between cities and suburbs. Finally, local zoning causes or aggravates major problems characteristic of segregated metropolitan areas, such as mismatches between housing opportunities and jobs for the poor, unequal educational opportunities, public service disparities, inequality in local revenue capacities, and the concentration of social pathologies within certain communities.

Tarr & Harrison, Legitimacy and Capacity in State Supreme Court Policymaking: The New Jersey Court and Exclusionary Zoning, 15 Rutgers L.J. 513, 556–57 (1984). *See also* Ellickson, Alternatives to Zoning: Covenants, Nuisance Rules, and Fines as Land Use Controls, 40 U.Chi. L. Rev. 681, 704 (1973) (concluding that exclusionary zoning "may cause substantial inefficiencies by widely separating housing for working-class families from industrial job opportunities"); Schill, The Federal Role in Reducing Regulatory Barriers to Affordable Housing in the Suburbs, 8 J. L. & Politics 703, 720–21 (1992) (arguing that exclusionary zoning has contributed to the concentration of poverty in inner cities, with resulting social isolation and social problems).

Professor Briffault emphasizes that exclusionary zoning can have regional effects.

> [L]ocal zoning autonomy often results in the promotion of local parochialism and a commitment to the preservation of community status regardless of the cost to other localities and to the balanced development of a region. "Community character" is often a code phrase for the local preference for expensive homes and the affluent people who can afford to own them. Inexpensive houses, apartments, rentals, public or publicly subsidized housing and mobile homes, and the people who would reside in these sorts of dwellings, are often considered inconsistent with the character of the community or the character to which the community aspires. Local zoning will have external effects as these unwanted residents, and many industrial and commercial uses as well, are displaced onto neighboring communities, or, in areas where exclusionary zoning is the norm, driven from the region.

By enabling some localities to insulate themselves from the economic and social costs of growth and from poorer people and their problems, local land use authority may reinforce the class and cultural differences that drive communities apart and breed interlocal suspicion, tension and conflict.

Briffault, Our Localism: Part I—The Structure of Local Government Law, 90 Colum. L. Rev. 1, 58 (1990). Thus, exclusionary zoning in a single municipality might not be highly problematic—people in need of affordable housing could look elsewhere—but it is usually a regionwide phenomenon, especially in suburbs. In Professor Sager's evocative phrase, many suburbs have become "tight little islands." Sager, Tight Little Islands: Exclusionary Zoning, Equal Protection, and the Indigent, 21 Stan. L. Rev. 767 (1969). Thus, some municipalities have kept the supply of affordable housing artificially low; where housing can be found, the prices are relatively high. *See also* Ellickson, Suburban Growth Controls: An Economic and Legal Analysis, 86 Yale L.J. 385, 402–05 (1977) (explaining that restrictive zoning will increase housing prices in other municipalities).

The problem of exclusionary zoning is part of a larger urban crisis. One author has written:

The United States has long faced two very different urban dilemmas. One is the fact that all U.S. metropolitan areas have large numbers of very poor, usually disproportionately minority, households; households suffering not just from poverty, but from many attendant social problems. * * * [T]he other dilemma is that the natural locational forces of U.S. metropolitan areas, in combination with the effects of jurisdictional fragmentation, conspire to keep most poor households in the central cities. * * *

Under present arrangements dealing with poverty is mostly a municipal concern. * * * The need to provide an expensive array of social, health, and housing services for the poor keeps cities from lavishing more money and attention on education, parks, and roads. Education, for example, consumes about half of most suburban budgets, but rarely more than a third of most central cities'. And the cities' lower level of school funding must be expended on more educationally intractable pupils. * * *

In most states, "home rule" has devolved zoning and subdivision regulations to incorporated municipal governments, giving suburban jurisdictions * * * the power to regulate the kinds of housing and business they will permit within their borders. * * * As a result of these stratagems, all U.S. metropolitan areas are intensely segregated by race. * * *

Thus, what American urban policy really amounts to is a kind of Faustian bargain struck by the leaders of the cities and the residents of the expanding suburbs: the cities agree to serve increasingly as the poorhouses of the metropolitan community, as long as the suburbanites—with Washington and the state capitals

acting as brokers and intermediaries—underwrite the extra costs
this role imposes.

Salins, Cities, Suburbs, and the Urban Crisis, Pub. Interest, Fall 1993, at
91, 92–99.

Courts face difficult problems in trying to address claims that municipal policies are improperly exclusionary. First, there often is little textual
basis in state statutes or state constitutions to establish a municipal
obligation to refrain from exclusionary zoning. State zoning enabling acts
often require zoning ordinances to advance the "general welfare," but most
courts read this phrase to mean the general welfare of residents *in the
excluding jurisdiction*, not outsiders. Few legislatures have overridden this
interpretation. Although state constitutional "due process" and "equal
protection" clauses may be (and sometimes are) broadly read to protect
landowner/developers and excluded persons, home rule provisions favoring
local autonomy, statutory, and constitutional provisions making zoning
presumptively valid, and a tradition of deference to municipalities dating
back to *Euclid*, have made most courts reluctant to invent new constitutional obligations and rights. Judicial forays in this area look illegitimate;
many people believe courts are just making up the rules as they go along, in
derogation of democratic processes.

Second, courts face serious practical problems in adjudicating exclusionary zoning claims. It is difficult to decide when a set of municipal
policies, taken together, are improperly exclusionary. There are no clear
criteria to define exclusionary zoning (again, the statutory and constitutional texts provide no guidance), and to some extent *all* zoning is exclusionary. In addition, courts lack effective remedial tools to deal with
exclusionary zoning. Courts have no ability to raise taxes, and no technical
ability to undertake land use planning. Remedying exclusionary zoning is a
daunting and perhaps futile task for courts, and consequently, few courts
have developed doctrines of exclusionary zoning. Notable exceptions include
courts in Pennsylvania, New Jersey, and New Hampshire, and their experiences highlight the institutional limitations of courts in addressing complex
social problems.

Although many state legislatures have enacted programs that encourage the development of low-income housing,[23] few have directly addressed
the problem of exclusionary zoning. State legislatures generally have been
reluctant to interfere with local autonomy in land use regulation. Legisla-

---

23. *See* Salsich, Urban Housing: A
Strategic Role for the States, 12 Yale L. &
Pol'y Rev. 93, 96–106 (1994); Javor, Affordable Housing: An Attorney's Guide to Key
Issues and Governing Statutes: Part I, 17
Real Prop. L. Rptr. 329 (1994) (discussing
general plan requirements, growth controls,
and environmental issues related to affordable housing); Javor, Affordable Housing: An
Attorney's Guide to Key Issues and Governing Statutes: Part II, 18 Real Prop. L. Rptr. 1
(1995) (discussing federal and state financing
programs and finance issues related to affordable housing). These programs include housing trust funds to subsidize construction
(through grants and low-interest loans) and
general plan requirements for inclusionary
zoning in new residential developments.

tures in a few states, including, New Jersey, Massachusetts, Rhode Island, and Connecticut, have made some modest efforts.

————————

1. *Political Models of Exclusionary Zoning.* How would exclusionary zoning policies arise under each of the main political theories—pluralism, republicanism, public choice theory, and the Tiebout Hypothesis? Which theory best explains the proliferation of zoning restrictions that have exclusionary effects?

Does the process by which exclusionary policies arise affect their legitimacy as a matter of law or policy? For example, to what extent might republicanism provide support for some types of zoning restrictions that have exclusionary effects? Would republican theorists defend zoning restrictions that have strong exclusionary effects if they were the result of a genuine collective decisionmaking dialogue? Should it matter whether exclusionary zoning results from attempts to maximize property values as opposed to the attempt to achieve a desired community ambiance?

2. *Tragedy of the Commons.* Is exclusionary zoning another form of the "tragedy of the commons," *supra*, pp. 17–19?

3. *Tiebout Hypothesis.* Doesn't the problem of exclusionary zoning reflect a breakdown of a key assumption of the Tiebout Hypothesis, *supra*, pp. 895–96? Do suburban communities have any incentive to address the problem of exclusionary zoning? Or are their incentives to send the social costs associated with low- and moderate-income housing outside of their community—to the social commons?

4. *Regional Land Use Policies.* To what extent is exclusionary zoning the result of making land use regulations a purely local matter? Would region-wide zoning reduce the amount of exclusionary zoning? Would enlarging jurisdictions undermine other assumptions of the Tiebout model?

5. *State and Federal Land Use Policies.* Why is there so little state or federal legislation barring or limiting exclusionary zoning? Why don't landowner/developer groups who, along with excluded people bear the costs of exclusionary zoning, organize at the state or national level to obtain remedial legislation? Could the problem also be that even in the most urbanized states, a solid majority of the population live in suburban communities. Schill, The Federal Role in Reducing the Regulatory Barriers to Affordable Housing in the Suburbs, 8 J. L. & Politics 703, 726–27 (1992) (citing census data showing that even in the most highly urbanized states, such as California and Connecticut, less than 40% of the population live in central cities and more than 55% live in suburbs).

6. *Exclusionary Covenants.* Suppose that the state courts or legislature abolished exclusionary zoning. Would homeowners just use private covenants to achieve the same ends?

How is exclusionary zoning any different from the restrictions found in many common interest communities, discussed in Chapter IV.C, that effectively limit access? Are private exclusionary policies and practices any more defensible than public policies that have the same effects?

---

a. FEDERAL COURTS

Because housing is all but essential for human survival, some people have argued that there is, or should be, a federal constitutional right to housing, or at least that the Equal Protection Clause should invalidate municipal policies that reduce housing opportunities for racial or economic groups.[24] The federal courts have, however, rejected virtually all exclusionary zoning claims.

The first argument—that the Constitution should provide a right to housing—is problematic because there is no textual basis for a right to housing in the federal Constitution. Nothing in the Constitution mentions housing or suggests that government should have such an affirmative obligation. Moreover, an affirmative constitutional right against the government would be inconsistent with the other provisions in the Bill of Rights, which are negative rights restricting government action.

In *Lindsey v. Normet*, 405 U.S. 56, 92 S.Ct. 862, 31 L.Ed.2d 36 (1972), the Supreme Court eliminated any possibility that it would endorse a constitutional right to housing. In that case, two tenants challenged an Oregon unlawful detainer law, which barred tenants from raising uninhabitability as a defense in a suit for possession for nonpayment of rent. In rejecting the tenants' claim, the Court noted, with unintended ironic reference to Anatole France, that the unlawful detainer statute "potentially applies to all tenants, rich and poor, commercial and noncommercial." *Id.* at 70, 92 S.Ct. at 872. So long as the Oregon statute was "rationally related" to a legitimate government purpose, it would be upheld; greater judicial scrutiny of the Oregon statute was not required because the interest at stake—decent housing—was not constitutionally significant.

24. A constitutional right to housing would impose on the government (and perhaps the state and municipal governments through the Fourteenth Amendment) the obligation to ensure that every person is properly housed. The government would become a housing agency of last resort.

There is a longstanding policy debate about the wisdom of rights to housing (and other welfare benefits), which we discussed in Chapter IV, *supra*, pp. 709, 712–21. *See* Berger, Beyond Homelessness: An Entitlement to Housing, 45 U. Miami L. Rev. 315 (1990) (arguing for a statutory entitlement to housing); Michelman, Welfare Rights in a Constitutional Democracy, 1979 Wash. U.L.Q. 659 (arguing for unconditional welfare rights); Ellickson, The Untenable Case for an Unconditional Right to Shelter, 15 Harv. J.L. & Pub. Pol'y 17 (1992) (arguing that unconditional welfare rights would substantially reduce individuals' incentives to work and would, by reducing the total economic productivity of society, hurt poor people); Weicher, Private Production: Has the Rising Tide Lifted All Boats?, in Housing America's Poor 45 (P. Salins ed. 1987) (arguing the private production of housing has been the primary, and largely successful, mechanism for increasing the quantity and quality of housing for the poor in the United States).

We do not denigrate the importance of decent, safe, and sanitary housing. But the Constitution does not provide judicial remedies for every social and economic ill. We are unable to perceive in that document any constitutional guarantee of access to dwellings of a particular quality, or any recognition of the right of a tenant to occupy the real property of his landlord beyond the term of his lease without the payment of rent or otherwise contrary to the terms of the relevant agreement. Absent constitutional mandate, the assurance of adequate housing and the definition of landlord-tenant relationships are legislative, not judicial, functions.

Id. at 74, 92 S.Ct. at 874.

A year after *Lindsey v. Normet*, the Court made clear that purposeful economic discrimination would not receive serious constitutional scrutiny. In *San Antonio Independent School District v. Rodriguez*, 411 U.S. 1, 93 S.Ct. 1278, 36 L.Ed.2d 16 (1973), a case challenging a state school financing system on equal protection grounds, the Court held that unlike race, statutory distinctions based on wealth were not a classification that required "strict scrutiny" by a reviewing court. In other words, so long as a statute is rationally related to a legitimate governmental purpose (a standard that is almost trivially easy to meet), it will be upheld even though it treats people differently on the basis of their wealth. Under this standard, zoning ordinances that deliberately exclude persons on the basis of their wealth would very likely survive constitutional challenge.

Race-based constitutional challenges have not fared much better. In *James v. Valtierra*, 402 U.S. 137, 91 S.Ct. 1331, 28 L.Ed.2d 678 (1971), the Court upheld a California constitutional provision that required local governments to submit all proposals for low-income housing to a local referendum. Although this requirement did not apply to other housing or land use decisions, and despite an argument that the requirement would have a disproportionate impact on racial minorities, the Court upheld the provision as being racially neutral and thus not in violation of the Equal Protection Clause. *Id.* at 141–42, 91 S.Ct. at 1333–34. *See also City of Eastlake v. Forest City Enterprises*, 426 U.S. 668, 96 S.Ct. 2358, 49 L.Ed.2d 132 (1976) (rejecting a due process challenge to a municipal ordinance requiring that certain land use decisions be approved by a super-majority in a city-wide referendum).

Several years after *Valtierra*, the Court rejected a challenge to a housing ordinance that allegedly had a disproportionate impact on racial minorities. In *Village of Arlington Heights v. Metropolitan Housing and Development Corp.*, 429 U.S. 252, 97 S.Ct. 555, 50 L.Ed.2d 450 (1977), the Metropolitan Housing Development Corporation (MHDC), a non-profit developer, petitioned the Village to rezone 15 acres to allow it to build 190 units of multi-family, low-income rental housing.

Many residents vigorously opposed the rezoning,[25] and the Village Board of Trustees denied MHDC's application to change the zoning. MHDC

---

25. Residents opposed the rezoning on the grounds that the housing would likely be racially integrated; that rezoning (regardless of the change in racial demographics) would

sued on behalf of potential residents, claiming that the denial violated the
Equal Protection Clause of the Fourteenth Amendment. The Supreme
Court upheld the Village's decision because there was no evidence that the
Village Board (as opposed to the residents) acted with discriminatory
intent. Quoting *Washington v. Davis*, 426 U.S. 229, 242, 96 S.Ct. 2040,
2049, 48 L.Ed.2d 597 (1976), the Court stated " 'Disproportionate impact is
not irrelevant, but it is not the sole touchstone of an invidious racial
discrimination.' Proof of racially discriminatory intent or purpose is required to show a violation of the Equal Protection Clause." Although
MHDC did not need to show that the challenged governmental action
rested solely on a racially discriminatory purpose, or even that that purpose
was dominant or primary, 429 U.S. at 265, 96 S.Ct. at 2059, MHDC's
constitutional claim was rejected because MHDC "failed to carry [its]
burden of proving that discriminatory purpose was a motivating factor in
the Village's decision." *Id.* at 270, 96 S.Ct. at 2062.

The Court also has restricted standing to bring exclusionary zoning
cases. In *Warth v. Seldin*, 422 U.S. 490, 507–08, 95 S.Ct. 2197, 2209–10, 45
L.Ed.2d 343 (1975), the Court held that low-income residents who lived
outside the jurisdiction had no standing in federal court to challenge the
jurisdiction's exclusionary policies unless they could show that they had a
concrete interest in a particular development project barred by the exclusionary policies. Absent such a specific injury, the non-residents suffered
only "the consequences of the economics of the area housing market,
rather than of [the municipality's] assertedly illegal acts." *Id.* at 506, 95
S.Ct. at 2209. Professor Briffault wrote:

> *Warth* is the perfect procedural complement to *Belle Terre*, *Arling-
> ton Heights* and the other substantive local zoning cases. Local
> land use regulations receive the deference normally accorded to
> government action, and the ordinary means of attacking local
> zoning will be the political process. Outsiders unable to participate
> in local politics will usually lack standing to challenge local zoning
> in courts; even if they do have standing, they usually will have no
> substantive claim. In all but the most egregious cases involving
> clear racial discrimination or other invidious attacks on estab-
> lished constitutional rights, the locality can exclude. Each locality
> is treated as a distinct governmental unit; the cumulative effect of
> numerous localities in a region adopting such measures adds
> nothing to the case for standing or on the merits. Localities have
> the freedom to pursue local self-interest, without any duty to take
> into account the effects of local land use regulation on excluded
> nonresidents or the economy of the region as a whole.

affect property values; that residents had bought their property in reliance on the ex-isting zoning of surrounding property; and that multi-family zoning at this location was inconsistent with the local land use plan.

The Village was not the least bit inte-grated. Of the Village's 64,000 residents, only 27 were African–Americans. Roughly 18% of the Chicago area population were minorities, as were 40% of the people eligible to be residents of the low-income housing develop-ment.

Briffault, Our Localism: Part I—The Structure of Local Government Law, 90 Colum. L. Rev. 1, 108–09 (1990).

Finally, in *Hills v. Gautreaux*, 425 U.S. 284, 96 S.Ct. 1538, 47 L.Ed.2d 792 (1976), the Supreme Court restricted the lower federal courts' remedial powers when the constitutional violation was undisputed. In *Gautreaux* the district court found that the federal government deliberately located public housing in black neighborhoods in order to avoid placing black families in white neighborhoods, in violation of the Civil Rights Act and the Due Process Clause. 296 F.Supp. 907 (N.D.Ill.1969), *aff'd* 448 F.2d 731, 739 (7th Cir.1971).[26] The Supreme Court held that while the trial court could order the federal Department of Housing and Urban Development to build housing only in the suburbs, "an order directed solely to HUD would not force unwilling localities [*i.e.*, suburbs] to apply for assistance under [federal housing programs] but would merely reinforce the regulations guiding HUD's determination of which of the locally authorized projects to assist with federal funds." 425 U.S. at 303, 96 S.Ct. at 1549. Although local approval is not required for federal projects, such projects must conform to local zoning and land use restrictions. *Id.* at 305, 96 S.Ct. at 1550. Thus, a remedial decree "would neither force suburban governments to submit public housing proposals to HUD nor displace the rights and powers accorded local government entities under federal or state housing statutes or existing land-use laws." *Id.* at 306, 96 S.Ct. at 1551. *See* Fuerst & Petty, Public Housing in the Courts: Pyrrhic Victories for the Poor, 9 Urb. Law. 496, 508–11 (1977) (arguing that courts lack the ability to force comprehensive social change).

b. PENNSYLVANIA

In contrast to the federal courts, the Pennsylvania Supreme Court marched into the exclusionary zoning thicket, hoping to establish straightforward criteria and remedies. The Pennsylvania decisions striking down certain zoning ordinances are grounded in substantive due process, *i.e.*, the justifications for the land use restrictions do not fall within the state's definition of the police powers. The decisions deal with two kinds of zoning problems—large lot zoning and exclusion of certain uses, such as apartment buildings.

The first important case was *National Land & Investment Co. v. Easttown Township Board of Adjustment*, 419 Pa. 504, 215 A.2d 597 (1965), in which the court held that a four-acre minimum lot size violated substantive due process. The court understood the difficulty of deciding such cases.

---

26. The Seventh Circuit's holding was based on § 601 of the Civil Rights Act of 1964 (which prohibits racial discrimination in federally assisted housing programs, including public housing) and the Fifth Amendment. The Court could not base its holding on the Fourteenth Amendment because that provision, by its express terms, applies only to the States. Although the Fifth Amendment does not have an Equal Protection Clause, the Supreme Court previously ruled that the Fifth Amendment has an "implicit" equal protection component that applied to the federal government. *Bolling v. Sharpe*, 347 U.S. 497, 74 S.Ct. 693, 98 L.Ed. 884 (1954).

The greater amount of land [per housing unit], the more room for children, the less congestion, the easier to handle water supply and sewage, and the fewer municipal services which must be provided. At some point along the spectrum, however, the size of the lots ceases to be a concern requiring public regulation and becomes simply a matter of private preference. The point at which legitimate public interest ceases is not a constant one, but one which varies with the land involved and the circumstances of each case.

419 Pa. at 524, 215 A.2d at 608. The court, however, rejected the township's arguments that the large-lot zoning was justified by inadequate sewerage capacity and the fact that its roads were close to capacity. "Zoning provisions may not be used * * * to avoid the increased responsibilities and economic burdens which time and natural growth invariably bring." 419 Pa. at 528, 215 A.2d at 610. Nor did the court find adequate the township's desire to maintain the rural character of the area and to conserve open space.

A zoning ordinance whose primary purpose is to prevent the entrance of newcomers in order to avoid future burdens, economic and otherwise, upon the administration of public services and facilities can not be held valid. * * * What basically appears to bother intervenors is that a small number of lovely old homes will have to start keeping company with a growing number of smaller, less expensive, more densely located houses. It is clear, however, that the general welfare is not fostered or promoted by a zoning ordinance designed to be exclusive and exclusionary.

419 Pa. at 532–33, 215 A.2d at 612.

Five years later, in *Appeal of Kit–Mar Builders, Inc.*, 439 Pa. 466, 268 A.2d 765 (1970), the supreme court declared invalid zoning ordinances that imposed two- and three-acre minimum lot sizes. Citing *National Land*, the court declared that the adequacy of sewage disposal facilities was "irrelevant." "[C]ommunities must deal with the problems of population growth. They may not refuse to confront the future by adopting zoning regulations that effectively restrict population to near present levels. It is not for any given township to say who may or may not live within its confines, while disregarding the interests of the entire area." 439 Pa. at 474, 268 A.2d at 768–69.

That same year, in *Appeal of Girsh*, 437 Pa. 237, 263 A.2d 395 (1970), the supreme court held that a zoning ordinance totally excluding apartment buildings from the municipality violated state due process requirement. Citing *National Land*, the court rejected the municipality's arguments that it was necessary to limit population increases that would strain municipal services and roads and that would clash with the existing scheme of residential development. 437 Pa. at 243–44, 263 A.2d at 398. The township

may not permissibly choose to only take as many people as can live in single-family housing, in effect freezing the population at near present levels. Obviously if every municipality took that view, population spread would be completely frustrated. Municipal services must be provided somewhere, and if [the township] is a logical place for development to take place, it should not be heard to say that it will not bear its rightful part of the burden.

437 Pa. at 244–45, 263 A.2d at 398–99. *See also Township of Willistown v. Chesterdale Farms, Inc.*, 462 Pa. 445, 341 A.2d 466 (1975) (striking down an ordinance that substantially excluded apartment buildings from the township).

Surrick v. Zoning Hearing Board

Supreme Court of Pennsylvania, 1977.
476 Pa. 182, 382 A.2d 105.

■ NIX, JUSTICE.

This is an appeal from an order of the Commonwealth Court, *Surrick v. Zoning Hearing Bd. of Twp. of Upper Providence*, 11 Pa.Cmwlth. 607, 314 A.2d 565 (1974), affirming an order of the Court of Common Pleas of Delaware County which upheld the denial of appellant, Robert B. Surrick's, application for variance from the terms of the Zoning Ordinance of Upper Providence Township, Ordinance No. 34 of 1952, as amended, by the Zoning Hearing Board (Board) of Upper Providence Township. The dispositive issue is whether the township ordinance unconstitutionally excludes multi-family dwellings. * * *

* * * Appellant sought to build apartments and townhouses on a 16.25 acre tract of land (four acres owned by appellant; 12.25 acres under agreement of sale with zoning contingency). The tract is located in an area designated A–1 Residential under the township ordinance, which permits only single family dwellings on one-acre lots. Appellant initially had applied to the Board of Supervisors of the Township to rezone the 12.25 acre tract to B–Business, the only ordinance classification permitting multi-family housing, to develop the site for apartments. The requested rezoning was denied after hearing held on September 2, 1971. Thereafter, appellant revised his plans to include the four acres of ground owned by him. He sought building permits, which were denied by the Building Inspector. An appeal was then taken to the Board requesting a variance and including a challenge to the constitutionality of the ordinance. The Board held hearings and subsequently denied the requested variance. It was this denial which ultimately resulted in the instant appeal.

Upper Providence Township is a western suburb of Philadelphia, located about 12 miles from the center of the city. Providence Road bisects the township along a roughly north-south axis, and Route 1, a limited access highway, intersects Providence Road cutting across the southern quarter of the township in a generally east-west direction. The 1970 census set the township's population at slightly over 9,200; the total acreage of the township is approximately 3,800 acres. Approximately one-quarter of the township land is undeveloped.

The zoning ordinance in question has classified 43 acres, or 1.14% of the total township acreage, as a B district; in this B district apartments are permitted along with other essentially commercial uses, and the record shows that the B district is already substantially developed. Except for a three-block stretch of B district farther south in the township, most of the B district extends eight to ten blocks from the intersection of Sandy Bank Road and Providence Road north along Providence Road and ends at the intersection of Rose Tree Road and Providence Road. Appellant's tract is just north of this intersection. The width of this portion of the B district is 175 feet on either side of Providence Road.

Article I Section 1 of the Pennsylvania Constitution protects the citizen's right to the enjoyment of private property, and governmental interference with this right is circumscribed by the due process provisions of the Fifth and Fourteenth Amendments to the United States Constitution. U.S.Const. amends. V, XIV; Pa.Const. art. 1, § 1; *Girsh Appeal*, 437 Pa. 237, 241 n. 3, 263 A.2d 395, 397 n. 3 (1970). In reviewing zoning ordinances, this Court has stated that an ordinance must bear a substantial relationship to the health, safety, morals, or general welfare of the community. *National Land and Investment Co. v. Easttown Twp. Bd. of Adjustment*, 419 Pa. 504, 522, 215 A.2d 597, 607 (1965), citing, *inter alia*, *Glorioso Appeal*, 413 Pa. 194, 196 A.2d 668 (1964). Thus, without expressly labelling it as such, this Court has employed a substantive due process analysis in reviewing zoning schemes and has concluded implicitly that exclusionary or unduly restrictive zoning techniques do not have the requisite substantial relationship to the public welfare. *See Concord Twp. Appeal [Appeal of Kit–Mar Builders, Inc.]*, 439 Pa. 466, 268 A.2d 765 (1970); *Girsh Appeal, supra.*

In *Twp. of Willistown v. Chesterdale Farms, Inc.*, 462 Pa. 445, 341 A.2d 466 (1975), this Court reaffirmed its conviction that suburban communities which find themselves in the path of urban-suburban growth cannot establish residential enclaves by excluding population growth. *Willistown* in fact was no departure from precedent but merely a culmination of prior case law which had invalidated zoning techniques which seriously impeded or effectively "zoned out" population growth. *See National Land and Investment Co. v. Easttown Twp. Bd. of Adjustment, supra* (invalidating a four acre lot minimum); *Girsh Appeal, supra* (invalidating a zoning ordinance which totally excluded apartments); *Concord Twp. Appeal, supra* (invalidating two and three acre lot minima). In *Willistown*, this Court was confronted with a zoning ordinance amendment which permitted multi-family dwellings on 80 acres out of a total of 11,589 acres in the township. In striking down this land-use scheme as "tokenism" and thus exclusionary, we extended the prohibition in *Girsh* to include not only total exclusion of multi-family dwellings but also partial exclusion, or "selective admission." *Twp. of Willistown v. Chesterdale Farms, Inc.*, 462 Pa. 445, 448–49, 341 A.2d 466, 468 (1975). In so holding, we set forth the following rationale:

The implication of our decision in *National Land* is that communities must deal with the problems of population growth. They may not refuse to confront the future by adopting zoning regulations that effectively restrict population to near present levels.... *Id.* at 449, 341 A.2d at 468, quoting, *Concord Twp. Appeal*, 439 Pa. 466, 474, 268 A.2d 765, 768–69 (1970).

This Court's ruling in *Willistown* rested upon the premise of *Girsh* that where a municipal subdivision "is a logical place for development to take place, it should not be heard to say that it will not bear its rightful part of the burden." *Appeal of Girsh, supra,* 437 Pa. at 245, 263 A.2d at 399. It also embraces the more basic proposition that a political subdivision cannot isolate itself and ignore the housing needs of the areas surrounding it. To implement these concepts, we adopted the "fair share" principle, which requires local political units to plan for and provide land-use regulations which meet the legitimate needs of all categories of people who may desire to live within its boundaries. * * *

Some commentators have expressed concern that judicial adoption of the "fair share" test will thrust courts into the role of super boards of adjustment, thereby usurping a function that is more properly legislative or administrative in nature.[27] Such concern shows a misconception of what we contemplate our role will be. In establishing the "fair share" standard, this Court has merely stated the general precept which zoning hearing boards and governing bodies must satisfy by the full utilization of their respective administrative and legislative expertise. We intend our scope of review to be limited to determining whether the zoning formulas fashioned by these entities reflect a balanced and weighted consideration of the many factors which bear upon local and regional housing needs and development.

* * * The initial inquiry must focus upon whether the community in question is a logical area for development and population growth. *Girsh Appeal, supra; National Land and Investment Co. v. Easttown Twp. Bd. of Adjustment, supra.* The community's proximity to a large metropolis and the community's and region's projected population growth figures are factors which courts have considered in answering this inquiry. *Waynesborough Corp. v. Easttown Twp. Zoning Hearing Bd.*, 23 Pa.Cmwlth. 137, 143, 350 A.2d 895, 898 (1976).

Having determined that a particular community is in the path of urban-suburban growth, the present level of development within the particular community must be examined. Population density data and the percentage of total undeveloped land and the percentage available for the development of multi-family dwellings are factors highly relevant to this inquiry. *Twp. of Willistown v. Chesterdale Farms, Inc., supra; National Land and Investment Co. v. Easttown Twp. Bd. of Adjustment, supra;*

27. *See, e.g.,* Ellickson, Suburban Growth Controls: An Economic and Legal Analysis, 86 Yale L.J. 385, 492 (1977); Payne, The Delegation Doctrine in the Reform of Local Government Law, 29 Rutgers L.Rev. 803 (1976).

Waynesborough Corp. v. Easttown Twp. Zoning Hearing Bd., supra; *DeCaro v. Washington Twp.*, 21 Pa.Cmwlth. 252, 254, 344 A.2d 725, 726 (1975).

Assuming that a community is situated in the path of population expansion and is not already highly developed, this Court has, in the past, determined whether the challenged zoning scheme effected an exclusionary result or, alternatively, whether there was evidence of a "primary purpose" or exclusionary intent to zone out the natural growth of population. *Twp. of Willistown v. Chesterdale Farms, Inc., supra*, citing, *National Land and Investment Co., supra*; *Concord Twp. Appeal, supra*. Because the *Willistown* "fair share" test compels judicial examination of the actual effect of a zoning ordinance upon the availability of multi-family dwellings, evidence of exclusionary motive or intent, whether direct or circumstantial, is not of critical importance. Thus, *Willistown* marked an implicit departure away from judicial inquiry into the motives underlying a particular zoning ordinance. Our primary concern now is centered upon an ordinance's exclusionary impact.

In analyzing the effect of a zoning ordinance, the extent of the exclusion, if any, must be considered. Is there total exclusion of multi-family dwellings, which we disapproved in *Girsh Appeal, supra*, or is the exclusion partial? If the zoning exclusion is partial, obviously the question of the ordinance's validity is more difficult to answer. In resolving this issue, once again the percentage of community land available under the zoning ordinance for multi-family dwellings becomes relevant. This percentage must be considered in light of current population growth pressure, within the community as well as the region, and in light of the total amount of undeveloped land in the community. Where the amount of land zoned as being available for multi-family dwellings is disproportionately small in relation to these latter factors, the ordinance will be held to be exclusionary.[28]

It now remains to apply this analytical matrix to the facts of the instant case to ascertain if the ordinance in question reflects the proper consideration of the above-discussed factors. There can be little doubt that Upper Providence Township is a logical area for development and population growth. This conclusion is supported by the fact that the township is located a mere twelve miles or so from Philadelphia and is situated at the intersection of two main traffic arteries, one of which, Route 1, is a direct link with the city. *See Girsh Appeal, supra*; *National Land and Investment Co. v. Easttown Twp. Bd. of Adjustment, supra*; *Waynesborough Corp. v. Easttown Twp. Zoning Hearing Bd., supra*. The record shows that the township is not a high density population area; roughly one-quarter of the township land is undeveloped. Thus the township's present level of development does not preclude further development of multi-family dwellings.

---

28. We hasten to emphasize that the factors discussed thus far in no way comprises an exhaustive list. Nor is any one factor necessarily controlling. We anticipate that zoning boards and governing bodies, in the exercise of their special expertise in zoning matters, will develop and consider any number of factors relevant to the need for and distribution of local and regional housing.

The zoning ordinance in question results in a partial exclusion of multi-family dwellings, providing, as it does, 1.14% of the township land for development of multi-family dwellings. It is also significant that multi-family dwellings are only one of more than a dozen other uses permitted on this fraction of land. Therefore, this land is not set aside for the exclusive use of multi-family dwellings; development of such dwellings must compete with the other uses permitted in the B district. The above analysis leads inescapably to the conclusion that the facts of the instant case are legally indistinguishable from those in *Willistown*.[29] Thus we hold that Upper Providence Township has not provided a "fair share" of its land for development of multi-family dwellings. *Twp. of Willistown v. Chesterdale Farms, Inc., supra.*

We therefore direct that zoning approval for appellant's land be granted and that a building permit be issued conditional upon appellant's compliance with the administrative requirements of the zoning ordinance and other reasonable controls and regulations which are consistent with this opinion. *Id.*

---

1. *Criteria for Exclusionary Zoning.* Do the decisions in *National Land* and *Kit-Mar* help to decide the "next" large-lot case, in which the zoning ordinance requires a 1.5–acre minimum lot size? What is a principled basis—or at least a workable set of criteria—upon which to decide large lot zoning cases?

2. How does the *Surrick* court frame the exclusionary zoning question? What are the relevant criteria? Is the reviewing court expected to analyze these criteria in a quantitative manner? By what criteria is the court to decide whether the amount of land available for multi-family dwellings is "disproportionately small" to the "current population growth pressure" and the "total amount of undeveloped land"? The court speaks in terms of regional population growth pressure as well as population growth pressure within the community. What is the significance of this focus?

3. *Basis for Decision.* What is the legal basis for the decision in *Surrick*? Whose rights does the opinion vindicate? What is the right that the court upholds?

29. Appellees properly note that a presumption of validity attaches to any challenged zoning ordinance. Nevertheless, this presumption is rebuttable and was never intended to foreclose full judicial review of constitutional issues. *See National Land and Investment Co. v. Easttown Twp. Bd. of Adjustment, supra*, 419 Pa. at 522, 215 A.2d at 607. Where, as in the instant case, the facts show an obvious dearth of land zoned as available for multi-family dwellings, the proponents of the zoning ordinance must put forth adequate justification for this zoning-created scarcity. Appellee's concerns about population burdens, water supply, and the environment, while understandable, do not justify the fraction of land now open for development of multi-family housing.

4. *Takings.* Recall the Ellickson excerpt in the previous section on growth controls, *supra*, pp. 968–73. Would Ellickson have upheld the restrictions in *Surrick*, or would he have found a taking? What additional information would you need in order to decide?

Fernley v. Board of Supervisors of Schuylkill Twp.

Supreme Court of Pennsylvania, 1985.
509 Pa. 413, 502 A.2d 585.

■ HUTCHINSON, JUSTICE.

Appellants, owners of 245 acres of undeveloped land in Schuylkill Township in Chester County, appeal a Commonwealth Court, 76 Pa. Cmwlth. 409, 464 A.2d 587 order affirming the Court of Common Pleas of Chester County. The Court of Common Pleas, in turn, had affirmed the decision of the Board of Supervisors of Schuylkill Township denying appellants' application for a curative amendment which challenged the total prohibition of multi-family dwellings contained in the Township's zoning ordinance on exclusionary grounds and sought the establishment of a new residential district in which appellants could construct garden apartments, townhouses and quadraplexes. We now reverse Commonwealth Court and hold that Schuylkill Township's zoning ordinance is impermissibly exclusionary because it totally prohibits the construction of multi-family dwellings.

The zoning ordinance in effect at the time appellants filed for a curative amendment established five residential districts, the least restrictive of which was designated R4–Residential and permitted single family dwellings on lots having a minimum area of 15,000 square feet. Zoning Ordinance of 1955, as amended, § 676(1). Appellants' property was classified under the zoning ordinance as A–Agricultural. Section 302(1) of the ordinance provided for a minimum lot size of five acres in that district. Two-family detached dwellings were permitted but only on lots of ten acres or more. *Id.* at § 301(2). Moreover, dwellings existing at the time the ordinance was adopted in 1955 could be converted to accommodate no more than three families. *Id.* at § 301(1). The zoning ordinance otherwise prohibited multi-family homes.

On this appeal, appellants challenge Commonwealth Court's conclusion that the zoning ordinance's absolute prohibition of multi-family housing is not unconstitutionally exclusionary because Schuylkill Township is not a logical area for growth and development, and, therefore, no one has been excluded.[30] In reaching its conclusion, Commonwealth Court employed the "fair share" analysis first announced in *Surrick v. Zoning Hearing Board*, 476 Pa. 182, 382 A.2d 105 (1977), which, until its decision, had been

---

30. One of the Board of Supervisors' key findings of fact is that Schuylkill Township is not in the path of urban-suburban development. This finding was affirmed on appeal by the Court of Common Pleas.

applied only in cases involving zoning regulations which partially, not totally, ban a particular type of housing stock. We are now confronted with the question of whether a fair share analysis must be employed to assess the exclusionary impact of zoning regulations which totally prohibit a basic type of housing. We hold that the fair share analysis is inapplicable to this Schuylkill Township zoning ordinance which absolutely prohibits apartment buildings.

A zoning ordinance is presumed constitutional and anyone challenging it bears a heavy burden of proving its invalidity. *Miller & Son Paving, Inc. v. Wrightstown Township*, 499 Pa. 80, 89, 451 A.2d 1002, 1006 (1982); *Schubach v. Silver*, 461 Pa. 366, 380, 336 A.2d 328, 335 (1975). Where the challenger proves a total prohibition of a legitimate use, the burden shifts to the municipality to establish that the prohibition promotes public health, safety, morals and general welfare. *Beaver Gasoline Co. v. Zoning Hearing Board*, 445 Pa. 571, 576, 285 A.2d 501, 503 (1971); *Ellick v. Board of Supervisors*, 17 Pa. Commw. 404, 410, 333 A.2d 239, 243–44 (1975). Moreover, the constitutionality of a zoning ordinance which totally excludes a legitimate use is regarded with circumspection and, therefore, such ordinance must bear a more substantial relationship to a stated public purpose than a regulation which merely confines that use to a certain area within the municipality. *Appeal of Elocin, Inc.*, 501 Pa. 348, 351–52, 461 A.2d 771, 772–73 (1983); *Appeal of Girsh*, 437 Pa. 237, 242–43, 263 A.2d 395, 397–98 (1970). *See Beaver Gasoline Co. v. Zoning Hearing Board*, 445 Pa. at 574, 285 A.2d at 503 (total ban on gasoline service stations); *Exton Quarries, Inc. v. Zoning Board of Adjustment*, 425 Pa. 43, 59, 228 A.2d 169, 179 (1967) (total ban on quarries).

The "fair share" test,[31] enunciated in *Surrick, supra*, was judicially developed as a means of analyzing zoning ordinances which effect a partial ban that amounts to a *de facto* exclusion of a particular use, as distinguished from those ordinances which provide for a total or *de jure* exclusion. The *de facto* exclusionary doctrine "was intended to foster regional growth by requiring communities located on the fringes of the metropolitan areas to absorb the 'increased responsibility' and 'economic burdens' which time and natural growth invariably bring." *Hammermill Paper Co. v. Greene Township*, 39 Pa. Commonwealth 212, 219, 395 A.2d 618, 621 (1978) (citing *National Land and Investment Co. v. Easttown Township Board of Adjustment*, 419 Pa. 504, 215 A.2d 597 [1965]). *See Surrick*, 476 Pa. at 189, 382 A.2d at 108; *Willistown v. Chesterdale Farms, Inc.*, 462 Pa. 445, 448–49, 341 A.2d 466, 468 (1975). Cases involving *de facto* or partially exclusionary zoning turn on the question of whether the provision for a particular use in the ordinance at issue reasonably accommodates the immediate and projected demand for that use. In these cases certain factors

---

31. The "fair share" analysis requires the reviewing court to determine whether "the zoning formulas fashioned by [local zoning hearing boards and governing bodies] reflect a balanced and weighted consideration of the many factors which bear upon local and regional housing needs and development." *Surrick v. Zoning Hearing Board*, 476 Pa. at 191, 382 A.2d at 109–10.

influencing population growth become relevant to the question of whether a zoning ordinance which already allows a particular and basic type of housing stock in designated areas is nevertheless impermissibly exclusionary because the amount of housing of that type permitted under the ordinance is unfairly limited when compared to the immediate and projected demand for it. *See Surrick*, 476 Pa. at 194, 382 A.2d at 111.

Considerations underpinning the fair share principle are irrelevant when the challenged zoning regulation totally excludes a basic form of housing such as apartments. It is true that demand for apartments often derives from the pressure of regional population growth. *See, e.g., Appeal of Girsh*, 437 Pa. at 244, 263 A.2d at 398 (township could not be permitted to "choose to only take as many people as can live in single-family housing, in effect freezing population at near present levels"). Similarly, permitting any type of new construction within a municipality will, ordinarily, result in an increase in that community's population.

However, demand for housing is not necessarily correlated to population growth. Regardless of projected growth patterns, there may be many families who presently desire to make their home in Schuylkill Township but who are effectively zoned out of the community because they cannot afford to purchase either a single-family house or a duplex. Accordingly, Schuylkill Township's contention that its zoning ordinance does not exclude anyone because population projections show little or no growth in the community is untenable. Because the Township has failed to establish that the total exclusion of apartments serves a legitimate public purpose, the zoning ordinance is unconstitutional insofar as it fails to provide for apartments or for other types of multi-family housing.

We must next determine the judicial relief to which appellants are entitled. Appellants contend that they are entitled to definitive relief, *i.e.*, automatic and total approval of their development plan. Conversely, the appellee argues that appellants' remedy is limited to the additional development rights provided them under the amendment passed by the Township in 1975 for the purpose of curing any constitutional infirmity created by the total ban on multi-family housing contained in the zoning ordinance as originally enacted.

In *Casey v. Zoning Hearing Board*, 459 Pa. 219, 228, 328 A.2d 464, 468 (1974), we observed that "an applicant, successful in having a zoning ordinance declared unconstitutional, should not be frustrated in his quest for relief by a retributory township." Accordingly, we held that a zoning provision adopted by a municipality which cures the constitutional infirmity but which was not considered or advertised prior to the filing of the challenger's application for review of the zoning ordinance, may not be given effect for purposes of fashioning the appropriate relief to be awarded to the successful challenger. *Id.* at 229, 328 A.2d at 469.

In reaching this determination, we reasoned that to hold otherwise:

would effectively grant the municipality a power to prevent any challenger from obtaining meaningful relief after a successful attack on a zoning ordinance. The municipality could penalize the successful challenger by enacting an amendatory ordinance designed to cure the constitutional infirmity, but also designed to zone around the challenger. Faced with such an obstacle to relief, few would undertake the time and expense necessary to have a zoning ordinance declared unconstitutional.

Id. at 228, 328 A.2d at 468. Accordingly, *Casey* governs the instant litigation and mandates that appellants be permitted to develop their property as proposed, subject to certain reasonable restrictions, regardless of how that land is currently zoned.

Nevertheless, we believe that approval of the developer's plan is not automatic but, instead, must be predicated on the suitability of the proposed site and various health and safety considerations.

* * *

Therefore, we reverse the Commonwealth Court's order and remand the record to the Court of Common Pleas for approval of appellants' proposed development unless the appellee can show that appellants' plan is incompatible with the site or reasonable, pre-existing health and safety codes and regulations relating to lands, structures or their emplacement on lands which the court determines apply to the development plan.

---

1. *Fair Share Analysis.* Why does the *Fernley* court abandon the "fair share" analysis when a municipality totally excludes a particular use, such as apartment buildings?

What analysis does the *Fernley* court use in place of the fair share analysis? Who bears the burden of proof when a use is totally excluded? What is the substantive standard? What social policy does the *Fernley* holding advance?

Should *Fernley* have been decided differently if the municipality had excluded not apartments but mobile home parks and the developer had wanted to create a mobile home park?

2. *Criteria.* Do the holdings in *Surrick* and *Fernley* give municipalities and developers clear criteria for adopting ordinances and deciding whether to challenge them? Are courts inherently handicapped in providing such clear direction when the underlying criterion is as fuzzy as due process? Will municipalities be able to avoid the impact of these holdings? How?

3. *Remedy.* What is the remedy in *Fernley*? Is the remedy adequate?

4. *Interests of Excluded Residents.* What is the underlying concern of the Pennsylvania Supreme Court in *Fernley* and other cases? If the court is concerned not just with the property rights of developers, but also with consumers' demand for more housing, do the holdings in these cases adequately address this concern? Notice that consumers are not represent-

ed in this litigation. Are developers an adequate proxy to represent consumers' interests?

5. *Municipality's Interests*. What is wrong, if anything, with a town wanting to exclude certain uses, such as apartment buildings or mobile home parks? Are homeowners' concerns about property values irrelevant or illegitimate (keep in mind that the family home is the single largest financial investment for most Americans)? Are concerns about congestion and population density irrelevant?

6. *Takings*. How would Ellickson have decided this case?

———————

c.   NEW JERSEY

The chief difficulties with the Pennsylvania exclusionary zoning doctrine are the indeterminacy of the criteria for a violation and the limited, case-by-case remedy. Municipalities that want to conform to the state constitution can not readily conform their ordinances to the vague, judge-made constitutional standards. Municipalities that want to evade the standards often are able to do so; developers and excluded residents can not easily decide whether to undertake the financial and emotional burdens and risks of extended litigation.

Despite the need for a more comprehensive approach to exclusionary zoning, statewide elected officials generally have been unwilling to attempt to either define or remedy the problem. Their reluctance in part stems from the fact that residents who enjoy the benefits of exclusionary zoning have greater economic and political resources than people who are disadvantaged by exclusionary practices. State politicians who press for broad reform of local land use practices risk becoming an endangered species.

In this context, the New Jersey Supreme Court undertook comprehensive, state-wide reformation of local exclusionary practices. Known collectively as the *Mount Laurel* litigation, these cases forced the state courts into the minutiae of land use administration and housing policy, thereby raising serious questions about the capacity and legitimacy of the courts to undertake these reforms. *See generally* D.L. Kirp, J.P. Dwyer, & L.A. Rosenthal, Our Town: Race, Housing, and the Soul of Suburbia (1995).

i.   *Mount Laurel I*

In the early 1970s, two public interest groups (Suburban Action Institute in northern New Jersey and Camden Regional Legal Services in southern New Jersey) and several developers brought suits in state courts challenging suburban zoning ordinances as unconstitutionally exclusionary. The complaints alleged both economic and racial discrimination and claimed that suburban towns had a state constitutional obligation to permit a "fair share" of the regional need for low- and moderate-income housing.

Most of the defendant towns readily acknowledged the economic discrimination inherent in their zoning ordinances, but they justified the ordinances on the ground that low- and moderate-income housing absorbed more local resources (*e.g.*, to pay for sewers, police, schools, and welfare) than it generated in property taxes. Fiscal zoning, as it was commonly called, was necessary to protect towns financially; as most tax revenues in New Jersey were raised and spent locally (in the form of property taxes), localities that did not control the cost of social services risked disproportionately high tax rates. Their authority to engage in fiscal zoning was reinforced by a long tradition of "home rule," which granted municipalities considerable autonomy in land use matters. Moreover, as the municipalities correctly pointed out, there was no federal or state right against economic discrimination. *See San Antonio Independent School District v. Rodriguez*, 411 U.S. 1, 93 S.Ct. 1278, 36 L.Ed.2d 16 (1973). The towns denied that they engaged in racial discrimination, but many people privately acknowledged a strong undercurrent of racism; more than a few people in the largely white suburban towns did not want black and Hispanic residents from cities such as Newark or Camden.

A few trial courts held the ordinances unconstitutional and required the towns to amend their zoning ordinances to permit construction of low- and moderate-income housing. The towns appealed. The first case to reach the New Jersey Supreme Court came from a Camden suburb, Mount Laurel.

Mount Laurel was founded before the Civil War. It had a small community of black residents whose forebears had escaped from slavery (the town was a stop on the Underground Railroad) and who had fought for the Union in the Civil War. Until the 1950s, the township land was primarily agricultural, and the black residents worked as tenant farmers.

In 1950, the township population was under 3000. Because of post-war suburban growth—fueled by the federal highway construction program (which enabled people to live farther from work), residential mortgage subsidies programs, and the growing unattractiveness of urban centers (*e.g.*, decaying infrastructure, shrinking property tax base, and increasing crime) and the corresponding attractiveness of suburbs—Mount Laurel's population doubled by 1960 and again by 1970.[32] The township was quickly

32. *See generally* Ford, The Boundaries of Race: Political Geography in Legal Analysis, 107 Harv. L. Rev. 1843, 1060–78 (1994) (describing the state role in facilitating local exclusionary policies); Frug, The Geography of Community, 48 Stan. L. Rev. 1047, 1070–72 (1996) (arguing that state policies granting municipalities land use authority and the opportunity to incorporate and avoid annexation promoted suburbanization); Schill & Wachter, The Spatial Bias of Federal Housing Law and Policy: Concentrated Poverty in Urban America, 143 U. Pa. L. Rev. 1285 (1995) (discussing the impact of federal public housing and mortgage assistance programs in concentrating low-income households in urban centers and facilitating middle class flight to the suburbs); O'Connell, The Federal Role in the Suburban Boom, in Suburbia Re-examined (B. Kelly ed., 1989) (discussing impact of federal mortgage insurance programs, tax policies, highway construction programs, and water and sewer infrastructure programs on suburbanization); K.T. Jackson, Crabgrass Frontier: The Suburbanization of the United States 195–30, 248–51

becoming home for commuters and light industry as farmers sold their land to developers. The new residents, now fearful of losing the small town character of Mount Laurel, adopted a zoning ordinance in 1964 that effectively prohibited low- or moderate-income housing, such as trailer parks or apartment buildings.[33]

In the late 1960s, several black residents in Mount Laurel formed a non-profit organization, acquired a federal grant to help subsidize the construction of 50 low-income garden apartments, and sought a variance to permit construction of the apartments. The town denied the variance. Shortly thereafter, Camden Regional Legal Services, representing several individual plaintiffs and two civil rights organizations, filed suit challenging the constitutionality of the ordinance. Much to everyone's surprise, the trial court held the ordinance unconstitutionally exclusionary under the state constitution.

The *Mt. Laurel* case reached the New Jersey Supreme Court in the early 1970s. The court did not address the plaintiffs' claims of racial discrimination,[34] but it unanimously held that Mount Laurel's zoning ordinance barred residents on the basis of their economic status in violation of state constitutional provisions for equal protection and due process. After describing the exclusionary impact of the town's zoning ordinance, and fully recognizing that its decision would affect numerous towns in the state, the court wrote:

> We conclude that every [developing] municipality must, by its land use regulations, presumptively make realistically possible an appropriate variety and choice of housing. More specifically, presumptively it cannot foreclose the opportunity of the classes of people mentioned for low and moderate income housing and in its regulations must affirmatively afford that opportunity, at least to the extent of the municipality's fair share of the present and prospective regional need therefor. These obligations must be met unless the particular municipality can sustain the heavy burden of demonstrating peculiar circumstances which dictate that it should not be required to do so.

Southern Burlington County NAACP v. Township of Mount Laurel, 67 N.J. 151, 174, 336 A.2d 713, 724–25 (1975) (*Mt. Laurel I*). The court emphasized that its holding derived not only from state constitutional requirements of

---

(1985) (describing the role of federal mortgage programs, public housing programs, and highway construction programs in concentrating the poor in central cities and facilitating the movement of the middle class to the suburbs).

33. The ordinance included a zone for multi-family housing, but that housing was limited to senior citizens and included building restrictions that made the price unaffordable for low- and moderate-income families.

The town had also approved a planned unit development, which included multi-family housing, but those units would also be priced beyond the means of low- and moderate-income families.

34. The Court accepted at face value the town's representation that the regulatory scheme was not adopted with any intent to discriminate on the basis of race. 67 N.J. at 159, 336 A.2d at 717.

due process and equal protection, but also from the requirement that zoning must further the "general welfare."

It is plain beyond dispute that proper provision for adequate housing of all categories of people is certainly an absolute essential in promotion of the general welfare required in all local land use regulation. Further the universal and constant need for such housing is so important and of such broad public interest that the general welfare which developing municipalities like Mount Laurel must consider extends beyond their boundaries and cannot be parochially confined to the claimed good of the particular municipality. It has to follow that, broadly speaking, the presumptive obligation arises for each such municipality affirmatively to plan and provide, by its land use regulations, the reasonable opportunity for an appropriate variety and choice of housing, including, of course, low and moderate cost housing, to meet the needs, desires and resources of all categories of people who may desire to live within its boundaries. Negatively, it may not adopt regulations or policies which thwart or preclude that opportunity.

67 N.J. at 179, 336 A.2d at 727–28.

Regarding the remedy, the court wrote:

The township is granted 90 days from the date hereof, or such additional time as the trial court may find it reasonable and necessary to allow, to adopt amendments to correct the deficiencies herein specified. It is the local function and responsibility, in the first instance at least, rather than the court's, to decide on the details of the same within the guidelines we have laid down. * * *

* * * Courts do not build housing nor do municipalities. That function is performed by private builders, various kinds of associations, or, for public housing, by special agencies created for that purpose at various levels of government. The municipal function is initially to provide the opportunity through appropriate land use regulations and we have spelled out what Mount Laurel must do in that regard. It is not appropriate at this time, particularly in view of the advanced view of zoning law as applied to housing laid down by this opinion, to deal with the matter of the further extent of judicial power in the field or to exercise any such power. * * * The municipality should first have full opportunity to itself act without judicial supervision. We trust it will do so in the spirit we have suggested, both by appropriate zoning ordinance amendments and whatever additional action encouraging the fulfillment of its fair share of the regional need for low and moderate income housing may be indicated as necessary and advisable.

67 N.J. at 191–92, 336 A.2d at 734.

1. *Purpose of the Doctrine*. What precisely are the New Jersey Supreme Court's underlying concerns? Is it the amount of low-income housing in the state? Is it the geographical distribution of low-income housing? Is it economic segregation? Why did the court decline to address the alleged racial discrimination? Why is economic segregation of such serious concern to the court? Does the court's concern flow from the failure of the state legislature to address these issues directly?

2. *State v. Federal Law*. Why did the plaintiffs base their claims on state constitutional law and not federal constitutional law?

3. *Scope of the Doctrine*. Which types of municipalities are subject to the *Mount Laurel* doctrine? What are the obligations of these municipalities? Will either municipalities, plaintiffs, or courts be able to decide easily whether the municipalities need to comply or have complied with the decision?

4. *Remedy*. What is the court's remedy? In terms of giving cities and potential plaintiffs guidance in the future, what are the weak points in the decision? In other words, where are the doctrinal ambiguities that will produce delay and litigation rather than housing?

Do you think that the court's remedy will produce the results that the court desires? In what respects is the court handicapped in imposing a more detailed remedy? What are the strengths of a court-designed solution? What are the potential costs of a court-designed solution?

---

ii. *Mount Laurel II*

There was both considerable apprehension and optimism about *Mount Laurel I*. Each side initially believed that the standards and remedies announced in the decision would be implemented quickly and would profoundly affect land use practices. Each side, however, seriously underestimated the importance of inertia and overestimated the court's ability to implement its original decree.

After the case was remanded to the superior court, the township amended its zoning ordinance to permit some low- and moderate-income housing, but the sites were, for all practical purposes, not capable of residential development.[35] The public interest groups (now represented by

---

35. The township rezoned 3 areas of land, a total of ¼ of one percent of the land in the township, for a potential total of 131 housing units. The first area was owned by an industrial developer, was entirely surrounded by industrial development, had no water or sewer connections, and was located in a flood plain. The second area was only 7 acres and thus probably too small to develop profitably. In addition, there were no water or sewer connections, and the land was located in a low-lying area that would require expensive improvements before it could be developed. The third area was part of the already approved (although not yet constructed) planned unit development for upper-middle class residents. Rezoning this third area permitted, but did not require, the developer to build 10% of the units as low- and moder-

the state Public Advocate) argued at a new trial that the rezoning was constitutionally inadequate. In addition, a developer intervened to challenge the township's total prohibition on mobile homes.

The trial court ruled against the public interest groups' claims but inexplicably ruled in favor of the trailer park developer. The judge eventually ordered the township to grant the developer a building permit for a 450–unit mobile home park so long as 20% of the units were reserved for low- and moderate-income residents. The township and the Public Advocate appealed.

In the meantime, developers and public interest groups had filed suit against several northern New Jersey suburbs on the ground that their zoning ordinances did not comply with the state supreme court's decision in *Mount Laurel I*. On the basis of that decision, superior court judges declared several town zoning ordinances unconstitutional. The towns appealed and all of the cases were consolidated for argument before the state supreme court in 1980.

After a delay of more than two years (during which time virtually all exclusionary zoning litigation in the trial courts ceased), the supreme court issued a unanimous decision, *Southern Burlington County NAACP v. Township of Mount Laurel (Mount Laurel II)*, 92 N.J. 158, 456 A.2d 390 (1983). The court plainly was angry.

> Mt. Laurel remains afflicted with a blatantly exclusionary ordinance. Papered over with studies, rationalized by hired experts, the ordinance at its core is true to nothing but Mount Laurel's determination to exclude the poor. Mount Laurel is not alone; we believe that there is widespread non-compliance with the constitutional mandate of our original opinion in this case.
>
> To the best of our ability, we shall not allow it to continue. This Court is more firmly committed to the original *Mount Laurel* doctrine than ever, and we are determined, within appropriate judicial bounds, to make it work. The obligation is to provide a realistic opportunity for housing, not litigation, We have learned from experience, however, that unless a strong judicial hand is used, *Mount Laurel* will not result in housing, but in paper, process, witnesses, trials and appeals. We intend by this decision to strengthen it, clarify it, and make it easier for public officials, including judges, to apply it.

Id. at 198–99, 456 A.2d at 410. A little later in the opinion , the court wrote:

> It is obvious that eight years after *Mount Laurel I* the need for satisfaction of this doctrine is greater than ever. Upper and middle income groups may search with increasing difficulty for housing within their means; for low and moderate income people, there is nothing to search for.

ate-income units. The developer had no intention of building such units.

Id. at 211–12, 456 A.2d at 416–17.

The court acknowledged that its earlier opinion left significant doctrinal ambiguities that generated further litigation and delay. For example, there was no definition of a "developing" municipality or of a "region," no process to establish "fair share," and no description of a town's obligation to "affirmatively afford" an opportunity to provide low- and moderate-income housing. *Id.* at 205, 456 A.2d at 413. In the court's view, the basic "doctrine is right but its administration has been ineffective." *Id.* at 158, 456 A.2d at 411.[36]

In an effort to give clear direction to towns, developers and potential residents, the court specified in great detail both the substantive requirements and the process to be used in implementing the doctrine. First, every municipality must provide "a realistic opportunity for decent housing for at least some part of its resident poor who now occupy dilapidated housing" (the so-called "indigenous poor"). *Id.* at 214, 456 A.2d at 418.

Second, a municipality's obligation to provide "a realistic opportunity for a fair share of the region's present and prospective low- and moderate-income housing need" is determined by the State Development Guide Plan (SDGP) rather than a vague definition of "developing municipality." *Id.* at 215, 223–48, 456 A.2d at 418, 422–36.[37] If the SDGP (which was developed by a state agency) designated a municipality as being a "growth area," the municipality is obligated to meet the *Mt. Laurel* obligation. The court hoped that the use of the SDGP would reduce the possibility of conflict with the legislative and executive branches concerning the location of growth in the state. *Id.* at 215, 456 A.2d at 418. *See also* Tarr & Harrison, Legitimacy and Capacity in State Supreme Court Policymaking: The New Jersey Court and Exclusionary Zoning, 15 Rutgers L.J. 513, 523 (1984).

Third, a town's compliance with its constitutional obligation is determined by an objective standard of compliance; good faith efforts to encour-

---

36. The court also tried to clarify the constitutional basis for the doctrine. The court reiterated that local zoning power must be

exercised for the general welfare. When the exercise of that power by a municipality affects something as fundamental as housing, the general welfare includes more than the welfare of that municipality and its citizens: it also includes the general welfare—in this case the housing needs—of those residing outside of the municipality but within the region that contributes to the housing demand within the municipality. * * * In particular, those regulations that do not provide for a fair share of the region's need for low and moderate income housing conflict with the general welfare and violate the

state constitutional requirements of substantive due process and equal protection. * * *

It would be useful to remind ourselves that the doctrine does not arise from some theoretical analysis of our Constitution, but rather from underlying concepts of fundamental fairness in the exercise of governmental power.

Id. at 208–09, 456 A.2d at 415.

37. The SDGP did not exist when the court decided *Mt. Laurel I.* To ensure that the SDGP remained a valid basis for defining the *Mt. Laurel* obligation, the *Mt. Laurel II* court wanted the government to revise the SDGP by January 1, 1985 and every three years thereafter. *Id.* at 242–43, 456 A.2d at 432–33.

age construction of low- and moderate-income housing would not be sufficient. 92 N.J. at 215–16, 220–22, 456 A.2d at 419, 421–22. In addition, towns were required to remove land use restrictions "that are not necessary to protect health and safety," *id.* at 259, 456 A.2d at 441, and to offer "affirmative inducements to make the opportunity [for low- and moderate-income housing] real," *id.* at 261, 456 A.2d at 442. The court described the inducements as encouraging or requiring the use of available federal or state housing subsidies and adopting one of the "inclusionary" zoning methods, including incentive zoning (offering a developer relaxation of zoning laws, such as density limits, in exchange for construction of low-income housing), and mandatory set-asides (requirements that developers include a minimum number of lower-income units in their projects). *See id.* at 261–74, 456 A.2d at 443–50.

Fourth, the decision authorized the Chief Justice to appoint three trial court judges to determine and allocate the fair share of affordable housing to regions and municipalities, to hear challenges to exclusionary zoning ordinances, and to oversee the promulgation and enforcement of conditions to guide and control residential development. *Id.* at 216–17, 253–58, 456 A.2d at 419, 439–41. The judges were authorized to impose a number of remedies, including orders to revise the zoning ordinance; enjoin development until the municipality rezoned or low-income housing was built; declare void all or part of a zoning ordinance; and require municipal approval of pending applications to build low-income housing. *Id.* at 281–92, 456 A.2d at 453–59. The court also endorsed the "builder's remedy," under which builders who successfully challenged a zoning ordinance under the *Mt. Laurel* doctrine and proposed a development that included a large amount of low-income housing (20%) would get a court order allowing construction. *Id.* at 279–81, 456 A.2d at 452–53. Each judge could appoint a special master (who in practice would be a professional planner) to assist him in formulating builders' remedies, revising zoning ordinances, and making land use decisions. *Id.* at 279–88, 456 A.2d at 452–55.

Mt. Laurel II plunged the lower courts into active supervision of local land use regulation and it transformed the trial courts into super-administrative agencies.[38] By 1985, developers had filed over 100 suits in order to reap the economic benefits of the builders' remedy. In the economic climate of the early 1980s, developers could make enough profit on the market rate units (80% of the total in any development) to more than offset the losses on the low- and moderate-income units. *Mt. Laurel II* thus harnessed the developers' profit motive, and effectively sidestepped the absence of federal, state, or local funds. The court hoped that markets, properly primed with off-budget subsidies from the developers, would overcome the inertia of state and local politics.

38. The supreme court acknowledged this unusual role and the practical limitations of judicial intervention, but justified it by noting that "In the absence of adequate legislative and executive help, we must give meaning to the constitutional doctrine in the cases before us through our own devices, even if they are relatively less suitable." *Id.* at 417–18.

No other state court has fully embraced the *Mt. Laurel II* solution, although a few courts have adopted the underlying fair share principle, or at least required municipalities to weigh regional housing needs as one of the criteria used to review the validity of zoning ordinances.[39] The case closest to *Mt. Laurel II* is *Britton v. Town of Chester*, 134 N.H. 434, 595 A.2d 492 (1991), where a developer of low- and moderate-income housing successfully challenged an ordinance that substantially restricted the ability to build affordable housing. The ordinance restricted multi-family residences to only a tiny fraction of available land, required proposed projects to obtain the approval of the town planning board but did not specify criteria for approval, and required the developer to pay for the services of an engineer, a hydrologist, and other professionals needed to assist the planning board. The state supreme court's analysis was based on the enabling act requirement that municipalities exercise their zoning powers for the "general welfare of the community"; according to the court, the community included not just the town but also the broader region. Since the ordinance did not provide for the broader housing needs of the region, it was invalid. *Id.* at 439–41, 595 A.2d at 495–96.

The New Hampshire Supreme Court ordered the town to amend its zoning ordinance and upheld the trial court's order imposing a builder's remedy, "both to compensate the developer who has invested substantial time and resources in pursuing this litigation, and as the most likely means of insuring that low- and moderate-income housing is actually built." *Id.* at 443, 595 A.2d at 497. *Britton* thus differs from *Mt. Laurel II* in several important respects: the substantive right was statutory rather than constitutional, the town and not the trial court was expected to amend the ordinance, the builder's remedy was discretionary rather than mandatory, and there was no elaborate, state-wide, judicial mechanism to quantify and allocate fair share obligations.

A few state legislatures have adopted provisions to restrict exclusionary zoning and some have codified the principle of fair share. Massachusetts adopted a procedural approach: nonprofit developers of affordable housing may appeal a local land use decision to a state board of appeals. *See* Mass. Ann. Laws ch. 40B, §§ 20–23 (establishing a special state procedure

---

39. *See, e.g., Britton v. Town of Chester*, 134 N.H. 434, 439–41, 595 A.2d 492, 495–96 (1991) (declaring invalid a zoning ordinance that failed to provide for regional housing needs; ordering the town to amend its zoning ordinance, and ordering a builder's remedy); *Surrick v. Zoning Hearing Board*, 476 Pa. 182, 189–91, 382 A.2d 105, 108–10 (1977) (accepting the *Mt. Laurel* fair share principle as a "general precept," but declining to impose the detailed, quantitative remedies in *Mt. Laurel II*); *Associated Home Builders of Greater Eastbay, Inc. v. City of Livermore*, 18 Cal.3d 582, 607–11, 135 Cal.Rptr. 41, 55–58, 557 P.2d 473, 487–90 (1976) (suggesting in dicta general criteria to determine whether a zoning ordinance adequately considered regional housing needs, but declining to adopt the *Mt. Laurel II* doctrine); *Arnel Development Co. v. City of Costa Mesa*, 126 Cal. App.3d 330, 340, 178 Cal.Rptr. 723, 729 (1981) (invalidating a zoning ordinance that would have banned multi-family housing on the ground that the ordinance did not adequately weigh regional housing needs as required by *Associated Home Builders*); *Robinson Twp. v. Knoll*, 410 Mich. 293, 302 N.W.2d 146, 149 (Mich. 1981) (striking down an ordinance banning mobile homes).

for public agencies and nonprofit organizations to submit proposals to build low-income housing projects in cities where less than 10% of the housing units are for low- or moderate-income families); R.I. Gen. Laws §§ 45–53–1 to 45–53–8 (following the Massachusetts approach). *See generally* Stockman, Anti-Snob Zoning in Massachusetts: Assessing One Attempt at Opening the Suburbs to Affordable Housing, 78 Va. L. Rev. 535 (1992). Other states impose substantive standards on municipal planning agencies. *See, e.g.,* Or. Rev. Stat. §§ 197.005–197.860 (establishing criteria for the municipal general plan, which is subject to review by a state planning agency, and requiring each municipality to zone an adequate amount of land for its share of regional housing needs); Cal. Gov't Code § 65915 (requiring municipalities to provide density bonuses to developers who set aside a percentage of new units for affordable housing); Cal. Gov't Code §§ 65583–65584 (requiring the housing element of each municipal general plan to provide for its fair share of regional housing needs).

---

1. *Municipal Response to the Decision.* Do you think that *Mt. Laurel II* will cause more low- and moderate-income housing to be built?

Under *Mt. Laurel II*, could towns rezone to build only housing for senior citizens? Would this be an evasion of the decision?

2. *Developer Response to the Decision.* Do you think that developers will build rental housing when they invoke the builders' remedy? Would it be problematic if they did not? Do you think developers will try to make side deals with municipalities by threatening litigation but settling with an agreement *not* to build low-income housing?

3. *Builders' Remedy.* Does the availability of the builders' remedy give developers an unreasonable advantage over towns?

4. *Political Consequences.* What are the possible political consequences of the *Mt. Laurel II* decision? Would you expect the legislature to become more active in shaping housing policy? Are there any possible consequences for the state judiciary?

5. *Other Approaches.* Do any of the other state approaches to planning to provide housing for low-income families seem preferable to the *Mt. Laurel II* approach? Why or why not?

---

iii.   Mount Laurel III and Legislative Reform

The three *Mt. Laurel* trial judges moved quickly to devise a formula to determine and allocate "fair share" numbers to towns. In short order, the courts began to obtain settlements in cases and impose judgments in others. One developer attorney colorfully, if crudely, declared that successfully suing towns under the doctrine was as easy as "clubbing baby harp seals."

Many of the judgments seemed unobjectionable, but some were unfathomable. One of the most notorious cases involved Cranbury, a semi-rural town of 2000 people and about 700 houses, many of which were on the state and national registry of historic buildings. The trial judge imposed a fair share number of 816 units, which with the builders' remedy would produce 4080 new housing units.

Many governmental officials were outraged by *Mt. Laurel II*. At least two town mayors threatened to go to jail rather than obey the court mandates. Governor Kean reportedly called the *Mt. Laurel* decision "communistic." Republican legislators proposed a constitutional amendment to eliminate state court jurisdiction over zoning cases. In non-binding referenda held in 220 towns across the state in the fall of 1985, voters favored the constitutional amendment by a 2–1 ratio, and in some towns by a 5–1 ratio. There was an unprecedented and concerted (although barely unsuccessful) attempt to deny the chief justice (who authored *Mt. Laurel II*) reconfirmation for another term.

Meanwhile, in the midst of all the rhetoric, Republican Governor Kean and Democratic Senator Lynch (who was simultaneously the President of the Senate and the Mayor of New Brunswick) quietly hammered out a legislative compromise. In the summer of 1985, the New Jersey legislature enacted the Fair Housing Act. N.J. Stat. Ann. §§ 52:27D–301 to 329. *See generally* Salkin & Armentano, The Fair Housing Act, Zoning, and Affordable Housing, 25 Urban Law. 893 (1993); Hughes & Vandoren, Social Policy Through Land Reform: New Jersey's Mount Laurel Controversy, 105 Pol. Sci. Q. 97 (1990); Colloquium, Mount Laurel and the Fair Housing Act: Success or Failure?, 19 Fordham Urban L.J. 59 (1991). The Act adopted the basic outline of the *Mount Laurel* doctrine and gave responsibility for its implementation and enforcement to a newly created administrative body, the Council on Affordable Housing (COAH). §§ 305–306. Under the Act, COAH has wide discretion to define housing regions, determine the present and future need for housing, and promulgate criteria and guidelines to assist municipalities in determining their fair share of the affordable housing need. § 307. The Act, however, eliminated the "builders' remedy" against "participating municipalities" that meet the statutory deadlines for filing housing elements. §§ 309, 328.

Municipalities may comply with the statute by submitting a resolution of participation, the housing element of the general plan,[40] and a fair share housing ordinance for approval by the COAH. §§ 309–311. If COAH certifies the housing element and zoning ordinances as meeting the statutory fair share requirements, the municipality is exempt from exclusionary zoning litigation for six years. § 313.[41] Subject to COAH approval, a

40. The municipality has wide discretion in choosing the methods to implement the housing element. §§ 310–311. In the event of disagreement over the zoning ordinance, the statute provides for mandatory mediation.

41. If someone objects to a proposed certification, the parties must submit to mediation. § 315. An objecting party may seek judicial review only after completing mediation. Certified ordinances have a presumption of validity and the burden of proof is on the

municipality may also enter into a regional contribution agreement (RCA) wherein municipalities can trade up to 50% of their low-income housing allocation to another municipality within the same region. § 312. In practice, receiving municipalities are urban areas that are paid to take the obligation; these urban centers use the money for rehabilitation of existing housing. By 1994, COAH had approved 170 RCAs involving $75 million and 4000 rehabilitated units. D.L. Kirp, J.P. Dwyer, & L.A. Rosenthal, Our Town: Race, Housing, and the Soul of Suburbia 161–62 (1995).

Several municipalities sought to have their cases transferred to COAH,[42] but the *Mt. Laurel* judges denied the motions on the ground that transfers of pending cases close to settlement would result in "manifest injustice" in violation of the Act. The municipalities appealed, but so did the *Mt. Laurel* plaintiffs, on the ground that provisions eliminating the builders' remedy and permitting RCAs violated the state constitution.

In *Hills Development Corp. v. Township of Bernards (Mount Laurel III)*, 103 N.J. 1, 510 A.2d 621 (1986), the court firmly endorsed the Act as a constitutional vindication of the original *Mount Laurel* doctrine. The court emphasized its preference, stated in *Mount Laurel II*, for legislative action over judicial activism and concluded that it was possible that the Act would result in more low-income housing than the courts could achieve. Although the court reserved the option to re-enter the fray if the Act failed to meet the *Mount Laurel* goal, the court largely abdicated its role to COAH. *Id.* at 23–24, 510 A.2d at 633. At the end of the opinion the court stated:

> No one should assume that our exercise of comity today signals a weakening of our resolve to enforce the constitutional rights of New Jersey's lower income citizens. The constitutional obligation has not changed; the judiciary's ultimate duty to enforce it has not changed; our determination to perform that duty has not changed. What *has* changed is that we are no longer alone in this field. The other branches of government have fashioned a comprehensive statewide response to the *Mount Laurel* obligation. This kind of response, one that would permit us to withdraw from this field, is what this court has always wanted and sought. It is potentially far better for the state and for its lower income citizens.

Id. at 65, 510 A.2d at 655. Since enactment of the Fair Housing Act, the New Jersey Supreme Court has occasionally ruled on COAH regulations, *see, e.g., In re Township of Warren*, 132 N.J. 1, 622 A.2d 1257 (1993) (declaring invalid an ordinance providing a preference for local residents and employees), but it has mostly avoided exclusionary zoning litigation.

---

challenging party to show by clear and convincing evidence that an ordinance does not meet the statutory standards. §§ 316, 318.

42. The Act mandated the transfer to COAH of all cases commenced within 60 days before the effective date of the Act. All previously filed and undecided cases were also to be transferred unless the transfer would result in "manifest injustice" to any party involved in the litigation. § 316.

In practice, the Act and the corresponding regulations have diluted the substantive mandate of the original *Mt. Laurel* doctrine. Under COAH's regulations, the estimated statewide need for affordable housing dropped by 50%; in subsequent regulations, the statewide need dropped by another 50%. In many jurisdictions, the fair share numbers dropped by 80–90%. In addition, the declining housing market in the late 1980s eliminated developers' incentives to build low and moderate income housing as part of their developments.

----

1. *Statutory v. Constitutional Rights.* To what extent does the New Jersey Fair Housing Act codify the judicial rights and remedies in *Mt. Laurel I* and *Mt. Laurel II*? In what ways does the legislation fall short of the constitutional doctrine? Do you think that the legislature erred in eliminating the builders' remedy for participating municipalities? Do you think that the court was right to uphold the elimination of the remedy?

2. *Administrative v. Judicial Control.* Do you think that the legislature's creation of COAH is an improvement over the *Mt. Laurel II* judicial administration? Do you think the Fair Housing Act has the potential to produce a significant amount of low-income housing?

3. *Regional Contribution Agreements.* What do you think about the statutory provision authorizing regional contribution agreements (RCAs)? Is your answer affected by the fact that a substantial amount of affordable housing built in the last few years is rehabilitated rental housing in urban areas funded by RCAs?

4. *Judicial Role in Policy Formation.* Does the enactment of the Fair Housing Act suggest that litigation was a wasteful strategy to produce additional low-income housing? *Cf.* G. Rosenberg, The Hollow Hope: Can Courts Bring About Social Change? (1991).

E. FLEXIBILITY IN LAND USE CONTROLS: THE EVOLUTION FROM TECHNOCRATIC RATIONALITY TO BARGAINING

In principle, zoning should be based on comprehensive land-use planning. Planners would collect relevant data on the current state of the community (*e.g.*, population size and distribution; location, amount and characteristics of undeveloped land; adequacy of infrastructure; and type, location, and amount of commercial and industrial development), make predictions about future changes and needs affecting land use, and identify goals for the rational development of the community. Comprehensive planning would be free of politics; professional planners would make the basic judgments. The comprehensive plan would then be implemented through zoning.

In practice, comprehensive land use planning often has been irrelevant in municipal land use decisions. Although most states require municipalities to prepare a comprehensive plan, many if not most municipalities pay only cursory attention to their general plans; the important decisions are made in the zoning ordinance or its various administrative adjustments (*e.g.*, variances, conditional use permits). In part planning cannot achieve its own technocratic goals, and in part it is in tension with *ad hoc*, politically driven decisions characteristic of zoning, zoning amendments, and administrative exemptions from the zoning ordinance.

1. THE EVOLUTION AND DEMISE OF COMPREHENSIVE PLANNING

Municipal planning in this country dates from the colonial era, when William Penn commissioned a street plan for the development of Philadelphia. As the growth of cities in the mid to late 19th century brought increasing congestion, disease, and generally poor living conditions, many towns and cities adopted and implemented narrowly focused plans for future infrastructure needs, such as municipal water supply and sewerage. Peterson, The Impact of Sanitation Reform upon American Urban Planning, 1840–1890 in Introduction to Planning History in the United States 13–25 (D. Krueckeberg, ed. 1983). These plans, however, were for specific needs and were not comprehensive plans for community development.

Comprehensive municipal land use planning first received serious national attention at the 1909 First National Conference on City Planning and the Problems of Congestion. At that and subsequent conferences, urban planners and landscape architects emphasized the need for comprehensive urban planning to identify potential land use problems, specify land use goals, and identify the means to prevent potential problems and achieve these goals. In 1928, the U.S. Department of Commerce published a model enabling act for planning—the Standard City Planning Enabling Act—that would give municipalities authority to engage in land use planning. Although the model act itself was not widely adopted, N. Williams, Jr., American Planning Law: Land Use and the Police Power, § 18.01 (1988), many larger cities eventually established planning departments and developed comprehensive land use plans. The 1954 amendments to the Federal Housing Act, which required municipalities to adopt land use plans to qualify for federal slum clearance funds, further encouraged municipalities to undertake systematic land use planning. Q. Johnstone, The Federal Urban Renewal Program 25 U. Chi. L. Rev. 301, 337–41 (1958).

Today, all states have authorized municipalities to engage in land use planning, and about half of the states make land use planning a prerequisite for zoning. The end product of planning is the comprehensive plan (also called a general plan or a master plan).[1]

---

1. Land use planning is not solely the province of municipalities. The federal government, for example, requires federal agencies to engage in planning with regard to federal lands. *See, e.g.,* Wilderness Act, 16 U.S.C. §§ 1131–1136 (establishing the National Wilderness Preservation System); Wild and Scenic Rivers Act, 16 U.S.C. §§ 1271–

Although specific requirements vary substantially from state to state, comprehensive plans frequently are organized around "elements." Most planning enabling acts require general plans to have elements for infrastructure, transportation, and land use, and in some states plans must contain additional elements, such as for housing, open space, historic preservation, and energy conservation. Many planning codes permit comprehensive plans to have additional optional elements, such as for community renewal, flood control, or conservation. *See, e.g.,* Ky. Rev. Stat. § 100.187 (community renewal, flood control, pollution, conservation, regional impact, historic preservation); Wash Rev. Code Ann. §§ 36.70.340–36.70.350 (conservation, solar energy, recreation, capital improvements); P.W. Salsich, Jr., Urban Housing: A Strategic Role for the States, 12 Yale L. & Pol'y Rev. 93, 105–06 (1994) (listing states encouraging or requiring adoption of plans with low-income housing elements).

Many states subject general plans to judicial review to ensure compliance with statutory requirements. *See, e.g.,* Wis. Stat. § 66.023(9) (planning department's decision to adopt or amend a plan is subject to judicial review); *Buena Vista Gardens Apartments Ass'n v. City of San Diego Planning Dep't,* 175 Cal.App.3d 289, 298, 220 Cal.Rptr. 732, 737 (1985) (requiring actual compliance with statutory planning requirements); *but see City of Jacksonville v. Wynn,* 650 S.2d 182, 185–86 (Fla.App.1995) (statute "was not intended to broadly justify a judicial challenge to the validity of a comprehensive plan"). In some states, a state court may enjoin a municipality from subdividing property if it does not have a valid comprehensive plan, thereby effectively blocking significant development projects. For example, in *Camp v. Board of Supervisors,* 123 Cal.App.3d 334, 358–61, 176 Cal.Rptr. 620, 635–37 (1981), the court upheld an injunction enjoining the county from approving any zoning changes or subdivision maps until it adopted a valid plan. In Maine, the state Land Use Regulation Commission may adopt a moratorium on the issuance of development permits if it finds that the comprehensive plan or zoning scheme is "inadequate to prevent serious harm from residential, commercial or industrial development in the affected geographic area." Me. Rev. Stat. § 685B.[2]

Comprehensive land use planning is difficult under the best of circumstances. It is virtually impossible to predict important changes in technology, the local economy, or even demographics. It is equally difficult to predict changes in public values; the public demand for environmental protection, including open space, exemplifies such important shifts. Even if planners had perfect information, they would face a daunting task in

1287 (establishing the National Wild and Scenic River System); National Marine Sanctuaries Act, 16 U.S.C. §§ 1431–1445a (requiring protection of marine areas having special national significance and value); Federal Land Policy and Management Act, 43 U.S.C. §§ 1701–1784 (requiring the Bureau of Land Management to manage federal lands "on the basis of multiple use and sustained yield"); Multiple–Use Sustained Yield Act of 1960, 16 U.S.C. §§ 528–531 (governing management of the national forests).

2. Adoption of the general plan may also be subject to environmental review. *See, e.g.,* N.Y. Town Law § 272–a(8); Cal. Pub. Res. Code §§ 21000–21177.

making judgments that would usefully guide community development over a period of a decade or more. As Professor Lindblom has explained,

> No person, committee, or research team, even with all the resources of modern electronic computation, can complete the analysis of a complex problem. Too many interacting values are at stake, too many possible alternatives, too many consequences to be traced through an uncertain future—the best we can do is achieve partial analysis or, in Herbert Simon's terms, a "bounded rationality."

Lindblom, Still Muddling, Not Yet Through, 39 Pub. Admin. Rev. 517, 518 (1979); *see also* Lindblom, The Science of "Muddling Through", 19 Pub. Admin. Rev. 79 (1959). Of course, the actual conditions for urban planning are less than ideal; land use planners must make do with inadequate information and limited planning resources. Finally, comprehensive planning, with its emphasis on technocratic expertise, conflicts with political values of public participation in public decision making; rational planning is under constant pressure to succumb to popular demands and political expediency.

In the 1950s and 1960s, community land use plans often focused unrealistically on long-term development and contained a meaningless wealth of detail. Land use regulators—the people who had to adopt zoning ordinances and rule on applications for variances and conditional use permits—simply ignored them. *See* A. Altshuler, The City Planning Process (1965) (concluding that comprehensive planning did not have much impact on land use decisions in the Twin Cities); D.R. Mandelker, The Zoning Dilemma 61 (1970) (many comprehensive plans "project to a fixed 'end state' as much as twenty to thirty years forward in time, with no attempt to indicate what zoning steps should be taken intermediate to the achievement of the goals ultimately projected"). These studies suggest that land use plans should focus on short- and mid-term land use problems, and that they should be continually revised to take account of new information, evolving community values, and changing facts.

Even with more modest aims, there is evidence that professional planning cannot resolve basic conflicts and that often planning may be a disguise for backroom bargaining. In an illuminating study of land-use planning for a regional shopping center in Lexington, Kentucky, Professor Tarlock concluded:

> This study indicates that enabling legislation requiring adoption of community development use plans as a basis for regulation will not insure rational decisions. The decisions of the Planning Commission cannot be considered rational, if the term is defined as a thorough and objective consideration of a series of proposed alternative choices according to the previously agreed upon criteria. The initial choice of the non-included site was based on reasons which sharply deviated from the criteria the previously adopted plans deemed relevant. * * *

* * * [T]he Lexington experience raises the question whether the planning process can be trusted to produce decisions which result in a net gain to the community rather than conferring monopoly status on certain classes of uses [or] individuals. I would suggest that the timing policy made it possible to define the general welfare to benefit narrow segments of the community to the detriment of large, politically powerless groups. The recommendations were used by the Commission to justify pre-existing value preferences for special groups and individuals. There was little evidence that the plans considered the actual impact of increased retail competition on the long-run dislocations. No effort was made to substantiate the vague references to the danger of blight or the shrinkage of the property tax base.

Tarlock, Not in Accordance with a Comprehensive Plan: A Case Study of Regional Shopping Center Location Conflicts in Lexington, Kentucky, 1970 Urb. L. Ann. 133, 168, 180.

Professor Mandelker's study of the planning process in King County, Washington, concluded that the comprehensive plan was rife with "ambiguities and omissions." The Zoning Dilemma 163 (1970).

The plan compromised. It committed the county to an allocation of urban centers of concentration at specified points at the county level, but at the same time opted for a development model capable of being applied on a neighborhood scale at any point within the county. Moreover, the commitment to urban center concentrations was not firm. * * * Add to this circumstance the fact that the plan had no policy on the size, character, rate and priority of development of the urban centers that were tentatively selected, and we can conclude that the zoning authorities were left without effective guidelines. In short, nothing in the comprehensive plan firmly told the zoning agencies which were the preferred locations for apartment development.

Id. at 163–64. Mandelker concludes that the core problem is that land use planning inherently involves value-laden conflicts between community control and the individual freedom of property owners. "We are simply not sure of the values we wish to implement in our urban policies. Until we are, we can continue to expect the planning and zoning process to be deeply troubled by ambiguity and ambivalence." Id. at 188.

Planning remains a part of the land use decisionmaking process of many municipalities, but its significance is often overshadowed by the adoption of zoning ordinances and their amendments by the granting of administrative exceptions, and by municipality-developer agreements tailored to individual projects.

2. Legislative and Administrative Flexibility in Zoning

Euclidean zoning, with its careful segregation of conflicting land uses (e.g., single family homes, apartment buildings, retail stores, light industry, heavy industry), was designed for a nearly static world. Development would proceed in appropriate zones, and small adjustments to the zoning ordinance would be necessary only in unanticipated cases of hardship. Euclidean zoning assumed that regulators could predict well into the future the proper layout of a city, and that they could anticipate and through zoning restrain and even shape the direction of market forces.

The Euclidean vision of zoning substantially underestimated the impact of a growing economy and rapidly changing technologies on private preferences and municipal needs, overestimated the ability of officials to anticipate market demand for new land uses, and underestimated the vulnerability of zoning and government regulators to market demand and political pressure. In the face of a dynamic economy and growing urban and suburban populations, municipalities regularly had to adjust the zoning scheme; the only question was whether the changes would be more the product of rational, comprehensive planning, or the result of *ad hoc* bargaining.

Professor Mandelker maintains that many zoning authorities are reactive to development proposals rather than engaged in careful planning.

> Especially in urbanizing areas, zoning authorities may pursue a policy of watchful waiting. They put aside any meaningful advance zoning, and rely for their zoning policy on zoning changes which are made in response to applications from individual developers. These changes may be made by a variety of techniques, ranging all the way from use variances, through conditional uses and exceptions, to the simple zoning amendment.

D.R. Mandelker, The Zoning Dilemma 103–04 (1970).

As Mandelker indicated, municipalities have a variety of devices with which to adjust the zoning scheme. They can grant a variance, grant a conditional use permit, amend the zoning ordinance, or even authorize a development that meets none of the Euclidean zoning criteria but is governed by a detailed developer agreement specifying conditions for the project to proceed. Inherent in these devices for flexibility is the opportunity for bargaining—for the municipality to demand exactions (*e.g.*, dedications of streets or parks, or cash payments) or to make concessions (*e.g.*, relax zoning restrictions to attract business).

Bargaining over land use restrictions is not new; municipalities have been extracting subdivision exactions from developers for decades. But bargaining has become more widespread and far reaching in recent years, and as bargaining over the "price" for the right to develop has increased, questions about equity, efficiency, governmental sovereignty, and corruption have intensified.

The following materials look first at the devices for flexibility in land use regulation and then consider the proper role of bargaining over municipal land use decisions.

a.   VARIANCES

In every state, the landowner may petition a local administrative agency (*e.g.*, the board of zoning appeals) for a variance from zoning restrictions. State statutes use a variety of formulations, but the essential criteria are that the existing zoning restriction causes the landowner to suffer a special hardship, and that granting a variance will not undermine the purposes of the original zoning classification. For example in *Otto v. Steinhilber*, 282 N.Y. 71, 76, 24 N.E.2d 851, 853 (1939), the court held that "unnecessary hardship" requires a showing that the land as zoned cannot yield a reasonable return, that the hardship is due to unique circumstances and not general conditions in the area, and that the use will not alter the essential character of the locality. *See also Carbonneau v. Town of Exeter*, 119 N.H. 259, 263, 401 A.2d 675, 678 (1979) (that the landowner could use his land more profitably does not meet the "undue hardship" standard).

Most variances fall into two categories: *area variances*, which involve relaxation of size restrictions (*e.g.*, height limits, setback requirements, and minimum lot size requirements), and *use variances*, which permit otherwise prohibited uses (*e.g.*, retail stores). Courts and legislatures tend to impose stricter substantive criteria for the approval of use variances. *See, e.g.*, Ind. Code §§ 36–7–4–918.5(3), 36–7–4–918.4(4) (requiring a showing of "practical difficulties" for area variances and "unnecessary hardship" for use variances). Some legislatures have imposed additional procedural obstacles for use variances. In Delaware, for example, the city council, rather than the board of adjustment, must vote on any proposed use variance. Del. Code tit. 9, § 1352(d). In New Jersey, two-thirds of the board must approve a request for a use variance. N.J. Stat. Ann. § 40:55D–70(d). Some states bar use variances altogether on the ground that a change in permitted use requires a zoning ordinance amendment. *See, e.g.*, Ark. Stat. Ann. § 14–17–209(h) (the board of adjustment "shall not permit, as a variance, any use in a zone that is not permitted under the ordinance"); *Bradley v. Zoning Board of Appeals*, 165 Conn. 389, 392, 334 A.2d 914, 916 (1973) (to allow variances for uses not otherwise permitted in the zoning ordinance "would fly in the face of that clearly expressed policy").

b.   CONDITIONAL USES/SPECIAL EXCEPTIONS

Conditional uses, often called special exceptions, were created "to meet the problem which arises where certain uses, although generally compatible with the basic use classification of a particular zone, should not be permitted to be located as a matter of right in every area included within the zone because of hazards inherent in the use itself or special problems which its proposed location may present." *Zylka v. City of Crystal*, 283 Minn. 192, 196, 167 N.W.2d 45 (1969). It is easier for an applicant to obtain a conditional use permit than to obtain a variance. *See, e.g., Inland Const. Co. v. City of Bloomington*, 292 Minn. 374, 379, 195 N.W.2d 558, 562 (1972) (the criteria to obtain a conditional-use permit is "much lighter" than the criteria required to obtain a variance). Consequently, most courts more readily uphold decisions to grant a conditional use permit, and more carefully scrutinize decisions to deny a conditional use permit. *See, e.g., Board of Supervisors of Benton Township v. Carver County Board of Commissioners*, 302 Minn. 493, 499, 225 N.W.2d 815, 819 (1975) ("there is a heavier burden required on the part of those who challenge the *approval* of a conditional-use permit, as compared to the degree of proof required of a landowner whose application is denied"). The reason is that the local legislature already has determined that conditional uses are compatible with other uses in the zone.

> Because * * * [conditional] uses are generally compatible with the design of the zone the possibility that a permitted use will not comport with the comprehensive plan is not as great as it is when a variance or amendment is sought. * * * [T]he ordinance itself reveals the legislative plan. * * * The suspicion which is cast upon the approval of a change involving an incompatible use * * * is not warranted where the change has been anticipated by the governing body.

Archdiocese of Portland v. County of Washington, 254 Or. 77, 84–85, 458 P.2d 682, 685–86 (1969).

c. ZONING AMENDMENTS

Every zoning enabling act permits the local legislature to amend the zoning ordinance, and in general courts show substantial deference in reviewing such enactments. For example, in *Lockard v. City of Los Angeles*, 33 Cal.2d 453, 461, 202 P.2d 38, 42–43 (1949), the court held that it would uphold rezoning "unless the regulations have no reasonable relation to the public welfare. * * * [A court] will not substitute its judgment for that of the zoning authorities if there is any reasonable justification for their action." Most courts place the burden of proof on the party challenging the validity of the rezoning, although a few states require the municipality to demonstrate that the original zoning classification was a mistake or that changed conditions on nearby parcels support the rezoning. *See, e.g.,* Md. Ann. Code art. 66B, § 4.05(a) (the local legislature can adopt a zoning amendment finding either "a substantial change in the character of the neighborhood" or a "mistake in the existing zoning classification").

Ballot Measures. Local citizen groups often resort to ballot measures to overturn zoning amendments or to adopt amendments that the local legislature has refused to adopt. Ballot measures are the antithesis of the technocratic model of land use planning, and consequently in some states they are subject to closer judicial review than legislatively enacted amendments.

Often focused on a single tract of land whose potential development is hotly contested, the typical ballot measure contains none of the characteristics associated with planning: expert collection and analysis of data, and identification and gradual adjustment of long-term goals representing an integrated view of the community. Public participation in the usual sense— public hearings—gives way to popular control; compromise and accommodation of competing concerns characteristic of legislative processes are replaced with an up-or-down vote. Ballot measures may be useful in that they break the political and legislative deadlock that perpetuates the *status quo*, and they may provide a useful check on a legislature imposing unwanted change in the community. Or they may produce uninformed, *ad hoc* land use decisions. *See generally* Orman, Ballot-Box Planning: The Boom in Electoral Land–Use Control, 25 Public Affairs Report No. 6 (Dec. 1984); Note, Urban Blight Meets Manifest Destiny: Zoning at the Ballot Box, the Regional Welfare, and Transferable Development Rights, 85 Nw. U.L. Rev. 519 (1991).

Several state courts have held that voters may enact zoning amendments by initiative and that they may decide by referendum whether to approve or disapprove legislative adopted amendments.[3] These courts reason that since adoption of the initial zoning ordinance was a legislative act that could have been subject to the initiative or referendum processes, zoning amendments, no matter how minor, are also subject to the initiative and referendum processes. *See, e.g., Margolis v. District Court*, 638 P.2d 297, 304 (Colo.1981) ("It seems entirely inconsistent to hold that an original act of general zoning is legislative, whereas an amendment to that act is not legislative"). These courts also emphasize that ballot measures are "a direct check on the exercise or non-exercise of legislative power by elected officials." *Id.* at 303. They brush off concerns that ballot measures may lead to irrational decisions. "The wisdom [of upholding ballot measures] may be questioned in that all zoning changes made in his fashion are subject to the whims of a referendum and to the vicissitudes of the electorate. The other side of the coin is that this is a power that the people have reserved [in the state constitution]." *Florida Land Co. v. City of Winter Springs*, 427 So.2d 170, 174 (Fla.1983).

Other courts conclude that zoning amendments are administrative rather than legislative and therefore are not the proper subject of ballot measures. *See, e.g., Leonard v. City of Bothell*, 87 Wash.2d 847, 850–51, 557 P.2d 1306, 1309 (1976); *Forman v. Eagle Thrifty Drugs and Markets*, 89 Nev. 533, 537–38, 516 P.2d 1234, 1237 (1973). Although these courts base their decisions on the ground that zoning amendments are administrative rather than legislative acts (which is more of a conclusion than a reason), the courts are plainly concerned that voters may not adequately study ballot provisions and may be influenced by intense and misleading publicity that oversimplifies or distorts the important issues.

Amendments to the zoning code or rezone decisions require an informed and intelligent choice by individuals who possess the expertise to consider the total economic, social, and physical characteristics of the community. Respondent's planning commission and city council normally possess the necessary expertise to make these difficult decisions. * * * In a referendum election, the voters

---

3.   There are no serious federal constitutional obstacles to rezoning through the ballot box. *See Eastlake v. Forest City Enter-* *prises, Inc.*, 426 U.S. 668, 679, 96 S.Ct. 2358, 2364, 49 L.Ed.2d 132 (1976) (rejecting a due process challenge).

may not have an adequate opportunity to read the environmental impact statement or any other relevant information concerning the proposed land-use change.

Leonard v. City of Bothell, 87 Wash.2d 847, 557 P.2d 1306, 1311 (1976). Because of its all-or-nothing nature, the initiative process does not allow voters to weigh tradeoffs, balance competing concerns, and make compromises.

Consistency With the General Plan. Some jurisdictions statutorily require zoning amendments to be consistent with the comprehensive plan. *See, e.g.,* Ariz. Rev. Stat. Ann. § 9–462.01F (zoning ordinances "shall" be consistent with the general plan); N.J. Stat. Ann. § 40:55D–62(a) (zoning "shall * * * be substantially consistent with the land use plan element and the housing plan element," but providing a procedure to adopt inconsistent zoning ordinances). When a zoning amendment is not consistent with the comprehensive plan, the court often must invalidate inconsistent zoning provisions or uphold a municipality's refusal to rezone land inconsistent with the plan. *See, e.g., Lesher Communications, Inc. v. City of Walnut Creek*, 52 Cal.3d 531, 544, 277 Cal.Rptr. 1, 802 P.2d 317, 324–25 (1990) (striking down a zoning amendment that would have limited development in conflict with the comprehensive plan); *City of Mounds View v. Johnson*, 377 N.W.2d 476, 478–79 (Minn.App.1985) (upholding denial of rezoning from residential to commercial use because proposal had no rational relation to the goals of the comprehensive plan).

Most courts have declined to imply a consistency requirement in the absence of a statutory mandate. For example, in *Nottingham Village, Inc. v. Baltimore County*, 266 Md. 339, 354, 292 A.2d 680, 687–88 (1972), the court held that the zoning ordinance need not conform to the master plan as it was only a guide. *See also West Hill Citizens for Controlled Development Density v. King County Council*, 29 Wash.App. 168, 172, 627 P.2d 1002, 1004 (1981) (a comprehensive plan is just a "blueprint"; it should "not be considered other than * * * a guide to the later development and adoption of official controls"). Some other courts simply hold that the zoning ordinance *is* the general plan. *Bell v. City of Elkhorn*, 122 Wis.2d 558, 566, 364 N.W.2d 144, 148 (1985); *Dawson Enters., Inc. v. Blaine County*, 98 Idaho 506, 510, 567 P.2d 1257, 1261 (1977). *See generally* D.R. Mandelker, The Zoning Dilemma 57–58 (1970).

Spot Zoning. Although a court normally will defer to the local legislature's decision to amend a zoning ordinance, a court will more carefully scrutinize a seemingly *ad hoc* rezoning—called spot zoning—that favors the owner of the rezoned parcel (normally by permitting a more intensive use) and that injures neighboring landowners. For example, in *Anderson v. City of Seattle*, 64 Wash.2d 198, 201, 390 P.2d 994, 996 (1964), the court invalidated a zoning ordinance amendment that rezoned a single parcel to permit construction of an apartment building; the court based its holding on its conclusion that the apartment building would depreciate the value of existing detached homes across the street.

In reviewing a claim of spot zoning, courts not only consider the negative spillovers to nearby landowners, but also often weigh the wider public benefits of the rezoning. For example, in *Woodland Estates, Inc. v. Building Inspector of Methuen*, 4 Mass.App.Ct. 757, 760–61, 358 N.E.2d 468, 471 (1976), the appellate court upheld the creation of a small zone for a hospital, carved out of a larger residential zone, in part because the hospital would treat several thousand local residents each year. In *Save Our Rural Environment v. Snohomish County*, 99 Wash.2d 363, 368–69, 662 P.2d 816, 819 (1983), the court upheld a rezoning to permit a business park because it would provide "a flexible means to broaden the industrial base of the region and to produce energy and travel time savings for employees."

The doctrine of spot zoning has an *ad hoc* quality, not unlike the evil it seeks to prevent; the criteria for spot zoning are vague and their application to specific cases difficult to predict. Virtually all rezonings to a more intensive use favor the rezoned landowner, and most development projects both injure and benefit other landowners. Underlying the spot zoning cases are concerns that politically driven, *ad hoc* rezoning is inconsistent with the ideals of comprehensive, technocratic planning, that spot zoning may defeat the neighbors' justified expectations without any compensating benefits, and perhaps that the rezoning is the product of favoritism or even corruption.

Downzoning. Municipalities may also "downzone" land to permit only less intensive uses, such as agricultural uses or open space. Landowners whose land has been downzoned may claim a taking, although such claims may be difficult to prove if the resulting zoning classification leaves landowners some economically viable use for their land. For example, in *Tim Thompson, Inc. v. Village of Hinsdale*, 247 Ill.App.3d 863, 887–89, 187 Ill.Dec. 506, 523–25, 617 N.E.2d 1227, 1245–46 (1993), a zoning amendment barred the landowner from building three separate houses on its land. Relying on *Penn Central*, *supra*, pp. 325–44, the court held that even though the landowner could not realize as much profit as it originally anticipated when it purchased the land, its claim for inverse condemnation failed because it did not allege that it had no economically viable use for the rezoned property.

More likely, landowners will challenge the rezoning as being inconsistent with the comprehensive plan. In addition, in many states, the landowner may claim immunity from the rezoning under the "vested rights" doctrine. That doctrine holds that a landowner is not subject to zoning revisions if the municipality issued the landowner a building permit before the rezoning, the landowner acted in good faith in obtaining the permit, and the landowner substantially relied on the original zoning. The doctrine thus protects certain well-defined expectations from sudden changes in land use regulations. D.R. Mandelker, Land Use Law 234–44 (3rd ed., 1993).

Contract Zoning. Most instances of rezoning involve bargaining between the developer and the municipality. The developer (who may own the land or have an option to purchase the land if she obtains the favorable rezoning) needs a rezoning to proceed with the project and the municipality wants to extract valuable concessions (*e.g.*, dedications of facilities or land, such as a public park) from the developer. Of course, if the municipality were competing with other jurisdictions for more development, it may offer developers concessions (*e.g.*, relaxation of land use restrictions, property tax reductions) to attract the development.

Many legislatures and courts have erected barriers to such bargaining. The primary legal argument against bargaining is that the municipality may not bargain away its police power to serve private interests. For example in *Houston Petroleum Co. v. Automotive Products Credit Ass'n*, 9 N.J. 122, 87 A.2d 319, 322 (1952), the court wrote that "[c]ontracts * * * have no place in a zoning plan and a contract between a municipality and a property owner should not enter into the enactment or enforcement of zoning regulations." In *Dacy v. Village of Ruidoso*, 114 N.M. 699, 703–04, 845 P.2d 793, 797–98 (1992), the court held that contract zoning is illegal if the municipality is a party to a bilateral contract or to a unilateral contract in which the municipality promises to rezone in return for some action or forbearance by the landowner. In other words, the municipality may not bind itself to rezone a piece of property.

Courts are more tolerant when the landowner agrees unilaterally to the restrictions, and the city subsequently rezones the property with the restrictions as part of the rezoning. In *Collard v. Incorporated Village of Flower Hill*, 52 N.Y.2d 594, 601, 421 N.E.2d 818, 821, 439 N.Y.S.2d 326, 329–30 (1981), the court stated that although it would be improper for a city to bargain away its police power, rezoning with conditions is valid "absent proof of a contract purporting to bind the local legislature in advance to exercise its zoning authority in a bargained-for manner." Since the city was not legally committed to rezoning the land, and since in principle it could later change its mind, no improper bargaining had taken place. *See also Church v. Town of Islip*, 8 N.Y.2d 254, 259, 168 N.E.2d 680, 683, 203 N.Y.S.2d 866, 869 (1960) (upholding rezoning in part because "the record does not show that there was any agreement in the sense that the owners made an offer accepted by the board"; rather, the town required the developer to meet certain conditions restricting the use of their property before it could be rezoned).

Some state statutes expressly permit conditional zoning. For example, an Arizona statute provides:

> The board may approve a change of zone conditioned on a schedule for development of the specific use or uses for which rezoning is requested. If at the expiration of this period the property has not been improved for the use for which it was conditionally approved, the board * * * shall schedule a public hearing to grant an extension, determine compliance with the schedule for development or cause the property to revert to its former zoning classification.

Ariz. Rev. Stat. Ann. § 11–832. *See also* Idaho Code § 67–6511A (authorizing the municipality to require a developer to make a written commitment
concerning the use of a parcel that the municipality may subsequently
rezone). Obviously, the specified conditions may be the subject of intense
bargaining between the developer, the municipality, and others (*e.g.*, environmental groups, neighborhood groups).

d. PLANNED UNIT DEVELOPMENTS (PUDS)

Euclidean zoning assumes that certain kinds of uses are incompatible
and should be segregated, that densities should be uniform (as a consequence of the statutory requirement for uniform regulations within a zone),
and that development will (and perhaps should) occur one structure at a
time. Euclidean zoning, however, tends to produce uniform, even monotonous land use patterns. *See generally* J. Jacobs, The Death and Life of
Great American Cities (1961) (advocating land use policies that promote a
diversity of uses—public spaces, residences, retail stores, cultural facilities
and entertainment—to create and maintain the vitality of municipal life).

Whatever its merits, Euclidean zoning is particularly ill-suited for large
residential development projects. Euclidean zoning makes it difficult to
include both single-family and multi-family residences as well as retail
stores within a single development, and it leaves little incentive to conserve
open spaces or environmentally sensitive areas. In *Chrinko v. South Brunswick Township Planning Board*, 77 N.J.Super. 594, 187 A.2d 221 (1963), a
case in which neighboring landowners challenged an ordinance authorizing
"cluster zoning," the court wrote:

> Zoning ordinances in rapidly growing municipalities may be
> founded on an outmoded concept that houses will be built one at a
> time for individual owners in accordance with zoning regulations,
> with latitude for variances in hardship or other exceptional cases,
> and that the municipality can take steps whenever warranted to
> acquire school, park and other public sites. Such a gradual and
> controlled development is not practicable in many municipalities
> today. Confronted with a subdivision plan for several hundred
> homes in a tract meeting all water drainage, sanitation and other
> conditions, a municipality must anticipate school needs but with-
> out lands set aside for that purpose; it must anticipate a large
> population concentration without recreation areas, parks or green
> spaces, or lands for firehouses or other public purposes.

Planned unit developments (PUDs) provide an alternative to the
standard Euclidean zoning. PUDs generally require rezoning a large parcel
of undeveloped land to permit development of a self-contained residential
community, including related uses, such as retail stores. PUDs commonly
cluster residences while keeping the overall average density the same as in
a single-family residential zone. Cluster zoning produces more open space
(in the form of parks, playgrounds, golf courses, or undeveloped land) and
reduces the cost of building roads and installing utilities. PUDs also reduce
the monotony of more uniform residential development.

PUDs were first developed in the 1920s, but were not widely used until the 1960s. *See* Symposium: Planned Unit Development, 114 U. Pa. L. Rev. 3 (1965). Although many courts have held that municipalities may adopt PUD ordinances without special enabling legislation, *see, e.g., Cheney v. Village 2 at New Hope, Inc.*, 429 Pa. 626, 637–38, 241 A.2d 81, 86–87 (1968) (given the broad power to zone for a wide range of uses the council had adequate authority to create a PUD district), several states have adopted enabling acts. The Nebraska statute is typical:

(1) [the] city shall have the power to include within its zoning ordinance, provisions authorizing and regulating planned unit developments. * * * [P]lanned unit developments shall include any development of a parcel of land or an aggregation of contiguous parcels of land to be developed as a single project which proposes density transfers, density increases, and mixing of land uses, or any combination thereof, based upon the application of site planning criteria. The purpose of such ordinance shall be to permit flexibility in the regulation and land development, to encourage innovation in land use and variety in design, layout, and type of structures constructed, to achieve economy and efficiency in the use of land, natural resources, energy, and the provision of public services and utilities, to encourage the preservation and provision of useful open space, and to provide improved housing, employment, or shopping opportunities particularly suited to the needs of an area.

(2) An ordinance authorizing and regulating planned unit developments shall establish criteria relating to the review of proposed planned unit developments to ensure that the land use or activity proposed through a planned unit development shall be compatible with adjacent uses of land, the capacities of public services and utilities affected by such planned unit development, and to ensure that the approval of such planned unit development is consistent with the public health, safety, and general welfare of the city, and is in accordance with the comprehensive plan.

(3) Within a planned unit development, regulations relating to the use of land, including permitted uses, lot sizes, setbacks, height limits, required facilities, buffers, open spaces, roadway and parking design, and land-use density shall be determined in accordance with the planned unit development regulations specified in the zoning ordinance. The planned unit development regulations need not be uniform with regard to each type of land use.

(4) * * * In approving any planned unit development, a city may, by covenant, by separate agreement, or otherwise, impose reasonable conditions as deemed necessary to ensure that a planned unit development shall be compatible with adjacent uses of land, will not overburden public services and facilities, and will not be detrimental to the public health, safety, and welfare. Such condi-

tions or agreements may provide for dedications of land for public purposes.

Neb. Rev. Stat. § 19–4401.

Although PUDs are subject to the municipality's PUD ordinance, the specific conditions governing a particular PUD normally are contained in a negotiated, detailed agreement between the developer and the approving agency (*e.g.*, the planning commission).[4] In *Rutland Environmental Protection Ass'n v. Kane*, 31 Ill.App.3d 82, 334 N.E.2d 215 (1975), the court rejected a claim that the zoning was improperly the product of negotiations and bargaining; "the overall aims of [PUD] zoning cannot be accomplished without negotiations and * * * conferences are indeed mandated by the regulating ordinance." *Id.* at 86, 334 N.E.2d at 219.

Problem

Moses Cohen owns seven bagel shops in the San Francisco metropolitan area, called Moses' Bagels. The shop on Onalos Street in Berkeley serves take-out food only; aside from a small park bench on the sidewalk in front of the store, there is no place for customers to sit and enjoy their food. When the small eye glasses store next door recently went out of business, Cohen decided to expand his shop to provide indoor seating for his customers.

The Onalos Street shop is located in a small commercial district about three blocks long. The district includes a bakery, two restaurants, a fresh produce store, a drug store, a barber shop, a craft shop, a hardware store, and a gardening shop. The commercial district is entirely surrounded by residences, including a mix of single-family houses and small apartment buildings. There is a large middle school and public park nearby, and a more substantial commercial district lies 7 blocks to the west and another one is 10 blocks to the north.

The Onalos Street commercial district has been zoned for small commercial stores. The express purpose of the zoning is to ensure (1) that the retail establishments are small (no more than 3000 square feet, height not to exceed two stories), (2) that they are of comparable size, so that one store does not dominate, and (3) that there is a mix of types of retail establishments that primarily serve the local neighborhood.

To expand into the former eye glasses store, Moses' Bagels would have to get a variance or a rezoning; the expanded shop would well exceed 3000

---

4. Although the local legislature must rezone the land to permit a PUD, normally the local legislature delegates authority to approve the details of the PUD to an administrative agency, such as the planning commission. *See Cheney v. Village 2 at New Hope, Inc.*, 429 Pa. 626, 241 A.2d 81 (1968) (upholding the delegation). *But see Lutz v. City of Longview*, 83 Wash.2d 566, 570, 520 P.2d 1374, 1377 (1974) (invalidating a delegation because the local legislature authorized a "floating zone" and did not rezone a particular parcel of land for the PUD).

square feet, and arguably it would become more like a restaurant, thereby undermining the diversity of uses in the commercial district. After the city posted appropriate public notices of the proposed change, a group of neighbors informed the city of their opposition to the change. Because Moses' Bagels is a well-known and popular bagel shop attracting clientele from outside the neighborhood, the neighbors were concerned about increased traffic congestion, noise, and air pollution. They noted that the expanded shop would not provide parking, so there also would be increased pressure on already scarce on-street parking. The neighbors opposing the shop have not expressed any desire for exactions from Moses' Bagels. That is, they do not think they can be adequately compensated for the perceived harm to their community, and they are not interested in bargaining over the conditions for a variance or a rezoning.

Cohen points out that other neighborhood residents have expressed their support for the shop, that he employs local residents, and that having an expanded store would be better than having a vacant store in the commercial district. He also disputes that there would be any noticeable impact on traffic, noise, or air pollution. The busiest traffic during the week occurs on weekend mornings, when local residents come by to get fresh bagels and schmooze. There is always ample parking on the street at those times because the other businesses are not yet open.

1.   What theory of politics seems to be at work here? To what extent does the freerider problem affect the organization of interests?

2.   How should the city approach the resolution of this dispute? That is, what theory of politics should the mayor foster? What pressures will she face? How are the politics likely to play out?

3.   Should Moses' Bagels seek a variance or a rezoning? What are the standards for obtaining each? Which one is more vulnerable on judicial review?

4.   Suppose that the city believes that the objecting neighbors' complaint has some merit, but that overall it would be best for the neighborhood and the city to let the bagel shop expand. May the city enter an agreement with Moses' Bagels in which it agrees to approve the development (*i.e.*, rezoning or variance) in exchange for conditions on the use of the establishment? If not, what can the city do to ensure that the bagel shop mitigates some of the harm that its expanded operations will cause?

---

3.   CONFLICT OF INTEREST, CORRUPTION, AND BARGAINING

To a significant extent, bias and even conflict of interest are inherent in municipal land use decisions. Land use decisions are local in nature and the decisionmakers frequently live in the affected community. As a consequence, decisionmakers often have first-hand knowledge of the issues, and in some cases they have reached some judgment before the formal decisionmaking process has begun. Decisionmakers may be financially affected by the outcome, may have had *ex parte* contacts with the parties, or even may have received campaign contributions or outright bribes from the parties. *See* S.L. Elkin, City and Regime in the American Republic 36–82 (1987) (arguing that city officials are biased in favor of land use development in order to improve municipal finances, secure campaign funds, and retain office).

Land use decisions are often unabashedly political; professional planners have a role in land use decisions, but the wishes of landowners, interest groups, and elected officials are also important and frequently decisive determinants. Land use decisions unavoidably involve conflicting values and require the exercise of discretion. The role of politics is magnified because many land use decisions are the product of *ad hoc* decisionmaking and dealmaking rather than the product of comprehensive planning. *See* Rose, Planning and Dealing: Piecemeal Land Controls as a Problem of Local Legitimacy, 71 Cal. L. Rev. 837, 841 (1983).

a. CONFLICT OF INTEREST AND CORRUPTION

Close judicial scrutiny of land use decisions, including prohibitions of spot zoning and contract zoning and requirements that zoning be consistent with the comprehensive plan, in part reflects a distrust of local land use politics and a suspicion that officials may be engaged in self-dealing.

Many state legislatures address these issues through conflict-of-interest statutes, which may require decisionmakers to reveal their conflicts of interest, or which may require them to recuse themselves from decisions in which they or family members have a financial interest. *See, e.g.*, Ind. Code Ann. §§ 36–7–4–223, 36–7–4–909 (covering planning commissions and boards of zoning appeals); Ariz. Rev. Stat. Ann. § 11–222 ("a supervisor shall not vote upon any measure in which he, any member of his family or his partner, is pecuniarily interested"). *See generally* Cordes, Policing Bias and Conflicts of Interest in Zoning Decisionmaking, 65 N.D.L. Rev. 161 (1989) (urging the adoption of regulations to limit conflicts of interest in zoning decisions).

Some courts have required or upheld the recusal of *administrative* officials who have a financial interest in land use decisions, even absent a conflict-of-interest statute. *See, e.g., Montgomery County Board of Appeals v. Walker*, 228 Md. 574, 580, 180 A.2d 865, 868 (1962) (affirming a board member's decision to recuse himself because "public policy requires that personal or pecuniary interests that would constitute a possible factor of influence in regard to his official actions should be nonexistent"). Only a few courts, however, require recusal of *legislative* officials who may have a conflict of interest, absent a statute prohibiting conflicts of interest for such officials.

Schauer v. City of Miami Beach

Supreme Court of Florida, 1959.
112 So.2d 838.

■ THOMAS, JUSTICE.

Suit had been instituted in the circuit court for declaratory decree, injunction and other relief and had culminated in a final decree declaring invalid Ordinance No. 1253 of the City of Miami Beach, which amended Ordinance No. 289 of the city, and enjoining enforcement of it.

It was the purpose of the amendatory ordinance to effect a change in the zoning of a large area so that it would not be restricted to use as sites for private residences but could be used as locations for multiple-family buildings and hotels. To pass the ordinance required the affirmative vote of five of the seven members of the city council. Of the five approving votes one was cast by S. J. Halperin who will gain $600,000 by reason of the increase in value of property owned by him in the territory.

The chancellor held, in effect, that because of his interest in the property affected, the councilman was disqualified to vote on the enactment of the ordinance and that, therefore, it failed to carry, hence was unenforceable.

An appeal was taken to the District Court of Appeal, Third District, and that court in a unanimous opinion reversed the decision of the chancellor. * * *

Adverting to the opinion of the district court of appeal, we find that one basic question was presented to it, namely, whether or not a court may investigate the motive of a council in voting for amendment of a zoning ordinance when the power to enact is vested in the council and is exercised in accordance with law. The court stated its understanding that the motives of a governing body of a municipality in adopting an ordinance of legislative character are not subject to judicial inquiry while actions of judicial tribunals or bodies acting quasi-judicially can be reviewed. * * * Then the court announced the opinion that the passage of the original zoning ordinance as well as the amending ordinance were the exercise of a legislative function. We agree with the conclusion * * *.

It is obvious to us that the enactment of the original zoning ordinance was a legislative function and we cannot reason that the amendment of it was of different character.

In its opinion the district court referred to abundant respectable authority for the position that once the legislative nature of the action is established the barrier against judicial incursion is erected. For instance, it was written in *Angle v. Chicago, St. P., M. & O. R. Co.*, 151 U.S. 1, 18–19 (1894), * * * that "whenever an act of the legislature is challenged in court the inquiry is limited to the question of power, and does not extend to the matter of expediency, the motives of the legislators, or the reasons which were spread before them to induce the passage of the act." As a reason for the rule the court continued: "It would not be seemly for either of the three departments [of the government] to be instituting an inquiry as to whether another acted wisely, intelligently, or corruptly."

* * *

We cannot agree that the * * * action claimed now to have been improper justif[ies] our interfering with the action of the city council on the theory that one of the councilmen should not have voted at all on the question of the adoption of the amending ordinance since he, admittedly, would gain if the ordinance passed. Such a conclusion would result in judicial investigation of legislation to determine what personal interest legislators had when their votes were cast, on the theory that those who had a personal interest in the outcome violated public policy by casting their votes. This theory we reject.

* * *

We have not discovered in the record that the council lacked power to amend the zoning ordinance or illegally exercised it; nor have we found evidence of fraud or overreaching. At the worst the councilman had a selfish interest, possibly with others similarly situated, in changing the status of his property to his financial advantage. But this human quality did not amount to fraud or overreaching. No attempt was made by him to conceal his interest; on the contrary he stated publicly that he would benefit greatly by the adoption of the ordinance.

Aside from the reasons for the general rule given in the cited cases, that is, the preservation of the independence of the three branches of government, it is not difficult to picture the havoc that would be wrought in legislative bodies if each member of them could by decree of the judiciary be declared disqualified to participate in any legislation that affected a class, race, creed, business, profession, occupation, association or trade to which he belonged.

Upon scrutiny of the opinions of this court and the District Court of Appeal, Third District, we come inescapably to the conclusion that no conflict has arisen on the same point of law so the petition for certiorari is—

Discharged.

■ ROBERTS, JUSTICE (dissenting).

* * *

To give judicial approval to conduct so obviously opposed to the traditional standards of morals and ethics required of our public officials is to admit a failure in our judicial system; and I, for one am unwilling to concede that an ordinance enacted under such circumstances is beyond the reach of the judicial process.

* * *

Legal sanction for the action of the councilman in casting the deciding vote in an official matter by which he stood to gain some $600,000 is sought in the well settled rule that the motives of the members of a legislative body in enacting a particular law are the sole concern of the legislators and the electors who elected them to office, and not of the courts. The impracticability of any other rule, insofar as a state legislature is concerned, is obvious. The dangers inherent in the application of this rule to a governmental agency that exercises both quasi-legislative and quasi-judicial powers are equally apparent. * * *

[A]ll the cases agree that a personal or financial interest disqualifies a member of a municipal council from participating in official action of a quasi-judicial nature. * * * It is equally well settled that the courts are not required to assume a "hands-off" attitude where the validity of a contract made by the City is brought into question because of a financial interest therein on the part of councilmen, even though the contractual arrangement was in the form of an ordinance. *City of Coral Gables v. Coral Gables, Inc., supra*, 160 So. 476 (1935). And it is my firm conviction that, in those cases where official action of a municipal body must be based on what is commonly thought of as a "judicial" inquiry, the courts are authorized to and should intervene to determine whether the preliminary judicial inquiry was made by a completely disinterested and impartial body, even though the official action partakes sufficiently of a "legislative" character to require the enactment of an ordinance or resolution to effect it.

Amendments to comprehensive zoning ordinances to take care of hardship cases, or to meet changes in the character of the neighborhood, are typical of this type of quasi-legislative-judicial municipal activity. It is well settled that the enactment of a comprehensive zoning ordinance is the exercise of a legislative and governmental function; and this court holds with the majority of other courts that the amendment of a zoning ordinance, including the granting of a variance to permit a non-conforming use because of an alleged "unnecessary hardship", is sufficiently legislative in character to require that it be done by the city's legislative body and not by a zoning board of appeals. * * *

The strict disinterestedness that should be required of municipal councilmen is particularly important in zoning cases, since this court is committed to the rule that if the zoning determination made by the City Council is "fairly debatable", it should not be disturbed by a court. *See City of Miami Beach v. Wiesen*, Fla.1956, 86 So.2d 442. And it is only in rare cases that a zoning determination by a City is stricken down by the courts as being not "fairly debatable" as to its reasonableness.

This court said in *City of Coral Gables v. Coral Gables, Inc., supra*, 160 So. 476, 478, that

> Whether in the form of ordinances or resolutions the acts of municipal corporations may be looked into by the courts to determine whether they were legally exercised, or whether the purpose accomplished by them was within the scope of its power, or whether they were in fact consummated through fraud or over-reaching.

The fraud referred to was not actual intentional fraud, but fraud in the contemplation of the law, or "legal" fraud. And, in my opinion, when a councilman, having an acknowledged financial interest in the passage of an amendatory zoning ordinance of the type here involved, casts the deciding vote in favor of the passage of such ordinance, he is not only guilty of a breach of faith in the exercise of the quasi-legislative and quasi-judicial powers entrusted to him, he has also committed a legal fraud against the people who trusted him. And to hold that the courts are powerless to intervene and invalidate an ordinance enacted in such circumstances would not, in my opinion, be in harmony with the decision of this court in the *Coral Gables* case, *supra*.

For the reasons stated, I would quash the judgment of the District Court of Appeals with directions to enter its order affirming the judgment of the Circuit Court vitiating the adoption of the ordinance in question.

I therefore respectfully dissent.

———————

1. Why did the court refuse to invalidate the zoning ordinance in this case?

Are there any circumstances under which the court would review a municipal zoning decision? What does the majority mean by "fraud"? What circumstances would constitute fraud in a rezoning case?

2. The dissent agrees with the majority that the court cannot review state legislative decisions, but concludes that it can review municipal zoning decisions. What is the basis for this distinction? What does the dissent mean by "fraud"?

3. Do you agree with the premise of both opinions that courts should not review state legislative decisions? How relevant is the consideration that the state legislature—unlike a state agency, whose decisions normally are subject to judicial review—is popularly elected and thus accountable to voters in the next election? If that is a substantial consideration, what is the basis to review municipal zoning decisions? Should the analysis turn on whether the municipal decision is characterized as legislative, quasi-legislative, or quasi-judicial? Do any of the political theories—pluralism, republicanism, or public choice theory—suggest a reason for judicial review?

———————

Fleming v. City of Tacoma

Supreme Court of Washington, 1972.
81 Wash. 2d 292, 502 P.2d 327.

■ STAFFORD, JUSTICE.

This case involves an alleged conflict of interest on the part of a city councilman who voted in favor of a zoning amendment.

In March 1969, the application of certain land developers, for a zoning reclassification of four parcels of real property in the vicinity of the Narrows Bridge in the city of Tacoma, was placed on the agenda of the Tacoma Planning Commission. The City of Tacoma and the land developers are appellants herein. The proposal sought to change the area from R–1 and R–2, single family residence districts, to an R–3 and R–5 PRD, multiple family planned residential development district. The primary purpose was to authorize construction of a high-rise condominium although the requested reclassification would also have permitted construction of town houses and retirement homes as well. The planning commission recommended approval, subject to certain conditions.

On July 1, 1969, the Tacoma City Council held a public hearing on the proposed rezoning. At its conclusion, the council concurred with the planning commission's recommendation and, by a 5–4 vote, directed the city attorney to prepare an ordinance to rezone the area. Councilman Murtland voted with the majority.

At the first reading of the ordinance on August 19, 1969, another public hearing was held. Respondent and neighbors living adjacent to the property to be rezoned presented testimony in opposition to the application. They claimed the proposed high-rise condominium would obstruct their view of Puget Sound and would be detrimental to the value of their property because covenants running with the land restricted use to single family dwellings whereas the property under consideration for rezoning was not similarly restricted. The neighbors also alleged that the proposal constituted spot zoning.

On August 26, 1969, the ordinance came on for the second and final reading. Respondent and the other neighboring property owners again protested the probable loss of property value. Councilman Murtland suggested further study of the effect of the ordinance upon the abutting property which was burdened with restrictive covenants. The council refused and a vote was called. The ordinance lost by a tie vote of 4–4, Councilman Murtland voting against it. Having voted with the prevailing side, Councilman Murtland was empowered to move for reconsideration of the ordinance.

At the next council meeting, Councilman Murtland moved to reconsider. The motion passed 6–3, Councilman Murtland voting with the majority. As a result, consideration of the ordinance was placed on the council's September 17 agenda. On September 17 the ordinance passed by a vote of 6–3. This time Councilman Murtland voted in favor thereof. The meeting was adjourned about 10 p.m., September 17, 1969.

On September 19, less than 48 hours after the final vote, Councilman Murtland, now acting as attorney for the successful land developers, wrote to the Secretary of State asking whether the name Bridgeview Development Company was available for his clients' corporate use. On September 26, 1969, articles of incorporation for the Bridgeview Development Company were executed by the land developers in the law office of Councilman Murtland. They were approved by the Secretary of State on October 1,

1969. The ordinance became law on October 2, 1969. Mr. Murtland remained a city councilman until well after the events here involved.

Thereafter, respondent applied for a writ of certiorari alleging, *inter alia*, that the rezone was illegal because (a) the council failed to consider the ordinance's effect on abutting property which was burdened with restrictive covenants, and (b) the rezone constituted spot zoning. Following a hearing the trial court orally denied the writ. Thereafter respondent moved for reconsideration of the court's oral decision, alleging new evidence of a possible conflict of interest on the part of Councilman Murtland.

After a hearing on the conflict of interest issue, the trial court entered judgment against respondent on those matters contained in the original writ application but held the ordinance was invalid because it would appear to third persons "that a conflict of interest and impropriety existed in the action of the council ... during passage of [the] Ordinance." Although the court specifically found that no actual conflict of interest existed, it also found that:

> by reason of the representation of the applicant [developer] by Councilman Murtland two days following the final vote on [the] ordinance ... that the public has not been afforded the action and decision of a public official that is free of suspicion of unfairness or temptation to which they are entitled in the passage of zoning reclassification ordinances.

We have long passed the time when one may use his land as he wishes provided it creates no nuisance. The concentration of population and the infinite variety of modern land uses necessitate effective land use planning. The restrictions on use, inherent in zoning, insure that if one uses his property in a way harmonious with the existing zoning codes, he will be free from the danger that the future use of his neighbor's land might be detrimental to or foreclose his own established use. Decisions which amend or change conditions under existing zoning laws therefore require an extremely sensitive balance between individual rights and the public welfare. The process by which such decisions are made must not only be fair but must appear to be fair to insure public confidence therein.

In recent years we have adopted the appearance of fairness doctrine in zoning decisions. Three cases in particular have developed the essential guidelines.

In *Smith v. Skagit County*, 75 Wn.2d 715, 739, 453 P.2d 832 (1969), we said:

> the law requires a hearing of any sort as a condition precedent to the power to proceed, it means a fair hearing, a hearing not only fair in substance, but fair in appearance as well.... Where the law expressly gives the public a right to be heard ... the public hearing must, to be valid, meet the test of fundamental fairness, for the right to be heard imports a reasonable expectation of being heeded. Just as a hearing fair in appearance but unfair in sub-

stance is no fair hearing, so neither is a hearing fair in substance but appearing to be unfair.

In *Smith* we focused our attention upon defects in the hearing itself rather than upon motives of the members who conducted the hearing. We held that hearings before the county planning commission and board of county commissioners failed to meet the test of fairness.[5] We were particularly disturbed by the planning commission's closed executive session to which proponents were invited and opponents excluded, and by the county commissioners' refusal to allow opponents to present their views on certain occasions. Additionally, there was a sharp contrast between the deliberative consideration given the original zoning and the hasty consideration given its amendment.

In two subsequent cases we shifted our attention from hearing procedures to the motives of those who conducted them. In *Chrobuck v. Snohomish County*, 78 Wn.2d 858, 480 P.2d 489 (1971), we held that hearings before the county planning commission lacked an appearance of fairness because a member thereof had close prior social and business connections with a proponent of the rezone and his successor had publicly supported the proponent's position prior to his appointment. We were critical of the fact that even though the challenged commissioner had not voted, he had participated in the commission's deliberations. Similarly, in *Buell v. Bremerton*, 80 Wn.2d 518, 495 P.2d 1358 (1972), we held that hearings before a city planning commission lacked an appearance of fairness because one of its members owned property that appreciated in value as a result of the decision. In *Buell* there was a question as to whether the commission member had actually voted. We held, however, that even if he had not voted there was a possible conflict of interest because the value of his own property had been appreciated by the rezone. We therefore invalidated the planning commission's actions, stating at page 525:

> The fact that the action carried without the necessity of counting his vote is not determinative. The self-interest of one member of the planning commission infects the action of the other members of the commission regardless of their disinterestedness.

The challenged actions in both *Chrobuck* and *Buell* were taken by administrative bodies.

In the past we have examined the motives of administrative officers when reviewing their decisions in zoning matters. On the other hand, we have refrained from such an examination of legislative bodies, *i.e.*, boards of county commissioners or city councils, when acting pursuant to statutes

---

5. *Smith v. Skagit County*, 75 Wn.2d 715, 741, 453 P.2d 832 (1969):

The test of fairness ... in public hearings conducted by law on matters of public interest ... is whether a fair-minded person in attendance at all of the meetings on a given issue, could, at the conclusion thereof, in good conscience say that everyone had been heard who, in all fairness, should have been heard and that the legislative body required by law to hold the hearings gave reasonable faith and credit to all matters presented, according to the weight and force they were in reason entitled to receive. * * *

regulating zoning. We have held that while so acting they are exercising legislative powers and therefore we will not, in the absence of fraud, inquire into the motives of their members. *Lillions v. Gibbs*, 47 Wn.2d 629, 632, 289 P.2d 203 (1955). The question here is whether we should continue in that vein or whether we should extend the appearance of fairness doctrine to encompass an examination into the motives of city councilmen and county commissioners when acting in a legislative capacity upon zoning amendments.

Generally courts will not inquire into the motives of legislative officers acting in a legislative capacity. *Goebel v. Elliott*, 178 Wash. 444, 35 P.2d 44 (1934); *Cornelius v. Seattle*, 123 Wash. 550, 213 P. 17 (1923); 1 C. Antieau, Municipal Corporation Law § 5:15 (1968); 5 E. McQuillin, The Law of Municipal Corporations § 16.90 (3d ed. 1969 rev. vol.); Annot., 32 A.L.R. 1517 (1924). The rule follows from the doctrine of the separation of powers. *Angle v. Chicago, St. P., M. & O. Ry.*, 151 U.S. 1, 18–19 (1894). The rule's wisdom is stated in *Schauer v. Miami Beach*, 112 So. 2d 838, 841 (Fla. 1959):

> Aside from the reasons for the general rule given in the cited cases, that is, the preservation of the independence of the three branches of government, it is not difficult to picture the havoc that would be wrought in legislative bodies if each member of them could by decree of the judiciary be declared disqualified to participate in any legislation that affected a class, race, creed, business, profession, occupation, association or trade to which he belonged.

Although a majority of courts follow the rule in the zoning context, we are convinced that zoning amendments or zoning reclassifications are sufficiently distinguishable from other legislative functions that an exception to the general rule is desirable.[6]

Zoning decisions may be either administrative or legislative depending upon the nature of the act. *See Durocher v. King County*, 80 Wn.2d 139, 492 P.2d 547 (1972). But, whatever their nature or the importance of their categorization for other purposes, zoning decisions which deal with an amendment of the code or reclassification of land thereunder must be arrived at fairly. The process by which they are made, subsequent to the adoption of a comprehensive plan and a zoning code, is basically adjudicatory.

Generally, when a municipal legislative body enacts a comprehensive plan and zoning code it acts in a policy making capacity. But in amending a zoning code, or reclassifying land thereunder, the same body, in effect, makes an adjudication between the rights sought by the proponents and those claimed by the opponents of the zoning change. The parties whose

---

6. *See* Note, 57 Mich. L. Rev. 423 (1959). Other jurisdictions have reached a similar result by classifying the actions of a city council in passing a rezoning amendment or granting a planned residential development permit as an administrative action. *See, e.g., RK Dev. Corp. v. Norwalk*, 156 Conn. 369, 242 A.2d 781 (1968); *Aldom v. Roseland*, 42 N.J. Super. 495, 127 A.2d 190 (1956).

interests are affected are readily identifiable. Although important questions of public policy may permeate a zoning amendment, the decision has a far greater impact on one group of citizens than on the public generally.

Another feature of zoning amendment decisions, which distinguishes them from other types of legislative action, is their localized applicability. Other municipal ordinances which affect particular groups or individuals more than the public at large apply throughout an entire geographic area within the municipal jurisdiction, whereas ordinances that amend zoning codes or reclassify land thereunder apply only to the immediate area being rezoned.

Finally, legislative hearings are generally discretionary with the body conducting them, whereas zoning hearings are required by statute, charter, or ordinance. The fact that these hearings are required is itself recognition of the fact that the decision making process must be more sensitive to the rights of the individual citizen involved.

In light of these distinctions, it is appropriate to apply the appearance of fairness doctrine to all hearings, conducted by a municipal legislative body, which are aimed at amending existing zoning codes or reclassifying land thereunder. Not only must the hearings appear fair, but the motives of the persons conducting the hearings and voting therein must be above reproach. We expressly overrule that portion of *Lillions v. Gibbs, supra*, which states the contrary rule. We now hold that members of municipal legislative bodies who conduct such hearings must, as far as practicable, be open-minded and free of entangling influences. As we said in *Buell v. Bremerton, supra* at 523, they must be "capable of hearing the weak voices as well as the strong. . . . It is important not only that justice be done but that it also appear to be done . . ."

In this case there is direct, tangible evidence that a city councilman was employed by the successful proponents of a zoning amendment, for which the councilman voted in the majority. While the evidence goes only so far as to show the councilman's employment, less than 48 hours after the critical vote on the rezoning application, the inference that such employment was arranged before the vote cannot be ignored. As the trial judge stated in his oral opinion:

> I will go out of my way here to say that I believe Mr. Murtland when he said there was no contact regarding employment before the 19th of September. I believe it because I have known him for twenty-five years, and my experience observing him is that this is not the type of thing that he would tell us anything other than the truth on. The problem is that's what I believe. That is not what the Relators believe, I am sure of that. That is not what the Relators believe, and that is not what the average person looking at the process of what has transpired would be inclined to believe.

> The time coincidence is devastating. It is unfortunate this probably has taken place because this was one of those days that we all have where a problem arose and a man just didn't think

about the whole implications of what he was doing. The appearance of conflict of interest is here. The appearance of conflict of interest is so strong that I am sure those who oppose the zoning and who thought this thing through will never, never believe that somehow this wasn't kind of wired before the final vote was taken.

We agree with the trial court. The proceedings in which the questioned zoning amendment was enacted is permeated with an appearance of unfairness by Councilman Murtland's conduct. We therefore hold that the ordinance is invalid, notwithstanding that Councilman Murtland's vote was unnecessary for passage.

　　* * *

The trial court is affirmed.

---

1.   The court extends the "appearance of fairness" standard to municipal zoning decisions. The court's rationale is based on its judgment that rezoning is different from other municipal decisions, and therefore requires closer judicial scrutiny. What is the court's reasoning? Do you find it persuasive?

2.   What are the relevant criteria to decide whether there is an "appearance of fairness" in a particular decision? Will this standard be easy to apply?

3.   Which approach will produce better land use decisions—disclosure of any potential conflict of interest (which *Schauer* suggests would prevent fraud) or recusal of any municipal legislator whose participation would undermine "appearance of fairness" (which *Fleming* requires)? Are there other possible standards?

Conflict-of-interest statutes reduce the opportunities for corruption, but they cannot eliminate it. Many land use decisions create substantial wealth by authorizing large development projects, but even relatively small decisions create opportunities for corruption. Coupled with the broad governmental discretion and dealmaking that typifies most significant land use decisions, corruption seems almost inevitable. *See* G. Amick, The American Way of Graft 77–100 (1976) (giving examples of corruption in local land use regulation, including conflict of interest, campaign contributions, and bribery); J.S. Gardiner & T.R. Lyman, Decisions for Sale: Corruption and Reform in Land–Use and Building Regulation (1978) (discussing several land use cases involving extortion and bribes, including cash payments and campaign contributions). Karkkainen, Zoning: A Reply to the Critics, 10 J. Land Use & Envt'l L. 45, 59–60, 86–89 (1994) (citing various instances of corruption in land use decisions). Gardiner and Lyman argue that greater professionalization—increased use of planners, for example—and more transparent decisionmaking—making information, meetings, and decisions public and encouraging public participation—would help to combat corruption.

b.   BARGAINING FOR EXACTIONS: SUBDIVISION EXACTIONS, IMPACT FEES, LINKAGE PROGRAMS, AND INCLUSIONARY ZONING

One must be careful, however, to distinguish corruption from bargaining more generally. Professor Fischel argues that

> The problem with bribing the official is not that money is being paid but that it is being paid to the wrong party. Zoning is a collective community entitlement, not a personal one. If the developer is willing to pay for a rezoning, he should pay the proper owners of the entitlement. Aside from the inequity of a system of bribes, there is an efficiency problem The bribe to a single person will usually be too small. This is because there are neighborhood effects from most developments, so that many people will be affected simultaneously. The well-being of all those affected must be considered. * * * If we are to have a market for zoning, the market must be arranged so that some approximation of a solution to the public goods problem must be reached. Just compensating some party, who may not even be affected by the development, is insufficient.

W.A. Fischel, The Economics of Zoning Laws 72 (1985).

Bargaining is a regular feature of land use decisions. Putting aside corruption, bargaining turns on the relative positions of the parties (*e.g.*, does the municipality desperately want additional development, or would it just as soon do without new development; does the municipality offer unique features that developers cannot find elsewhere, or must it compete with other jurisdictions). In some communities, especially larger cities that need economic growth to generate tax revenues and provide jobs, municipal officials are likely to offer developers a variety of economic incentives to attract development, including relaxation of land use restrictions (*e.g.*, through variances, rezoning), infrastructure (roads, sewer lines), tax incentives (*e.g.*, waiver of property taxes for a period of time), and assistance in assembling suitable parcels for development (*e.g.*, through eminent domain). But in other communities, where development is more desirable, municipal officials are able to demand concessions from developers. These concessions (usually called exactions) may include dedications of infrastructure (*e.g.*, roads, parks, school buildings), and payments of "in-lieu" fees (thereby giving developers an option to provide either dedications or fees), impact fees (designed to cover the costs of development), and linkage fees (designed to pay for low-income housing that the development will directly or indirectly displace).

Vicki Been, "Exit" As a Constraint on Land Use Exactions: Rethinking the Unconstitutional Conditions Doctrine

91 Columbia Law Review 473, 482–83 (1991).

The main reason municipalities impose exactions upon development is, of course, to shift to the developer the costs of the public infrastructure that the development requires. But exactions serve a variety of other purposes as well. First, by forcing the developer and its customers to assume or share in the costs of infrastructure, exactions induce a more efficient use of the infrastructure. Second, exactions serve to mitigate the negative effects a development may have on a neighborhood, such as increased traffic congestion, noise, and environmental degradation. In serving this purpose, exactions again encourage efficiency by forcing the developer and its customers to internalize the full costs of the harms that the development causes.

Third, exactions serve as growth enablers: in areas that are growing so rapidly that the government cannot provide public facilities fast enough, exactions allow growth that might otherwise be stalled by growth control measures. Or, in areas in which a particular development, or growth in general, is controversial, a local government that favors a project may use exactions to counter or "buy off" opposition. Fourth, a local government may use exactions to try to discourage all growth, or to prevent certain kinds of development, such as low- and moderate-income housing, in order to preserve the exclusiveness of a community or to preserve its fiscal position.

Finally, exactions may be used either to redistribute wealth from the developer or its customers to others, or to prevent the developer from appropriating wealth created by the activities of the local government. A community may impose exactions as a means of capturing part of the developer's profit. Or, in some markets, a community may adopt exactions in order to inflate the price of existing housing and thereby allow the current residents to profit at the expense of newcomers. On the other hand, a community may use exactions to recapture from the developer part of the value added to land by improvements financed by the community.

––––––

As Professor Been points out, the majority of municipalities, especially those in growth areas, seek exactions from developers. Been, "Exit" As a Constraint on Land Use Exactions: Rethinking the Unconstitutional Conditions Doctrine, 91 Colum. L. Rev. 473, 481 n. 42 (1991) (citing surveys showing that 89% of all communities require dedications and that 58% require some type of fees). Most municipalities employ a formula to determine the amount of the exaction, but a significant fraction determine exactions through case-by-case negotiations. *Id.* at 481 n. 43. There is substantial variation in the amount of exactions obtained. *Id.* at 482.

The following is a brief typology of exactions. Beware that courts and legislatures do not always make such fine distinctions (*e.g.*, a court may label *all* fees as "impact fees").

Subdivision Exactions. Subdivision controls and conditional rezoning frequently require dedications of public infrastructure, such as streets, parks, sewers, storm drains, and schools.

Subdivision dedications are not new. Subdivision statutes have long required developers to provide on-site infrastructure in exchange for subdivision approval. Smith, From Subdivision Improvement Requirements to Community Benefit Assessments and Linkage Payments: A Brief History of Land Development Exactions, 50 L. & Contemp. Probs. 5 (1987). Courts have upheld such exactions against constitutional challenge on the grounds that the development caused the need for the improvements and that the improvements would specially benefit the subdivision. *See, e.g., Brous v. Smith*, 304 N.Y. 164, 106 N.E.2d 503 (1952) (upholding a requirement to dedicate streets); *Crownhill Homes, Inc. v. City of San Antonio*, 433 S.W.2d 448 (Tex.Civ.App. 1968) (upholding a requirement to dedicate water mains).

Off-site dedications may be more problematic because the statutory authority for off-site exactions is less clear. *See, e.g., Cherry Hills Resort Development Co. v. Cherry Hills Village*, 790 P.2d 827 (Colo.1990) (finding no statutory authority for conditions requiring additional fire equipment and improvements at a nearby intersection); *Hylton Enters. v. Board of Supervisors*, 220 Va. 435, 440, 258 S.E.2d 577, 580 (1979) (finding no statutory authority to require a subdivider to construct improvements to existing public roads). Courts and legislatures are also concerned that the relationship between the development and the exaction may be too tenuous. *See, e.g., Liberty v. California Coastal Comm'n*, 113 Cal.App.3d 491, 502, 170 Cal.Rptr. 247, 254 (1980) (declaring invalid exactions that would provide free parking for the benefit of the general public); Cal. Gov't Code § 65909 (requiring the dedication to be "reasonably related" to the use of the property for which the building permit is requested). Although the cases and statutes do not clearly articulate the underlying concern, it appears to stem from a suspicion that the municipality may demand exactions far in excess of the social costs of the development project. We will return to this concern below in analyzing *Dolan v. City of Tigard*, 512 U.S. 374 (1994).

Some state legislatures authorize municipalities to assess fees in lieu of subdivision dedications. *See, e.g.,* Colo. Rev. Stat. § 30–28–133(4)(a) (authorizing dedications and in-lieu payments for parks and schools); Cal. Gov't Code § 66477 (authorizing dedications and in-lieu payments for parks and recreational facilities); N.J. Stat. Ann. § 27:1C–7(d) ("any development which has received preliminary approval * * * shall be liable for the payment of offsite transportation improvements"). Absent statutory authorization, many courts strike down exactions of in-lieu fees. *See, e.g., City of Montgomery v. Crossroads Land Co.*, 355 So.2d 363, 364–65 (Ala.1978) (although the statute allows cities to require "adequate and convenient open spaces for recreation," there is no authority to require payment of a fee in lieu of a dedication of land); *Admiral Development Corp. v. City of Maitland*, 267 So.2d 860, 863 (Fla.App. 1972) (no statutory authority to require a subdivider pay an in lieu fee of 5% of the gross value of the land).

Impact Fees. Municipalities increasingly impose "impact fees" on all kinds of developments, not just those requiring subdivision approval, to help finance a range of municipal facilities that may be required as a result of development, such as construction or expansion of water and sewerage facilities. *See generally* Bauman & Ethier, Development Exactions and Impact Fees: A Survey of American Practices, 50 Law & Contemp. Probs. 51 (1987). Many states have enacted statutes specifically authorizing impact fees. *See, e.g.,* Cal. Gov't Code §§ 66000–66007 (establishing criteria and procedures for municipalities to require payment of fees as a condition for approval of a development project); Tex. Local Gov't Code §§ 395.001–395.025 (authorizing municipalities to require payment of impact fees to pay for capital improvements or facility expansions). In other states, courts have found adequate authority in statutes that authorize user fees for the maintenance and construction of public facilities. *See, e.g., Coulter v. City of Rawlings*, 662 P.2d 888, 896 (Wyo.1983) (upholding sewer connection and meter placement fees as implicitly allowed by state statutes granting municipalities the power to "provide and regulate the construction and use of sewers and mains" and to assess costs in compliance with the regulations).

State courts have generally upheld impact fees so long as there is an adequate relation between the fee and the additional burden imposed on public facilities. *See, e.g., St. Johns County v. Northeast Florida Builders Ass'n*, 583 So.2d 635, 637 (Fla.1991) (upholding fees to build new schools because there is a rational nexus between the need for additional capital facilities and the growth in the population generated by the subdivision); *Blue Jeans Equities West v. City and County of San Francisco*, 3 Cal. App.4th 164, 172, 4 Cal.Rptr.2d 114, 119 (1992) (upholding the public transit impact development fee); *Balch Enterprises, Inc. v. New Haven Unified School Dist.*, 219 Cal.App.3d 783, 792–95, 268 Cal.Rptr. 543, 547–49 (1990) (upholding a trial court finding that the "school facilities fee" was not adequately related to demonstrated school needs caused by new development).

Linkage Programs. Linkage programs are a more recent innovation. They presume that new commercial development will either displace existing private land uses or create new demand for particular land uses— normally low- and moderate-income housing—that the market will not supply. Municipal ordinances usually require the developer to pay fees reflecting the cost of housing construction, although some programs give the developer the opportunity to provide the housing directly. The municipality deposits the linkage fees in a fund dedicated to the construction of low- and moderate-income housing. *See generally* Collin & Lytton, Linkage: An Evaluation and Exploration, 21 The Urban Law. 413 (1989).

Some state statutes expressly authorize linkage fee programs, and some state courts have found implied authority. *Blagden Alley Ass'n v. District of Columbia Zoning Comm'n*, 590 A.2d 139, 145 (D.C.App.1991) (finding implied authority for linkage fees to pay for off-site housing); *but see San Telmo Associates v. City of Seattle*, 108 Wash.2d 20, 735 P.2d 673 (1987) (finding no implied authority to impose a fee on owners of low-income rental housing who convert the property to non-residential uses). Where there exists adequate authority, courts have upheld linkage fee ordinances so long as the city can demonstrate a rational connection between the fee and the social problem caused by the new development. *See, e.g., Terminal Plaza Corp. v. City & County of San Francisco*, 177 Cal.App.3d 892, 223 Cal.Rptr. 379 (1986) (upholding a linkage fee imposed on owners of residential hotels who seek to convert their property to other uses, equal to 40% of the cost of constructing an equal number of new units).

San Francisco Planning Code (1997)

313.2. **Findings**. The Board hereby finds and declares as follows: Large-scale office developments in the [City] have attracted and continue to attract additional employees to the City, and there is a causal connection between such developments and the need for additional housing in the City, particularly housing affordable to households of low and moderate income. Office uses in the City are benefitted by the availability of housing for persons employed in such offices close to their place of employment. However, the supply of housing units in the City has not kept pace with the demand for housing created by these new employees. Due to this shortage of housing, employers will have difficulty in securing a labor force, and employees, unable to find decent and affordable housing, will be forced to commute long distances, having a negative impact on quality of life, limited energy resources, and already overcrowded highways and public transport.

There is a low vacancy rate for housing affordable to persons of lower and moderate income. In part, this low vacancy rate is due to factors unrelated to large office development, such as high interest rates, high land costs in the City, immigration from abroad, demographic changes such as the reduction in the number of persons per household, and personal, subjective choices by households that San Francisco is a desirable place to live. This low vacancy rate is also due in part to large office developments which have attracted and will continue to attract additional employees and residents to the City. Consequently, some of the employees attracted to these large office developments are competing with present residents for scarce, vacant affordable housing units in the City. Competition for housing generates the greatest pressure on the supply of housing affordable to households of lower and moderate income. In San Francisco, office or retail uses of land generally yield higher income to the owner than housing. Because of these market forces, the supply of these affordable housing units will not be expanded. Furthermore, Federal and State housing finance and subsidy programs are not sufficient by themselves to satisfy the lower and moderate income housing requirements of the City.

    * * *

It is desirable to impose the cost of the increased burden of providing housing necessitated by such office development projects directly upon the sponsor of new development generating the need through a requirement that the sponsor construct housing or pay a fee to the City to subsidize housing development as a condition of the privilege of development and to assist the community in solving those of its housing problems generated by the development.

313.3.   **Application**.

(1) This ordinance shall apply to office development projects proposing the net addition of 25,000 or more gross square feet of office space.

    * * *

313.4.   **Imposition of Housing Requirement**.

(a) * * * The conditions [for approval of applications for office development projects] shall require that the applicant pay a housing developer to construct housing or pay an in-lieu fee to the City Controller which shall thereafter be used exclusively for the development of housing affordable to households of lower or moderate income.

    * * *

(g) The sponsor of any office development project subject to this Ordinance shall have the option of:

    (1) Contributing a sum equal to or greater than the in-lieu fee according to the formula set forth in Section 313.6 to one or more housing developers who will use the funds to construct housing units pursuant to Section 313.5; or

    (2) Paying an in-lieu fee to the Controller according to the formula set forth in Section 313.6; or

    (3) Combining the above options pursuant to Section 313.7.

313.5.   **Compliance Through Payment to Housing Developer**.

(a) If the sponsor elects to pay a sum equivalent to the in-lieu fee to one or more housing developers to meet the requirements of this ordinance, the housing developer(s) shall be required to construct at least the number of housing units determined by the following formula:

Net Addition Gross Sq. Ft. Office Space x .000386 = Housing Units

Sixty-two percent of those housing units required to be constructed under the above formula must be affordable to qualifying households continuously for 50 years. * * *

313.6. **Compliance Through Payment of In–Lieu Fee**.

(a) Commencing on January 1, 1995, the amount of the fee which may be paid by the sponsor of an office development project in lieu of developing and providing the housing required by Section 313.5 shall be computed as follows:

Net Addition Gross Sq. Ft. Office Space x $7.05 = Total Fee

* * *

313.7. **Compliance Through Combination of Payment to Housing Developer and Payment of in Lieu Fee**. The sponsor of an office development project may elect to satisfy its housing requirement by a combination of paying money to one or more housing developers under Section 313.5 and paying a partial amount of the in-lieu fee to the Controller under Section 313.6. * * *

313.12. **Affordable Housing Fund**. All monies contributed pursuant to Sections 313.6 or 313.7 * * * shall be deposited in the special fund maintained by the Controller called the Citywide Affordable Housing Fund ("Fund"). The receipts in the Fund are hereby appropriated in accordance with law to be used solely to increase the supply of housing affordable to qualifying households subject to the conditions of this Section. * * * No portion of the Fund may be used, by way of loan or otherwise, to pay any administrative, general overhead, or similar expense of any entity. * * *

———

Inclusionary Zoning. Inclusionary zoning describes a set of techniques to encourage or even require residential developers to include low- and moderate-income housing as part of the overall housing development. Inclusionary zoning normally involves an exchange: a residential developer agrees to build a percentage of its units for low- and moderate-income families in exchange for the municipality's relaxation of land use requirements, such as density limits, street widths, and uniformity requirements. Some ordinances permit payment of fees in lieu of construction. Such housing is sold at steeply discounted prices to income-qualified buyers, and covenants running with the land ensure that the housing will remain deeply discounted when resold.

Some state statutes expressly authorize municipalities to engage in inclusionary zoning. *See, e.g.,* Conn. Gen. Stat. § 8–2g (authorizing a special exemption from density limits for affordable housing); Md. Ann. Code art. 66B, § 12.01 (authorizing local legislatures to "[i]mpose inclusionary zoning and award density bonuses to create affordable housing units"); N.Y. Town Law § 261–b (authorizing incentives, such as adjustments to density, area, height, open space, use, or other requirements in exchange for low- and moderate-income housing). A few others strongly encourage or even require municipalities to employ inclusionary zoning techniques. *See, e.g.,* N.J. Stat. Ann. §§ 52:27D–311(a)(1) (requiring municipal housing elements to contain set asides or density bonuses "as may be necessary to meet all or part of the municipality's fair share''); Cal. Gov't Code § 65915 (requiring municipalities to award density bonuses to developers who restrict a percentage of new units for affordable housing). Municipalities, in turn, have adopted ordinances requiring mandatory ''set-asides'' (requirements to dedicate a percentage of new housing units as low- and moderate-income housing), although they usually permit the developer to satisfy its obligation with in-lieu payments or off-site construction of affordable units.

San Francisco Subdivision Code (1997)

1341. Low and Moderate Income Occupancy.

(a) In all subdivisions involving 50 or more lots or units, except for condominium or cooperative conversion subdivisions, the subdivider shall make available 10 percent of the units for low and moderate income occupancy provided that the Department of City Planning finds that governmental subsidies for such occupancy are available to the subdivider. * * *

(b) In all condominium or cooperative conversion subdivisions with five or more lots or units, the subdivider shall make available 10 percent of the lots or units for rental or for purchase by households of low or moderate income. * * *

(c) If the units are to be made available for purchase, then the sales prices of such units shall not exceed 2.5 times the annual median income [of] low or moderate income households * * *. Any low or moderate income household which purchases a dwelling pursuant to this Section shall grant a right-of-first-refusal, to the City and County of San Francisco * * * to repurchase the dwelling from the initial purchaser at the original price plus the cost of any improvements paid for by the owner, plus an increase proportionate to the increases in the housing component of the ''Bay Area Cost of Living Index, U.S. Dept. of Labor,'' over the intervening time period. * * *

(d) If the converted units are to be for rental, then the rent in such units shall not exceed the rent charged at the time of filing the application for conversion, or the maximum rent that would be allowed so as to keep the unit within moderate income housing stock, whichever rent is lower. * * *

(e) * * * Units made available for rental pursuant to Subsection (d) above shall remain as rental units for no less than 20 years, provided, however, that such rental units may be sold by the original subdivider or any subsequent owner during such 20-year period at a price not exceeding the price at which the City and County of San Francisco would be entitled to repurchase the unit if exercising its right of first refusal under Subsection (c) above * * *.

(f) As an alternative to the provisions of Subsections (b) and (c) above, the subdivider shall make a bona fide agreement, satisfactory to the Department of City Planning, to construct or cause to be constructed within a period commencing 18 months prior to the date of filing the application for conversion and ending 18 months after filing of the final or parcel map, or to provide through other means, the same number of units and under the same conditions as would be required for low or moderate income occupancy under the provisions of Subsections (b), (c), and (d) above, in areas approved by the Department of City Planning as being non-impacted with assisted housing.

(g) As a further alternative to the provisions of Subsections (b), (c), and (f) above, the subdivider shall pay to the City and County of San Francisco an amount equal to 10 percent of the difference between the aggregated total of the proposed market rate sales prices, * * * and the aggregate total of the sales prices if the units were to be sold at moderate-income sales prices * * *

(h) Funds collected pursuant to Subsection (g) above, shall be deposited into the Housing Development Fund, which fund is to be used for persons and households of low or moderate income.

1343.   Policies and Procedures for Use of the Housing Development Fund. * * *

(2) Eligible Uses of the Fund.

(a) Monies from the Fund may be made available to nonprofit housing corporations for the acquisition of available and feasible sites for developing low and moderate income housing and the rehabilitation or existing sites for low and moderate income housing.

(b) Monies from the Fund may be used for costs incident to the acquisition or rehabilitation of property, including, but not limited to, architectural and engineering costs.

(c) Any developer receiving monies form this Fund shall ensure that a minimum of 51 percent of the units in the project are made available to persons and families of low and moderate income.

Despite their attraction as a means to generate funding for low- and moderate-income housing, linkage fee programs and inclusionary zoning techniques have come under heavy attack by public policy analysts. One debate concerns whether there is any significant causal connection between new commercial development and increased demand for low- and moderate-income housing. *See* Fischel, The Economics of Land Use Exactions: A Property Rights Analysis, 50 Law & Contemp. Probs. 101 (1987) (concluding that the connection is tenuous at best); Kayden & Pollard, Linkage Ordinances and Traditional Exactions Analysis: The Connection Between Office Development and Housing, 50 Law & Contemp. Probs. 127 (1987) (concluding that downtown development projects increase the demand for low-income housing).

Another set of critics maintains that linkage fees tax the production of new housing, and thereby increase housing prices and limit the housing opportunities of moderate-income families. W.A. Fischel, The Economics of Zoning Laws 327–29 (1985); Ellickson, The Irony of "Inclusionary" Zoning, 54 S. Cal. L. Rev. 1167 (1981). Ellickson argues that inclusionary zoning is not equitable and does not achieve its intended purposes.

> Inclusionary zoning, as it is usually practiced, is a misguided undertaking that is likely to aggravate the housing crisis it has ostensibly been designed to help solve. As a program of income redistribution, inclusionary zoning makes no sense. Although nominally aimed at benefiting low- and moderate-income families, almost all inclusionary units have in fact been bestowed on families in the middle third of the state's income distribution. Because only a small percentage (at most) of the members of the class of eligibles can hope soon to obtain units, inclusionists must resort to lotteries and queues to select the few lucky beneficiaries of handsome housing grants.

> Government distribution of massive subsidies to a few arbitrarily designated members of the middle class might be defensible if this redistribution produced important benefits to the larger society. The only possible social gains from inclusionary zoning are the intangible benefits flowing from the economic integration of new buildings and subdivisions. Yet even the social critics who have pushed most strongly for greater residential mobility doubt that economic integration at the block and building level is in the interest of the members of *any* income group. Moreover, inclusionary zoning as currently practiced will have only a trivial effect on the amount of economic integration in residential neighborhoods.

> The costs of inclusionary zoning, by contrast, are large and tangible. Inclusionary zoning involves in-kind housing subsidies, a method increasingly viewed as one of the most inefficient forms of income redistribution. Inclusionary zoning can also constitute a double tax on new housing construction—first, through the burden of its exactions; and second, through the "undesirable" social environment it may force on new housing projects. In the sorts of housing markets in which inclusionary zoning has been practiced, this double tax is likely to push up housing prices across the board, often to the net injury of the moderate-income households inclusionary zoning was supposed to help. The irony of inclusionary zoning is thus that, in the places where it has proven most likely to be adopted, its net effects are apt to be the opposite of the ones advertised.

Id. at 1215–16.

c.   FEDERAL CONSTITUTIONAL CHALLENGES TO EXACTIONS

Landowners have challenged exactions as violating constitutional prohibitions on takings. Until 1987, the Supreme Court had not addressed the
issue, effectively leaving the matter to state courts. State courts generally
upheld the exactions so long as municipalities could demonstrate some
relationship between the type and amount of the exaction and the social
problem created by the proposed land use. State court decisions, however,
varied significantly in the precise showing required.

In 1987, the Supreme Court decided the first of two important exaction
cases. In *Nollan v. California Coastal Comm'n*, 483 U.S. 825, 107 S.Ct.
3141, 97 L.Ed.2d 677 (1987), the Coastal Commission required the landowners to dedicate a public easement across their property in exchange for
a building permit. The Commission justified the need for the easement on
the ground that the proposed house would impair the public's ability to see
the beach from the road and thus would create a "psychological barrier"
preventing the public from using the beach.

The *Nollan* opinion began with the proposition that if the Commission
had simply required the landowners to dedicate an easement to increase
public access to the beach, a taking would have occurred. *Id.* at 830, 107
S.Ct. at 3145. "We think a 'permanent physical occupation' has occurred,
for purposes of that rule, where individuals are given a permanent and
continuous right to pass to and fro." *Id.* at 832, 107 S.Ct. at 3146. The
Court emphasized that the right to exclude is one of the most important of
the rights that constitute property.

The Court recognized, however, that the case involved not a bare
dedication, but a dedication in exchange for a building permit. If the
Commission could deny permission to develop because of the negative
impact of the development, it could impose appropriate conditions on its
approval of the development.

> The Commission argues that a permit condition that serves
> the same legitimate police-power purpose as a refusal to issue the
> permit should not be found to be a taking if the refusal to issue
> the permit would not constitute a taking. We agree. Thus if the
> Commission attached to the permit some condition that would
> have protected the public ability to see the beach notwithstanding
> construction of the new house—for example, a height limitation, a
> width restriction, or a ban on fences—so long as the Commission
> could have exercised its police power * * * to forbid construction
> of the house altogether, imposition of the condition would also be
> constitutional. Moreover, * * * the condition would be constitu-
> tional even if it consisted of the requirement that the Nollans
> provide a viewing spot on their property for passersby with whose
> sighting of the ocean their new house would interfere. Although
> such a requirement, constituting a permanent grant of continuous
> access to the property, would have to be considered a taking if it
> were not attached to a development permit, the Commission's

assumed power to forbid construction of the house in order to protect the public's view of the beach much surely include the power to condition construction upon some concession by the owner, even a concession of property rights, that serves the same end. If a prohibition designed to accomplish that purpose would be a legitimate exercise of the police power rather than a taking, it would be strange to conclude that providing the owner an alternative to that prohibition which accomplishes the same purpose is not.

The evident constitutional propriety disappears, however, if the condition substituted for the prohibition utterly fails to further the end advanced as the justification for the prohibition. When that essential nexus is eliminated, the situation become the same as if California law forbade shouting fire in a crowded theater, but granted dispensations to those willing to contribute $100 to the state treasury. While a ban on shouting fire can be a core exercise of the State's police power to protect the public safety, and can thus meet even our stringent standards for regulation of speech, adding the unrelated condition alters the purpose to one which, while it may be legitimate, is inadequate to sustain the ban. Therefore, even though, in a sense, requiring a $100 tax contribution in order to shout fire is a lesser restriction on speech than an outright ban, it would not pass constitutional muster. Similarly here, the lack of nexus between the condition and the original purpose of the building restriction converts that purpose to something other than what it was. The purpose then becomes, quite simply, the obtaining of an easement to serve some valid governmental purpose, but without payment of compensation. Whatever may be the outer limits of "legitimate state interests" in the takings and land-use context, this is not one of them. In short, unless the permit condition serves the same governmental purpose as the development ban, the building restriction is not a valid regulation of land use but "an out-and-out plan of extortion."

Id. at 836–37, 107 S.Ct. at 3148.[7]

In other words, to survive a constitutional challenge after *Nollan*, an exaction must mitigate the specific adverse impacts caused by the development. *See generally* Delaney, Gordon & Hess, The Needs–Nexus Analysis: A Unified Test for Validating Subdivision Exactions, User Impact Fees and Linkage, 50 Law & Contemp. Probs. 139 (1987). In response to the *Nollan* holding, municipal planners now generate "nexus reports," which are designed to insulate the exaction from judicial review by demonstrating the

7.   Under the facts of this case, since the alleged government interest was to preserve the view of the ocean, the required dedication of an easement along the ocean (which did not enhance the view that was blocked) was insufficiently connected to the government purpose to survive a takings challenge. *Id.* at 838–40, 107 S.Ct. at 3149–50. There was not, in the language of the case, an adequate "nexus."

connection between the exaction and the local government's purpose in
imposing the exaction.[8]

Vicki Been, "Exit" As a Constraint on Land Use Exactions: Rethinking the Unconstitutional Conditions Doctrine

91 Columbia Law Review 473, 486–92, 504, 509–10 (1991).

The *Nollan* Court's concern that a municipality will use its power over
land use to "extort" cash or property from developers stems from the
theory that conditions may not be enforced when they are imposed for
"bad" purposes. That theory holds that "[a]cts generally lawful may
become unlawful when done to accomplish an unlawful end, and a constitutional power cannot be used by way of a condition to attain an unconstitutional end."[9] Proponents of the extortion theory usually argue that unlawful purposes can be identified through a nexus test similar to *Nollan*'s
requirement that the challenged condition substantially serve the same
purpose as a denial of the unconditioned benefit would serve.

An initial difficulty with the theory, and with its tool the nexus test, is
the fuzziness of the concept of a "bad" purpose. A purpose can be "bad"
for at least two reasons: because it is not a legitimate state interest; or
because, although a legitimate state interest, it is not sufficiently related or
germane to the purpose which an exercise of the greater power would
serve.

Under either interpretation, the major flaw of the nexus test, in the
context of land use exactions, is that it ignores the role that exactions play
as "damages" for the injuries that developments cause to the public. The
Court repeatedly has held that a state, or a local government in its stead,
may regulate certain land uses that would harm the public's health, safety,
or welfare without incurring an obligation under the fifth amendment to
pay just compensation for the property. When it seeks to regulate such
harms, land use regulation is analogous to nuisance law, which recognizes
that in some circumstances it may be most efficient to allow a land use that

---

8. State legislatures have imposed similar requirements. For example, Cal. Gov't
Code § 66001 requires municipalities exacting impact and linkage fees to:

    (1) Identify the purpose of the fee.

    (2) Identify the use to which the fee
is to be put. * * *

    (3) Determine how there is a rea-
sonable relationship between the fee's
use and the type of development project
on which the fee is imposed.

    (4) Determine how there is a rea-
sonable relationship between the need

for the public facility and the type of
development project on which the fee is
imposed.

    (5) * * * determine how there is a
reasonable relationship between the
amount of the fee and the cost of the
public facility or portion of the public
facility attributable to the development
on which the fee is imposed.

9. *Western Union Tel. Co. v. Foster*, 247
U.S. 105, 114 (1918).

would constitute a nuisance, but impose damages upon the user in order to force it to internalize the costs of the activity. Similarly, it may be most efficient for local governments to waive land use regulations upon the payment of exactions. If the local government refuses to allow an otherwise prohibited land use in exchange for payment of exactions, it may prevent development that would be socially beneficial. On the other and, if the local government allows a developer to build a project that imposed costs upon the community without requiring exactions to compensate for those costs, the developer is likely to produce more housing units (or commercial, office, or industrial space) than is efficient because the true cost of the development will not be reflected in the ultimate price of the product. In addition, the developer will be less likely to take precautions in building the project that could efficiently mitigate the development's costs to the public.

Land use exactions thus serve an important and legitimate purpose by creating incentives for developers to take the efficient level of precaution against harm and by forcing developers to consider all costs in determining how much to develop. That function is served regardless of how the exactions are then spent; indeed, the exactions would transmit the right incentives even if the money or other resources were then burned. If the nexus test is intended to signal situations in which the real purpose of the condition is not a legitimate state interest, then, it is grossly overinclusive because it brands as illegitimate the legitimate interest the local government has in requiring the developer to internalize the full costs of the development.

* * * Justice Scalia may have intended the germaneness requirement of *Nollan* to ensure [a] "cause-and-effect" relationship * * *: if an exaction serves to remedy a harm caused by the development, it presumably is fair; but if the exaction is not germane, the causal connection that guards against unfairness and arbitrariness in the regulatory process is lacking.

The fact that the development is not the proximate cause of the harm remedied by the exaction does not mean, however, that the developer is being unfairly singled out to bear a burden for which the developer is not responsible. By developing its property in a manner inconsistent with land use regulation, a property owner causes some "social evil" that the regulation seeks to prevent. It is therefore fair to ask the property owner to pay for the damages caused by the use of the property. Whether those damages are then spent in some way unrelated to the harm is irrelevant to the question of causation.

* * *

[However, the] incentive problem posed by the absence of a nexus is clear: if the government is allowed to spend the exaction in any way it chooses, the government will have an incentive to impose land use regulations not because it is truly concerned about the damage that development will cause the public, but because it sees the "sale" of exemptions from the regulation as a source of funds, or because it sees the exemptions as a form of capital that it can use to grant favors to its supporters. Requiring a local government to spend exactions on projects that are germane to the harm that the development causes limits the potential profit from overregulation and thereby helps to ensure the efficient level of regulation. The germaneness requirement also reduces the number of interest groups likely to pressure government to overregulate. If factions such as those that want better subways and those that want more playgrounds see that exactions are a source of funds for those projects, they will seek to persuade the government to overregulate, then ask the government for a share of the proceeds from the sale of the regulation. If exactions may be spent only for germane projects, on the other hand, the number of rent-seekers that may be able to appropriate the benefit of the exaction is significantly reduced, and the pressure to overregulate will decrease accordingly.

* * *

[L]and use exactions pose two dangers: exactions allow municipalities to redistribute wealth by charging the developer more than the costs of the harm that the development is causing, and transferring that overcharge to others; and exactions may encourage the government to overregulate in order to give itself a way of raising money or other benefits. * * * [O]verregulation has consequences beyond redistribution. Unnecessarily stringent regulation may prevent development that would have been socially beneficial. Further, the sales or trades that overregulation makes possible eventually may lead to underregulation: municipalities will become so dependent upon exactions as a way to balance their budgets without the political difficulties of tax increases that they will sell development too cheaply and thereby provide insufficient protection against the harms that development may impose upon a community.

[Explicitly invoking the Tiebout Hypothesis, Professor Been examines whether municipalities face competitive pressures that would obviate the need for the nexus requirement.]

A community faces competition from several sources when it imposes exactions. First, the community must compete with other jurisdictions if it wants to encourage development because a developer dissatisfied with a community's exactions policy can take the project to another jurisdiction that offers better terms. In some parts of the country, the municipality must compete not only with existing neighboring jurisdictions, but also with potential new jurisdictions because a developer can seek to have its site incorporated as a new jurisdiction.

Second, the community must compete with its own electorate. In many jurisdictions, a developer can bypass the local government and go directly to the voters, seeking approval of the project through an initiative measure, or asking the voters to veto the local government's adverse policy through a referendum. * * * Even when developers cannot go directly to the voters for land use approval, developers can use the threat that they will leave the community to seek to persuade voters that they should turn out of office leaders who block the development.

Third, the community must compete with higher levels of government. States unwilling to lose projects to other states may strong-arm towns that balk at accepting a developer's terms or may impose limits upon local governments' ability to block development or levy exactions. Or the federal government may step in, offering to allow development on land that it owns.

Finally, a community must contend with competition from the private sector because a developer can invest the money it would spend on a development project in some other capital-seeking enterprise. Or the developer may shift its investment to development projects such as commercial or industrial buildings that typically are subject to fewer exactions than housing development.

[Been then points to some evidence for intra-municipality competition, including that exactions in many communities are lower than the actual costs of required infrastructure improvements, that surveys reveal that communities compete for development, and that in many metropolitan areas there are numerous municipalities giving residents and developers choices.]

In any imperfectly competitive market, there are costs to relying on competition to regulate contractual relationships. But there are disadvantages as well in permitting the judiciary to police those relationships. Indeed, the unconstitutional conditions doctrine, in the form of the *Nollan* nexus test * * * is quite costly. First, it will prevent local governments from spending exactions for something other than a remedy for the harm at issue, even when that course would be most efficient. It may be that there is no practical way to remedy a particular harm if the development is allowed; if building a high-rise will cast a shadow over a large portion of Central Park, for example, there may be no technologically feasible way to have both a high-rise and a sunny park. Or the remedy for the harm may be more costly than the value of preventing the harm; Justice Scalia's idea of a viewing spot on property that blocks visual access to the ocean may strike the municipality as unworkable because the cost of maintaining the viewing spot, enforcing the public's right to use the spot, and resolving disputes that may arise over such access may be higher than the value the public receives. A community then can quite justifiably seek a "second best" solution: a benefit that substitutes or makes up for the harm for which there is no feasible or cost-effective solution. That the municipality accepts a substitute remedy does not signal that the municipality was overregulating; it shows instead that the municipality acts rationally by trying to maximize the benefits that its citizens will receive in payment for the harm they must suffer. But the nexus test prevents substitute remedies.

The nexus test also raises the possibility that judges will substitute their value judgments for the judgments of the legislature under the guise of assessing the closeness of the fit between an exaction and the purposes for which development might have been denied. The calculation of harms caused by a development, and the allocation of costs among new developments, or between new residents and existing residents, is fraught with complexities for which judges enjoy no special competence. Those calculations, as well as the judge's initial determination of the legislature's purposes, leave plenty of room for a judge to substitute her notion of the public good for that of the legislature. Finally, the nexus requirement has the cost of chilling local governments' creative attempts to resolve the pressing problem of harmonizing demands for economic development with the goals of preserving the environment and improving the quality of life within the community.

---

1. In *Commercial Builders of Northern California v. City of Sacramento*, 941 F.2d 872 (9th Cir.1991), developers challenged an ordinance requiring them to pay an impact fee to finance low-income housing. The fee was expected to raise about $3.6 million annually, about 9% of the projected annual cost of needed low-income housing for the city. The city maintained that the fee was necessary to help it deal with the expected influx of new employees who would move to the city because of the commercial development. Relying on *Nollan*, the majority upheld the impact fee, based on a nexus report that projected the impact of the proposed development on housing needs. The dissenting opinion argued that

> Sacramento's ordinance is a transparent attempt to force commercial developers to underwrite social policy. Apparently, legislators find it politically more palatable to exact payments from developers than to tax their constituents. * * * The new workers attracted by the new jobs associated with the new development surely will increase the demand for all manner of goods and services. If Sacramento has shown a sufficient causal connection in this case, we can be expected next to uphold exactions imposed on developers to subsidize small business retailers, child-care programs, food services and health-care delivery systems.

Id. at 876–78. Is the dissenting opinion correct? Could a city, armed with an adequate nexus report, demand exactions for "small business retailers, child-care programs, food services and health-care delivery systems"? What, if anything, is wrong with that?

2. Professor Been argues that the only possible purpose of the nexus test is to ensure that municipalities are not overregulating. Her point is that if overregulation (extortion, in Justice Scalia's terms) is not a serious problem, the municipality *should* be able to use the exaction for *any* purpose. The real issue as far as efficiency is concerned is that the developer be charged the right amount (for the social costs of development), not how the municipality spends it. The court should not care if the municipality would rather have a beach easement than a viewing spot, so long as each exaction is no greater than the cost of the development on society. Been argues that municipalities are under substantial competitive pressures and consequently are unlikely to overregulate.

Can you think of circumstances where a municipality does not face competitive pressures, and thus is likely to overregulate? Can a court adequately distinguish competitive from non-competitive circumstances, and thus impose a nexus test only on the later? If not, should a court abandon the nexus text completely, or apply it across the board?

***

Dolan v. City of Tigard

512 U.S. 374, 114 S.Ct. 2309, 129 L.Ed.2d 304 (1994).

■ CHIEF JUSTICE REHNQUIST delivered the opinion of the Court.

Petitioner challenges the decision of the Oregon Supreme Court which held that the city of Tigard could condition the approval of her building permit on the dedication of a portion of her property for flood control and traffic improvements. 317 Ore. 110, 854 P.2d 437 (1993). We granted certiorari to resolve a question left open by our decision in *Nollan v. California Coastal Comm'n*, 483 U.S. 825 (1987), of what is the required degree of connection between the exactions imposed by the city and the projected impacts of the proposed development.

I

The State of Oregon enacted a comprehensive land use management program in 1973. Ore. Rev. Stat. §§ 197.005–197.860 (1991). The program required all Oregon cities and counties to adopt new comprehensive land use plans that were consistent with the statewide planning goals. §§ 197.175(1), 197.250. The plans are implemented by land use regulations which are part of an integrated hierarchy of legally binding goals, plans, and regulations. §§ 197.175, 197.175(2)(b). Pursuant to the State's requirements, the city of Tigard, a community of some 30,000 residents on the southwest edge of Portland, developed a comprehensive plan and codified it in its Community Development Code (CDC). The CDC requires property owners in the area zoned Central Business District to comply with a 15% open space and landscaping requirement, which limits total site coverage, including all structures and paved parking, to 85% of the parcel. CDC, ch. 18.66. After the completion of a transportation study that identified congestion in the Central Business District as a particular problem, the city adopted a plan for a pedestrian/bicycle pathway intended to encourage alternatives to automobile transportation for short trips. The CDC requires that new development facilitate this plan by dedicating land for pedestrian pathways where provided for in the pedestrian/bicycle pathway plan.

The city also adopted a Master Drainage Plan (Drainage Plan). The Drainage Plan noted that flooding occurred in several areas along Fanno Creek, including areas near petitioner's property. The Drainage Plan also established that the increase in impervious surfaces associated with continued urbanization would exacerbate these flooding problems. To combat these risks, the Drainage Plan suggested a series of improvements to the Fanno Creek Basin, including channel excavation in the area next to petitioner's property. Other recommendations included ensuring that the floodplain remains free of structures and that it be preserved as greenways to minimize flood damage to structures. The Drainage Plan concluded that the cost of these improvements should be shared based on both direct and indirect benefits, with property owners along the waterways paying more due to the direct benefit that they would receive. CDC Chapters 18.84, 18.86 and CDC § 18.164.100 and the Tigard Park Plan carry out these recommendations.

Petitioner Florence Dolan owns a plumbing and electric supply store located on Main Street in the Central Business District of the city. The store covers approximately 9,700 square feet on the eastern side of a 1.67–acre parcel, which includes a gravel parking lot. Fanno Creek flows through the southwestern corner of the lot and along its western boundary. The year-round flow of the creek renders the area within the creek's 100–year floodplain virtually unusable for commercial development. The city's comprehensive plan includes the Fanno Creek floodplain as part of the city's greenway system.

Petitioner applied to the city for a permit to redevelop the site. Her proposed plans called for nearly doubling the size of the store to 17,600 square feet, and paving a 39–space parking lot. The existing store, located on the opposite side of the parcel, would be razed in sections as construction progressed on the new building. In the second phase of the project, petitioner proposed to build an additional structure on the northeast side of the site for complementary businesses, and to provide more parking. The proposed expansion and intensified use are consistent with the city's zoning scheme in the Central Business District. CDC § 18.66.030.

The City Planning Commission granted petitioner's permit application subject to conditions imposed by the city's CDC. The CDC establishes the following standard for site development review approval: "Where landfill and/or development is allowed within and adjacent to the 100–year floodplain, the city shall require the dedication of sufficient open land area for greenway adjoining and within the floodplain. This area shall include portions at a suitable elevation for the construction of a pedestrian/bicycle pathway within the floodplain in accordance with the adopted pedestrian/bicycle plan." CDC § 18.120.180.A.8. Thus, the Commission required that petitioner dedicate the portion of her property lying within the 100–year floodplain for improvement of a storm drainage system along Fanno Creek and that she dedicate an additional 15–foot strip of land adjacent to the floodplain as a pedestrian/bicycle pathway.[10] The dedication required by that condition encompasses approximately 7,000 square feet, or roughly 10% of the property. In accordance with city practice, petitioner could rely on the dedicated property to meet the 15% open space and landscaping requirement mandated by the city's zoning scheme. The city would bear

---

10. The city's decision includes the following relevant conditions: "1. The applicant shall dedicate to the City as Greenway all portions of the site that fall within the existing 100–year floodplain [of Fanno Creek] (*i.e.*, all portions of the property below elevation 150.0) and all property 15 feet above (to the east of) the 150.0 foot floodplain boundary. The building shall be designed so as not to intrude into the greenway area."

the cost of maintaining a landscaped buffer between the dedicated area and the new store.

Petitioner requested variances from the CDC standards. Variances are granted only where it can be shown that, owing to special circumstances related to a specific piece of the land, the literal interpretation of the applicable zoning provisions would cause "an undue or unnecessary hardship" unless the variance is granted. CDC § 18.134.010. Rather than posing alternative mitigating measures to offset the expected impacts of her proposed development, as allowed under the CDC, petitioner simply argued that her proposed development would not conflict with the policies of the comprehensive plan. The Commission denied the request.

The Commission made a series of findings concerning the relationship between the dedicated conditions and the projected impacts of petitioner's project. First, the Commission noted that "[i]t is reasonable to assume that customers and employees of the future uses of this site could utilize a pedestrian/bicycle pathway adjacent to this development for their transportation and recreational needs." City of Tigard Planning Commission Final Order No. 91–09 PC. The Commission noted that the site plan has provided for bicycle parking in a rack in front of the proposed building and "[i]t is reasonable to expect that some of the users of the bicycle parking provided for by the site plan will use the pathway adjacent to Fanno Creek if it is constructed." In addition, the Commission found that creation of a convenient, safe pedestrian/bicycle pathway system as an alternative means of transportation "could offset some of the traffic demand on [nearby] streets and lessen the increase in traffic congestion."

The Commission went on to note that the required floodplain dedication would be reasonably related to petitioner's request to intensify the use of the site given the increase in the impervious surface. The Commission stated that the "anticipated increased storm water flow from the subject property to an already strained creek and drainage basin can only add to the public need to manage the stream channel and floodplain for drainage purposes." Based on this anticipated increased storm water flow, the Commission concluded that "the requirement of dedication of the floodplain area on the site is related to the applicant's plan to intensify development on the site." The Tigard City Council approved the Commission's final order, subject to one minor modification; the City Council reassigned the responsibility for surveying and marking the floodplain area from petitioner to the city's engineering department.

[Petitioner appealed to the Land Use Board of Appeals and the state courts on the ground that the dedication requirements constituted an uncompensated taking. Both the agency and the courts rejected that argument].

II

The Takings Clause of the Fifth Amendment of the United States Constitution, made applicable to the States through the Fourteenth Amendment, *Chicago, B. & Q.R. Co. v. Chicago*, 166 U.S. 226, 239 (1897), provides: "[N]or shall private property be taken for public use, without just compensation." One of the principal purposes of the Takings Clause is "to bar Government from forcing some people alone to bear public burdens which, in all fairness and justice, should be borne by the public as a whole." *Armstrong v. United States*, 364 U.S. 40, 49 (1960). Without question, had the city simply required petitioner to dedicate a strip of land along Fanno Creek for public use, rather than conditioning the grant of her permit to redevelop her property on such a dedication, a taking would have occurred. *Nollan, supra,* 483 U.S., at 831. Such public access would deprive petitioner of the right to exclude others, "one of the most essential sticks in the bundle of rights that are commonly characterized as property." *Kaiser Aetna v. United States,* 444 U.S. 164, 176 (1979).

On the other side of the ledger, the authority of state and local governments to engage in land use planning has been sustained against constitutional challenge as long ago as our decision in *Euclid v. Ambler Realty Co.,* 272 U.S. 365 (1926). "Government hardly could go on if to some extent values incident to property could not be diminished without paying for every such change in the general law." *Pennsylvania Coal Co. v. Mahon,* 260 U.S. 393, 413 (1922). A land use regulation does not effect a taking if it "substantially advance[s] legitimate state interests" and does not "den[y] an owner economically viable use of his land." *Agins v. Tiburon,* 447 U.S. 255, 260 (1980).[11]

The sort of land use regulations discussed in the cases just cited, however, differ in two relevant particulars from the present case. First, they involved essentially legislative determinations classifying entire areas of the city, whereas here the city made an adjudicative decision to condition petitioner's application for a building permit on an individual parcel. Second, the conditions imposed were not simply a limitation on the use petitioner might make of her own parcel, but a requirement that she deed portions of the property to the city. In *Nollan, supra,* we held that governmental authority to exact such a condition was circumscribed by the Fifth and Fourteenth Amendments. Under the well-settled doctrine of "unconstitutional conditions," the government may not require a person to give up a constitutional right—here the right to receive just compensation when property is taken for a public use—in exchange for a discretionary benefit conferred by the government where the property sought has little or no relationship to the benefit. *See Perry v. Sindermann,* 408 U.S. 593 (1972); *Pickering v. Board of Ed. of Township High School Dist.,* 391 U.S. 563, 568 (1968).

Petitioner contends that the city has forced her to choose between the building permit and her right under the Fifth Amendment to just compen-

---

11. There can be no argument that the permit conditions would deprive petitioner "economically beneficial us[e]" of her property as she currently operates a retail store on the lot. Petitioner assuredly is able to derive some economic use from her property. *See,* *e.g., Lucas v. South Carolina,* 505 U.S. 1003, 1015–16 (1992); *Kaiser Aetna v. United States,* 444 U.S. 164, 175 (1979); *Penn Central Transportation Co. v. New York City,* 438 U.S. 104, 124 (1978).

sation for the public easements. Petitioner does not quarrel with the city's authority to exact some forms of dedication as a condition for the grant of a building permit, but challenges the showing made by the city to justify these exactions. She argues that the city has identified "no special benefits" conferred on her, and has not identified any "special quantifiable burdens" created by her new store that would justify the particular dedications required from her which are not required from the public at large.

III

In evaluating petitioner's claim, we must first determine whether the "essential nexus" exists between the "legitimate state interest" and the permit condition exacted by the city. *Nollan*, 483 U.S., at 837. If we find that a nexus exists, we must then decide the required degree of connection between the exactions and the projected impact of the proposed development. We were not required to reach this question in *Nollan*, because we concluded that the connection did not meet even the loosest standard. 483 U.S., at 838. Here, however, we must decide this question.

A

We addressed the essential nexus question in *Nollan*. The California Coastal Commission demanded a lateral public easement across the Nollans' beachfront lot in exchange for a permit to demolish an existing bungalow and replace it with a three-bedroom house. 483 U.S., at 828. The public easement was designed to connect two public beaches that were separated by the Nollans' property. The Coastal Commission had asserted that the public easement condition was imposed to promote the legitimate state interest of diminishing the "blockage of the view of the ocean" caused by construction of the larger house.

We agreed that the Coastal Commission's concern with protecting visual access to the ocean constituted a legitimate public interest. *Id.*, at 835. We also agreed that the permit condition would have been constitutional "even if it consisted of the requirement that the Nollans provide a viewing spot on their property for passersby with whose sighting of the ocean their new house would interfere." *Id.*, at 836. We resolved, however, that the Coastal Commission's regulatory authority was set completely adrift from its constitutional moorings when it claimed that a nexus existed between visual access to the ocean and a permit condition requiring lateral public access along the Nollans' beachfront lot. *Id.*, at 837. How enhancing the public's ability to "traverse to and along the shorefront" served the same governmental purpose of "visual access to the ocean" from the roadway was beyond our ability to countenance. The absence of a nexus left the Coastal Commission in the position of simply trying to obtain an easement through gimmickry, which converted a valid regulation of land use into "an out-and-out plan of extortion." *Ibid.*, quoting *J.E.D. Associates, Inc. v. Atkinson*, 121 N.H. 581, 584, 432 A.2d 12, 14–15 (1981).

No such gimmicks are associated with the permit conditions imposed by the city in this case. Undoubtedly, the prevention of flooding along Fanno Creek and the reduction of traffic congestion in the Central Business District qualify as the type of legitimate public purposes we have upheld. *Agins, supra*, 447 U.S., at 260–262. It seems equally obvious that a nexus exists between preventing flooding along Fanno Creek and limiting development within the creek's 100–year floodplain. Petitioner proposes to double the size of her retail store and to pave her now-gravel parking lot, thereby expanding the impervious surface on the property and increasing the amount of stormwater run-off into Fanno Creek.

The same may be said for the city's attempt to reduce traffic congestion by providing for alternative means of transportation. In theory, a pedestrian/bicycle pathway provides a useful alternative means of transportation for workers and shoppers: "Pedestrians and bicyclists occupying dedicated spaces for walking and/or bicycling . . . remove potential vehicles from streets, resulting in an overall improvement in total transportation system flow." A. Nelson, *Public Provision of Pedestrian and Bicycle Access Ways: Public Policy Rationale and the Nature of Private Benefits* 11, Center for Planning Development, Georgia Institute of Technology, Working Paper Series (Jan. 1994). *See also*, Intermodal Surface Transportation Efficiency Act of 1991, Pub.L. 102–240, 105 Stat. 1914 (recognizing pedestrian and bicycle facilities as necessary components of any strategy to reduce traffic congestion).

B

The second part of our analysis requires us to determine whether the degree of the exactions demanded by the city's permit conditions bear the required relationship to the projected impact of petitioner's proposed development. *Nollan, supra*, 483 U.S., at 834 quoting *Penn Central*, 438 U.S. 104, 127 (1978) ("'[A] use restriction may constitute a taking if not reasonably necessary to the effectuation of a substantial government purpose'"). Here the Oregon Supreme Court deferred to what it termed the "city's unchallenged factual findings" supporting the dedication conditions and found them to be reasonably related to the impact of the expansion of petitioner's business. 317 Ore., at 120–121, 854 P.2d, at 443.

The city required that petitioner dedicate "to the city as Greenway all portions of the site that fall within the existing 100–year floodplain [of Fanno Creek] * * * and all property 15 feet above [the floodplain] boundary." In addition, the city demanded that the retail store be designed so as not to intrude into the greenway area. The city relies on the Commission's rather tentative findings that increased stormwater flow from petitioner's property "can only add to the public need to manage the [floodplain] for drainage purposes" to support its conclusion that the "requirement of dedication of the floodplain area on the site is related to the applicant's plan to intensify development on the site." City of Tigard Planning Commission Final Order No. 91–09 PC.

The city made the following specific findings relevant to the pedestrian/bicycle pathway: "In addition, the proposed expanded use of this site is anticipated to generate additional vehicular traffic thereby increasing congestion on nearby collector and arterial streets. Creation of a convenient, safe pedestrian/bicycle pathway system as an alternative means of transportation could offset some of the traffic demand on these nearby streets and lessen the increase in traffic congestion."

The question for us is whether these findings are constitutionally sufficient to justify the conditions imposed by the city on petitioner's building permit. Since state courts have been dealing with this question a good deal longer than we have, we turn to representative decisions made by them.

In some States, very generalized statements as to the necessary connection between the required dedication and the proposed development seem to suffice. *See, e.g., Billings Properties, Inc. v. Yellowstone County*, 144 Mont. 25, 394 P.2d 182 (1964); *Jenad, Inc. v. Scarsdale*, 18 N.Y.2d 78, 271 N.Y.S.2d 955, 218 N.E.2d 673 (1966). We think this standard is too lax to adequately protect petitioner's right to just compensation if her property is taken for a public purpose.

Other state courts require a very exacting correspondence, described as the "specifi[c] and uniquely attributable" test. The Supreme Court of Illinois first developed this test in *Pioneer Trust & Savings Bank v. Mount Prospect*, 22 Ill.2d 375, 380, 176 N.E.2d 799, 802 (1961).[12] Under this standard, if the local government cannot demonstrate that its exaction is directly proportional to the specifically created need, the exaction becomes "a veiled exercise of the power of eminent domain and a confiscation of private property behind the defense of police regulations." *Id.*, at 381, 176 N.E.2d, at 802. We do not think the Federal Constitution requires such exacting scrutiny, given the nature of the interests involved.

A number of state courts have taken an intermediate position, requiring the municipality to show a "reasonable relationship" between the required dedication and the impact of the proposed development. Typical is the Supreme Court of Nebraska's opinion in *Simpson v. North Platte*, 206 Neb. 240, 245, 292 N.W.2d 297, 301 (1980), where that court stated: "The distinction, therefore, which must be made between an appropriate exercise of the police power and an improper exercise of eminent domain is whether the requirement has some reasonable relationship or nexus to the use to which the property is being made or is merely being used as an excuse for taking property simply because at that particular moment the landowner is asking the city for some license or permit." Thus, the court held that a city may not require a property owner to dedicate private property for some

---

12. The "specifically and uniquely attributable" test has now been adopted by a minority of other courts. *See, e.g., J.E.D. Associates., Inc. v. Atkinson*, 121 N.H. 581, 585, 432 A.2d 12, 15 (1981); *Divan Builders, Inc. v. Planning Bd. of Twp. of Wayne*, 66 N.J. 582, 600–601, 334 A.2d 30, 40 (1975); *McKain v. Toledo City Plan Comm'n*, 26 Ohio App.2d 171, 176, 270 N.E.2d 370, 374 (1971); *Frank Ansuini, Inc. v. Cranston*, 107 R.I. 63, 69, 264 A.2d 910, 913 (1970).

future public use as a condition of obtaining a building permit when such future use is not "occasioned by the construction sought to be permitted." *Id.*, at 248, 292 N.W.2d, at 302.

Some form of the reasonable relationship test has been adopted in many other jurisdictions. *See, e.g., Jordan v. Menomonee Falls*, 28 Wis.2d 608, 137 N.W.2d 442 (1965); *Collis v. Bloomington*, 310 Minn. 5, 246 N.W.2d 19 (1976) (requiring a showing of a reasonable relationship between the planned subdivision and the municipality's need for land); *College Station v. Turtle Rock Corp.*, 680 S.W.2d 802, 807 (Tex.1984); *Call v. West Jordan*, 606 P.2d 217, 220 (Utah 1979) (affirming use of the reasonable relation test). Despite any semantical differences, general agreement exists among the courts "that the dedication should have some reasonable relationship to the needs created by the [development]." *Ibid. See generally*, Morosoff, *Take My Beach Please!: Nollan v. California Coastal Commission and a Rational–Nexus Constitutional Analysis of Development Exactions*, 69 B.U.L.Rev. 823 (1989); *see also Parks v. Watson*, 716 F.2d 646, 651–653 (CA 9 1983).

We think the "reasonable relationship" test adopted by a majority of the state courts is closer to the federal constitutional norm than either of those previously discussed. But we do not adopt it as such, partly because the term "reasonable relationship" seems confusingly similar to the term "rational basis" which describes the minimal level of scrutiny under the Equal Protection Clause of the Fourteenth Amendment. We think a term such as "rough proportionality" best encapsulates what we hold to be the requirement of the Fifth Amendment. No precise mathematical calculation is required, but the city must make some sort of individualized determination that the required dedication is related both in nature and extent to the impact of the proposed development.[13]

JUSTICE STEVENS' dissent relies upon a law review article for the proposition that the city's conditional demands for part of petitioner's property are "a species of business regulation that heretofore warranted a strong presumption of constitutional validity." But simply denominating a governmental measure as a "business regulation" does not immunize it from constitutional challenge on the grounds that it violates a provision of the Bill of Rights. In *Marshall v. Barlow's, Inc.*, 436 U.S. 307 (1978), we

13. Justice Stevens' dissent takes us to task for placing the burden on the city to justify the required dedication. He is correct in arguing that in evaluating most generally applicable zoning regulations, the burden properly rests on the party challenging the regulation to prove that it constitutes an arbitrary regulation of property rights. *See, e.g., Euclid v. Ambler Realty Co.*, 272 U.S. 365 (1926). Here, by contrast, the city made an adjudicative decision to condition petitioner's application for a building permit on an individual parcel. In this situation, the burden properly rests on the city. *See Nollan*, 483 U.S., at 836. This conclusion is not, as he suggests, undermined by our decision in *Moore v. East Cleveland*, 431 U.S. 494 (1977), in which we struck down a housing ordinance that limited occupancy of a dwelling unit to members of a single family as violating the Due Process Clause of the Fourteenth Amendment. The ordinance at issue in Moore intruded on choices concerning family living arrangements, an area in which the usual deference to the legislature was found to be inappropriate. *Id.*, at 499.

held that a statute authorizing a warrantless search of business premises in order to detect OSHA violations violated the Fourth Amendment. *See also Air Pollution Variance Board of Colo. v. Western Alfalfa Corp.*, 416 U.S. 861 (1974); *New York v. Burger*, 482 U.S. 691 (1987). And in *Central Hudson Gas & Electric Corp. v. Public Service Comm'n of N.Y.*, 447 U.S. 557 (1980), we held that an order of the New York Public Service Commission, designed to cut down the use of electricity because of a fuel shortage, violated the First Amendment insofar as it prohibited advertising by a utility company to promote the use of electricity. We see no reason why the Takings Clause of the Fifth Amendment, as much a part of the Bill of Rights as the First Amendment or Fourth Amendment, should be relegated to the status of a poor relation in these comparable circumstances. We turn now to analysis of whether the findings relied upon by the city here, first with respect to the floodplain easement, and second with respect to the pedestrian/bicycle path, satisfied these requirements.

It is axiomatic that increasing the amount of impervious surface will increase the quantity and rate of storm-water flow from petitioner's property. Therefore, keeping the floodplain open and free from development would likely confine the pressures on Fanno Creek created by petitioner's development. In fact, because petitioner's property lies within the Central Business District, the Community Development Code already required that petitioner leave 15% of it as open space and the undeveloped floodplain would have nearly satisfied that requirement. But the city demanded more—it not only wanted petitioner not to build in the floodplain, but it also wanted petitioner's property along Fanno Creek for its Greenway system. The city has never said why a public greenway, as opposed to a private one, was required in the interest of flood control.

The difference to petitioner, of course, is the loss of her ability to exclude others. As we have noted, this right to exclude others is "one of the most essential sticks in the bundle of rights that are commonly characterized as property." *Kaiser Aetna*, 444 U.S., at 176. It is difficult to see why recreational visitors trampling along petitioner's floodplain easement are sufficiently related to the city's legitimate interest in reducing flooding problems along Fanno Creek, and the city has not attempted to make any individualized determination to support this part of its request.

The city contends that recreational easement along the Greenway is only ancillary to the city's chief purpose in controlling flood hazards. It further asserts that unlike the residential property at issue in *Nollan*, petitioner's property is commercial in character and therefore, her right to exclude others is compromised. The city maintains that "[t]here is nothing to suggest that preventing [petitioner] from prohibiting [the easements] will unreasonably impair the value of [her] property as a [retail store]." *PruneYard Shopping Center v. Robins*, 447 U.S. 74, 83 (1980).

Admittedly, petitioner wants to build a bigger store to attract members of the public to her property. She also wants, however, to be able to control the time and manner in which they enter. The recreational easement on the Greenway is different in character from the exercise of state-protected rights of free expression and petition that we permitted in *PruneYard*. In *PruneYard*, we held that a major private shopping center that attracted more than 25,000 daily patrons had to provide access to persons exercising their state constitutional rights to distribute pamphlets and ask passersby to sign their petitions. *Id.*, at 85. We based our decision, in part, on the fact that the shopping center "may restrict expressive activity by adopting time, place, and manner regulations that will minimize any interference with its commercial functions." *Id.*, at 83. By contrast, the city wants to impose a permanent recreational easement upon petitioner's property that borders Fanno Creek. Petitioner would lose all rights to regulate the time in which the public entered onto the Greenway, regardless of any interference it might pose with her retail store. Her right to exclude would not be regulated, it would be eviscerated.

If petitioner's proposed development had somehow encroached on existing greenway space in the city, it would have been reasonable to require petitioner to provide some alternative greenway space for the public either on her property or elsewhere. *See Nollan*, 483 U.S., at 836 ("Although such a requirement, constituting a permanent grant of continuous access to the property, would have to be considered a taking if it were not attached to a development permit, the Commission's assumed power to forbid construction of the house in order to protect the public's view of the beach must surely include the power to condition construction upon some concession by the owner, even a concession of property rights, that serves the same end"). But that is not the case here. We conclude that the findings upon which the city relies do not show the required reasonable relationship between the floodplain easement and the petitioner's proposed new building.

With respect to the pedestrian/bicycle pathway, we have no doubt that the city was correct in finding that the larger retail sales facility proposed by petitioner will increase traffic on the streets of the Central Business District. The city estimates that the proposed development would generate roughly 435 additional trips per day.[14] Dedications for streets, sidewalks, and other public ways are generally reasonable exactions to avoid excessive congestion from a proposed property use. But on the record before us, the city has not met its burden of demonstrating that the additional number of vehicle and bicycle trips generated by the petitioner's development reasonably relate to the city's requirement for a dedication of the pedestrian/bicycle pathway easement. The city simply found that the creation of the pathway "could offset some of the traffic demand ... and lessen the increase in traffic congestion."[15]

14. The city uses a weekday average trip rate of 53.21 trips per 1000 square feet. Additional Trips Generated = 53.21 x (17,600–9720).

15. In rejecting petitioner's request for a variance from the pathway dedication condition, the city stated that omitting the planned section of the pathway across petitioner's property would conflict with its adopted policy of providing a continuous pathway system. But the Takings Clause requires the city to implement its policy by condemnation unless the required relation-

As Justice Peterson of the Supreme Court of Oregon explained in his dissenting opinion, however, "[t]he findings of fact that the bicycle pathway system '*could* offset some of the traffic demand' is a far cry from a finding that the bicycle pathway system *will*, or is *likely to*, offset some of the traffic demand." 317 Ore., at 127, 854 P.2d, at 447 (emphasis in original). No precise mathematical calculation is required, but the city must make some effort to quantify its findings in support of the dedication for the pedestrian/bicycle pathway beyond the conclusory statement that it could offset some of the traffic demand generated.

IV

Cities have long engaged in the commendable task of land use planning, made necessary by increasing urbanization particularly in metropolitan areas such as Portland. The city's goals of reducing flooding hazards and traffic congestion, and providing for public greenways, are laudable, but there are outer limits to how this may be done. "A strong public desire to improve the public condition [will not] warrant achieving the desire by a shorter cut than the constitutional way of paying for the change." *Pennsylvania Coal*, 260 U.S., at 416.

The judgment of the Supreme Court of Oregon is reversed, and the case is remanded for further proceedings consistent with this opinion.

It is so ordered.

■ Justice Stevens, with whom Justice Blackmun and Justice Ginsburg join, dissenting.

* * *

Certain propositions are not in dispute. The enlargement of the Tigard unit in Dolan's chain of hardware stores will have an adverse impact on the city's legitimate and substantial interests in controlling drainage in Fanno Creek and minimizing traffic congestion in Tigard's business district. That impact is sufficient to justify an outright denial of her application for approval of the expansion. The city has nevertheless agreed to grant Dolan's application if she will comply with two conditions, each of which admittedly will mitigate the adverse effects of her proposed development. The disputed question is whether the city has violated the Fourteenth Amendment to the Federal Constitution by refusing to allow Dolan's planned construction to proceed unless those conditions are met.

The Court is correct in concluding that the city may not attach arbitrary conditions to a building permit or to a variance even when it can rightfully deny the application outright. I also agree that state court decisions dealing with ordinances that govern municipal development plans provide useful guidance in a case of this kind. Yet the Court's description of the doctrinal underpinnings of its decision, the phrasing of its fledgling test of "rough proportionality," and the application of that test to this case run

ship between the petitioner's development
and added traffic is shown.

contrary to the traditional treatment of these cases and break considerable and unpropitious new ground.

I

Candidly acknowledging the lack of federal precedent for its exercise in rulemaking, the Court purports to find guidance in 12 "representative" state court decisions. To do so is certainly appropriate. The state cases the Court consults, however, either fail to support or decidedly undermine the Court's conclusions in key respects.

First, although discussion of the state cases permeates the Court's analysis of the appropriate test to apply in this case, the test on which the Court settles is not naturally derived from those courts' decisions. The Court recognizes as an initial matter that the city's conditions satisfy the "essential nexus" requirement announced in *Nollan v. California Coastal Comm'n*, 483 U.S. 825 (1987), because they serve the legitimate interests in minimizing floods and traffic congestions. The Court goes on, however, to erect a new constitutional hurdle in the path of these conditions. In addition to showing a rational nexus to a public purpose that would justify an outright denial of the permit, the city must also demonstrate "rough proportionality" between the harm caused by the new land use and the benefit obtained by the condition. The Court also decides for the first time that the city has the burden of establishing the constitutionality of its conditions by making an "individualized determination" that the condition in question satisfies the proportionality requirement.

[Justice Stevens then argues that the state cases support *Nollan*'s nexus requirement, but do not support the Court's new rough proportionality test. He also argues that the state cases consider the impact on the entire parcel, not just the portion affected.]

II

It is not merely state cases, but our own cases as well, that require the analysis to focus on the impact of the city's action on the entire parcel of private property. In *Penn Central Transportation Co. v. New York City*, 438 U.S. 104 (1978), we stated that takings jurisprudence "does not divide a single parcel into discrete segments and attempt to determine whether rights in a particular segment have been entirely abrogated." *Id.*, at 130–131. Instead, this Court focuses "both on the character of the action and on the nature and extent of the interference with rights in the parcel as a whole." *Ibid. Andrus v. Allard*, 444 U.S. 51 (1979), reaffirmed the nondivisibility principle outlined in *Penn Central*, stating that "[a]t least where an owner possesses a full 'bundle' of property rights, the destruction of one 'strand' of the bundle is not a taking, because the aggregate must be viewed in its entirety." *Id.*, at 65–66. As recently as last Term, we approved the principle again. *See Concrete Pipe & Products, Inc. v. Construction Laborers Pension Trust*, 508 U.S. 602, 643 (1993) (explaining that "a claimant's parcel of property [cannot] first be divided into what was taken and what was left" to demonstrate a compensable taking). Although limitation of the right to exclude others undoubtedly constitutes a significant infringement upon property ownership, *Kaiser Aetna v. United States*, 444 U.S. 164, 179–180 (1979), restrictions on that right do not alone constitute a taking, and do not do so in any event unless they "unreasonably impair the value or use" of the property. *PruneYard Shopping Center v. Robins*, 447 U.S. 74, 82–84 (1980).

The Court's narrow focus on one strand in the property owner's bundle of rights is particularly misguided in a case involving the development of commercial property. * * *

The exactions associated with the development of a retail business are likewise a species of business regulation that heretofore warranted a strong presumption of constitutional validity.

* * * The city of Tigard has demonstrated that its plan is rational and impartial and that the conditions at issue are "conducive to fulfillment of authorized planning objectives." Dolan, on the other hand, has offered no evidence that her burden of compliance has any impact at all on the value or profitability of her planned development. Following the teaching of the cases on which it purports to rely, the Court should not isolate the burden associated with the loss of the power to exclude from an evaluation of the benefit to be derived from the permit to enlarge the store and the parking lot.

The Court's assurances that its "rough proportionality" test leaves ample room for cities to pursue the "commendable task of land use planning,"—even twice avowing that "[n]o precise mathematical calculation is required,"—are wanting given the result that test compels here. Under the Court's approach, a city must not only "quantify its findings," and make "individualized determination[s]" with respect to the nature and the extent of the relationship between the conditions and the impact, but also demonstrate "proportionality." The correct inquiry should instead concentrate on whether the required nexus is present and venture beyond considerations of a condition's nature or germaneness only if the developer establishes that a concededly germane condition is so grossly disproportionate to the proposed development's adverse effects that it manifests motives other than land use regulation on the part of the city. The heightened requirement the Court imposes on cities is even more unjustified when all the tools needed to resolve the questions presented by this case can be garnered from our existing case law.

III

Applying its new standard, the Court finds two defects in the city's case. First, while the record would adequately support a requirement that Dolan maintain the portion of the floodplain on her property as undeveloped open space, it does not support the additional requirement that the floodplain be dedicated to the city. Second, while the city adequately established the traffic increase that the proposed development would generate, it failed to quantify the offsetting decrease in automobile traffic that the bike path will produce. Even under the Court's new rule, both defects are, at most, nothing more than harmless error.

In her objections to the floodplain condition, Dolan made no effort to demonstrate that the dedication of that portion of her property would be any more onerous than a simple prohibition against any development on that portion of her property. Given the commercial character of both the existing and the proposed use of the property as a retail store, it seems likely that potential customers "trampling along petitioner's floodplain," are more valuable than a useless parcel of vacant land. Moreover, the duty to pay taxes and the responsibility for potential tort liability may well make ownership of the fee interest in useless land a liability rather than an asset. That may explain why Dolan never conceded that she could be prevented from building on the floodplain. The City Attorney also pointed out that absent a dedication, property owners would be required to "build on their own land" and "with their own money" a storage facility for the water runoff. Dolan apparently "did have that option," but chose not to seek it.
* * *

The Court's rejection of the bike path condition amounts to nothing more than a play on words. Everyone agrees that the bike path "could" offset some of the increased traffic flow that the larger store will generate, but the findings do not unequivocally state that it will do so, or tell us just how many cyclists will replace motorists. Predictions on such matters are inherently nothing more than estimates. Certainly the assumption that there will be an offsetting benefit here is entirely reasonable and should suffice whether it amounts to 100 percent, 35 percent, or only 5 percent of the increase in automobile traffic that would otherwise occur. If the Court proposes to have the federal judiciary micro-manage state decisions of this kind, it is indeed extending its welcome mat to a significant new class of litigants. Although there is no reason to believe that state courts have failed to rise to the task, property owners have surely found a new friend today.

IV

[Justice Stevens argues that the Court's opinion applies a rejected due process theory. As a result, the Court improperly puts the burden of proof on the city to justify the conditions.]

In our changing world one thing is certain: uncertainty will characterize predictions about the impact of new urban developments on the risks of floods, earthquakes, traffic congestion, or environmental harms. When there is doubt concerning the magnitude of those impacts, the public interest in averting them must outweigh the private interest of the commercial entrepreneur. If the government can demonstrate that the conditions it has imposed in a land-use permit are rational, impartial and conducive to fulfilling the aims of a valid land-use plan, a strong presumption of validity should attach to those conditions. The burden of demonstrating that those conditions have unreasonably impaired the economic value of the proposed improvement belongs squarely on the shoulders of the party challenging the state action's constitutionality. That allocation of burdens has served us well in the past. The Court has stumbled badly today by reversing it.

I respectfully dissent.

---

1.   What is the Court's standard defining the constitutionally required relationship between the state's interest and the exaction? Do you agree with the Court's substantive standard? If not, what would you choose instead? What is the dissent's proposed standard? Do you agree with the dissent that the majority opinion is just a "play on words"—a harmless failure by the trial court to say "would" instead of "could?"

2.   Which party bears the burden of proof—the landowner or the government?   On what issues?

3.   To what types of cases does this standard apply? For example, does it apply to rezoning cases? Does it apply to impact or linkage fees imposed on all new developers? Should there be a difference?

4.   Do you agree with the Court's analysis regarding the dedication of the "greenway"? What did the city want? How was its desire for the dedication related to its concern about flooding?

5.   Do you agree with the Court's analysis regarding the dedication for the bicycle pathway? What does the Court require the city to demonstrate in order to survive the constitutional challenge?

6.   Some observers have expressed concern that the heightened scrutiny required by *Nollan* and *Dolan* would impede local jurisdictions intent on raising capital for new public facilities or compelling developers to construct low-income housing. *See, e.g.,* Michelman, Takings, 1987, 88 Colum. L. Rev. 1600, 1614 n.63 (1988). Do you think this concern is substantial? Do you think this concern is legitimate?

7.   Would Professor Been, who raised a substantial challenge to the *Nollan* nexus test, also oppose the *Dolan* rough proportionality test?

Problems: Exactions and Bargaining

1.   Reread the Moses' Bagels problem, *supra*, pp. 1019–20. Suppose that city officials have decided tentatively to approve the project, but that they want to condition the approval on the bagel shop's agreement to compensate the neighbors or the city in some fashion for the harm that the expansion of the shop will cause.

a.   What are the constitutional standards for such exactions? Who bears the burden of proof on different factual issues?

b.   What sorts of conditions can the city impose on the operation of the bagel shop? Recall that there is no room for additional parking (that is, given existing land uses, the shop cannot provide additional parking), and that there is nothing Moses' Bagels can do directly to address the problems of traffic congestion, noise, and air pollution. Can the city require Moses' Bagels to pay for a new traffic light and the cost of painting new cross walks at nearby intersections? Can the city require Moses' Bagels to pay a transit impact fee that would be deposited in a municipal fund for road-improvement projects throughout the city? Can the city require donation of 250 bagels each week to the municipally funded Homeless Outreach Project? What would Professor Been say about these proposed exactions?

c. Should the city engage in negotiations with Moses' Bagels? Or should it just rule on the requested rezoning or variance and attach what it sees as appropriate conditions? If the city engages in negotiations, should the objecting neighbors be brought into the negotiations? Should the city also bring in the neighbors who support the expansion? What about the other store owners, who may have strong feelings (either for or against) the expansion?

2. A developer owns 111 acres of rural land that he intends to subdivide into 25 lots and develop as residences of various sizes ranging from 2 acres to 19 acres. The development plans do not include any provision for a public sewer system or domestic water supply system. The developer plans to install individual septic sewer systems and wells for each house. To proceed with his project, the developer needs to have the land rezoned.

Some neighbors complained that the proposed plans (particularly the lack of connection to public water supplies and a public sewerage system) would devalue the homes in other residential subdivisions in the vicinity. The local legislature considered these complaints and rezoned the land, but imposed conditions that the developer provide and dedicate public sewer and water supply systems.

The developer claims that the conditions violate *Nollan* and *Dolan*. Is he right? What additional facts would you need to have to decide? *See Marshall v. Board of County Commissioners of Johnson County,* 912 F.Supp. 1456 (D.Wyo.1996).

3. Chesterfield County adopted an ordinance requiring an impact fee of $5000 for every residential lot developed within the city limits. The amount was based on a county-wide survey of the average costs of providing municipal facilities, such as roads, schools, and parks. The county deposited the collected fees in the general fund.

A builders' association has challenged the ordinance as a violation of the principles set forth in *Nollan* and *Dolan*. Is the association correct? *See National Association of Home Builders of the United States v. Chesterfield County,* 907 F.Supp. 166 (E.D.Va. 1995).

4. The City of Seattle adopted an ordinance that required landlords who demolished or substantially remodeled their apartment buildings to pay $1000 toward the relocation costs of each of their tenants (the city would contribute another $1000). The amount was based on a telephone

survey of four moving companies who quoted approximate prices for moving a one-bedroom apartment. The stated purposes of the ordinance are to encourage economic opportunity for all citizens, to promote the availability of housing, and to preserve existing housing stock.

A group of landlords challenge the validity of the ordinance under *Nollan* and *Dolan*. Is the ordinance valid? *See Garneau v. City of Seattle,* 897 F.Supp. 1318 (W.D.Wash. 1995).

Review Problem:
Background Legal Rules, Social Norms, Markets,
and Political Institutions

Portopolis is a medium-sized city. It is the largest city in its region, and as such is the cultural, political, and economic center of the region. It is surrounded by two dozen suburbs, mostly bedroom communities. To the north of Portopolis and the suburbs are foothills and then a small mountain range. To the east and south are agricultural lands. To the west is the ocean. There are virtually no local, state, or federal lands in the region except for a state park in the mountains.

Portopolis is home to the state's largest public university as well as a large aerospace company and a new high-tech industry clustered around a giant software manufacturer. The long-term economic prospects of the region are bright. Because of the potential job growth and the recreational and environmental attractions of the area, the population is expected to grow substantially if unchecked.

The agricultural land in the region is worth considerably less than if the same land were sold for commercial or residential development. Both commercial and residential developers have begun to talk to farmers and other large landholders, and a few developers have taken out options on some large parcels; others will surely follow. At present, the undeveloped land is unzoned and not subject to any system of private servitudes. Most of the land is in unincorporated areas of the county.

Some civic leaders have become concerned about the region's future development. On the one hand, they welcome economic growth. They want the potential benefits of development—increased tax base and greater cultural and social amenities (*e.g.*, more and better libraries, museums). At the same time, they are concerned about the potential long-term costs of urban sprawl—*e.g.*, polluted air and water, gridlocked traffic, reduced amount of open space, and a depleted urban center. Newspaper stories about the ill effects of urban sprawl in cities like Los Angeles and Phoenix, *see, e.g.,* Timothy Egan, *Urban Sprawl Strains Western States,* New York Times at 1 (Dec. 29, 1996), have led editorial writers and talk show hosts to coin and repeat the slogan "No LA".

The civic leaders want to explore broad approaches to reach an appropriate balance.

1. In what ways are the problems faced by Portopolis analogous to those discussed by Hardin, *supra* pp. 17–19? To what extent does the model suggested by Demsetz, *supra* pp. 49–53 bear on this problem?

2. Consider the different institutions that we have studied in this course—background legal rules, social norms, markets, and politics.

What is the probable outcome if Portopolis relies only on background legal rules?

Can social norms play a significant role in addressing the problems associated with urban sprawl? What characteristics of the situation in Portopolis limit the usefulness of social norms?

Can structured markets play a significant role? For example, should Portopolis and surrounding suburbs promote or mandate development through common interest communities? What are the shortcomings or limitations of common interest communities in dealing with urban sprawl? Alternatively, should the municipalities begin to purchase undeveloped land for parks or open space? Should they begin to subsidize farmers (through tax breaks or direct cash subsidies) under long-term contracts as a means to reduce growth in undeveloped areas?

Should Portopolis pursue a political solution—land use planning and zoning? Does the segmentation of the region into two dozen municipalities pose a serious obstacle to a zoning solution? How can this problem be overcome?

3. Suppose that the mayor of Portopolis decides to pursue a political solution. How should the mayor proceed? Should she begin by appointing a task force of land use experts to propose a land use plan for the region? Should she appoint a task force consisting of representatives of major interest groups, such as farmers, industry, homeowners, and developers and instruct them to come up with a plan? Or should she hold public meetings and conduct surveys as a means to involve the general public?

If a proposed plan is developed, should she seek approval through the local legislature or through ballot measures?

INDEX

1–56662–533–5

9 781566 625333
90000

†